D0883261

Modern French
Culinary Art

HENRI-PAUL PELLAPRAT

Modern French Culinary Art

THE PELLAPRAT OF THE 20th. CENTURY

This edition edited by **JOHN FULLER** F.H.C.I., F.R.S.H.,
formerly Rank Organisation Professor of Hotel Management, and Director, Scottish Hotel School, University of Strathclyde

IITED

FIRST
PUBLISHED IN THIS EDITION, 1967

ÉDITIONS KRAMER, SWITZERLAND
TEXT PRINTED IN GREAT BRITAIN
BY C. TINLING & CO. LTD. LIVERPOOL
ILLUSTRATIONS PRINTED IN SWITZERLAND
BY IMPRIMERIE CENTRALE,
LAUSANNE
ISBN 0 00 435143 6

Fifth Impression 1972

Contents

Introduction to the first French edition

by H.-P. PELLAPRAT (1869-1949)

After thirty years' teaching experience in the "Cordon Bleu de Paris" cookery and confectionery schools and publishing a number of professional works I wished to use the leisure of retirement—earned by fifty-three years' work of various kinds in the kitchens of France and other countries—by compiling a book for the housewife containing all she needs to know about cookery and related matters.

In this book I have dealt with the question of menus, which are always difficult to work out, with the serving of wine, with serving at table and with the necessary materials and supplies for the kitchen. I have given practical and economic advice, explaining the whys and wherefores of various cooking methods. In a word, I have tried, in the pages which follow, to remain the teacher I have been to thousands of pupils during the last thirty years.

I have also given some forty menus, selected from these pages, some suitable for every day use, others for small but special dinners, others for receptions and ceremonial banquets.

Good entertaining is one of the housewife's duties. To help her in this task I have added some more extravagant dishes to each chapter. Moreover, to make the explanation clearer, colour plates of the major dishes have been inserted, which will certainly encourage readers to complete their dishes to their entire satisfaction.

I have tried to produce a work of lasting value in a field which is overcrowded, though rarely by qualified professionals. I was apprenticed in 1882 *and never took off my white coat again; I did pastry-making, confectionery and cookery; I have practical experience of canning, ice-making, chocolate making, industrial biscuit-making. I therefore believe, without vanity, that I have the right to be called an all-round craftsman and to be qualified to teach the things I know, unlike the many charlatans who pose as professors of a science they have never learned.*

The recipes in this book have not been taken from my imagination. I have tried every one of them out on the stove, and those for foreign dishes come from highly esteemed authors. Considerable space is given to ways of using up left-overs, a major factor in the domestic economy; and I believe I have fulfilled the aim I set myself when I started to write this book, that is, to give the housewife the most all-round training possible.

While "L'Art culinaire moderne" does not contain everything I should have liked to see in it—three volumes would not have been enough for that—it does at least contain most of what a housewife should know. She may rest assured that I have done all I can to help her and to teach and propagate an art very dear to my heart—that of the good, the best French cuisine.

Before concluding I would like to thank the Comptoir Français du Livre for undertaking the publication of "L'Art culinaire moderne". It is due to its distinguished editor-publisher, Mr. J. Kramer, that it has been possible to illustrate this book so well and so profusely, and that I have been enabled to contribute my stone to the monument to French cookery which the great Carême started to build.

Paris, April 1935

Une Bible de la Cuisine

by CURNONSKY, *Prince élu des Gastronomes*

Curnonsky, born Maurice Edmond Saillant, was "elected" Prince of Gastronomes in 1927, possibly following acclamation by fellow gourmets, writers and through a journal referendum. Despite his title's obscurity, there is no doubt of his dominance in French gastronomy for over almost three decades until his death in 1956. His judgement of chefs, their work and their books was, if favourable (as in Pellaprat's case), regarded as ultimate recognition. (EDITOR).

With the unanimous agreement of many people, and even the French who love so much to disparage themselves, French cuisine is undoubtedly the best in the world. This is because of its natural products, as well as for the diversity of its dishes, of its food, of its specialities, and above all because of the talent and integrity of its chefs and *cordon bleus*. Its eminent superiority, its excellence has never been disputed; famous hotels throughout the world are honoured to have French chefs.

France's innumerable recipes have inspired a whole library. Since the famous "Viandier du Grand Maistre queux Guillaume Tirel, dit Taillevent" (published 600 years ago) our culinary literature remains incomparably enriched with true works of art.

Here is one of the most perfect and most authentic.

It is a great honour and a joy to preface a new and splendid edition of a book known to all gourmets; and all gourmets agree in considering this a classic of the table. *L'Art culinaire moderne* is the work of a great cook, of an impeccable master of technique, and of a perfect artist in love with his work.

Henri-Paul Pellaprat is one of the masters of this magnificent generation of chefs who during half a century have carried so high the prestige, and we may add, have procured and ensured the glory of, high class French cuisine: Escoffier, Phileas Gilbert, Guerot, Prosper Montagne, Mourier, Carton, Nignon, Tony Girod, Prosper Salles, Burtin, Reboul, Gimond, Ninlias, Dumont-Lespine, Wernert, Herbodeau, Casimir Moisson, Delaunay, Falcoz, Chosson, Duplat, Argentier, Dreneau, Caillat, and the three Grioix, and the four Bouzy. I could name at least twenty other worthy successors of the famous Antonin Carême who have made France the paradise of gastronomy. Those who remain of this incomparable assembly are today, like me, almost octogenarians. But it seems that work and love of the culinary profession confers long life, for these great workers have kept a vitality and a spirit that many young people could envy.

As to Pellaprat, whom we had the grief to lose in 1949, he leaves a considerable work and a *great book*: here it is.

His biography may be summarised in a few lines, for his life was a model of unity and probity, consecrated wholly to his Art, the life of an admirable artist who knows all there is to know about his work.

Henri-Paul Pellaprat, born in Paris in 1869, began with a three-year apprenticeship in pastry-making, following the rule of the Master, Auguste Escoffier, who believed that a cook should be, first of all, a pastry-cook. After this, he worked for a year in confectionery with Forest at Bourges. Finally, he started cooking in Paris at the Café de la Paix, with the famous Père Lepy. From there he went on to La Maison Dorée with the great chef Casimir Moisson. Next he worked with Bignon, with Maire, and with Prillard. He did his military service at Verdun going through most of France and part of Europe. He then entered the schools of the Cordon Bleu as a teacher.

He was mobilised in 1914 and was discharged in 1915, on account of his family (at 46 he had seven children). As the Cordon Bleu school was closed, he became chef at Lucas, then at the Terminus Denain. After the war, he took up once more his work at the Cordon Bleu and remained there until 1932, when he retired. This early decision was a stroke of good luck for French cookery, because our good master being unable to remain inactive, employed his leisure time in writing his culinary treatises which are authoritative works: *La Cuisine au vin*, in collaboration with Raymond Brunet, the famous oenophile (1934), *Les Sandwichs et les Pains fourrés* (1934), *La Pâte feuilletée* (puff pastry) (1932).

In 1935 appeared the first edition of *L'Art culinaire moderne*. Then as now, it is a real encyclopaedia of table and cuisine. It summarises the essentials of all kinds of cookery, and first of all, of the four types of French cookery: *Haute Cuisine* (high class cookery)—one of the ornaments of France. *Bourgeoise Cuisine*—the triumph of our cordons bleus and housewives. Pellaprat is a fervent feminist who pays homage to the finesse, grace and simplicity which women's culinary rivalry has brought to French cookery. *French Regional Cuisine*—unique in the world, because of its diversity, richness, and the originality of its innumerable local dishes and specialities. Finally, *Impromptue Cuisine*, the simplest and quickest ways of using whatever is at hand. Pellaprat makes most judicious choice from the innumerable recipes of these four types of cookery.

But one of the rare attractions of this book is that Pellaprat, unparalleled cook and teacher, is also a master of pastry-making and confectionery—still exquisite jewels in French cuisine. Moreover, Pellaprat is no xenophobe and hopes to see his book universally read and used. *L'Art culinaire moderne* also contains, therefore recipes for many of the best foreign dishes.

Pellaprat may indeed glory, and with justice, in having attained his end; to be as completely as possible the household educator.

This book's recipes are not fanciful. They can stand the actual test of preparation as he himself said. They are all practical and reliable, and they all possess an eminently French quality, of being written in a clear, precise, intelligible, direct and neat style. "What is well-conceived expresses itself clearly . . ."

When the first edition of this book appeared, the great chef Phileas Gilbert wrote to his colleague and friend Pellaprat a letter of enthusiastic praise from which I should like to quote a passage:

"I am convinced that your book will be welcomed, because following your instructions, any novice of a housewife will be able, once having studied a recipe, to carry out its directions; she will have understood it, for the descriptive form that you have adopted can be understood by everybody". Gilbert's forecast has been realised.

This beautiful book has obtained a success without precedent in culinary literature. At the same time as to its author, it is only just to pay homage to its first editor, Jacques Kramer, whose bold initiative resulted in an incomparable work of art in book publication. Such pioneer presentation made this great book, a unique monument to the glory of Culinary Art.

Curnonsky

Prince-Elect of the Gastronomes
Founder-President of the Academie des Gastronomes

Pellaprat - The Man and the Book

by JOHN FULLER, formerly Rank Organisation Professor of Hotel Management and Director, Scottish Hotel School, University of Strathclyde

The literature of cookery reveals enduring principles in the preparation of dishes whether they are applied by the professional chef or the housewife. Techniques vary, of course, often considerably, when professional chefs apply their craft in changing hotel or restaurant situations. In these circumstances, cooks' methods are further conditioned by the organisation of professional kitchens themselves to meet the demands of cooking for larger numbers often in quick succession.

Because of variations in organisation and technique between hotel-restaurant kitchen and housewives' kitchen some cooks may overlook much common ground in good cookery between the two. The gulf between professional chef and *cordon bleu,* or good woman cook, often seems too wide and too deep to be bridged.

It is, however, noticeable, certainly during and since the nineteenth century, that eminent chefs have made strong efforts to communicate with domestic cooks. Great chefs, particularly, have sought to participate in lifting cookery standards in the home through training. At the same time, those women who have been similarly concerned with training to improve cookery in domestic science or home economics colleges and schools have generally been responsive to such approaches from professionals.

In France the gulf between women domestic cooks and professional chefs in hotel-restaurant kitchens has never, perhaps, been so marked as in this country. Restaurant cuisine in that country clearly owes much to the respect of French *cuisiniers* for dishes evolved from the home environment and for *cordons bleus*—fine women cooks. Professional cuisine in France is, indeed, openly derived from domestic sources—folk cookery, bourgeois cookery and even the cookery of poverty.

Henri-Paul Pellaprat has by his work staked a claim as a significant figure in the history of communication between *chefs de cuisine* and *cordons bleu* and in instructing professional cook and housewife alike. Pellaprat was a pioneer in the pre-World War II era in carrying to the home cook the skills of the professional chef. He has significance not only for successfully imparting his expertise to housewives and domestic cooks during most of his later life, but because at the same time, he retained the respect and admiration of his professional colleagues. His published works, of which *L'Art culinaire moderne* is his most substantial, have long enjoyed the distinction of being consulted and used by chefs throughout the western world. At the same time these same works have enjoyed enormous popularity with hostesses who now so often are cooks also in the home.

Born in the Victorian age, Pellaprat's greatest and most productive period was the era between the two World Wars. Curnonsky, the gastronomic writer accepted as an authority in France by gourmet and chef alike, sketches Pellaprat's career in his preface to *L'Art culinaire moderne* which he hails as "une bible de cuisine". Endorsement by Curnonsky who had been elected "Prince des Gastronomes" was recognition indeed.

From Curnonsky's biographical note (page *ix*) we see that Pellaprat bridges, therefore, not only domestic and professional cookery, but also the former culinary-elaborate Edwardian era and the present. His authority as a master chef stems from varied experience during his own career. Personal skill and qualifications from this experience substantiate his claim and his desire to teach the art which he loved.

His wish to teach came to realisation more in the domestic than in the professional situation. In the early years of the twentieth century, organised schools of professional training for chefs and hoteliers had not, of course, reached their present stage of development. Indeed, they hardly existed. Pellaprat, therefore, entered teaching through the Cordon Bleu de Paris where he headed the cookery and pastry schools for thirty years and helped build its fame as the Mecca for women cooks of ambition and merit. During this time his work, though directed primarily at aspiring women *cordons bleus,* also attracted some men pupils. He reached and "taught" chefs in the trade, however, by less direct means—through his books.

As a teacher, Pellaprat learned to organise his craft knowledge for absorption by the learner. His writings, thus informed by years of experience with pupils, proved highly acceptable amongst others learning or seeking advancement.

He was a versatile and gifted writer. When his works began to appear in the pre-war 1930s, continuing in print until the present day, they had the distinction (like those of Carême, Soyer, Escoffier and Francatelli) of being accepted by good cooks everywhere—in homes or hotels.

L'Art culinaire moderne, written in his retirement, represents the culmination of Pellaprat's skills, knowledge and ideals. He hoped and believed that household cookery could and should enrich itself by absorbing much of what, heretofore, had been regarded as exclusively within the compass of the professional chef. In *L'Art culinaire moderne* he aimed to assemble together all that he knew, and all that he could acquire, about kitchen and cookery skills and practice. He sought to include, too, those things ancillary to his craft—menu composing, wine service, table setting and floral arrangements. "I would like to present a lasting work in a field where so many books circulate but where they are so seldom written by qualified professionals," he declared.

That his book has been in continuous print in many languages besides English and French since that time helps demonstrate the achievement of that aim.

His work and his writing contribute significantly to breaking down the remaining "mystique" which still lingered in France (and in other parts of Europe) about fine cooking; the idea that this was secret knowledge known only to a favoured few professional *maîtres.* Pellaprat moved away from the tradition or vogue that had been established by French masters in which recipes were written in vague technical terms understandable only to professional initiates. His devotion to "popularising" classical and traditional cookery, though wholly acceptable and fashionable today, represented in his own time a new way of thinking in male-dominated French culinary circles.

Like Escoffier, Pellaprat valued and sought to develop simplicity especially in simplifying and explaining elaborate culinary jargon but also in simplifying dishes themselves. "Simplicité de la cuisine ne doit pas excluse la qualité" ('simplicity in cookery should not exclude quality') was one of his tenets. Yet he may also be regarded as a professional descendant of the great Carême, who worked for a time in Regency England, in that he appropriately valued "presentation" and did not hesitate to offer to "simple cooks", the opportunity to dress and present dishes attractively and sometimes, indeed, in splendid dramatic and exciting form.

Yet, however elaborate, Pellaprat's work never descends to mere fantasy. His recipes are those of a practical cook and teacher—conditioned by his knowledge of the limitations yet aspirations, of learners.

However great may be the culinary practitioners of the past and however immortal their written works may become, their recipes are used by cooks, whether professional or domestic, in changing conditions affected by social, economic and technological factors. Food commodities themselves change with new forms of horticulture and husbandry and new techniques in packaging and marketing. Cookery is a highly absorbent craft which continues to grow. Clearly *L'Art culinaire moderne*, this last and greatest work of Pellaprat's published in the 20th century, embodies so much of what is fundamental to modern cookery concepts that it was vital that it should not be allowed to "date". In 1935, Jacques Kramer edited *L'Art culinaire moderne* with the intention of conserving all that was enduring in Pellaprat's work—his watch on traditions, his feeling for simplification and his keen interest in foreign specialities. Pellaprat recognised evolution in his craft. He would rejoice that his successors as culinary masters and teachers were co-opted under Jacques Kramer (and later his son René Kramer) to keep *L'Art culinaire moderne* under constant revision. Such revision reflects changes without the book losing its basic tradition, "flavour" and its ultimate goals.

This new British edition is especially rich in pictures with more than decorative value. Illustrations in Pellaprat have been, and remain, an important "self-teaching" aid—guiding cooks in "finish" and the presentation of fine fare. Now in 1968, this new British edition must continue to merit its sub-title *The Pellaprat of the 20th. Century*. The text has been remodelled and the book's concept adapted to today's needs. *All* illustrations are new, engraved and printed in photogravure; a task occupying specialists in many countries—many months.

The editorial team have sought to remain faithful to Pellaprat's work. Many classical recipes remain unchanged because their timeless quality merits their permanent place in culinary literature. But new material includes recipes from internationally known chefs in many parts of the world. Recipes have been adapted to British weights and measures and some changes and additions made. For this revision, Pellaprat's admirers in several countries, well-known chefs, specialists and gastronomic authors, conformed in a basic approach to justify the modernity of the title whilst retaining Pellaprat's original concept.

This new British edition owes much to earlier work by eminent continental revisers recruited by René Kramer, who inherited his father's respect and enthusiasm for *L'Art culinaire moderne*.

The British team who helped prepare this revision include not only chefs but specialists in nutrition, wine, equipment and commodities and whose names are listed in the Acknowledgement on page xiv.

The result, like its recent French and other continental editions, is a fusion of effort in which Pellaprat and his successors have the support of other specialists—not least those from printing and book production. All who have collaborated as a British team in this up-to-date version, have accepted that Pellaprat's work, however adapted to British usage, must retain its blend of Gallic and international flavour. They hope *L'Art culinaire moderne* will continue long into this century to serve, as it has for long in the century's earlier years, its readership of chefs and housewives, students of cookery and experienced amateurs alike.

Glasgow, 1967.

Acknowledgments

We should like to thank and acknowledge all those contributors who have lent their valuable help and vast experience in bringing Pellaprat's classic book up to date.

The technical editing of *L'Art culinaire moderne* was carried out by:
Professor JOHN FULLER, F.H.C.I., F.R.S.H., *formerly Director of the Scottish Hotel School,*
and WILFRED J. FANCE, F.INST.B.B.
and the Staff of the Scottish Hotel School, University of Strathclyde:
ALEXANDER J. CURRIE; JOSEPH HOUSTON; CHARLES K. JARVIE; JOHN MCKEE;
IAIN T. MARSHALL; EDWARD RENOLD; PETER R. SHILL; GORDON SINCLAIR

This edition has been adapted to suit the needs of the British housewife by
the editorial staff of William Collins Sons & Company Limited, Glasgow:
ANTONY ATHA, *Managing Editor;* PATRICIA M. BATEMAN, *Cookery Editor;*
CHRISTINE WATT, *Home Economist*

Acknowledgment for contributions and assistance is also gratefully made to:
Mesdames G. CONACHER, COLETTE GUÉDEN, A. JACKSON, LUCIA MAZZUCCHETTI, S. WHITTINGHAM; Mesdemoiselles MADELEINE DECURE, HELGA LUND, RUTH OLIVER; Messieurs ALEX ALLEGRIER, FRANÇOIS D'ATHIS, WALTER BICKEL, PIERRE BOUTINES, PINO BRAGUTI, OCTAVE BRUST, FRANCO CORPORA, CLAUDE DESARZENS, JEAN DOREAU, MARC FATIO, DAGOBERT FEHLMANN, WERNER FISCHER, GIUSEPPE FONTANA, HERBERT GÖMÖRI, CHARLES GOETZ, R. GOODWIN, CÉSAR GOSI, MARCO GUARNORI, ROGER GUILLAUME, JEAN GUINOT, GEORGES GUTH, PAUL HEINZ, ARTHUR HOPE, HUBLET, P. W. KING, RENÉ KRAMER, RENÉ LACROIX, FRED LAUBI, LEONE LEGNANI, JEAN LIBAN, XAVIER MAIER, PHILIPPE MARNIER-LAPOSTOLLE, PIERRE MENGELATTE, FLAVIEN MONOD, LUIGI MORANDI, BRUNO MOSCA, FRANCO PURICELLI, GILBERT ROHRER, NATALE RUSCONI, HERBERT SEIDEL, CHARLES VAUCHER, STEFANO ZACCONE, FRANCO ZECCA

Each of these names represents concrete work, suggestions, ideas. The whole forms

L'Art culinaire moderne

How to use this book

While all the recipes in this book have been carefully edited and made as simple to follow as possible, it is important to approach each recipe in the proper manner. Many of the culinary terms and techniques referred to will be familiar to you but, in case of doubt, you should consult the specific chapters for a more detailed explanation. It is important, at all times, to read over a recipe carefully—several times if necessary—then, to assemble all the materials and ingredients involved and to carry out the preliminary ground work such as sauce making, the cleaning and preparation of vegetables and the assembly of the desired garnish. The following is an example of how individual recipes should be tackled.

Noix de Veau à l'Ancienne * *Cushion of Veal à l'Ancienne*

For 15 *persons:* 4½ *lb cushion of veal;* 2 *carrots;* 2 *onions;* 1 *lb Fine Forcemeat quenelles;* ½ *lb sliced mushrooms;* 30 *cocks' combs and* 30 *chicken livers;* ⅛ *pint sauce Suprême;* ⅛ *lb bacon.* Cooking time: 3 hours.

Cushion of Veal: see Veal Chapter, preliminary notes on *Noix de Veau.*

Fine Forcemeat quenelles: see chapter on Basic Preparations and Ingredients, section dealing with Forcemeats and Quenelles.

Sauce Suprême: for method of preparation see Sauce chapter.

Cooking time: This refers to the amount of time required to braise the meat. At best this can only be an approximate time and due allowance should always be made for the variable factors involved in any form of cooking. These include the quality and cut of the meat, personal preference in the degree of "doneness" of the meat, and variable oven temperatures.

Lard a small, prime cushion of veal. Place in a *cocotte* with the sliced vegetables and *moisten* with little stock. *Braise* very slowly in a warm oven, 350°F or Gas Mark 3. Prepare a *garnish* of Fine Forcemeat *quenelles,* sautéed mushrooms, cocks' combs and chicken livers, all bound with the *sauce Suprême.* Let the veal cool slightly. Using a small sharp knife, make a round incision about 4/5 inch from the edge—do not cut right through to the bottom—and remove a large cylinder of meat to form a hollow which is then filled with the garnish. Make a lid with a slice cut from the top of the meat which has been removed so that the veal appears to be intact. Arrange decoratively on a large dish. Skim all the fat from the cooking liquid, strain and pour over the veal. Slice the remains of the inner cylinder and place around the meat.

Larding: Consult the Glossary of Cooking Terms.

Cocotte: Consult the Glossary of Cooking Terms.

Moisten: Consult the Glossary of Cooking Terms.

Braise: Refer to *Braising* in the Culinary Craft chapter in the section dealing with methods of cooking.

Garnish: Consult the section dealing with Garnishes.

N.B. In order to avoid tedious repetition, we have replaced with a black square symbol the name of the basic material of the main recipe, where a number of derivative recipes are given. Thus you will find:

Noix de Veau * *Cushion of Veal*

⊡ à l'Ancienne

⊡ Braisée à la Breban

⊡ Braisée à la Gendarme

⊡ Judic, etc.

Entertaining, like cooking, is an art and the secret of success lies in your natural, unharassed approach as host or hostess. Successful entertaining demands careful preparation. The quality of the dishes, the subtlety of the table decorations, the choice of menu and wine, all require the same care and attention as the good cook will give to the dishes themselves. When planning a meal you should remember that guests, no matter how eminent, shrink from ostentation. You should avoid the impression of great effort and you should always aim to put your guests at their ease.

The good hostess puts herself in the position of others and thinks in advance of what they would enjoy. She will always remember their dislikes and take charge, for however short a time, of their enjoyment. Some people feel happier in rather formal surroundings, seated before a sophisticated table, laid with linen, crystal and silver. Others attach more importance to the freshness of the flowers and a more informal approach. However, what is always appreciated by everyone is the personal note and the attentions that remind the guests that everything has been done for their pleasure, their comfort and their relaxation. Do not make these considerations an excuse for an excessive display of your material possessions and remember to leave sufficient room at the table for each guest. It is better to have two guests fewer and not to squash either objects or people. Attention must also be paid to ventilation and temperature. Always check the freshness of the air, the temperature of the dining area and proper degree of heat or chill for food, wines and plates. The table must be big enough for glasses, plates, covers and various accessories not to be cramped.

In the past the centrepiece consisted of large, silver ornaments. These can still be used for very traditional receptions but nowadays flowers, possibly reflected in a discreet mirror mat, are preferable as they are always available and can be either simple or sumptious. You do not have to confine your flowers exclusively to the centre of the table. However, if the flowers are set individually they must not engulf the place settings; a table turn ed into a greenhouse or a high-class florist's display is out of place. Nor should the flowers be too strongly scented, otherwise they may drown or form dubious alliances with the subtle odours of well-cooked food.

Proper lighting lends the finishing touch to the table and to the whole of the room. Wherever possible, the gentle light of candles should be used in the evening. Candelabras and chandeliers give a table a sparkle and shimmer for which there is no substitute but this does not mean that you cannot use either indirect or filtered electric light. Remember that changes in table accessories and décor stimulate the appetite as much as do changes in seasonings. Soup can be served from tureens or in cups. Serve salads in bowls, on plates or crescent-shaped "bone plates," and if you are looking for variety replace individual vegetable dishes with an outsize platter holding several vegetables attractively garnished. You should always vary the décor to suit the occasion and your individual taste.

THE FORMAL DINNER

Even if the number of guests is small, dinner always involves a degree of formality. In addition to general considerations on the care required for a well-regulated dinner, here are some specific pointers to facilitate correct table setting.

The most formal way of laying the table is with a white linen cloth and in former days this was *de rigeur*. The next more formal method is with mats on a plain, polished wood surface. Today scientific advances in the realms of furniture making have provided us with heat- and stain-resistant table surfaces which combine ease of service and visual appeal and there is no reason why these should be ignored.

All glasses are placed in a row behind the plate; water and wine glasses are to the right of the setting with water glasses being filled to the three-quarter mark, while wine glasses are left empty.

There are certain rules about the placing of silver and tableware. All forks are placed to the left except the very small fish fork which goes to the right. Place silver that is to be used first, farthest away from the plate. You should not have more than three pieces of silver at either side. Any other silver can be brought in on a small tray as required. Dishes and tableware should be simple in form and not too pronounced in pattern or colour. These can then be combined without fear of clashing with the varied linens, fruits and flowers, and, most important, varied food.

The place setting for dinner is as follows:

Flat plate on which the napkin is laid.

Soup plate. This is handed, ready filled, when the guests are seated, unless the soup is cold, in which case the plate is set in place beforehand and a tureen passed round from which the guests help themselves.

Table knife, cutting edge turned towards the inside of the cover setting.

Fish knife.

Soup spoon. In France, the convex side is laid uppermost. In Great Britain and the United States, the hollow side is turned up. The same applies to forks.

Oyster or *melon fork* if required.

Table fork, changed with each dish, together with the plate.

Fish fork.

Dessert knife and other cutlery. These are sometimes placed between the plate and the glasses. In France, they are more frequently brought in on the dessert plate. They must never be placed crosswise. The fruit knife and fork and the last dessert plate are laid on either side of the finger bowls.

Individual butter dish with knife. This may be replaced by a side plate on which the butter, the knife and the bread is also placed. A *salad plate* is sometimes laid on the left of the *flat plate*.

Water glass

Red wine glass.

White wine glass.

Champagne glass.

Port glass.

The lower edges of cutlery on either side of the plate must be aligned. The dessert cutlery on the plate is brought into line with the latter.

One rule of good etiquette, rarely observed nowadays, said that butter should not be served with rolls at dinner and that rolls should be laid on a table napkin. For a formal luncheon today, a butter plate is placed to the left of the service on a level with the water glass. This is removed before the sweet is served, or at least after the salad course, is finished. Napkins are folded simply, without any attempt at elaboration, and put on the plates, unless the soup is brought in before the guests arrive; in that case, like the bread, the napkins are put on the left plate. Place cards should be placed at the back of the plate, next to the glasses. For a large dinner, involving many guests, it is usual for the hostess to write out the menus herself.

Salt and pepper pots (desirably 1 set per 2 to 4 persons), are set on the table. Mustard and other condiments are normally passed from the sideboard as required.

Setting the dessert spoon and fork in place above the plate is acceptable at an informal luncheon and usually indicates that finger bowls will not be used.

When it is time to serve coffee, cups and saucers are placed to the right, the spoon in the saucer behind the cup, parallel to the cup handle, which is turned to the diner's right. It is entirely optional whether the entire coffee service is served directly on to the table after dessert or poured individually by a servant from a tray; or for that matter whether the coffee service, together with cups and liqueurs, is carried into the drawing-room when the guests leave the table. Since smoking lessens the sensitivity of the palate it is correct to wait until coffee has been served before placing ash trays and cigarettes before the guests.

Guests of honour if female are seated to the right of the host and if male to the left of the hostess. Food is offered first to the female guests of honour. If there is no special guest of honour you may want to reverse the serving order of each course so that the same people are not always served last. Plates are usually removed from the right and placed and passed from the left.

Although strictly speaking, *demitasse* coffee should be served black, most people provide sugar and cream, and this is nowadays considered correct.

INFORMAL DINING

When trained staff disappeared from the homes of Britain, the pattern of entertaining changed. Few people can nowadays afford to keep servants and entertaining has become restricted to what the hostess can accomplish herself. This, together with modern eating habits, has restricted the number of courses at dinner to three or four and has changed the shape of the menu.

Multiple courses which involve constant last-minute attention in the kitchen by the hostess defeat the object of relaxed and effortless entertaining and the guests will be left standing around not knowing whether to offer to help or not. Menus should be planned so that most of the cooking can be done in advance and the amount that has to be attended to at the last minute, is kept to a minimum.

The first thing when compiling a menu for home entertaining is to choose the main course and then plan the rest of the meal around it. The main course can be meat, fish or game, in season, and much the easiest is a casserole dish that can be cooked the day before and even improves with reheating. That done, the hostess can tackle the rest of the menu, bearing in mind certain proven rules. These are: never serve a meal where the dishes won't wait no matter how exquisite your *soufflés*; never serve a meal with too many elaborate dishes; never serve a meal with two dishes of the same type, for instance, two egg dishes; never serve a meal with strongly contrasted tastes; and never serve a meal where all the dishes are one colour. Blend and subtle distinction, within the limits of your purse, your time and your skill as a chef, are the aims of the modern hostess.

Informal dining does not mean breaking all the rules of etiquette. It implies a judicious bending. It is a help if your first course can be *pâté* or smoked salmon which can be set on the table before the guests arrive, or if you have a hot plate in the dining-room, hot soup which can keep warm while you wait for your guests. If you are having a joint you can also carve this just in advance of service, then it can be rearranged in slices on a platter and handed to each guest. During the course of the meal the host will serve wine which he first tastes himself and then passes to the guest on his left and so on round the table.

A large trolley is a useful thing to have as you can place on it the dishes you have used for the first course and it can also carry the vegetable plates and gravy boats which obtrude on the table in any case. You can also put the salad bowl, dessert and cheese on a trolley or sideboard if you have one. Correctly speaking, salad and dessert should be served in individual portions for formal lunches and dinners. Cheese should be passed round on a large board. But for dining at home it is much simpler to have a large communal bowl for salad and the dessert in a single dish from which everyone can be served.

After salad the table should be cleared and dessert served with only the hostess rising, and it is optional whether coffee is served at table or in the drawing-room.

PRE-DINNER DRINK

It is usual when you are giving a dinner party to serve your guests with drinks before as this will allow everyone to arrive, be introduced and talk for some minutes. Formerly only sherry was served but nowadays a cocktail or a longer mixed drink such as gin and tonic is more usual. You should always have non-alcoholic drinks like tomato juice for anyone who wants. It is usual to hand round cocktail biscuits or savoury *canapés*. These should be carefully prepared and the preliminaries should not be allowed to drag on indefinitely. Too much drink will dull the palates of your guests and lessen their appreciation of your culinary efforts.

Menus

The great traditional menus of ten to twelve courses belonged to the past. Nowadays these elaborate menus have vanished as the result of changing customs, social and economic necessity and even the demands of health and beauty and a menu even of six to seven courses has become exceptional. When serving dinner there was a strict order of dishes and the composition of a grand traditional menu was roughly as follows:

SOUP Usually a clear or thickened soup.

HOT HORS D'ŒUVRE

COLD HORS D'ŒUVRE

FISH

A REMOVE OF MEAT, POULTRY OR GAME Usually a roasted joint or bird or braised meat with garnish.

ENTRÉE Many dishes could be served as *entrée*, but it was usually a dish in a sauce.

ROAST Usually poultry or game. The roast was, and is, accompanied by a green salad but this may also be served separately.

SORBET With menus of many courses it was obligatory to serve a sorbet after the roast (or after the *entrée* if a cold *entrée* was not to be featured after the roast) to cleanse the palate for the next courses.

COLD ENTRÉE This could be *foie gras pâté* or *parfait*, a lobster or crayfish *en Belle Vue*, cold chicken or some other decorated cold dish.

SIDE DISHES These included not only sweets and ices but also vegetables and cheese.

DESSERT AND FRUIT

The following menu, described as a "simple dinner" at the beginning of the nineteenth century, is taken from Antonin Carême's book *The French Maître d'Hôtel*. It consisted of two soups, two *hors d'œuvre* of Russian *canapés*, two removes, two soups, *twenty* entrées, four different roasts, two large and two medium-sized dishes and sixteen smaller side dishes or *entremets* consisting of eggs, vegetables and sweets.

Towards the middle of the nineteenth century radical deletions began to appear, as can be seen from this menu for a dinner at the court of Napoleon III.

Dinner at the Tuileries on 1st February, 1858,

Potage printanier
Riz au consommé
Turbot, sauce Homard et Hollandaise
Filet de bœuf à la Jardinière
Grenadins mignons de poularde
Faisan à la Perigeux
Chaudfroid de perdreau
Casseroles de riz à la Toulouse
Pâtés de foie gras de Strasbourg
Chevreuil
Bécasses
Canetons de Rouen
Asperges en branches
Haricots verts
Gâteau mille feuilles Pompadour
Gelée d'orange et mandarine
Timbale à la Châteaubriand
Corbeille d'abricots au riz

At the beginning of the twentieth century, the number of dishes was again reduced. The menu, even at a banquet, looked something like this.

One thick or clear soup,
One fish,
One remove or entrée,
One roast, usually accompanied by a salad,
One vegetable dish,
One side dish, hot or cold, followed by an ice,
Dessert.

At very elegant dinners, a cold *hors d'œuvre* was served, contrary to general usage, such as caviar, melon or oysters. A single dish was served for each course and this constituted the main simplification.

The remarkable simplification of menus in the second half of the twentieth century should be noted. Even on the occasion of the marriage of King Baudouin of the Belgians to Dona Fabiola de Mora y Aragon on 13th December, 1960, only the following simple meal was served:

Consommé Diane
Homard aux aromates
Selle de marcassin Nesselrode, Purée de marrons
Délice de foie gras de Strasbourg, Gelée au Xérès
Parfait Royal

Luncheon given by the disciples of Antonin Carême, 1959,

Parfait de foie gras
Sole soufflée Abel Luquet
Selle d'agneau Antonin Carême
Sorbet Cointreau
Aiguillettes de caneton nantais (froid) à l'orange
Fromage
Omelette duc de Praslin

Luncheon given at the Jean-Drouant Hotel School, Paris,

Terrine Lucullus maison toast
ou
Saumon rose à la russe, sauce mayonnaise
Poularde royale aux morilles
ou
Entrecôte grillée maître d'hôtel
Jardinière de légumes
Salade
Fromages assortis
Dessert aux choix

Dinner given by the French Culinary Academy, in honour of Monsieur Eugene Lacroix at Lucas Carton, Paris,

Truite saumonée, sauce l'Ermitage
Côte de bœuf rôtie, pommes macaire
Timbale de ris de veau aux petits pois
Terrine Brillat-Savarin, cœurs de laitues
Délices de France
Pêche Madeleine
Rocher de glace vanille
Petits fours
Pouilly Fuissé 1956
Château Montrose 1937
Champagne Irroy 1950

All these menus show that while the number of dishes offered has decreased considerably and some changes have been made in the composition of dishes, the basic construction or pattern of the menu has not changed

However, there have been major changes of detail. Before going into these, one should explain what an *entrée* was in a traditional menu. The *entrée* has never meant, as one might be tempted to believe, the first dish on a menu. In a traditional menu, without any exception whatsoever, the *entrée* follows the dish known as a remove, which was served after fish, if fish appeared on the menu. In principle, an *entrée* should be a hot dish in a white or brown sauce although at a formal dinner it is possible to serve a cold dish instead. While this principle should be followed for formal dinners, in practice, in certain restaurant menus a choice of several "main" courses are listed as *entrées.*

The most important changes that have taken place in menus are the result of the present-day way of life. Few people wish to spend a long time at table. Nor does anyone wish to put on weight. A large joint is no longer as popular as it used to be, especially at luncheon. Small, easily digestible dishes are preferred—quickly sautéed meat, poultry or grills. Stews or *ragoûts* have become less popular. People want a light meal with plenty of vegetables, salad and fruit. In fact, a meal which does not make one feel overfed and makes it possible to resume work afterwards without any difficulty.

Present Day Luncheon Pattern

There are no absolute rules, but in practice a present-day luncheon may look like this:

1. A cold *hors d'œuvre*, an egg dish or fish or a *pasta* or rice dish or soup.
2. A hot meat dish (or *entrée*) or a grill, garnished. A fish dish or egg dish (especially omelette) may be featured if not chosen for the opening course. In summer cold meat may be served, accompanied by salad.

The meal may be completed by:

3. Sweet or dessert, such as ice or stewed fruits, pastry or fresh fruit.
4. Cheese—optional (on the continent this is nowadays often served before the sweet. It also suits those who wish to continue to drink red wine, served with the meat course, with their cheese).

Dinner or Evening Meal

Dinner, or the evening meal, may be more substantial, since time is not so limited. In spite of this, dinners now are far less rich than they used to be. A dinner usually consists of:

1. Clear or thick soup (usually a cream soup) or a small cold *hors d'œuvre* (normally a a "single" *hors d'œuvre*).
2. Fish course or a small *entrée* or a dish of garnished vegetables.
3. A roast garnished with vegetables (and/or salad). When the *entrée* is substantial a small cold dish with salad may be served instead.
4. A sweet course or dessert or fresh fruit.

In Britain some people like a savoury as a final course, and on the continent many people like to finish with cheese.

Normally dinner would only be three courses on everyday occasions and a menu of four or five courses would only be served at a dinner party or formal banquet.

MENU PLANNING

A correct menu, gastronomically speaking, is more difficult to compose than one might think. There are some fundamental concepts which must be borne in mind. Here are the most important:

1. Do not serve the same meat or poultry twice on one menu, even if they are prepared in different ways.
2. Ensure a variety of colours of food and that predominant colours are alternated by courses. Thus you will not serve two white or two brown sauces in succession, for example, if there is a fish in a white sauce it must not be followed by chicken in a white sauce.
3. Vary garnishes from course to course. If serving mushrooms, tomatoes or artichoke bottoms as garnish for a fish dish, do not serve them again with the meat or poultry, nor even as a separate vegetable course. You may, however, use truffles to garnish a cold dish, even when they have already accompanied a previous dish.
4. Vary methods of cooking. Do not follow a boiled or poached fish by a boiled chicken. An exception may be made if the menu is a very long one but this is permissable only if dishes cooked in other styles have intervened.
5. Take into account the time of year and attendant weather conditions, for example, keep thick and nourishing soup for a cold winter's day. Similarly, restrict fat or filling dishes for winter service.
6. Choose vegetables in season, when they are better flavoured and usually cheaper. Avoid serving dried or tinned vegetables during or immediately after the season of the fresh one. When the asparagus season is just over, for example, do not feature tinned asparagus unless it is especially requested. While this rule must be remembered, bear in mind that there are now excellent deep-frozen vegetables, thus making it possible to have fresh-tasting vegetables all the year round.

▲ *A continental breakfast table*

A family luncheon table ▼

▲ *A formal dinner table*

The traditional elegance of a restaurant ▼

7. Do not begin a meal with fruit such as grapefruit or melon if you mean to end with a fruit sweet or dessert.
8. Do not start a meal with *hors d'œuvre* if you mean to end with a savoury.
9. Vary texture. Do not follow a hash or minced meat dish with a milk pudding, nor start with a cream soup if you plan to include a creamed dish or a dish accompanied by a cream sauce later in the menu.
10. Rich savoury dishes such as roast duck, goose or pork need the accompaniment of a tart or piquant sauce to offset their richness and to aid digestion. Fatless white fish, for example, cod, haddock, turbot and whiting, require a piquant emollient sauce (one containing a high proportion of butter or oil), such as *sauce aux Câpres* or *Tartare.*
11. In choosing desserts, remember that a light dessert best follows a hearty meal and vice-versa.
12. Avoid a menu of exclusively cold dishes even in warm weather.
13. Every menu should be written in clear and comprehensible language, though some "French" titles for dishes may be retained on fine menus.
14. Every menu should be correctly written, without a single error. A hand-written or typed menu (top copy) is always pleasanter than a mimeographed one.

Planning Methods for Special Occasions

The rules above apply not only to daily meals but even more to formal dinners. Composing grand menus for special functions demands further thought and care, for example, a chef must bear in mind not only his customers' wishes, the cost of material, the selling price, the time of year, but many other considerations as well. A wedding breakfast will differ in form from the closing banquet of a scientific congress. A hunting breakfast has a different character from a diplomatic dinner. The domestic hostess will not have all these demands to meet but she may well have to plan a meal for an extra special occasion. Even on the most formal occasions, however, it is unusual to go beyond the items listed below:

1. A small portion of a quality soup (usually cream soup) or a fine *consommé* (clear soup) served in cups. At large, official dinners a cold single *hors d'œuvre* may be served before the soup, such as caviar, oysters or *foie gras parfait.*
2. Fish or shellfish.
3. An *entrée* of meat or poultry garnished with vegetables.
4. Roast meat (a fine cut such as beef fillet), game or poultry with accompanying vegetables and salad.
5. Sweet dessert (usually with *petits fours*).
6. Possibly a dainty savoury (cheese may also be offered but it is not the normal custom in formal dinners).
7. Fresh fruit.

While salad, vegetables and fruit must be included in all meals, the question of cheese at large formal dinners is a controversial one. As noted, many continentals contend that cheese must be served before the sweet, but equally many connoisseurs maintain that cheese is out of place at a sumptuous dinner.

Planning Parties

When menu-planning for parties remember:

1. To plan the food for the people you are entertaining, avoiding, if possible, any personal dislikes.

2. If you are entertaining foreign visitors try to include one of our typical national dishes.
3. Develop a repertoire of dishes you feel at ease in preparing and can cook with confidence. Add, then, a few new specialities to this list each year.
4. Do keep a record of the parties you give and the guests who attend each one. In this way you can be sure you will not repeat your menus and serve the same people the same dishes each and every time.
5. Always try out new dishes first on the family to test their reaction.
6. Timing—always aim to have at least two courses that need no last minute attention at all.
7. The choice of dishes both in type and number must have a relation to the skill of the cook, the help available and the equipment in the kitchen.

A SELECTION OF MENUS

Here are a few menus, some simple and some more complicated, devised largely in the continental tradition but adapted for British use. They have been devised for the season of the year or for a particular occasion.

Spring

Luncheons

Avocado pear with sea food
Noisettes of lamb Salvatore
Cheese
Fruit Salad

Dinners

Chicken Consommé, Cheese straws
Fresh asparagus, Hollandaise sauce
Saddle of venison à l'Allemande
Chicory Salad
Charlotte russe

Summer

Hors d'œuvre plate
Entrecôte Steak Vert Pré
Heart of lettuce salad
Cheese
Strawberries and cream

Cream soup Ilona
Crayfish tails au gratin
Coq au Riesling
Noodles Alsacienne
Salade à Béatrice
Chilled raspberry soufflé

Autumn

Poached eggs Massena
Boiled brisket of beef Flamande
Cheese
Syllabub

Consommé Madrilène
Quenelles of whiting à la Lyonnaise
Pheasant Vallée d'Auge
Salade Mercédès
Pear Cardinal

Winter

Artichokes à la Grecque
Escalopes of Sweetbread Jérôme
Cheese
Profiteroles au Chocolat

Lobster cocktail
Cream of Chicken Soup
Saddle of hare à la Bergère
Bombe glacée Diane

Theatre Meals

Before

Assorted canapés
Consommé Julienne
Smoked salmon
Chicken à la Financière
Garden peas à la Française
Creamed potatoes
Peach melba
Coffee

After

Fruit juice or
Tomato soup
Veal noisettes
Sauté potatoes
Broccoli
Fresh fruit salad
Coffee

Dinner Menus

Soup à la Portugaise
Fillets of sole Meunière
Capon in Reisling
Noodles à l'Alsacienne
Beatrice Salad
Chocolate soufflé
Cheese

Vegetable consommé
Paupiettes of sole Daumont
Grilled steak
Braised celery
Matchstick potatoes
Orange tart
Cheese

Onion soup Gratinée
Filets of sole Monte Carlo
Pork chops à la Normande
Creamed potatoes
French beans à la Portugaise
Norwegian Surprise Omelette
Cheese

Avocado Cocktail
Tunny fish à l'Indienne
Veal fricassée
Stuffed tomatoes à la Hussarde
Broccoli
Mille Feuilles
Cheese

Lunch Menus

Soup Crécy au Riz
Sautéed veal Marengo
French beans
Macaire Potatoes
Tangarines Côte d'Azur

Artichauts with sauce Vinaigrette
Chicken suprême Maryland
Green salad
Sauté potatoes Maître d'Hôtel
Strawberry tart

Afternoon Teas

Ham sandwiches
Salmon sandwiches
Mixed fruit barquettes
Gâteau Hongrois
Apricot preserves
Brown bread
Tea

Tomato sandwiches
Chicken sandwiches
Scones
Assortment of small cakes
Brown bread
Black cherry jam
Tea

Breakfast Menus

Fruit juice
Cereal
Smoked Fish
Fried bacon and mushrooms
Toast and rolls
Tea or coffee

Grapefruit
Cereal
Omelette
Croissants
Marmalade
Tea or coffee

Fruit juice
Cereal or porridge
Scrambled eggs and grilled bacon
Toast and hot rolls
Honey and marmalade
Tea or coffee

Cereal
Stewed fruit
Bacon and sausage
Hot toast and rolls
Honey
Tea or coffee

Wedding Breakfast

Canapés riches
Cream of Asparagus soup
Salmon steaks Louis XVI
Breasts of guinea fowl with lychees
Palm shoots à la Milanese
Almond soufflé, Zabaglione with port

Diplomatic Dinner

Clear turtle soup with sherry
Fillets of sole Atelier
Saddle of lamb Richelieu
Lettuce hearts with celery
Slices of duck in aspic with oranges
Savarin Othello

Closing dinner for a Congress

Melon cocktail
Devilled clear soup
Red mullet à la Niçoise
Spit-roasted chicken
Green peas à la Française
Cress and beetroot salad
Kirsch parfait
Barquettes Cadogan

CHRISTMAS MENUS

These should include all the traditional dishes of Christmas.

Christmas Day

Breakfast

Orange, grapefruit or pineapple juice
Cereal
Boiled eggs, hot rolls or toast
Black cherry jam
Oxford marmalade
Tea or coffee

Dinner

Cocktail de Melon à l'Americaine or
Crême d'Orge
Roast Turkey
Prune stuffing
Bacon rolls
Bread sauce
Gravy
Cranberry sauce
Glazed chestnuts
Cauliflower, Brussels sprouts, roast potatoes
Christmas pudding
Brandy sauce or Brandy butter
Mince pies

For a light lunch or supper

Onion soup with grissini
Salad Tonnello, lettuce
Bavarois à la Crême

One of the most satisfactory ways of entertaining a large number of people is to give a buffet supper party. These vary enormously in their scale and intention. The simplest type of buffet meal is a barbecue or a Wine and Cheese party, while the grandest is a full scale reception at a hotel.

Barbecues and Wine and Cheese parties are both easy ways of entertaining your friends and the number of people you have at any time will depend entirely on the facilities you have available. The common factor to both is that the menu is reduced to the simplest possible ingredients which means less trouble and effort in the kitchen.

Barbecues can be elaborate and you can if you are adventurous, cook chicken, wrapped in foil (*en papillote*) with sauce and salad served separately as a variant to the usual sausages and chops. Fruit or fruit salad can take the place of dessert, with beer or wine to drink or a cup depending on the tastes and age of your guests.

Mostly buffets will take the place of a dinner party. In these cases you can make the food as simple and grand as you wish and it is often an opportunity for you to provide a glamorous array of cold dishes which show your ability as a chef. It is a good idea too, to have one hot dish. The easiest to start with is hot soup which you can keep warm on a hot plate but you can provide a large casserole with rice as an accompaniment or maybe just baked potatoes to go with cold meat.

PLANNING A BUFFET

Whatever you choose as the main dish for a meal, plan a menu that has a good balance. Certain cakes and puddings or savoury flans manage to look a complete mess when more than a few helpings have been removed. Food that has to be carved by the guests is not a good idea and turkeys and beef should always be carved in advance. A large but shallow cake is always preferable to a thick, towering one on a buffet table. To avoid the pitfall of having your carefully arranged table look like the aftermath of a battle, cater generously, as guests are apt to take larger helpings than normal. Where there is any danger of over-crowding the serving surface, use two tables.

Remember chairs for the guests to sit on and tables where they can put their food as it is more difficult for a guest to attempt to carry on conversation while holding a drink in one hand and a plate of food in the other. Small tables are ideal for this but chairs round the walls or cushions may do as well. The room in which the buffet is to be held (preferably not the same one in which the host receives his guests) must be cleared of small pieces of furniture which may cause people to trip. The buffet should be laid out on a long, narrow table covered with a white damask cloth reaching down to the floor. The table should be neither too high nor too low in order to make service easier. A second smaller table should be set aside for drinks which will be handed round to the guests.

If possible, try to have one fairly skilled barman, amateur or professional, to look after the distribution of the drinks. No matter how informal the gathering, people do tend to shy away from the task of selecting and pouring drinks for themselves. If all the guests are seated together, wine may be poured either directly by the host, who will also hand round the glasses, or wine may be passed in its bottle with each guest pouring his own into the glass at his place. The same self-catering technique can be used to hand round coffee.

The table decorations are important. The buffet table should correctly be covered with a white damask cloth. However, this tends to be formal in effect while entertaining should be merry and light-hearted. Moreover, anything spilt stands out distinctly against a white background and upsets and spillage are unavoidable at buffets. In recent years, guided by a strong Danish influence, the tendency has been to emphasise the essentially informal nature of this gathering by using mats or gay linens.

Table decorations need not be costly but they should be imaginative. Arrange some flowers on the buffet table behind the food and for an evening party use candles to create a graceful atmosphere. Above all make sure that your decorative piece on the main buffet table is standing on a very solid base or it may be upset. It is much better to remove flimsy floral decorations and ornaments to individual tables where people sit down to eat and have time to admire the overall effect of the room and its décor.

Lastly a word on procedure; guests may form a line at one end, pick up plates which have been stacked within convenient reach of the foods, either serve themselves or be given servings from main dishes. Secondary dishes, such as buttered rolls, salads, relishes, are placed on the adjacent dining tables. Soiled dishes are returned to the buffet table and promptly put out of sight. The necessary silver should be attractively arranged, not piled, near the plates while napkins may be neatly sandwiched between the plates. If your tableware has a predominant colour theme then often it is a good idea to have the napkins either in a strongly contrasting shade or in a colour which is a shade lighter or darker than the main colour but tones in with it. Make an effort to have everything both convenient and inviting. A well-arranged buffet table is a delight to the eye and an invitation to the palate.

Many recipes and suggestions for simple dishes will be found in the chapters on cold *hors d'œuvre*, cold eggs and mixed salads. Skill, taste and experience will enable you to choose many fine cold dishes ranging from fish to game which will give great pleasure to everyone. Fruit salads, cold *zabaglione*, charlottes, *savarins*, *parfaits* and ices will be the favourite desserts. Do not forget *petits fours* and cakes.

If you have more than ten guests, prepare two plates of each dish.

Choose the drinks to suit the dishes and the time of day; at the end of the morning and at lunch time serve vermouth, sherry, Bellini cocktails, white and *rosé* wine, or champagne; in the evening, all apéritifs, cocktails, wines, fruit juice and minerals.

FORMAL BUFFET

The most formal buffets are those which are held in hotels, at public functions, or when the host is entertaining a large number of people. In a first class hotel it is always an occasion of great brilliance (*see illustrations on pp.* 26 *and* 27).

The chef and some of his assistants, or the waiters, will stand behind the buffet tables to serve the guests. Their number will depend on the number of guests, who will themselves choose the dishes they want. Fish, poultry, crustaceans and game, are presented on the same types of plate as this helps to avoid confusion. Soup is optional, being hot or cold according to the time of year. If there is only one dessert provided (e.g. *Oranges Riviéra*) it will be served to the guests in portions.

The drinks will be offered in the appropriate glasses placed on silver trays and handed round by waiters. Some guests prefer to sit down to eat in which case the waiters will go round pouring out wine for each place setting, as requested by the guests. Beer is not usually served unless a guest specially requests it.

A selection of dishes for Formal Buffets

The following recipes will be found in the relevant sections (*see index*).

Hors d'œuvre Cocktails

Crustacés * *Shellfish*

All cold rock lobster and lobster dishes given in the chapter on cold shellfish dishes are suitable for use at a formal buffet.

Poissons d'Eau * *Freshwater Fish*

Salmon Bellevue.
Salmon steaks Moscow.
Smoked salmon cornets *à la Russe.*
Smoked salmon rolls Rosa Branca.
All cold salmon dishes.
Trout: All trout dishes which are sufficiently decorative may be used.

Darnes de Saumon Louis XVI * *Salmon Steaks Louis XVI*

For 20-22 persons: 2 fillets of salmon of about 2¼ lb without skin or bones, poached for 12-15 *minutes; 50 prawn tails;* 20-30 *small tomatoes;* 11 *oz mousse of pimento* (½ *lb pimento* (*red pepper*) *purée,* 3 *oz aspic jelly*); 22 *half quail eggs;* 22 *black* (*Spanish*) *half olives;* 22 *poached mushroom caps;* ½ *lb red salmon caviar; melon balls scooped out with a spoon;* 1½ *lb vegetable julienne;* ½ *pint Mayonnaise;* ¾ *pint Mayonnaise Collée;* ¾ *pint aspic jelly. For decoration: mushrooms; black olives; tangerine segments; crayfish tails; gulls' eggs; leek; tomatoes; red peppers;* 1¾ *pints sauce Chantilly or sauce Verte.*

Wrap the salmon fillets in buttered paper and place them on a rimmed deep tray. Poach in a little *court-bouillon*, in the oven, till just done. Leave to grow quite cold under slight pressure. Bind the vegetable *julienne* with the *Mayonnaise* and 3½ oz half-set aspic. Fill into a round, fairly shallow mould and leave to set in a cool place. Turn out on to the middle of a large round dish. Cover entirely with *Mayonnaise Collée*. Decorate with the mushrooms, black olives, tangerine fillets, halved gulls' eggs, leek, tomatoes and glaze with aspic. Dress the crayfish tails all round the salad and glaze them with a glazing brush. Cut the salmon into very even slices, and garnish each slice with a mushroom cap and place a small spoonful of red caviar on top. Glaze with aspic. Dress the salmon steaks around the salad, rounded end pointing inwards. Place small tomatoes filled with pepper *mousse* on the outer edge, between the pointed ends. Garnish each tomato with half a quail's egg garnished with half a black olive. Glaze. Finish off with a ring of glazed melon balls. Serve *sauce Chantilly* or *sauce Verte* separately. (*See illustration p.* 27).

Poissons de Mer * *Sea Fish*

Cod *à la Russe*
Fillets of sole Floralies.

Bœuf Froid * *Cold Beef*

Glazed beef *en Berceau.*
Fillet of beef Rothschild.
Fillet of beef *à la Russe.*
Fillet of beef Vintner.
Ox tongue Karachi.
Ox tongue Princess.

Veau Froid * *Cold Veal*

Glazed topside of veal *Grand-mère.*
Cold saddle of veal

Porc Froid * *Cold Pork*

Ham cornets Astor.
Andalusian style ham.
All the more elegant cold ham dishes.

Roulade de Jambon * *Savoury Ham Roll*

For 50-60 slices: 8 eggs; ½ lb flour; ¼ lb butter; ¼ oz salt; ½ lb purée of boiled ham; ¼ pint whipped cream; ¼ pint aspic jelly; 1 tablespoon brandy. Cooking time: 8-10 minutes.

Whisk the eggs and salt in a double boiler and continue until the mixture draws threads. Then whisk till cold. Gently mix in the flour and melted butter, pouring in the latter in a thin stream. Fold lightly, so as not to make the mixture heavy. Spread on a buttered and floured baking sheet, about ⅛ inch thick and bake in a hot oven, 425° F or Gas Mark 7, for about 10 minutes. Remove from baking sheet immediately and leave to cool, covered by a slightly moistened cloth. Season the ham *purée* with paprika and brandy and combine with the half-set aspic and whipped cream. Spread this *purée* quickly on to the sponge, roll up and put in a cool place. When the *purée* is quiet cold cut into slices about ⅜ inch thick.

Volaille * *Poultry*

Poultry *ballotines* and galantines.
Poultry *chaudfroid.*
Selection of poultry and pies.

Choix de Volaille et de Pâtés * *A Selection of Cold Poultry and Pâtés*

For 20-30 *persons:* 1 *cold roast chicken;* 1 *cold roast pheasant;* 1 *cold roast duck;* 1 *Chicken Pâté en croûte;* 1¼ *lb foie gras mousse;* 3 *lb Waldorf salad;* 8 *peeled, deseeded and quartered tomatoes;* 10 *turned mushrooms; some strips of red pepper;* 10 *small slices of Chicken Galantine;* 6 *oz foie gras cream;* 5 *or* 7 *truffles surprise;* 10 *small halved green peppers prepared à la grecque* (*Greek style*), *garnished with a salad of diced mushrooms, gherkins, cooked chicken and crushed tomatoes, marinated wtih Vinaigrette and a little tomato ketchup;* 3 *hardboiled egg whites;* 5 *quartered tomatoes;* ¾ *pint aspic;* 1 *sculpture in butter;* 1 *bunch of grapes.*

Remove the breasts and breastbone of the ducks. Fill the carcase with the *foie gras mousse* and cover symmetrically with the flesh of the quartered tomatoes. Place a line of round slices of white or hardboiled egg down the centre. Glaze with aspic. Slice the duck breasts diagonally and place them on slices of Galantine spread with *foie gras mousse*; glaze with aspic. Remove the breasts and the breastbone of the chicken. Fill the carcase with Waldorf salad in a dome and arrange the sliced breasts on top. Place the turned mushrooms in the centre with a line of red pepper strips on top and glaze with aspic. Glaze the pheasant with aspic and cut about 10 slices of the Chicken *Pâté*. Place the butter sculpture at one end of a long dish with the chicken, duck, pheasant and Chicken *Pâté* in front of it. Place the bunch of grapes between the duck and the sculpture. Garnish lengthwise with slices of pie, stuffed peppers, the slices of duck decorated with a tomato slice and a pointed sliver of hardboiled egg white, the truffles cut in quarters and the quarter tomatoes filled with Waldorf salad and glazed with aspic. (*See illustration p.* 25).

Suprême de Dindonneau Champs-Elysées * *Turkey Breasts Champs-Elysées*

For 20-30 *persons: the breasts of a* 9-10 *lb roast turkey;* 30 *slices of Chicken Galantine;* 40-50 *radishes cut into rosettes;* 30 *tangerine slices;* 30 *half pistachios;* 15-20 *tomatoes, peeled and scooped out;* 2 *lb Waldorf salad;* 15-20 *slices cooked celeriac;* 10 *artichoke bottoms;* ½ *lb red pepper julienne;* 7 *truffles surprise;* 1 *tartlet case baked blind;* ¾ *pint aspic.*

Season the inside of the tomatoes. Marinate the celeriac slices, artichoke bottoms and pepper *julienne* separately in oil, vinegar, pepper and salt. Drain well. Fill the tomatoes with Waldorf salad. Place them on the celeriac slices and glaze with aspic. Fill the artichoke bottoms with pepper *julienne* and glaze them too with aspic. Glaze the truffles with aspic and place them in a ring in the middle of a round dish. In the middle of this ring place the tartlet filled with Waldorf salad. Around the truffles place first the artichoke bottoms, then the stuffed tomatoes on celeriac slices and lastly the slices of Chicken Galantine. On each place a fine slice of turkey breast, cut diagonally. Decorate these with a tangerine slice and half a pistachio. Glaze with aspic. Finish off with an outer ring of radishes cut into rosettes. (*See illustration p.* 25).

Foie Gras

Foie gras medallions and *mousse*

Gibier * *Game*

Glazed wild duck.
Glazed pheasant.

Selle de Chevreuil Grand-Duché * *Saddle of Venison*

For 18-20 *persons:* 1 *saddle of venison, about* 6½ *lb;* 24 *round slices of poached apple, decorated with half a cherry and a small piece of truffle;* 4 *pineapple slices;* 24 *truffle flakes;* 20 *cooked artichoke bottoms;* ¾ *lb julienne of marinated green peppers;* 6 *truffles surprise;* 32 *fluted and marinated mushrooms;* 8 *tartlet cases baked blind;* 10 *oz Waldorf salad;* 1⅞ *pints aspic.* Cooking time of saddle: 40-45 minutes.

Roast the saddle, keeping it underdone. Let it cool. Remove the fillets from the bone and cut into thin diagonal slices. Replace the slices on the carcase so that they overlap. Cut each pineapple slice into 8 triangles and arrange them in place of the vertebrae, which has been removed. Arrange them close to one another with a tiny piece of truffle on each. Glaze the whole of the saddle with aspic. Fill the tartlets with Waldorf salad. Glaze these tartlets, also the truffles, the apple slices and the mushrooms. Fill the artichoke bottoms with the marinated green pepper and prepare triangular wedges of aspic *croûtons.*

Presentation: Line a large rectangular dish with a thin coating of aspic. When set, place the saddle of venison in the centre. Place apple slices down each side and a truffle flanked by 2 mushrooms at each end. Place the artichoke bottoms and aspic *croûtons* on either side of the saddle, and the tartlets garnished with Waldorf salad at each end. Place a truffle surrounded by 7 fluted mushrooms in each corner. Cumberland sauce may be served with it if desired. (*See illustration p.* 28).

Galantine de Selle de Chevreuil Renoir * *Saddle of Venison Galantine*

For 15-18 *persons: lardons;* ¼ *pint brandy;* 6 *each coriander seeds, black peppercorns, juniper berries;* 1 *clove;* ½ *bay leaf;* 1 *tablespoon chopped parsley;* 2 *tablespoons olive oil;* 2 *fillets of venison;* ½ *lb bacon;* 1½ *lb Mousseline forcemeat made with venison trimmings; Waldorf salad.* Cooking time of the venison: 35-40 minutes.

Lard the fillets with thick lardons marinated in brandy and spices. Butter a long mould with a rounded bottom thoroughly, and bard with thin slices of bacon. Cover the bottom and sides of the mould with a thick layer of forcemeat. Insert the fillets of venison and cover with forcemeat. Knock the bottom of the mould on the table several times to spread and settle the forcemeat. Cover with lightly buttered paper and poach in the oven in a water-bath. Keep the fillets underdone. Keep in a cold place for at least 6 hours before slicing. Cut a slice of 5-6 oz per person and glaze with aspic as desired. Serve with the Waldorf salad allowing approximately ¼ lb for each person.

Pâtés

Salades

The most decorative, subtle and lightest mixed salads.

Fruits

Baskets of fruit with a generous selection, well decorated.

Desserts

Charlotte Royale.
Charlotte Russe.
Oranges Riviéra.
Savarins.
Cold *Zabaglione.*
Ices, iced *coûpes, parfaits* and ice puddings.

Pâtisserie et Confiserie * *Pastry and Confectionery*

Appropriate cakes (wedding, anniversary).
Dry and iced *petits fours.*
Dipped crystallised fruit.
Chocolates.
Handmade sugar basket.
Croquembouche with *Choux* pastry.

COCKTAIL BUFFET

If you are having a cocktail party you will usually serve *canapés* and light refreshment at the same time. The more subtle and colourful these are, the more they will be appreciated. Use plates and trays that can be passed easily without being a nuisance to the guests.

The following is a good selection:
Small puff pastry fancies with anchovy, cheese, caraway seeds, ham.
Smoked eel *canapés* with pickled cucumber, carolines (small *choux* pastry cases piped with

▲ *A selection of Cold Poultry and Pâtés, p. 22*

Suprême de Dindonneau Champs-Elysées, p. 22 ▼

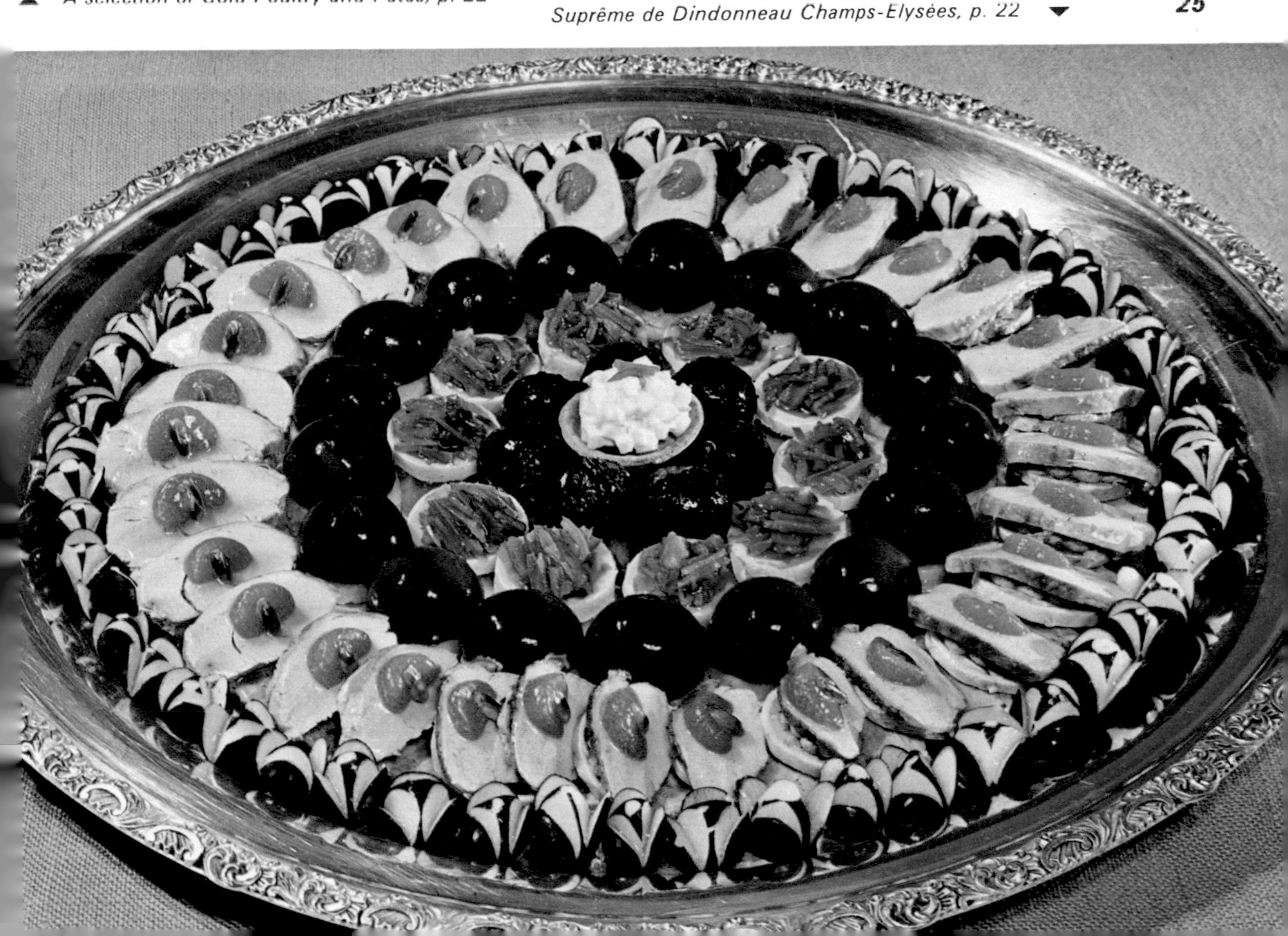

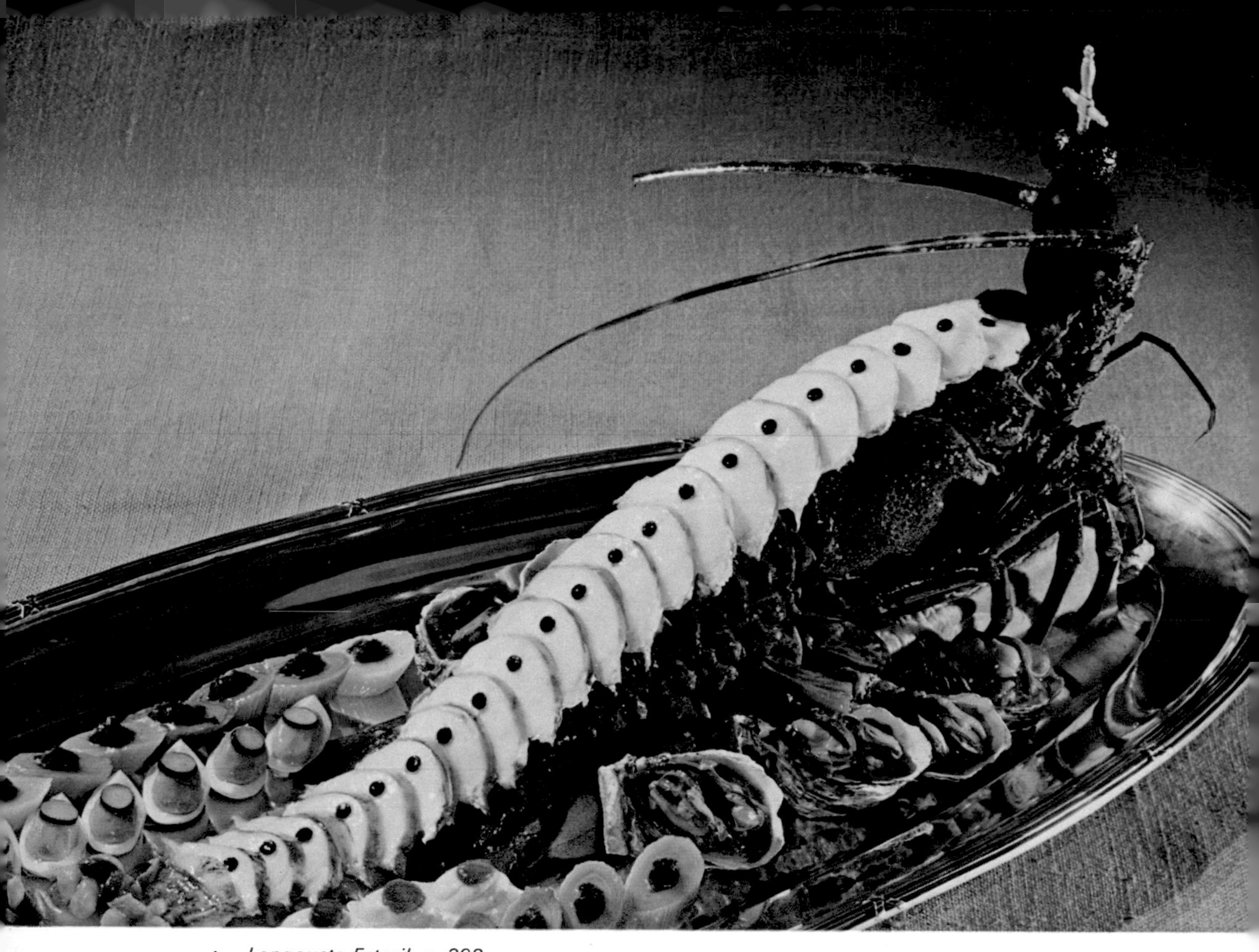

▲ *Langouste Estoril, p. 398*

▲ *Darnes de Saumon Louis XVI, p. 20*

A selection of dishes for Formal Buffets, pp. 20-24 ▼

▲ *Selle de Chevreuil Grand-Duché, p. 23*

Oranges Riviéra, p. 794 ▼

savoury *purées*), *canapés* of cured or smoked meats with stuffed olives, raw ham *canapés* with gherkins, cheese cubes sprinkled with caraway seeds and garnished with the white of hardboiled egg.

Puff pastry *barquettes* filled with truffled chicken salad, *canapés* of white bread spread with Gervais cheese, *canapés* of brown bread with slices of tomato and Emmenthal cheese sprinkled with paprika; slices of apple cooked slowly in butter and wrapped in slices of lean, grilled bacon. *Canapés* of shrimps and fresh butter, cornets of smoked ham filled with Gervais cheese, *canapés* of hardboiled eggs and caviar.

Grapefruit skewered with slices of *salami*, round slices of gherkins and pickled cucumbers, small cocktail onions pickled in vinegar, green peppers, cheese cubes dusted with paprika. Surround with small pieces of puff pastry cut in fancy shapes.

Grapefruit skewered with black olives, radishes, slices of pickled cucumber, cubes of cheese dusted with paprika. Surround with small pieces of puff pastry cut in fancy shapes.

Red cabbage skewered with crayfish tails, black olives, stuffed olives, small radishes, small celery hearts, garnish of small pieces of puff pastry cut in fancy shapes and chipolata sausages.

Slices of fresh cucumber covered with salmon, small *canapés* of brown bread spread with creamed cheese with a slice of tomato on top, *canapés* of bread spread with salmon *mousse* and Petit Suisse cheese.

Puff pastry *barquettes* filled with truffled lobster salad, *gorgonzola* and creamed *gruyère* mixed with diced brown bread and served in paper cases. *Canapés* of wholemeal bread, buttered and spread with cheese, with a garnish of red pimentos.

Thin slices of buttered white bread covered with slices of tomato topped with a small artichoke bottom, slices of cheese garnished with sweet peppers.

Salted almonds.

DANISH BUFFET

One of the common features of Scandinavian cuisine is the *smorrgasbord*. This idea has come over from Scandinavia within the last few years and its popularity has spread at an astonishing rate. The "sandwich table" or *smorrgasbord* can vary from just a few sandwiches to every variety of food imaginable, from herring, smoked eels, colourful vegetables, to a wide variety of cheeses. This "cold" table is usually served in small pottery bowls and dishes and provides an ideal setting for a summer party or a light luncheon. The point to remember is that this type of buffet must be presented as attractively and decoratively as possible and there is no limit to the extent to which an imaginative hostess can exercise her powers as long as she does not mix strong, individually flavoured, basic food—fish with fruit, or meat with cheese.

Here are a selection of typical dishes that can be served as a *smorrgasbord*.

Sliced roast pork garnished with pickled cucumbers, lettuce hearts and sliced tomatoes.

Sliced pickled tongue with lettuce hearts.

Cold sliced roast beef garnished with fresh cucumber.

Sliced boiled ham garnished with fresh cucumbers.

Danish caviar, chopped onions, parsley and radishes.

Hardboiled egg *Mayonnaise* garnished with tomatoes, asparagus and lettuce leaves.

Prawn salad with cocktail sauce, surrounded with lettuce leaves.

Julienne of pickled tongue and (red beet) beetroot bound with *Mayonnaise*, garnished with cucumbers, tomatoes and sliced, sweet peppers.

Salad of asparagus tips in *Chantilly mayonnaise.*

Sea food salad with *Chantilly mayonnaise* seasoned with ketchup and garnished.

Quartered hardboiled eggs and sliced tomatoes, garnished with parsley.

Asparagus tips.

Cornets of smoked salmon with asparagus tips and parsley.

Small steaks *Tartare* on lettuce leaves, egg yolks and salt served separately.

A sliced wholemeal, white and brown bread with fresh butter.

Small pickled onions, black olives, radishes, gherkins and pickles.

Small fillets of cold pork garnished with orange quarters.

Danish *pâté de foie* in aspic garnished with lettuce leaves and slices of grilled bacon.

Herring salad Gripsholm (pickled herrings, diced apple and cucumber, *Mayonnaise*, double cream and horseradish).

Sardines marinated with ketchup.

Tinned herrings.

Salad of herrings, cucumbers and *macédoine* of vegetables with sweet and sour sauce.

Matjes herrings garnished with onion rings.

Smoked mussels in *Mayonnaise.*

Pickled herrings garnished with gherkins and cucumber.

Drinks: For a reception in the country, first serve an apéritif and in summer, Bellini cocktails; with the buffet white and *rosé* wine, Danish beer, fruit juice, minerals.

Cooking has been called "an art that requires the discipline of the sciences", and so it follows that the good cook, no matter how much natural flair he or she demonstrates in the preparation and handling of foodstuffs, still requires a deeper understanding of the skills which are used daily in the kitchen. This knowledge will improve the dexterity of the chef and a better appreciation of the culinary craft will mean that basic kitchen processes will be executed with more care and accuracy, which will result in more outstanding dishes.

There are few foods which do not require further elaboration by way of cooking and few which are consumed in their natural raw state for best appreciation of their particular taste. Most foods may be treated by a variety of methods of heat transfer or cooking. It would be much simpler if there was only one method of cooking which could be applied to all foodstuffs, but appreciation of the various methods of cooking will prove that it is necessary to good cooking to acquire and understand these basic skills and the different processes that are involved in using them.

BOILING

Strictly speaking, there are very few occasions in the kitchen when food is actually "boiled". Most of the time we are referring to the simmering process. The practical difference between these two terms can be measured by the amount of surface movement of water, or ebullition, which is set up by the rapidity of the convection currents. The difference in water temperature is almost negligible—rapid boiling takes place at a temperature of 212° F or 100° C, while simmering requires a drop of three or four degrees of temperature to around 200° F or 97° C. Here the surface of the liquid is merely agitated whereas in rapidly boiling water the speed of water evaporation is stepped up without raising the cooking temperature of the water or liquid. (Beyond 212° F, water changes character and becomes steam). The result is that in rapidly boiling water delicately textured foods such as fish, potatoes, peas and beans are broken up by the bubbling action and should therefore be simmered. Meats boiled at 212° F become tough and unpalatable; so also do eggs. Simmering is essential to eliminate loss of nutrients, loss of character and colour and also loss of texture and flavour of the food.

If we put meat in cold or lukewarm water and then raise the temperature to 212° F, much of the protein content and valuable meat juices will be allowed to pass into the water. This will appear as scum on the surface of the water and the resultant meat broth will be strong and tasty. The meat itself will suffer by a corresponding loss of flavour and proteins. If you want to seal in the juices and flavour then the meat should be immersed in boiling water which helps seal off the surface pores. Cooking is then continued at simmering point, about 200° F, during which process the toughest meat becomes tender and the shrinkage and weight loss inherent in any cooking process is reduced to a minimum. Vegetables after their preliminary preparation should be placed—initially at least—in boiling water. This will set the natural dye which gives them their individual and distinctive colouring. Here cooking is continued at the simmering point.

On the rare occasions when rapid boiling is recommended, this is done to produce violent evaporation and is used for the reduction of wine or stock for glazes. This will produce a small quantity of concentrated "jus" or gravy.

STEAMING

In steaming the heat is transferred by steam and not water. As a method of cooking it is often ideal. The texture of the food is generally lighter and more digestible than foods cooked by any other method. This greater palatability is produced by the unique effect of steam on food. Nothing other than fat is dissolved out of the food cells. Little or no water is absorbed leaving the food full of flavour with all its nourishing properties preserved. Colouring matter is not dissolved or radically altered by steam and the loss in appetizing aroma is slight. The sole drawback is that this is an appreciably slower method of cooking than most.

Steaming may mean cooking *directly* with steam from boiling water or *indirectly* by placing the food in a covered container which is set over the source of steam and the food is cooked in the steam of its own juices. The direct method of immersing a food container or enamel bowl in a saucepan which is three-quarters filled with boiling water, usually demands that the food, possibly small sections of poultry, meat or whole English puddings, be protected by wrapping in greaseproof paper; otherwise the condensed particles of moisture which form will fall back on to the food making it soggy.

The essential points to note with both types of steaming are to maintain the rate of water evaporation by keeping the water boiling steadily—when necessary add fresh boiling water—and to ensure that the steamer should have a tightly fitting lid to prevent the escape of steam.

STEWING, COOKING A L'ÉTUVÉE OR CASSEROLING

Cooking *à l'étuvée* or slow stewing and casseroling, as processes of cooking, can be compared with steaming since all involve cooking by the prolonged action of moist steam. The differences are that in these forms of gentle cooking both steam and a little liquid (water, stock, wine, etc) and sometimes fat are used as the heat transfer agent and that the whole process takes place in a closed dish. Such stewing is essentially a long slow cooking process suitable for the tougher and cheaper cuts of meat, shin of beef or scrag-end-of-neck mutton. It differs from boiling in that a comparatively small amount of liquid is used. This liquid or stock must be in the correct proportion to the quantity of meat to be stewed, not only to obtain a full-bodied, well-flavoured gravy but also to ensure that the self-basting action as the steam condenses on the tight-fitting lid is maintained at regular intervals. Since this is a long, slow process it is essential to have a well-fitting lid as this will minimise the loss of evaporated liquid and juices.

A certain amount of confusion exists between the terms "casseroling" and "stewing" and "cooking *à l'étuvée*", but in fact *en casserole* and *à l'étuvée* are synonymous as regards a description of a method of cooking. In Britain, however, we tend to use the term "stewing"

Illustrated Culinary
Techniques

TURBOT

Halve the turbot lengthwise cutting directly through the fish head.

Cut off the fins with a pair of good strong scissors.

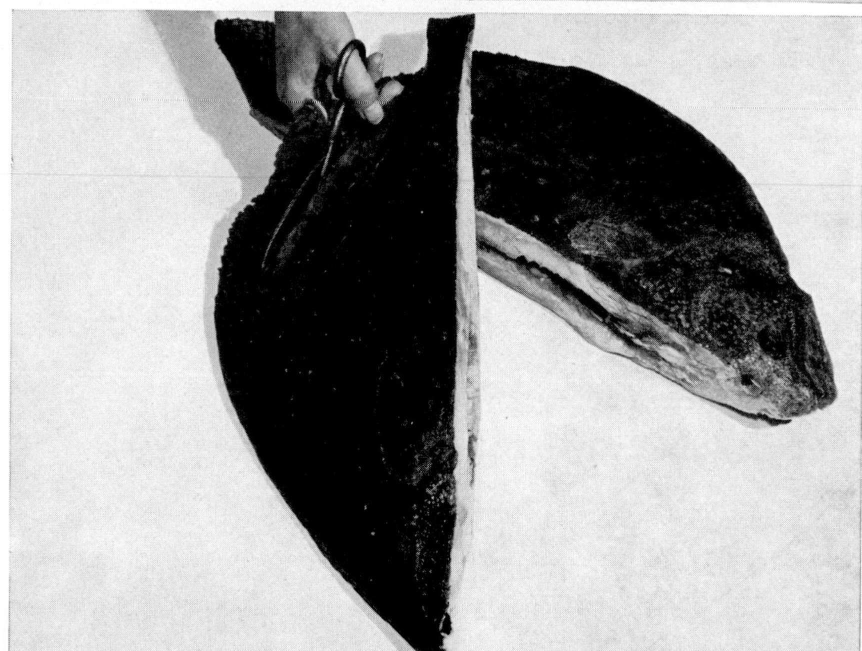

Slice each section into *darnes* or fish steaks according to the required thickness.

SOLE

Remove the outer skin from both sides of the fish. Beginning at the tail and with a sharp, tearing movement, strip off the skin.

Detach the four fillets from the backbone by sliding a sharp, flexible knife along the bone from head to tail. Use long, sweeping strokes of the knife.

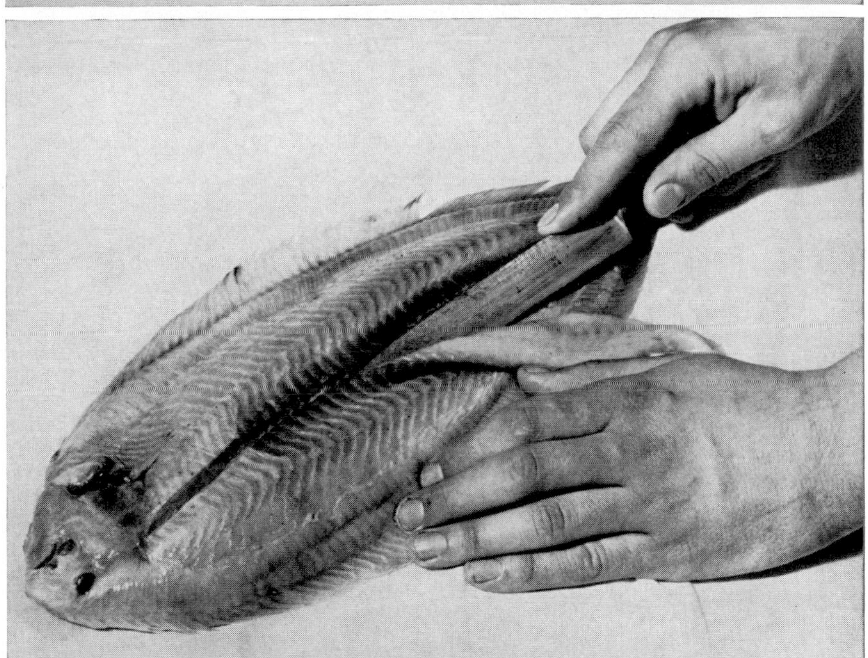

Fold the fillets and place in a buttered *sautoir* with some chopped shallots and fluted mushroom caps. The fillets are now ready to be poached.

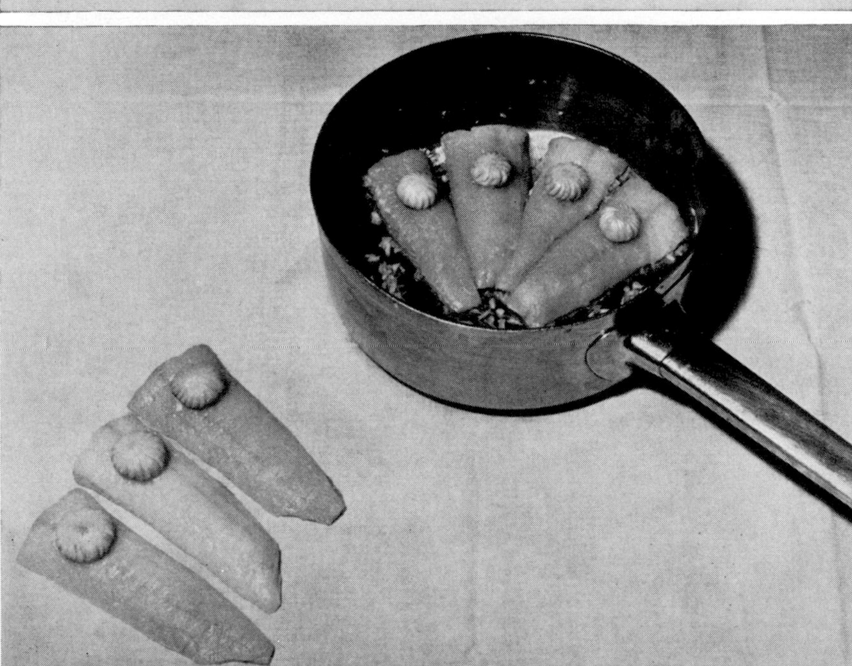

SOLE COLBERT

Place the cooked sole on a dish and remove the backbone which should lift out easily if the fish is properly cooked. Garnish with small pats of *maître d'hôtel* butter.

SHELLFISH

A selection of Dublin Bay prawns served as *hors d'œuvre* or *entrées*.

SCALING LARGE FISH e.g. SALMON

Cut off the fins with sharp scissors. Run a firm knife or fish scraper along the surface of the fish to remove the loose coating of scales. Hold the blade flat to avoid cutting the skin.

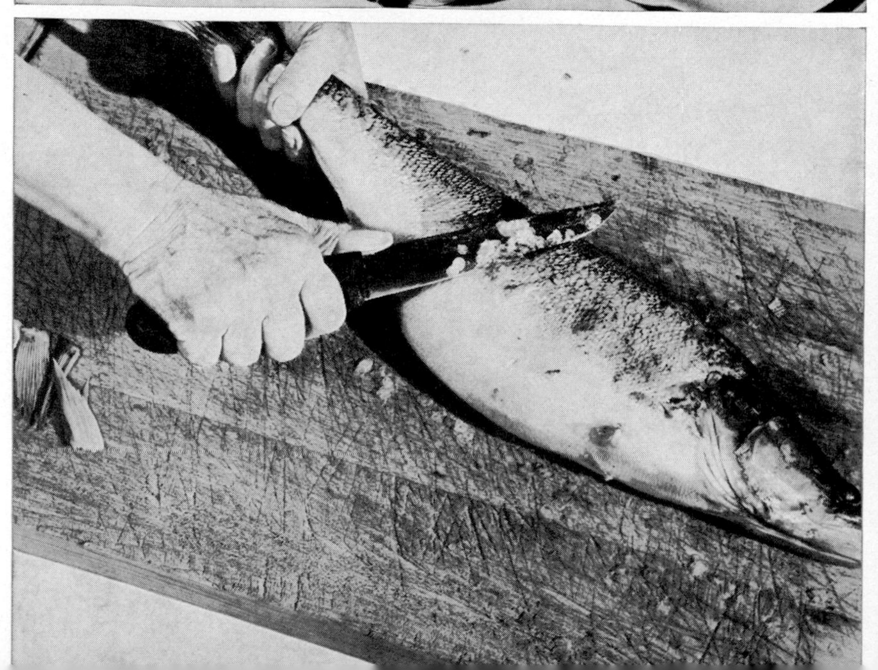

SCALING LARGE FISH e.g. SALMON

The fish head should be cut off just behind the gills. Angle the blade slightly.

The fish may be gutted from the opening behind the gills instead of splitting open the stomach. Insert the curved tip of a skimming ladle through the opening and draw out the intestines.

Fish cutlets and the whole washed fish ready for poaching.

CRAWFISH OR SPINY LOBSTER

Tie the living crawfish to a small plank of wood. This prevents the shell curling up after cooking and so makes it easier to remove the flesh in one piece.

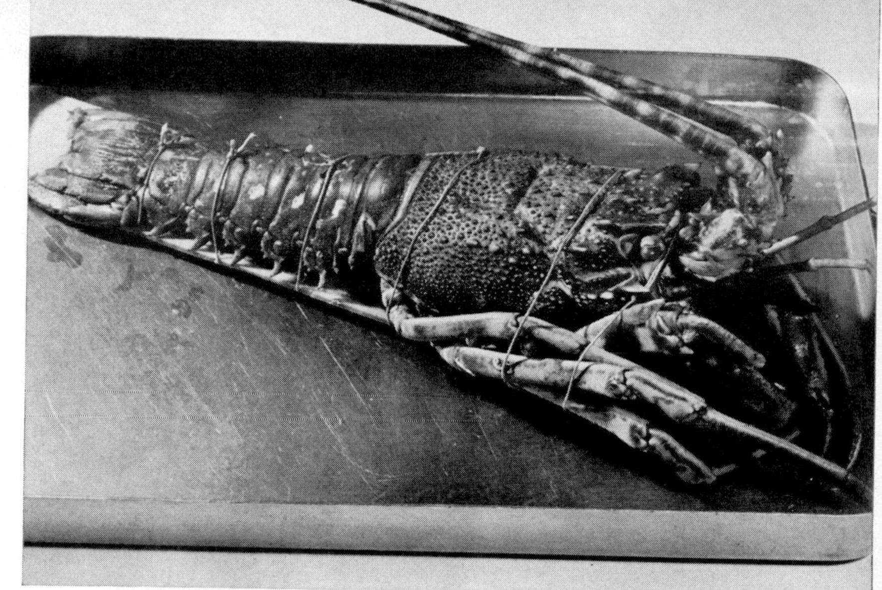

Cook and allow to cool down completely. Make two incisions in the underside with scissors.

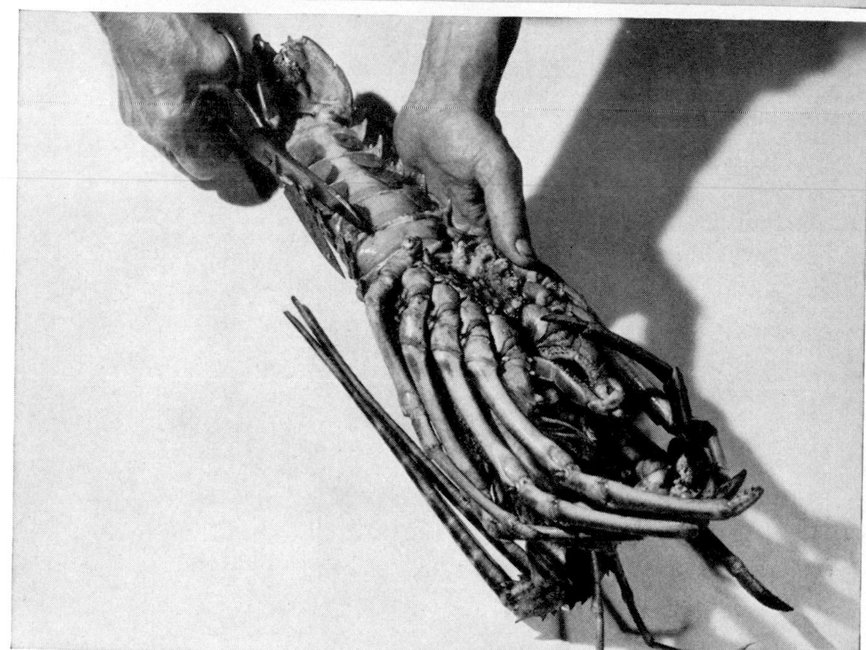

Bend the shell back a little and ease out the flesh carefully.

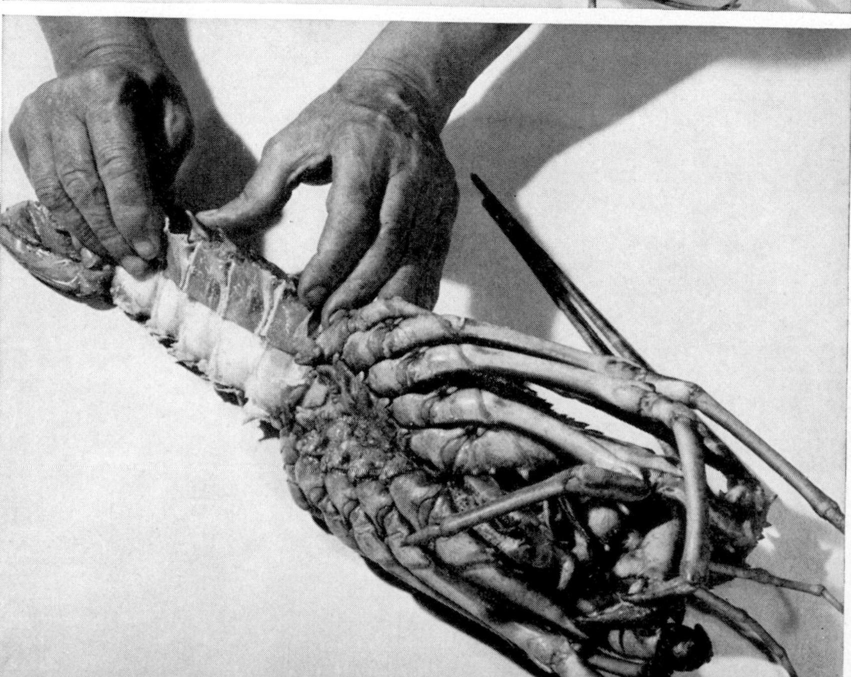

CRAWFISH OR SPINY LOBSTER

The flesh should be removed in one piece.

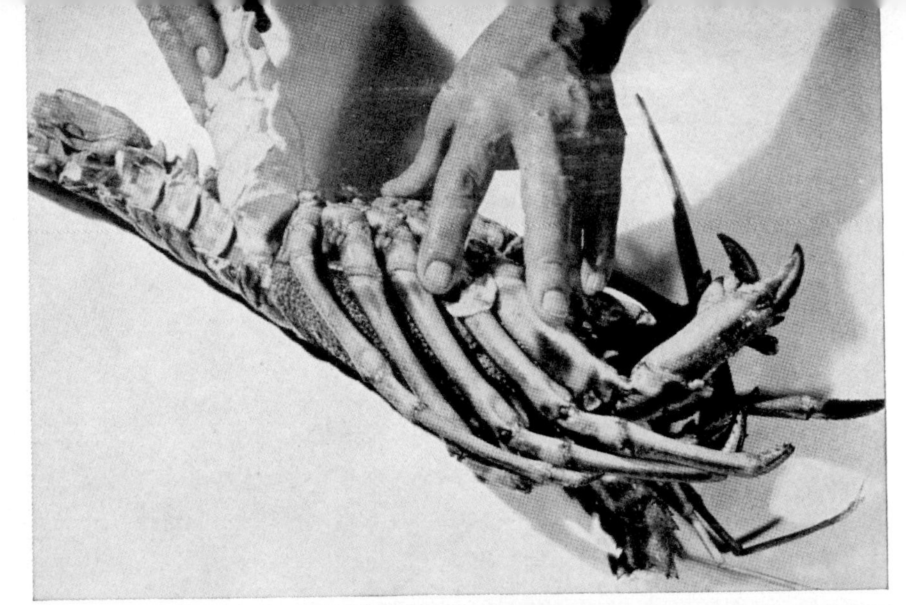

Divide the crawfish meat into neat, small pieces. The shell should be left completely intact and may be used for decoration.

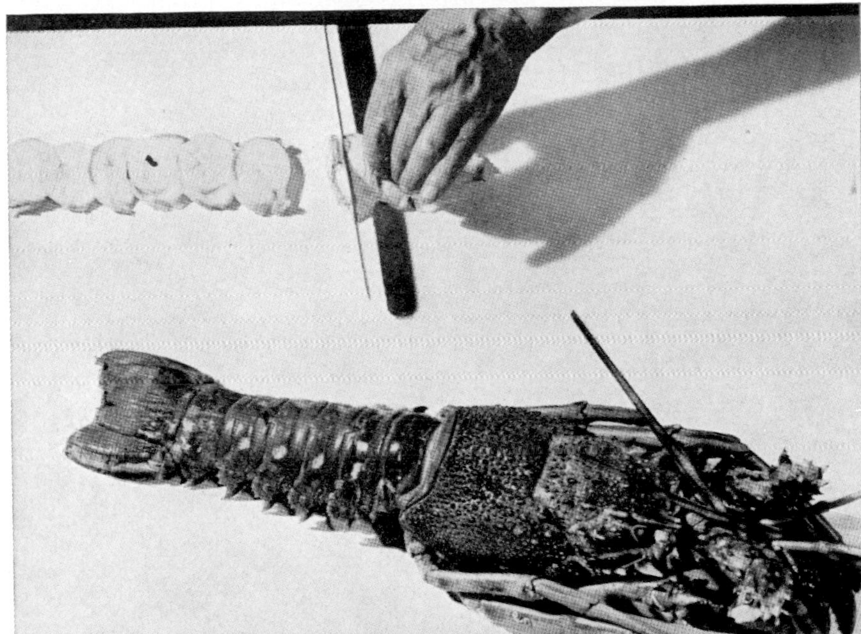

QUENELLES

Quenelles are made in a variety of shapes and sizes. They may be piped from a savoy bag straight into boiling, salted water, piped into very small bulbs on to a flat pan or moulded with spoons into shapes of various sizes.

RAVIOLI

Roll out the noodle paste into a thin rectangle about ⅛th of an inch thick. Divide one half of this into squares. Pipe the meat filling on to the centre of each square. Moisten slightly the other half of the pastry.

Fold this remaining half over the meat-filled squares. Press it down with your hand and with the flat of a pastry cutter to make it stick. Cut out the ravioli with the wheeled edge of the pastry cutter.

POTATOES

Potatoes cut and shaped in various designs prior to cooking.

POTATOES

Piped Duchess potatoes using various types of nozzles. These potatoes can be eaten without further cooking or they may be deep-fried or baked.

GARNISHES

An assortment of decorated cold boiled eggs. These can be used to garnish main dishes but are mainly used as cold *hors d'œuvre*.

The preparation of vegetable garnishes ready for cooking.

PUFF PASTRY

Make a well in the centre of the flour and to this add a small knob of butter (about 2 ounces) which has previously been mixed with an equal quantity of flour.

Add the water and a pinch of salt and mix to a firm and pliable paste.

Shape the paste into a ball. Make two incisions in the paste as shown.

PUFF PASTRY

Butter and paste ready to be combined.

Place the butter in the centre of the rolled pastry and envelope with the four pastry flaps.

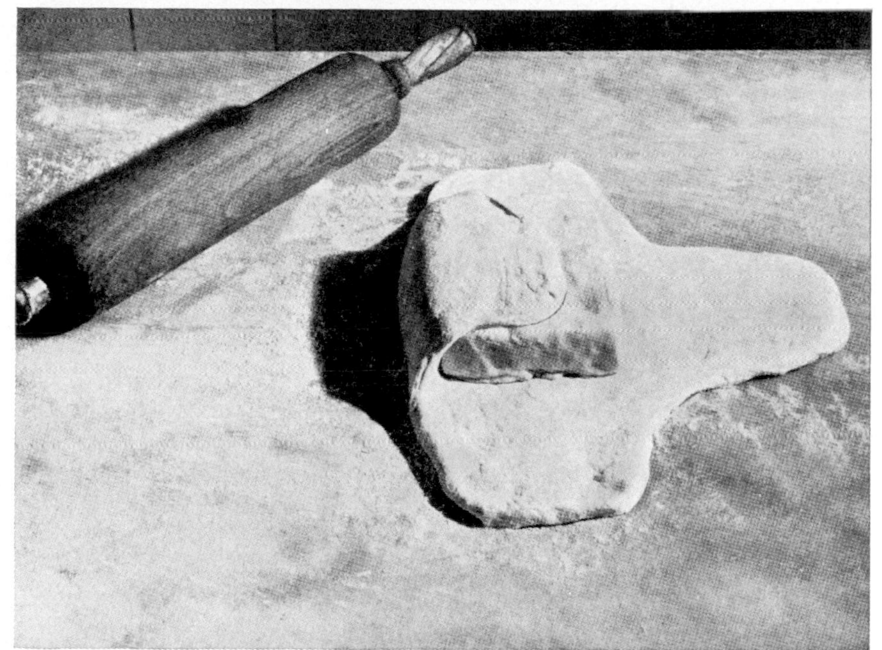

The pastry should be rolled out and folded as illustrated.

PUFF PASTRY

Roll out the pastry into a rectangle about $\frac{1}{4}$ of an inch thick. Bend the two outer edges back to meet in the centre of the pastry.

PALMIERS

Roll out the puff pastry thinly and fold over four times sprinkling with sugar between folds and press down. Now slice the pastry, and place on a lightly moistened baking tray and bake.

The baked *palmiers* ready for further decoration and filling

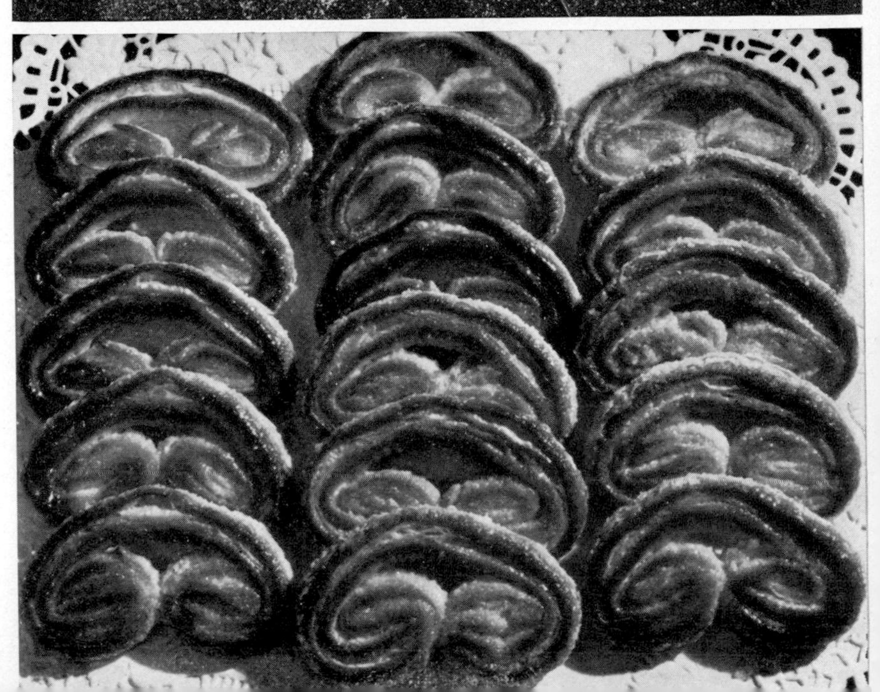

THE CLASSIC VOL-AU-VENT CASE

Cut out a large circular section of puff pastry. Prick the surface and lightly dampen the edges.

Cut out a ring from another circle of puff pastry of equal diameter. Join these two pieces edge to edge. Score the ring and brush with beaten egg. The unused interior section will serve as a lid and should be brushed with egg and baked at the same time.

The baked *vol-au-vent* cases ready to be filled.

THE MODERN VOL-AU-VENT CASE

Make a ball with some scraps of paper enveloped in a piece of tissue paper and tied up with string. Cut out a circular disc of fairly thin puff pastry. Place the paper ball in the centre and glaze the edge with beaten egg.

Cover this with another disc, larger and thicker. Seal the two edges well. Prick the cap.

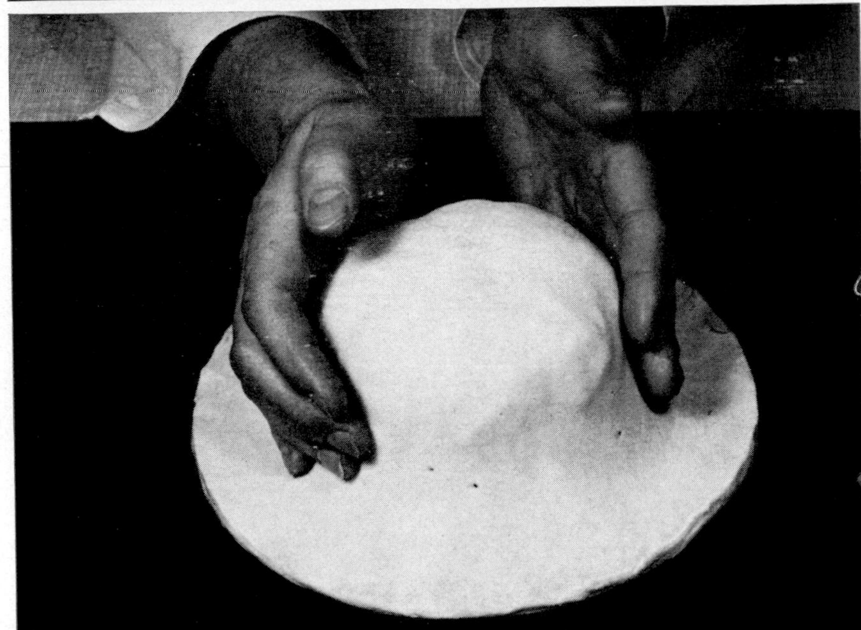

Glaze with beaten egg. Cut out four long strips of pastry and arrange around the cap and edges

THE MODERN VOL-AU-VENT CASE

Cut out another thicker ring of puff pastry and seal into position.

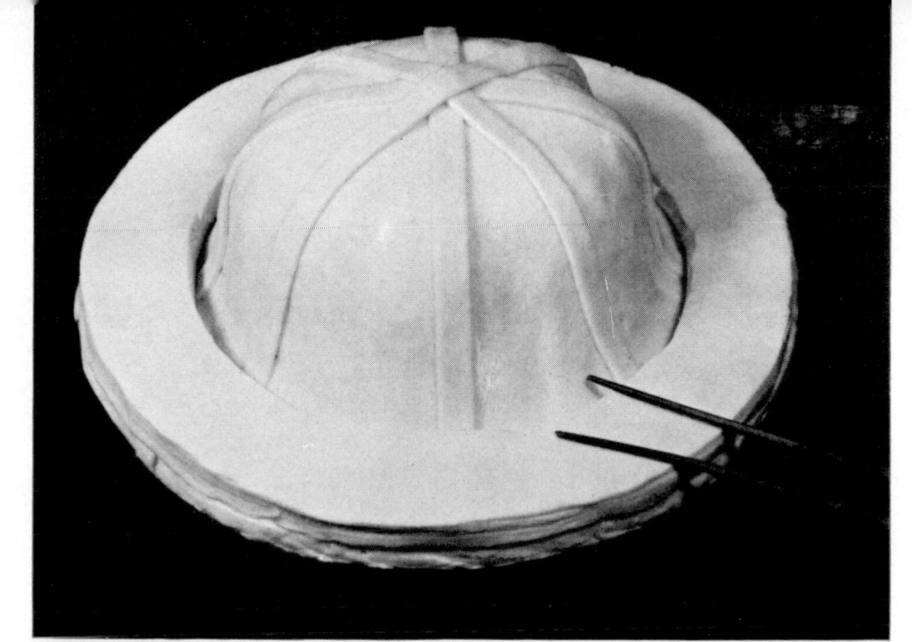

Decorate the *vol-au-vent* with various pastry designs, made with the help of a pastry cutter. Place a decorative crown on top of the cap to mark out the opening. Prick the paste with a fine needle in several places to prevent its splitting open while baking. Glaze again and bake in a very hot oven.

After baking cut round the inside edge of the upper crown—this will then become the pastry lid. Snip the paper ball with scissors and gently lift out the paper and string.

LARDING

Upper—Insert strips of bacon lengthwise right through the body of the meat.
Centre—Here the lardons are inserted crosswise (suitable for a saddle of kid or veal).
Lower—Lard lengthwise but closer to the surface (suitable for beef or veal fillets).

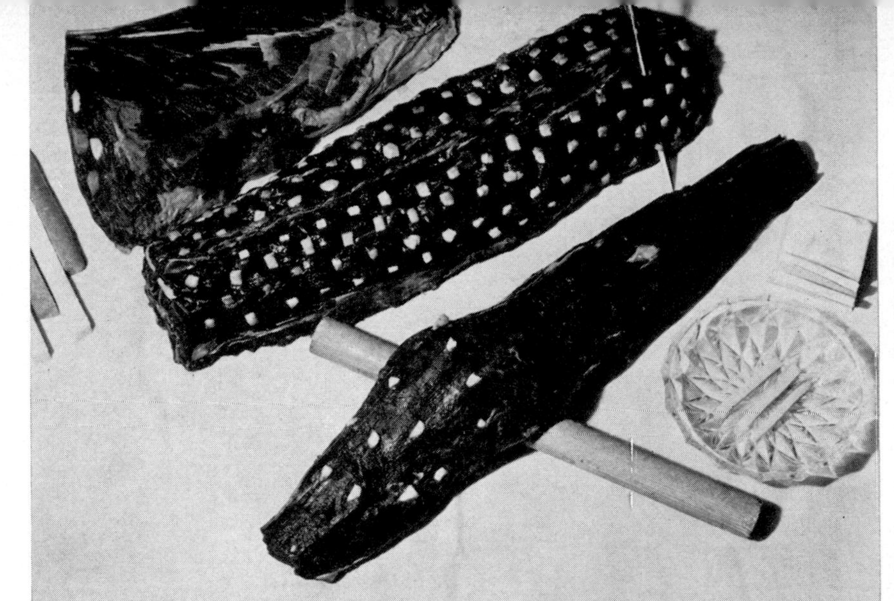

PAUPIETTES

Trim the meat into a neat oblong and gently flatten. Coat with stuffing.

Roll up the *paupiettes* and secure with string.

GRILLED CHICKEN

Remove the entrails from the chicken and split down the centre of the breast bone with a very sharp knife. Now remove the breast bones.

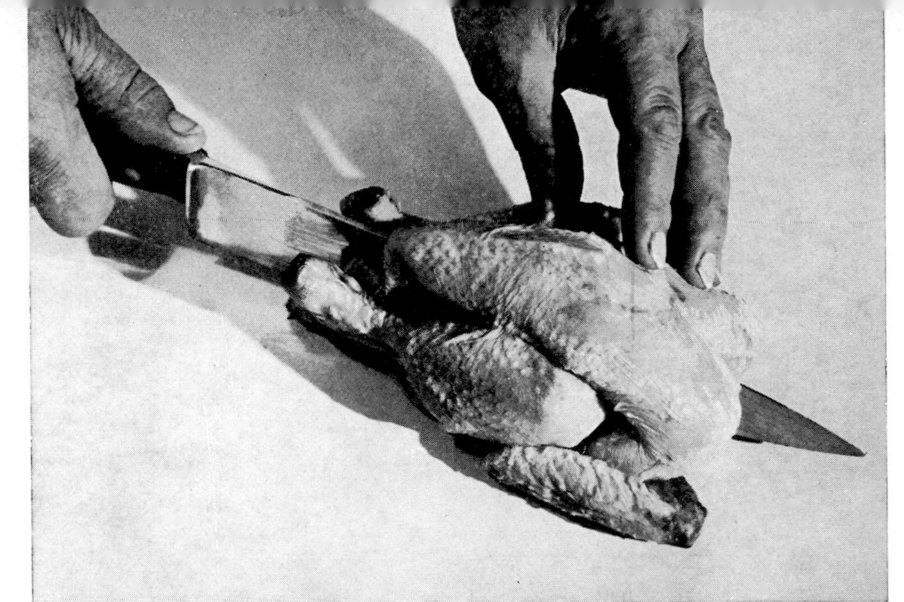

Flatten the chicken to give it a regular shape and more even surface.

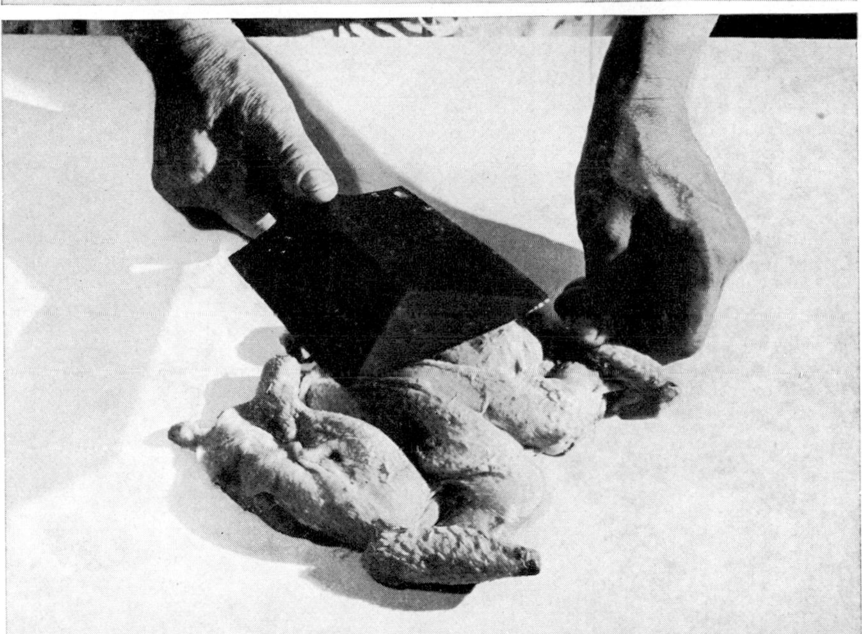

Insert the drumsticks into the skin. The chicken must retain this shape both before and after cooking.

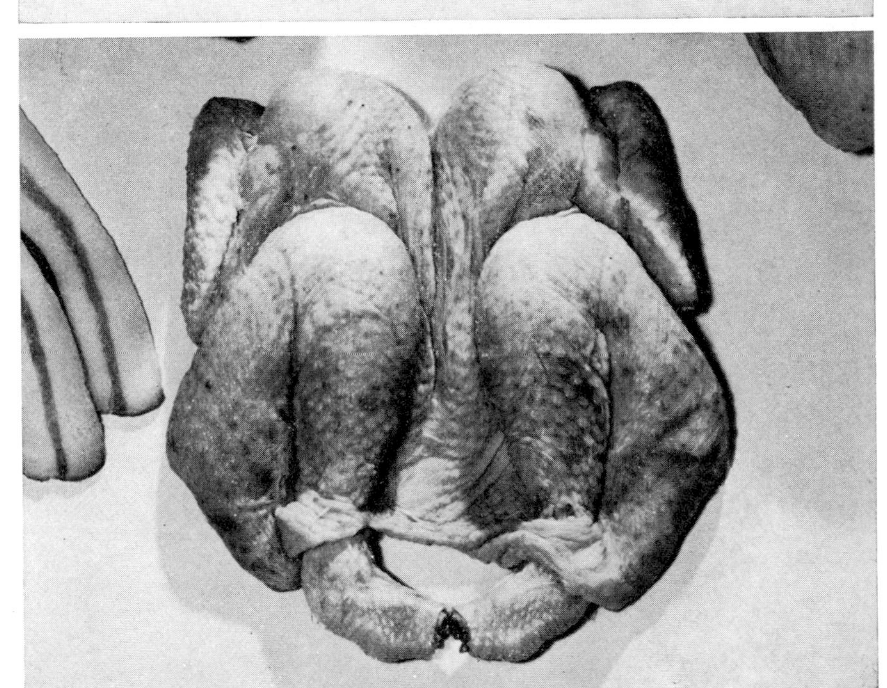

A JOINTED RAW CHICKEN

Drumsticks and top of the leg, wings or *suprêmes* and the back cut in two and trimmed.

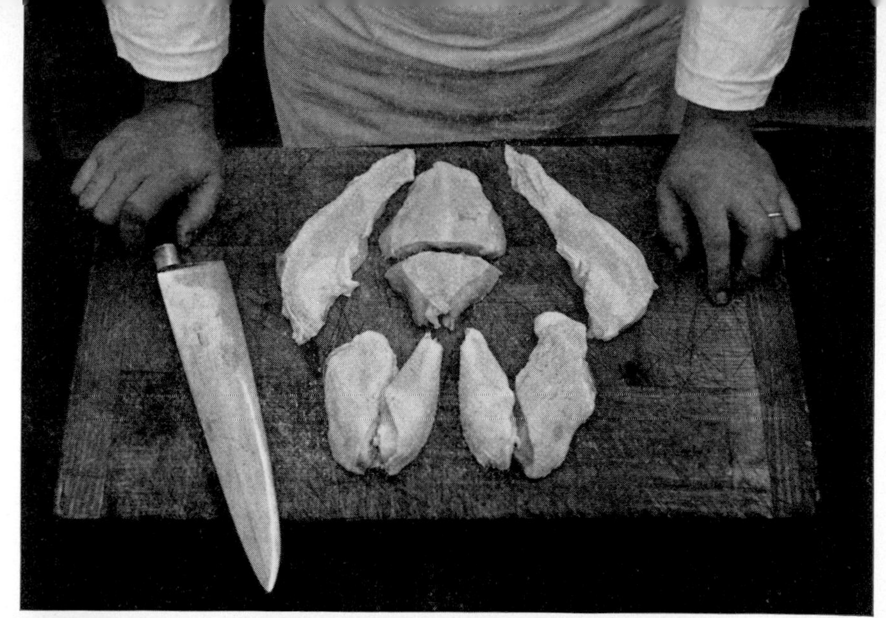

Trimmings: head, carcase, feet, neck and winglet.

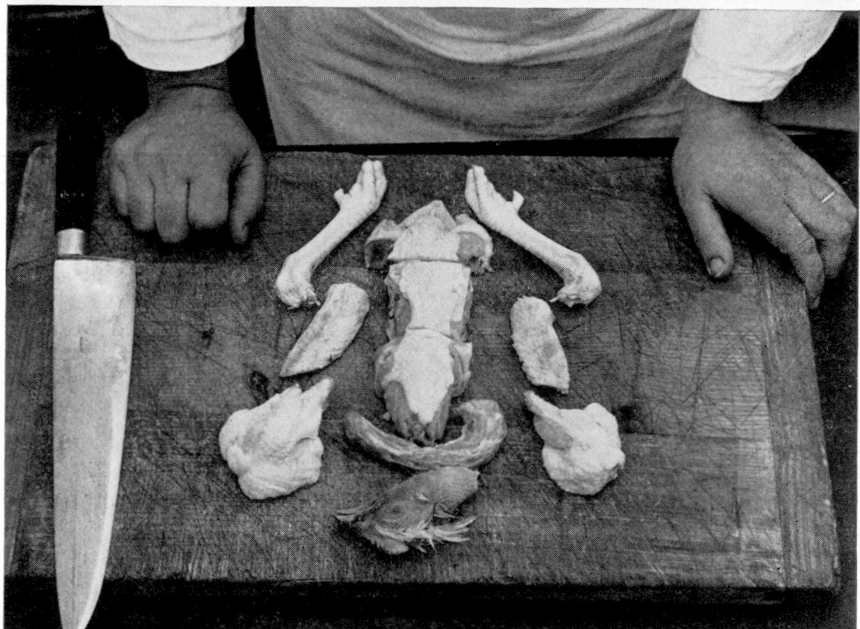

SUPRÊME OF CHICKEN

The *suprême* is the white flesh of the chicken, carved from either side of the breast bone. Often this will include both the breast and the wings. In the case of a larger bird the breast alone will form the *suprême*. It is best cooked by placing in a shallow buttered pan.

COLD STUFFED PHEASANT OR CHICKEN

Truss and bard the fowl prior to roasting.

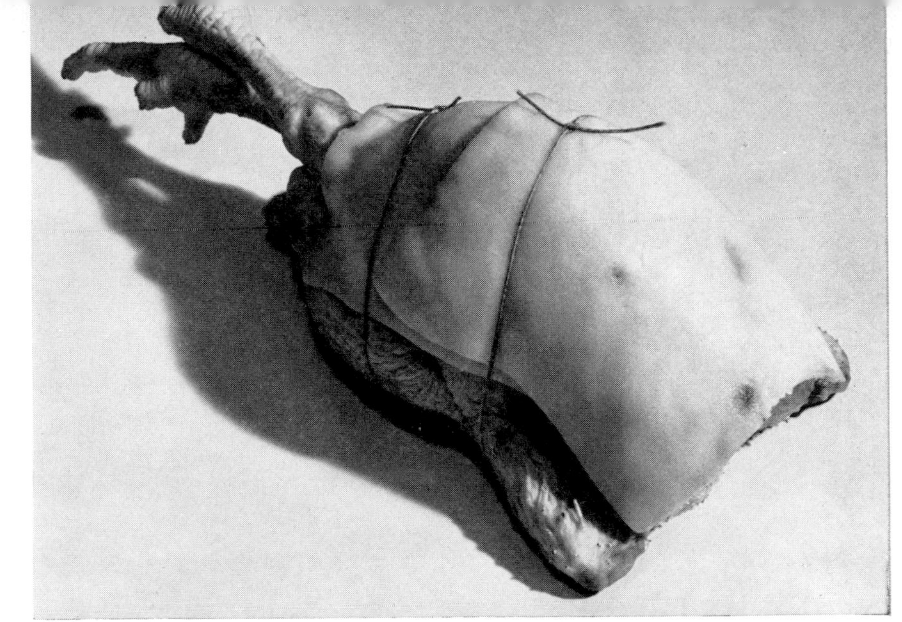

Roast the chicken and allow it to become quite cold. Slice away the breasts in one single piece and lift out the breast bone with a pair of scissors.

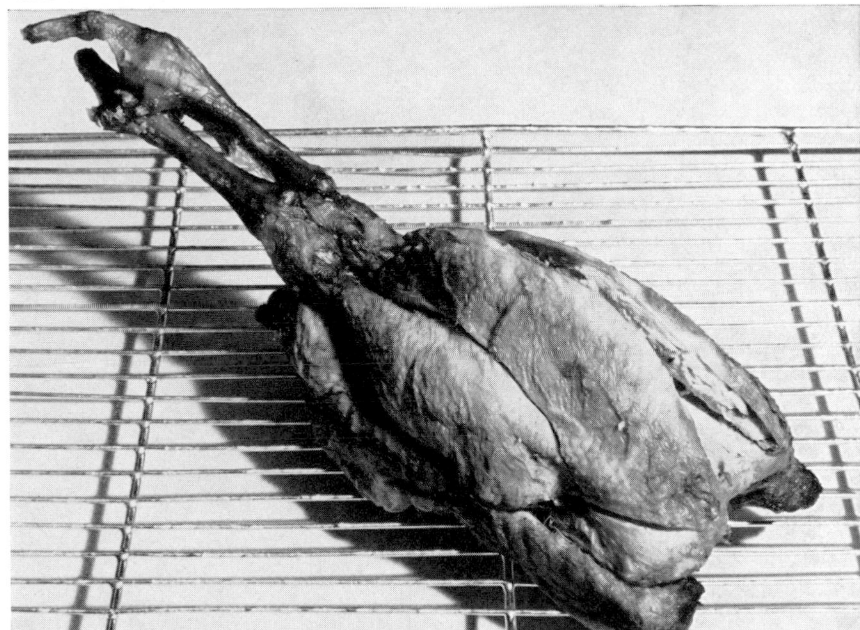

Fill the breast cavities with stuffing and shape the stuffing to resemble the original shape of the breast.

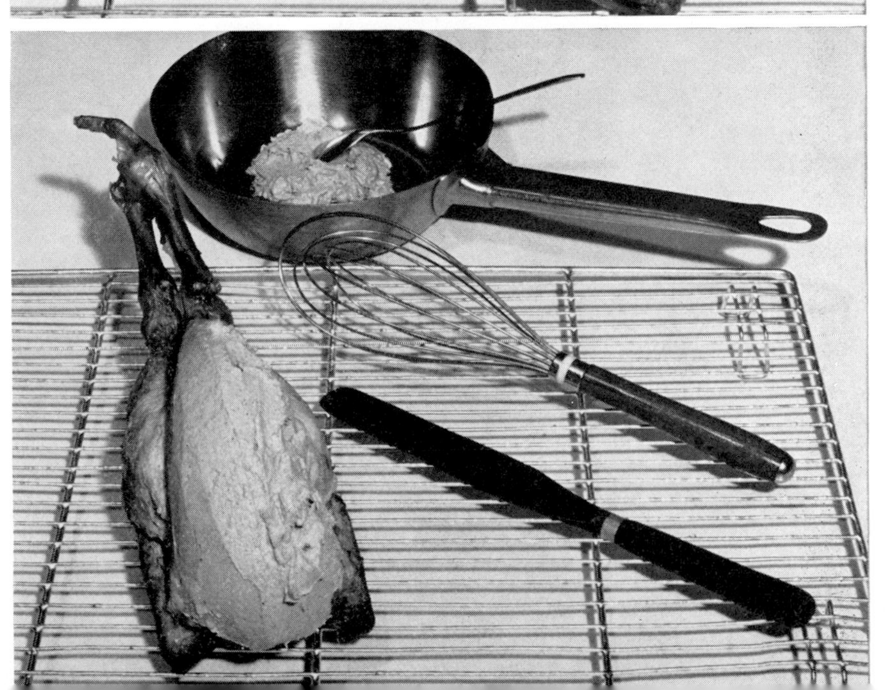

COLD STUFFED PHEASANT OR CHICKEN

Slice the breast thinly and insert each slice into the stuffing. They will overlap slightly.

Pipe little knobs of stuffing in between the breasts using a round plain nozzle.

Decorate along this centre line of stuffing with a row of fluted, poached mushrooms.

COLD STUFFED PHEASANT OR CHICKEN

For a colourful effect decorate the mushroom cap with a piece of red pepper or tomato.

Carefully glaze the entire dish with aspic.

The final view—the chicken is now ready to be served in all its glory.

PÂTÉ EN CROÛTE

Roll out the pie pastry to a thickness of $\frac{3}{8}$ of an inch, flour lightly and mark out the shape of the base of the pie tin on it four times.

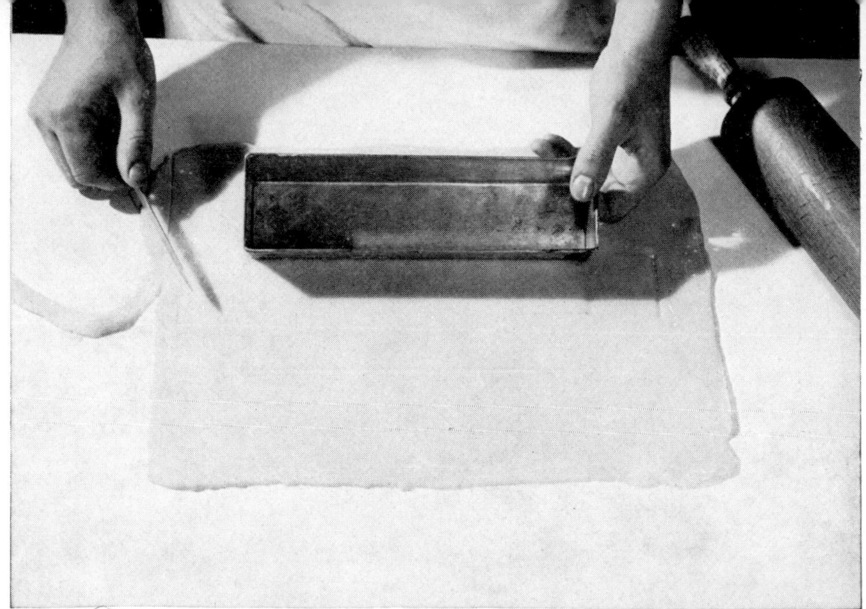

Cut off one of the four portions and set it aside to make the lid.

Line a greased, floured pie tin with the remaining pastry.

PÂTÉ EN CROÛTE

Ease the pastry gently into place using a ball of pastry; the pastry must overlap the mould.

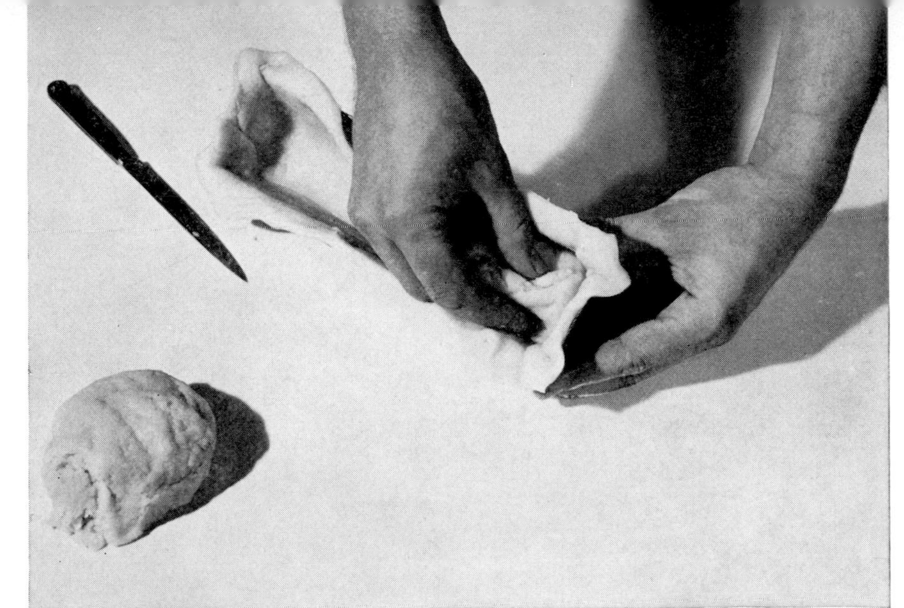

Line the mould with thin slices of fat bacon; half fill with the stuffing.

On top of this place fillet of meat (kid, hare, veal) which was previously marinated in brandy and spices.

PÂTÉ EN CROÛTE

Now fill with the remainder of the stuffing, cover it with a thin slice of bacon and fold the pastry over this.

Moisten the edges of the pastry and cover with the thinly rolled pastry lid, previously set aside. Seal these edges.

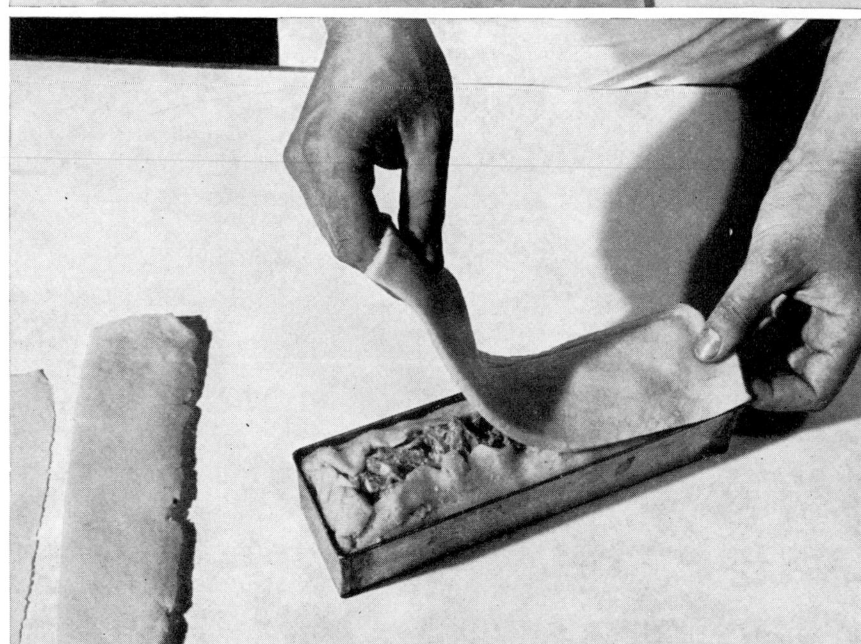

With special pastry tongs pinch these edges together. This will strengthen the seal and lend a more decorative effect.

PÂTÉ EN CROÛTE

Decorate according to your own taste. Make an opening to allow the steam to escape. Glaze the whole with beaten egg.

TURNED OR FLUTED MUSHROOMS

Shape the surface of the raw mushroom caps using a small sharp knife.

ASPARAGUS

Beginning at the tip gently and thinly scrape the asparagus. Tie them into neat, even, bundles.

POTATO RINGS

On a sheet of greaseproof paper, pipe the duchess potato mixture into small crown-shaped rings.

Drop these into hot fat and lift out the paper by the edge.

When they reach the correct golden colour on one side, turn them over and brown the other.

STUFFED PEPPERS

Prepare any rice-based filling of your choice. Pipe this into the peppers.

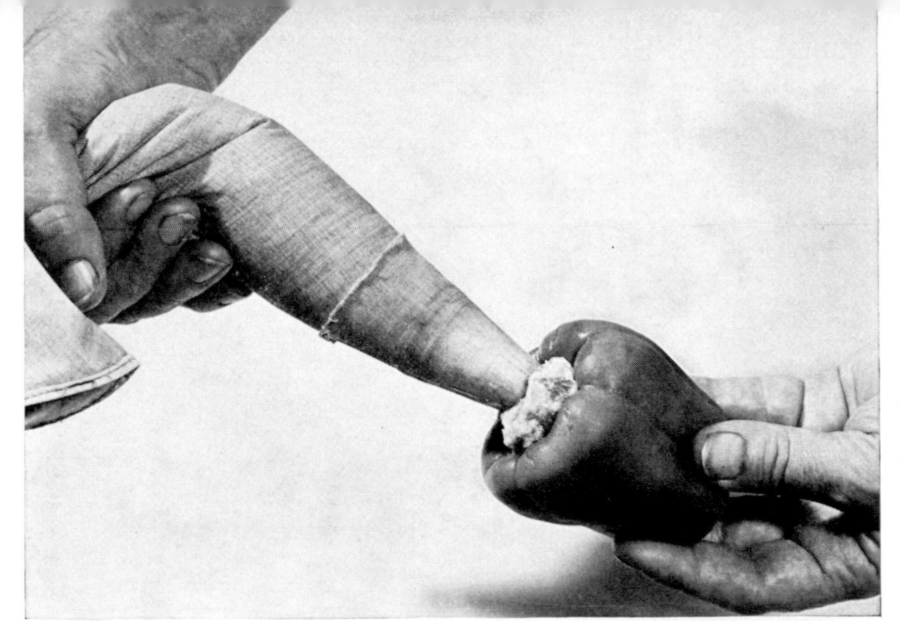

After cooking, these attractive slices may be used as a hot garnish.

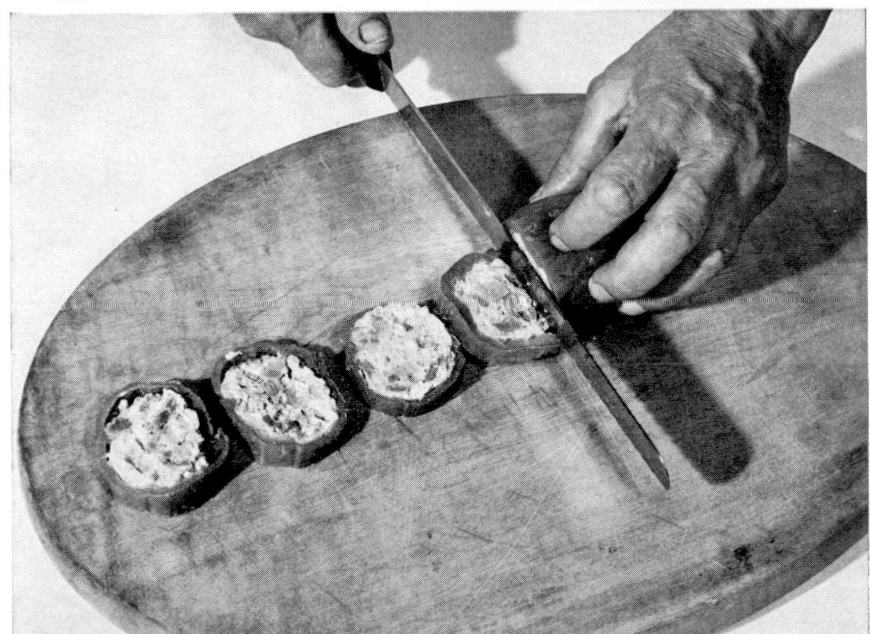

Halve some sweet red peppers. Fill with the *terrine* stuffing of your choice. Serve them either as cold *hors d'œuvres* or as a garnish for a cold dish.

PIPING

Piping *choux* pastry with various star or plain nozzles.

Small, baked individual *Saint-Honoré* cakes coated with apricot glaze, and piped with cream.

Piping melted chocolate for decoration on biscuits, using a paper piping bag.

PETITS FOURS

Roll out the *sablé* paste and cut out small rounds using a fluted cutter.

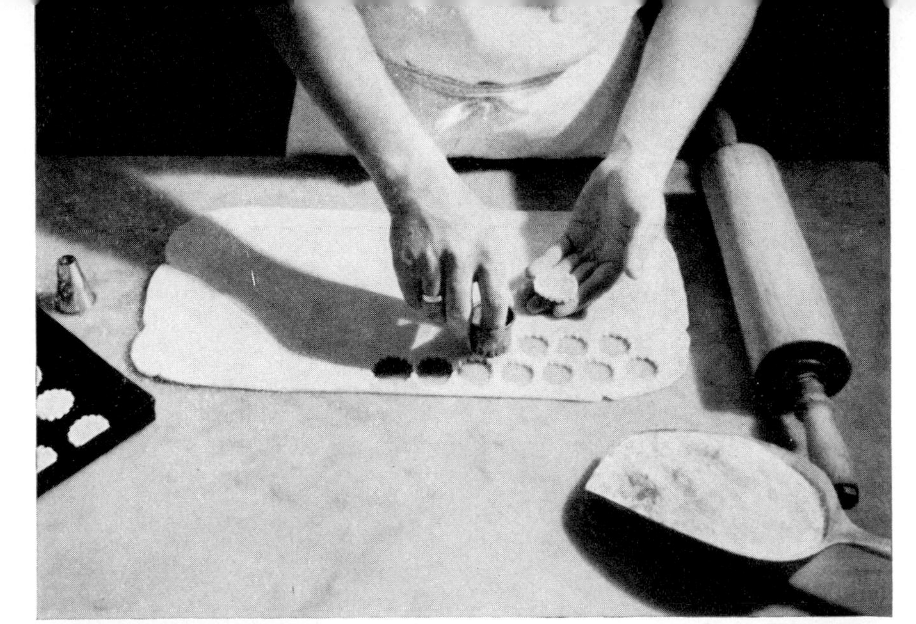

With a plain nozzle cut out the centres of half the prepared batch. Brush these rounds with beaten egg and milk and press into very finely chopped almonds. Bake in a very hot oven for about 10 minutes.

When cool, pipe a circular design of chocolate butter cream on the base of each biscuit.

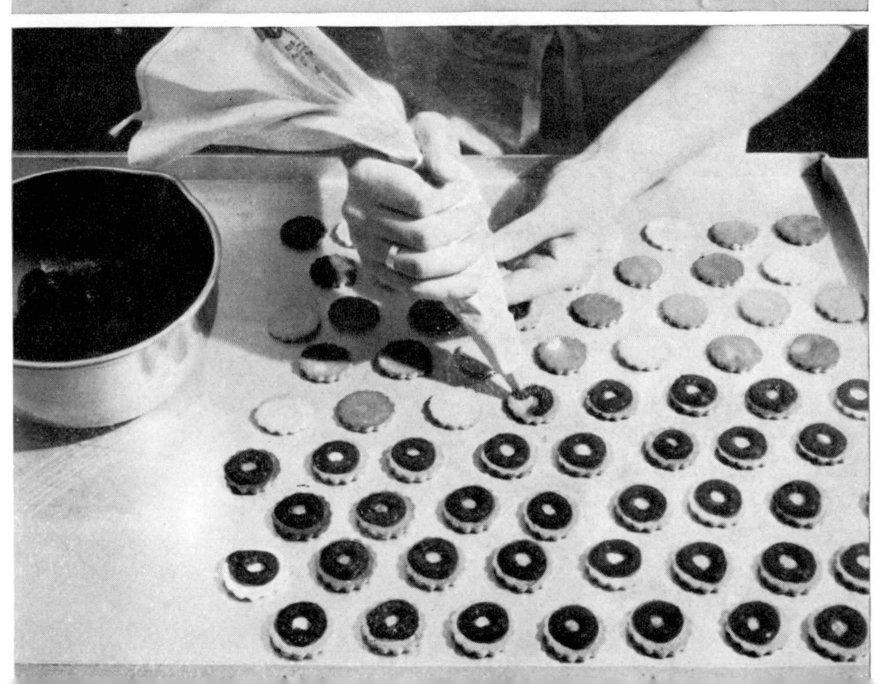

PETITS FOURS

Sandwich both halves of the biscuits together and pipe into the centre a round of coloured fondant icing.

GÂTEAU DE LA FORÊT-NOIRE

Divide the cake into 3 equal parts. Spread a layer of thickened, stewed morello cherries over the base and cover this with a layer of Kirsch-flavoured, whipped cream. Cover this with the second layer of cake which in turn should be covered with cream only. Top with the third layer.

Coat the top and sides with more of the whipped cream and sprinkle the sides with crumbled chocolate shavings. Use a savoy bag and star tube to decorate and top each star of cream with a *glacé* cherry. Fill the centre with chocolate shavings and lightly dust with castor sugar.

DOBOS TORTA

Prepare 6 discs as indicated in the recipe. Coat one of these discs with the caramel and cut into triangular wedges.

Sandwich each layer with chocolate butter cream. Coat the top and sides with more butter cream.

Smooth the top and mark the sides with a serrated palette or fork.

DOBOS TORTA

Pipe whirls of butter cream from the centre to the edge. Arrange the reserved triangles in between each of these whirls at an angle. The base may be decorated with finely chopped almonds.

BABAS

Unmould the *babas* and place on a baking tin. Soak with plenty of rum-flavoured syrup.

With a spatula carefully turn over the *babas* and lay on a wire cooling tray. Complete with reduced apricot *purée*.

GÂTEAU MEXICAIN

Halve the cake carefully and spread a thick layer of butter cream over the bottom layer. Replace the top half of the cake and glaze with reduced apricot *purée*, both the top and sides.

Spread the warm icing over the cake. Smooth off the top with a palette knife.

Fill an icing bag with royal icing and pipe across the surface of the cake parallel lines of icing.

GÂTEAU MEXICAIN

Break up these lines by running the edge of a palette knife in the opposite direction. Let the first stroke run from top to bottom and the second from bottom to top. The final effect is a feather-like regular pattern.

For this circular design—fill the icing bag with royal icing and mark out a spiral design, beginning at the centre.

With a sharp knife mark off a straight line running from the centre to the edge. Now reverse the direction—from edge to centre—and draw out another straight line. Keep the space between these alternating designs regular.

Carving, Slicing and Flambéing

SOLE MEUNIÈRE

Carefully and firmly hold the cooked sole in position with a fork while with a spoon you ease the outer bones.

Remove the scraps of bone and skin from the dish.

The fillet must not be allowed to break up. To prevent this hold the fish with a fork wedged against the side bones. Now ease the fillet away from the main backbone — gently pulling with the spoon and guiding with the fork. Remove the remaining three fillets in a similar fashion.

SOLE MEUNIÈRE

Collect the scraps onto a separate plate. Serve the sole *meunière* on a warmed plate.

CHÂTEAUBRIAND

Slide a carving knife under the meat. Using a fork as a support, lay the steak on a carving board.

Before carving calculate the number of slices required (normally six between two people) to help you judge the thickness of each slice. Control the meat by holding with the back of a fork. Using the minimum of pressure to allow the meat juices to remain within the steak, slide the knife into the meat. Carve at a slight angle.

CHÂTEAUBRIAND

The steak is now replaced on the serving dish. To do this, slide the knife under the meat while the last slice is held in position with the back of a fork.

Serve the first two slices together to form one serving. After this one slice per person is a sufficient quantity.

SADDLE OF HARE

Insert a fork in the backbone, lift the saddle with the aid of a spoon, drain and place on a carving board.

SADDLE OF HARE

Hold the saddle in the centre with a fork detach the fillets with a spoon.

The cooked hare should come away from the bone quite easily.

Remove the second fillet in a similar fashion.

SADDLE OF HARE

Now carve the fillet into four slices of equal thickness. Carve on the slant and try not to press too heavily on the knife. Simply slide it along the length of the meat.

ROAST CHICKEN

Lift up the chicken with the point of a carving knife and fork. Drain off excess fat and juices—these will later form the gravy. The chicken should be placed on its back on a carving board.

To remove the wing tips, hold down the wing with a fork and carve off the tips at the joint.

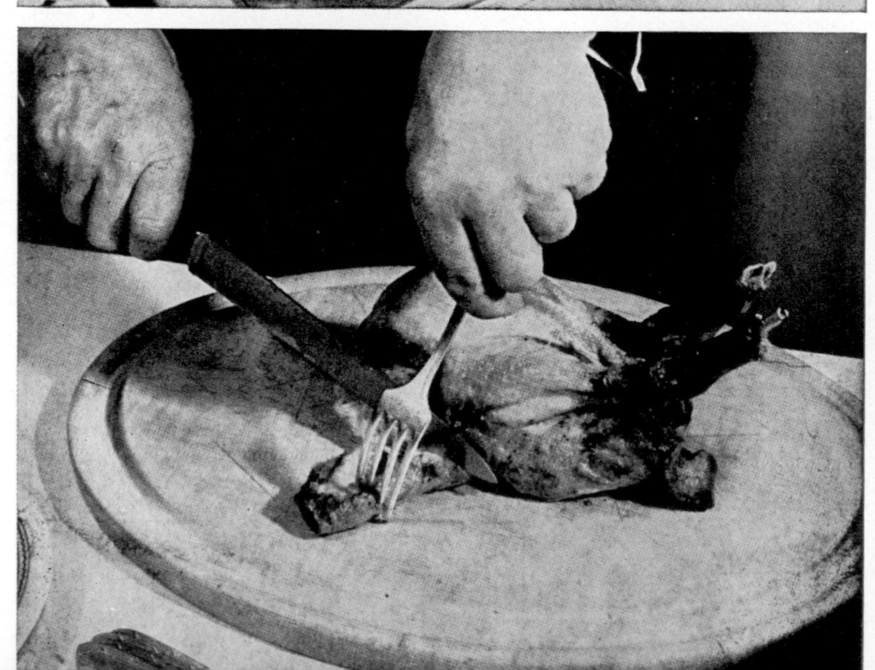

ROAST CHICKEN

To carve the leg and drumstick lay the chicken on its side. A fork wedged between the right leg and the drumstick will maintain this position. Separate the leg from the wing with a deep incision.

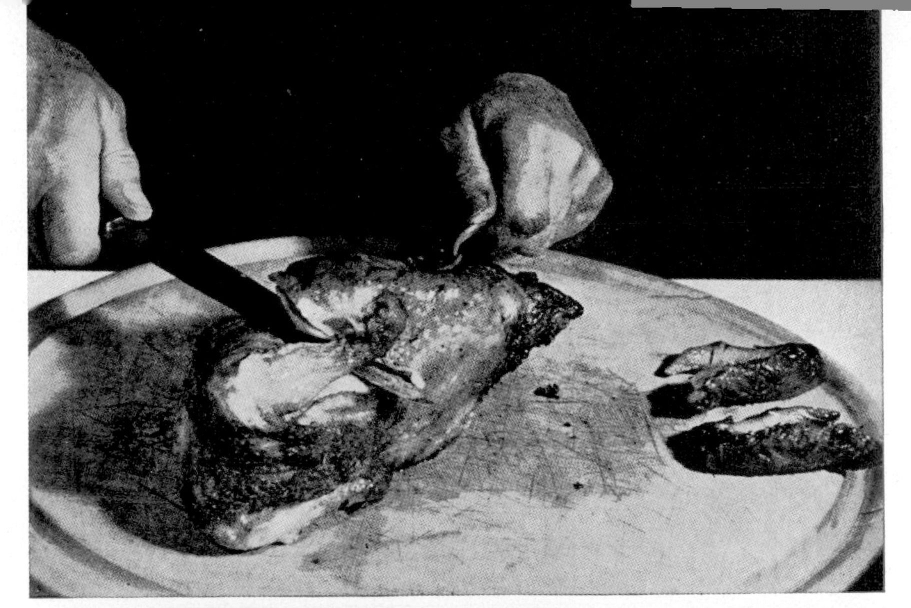

Pulling gently with the fork ease away the leg while holding down the body of the chicken with the blade of a knife.

Repeat these steps to carve the second leg.

Sit the bird on its back again and hold in position with a fork. Carve the wing at the joint.

Removing the rump or "parson's nose".

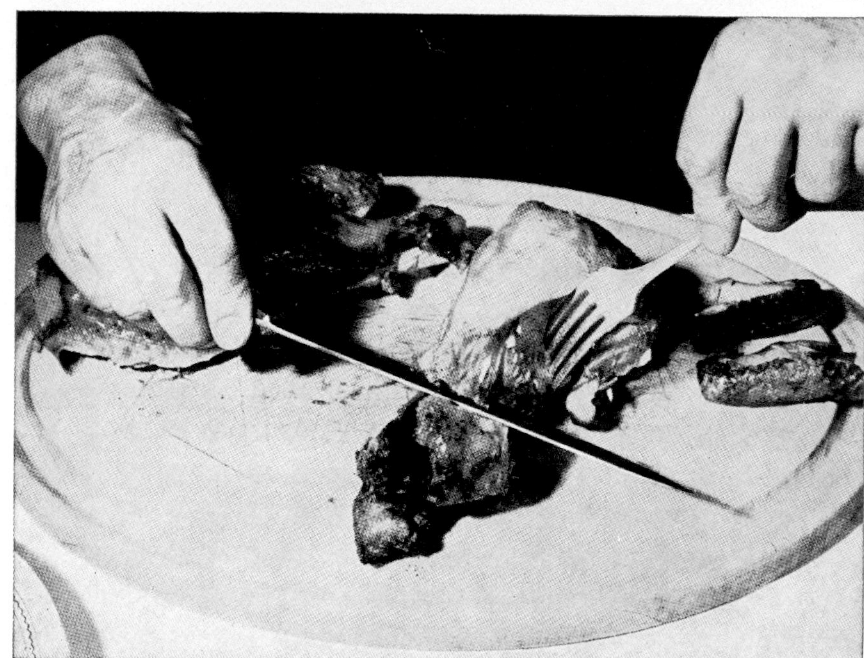

The removal of the second wing.

ROAST CHICKEN

To carve the tender, white flesh of the breast lay the chicken on its side again. Slice down the breast bone.

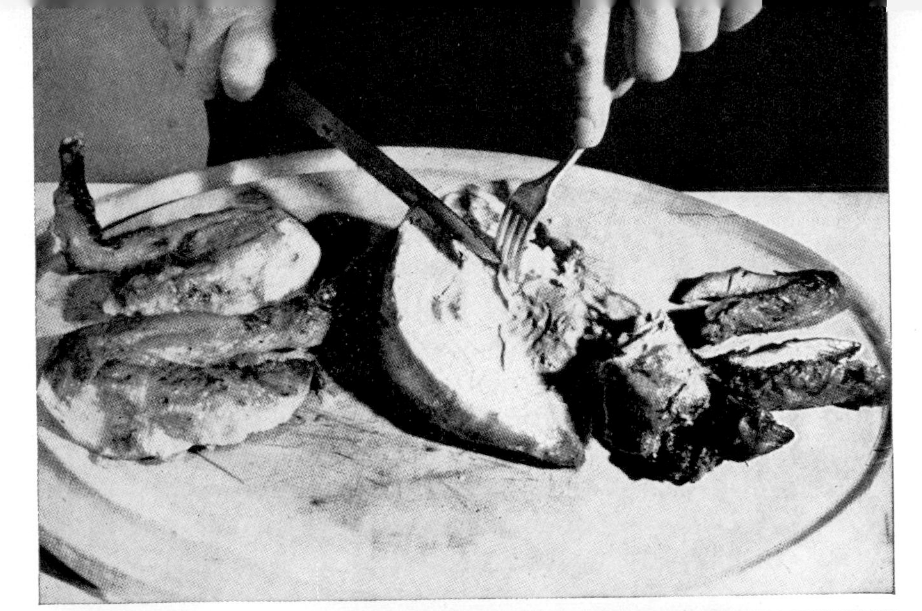

The breast will slice away easily. Sometimes with a really fat and plump bird the breast can be sliced into two pieces.

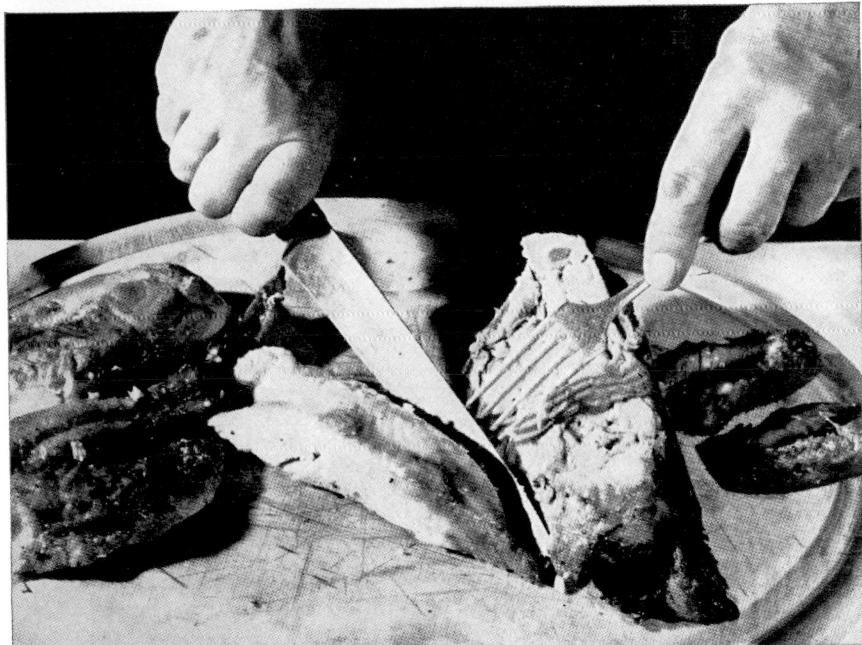

Cut through the leg and drumstick at the joint.

SEGMENTING AN ORANGE

Mark out a circle at the top and bottom of the orange. Cut one circle off and invert it, impale it on a fork and insert the latter into the other end of the orange.

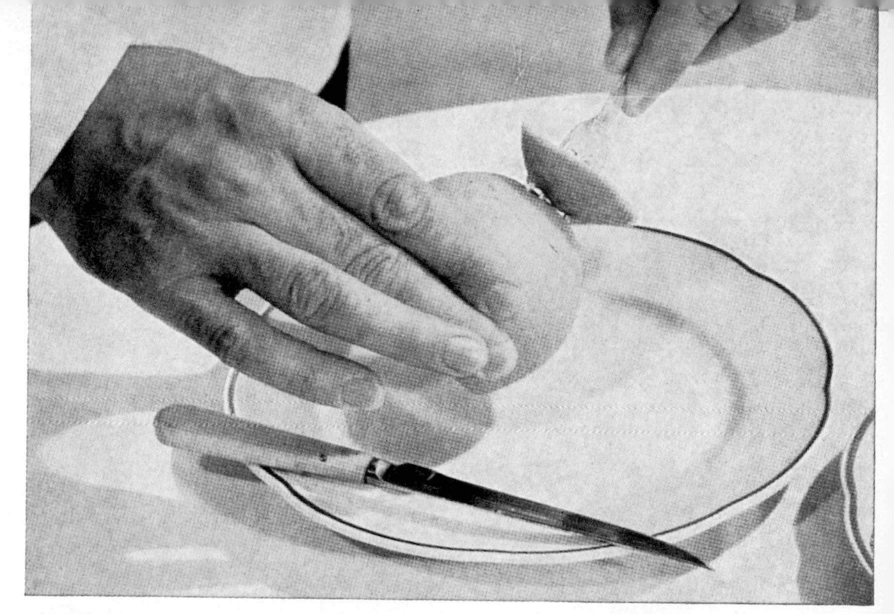

Peel the orange but only as far as the beginning of the second circle.

Cut the orange into very thin slices. Moisten these with the juice squeezed from the two circles.

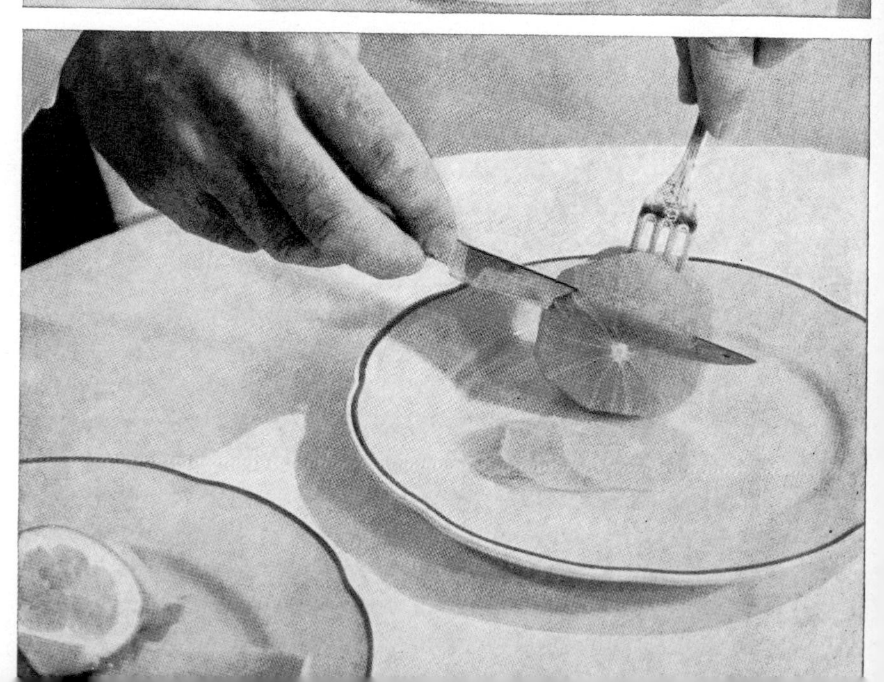

SEGMENTING AN ORANGE (2nd method)

Impale a fork into one end of the orange and cut off a small circle of rind from the other. With a spiral sawing movement peel away the rind and pith to expose the flesh. Make the fruit revolve by turning the fork.

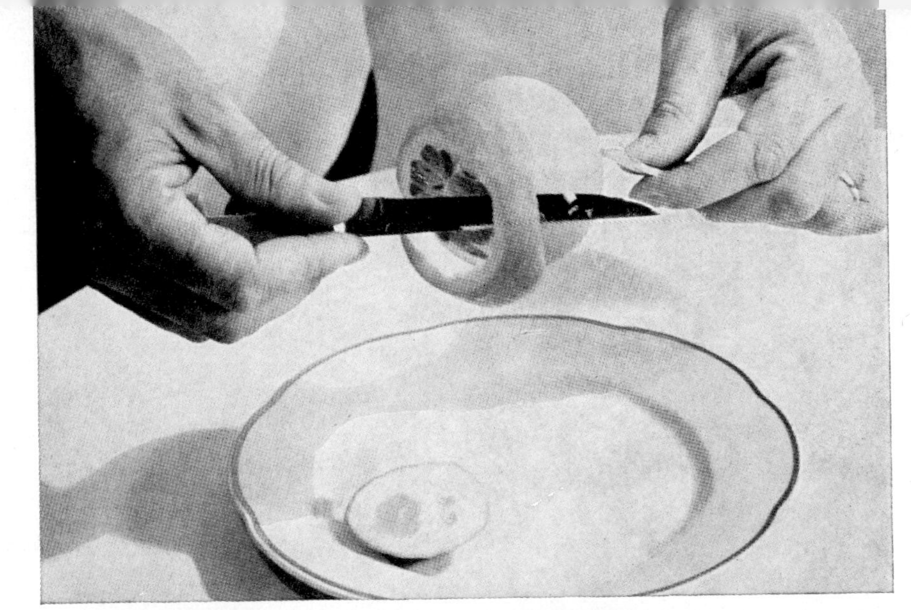

Cut out each slice individually taking care to remove the white membrane.

Arrange these segments on a plate and moisten with the juice from the segments.

CRÊPES SUZETTES

Take two oranges, one lemon and twenty-four lumps of sugar (proportions for four people). Using a napkin to avoid touching them with the hands rub the lumps of sugar well over the peel of the oranges.

Crush the sugar and mix with a generous amount of butter. Allow to melt.

Continue shaking the pan until the mixture begins to caramelise.

CRÊPES SUZETTES

Add the orange and lemon juice. Cook this briskly. The sauce must be oily.

Place the *crêpes* into this sauce and arrange around the pan so that they overlap slightly—having previously double-folded these into neat triangular shapes.

Allow the *crêpes* to soak up this rich sauce and turn them over repeatedly.

CRÊPES SUZETTES

Flambé or flame the *crêpes* with Grand-Marnier.

Arrange these on warmed plates and unfold.

Coat with some of the remaining fruit sauce. There are several methods of preparing *crêpes suzettes* but the basic principles remain constant.

rather more loosely, for example in regard to stewed fruits and "top of the stove" dishes like Irish stew. Centuries ago in Europe it was discovered that a certain earthenware, glazed pot was ideally suited to stewing. This, the "casserole", was not only economic in its use of fuel and easy to handle, but it could also stand up well to long hours of constant heat application without breaking or letting food burn. In those days it was the practice to sit these at the side of the fire to simmer away safely for hours.

Today, many stews are called casserole dishes and the casserole need not necessarily be of pottery. The most popular varieties for the housewife are those which are practical and pretty enough for carrying from oven to table. They may be of stainless steel, heat-resistant glass, fire-proof porcelain, copper or enamelled iron. They may be brought to the simmering point on top of the stove, then transferred to the oven. But whatever the guise or name, the principle of cooking *à l'étuvée* is employed for all.

SPIT ROASTING

True spit roasting, as practised in medieval kitchens, involved cooking by radiant heat. The meat was roasted over a large fire, rotating on a spit, until it was cooked. It was an admirable method of cooking as the succulent meat juices were sealed within the meat and the rotation of the spit caused the joint to baste itself, resulting in a fine flavour. It was, regrettably, rather time and fuel consuming and the meat had a tendency to shrink. For convenience, oven roasting or baking has superseded the old method. Since it is both the simplest and the tastiest method of cooking, it deserves to become a more popular method again. There are several models of the new style eye-level spits on the market today. Some of these work on the infra-ray basis.

OVEN ROASTING

Classic spit roasting relies on a free circulation of air around the meat. In oven roasting there is naturally little entrance of air and meagre ventilation, so that the heat is transferred by two direct agents, hot air trapped in the oven and roasting fat. The effect is much the same as in steaming, for no substances other than melting fat pass out of the meat into the roasting pan. The two heat transfer agents, fat and hot air, have an identical effect on the meat cells; at the same time the roasting fat enriches the meat. Just as with other methods of cooking there is a vitamin loss and some of the goodness of the food passes into the surrounding heat agent, in this case, the roasting fat. To compensate, roasting causes the formation of a new substance called *assamar* which gives the surface of the roast its brown crust and special flavour. If roasting continues at too high a temperature, this substance burns and causes an unpleasant taste. To prevent this charring, check evaporation and undue shrinkage and also to improve the flavour, the roast should be basted every 15-20 minutes with its own juices and roasting fat.

It is important to expose the meat to a high temperature, 450° F, for the first ten minutes to bring about a rapid searing of the surface of the meat which will help seal in the juices. The heat is reduced once the crust has formed and the meat is cooked till done at a temperature of 300-350° F. If cooking is completed at higher temperatures the shrinking of the roast will be pronounced.

For oven roasting the ventilation of the oven is very important. The steam collecting in the closed oven has the effect of moist heat. If the joint is to be crisp, a good top heat and efficient steam removal must be ensured. When possible, sit the food to, be roasted on a trivet or rack to allow hot air to circulate freely; this will prevent meat from soaking in the fat and becoming soggy. Alternatively, raise the joint from the bottom of the roasting pan by sitting it on a bed of root vegetables.

There are several methods of oven roasting in common use today. Apart from the method described above you may prefer to *slow roast* your joint. This method is particularly suited to less tender cuts of meat and it is difficult to overcook meat when using it. Slow roasted meat cuts are placed in an oven heated to 250° F and the temperature is kept constant throughout the cooking period which is usually one and a half times the normal cooking time. Advocates of this method claim that shrinkage is less and poor quality meat is made tender.

Some people prefer their meat to be slightly underdone inside with a crisp, well-browned exterior. So they expose their roast for a shortish period in a high temperature oven 450° F-475° F or Gas Mark 8-9. When using this latter method be careful to select only tender, fine quality cuts of meat.

One of the most difficult aspects of roasting is trying to calculate the cooking time. Suitable allowance must be made for the size of the joint, the amount of bone, the composition and distribution of the muscle and fat, and most important, the chosen method of roasting. Unless you are using a proper meat thermometer, most people rely on the standard allowances of minutes per pound of meat and there is a chart provided at the beginning of the meat, game and poultry chapters for this purpose. A meat thermometer will indicate, when pushed into the thickest part of the joint, the internal temperature and whether the roast is rare, medium or well done.

GRILLING

In grilling, hot air is also the heat transfer agent and the principles underlying the method of grilling are the same as when roasting. Grilling can be carried out over a glowing and smokeless fire, beneath the glowing reflector of a gas grill or over a hot grid or gridiron. The major difference between roasting and grilling is that this is a very quick method of cooking throughout which a high degree of heat is maintained. Grilled meat should be juicy and tender when cut and have a slightly puffy appearance caused by the sealing in of the meat juices as a result of the application of intense heat.

Grilling is usually confined to smaller pieces of meat, such as cutlets, *tournedos*, steaks and so on, smaller fish, soles, trout, whiting, fish steaks, fillets of fish and small poultry and game, sometimes halved or cut up according to size. The individual pieces are lightly brushed with oil or clarified butter or chicken or veal fat before they are placed on the grill. It is better to season them afterwards. The grill must have a clear radiant heat and must be turned on beforehand in order to seal off the surface juices. Fish, especially flat fish, should be floured before they are brushed with oil; this speeds up the formation of a protective crust and reduces the danger of their breaking up. Fish and poultry are sometimes egged and breadcrumbed before being dipped in oil or clarified butter. Wherever the pieces are first floured or egged and breadcrumbed, it is best to use a double-side hinged or scissor-type wire grill which must first be well heated and oiled. The food item can be secured between the sides and the whole apparatus turned rather than individual pieces. There is less danger of damage.

With a well-finished grill one should see the criss-crossed or trellisl-ike pattern upon the finished article. This is achieved quite simply by placing the article to be grilled upon the grill on the diagonal and then changing its position to the opposite diagonal; upon turning, the same process applies to the other side. The majority of grills are more succulent when kept underdone or pink coloured in the centre with the exception of all pork products which must be well cooked. Particular care should be taken when grilling fish as this becomes dry if it is overcooked. During grilling the pieces should be brushed with either oil, butter, chicken, or veal fat from time to time.

SHALLOW FRYING OR SAUTÉING

Properly sautéed or shallow fried food requires attention and skill in cooking and consistently good results are not easily obtained. To *sauter* correctly, food must be completely if briefly cooked. This may form a preliminary step in the preparation of food for more complex dishes requiring another style of cooking, be it slow roasting or casseroling. It is more commonly regarded as a method of cooking small pieces of fish, meat, game or poultry in an open *sauter* or frying pan or *plat à sauter* with a small amount of fat on top of the stove. Since the fat may be raised to a very high temperature without risk of burning this is often the quickest method of cooking but its very speed of execution demands constant attention by the cook. Direct heat only reaches the underside of the food so that after a certain period it has to be turned.

The fat itself is not important. It may be butter, lard, oil or rendered animal fat. What is important, however, is the amount of fat used and the temperature of the fat. When sautéing, the food must always be placed in shallow hot fat. If the fat is not hot enough the proteins will escape and the food will absorb much of the surrounding fat and become tasteless and soggy, without goodness or flavour. If there is too little hot fat, it will be difficult to prevent the food from sticking to the bottom of the pan. If too much, it will be difficult to toss or *sauté* the food without splashing hot fat and you are likely to be deep frying the food not sautéing it.

In the process of cooking *à sauter* certain aromatic roasting substances develop in the bottom of the pan. These are formed by the slight loss of meat juice which collects in the bottom of the pan and this becomes lightly caramelised. Care should always be taken to see that these juices merely caramelise and do not become too dark and bitter. After the food has been removed from the pan and the surplus fat poured off, the pan can be deglazed or rinsed with stock or this residue can be scraped up and mixed with some liquid—usually wine or stock, boiled down and used to make a sauce. If it is too dark the sauce will be bitter.

While sautéing is used basically as a preliminary step in the preparation of vegetables for soups and sauces and to cook lean and tender fillets of meat or fish, it may also be used to complete cooking and to flavour or to provide finish for garnishes such as *sauté* potatoes, tomatoes or mushrooms.

DEEP FRYING

With this method very often the results are more predictable and controllable than with sautéed foods. It is almost invariably less greasy and more digestible. Well-fried food should be golden or light brown in colour, free from grease and crisp on the outside. This is not too difficult to obtain provided that certain logical precautions are taken.

Use a deep frying thermometer to assess the temperature of the fat, or use the *bread* test. This is simply a rough but fairly accurate test to gauge the cooking temperature of the oil or fat without the use of a thermometer. Drop a small cube of bread into the fat. Count slowly up to sixty. If the fat is hot enough—about 375° F is satisfactory for frying most foods—the cube will be evenly browned and crisply fried at the end of this time. Never try to fry too much food in too small a quantity of fat since this will lower the temperature of the fat immediately. As with sautéed foods too low a temperature of fat means grease-laden food. Use the best oil, rather than fat, since this can be raised to a higher temperature without risk of burning and keep the oil in good, clean condition by straining after use. Deep fat frying requires a strong deep pan or kettle filled to a little more than the half-way mark with oil. A wire frying basket which should fit snugly inside the frying kettle is almost indispensable. With this you can safely immerse the food in the hot fat and lift it out again when cooked.

If the food to be deep fried is properly treated, the crust formation should be uniformly distributed all over the piece in question. To achieve this the heat must be regulated according to the nature of the food to be fried. It is usual to deep fry only smaller pieces, regardless of whether these be fish, meat, potatoes, vegetables or other foodstuffs. Breadcrumbed pieces with a soft filling, especially *croquettes*, must be fried in hot fat, 375°-400° F so that a protective crust is formed immediately, preventing the filling from running out. Some items, such as straw and matchstick potatoes and game chips are fried in one continuous process; whereas *soufflé* and French fried potatoes are first fried in only moderately hot fat, 330°-350° F, to cook the inside thoroughly. They are then returned to a hotter fat, 375°-400° F, to finish cooking and to become crisp and golden coloured.

COOKING À LA POÊLE

Cooking *à la poêle* or *pot-roasting* is a combination of roasting and casseroling. It is used mainly for tender meat, such as fillet of beef, saddle, leg and silverside of veal, white poultry and game. Place a layer of lightly browned slices of celery, carrots and onions and some ham trimmings in the bottom of a dish of suitable size. Place the seasoned meat or poultry on top, pour plenty of melted butter over it, cover, and place in a moderate oven. Baste with butter from time to time and when almost cooked remove the lid, so that the surface can brown. Remove the meat, reduce the residue with good stock or other liquid, skim off surplus fat and boil till clear. Do not remove the vegetables first but strain after boiling. Care must be taken to see that the vegetables do not burn during cooking, otherwise the sauce will be bitter.

À la poêle cooking is traditionally carried out in an oven, except for the small special cuts. These may be small pieces of meat or very small birds, which are prepared in the same way, but cooked in a lidded, fire-proof casserole or *cocotte* of porcelain, earthenware, glass or copper, on top of the stove and served in the same dish.

BRAISING

Braising is one of the most frequently used methods of cooking but is only rarely done properly. All too often one is offered a piece of brown meat with all the goodness boiled out of it instead of a piece of braised meat. The main characteristic of good braising is proper crust formation. The meat should be placed in very hot shallow fat and browned evenly all over, including the ends. This forms a protective crust, which prevents the juices from running out. During the browning process, aromatic substances and flavours are formed, which combine with the fat and are dissolved in the bottom of the pan and distributed when liquid is added. The liquid (water, stock, wine, sauce, etc.,) should come only about one quarter of the way up the joint after the joint has been placed upon a lightly fried bed of vegetables. Cover the dish and allow to complete cooking slowly in a warm oven, about 350° F or Gas Mark 3. The joint should be turned several times; it is best to let the liquid reduce down until it is drawing the fat from the meat, turn the meat in it several times, and fill up with fresh liquid. The pan should not be opened for lengthy periods, nor should the liquid be allowed to boil up violently.

A really good braised joint can only be cooked in a well-sealed dish in the oven at moderate heat, 350° F, because here the outside heat can penetrate from all sides. Each joint should not weigh more than 5-9 pounds. If necessary, larger pieces can be carefully browned in a tilting pan, and then braised with the necessary liquid and seasonings. It must, however, be possible to close the pan with a tightly fitting cover.

BAKING

Fine hot sweets, puddings, *soufflés*, fine pastry, bread and rolls are baked in the oven, hot air being the heat transfer agent. The crust forms only on those parts directly exposed to the hot air, for example, the top of *soufflés* and puddings, unless the bottom heat is so great that it penetrates the tins or moulds to an excessive degree. Since dry heat dries out dough to a considerable extent, steam is sometimes fed into baking ovens when bread or rolls are being baked, not only to keep the surface smooth and shiny, but to ensure the crust does not become tough and rubbery.

POACHING

The best definition of poaching is slow boiling at simmering point; the liquid must not be allowed to boil up and should remain at a constant temperature of 200° F. The effects of poaching on food are almost identical with those of boiling.

Poaching is used for large fish, large birds, ham, and so on, and also for small fish and fillets of fish and small pieces of meat and poultry. Large fish such as salmon, and turbot are placed in a fish kettle of appropriate size in cold water or seasoned stock, brought slowly to the boil and then poached till cooked. Small fish, fillets of fish, chicken breasts, etc., are placed in a shallow, buttered dish and seasoned. A little liquid (wine or stock) is added; they are covered with buttered paper and cooked in the oven until done.

AU GRATIN COOKING

Au gratin cooking involves the formation of a crust on top of the dish being cooked. There is a complete and correct cooking method and also a quick one and a light one. In the first method the raw food, usually cut in pieces, is placed in a buttered or fire-proof dish, the bottom of which has been lightly covered with sauce. There must be enough sauce for the food to cook in it, but during cooking the sauce must only bind and cover, and not become soupy from escaping juices. The food must be thoroughly baked and the crust formed at the same moment. This means that perfect *au gratin* cooking can only be done in the oven.

In the case of quick *au gratin* cooking the method is the same as before, except that the food is cooked first. These dishes can be browned either in a hot oven or under a salamander or grill.

The light *au gratin* method is the one employed most frequently. It is used mainly for *pasta* bound with a sauce, vegetables and fish, and sprinkled with grated cheese or bread-crumbs, or a mixture of both, and with melted butter. If the cheese is to melt slowly and combine with the butter, the heat must not be too great. Place these dishes in a moderate oven, or under a grill at slightly reduced heat, in order to obtain even browning of the surface.

GLAZING

Glazing and *au gratin* cooking are often confused, although they are two entirely different methods. The latter consists of browning the surface of a dish covered with a rich, buttered sauce. Since heavily buttered sauces curdle very easily, first fill a larger, flat dish with cold water, place the dish containing the food in it and brown the surface at great heat under the grill.

The other method involves coating the surface of the dish with sauce, usually *sauce Mornay*, sprinkled with grated cheese and melted butter. Under the heat of the grill, the melting cheese and butter combine to give a fine brown crust.

Kitchen Equipment

Kitchen equipment must be chosen with care. Your choice must be governed by the amount of money you wish to spend and also by the room you have in which to store it and the use you are going to make of it. Kitchen equipment is used more than anything else in the house and so you should pay close attention to ease of handling, cleaning, servicing and safety.

Cookers

This is the most important item of equipment in the kitchen. Cookers can be solid fuel, gas, electricity or oil, but for most people the choice will be between gas and electricity. Whatever you choose it should be large enough to suit the requirements of your household and should combine durability with strength and easy replacement of parts. A cooker which has a simple design will be easier to keep clean. Have the cooker positioned in a good light, away from draughts, and keep it clean for maximum efficiency. It may be necessary to fit an extractor fan in the kitchen to avoid unpleasant smells.

Saucepans

You will need saucepans of varying capacity, but choose those which will best fit the burner of your cooker and which have tight-fitting lids. If space is limited in your kitchen, choose pans which nest well. Pans of heavy gauge (thickness) will spread heat more evenly and will therefore help prevent scorching. These are a better buy than cheap, light pans which will buckle under intense heat. Insulated handles are useful. Make sure that the lining of the pan is smooth and the pan is rounded at the junction of sides and bottom as it is so very awkward to scrape food from straight-sided pots.

The material of pots and pans as well as their size and shape is very important.

Heavy aluminium has good heat diffusion and is very popular but should not be cleaned with harsh soaps or alkalis. Use scourers and scouring powders cautiously as these abrasives may eventually cause pitting and discolouration which will ultimately affect the colour of the foods.

Copper is best in heavier gauges since it gives quick, even heat distribution but, as it is affected by acids, it must be well-tinned or lined with stainless steel on the inside.

Stainless steel is the easiest to keep clean but is a poor conductor of heat. Often this is offset by thinning down the gauge. Regrettably, this has the adverse effect of producing hot-spots and food cooked on it is apt to burn easily.

Iron has low heat conductivity, it rusts easily and discolours with acid foods. To treat new iron frying pans, grease well and place in a hot oven (450° F) for 30 mins. then scour with steel wool before using.

Greaseless or *non-stick* pans are useful for people on fat-free diets, but they do need care in handling so always use a wooden spoon or spatula as metal tends to remove the non-stick coating.

It would be true to say that there is probably no single metal which provides the complete answer. However, there are on the market now a number of brands of cooking-ware with good flat bases which combine metals to take advantage of the good diffusion of aluminium, the quick conductivity of copper and non-corrosiveness of stainless steel.

Tempered glass and *porcelain enamel* are used for oven-to-tableware and and look most attractive. However, care is needed in their use and they are easily cracked. Both are poor conductors of heat.

Earthenware is a poor conductor of heat, but glazed or unglazed earthenware holds heat well and does not discolour foods. Like glass it is heavy and breaks easily with sudden temperature changes.

Tinware, tinned steel, and *aluminium* are used for cake and baking tins. These turn dark with use but have good heat conductivity. They are usually greased or lined before use.

Plastics are used for storage containers and cannot be washed in boiling or very hot water. Surfaces of all plastic materials retain grease so do not try to whip up egg whites in a plastic bowl.

One or two hints about the use and care of *baking tins* are appropriate here. Make sure that you choose cake and baking tins appropriate in size to the use you have in mind; this is especially important when baking or braising. Do not put unfilled saucepans on high heat unless they have fat or liquid in them as this will warp them.

Knives

Personal tools in the kitchen include knives, which should be of best quality steel, strongly made and always sharp, and always carefully looked after by the cook. The four essential knives are:

The "*couteau d'office*" or small knife which has a 3-4 inch blade and is used for the general preparation of vegetables.

The *filleting* knife with a flexible 6-7 inch blade and a sharp point. This is used for filleting fish and other jobs for which a larger knife would be too heavy.

The *kitchen* knife with an 8-10 inch blade which is ideal for chopping vegetables, slicing root vegetables, and cutting up meat.

The *palette* knife with a 7-8 inch flexible blade and rounded end. This is used for pastry work and turning food when frying.

TO KEEP KNIVES IN GOOD CONDITION it is necessary to have a good carborundum and steel. The best knives are the French type which means that the blade and handle are forged from one piece of metal.

POINTS TO NOTE WHEN USING A KNIFE

Work on a level wooden chopping board.

Use a good sharp knife with the cutting edge level.

Use a knife which is large enough for the task.

Use the correct knife for the purpose for which it was intended.

When slicing vegetables use the heel of the knife, the tip should rest on the board all the time during the slicing process.

Hold the piece of the vegetable with the left hand with the wrist resting on the board

and the fingertips tucked in. This ensures the left hand holding the article is firm and steady.
Put corks on the ends of fine kitchen knives. This will prevent them bending.

Basic Equipment

AMONG THE BASIC EQUIPMENT IN ANY KITCHEN ARE scales, measures, and measuring spoons as the right balance of ingredients is required if a dish is to be a success.

strainers: pointed, (conical) and round types
flexible spatulas
sieves: hair (or nylon) and wire
graters
variety of wooden spoons
rolling pin
mincing machine
potato peeler, apple corer
pastry and vegetable cutters
ladles and scoops
larding and trussing needles
Savoy bag and tubes
icing tubes of various shapes and sizes
kitchen scissors
cooking tongs
cooling wires
ice machine
pot stands
marble slab
whisks: large balloon and fine sauce whisks
moulds: *savarin*, fluted timbale, *bombe*, charlotte, *brioche* and raised pie moulds, also a loose-bottomed cake tin, a fluted and plain flan ring
various small moulds: boat-shaped, *dariole*, cornet *brioche*, shell, and tartlet moulds
a large metal spoon for skimming
Chefs' forks: these have two long prongs
wire salad basket
sugar boiling thermometer
a champignon (wooden "mushroom") for passing *purées* through wire sieves
frying pan, egg pan, saucepan with a steamer, fish kettle with drainer and lid
omelette pans and preserving pans

MISCELLANOUS KITCHEN EQUIPMENT INCLUDES

flannel jelly bag
a roll of butter muslin
a special cloth kept for drying fish
non-fluffy kitchen cloths
kitchen paper and greaseproof paper
canisters and a rack for spices, these should be arranged in alphabetical order for quick identification
An electric mixer with a liquidiser attachment is a most valuable accessory if you can afford it.

Glossary of Cooking Terms

Abaisser — To extend pastry with a rolling pin.

Agar-agar — Edible seaweed used in place of gelatine for pastilles, fine confectionery, etc.

Aiguillette — Long, thin vertically cut slices of meat cut from the breasts of poultry and game. Fish fillets cut in similar shaped slices for breadcrumbing or shallow frying.

Aile — The wing (including the breast) of poultry.

Angelica — Candied stem of the angelica plant.

Animelles — Lamb's fry.

Appareil — The various ingredients blended together for a certain preparation.

Aromates — Spices and aromatic herbs and vegetables.

Arrowroot — Edible starch obtained from the maranta plant.

Aspic — A clear brilliant jelly made from stock used for glazing or decorating cold dishes of fish, poultry, game or meats.

Au or Aux — With or cooked with.

Au Blanc — To retain whiteness, for example, by cooking vegetables in a "*blanc*", a flour and water paste of thin sauce consistency.

Au Bleu — Fish (especially trout) cooked immediately it has been killed in *court-bouilllon* or boiling water when the skin acquires a bluish tinge.

Au Maigre — Dishes without meat or meat stock.

Bain-Marie — A utensil for keeping foods hot and a gentle method of cooking. It usually consists of a fairly large shallow vessel containing hot water into which are placed smaller pans containing food such as sauces, stews and soups. In the domestic kitchen a double saucepan could be used. Sometimes food which is to be cooked at a very low temperature, for example custards, may be placed in a baking tin half-filled with hot water in the oven. This will prevent the food from over-heating and spoiling.

Ballotine — Piece of meat, poultry or bones, stuffed and rolled up—usually served hot.

Bard — To cover poultry, game, meat and sometimes fish with thin slices of pork fat or unsmoked bacon to prevent scorching and add moisture.

Barquette — A boat-shaped pastry tartlet.

Baste — To moisten, by pouring over the pan juices with fat or liquid, while cooking.

Bâtons Thin strips, about the size of a matchstick.

Beard To remove the "beard" from oysters or mussels: to remove fins and small fin bones from fish.

Bèche de Mer Sea slug or sea cucumber. Used as a garnish for soup.

Beurre-Manié Butterpaste. A mixture of four ounces of butter kneaded with three ounces of flour. Used for thickening sauces, vegetables, etc.

Bind To thicken with flour or other starch. You may also "bind" with eggs, cream, etc.

Bisque The name given to a thick, rich fish or shellfish soup.

Blanch (a) To cook in boiling water for a few minutes, then to plunge into cold water, e.g. to stiffen sweetbreads or scallops prior to cooking.
(b) To whiten or reduce the strong flavour of food by putting it in cold water, then bringing it to the boil.
(c) To remove excess saltiness from and to clean bacon and salt pork.

Blind Baking a hollow pastry case, flan, *barquette*, etc., using a temporary filling of haricot beans which are later discarded.

Blond (à) To shallow fry in butter, oil or fat to a very pale straw colour.

Bouchée A small puff pastry case.

Bouillon A rich strong clear stock of game, poultry, meat or vegetables.

Brunoise A mixture of vegetables chopped or finely shredded and cooked in butter or other fats; it is used in forcemeats, sauces, etc.

Buisson (en) Arranged in a cluster, bunch or pyramid. Fried smelts, sprats, anchovies, shrimps or crayfish are often arranged *en buisson.*

Canapé Small fancy-cut slices of bread which can be buttered, fried or toasted and used as a base for a savoury or *hors d'œuvre.*

Caramel Burnt sugar used for colouring gravies, etc.

Caramelise To melt sugar and cook till it reaches a straw or darker brown colour.

Casserole An ovenproof earthenware, porcelain or metal vessel with a lid. Food cooked *en casserole* is usually served at the table with its prepared contents.

Cassolette A small porcelain casserole for the service of individual eggs, shellfish, meat, poultry, etc.

Chaudfroiter To coat cooked meat, game, poultry, fish, etc., with a suitable sauce then with aspic jelly.

Chemiser To coat thinly the interior of moulds with a film of savoury or sweet jelly, meat or fish forcemeat or ice-cream, thus providing a coating for the main filling ingredient.

Chiffonade Shredded lettuce, sorrel, spinach, etc.

Chinois A wire sieve or strainer, conical in shape.

Chorizos Small highly seasoned Spanish sausages with a strong garlic content.

Ciseler To slash lightly with a sharp knife making incisions along the thick parts of the backs of such fish as trout, herring etc. to facilitate their cooking.
To shred into coarse *julienne* such vegetables as sorrel and lettuce.

Clarify To clear stock with crushed egg shells, slightly beaten egg whites and minced raw meat, the stock is brought to the boil, then cooled and strained.

Cloche A dome-shaped silver or glass cover. Essential equipment for mushrooms or chicken *sous cloche*.

Cock's Combs Cock's combs soaked in water to remove blood, lightly heated to facilitate their skinning, then poached in lemon juice, stock and butter.

Cocotte An ovenproof porcelain, earthenware or metal vessel with a lid for cooking individual dishes. Smaller *cocottes* are used for individual baked eggs.

Concasser To chop coarsely (especially tomatoes, after peeling and deseeding).

Contiser Incising pieces of fish, meat or poultry with a sharp knife to allow slices of truffle or mushrooms to be inserted.

Coucher To arrange the main ingredient on a bed or layer of one of the garnishing elements, such as spinach, noodles, etc.

Couverture A type of chocolate.

Crème Butter cream or Custard cream.

Croustades Deep scalloped tartlet pastry cases or hollowed out bread rolls for filling with various meats, sweetbreads and ragoûts.

Croustadines Shallow puff pastry cases of different shapes, oval, round, diamond and oblong.

Croûte A thick slice of bread, either fried or toasted, upon which small birds and *entrées* are served.

Croûtons Small cubes of bread fried in butter and used as a garnish for soups. Also various shapes of sliced bread fried in butter or oil or toasted and used as a garnish for fish and *entrées*.

Cuisson The liquor in which ingredients have been cooked.

Dariole Small, individual moulds.

Darne Thick, middle-cut of fish such as salmon or cod.

Deglaze To dilute with liquid (wine, stock, etc.) the pan sediment after cooking, especially after sautéeing or roasting.

Dégorger To soak certain foods in water to draw out the strong flavours or improve their colour. Also to remove coagulated blood from foods.

Degraissis The clarified fat from stocks.

Demi-glace Brown sauce, semi-clear and glossy.

Détendre To dilute to a thinner consistency.

Détrempe A paste of flour mixed with water or egg white, principally used for sealing casseroles hermetically.

Devil To season highly with a hot condiment such as cayenne or mustard.

Dorer To gild or to brush with beaten egg and bake to a golden colour.

Dry Duxelles Dry *duxelles*—two ounces chopped shallots stewed in one ounce of butter. One pound of finely chopped mushrooms added, then cooked until all moisture has evaporated. This mixture is used to flavour poached fish and shellfish and to garnish various dishes.

Escalope Very thin slices.

Etouffer To cook very slowly in very little liquid with a tightly fitting lid.

Etuver To cook slowly, without liquid, in butter, oil or fat and with a tightly fitting lid.

Farce Forcemeats and stuffings.

Fécule Starch flour usually but also cornflour or arrowroot.

Flambé Flamed; sprinkled with brandy or similar spirit and ignited.

Fleurons Small pieces of puff pastry, usually crescent shaped, used in garnishing, especially of fish dishes.

Fold To blend a light mixture gently into a heavier mixture, e.g. beaten egg whites.

Foncer To line flan rings and moulds with pastry, or to line braising pans with a layer of *mirepoix* prior to braising meat, etc.

Fondre To melt; usually to cook small garnishes under cover in butter or oil.

Fonds (a) Basic stocks (b) Bottoms, for example, of artichokes.

Fontaine *Faire la fontaine*—to make a well in a heap of flour on a marble top or pastry board before making pastry.

Forcemeat (*Les Farces*). Finely chopped meat or fish seasoned and used as a stuffing or garnish or in the making of other dishes.

Fraiser To knead or blend butter, sugar, etc., into flour with the palm of the hand downwards on a flat surface.

Frapper To chill. *Frappé* . . . iced.

Fricassée A white stew of white meats such as chicken, veal and rabbit. The meat is sautéed until barely coloured with cooking continued in a sauce.

Friture The special pan used for deep frying; also the name given to certain foods cooked by the deep frying method.

Fumet Concentrated stock of fish, game or poultry.

Galantine Boned meat or poultry, stuffed, rolled and cooked in gelatinous stock

Galette A small, flat cake of pastry, potato, etc.

Garnish See *Garniture* and section dealing with Garnishes.

Garniture The garnish; food items dressing the dish.

Glaze To give a golden coloured skin to heavily buttered sauces under the grill or in fierce oven.
To brush meat preparations with heavily reduced stocks to give a brilliant, shiny appearance.
To dust heavily with icing sugar, to pass through a hot oven until the sugar coating is translucent.
To envelope in fondant icing.
To dip fruits or marzipan in sugar cooked to the crack.

Gratin (au) Browning under the grill or quickly in the oven. Dishes cooked in this style are normally sprinkled with breadcrumbs, butter and possibly grated cheese. (*See Culinary Craft*, p. 85.)

Hachis Minced meat.

Hang A process by which meat is hung for a period of time depending on the type of meat, poultry or game to render the flesh tender.

Hors d'œuvre — Appetiser course opening a meal (normally luncheon). Frequently a variety of cold, piquant items but also "single" *hors d'œuvre* such as smoked salmon and hot *hors d'œuvre* of assorted, tiny savoury items.

Julienne — Fine or medium-sized strips of vegetables, meats, poultry of about one inch in length.

Jus — Unthickened gravy or the natural juices.

Lard — "To lard"—to introduce small or large pieces of dry salted pork fat or fat bacon by a special needle to enrich certain joints of meat, poultry and game before cooking.

Lardons — Small strips of fat bacon for larding purposes. Small or medium-sized cubes or *bâtons* of streaky bacon for *garniture.*

Liason — The binding or thickening agent used in soups and sauces. This may be egg yolks, *beurre manié,* roux or blood.

Losange — Lozenge or diamond shape.

Lustrer — To glaze or make brilliant by coating with aspic.

Macédoine — A variety of multi-coloured fruits or vegetables cut into small, even cubes and used for fruit salad or, in the case of vegetables, for a garnish or *hors d'œuvre.*

Macerate — To soak fruit in syrup, liquor, brandy, etc.

Marinate — To marinate—to steep pieces of meat in a prepared liquid of wine, water and *aromates* to both tenderise and flavour. Smaller pieces may be marinated in lemon juice, wine, spirits or oil with the addition of *aromates.* (*See Marinades,* p. 113.)

Marmite — A deep earthenware casserole in which certain broths are cooked and served.

Marzipan — A confection of almonds and sugar.

Mask — To cover or mask over with a sauce.

Matignon — Equal quantities of small, fine slices of carrot, onion, and raw ham with one-third of celery, a sprig of thyme and bay leaf. These are all stewed in butter, finished with Madeira or sherry and cooked to a soft or *purée* consistency.

Médaillon — A round slice of meat, poultry, game or fish.

Mie de Pain — Crumbs of bread without crust; fresh, white breadcrumbs.

Mijoter — To stew in sauce at a low temperature for a lengthy period.

Mirepoix — A basic flavouring prepared by frying roughly cubed onions, carrots, celery and raw ham. It is used for soups, sauces and braised dishes.

Moisten — To cover with liquid (stock, wine, etc.) or to add a specific amount of liquid as directed in the recipe.

Monter — To aerate by whisking or beating egg whites, cream, etc. *Monter au beurre*—to finish a sauce by beating whilst adding "nuts" of butter.

Moule — Mould. There are many varieties of moulds, such as *moule à baba* (baba mould), *à charmière* (hinged), etc.

Mousse — A light, aerated mixture of eggs, cream and gelatine which can be savoury (meat, poultry, game or fish) or sweet, (fruit *purée,* chocolate etc.).

Napper — To coat lightly with sauce, custard or aspic.

Noisette Butter This is butter which has been heated until it acquires a pale brown colour and nutty aroma. It is often called simply Brown butter.

Noisettes Small round pieces of meat without bone cut from the loin and best-end-of-mutton or lamb.

Panache A mixture of at least two different varieties of vegetables.

Panada A binding agent, commonly a thick mixture of flour, butter and a little liquid. It is also used as a foundation for *soufflés*. (*See Panada*, p. 115.)

Paner To coat with egg and breadcrumbs; to cover with breadcrumbs, cake crumbs or chopped nuts.

Papillote (en) Paper or foil cases in which food is cooked or served.

Pare To pare, peel or cut off the outside skin of a fruit or vegetable with a knife or parer (peeler). Also to trim to the desired shape or form.

Parings The trimmings which are left after peeling and shaping.

Pâte Pastry, dough.

Pâté Originally a meat or fish dish enclosed in pastry, now extended to meat or fish mixtures baked in a mould or loaf tin and served cold. (*See Pâtés.*)

Paupiette A thin slice of meat or fillet of raw fish, folded or rolled and normally filled with stuffing before cooking.

Paysanne Vegetables cut in small thin slices. (*See Garnishes*, p. 131.)

Pinch To crimp pastry, usually with a special utensil, in order to join or decorate the pastry edges.

Poach To cook gently in a liquid just at or below the point of boiling. (*See Poaching*, p. 85.)

Poêler To pot roast upon a bed of root vegetables in a roasting pan, tightly covered with a lid. (*See Cooking à la Poêle*, p. 84.)

Point The point of a small knife inserted into a finely powdered condiment such as cayenne pepper, and removed, leaving only a minute quantity on the knife.

Pot-au-Feu Popular, traditional beef broth.

Pré-Salé Describes lamb or mutton reared on salt marshes. (*See Mutton and Lamb.*)

Purér To mash solid foods by rubbing through a sieve, pounding in a mortar, or putting through the liquidiser of an electric blender. A *purée* of anything is food which has been so treated.

Quenelles Forcemeats shaped with different utensils and cooked. (*See Quenelles*, p. 118.)

Refresh To place fruit, meat and vegetables which have been previously blanched, under cold running water.

Raspings Breadcrumbs prepared from the oven-dried crusts of bread.

Réchauffé A dish made with previously cooked food which is reheated.

Reduce To reduce stocks, sauces, to their required consistency and flavour by boiling or simmering uncovered.

Repère A paste usually of flour and water for sealing casseroles when the contents must be tightly closed.

Revenir	To colour quickly in hot fat, usually prior to moistening with stock or sauce.
Roux	A thickening for soups and sauces, made of melted butter and flour cooked together. It can be white, straw or brown in colour. (*See Roux*, p. 120.)
Royale	A savoury custard of eggs variously coloured and flavoured. It is poached and cut in various shapes for garnishing soups, especially *consommés*.
Saignant	Underdone meat.
Saisir	To seize. To commence cooking with a fierce heat.
Salmis	Game stew.
Salpicon	Various ingredients cut into small dice and bound with a sauce. These are used to fill *vol-au-vent* cases, *bouchées*, *canapés* and used to make *croquettes*, rissoles. Various *glacé* fruits cut into small dice, macerated in liqueurs preceding their incorporation into various ices, cream and *bavaroises*.
Saupoudrer	To sprinkle with dry materials such as salt, seasonings, grated cheese breadcrumbs and sugar, as distinct from liquids.
Sauté	To shallow fry lightly in hot fat, shaking the pan frequently. (*See Sautéing*, p. 83.)
Sauteuse	A shallow, sloping sided saucepan of various sizes.
Sautoir	A deep *sauté* pan.
Sear	To brown and seal the outer surface of meat and poultry in hot fat for a few minutes on each side. This forms a coating or skin on the outside and helps prevent juices from being lost during the ensuing cooking process.
Singer	To sprinkle, usually meat, with flour and brown rapidly without cooking in the oven as a preliminary step in braises and similar dishes.
Soubise	A *purée* of onions enriched with cream.
Spaetzle	A noodle dough which has been pushed through a special sieve and boiled in water.
Spatula	A flat, wooden spoon.
Stiffen	To cook meat, poultry and oysters by brief heating in butter or liquid without colouring or completely cooking.
Suprêmes	Boneless breasts of poultry and game; also a term used for fillets of fish.
Sweat	To stew gently, without colouring, in butter with added seasoning so that the ingredients may cook in their own essences or juices.
Tabasco	Brand name of a hot, pungent, pepper sauce, originating in Louisiana, U.S.A.
Tammy	A sieve or "tammy", for example, *tamis de crin*—a hair sieve or *tamis de fer*—wire sieve.
Tarhonya	Hungarian noodle dough prepared and cooked as *spaetzle* and used for garnishing goulashes.
Timbale	A drum shaped mould; a drum shaped silver serving dish.

Tomber à Glace	To evaporate a stock to a syrupy consistency, that is, to make a glaze.
Tomatoes Concassée	Tomatoes skinned, deseeded and coarsely chopped.
Tomatoes Fondues	Concasséd tomatoes, gently stewed in butter or oil, with a little chopped shallot, until the moisture has evaporated and the product becomes a firm pulp. (*See Fondue de Tomates*, p. 119.)
Tragacanth	A vegetable gum or mucilage used in confectionery production.
Trancher	To carve or slice.
Travailler	To work and mix thoroughly and for a long period.
Tronçons	Thick slices or steaks of fish, including the bones, from larger fish such as turbot, brill or halibut.
Truss	To truss—to tie together poultry; to insert the claws of crayfish into their bodies for decorative purposes.
Turn	The rolling and folding of puff pastry. To shape with a knife into barrel or olive shapes.
Vanner	To stir sauces occasionally to prevent the formation of a skin.
Veil	To top cold sweet dishes with spun sugar.
Velouté	A foundation white sauce made from fish, poultry, meat and stocks; white soup of similar foundations.
Verjus	Verjuice—juice of sour unripe fruit, usually grapes.
Vesiga	The dried spinal marrow of the sturgeon. Essential ingredient in the preparation of *coulibiac* or Russian fish pies.
Zest	The "zest" is the outer, coloured rind of citrus fruits, which is thinly pared off (without any pith) for flavouring and garnishing.
Zucchini	A species of very small vegetable marrows used when immature.

Many of the very basic cooking materials which are included in nine out of ten recipes become so familiar and well-used that we sometimes forget that they deserve just as much consideration as the more unusual ingredients. Success in cooking depends to a great extent upon the knowledge and understanding of these basic materials, how to choose, prepare and use them. Armed with this knowledge it is easier to understand how such basics as flour, raising agents, fats, sugars and vegetables react in cooking and how to treat them to achieve the best results.

MILK AND DAIRY PRODUCTS

Milk occupies among foods an almost unique position in that it is a substance specifically designed to satisfy the nutritive demands of rapid growth. However, it must be remembered that the composition of cows' milk is not constant throughout the year, and that during winter and early spring, certain nutrient levels, for example, vitamins A and D fall rapidly. Vitamin C, a constant with milk straight from the cow, may be lost in various proportions during processing.

There are very strict regulations governing the sale of milk in this country. Various processes, for example, heat treatment, ensure that the milk is safe since milk can be a dangerous carrier of disease. When buying milk read the label first to see which type it is. It will probably be one of the following:

Pasteurised milk. This milk is collected in bulk from a number of dairy farmers. It is pasteurised by heating and retaining at a temperature of 150°F for 30 minutes or at 161°F for 15 seconds. At these time-temperature relationships certain germs are destroyed which ensures that the milk is safe.

Tuberculin tested milk is sometimes more expensive but has an excellent flavour. It is milk from certain tested and controlled herds, which must pass the tuberculin test (free from the tuberculin germ). This is the best milk to set for cream and to use for cheese and junkets as the necessary souring process proceeds quickly and naturally. The majority of pasteurised milk sold today is from T.T. herds in which case it will be labelled T.T. (Pasteurised).

Homogenised milk, mainly used by the catering trade, is milk which is processed to distribute the cream throughout the bottle of milk. There is, therefore, no "cream line". It keeps better and is considered to be more "creamy".

Sterilised milk. This is always homogenised; T.T. and pasteurised are sometimes treated in this way too. Sterilised milk is heated in the bottle and maintained at not less than 212°F for twenty to thirty minutes; it is then sealed. It tends to have a more creamy colour than other types of milk and some people say that it has a cooked flavour, but it does keep well.

Jersey and Guernsey milk must come from cows of these breeds. They give a rich creamy milk which is usually more expensive. The dairy will usually distinguish them by the use of a different coloured top.

In addition to milk itself there are other milk by-products which are used in cooking.

Skim-milk, which is whole milk with the cream skimmed off, still retains considerable nutritive value despite the loss of cream.

Butter-milk is the liquid residue left when milk or cream has been churned. Low in fat content like skim-milk, butter-milk has a sour flavour and is used for making scones.

Dried full-cream milk is milk from which the water content has been removed. It is used mainly in infant feeding.

Dried skim-milk, with the water and fat removed, is deficient in the fat-soluble vitamins but it is nevertheless nutritious and useful for cooking.
There are many well-known preserved milk products such as evaporated milk and condensed sweetened milk.

Sour-milk is required in a number of recipes.
Untreated or raw milk will sour naturally after approximately 2-3 days, although the time taken for it to sour will depend upon the place where the milk is kept, whether the milk was cooled after milking, and also upon climatic conditions. If you wish to sour milk, leave the milk standing in a warm room, or alternatively it can be soured by a "starter". A small amount of sour milk left over from a previous batch being stirred into the fresh milk.

Whey is the thin water fluid left after cheese-making. It contains no fat.

When boiling milk use a thick saucepan, preferably one kept exclusively for the purpose, and always rinse the pan first, with cold water.

Reduced milk may be called for in a recipe. To obtain this, simmer the milk until it is reduced in quantity, usually by half.

Milk should be stored in the refrigerator or in a cool dark place. Scald and rinse very thoroughly all vessels used for milk and never add a fresh milk supply to an earlier one. Milk absorbs other flavours so it should be kept covered and away from strong-smelling foods, especially in all-purpose refrigerators.

Milk is the raw material from which cream, butter, cheese and other dairy products are made. Single cream has a minimum fat content of 18% and will not whip on its own. It is widely used in cooking as it does not separate so easily when added to hot foods. Double cream has a minimum fat content of 48%.

Sour cream is cream that has fermented. This is a natural process and occurs after 2-3 days. It is due to the lactic acid bacterial constituents of the cream itself.

Yoghourt and *Kafir* are products made from fresh milk to which a lively organism, sensitive to temperatures, is introduced. This culture must be incubated in high quality milk which is heated to 180°, then cooled to 110°. The milk thickens and becomes slightly sour.

SOLID FATS

Butter is considered superior to other fats because of its flavour characteristics. This distinctive flavour is imparted to all foods cooked in it and all baked foods containing butter so it is used whenever possible in preference to all other fats. When butter turns rancid it has a strong unpleasant smell and flavour. Always keep butter away from strong-smelling foods at refrigerated temperatures.

New Zealand and *Australian* butters, which may be salted or unsalted, have a mild and delicate flavour and are bright yellow in colour. Use for pastry and biscuits.

Dutch and *Danish* butters are made from cream which has been ripened. They may also be salted or unsalted. They have a fuller flavour and a finer texture. Use especially for cakes.

Beef-fat (dripping) is a natural solid fat made by rendering the fats contained in beef.

Lard is one of the purest fats as it contains little or no water at all. It is the rendered fat from pork.

Suet is obtained from the fat surrounding the kidneys of animals. Beef suet is the most commonly used in recipes calling for suet.

Margarine is a manufactured fat made from oils usually, but not necessarily, of vegetable origin and also milk, colouring and vitamins A and D which must be added. The amount of vitamins added are governed by law, in fact margarine may be a superior source of vitamin D than butter, but butter often contains more vitamin A.

LIQUID FATS

Vegetable oils are pressed from various seeds and fruits, for example, corn, olive and soya bean, sesame and sunflower. There are also nut oils such as groundnut and coconut.

Olive Oil is used a great deal in cooking, especially for frying and salad dressings. The best olive oil is cold-pressed virgin oil. It has a fine, fruit taste and a greenish colour. It does not go rancid quickly. The most common type of olive oil sold in this country is hot-pressed olive oil. It is lighter in colour and becomes rancid more quickly than the virgin oil. Olive oils are like wines in that their flavours are affected by the soils in which they are grown. Greek, Spanish and Italian oils all have a distinctive flavour imparted by the soils of their native countries.

Edible oils, especially olive oil, must not be kept in too cold a place, otherwise they will congeal. It is better to store oils in a cool, dark, place in sealed bottles.

Most of the processed oils are bland in flavour, have high smoking points and are therefore useful for deep frying. Care must be observed with their handling; daily filtering increases their working lives. All fats are perishable and should be kept away from foods with a strong smell, as fats readily absorb flavours. Either keep fats in the refrigerator or else in a cool place. They should be kept covered either in their own wrapper, or in foil or in a plastic box with a lid. Fats also need to be kept away from strong lights and heat both of which help to turn them rancid.

Nutritionally, fats and oils are a concentrated source of energy and stored in the body help to protect us from cold. They also have a high "satiety" value which means a meal containing fat gives a more satisfying feeling than a fatless one.

CEREALS AND THEIR PRODUCTS

Cereals include rice, wheat, sweetcorn or maize, barley, oats, rice, millet and buckwheat. As cereals are the seeds from which a new plant will be grown, they are a concentrated source of nutrients. The chief one is carbohydrate (starch), but cereals also contain small amounts of protein, fat, mineral salts, and vitamins. They are also cheap and easy to produce so one or more of them forms the staple diet of most countries of the world.

Wheat Flour contains gluten and is the most widely consumed flour in the world. This protein forms a small proportion of each grain of wheat. Since gluten becomes viscous when moistened, it has the ability to turn flour and water into a sticky dough or paste. We distinguish between two kinds of wheat flour—"strong" and "weak". Strong flour contains more gluten and is therefore more suited to the making of bread, puff pastry, etc. Weak flours are better reserved for biscuits, scones, cakes and short pastry. Durum wheat is a variety originally grown in Italy—it gives an exceptionally strong flour and is used for making *pasta*. Heat sets the gluten rigidly forming the structure of bread.

There are many different flours sold and it is important to choose the right one for each purpose:

General purpose flour or household flour is known as *plain* flour. Suitable for most purposes, it is used for thickening sauces, making scones, plain cakes, fruit cakes, rich yeast mixtures, short crust pastry, steamed and baked puddings.

Soft flour is for light cakes, biscuits and short pastry. If soft flour is unobtainable a mixture of 7 oz of general purpose flour and 1 oz of cornflour can be used.

Bread flour is strong flour, i.e., flour with a high gluten content and is used for plain breads, buns and puff pastry.

Self-raising flour can be bought brown or white. This is a fairly soft flour containing a controlled amount of baking powder.

In addition there are two main types of *brown* flour sold, a *refined wholemeal* flour which contains a large proportion of the original grain with the bran and germ of the wheat removed, and a *coarse texture whole wholemeal* flour which is made from whole wheat grain. This is usually coarsely ground and is unsuitable for baking.

Do not store flour in the original paper bag because it is affected by steam and could become damp and spoil. Keep flour in a cool, dark place in a covered container.

OTHER CEREALS

Rye. This is used in Germany and Scandinavia for bread-making and distilled spirits. It is generally speaking unsuitable for bread as it is low in gluten.

Oats, which contain a larger proportion of fat, are made into flour, oatflakes and semolina.

Barley is used for making beer and also milled to produce flour, semolina and flakes.

Millet is milled and like wheat flour can be used to thicken soups and sauces.

Maize is used for cornflakes and the young corncobs are boiled or grilled and served as a vegetable with butter.

Rice is the most important cereal after wheat. It is the staple diet of many countries in the Eastern Hemisphere, although it has the highest carbohydrate content and the lowest proportion of protein, fat and mineral elements. The rice grain is milled to remove the outer bran layers and the germ. The most commonly used varieties are the round grain type of rice of which *Carolina* is the best known and long-grained *Patna* rice.

Carolina rice is of short or medium length. These grains have a tendency to stick together when cooked so it is better to use them for puddings.

Of long grained rice *Patna* is the best known, with its thin, elongated grains and rounded ends. The grains stay separated when cooked so it is used for boiled rice, savoury dishes and for stuffings, and moulded rice recipes.

There are also other types of rice named by their country of origin.

Siam rice, which has long thin transparent grains, is of superior quality.

Mexican rice, has hard thick transparent grains and is of good quality.

Italian rice, from Vialone or Ostiglia, has round grains often surrounded by a thin brown band and is rarely glazed. It is also of good quality.

Par-Boiled rice has the advantage that it has been partly cooked under steam pressure before milling so it contains more minerals and vitamins than milled white rice. It also absorbs more water during cooking and remains separate and fluffy.

Brown rice has had only part of the bran layers removed, thus it is more nutritious than milled white rice. It also takes longer to cook, has more flavour and absorbs more water; however the brown appearance may spoil the look of some dishes.

Wild rice is not a true rice and needs special recipes.

Rice Flour is used for thickening soups, etc., but it contains no gluten so it is not suitable for bread-making. There are also many types of rice breakfast cereals on the market.

Rice is easy to store and should be kept in a dry place.

Other types of flour on the market used in cooking include *cornflour*, which is a highly refined flour milled from corn. Its very fine texture is suitable for thickening and also for pastry-making and infant foods.

Buckwheat flour is used alone or mixed with wheat or oatmeal flour, then used for bread and pastries, *blinis* and other pancakes.

Starch is also obtained from other plants apart from cereals, such as arrowroot, from tropical plants and is used for thickening purposes.

Potato flour is a coarse flour with a less delicate flavour; it is normally used in combination with other flours.

Tapioca is starch extracted from Kassava roots; it is very white and is used in soups and puddings.

Soya flour from the soya bean has a high protein and fat content.

Sago is derived from an Indian palm and is used for soups and puddings.

Nut meal is made from finely ground dry nut meal and is used in *gâteaux* making.

SUGARS

Sugar is one of the two sources of carbohydrate. It is sweet-tasting and a most important source of calories. Most of our cooking is done with sugar obtained from one of two sources, either the sugar cane or the sugar beet. Chemically and in taste and appearance there is no difference between the two. When raw sugar is extracted from the cane or beet it contains many impurities so it is cleaned and highly refined to produce a number of varieties of sugar. The various types of sugar differ in their purity, colour and size of grain.

Granulated sugar is the cheapest white sugar and is suitable for most cooking purposes.

Castor sugar is a fine sugar separated from the coarse by sifting. It dissolves readily and therefore appears sweeter. Use it for fine cake-making especially for creaming mixtures and also for sweet pastry making.

Cube or Loaf sugar is made of granulated sugars moulded and cut into various sizes; it is used for beverages, for rubbing over the zest of citrus fruits and for caramel making.

Coffee sugar or crystals are very large crystals which dissolve slowly. Sometimes they are coloured.

Preserving sugar is also in very large crystals and is used in the preservation of fruit and jams.

Demerara sugar is brown crystalline sugar with a strong flavour.

Icing sugar is white sugar which has been passed through a fine mill. It is best used for icings, biscuits and desserts where a fine texture is required. It lumps easily and should always be sifted before use.

Moist sugar is light or dark brown sugar of a fine sandy texture.

Golden Syrup is made from the liquid residue which is left after the sugar crystals have been removed during refining.

Black Treacle is similar to syrup but it contains a smaller proportion of pure sugar substances and has a dark colour and strong flavour.

Molasses are made from a mixture of sugar and syrup formed during the refining process. It is dark brown in colour and is used for cattle food and by distillers.

Sugar should be stored in a dry well-ventilated place since it is easily affected by smell and damp.

VINEGAR

The choice of the right type of vinegar can make a great difference in cooking, as different vinegars have a sharp, rich, or mellow flavour. All vinegars are basically acetic acid, which may be brewed with beer, wine or cider. The following guide may help you to make the right choice for the particular purpose you have in mind;
Distilled white vinegar is *malt* vinegar which has been distilled to remove the brown colour. It is used in pickling, and where it is important to keep the food white.

Cider vinegar is based on cider, whilst malt vinegar is made from beer and has the stronger flavour.

Non-brewed vinegar is made from pure acetic acid and lacks the flavour and *bouquet* of brewed vinegars.

Wine vinegars are made from red or white wines and are the blandest in flavour.

Herb vinegars are made by using any of the above vinegars with individual herbs like tarragon in the proportion of 3 tablespoons of fresh herb leaves per quart of vinegar. After 4 weeks of steeping filter the vinegar, re-bottle in sterilised containers and keep tightly corked. For garlic vinegar crush the garlic, and leave in the vinegar for only 24 hours.

LEAVENING OR RAISING AGENTS

These are substances used to lighten the texture and consistency of baked mixtures. They depend upon the expansion of gases when heated. These gases may be air or carbon dioxide. Some mixtures depend for their lightness entirely upon the incorporation of air which is either beaten in, folded in, or added via beaten eggs, for example, sponges, batters, cakes without raising agents, *choux* pastry, meringues.

Carbon Dioxide is a raising agent produced by the use of baking powder either added to plain flour or that already added to self-raising flour. You can make your own baking powder by mixing bicarbonate of soda and cream of tartar. Sometimes soda is used alone as in soda bread and scones. Plain cakes of all kinds can be made satisfactorily with self-raising flour but there is too much raising agent in it for rich cakes, especially those containing plenty of eggs. Too much raising agent spoils both the texture and flavour of a cake and it is important in this respect to follow the advice of the recipe. When baking powder is added it should always be thoroughly sifted with the flour. Bicarbonate of soda is usually dissolved in milk or water, and is used in recipes which include acids like sour milk, lemon juice and vinegar. The chemical action between the acid and the bicarbonate of soda also produces carbon dioxide gas. Usually these recipes also contain some strong flavouring ingredient like syrup, treacle, or cocoa to disguise the brown colour and strong flavour imparted by the soda.

Yeast, like eggs and baking powder, is a leavening agent but it differs from the latter in that it is a living organism. As it grows it multiplies and produces carbon dioxide gas. In order to grow however it needs food, warmth, and moisture. It obtains food from the sugar used in mixing, warmth from the kitchen, utensils, and the place in which it is put to prove, and moisture from the water or milk used in mixing the dough. If the yeast lacks any one of these conditions the dough will not rise. Remember too that extreme heat kills but too much sugar, salt, or cold will inhibit the yeast.

There are three main types of yeast available to the housewife. *Compressed* yeast or *German* yeast is the most widely used. It is fawn in colour, crumbly in texture and if fresh should have a pleasant rather alcoholic smell. It should be quite free from brown or black specks which would indicate staleness. It will cream quickly with the sugar to become a thin fawn liquid. Store in a cool place, if necessary, but it is better to use as fresh as possible. Allow ½ ounce yeast in quantities up to 1 lb flour, 1 oz up to 3 pounds flour and 2 ounces up to 7 pounds flour.

Brewers yeast is in liquid form.

Dried yeast is in the form of small hard pellets. This yeast has to be steeped for several hours before use. It is more concentrated than compressed yeast and approximately half the amount is required.

When you are making rich yeast mixtures or yeast cake mixtures such as Danish pastry, *Savarin*, *Baba*, you will probably notice that due to the presence of large amounts of sugar, eggs, and fruit the action of the yeast is slowed down and they take longer to rise.

NUTS

Nuts are rich in fat and protein and are used largely in vegetarian cookery to take the place of meat. They are useful for their oils which carry their flavour, their texture for garnishing and to bring variety to foods.

Almonds are in two varieties, sweet and bitter, and are used for *torten*, almond paste, etc. A rich source of protein, fat and some vitamins and minerals, they are blanched and may be salted or toasted.

Brazil nuts have an exceptionally hard shell, so care is needed when cracking them to avoid breaking the kernel. They are also rich nutritionally.

Cashews. This nut is kidney shaped, it is softer and sweeter than most other nuts.

Chestnuts. The sweet variety are eaten and it is better to buy the larger size as they are easier to peel. Dried chestnuts are sold in Oriental shops and also chestnut flour. In some shops the tinned variety of water chestnuts are also available. Chestnuts are used for stuffings, as a vegetable and in confectionery. Water chestnuts are used for *hors d'œuvre*, vegetables and as salads.

Hazelnuts or *filberts* have a sophisticated flavour. Used in *gâteau* making.

Peanuts can be very useful if you appreciate the flavour. They are usually sold either unroasted and shelled or unshelled, or roasted and shelled and salted; they can be used for garnishing. Peanuts have a higher protein content than most other nuts.

Pistachio nuts are very small with a delicious flavour and delightful green colour; they are used for *farces* and *pâtés* and to garnish sweet dishes.

Pumpkin, squash, melon and *sunflower* seeds are all nutritionally valuable, have a good flavour and can be roasted.

Walnuts are probably the most familiar and most easily available type of nut. When unripe they are pickled, but they are sold ripe both with and without the shell.

Nuts should be kept and stored in their shells to protect them from light, heat, moisture and air which tend to cause rancidity. If they are already shelled store them tightly covered in a cool, dark, dry, place. To *blanch* nuts pour boiling water over the shelled nuts and allow to stand up to one minute. Drain, and pour cold water over them then pinch or rub off skins. To *roast* or *toast* nuts place them blanched or unblanched in an oven set at 300° F or Gas Mark 3; turn them frequently to avoid scorching. Do not overtoast. To chop nuts use a chopping knife and board, if larger pieces are needed simply break with the fingers.

Nuts may be ground with a special grater which shreds or grates them sharply so that no oil is lost.

DRIED FRUITS

Dried fruits have a high calorie value and nutritive value. This is because 5½ pounds of fresh apricots will yield 1 pound when dried. They are a concentrated foodstuff.

Dates, figs, apples, peaches, plums, apricots, currants and raisins are among the most popular dried fruits. They should all be stored in a cool place, tightly covered. Raisins are dried grapes and there are a number of different types; white raisins such as Muscatel are specially treated to retain their lovely colour.

Dried fruits may be plumped before being used. This is done by soaking them in the liquid in which they are to be cooked for 10-15 minutes before use.

When chopping small fruits use a portion of the flour called for in the recipe and they will be easier to chop.

CHOCOLATE AND COCOA

Both chocolate and cocoa come from the ever-green trees of the *genus Theobroma Cacao* "food of the Gods". They are both made from the cocoa bean but chocolate contains more cocoa butter and sugar.

Chocolate must be heated carefully over hot—never boiling—water; if it is over-heated it will become hard, white and fudgy. When grating chocolate, it is advisable to chill it first.

Chocolate is used in many sweet recipes for flavouring and decorating. Bitter American chocolate, which unfortunately is difficult to obtain in Britain, has no sugar added and is the strongest and best for cooking. Bitter French and English chocolate, of which several makes are available, does have sugar added.

Cocoa is used for flavouring foods and as a beverage. Both cocoa and chocolate contain fat, carbohydrate and iron.

In this country we differentiate between *couverture* and bakers' chocolate (ordinary cooking chocolate). *Couverture* contains pure cocoa butter, is more expensive and has to be tempered before use; one has to be experienced to do this. Bakers' chocolate generally made from palm kernel oil can be used at any temperature within limits and does not have to be tempered and thus is easy to use. Both can be bought either plain or milk. If *couverture* is not available use good quality plain chocolate.

SALT

Salt has many powers—the correct balance between salt and water in the body is essential to life itself. It also has great powers of preservation such as brining and curing meats.

The power of salt to heighten the flavour of other foods is its greatest culinary asset. It has many diverse effects upon foods being cooked so it must be used with care. It should be used sparingly, if at all, at the start of any cooking in which liquids will be greatly reduced, for instance, stocks, soups and sauces. A general rule to follow is that salt should be added towards the end of the cooking time and that seasoning should be corrected just before serving. Remember that it is far easier to add salt than to remove it, so calculate the amount you need with care. Also many foods contain salt, for example, sea-fish, celery and carrots. The following are the most common salts available to the housewife:

Rock salt is grey or pinkish brown in colour, as it is unrefined. It consists of small crystals which can be freshly ground by the cook for use at the table.

Block salt is sold in large bars or blocks and can be crushed before use. It is the best salt to use in the kitchen as it is purer than table salt.

Table salt is very fine salt which has been mixed with dehydrators to keep it free-flowing.

Iodised salt is recommended for use in certain areas where the water or soils are lacking in this essential mineral.

Brine is a solution of salt and water, preferably soft water. A 10% brine solution which is about the strongest used in food processing is made by dissolving 6 tablespoons salt in a quart of liquid.

Basic Preparations

STOCKS

The primary foundation preparation is stock or *les fonds*, which can be said to contain the character of the *cuisine*. It is the essential ingredient of sauces which are the traditional glory of French cooking. It is also the essential ingredient of soups, aspics and glazes, and is used for braising meats and many recipes.

Stock is the liquid in which meat, bones, fish or vegetables have simmered. The soluble nutrients and flavouring constituents gradually dissolve into the water during the long slow cooking process. As a general rule stock consists of the lean, gelatinous parts of meat with a proportion of bone and fresh vegetables, which need not necessarily be young and expensive, as trimmings and coarse stalks can be used.

When making stock avoid using too much seasoning or any foods which have a strong or a bitter flavour as these would overpower the characteristic flavour of meat stock—no one flavour should predominate. Do not use starchy substances such as old gravy, sauce or bread since these would sour the stock. Salt meat or very fat meat should not be used either. When seasoning stocks it is better to use whole spices like peppercorns, allspice, coriander, celery seeds and bay leaf, but only in small quantities. These are strong and pungent spices and should be used with discretion. Mace, paprika and cayenne should be added in very small pinches. Salt should be used sparingly as the stock will be reduced and therefore concentrated. Be sure to use a *bouquet garni*, an onion stuck with cloves is often included for flavouring purposes, and so also are one or two leeks.

When preparing foods for the stockpot always blanch bones for white stock; chop all bones and leave the vegetables whole to avoid clouding. Then cover all the ingredients with cold water and bring gradually to the boil. Lower the heat and simmer gently, skimming away all the white scum at the start of and during the cooking.

Meatless stock is used in vegetarian cookery and consists of a mixture of thinly sliced vegetables, carrots, celeriac, onions, browned in vegetable fat and moistened with water. It is seasoned with parsley, thyme and bay leaf. Other specialised stocks include *consommé*, white or brown thickened stocks, chicken stocks, game and veal stocks.

It is more practical in private households to make stock in large quantities and store it in the refrigerator or in a covered vessel in a cool place. You will find, therefore, that the average quantity for stock given in the following recipes is for 8 pints.

Unless carefully watched, stock will turn sour all too easily, particularly in hot weather. Meat deteriorates very quickly and vegetables soon ferment. As soon as the stock is removed from the heat, lift out the meat and the now flavourless vegetables. Remove the congealed fat from the stock after it has become cold. Another useful tip is to boil up the stock daily in summer and every second day in winter.

Fond Blanc Ordinaire * *Plain White Stock*

White stock is a colourless *bouillon* made from unbrowned meat and bones (including chicken) and vegetables. It is used as a basis for many soups and meat dishes and to make white sauces, for example, white stews (*Blanquettes*), *veloutés* and for poaching poultry.

To make 8 *pints:* 1 *lb shin of beef or shoulder of veal;* 4 *lb knuckle of veal;* 4 *lb chicken giblets and carcase;* ½ *lb carrots;* ½ *lb onions;* ¼ *lb leeks;* 1 *large bouquet garni;* ½ *oz salt;* 12 *pints water.* Cooking time: about 4 hours.

Bone and tie up the meats; crack the bones and place them with the meat in a large pan or stockpot. Add the chicken giblets and the carcase and cover with the water. Bring to the boil and skim away the scum constantly for 5 minutes. Then add the washed and prepared vegetables, herbs and seasonings. Skim off accumulated scum and fat occasionally. If the level of the liquid evaporates below the level of the ingredients add more *boiling* water. Simmer for 4 hours over low heat never allowing the liquid to boil. Remove from heat. Add a little cold water to aid settlement, cool then skim off fat and strain through muslin.

NOTE. Raw veal releases a considerable quantity of grey and granular scum that can cloud your stock if it is not completely removed. The easiest way to deal with this problem is to blanch the veal first before proceeding to make stock. Place the boned and tied veal and the raw, cracked veal bones in a large stockpot. Cover with cold water, bring to the boil and skim constantly for 5 minutes. Drain and rinse the bones and meat under cold water to remove all the scum. Rinse the stockpot clean and proceed according to the recipe instructions.

▣ Blanc de Volaille * *White Chicken Stock*

Proceed as for Plain White stock but add a medium-sized chicken, weighing about 3 lb, or an additional 2 lb of chicken carcase and giblets. The chicken may be removed when tender and served separately and the stock simmered for the remainder of the time.

▣ Brun Clair * *Clear Brown Stock*

Brown stock is made from beef or veal, the bones and vegetables are browned in a roasting tin in the oven. It is used to make brown sauces, braised meat and brown stews.

To make 8 *pints:* 5 *lb lean beef, usually shin;* 6 *lb knuckle of veal;* 2 *lb beef and veal bones;* 1 *lb rind of salt pork, blanched;* ½ *lb knuckle of ham, blanched;* 2 *oz fat;* ½ *lb carrots;* ¾ *lb onions;* 1 *large bouquet garni;* 1 *large clove of garlic;* ½ *oz salt;* 14 *pints water.* Cooking time: about 8 hours.

Cut the meats and pork rind into large pieces. Crack the beef and veal bones into small pieces. Slice the carrots and onions. Cook everything gently for a few minutes, including the bones, in the hot fat. When the ingredients are lightly browned, add 4 pints of water. Simmer 1 hour, with the pan partially covered, add the remainder of the water, and the herbs and garlic and simmer over low heat for 6-7 hours, skimming from time to time. Cool and remove the meat and bones. Finally skim off fat and strain through muslin. Never allow the liquid to boil as the stock will become cloudy.

Fond Brun de Veau * *Brown Veal Stock*

To make 8 pints: 6 lb shoulder of veal; 2 lb knuckle of veal; 2 lb veal bones; 3 oz fat; ½ lb carrots; ½ lb onions; 1 *large bouquet garni; ½ oz salt;* 14 *pints white stock.* Cooking time: about 6 hours.

Tie up the meat with string, spread with fat, season, and brown on top of the stove. Saw or chop the bones into manageable pieces (about 4-inch lengths). Line a pan with sliced vegetables, add the bones, place the browned meat on top and complete with the *bouquet garni.* Cover and sweat for 15 minutes. Add 3½ pints of the white stock and simmer for 1 hour with the saucepan partially covered with a lid. Then add another 4 pints of the white stock and simmer again for 1 hour. Add the remainder of the stock. Bring to the boil, skim, add salt and simmer for 6 hours over low heat. Cool and remove meat and bones. Skim off fat and strain through muslin. Use for making brown sauces, braising meat and vegetables and for making *consommé.*

⊡ **de Gibier** * *Game*

To make 5 pints: 2 lb hare heads and venison trimmings or bones; 4 lb game or game trimmings, in small pieces; ¼ lb leeks; ¼ lb carrots; 2 oz onion; 2 oz celery; ¼ lb mushroom trimmings; 6 juniper berries (if available); 3 cloves; 1 small bay leaf; ¾ oz salt; 9 pints water. Cooking time: about 3 hours.

Brown the game, hare heads, venison trimmings and bones in a roasting tin in the oven. Remove to the stockpot. Add water, bring to the boil, simmer, skimming occasionally. After 10 minutes, add the diced vegetables, mushroom trimmings, the juniper berries, the cloves, bay leaf and a little salt. Cook over low heat for 2½-3 hours, skimming as required. Remove from heat. Add a little cold water to settle the stock and skim. Strain through muslin.

⊡ **de Poisson** * *Fish Stock*

Fish stock is made from fish bones and trimmings, chopped onions, parsley, thyme, bay leaf, lemon juice and mushrooms. The liquid used can be augmented with up to an equal quantity of white wine. Fish stock is usually only simmered for about half an hour, as prolonged simmering would make the stock bitter and too strong. It is then used to make sauces which are served with fish (e.g. *sauce Normande, sauce Vin Blanc*), and to moisten braised or poached fish.

To make 4 pints: 6 lb bones and trimmings from different kinds of fish; ¼ lb sliced onions; ½ lb mushroom stalks; 1 oz parsley stalks; a few drops of lemon juice; 1 bay leaf; ⅛ oz salt; 4 pints water; 2 pints dry white wine.

Wash the fish trimmings and place the ingredients in the stockpot and season. Cover partially, bring to the boil slowly and skim. Reduce the heat and simmer slowly for half an hour. Strain through muslin. Use for poaching and braising fish, for fish stews and fish sauces.

⊡ **de Poisson au Vin Rouge** * *Fish with Red Wine*

Proceed as for Fish stock but moisten with 4 pints red wine and 2 pints water.

Jus au Coulis de Veau * *Veal or Meat Gravy*

To make 4 pints: $\frac{1}{2}$ lb veal (or meat) trimmings; 1 large carrot; 1 large diced onion; $\frac{1}{8}$ oz salt; $\frac{1}{4}$ lb flour; $\frac{1}{2}$ pint brown veal stock; $\frac{1}{2}$ pint white wine; aromatic vegetables such as celery, turnips and onions, to taste; 7 pints water. Cooking time: about 1 hour.

Tie up the meat with string then brown all the ingredients in a large saucepan on top of the stove. Sprinkle with flour and cook for a few minutes, stirring with a wooden spoon. Add white wine, scrape the base of the pan thoroughly and stir to acquire the colour and flavour. Reduce by half. Add stock and water and cook for 1 hour over low heat, skimming occasionally. Remove from the heat, cool and settle by adding a little cold water. Skim and strain through a muslin. Use for making gravy and as a liquid to deglaze the pan or tin in which meat has been cooked.

⊡ de Veau Lié * *Thickened Veal Gravy*

To make 1 pint: 4 pints brown veal stock; 1 oz potato flour; 3 tablespoons clear brown stock.

Reduce the brown veal stock by a quarter. Thicken with the potato flour (or cornflour) which has been mixed with the cold, clear brown stock. Strain through muslin. Serve as gravy for roast meat or use as a sauce.

⊡ de Veau Tomaté * *Tomato flavoured Veal Gravy*

To make $2\frac{1}{2}$ pints: 5 pints brown veal stock; 3 teaspoons tomato concentrate or paste.

Combine the brown veal stock and the tomato concentrate and reduce by half. Strain through muslin.

ESSENCES

Essences are obtained by boiling certain stocks, for example, game, chicken and fish, until they are reduced by one half the volume. Essences are not needed if the stocks have sufficient taste of their own and are used only to improve those which would otherwise be insipid.

GLAZES

Glazes are very intensive reductions of clear meat or game stocks. The stock is reduced until it is of a syrupy consistency and will coat a spoon without running off. Great care must be taken to get perfectly transparent glazes, so include a large proportion of bones rich in gelatine, for example knuckle of veal, in the stock. Be careful not to reduce the stock too much and so lose the delicate flavour.

Glazes are used for coating certain dishes, for instance *chaudfroid* of game and joints of meat to improve the flavour and make them look attractive. Glazes are used like essences to lend body to a sauce or preparation.

ASPIC JELLY

The most delicious aspic jellies or *gelées* are greatly reduced stock, made from the gelatinous portions of chicken, meat, or veal. Strictly speaking the reduced liquid should set of its own accord. Aspic should be brilliantly clear and have a well-seasoned slightly piquant flavour. If it is not sufficiently clear it will be necessary to clarify the aspic. The stock for aspic or *gelée* should be of the same general base as the food which is to be coated or moulded. Aspic is used for many cold dishes either as an ingredient or an accompaniment, and to make cold food look attractive and appetising.

Gelée Claire I * *Clear Aspic I*

To make 4 *pints:* 2½ *lb shin beef;* 1¼ *lb knuckle of veal;* ¼ *lb pork or bacon rinds;* 1 *calf's foot;* 2½ *lb knuckle of veal bones;* 4 *carrots;* 3 *leeks;* 2 *onions;* 1 *large bouquet garni;* 10 *peppercorns;* 1 *sprig of thyme;* 1 *bay leaf.* Cooking time: 4-5 hours.

Blanch the bacon rinds and the calf's foot, starting them in cold water. Boil for 5 minutes. Skim well, then rinse in cold water. Place all the meats in a tall stewpan in cold water. Bring to the boil, skim well and add the roughly chopped vegetables and the seasonings. Simmer 4-5 hours skimming regularly and taking great care that it does not boil but just simmers gently. Remove all fat and strain. If the aspic is to be used for chicken, add giblets or a whole chicken after 3 hours' cooking.

Gelée Claire II * *Clear Aspic II*

To make 8 *pints:* 4 *lb veal bones in small pieces;* 3 *calf's feet, split in* 2 *and tied up with string;* ⅛ *lb bacon rinds;* 4 *carrots;* 2 *leeks;* ⅛ *lb celery;* 3 *medium-sized onions;* 1 *bouquet garni;* 8 *peppercorns;* 12 *pints water.* Cooking time: 4-5 hours.

Place the calf's feet and bacon rinds in cold water. Blanch for 5 minutes and rinse in cold water. Place the calf's feet, bacon rinds and bones in 12 pints cold water and bring to the boil. Add the vegetables, knuckle of veal, *bouquet garni* and peppercorns. Salt moderately and simmer gently over very low heat skimming regularly. After cooking, the knuckle of veal may be removed and used for another dish. Remove fat and strain. For chicken aspic add very finely chopped chicken or a small whole chicken which is removed when cooked.

▣ Brune * *Brown Aspic*

Same recipe as for Clear Aspic II, but chop up and fry all the meat and vegetables except the calf's feet and bacon rinds until they are brown. Then proceed and cook as above. After cooking, remove all fat and strain. If the aspic is to be used with game, add some bones of the game or an old game bird.

▣ à l'Estragon * *Tarragon Aspic*

Add a spring of chopped tarragon when clarifying the aspic. (*See* p. 112.)

Gelée Maigre de Poisson * *Fish Aspic*

1 lb white fish; 1 lb bones of gelatinous fish; 1 small bouquet garni; 2 shallots; ¼ lb sliced onions; the green of one leek, sliced; 4 pints water; peppercorns; half a bay leaf; 2 cloves.

Place all the ingredients in a saucepan and bring to the boil. Lower the heat at once and simmer slowly for 30 minutes, skim and strain through a cloth. This aspic is clarified in the same way as other aspic jellies, but without the addition of meat. (*See below*)

⊡ au Porto, Madère * *Madeira, Port Aspic*

Add ¼ pint of the wine to 2 pints of cold clarified aspic while it is still liquid.

Base de Gelatine * *Quick Aspic using Gelatine*

In hot weather or when time is short, aspic may be made with stock to which gelatine has been added to set it. Either leaf or granular gelatine may be used but the leaf variety is recommended. The stock may be *bouillon*, from *pot-au-feu*, and from chicken, game or fish stock. The proportions to use are 10 sheets of French leaf gelatine (which should weigh 1 oz) to set 1 pint of liquid firmly. For a less solid result, 5 leaves, weighing approximately ½ oz will just set 1 pint of liquid. Gelatine should always be soaked before use, until it is soft. It should then be added to the warmed stock and clarified as specified.

Clarification de la Gelée * *Clarification of Aspic*

4 pints cold aspic; ½ lb lean, chopped beef; the green of a leek, sliced; ¾ oz chervil; 2 egg whites.

Before commencing the clarification make sure that all traces of fat have been removed from the stock and all equipment is free from grease. Place the meat, egg whites, chervil and sliced leek in a bowl and beat up together, then add the aspic. Pour this mixture into a saucepan and bring to the boil, stirring gently. Stop stirring as soon as the mixture boils and allow to stand for 15 minutes. Strain through muslin which has been wrung out in cold water.

NOTE: Leek and chervil do not contribute to the clarification process but it is convenient at this stage to complete the flavouring and adjust the seasoning.

COURT BOUILLON

Court bouillon is a special cooking liquor made from water, vegetables, herbs and wine or wine vinegar. It is used for boiling or poaching fish. It is not actually a stock in itself but rather a light stock which can yield a liquor from which a stock or sauce may be created. *Court bouillon* is nearly always prepared in advance and may be used several times provided it is strained and stored in a cool place. Large fish are always started in cold *bouillon*, whereas small fish or pieces are placed in the hot liquor. Fish intended for use with cold dishes are removed from the liquor while it is still lukewarm and covered with a moist cloth to prevent the surface from drying out. The proportions for *court bouillon* can be multiplied or divided according to the size of the fish or fish kettle in which it is prepared. When cooking fish, the liquid must not be allowed to bubble briskly when it has once come to the boil, since the flesh of the fish would fall apart. The fish kettle is therefore drawn to one side and the liquor maintained at simmering point. Crustaceans, such as lobsters, crayfish and crawfish, are cooked in salt water only, without any seasoning and must be boiled gently throughout the entire cooking time.

Court Bouillon I

For whole salmon, salmon trout, crawfish and lobster: 8 *pints water;* 1 *lb sliced carrots;* 1 *lb sliced onions;* 1 *sprig thyme;* 2 *small bay leaves;* 2 *oz parsley stalks;* ⅓ *pint wine vinegar;* 1 *oz salt;* 1 *dozen crushed peppercorns, added* 10 *minutes before the Court Bouillon is strained.* Cooking time: 1 hour.

Place all the ingredients in a large saucepan or fish kettle. The liquid is brought to the boil, skimmed and boiled for about 45 minutes. After cooking, strain through muslin and use either hot or cold depending on the type of fish to be cooked.

Court Bouillon II

For trout, carp, fish soups and crawfish: 4 *pints dry white wine;* 4 *pints water;* 5 *sliced shallots;* ¾ *lb sliced carrots;* ¾ *lb sliced onions;* 2 *oz parsley stalks;* 1 *sprig thyme;* 1 *bay leaf;* 1 *oz salt;* 1 *dozen crushed peppercorns, added* 10 *minutes before the Court Bouillon is strained.* Cooking time: 30 minutes.

Proceed as above, but only boil the liquid for about 30 minutes.

Court Bouillon III

Used for large pieces of turbot and brill. Cover the fish entirely with cold water; then add ¼ pint milk, a slice of peeled lemon and ½ ounce of salt per 1¼ pints of water.

MARINADES

A marinade is a seasoned liquid used for macerating (steeping) certain kinds of meat, especially game such as hare and venison, prior to cooking. Its purpose is to impregnate the piece with flavour and tenderise the meat. In some cases a marinade may be used to preserve the meat for a short time. The time taken for marinating depends on the nature and size of the piece. In winter large cuts such as thick roasts may take up to 6 days; in summer 2-3 days is normal. Smaller cuts such as meat for shish-kebabs may only require a few hours marinating time. Do not discard the marinade after use since it may be required for making a sauce as part of the recipe.

Marinades should be made in non-metal containers such as earthenware or glass vessels because of the corrosive action of acids on metal. Nowadays it is no longer necessary to marinate saddle of venison or saddle of hare in order not to change the very fine flavour of these meat cuts. On the other hand one may, although it is not always necessary, marinate the less fine cuts of hare and large game. To enhance the flavour of mutton, the addition of a little rosemary is recommended and for venison, the inclusion of a few juniper berries and basil. Again in any marinade, red wine may supplant white wine and the ratio of wine to vinegar may be varied according to taste.

Marinades may be raw or cooked. The cooked variety makes its flavour more available to the food and should be prepared in advance and used cold.

Marinade Crue * *Uncooked Marinade*

3 carrots; 2 onions; 3 shallots; peppercorns; 2 cloves; parsley stalks and thyme; 1 bay leaf; ¼ pint vinegar; ¾ pint red or white wine; 4 dessertspoons oil.

Place the meat to be marinated in a deep dish. On top place the sliced onions and shallots, a pinch of crushed peppercorns, a few juniper seeds, cloves, parsley, thyme, and bay leaf. Salt lightly and add the wine and vinegar. Baste the top of the meat with oil to prevent the part which is not submerged from turning black. Put in a cool place and turn the meat over several times. Small pieces (cutlets, *noisettes*) should marinate 24 hours and larger pieces such as haunch of venison for 2-3 days depending on the size of the piece.

⊡ Cuite * *Cooked Marinade*

The same ingredients as for uncooked marinade, but cook the vegetables in wine and vinegar, increasing the amount of the latter slightly to allow for evaporation during the cooking period which takes 1 hour. If in a hurry, the cooked, boiling marinade may be poured over the meat—provided that it is very fresh. In this way a perfectly marinated haunch of venison can be obtained in 24 hours and small pieces in 4-5 hours. Legs of mutton and mutton cutlets are sometimes marinated in this way and then known as "venison style" cutlets or leg.

⊡ pour Petites Pièces de Venaison * *Marinade for Small Pieces of Venison*

To make venison cutlets and *noisettes* very tender it is sufficient to marinate them for 1 hour before cooking in olive oil, salt and pepper. They should be turned twice. It would be a pity to spoil the flavour of these prime pieces with vinegar and lemon juice.

BRINES

Brine is a solution of salt and water, to which sugar, saltpetre, and *aromates* are often added. Its purpose is to preserve food from spoilage by bacteria. It is important to soak food which has been preserved in brine very thoroughly before use to remove excess saltiness.

Saumure pour Langue de Bœuf * *Brine for pickling Ox Tongue*

8 pints water; 5 lb of kitchen salt; 3 oz saltpetre; ½ lb sugar; 1 pinch of peppercorns and juniper seeds, thyme and bay leaf.

Boil all the ingredients together. Allow the mixture to cool and place in it a very fresh raw egg, in the shell. The egg should float. If the egg sinks, continue adding salt until it does float. Prick the tongue, beat it well to expel the air from the meat. Rub it thoroughly with a mixture of 9 oz fine salt and half an ounce saltpetre and prick thoroughly all over the surface. Pour the very cold brine over the tongue, which must be fresh and well trimmed. Leave in the brine 8-9 days, according to size.

Saumure à Sec * *Dry Pickle*

Tongue can also be pickled without using any liquid. Prepare the tongue as indicated (*see* p. 114) that is, prick and beat thoroughly. Roll in 7 oz fine salt mixed with 2 oz sugar and 1 oz saltpetre. Place in a wooden or earthenware tub on the bottom of which a layer of kitchen salt has been spread (allow 1 oz of saltpetre to each 2 lb of kitchen salt). Place a board on top held down by a heavy weight. At the end of a few days enough liquid will have formed to cover the tongue. It takes 6 days to produce a half-salted tongue and 11-12 days before it is ready for boiling as pickled tongue. Soak in running water for 24 hours before cooking or if this is impractical, change the water very frequently.

⊡ pour Pièces de Boucherie * *Heavy Brine*

To make 17 *pints:* 16 *pints water;* 10 *lb salt;* 5 *oz saltpetre;* $\frac{3}{4}$ *lb brown sugar.*

Cook all the ingredients together briskly. The brine is ready when a peeled potato dropped into it floats just below the surface. If it sinks to the bottom, there is not enough salt and more must be added. If it floats on the surface, there is too much salt and more water must be added. Cool and pour into the brine tub, which is usually of stone or earthenware, with a grill at the bottom on which to lay the meat, which must be perfectly trimmed and deeply pricked with a large needle. For a piece of 10-11 lb allow a pickling time of 8 or 9 days. This brine is used for large pieces of meat.

FORCEMEAT (STUFFINGS) AND PANADAS

There are many types of forcemeat, *farces* and stuffings in French *cuisine.* They are used in a variety of ways; for making *quenelles*, *mousses*, *mousselines*, *zephyrs*, *pâtés*, *vol-au-vents*, garnishes, *canapé* spreads, *galantines*, for stuffing breast of lamb or veal, poultry, game, fish, vegetables and eggs. Forcemeats are made of meat, poultry and close-grained fish, finely ground or puréed and mixed with seasonings.

PANADE * *PANADA*

The preparation of some types of forcemeat requires the addition of a panada. Panada is a thick paste made of flour and water or milk, and a small amount of butter. The panada is cooked and used as a binding agent in forcemeat mixtures and also to give them body. In the past, panada was made entirely with bread, but now a very thick paste made with flour and water or milk is preferred since it makes *quenelles* lighter and more delicate.

⊡ à la Farine * *Flour*

To make 1 *pound:* $\frac{1}{2}$ *pint water;* 2 *oz butter;* 5 *oz flour; a pinch salt.*

Put the salt, water and butter into a saucepan and bring to the boil then remove from the heat. Add all the flour at once, stir well with a wooden spoon and return to the heat, drying the panada by stirring with a spoon over the heat. Remove from the heat, spread out on a sheet of buttered paper and leave to cool thoroughly. Mix with finely minced meat, chicken, game or fish as specified in each recipe.

⊡ au Lait * *Milk*

Same method as for Flour Panada but using milk instead of water.

Panade aux Oeufs * *Egg Panada*

To make 1 lb: ½ pint milk; 3 oz flour; 4 egg yolks; 3 oz melted butter; salt, pepper, grated nutmeg.

This is used for fish and poultry. Put all the ingredients except the milk into a saucepan and mix with a wooden spoon. Gradually add the boiling milk. Dry out the panada by stirring it over the heat for about 5 minutes. Spread out, butter the surface and leave to cool.

LES FARCES * *FORCEMEAT*

⊡ **Fine** * *Fine Forcemeat for Quenelles*

¾ lb topside of veal or white meat of poultry, with sinews and fat removed; 2 oz Egg panada; ¼ pint of cream; ¼ lb butter; 3 egg whites; salt, pepper and nutmeg.

Finely grind the meat and pound in a mortar. Add the seasonings and soft butter and beat well using a wooden spoon. Beat in the egg whites and the chilled panada. Pass through a sieve and chill. Beat in the cream adding half a tablespoonful at a time and adding only enough for the mixture to hold its shape while poaching. The consistency of the forcemeat may be checked by poaching a *quenelle* in boiling water. If the forcemeat crumbles when lightly touched, add another one or two egg whites. Keep in a cool place until required.

⊡ **pour Galantines** * *for Galantines*

¾ lb lean pork; ¾ lb lean veal; 1¾ lb fat bacon; 1 oz salt and white pepper, mixed.

Finely mince the meat and bacon, season and pass through a sieve.

⊡ **pour Galantines de Gibier** * *for Game Galantines*

½ lb veal; ½ lb pork; 1 lb game; 2 lb fat bacon; 4 eggs; 1 oz salt anp pepper, mixed.

Finely mince the meat and bacon. Season and add the eggs—one by one—then sieve.

⊡ **à Gratin**

¼ lb green (unsmoked) fat bacon; ½ lb liver (poultry, game or veal); 1 oz shallot, chopped; parsley, thyme, bay leaf, salt and pepper.

Cut the bacon in small dice and cook over low heat until all the fat has melted and is sizzling. Then add the chopped liver. Brown it, season and *sauté* for another 2 minutes and remove from the stove. Mince or grind the whole mixture and pass it through a sieve and beat well with a wooden spoon. Keep cool in a container and cover with oiled paper.

Farce Mousseline * *Mousseline Forcemeat*

½ lb veal; 2 fl oz fresh double cream; ½ oz salt and pepper; 1 egg white.

Mince and pound the veal in a mortar with the seasoning and gradually incorporate the egg white. Pass through a sieve, transfer to a bowl which has been placed over crushed ice. Beat until the meat is cold then beat in the fresh cream—a little at a time. The quantity of cream will vary with the ingredients used. Experiment until the desired soft but firm consistency of the forcemeat is obtained. Chill thoroughly before use. The mixture may be used for stuffing poultry, fish etc. For fish replace the veal with pike.

▣ pour Pâtés * *for Pâtés*

1 lb fresh lean pork, from the shoulder or neck; 1 lb fresh fat bacon; salt; 1 oz spiced salt.

Coarsely dice the meat and bacon. Mince the whole finely, add salts and pass it through a sieve.

▣ de Poisson * *Fish*

For fish galantines and pâtés: ½ lb raw pike, without skin and bone (whiting or fresh haddock may be substituted); ½ lb Egg panada; salt, pepper, nutmeg; 2 whole eggs and 1 egg yolk.

Mince the fish finely and pound in a mortar with the seasoning. Incorporate the panada. Work with a wooden spoon, adding the eggs one by one. Pass through a sieve and mix thoroughly again in a bowl.

▣ à Quenelles à la Panade * *Quenelle Forcemeat with Panada*

10 oz topside of veal or white meat of poultry, with all sinews and fat removed; 5 oz Flour panada; 5 oz butter; 2 eggs; 2 egg yolks; salt, pepper and nutmeg.

Pound the meat to a *purée* in a mortar, season and beat well. Add the cold panada and beat it into the meat with a wooden spoon, incorporating the butter at the same time. When the mixture is homogenous, add the eggs one by one and beat well after each addition. Pass through a sieve and mix thoroughly again in the bowl. Check the consistency of the forcemeat by poaching a *quenelle* in boiling water. If the forcemeat crumbles when lightly touched, add another one or two egg yolks. Keep in a cool place until required.

▣ Zéphyr

As for *Farce Mousseline* above with the addition of another 3 oz of whipped cream. It is usually cooked in a small, buttered mould in a *bain marie* (water-bath) and coated with sauce. *Zéphyrs* can be made of fish, poultry, game, ham, etc.

LES QUENELLES * *QUENELLES*

Once eaten never forgotten is the texture of a well-made *quenelle*. Success lies partly in the mixing and partly in the shaping. They are mixtures of minced and pounded meat which may be veal, chicken, game or fish, together with butter, seasonings, eggs and sometimes cream.

There are a number of methods of shaping the *quenelles*—by hand, with a piping bag, with a spoon or in moulds. They are cooked uncovered in simmering water or stock, but care should be taken to ensure that the liquid does not boil rapidly or the *quenelles* will break.

◘ à la Cuiller * *Moulded by Spoon*

These *quenelles* are shaped by soup, dessert or coffee spoon (depending on the desired size). Here is one trick of the trade to be learnt when shaping these *quenelles*. Have ready a large buttered *sauté* pan, a small pan of boiling water and 2 spoons. Dip one spoon in the boiling water while filling the other generously with the *quenelle* mixture. Then use the blade of a knife to smooth the *quenelle* in a dome shape. Then take the other spoon out of hot water and loosen the *quenelle* without spoiling its shape. Place the egg shaped *quenelle* in the buttered pan and continue with the rest of the *quenelles* always dipping one spoon in hot water. Leave room for the *quenelles* to expand.

◘ Décorées pour Garniture * *Moulded for Garnishing*

Quenelles may also be shaped in *barquette* (boat-shaped) or tartlet moulds. Butter the moulds generously and decorate with a simple design, using pieces of truffle, pimento or olives. Fill with plenty of forcemeat making sure that there are no gaps along the sides. Place everything, including the mould into boiling salted water and poach as for other *quenelles*. They will unmould themselves and float to the surface.

◘ à la Main * *Moulded by hand*

Flour a board, divide the forcemeat into small pieces of about ½ oz with a coffee spoon. Flour your hands and roll the *quenelles* with the fingers straight. Either shape them like small sausages or else in circles. Poach for 8-10 minutes in boiling water. Drain.

◘ à la Poche * *Piped*

Butter the bottom of a fire-proof dish lightly. Place the forcemeat in a piping bag with a round plain nozzle of appropriate size and pipe strips of forcemeat side by side. Pour boiling water carefully down the sides to cover them. Add salt and poach without boiling for 8-10 minutes. Drain.

◘ à Potage * *for Soup*

These are made with a piping bag using a very small nozzle. Pipe the forcemeat into a buttered fire-proof dish in a zig-zag movement to give the *quenelles* a slight curl. These are called *quenelles de cherilles* (caterpillars). Pour boiling water over carefully and poach for 3 minutes. *Quenelles* may be made in various colours by the addition of a few drops of green, carmine or any other artificial colourant.

VARIOUS BASIC PREPARATIONS

There are certain basic preparations or *appareils* which are employed in the preliminary stages of many dishes. Those listed below are used frequently and they are explained here in order to avoid over-loading the recipes with repetitious information.

Duxelles Graisse * *Rich Duxelles*

¼ lb mushrooms; ½ oz butter; 2 tablespoons finely chopped onions; 1 tablespoon finely chopped shallots; 2 oz lean minced ham; 2 tablespoons concentrated tomato purée; salt and pepper.

Wash and finely chop the mushrooms and squeeze them in a cloth to extract the moisture. Then cook in butter with the shallots and onions until they begin to brown. Add the ham and tomato *purée*, salt and pepper. Allow to simmer for a few minutes, then place in a bowl covered with oiled paper. Cool and store in a covered jar in the refrigerator to use as needed.

Duxelles Maigre * *Meatless Duxelles*

As above but omit the ham.

Fondue de Tomates ou Portugaise * *Tomato Fondue*

A *fond* is often used as a basis for a braise. Tomato *fondue* is made of very ripe tomatoes peeled, deseeded, quartered or chopped and cooked in butter with onions, shallots and crushed garlic until the pulp is firm. The mixture may be seasoned with paprika, saffron or tarragon or green pepper. It is served as an accompaniment to eggs, fish, meat and poultry dishes and to fill small tart shells.

1 *lb tomatoes; a clove of crushed garlic;* 2 *oz chopped shallots;* 1 *oz butter; pinch salt; a pinch of ground black pepper;* ½ *teaspoon sugar; chopped parsley.* Cooking time: 10 minutes.

Brown shallots in butter, add the prepared tomatoes, garlic and seasonings. Cook slowly over low heat, stirring with a wooden spoon until all the liquid is reduced. Sprinkle with chopped parsley.

Mirepoix

This is a mixture of vegetables cut in dice and used as a basis of a braise or to improve the flavour of sauces and gravies.

1 *carrot;* 1 *stick celery;* 2 *shallots or* 1 *medium onion;* 2 *sprigs parsley; half a bay leaf; a sprig of thyme;* 2 *oz ham; salt and ground black pepper.* Cooking time: 7-8 minutes.

Cut all ingredients in small dice and brown slowly with herbs in the butter. Cool, and store in a covered jar in the refrigerator to use as required.

Matignon

This is used for the same purposes as *Mirepoix* and the same ingredients are used, except that the ham is replaced by lean bacon and the ingredients are cut into a *julienne* instead of dice.

Montglas

Montglas is used to stuff lamb cutlets or is served in tartlet shells or very small *vol-au-vents.*

¼ lb pickled tongue; ¼ lb cooked mushrooms; 1 *oz truffles; ⅛ pint Demi-glace;* 2 *oz Madeira; salt and pepper.*

Cut into a *julienne*, the pickled tongue, cooked mushrooms and the truffles which have been cooked in Madeira. Bind this *julienne* with ⅛ pint of *Demi-glace* plus the Madeira in which the truffles were cooked and reduce to a thickish consistency. Season and allow to cool before using. *Foie gras purée* may be used to bind the *Montglas* instead of *Demi-glace.*

ROUX * *ROUX*

Roux, the most common liaison for savoury sauces, may be white, blond or brown. All of these general types consist of the same basic ingredients but change in character and colour according to the length of the cooking time. *Roux* is usually made of nearly equal quantities of flour and butter, the proportions varying slightly according to the fat used. A properly cooked *roux* will keep well in a jar in the refrigerator, providing that no other ingredients—apart from butter and flour—have been added. It is useful to make up a pound of *roux*, store it and use as required. Butter, preferably unsalted butter, should be used to make the *roux* although clarified salt butter may be substituted. The flour should be dry and of good quality.

▣ Blanc * *White Roux*

Roux Blanc is used to thicken *veloutés* of white poultry, such as chicken, turkey and veal, and also for *sauce Béchamel* and *sauce Crème.*

For 2 *pounds of roux:* 1 *lb butter;* 1 *lb* 2 *oz flour.*

Melt the butter slowly in a saucepan (preferably a white-lined saucepan). When it has just melted, draw the pan off the heat and add the sifted flour. Stir until the mixture is smooth. Cook the *roux* in a cool oven, 200° F or Gas Mark 2, until the texture becomes of a sandy nature but do not allow the *roux* to colour.

▣ Blond * *Blond or Straw-Coloured Roux*

Roux Blond is made from the same ingredients and cooked using the same method as *Roux Blanc.* However, it is cooked in the oven a little longer until it turns a very pale straw colour. Use to thicken *veloutés* of pheasant, partridge and guinea fowl, and also for piquant sauces and soups.

▣ Brun * *Brown Roux*

Using the same ingredients and cooking method as *Roux Blanc*, cook the *roux* until it is a fine light brown in colour and has acquired a nutty aroma. It is used for brown sauces, notably *sauce Espagnole.*

Les Socles * *Bases*

In the past, set pieces were prepared in which the main item disappeared beneath all the accessories and decorations. Nowadays the presentation has become very simple.

Nevertheless it is sometimes indispensable, especially when presenting certain cold pieces, to raise the main item on a *socle* or base.

These *socles* may be cut or moulded in all sorts of shapes—as a square or a rectangle, as steps or a fan, etc. In most cases the bottom of the dish must first be lined with a mirror of jelly.

Socles are made of rice of ordinary quality or cut out of dry bread.

Rice *socles* are made as follows: Thoroughly wash 1½ to 1¾ lb of rice. Blanch it, rinse it, then cook very slowly with a little water for 45 minutes. It must become dry and hard. Pound this mixture or pass it through the mincer, knead it by hand on a moistened marble slab like a dough in order to give it body. Then shape the base with moistened hands. By way of example, for a long fish, give the base the shape of a slightly hollow boat, so that the fish will keep upright if it is placed on its belly. For a bird make a heart shaped base or a plain round one, some 2 to 3 inches thick.

These rice bases have a tendency to turn black. They must be wrapped in a damp cloth and kept in a cool place.

Spices and Herbs in the Kitchen

SPICES

Aniseed

Origin Mediterranean. One of the sweetest-smelling herbs, surrounded by a wealth of folk lore. This delicate plant is grown mainly for the seed which is used extensively in cooking and in the manufacture of liqueurs, particularly anisette. The feathery leaves of the plant may be included in salads and used as a garnish.

Soups, meats, sweet pastry, rolls, fruit tarts.

Cardamom

Origin India and Ceylon. From the perennial plant Cardamom comes the small, oddly shaped seeds which, when crushed, emit a cool eucalyptus-scented flavour.

Sausages (black pudding), curries, pastries, syrups and mixed spices. When serving black coffee, crush a few seeds and pass round with coffee crystals.

Cinnamon

Origin Ceylon. The bark of the cinnamon tree. One of the oldest and most valued spices known to man. Its predominant scent, fine, delicate and aromatic, comes from oil of cinnamon which is extracted from the bark. Regarded as having preservative and medicinal qualities, its uses in cooking are numberless.

Fine pastries, infusions for various drinks and syrups, chocolate, hot and cold sweets. Mixed spices.

Cloves

Origin Moluccas, Zanzibar. These, the dried flower-buds of an evergreen tree, resemble little brown nails or thorns. Their delicious, pungent flavour has become indispensable in the preparation of many dishes. From it is extracted oil of cloves, a powerful antiseptic. Cloves may be used either whole or ground.

Baked leg of ham is traditionally studded with cloves, fruit compotes and pies (e.g., apple), marinades, soups, preserves and sauce flavouring.

Coriander

Origin Mediterranean and Orient. These small, ovular seeds come from a tall annual plant which has delicate, pink-edged flowers. Coriander has a pleasantly sharp flavour which has long been appreciated by cooks. Store these grains in an air-tight jar and grind only at the last moment.

Hors d'œuvre, herring preparation, fish marinades, sauces, curries, soups, vegetables, some fish recipes.

Caraway

Origin European. This ancient spice comes from the seed of a biennial plant whose roots are also edible after boiling. Throughout the ages many magical qualities have been ascribed to the caraway including the belief that it prevents infidelity in love. Whatever the authenticity of these tales, it certainly aids digestion.

A variety of culinary uses, especially Austrian specialities, cake and bread preparations, cheeses; also soups, vegetables and some fish recipes.

Curry

Curry powder is a blend of many spices. It is not simply one spice. In Eastern countries the practice of cooking with curry powder has been in favour for countless centuries and even today most Indian families will select their own aromatic seeds to grind their powder fresh for each day. Depending on the type and strength of seeds selected and blended the curry powder will be hot, mild, medium or sweet.

Curry Paste is basically the same type of blended seeds with the addition of vegetable oil, some vinegar and a little crushed garlic. This mixture is cooked slowly for a few minutes, then sealed down.

Accompaniments

Certain side dishes are traditionally offered with a curried meal; carefully cooked rice; relishes; mango chutney; grated fresh coconut; shredded Bombay duck (dried Indian fish) and salted nuts.

Curry Powder

This is a good recipe, which the individual can vary at will by changing the quantities of the various spices. Dry grains in gentle heat before grinding.

Cardamom 1¼ pounds; Cayenne 1 ounce; mace 1 ounce; fenugreek 1¼ pounds; white pepper 2 ounces; clove 1 ounce; ginger 2 ounces; celery seed 1 ounce.

Curcuma

Origin Asia Minor and China. The aromatic smell of this plant is slightly reminiscent of ginger. If used to excess the taste becomes bitter. When sieved, it is known as Indian saffron. The pulverised roots yield turmeric.

Sometimes used as an ingredient of curry powder; substitute for saffron in colouring rice, piccalilli, chutneys.

Fenugreek

Origin Southern Europe and Asia Minor. A clover-like seed claiming medicinal properties. The flavour and fragrance resembles that of honey.

Pastries, syrups, spices.

Ginger

Origin China. Coming from a tuberous root, grown in tropical Asia it is used in our kitchens in many forms. Sometimes it is ground, sometimes it is crystallised and occasionally it is preserved in syrup. Whatever the guise, its rich, clean tang has been and always will be appreciated by spice lovers.

Young shoots are preserved in syrup and crystallised. Older stems are dried and ground into powder. Cakes, pastries.

Mustard

The mustard seed is unique among spices. It has been treasured as a condiment and digestive stimulant since earliest times. Oddly enough, its hot and piquant flavour can only be appreciated when released by the addition of a liquid such as milk, water or dry white wine to the powdered mustard. Then it forms a sharp, delicious paste which should be allowed to stand for a short period to enable its flavour to develop.

Sauces, hors d'œuvre, preserves, pickles.

Mace

Origin East Indies. This mild, fragrant spice forms the outer coating of the nutmeg seed. Naturally reddish in colour, mace develops a light orange hue when dried for commercial use. Not surprisingly it resembles its sister spice, the nutmeg, in odour and flavour but mace is more pungent.

Potatoes, potato-based soups, vegetables, milk pudding, pastries, syrups.

Nutmeg

The popularity of this spice is attributed to its pleasantly crisp and dry qualities and as an aid to good digestion. Of slightly ovular form, the nutmeg is at its best when freshly grated and is far superior to the commercially ground variety.

In mixed spices for cakes and puddings, grated to top junkets and light milk puddings.

Peppercorns

Origin East Indies. Pepper has been valued from earliest times as a most precious spice. Indeed in the Middle Ages it formed part of the currency of the times, levies of pepper along with dowries and taxes being a common occurrence. From the same vine comes both the black and the white peppercorns.

Black Peppercorns

After picking, the berries of this vine are dried in the hot sun. In the process they become dark in colour, wrinkled—and are very hot to the palate.

All culinary uses and with other spices.

White Peppercorns

With the removal of the dark outer husk, there remains a smooth, cream-coloured core. This is the white peppercorn which is similar to but milder in flavour than the black peppercorn. The aromatic flavour of the peppercorn is better appreciated if freshly ground in a peppermill.

Paprika

Origin Asia Minor and Central America. This sweet and fragrant spice with its slightly earthy smell comes from a specially cultivated, mild, sweet capsicum. When fully ripened it is deseeded, dried and ground and is a vibrant red in colour. Originally native to Central America, it is now cultivated in different parts of Europe and America. Indeed the best variety comes from Hungary, the Hungarian or rose paprika. It is valuable as a flavouring for delicately textured food such as crab, chicken and cream sauces.

Soups, sauces, casseroles, goulash, fish, meat and vegetable preparations.

Pimento

Origin West Indies. Symbolic of compassion, the Pimento or Jamaica Pepper is ground from the small sun-dried berries of the allspice tree. The pungent and sharply aromatic taste of this spice, also called the *allspice,* appears to be a combination of cinnamon, cloves and nutmeg. It is not however, a mixture of these three spices. In ground form it acts as a delicious baking spice.

Various cakes etc., spices, brines, pickles.

Poppy Seeds

Origin Europe and Asia Minor. Do not confuse these with seeds of the opium-bearing poppy. Poppy seeds are not renowned for their narcotic effect. These tiny grains, with a mild, nut-like flavour, come from a species of poppy which grows wild in most parts of Europe. Apart from their famed gritty texture, the poppy seed is a natural source of minerals and claims several medicinal properties. It is available either in whole or ground form.

Bread, rolls, white sauces for vegetables, all desserts and pastries, sprinkled over buttered noodles and creamed potatoes.

Saffron

Origin Italy and Asia. Logically enough, this, the world's costliest spice, is said to be symbolic of the necessity to guard against excess. Only the orange-coloured and hand-picked stigmas of a special crocus flower, the *Crocus sativus* are utilised. It takes many hundreds of thousands of these stigmas to make one pound of saffron. So this golden coloured spice with its slightly bitter aroma has been prized since Biblical times not only as a deliciously aromatic spice and food colourant but also as a dye and medicine.

Soups, sauces, risottos, bouillabaisse, pastries, preserves.

Vanilla (Pod)

From a Central American orchid comes the vanilla bean, the most fragrant of all the culinary spices. The long, flat seed pods when dried have a sweet and permeating savour which makes it an excellent spice for all desserts and particularly in ice cream. To make vanilla sugar, split a piece down the centre and store in a sugar container; this will keep the pod dry and clean while also scenting the sugar. For a stronger flavour, pulverise 1½ ounce or 2 whole vanilla beans in a mortar with ¼ pound of sugar lumps, then pass through a very fine-meshed sieve. You may use an electric blender for this but if you do so, allow the pulverised mixture to stand in a closed jar for a day or so before sieving it. The same piece of vanilla bean may be used several times.

HERBS

Artemisia

Principally in the preparation of pork, duck and geese dishes.

Origin Asia Minor and Europe. There are many varieties of this perennial herb. Sometimes we know it as wormwood or southern wood but more commonly refer to it as mugwort. This herb with its intensely bitter taste has a fascinating history throughout the annals of folk lore and has become symbolic being credited with certain mystic qualities of man's bitterness towards life. Certainly its strangely antiseptic odour does act as an effective moth repellent. Only the dried flowers and stalk are of culinary value.

Basil

Soups, casseroles; stock making; pasta and rice dishes; most vegetables, especially eggplant.

Origin Europe, Asia Minor. One of the most delicate and fragrant of herbs, basil comes from a handsome green-leaved plant which has figured prominently over the years in Greek, Italian and French cooking. The chopped green leaves make an excellent addition to any salad and it combines particularly well with tomatoes. The Italians for whom it symbolises love use it generously in their pasta dishes and its distinctive flavour marries well with a variety of vegetables. The most famous sauce made with basil is *pesto.*

Bay Leaves

Bouquet garni; stock making; soups, casseroles, and marinades.

Origin Europe and Asia Minor. This is the leaf of the laurel tree, famed throughout history as a symbol of glory, particularly to the heroes of Ancient Greece and Rome who were crowned with wreaths of laurel to mark their daring exploits. In modern continental cookery few meat dishes whether stewed or braised, or soups, would be without some hint of its pleasing aromatic scent. It is a foundation flavour of *la bonne cuisine.*

Borage

This aromatic herb, tasting rather like cucumber, is often grown by bee keepers to attract bees which seem to relish its scent. The young leaves may be added to salads and pickles while the flowers are used principally nowadays as a garnish for fruit cups.

Salads, summer drinks, wines and Pimm's Cup.

Chervil

The delicate fern-like leaves of this member of the carrot family closely resemble parsley leaves. There the resemblance ends. Chervil has a unique flavour vaguely reminiscent of aniseed. Along with tarragon, parsley and chives it forms part of the traditional "*quatre fine herbes*".

Soups, sauces, salads and decoration of cold dishes, because of its pleasingly shaped leaves and stalks. Excellent in omelettes with cream cheese.

Chives

Origin Asiatic. The most delicate member of the onion family, chives have fine tubular leaves with a mild flavour which is slightly reminiscent of garlic. Whenever a touch of raw onion is called for in a recipe chives may be safely—and advantageously—inserted. They are useful too in a garnish.

Cold sauces and soups, salads, butter, cream cheese, meat and fish dishes. Only the leaves are used.

Dill

Both the leaf and seed of this yellow-flowering plant have immense practical value in the kitchen. Its fresh, fern-like leaves are excellent with cucumber and sour cream and when chopped blends well with eggs and light cream cheeses. Dill seeds are sometimes used as an alternative to caraway seeds being of a similar if milder flavour.

Soups, sauces, sauerkraut, crayfish, salads, decoration of cold dishes, pickled gherkins, and cucumbers, bread, rolls, fruit flans. Excellent in sauces for fish and vegetables.

Fennel

There are several varieties of fennel but Florence fennel having more tender and delicate leaves is the wisest choice in the kitchen. Almost the entire plant from its fleshy base to its lacy leaves can be put to good culinary use. The bulb is delicious when sliced and eaten raw, much the same way as with celery. Use the leaves with any fish dish either directly or in the accompanying sauce. Reminiscent of aniseed, the crisp and nut-like flavour of the broad, white stalks are best appreciated when thinly sliced and added to green salads. The fennel seed, a necessary ingredient in certain liqueurs, are also scattered on top of rolls, fruit tarts and in cheese mixtures.

Leaves. Sauces (hot and cold), decoration of cold dishes. Bulbous root as vegetable, a garnish and hors d'œuvre, pork, liver and kidney dishes; fish, pickles.

Garlic

A member of the lily family. Unless whole garlic cloves are used subtly as in *soup à l'ail* or *chicken à l'ail*, most British people tend to be rather shy of including the strong, permeating aroma of garlic in their food. Devotees relish the virile, positive savour but for the average consumer it should be used with discretion. Then its flavour will enhance, without overpowering, the taste of a dish.

Nearly all savoury culinary preparations; must be used with discretion.

Horseradish

Despite its inelegant name, this useful herb is much admired for its hot peppery taste which is most suitable as an alternative to pickles and mustard. To appreciate its fiery tang use freshly grated.

Hot and cold sauces; when grated it is usually combined with cream or possibly vinegar and used for meat dishes, preserves and pickles, as accompaniment to roast beef, in combination with grated raw beetroot or alone in cold sauces for cold fish e.g., smoked trout, gefullte fisch.

Juniper Berries

These deep blue-purple tinged berries are the dried fruit of an evergreen tree found in most parts of Europe and, oddly enough, the Arctic regions. Its bitter-sweet flavour is most commonly associated with the manufacture of gin to which it lends its characteristic juniper aroma. Only a small quantity of berries (about nine) are needed to impart the correct flavour. Since these are a soft fruit they are easily crushed with the back of a spoon.

Sauerkraut; game and pork preparations; boar's head; sauces; gin; coleslaw, stuffing for domestic fowl and game.

Lovage

The strong celery flavour of this herb used to be more popular than it is now. It has been included in cordials and can be candied like Angelica.

Soups, pork preparations, roast beef and mutton, salads.

Marjoram

This aromatic herb of a thousand uses belongs to the mint family and has long been in favour with chefs who admire its delicately-scented, soft, greyish leaves. It closely resembles oregano, but is more delicate and sweeter. Of the many varieties of this herb sweet marjoram is the most popular and highly recommended. Combined with other herbs and ingredients it makes a delicious stuffing especially suited to savoury dishes. There are many popular stories attached to marjoram, one belief being that it brings peace and happiness, another that it symbolises blushes.

White meat and poultry stuffings, farce for tomatoes, egg plant, etc.

Mint

While there exist many varieties of mint, only spearmint and peppermint are worthy of culinary consideration. Its fresh, cool taste combines well with such vegetables as carrots, peas and new potatoes and adds an interesting touch to mixed green salads. It is an enormously versatile herb recommended not only as a relish but also as an aid to the digestion.

Soups, mint sauce and mint jelly, potatoes, vegetables, vinegars, salads, yoghourt. Infusions and cold drinks.

Oregano or Wild Marjoram

Oregano, a handsome and leafy member of the mint family, grows wild on the hills around the Mediterranean coast. Indeed oregano means "joy of the mountains", from the Greek "orus" (a mountain) and "gamus" (joy), and can be used to advantage in the robust dishes of Mediterranean origin. The hot pungent impact of this herb has been of special delight to Italian cooks who flavour their traditional *pizzas* and *pasta* dishes with a discretionary pinch, while Spaniards find its more potent aroma well suited to some of their classic sauces.

Tomato dishes, mushrooms, meat (especially veal and beef), cream sauces, cheese and egg mixtures.

Parsley

One of the most popular herbs and the easiest to grow, parsley is indispensable in the preparation of the *bouquet garni*, beloved by good cooks everywhere, and in dishes prepared "*aux fines herbes*". It has been cultivated for thousands of years and a wealth of legends and superstitions has grown round this herb, more so than any other. Boasting certain health-bringing qualities, it is specially recommended as a tonic for the kidneys. There are two varieties commonly recognised, the curly and the flat-leaved parsley.

Soups, sauces, fish, quenelles, meat, vegetables, potatoes. When finely chopped use as a garnish, especially for egg dishes.

Rosemary

A Mediterranean evergreen herb of the mint family, rosemary or "dew of the sea" flourishes best in coastal areas. The bracing and tonic effect of the leaves is so impressive that in former times it was reputed to be a scalp stimulant and hair restorer. In any event a wealth of herbal lore still surrounds rosemary, its origin and uses. Certainly its pungent scent is excellent with lamb and chicken as also with certain green vegetables—green beans, asparagus and tomatoes. After drying, the leaves become brittle and are readily chopped or crumbled.

Pork, lamb, mutton, infusions, vinegars, fish soups, sauces, risottos, sausages, duck and geese.

Sage

This hardy, sun-loving plant is believed to possess many healing properties, not the least interesting being a claim to promote longevity. The strong and fragrant odour of this remarkable plant combines admirably with pork dishes. Its fame in Britain is probably based upon its association with the classical stuffing of sage and onion for roast, pork, goose and duck.

Fish preparations, especially tench, pork, geese, duck, Italian specialities, pickling brines and marinades, sausages, cheese dishes.

Savory

Whether of the summer or winter variety, savory adds a delicious and compelling aroma to most dishes whose base is either beans, peas or lentils. This is another native plant of the Mediterranean countries whose hot and rather peppery flavour is savoured and enjoyed in many other parts of the world.

Broad beans, French beans, peas, mushrooms, soups, sauces, meats, preserves.

Shallot

Another famous member of the onion family but with a much finer taste, the shallot seems to possess a mild flavour and aroma which is an ideal blend of garlic, spring onion and onion.

Many culinary uses, especially fish, small meats, poultry and sauces.

Spring Onions

Called "scallions" in America and known as "green onions", these are a delectable member of the onion family. Of an infinite variety of uses, spring onions are best appreciated when completely fresh. They are, in fact, the tender seedlings of the onion plant and are completely edible from root to green stem.

Peas, salads, egg dishes, numerous uses in the kitchen, cream cheese, mayonnaise, and herb butter.

Tarragon

The "little dragon" or "*estragon*" of the kitchen, so called because of its serpentine root formation. This is a fragrant herb, with both taste and smell reminiscent of aniseed; it is complementary to poultry, veal and egg dishes. When using the dried herb use only one teaspoonful—unless otherwise directed by the recipe—for its extremely potent flavour should be included with discretion. The attractive, elongated leaves are often used for decorative designs and garnishes, particularly with the cold buffet.

Soups, sauces (especially Béarnaise), butter, eggs, fish, meat and poultry dishes, mustard, preserves and vinegar.

Thyme

The delicate, warm fragrance of thyme has been treasured from Medieval times. The English variety is a handsome grey-green plant often found in rock gardens. Since it is a moderately potent herb you may be quite generous when using it. It can be bought either whole or in ground form.

For most culinary preparations, soups, sauces, fish, meats, vegetables, potatoes, marinades, brines, pickles, preserves and vinegar.

Wormwood

A plant growing over 3 feet high with branch-like stalks and small feathered leaves which are hairy underneath and have a whitish shimmer. Strangely, the root leaves are trebly feathered, the stalk leaves doubly and the top leaves at the ends of the stalks only slightly feathered. The tips of the plant and the flowers, which are used for seasoning, have a strong spicy smell and a very bitter taste. (See *Artemisia*.)

Used less for cooking than for flavouring and to make vermouth, wine and liqueurs. Also pork, duck and geese dishes.

Garnishes

Garnishes are a traditional part of French cooking. They are sometimes named after the place of origin, the person who invented them, or perhaps a special occasion. The object of a garnish is to add colour, flavour, interest and texture to foods. A garnish may be an integral part of a dish, or simply a sprig of watercress.

Colour is added to dishes which are basically colourless, such as white soups and fish. Thus we find that black truffles are often used to decorate white fish dishes.

Foods with uninteresting shapes are also helped considerably by garnishes with plenty of form and character of their own, such as parsley at the simplest level, the design and shape of slices of lemon or tomato, shaped pieces of toast, fried bread or pastry; these last items provide a change of texture which is very welcome with soft foods.

Garnishes are also used to add flavour to dishes. This will either complement the original flavour of the dish or provide a contrast.

The choice and suitability of the garnish must be left greatly to individual taste and judgement. For hot food the garnish should be simple so that the food can be served quickly, whereas for cold food one of a more elaborate nature can be used. Remember that over-garnishing detracts rather than contributes to the smart appearance of the food. One of the basic principles to note is that food being garnished should live up to the promise of its appearance so that you are able to say with truth that the food looks and tastes good.

Soup garnishes, for example, *consommé* garnishes, must be cooked before addition to the soup and anything of a starchy nature such as pasta, should be washed after cooking to avoid making the *consommé* cloudy. The garnish may be arranged round the edge of the main dish but take care that it does not become masked by gravy or sauce. Always have enough of the garnish to serve each person but do not over-garnish.

Serving Food

Neat and deft serving of food is important as it contributes greatly to the success of all dishes and this is particularly true of the very simple dishes which can look most uninviting if served in an untidy manner.

Always match the plates and dishes with the type and shape of food to be served. For example, it is traditional to serve aspic foods on highly polished silver, cheese on wood and bread rolls in a basket, since this background detail will accentuate the basic nature of the food.

When serving hot food both the dish and any accompaniments should be thoroughly heated in readiness for the food to be sent "piping hot" to the table. Certain foods require to be served very quickly and must not be kept waiting, for example, grilled foods, *soufflés*, batters, omelettes. Light hot after-dinner savouries should be placed on the table as quickly as possible after they are cooked.

Agnes Sorel

Chicken *Mousseline* Forcemeat with thin slices of sautéed mushrooms, poached in small baking tins; round slices of pickled tongue; thin slices of truffles; *sauce Allemande.* — *Suprême of chicken, poached chicken.*

Albuféra

The bird is stuffed with a mixture of *risotto* and diced truffle and *foie gras*; puff pastry cases filled with truffles in sauce; mushrooms; balls of chicken meat and cocks' kidneys, bound with *sauce Albuféra*; decorated with round slices of pickled tongue; *sauce Albuféra* served separately. — *Poached chicken.*

Algérienne

Sweet potato *croquettes*; small peeled and deseeded tomatoes, casseroled in oil; clear *sauce Tomate* with thin strips of red peppers added. — *Joints, roasted or sautéed.*

Alsacienne

Small pastry cases, filled with braised *sauerkraut* and garnished with round slices of ham on top; juice of the meat. — *Joints.*

Américaine

Collops or slices of lobster tail *à l'Américaine*; Lobster sauce; slices of truffle. — *Fish.*

Amiral

Oysters and mussels; mushrooms, preferably turned; crayfish tails; thin slices of truffle; *sauce Normande* mixed with Crayfish butter. — *Large fish, especially turbot and brill.*

Andalouse

Peppers halved and garnished *à la Grècque*; thick slices of scooped-out *aubergines*, fried in oil and decorated with tomato *concassé*; chipolata sausages; thickened gravy. — *Meat, poultry.*

Argentueil

White asparagus tips coated with *sauce Hollandaise.* — *Poultry, meat.*

Arlésienne

Slices of fried *aubergine*; tomatoes peeled, cut small and sautéed; French-fried onion rings; *sauce Demi-glace* flavoured with tomato. — *Tournedos and noisettes.*

Beaugency

Artichoke bottoms garnished with tomato *concassé*, topped with round slices of blanched beef marrow; *sauce Béarnaise.* — *Small pieces of sautéed meat.*

Beauharnais

Artichoke bottoms quartered and sautéed; stuffed mushroom caps; *Château* potatoes; *sauce Beauharnaise.* — *Small pieces of meat, sautéed or grilled.*

Belle Hélène

Flat asparagus *croquettes*; thin slices of truffle; thickened gravy. *Tournedos, noisettes.*

Berrichonne

Braised cabbage balls; whole chestnuts and glazed, small onions; small slices of bacon cooked with the cabbage; juice of the meat reduced with *sauce Demi-glace*. *Braised meat.*

Bonne Femme

The fish is poached in white wine and fish liquid with chopped shallot, finely cut mushroom and chopped parsley; the reduced liquid is mixed with a sauce of white wine and butter; it is then poured over the fish and glazed quickly. *Small fish, fillets of fish.*

Bouquetière

Small pieces of carrot and turnip, turned and glazed; French beans; peas; sprigs of cauliflower coated with *sauce Hollandaise*; *Château* potatoes; lightly thickened gravy. *Joints.*

Bourguignonne

Browned, diced bacon; mushrooms, quartered and sautéed; small glazed onions; gravy from the meat, always with red Burgundy added. *Braised beef and ham.*

Bruxelloise

Braised chicory; Brussels sprouts casseroled in butter; *Château* potatoes; light Madeira sauce. *Joints.*

Cardinal

Collops or slices of lobster tails and claws; slices of truffle; *sauce Cardinal.* *Fish.*

Castillane

Small nests of Duchess potatoes, garnished with tomato *concassé*, sautéed in olive oil; deep-fried onion rings; juice of the meat reduced and flavoured with tomato. *Joints, tournedos, noisettes, poultry.*

Catalane

Grilled tomatoes; artichoke bottoms; tomato-flavoured *sauce Demi-glace.* *Tournedos, noisettes.*

Chambord

Fish *quenelles* with truffles; truffles cut in olive shapes; carefully peeled mushroom caps; fried milt; crayfish cooked in *court-bouillon*; heart-shaped *croûtons*, fried in butter; *sauce Chambord.* *Whole braised fish.*

Chasseur

Mushroom caps filled with onion *purée*; Duchess potatoes; *sauce Hussarde.* — *Roast, small pieces of sautéed meat.*

Chipolata

Braised button onions and glazed carrots; chestnuts cooked in *consommé*; browned, diced bacon; chipolata sausages; meat juices reduced with *sauce Demi-glace.* — *Joints, poultry.*

Choisy

Braised lettuce halves; *Château* potatoes; reduced meat gravy enriched with butter. — *Tournedos, noisettes.*

Choron

Artichoke bottoms, garnished with green asparagus tips or peas tossed in butter; Noisette potatoes; *sauce Béarnaise*, flavoured with tomato. — *Sautéed meat tournedos.*

Clamart

Macaire potato; small pastry cases filled with peas *à la Française*; thickened veal gravy. — *Sautéed meat.*

Condé

Purée of kidney beans cooked in red wine with small strips of lean bacon; braising liquor reduced with *sauce Demi-glace.* — *Braised meat.*

Conti

Purée of lentils cooked with small strips of lean bacon; braising liquor reduced with *sauce Demi-glace.* — *Braised joints.*

Demidoff

Onion rings, crescent-shaped pieces of carrot and turnip (the vegetables normally grooved before slicing), tossed in butter; diced celery, casseroled with the bird in a covered fire-proof dish; half-moons of truffle added at the last moment. — *Poultry, game birds.*

Dieppoise

Shelled prawn tails; bearded mussels casseroled in white wine; white wine sauce with the *fumet* formed by reducing the fish poaching liquor. — *Small fish, fillets of fish.*

Doria

Cucumbers cut into the shape and size of olives, casseroled in butter; slices of lemon, peeled and deseeded. — *Fish cooked à la Meunière.*

Dubarry

Bouquets or balls of cauliflower, coated with *sauce Mornay*, sprinkled with cheese and cooked *au gratin*; liquid from the meat or clear stock. — *Joints, tournedos, noisettes.*

Financière

Mushroom caps; veal *quenelles*; thin slices of truffle; blanched stoned olives; cocks' crests and kidneys; *sauce Financière.* — *Joints, poultry.*

Flamande

Balls of braised cabbage, carrots and turnip; small boiled potatoes; small strips of bacon cooked with the cabbage; liquid from the braised meat. — *Braised or boiled meat, goose and duck.*

Forestière

Mushrooms sautéed in butter; browned, diced potatoes; dice of lean bacon, blanched and browned; *sauce Duxelle* reduced with the meat juice or with *sauce Demi-glace.* — *Joints, poultry.*

Godard

Veal forcemeat *quenelles* with chopped truffles and mushrooms; chicken forcemeat *quenelles* decorated with truffles and pickled tongue; fluted mushrooms; truffles cut in olive shapes; glazed lamb sweetbreads; *sauce Godard.* — *Large joints, poultry.*

Grand-Duc

Green asparagus tips bound with butter; thin slices of truffle; crayfish tails; *sauce Mornay.* — *Fish.*

Helder

Artichoke bottoms garnished alternately with buttered asparagus tips; Noisette potatoes and tomatoes *concassées*; *sauce Béarnaise.* — *Tournedos, noisettes, sautéed meat.*

Henry IV

Artichoke bottoms garnished with very small Noisette potatoes; clear meat stock poured over; *sauce Béarnaise.* — *Tournedos, noisettes.*

Hussarde

Mushroom caps filled with onion *purée*; Duchess potatoes; *sauce Hussarde.* — *Roasts, sautéed meat.*

Italienne

Artichoke quarters with chopped mushrooms; triangular *croquettes* of macaroni with cheese; *sauce Italienne.* — *Joints, poultry.*

Jardinière

Carrots and turnips turned to olive shape and glazed; French beans cut in lozenge shapes, kidney beans, peas, all glazed with butter; cauliflower coated with *sauce Hollandaise*; clear veal gravy. — *Joints.*

Joinville

Sauce Joinville mixed with large pieces of mushroom, crayfish tails and truffles; thin slices of truffle; crayfish tails. — *Fish.*

Judic

Braised lettuce halves; thin slices of truffle; cocks' kidneys; fine *sauce Demi-glace.*	*Tournedos, noisettes, poultry.*

La Vallière

Artichoke bottoms garnished alternately with buttered green asparagus tips; *Château* potatoes; *sauce Bordelaise.*	*Tournedos, small pieces of sautéed meat.*

Lorette

Asparagus tips or peas with butter; very small chicken *croquettes*; slices of truffle; thickened veal gravy.	*Tournedos, noisettes.*

Maillot

Shaped and glazed carrots and turnip; small glazed onions; braised lettuce; peas; French beans; gravy.	*Braised meat, especially ham.*

Maraîchère

Slices of salsify bound with a light *sauce Béchamel*; Brussels sprouts tossed in butter; *Château* potatoes; juice of the braised meat.	*Braised meat.*

Maréchale

The meat is dipped in melted butter and then in chopped truffle, or in a mixture of fine white breadcrumbs and chopped truffle; thin slices of truffle; green asparagus tips; peas with butter.	*Sliced veal sweetbreads, lamb chops, suprême of chicken.*

Margot (Reine)

See *Reine Margot.*

Marie-Louise

Artichoke bottoms garnished with 3 parts mushroom *purée* and 1 part onion *purée*; *sauce Madère* or gravy thickened with arrowroot.	*Sautéed meat and poultry.*

Mascotte

Artichoke bottoms braised in butter; potatoes cut in olive shapes and sautéed in butter; truffle balls; clear stock with white wine and veal juice.	*Tournedos, noisettes, poultry, always cooked in a casserole and surrounded by their garnishes.*

Massena

Artichoke bottoms bound with thick *sauce Béarnaise*; poached round slices of beef marrow placed on top of the meat; *sauce Tomate.*	*Tournedos, grills, small sautéed pieces.*

Mexicaine

Large mushroom caps grilled and garnished with *fondue* of tomatoes; small grilled peppers; well-seasoned tomato juice.	*Joints, poultry.*

Mirabeau

Anchovy fillets placed crosswise on the meat; a border of blanched tarragon leaves; stoned olives; Anchovy butter. *Grilled red meat.*

Montmorency

Artichoke bottoms garnished with a *macédoine* of mixed vegetables; bunches of green asparagus tips; *sauce Madère* mixed with meat juice. *Joints, poultry.*

Montreuil

Neatly shaped boiled potatoes coated with Shrimp sauce, placed round the fish; the fish coated with White Wine sauce. *Small fish, fillets of fish.*

Murat

The fillets are cut in large strips which are sautéed in butter and mixed with diced artichoke bottoms and diced potatoes sautéed in butter; garnished with slices of tomato, sautéed in butter, chopped parsley; lemon juice; a little clear meat stock; browned butter. *Fillets of fish.*

Nantua

Crayfish tails bound with *sauce Nantua*; thin slices of truffle; *sauce Nantua.* *Fish.*

Nicoise I

Fondue of tomatoes with garlic and chopped tarragon; anchovy fillets; black olives; lemon slices peeled and the pips removed; Anchovy butter. *Fish.*

Nicoise II

Fondue of tomatoes with garlic tip and chopped tarragon; French beans sautéed in butter; *Château* potatoes; thickened meat juice. *Joints, poultry.*

Normande

Oysters and mussels, bearded and poached; button mushrooms; shelled prawn tails; thin slices of truffle; shelled crayfish; sautéed gudgeons or small smelts; puff pastry *fleurons* (crescents); *sauce Normande.* *Fish.*

Orientale

Timbales of *Riz à la Grécque*; halved tomatoes braised in olive oil; sweet potato *croquettes*; *sauce Tomate.* *Poultry.*

Portuguaise

Small tomatoes garnished with *duxelles; Château* potatoes; *sauce Tomate.* *Joints, poultry.*

Princesse

Asparagus tips in cream sauce; slices of truffle; *sauce Allemande* with mushroom essence. *Veal sweetbreads, poultry.*

Provençale

Small casseroled tomatoes; mushroom caps garnished with *duxelles* and some garlic tips; *sauce Provençale.* *Joints, poultry.*

Rachel

Artichoke bottoms each garnished with a large slice of beef marrow and sprinkled with chopped parsley; *sauce Bordelaise.* *Tournedos and small joints.*

Régence I

Spoon-shaped *quenelles* of whiting forcemeat with Crayfish butter; poached oysters; mushroom caps; slices of truffle; poached milts; *sauce Normande.* *Fish.*

Régence II

Chicken *quenelles* shaped by spoons; large veal forcemeat *quenelles* decorated with truffles; small slices of *foie gras* sautéed; cocks' crests; truffles cut in olive shapes; mushroom caps; *sauce Allemande* with truffle essence. *Poultry and veal sweetbreads.*

Reine Margot

The bird is stuffed with fine chicken forcemeat and almond *purée*; small chicken *quenelles* with Pistachio butter; small chicken *quenelles* with Crayfish butter; *sauce Suprême* mixed with almond milk. *Poached poultry.*

Riche

Thin slices of lobster meat; slices of truffle; *sauce Victoria.* *Fillets of fish.*

Richelieu

Tomatoes and mushroom caps filled with *duxelles*; braised lettuce; *Château* potatoes; slightly thickened meat juice. *Joints, especially fillet of beef.*

Romaine

Small pastry cases filled with *Gnocchi à la Romaine*; spinach soufflé with anchovies, poached in baking tins; *sauce Romaine.* *Joints.*

Rossini

Small round slices of *foie gras*, lightly sautéed in butter; *sauce Demiglace* with truffle essence or *sauce Madère.* *Tournedos.*

Saint-Germain

Neatly shaped glazed carrots; small moulds of pea *purée*; small *Fondant* potatoes; *sauce Béarnaise*; juice from the meat. *Joints.*

Saint-Mandé

Base of *Macaire* potatoes; French beans; peas sautéed in butter; thickened meat juices. — *Joints.*

Sarde

Saffron rice *croquettes*; tomatoes stuffed with *duxelles*; slices of de-seeded cucumber garnished with *duxelles* and breadcrumbs and browned; light *sauce Tomate.* — *Joints.*

Talleyrand

Small pieces of macaroni mixed with butter, grated cheese, diced *foie gras* and truffle; *sauce Périgueux* with thin strips of truffle. — *Joints, poultry.*

Tortue (en)

Salpicon of veal *quenelles,* mushrooms, truffles, blanched and stuffed olives, gherkins, all bound with sauce; slices of veal tongue; slices of calf's brains; crayfish; French Fried eggs; heart-shaped fried *croûtons*; *sauce Tortue.* — *Calf's head.*

Toulousaine

Small chicken *quenelles*; small mushroom caps; small slices of veal and lamb sweetbreads; cocks' combs and cocks' kidneys; thin slices of truffle; *sauce Allemande* with mushroom essence. — *Poultry, vol-au-vents.*

Trouvillaise

Prawn tails; poached mussels; small fluted mushroom caps; Shrimp sauce. — *Fish.*

Tsarine

Cucumber turned to olive shapes, casseroled in butter; turned mushrooms; glazed *sauce Mornay.* — *Fish.*

Tyrolienne

French fried onion rings; tomatoes *Fondues*; *sauce Tyrolienne.* — *Grilled red meat.*

Valois

Large boiled potatoes; poached soft roes; dressed crayfish; *sauce Valois.* — *Fish.*

Vert-Pré

Potato straws; watercress; *Maître d'Hôtel* butter. — *Grills.*

Victoria

Small round slices of lobster meat; thin slices of truffle; glazed *sauce Victoria.* — *Fish.*

Viroflay

Artichoke bottoms quartered, sautéed and sprinkled with chopped parsley; spinach balls *Viroflay*; *Château* potatoes; thickened gravy. *Joints.*

Walewska

Small round slices of lobster tail meat; thin slices of truffle; *sauce Mornay* with lobster butter. *Fish.*

Zingara

Thin strips of mushrooms, ham, pickled tongue, and truffles; *sauce Demi-glace* flavoured with tomato and tarragon. *Veal, poultry.*

The making of sauces is one of the most important aspects of the French *cuisine* and it has been said that it is the main reason France enjoys supremacy in the kitchen.

The purpose of a sauce is to add to the appearance, flavour and texture of food. The perfect sauce should be absolutely smooth, glossy, full of flavour; rich but never greasy.

Basic sauces may be classified as basic brown sauces such as sauce *Espagnole* and sauce *Demi-glace* and basic white sauces such as *Velouté* and *Béchamel.* These sauces are made from stock either white or brown and upon these basic sauces depend most of the subsidiary sauces used in cooking. They are really "unfinished" sauces because they are used as a basic ingredient of so many other sauces and dishes. Another important basic sauce is "la sauce Tomate".

In the large kitchens of hotels and restaurants these basic sauces are prepared every morning so that they are ready to use for a variety of dishes in the course of the day. In case you have always imagined sauce-making to be a very elaborate and expensive business remember that once you have mastered the preparation of the basic sauces the door is open to the hundreds of derivatives of these basic sauces.

Sauce-making equipment includes a *bain-marie*, although in smaller households this will probably be a baking tin filled with hot water with smaller pans standing in it. You will find useful, a special spiral sauce whisk and small heavy saucepans.

Sauces may be thickened by the addition of one or more of the following ingredients: a *roux*; *beurre manié*; *à la fecule*—with some type of starch; *au sang* (blood); with egg yolk or with egg yolk and butter or cream; and thickening by reducing the quantity of the sauce. Whenever egg and cream are added to a sauce always mix them together first and add a little of the hot sauce gradually to this mixture, stirring all the time. When egg yolk alone is to be added to a sauce it should be mixed with a little cold liquid first and then the hot sauce stirred slowly into it. The sauce may then be reheated, but if possible it should not boil. Sauces can be made in advance and kept hot in the *bain-marie* or over hot water in a double boiler. The basic sauce mixtures, such as the *Velouté* and *Demi-glace*, can be made in large quantities, stored in the refrigerator or deep freeze and then used as required.

When serving sauces remember only one rich sauce should be served at any one meal and that the amount of sauce should be small in proportion to the amount of food.

LES SAUCES DE BASE BRUNES * *BASIC BROWN SAUCES*

Basic Brown Sauces are composed of a butter and flour *roux* cooked until it becomes a nut brown colour. Then Brown stock is slowly added to the cooked *roux*. The sauce is skimmed frequently and simmered for a considerable length of time in order to develop the flavour and reduce the sauce to the correct consistency.

Sauce Espagnole (Classical Method)

For 4 pints: 9 oz brown roux; 8 pints light brown stock; ¼ lb carrots; ¼ lb onions; ¼ lb streaky bacon; ½ lb concentrated tomato purée or 2 lb tomatoes; 1 sprig of thyme and 1 small bay leaf; ¼ pint white wine.

Make a *mirepoix* with the onions and carrots and sweat these gently with the bacon in a marmite. Add the thyme and bay leaf. Moisten this with the white wine. Then add the *roux* which should be light brown in colour and the brown stock which should be warm. Whisk until smooth, raise to the boil then simmer very gently for 2 hours, skimming the sauce frequently. Pass the sauce through a tammy cloth or fine *chinois.* Cook for a further 2 hours skimming frequently. Sieve the sauce again and leave it to cool stirring constantly until it has cooled completely. The next day cook the sauce for a further 2 hours adding the ½ lb concentrated tomato *purée* or 2 lb fresh tomatoes. Sieve. This sauce will keep well for 8-14 days if kept cool or refrigerated. If it is necessary to make a *sauce Espagnole* in less time, the tomatoes can be added during the second cooking. When this is done the sauce is less concentrated and does not keep for so long.

⊡ Espagnole (Modern Method)

For 4 pints: 9 pints water or light stock; 4 lb beef bones and 2 lb veal bones cut in small pieces; ½ lb bacon rind or scraps of fat bacon, blanched and diced; ¼ lb carrots; ¼ lb onions; 1 large clove garlic; 1 bouquet garni; ¼ pint tomato purée or 1 lb fresh tomatoes; ¼ lb fat; 5 oz flour; ¼ lb mushroom trimmings.

Brown the bones lightly in the oven with the fat. Chop the carrots and onions and add them to the bones with the bacon fat, and let them brown with the bones. Sprinkle the flour over them, mix it well, and let the flour colour. Do not let it become too dark or the sauce will be bitter. Add the water or stock if you require a sauce of extra strength. Whisk and bring to the boil. Season lightly, add the garlic, the *bouquet garni* and the mushroom peelings. Simmer on a gentle heat for 5 hours. Chop the tomatoes finely and cook them in the oven long enough for most of their moisture to evaporate or, if you are using tomato *purée,* heat it gently in the oven. Mix the tomatoes with the sauce and let the sauce simmer for a further 5 hours, skimming frequently. Strain everything through a *chinois,* and stir constantly while the sauce cools. Cover with a layer of greaseproof paper. *Sauce Espagnole* will keep for 8 days in a refrigerator.

⊡ Demi-glace

For 1 pint: 1 pint brown stock; 1 pint sauce Espagnole.

Add the rich brown stock to the *sauce Espagnole.* Simmer until the quantity is reduced by half, skimming repeatedly during the process. Strain into a bowl or jar and store in a cool place until required.

LES SAUCES DE BASE BLANCHES * *BASIC WHITE SAUCES*

Generally speaking, white sauces play a larger part in cooking than brown sauces and have the advantage of being made more quickly. In order to make a very smooth white sauce which is free from lumps, the *roux* is only cooked until the flour has lost its raw taste but is still white in colour. It should always be allowed to cool a little before the hot liquid is added and stirred smooth with a whisk. It is better not to add all the liquid at once, for if the sauce is too thick it is always possible to thin it with a little more liquid. White sauces should not be made in aluminium saucepans, since stirring with a whisk in such a saucepan tends to give the sauce a greyish tinge. The two basic white sauces are the famous *Velouté* and *Béchamel*. *Velouté* may be moistened with almost any type of white stock, whereas for *Béchamel* only milk may be used.

Sauce Allemande

For 2 pints: 2 pints chicken or veal stock; 2 pints chicken or veal Velouté; ¼ pint mushroom liquor; 6 egg yolks; ½ pint cream; ¼ lb unsalted butter; juice of half a lemon. Cooking time: 15 minutes.

Add the stock to the *Velouté* and reduce by half. Beat together the egg yolks, cream, mushroom liquor and lemon juice. Pour some of the reduced stock into this mixture, whisk together, then tip all the ingredients back into the original pan. Whisk vigorously until the sauce is thick enough to coat a spoon. Add the unsalted butter. Strain through a tammy or fine sieve.

▣ Béchamel

For 2 pints: 3 oz butter; 3 oz flour; 2 pints milk. Cooking time: 15 minutes.

Make a *roux* with the butter and flour using slightly more butter than flour—it is essential that the proportion of butter to flour is marginally greater. Cook for a few minutes over a gentle heat. Warm the milk and then add it to the *roux* about a third at a time. Bring the sauce to boiling point stirring all the time. Season with salt and pepper. Strain. The sauce should be cooked very gently to avoid burning.

▣ Suprême * *Creamy Chicken*

For 2½ pints: 2 pints chicken Velouté; 2 pints chicken stock; ½ pint cream; ¼ pint mushroom liquor; ¼ lb butter. Cooking time: 15 minutes.

Boil the *Velouté*, stock and mushroom liquor together over a fierce heat until it is reduced by half, stirring constantly. Add the half pint of cream gradually. Remove from the heat, blend in the butter and strain.

▣ Velouté

For 2 pints: 3 oz butter; 3 oz flour; 2 pints white veal, chicken or fish stock. Cooking time: 35 minutes.

Make a white *roux* with the butter and the flour and do not allow it to colour. Add the stock, stirring constantly, bring to the boil and continue cooking slowly for another 30 minutes. It is only seasoned very lightly since it is the basis for a number of white sauces. As soon as it is cooked remove all fat and strain into a bowl. Butter the top to prevent a skin forming.

LES SAUCES TOMATES * *BASIC TOMATO SAUCES*

Tomato sauce requires a cooking time of about one and a half hours to develop its full flavour.

⊡ Tomate * *Tomato*

For 2 pints: 2 pints brown stock; ½ pint tomato purée; 2 oz butter; 2 oz flour; ¼ lb onion; ¼ lb carrot; ¼ lb celery; 2 oz bacon trimmings; 1 bay leaf; 1 sprig of thyme. Cooking time: 1½ hours.

Make a *mirepoix* with the onions, carrots, celery, bacon scraps, bay leaf and thyme. Add the flour and cook over a low heat for 5 minutes stirring constantly. Add the tomato *purée* and stir well. Add the stock, cover and cook the sauce slowly for 1 hour, if possible in the oven. Strain, season lightly, and add a pinch of sugar, and the butter. If the sauce is too thick, thin with stock as required.

⊡ aux Tomates Fraiches * *with Fresh Tomatoes*

Replace *purée* by 3 lb of fresh tomatoes. Prepare as in preceding recipe, add tomatoes crushed together and cook for 25 to 30 minutes. Do not cook tomatoes or *purée* too long, as *sauce Tomate* made from fresh tomatoes will begin to darken in colour and become acid after half an hour.

⊡ aux Tomates Fraiches à l'Italienne

For 2 pints: 2 lb fresh tomatoes; ¼ lb onions; 2 oz carrots; 2 oz lean, smoked bacon; 1 bouquet garni; 2 oz butter; 2 oz flour; 2 pints stock. Cooking time: 1½ hours.

Start frying the carrots, onions and coarsely diced bacon in butter, sprinkle with flour and, as soon as the ingredients begin to change colour, add the tomatoes and mix together. Add the stock, season, add the *bouquet garni* and cook in a very cool oven, 250° F or Gas Mark ½, for 1 hour. Pass through a conical sieve, add more seasoning if required and finally add a lump of sugar and a knob of butter. This sauce is even better if the tomatoes have first been braised in the oven until all the juice has evaporated.

LES SAUCES BRUNES COMPOSÉES * *DERIVATIVE BROWN SAUCES*

Most of the brown sauces are based on the *Demi-glace*, so it is advisable to make up a large quantity of this and store it to use as required for the derivative sauces. In this section you will find the principal composed or derivative brown sauces which are often combined with the cooking liquor of the dishes they are to accompany.

⊡ Bordelaise ou à la Moelle * *Marrow*

For ½ pint: 1 shallot; ¼ lb beef marrow; ¼ pint red wine; 6 peppercorns; 1 sprig thyme; ½ pint Demi-glace; 1 oz butter. Cooking time: 25 minutes.

Toss the chopped shallots briefly in butter, reduce with the red wine, add the crushed peppercorns and the thyme and reduce to almost nothing. Add *Demi-glace*, cook slowly for

15 minutes, skim off the fat, strain, and stir in 3 oz of the marrow cut in dice. Let the sauce simmer slowly for a further 10 minutes. Crush the remaining marrow and add to sauce which here replaces the butter. This sauce is served with *tournedos* and rump steak.

The best slices of marrow are not added to the sauce but poached in lightly salted water, placed on the meat and the sauce poured on top.

Sauce Bourguignonne I * *Burgundy Sauce I*

For ½ pint: ¾ pint Demi-glace; 2 oz shallots; bay leaf; 1 pint red wine; 6 crushed peppercorns; ¼ lb butter. Cooking time: 20 minutes.

Chop the shallots finely and *sauté* them in butter. Add the red wine with the peppercorns and bay leaf and reduce by two-thirds. Add the *Demi-glace* and cook until the sauce is reduced by half. Strain through a cloth. Add 2 oz of butter just before serving.

If this sauce is to accompany sautéed meat or game it should be made in the pan in which the meat is cooked.

▣ Bourguignonne II * *Burgundy II*

For 1 pint: 2 pints red wine; 1 oz shallots; a bouquet garni; 6 crushed peppercorns; salt; 2½ tablespoons beurre manié; 2 oz butter. Cooking time: 15 minutes.

Chop the shallots finely and add them with the peppercorns and *bouquet garni* to the wine. Bring to the boil and reduce by half. Whisk in the *beurre manié*, drop by drop, until the sauce is smooth and thick. Remove from the heat, strain and add the butter at the last moment. This sauce is for poached eggs. Mushroom trimmings may be added to both the above sauces.

▣ aux Champignons * *Mushroom*

For ¾ pint: 1 pint Demi-glace; ½ lb mushrooms; ½ pint mushroom stock; 2 oz butter. Cooking time: 15 minutes.

Reduce stock and *Demi-glace* to ¾ pint. *Sauté* the mushrooms in a little butter, add to the sauce and enrich with butter.

▣ Charcutière

For 1 pint: 1 pint Demi-glace; ¼ lb chopped onion; 1½ oz mustard; ½ pint white wine; ¼ lb gherkins; 1 oz butter. Cooking time: 20 minutes.

Stew the onions in the butter, add the wine, reduce by half, add *Demi-glace* and simmer to 1 pint. Cut the gherkins in coarse *julienne*. Remove sauce from the heat, add the mustard and gherkins. Usually accompanies pork chops.

▣ Chasseur

For ¾ pint: 1 pint Demi-glace; 1 oz minced shallot; ½ lb sliced mushrooms; ½ pint white wine; ½ lb fresh tomato purée; 2 oz butter; 1 oz chopped parsley and tarragon. Cooking time: 20 minutes.

Melt the butter and add the shallots, cook gently then add mushrooms. Add white wine and reduce by half. Add 1 pint *Demi-glace* and tomatoes and boil for a few minutes. When cooked, add butter and the chopped parsley and tarragon.

Sauce Chaudfroid Brune * *Brown Chaudfroid Sauce*

For 1 *pint:* 1 *pint Demi-glace;* ¾ *pint beef aspic; a small glass of sherry or Madeira;* 3 *tablespoons truffle essence* (*optional*). Cooking time: 30 minutes.

Add the truffle essence to the *Demi-glace* and reduce over a high heat to a half, adding the aspic little by little. Season with sherry or Madeira and strain. Let the sauce cool stirring constantly. Coat the meat or game with the *Chaudfroid* when it is cold but has not begun to set.

⊡ Chaudfroid de Gibier * *Game Chaudfroid*

Follow the same recipe as for Brown *Chaudfroid* sauce, replacing the brown aspic with game aspic.

⊡ Chevreuil

For 1 *pint:* 1 *pint sauce Poivrade;* ¼ *pint red wine.*

Reduce the *sauce Poivrade* by a third adding the red wine little by little. Season with cayenne and strain.

⊡ Colbert

For ½ *pint:* ½ *lb butter;* ¼ *pint meat glaze; chopped parsley and tarragon; juice of* 1 *lemon.*

Mix the melted butter and meat glaze together and leave to cool. Add the herbs, lemon juice, salt and pepper. Accompanies grilled meat and fish.

⊡ Diable * *Devilled*

For 1 *pint:* 2 *shallots;* ¼ *pint dry white wine;* 1 *teaspoon concentrated tomato purée;* 1 *pint Demi-glace; Worcester sauce.* Cooking time: 15 minutes.

Brown the chopped shallots lightly in butter, add the wine and reduce slowly by half. Add the *Demi-glace* and the tomato *purée*, cook for 5 minutes, season with a generous dash of Worcester sauce and cayenne pepper and add a little chopped chervil. Accompanies chicken and grilled pigeon.

⊡ Duxelles

For 1 *pint:* 1 *oz chopped shallot;* ¼ *lb duxelles of mushrooms;* ¾ *pint sauce Espagnole;* 1 *oz chopped parsley;* ¼ *pint Tomato sauce;* ¼ *pint white wine;* 1 *oz butter.* Cooking time: 25 minutes.

Stew shallots in the butter, add wine and reduce by half and sieve. Add the mushrooms prepared as *duxelles, Espagnole* and Tomato sauces, bring to the boil and simmer for 20 minutes; stir constantly. Add the parsley at the last moment. This sauce accompanies fine pieces of meat, chicken and eggs.

Sauce Estragon * *Tarragon Sauce*

For ¾ pint: ¼ pint white wine; 1 pint Demi-glace; tarragon. Cooking time: 20 minutes.

Boil up white wine, add 2 sprigs tarragon, cover and allow to simmer for about 10 minutes. Strain the wine, add the *Demi-glace* and reduce to a syrupy consistency. Complete sauce with a large pinch of freshly chopped tarragon leaves.

▣ Financière

For 1 pint: 1 pint Demi-glace; ⅛ pint truffle essence; 2 tablespoons Madeira Cooking time: 15 minutes.

Reduce sauce by one-third, remove from heat, add essence and Madeira. Strain. This sauce is rarely used by itself; its main purpose is to bind garnish *à la Financière.*

▣ Grand-Veneur

Make a light *sauce Poivrade* and shortly before serving thicken with a few tablespoons of hare's blood. Keep warm but do not allow to boil again. Serve with saddle of hare or venison.

▣ Italienne

For 1 pint: ¼ lb mushrooms; 2 oz boiled ham; 1 shallot; ¼ pint white wine; 1 tablespoon oil; ¼ pint tomato purée; 1 pint Demi-glace. Cooking time: 15 minutes.

Chop the mushrooms finely and sweat them in oil. Add the chopped shallot and ham, very finely diced. Add the white wine and reduce by half. Add the *Demi-glace*, tomato *purée* and a little chopped parsley and simmer until the sauce has reached the consistency of light syrup. Adjust the seasoning. This sauce accompanies small portions of meat or fowl.

▣ Lyonnaise * *Onion*

For 1 pint: ¼ lb onions; 2 oz butter; ¼ pint dry white wine; 1 pint Demi-glace.

Toss the sliced onions in butter without colouring. Add the white wine and reduce to half the volume. Add the *Demi-glace*, cook for another 10 minutes and serve with meat, vegetables and especially artichokes. Strain or not, as desired.

▣ Madère * *Madeira*

For 1 pint: ⅛ pint Madeira; 1 pint Demi-glace; 1 oz meat glaze; 1 oz butter. Cooking time: 15 minutes.

Place Madeira and meat glaze in a casserole and reduce to half the volume. Add 1 pint *Demi-glace*, boil for a few minutes, remove from the heat, season, and stir in butter. This sauce accompanies pork, especially ham, and beef.
NOTE. Madeira and other wines used for sauces should first be reduced so that the alcohol can evaporate, otherwise the sauce will taste acid or of mulled wine.

Sauce Matelote

For 1 *pint:* 1 *pint Demi-glace;* ½ *pint fish stock;* ¼ *lb butter;* 6 *peppercorns;* 1 *bay leaf;* ½ *pint red wine;* 1 *oz shallots;* 2 *oz mushroom trimmings;* 1 *sprig thyme.* Cooking time: 15 minutes.

Chop the shallots and melt them in a little butter. Add peppercorns, bay leaf, thyme, fish stock and wine and reduce by a half. Add the *Demi-glace* and simmer until the sauce has thickened. Strain and stir in the remaining butter. This sauce accompanies fish.

⊡ Moscovite

A pint of *sauce Poivrade* with an infusion of a few crushed juniper berries garnished with 2 oz chopped roast cashew nuts or almonds and 2 oz currants plumped in hot water. This is a special sauce for game.

⊡ Périgueux * *Truffle*

For 1 *pint:* 1 *pint Demi-glace;* ½ *pint thickened gravy;* 2 *fl oz truffle essence;* 2 *oz chopped truffle;* 2 *fl oz Madeira.* Cooking time: 15 minutes.

Reduce *Demi-glace* and thickened gravy to ¾ pint. Remove from the heat, add the truffle essence, truffles and Madeira.

⊡ Piquante * *Sharp*

For 1 *pint:* 2 *oz shallots;* ½ *pint mild wine vinegar;* 2 *oz gherkins;* 1 *pint Demi-glace;* 2 *oz butter.* Cooking time: 15 minutes.

Chop the shallots and toss them quickly in butter. Add the vinegar and reduce to a quarter. Combine with *Demi-glace* and cook slowly for 15 minutes. Add the gherkins cut in slices or strips and a little chopped parsley and do not let the sauce boil again. This sauce accompanies pork and boiled beef.

⊡ Poivrade * *Pepper*

For ¾ *pint:* ½ *lb game trimmings;* 1 *carrot;* 1 *medium-sized onion;* 4 *parsley stalks; a sprig of thyme; half a bay leaf;* ½ *pint vinegar;* ¼ *pint marinade;* 6 *peppercorns;* 1 *pint Demi-glace.* Cooking time: 1½ hours.

Brown the chopped game trimmings in oil. Add the sliced vegetables and herbs. When everything is well-browned, add the vinegar and reduce almost completely. Moisten with the *Demi-glace* and the marinade. Add 6 crushed peppercorns and cook very slowly for 1 hour. Skim well to remove surface fat, strain and season highly.

⊡ Porto * *Port Wine*

Follow the same recipe as for *sauce Madère*, replacing the Madeira with Port.

Sauce Provençale

For 1 *pint:* 1 *lb tomato concassé;* ½ *pint olive oil;* 2 *crushed cloves garlic;* 1 *tablespoon chopped parsley.* Cooking time: 20 minutes.

Fry the tomatoes in the oil. Add salt and pepper and mix in the garlic. Simmer the sauce for 20 minutes with the lid on the pan. This sauce is also known as *Fondue de Tomates* or melted tomatoes.

⊡ Robert

Take one pint *sauce Piquant* which has been made with half vinegar and half white wine instead of white wine only. Add a teaspoon of mustard paste at the last moment. Do not allow the sauce to boil again. Serve with grilled pork cutlets.

⊡ Romaine

For 1 *pint:* 2 *oz castor sugar;* ½ *pint vinegar;* 2 *oz currants;* 2 *oz cashew nuts or almonds;* 1 *pint Demi-glace;* ½ *pint brown game stock.* Cooking time: 25 minutes.

Caramelise the sugar lightly without water, add the vinegar and reduce almost entirely. Add the *Demi-glace* and game stock and cook slowly for 15 minutes. Ten minutes before serving add the currants which have been soaked in hot water and the sliced, roasted cashew nuts or almonds. Serve with braised beef, calf's tongue or venison.

⊡ Rouennaise

For ½ *pint:* 2 *oz shallots;* ¼ *pint red wine;* 2 *raw duck livers;* ½ *pint Demi-glace;* 2 *oz butter.* Cooking time: 15 minutes.

Chop the shallots and toss them in the butter. Add the red wine and reduce almost entirely. Add the *Demi-glace*, cook slowly for a few minutes and add a little chopped parsley. Pass the livers through a fine sieve and stir into the hot sauce when about to serve. Season well and do not allow to boil again. Accompanies duck.

⊡ Salmis * *Game*

For 1 *pint:* 1 *onion;* 1 *shallot;* 1 *small clove garlic;* ½ *bay leaf;* 1 *sprig thyme;* a *few parsley stalks;* ½ *pint red or white wine;* 1 *tablespoon oil; bones of two snipe or partridge or* 1 *pheasant;* ½ *pint Demi-glace.* Cooking time: 30 minutes.

Chop the onion, shallot and parsley stalks coarsely and fry them in the oil until they are golden brown. Add the crushed garlic, thyme, and bay leaf and the wine and reduce to one quarter. Add the *Demi-glace* and cook slowly for 20 minutes. Take the bones from an underdone game carcase and crush them as finely as possible in a mortar and add to the sauce. Cook for a few minutes longer, then pass through a pointed sieve under heavy pressure. Season, reheat without bringing to the boil and pour over the dish.

Sauce Tortue * *Turtle Sauce*

This is a Madeira sauce boiled up with a little tomato *purée* and seasoned with an infusion of turtle herbs. These herbs can be bought, but one can make the infusion oneself with a pinch each of marjoram, rosemary, basil and a very little sage, pouring a little hot stock on top, covering and allowing to simmer. Do not allow to boil. Strain the infusion through a cloth. Serve this sauce with calf's head.

▣ Venaison

This is a *sauce Poivrade* for venison. Remove ¾ pint *sauce Poivrade* from the heat and add a ¼ pint double cream and 1 tablespoon redcurrant jelly.

▣ Zingara

For 1 *pint:* ¾ *pint Demi-glace;* ¼ *pint Tomato sauce;* 2 *fl oz mushroom essence;* 1 *oz cooked mushrooms;* 2 *oz pickled ox tongue;* 1 *oz truffle;* ¼ *pint white wine;* 2 *oz ham.* Cooking time: 25 minutes.

Cut the mushrooms, ham, tongue and truffles in *julienne*. Add the white wine to the mushroom essence, bring to the boil and reduce by half. Add the *Demi-glace* and Tomato sauce and cook for a few minutes. Add the *julienne*. Season with paprika and keep warm without allowing the sauce to boil. This sauce usually accompanies small pieces of veal and poultry.

SAUCES BLANCHES COMPOSÉES * *DERIVATIVE WHITE SAUCES*

Composite or derivative white sauces are derived from the two basic white sauces, *Velouté* and *Béchamel.* In many of the following recipes you will notice that the sauces are often enriched with one of the following ingredients:

Butter is the simplest of these embellishments; it enriches the flavour and texture and helps with the liaison of a sauce. Heavily buttered sauces should not be overheated.

Cream is added to soups and sauces to add richness but remember that cream tends to thin out a sauce, so make sure the sauce is of a fairly thick consistency before adding the cream.

Egg yolk and cream make sauces smooth and velvety. The important point to remember is that egg yolks must not be added to hot liquids. To avoid this mix the yolks with a little cold liquid first and then gradually pour the hot liquid over them, stirring constantly. Reheat the sauce and if necessary bring to the boil; once the egg yolks have been incorporated as indicated there should be no danger of the mixture curdling.

▣ Albuféra * *Poultry Cream*

For 1 *pint:* 1 *pint sauce Suprême;* 1 *oz meat glaze.*

This consists of *sauce Suprême* to which melted meat glaze has been added and seasoned with cayenne pepper. It is used only for poultry.

▣ Américaine

The sauce for *Homard à l'Américaine* (p. 391). Sometimes fillets of sole or other fish are accompanied by this sauce.

Sauce Anchois * *Anchovy Sauce*

½ pint sauce Béchamel or Normande or Fish Velouté; 2 oz Anchovy butter; 2 anchovy fillets.

Bring the basic sauce to the boil and gradually add the Anchovy butter. Pound the anchovy fillets in the mortar then sieve and add to the sauce. This sauce is served with egg and fish dishes.

⊡ Aurore

For 1 pint: ¾ pint Velouté; ¼ pint Tomato sauce; 2 oz butter. Cooking time: 5 minutes.

Bring the *Velouté* to the boil and add the Tomato sauce. Remove from the heat and stir in the butter. Season well. Use with egg, fish and poultry dishes.

⊡ Aurore Maigre

Prepare in the same way as above using a base of Fish *Velouté*.

⊡ Bercy

For 1¼ pints: 2 oz chopped shallots; ½ pint white wine; ½ pint fish stock; 1 pint Velouté made with fish stock; 2 oz butter; 1 tablespoon chopped parsley. Cooking time: 25 minutes.

Toss shallots briefly in half the butter, add the white wine and fish stock, and reduce to one-third the quantity. Add the *Velouté*, boil briefly, season well, remove from heat and add butter and chopped parsley. Special sauce for fish.

⊡ au Beurre dite Sauce Bâtarde

For 1 pint: 1 oz butter; 1 oz flour; 3 egg yolks; ¼ pint cream; ¼ lb butter; 1 tablespoon lemon juice; pinch salt; 1 pint water. Cooking time: 10 minutes.

Make a *roux* with the melted butter and flour. Pour 1 pint boiling water over this mixture all at once, add salt and whisk briskly. Thicken with the egg yolks which have been beaten up with the cream, and add the lemon juice. Strain through a cloth and whisk in the remaining butter away from the heat.

⊡ Café de Paris

For 1 pint: 2 oz Café de Paris butter; 1 pint fresh cream; 1 oz beurre manié. Cooking time: 5 minutes.

Warm the cream slowly in a pan. Add the *Café de Paris* butter and thicken with the *beurre manié*. Heat gently until well blended.

⊡ aux Caprês * *Caper*

A White Butter sauce to which 2 tablespoons of capers have been added for every pint of sauce.

Sauce Cardinal

For 1 pint: 1 pint Béchamel; ¼ pint cream; ¼ pint fish stock; 3 oz very red Lobster butter. Cooking time: 25 minutes.

Reduce the *Béchamel* with the fish stock and cream to 1 pint. Remove from the heat and stir in the Lobster butter. Season with cayenne pepper.

⊡ Chaudfroid Blanche * *White Chaudfroid*

For 1 pint: 1 pint Velouté; ½ pint stiff aspic jelly, made from veal or chicken stock; ¼ pint fresh cream.

Simmer the *Velouté* and reduce to a good consistency, gradually adding the aspic and the cream. Correct the seasoning and stir until almost cold and then coat the food as required.

⊡ Chaudfroid Aurore * *Pink Chaudfroid*

The same recipe as above with the addition of 4 tablespoons of tomato *purée.*

⊡ Chaudfroid Vert-Pré * *Green Chaudfroid*

1 pint White Chaudfroid sauce; 1 small handful spinach; half that quantity of cress; a few chervil and tarragon leaves.

Blanch chervil and tarragon for 2 minutes, cook spinach and cress in their own juice until soft. Refresh, squeeze out moisture thoroughly, pass through a fine hair sieve and do not add to sauce until cold, otherwise it will acquire an unpleasant greyish tinge.

⊡ Chivry * *Cream Sauce with Herbs*

For 1 pint: 1 pint sauce Suprême; ¼ pint white wine; tarragon; cress; chives; 2 oz Maître d'Hôtel butter. Cooking time: 15 minutes.

Boil up the white wine and add the herbs. Reduce by a half. Add the *sauce Suprême* and reduce to 1 pint. Beat in the butter away from the heat and strain.

⊡ Crème * *Cream*

For 1 pint: 1 pint Béchamel; ¼ pint cream. Cooking time: 15 minutes.

Add half the cream to the *Béchamel* and reduce to the desired consistency. Strain and add the remaining cream after the sauce has been removed from the heat.

⊡ Crème à l'Estragon * *Tarragon Cream*

For 1 pint: 1 pint Velouté; 1 oz tarragon stalks; 2 oz butter; teaspoon chopped, fresh tarragon; ¼ pint cream; ¼ pint white stock.

Bring the white stock to the boil and infuse the tarragon stalks for 15 minutes. Strain and add this liquid to the *Velouté* and cream. Reduce to 1 pint and garnish with the chopped tarragon. Stir in the butter away from the heat and butter the top to prevent a skin forming.

Sauce Crevette ou Joinville * *Shrimp or Prawn Sauce*

1 *pint velouté; ¼ pint cream; 2 oz peeled shrimps or prawns; 2 oz Shrimp butter*. Cooking time: 20-25 minutes.

Reduce *Velouté* and cream to 1 pint. Remove from the heat and stir in the prepared Shrimp butter, strain and garnish with the peeled shrimps. Season lightly with cayenne.

▣ Curry

For 1 *pint:* 1 *oz butter;* 1 *oz flour;* 2 *oz chopped onions;* 2 *medium-sized, peeled, cored and coarsely chopped apples; ½ oz curry powder;* 1 *crushed clove of garlic;* 1 *tablespoon concentrated tomato purée;* 1 *pint stock;* 1 *oz grated coconut or* 2 *fl oz coconut milk*. Cooking time: 1 hour.

Fry the onion in the butter until it is pale brown. Sprinkle the flour on top and cook for a few minutes. Add the curry powder and the apples, cook briefly, and stir in the stock. Add the tomato *purée*, the garlic and the coconut, salt lightly, stir and cook slowly for 35 to 40 minutes. Do not strain. Usually cooked at the same time as the dish with which it is to be served. Boiled rice is always served with curry dishes.

▣ Dieppoise

For 1 *pint:* 1 *pint sauce Vin Blanc; ¼ pint white wine; ¼ pint mussel cooking liquor;* 2 *oz butter.*

Mix the white wine and cooking liquor together, bring to the boil and reduce to the correct consistency. Add the butter and sauce *Vin Blanc* and garnish with bearded mussels and peeled shrimp tails.

▣ Gratin

For 1 *pint: ½ pint white wine; ½ pint fish stock;* 1 *pint Demi-glace; ¾ lb dried duxelles;* 3 *chopped shallots; ½ tablespoon chopped parsley.* Cooking time: 10 minutes.

Reduce the shallots, white wine and fish stock by half. Add the *duxelles* mixture and *Demi-glace* and simmer for 6 minutes. Add the chopped parsley. This sauce is used for fish and fillets of fish *au gratin.*

▣ Homard * *Lobster*

For 1 *pint:* 1 *pint Fish Velouté; ½ pint cream; ½ lb Lobster butter;* 1 *teaspoon paprika;* 2 *oz diced lobster.*

Reduce *Velouté*, cream and paprika to 1 pint, strain, remove from heat. Blend in the butter and chopped lobster.

Sauce Hongroise

For 1 *pint:* 1 *medium-sized chopped onion;* 1 *pint white wine;* 1 *pint Velouté;* 1 *teaspoon paprika;* 2 *oz butter.* Cooking time: 15 minutes.

Sweat the onion in the butter. Add the white wine and the *Velouté* and paprika, and reduce to 1 pint. Strain the sauce, season well and enrich with a little butter or cream. The sauce should have a pinkish tinge. This sauce accompanies egg, fish, poultry and white meat dishes.

⊡ Indienne * *Curry*

For 1 *pint:* 1 *medium-sized chopped onion;* 1 *oz butter;* 2 *fl oz coconut milk;* 1 *oz curry powder;* 1 *pint Velouté;* ¼ *pint cream; juice of half a lemon.* Cooking time: 15 minutes.

Cook the onion in the butter without allowing it to colour. Sprinkle the curry powder on top and allow the powder to cook for half a minute. Add the coconut milk and reduce by half. Add the *Velouté* (Fish *Velouté* for fish curries) and cook slowly for 10-12 minutes, the sauce should then be fairly thick. Strain, enrich with cream, season, and add the lemon juice.

Coconut milk: pour ½ pint hot milk over ½ lb grated coconut, fresh if possible. Cover and steep away from the heat. When cool press firmly through a cloth and only use the milk.

⊡ Ivoire

This is the same recipe as *sauce Albuféra.* Meat glaze gives the sauce a shiny appearance.

⊡ Marinière * *Mussel*

For 1 *pint:* 1 *pint sauce Bercy;* ¼ *pint mussel cooking liquor;* 3 *egg yolks; the juice of* ¼ *lemon;* ¼ *lb butter.* Cooking time: 12 minutes.

Reduce the mussel liquor and the *sauce Bercy* to 1 pint, and then bind in yolks of egg away from the heat. Complete the sauce with the butter and the lemon juice.

⊡ Matelote

For 1 *pint:* 1 *pint Fish Velouté;* ¼ *pint fish stock;* 1 *oz chopped shallots;* ¼ *pint white wine;* 1 *sprig thyme;* 1 *bay leaf;* 2 *oz mushroom trimmings;* ¼ *lb butter;* ¼ *pint cream;* 4 *crushed peppercorns;* 12 *small fluted mushrooms;* 12 *button onions.* Cooking time: 15 minutes.

Sweat the shallots in the butter. Add the peppercorns, bay leaf, thyme, fish stock and white wine. Reduce and add the *Velouté* and half the cream. Reduce to 1 pint. Meanwhile blanch the onions and mushrooms, then poach them keeping them as white as possible. Then strain the sauce, adjust the seasoning and complete with the rest of the cream together with the mushrooms and onions.

Sauce Mornay * *Cheese Sauce*

For 1 pint: 1 pint Béchamel; 2 egg yolks; 2 fl oz cream; 2 oz grated Parmesan or gruyère. Cooking time: 10 minutes.

Blend the egg yolks with the cream. Bring the *Béchamel* to the boil and blend it with the egg and cream mixture away from the heat. Fold in the grated cheese and heat the sauce until it is thick. Do not let the sauce boil.

▣ Moutarde * *Mustard*

This is a White Butter sauce with a little mustard or mustard powder added at the end.

▣ Nantua * *Crayfish*

For 1 pint: 1 pint Béchamel; 2 oz Crayfish butter; 4 crayfish tails. Cooking time: 20 minutes.

Make 1 pint *sauce Béchamel* and remove from the heat. Stir in the Crayfish butter and season well. Dice the crayfish tails and add them to the sauce as a garnish.

▣ Normande

For 1 pint: 1 pint Fish Velouté; 2 fl oz oyster liquor; 2 fl oz mushroom stock; 2 egg yolks; ¼ pint cream; 2 oz butter. Cooking time: 15 minutes.

Boil the *Velouté* with the oyster liquor and mushroom stock, and reduce slightly. Remove from the heat. Blend together the egg yolks and cream and pour the sauce into this mixture. Stir together over a low heat until the sauce thickens. Remove from the heat, season and enrich with the butter. This is a special sauce for *Sole à la Normande* and other fish dishes.

▣ aux Oeufs Durs * *Hardboiled Egg*

For 1 pint: 1 pint Béchamel; 2 hardboiled eggs.

Season the *Béchamel* with salt, pepper and lemon juice. Chop the hardboiled eggs coarsely and add them to the sauce. This sauce is specially suitable for boiled cod.

▣ Poulette

For 1 pint: 1 pint sauce Allemande; 2 fl oz mushroom essence; 2 oz butter; juice of ¼ lemon; 1 teaspoon chopped parsley. Cooking time: 15 minutes.

Reduce the *sauce Allemande* with the mushroom essence. Remove the sauce from the heat and complete with the butter, lemon juice and parsley.

▣ Ravigote

For 1 pint: ¼ pint white wine; 2 fl oz wine vinegar; 1 pint Velouté; 2 oz shallot butter; 1 oz chopped tarragon, chives and chervil. Cooking time: 10 minutes.

Reduce the wine and vinegar by half. Add the *Velouté* and reduce to 1 pint. Remove from the heat and blend in the butter and chopped herbs.

Sauce Riche

For 1 pint: 1 pint sauce Cardinal; 2 oz lobster flesh; 1 small truffle.

Cut the lobster flesh and the truffle in very small dice and add them to the *sauce Cardinal.* This sauce accompanies egg and fish dishes.

▣ Soubise * *Onion*

For 1 pint: ½ lb onions; ¾ pint thick sauce Béchamel; ½ pint cream; 1 oz butter. Cooking time: 1 hour.

Slice the onions, blanch them and then cook them in butter until they are soft. Add the thick *Béchamel,* cook for a few moments longer and then pass everything through a sieve. Boil the sauce up again, remove from the heat and complete with cream. Season well. This sauce is served with egg, mutton and lamb, and sweetbread dishes.

▣ Vénitienne

For 1 pint: 1 pint Velouté; ½ pint white wine; 2 fl oz tarragon vinegar; 1 chopped shallot; ¼ oz chervil leaves; 2 oz Maître d'Hôtel butter; 1 teaspoon chopped chervil and tarragon. Cooking time: 10 minutes.

Reduce the vinegar and wine with the chervil and shallot until it has almost completely evaporated. Boil the *Velouté* and stir it into this mixture. Remove from the heat, stir in the butter, season and complete with the chopped herbs. This is a special sauce for fish.

▣ Villeroi

For 1 pint: 1 pint sauce Allemande; 2 fl oz mushroom essence; 2 fl oz light stock. Cooking time: 10 minutes.

Blend the mushroom essence with the stock and *sauce Allemande* and reduce until the mixture coats the back of the spoon. Strain and stir until the sauce is cold. This sauce is used to coat food that is to be egged, breadcrumbed and deep fried. *Sauce Villeroi* which is to be used for fish dishes should be prepared with a *sauce Allemande* based on fish stock.

▣ Vin Blanc * *White Wine Sauce*

For 2 pints: 2 pints Fish Velouté; ½ pint fish stock; 5 egg yolks; ½ lb butter

Add the fish stock gradually to the *Velouté.* Reduce by a third over high heat. Remove from the heat and thicken with the egg yolks, stir in the butter and adjust the seasoning. Strain and butter the surface.

SAUCE FINES * *FINE BUTTER SAUCES*

This class of sauces includes *Hollandaise, Béarnaise* and *Mousseline*; these are all rich sauces which require an understanding of the following basic principles. Once you understand the principles behind the thickening of these sauces, which are thickened not with flour but with a liaison of egg yolks and butter you will be delighted with the results. Great care must be taken to heat and thicken the egg yolks over gentle heat. If they are not heated slowly and gradually they will become granular and over-cooking will produce scrambled eggs. You may prefer to use a *bain-marie* or double boiler to make these sauces at first, but take care that the water never reaches boiling point. Keep stirring the sauce all the time and then add the butter very, very slowly especially at first, so that the egg yolk has time to absorb the butter. If you add too much butter, especially at the beginning, the sauce will not thicken. You will probably find a wooden spoon or whisk the best utensil for making these sauces; do not forget to scrape the mixture from the sides and bottom of the pan as you stir.

Sauce Béarnaise

For 6 persons: 2 chopped shallots; 2 tablespoons tarragon vinegar; 4 crushed peppercorns; ½ lb butter; 3 egg yolks; ½ teaspoon chopped fresh tarragon; 1 teaspoon chopped chervil; 1 teaspoon lemon juice.

Put the shallots, the tarragon stalks, peppercorns and vinegar into the saucepan and reduce together. When the vinegar has almost completely evaporated, pass the mixture through a *chinois*. Cool this mixture then add it to the egg yolks and proceed as for *sauce Hollandaise*. When the sauce is completed, add the chopped tarragon, chervil and lemon juice and adjust the seasoning. This sauce accompanies grills, eggs, etc.

▣ au Beurre Blanc * *White Butter*

1 large chopped shallot; ¼ pint white wine or wine vinegar; ¼ lb butter.

Reduce the white wine or vinegar with the shallot to almost nothing, remove the shallot and allow the saucepan to cool. Work a little salt and pepper into the butter. Add the butter very gradually to the reduced wine, beating constantly with a whisk so that it does not melt completely.

This sauce is a speciality of Nantes and accompanies a dish of that region, *le brochet de la Loire*, which is boiled pike. The sauce is usually made with Muscatel wine, from the country around Nantes.

▣ Choron

Sauce Béarnaise to which is added 2 large tablespoons thick tomato *purée*.

▣ Foyot ou Valois

Sauce Béarnaise to which a walnut-sized lump of meat glaze is added. It is served with eggs and veal sweetbreads.

▣ Hollandaise

For 6 persons: 3 egg yolks; ½ lb butter; 3 large tablespoons cold water; 1 teaspoon lemon juice.

Melt the butter, it should only be lukewarm. Place the egg yolks and water in thick shallow saucepan or basin and place this in a *bain-marie*. Take great care that the *bain-marie* is over very low heat. Using a whisk, beat the sauce rapidly until it becomes thick and foamy. Remove from the heat and beat in the melted butter, a little at a time. Add lemon juice and season with salt, white pepper and cayenne, strain and keep the sauce lukewarm, if this is necessary, over heat. Serve with fish, shellfish and vegetables.

If the *sauce Hollandaise* should curdle, add 1½ tablespoons of boiling water, beating constantly to regain the emulsion.

Sauce Maltaise

¾ pint thick sauce Hollandaise; 2 large tablespoons blood-orange juice; the zest of the blood orange cut in julienne.

Blanch the zest for 2 minutes and add to the *sauce Hollandaise* with the orange juice. This sauce is served with asparagus.

⊡ Mousseline

As for a thick *sauce Hollandaise* with 3 tablespoons whipped cream folded in just before serving.

Foreign Sauces

In this section you will find some of the most popular British and foreign sauces which cannot be classified according to the previous sections.

Apple Sauce

A slightly sweetened apple *purée*, seasoned with cinnamon and served with roast pork, goose, duck and occasionally game.

Bread Sauce

For 6 persons: 2 oz fresh white breadcrumbs; ¾ pint milk; 1 small onion stuck with 4 cloves; ¼ pint cream; salt and pepper; 1 oz butter. Cooking time: 20 minutes.

Heat the milk slowly with the onion, salt and pepper for 10 minutes. Remove the onion and stir in the breadcrumbs and cook, stirring occasionally for a further 10 minutes. Complete the sauce with butter and cream. This sauce is served with roast poultry and game birds.

Cranberry Sauce

For 6 persons: ½ lb cranberries; 3 oz sugar. Cooking time: 12 minutes.

Wash the berries, add just enough water to cover them and boil them till they burst. Drain off and keep the juice and pass berries through a sieve. Sweeten slightly with the sugar and stir in as much of the juice as is needed to make a thick sauce. It is served cold with roast turkey or venison.

Cumberland Sauce

For 6 persons: ½ lb redcurrant jelly; 2 chopped shallots; the zest of ½ orange and ½ lemon cut in fine julienne; 2 tablespoons Port; juice of ½ orange; juice of ¼ lemon; ⅛ teaspoon mustard powder; one generous pinch ground ginger; one pinch cayenne pepper.

Blanch the zest and shallots for 3 minutes and drain. Pass the jelly through a sieve, mix with the Port, orange and lemon juice and season with the mustard, ground ginger and cayenne pepper. Finally add shallots and *julienne* and leave to stand for several hours. Serve with game dishes or all types of ham.

Horseradish Sauce

For 6 persons: ¾ pint whipped cream; 3 tablespoons grated horseradish; 1 pinch each of sugar, salt and paprika; 2 teaspoons vinegar; 1 teaspoon made mustard; 2 oz breadcrumbs.

Mix horseradish with the vinegar and breadcrumbs, season with sugar, salt and paprika and gently fold in whipped cream.

Mint Sauce

For 6 persons: 3 oz freshly chopped mint; 1 oz sugar; ¾ pint vinegar; ½ pint water.

Pour vinegar over chopped mint and leave to stand, add cold water and sugar. Serve cold with hot or cold roast mutton or lamb.

Piccadilly Sauce

For 6 persons: 1 pint Mayonnaise; 2 tablespoons sour cream; juice of ½ lemon; ½ teaspoon chopped fennel leaves; 1 dash Worcester sauce.

Mix the very thick *Mayonnaise* with the sour cream and lemon juice, season with the Worcester sauce and stir in chopped fennel. Serve with cold fish.

Sauce Smitane * *Russian Sour Cream*

For 6 persons: 1 large tablespoon chopped onion; 1 oz butter; ¼ pint white wine; 1 pint sour cream. Cooking time: 10 minutes.

Cook the onion with the butter, add the white wine and almost completely reduce. Add the sour cream and cook for 5 minutes, then season with pepper and lemon juice.

SAUCES FROIDES * *COLD SAUCES*

The sauces in this section include the simple cold sauces such as *Vinaigrette* and the more elaborate emulsion sauces such as *Mayonnaise*. The latter depend for their success on the principle that egg yolk will absorb a fatty substance such as oil, to form a thick, creamy emulsion. The making of these sauces is rather like making the fine butter sauces but in this case you do not have to warm the egg yolks and the process is simpler.

There are several points to remember when you are making the "*mayonnaise*" type of sauces. All the ingredients should be at normal room temperature. This includes allowing the eggs to reach this temperature, warming the oil if it has become cloudy or chilled and warming the mixing bowl in hot water before use.

Work the egg yolks for a minute or two with the spoon or whisk until they become sticky—this will help them to absorb the oil more readily. The oil must be added very gradually at first, drop by drop, until the egg yolk has time to absorb it. The oil may be added more quickly later on, once the sauce has begun to thicken and become rather like thick cream. Egg yolks are capable of absorbing only a certain amount of oil. If oil is added too rapidly, or, too much oil is added in proportion to the number of egg yolks used, the sauce will curdle. Generally speaking an egg yolk will absorb about 4 fluid ounces of oil, which is just under a quarter of a pint. Once these principles are understood and observed, you will find these sauces easy to make and delicious.

Sauce Aïoli * *Garlic*

For 6 persons: 6 cloves of garlic; 2 egg yolks; ½ pint oil; salt; pepper; lemon juice.

Pound garlic very finely in a mortar, add salt, pepper and egg yolks, add the oil in a thin stream very gradually as for *Mayonnaise* and from time to time add a few drops of lemon juice. Finally stir in a teaspoonful of boiling water to prevent sauce curdling.

▣ Andalouse

For 6 persons: ¾ pint Mayonnaise; ¼ pint very thick tomato purée; 2 oz diced red pepper.

Mix tomato *purée* with *Mayonnaise*, season and add red pepper cut in tiny dice. (Tomato ketchup can be substituted for *purée.*)

▣ Chantilly

For 4-5 persons: ¾ pint Mayonnaise; juice of a lemon; 3 tablespoons thick whipped cream.

Mix the lemon juice into the *Mayonnaise* and add the cream. This sauce is served with asparagus.

▣ Gribiche

For 4-5 persons: 3 hardboiled eggs; ½ teaspoon mustard; 1 tablespoon vinegar; ½ pint oil; 1 tablespoon capers and gherkins; 1 teaspoon chopped chervil, tarragon and parsley.

Pass the egg yolks through a sieve, mix with the mustard and vinegar, salt and pepper and combine with oil as for *Mayonnaise*. Chop the remaining ingredients finely and stir into the sauce.

▣ Ketchup à la Crème * *Tomato and Cream*

Flavour 1 pint double cream with a pinch of salt, paprika and 2 fluid oz tomato ketchup. Test for taste and finally add some lemon juice.

▣ Mayonnaise

For 6-7 persons: 3-4 egg yolks; 1 pint olive oil; salt and pepper; 1 small tablespoon vinegar; 1 teaspoon English mustard.

Stir egg yolks with a whisk in a bowl with salt, pepper, mustard and half the vinegar. Add the oil drop by drop, then in a very thin stream as the sauce begins to bind, stirring vigorously. Add a few drops of vinegar from time to time together with the oil. Then add the remainder of the vinegar and continue to stir until all the oil has been used and the sauce is thick and smooth. Lemon juice may be used instead of vinegar. Always keep the oil at room temperature; if it is too cold the *Mayonnaise* will curdle. Finally stir a tablespoon of boiling water into the *Mayonnaise*.

NOTE. Curdled *mayonnaise* may be restored by placing a tablespoon of boiling water in a clean bowl and adding the curdled *Mayonnaise* drop by drop, stirring constantly. Other causes of *Mayonnaise* curdling are too rapid addition of oil at the beginning, using oil which is too cold and too much oil for the number of eggs used.

Sauce Mayonnaise Collée * *Mayonnaise with Gelatine*

1 pint Mayonnaise; ⅓ pint aspic.

Blend together without whisking as this causes air bubbles. It is used to coat fish, poultry and certain meats. It is allowed to set for only a few minutes before decorating as it would soon become too solid and impossible to use. *Mayonnaise collée* can be melted, if it has set, by applying a gentle heat.

⊡ Moutarde à la Crème * *Mustard Cream*

For 5-6 persons: 2 oz mustard; salt; pepper; lemon juice to taste; ½ pint fresh cream.

Blend together the mustard, salt, pepper and lemon juice in a mixing bowl. Stir in the cream in the same way as oil is stirred into *Mayonnaise.*

⊡ Ravigote ou Vinaigrette

For 5-6 persons: ¾ pint oil; ¼ pint vinegar; ½ oz capers; chopped tarragon, parsley and chives; 3 oz chopped onions; salt and pepper.

Incorporate all ingredients together by stirring with a whisk. This sauce accompanies calf's head and other meat dishes.

⊡ Rémoulade

For 6 persons: 3 oz each capers and gherkins; 1 oz parsley and chervil; 2 oz purée of anchovies; 1 pint Mayonnaise.

Chop the herbs and mix with the anchovies. Blend into the *Mayonnaise* and season with salt and mustard.

⊡ Tartare

Prepare a *sauce Rémoulade* and incorporate the sieved yolks of 2 eggs and a level teaspoon of mustard.

⊡ Verte * *Green*

For 6 persons: 1 pint Mayonnaise; about ½ oz each of chervil, watercress and spinach; 1 sprig tarragon.

Blanch the watercress and spinach for 6-7 minutes. Blanch the tarragon and chervil for 1-2 minutes. Pass the herbs through a fine sieve and incorporate this *purée* with the *Mayonnaise*, season well.

⊡ Vincent

2 oz spinach; 1 pint Mayonnaise; 1 oz altogether of sorrel, watercress, tarragon, chervil, parsley, chive; 2 hardboiled egg yolks.

Blanch, cool, drain and dry the vegetables and herbs. Pound to a fine *purée* and sieve. Blend nto the *Mayonnaise* with the sieved egg yolks. Alternatively make a sauce of one part *sauce Verte;* one part *sauce Tartare.*

LES BEURRES COMPOSÉES * *SAVOURY BUTTERS*

Butter may be creamed with wine, mustard, herbs, egg yolks, meat, shellfish and nuts to produce appetising flavourings. These butter mixtures are used to baste food whilst it is being cooked, to enrich soups and sauces, as fillings for sandwiches and savouries, to accompany hot food and to garnish dishes.

Beurre d'Ail * *Garlic Butter*

¼ lb butter; 1 oz garlic.

Pound garlic, mix with the butter and pass through a fine sieve. Mould, chill and use as required.

⊡ d'Amande, Noisette, Pistache * *Nut*

¼ lb butter; 2 oz nuts (almonds, walnuts, etc.).

Peel the nuts and grind very finely with a few drops of water, gradually incorporate the butter and sieve.

⊡ d'Anchois * *Anchovy*

4 anchovy fillets; 3 oz butter.

Soak the anchovy fillets in milk, drain and dry them. Then pound them. Gradually incorporate the butter and strain.

⊡ Bercy

¼ pint white wine; 2 chopped shallots; 2 oz diced, poached and well-drained beef marrow; 3 oz softened butter; salt, pepper and lemon juice.

Boil the shallots with the white wine and reduce almost to nothing. Allow to cool a little, add the creamed butter and stir till smooth. Add the marrow and parsley and season with lemon juice, pepper and salt.

⊡ Café de Paris

2 lb butter; 2 fl oz tomato ketchup; 1 oz mustard; 1 oz capers; ¼ lb shallots; 1 oz parsley; 1 oz chives; pinch of marjoram; pinch of dill; pinch of thyme; 10 tarragon leaves; pinch of rosemary; 1 clove garlic; 8 anchovy fillets; 1 tablespoon brandy; 1 tablespoon Madeira; ½ tablespoon Worcester sauce; 1 tablespoon paprika; ½ tablespoon curry powder; pinch cayenne pepper; 8 peppercorns; juice of 1 lemon; zest of ½ lemon; zest of ¼ orange; just under ½ oz salt.

Put all the ingredients except the butter in a mixing bowl. Cover and leave to ferment slightly in the kitchen for 24 hours. Pound thoroughly, cream the butter and mix the *purée* into it. Store this butter in a covered dish in a cold place where it can be kept for several weeks.

Beurre Colbert

¼ lb butter; juice of ½ lemon; salt; pepper; ½ oz chopped tarragon; ½ oz meat glaze.

Incorporate all ingredients together.

▣ de Crevette * *Shrimp*

2 oz shelled shrimps; ¼ lb butter.

Pound the shrimps and incorporate the butter. Pass through a fine sieve.

▣ d'Ecrevisse * *Crayfish*

12 cooked crayfish; ½ lb butter.

Pound the crayfish flesh and shells, incorporate the butter. Pass through a *chinois* or tammy.

▣ d'Ecrevisse Cuit * *Cooked Crayfish*

The shells of 25 to 30 crayfish; ½ lb butter.

Break up the shells into short pieces and pass them through the grinder, or pound in a mortar. Mix in the butter. Heat in a saucepan until the butter is melted, stirring all the time. Cover with water, cook for a few more moments and gently press through a conical sieve into a dish. Leave to cool and place in the refrigerator until this butter has become firm.

▣ Escargots * *Snail*

½ oz shallots chopped and blanched; 1 clove garlic; ½ oz chopped parsley; ¼ lb butter; salt and black pepper.

Pound and sieve garlic and shallots. Blend *purée* with butter, chopped parsley and seasonings.

▣ d'Estragon * *Tarragon*

¼ lb butter; 2 oz tarragon leaves.

Blanch the tarragon for a minute, allow to cool, squeeze out all moisture and pound in a mortar. Add the butter and pass through a hair sieve.

▣ de Homard * *Lobster*

3 oz eggs and coral of lobster; 6 oz butter.

Pound the lobster coral and eggs and incorporate the butter. Sieve.

▣ de Langouste * *Crawfish*

Follow the same recipe as for Lobster butter.

Beurre Maitre d'Hotel * *Herb Butter*

3 *oz butter; the juice of ½ lemon; salt and pepper; ½ oz chopped parsley.*

Incorporate all ingredients together, chill and use for all types of grills.

⊡ Marchand de Vin

¼ *pint red wine;* 1 *teaspoon of chopped shallot;* 1 *oz meat glaze; ¼ lb butter; juice of ¼ lemon;* 1 *oz chopped parsley.*

Reduce red wine and shallots to one quarter, add meat glaze, melt, cool, incorporate butter, lemon juice and parsley.

⊡ Montpellier

2 *oz spinach leaves;* 2 *oz watercress leaves; ½ oz each of tarragon, parsley, chives, chervil and chopped shallot;* 1 *clove garlic; ½ oz of gherkins and capers;* 6 *anchovy fillets;* 3 *hardboiled egg yolks;* 3 *raw egg yolks; ¼ pint oil;* 1 *lb butter; salt, white pepper.*

Blanch and refresh herbs and vegetables and squeeze dry. Pound with the capers, anchovies, gherkins and cooked egg yolks, pass through a fine sieve and beat in the oil and raw egg yolks. Mix the butter with the *purée* and blend together, correct seasoning. Mould and use as required.

⊡ de Moutarde * *Mustard*

¼ *lb butter; 1½ oz mustard; salt and pepper.*

Incorporate all ingredients together.

COLD HORS D'ŒUVRES

There is nothing more tempting to the appetite than a well-arranged plate of *hors d'œuvre* which always add a variety of shape, colour and texture to the table. *Hors d'œuvre* are usually served only for lunch when they precede the soup course. In this case the soup will be a light one. If you are going to serve *hors d'œuvre* for dinner, omit the soup course. It is incorrect to serve both.

The purpose of the *hors d'œuvre* is to stimulate the appetite and for this reason skill and knowledge is required in presentation. Each item should be served on a separate dish or section of an *hors d'œuvre* dish, and of course should be neatly arranged. The food you choose will depend on the rest of the menu so that a careful balance of flavours is achieved.

There are two categories of *hors d'œuvre*, the cold dishes and the hot or small *entrées*.

Anchois * *Anchovies*

Anchovy fillets are often used for *hors d'œuvre*. They are packed into tins in a brine solution and it is advisable to soak in milk before use to remove excess saltiness.

Avocat de Fruit de Mer * *Avocados Stuffed with Sea Food*

For 4 persons: 2 avocado pears; 2 peeled prawn tails; 2 oz diced lobster; 3 diced scampi; 2 diced mushrooms; 4 cleaned oysters; 1 hardboiled egg; ¼ pint Mayonnaise; 1 tablespoon grated horseradish; ½ teaspoon mustard; 1 tablespoon ketchup; 1 tablespoon dry sherry; 2 tablespoons unsweetened, whipped cream; lemon juice; oil; salt; pepper.

Half the avocados lengthwise, remove the stone and scoop them out, leaving a quarter inch of flesh. Combine the lobster, prawns, scampi and raw mushrooms with the avocado flesh. Cover and allow to marinate in a cool place with lemon juice, olive oil, salt and pepper. Mix the *Mayonnaise* with mustard, ketchup and sherry. Check seasoning and add the whipped cream. Bind the *salpicon* of sea food with the sauce, fill the avocado halves with the mixture and sprinkle with chopped hardboiled egg. Place a cleaned oyster, lightly coated with aspic on top of each. Serve well chilled. (*Another version p.* 176).

BARQUETTES ET TARTELETTES FROIDES * *COLD PASTRY BOATS AND TARTLETS*

These pastry cases are prepared with Short pastry or from Puff pastry and are cooked blind and must not be allowed to colour. When they are cold they may be filled with a variety of mixtures which are to be found below and in the other chapters. (*See illustration p.* 173.)

▣ Beauharnais

Finely diced chicken bound with *Mayonnaise* containing chopped tarragon Decorate with truffle or tarragon leaves. Glaze with aspic.

▣ Marivaux

Diced prawns and mushrooms bound with *Mayonnaise*. Decorate with slices of hardboiled egg and chervil leaves. Glaze with aspic.

▣ Normandes

Diced, cooked fillet of sole and mussels bound with a white fish *sauce Chaudfroid*. Fill into pastry cases and mask with more sauce. Decorate with truffle and crayfish tails. Glaze with aspic.

▣ au Roquefort

For 6 persons: 12 *pastry boats or tartlets;* ¼ *lb Roquefort cheese;* 3 *oz butter;* ½ *glass Port;* 2 *tablespoons whipped cream;* ½ *pint Port wine aspic.*

Cream the butter, add the cheese, blend well with the Port and a little paprika, fold in the cream, pipe into the pastry cases using a star nozzle, allow to set. Glaze with Port wine aspic.

▣ Strasbourgeoise

Combine 4 parts *foie gras* with 1 part of butter and cream to a smooth paste. Spoon or pipe the mixture into pastry cases, decorate with a dainty slice of truffle. Glaze with aspic.

▣ de Thon * *Tuna*

Cream the tuna fish with oil, fill into pastry cases and decorate with anchovy fillets.

Bouchées de Gourmand

For 6 persons: 6 *Short pastry tartlet cases;* 12 *small round slices of tongue;* ¼ *lb piccalilli;* ½ *pint aspic.*

Fill the tartlets with piccalilli and place two slices of tongue on each. Glaze lightly with aspic and garnish with a little chopped aspic.

CANAPÉS

Canapés consist of a base made from small square, rectangular, oval or round slices of bread. They are either fried in deep fat, sautéed in butter, toasted or spread with plain butter or a butter mixture. Shortly before serving, they are spread with various seasoned mixtures or covered with thinly sliced fish, meat, poultry or cheese, all cut to fit the bread. *Canapés* may be garnished with parsley, watercress, truffles, olives, mushrooms, pimento, hardboiled eggs or anchovies. They may be served hot or cold and you should allow 2 to 3 of any one kind for each individual serving.

▣ aux Anchois * *Anchovy*

Use rectangular shaped *canapés* fried in oil. When cold spread a layer of Anchovy butter on top. Put chopped hardboiled egg white on one side, chopped hardboiled egg yolk on the other, and chopped parsley at the ends. Garnish centre with two crossed anchovy fillets in oil. Glaze with aspic. (*See illustration p.* 175).

▣ à l'Aurore

Butter *canapés*, cover with a slice of smoked salmon, sprinkle with sieved egg yolk. Place half a black olive in the centre of each.

▣ à la Bordelaise

Spread with Bercy butter. Garnish with a *salpicon* of cooked *cèpes* and ham. Decorate with shredded red pimentos.

▣ Bradford

Toast round slices of white bread and butter them. Sieve hardboiled egg yolks, blend with a little cream, season with salt, pepper, lemon juice and a little curry powder and spread the *canapés* with the mixture. Place a seasoned slice of tomato on top and sprinkle with diced gherkin.

▣ Cardinal

Use round slices of buttered toast. Spread with *Mayonnaise*, seasoned with pepper and paprika. Place in the centre of each a thin slice of lobster.

▣ au Caviar

Spread small round slices of white or brown bread with slightly salted butter. Cover with a thin layer of ice-cold caviar and place a quarter of a peeled lemon slice in the centre.

▣ aux Crevettes * *Shrimp Canapés*

Fry round slices of bread in butter. Cool, spread with Shrimp butter and dip in chopped hardboiled egg yolks. Place shrimp tails in a rose pattern on top and decorate the centre with a butter curl.

Canapés Divers * *Assorted Canapés*

The illustration shows *canapés* of squares of bread without crusts, buttered and garnished in various ways:
Softened butter, slice of white chicken meat, white asparagus tips.
Maître d'Hôtel butter, slice of pickled tongue, mixed pickles.
Anchovy butter, slice of salami, half slice of hardboiled egg.
Chive butter, slice of raw ham, asparagus tips.
Softened butter, slice of Chicken Galantine, mandarin segment.
Softened butter, creamed *gruyère* cheese, roasted half almonds.
Softened butter, steak *Tartare*, anchovy fillet, small pickled onion.
Mustard butter, slice of boiled ham, small piece of pineapple.
All these *canapés* are glazed with aspic jelly. (*See illustration p.* 174).

▣ Félicia

Fry small rectangles of bread in butter. When cold spread them with Mustard butter and sprinkle chopped ham on one half and chopped chicken on the other; the chicken may be replaced by hardboiled egg.

▣ au Fromage * *with Cheese*

Bind grated *gruyère* cheese with a little thick *Béchamel*, season with paprika and spread thickly on rectangular, seasoned, buttered white bread slices. Brown quickly under the grill or in a hot oven and serve hot or cold.

▣ Martine

Pass hardboiled egg yolks through a sieve and combine with a little soft butter, season with mustard and mix with chopped herbs. Spread this *purée* on round slices of toasted white bread, sprinkle coarsely chopped ham, hardboiled egg white and gherkins on top and press down lightly.

▣ Martinique

Use round pieces of bread spread with *Mayonnaise*. Garnish with one slice of tomato sprinkled with salt and top with a slice of banana dipped in lemon juice.

▣ Menagère

Fry small squares of bread in butter, leave to cool. Chop leftovers of beef very finely, mix with chopped hardboiled egg, some gherkins and herbs and bind with *Mayonnaise*. Cover the bread squares generously with the mixture and garnish with a slice of tomato.

▣ Niçois

Spread with Anchovy butter, garnish with a little heap of chopped tomatoes and top with a stoned olive. (*See illustration p.* 175).

▣ à l'Ostendaise

Fry round slices of bread in butter, cool, then spread with Mustard butter. On top place a large, cleaned, barely stiffened oyster which has been coated with thin mustard *Mayonnaise* when cold. Sprinkle chopped hardboiled egg yolk all round it.

▲ Melon en Perles, p. 182

Jambon à la Villandry, p. 524 ▼

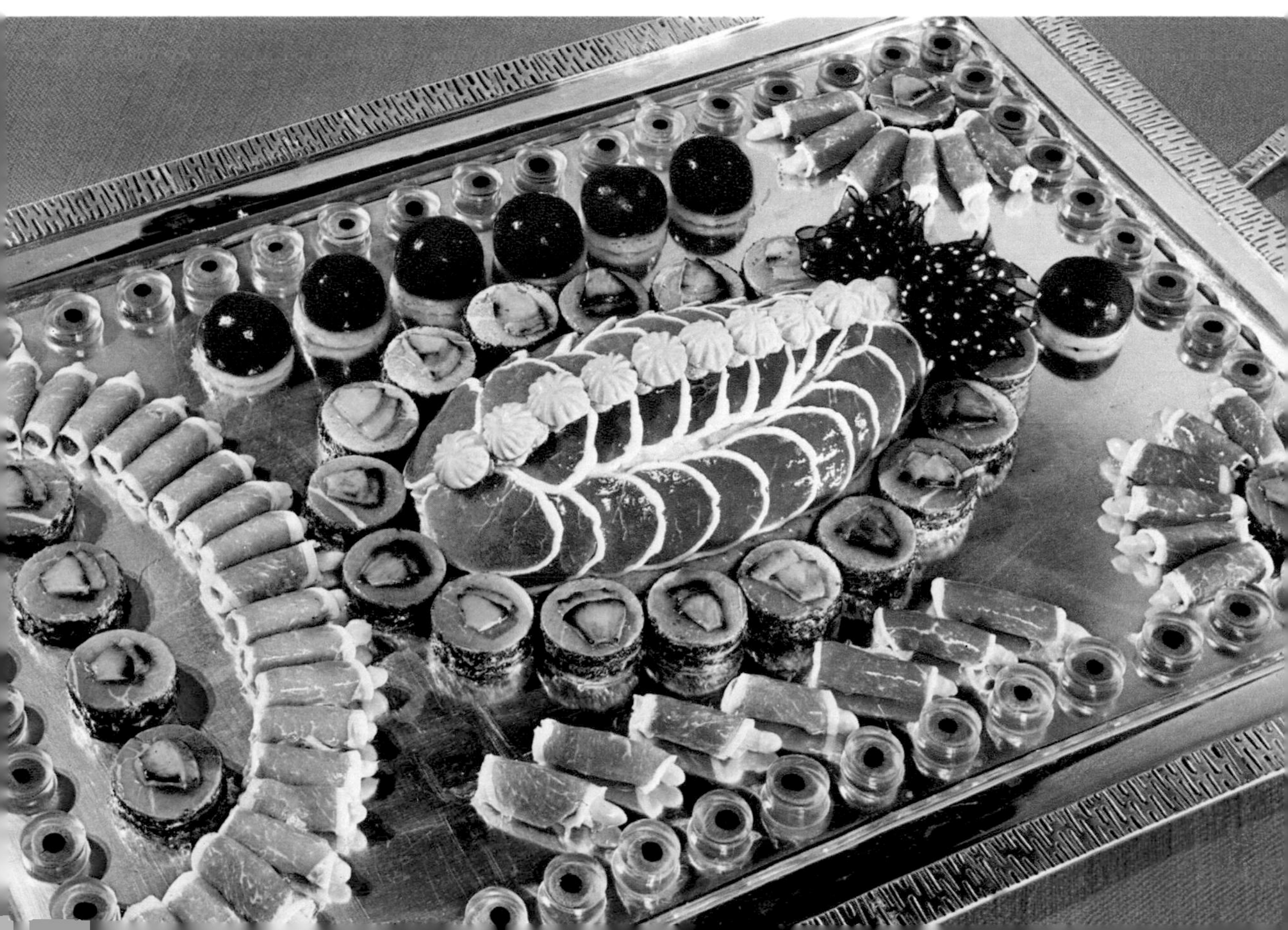

170 ▲ *Cocktail de Homard, p. 179*

Salade de Homard en Noix de Coco, p. 187 ▼

▲ A selection of Tomato hors d'œuvre, pp. 188-190

Tomates aux Ecrevisses et aux Scampi, pp. 189-190 ▼

▲ Cornets de Saumon Fumé, p. 194

Fish and Shellfish hors d'œuvre, pp. 192-194, 181 ▼

▲ *Vegetable hors d'œuvre, pp. 186 187*

Barquettes and Bouchées, p. 166 ▼

▲ Assorted Canapés, p. 168

A selection of Mixed Salad hors d'œuvre, pp. 185-186 ▼

▲ Canapés aux Anchois-Nicois-aux Asperges-Parisiens-Joinville, pp. 167-168, 177

Canapés Riches, p. 177 ▼

▲ Gourmandises, p. 181

Avocat de Fruit de Mer ▼

Canapés Parisiens

Rub hardboiled egg yolk through a sieve, mix with highly-seasoned mustard *Mayonnaise*, and spread this cream on round *canapés* fried in butter. Garnish centre with a sprig of watercress.

⊡ Riches

The illustration shows *canapés* on rectangles of bread without crusts, spread with softened butter and garnished in different ways:
Lobster, grapefruit segment, black olive.
Smoked salmon, Horseradish cream sauce.
Crayfish tails, lettuce.
Caviar, small lemon segment.
Smoked trout, *tomate concassé.*
Slice of turkey breast, small slice peach, half grape.
Foie gras parfait, tomato cut into a fan.
(*See illustration p.* 175).

⊡ Yvette

Spread rectangular pieces of white bread with horseradish butter, place two slices of sausage on top, garnish centre with a slice of hardboiled egg and decorate with an onion ring.

Cannelons au Camembert

For 6 *persons:* ½ *lb Puff pastry;* 1 *egg yolk;* 10 *oz grated Parmesan cheese;* 6 *oz Camembert;* 1 *tablespoon whipped cream.*

Roll out paste ⅛ inch thick, cut into strips 6 inches long and ½ inch wide. Roll strips around small wooden or tin cones or cream horn funnels. Brush with egg wash, sprinkle with the grated cheese and bake in a hot oven, 425° F or Gas Mark 7, for 10-12 minutes or until browned. Remove cones while the *cannelons* are still hot, allow to cool and fill with the *Camembert* which has been blended with the whipped cream to make it fluffy.

Caviar

This expensive *hors d'œuvre* is obtained from the eggs, which are called the roe, of the different varieties of sturgeon, a fish which is found in the Caspian and the Black Seas. The roe is removed from the fish as soon as it is caught. Caviar may be classified according to the variety of sturgeon.

Beluga is one of the most famous and best varieties of caviar. It comes from a very large sturgeon, called the Beluga, which has large grey eggs.

Ship is a type of Sturgeon which weighs from 30 to 120 pounds and produces medium-sized eggs.

Sevruga is another popular type and produces smaller grey eggs than the Beluga.

Russian caviars include: *Beluga Malossol*, a slightly salty caviar which is much esteemed for its flavour. *Parnaja Malossol*, a lightly salted caviar from sturgeon which are caught in winter.

Iraqui caviars include: *Shah* caviar which is also lightly salted and delicately flavoured. The best Rumanian caviar is *Icre Negre* which is lightly salted and well flavoured.

Caviar is highly perishable and must be kept cold until it is eaten. It can be served either in its original pot or carton or turned out on to a chilled glass dish. Whichever way it is served the container should be embedded in a bowl of cracked ice. Garnish with butterflies or wedges of lemon, Melba toast, butter balls and cayenne pepper. Keta or red caviar is obtained from salmon roe and should also be served cold with lemon, toast and butter.

Charcutérie

These are very often served as *hors d'œuvre.* Several types may be served together or with salad.

COCKTAILS HORS D'ŒUVRE * *VARIOUS COCKTAILS*

These comprise a great variety of mixed preparations, served in *coupes* or glasses and are always chilled. Like cocktails they originate in America.

▣ d'Avocat * *Avocado*

For 6 *persons:* 2 *avocado pears, not overripe;* ½ *pint tomato ketchup;* 1 *tablespoon oil;* 1 *tablespoon wine vinegar;* 1 *teaspoon grated horseradish;* 1 *teaspoon chopped parsley and chives;* ½ *teaspoon mustard;* ½ *teaspoon chopped shallots; dash Tabasco;* 6 *slices hardboiled egg; salt; pepper.*

Peel the avocados, open and remove the stones, cut the flesh in not too thin slices and macerate in the oil and vinegar, salt and pepper for at least half an hour. Mix the ketchup with the horseradish, chives and parsley, season with the mustard and Tabasco and lastly the liquor from the maceration. Blend the avocados well with the sauce and fill into six chilled cocktail goblets. Place a slice of egg in the centre of each and sprinkle with a few drops of ketchup.

▣ d'Ecrevisses * *Shrimp*

For 4 *persons:* 24 *to* 28 *crayfish tails;* 4 *small tomatoes; sauce as for Oyster cocktail;* ¼ *green capsicum;* 1 *hardboiled egg white.*

Peel and deseed the tomatoes and cut them into small dice. Cut the egg white and green capsicum into a fine *julienne.* Mix the crayfish tails, sauce and tomatoes together, arrange in 4 cocktail goblets, sprinkle the surface with the capsicum and egg. May also be prepared as for Lobster cocktails by reserving one or two crayfish tails as a garnish.

▣ de Homard I * *Lobster*

For 4 *persons:* ½ *lb diced lobster;* 4 *small, round lobster slices; half a lettuce heart;* 8 *white asparagus tips;* ¼ *pint thick Mayonnaise;* 1 *tablespoon grated horseradish;* 4 *tablespoons ketchup;* ½ *teaspoon mustard;* 1 *teaspoon chopped chervil and tarragon;* 1 *teaspoon brandy;* 1 *teaspoon sherry; generous pinch paprika; few drops of Tabasco sauce.*

Combine the *Mayonnaise* with the horseradish and the other condiments. Flavour with the brandy, sherry, paprika, Tabasco sauce and a pinch of salt. Bind the lobster with half the sauce. Shred the lettuce, distribute it among the chilled glasses and place the lobster *salpicon* on top. Place a lobster slice in the middle of each glass with an asparagus tip on either side. Coat with the remainder of the sauce.

Cocktail de Homard II * *Lobster Cocktail II*

For 4 persons: 1 *lobster, weighing about* 1½ *lb;* 4 *concasséed tomatoes;* 4 *fluted mushrooms;* 4 *lettuce leaves; brandy; tomato ketchup;* ¼ *pint tomato-flavoured Mayonnaise.*

Slice the lobster tail and dice the claws. Combine the claw meat with the well-drained *tomates concassés* and bind with the tomato-flavoured *Mayonnaise.* Place lettuce leaves in the bottom of 4 champagne glasses and fill with the mixture. Garnish each glass with 2 lobster slices and a mushroom. Sprinkle lightly with brandy and ketchup. (*See illustration p.* 170).

▣ d'Huitres * *Oyster*

For 4 persons: 20 *cleaned large oysters;* ¼ *pint Mayonnaise;* 1 *tablespoon grated horseradish;* 2 *tablespoons tomato ketchup; a few drops of lemon juice; a few drops of Worcester sauce;* a *dash of Tabasco sauce to taste; salt; chopped parsley.*

Mix the *Mayonnaise* with the other ingredients, except the parsley, correct the seasoning. Combine sixteen of the oysters with the sauce. Lightly mask the other four oysters with a little of the sauce. Serve the oysters in 4 cocktail or champagne glasses, place an oyster in the centre of each and sprinkle with chopped parsley.

▣ de Melon à l'Américaine

1 *small ripe Charentes melon; a pinch of salt and paprika; tomato ketchup; a little orange juice; a good sprinkling of brandy.*

Cut the melon in half, remove the seeds and scoop out the flesh into small balls; cover and chill. Blend the tomato ketchup, orange juice and brandy together, season. Do not allow the sauce to become too liquid. Serve the melon in iced glasses and garnish generously with the sauce.

▣ de Melon au Porto

Cut a circle out of the melon round the stalk and remove seeds through the hole. Pour in a glass of Port, Madeira, sherry or other fortified wine. Replace lid and keep melon in crushed ice for 2 hours before serving. (*See Illustration p.* 169).

CONCOMBRES * *CUCUMBERS*

Choose firm thick cucumbers for dishes where they are to be stuffed and peel thickly to remove the layer just beneath the skin which tends to be bitter.

▣ à l'Alsacienne

Peel the cucumbers, cut into 1 inch lengths. Scoop out the centre and marinate with *sauce Vinaigrette* for 3-4 hours. Fill with finely diced ham bound with thick cream or *sauce Crème,* seasoned and sprinkle with grated horseradish.

Concombres Garnis à la Danoise * *Danish Cucumbers*

2 small cucumbers; $\frac{1}{4}$ lb poached salmon; 2 oz pickled herring; 1 hardboiled egg; 1 oz butter; 1 tablespoon double cream; horseradish.

Prepare cucumber (*see* p. 179). Pound the salmon and pass through a sieve, combine this *purée* with the butter and cream; season well. Dice the herring and the egg and blend with the *purée* and a few drops of vinegar. Fill the prepared cucumber with the mixture and sprinkle with grated horseradish.

⊡ Renaissance

Prepare the cucumbers as above, but fill with a salad of finely diced spring vegetables bound with a little piquant *Mayonnaise* and seasoned with paprika.

COQUILLES * *SCALLOPS*

These are the natural scallop shells, emptied and cleaned and used as dishes for various preparations. You may, however, prefer to use artificial scallop shells of silver or porcelain.

⊡ de Langouste * *Rock Lobster or Crawfish*

For 6 persons: 6 shells; $\frac{3}{4}$ lb cooked slices of crawfish meat; $\frac{1}{2}$ pint Mayonnaise; 1 chopped hardboiled egg; a few capers; 1 lettuce.

Shred the lettuce and arrange in the shells, arrange the crawfish meat on the lettuce, mask with *Mayonnaise*, decorate with egg and capers.

⊡ de Poisson à la Parisienne

For 4 persons: 8 scallops; $\frac{1}{4}$ pint white wine; $\frac{1}{2}$ pint sauce Mornay; 2 shallots; 1 oz grated cheese.

Blanch the scallops whole for 10 minutes, then simmer till soft in white wine with chopped shallots, salt and pepper. Slice scallops, bind with well seasoned *sauce Mornay* and put into shells. Cover with sauce, sprinkle with grated cheese and butter and glaze under the grill until brown. Some sliced mushrooms or leftovers of boiled fish, lobster, crayfish, etc., can also be added to the scallops.

⊡ de Volaille Mayonnaise

For 6 persons: 6 scallop shells; 1 lb cooked poultry; 1 lettuce; $\frac{1}{2}$ pint Mayonnaise; 2 hardboiled eggs.

Line the bottom of the shells with lettuce and fill with thin slices of cold poultry. Mask with *Mayonnaise* and decorate each with slices of hardboiled egg and a wedge from the heart of the lettuce.

Crudités * *Assorted Raw Vegetables*

A selection of raw vegetables is often served—especially in the summer—as cold *hors d'œuvre*: globe artichoke, carrots, radishes, small tomatoes and celery may be served whole, cut up, sliced or grated with or without seasoning, either alone or with cold pork meats (*charcutérie*).

Crustacés * *Shellfish*

See shellfish section (*p.* 384) for suitable recipes.

Cygnes au Fromage * *Cheese Swans*

For 6 persons: 1 lb unsweetened Choux pastry. Filling: any of the following cheeses creamed to a piping consistency. Cheshire—Emmenthal—Dutch, although most cheeses available could be easily adapted.

Using a piping bag and 1 inch plain nozzle, pipe lines of *Choux* pastry about 2 inches long and 1 inch wide on a greased baking sheet and bake till dry in a hot oven, 400° F or Gas Mark 6. Do not use all the *Choux* pastry but reserve about 2 oz. Using a small nozzle, pipe the remainder of the paste into thin S-shapes about 1 inch long and ⅛ inch thick; bake till dry and crisp. When cool cut open along the top, fill with the creamed cheese and push in an S for a head.

Eventails au Parmesan * *Parmesan Fans*

For 6 persons: ½ lb flour; ½ lb butter; ½ lb grated Parmesan; 1 egg yolk; ⅛ pint cream. Cooking time: 8 minutes.

Make a pastry of all the ingredients except for a little of the egg yolk and the cheese, do not work it too much, and allow it to rest for a few hours. Roll out ¼ inch thick with a rolling pin and cut out biscuits about 5 inches in diameter. Cut each biscuit in four, making a fan shape, brush with egg yolk, sprinkle with grated cheese, bake in a hot oven, 400° F or Gas Mark 6 and serve hot or cold.

Foie Gras

See Poultry section (p. 529) for suitable recipes.

Gourmandises

These include:

Slices of cooked chicken *suprême* with pineapple and a dot of truffle.
Rolls of ham stuffed with creamed egg yolks and cucumber.
Galantine of chicken with sliced mushrooms.
Fillet of pork with piccalilli.
(*See illustration p.* 176).

Les Huîtres * *Oysters*

The best oysters are the English natives, the Belons and Cançales, the white and green Marennes, the Ostend oysters and the Dutch Imperials. The large Danish Limfjords, the Holsteins and the rather ugly green Portuguese are also very popular. It is usual to allow 6 oysters per person. They are opened at the last minute, placed on crushed ice and served with lemon segments and very thin brown bread and butter.

Légumes à la Grecque * *Greek-style Vegetables*

Globe artichokes, celery, mushrooms, fennel, endive stumps, onions, leeks may be prepared in this manner. For easy reference these recipes for the various vegetables prepared *à la Grecque* have been grouped together at the end of the cold *hors d'œuvre* section (*p.* 191).

LES MELONS * *MELONS*

Melon is a favourite *hors d'œuvre.* There are many varieties, the most popular being the *cantaloupe*, which itself has many varieties. The name of this melon is derived from Cantalupo, a formal papal residence near Rome. When the popes emigrated to Avignon in 1309, they brought with them some of these melons, which flourished exceedingly in Vaucluse. Hence was derived the famous *cavaillon* strain which we know as *cantaloupe.* A good melon must be heavy, the skin must yield easily to the pressure of the fingers and give off its aroma. Melon is usually served in slices, heavily chilled, with the seeds removed and dressed on crushed ice. It is served with castor sugar, although many people like it with freshly ground pepper. It is often served soaked in a fortified wine.

⊡ et Jambon de Parme * *Parma Ham*

Cut off the stalk together with a slice from the top of the melon and remove the pips and central pith through the hole with a spoon. Next use a spoon to scoop out the flesh of the melon in round pieces, still keeping the skin intact. Put the pieces back inside and pour in some sherry. Leave in a cool place for 2 hours. Serve on a silver dish garnished with rolls of Parma ham.

⊡ en Perles * *Melon Balls*

Cut a chilled melon in half and remove the seeds and central pith. With a round spoon scoop out the flesh into small spherical balls which are then dropped back into the chilled shell. Pour some Port over the pieces of melon. (*See illustration p. 169*).

LES MOUSSES * *MOUSSES and COLD SOUFFLÉS*

The basic mixture is the same in all cases. A *mousse* is made in a mould large enough for 6 to 8 persons. *Mousselines* on the other hand are shaped with a spoon, piped from a Savoy bag or made in small *quenelle*-shaped moulds. Small *soufflés* are prepared in small *cassolettes*, while large ones are made in a *soufflé* dish, above the rim of which is placed a band of paper which is removed before serving.

⊡ de Foie Gras Alexandra

For 6 *persons:* 10 *oz foie gras;* 2 *oz butter;* ¼ *pint cream;* 1 *pint aspic;* 1 *truffle; paprika; allspice.*

Cook the liver and make a *mousse* by mixing it with the butter, ⅛ pint aspic and the partially whipped cream. Season with salt, paprika and allspice. Leave in a cool place. Line an oval shaped mould with aspic. Decorate the bottom and sides with thin slices of truffle. Mix some diced truffle with the *mousse* and put into the mould. Fill to the brim with aspic and leave to set. Turn out on to a cold dish, cover with aspic and surround with chopped aspic.

⊡ de Jambon en Damier

For 6 *persons:* 1 *lb lean, cooked ham;* ¼ *pint sauce Chaudfroid Aurore* ¼ *pint fresh cream;* 2 *hardboiled eggs;* 1 *truffle;* 1 *pint Madeira aspic.*

Purée the ham and blend it with the *sauce Chaudfroid*, the partially whipped cream and a little melted Madeira aspic. Chill a shallow square mould and line it with the aspic.

Decorate it to resemble a chess board with small squares of egg white and truffle. Fill the mould first with the *mousse* and finally with the aspic and leave to set in a cool place. Turn out on to a dish. Garnish with chopped aspic and some small *croustades* filled with vegetable salad.

Mousse de Jambon Hongroise * *Hungarian Ham Mousse*

For 6-8 persons: 1 *lb purée of cooked ham;* ¼ *pint cream;* 1½ *oz tomato purée;* ½ *pint sauce Béchamel;* ¼ *lb butter; paprika;* 1 *pint Port aspic;* 2 *hardboiled eggs;* 1 *truffle.*

Mix thoroughly the *purée* of ham with the butter, cream, cold *Béchamel* and tomato *purée*. Season with paprika and add a little melted aspic. Line a charlotte mould with aspic decorate with the egg white and the truffle which are cut into the desired shapes. Nearly fill the mould with the *mousse* and top with the aspic. Leave in a cool place for 1 or 2 hours and then turn out on to a round dish. Garnish with chopped aspic.

▣ de Saumon * *with Salmon*

For 6 persons: ¾ *lb cooked salmon;* ½ *pint cream;* ½ *pint sauce Béchamel;* 1 *pint fish aspic.*

Purée the salmon and blend it with the *sauce Béchamel* and season well. Pass through a sieve and mix in ⅛ pint aspic and the partially whipped cream. Put in a mould previously lined with aspic and then proceed as above.

▣ de Volaille Fédora

For 6-8 persons: 14 *oz cooked poultry meat;* ½ *pint cream;* ½ *pint sauce Chaudfroid;* ½ *pint sherry aspic;* 2 *hardboiled eggs;* 2 *slices tongue;* 1 *truffle;* ½ *lb foie gras.*

Purée the poultry meat with the *sauce Chaudfroid* and pass through a sieve. Add a little melted aspic and the partially whipped cream and season to taste. Line a chilled charlotte mould with aspic, decorate with the egg whites, a little truffle and the tongue. Cover with a layer of *mousse*, then with a few slices of *foie gras* and some more *mousse* and, after adding a few more slices of truffle, finish with some more *mousse* to within ¾ inch of the top of the mould; this space is then filled with aspic. Put in a cold place till set and turn out on to a dish and garnish with crescents of aspic.

Œufs de Caille aux Cœurs de Palmiers * *Quails' Eggs with Palm Hearts*

20 *quails' eggs, cooked and shelled;* 1 *teaspoon chopped chervil and tarragon; small tin palm hearts;* 1 *large chopped shallot;* ½ *pint Mayonnaise;* 2 *tablespoons tomato ketchup; vinegar; oil; salt.*

Slice the hearts finely, macerate with the oil, vinegar and seasoning. Add the shallots and herbs to the *Mayonnaise*. Part fill 4 *cocottes* with the palm hearts, arrange 5 eggs in each mask liberally with the sauce.

LES OLIVES * *OLIVES*

Two different types of olives are served as *hors d'œuvre*: green olives, which have been picked before they are ripe and are first soaked in a potash dye and then in brine, and which have a firm, crisp flesh; black olives, which are similar except that they are very ripe. Olives which are to be stuffed should be fairly large; the stones are removed and replaced by the stuffing.

◘ aux Anchois * *with Anchovies*

Stuff the olives with a *purée* of anchovy fillets with or without the addition of tomato.

◘ à la Joinville

Stone the olives, stuff with Shrimp butter and serve on curly parsley. They are also used to garnish cold fish dishes.

◘ à la Sicilienne

½ lb olives; ¼ pint purée of fresh tomatoes and red peppers; 2 leaves of gelatine (approximately ⅛ oz).

Make a fairly thick *purée* of fresh tomatoes and red peppers, season well and mix with 2 leaves of gelatine which have been melted in a little water. When the *purée* starts to set fill the centre of stoned olives with it with the aid of a forcing bag and a round nozzle and leave to set. The filling must be bright red in order to make a good contrast with the green of the olives. These olives may also be used as garnish with cold meat dishes.

Oranges Farcies * *Stuffed Oranges*

For 4 persons: 4 medium-sized oranges; 2 oz cooked rice; 1 red pepper; 2 oz spring onion or 2 oz onion; 4 black olives; 2 olives stuffed à la reine; vinegar; olive oil; salt; ¼ teaspoon curry powder.

Cut off the upper third of the oranges. Scoop out the pulp and remove the pips, pith and membranes. Carefully clean the insides of the orange skins and crimp the edges. Remove the pips and pith from the peppers and shred the latter finely. Mix together with the rice, the finely chopped spring onions, orange pulp and coarsely chopped olives. Prepare *sauce Vinaigrette* containing the curry powder and pour over the other ingredients. Leave in a cool place for at least 30 minutes. Stir the mixture once more, test for taste and fill the orange skins. Decorate the tops with slices of stuffed olives *à la reine*. Serve on lettuce leaves.

Pamplemousses Farcis * *Stuffed Grapefruit*

For 4 persons: 2 medium-sized grapefruit; 1 small grapefruit; 6 oz cooked scampi; 3 oz cold poached mushrooms; ½ pint Mayonnaise; ¼ teaspoon English mustard powder; a good pinch ground ginger.

Cut the grapefruit into halves and trim the ends so that the halves stand upright. Scoop out the pulp and cut it into pieces, removing the pips and pith. Skin the small grapefruit, separate all the segments, remove the pith and keep on one side. Thinly slice the mushrooms and cut the scampi into thick pieces; soak these for a few moments in some grapefruit juice in a cool place. Thoroughly drain the pieces of grapefruit and mix with the scampi and drained mushrooms. Bind these together with the Mayonnaise seasoned with the mustard and ground ginger. Pour into the cleaned grapefruit skins and garnish each half with 2 segments of grapefruit.

Picholines * Pickled Olives

These are sold preserved in finest olive oil (*huile vierge*) and served as they are with a little of their marinade.

Poissons * *Fish*

There are many and varied fish *hors d'œuvre*. For convenience all the recipes are given at the end of the cold *hors d'œuvre* section on page 192.

Roulades au Fromage * *Cheese Wheels*

For 6 persons: ¼ lb butter; 6 large eggs; ¼ lb grated Parmesan cheese; 6 oz flour; salt; paprika; nutmeg. For the filling: ¼ pint sauce Béchamel; ¼ lb Camembert or Brie without its rind; 2½ oz butter; salt; paprika. Cooking time: 8-10 minutes.

Cream the butter and gradually mix in the egg yolks. Season with salt, paprika and nutmeg. Lightly fold in the stiffly whisked egg whites, the flour and grated Parmesan. Spread this mixture about ⅓ inch thick on a piece of buttered and floured greaseproof paper. Place on a baking sheet and lightly brown in a moderate oven, 350° F or Gas Mark 4, taking care that the mixture retains its creamy consistency. Leave till cool and then spread with the cream.
To make the filling: Push the cheese through a sieve and blend it with *Béchamel* which should still be warm. Season with plenty of paprika and a little salt. Add the butter and stir until the mixture is cold. Roll up the sponge with the filling inside like a Swiss roll, wrap it up in greaseproof paper and leave in a cold place. When serving, cut up into even slices ¾ inch thick. These rolls are often served with other cheese pastries.

SALADES * *SALADS*

There are two kinds of salads. The green salads, such as lettuce, escarole, endive, chicory which are usually prepared with an oil and vinegar dressing and served with joints. Mixed salads, consisting mainly of mixed vegetables, are usually bound with *Mayonnaise* and served with cold dishes.

⊡ en Assortiment * *Various Mixed Salads*

The salads are listed from left to right as they appear in the illustration on *p.* 174.

Fish salad: sole, turbot, tomatoes, small onions and truffles in *sauce Vinaigrette*.
Mayonnaise of fillet of venison with mushrooms.
Veal salad, ketchup, paprika.
Chicken *Mayonnaise* with asparagus tips and mushrooms.
Devilled salad: roast beef salad with piccalilli.
Marinated chicken fillets with peaches.
Beef salad with young vegetables.
Frankfurter salad: Frankfurter or Vienna sausages, salted cucumbers and tomatoes with mustard-flavoured *Mayonnaise*.
Alsatian salad: cheese, sausage and radishes.
Asparagus salad with *julienne* of ham and pickled tongue.
Lobster salad.

Salad of artichoke bottoms with *julienne* of smoked salmon.
Salad of scampi, tomatoes, hardboiled eggs, salted cucumbers.
Salad of mussels, cucumbers and tomatoes.
Salad of crayfish tails, artichoke bottoms and quail's eggs.
(*See illustration p.* 174).

Salade de Betterave * *Beetroot Salad*

Boil the beet for 1 hour in plenty of water, drain, and complete cooking in the oven. Cool, peel, slice thinly and prepare with pepper, salt, oil and vinegar—a little more of the latter than is usual with salads. When about to serve sprinkle some chopped egg white on top followed by some chopped parsley.

⊡ de Bœuf * *Beef*

This is a good use for leftover beef. Remove all fat, cut in small, thin slices, add a few thin gherkin slices and marinate with salt, pepper, oil, vinegar, chopped onion and herbs. Leave to stand 1-2 hours before using. When serving garnish with slices of hardboiled egg and gherkins.

⊡ de Céleri Blanc * *White Celery*

Remove the individual stalks from a tender, very white celery, wash well and remove the leaves. Cut in strips about 1½ inches long and slice these very thinly lengthwise. Serve with *sauce Rémoulade* or acidulated cream. Leave to stand for 2 hours and serve cold with chopped herbs sprinkled on top.

⊡ de Céleri-rave * *Celeriac*

For 6 *persons:* 2½ *lb very white celeriac;* 1 *pint Mayonnaise; mustard; juice of half a lemon.*

Peel the celeriac, and cut it into *julienne* or in very small dice. Blanch for 2 minutes in order to make it tender, cool and drain well. Marinate with lemon juice and very little salt for 1-2 hours. Then bind with *Mayonnaise* seasoned with mustard. Arrange in a salad bowl and sprinkle chopped herbs on top.

⊡ de Chou Blanc * *White Cabbage*

Finely shred the heart of a young fresh white cabbage and prepare with salt, pepper, finely chopped onions, oil and vinegar. Before serving, leave to stand so that seasoning can penetrate and serve cold. Or, toss the onions in oil with diced bacon, pour over cabbage while still hot and prepare salad with salt, pepper and vinegar.

⊡ de Chou-fleur * *Cauliflower*

Divide cooked cauliflower into rosettes, season in the usual way and arrange in an *hors d'œuvre* dish. Surround with small tomato slices or French beans and sprinkle the cauliflower with chopped hardboiled egg yolk. Leftover haricot beans, lentils, carrots, etc., can also be made into salad.

Salade de Chou Rouge * *Red Cabbage Salad*

Remove the outer leaves from a firm red cabbage and take only the more tender inside ones. Cut out the thick ribs and shred the leaves finely. For each 2 lb of red cabbage, dice 4 oz each of lean and fat bacon, brown lightly with 2 tablespoons of oil in a large saucepan and add the cabbage. Pour in ½ glass dry white wine and cook till half done, stirring constantly. Season with salt, pepper, a pinch of sugar, oil and vinegar and serve cold. If desired add some finely chopped onion.

▣ de Concombre * *Cucumber*

Use the long green cucumbers for salads, the short yellow ones are used for stuffing or as garnish. Peel the cucumber carefully lengthwise. Cut in half lengthwise, remove seeds, slice both halves thinly with a slicer or a knife and salt slightly in order to draw the water from the cucumber. Then squeeze out moisture and prepare with pepper (do not add more salt), vinegar, oil and mixed herbs.

Another Method

Peel cucumber, slice fairly thinly, arrange slices in *hors d'œuvre* dish so that they overlap and put in a cold place. When about to serve dust lightly with salt and pepper, sprinkle with oil and vinegar and with chopped herbs.

▣ de Homard en Noix de Coco * *Lobster and Coconut*

For 8 persons: 4 small coconuts, halved, and partly dried inside; 2 boiled lobsters, each weighing about 1½ lb; ½ lb asparagus cut in small sections; 6 oz thinly sliced mushrooms; ½ pint Mayonnaise; 2 fl oz tomato ketchup; ½ tablespoon brandy; ¼ pint aspic.

Remove the flesh of the lobster tails and cut into 8 slices. Open the claws and halve them lengthwise. Make a salad of the mushrooms, asparagus, lobster trimmings, *Mayonnaise*, ketchup and brandy. Season well. Fill the half coconuts with the salad, garnish with lobster slices and half a claw. Glaze with aspic. (*See illustration p.* 170).

▣ de Museau de Bœuf

Boil ox palate as soft as possible in the same way as calf's head. Cut in small, very thin slices and season with salt, pepper, oil, vinegar, chopped onions and herbs. Ox palate can also be bought ready cooked.

▣ de Poissons ou de Volaille * *Poultry or Fish*

Remove skin from cooked poultry and cut in thin slices. Arrange in a salad bowl on lettuce cut in strips, coat with *Mayonnaise,* and garnish with anchovy fillets, quarters of hardboiled eggs and quarter hearts of lettuce. Fish salad may be prepared in exactly the same way.

▣ de Pommes de Terre * *Potato*

Cook some potatoes in their jackets and then peel and either cut them into slices or dice. Season while still hot with oil, vinegar and mixed herbs. This is most important; it is the only way in which the potatoes absorb the *sauce Vinaigrette*; so much so that the *sauce Vinaigrette* may need to be diluted with a glass of hot water or white wine to keep the potatoes soft enough. Potato salad is better served while it is still warm. An alternative method is to bind the cooked, diced potatoes with *Mayonnaise*.

Salade de Queues d'Ecrevisses à l'Indienne * *Indian-style Shrimp Tail Salad*

For 4 persons: 2 small coconuts; 3 oz boiled rice; 1 small green pepper; 2 large tomatoes; 24 small crayfish tails; ½ pint Mayonnaise; ½ teaspoon curry; a generous tablespoon of mango chutney; 2 tablespoons of unsweetened whipped cream; lemon juice, oil, salt and pepper.

Saw the coconuts in half horizontally and saw a small piece off each end so that they will stand up. Remove about 2 oz of the flesh and grate it. Peel, deseed and dice the tomatoes. Cut open the pepper, remove the seeds and the white parts and cut in small dice. Marinate the rice, diced tomato and pepper and 16 crayfish tails for 30 minutes with the lemon juice, oil, salt and pepper. Spice the *Mayonnaise* with the curry powder, grated coconut and mango chutney. Add the whipped cream. Drain the marinated mixture, bind with *Mayonnaise* and fill the half coconuts with this salad. Garnish each one with 2 crayfish tails and coat lightly with aspic. Serve very cold.

▣ de Tomates * *Tomato*

Place medium-sized, firm, ripe tomatoes in boiling water for a few moments to facilitate peeling. Cut in not too thin slices, arrange in *hors d'œuvre* dishes so that they overlap, dust with salt and pepper, sprinkle with oil and vinegar, place very thin onion rings on top and sprinkle with chopped parsley.

Tapenade

This is a *purée* of highly seasoned black olives, bought ready prepared. It is used in the same way as anchovy paste, and prepared butters.

Tartelettes à la Tarnoise

For 6 persons: ½ lb unsweetened Short pastry; 1½ oz green, blanched, chopped olives; ¼ lb creamed gruyère cheese; 3 oz butter; 12 slices stuffed olives; 1 tablespoon sherry; ¼ pint aspic. Cooking time: 10 minutes.

Line the tartlet moulds thinly with the pastry and bake blind. Cream the butter, mix in the cheese, olives, sherry; blend well and season with salt and paprika. Fill the tartlets with this mixture using a star tube and piping bag; garnish each tartlet with a ring of stuffed olive. Chill. Glaze carefully with aspic.

TOMATES * *TOMATOES*

Preparation: Use medium-sized tomatoes with a regular shape. Skin them by dropping them into boiling water for a maximum of 10 seconds as this makes it very easy to remove the skins. Cut off the top and scoop out the inside of the tomato with a small spoon. Place the tomato upside down to drain. Season with salt and pepper. This is the basic preparation when the tomatoes are to be used as a garnish or decoration.

▣ à l'Andalouse

For 4 persons: 4 medium-sized tomatoes; 2 oz rice; 2 green Spanish peppers; 1 onion; ¼ pint Mayonnaise; 3 tablespoons oil; parsley. Cooking time for the rice: 16-18 minutes.

Scoop out the tomatoes as directed above. Season for ½ hour and drain. Cook rice in boiling water, drain and allow to cool. *Sauté* chopped onion and one Spanish pepper with the seeds removed in oil, without allowing them to brown. When everything is cooked, mix rice with onions, peppers and highly seasoned *Mayonnaise* and fill the tomatoes with the mixture. Remove seeds from the last Spanish pepper, cut it into very thin strips and scatter them on top of the tomatoes. Serve on a layer of parsley or lettuce leaves.

Tomates à l'Antiboise

3 *small tomatoes;* 3 *oz tuna fish in oil;* 1 *oz butter; lemon juice;* 2 *tablespoons Mayonnaise;* 1 *hardboiled egg.*

Hollow out the ripe but firm tomatoes through an opening around the stalk, season with salt, pepper and vinegar for 1 hour beforehand. Turn upside down and allow to drain. Crush the tunny with a fork and combine with the butter, salt, pepper and lemon juice and then the *Mayonnaise*. The *purée* must be creamy, finely crushed and well seasoned. Fill the tomatoes with it. Place on a dish garnished with parsley. Decorate with alternate slices of hardboiled egg yolk and white.

▣ à la Beaulieu

For 3 persons: 3 *tomatoes;* 2 *oz tunny fish in oil;* 1 *oz butter;* 2-3 *tablespoons Mayonnaise; lemon juice;* 1 *hardboiled egg;* 3 *black olives.*

Prepare tomatoes as above. Mash the tunny fish, mix with soft butter and *Mayonnaise*, and season with lemon juice, salt and pepper; this *purée* should be very creamy. Fill tomatoes with this stuffing, cover one half with finely chopped egg white and the other half with chopped egg yolk and place half a pitted black olive in the centre. (*See illustration p.* 171).

▣ aux Ecrevisses I * *with Shrimps*

Prepare tomatoes as above. Fill with 6 crayfish tails bound with paprika-seasoned *Mayonnaise*. Place on a bed of lettuce.

▣ aux Ecrevisses II

Fill the bottom of the hollow tomatoes with *Mayonnaise* and arrange the crayfish tails on top in a mound; glaze with aspic and garnish with pistachios. (*See illustration p.* 171).

▣ à l'Italienne

Cut off the tops of the tomatoes and scoop them out. Stuff with Italian salad. Garnish with whirls of *Mayonnaise* and slices of hardboiled egg.

▣ à la Mousmé

For 4 persons: 4 *medium-sized tomatoes;* ¼ *lb celeriac;* ¼ *lb Chinese artichokes;* 3-4 *tablespoons sauce Rémoulade.* Cooking time: 20 minutes.

Choose firm, ripe tomatoes, make a small opening on the top and scoop out. Season with salt, pepper and vinegar ½ hour before use. Fill with a salad of celeriac cut into fine strips and mixed with *sauce Rémoulade*. Garnish with the Chinese artichokes cooked in water and lemon juice, drained, and seasoned as for salad. Arrange tomatoes on lettuce leaves.

Tomates à la Murcie

2 *large tomatoes;* ¼ *lb diced cucumber; Vinaigrette; parsley; mixed herbs.*

Fill the tomatoes with cucumber salad mixed with herbs. (*See illustration p.* 171).

⊡ à la Parisienne

Scoop out small tomatoes, marinate inside and fill with a salad of diced lobster, crawfish, crayfish or Dublin Bay prawns bound with a few spoonfuls of thick *Mayonnaise.* Place each tomato on a bed of lettuce and serve cold.

⊡ Pêcheur

Cut a lid off the tomatoes and scoop them out. Fill with Russian salad. Garnish with a rosette of salmon and a round slice of gherkin. Arrange on lettuce leaves with lemon slices.

⊡ à la Russe

For 4 *persons:* 4 *medium-sized tomatoes;* 6 *oz Russian salad;* 3-4 *tablespoons Mayonnaise;* 1 *hardboiled egg.*

Prepare tomatoes as above. Fill with the Russian salad mixed with *Mayonnaise* and well-seasoned. Place a slice of egg on top and serve on a bed of lettuce. (*See illustration p.* 171).

⊡ aux Scampi

Fill the tomatoes with scampi salad and garnish with a cucumber ball. (*See illustration p.* 171).

⊡ à la Sévigné

8 *small tomatoes;* 2 *oz mushrooms;* 6 *oz chopped chicken;* 1 *small green pepper;* ½ *pint Mayonnaise.*

Dice the skinned chicken meat and the mushrooms, not too fine, and bind with the well-seasoned *Mayonnaise.* Cut tops of small, ripe, firm tomatoes, scoop them out, marinate inside for 30 minutes with salt, pepper and a few drops of vinegar, turn down and drain. Fill with the poultry mixture, rounding the top slightly. Sprinkle a very fine *julienne* of peppers on top and serve on an *hors d'œuvre* dish with curly parsley. They may also be used to garnish cold meat dishes. Any other poultry can be substituted for the chicken.

Viande Sechée * *Dried Meat*

Dried meat can be served as *hors d'œuvre* in the same way as pork meats (*charcutérie*). This is beef which has been dried in the mountain air (especially in Switzerland), salted and slightly smoked. It is served in wafer-thin slices which look rather like wood shavings.

VEGETABLES À LA GRÈCQUE

Many vegetables may be prepared *à la Grècque* and are very popular *hors d'œuvre.* The liquor in which the vegetables are cooked is the same for all the types of vegetables although the method of preparing the vegetables may differ. The vegetables should be allowed to remain in the liquid until very cold and should be served with a little of the cooking liquor.

Cooking Liquor: ¼ pint white wine; 2 fl oz olive oil; 1 sprig parsley; ¼ pint water; juice of 1 lemon; 1 small bay leaf; 6 peppercorns; 1 teaspoon salt.

Bring all ingredients to the boil in a saucepan large enough to hold the required quantity of vegetables. The vegetables can now be added when prepared.

Artichauts à la Grècque * *Greek-style Artichokes*

For 8 persons: 8 very small artichokes.

Trim artichokes, cut off the tips of leaves, wash and drain well. If large, cut into halves or quarters. Blanch in boiling, salted water with lemon juice added for about 10 minutes. Drain off water and add the cooking liquor as above, cover and cook for about 30 minutes or until artichokes are cooked but still crisp. Cool in the liquor.

▣ Céleri * *Celery*

For 8 persons: 2 lb celery hearts.

Wash, clean and blanch celery in boiling, salted water for 3 minutes. Drain and cut into 2 inch *bâtons.* Place in cooking liquor as above and cook for 5-10 minutes. Cool in liquor.

▣ Champignons et Cèpes * *Mushrooms*

For 6-8 persons: 1½ lb mushrooms.

Simmer the cooking liquor. Wash and blanch the mushrooms for 5 minutes. Add the mushrooms to the cooking liquor and cook slowly for 6-8 minutes. Cool in liquor.

▣ Champignons Pimentés

Take very large, firm mushrooms, clean, peel, wash and rub with lemon juice. Slice thinly, arrange in an *hors d'œuvre* dish and pour a marinade of lemon juice, oil, salt, cayenne pepper and a little mustard on top. These mushrooms remain raw.

▣ Fenouil * *Fennel*

For 6-8 persons: 1½ lb fennel roots.

Cut the fennel into quarters, blanch and cook as for Celery *à la Grècque.*

▣ Gourillons

For 6-8 persons: 2 lb endive; ½ lb fresh tomatoes.

Drain, trim and wash the endive. Blanch for 5 minutes. Cut into 1 to 2 inch *bâtons* and place in cooking liquor along with the tomatoes which have been skinned and quartered. Proceed as directed above.

Oignons à la Grècque * *Greek-style Onions*

For 10-12 *persons:* 1½ *lb button onions.*

Peel, wash, and blanch onions for 10 minutes. Drain off and discard the water. Heat cooking liquor and cook slowly for 5 minutes. Add onions and cook over moderate heat until onions are tender, 12-15 minutes. Cool in the liquor.

⊡ Poireaux * *Leeks*

For 6-8 *persons:* 2 *lb leeks.*

Trim and clean leeks, tie into neat bundles, blanch for 5 minutes and drain off cooking water. Cut into 2 inch lengths and place into cooking liquor, proceed as for Celery *à la Grècque*.

FISH HORS D'ŒUVRES

ANCHOIS * *ANCHOVIES*

⊡ à la Nîmoise

Allow 3 anchovies per person. Cut anchovy fillets in half lengthwise and arrange as a lattice in the middle of an *hors d'œuvre* dish. Sprinkle with oil and chopped hard-boiled egg yolk and garnish with very thin small half-slices of pickled beetroot.

⊡ de Norvège (Kilkis)

Allow 3 anchovies per person. Serve the anchovies in the marinade in which they are canned and arrange in an *hors d'œuvre* dish. Serve with bread and butter.

⊡ à la Russe

Arrange the anchovy fillets on a mixture of cold, diced, steamed potatoes and diced russet apples. Sprinkle with chopped chives and grated horseradish.

⊡ à la Toulonnaise

For 6 *persons:* 1 *lb hot Potato salad;* 9 *large anchovies in oil;* 9 *olives;* 3 *hardboiled eggs.*

Make a mound of warm Potato salad in the middle of an *hors d'œuvre* dish. Garnish all round with slices of the white hardboiled egg, discard the yolk, place a rolled-up anchovy fillet on each and place a stoned olive in the middle of each fillet.

NOTE: To obtain good round slices of egg white pour the egg white into small, buttered *baba* moulds, poach in the oven in a water-bath like a cream and allow to cool before turning out and slicing.

Eperlans ou Equilles Marinés

For 4 *persons:* 10 *oz smelts or sand-eels;* ¼ *pint white wine;* ¼ *pint oil;* 3 *tablespoons vinegar;* 3 *shallots;* ½ *teaspoon mustard powder mixed with* 1 *teaspoon water; flour; salt; pepper; parsley.*

Roll the clean smelts in flour, seasoned with salt and pepper and brown quickly on both sides in hot oil. Boil white wine with vinegar, sliced shallots, salt, pepper and a little chopped parsley for 5 minutes and stir in a teaspoon of mustard. Pour the marinade over the fish, boil up once more and then remove from the heat and chill.

HARENGS * *HERRINGS*

▣ Filets Lucas

Prepare in equal quantities some bananas and plain boiled potatoes cut into small dice, mix together and arrange in the bottom of an *hors d'œuvre* dish. Cut some raw marinated fillets of herring into three pieces lengthwise and arrange in trellis fashion on the potato and banana base. Sprinkle with white wine, vinegar and oil. Sprinkle with chopped parsley, garnish the border with overlapping slices of hardboiled eggs.

▣ Filets à la Russe

For 6 *persons:* 3-4 *raw herrings;* ¾ *lb cooking apples;* 1 *small tablespoon finely chopped onion; the juice of half a lemon;* 2 *fl oz white wine;* 2 *tablespoons oil; pepper.*

Peel and core apples and cut in very small dice. Add onion and lemon juice. Dip the herrings in boiling water for a moment, skin and neatly remove fillets, removing any bones. Arrange the apple mixture in an *hors d'œuvre* dish, place sliced fillets over them, sprinkle a little pepper on them and pour the white wine and oil on top.

▣ Frais Marinés * *Marinated Fresh*

For 6 *persons:* 6 *fresh herrings, cleaned and with heads removed;* ¼ *pint white wine;* 2 *fl oz vinegar;* 1 *medium-sized onion and* 1 *small carrot, both thinly sliced;* 2 *sliced shallots; a few peppercorns; a small bay leaf;* 1 *sprig thyme; a little parsley*. Cooking time: 15 minutes.

Boil the marinade for 5 minutes. Place the cleaned herrings in a deep fire-proof dish, pour the boiling marinade on top and poach for 10 minutes without allowing to boil. Leave to cool in the marinade and serve as they are.

Maquereaux Marinés * *Marinated Mackerel*

Made in the same way as Marinated Fresh Herrings.

Raviers de Poisson

Garnish the bottom of the *hors d'œuvre* dishes with a *julienne* of lettuce. Arrange on the lettuce a mixture of varieties of neatly diced, cooked fish bound with *Mayonnaise* which must be highly seasoned. Garnish with tomatoes, slices of hardboiled eggs and chopped herbs or onions.

Rollmops

Fillets of herring prepared as fresh marinated herrings. Serve rolled round gherkins. Hold in position with a cocktail stick.

Rougets-Barbets à l'Orientale

For 10 *persons:* 10 *red mullet weighing about each* ½ *lb;* 1 *lb tomatoes;* 1 *clove garlic;* 2 *fl oz white wine;* 2 *fl oz oil;* 1 *pinch saffron;* ½ *teaspoon chopped parsley; salt; pepper.*

Clean, wash and dry the red mullet, dip in seasoned flour and fry on both sides in hot oil until brown. Peel, halve and deseed the tomatoes, dice and let them soften in oil; add the crushed clove of garlic, chopped parsley, white wine, salt, pepper and saffron, boil up and pour over the red mullet. Put in a moderate oven, 350° F or Gas Mark 4, for 10 minutes until cooked. Arrange in *hors d'œuvre* dishes, pour the liquor over them as it is and serve very cold. Garnish to taste with half slices of tomato.

Sardines à l'Huile * *Sardines in Oil*

When serving sardines you should take care to present them as attractively as possible. They may be arranged in a fan on one half of a round dish, with chopped onions, capers, chopped hardboiled egg yolk, chopped parsley and chopped hardboiled egg white arranged on the other half. Between the sardines arrange half lemon slices with serrated edges and parsley and serve toast and butter on the side. A little lemon juice sprinkled on the sardine brings out the flavour.

Sardines à la Rovigo

For 6 *persons:* 12 *sardines;* ¼ *pint cold sauce Tomate;* 1 *sprig sage;* 1 *green pepper;* 1 *hardboiled egg white.*

Drain the sardines and serve on cold *sauce Tomate,* if possible made with fresh tomatoes and flavoured with sage. On top sprinkle first a very fine *julienne* of green peppers and then of hardboiled egg white.

SAUMON FUMÉ * *SMOKED SALMON*

The best smoked salmon comes from Scotland. The taste varies according to the cure. Smoked salmon is best served plain with lemon and brown bread and butter.

⊡ Cornets * *Smoked Salmon Horns*

For 6-12 *persons:* 2, 7 *oz tins tuna fish in oil;* 6 *oz softened butter; lemon juice; salt; ground black pepper;* 12 *slices smoked salmon;* 1 *lb mixed, cooked vegetables;* ½ *pint Mayonnaise; truffles or black olives.*

Mash tuna fish with oil in which it was tinned and mix with butter. Season to taste with lemon juice, salt and pepper. Put mixture through a sieve. Shape salmon slices into cornets and fill with the tuna fish and butter mixture using a teaspoon or piping bag fitted with a fluted tube. Chill. Mix vegetables with *Mayonnaise*, adding lemon juice, salt and pepper to taste. Mound in the centre of an *hors d'œuvre* dish. Flatten the top and chill. Shortly before serving arrange tuna-filled salmon cornets over the top of the salad, with the small ends pointed towards the centre. Garnish with truffle or black olive. If salad is not to be served immediately, glaze it over with aspic.

Roulades Rosa Branca

For 25 persons: 2¼ lb smoked salmon slices; 2½ lb asparagus tips; 15 *hardboiled eggs;* 2 *truffles;* 3 *tomatoes.*

Roll the wafer thin slices of smoked salmon round the asparagus tips. Decorate with slices of truffle. Garnish with halves of hardboiled egg, which are topped with a slice of tomato.

Sprats

These are small, smoked fish resembling herrings. Select very fat fish, dip in boiling water for a few seconds, skin, clean, cut off heads and arrange in an *hors d'œuvre* dish. Marinate with salt, pepper, chopped shallots and parsley, a dash of vinegar and a little white wine. But often they are served as they are, with fresh butter.

Crème de Thon à la Mirabeau

For 4 persons: small tin tuna fish; 3 *oz butter;* 2 *tablespoons Mayonnaise;* 2 *green olives;* 2 *medium-sized tomatoes; lemon juice.*

Mash tuna fish, mix with creamed butter and *Mayonnaise*. Season with salt, pepper and lemon juice. Arrange on oval dish in a heap and smooth top. Decorate with pitted, round olives and border with firm tomatoes, peeled and cut into eighths.

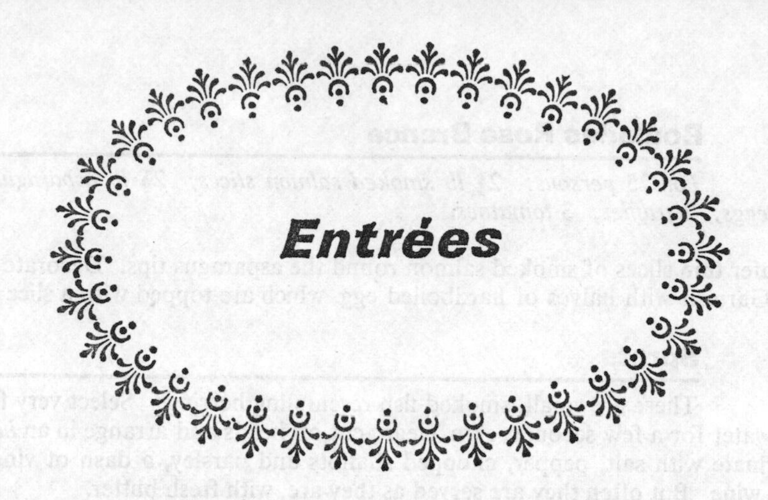

Entrées

It is difficult to distinguish between hot *hors d'œuvre* and *entrée* dishes. The main difference is in size, because for both dishes a variety of savoury mixtures and vegetables are used and they are served in flan cases, tartlet cases, Puff pastry cases and small fire-proof dishes. *Mousses, croquettes, soufflés, quiches* and *cromesquis* are some of the foods served for both purposes. When they are to be served as hot *hors d'œuvre* the items should be made in small individual dishes. Hot *hors d'œuvre*, like cold, are usually served at lunch and only occasionally at dinner when the soup course is omitted. When these preparations are served as small *entrées*, the size of the items and the amounts served are increased and these dishes may be part of the lunch or dinner menu.

Allumettes aux Anchois * *Anchovy Straws*

½ lb Puff pastry; 16 *anchovy fillets in oil; chopped hardboiled egg; chopped parsley*. Cooking time: 10-12 minutes.

Roll out Puff pastry in a strip less than ¼ inch thick and 3-3¼ inches wide. Turn the anchovy fillets in chopped hardboiled egg and chopped parsely. Place one fillet at the edge of the strip, roll it in the Puff pastry, making a complete turn, and cut it off. Wet the edge of the pastry so as to make it stick together. Cut one end of each strip in shape of a fish tail and the other on a slant. Place the sticks on a baking sheet sprinkled with a few drops of cold water, brush with egg and bake in a hot oven, 400° F or Gas Mark 6.

Allumettes au Parmesan * *Parmesan Straws*

¾ lb Puff pastry; ¼ lb grated Parmesan cheese; 1 *egg yolk*. Cooking time: 6-8 minutes.

Prepare Puff pastry as usual. Sprinkle with the grated cheese and a shake of cayenne when completing the last two turns. Then roll thinly into strips about 3 inches wide. Brush the top with egg, sprinkle with grated Parmesan and a shake of cayenne. Cut into pieces the width of a finger, place them on a baking sheet, and bake them in a hot oven, 400 °F or Gas Mark 6. Serve hot on a table napkin. Grated *gruyère* cheese may be used instead of Parmesan.

BARQUETTES * *PASTRY BOATS*

Barquettes and tartlets differ only in shape. At one time *barquettes* were used only for fillings of fish or shellfish, but this practice no longer survives. *Barquettes* are oval-shaped cases made with Short pastry (or scraps of Puff pastry) which are baked blind and then filled with the various *salpicons* or mixtures described below. They are then often reheated for a few minutes and served hot.

Barquettes à l'Américaine * *Lobster Barquettes*

Fill with a *salpicon* of lobster *à l'Américaine* sprinkled with toasted breadcrumbs.

▣ **aux Anchois** * *Anchovies*

Fill with a *salpicon* of anchovy fillets and mushrooms bound together with *sauce Béchamel.* Sprinkle with breadcrumbs and brown in a hot oven.

▣ **à la Bouquetière** * *Vegetable*

Fill with vegetable *macédoine* bound together with *sauce Béchamel.* Garnish with a small bunch of asparagus tips.

▣ **de Crevettes** * *Shrimps*

Bind the shrimps with *sauce Mornay,* fill into *barquettes,* mask with *sauce Mornay,* sprinkle with grated Parmesan and brown in a hot oven, 425° F or Gas Mark 7.

▣ **au Foie Gras**

Fill baked *barquette* cases with *foie gras purée* which has been blended over heat with a little white sauce. Mask with *sauce Velouté.*

Bâtons au Chester * *Cheshire Cheese Straws*

For 6 persons: 6 oz flour; ¼ lb butter; ¼ lb grated Cheshire cheese; 1 egg; 2 tablespoons cream; salt; paprika. Cooking time: 6-8 minutes.

Quickly mix all the ingredients into a fairly stiff paste. Season with salt and paprika and leave to stand for 2 hours. Roll out the paste to a thickness of ⅓ inch and cut up into strips 3 inches wide which are in turn cut up into small sticks ½ inch wide. Brush with egg and sprinkle with a little grated cheese. Bake in a moderate oven, 375° F or Gas Mark 4.

BEIGNETS * *FRITTERS*

Fritters—pieces of food coated with paste or batter and fried in very hot fat—are made with either unsweetened *Choux* pastry or Coating batter. They should be made at the last moment, and served hot.

▣ **Amandine** * *Almond*

For 6 persons: ¼ lb flour; 2 oz butter; 4 eggs; just under ½ pint water; 1 oz gruyère; 2 oz lean, cooked ham; 2 oz almonds. Cooking time: 3-4 minutes.

Make a *Choux* pastry in the following manner. Heat the water and butter in a saucepan with a pinch of salt. When the water is boiling rapidly tip in the flour all at once, remove from the heat and mix with a wooden spoon until the mass leaves the sides of the pan. Cool slightly. Add the eggs one by one beating well between each addition. Add the cheese, ham, seasonings and the peeled chopped and lightly-browned almonds. Mould the mixture with 2 spoons or pipe it with a plain tube into pieces the size of a walnut. Fry until golden brown and puffy in hot deep fat. Drain and serve immediately on a table napkin.

Beignets d'Anchois * *Anchovy Fritters*

Using very thin slices of bread without their crusts, make sandwiches containing anchovy fillets, cut into fingers. Dip in Coating batter and fry in hot deep fat.

◘ au Fromage * *Cheese*

For 6 persons: ½ pint water; 5 oz flour; ¼ lb butter; ¼ lb Parmesan cheese; 4 eggs; salt. Cooking time: 4-5 minutes.

Put water to boil with butter and salt. Add the flour and mix till mixture leaves the sides of the pan clean. Cool slightly and blend in eggs one at a time. Finally add cheese and adjust seasoning. Mould mixture with aid of a spoon or pipe with a plain tube into pieces the size of a walnut. Fry in deep fat and serve immediately.

◘ de Légumes * *Vegetable*

Cut up some vegetables (such as globe artichokes, asparagus tips, cauliflower, salsify) into slices, sticks or quarters. Marinate in a mixture of oil, lemon juice, salt, pepper and chopped parsley for about 30 minutes. Dip each piece of vegetable in Coating batter and fry.

◘ Pignatelli

¼ lb flour; 2 oz butter; 4 eggs; just under ½ pint water; 2 oz diced gruyère; 2 oz cooked diced ham; 2 oz skinned, sliced and toasted almonds. Cooking time: 3-4 minutes.

Make a *Choux* pastry as above with the flour, water, butter and eggs. Toss ham lightly in butter, cool and mix with the *Choux* pastry together with the cheese and the almonds. Shape into balls the size of a small apricot on a floured pastry board and fry in the same way as Almond Fritters, gradually increasing the temperature of the fat. Drain well, arrange on a table napkin and serve hot.

◘ de Poissons Divers * *Mixed Fish*

Cut any braised or poached fish into medium-sized pieces. Marinate with oil, lemon juice, salt, pepper, and chopped parsley for ½ hour. Dip each piece in Coating batter and deep fry.

Bonne-bouche Jurasienne * *Baked Cheese Puffs*

For 6 persons: ½ lb Puff pastry. For cheese filling: ¼ pint Béchamel; 1 egg yolk; 2 oz grated cheese; 1 tablespoon double cream; seasoning. Cooking time: 10 minutes.

Mix together all ingredients for the filling. Roll out Puff pastry ⅛ inch thick. For each *bonne-bouche* allow 3 layers of pastry, each 2 inches in diameter. The layers are placed one on top of the other, the centre layer having a hole 1 inch in diameter cut from its centre. Before positioning the third layer, fill this hole with the cheese mixture. Place the last layer on top and press down the edges, brush with beaten egg. Prick with a fork and bake for 10 minutes in a hot oven, 425° F or Gas Mark 7. Serve hot.

BOUCHÉES * *PUFF PASTRY CASES*

Roll out Puff pastry ½ inch thick. Cut into circles with a fluted pastry cutter not more than 2½ inches in diameter. Care should be taken not to twist the cutter when cutting the circles. Place them on a baking sheet which has been sprinkled with cold water. Make a circular cut with a pastry cutter barely 2 inches in diameter to mark the cover of the *bouchée* case. Brush the top lightly with egg and bake in a hot oven, 425° F or Gas Mark 7 for 15 to 18 minutes. Watch these cases while baking. They should be quite dry when they are baked. Remove the lid with the point of a small knife; this cover should come off quite easily. Remove any dough in the centre of the cases that is not quite cooked. Fill with any of the mixtures described below.

▣ à l'Américaine * *Lobster*

Diced lobster bound with *sauce Américaine.*

▣ à la Bouquetière * *Vegetable*

Macédoine of vegetables and *sauce Crème.*

▣ Chasseur * *Game*

Diced game, mushrooms and truffles bound with *sauce Madère.*

▣ de Crevettes ou Joinville * *Shrimp*

Shrimps and cooked white mushrooms diced in *sauce Crevette.*

▣ à la Dieppoise * *Shrimp and Mussel*

Diced shrimps and mussels in *sauce Vin Blanc.*

▣ à la Financière

Diced cocks' combs and kidneys, lambs' sweetbreads, mushrooms, small *quenelles,* stoned olives and truffles in *sauce Velouté.*

▣ Julienne * *Vegetable*

Julienne of vegetables stewed in butter bound with *sauce Crème.*

▣ Montglas

Diced *foie gras,* mushrooms, pickled ox tongue and truffles in *sauce Madère.*

▣ Nantua * *Crayfish*

Diced crayfish tails, mushrooms and truffles in *sauce Nantua.*

▣ Quatre-temps

Any fish leftovers, mushrooms, mussels and shrimps bound with *sauce Béchamel* or *sauce Crevette.*

Bouchées à la Reine * *Chicken and Mushroom Bouchées*

8 bouchée cases; ½ boiled, skinned fowl; ¼ lb mushrooms; 1 small truffle; ½ pint sauce Suprême.

Dice chicken, mushrooms and truffle and mix with the hot *sauce Suprême.* Fill into the hot cases, place the lid on top and serve at once. (*See illustration p.* 210).

Cannelons aux Oeufs Durs * *Egg-Filled Cornets*

For 6 persons: ¾ lb Puff pastry; 6 hardboiled eggs; ⅛ pint Béchamel. Cooking time of cornets: 10-12 minutes.

Roll out Puff pastry ⅛ inch thick and cut into strips ¼ inch wide and 6 inches long. Wrap the pieces round metal or wooden horn-shaped moulds (cream horn tins). Brush the surface with egg yolk beaten with milk. Place moulds 1 inch apart on greased baking sheets. Bake 10 minutes in a very hot oven, 450° F Gas Mark 8 or until pastry is golden. Remove moulds immediately by carefully twisting them free. Cool, fill with diced hardboiled eggs which have been bound with *Béchamel* and well seasoned.

CASSOLETTES * *SMALL INDIVIDUAL DISHES*

The *casolette* is a small fire-proof porcelain vessel in which food is cooked and served. They are used for *hors d'œuvre* or small *entrées* and are available in various shapes. For certain dishes a border of *Duchesse* potatoes is often piped round the rim through a star tube. A variety of fillings is given below.

⊡ Bouquetière

For 6 persons: ½ lb Duchesse potato mixture; ½ pint cream; 1 lb cooked macédoine of vegetables; 18 cooked asparagus tips. Cooking time: 5-10 minutes.

Pipe a border of *Duchesse* potatoes round the dish. Mix the *macédoine* with the cream, season and fill into individual *cassolettes.* Put in a hot oven, 425° F or Gas Mark 7, to brown the potatoes. Serve the *cassolettes* garnished with asparagus tips.

⊡ Deauville

For 6 persons: 1 lb diced, cooked lamb; 3 hardboiled eggs; ½ pint sauce Demi-glace; 3 tomatoes concassé.

Heat the lamb in the sauce, and spoon into 6 buttered, heated *cassolettes*, mask with tomatoes *concassé.* Garnish with half an egg.

⊡ à la Florentine

For 6 persons: ½ lb Duchesse potato mixture; ¾ lb diced, cooked chicken; ½ lb cooked leaf spinach; ½ pint chicken Velouté.

Garnish the bottoms of the *cassolettes* with the spinach heated in butter, complete filling with the chicken blended into the sauce, pipe a border of *Duchesse* potato around, brush with milk and brown in a hot oven for about 10 minutes.

Cassolettes à la Japonaise

For 6 persons: 24 hardboiled quails' eggs or 6 hardboiled hens' eggs; 1 tablespoon soya sauce; ¼ lb cooked mushrooms; 1 tablespoon Sake or dry sherry; ¼ lb smoked ham; ¼ teaspoon ground ginger; ½ pint Demi-glace; 2 oz butter.

Cut the ham and mushrooms into a fine short *julienne*, stew in butter, add the *Demi-glace*, cook for a few minutes, season with Sake or soya sauce and ginger. Shell the eggs, arrange in the *cassolettes* and mask generously with the sauce.

⊡ Mylord

For 6 persons: 10 oz cooked, diced game; a few fresh breadcrumbs; 6 oz cooked, diced ham; ½ pint sauce Salmis.

Heat the meat in the sauce and fill into the dishes. Fry the breadcrumbs in butter until golden and sprinkle on top. Place in a hot oven for about 10 minutes.

⊡ Opéra

For 6 persons: 10 oz diced, cooked ham; ¼ lb diced, cooked mushrooms; ¼ lb truffled foie gras; ½ pint sauce Salmis; ½ lb Duchesse potato mixture.

Blend the ham, mushrooms and *foie gras* with the sauce, fill into the *cassolettes.* Pipe six rounds of *Duchesse* potatoes, brush with beaten egg and bake in a hot oven until golden. Place upon the *cassolettes.*

⊡ Régence

For 6 persons: ½ lb Duchesse potato mixture; ½ pint chicken Velouté; 1 lb cooked chicken; 18 cooked asparagus tips; 1 truffle (optional); a little milk.

Mix the chicken and truffle and bind with the *sauce Velouté*, add salt and pepper. Pipe a border of *Duchesse* potatoes round 6 buttered *cassolettes*, and brush potatoes with milk. Fill with the chicken mixture. Brown in a hot oven, 400°F or Gas Mark 6. Garnish with a slice of truffle and the asparagus tips.

⊡ Saint-Hubert

For 6 persons: 1 lb any type of cooked game; ½ pint sauce Venaison; 1 fl oz Port; ½ lb Duchesse potato mixture; 6 mushroom caps. Cooking time: 5-6 minutes.

Purée the game, mix with warm sauce and flavour with Port. Heat slightly and fill *cassolettes* ¾ full. Cover *purée* with potato mixture, using a forcing bag and fluted nozzle, brown in a hot oven and put a mushroom cap in the middle.

⊡ Sultane

For 6 persons: 1 lb any type of cooked game; ¼ lb chestnut purée; ½ pint sauce Salmis (made from the bones); 1 truffle.

Trim the meat and mix with ⅓ the quantity of chestnut *purée*, add a few spoons of sauce, stir, season and keep warm in water-bath. Fill small china *cocottes* or a deep-cooked flan case of unsweetened Short pastry with the *purée*, coat with a little sauce and place a truffle slice on top or sprinkle with chopped pistachio nuts. Serve hot.

Cassolettes Suzanne

For 6 persons: 1 lb cooked poultry meat; ¼ lb mushrooms; 1 lb spinach; ½ pint Béchamel; 1 oz butter; 6 truffle slices; 6 pimento strips.

Boil the spinach briskly, cool, squeeze out well, *sauté* in butter and season. Use it to cover the bottoms of 6 *cassolettes* and on top place a coarse mince of poultry mixed with some chopped mushrooms and bound with well-seasoned *Béchamel.* Coat mince lightly with a little *Béchamel* and heat in a moderate oven, 375° F or Gas Mark 5, for 15 minutes. Garnish if desired with pimento and truffle slices. Serve hot.

Petits Choux au Fromage * *Cheese Puffs*

For 6 persons: 1 lb unsweetened Choux pastry; 1 egg; grated Parmesan; For the cheese filling: ¼ pint Béchamel; 1 egg yolk; ½ oz butter; 2 oz grated cheese; 1 tablespoon of cream. Cooking time: 10-12 minutes.

Put knobs of *Choux* pastry on a buttered baking sheet, brush with egg, sprinkle with grated cheese and bake in a hot oven, 425° F or Gas Mark 6, for 10 minutes. Cut a small hole underneath and fill with the cheese filling. These puffs can be served either hot or cold. Meanwhile prepare the cheese filling, heat the *Béchamel,* remove from the heat and stir in the egg yolk, cheese, butter and cream and season well with salt and cayenne.

COQUILLES * *SCALLOP SHELLS*

For these dishes one uses either scallop shells or their counterparts in porcelain or silver. The hot scallop shells are usually brushed with melted butter then a border of *Duchesse* potato is piped around the outer edge before filling with a variety of mixtures.

⊡ de Cervelles Sauce Mornay * *Brains with Mornay Sauce*

For 6 persons: 3 brains; ½ pint sauce Mornay; 2 oz grated cheese; ½ lb Duchesse potato mixture; 6 cooked mushroom caps.

Wash brains, remove membranes and soak ½ hour in cold water. Rinse, cover with fresh cold water, add salt and lemon juice or vinegar, cover and simmer 20 minutes. Drain and cool. Pipe the edges of the shells with *Duchesse* potato. Slice the cooked brains and place them in the scallop shells. Mask with the *sauce Mornay*. Sprinkle with cheese and breadcrumbs. Brown under a grill. Decorate each scallop with a mushroom cap.

⊡ de Crevettes * *Shrimps*

For 6 persons: ½ lb shelled, cooked shrimps; ½ pint Béchamel; 1 oz Shrimp butter; 2 oz grated cheese; ½ lb Duchesse potato mixture.

Pipe the edges of the shells with the *Duchesse* potato. Bind the shrimps with a mixture of the *Béchamel* and Shrimp butter. Season with a small pinch of cayenne pepper. Fill the shells, sprinkle with cheese and top with a knob of butter. Brown under a grill.

Coquilles de Gibier Duchesse * *Game with Duchesse Potato*

1 lb any type of cooked game; ¼ lb ham; ½ lb Duchesse potato mixture; ½ pint sauce Salmis; 1 truffle.

Pipe the edges of the shells with the *Duchesse* potato. Fill with a mixture of shredded game, ham and truffle. Mask with the game sauce. Brown in a hot oven for 5 minutes.

◻ de Homard Thermidor * *Lobster Thermidor*

For 6 persons: lobster, weighing about 1½ lb; 2 oz grated gruyère; 2 shallots; salt, pepper, cayenne; ¼ pint white wine; chopped parsley; ¼ pint cream; brandy; ¼ pint Béchamel; English mustard.

Cut the lobster in two lengthwise. Remove the inedible parts (the intestines and the bag in the head) and reserve the green and the coral for future use. Fry in oil to colour for 5-6 minutes, pour away the oil, add the chopped shallot and parsley; deglaze with brandy; add the wine and simmer, covered, for 20 minutes. Remove the flesh from the lobster and cut into large dice. Reduce the cooking liquor by half, blend in the cream, *Béchamel* and mustard, correct seasoning, stir until the sauce boils, pass through a sieve. Mix the flesh with a little sauce, fill into the shells, mask with the rest of the sauce, sprinkle with the cheese and brown in a very hot oven or under the grill.

◻ de Langouste Thermidor * *Crawfish Thermidor*

Same preparation as for Lobster *Thermidor*, but using crawfish.

◻ Saint-Jacques à la Diable * *Devilled Scallops*

For 6 persons: 1½ lb Duchesse potatoes; 2 lb scallops; 5 oz butter; dry white wine to cover (about 1 pint); 2 chopped shallots; 1 pint Béchamel; ½ teaspoon dry mustard; salt and black pepper to taste; dash cayenne; ¼ lb soft white breadcrumbs.

Pipe a border of *Duchesse* potatoes around the edge of 6 buttered scallop shells. Place scallops, 2 oz of the butter, wine, and chopped shallots in a saucepan. Bring to boiling point, reduce heat and simmer 8-10 minutes. Remove scallops. Strain the liquid and simmer it until the quantity has been reduced to one quarter its original amount. Add ⅔ of the *Béchamel* and strain the mixture through a fine sieve. Blend the mustard with 1 tablespoon water and let it stand 5 minutes, then add it to the sauce along with the rest of the seasonings. Slice the scallops and add to the mixture. Heat and spoon into the prepared scallop shells. Coat with remaining *Béchamel*. Melt remaining butter and mix with the breadcrumbs. Sprinkle over the tops of the prepared shells and brown under the grill, or bake in a moderate oven, 375° F or Gas Mark 4, for 15-20 minutes or until crumbs are brown.

◻ de Volaille Mornay * *Chicken with Mornay Sauce*

For 6 persons: 1½ lb cooked chicken; 2 oz grated cheese; ½ lb Duchesse potato mixture; 1 oz melted butter; ½ pint sauce Mornay. Cooking time: 8-10 minutes.

Pipe a border of *Duchesse* potatoes, mask the bottom of the shell with a little *sauce Mornay*, fill with the pre-heated chicken, mask with the sauce; sprinkle with the cheese and melted butter and brown in a hot oven, 400° F Gas Mark 6.

Coulibiac de Saumon à la Russe * *Russian Coulibiac*

For 8-10 *persons:* 1½ *oz Vesiga marrow from the back-bone of a sturgeon;* 1 *lb salmon;* ½ *lb semolina;* 1¼-1½ *lb Brioche dough or Puff pastry; salt and black pepper;* 3 *sliced hardboiled eggs;* ½ *tablespoon chopped parsley;* ½ *tablespoon chopped, fresh dill;* 2 *tablespoons chopped onion;* 3 *oz butter;* 1 *raw egg, beaten; sour cream; parsley sprigs;* 1 *whole tomato.*

Soak sturgeon marrow in cold water overnight. Cover and cook slowly 5 hours or until marrow is soft. Cool and cut in thin slices. Poach salmon, cool, remove skin and bones and flake the salmon. Cook semolina by boiling it in beef stock. Cool. Roll out dough or Puff pastry ¼ inch thick in a rectangle 12 × 8 inches. Spread half of the cooked semolina down the centre of the rectangle of dough and place half the vesiga on top. Sprinkle the salmon with salt and pepper and place this over the marrow. Arrange egg slices over salmon and sprinkle with parsley and dill. *Sauté* the onion in ½ oz butter and sprinkle over the egg slices. Add another layer of Vesiga and the remaining semolina. Turn the 2 sides of the dough up towards the centre over the filling—press together. Turn up the dough at the ends and press together. Place the roll seam side down on a lightly-greased baking sheet. Roll out the trimmings ¼ inch thick and cut into narrow strips and arrange in a lattice pattern over the roll. Make a hole in the centre of the top for the steam to escape, brush the surface with beaten egg and leave in a warm place for ½ hour. Bake in a hot oven, 400° F or Gas Mark 6, for 30 minutes or until browned. Remove from the oven, melt remaining butter and pour it into the hole in the top of the crust. Serve garnished with parsley sprigs and the whole tomato. Cut the roll into slices and serve with sour cream. (*See illustration p.* 209).

Crêpes au Roquefort * *Roquefort Cheese Pancakes*

For 6 *persons:* ¼ *lb flour;* 2 *eggs;* ½ *pint milk;* 2 *oz Roquefort;* 1 *oz melted butter*. Cooking time: 3-4 minutes for each pancake.

Prepare a smooth batter with the sifted flour, egg yolks and milk. Season with salt and paprika. Mix the sieved Roquefort and melted butter into the batter. Finally fold in the stiffly-whisked egg whites. Make the pancakes small and very thin. Serve them hot.

CROMESQUIS * *CROMESQUIS*

Cromesquis are a variant of *croquettes*. They are prepared in exactly the same way as *croquettes* except that *croquettes* are egg and breadcrumbed before deep frying, while *cromesquis* are often wrapped in a small pancake or rolled in thin bacon rashers before dipping into Coating batter and deep frying.

⊡ Bonne Femme

For 6 *persons:* 1 *lb finely diced cooked beef;* ½ *pint Velouté; Coating batter; seasoning;* ¼ *lb diced, cooked mushrooms;* 3 *egg yolks.*

Mix the mushrooms, beef and sauce together and bring to the boil. Continue cooking until the mixture leaves the side of the pan. Remove from the heat, blend in the egg yolks vigorously, one at a time and correct seasoning. Spread upon a buttered tray, cover with buttered paper and allow to cool. Mould into round *croquettes* 2¼ inches long, dip into Coating batter and deep fry.

Cromesquis à la Florentine * *Spinach Cromesquis*

For 6 persons: 1½ lb spinach; 1 oz butter; ¼ lb grated Parmesan; Coating batter; ½ pint reduced Béchamel; 6 thin, 4-inch pancakes.

Stew the spinach in butter, it should weigh 1½ lb when cooked. Mix the spinach with the cheese and *Béchamel,* and spread the mixture over the pancakes. Roll up like a Swiss roll, trim the ends square, cut into 2-inch lengths, dip into Coating batter and deep fry.

▣ de Légumes Divers * *Mixed Vegetables*

For 6 persons: 1½ lb mixed vegetables; ¼ lb grated Parmesan; ½ pint thick Béchamel; Coating batter; salt and pepper.

Dice the vegetables finely. Bind the vegetables with the *Béchamel* and proceed as for *Cromesquis à la Florentine.*

▣ aux Oeufs * *Eggs*

For 6 persons: 10 hardboiled eggs; ½ pint sauce Tomate; 2 raw eggs; parsley; ½ pint thick Béchamel; Coating batter.

Dice the hardboiled eggs, add the *Béchamel,* bring to the boil stirring constantly and cook until the mixture has a firm consistency. Beat in the raw eggs, finish cooking and spread on a buttered baking tray. Allow the mixture to cool. Shape into small eggs, dip in Coating batter; deep fry. Serve on a dish paper with fried parsley. Heat the *sauce Tomate* and serve it separately in a sauce-boat.

▣ à la Polonaise * *Meat*

These are made with various meats, but are always wrapped in a thin pancake before dipping in Coating batter and frying. Serve *sauce Tomate* separately.

▣ Saint-Hubert * *Game*

For 6 persons: 1½ lb diced game; 1 pig's caul; ½ pint Demi-glace; Coating batter.

Bind the game with the sauce over heat, season well. Cool, then mould into small oblongs 2 inches in length, wrap in pig's caul. Dip in batter and deep fry. Serve with *sauce Venaison* in a sauce-boat.

▣ à la Vladimir

For 6 persons: 1 lb cooked fillets of sole (or other white fish); ½ pint thick Velouté; 12 shelled cooked crayfish tails; ½ lb Duchesse potato mixture; 1 truffle; 12 thin, 3-inch pancakes; salt and pepper.

Dice the sole, crayfish and truffle, add to the sauce and bring to the boil. Spread on a buttered baking tray ¾-inch thick, cover with a buttered paper, cool, then mould into oblongs 2 inches long. Spread 12 pancakes with the *Duchesse* potato, place the fish in the centre, fold up, dip in Coating batter and deep fry. Serve with a sauce-boat of *sauce Normande.*

CROQUETTES * *CROQUETTES*

Croquettes may be made in various shapes. In general they are made in a sausage or cork shape about 2-3 inches long. They are usually made with a *salpicon* of meat (or poultry, etc.) and mushrooms. The following proportions are for 6 persons.

Put into a pan 1 lb finely diced meat or poultry, ½ lb diced, cooked mushrooms, moisten with 2 fluid oz of sherry, heat until the liquid has evaporated. Mix in ½ pint well reduced *Velouté*, bind with 2 egg yolks. Spread on a buttered tray, cover with a buttered paper and allow to cool and set.

Mould into *croquettes* 2½-inches long and ⅝-inch in diameter; egg and breadcrumb, reform. Unless it is stated to the contrary the instructions, the method, proportions and ingredients for other *croquettes* are the same as are in this basic recipe.

▣ de Bœuf * *Beef*

1 lb boiled beef; ½ pint Béchamel; ½ lb cooked mushrooms; 2 egg yolks.

Serve with *sauce Tomate.*

▣ Cressonnière * *Watercress*

1 lb cooked purée of watercress; ½ lb Duchesse potato mixture; ½ pint Béchamel; 2 egg yolks.

Serve with a parsley sauce made from *sauce Velouté.*

▣ de Foie Gras

1 lb diced, cooked foie gras; 2 fl oz sherry; 1 chopped truffle; ½ pint sauce Suprême; 2 egg yolks.

Serve with *sauce Périgueux.*

▣ de Fromage * *Cheese*

½ lb grated cheese; 2 egg yolks; 1 pint Béchamel; 2 whole eggs; mace.

Boil the *Béchamel* and reduce, then incorporate the yolks and whole eggs, finish cooking. Remove from heat and blend in the cheese. Season with a pinch of mace.

▣ de Gibier * *Game*

1 lb diced, cooked game; ¼ lb diced, cooked mushrooms; ½ pint well-reduced sauce Demi-glace; a little brandy.

Serve with *sauce Venaison.*

▣ de Homard * *Lobster*

1 lb diced, cooked lobster; 2 egg yolks; ½ lb diced, cooked mushrooms; pinch cayenne; ½ pint Béchamel.

Serve with *sauce Homard.*

Croquettes d'Huitres * *Oyster Croquettes*

1 lb diced, poached oysters; pinch cayenne; ½ lb diced, cooked mushrooms; 2 egg yolks; ½ pint Béchamel.

Serve with *sauce Normande*

◘ de Langouste * *Crawfish*

1 lb diced, cooked crawfish (rock lobster); ½ lb diced, cooked mushrooms; ½ pint Béchamel; 2 egg yolks.

Serve with *sauce Nantua.*

◘ Montrouge * *Ham and Mushroom*

¾ lb diced, lean, cooked ham; 2 egg yolks; ½ lb diced, cooked mushrooms; ½ pint thick Béchamel.

These are moulded into the shape of small eggs. Serve with *sauce Tomate.*

◘ de Poisson * *Fish*

1¼ lb diced, cooked fish; 2 egg yolks; ½ pint thick Béchamel; juice of one lemon.

Serve with *sauce Joinville* or *Homard.*

◘ de Volaille * *Poultry*

For 6 persons: 1 lb cooked chicken; 6 oz cooked mushrooms; ½ pint thick sauce Béchamel; 2 egg yolks; 1 egg; breadcrumbs.

Serve with *sauce Tomate.*

CROUSTADES * *PASTRY CASES*

These are small cases prepared from pastry or *Duchesse* potato. *Croustades* take their names from the various fillings as do *barquettes*. They are generally served hot.

◘ à l'Alsacienne

Spread a layer of *Duchesse* potato on a buttered baking tray, 2-inches thick. Allow to cool, then cut out rounds of 2-inches in diameter with a cutter; egg and breadcrumb, mark the lid with a 1¾-inch round cutter and deep fry. Remove the lid and then the interior, leaving a shell ¼-inch thick; fill with braised *sauerkraut* and top with slices of Strasbourg sausage.

◘ Cardinal * *Prawn*

Prepare a *salpicon* of Dublin Bay prawn tails previously cooked in a *court bouillon*. Blend into a *sauce Béchamel* enough Crayfish or Lobster butter to both flavour and colour the sauce, then mix in the *salpicon* and fill into the *croustades*. Lobster or crawfish can be substituted for the prawns.

Croustades Forestière

Prepare *croustades* with *Duchesse* potatoes (see *Croustade à l'Alsacienne*). Fry in butter, flavour with finely-chopped herbs and bind with *Demi-glace*. Fill into the *croustades*. Prepare some fine lardons and chopped onions, blanched and fried in butter. Blend and arrange on top of each *croustade*.

▣ de Gnocchi à la Parisienne

For 6 persons: 5 oz Choux pastry (unsweetened); ½ pint Béchamel; 5 oz grated gruyère cheese.

Add 4 oz of *gruyère* to the *Choux pastry*, mould into small balls and poach in boiling salted water. Drain, bind with the *Béchamel*, season, remove from the heat; fill into *croustades*, sprinkle with cheese and melted butter and gratinate for 8-10 minutes in a hot oven, 450° F or Gas Mark 8.

▣ d'Oeufs Durs * *Hardboiled Eggs*

Dice the eggs and mix with cream or *Béchamel*. Make *croustades*, *vol-au-vent* cases or *bouchées* with Puff pastry or use Short Crust pastry for *timbales* or *croustades*.

▣ à la Reine

Prepare the *croustades* from Puff pastry in fancy tartlet moulds, cook blind and do not allow them to colour. Fill with a *salpicon* of chicken and mushrooms bound with *sauce Crème*. Mask with *sauce Mornay*. Sprinkle with grated cheese and melted butter and gratinate in a hot oven, 425° F or Gas Mark 7, for 8-10 minutes.

Croûtes aux Champignons * *Savoury Mushrooms*

For 6 persons: 2½ lb mushrooms; ¾ pint sauce Suprême.

Clean, wash and slice the mushrooms. Cook them in butter with salt and lemon juice until soft. Bind with the *sauce Suprême*. Simmer for 8-10 minutes and season with freshly-ground pepper and a small pinch of cayenne pepper. Serve on Short Crust pastry bases or on slices of bread fried in butter.

Délices de Manon

For 6 persons: ½ pint Pancake batter; 1 gaufre (or waffle) iron the size of a small fancy dariole mould.

Heat some oil and immerse the iron in the oil. When at frying heat, remove the iron by the handle, dip into the batter, leaving sufficiently long for the mould to be well coated with batter. Return to the frying oil, fry to a light golden colour, gently loosen the shell from the iron and continue frying until crisp and golden. Remove, drain and keep hot. Do not fill until the last moment. Usual fillings are sweetbreads, *quenelles*, crayfish tails, mushrooms, truffles, etc, bound with *sauce Sûpreme* or the respective creamed sauce.

▲ Vol-au-Vent Moderne, p. 232

Coulibiac de Saumon à la Russe, p. 204 ▼

▲ *Bouchées à la Reine, p. 200*

Quiche à la Lorraine, p. 221 ▼

▲ *Gnocchi en Croustades à la Parisienne, p. 218*

Pizzas, p. 238 ▼

 ▲ Ravioli di Carne, p. 239

Tortellini de Ricotta, p. 242 ▼

▲ *Delizie alla Romana, p. 235*

Tagliatelle Verdi alla Bolognese, p. 242 ▼

▲ *Riz à la Grecque, p. 240*

Risotto alla Milanese, p. 240 ▼

▲ Risotto con Funghi, p. 239

Spaghetti Carbonara, p. 241 ▼

▲ *Spaghetti alla Vongole, p. 242*

Lasagne alla Casalinga, p. 236 ▼

Diablotins à la Normande

3 oz butter; 1 oz plain flour; 1 oz rice flour; 3½ fl oz milk; ¼ lb Camembert (without crust); salt, cayenne.

Melt butter in pan, stir in flours, stir in milk gradually, then add *Camembert* and seasoning and bring the mixture to the boil stirring constantly. When mixture is very thick turn it out on to a tray and allow to cool. It will become solid and can be cut or moulded into small round biscuit shapes approximately ¾-inch thick. These are then floured and egg-and-breadcrumbed and fried golden brown in deep fat.

Duchesse au Chester

For 6 persons: 5 oz flour; ¼ lb butter; ½ pint water; 5 eggs; salt; 1 egg yolk; 1 oz grated cheese; ½ pint cheese filling as for Fondants au Chester. Cooking time: about 45 minutes.

Make a *Choux* pastry with the flour, butter, water and the 5 eggs. Using a savoy bag fitted with a star nozzle, pipe this paste out on a lightly-greased baking sheet in oval shapes about 2½ inches × 1½ inches. Brush lightly with egg yolk, sprinkle with grated cheese and brown in the oven, 400° F or Gas Mark 6, for about 35 minutes. When the puffs are crisp and dry, remove from the oven, slit them open immediately on one side, cool and using a piping bag, fill with the cheese filling mixture. Serve very hot.

Éclairs au Fromage * *Cheese Éclairs*

For 6 persons: the basic Choux pastry as for the previous recipe. For the cheese filling: ¼ pint sauce Béchamel; 2 egg yolks; 3 oz grated Cheshire, Parmesan, Dutch or gruyère cheese; 2 tablespoons cream; 2 oz butter; salt, paprika. Cooking time: 45 minutes.

Pipe *éclairs* of *Choux* pastry on to greased tray. They should measure about 2¾-inches × 1-inch. Brush with the egg yolk, sprinkle with the grated Parmesan and bake in a hot oven, 400° F or Gas Mark 6. Heat the *sauce Béchamel*, cheese, egg yolks, cream, salt and paprika until thick. The filling must be highly seasoned. Remove from heat and complete with butter. When the *éclairs* are cooked, remove from the oven, split open immediately on one side and pipe in the cold filling. These *éclairs* may be served either hot or cold.

Fondants au Chester

For 6 persons: 6 oz grated Cheshire cheese; ¼ pint thick cold Béchamel; 1 egg yolk; ½ lb Puff pastry trimmings. Cooking time: 10-12 minutes.

Prepare the Cheshire cheese filling. Mix cheese with the *Béchamel* and the egg yolk and season with cayenne pepper. Roll out the Puff pastry ⅛-inch thick, cut strips 3-inches long by 2-inches wide. Well fill these pieces, except for a strip at the edge, with the cheese filling, roll up, moisten the ends, and press down in order to enclose the filling. Bake in a hot oven, 425° F or Gas Mark 7, and serve very hot.

Galettes au Parmesan * *Parmesan Biscuits*

Proceed in the same way as for Chester cakes (*p.* 234), replacing the Cheshire cheese with Parmesan.

Gnocchi en Croustades à la Parisienne

For 6 persons: Choux pastry made with 5 oz flour; ¼ lb butter; ½ pint water; pinch salt; 4 eggs; 6 oz grated gruyère cheese; ½ pint not too thick Béchamel; 1 oz butter. Cooking time: 35 minutes.

Mix the *Choux* pastry thoroughly with half the cheese, shape into small balls and poach for 10 minutes in salt water without allowing to boil. Drain the *gnocchi* well, simmer for a few minutes in thin *Béchamel*, remove from the heat and carefully fold in 2 oz grated cheese. Place the *gnocchi* in a buttered baking dish. Sprinkle with a little grated cheese and melted butter, brown in a moderate oven, 375° F or Gas Mark 4. Tartlets or *croustades* can also be used instead of the baking dish. (*See illustration p.* 211).

Gougère

For 6 persons: 5 oz flour; ¼ lb butter; 4 eggs; ½ pint water; ¼ lb gruyère cut in tiny dice; 2 oz gruyère cut in small thin slices. Cooking time: 15-20 minutes.

Make a *Choux* pastry and fold into diced cheese. Using a forcing bag and a large round plain nozzle, pipe a ring on a slightly-greased baking sheet, cover evenly with the sliced cheese, bake in a hot oven, 425° F or Gas Mark 7, and serve at once.

Macaroni au Fromage * *Macaroni Cheese*

For 6 persons: 1 lb macaroni; 5 oz grated Parmesan or gruyère cheese; 2 oz butter.

Cook the macaroni in boiling salted water, drain well and season with salt, pepper and grated nutmeg. Mix in 4 oz cheese and serve in a deep dish sprinkled with the rest of the cheese.

▣ au Gratin

For 6 persons; 1 lb macaroni; ¼ lb grated gruyère cheese; 2 oz butter; ½ pint Béchamel. Cooking time: 10-15 minutes.

Cook macaroni as above, bind with butter and *Béchamel* and mix with 3 oz grated cheese. Put in a baking dish, sprinkle with remaining grated cheese, a few breadcrumbs and melted butter, and brown in a hot oven, 450° F or Gas Mark 8, for about 10 minutes.

▣ à la Niçoise

For 6 persons: 1 lb macaroni; 1 lb tomatoes; 3 anchovies; 2 oz grated cheese; 2 oz butter; 1 clove of garlic. Cooking time: 10-15 minutes.

Toss boiled macaroni in butter, add skinned and diced tomatoes, crushed garlic and chopped anchovies. Toss together till well blended, and serve with grated cheese.

Mille-Feuilles à la Briarde

For 6 persons: ½ lb Puff pastry; ¼ lb ripe Brie cheese; 3 oz butter; 2 tablespoons whipped cream; 2 fl oz brandy; paprika; ¼ lb roasted, ground and sieved hazelnuts. Cooking time: 5-6 minutes.

Roll out the pastry to a thickness of ⅛-inch and cut out 24 round biscuits 2-inches in diameter. Prick them in several places and bake them until they are crisp. Allow to cool.

Cream the butter and mix it with the sieved *brie*. Flavour the cheese mixture with brandy and paprika and lightly fold in the whipped cream. Sandwich the biscuits together in fours with the cheese mixture, press down gently and leave to set in a cold place. Trim the sides, coat them with a thin layer of the cheese mixture and sprinkle with the sieved hazelnuts. Finally pipe a small whirl of cheese mixture on top.

MOUSSES DE VOLAILLE * *POULTRY MOUSSES*

⊡ à la Florentine

For 6 *persons:* 1¼ *lb Mousseline forcemeat;* 1 *pint sauce Mornay;* 2 *lb spinach;* 2 *oz finely grated cheese;* 2 *oz butter; seasoning.* Cooking time: 30-35 minutes.

Cook spinach in boiling salted water, drain well and toss in butter and line the bottom of a round dish with it. Fill the forcemeat into a buttered charlotte mould and poach in a water-bath. Unmould on to the bed of spinach. Coat *mousse* with *sauce Mornay*, sprinkle with the grated cheese and glaze under a hot grill.

⊡ Nantua

For 4-5 *persons:* 1¼ *lb Mousseline forcemeat;* 12 *slices truffle;* 18 *crayfish tails;* 1 *pint sauce Nantua.* Cooking time: 30-35 minutes.

Poach the forcemeat in a buttered charlotte mould, unmould on a round dish, garnish the top with the slices of truffle, surround with the crayfish tails. Mask *mousse* and crayfish with the *sauce Nantua*. Serve the surplus sauce in a sauce-boat.

⊡ Sauce Suprême

For 6 *persons:* 1¼ *lb Chicken Mousseline forcemeat;* 1 *pint sauce Suprême.* Cooking time: 30-35 minutes.

Fill the forcemeat into a buttered *timbale* mould, poach in a *bain-marie* (water-bath), allow to rest for a short time and turn out on a round dish. Mask with the *sauce Suprême* and garnish with Puff pastry *fleurons*.

MOUSSELINE DE VOLAILLE * *SMALL POULTRY MOUSSES*

⊡ Balaton

1¼ *lb Chicken Mousseline forcemeat;* 2 *red capsicums* (*skinned, deseeded, cut into julienne and stewed in butter*); ½ *lb cooked noodles;* ¾ *pint sauce Suprême, well-seasoned.*

Mould the *mousseline* with tablespoons and poach in chicken stock for 10 minutes. Drain and place the poultry *mousses* on a round dish and mask with the sauce. Mix the noodles and capsicums together with the butter and garnish the centre of the dish.

Mousseline de Volaille à la Florentine

For 6 persons: 1¼ lb Poultry Mousseline forcemeat; 2 lb leaf spinach blanched and lightly cooked in butter; 1 pint sauce Mornay; 2 oz grated cheese; 1 oz butter. Total cooking time: 25 minutes.

Fill 12 small buttered moulds with the forcemeat and poach in a *bain-marie.* Turn out, drain and put the *mousselines* on a layer of the spinach in a shallow ovenproof dish. Mask with the *sauce Mornay,* sprinkle with the cheese and a little melted butter and brown in a hot oven, 425° F or Gas Mark 7, for about 10 minutes.

Palets Prinsky

For 6 persons: ½ lb Choux pastry; ¾ pint Béchamel; 6 oz gruyère cheese. Cooking time: 15-20 minutes.

Blend 3 oz of the cheese into the *Choux* pastry and pipe in two long, 2-inch wide, straight bands on a baking sheet and cook until fairly dry, at 400° F or Gas Mark 6; this should take about 15-20 minutes. Mix the rest of the cheese into the *Béchamel* and season well. Spread a thick layer upon the band of the cooked *Choux* pastry, cover with the other band of *Choux* pastry, cut into strips about ¼-inch wide, spread both sides with the *Béchamel,* roll in dry white breadcrumbs, egg-and-breadcrumb and shallow fry in oil and butter. Drain and serve on a table napkin or suitable dish.

PILAF * *PILAF*

▣ d'Agneau à la Syrienne * *Lamb*

For 5 persons: 1½ lb lamb, without bones or trimmings; 2 tablespoons tomato purée; 2 oz flour; 1 bouquet garni; 1 stick of cinnamon; paprika; 1 pint stock (optional); ½ lb rice; 1 large onion. Cooking time: 1½-2 hours.

Sweat the chopped onion in mutton fat. Chop the lamb coarsely and add it to the fat and toss when brown. Dust with flour, and add salt and a generous pinch of paprika. Add 1 pint water or stock, the tomato *purée,* the herbs and the cinnamon, stir and cook slowly till tender. Season well, remove herbs and cinnamon and serve the lamb in a ring of very dry, boiled rice.

▣ de Langouste ou Homard * *Lobster*

For 6 persons: 1 lb cooked crawfish or lobster meat; ½ lb rice; 2 oz butter; 1 pint sauce Cardinal. Cooking time for the rice: 17-18 minutes.

Prepare *Pilaf* rice (*p.* 679). Press the rice round the sides of a well-buttered conical mould. Fill the space in the centre of the mould with the meat of the lobster, which has been cut into small pieces, and simmered in butter for a few minutes. Cover with rice, pack down, and turn out on a round dish. Pour a little sauce around, and decorate with the legs. Serve the rest of the sauce separately. Rice can also be moulded in a *dariole* or *savarin* mould.

▣ de Mouton à la Ménagère * *Mutton*

For 6 persons: ½ lb boned mutton; 36 small onions; 3 oz tomato purée; pinch of saffron; ½ lb rice.

Prepare a Navarin of Mutton (*p.* 493), but leave out the vegetables and add the saffron, tomato *purée* and small onions. Prepare the rice *Pilaf* (*p.* 679). Serve surrounded by the rice.

Pilaf de Rognons de Veau * *Calf's Kidney Pilaf*

For 6 persons: ½ lb rice; 1 chopped onion: ½ lb calves' kidneys; ½ pint tomato-flavoured Demi-glace. Cooking time for the kidneys: 5 minutes.

Prepare the kidneys, removing the fat cores and dice finely; *sauté* them in very hot butter over a high heat. As soon as the meat starts to brown, sprinkle it with salt, pepper and a pinch of curry powder; pour in the tomato-flavoured *sauce Demi-glace* and, as soon as it has boiled for a moment, remove from the heat. Serve the kidneys surrounded by the *pilaf* of rice.

▣ de Volaille à l'Orientale

For 6 persons: 1 *roasting chicken, weighing about* 4 *lb;* 3 *oz onions;* ½ *lb rice;* ½ *lb tomatoes;* 2 *peppers;* 1½ *pints stock.* Cooking time: 1½ hours.

Cut up the chicken into small pieces and fry in butter with the chopped onion. When the chicken turns brown, add the rice and fry again for a few moments; pour in the chicken stock. Skin, quarter and remove the seeds from the tomatoes and add to the mixture together with salt, pepper, saffron and a *bouquet garni.* Add the finely sliced peppers and cook until the chicken is tender.

Pouding au Fromage * *Cheese Pudding*

For 6 persons: 4 *slices bread,* ½*-inch thick without crusts;* 8 *thin slices gruyère cheese;* 4 *eggs;* 1 *pint milk;* 2 *oz butter.* Cooking time: 20-25 minutes.

Lightly butter an oval baking dish. Cut the slices of bread in half and cut the cheese so that it is the same size as the bread. Arrange cheese and bread alternately in the baking dish so that they overlap. Beat the eggs, mix with the milk and season with salt and pepper. Pour this mixture slowly over the bread and cheese so that the bread absorbs it and does not float. Cover with dabs of butter and bake in a moderately hot oven, 375° F or Gas Mark 4, for 20-25 minutes.

QUICHE * *SAVOURY CUSTARD FLANS*

▣ à la Lorraine * *Cheese and Bacon*

For 6 persons: ¾ *lb unsweetened Short Crust pastry;* 6 *oz blanched bacon;* 2 *oz gruyère cheese;* 3 *eggs;* ¾ *pint milk.* Cooking time: about 25 minutes.

Place a lightly-buttered flan ring on a baking sheet and line with unsweetened Short pastry. Prick the bottom a few times with a fork and cover with very thin slices of grilled bacon. Cover the bacon with thin slices of cheese and on top of this pour egg milk which has been made from the well-beaten eggs, the milk, salt, and pepper. Place in a hot oven, 400° F or Gas Mark 6, bake and serve hot. It can be made with either cheese or bacon alone, but the egg milk is compulsory. It tastes best when the milk is replaced by a thin cream or a mixture of half cream and half milk. (*See illustration p.* 210).

▣ aux Oignons * *Onions*

For 6 persons: ¾ *lb unsweetened Short Crust pastry;* 2 *lb onions;* 2 *oz butter;* 2 *eggs;* ½ *pint milk.* Cooking time: about 25 minutes.

Slice onions thinly and simmer in the butter without allowing them to brown. Lightly butter a flan ring, place on a baking sheet and line with unsweetened Short pastry. Fill with the onions when they are cool, pour on egg milk made with the well-beaten eggs mixed with the milk and the salt and pepper and bake in a hot oven, 400° F or Gas Mark 6.

Quiche aux Poireaux * *Leek Flan*

For 6 persons: ¾ lb unsweetened Short Crust pastry; ½ lb leeks (white part only); 2 oz butter; 2 eggs; ½ pint milk. Cooking time: about 25 minutes.

Slice the leeks thinly, blanch for 5 minutes and simmer in butter till tender, then proceed as for Onion Flan.

Ramequins

For 6 persons: 5 oz flour; ¼ lb butter; ½ pint water; 5 eggs; salt; 1 egg yolk; ¼ lb grated gruyère; 2 oz finely diced gruyère.

Make a *Choux* pastry with the ingredients other than the cheese and mix in the grated cheese. Using a forcing bag and round nozzle, pipe buns the size of a small apricot on a baking sheet, brush with egg yolk and sprinkle diced cheese on top. Bake in a moderate oven, 375° F or Gas Mark 5, for 20-25 minutes and serve very hot.

RISSOLES * *RISSOLES*

Rissoles may be served as *hors d'œuvre* or *entrées*. They may be of varying sizes and shapes, for instance, round or half-moon shaped, and are encased in an envelope of Short pastry or Puff pastry. If enclosed in unsweetened *Brioche* dough, they are known as rissoles *à la Dauphine*. Rissoles are made of a *salpicon* of poultry, game and mushrooms and are nearly always fried although they can be baked.

For 8 rissoles: use ½ lb paste, which is rolled out in a fairly thin strip and cut out with a fluted pastry cutter 3-inches in diameter. Place the *salpicon* in the middle of each piece of paste, brush half-way round the edge with egg, fold over and press the edges together. Fry and serve very hot. Listed below are details of various fillings sufficient for 8 rissoles.

▣ Bergère

½ lb salpicon of braised sweetbreads and cooked mushrooms; 1 pint very thick Béchamel.

Blend together. Proceed as above.

▣ Bohémienne

½ lb salpicon of foie gras and truffle; ¼ pint well-reduced Demi-glace.

Proceed as before.

▣ Cendrillon

½ lb salpicon of cooked poultry and truffle; ¼ lb foie gras purée.

▣ Fermière

½ lb mixture of finely diced vegetables and ham, tossed in butter; ¼ pint thick Demi-glace.

Rissoles au Foie Gras

¾ lb truffled foie gras purée.

◘ aux Morilles * *with Morels*

½ lb salpicon of morels stewed in butter; ¼ pint very thick Béchamel.

◘ Nantua

½ lb salpicon of crayfish tails; ¼ pint very stiff Béchamel, seasoned with a pinch of cayenne pepper and Crayfish butter.

◘ Pompadour

½ lb salpicon of tongue; cooked mushrooms and truffle; ¼ pint well-reduced Demi-glace.

◘ à la Reine

½ lb salpicon of cooked poultry; ¼ pint very thick Béchamel.

Rissolettes

A thick slice of bread is toasted and covered with minced or finely diced ingredients. It is then browned in the oven.

Riz Valencienne * *Rice Valenciana*

For 6 persons: 1 lb carolina rice; ¼ lb chopped onions; ¼ lb raw ham cut into julienne; ¼ lb sliced mushrooms; 2 sweet red peppers cut into strips; 2 cooked artichoke bottoms cut in slices; 6 very small poached pork sausages (chipolatas); about 2½ pints stock; 2 oz butter. Cooking time: 30 minutes.

Brown the onions lightly in butter. Add the rice and stir for a minute or two to allow the rice to absorb the butter. Add the stock and the ham and cook in a moderate oven, 375° F or Gas Mark 4, with a lid on. When the rice is cooked it should be soft and a little creamy. Meanwhile cook the mushrooms, artichoke bottoms and the red peppers in butter and stir into the rice with a fork. Arrange the rice in a vegetable dish and garnish with the poached chipolatas.

Sacristains au Fromage * *Cheese Straws*

½ lb Puff pastry; 3 oz grated cheese; 2 eggs. Cooking time: 10-12 minutes.

Roll out the pastry ¼-inch thick into a rectangle 12-inches by 8-inches. Beat the eggs and brush the surface, sprinkle with the cheese. Cut the pastry crosswise into strips ½-inch by ¾-inch wide. Shape them like corkscrews by taking one end of the strip in each hand and giving it a twist. Place on baking sheets and bake in a hot oven, 400° F or Gas Mark 6, until they are golden brown.

SOUFFLÉS * *SOUFFLÉS*

⊡ de Cervelle * *Brain*

For 6 *persons:* ¼ *pint thick Béchamel;* ½ *lb sieved brains;* 3 *eggs; salt; pepper; mace.* Cooking time: 20-25 minutes.

Reduce the *purée* of brains to a firm consistency, add the *Béchamel*, blend together. Season, remove from heat and incorporate the egg yolks one by one, then carefully fold in the whipped egg whites. Fill into a well buttered *soufflé* case or *timbale* mould and cook in a moderate oven, 375° F or Gas Mark 4, and serve immediately.

⊡ de Crevettes * *Prawn*

For 6 *persons:* ½ *lb shrimp purée;* ¼ *lb diced shrimp tails;* 3 *eggs;* ¼ *pint Béchamel; salt; pepper; mace.* Cooking time: 20-25 minutes.

Proceed as for *Soufflé de Cervelle.* Mix in the diced shrimps before folding in egg whites.

⊡ de Crustacés * *Shellfish*

For 6 *persons:* ¼ *pint thick sauce Béchamel;* ½ *lb shellfish purée;* ¼ *lb salpicon of shellfish;* 3 *eggs; salt, pepper, nutmeg.*

Proceed in the same way as for Shrimp or Brain *Soufflé.*

⊡ d'Epinards * *Spinach*

For 6 *persons:* ½ *lb cooked spinach purée;* 3 *eggs; salt; pepper.* Cooking time: 20-25 minutes.

Dry the *purée* well by stirring it over heat until most of the liquid has evaporated. Remove from the heat, blend in the yolks one by one, then carefully fold in the whipped whites with a metal spoon or spatula. Fill into a well-buttered porcelain *soufflé* dish and cook in a hot oven, 400° F or Gas Mark 6. Serve immediately.

⊡ d'Epinards à la Florentine

Proceed as for Spinach *Soufflé*, with the addition of 3 oz grated Parmesan.

⊡ d'Epinards à la Romaine

Proceed as for Florentine *Soufflé* with the addition of 4 or 5 finely diced anchovy fillets.

⊡ de Foie Gras Chaud

For 4-5 *persons:* 3 *oz lean veal;* 1-2 *truffles;* ½ *lb raw foie gras;* ½ *pint thick cream;* 5 *eggs.* Cooking time: about 25 minutes.

Pound the veal, season with salt and pepper, add the raw *foie gras*, 2 whole eggs and 2 egg whites. Put the mixture through a very fine hair sieve and then mix with a wooden spoon over ice. Gradually incorporate the fresh cream, only add a small amount at a time, so that the mixture gradually thickens. Then add 3 stiffly-beaten egg whites. Place ⅓ of this mixture into a buttered *timbale* mould or *soufflé* dish. Then add a layer of cooked sliced truffles, another layer of *soufflé* mixture, a final layer of truffles and the remaining *soufflé* mixture. Cook the *soufflé* in a water-bath in a moderate oven, 375° F or Gas Mark 4. Serve immediately with *sauce Périgueux.*

Soufflé au Fromage * *Cheese Soufflé*

2 oz butter; 1 oz flour; ½ pint milk; 4 eggs; ¼ lb grated gruyère cheese. Cooking time: 20-22 minutes.

Melt the butter, mix in the flour and gradually add the milk. Season with salt and a pinch of cayenne pepper and, stirring constantly with a whisk, stir into a thick mixture resembling *Béchamel.* When it boils remove from heat and add 3 oz grated cheese, a pinch of grated nutmeg and the egg yolks. Still away from the heat, gently fold in 4 stiffly beaten egg whites with a metal spoon. Three-quarters fill a buttered *soufflé* dish sprinkled with grated cheese. Bake in a moderate oven, 375° F or Gas Mark 4, and serve at once. The mixture can also be baked in small *cocottes,* which will take about 8 minutes to cook.

▣ de Gibier * *Game*

For 4 persons: ½ pint thick Béchamel; 3 eggs; ½ lb cooked game purée; few tablespoons game cooking liquor. Cooking time: 20-25 minutes.

Mix game with *Béchamel* and game stock, season highly and mix with 3 egg yolks and then gently fold in 3 stiffly beaten egg whites. Three-quarters fill a buttered *soufflé* dish with the mixture and bake in a hot oven, 400° F or Gas Mark 6. Serve immediately.

▣ de Jambon * *Ham*

For 6 persons: ½ lb purée cooked ham; ¼ pint Béchamel; 2 fl oz cream; salt, pepper; 3 eggs.

Mix the *Béchamel* with thc ham and cream. Proceed as for recipe above.

▣ de Poisson * *Fish*

For 6 persons: ¾ lb flaked fish cooked in butter or poached in white wine and sieved; ½ pint thick Béchamel; 3 eggs; salt, pepper.

Proceed in the same way as in the preceding recipes.

▣ de Pommes de Terre * *Potato*

For 3 persons: ½ lb potatoes; 1 oz butter; ¼ pint cream; 3 eggs. Cooking time: 20-25 minutes.

Peel, boil, drain and *purée* the potatoes, add the butter and dry in a saucepan over heat, season with salt and pepper and stir to a thick *purée* with a little of the cream. Remove from heat, combine with 3 egg yolks and then gently fold in the stiffly beaten egg whites. Place in a buttered *soufflé* dish and bake in a moderate oven, 375° F or Gas Mark 4.

▣ de Pommes de Terre au Fromage * *Potato and Cheese*

Follow the above recipe, but add to the mixture 3 oz of grated cheese, preferably Parmesan or *gruyère.*

Soufflé de Volaille * *Poultry Soufflé*

For 6 persons: 2 *oz flour;* 2 *oz butter;* ¼ *pint single cream and chicken stock;* 4 *large eggs, separated;* ½ *teaspoon salt; pepper;* 1 *lb finely chopped cooked chicken;* 1 *teaspoon lemon juice.* Cooking time: 30-40 minutes.

Make a *roux* with the flour and butter, add cream and chicken stock and cook over low heat until sauce is smooth. Remove from the heat, cool a little and beat in the egg yolks, add the seasonings, lemon juice and chicken. Whisk egg whites until stiff then carefully fold into a buttered, prepared *soufflé* dish. Bake in a moderate oven, 375° F or Gas Mark 4.

TARTELETTES * *PASTRY TARTLETS*

These are very similar to *barquettes* (*p.* 196). They are round pastry cases made of Short pastry (or scraps of Puff pastry) which are baked blind and are then filled with the various *salpicons* or mixtures described below.

▣ Agnès Sorel

Bake blind some tartlet cases made of Short pastry or Puff pastry and take them out of the oven as soon as they begin to turn golden coloured. Line the tartlet cases with finely-minced chicken stuffing ⅛-inch thick. Fill with a *salpicon* of tongue, poultry and truffle bound together with a chicken *Velouté.* Cover with some more chicken stuffing, again-⅛ inch thick. Put in a moderate oven for 8 to 10 minutes. Garnish with a round slice of tongue and a slice of truffle. Mask with Madeira-flavoured *sauce Demi-glace.*

▣ Argenteuil

Fill with a poultry and asparagus *purée.* Bake in the oven and decorate with asparagus tips which have been tossed in butter.

▣ Danoises

Fill with a salmon *purée,* mask with *sauce Mornay* and sprinkle with grated cheese. Brown in the oven.

▣ Marion Delorme

½ *lb Puff pastry;* 6 *oz cooked chicken;* ¼ *lb very finely chopped, raw mushrooms;* ¼ *pint thick sauce Béchamel;* 3 *egg yolks; seasoning.* Cooking time: 10-12 minutes.

Line small tartlet tins with thinly rolled pastry. Mix chicken, sauce, mushrooms and seasonings together in a saucepan, stir and cook for 3 to 4 minutes. Remove from the heat and beat in the egg yolks. Spoon into the tartlet cases and bake in a hot oven, 425° F or Gas Mark 7. Serve hot.

▣ à la Milanaise

For 12 *tartlets:* ½ *lb Pâte Brisée;* ¼ *lb cooked and finely chopped macaroni;* 1 *oz each of pickled tongue, ham, mushrooms and truffles, if desired;* 2 *oz grated gruyère cheese; a little thick, well-seasoned sauce Tomate.* Cooking time: 10 minutes.

Line the moulds with the thinly rolled out paste, prick well and bake in a hot oven. Cool. Chop the filling ingredients, add enough sauce to bind, season well and heat for a few minutes. Spoon into the tartlet cases. Sprinkle a little grated cheese on top of each. Put into hot oven for a few minutes and serve hot.

Tartelettes à la Roumaine

For 6 persons: ½ lb Pâte Brisée; ½ lb Choux pastry; 2 oz grated cheese. Filling: ½ pint sauce Béchamel; 2 egg yolks; 2 oz grated cheese. Cooking time: 20 minutes.

Line 3-inch tartlet tins with a thin layer of the paste. Mix the *Choux* pastry with the 2 oz of cheese and put this paste into a piping bag fitted with a small round nozzle. Pipe three rings of cheese paste on top of one another in each unbaked tartlet. Mix the sauce, remaining cheese and egg yolks and cook over low heat stirring constantly until the egg yolks thicken. Fill the centre of the tarts with this mixture. Bake in a hot oven, 400° F or Gas Mark 6. Serve hot.

▣ Suisses

For 12 tartlets: ½ lb Puff pastry; ½ pint thick sauce Béchamel; 2 *eggs;* 2 *oz grated Parmesan cheese;* 2 *Petit Suisse cheeses; mustard.* Cooking time: 10 minutes.

Heat the *Béchamel* to the boil. Remove from the heat and add the eggs, *Petit Suisse* cheeses and the grated cheese, stirring all the time. Season highly, add mustard and allow to cool. Line small tartlet moulds thinly with the Puff pastry. Fill to within ¼-inch from the rim of the moulds with the prepared mixture. Bake in a very hot oven, 450° F or Gas Mark 8, and serve immediately, while the tartlets are still puffed up.

Tartines Marquises

Prepare 8 pieces of toast ½-inch thick and 2½-inches wide. Cover with a mixture of ¼ pint *sauce Béchamel*, 2 egg yolks and 3 oz grated *gruyère*. Fry in very hot fat with the mixture side uppermost, until crisp.

TIMBALES * *TIMBALES*

▣ Agnès Sorel

For 8 timbales: ½ lb Fine forcemeat; ½ lb salpicon of pickled tongue, chicken and truffle bound with sauce Velouté; 8 *rounds of pickled tongue;* 8 *rounds of truffle or halved black olives.*

Butter eight small moulds, put a round of truffle on the bottom and a round of tongue over this. Add a layer of Fine forcemeat, then the *salpicon* and complete with a layer of the forcemeat. Poach in a moderate oven for 20 minutes in a water-bath. Unmould and serve with a *sauce Demi-glace.*

▣ Christina

For 8 individual portions: 8 slices of truffle; ½ lb Fish quenelle mixture; ¾ lb salpicon of lobster and mushrooms bound together with sauce Cardinal. Cooking time: 20 minutes.

Place a slice of truffle at the bottom of each mould. Line with the *quenelle* mixture, fill with the *salpicon* and complete with some more *quenelle* mixture. Poach as above. Turn out of the moulds and serve with the *sauce Cardinal.*

Timbales Maréchale

For 8 persons: 8 slices of truffle; ½ lb Fine forcemeat; ¾ lb salpicon of tongue. Cooking time: 15 minutes.

Proceed in the same way as for the preceding recipes. Serve with *sauce Périgueux.*

◘ Virgile

For 8 persons: 6 oz rabbit meat; 3 oz Panada; 3 oz butter; 2 eggs; ½ lb cooked game; 3 oz mushrooms; 1 truffle; 3 oz asparagus tips; ½ pint sauce Poivrade; a little thick Brown sauce prepared from the game bones. Cooking time: 15 minutes.

Butter the moulds and sprinkle with chopped truffles. Mince the rabbit meat very finely, add the Panada and eggs. Line the moulds with half this mixture, then add a layer of the *salpicon* of cooked game, chopped mushrooms and asparagus bound together with a little Brown sauce. Cover with the remaining rabbit panada and poach in a water-bath in a moderate oven. Turn out and serve with *sauce Poivrade.*

◘ Washington

For 6-8 persons: ½ lb raw chicken meat; 3 oz Panada; 3 oz butter; 2 eggs; ¼ lb tip of pickled tongue; 6 oz mushrooms; 1 pint sauce Madère. Cooking time: 10-12 minutes.

Butter *baba* moulds and sprinkle plenty of chopped tongue inside. Line with chicken forcemeat prepared from the chicken, Panada and eggs, fill with a *salpicon* of mushrooms and tongue lightly bound with a little of the sauce, cover with forcemeat and poach as above. Serve on a round dish surrounded with *sauce Madère* and serve remainder of sauce separately.

Petites Timbales à la Courtisane

For 6 persons: 14 oz cooked chicken; 5 oz mushrooms; ½ pint sauce Béchamel; 3 egg yolks; 12 pancakes. Cooking time: 10 minutes.

Make 12 very thin, unsweetened pancakes. From these pancakes cut out 12 rounds the same size as the base of the moulds and the same number of strips for lining the sides of the moulds. Mash the cooked chicken together with the salt, pepper and *sauce Béchamel* until the mixture is creamy. Pass through a sieve. Mix in a few finely diced mushrooms and the 3 egg yolks. Fill the *timbales* with this mixture and poach in a water-bath in a moderate oven, 375° F or Gas Mark 4. Turn out the moulds and serve with *sauce Soubise.* These are also known as *Timbales à la Païva.*

Petites Timbales Régina

For 16 persons: 6 oz pike or whiting; 3 oz Panada; 3 oz butter; 2 whole eggs; 1 egg white. Garnish: 1 truffle; 1½ pints mussels; 6 oz prawns or shrimps; ¼ lb mushrooms; 1 pint sauce Crevette. Cooking time: 10-12 minutes.

Prepare a forcemeat with the fish, Panada, eggs and seasoning in the same way as a veal forcemeat is prepared. Cook the mushrooms, shrimps and mussels whole. When they are cold bind with *sauce Crevette*. Butter small *timbale* moulds and decorate the sides and base with truffle, shrimps and mussels. Fill with the fish forcemeat and poach as above. Serve with the remaining *sauce Crevette*.

GRANDES TIMBALES EN CROÛTES • *LARGE TIMBALES IN A PASTRY CRUST*

⊡ à la Financière

For 6 persons: ¾ lb Pie pastry; ¼ lb lamb's sweetbreads; ¼ lb chicken quenelles; ¼ lb mushrooms; ¼ lb cocks' combs and kidneys; 24 olives; 1 truffle; 3 tablespoons Madeira; 1 pint sauce Demi-glace; butter.

Butter a *timbale* or raised pie mould and line with pastry, leaving enough for a lid. Prick the bottom with a fork, put a piece of greaseproof paper and baking beans or rice in the bottom and bake blind in a hot oven for 20 minutes without allowing the case to colour. Decorate the lid and bake at the same time. Meanwhile prepare and cook all the filling ingredients; mix with Madeira. When the case is cooked, remove paper and beans, and pour in the filling. Replace the lid and cook for about 10 minutes.

⊡ aux Fruits de Mer

For 6 persons; 1¼ lb Pie pastry; ¾ lb fillets of sole; ½ lb Fish forcemeat; 4 scampi; ¾ pint mussels; 6 oz poached mushrooms; ¼ pint white wine; 1 oz butter; ¾ pint sauce Vin Blanc.

Bake a *timbale* case blind, as above. Cook the mussels in their own juice just until they open. Shell and beard them. Fillet soles, trim fillets, flatten them, spread thinly with part of the forcemeat mixed with chopped parsley, roll up and poach in white wine. Prepare some *quenelles* with the rest of the forcemeat and carefully poach in simmering water. Cut the scampi in four, brown in butter and cut the mushrooms in four, cut the soles into slices and mix together with the mushrooms, mussels, scampi and *quenelles*. Reheat everything together and bind with the *sauce Vin Blanc*. Fill the cooked *timbale* case with this *salpicon*. Replace the lid and reheat in a moderate oven for about 5 minutes. Meanwhile add the mussel and fish cooking liquors to the rest of the sauce and serve it separately.

⊡ de Macaroni à l'Ancienne

For 6 persons: ¾ lb Pie pastry; ½ lb macaroni; ¼ lb foie gras; 2 truffles; 1½ oz Parmesan (*optional*); *1 pint sauce Madère*. Cooking time: 40 minutes.

Line a *timbale* with pastry dough, not too thinly and fill with a cold mixture of broken boiled macaroni, sliced, poached *foie gras*, cheese and truffle, lightly seasoned and bound with thick *sauce Madère*. The filling must be cold otherwise it would spoil the pastry. Close with a round lid of dough, moisten with water and press down very firmly. Bake in a hot oven, 425° F or Gas Mark 7. Turn out carefully on a round dish and serve with the remainder of the *sauce Madère*.

NOTE: *Timbales* can be filled to taste with veal or chicken. Garnish with a little of each of the filling ingredients, bound with sauce and well cooled. If it were filled while hot, the dough would be soaked, lose shape and might break when turned out.

Timbale à la Milanaise

For 6 persons: ¾ lb Pie Pastry; 6 oz macaroni; 2 oz poached mushrooms; 2 oz boiled lean ham; 2 oz red pickled tongue; 1 small truffle; 3 oz grated Parmesan; ½ pint fresh sauce Tomate. Cooking time: about 30 minutes.

Line a *timbale* very carefully with Pie pastry, pressing it down well against the sides and into the corners. Cut off straight at the top. Prick the bottom several times and bake blind. Bake in a hot oven for 20 minutes, then remove peas and paper so that the inside of the crust can dry. At the same time cut out a round lid of Pie pastry to fit the crust, brush with egg, decorate with leaves and other garnishes in dough, brush with egg again and bake slowly till brown. Drain the boiled, broken macaroni, toss with butter, mix with *julienne* of mushrooms, tongue, ham and truffle and bind with grated cheese and *sauce Tomate*. Fill into pastry case, put on lid and serve very hot.

⊡ Sully

For 6 persons: ¾ lb Pie pastry; ½ lb sausage meat; ¼ lb blanched lamb's sweetbreads; ¼ lb chicken quenelles; ¼ lb mushrooms; 24 olives; 1 truffle; ¼ lb cocks' combs and kidneys; 1 pint sauce Demi-glace; 3 tablespoons Madeira; butter. Cooking time: 40-50 minutes.

Roll strips of pastry to make ropes resembling large macaroni. Grease a mould with plenty of butter and coil the ropes end to end round the sides from bottom to top. Season the sausage meat with mixed herbs, salt and pepper. Chop the sweetbreads, cocks' combs and kidneys, and mushrooms. Mix with the sausage meat, *quenelles*, stoned olives and truffle, bind with Madeira and a little *sauce Demi-glace* if necessary. After dipping the fingers in water, spread the stuffing against the sides of the mould between the ropes of pastry. Cover with a pastry lid and bake in a moderate oven, 375° F or Gas Mark 4. Serve hot with a sauce separately.

GRANDES TIMBALES SANS PÂTE * *LARGE TIMBALES WITHOUT A PASTRY CRUST*

There are no general rules: each *timbale* is prepared in its own special way.

⊡ Ambassadrice

For 6 persons: 15 slices red pickled tongue; 1 truffle; 14 oz Quenelle Forcemeat with Panada; 6 oz cooked chicken meat; 6 oz poached mushrooms; 6 oz poached foie gras; 6 oz white braised calf's sweetbreads; 1 pint sauce Madère. Cooking time: 45 minutes.

Butter a *timbale* and line the whole of it with round slices of tongue, about 1½-inches across. Cut a round hole in the centre of each slice and fill it with a truffle dot of the appropriate size. Let the butter harden on ice or in the refrigerator so that the decoration does not slip, and then line the mould with a thick layer of *Quenelle* Forcemeat with Panada spreading it evenly with the back of a moistened spoon. Fill the centre with a *salpicon* of diced sweetbreads, mushrooms and *foie gras,* bound with cold *sauce Madère.* Close with forcemeat and poach in a water-bath in a moderate oven covered with a sheet of buttered paper. When cooked turn out on a round dish and pour *sauce Madère* round it.

Timbale Beckendorf

For 6 persons: ½ lb medium-sized macaroni; 1¾ oz butter; ¾ pint sauce Tomate; 3 egg yolks; 5 oz smoked salmon; ¼ lb mushrooms; breadcrumbs; ¾ pint reduced and strained tomato juice. Cooking time: 25-30 minutes.

Boil the macaroni, drain it and mix with a little butter. Stir in a rather thick *sauce Tomate* and add seasoning. When the mixture comes to the boil, remove from the heat and add the egg yolks. Finely slice the smoked salmon and mix it with the macaroni. Now add the finely sliced mushrooms, which have been cooked in butter and browned under the grill. Brush a *timbale* mould with butter and sprinkle with breadcrumbs. Fill with the macaroni mixture. Cook in a *bain-marie* in a moderate oven, 375° F or Gas Mark 4. Turn out of the mould and serve with the reduced and strained tomato juice containing plenty of butter.

▣ à la Bisontine

For 6 persons: 1 lb Veal Quenelle forcemeat; ¼ lb sweetbreads; 3 oz small chicken quenelles; 3 oz cocks' combs and kidneys; 1 truffle; 18 crayfish tails; ½ pint sauce Velouté; 3 oz morels or mushrooms; 3 oz Crayfish butter; ½ pint sauce Nantua. Cooking time: 40-50 minutes.

Line a *timbale* or deep sponge cake tin, with a fairly firm veal forcemeat. Fill the inside with a *salpicon,* chicken *quenelles,* calf's sweetbreads, truffles, morels and crayfish tails, bound with cold *Velouté;* this *salpicon* must also be cold. Cover with forcemeat and poach in a water-bath. Turn out on a round dish, cut out a round section of forcemeat about two inches across in the centre of the top and pour in the hot Crayfish butter through it. Replace forcemeat and serve *sauce Nantua* separately.

▣ Orloff

For 6 persons: 1½ paper-thin, unsweetened pancakes; 3 oz semolina; 4 eggs; 10 oz cooked chicken (leftovers); ¼ lb ham; 1 pint bouillon; ¼ lb mushrooms; ½ pint sauce Velouté; ½ pint sauce Soubise. Cooking time: 20-30 minutes.

Butter a *gâteau* tin and line with halved, overlapping pancakes in such a way that the points meet in the middle of the bottom and the ends fold over the edge. Boil the semolina in *bouillon,* season, remove from heat, thicken with 2 egg yolks and let it cool slightly. Dice the chicken, ham and mushrooms finely, bind with *Velouté* and also fold in 2 egg yolks. Fill the bottom of the tin with half the semolina mixture and smooth. Place the chicken mixture on top, cover with the semolina and fold in pancakes over it. Cook in a water-bath in a moderate oven, 375° F or Gas Mark 4. Turn out and serve with *sauce Soubise.*

▣ Régina

For 6 persons: ¼ lb truffles; 1 lb Fish forcemeat; 10 oz fillets of sole; 1½ pints mussels; 6 oz mushrooms; ¼ lb shrimps; ½ pint sauce Crevette; 2 pints sauce Nantua. Cooking time: 40-50 minutes.

Butter a *timbale* and decorate sides with truffles. Line with Fish forcemeat and fill with a cold *salpicon* of cooked fillets of sole, mushrooms, bearded mussels and shrimps or crayfish tails, bound with cold *sauce Crevette.* Cover with forcemeat, poach in a water-bath in the oven, turn out on a round dish and serve with *sauce Nantua.* This can also be made in small *baba* moulds, but then the *salpicon* must be cut correspondingly small.

Vol-au-Vent

For 6 persons: 1 *lb Puff pastry.*

For the preparation see *Illustrated Culinary Techniques*. When the cases have been baked, fill, according to taste, with the same mixtures as are used for *bouchées*. (*See illustration p.* 209).

FOREIGN SPECIALITIES

Angels on Horseback

32 *oysters;* ½ *lb bacon;* 8 *slices of toast,* 1½*-inches wide* × 3*-inches long;* 1½ *oz butter*. Cooking time: 5-6 minutes.

Stiffen the oysters without letting them boil and drain well. Wrap each one in a small, very thin slice of bacon, spear 4 on a skewer, grill, place on buttered toast and lightly dust with cayenne pepper. (*Great Britain*)

Beurrecks * *Turkish Cheese Croquettes*

10 *oz Noodle dough;* ½ *pint very thick Béchamel;* 6 *oz very dry cream cheese;* 1 *egg;* 2 *tablespoons oil;* 6 *oz fine white flour*. Cooking time: 3-4 minutes.

Make *Béchamel* the thickness of *Choux* pastry and allow to cool till lukewarm. Then mix with the strained, very dry cream cheese and season well with salt and pepper. Shape first into balls the size of a small plum and then roll these into cigar shapes on a floured table. Roll out Noodle dough $\frac{1}{10}$ inch thick. Cut into pieces about 2 × 3 inches, moisten, place one of the rolls on each, roll up and press down both ends. Egg and breadcrumb each one and fry till golden in deep fat. Serve on a napkin with a sauce of fresh tomatoes made without flour, and seasoned with lemon.

Blinis Russes * *Buckwheat Pancakes*

1 *lb sifted buckwheat flour;* ½ *oz yeast; about* 1 *pint lukewarm milk;* 2 *eggs;* 3 *tablespoons whipped cream; butter for frying*. Cooking time of blinis: 4-5 minutes.

Dissolve yeast in the lukewarm milk and mix with the flour, add egg yolks and salt, cover, and allow to rest for 3-4 hours. If necessary add some more milk or cream, the consistency should be that of thick Pancake batter. When the mixture has risen well, beat thoroughly and gently fold in the stiffly beaten egg whites followed by the whipped cream. Heat a small pan together with melted butter, fry *blinis* light brown on both sides and coat them with butter. Serve with caviar with melted butter and sour cream (*smihtana*). Instead of serving with caviar, coarsely chopped harboiled egg or small pieces of smoked salmon can be mixed with the dough before frying. They are then also served with melted butter and sour cream. (*Russia*)

Brochettes à la Suissesse * *Ham and Cheese Skewers*

Cut some thin slices of raw, smoked gammon 2 inches in diameter. *Sauté* them in butter. Cut some slightly smaller pieces of *gruyère* ¾-inch thick. Put alternate slices of ham and cheese on skewers. Coat twice with egg and breadcrumbs and fry in hot fat. Serve piping hot on the skewers. (*Switzerland*)

CANNELLONI * *CANNELLONI*

⊡ alla Casalinga

For 8 *persons:* ½ *lb cannelloni;* 14 *oz cooked, minced beef*; ¼ *lb cooked mushrooms;* ¼ *lb grated cheese;* 1 *pint Tomato-flavoured Gravy.* Cooking time: 8 minutes to poach the *cannelloni;* 15-18 minutes to simmer the *cannelloni* in the gravy.

The filling may be made with remains of cooked beef, minced and mixed with chopped mushrooms, chopped onion and parsley, a little Tomato sauce and an egg; if pork is used, omit the egg. Cook the *cannelloni* in salted, boiling water. When it is about three-quarters cooked, drain well on a cloth. Stuff the *cannelloni* with the filling, using a piping bag and a plain round tube. Roll the *cannelloni* up with the stuffing in the middle and place in a buttered baking dish. Sprinkle with grated cheese, add Tomato Gravy, and more cheese. Place in a moderate oven to brown, simmering slowly to finish cooking.

The stuffed *cannelloni* may also be simmered in Tomato sauce without cheese. They are then arranged on a long dish, covered with diced tomatoes simmered in butter, and sprinkled with chopped parsley. The Tomato Gravy is poured around the *cannelloni* and the grated cheese is served separately. *(Italy)*

⊡ César

For 10 *persons:* 1¾ *lb Mozzarella or soft cheese;* ½ *pint sauce Béchamel;* ¼ *lb ham;* 1½ *oz Parmesan cheese;* 10 *eggs;* 9 *oz flour;* 1¾ *pints milk;* 9 *oz butter;* 2 *oz oil; nutmeg. For the pancakes:* 5 *eggs;* 5 *oz flour;* 1¼ *pints milk;* 1 *oz butter.* Cooking time: 20 minutes.

Make 10 very thin pancakes. Meanwhile, with a spatula mix the cold *sauce Béchamel* with 2 egg yolks, the ham and diced cheese, adding a pinch of salt and ground nutmeg and the grated Parmesan. Spread this mixture on the pancakes and roll them up. Cut them diagonally into pieces about 2½-inches long so as to obtain 3 to 4 *cannelloni* per person. Prepare a *sauce Béchamel* with 9 oz butter, 9 oz flour, and 1¾ pints milk. Stir 8 egg yolks into the hot sauce. Fold in the stiffly whisked egg whites. Put half of this sauce in a shallow, ovenproof dish, arrange the *cannelloni* on top, cover with the remainder, sprinkle with grated Parmesan and brown in the oven for 20 minutes. *(Italy)*

⊡ al Formaggio

For 10 *persons:* 1½ *lb flour;* 3 *eggs;* 2 *tablespoons oil;* ¼ *pint water;* 14 *oz cream cheese;* 3½ *oz finely diced gruyère;* 7 *oz grated Parmesan cheese;* 7 *oz butter.* Cooking time: 15 minutes.

Prepare the same dough as for *lasagne. Lasagne* are strips of flat macaroni cut up into pieces about 6 inches square which are poached in boiling water, drained and dried on a cloth. (*See p.* 676).

For the filling: blend together the cream cheese, 1 egg yolk, the diced *gruyère*, 5 oz grated Parmesan and the salt and pepper. Spread strips of this mixture on the squares of dough which are then rolled up. Arrange the *cannelloni* in a buttered ovenproof dish, sprinkle with grated cheese and add knobs of butter on top. Put in a very hot oven, 425° F or Gas Mark 7. *(Italy)*

Cannelloni alla Ligure

For 10 persons: 2½ *lb flour;* 8 *eggs;* ¼ *pint oil;* 14 *oz veal, marinated in Marsala;* ½ *lb ham or leftovers of pork;* ½ *lb giblets;* ½ *lb Parmesan cheese;* ½ *lb spinach;* 3 *oz marjoram;* 1 *lb sliced fresh cèpes or mushrooms; sprig basil.* Cooking time: 1½ hours.

Make a well in the flour and pour in the eggs, oil and a little salt. Mix thoroughly. Leave to stand for ¾ hour. Roll out the dough and cut up into oblongs, 1½-inches wide and 2½-inches long. For the filling: fry the marinated veal, ham or pork and giblets in butter, adding a pinch of marjoram, a few basil leaves, the Parmesan and the spinach. Mince all these ingredients very finely. Poach the pieces of dough in salt water containing a little oil. Leave to cool down, drain on a cloth and fill with the prepared filling mixture using a Savoy bag. Mask with *sauce Béchamel* and garnish with the *cèpes* and basil leaves. Brown in a hot oven for about 10 minutes and serve very hot. *(Italy)*

▣ alla Lombarda

For 8 *persons:* ½ *lb cannelloni;* 1 *lb minced beef;* ¼ *lb cooked cèpes or mushrooms;* ¼ *lb Parmesan cheese;* ¾ *pint Tomato-flavoured Veal Gravy.* Cooking time: for boiling the *cannelloni*: 8 minutes; for simmering the stuffed *cannelloni:* 15-20 minutes.

The stuffing for the *cannelloni* may be made with leftover meat which is minced and mixed with mushrooms, *sauce Tomate*, mixed herbs and eggs. The eggs are omitted if pork is used. Boil the *cannelloni* in water containing a tablespoonful of oil. Take it out when it is three-quarters cooked, drain it on a cloth and, using a Savoy bag, fill with the stuffing. Roll the *cannelloni* up and arrange it in a shallow, ovenproof dish. Sprinkle with Parmesan, cover with the tomato-flavoured Veal gravy and sprinkle with some more cheese. Brown and then simmer the *cannelloni* until it is cooked. *(Italy)*

Chester Cakes

5 *oz flour;* ¼ *lb butter;* ¼ *lb grated Cheshire cheese;* 2 *egg yolks. Filling:* ¼ *pint Béchamel;* 1 *egg yolk;* 1 *oz butter;* 1¾ *oz grated Cheshire cheese.* Cooking time: about 10 minutes.

Make a fairly firm dough with the flour, the butter, the cheese, the egg yolks, a few drops of water, a pinch of salt and cayenne pepper and allow to rest for 1 hour. Roll out dough about ¼-inch thick and cut out biscuits 2-inches across with a plain or scalloped cutter, arrange on a baking sheet and bake in a moderate oven, 375° F or Gas Mark 4. Fill these biscuits in pairs with a cream made from the thick, hot *Béchamel*, the egg yolk, the butter and the grated cheese seasoned with salt and cayenne pepper. Serve very hot. *(Great Britain)*

Chester Soufflé

For 6 *persons:* 2 *oz butter;* 1¾ *oz flour;* ½ *pint milk;* ¼ *lb grated Cheshire cheese;* 4 *egg yolks;* 5 *egg whites; salt; paprika; nutmeg.* Cooking time: 20-25 minutes.

Melt the butter and mix in the flour, add the milk and stir. Season with a pinch of salt, paprika and nutmeg. Stir over heat until the mixture reaches the consistency of a thick *sauce Béchamel.* Remove from the heat and add first the cheese and the egg yolks and then the stiffly whisked egg whites. Butter a *soufflé* dish, sprinkle it with cheese and fill three-quarters full with the mixture. Bake in a moderate oven, 375° F or Gas Mark 4-5, and serve immediately. Individual *soufflés* can be made if required, in which case the cooking time is 8 to 10 minutes. *(Great Britain)*

Délices Helvétia * *Swiss Delights*

Whisk stiffly 2 egg whites and mix in 5 oz grated *gruyère* and a small pinch of cayenne pepper. Make the mixture into little balls, coat with egg and breadcrumbs and fry in fairly hot fat. Serve immediately. (*Switzerland*)

Delizie alla Romana * *Rome Delights*

For 10 persons: 1½ lb spaghetti; 1¾ pints sauce Béchamel; ½ lb raw or cooked, diced ham; 1 lb raspings; ¼ lb Parmesan cheese; oil; ¾ pint meat gravy; nutmeg.

Boil the *spaghetti*, drain and add the *sauce Béchamel*, grated Parmesan and nutmeg. Mix together and pour on to an oiled baking tray to a uniform thickness of about 2½-inches. Leave to cool. With a pastry cutter or a glass cut out pieces about 2½-inches in diameter. Coat with egg and breadcrumbs. Using a small tube pastry cutter, cut out the middle of each piece. Roll out the rest of the dough to a thickness of ¼-inch and cut out some pieces of the same diameter as the first pieces. Fry all the pieces in oil. Brown the diced ham in the meat gravy and pour into the hollow pieces, and place the flat pieces on top. Serve with a bunch of fried parsley. (*See illustration p.* 213). (*Italy*)

Devilled Jumbo Shrimps

For 6 persons: 30 peeled jumbo shrimps (or Dublin Bay prawns); 2 eggs; 8 oz breadcrumbs; pepper and mustard. Cooking time: 3-4 minutes.

Season the beaten eggs with a tiny pinch of cayenne pepper and a little mustard powder. Egg and breadcrumb the shrimps and fry in hot, deep fat. Serve on a suitable dish sprinkled with lemon juice and parsley. (*North America*)

Fish Balls

1 lb potatoes; 1 lb boiled fish without waste (e.g. cod, haddock, turbot); 4 eggs; 1½ oz butter; ¾ lb white breadcrumbs; parsley.

Flake the boiled fish and pre-dry in oven. Drain the freshly boiled potatoes well, strain, mix with the butter, add two eggs, and dry well over heat. Add dried fish, season well and leave to cool. With this mixture make slightly flattened balls the size of an apricot on a floured table, egg and breadcrumb and fry golden brown in very hot, deep fat. Serve with fried parsley and *sauce Tomate*. Also served for breakfast. (*Great Britain*)

Fritto Misto * *Mixed Fried Veal*

Deep fry very small pieces of calf's head, slices of calf's brains and sweetbreads, all previously boiled; small, round pieces of calf's liver; thick slices of raw calf's marrow; small, boiled, halved artichoke bottoms; very small boiled potatoes and small pieces of white bread, all egged and breadcrumbed. Drain well, serve with fried parsley and lemon slices. (*Italy*)

Gnocchi alla Romana

For 6 persons: 3 oz semolina; ¾ pint milk; ¼ lb grated gruyère; ¾ oz raspings; 1 oz melted butter. Cooking time for the semolina: about 10 minutes.

Cook the semolina in the milk, adding salt and pepper. When the cooked semolina becomes like thick porridge, remove from the heat and add *gruyère*. Spread on a buttered and floured baking tray. Leave to cool. With a pastry cutter, cut out some crescent-shaped pieces and arrange these on an ovenproof dish. Sprinkle with cheese and raspings and pour melted butter over. Brown quickly. (*Italy*)

LASAGNE * *LASAGNE*

⊡ alla Casalinga

For 10 *persons:* 2¼ *lb Lasagne (flat macaroni);* 1¾ *pints sauce Crème;* ½ *lb grated Parmesan cheese;* 3 *oz butter. For the sauce:* ½ *lb coarsely minced meat;* 1 *oz dried cèpes or mushrooms;* ½ *onion;* ½ *carrot;* ¾ *oz butter;* ¼ *pint oil;* 3 *oz Marsala;* 1 *tablespoon condensed tomato purée;* 1 *tablespoon flour.* Cooking time: 1¼ hours.

First prepare the sauce. Chop finely the onion and carrot, cook these in butter and oil until golden coloured, add the meat and fry together. Pour in the red wine and the tomato *purée*. Reduce and mix a tablespoon of flour with a little Marsala and gradually add to the tomato mixture. Add the unthickened meat gravy. Finally put in the roughly chopped *cèpes* and cook for 45 minutes. Cook the *Lasagne*. Combine the meat mixture with the *sauce Crème*. Spread a layer of this sauce at the bottom of an ovenproof dish and cover with a layer of *Lasagne* which is then sprinkled with Parmesan and brushed with the melted butter. Fill the dish with alternate layers of sauce and buttered *Lasagne* with cheese. Sprinkle with Parmesan and cook in a *bain-marie* in a hot oven for 20 minutes. (*See illustration p.* 216). (*Italy*)

⊡ alla Ligure

For 10 *persons: Lasagne dough* (2¼ *lb flour;* 4 *eggs and* ¼ *pint oil);* 3 *oz butter;* 1¾ *oz dried cèpes or mushrooms;* ¾ *lb sausage meat;* 4 *fl oz white wine;* ¼ *pint sauce Tomate;* ½ *pint meat gravy;* ½ *pint sauce Béchamel;* 1 *finely chopped onion;* 3 *oz Parmesan cheese.* Cooking time : 2 hours.

Cook the onion in butter until it is golden coloured; add the *cèpes*, which have been swollen in water and then chopped, and the sausage meat and fry lightly together. Pour in the white wine and reduce. Stir in the *sauce Tomate* and the meat gravy and simmer for 20 minutes. Whisk in the *sauce Béchamel*. Make the *Lasagne* dough and cut up into 2-inch squares. Cook these, put them in cold water to cool down and drain them on a cloth. In an ovenproof dish put a layer of sauce and a layer of *Lasagne* sprinkled with Parmesan. Repeat this three times. Cover all over with sauce, sprinkle with Parmesan and top with small leaves of basil. Brown in a *bain-marie* in a hot oven. (*Italy*)

⊡ Verdi alla Ricotta * *Green Lasagne with Cream Cheese*

For 10 *persons:* 2¼ *lb Lasagne;* 1 *lb cream cheese;* 2 *oz butter;* ¼ *lb Parmesan cheese; nutmeg.* Cooking time: 15 minutes.

Beat up the cream cheese with a spatula, gradually adding a pinch of pepper, a pinch of nutmeg and 2 tablespoons of boiling water. Continue beating up until the cheese becomes light and creamy like a *soufflé*. Meanwhile poach the *Lasagne* in a large quantity of boiling salt water, drain it and put it in an ovenproof dish in layers alternating with the cream cheese mixture. Finally pour melted butter all over, sprinkle with Parmesan and brown for a few minutes in a hot oven. (*Italy*)

MACCHERONI * *MACARONI*

⊡ alla Meridionale

For 10 *persons:* 2¼ *lb macaroni;* 1¼ *lb aubergines;* ½ *pint sauce Tomate;* 10 *oz butter;* 6 *oz flour;* 7 *fl oz oil;* 7 *oz grated Parmesan cheese;* 10 *thin,* 1-*inch squares of mozzarella or other soft cheese.* Cooking time for the macaroni: 20 minutes.

Peel the *aubergines*, cut them into thin slices, flour them and fry in hot oil. Cook the macaroni, drain and add *sauce Tomate* and butter. Into an ovenproof dish put a layer of macaroni and then one of *aubergine* and grated Parmesan; repeat, finishing with a layer of *aubergine*. Cover with *sauce Tomate* and place the slices of cheese on top. Brush with melted butter and sprinkle with Parmesan. Brown in a *bain-marie* in a hot oven. *(Italy)*

Maccheroni alla Milanese

For 4 persons: ½ *lb macaroni;* 1¾ *oz each of ham, pickled tongue and mushrooms, cut in fine julienne;* ½ *pint sauce Demi-glace with tomato;* 3 *oz grated cheese;* 3 *oz butter.*

Boil macaroni in the usual way. Heat the *julienne* with a walnut of butter and bind with a little *Demi-glace*. Bind the macaroni with the butter and the grated cheese, pour into a serving dish, make a hollow in the middle and fill *julienne* into this. Pour the remainder of the sauce round it. The sauce and garnish can also be mixed with the macaroni when serving. *(Italy)*

▣ alla Napoletana

For 5 persons: 10 *oz macaroni;* ½ *lb minced beef;* ¼ *pint sauce Tomate;* 3 *oz grated cheese.*

Mince meat very finely, heat with the sauce and season well. Boil macaroni in the usual way. Sprinkle grated cheese over the bottom of a baking dish, fill with layers of macaroni, grated cheese and meat, cover with sauce, put in a hot oven for a few minutes and serve at once. *(Italy)*

Oyster Brochettes * *Oysters on Skewers*

For 6 persons: 18 *oysters;* 18 *small mushroom caps;* ¼ *lb bacon;* 6 *oz white breadcrumbs;* 1-2 *eggs;* 1 *tablespoon oil;* ¼ *lb Maître d'Hôtel butter.* Cooking time: 5-6 minutes.

Stiffen the oysters, wrap in small thin slices of bacon and place 3 on a skewer alternately with 3 mushroom heads. Egg and breadcrumb, grill, dust lightly with salt mixed with a generous pinch of cayenne pepper and serve with the *Maître d'Hôtel* butter.

Paella

For 8 persons: 1 *chicken;* 12 *crayfish;* 1¾ *pints cockles;* 1¾ *pints mussels;* 1 *lb cuttlefish or squid;* ½ *lb prawns;* 12 *chipolata sausages;* 4 *globe artichoke bottoms;* 4 *onions;* 6 *tomatoes;* 6 *cloves of garlic;* 1 *medium-sized tin peas;* 1 *lb rice;* 1¾ *pints olive oil.*

This Spanish national dish constitutes a meal in itself. It is prepared in a large, fairly deep pan. Cut up the chicken into fairly small pieces and brown these in oil in the pan. Cook the cleaned crayfish in the same way. Steam the cockles and mussels until they open, discard the cockle shells but keep those of the mussels and also the cooking liquor, which is then strained. The squid must first be cooked in water and then fried in oil. The artichoke bottoms are lightly cooked, cut up into six pieces and then fried in oil. Cook all these ingredients in the pan one after the other, keeping those already cooked on a dish. Chop the onions and garlic and fry in oil until golden coloured. Add the peppers, if they are fresh, then the tomatoes, which have been skinned, deseeded and chopped up, and finally the chopped mixed herbs. Fry these ingredients until they form a *purée*. Now arrange evenly round the edge of the pan first the pieces of chicken, then the sausages, squid and artichoke, keeping these ingredients to the edges. Wash the rice in tepid water and spread evenly over the middle if possible without stirring. Pour in the cooking liquor from the shellfish in which the saffron has been dissolved, season well with salt and pepper and, if necessary, put a little more tepid water over the rice. While the rice is cooking, put the crayfish on top in such a way as to indicate the portions. Garnish with the mussel shells filled with peas and cockles and insert the mussels into the prawns. By this time the rice should be cooked and ready to serve. *(Spain)*

PIZZA * *PIZZA*

▣ Margherita

For 6 persons: 6 portions Pizza dough; ½ lb skinned, deseeded tomatoes; ½ lb Mozzarella cheese; 1¾ oz grated Parmesan cheese; 12 basil leaves.

Put the tomatoes on the pieces of *Pizza* dough, season with pepper, cut the *Mozzarella* into slices and place these on top of the tomatoes. Sprinkle with Parmesan and oil and bake in a moderate oven, 375° F or Gas Mark 4. (*See illustration p.* 211). *(Italy)*

▣ alla Marinara

For 6 persons: 6 portions Pizza dough; ½ lb skinned, deseeded tomatoes; ½ lb Mozzarella cheese; 6 cloves garlic.

Prepare in the same way as *Pizza Margherita.* (*See illustration p.* 211). *(Italy)*

▣ Quattro Stagioni

For 6 persons: 6 portions Pizza dough; each pizza has four 'compartments' filled respectively with the following ingredients: (1) *2 oz cèpes;* (2) *2 oz whole cleaned mussels;* (3) *½ lb ham and 10 stoned olives;* (4) *¼ lb scampi or prawns.*

Prepare in the same way as *Pizza Margherita*, but with the ingredients given above. *(Italy)*

▣ San Domenico

For 6 persons: 6 portions Pizza dough; ½ lb skinned, deseeded tomatoes; ½ lb Mozzarella cheese; 2 oz Parmesan cheese; 6 anchovies; 6 cloves garlic; marjoram.

Arrange the tomatoes on the pieces of *Pizza* and season with pepper. Cut the *mozzarella* into thin slices and place them on top of the tomatoes; place the anchovy fillets criss-cross on the cheese and top with the cloves of garlic. Sprinkle with Parmesan and marjoram and pour oil over before baking in a moderate oven. *(Italy)*

▣ alla Siciliana

For 6 persons: 6 portions Pizza dough; ½ lb skinned, deseeded tomatoes; ½ lb Mozzarella cheese; 6 anchovies; marjoram; 6 tablespoons capers; 6 stoned olives.

Proceed in the same way as for *Pizza San Domenico.* *(Italy)*

RAVIOLI * *RAVIOLI*

▣ di Carne

For 6 persons: ¾ lb Noodle paste; 1 lb forcemeat; ½ oz butter; ¼ lb Parmesan.

The forcemeat may be prepared with any type of cooked leftover meat or poultry, which has been very finely minced and mixed with finely chopped mushrooms, chopped herbs, grated lemon rind and moistened with a little *bouillon* or other stock. Prepare ravioli from Noodle paste. Fill and poach the ravioli in salted water for 20-30 minutes. Drain and put on a plate, sprinkle with butter and Parmesan. Ravioli may be served as they are, with butter, cheese, *sauce Tomate* or *Demi-glace* with tomato. *See* (*illustration p.* 212).

▣ di Spinaci

For 6 persons: ¾ lb Noodle dough; 2 lb spinach; 1½ oz butter; 1½ oz Parmesan; ¼ lb grated gruyère; 2 egg yolks; 1 pint sauce Tomate. Cooking time for ravioli: 25 minutes.

Boil spinach, drain, squeeze out all moisture and pass several times through the finest blade of the mincer. Heat with a small piece of butter, season well, remove from heat and mix with the egg yolks and plenty of grated cheese. Roll out the Noodle dough into 2 square pieces about ⅛-inch thick and moisten slightly with water. Put small mounds of spinach the size of a hazelnut at regular intervals on one piece of dough with a forcing bag and a round nozzle and cover with the second piece of dough. Press down dough around each mound and cut regular squares with a pastry wheel. Poach the ravioli for 25-30 minutes without allowing poaching liquid to boil, drain well. Then heat for a short time in the sauce, place in a baking dish sprinkle with plenty of grated cheese and brown in a hot oven for a few minutes.

RISOTTO * *RISOTTO*

▣ con Frutte di Mare * *with Sea Food*

For 6 persons: 1 lb rice; 1 lb mussels; ½ lb prawns; ¼ pint Cognac or ½ pint white wine; ½ pint cream; 1 pint oil; 1½ oz butter; 3 oz Parmesan; ½ onion; 1½ pints bouillon.

Clean the mussels and brush them thoroughly in running water. Leave them to soak for 1 hour. Put them in a casserole with a little water; cook until they open. Remove the beard and pour the cooking liquor through a muslin cloth. Shell the prawns and scampi. Cook the onion in oil and butter until soft but do not brown, mix in the rest of the sea food, the white wine or Cognac, the washed rice, the mussel liquor and the *bouillon.* Just before the completion of cooking time add the cream and Parmesan. (*Italy*)

▣ con Funghi * *with Mushrooms*

For 10 persons: 1¾ lb rice; 3¼ pints bouillon; 3 oz grated Parmesan cheese; 2 oz butter; ½ onion; 3 fl oz oil; 3 fl oz white wine; ½ lb cèpes or mushrooms. Cooking time: 20-25 minutes.

Cook the chopped onion in oil and a little butter until it becomes golden in colour. Pour over the white wine and reduce. Gradually add the rice, the sliced *cèpes* and the *bouillon.* Cook. Add the rest of the butter and the cheese. Remove from the heat and mix well. (*See illustration p.* 215).

Risotto alla Milanese

For 6 persons: 1 *lb rice;* 3 *oz chopped onion;* 2 *oz butter;* 2 *oz grated Parmesan cheese;* 1½ *oz each julienne of ham, red tongue and mushrooms;* 1 *oz julienne of truffle; saffron; white stock;* ½ *pint sauce Demi-glace with tomato.* Cooking time: 20 minutes.

Prepare the *risotto* as for *Piemontese.* When it is cooked add the grated cheese, a lump of butter, *sauce Demi-glace, julienne* of ham, tongue, mushrooms and truffle, and mix in with a fork. The *julienne* may also be bound with a little *sauce Demi-glace*, served in the middle of the rice, and the remaining *sauce Demi-glace* poured all around. (*See illustration p.* 214).

▣ con Ostriche

For 6 persons: 1 *lb rice;* 36 *oysters;* 3 *oz butter;* 1¾ *oz Parmesan cheese;* 4 *tablespoons oil;* ½ *pint white wine;* ½ *onion, finely chopped;* 2½ *pints bouillon.* Cooking time: 20 minutes.

Open the shells and take out the oysters (*see p.* 399), which are put together with their liquor into an earthenware dish. Meanwhile fry the onions in oil and butter until golden coloured, add the rice and brown lightly. Pour in the white wine and gradually add the *bouillon* and oyster liquor. After 15 minutes, put in the oysters, cook for another 5 minutes, remove from the heat and add a knob of butter and the grated Parmesan. (*Italy*)

▣ alla Piemontese

For 6 persons: ¾ *lb rice;* 1 *large chopped onion;* 1¼ *pints bouillon;* 2 *oz butter;* 2 *oz grated Parmesan;* 2 *tablespoons tomato purée.* Cooking time: 18 minutes.

Sweat the chopped onion in butter, add the rice and cook till it is well-buttered and glossy. Add the *bouillon* in small quantities, allowing rice to absorb liquid before adding more. Season the rice, cover and simmer gently till tender. Shortly before the rice is completely ready add the tomato *purée*, but this is optional. Finally gently mix the cheese with the rice. (*Italy*)

▣ Guiseppe Verdi

For 6 persons: ½ *onion;* 5 *oz butter;* 1¼ *lb rice;* 2¼ *pints bouillon;* ¼ *lb mushrooms;* ¼ *lb asparagus tips;* ¼ *lb raw ham;* ¼ *lb skinned tomatoes;* ¼ *lb Parmesan cheese;* ¼ *pint cream.* Cooking time: 18 minutes.

Cook the onion in butter until it is golden coloured and then add the mushrooms, asparagus tips, thinly sliced raw ham and the skinned and diced tomatoes. Proceed in the same way as for previous *risotto* recipes. Stir in the cream before serving. (*Italy*)

Riz à la Grecque * *Greek-style Rice*

For 10 persons: 1¾ *lb rice; knob of butter;* 3 *oz oil;* 3½ *pints bouillon;* 2 *cloves garlic;* 2 *bay leaves;* 2 *oz marinated tongue;* 2 *oz ham;* 1 *oz pickled red peppers;* 1 *oz pickled mushrooms;* 2 *oz peas;* ½ *onion.* Cooking time: 15 minutes.

Fry the onion until it is golden coloured, add the rice and brown lightly. Pour in the *bouillon* and put in the garlic and bay leaves. Bake in a moderate oven, 375° F or Gas Mark 4, test the rice to see if it is tender and thoroughly cooked, add all the other ingredients which have been finely diced. The rice should be served very hot. (*See illustration p.* 214).

Soufflé Helvétia

The same mixture as for Cheese *soufflé* but only using two stiffly-beaten egg whites. Place in buttered, deep tartlet moulds, place the moulds in a baking tin in which a little water has been poured and poach in a moderate oven, 375° F or Gas Mark 4, for 8 to 12 minutes until they have risen well. Turn out on a buttered baking dish, pour plenty of fresh cream on top, sprinkle with grated cheese and brown and allow to rise again in a hot oven.

SPAGHETTI * *SPAGHETTI*

⊡ Carbonara

For 10 persons: 1½ *lb spaghetti;* 3 *oz butter;* ½ *lb cooked ham;* 3 *egg yolks;* ½ *pint cream.* Cooking time: 30 minutes.

Cook the *spaghetti* first and keep it hot. Melt the butter and add the shredded ham and the cream. Reduce. Remove from the heat and stir in the egg yolks. Pour this sauce over the *spaghetti* and mix together. (*See illustration p.* 215). (*Italy*)

⊡ con Carciofi * *with Globe Artichokes*

For 12 persons: 2¼ *lb spaghetti;* 8 *young globe artichokes;* ¼ *pint oil; knob of butter;* ½ *onion;* 4 *eggs;* ¼ *lb grated Parmesan cheese;* 1 *lemon.* Cooking time: 15 minutes.

Prepare the artichokes by cutting off the tops of the leaves and stalks and by slicing thinly and dipping in water containing lemon juice. Fry the onion in butter and oil, add the sliced artichoke and season. Pour in some water to facilitate the cooking which should be brisk so that the water evaporates quickly. In a mixing bowl beat up the eggs and add the salt and half the grated Parmesan. Boil the *spaghetti* in plenty of salt water, drain and put into the mixing bowl and start to mix together. Add the cooked artichokes and continue mixing. Serve on a dish and sprinkle with grated Parmesan just before serving. (*Italy*)

⊡ alla Marinara * *with Shellfish*

For 6 persons: 2¼ *lb spaghetti;* 1 *lb shelled shellfish;* ¾ *lb tomatoes;* ¼ *pint olive oil;* 1 *teaspoon anchovy purée;* ½ *clove garlic;* ½ *onion;* ¾ *pint sauce Béchamel; sprig basil; parsley; bay leaf;* ½ *red pepper.* Cooking time: 20 minutes.

Fry the finely chopped onion and garlic in oil until they are golden coloured. Mix in the anchovy *purée*. Add the mixed shellfish (clams, mussels, prawns), the red pepper, half a bay leaf, the skinned and diced tomatoes and finally salt and pepper. Reduce and add the basil and parsley. Pass through a sieve and stir in the *sauce Béchamel*. Cook the *spaghetti*, drain and mix in the butter and sauce. Put the *spaghetti* in an ovenproof dish and brown in the oven. (*Italy*)

⊡ Montanara

For 4 persons: 1 *lb spaghetti;* ¼ *lb salt pork;* 2 *oz butter;* 1 *lb tomatoes;* ¼ *lb diced gruyère cheese;* 1 *onion;* ¼ *pint dry white wine; garlic; sprig basil.* Cooking time for the sauce: 12 minutes.

Crush the garlic and fry in the oil and butter until golden coloured. Remove garlic from the pan, and fry the grated or finely chopped onion and diced salt pork in this pan. Then pour in the white wine and allow to evaporate. Add the chopped tomatoes and basil leaves. Stir all the time while reducing the liquor. Cook the *spaghetti* in salt water, drain and add the sauce. Sprinkle with *gruyère*. (*Italy*)

Spaghetti alla Napoletana * *Spaghetti with Tomato Sauce*

This is *spaghetti* served with *sauce Tomate.* (*Italy*)

⊡ alla Vongole * *with Mussels or Clams*

For 10 persons: 2¼ *lb spaghetti;* 2¼ *lb skinned, finely chopped tomatoes;* 2 *tablespoons condensed tomato purée;* ¾ *lb shelled mussels;* 2 *oz butter;* ¼ *pint oil;* ½ *oz sugar;* ½ *onion;* 3 *cloves garlic; salt and pepper;* ½ *oz finely chopped parsley.*

To prepare the sauce: fry the finely chopped onion in half the oil and butter until golden coloured, add the tomatoes and the condensed tomato *purée* and cook for 5 minutes. Add the sugar, cook for another 10 minutes, evaporate the water and strain. Keep hot. Fry the whole cloves of garlic in remaining oil and then take them out of the pan. Now put in the mussels, parsley and the prepared *sauce Tomate*, simmer for 5 minutes and add pepper. Boil the *spaghetti*, drain and mix in half of the sauce. Serve the rest of the sauce separately. (*See illustration p.* 216). (*Italy*)

Tagliatelle Verdi alla Bolognese * *Green Noodles with Cream Cheese*

For 10 person: 1½ *lb flour;* 4 *eggs;* ¼ *pint oil;* 2 *fl oz water;* 1 *lb spinach purée;* ½ *pint sauce Bolognaise.*

Blend together the flour, eggs, oil, water and spinach *purée.* Roll out this dough as thinly as possible and let it dry. Cut into very fine strips about ⅜-inch wide, poach them, drain and then stir over heat in a buttered saucepan for 5-6 minutes. Mix in the *sauce Bolognaise.* (*See illustration p.* 213). (*Italy*)

Tortellini de Ricotta * *Lasagne with Cream Cheese*

For 10 *persons:* 1 *lb cream cheese;* 2 *oz gruyère;* 2 *egg yolks;* 2 *oz grated Parmesan cheese;* ½ *lb butter; Lasagne dough.*

Roll out *Lasagne* dough as thinly as possible and cut it up into 2½-inch squares. Mix all the ingredients and put a spoonful on each of half the squares. Brush the dough round the filling with water and place another square on top. Press down firmly on all sides. Poach in salt water for 6-7 minutes. Drain, sprinkle with Parmesan cheese and brush with *Noisette* butter. (*See illustration p.* 212). (*Italy*)

Welsh Rarebit

4 *slices toast without crust;* ½ *lb Cheshire cheese;* 3 *tablespoons Pale Ale;* Cooking time: 5 minutes.

1. Cut cheese in small dice, pour beer on top, season with a small pinch of cayenne and a little mustard, melt very gently over low heat and immediately pour over the hot buttered toast. Cut in half and serve at once.

2. Partially toast bread after cutting off crusts, place a slice of cheese on top, dust with mustard and a little cayenne pepper and grill quickly.

When a meal has several courses, soup is usually the first—unless preceded by cold *hors d'œuvre*. The soup can therefore be considered an indication of the nature of the culinary pleasures to come. Even a mediocre meal appears tolerable if the beginning, the soup, was good.

In France, soup making is very important and undertaken with care using fresh, perfect ingredients. All soups must be well-seasoned, for an insipid soup without character is a bad start to any meal. Good soup is easy to make but can only be as good as the ingredients you put into it. Once soup comes to the boil, let it simmer steadily, unless otherwise indicated in the recipe; if boiled too fast a cloudy soup will result. Do not allow soup thickened with egg yolk or cream and egg yolk to come to the boil or it will curdle. When a recipe for white or light-coloured soups calls for frying the vegetables do not allow them to colour. The nutritive value of soups is not normally very high but this will depend upon the ingredients used; obviously, thickened soups and *purées* will have a higher nutritive value than clear soups and *consommés*.

A most important point in soup-making is that cold soups should be icy cold and served in soup cups while hot soups should be served very hot in heated cups or bowls. Serve about half a pint of soup per person, but a little less if the soup is very thick or forms part of a very substantial meal.

Soups need time and trouble to make but the methods described in the following recipes have been set out as clearly as possible. You will find a large number of different types of soup in the ensuing section including the basic soups such as *Pot-au-Feu* which may be served for family meals as it stands or used as an ingredient for a richer soup. There is also a special section on French regional and Peasant soups which enjoy such popularity all over the world.

Soups can be divided into 3 categories:

Clear soups and *Consommés*,

Cream and Thickened soups,

Thickened Vegetable soups and *Purées*.

BASIC SOUPS

These soups form the rich basis or stock for most of the soup recipes which follow in this chapter. They may be served as they are, accompanied by bread or potatoes, because they are substantial and constitute a meal in themselves.

Grande Marmite * *Bouillon*

This is a soup made by simmering meat, poultry and vegetables together. When cooked the meat is removed, chopped and replaced in the dish. Its name comes from the tall earthenware pot or "*marmite*" in which the soup is cooked and served.

For 3½ pints bouillon: 1¼ lb of lean beef; 1 shin of beef, with bone; 2 leeks and 1 celery stalk tied together; 1 small turnip; 2 large carrots; 1 onion stuck with one or two cloves; 1 clove of garlic; 1 sprig of thyme; ½ a bay leaf; 4½ pints water. Cooking time: 3½ hours.

Cover the meat with the water, bring to the boil, skim, add the vegetables and herbs. Simmer gently until all ingredients are tender. Cool, remove meat and bones and strain through a cloth.

Consommé (Clarification) * *Basic Consommé*

Both hot and cold *consommés* must be clarified before they are served. Clarification removes cloudiness from the stock and to some extent it strengthens the flavour.

For 3½ pints of consommé; ¾ lb lean minced beef; 2 egg whites; the white of 1 leek; 1 carrot; chervil; 3½ pints bouillon or Pot-au-Feu. Cooking time: 50 minutes.

Skim the *bouillon* or stock very thoroughly so that it is entirely free from fat. Place any uncooked bones and carcases indicated in specific recipes with the vegetables in a roasting tin with a small amount of fat. Brown in the oven. Mix the minced beef and egg whites thoroughly with a little cold stock. Drain the browned bones free of fat and place in a thick-bottomed saucepan. Add the clarifying agents, that is, the mince and egg whites and gradually mix in remaining stock. Stir well and bring to boil. Simmer the *consommé* slowly for 50 minutes. Carefully remove all fat and strain gently through muslin into a clean pan. Bring to the boil and remove all grease with a piece of soft tissue paper. Strain through muslin and season to taste.

⊡ de Gibier * *Game Consommé*

For 6 persons: 1 pheasant; 2 egg whites; a mirepoix consisting of 1 carrot, 1 white of leek, 1 onion and 1 piece of celery; 3 juniper berries; 1 oz mushroom trimmings; 1 sprig rosemary; 3 pints game stock.

Bone the bird and mince the flesh very finely, then brown the bones and *mirepoix* in the oven. Proceed as for basic *consommé* substituting the game flesh for minced beef. The mushroom trimmings or peel should be well washed and added before cooking. Garnish this *consommé* with a *julienne* of 6 oz of cooked game or game *quenelles*.

⊡ de Poisson * *Fish Consommé*

For 3½ pints of clear fish consommé; 1 lb of minced pike or whiting; 3 oz shredded white of leek; 1 oz parsley stalks; ¼ lb mushroom trimmings; 2 egg whites; 1 pint white wine; 4 pints fish stock.

Thoroughly mix together the fish, egg whites, wine, parsley and mushrooms, then blend in the fish stock; bring carefully to the boil, simmer for thirty minutes and strain through muslin. Season and garnish with 6 oz small white fish *quenelles*.

Consommé de Volaille * *Poultry Consommé*

For 6 persons: ¾ lb lean minced beef; 1 *carrot;* 1 *white of leek;* 1 *chicken browned in the oven;* 1 *lb roast chicken carcases;* 2 *egg whites;* 4½ *pints bouillon;* 1 *onion;* 1 *stalk celery.*

Shred the leek and carrot, add the meat and egg white, mix thoroughly, blend in the stock. Bring to the boil, and add the chicken carcases. Simmer and strain through muslin. Season and garnish with 6 oz *julienne* of white cooked chicken meat or chicken *quenelles.*

Petite Marmite

This is virtually the same dish as *Grande Marmite* except that the soup is served in individual pots.

For 6 persons: ½ lb silverside of beef; ½ lb flank beef; 1 *small boiling chicken with giblets;* 1 *marrow bone;* 1 *large carrot; ½ small turnip;* 1 *white of leek;* 1 *onion; half a head of celery; ½ small cabbage;* 4½ *pints beef bouillon.* Cooking time: 3 hours.

Brown the chicken for about 20 minutes, drain well and put in a *marmite* or large deep casserole together with the meat and bones and stock. Bring slowly to the boil and allow to simmer. Meanwhile turn the carrots and turnip to the shape of small olives. Slice the leek, celery and cabbage, add to the pot and continue to cook. When the meat is tender, remove and either slice or cut it into small cubes. Slice the chicken meat and discard the giblets. Return the meats to the pot, skim off the fat and season. The marrow bone may be served in the pot if liked. This soup is served with thin slices of toast.

Pot-au-Feu Simple

Thick soup made with meat and vegetables. When cooked the soup is strained and the meat and vegetables served as a second course after the soup.

5 *lb beef bones; ¾ lb beef (shoulder, flank, silverside);* 1 *large carrot;* 1 *browned onion; ¼ lb white of leek; small piece turnip;* 1 *stick celery;* 1 *bouquet garni;* 4½ *pints cold water.* Cooking time: 3 hours.

First place bones in cold water and bring to the boil. Skim and add salt. Add vegetables, meat and other ingredients. Skim once more and simmer slowly for 2½-3 hours. The meat is placed in boiling water so that the pores close at once, and the flavour and nutrients are kept in the meat. A boiling fowl or the trimmings from a roasting fowl can be added to the *Pot-au-Feu.* Bread *croûtons* should be served separately, otherwise they become soggy and unattractive.

Croûte au Pot

This is a more elaborate *Pot-au-Feu,* the same recipe is used as above with the addition of quarter pound of white cabbage. The vegetables are not added until half-way through the cooking time, and are usually turned into small olive shapes. When cooking time is completed the soup may be strained and the meat sliced, the vegetables and meat are then returned to the pan and the soup served sprinkled with chopped parsley and *croûtons.* The *croûtons* should be diced French bread with the fat from the *bouillon* poured over and browned in the oven or toasted. Alternatively the *croûtons* may be sprinkled with grated *gruyère* cheese and served floating in the soup or separately.

HOT CONSOMMÉS

Consommés are the boiled and seasoned stock of fish, poultry, meat, game or vegetables. It should be clear and varies from a pale golden colour to a rich amber. It may be garnished with dices of the appropriate meats, or with pasta, *croûtons* or egg *royale*. *Consommé* makes an excellent start to a meal because it stimulates the appetite more, perhaps, than any other type of food. 3½ pints of Basic *consommé* is used for all these recipes and will serve six people.

◘ Aurore

2 oz tapioca; 2 tablespoons tomato purée; 2 hardboiled egg yolks rubbed through a sieve.

When clarifying the *consommé* add the tomato *purée*, then boil up with the tapioca. Sprinkle with a little egg yolk when serving.

◘ à la Basquaise

1 tablespoon julienne of peppers or pimentos; 1 tablespoon diced tomatoes; 1 tablespoon cooked rice; chervil.

Add this garnish to the hot *consommé*.

◘ Brunoise

A brunoise composed of: 2 large carrots; ¼ lb turnip; the white of a leek and a stalk of celery; 1¾ pints Basic consommé.

Sweat the vegetables in butter for 25 minutes. Add salt and a pinch of sugar, mix with the Basic *consommé*, bring to the boil then simmer for ten minutes. Serve sprinkled with chopped parsley.

◘ Célestine

3 small savoury pancakes; chopped chervil.

Cut the pancakes in very thin, narrow strips and add to Poultry *consommé* together with the chervil just before serving.

◘ Colbert

2 oz carrots; 2 oz turnip; 1 oz green peas; 1 oz French beans; 6 eggs. Cooking time: 30 minutes.

Cut the vegetables in small dice, then cook each vegetable separately in boiling salted water. Add to the *consommé* and simmer slowly for ten minutes. Poach an egg for each person in *bouillon* and serve with the *bouillon*.

Consommé Diablotins

¼ pint thick Béchamel; 2 oz grated Parmesan; cayenne pepper; 20 rounds bread.

Dry the bread in the oven. Mix the cheese with the *Béchamel* and then heap on to the slices of bread. Season with cayenne. Gratinate in the oven and serve separately with the Basic *consommé.*

▣ à la Florentine

Beat up two whole eggs and stir them into boiling Poultry *consommé.* Add two tablespoons of cooked rice and some feathery leaves of chervil.

▣ Julienne

2 *oz carrot;* 1 *oz turnip;* 1 *onion; the whites of two leeks;* 2 *oz cabbage.* Cooking time: 40 minutes.

Cut all the vegetables into short, very thin strips. Mix, place in a casserole in which a little butter, or better still, the fat skimmed from the stock, has been heated, season with salt and a pinch of sugar and cover with a buttered piece of paper. Put on the lid and simmer slowly at moderate heat at the side of the stove or till the vegetables are tender and the liquid has evaporated. Place in the Basic *consommé,* boil for a few minutes and serve with pieces of chervil leaves.

▣ Mimosa

2 *oz tapioca;* 2 *oz French beans;* 1 *green Royale garnish;* 1 *hardboiled egg.*

Garnish the *consommé* with the cooked tapioca, the sliced beans, the diced *Royale* and the egg white cut in strips. Rub the egg yolk through a sieve and scatter over soup when serving it; it should float on top.

▣ Mosaïque

2 *oz carrot;* 1 *oz turnip;* 2 *oz peas;* 2 *oz French beans;* 1 *small truffle;* 1 *oz pickled tongue;* 1 *hardboiled egg white.*

Cut the vegetables in small dice and cook in *bouillon.* Add the diced truffle, tongue, egg white and vegetables to the Basic *consommé* when ready to serve.

▣ Mousseline

3½ *pints Consommé;* 3 *oz tapioca;* 3 *egg yolks; fresh cream.* Cooking time: 10 minutes.

Cook tapioca with the ½ pint *Consommé.* Stir egg yolks with cream, pour boiling soup on top stirring all the time.

▣ Niçoise

2 *oz deseeded, peeled and diced tomatoes;* 2 *oz boiled sliced French beans;* 2 *oz diced boiled potatoes.*

Place diced tomatoes and all other ingredients in hot Poultry *consommé* and scatter chervil leaves on top.

Consommé à l'Orge Perlé * *Consommé with Pearl Barley*

$1\frac{1}{2}$ *oz pearl barley*. Cooking time: 2 hours.

Wash and blanch the barley thoroughly. Cook in *bouillon* and serve in the boiling *Consommé*.

⊡ à la Parisien

This is a *Poultry consommé* containing some *Royale* (egg custard) and diced vegetables.

⊡ au Parmesan

2 *eggs;* $1\frac{1}{2}$ *oz Parmesan cheese;* $1\frac{3}{4}$ *oz flour; salt and pepper*. Cooking time: 5 minutes.

Blend the egg yolks, salt, pepper and Parmesan together. Fold in the stiffly whisked egg whites together with the flour. Spread a thin layer of this mixture on a sheet of greaseproof paper. Bake in a very hot oven, 425° F or Gas Mark 7, and leave to cool. Cut up into diamond-shaped pieces and put them in the soup just before it is served.

⊡ aux Perles du Japon * *with Sago*

3 *pints Consommé;* 2 *oz pearl barley or sago or salep*. Cooking time: 15 minutes.

If the *Consommé* is to remain clear, the pearl barley is first blanched for 3 minutes, then put into a sieve and boiling water poured through and only then is it cooked in the soup. Sago and salep can be put directly into the *Consommé*.

⊡ aux Profiteroles

$\frac{1}{4}$ *pint Choux pastry;* 1 *oz grated Parmesan*. Cooking time: 8-10 minutes.

Mix *Choux* pastry with cheese. Using a forcing bag and a small round nozzle, pipe tiny *profiteroles* on to a lightly buttered baking sheet and bake in a hot oven, 425° F or Gas Mark 7, till crisp. Only place in *Consommé* when about to serve.

⊡ aux Quatre Filets

Cut 2 oz each of poultry, tongue, mushrooms and truffle, place in *Consommé* and boil for a few minutes.

⊡ Queue de Bœuf * *Oxtail*

For 6 persons: $1\frac{1}{2}$-2 *lb oxtail;* $\frac{1}{2}$ *lb knuckle of veal;* $\frac{1}{4}$ *lb carrots;* 2 *oz turnips; white of* 1 *leek;* 1 *browned onion stuck with cloves;* $\frac{1}{2}$ *lb lean chopped beef*. Cooking time: 5 hours.

Chop oxtail and veal into small pieces, brown well in a pan with hot fat. Drain and place in a pan with the vegetables. Add 3 pints stock. Bring to boil and simmer. Remove vegetables, except onion, when cooked and cut into dice. Remove oxtail when tender and dice. Brown chopped beef in another pan, strain oxtail stock over this. Boil and simmer for one hour. Carefully remove all fat and strain through muslin. Season, add diced vegetables and oxtail.

Consommé à la Royale

This quantity is suitable for 3½ pints of Consommé or 10 persons: 3 whole eggs; 8 fl oz Bouillon; salt and pepper. Cooking time: 30 minutes.

Royale is a garnish which can be used in any soup. Beat the eggs well, season with salt and pepper, stir in hot stock and pour through a pointed strainer. Pour into a lightly-buttered beaker-shaped mould, place in a water-bath and poach in the oven like a cream. The water must remain hot but must not boil. The *Royale* is ready when a skewer pushed into it is dry when withdrawn. Allow to cool completely and cut into dice, slices, or any desired shape with a cutter. Place carefully in the soup and sprinkle a little chopped chervil on top. *Royale* can be used for clear and thick soups.

▣ au Tapioca

3½ pints Consommé; 3 oz tapioca. Cooking time: 10 minutes.

Sprinkle the tapioca into the boiling soup and cook slowly.

▣ au Vermicelle, aux Pâtes d'Italie * *with Vermicelli or Noodles*

Cooking time: 10 minutes.

Vermicelli or any type of Italian pasta may be added to *Consommé* in the proportions of ¼ lb pasta to 3½ pints of *Consommé*. The pasta should be washed and blanched, then sprinkled into the boiling *Consommé* and cooked very slowly. Grated Parmesan may be served separately.

▣ Xavier

2 oz flour; 2 eggs; 3 tablespoons fresh milk.

Mix a batter with the flour, whole eggs, a pinch of salt, a pinch of chopped chervil and the milk. Pour this mixture into the boiling *Consommé* through a coarse strainer. Cook gently; the paste should be in threads like vermicelli.

COLD CONSOMMÉS

For 6 persons

In summer, or for cold buffets, *Consommé* is usually served cold. The *Consommé* should be well seasoned and rich enough to jelly when cold. Serve chilled in *Consommé* cups.

Consommé à l'Estragon * *with Tarragon*

Allow a small bundle of tarragon to simmer—not boil—for a few minutes in hot *consommé*. Serve cold with very small piece of fresh chopped tarragon in each cup.

Consommé au Madère, au Porto * *with Madeira, Port*

One part of a fortified wine such as Madeira, Port, Marsala or sherry may be added to 10 parts of Poultry *Consommé*.

Consommé Madrilène

4½ *pints beef Consommé;* ¾ *lb lean minced beef;* 1½ *lb tomatoes;* 2 *egg whites; chervil leaves;* ¼ *lb red pepper.*

Skim the fat from cold *consommé* made using the basic recipe (*p.* 244). Chop 1 lb tomatoes and pepper coarsely, mix well with the beef and the egg whites and slowly pour the cold *Consommé* over them. Boil up, and simmer for thirty minutes. Strain the soup, carefully skimming off the fat, and serve in cups with a garnish of ½ lb of peeled, deseeded, diced raw tomatoes and chervil leaves. To enable it to set easily the stock from a split calf's foot may be added. The soup should be served cold and slightly jellied.

THICKENED AND CREAM SOUPS

These soups can be divided into 2 categories—those with a basis of wheat, oats, rice, barley or cornflour—and those which need a vegetable *purée*, potatoes, haricot or other beans, peas or lentils as a thickening.

In addition there is another kind of cream soup for which the thickening qualities of the vegetables are not enough and where some type of flour must be used, for example, asparagus, lettuce and cress. Thick soups should not be served as the first course of a heavy meal.

BASIC CREAM SOUPS

For 6 persons

These soups may be served as they are or used as a basis for more elaborate soups. They both thicken and flavour the derivative soups.

Crème d'Avoine * *Cream of Oatmeal*

¼ *lb oatmeal;* 1½ *pints Bouillon or stock;* 2½ *pints milk;* 2 *fl oz fresh cream.* Cooking time: 1 hour.

Boil 1¾ pints milk and mix it with the *Bouillon*. Stir the oatmeal into the rest of the cold milk and pour into the boiling liquid. Simmer for an hour, strain, add the cream (or butter) and small fried *croûtons*.

Crème d'Orge * *Cream of Barley*

Same method as for Cream of Rice soup but using barley instead of rice flour. Blanch 3 oz of pearl barley thoroughly, boil for at least 45 minutes in stock, strain, and add to soup. Rice flour, and to a lesser degree barley flour, form the basis of most cream soups.

Crème de Riz * *Cream of Rice*

2 *oz butter;* 3 *oz rice flour;* 2 *egg yolks;* ⅛ *pint cream;* ½ *pint milk;* 2½ *pints stock.* Cooking time: 45 minutes.

Stir the rice flour into the melted butter and cook this *roux* for a moment. Add the veal or beef stock, stir well and cook for 40 minutes at low heat. Add milk, season and cook another 5 minutes. Mix the egg yolks and cream in the soup tureen and pour the hot soup on top, stirring continuously.

CREAM SOUPS

These soups are based on one of the above basic soups, they are flavoured according to their type and then thickened and enriched with egg yolks, cream and sometimes butter as well. The best way to add eggs or cream to a soup is to mix them together with a little cold liquid first of all and then add a small amount of hot soup to this and mix carefully. The egg and cream mixture may then be added to the remaining soup stirring all the time and the soup is then reheated. After the addition of butter, egg yolks and cream, the soup should not boil. All proportions are for 6 persons.

Crème Andalouse

½ lb onions; 2 lb tomatoes; 2 oz rice flour or semolina; 2 oz butter; 2 pimentos; 3 tablespoons fresh cream; 3½ pints Bouillon; 1½ oz rice Cooking time: 45 minutes.

Slice the onions finely and fry in butter, add 1½ lb of the tomatoes and cook them for a few minutes with the onions. Sprinkle the rice flour over and cook this for a few minutes. Moisten with the *bouillon,* season, and simmer slowly. Meanwhile boil the 1½ oz rice, rinse and keep it on one side. Peel and deseed the remaining tomatoes and put together with the pimento into the *julienne*, cook slowly in butter. When everything is tender, sieve the soup and mix in the cream and butter. Garnish with the cooked rice, the pimento and tomatoes.

⊡ d'Asperges * *Asparagus*

2 oz butter; 2 oz rice flour; 2 oz fresh cream; 2 egg yolks; 2½ pints stock; ½ pint milk; 1 lb asparagus. Cooking time: 1 hour.

Make a light *roux* with the butter and rice flour and cook for 2 minutes and add stock. Cut tips of asparagus and cook separately. Add the green part of the asparagus after blanching it for five minutes and cook at low heat for 1 hour. Season well, strain through a sieve, and boil up again with the milk. Thicken with the egg yolk and cream and add the butter and garnish with the asparagus tips.

⊡ Bisque d'Écrevisses * *Crayfish*

24 crayfish; 3 oz butter; 2 oz rice flour; 1 small carrot; 1 medium-sized onion; 2 shallots; 1 sprig thyme; half a small bay leaf; 6 parsley stalks; 2 fl oz brandy; 3 fl oz white wine; 3½ pints stock; 2 fl oz cream. Cooking time: 1 hour.

Cut carrots, onions, shallots and parsley stalks into fine *mirepoix*, fry lightly in butter, add washed and cleaned crayfish, thyme and bay leaf, *sauté* for a few minutes, flambé with the brandy, reduce with the white wine, season, cover and boil 8-10 minutes. When cool, remove crayfish tails, remove and throw away intestine and crush all shells. Add this *purée* to a Cream of Rice soup made with the stock and rice flour and cook slowly for a further 10 minutes. Press through a fine wire sieve so that none of the juice is lost, heat up again, add the cream and enrich with the rest of the butter. The crayfish tails are put in the soup whole or diced.

In a number of countries it is illegal to remove the intestine of live crayfish or to fry them alive. Before browning, it is therefore advisable to throw them into boiling water for a few minutes until they are dead and then to remove the intestine before sautéing.

Crème Calcutta

Cream of Rice soup plus 1 *lb onions;* $1\frac{3}{4}$ *oz butter;* 3 *oz rice;* 1 *heaped teaspoon curry powder*. Cooking time: 1 hour.

Slice the onions, blanch, drain well and cook in butter. Dust with curry powder, brown well, add rice soup and cook till done at low heat. Strain through a fine sieve, boil up again with the milk and thicken with cream only. Boil rice separately, drain well and use as a garnish.

⊡ Capucine (aux Champignons) * *Mushroom*

$2\frac{1}{2}$ *pints white stock;* 3 *oz butter;* $2\frac{1}{2}$ *oz rice flour;* $\frac{3}{4}$ *lb fresh, very white mushrooms;* 2 *egg yolks; the juice of* 1 *lemon*. Cooking time: 45 minutes.

Make a Cream of Rice soup with the stock, 1 oz butter and rice flour. Wash and peel the mushrooms and press them quickly through a fine wire sieve. Cook them in remaining butter with the lemon juice until all liquid has evaporated. Mix with the rice soup and cook another 15 minutes. Bind with egg yolks and cream and garnish with fried bread cubes. Instead of thickening the soup with eggs and cream it may be completed with a little milk and fresh butter.

⊡ de Céleri-Rave * *Celeriac*

$\frac{3}{4}$ *lb celeriac;* $2\frac{1}{2}$ *pints Cream of Rice soup;* 1 *oz butter;* 2 *egg yolks;* $\frac{1}{2}$ *pint fresh cream*. Cooking time: 40 minutes.

Wash, peel and cut the celeriac in quarters. Sweat in butter but do not allow it to brown or colour at all. When tender remove a third of the celeriac and cut into dice; this is reserved for garnish. Sieve the rest of the celeriac and add to the Cream of Rice. Boil for 5 minutes, skim, strain and season. Thicken with egg yolk and cream and garnish with the remaining diced celeriac. Serve with *croûtons*.

⊡ à la Châtelaine (aux Artichauts) * *Artichoke*

$1\frac{1}{2}$ *oz butter;* 2 *oz flour;* 4 *raw artichoke bottoms;* $\frac{1}{2}$ *pint milk;* $1\frac{3}{4}$ *pints stock;* 2 *fl oz cream;* 2 *egg yolks*. Cooking time: 30 minutes.

Make a light *roux* with the butter and flour, add stock and the sliced artichoke bottoms which have first been cooked in butter. Cook slowly for 30 minutes and stir through a fine sieve. Stir the egg yolks well with the cream and milk and thicken the soup with them. Garnish with fried bread cubes or egg custard (*Royale*).

⊡ de Chicorée ou Colbert * *Endive*

Proceed as for Cream of Asparagus with very green endive. Finish with or without thickening, but with a little cream or butter. Garnish with fried *croûtons* or with egg custard (*Royale*).

Crème Clamart * *Cream of Pea*

2 lb freshly shelled peas; 2 oz rice; the white of 2 leeks; 2 oz butter; 3 pints stock or bouillon; 1 lettuce; 2 egg yolks; ½ pint milk; 2 fl oz cream. Cooking time: 45 minutes.

Sweat the peas and sliced leeks in butter for a few minutes then cover with stock. Bring to the boil and cook till peas are tender. Meanwhile boil the rice in salted water, drain, rinse and keep on one side. Sieve the soup, boil up with the rest of the stock, skim and season and thicken with egg yolks and cream. Garnish with a *chiffonade* of blanched lettuce.

▣ Dubarry * *Cauliflower*

1 lb cauliflower; 2 oz flour; 2 oz butter; 2½ pints stock; 2 oz white of leek; ½ pint milk; ¼ pint fresh cream; 2 egg yolks. Cooking time: 40 minutes.

Cook a few small cauliflower sprigs separately as garnish. Slice the leek and sweat in butter. Add the flour and make a light *roux*, add the stock, boil up and add blanched cauliflower. Cook 35 minutes, season well and stir through a sieve. Boil up again with the milk. Thicken with egg yolks and cream and serve with garnish of cauliflower sprigs.

▣ à la Fréneuse * *Turnip*

Made in the same way as Cream of Cauliflower but using ¾ lb strongly blanched sliced white turnips and ¼ lb potatoes instead of the latter. Garnish with fried *croûtons.*

▣ de Laitue * *Lettuce*

Proceed as for Cream of Chicory but using two blanched lettuces.

▣ de Mais * *Corn*

¼ lb cornflour; 3 pints stock; ½ pint milk; 2 egg yolks; 2 fl oz cream; ½ lb corn on the cob; 2 oz butter.

Boil the corn in salted water till soft. Make a *roux* with the butter and cornflour and slowly add the milk and *bouillon,* bring to the boil stirring constantly. Remove kernels from the corn and place in the soup. Cook for thirty minutes and strain. Mix the egg yolks and cream together and gradually add the soup. Return to the saucepan to heat through.

▣ Nivernaise * *Carrot*

1½ lb carrots; 3 pints Cream of Rice; ¼ pint fresh cream. Cooking time: 1 hour.

Make a *brunoise* with ¼ lb carrots. Slice the remainder and cook slowly in butter. Finish cooking in the Cream of Rice. Pass through strainer. Thicken with cream when about to serve. Garnish with the *brunoise.*

Crème Portugaise * *Cream of Tomato*

1 *medium-sized onion;* 1 *medium-sized carrot;* 2 *oz bacon;* 1¼ *lb fresh tomatoes;* 2 *oz butter;* 2 *oz flour;* 2 *oz cooked rice;* 1 *bouquet garni;* 2½ *pints stock;* 2 *oz cream; salt; sugar.* Cooking time: 45 minutes.

Cut bacon, onion and carrot in small dice and fry lightly. Add flour, stir until brown. Cut the tomatoes (which should be ripe) in quarters and add them to the *roux*. Pour on stock, stir well, season with salt and a pinch of sugar, add the *bouquet garni* and cook slowly for 45 minutes. Stir through a sieve, boil up again, if necessary thin with a little stock, bind with the cream and garnish with boiled rice.

▣ **à la Reine** * *Chicken*

2½ *pints Cream of Rice soup;* 2 *oz butter; white chicken meat;* 2 *egg yolks;* 2 *oz fresh cream.* Cooking time: 30 minutes.

Make the Cream of Rice soup with chicken stock, if possible from a boiling fowl. Remove the breast of chicken, cut one half in small dice or strips, pound the other finely, mix with a little butter and rub through a fine sieve. Add the *purée* to the soup, boil up briefly. Again, skim and strain, season well and bind with egg yolks and cream. Garnish with the diced chicken.

▣ **à la Rohan** * *Cauliflower*

A thin cauliflower soup, thickened with 3 oz of tapioca.

▣ **à la Saint-Hubert** * *Game*

3 *pints stock (game if possible);* 2 *oz butter;* 2 *oz rice flour; carcases and trimmings of roast game;* 6 *oz diced cooked game.* Cooking time: 1½ hours.

Pound carcases and trimmings very finely and fry in butter until they are golden brown. Mix in the flour and brown it, add stock, boil up and skim. Then strain, thicken with egg yolks and serve with the diced game meat as a garnish.

▣ **Solférino** * *Vegetable*

¼ *lb butter;* 2½ *oz rice flour;* 1 *lb fresh tomatoes;* 2 *carrots;* 1 *turnip;* 3½ *pints Cream of Rice soup.* Cooking time: 1 hour.

Peel the tomatoes and *sauté* in butter, boil the Cream of Rice soup, add the tomatoes and cook very slowly. Meanwhile using a scoop cut out tiny balls of carrots and turnip and boil in *bouillon*. When they are cooked, drain and *sauté* in butter. Strain the soup, season, reheat and enrich with butter, then garnish with the vegetable balls. Sprinkle the soup with chopped chervil.

THICKENED VEGETABLE SOUPS OR PURÉES

A sieve or special vegetable *moulinette* may be used to *purée* vegetables for soup, but do not forget to scrape the *purée* from underneath the sieve. The liquidiser attachment of the electric mixer is certainly a time saver but it does tend to spoil the texture of the vegetables and reduce them to a rather pulpy mass. These soups are usually enriched with butter just before serving.

Potage Ambassadeur

This consists of *Potage Saint-Germain* garnished with 2 tablespoons each of sorrel and lettuce *chiffonade* tossed in butter and 2 oz rice cooked in bouillon.

◘ Chantilly

3½ pints stock; ¾ lb lentils; 1 *bouquet garni;* 1 *onion stuck with* 2 *cloves; ¼ lb bacon rinds or fat bacon; 4 fl oz fresh cream;* 3 *oz small chicken quenelles; 4 pints bouillon;* 2 *oz butter; seasoning.*

Soak the lentils overnight. Next day cook the lentils with the bacon, onion and *bouquet garni.* Then add stock, boil and skim and simmer for 45 minutes. Strain, season, add cream and garnish the soup with *quenelles.*

◘ Chevrière

¾ lb kidney beans; 4 *pints stock; ½ lb onion; ¼ lb butter; ¼ pint cream; seasoning.*

Slice onions and carrots, sweat in half the butter. Wash and drain the beans, add stock, bring to the boil and simmer till tender. Sieve, boil up, season and complete with butter and cream. Serve with fried *croûtons.*

◘ Condé

Make in the same way as *Potage Soissonnais* but correct consistency with red wine and complete with butter.

◘ Crécy au Riz

¼ lb lean bacon; 1 *onion;* 2¼ *lb carrots; ¼ lb rice;* 4 *pints stock;* 2 *oz butter;* 2 *fl oz cream.* Cooking time: 1¼ hours.

Brown the diced bacon and sliced onions well in the butter, add the sliced carrots, cover the pan and cook for a few minutes at low heat. Fill up with the stock, add half the rice, season, cover, simmer slowly for 1 hour. Boil the remaining 2 oz of rice separately in salted water for the garnish. Pass the soup through a very fine sieve, boil up, season well, correct consistency with more stock, complete with cream and garnish with rice.

◘ Cressonière

½ lb onions; 2 *bunches watercress;* 1 *bouquet garni;* 2 *lb potatoes;* 4 *pints white stock;* 2 *oz butter;* 1 *white of leek; ¼ pint cream.* Cooking time: 1 hour.

Shred onions and leek finely, sweat in butter without colouring. Slice potatoes and add to vegetables with *bouquet garni,* cover with stock, bring to the boil, skim and add the well washed watercress. Boil quickly to break down the potatoes. When cooked, strain, reboil, season and garnish with cream and blanched watercress leaves.

◘ Darblay

This consists of *Potage Parmentier* garnished with a *julienne* of 2 oz each of carrots, leeks and lettuce tossed in butter. Sprinkle a little chopped chervil on top.

Potage Faubonne

This consists of *Potage Soissonnais* garnished with a *julienne* of 2 oz each of carrot, turnip, and the white part of leek which have been cooked in butter. Sprinkle chervil leaves on top.

⊡ Fontanges

This consists of *Crème Clamart* garnished with a *chiffonnade* of sorrel and lettuce cooked in butter.

⊡ Garbure

6 oz carrots; 6 oz turnips; ¾ lb potatoes; ¾ lb cabbage; 1 oz haricot beans; 3 oz butter; 3 pints stock; rounds of bread; grated cheese.

Soak beans in water overnight, slice all other vegetables finely. Sweat in butter. Then add stock, boil and skim. Cook beans in water separately, take some of the vegetables from soup when cooked, chop finely and reserve for *croûtons*. When beans are tender add to the soup, boil up and sieve. Reboil, skim and season. Spread vegetable *purée* on *croûtons*. Sprinkle with cheese and brown under the grill. Serve these apart from the soup.

⊡ Germiny

3 pints chicken stock; ½ pint cream; 6 egg yolks; 2 oz shredded sorrel; 2 oz butter; Cheese Straws.

Wash sorrel very thoroughly and cook in the butter. Beat egg yolks and cream and pour boiling stock on to the cream stirring constantly. Return to the heat and cook slowly without boiling. When thickened add the sorrel, season and serve the Cheese Straws apart.

⊡ Lamballe

This consists of *Potage Saint-Germain* with the addition of 3 oz tapioca cooked in *bouillon*.

⊡ Longchamps

This consists of *Potage Fontanges* with the addition of ¼ lb vermicelli cooked in water.

⊡ Marigny

This consists of *Potage Saint-Germain* garnished with ¼ lb peas, ¼ lb haricot beans, and one lettuce cut in *chiffonade*. All the vegetables are cooked in butter.

⊡ Parmentier

3 leeks; 2½ lb potatoes; 2 oz butter; 1 bouquet garni; 2½ pints stock or water; 2 fl oz cream. Cooking time: 1 hour.

Slice the leeks and brown well in butter. Add the sliced potatoes and the *bouquet garni* salt lightly, just cover with water and simmer slowly till very soft. Remove herbs, pass through a fine sieve, add more water if necessary to make a bland soup, boil a few minutes longer, season, and complete with cream. Serve with fried *croûtons*.

Potage Paulette

Made as for *Potage Soissonnais* and garnished with chopped lettuce and sorrel leaves cooked in butter; chervil leaves and cream are added at the last moment.

▣ Saint-Germain

1 *lb dried green split peas;* 1 *carrot;* 1 *onion;* ¼ *lb bacon trimmings;* 2 *cloves;* 1 *bouquet garni;* ¼ *lb butter;* ¼ *pint cream;* 4 *pints chicken, veal or white stock.* Cooking time: 1½ hours.

Soak peas overnight in cold water, bring to the boil in water, skim and drain. Put the chopped vegetables together with the peas, diced bacon and *bouquet garni* into a saucepan and sweat slowly for one hour and mix in the stock, bring to the boil, season with sugar and salt. Remove from the heat and add the butter and cream. Serve with fried *croûtons.*

▣ Soissonais

¾ *lb dried beans or* 1½ *lb fresh beans;* 1 *onion;* 1 *carrot;* 2½ *pints stock;* ½ *pint milk;* 2 *oz butter;* 2 *fl oz cream.* Cooking time: about 1½ hours.

Wash dried beans beforehand and soak for 2 hours. Just cover with water, together with the carrot and onion, season and cook till soft. Pass through a fine sieve, dilute with the milk and stock and if necessary boil up again, season, and enrich with the cream and butter. Garnish with *croûtons.*

▣ Vélours

This consists of *Potage Crécy* garnished with two tablespoons of tapioca which have cooked separately in stock.

FISH SOUPS

French cooks prefer to use the more delicately flavoured fish such as cod, hake, haddock, halibut, pike, sole and eel for making fish soups. Fish soup should be cooked below boiling point and only for about 25-30 minutes, otherwise the taste of fish becomes too pronounced. The basis of these soups is a Fish *velouté*, which is made from white *roux* and fish stock; the method is given below. Fish soups are usually fairly quick soups to make because of their short cooking time.

Stock or Fumet for Fish Soups

This is the stock gained by simmering fish trimmings or a quantity of white fish. Oily fish such as mackerel and herring should not be used as the resultant flavour would be too strong.

To make 4 *pints:* 1 *lb trimmings and bones of fish such as sole, turbot, brill, whiting, hake, cod or pike;* 1 *large sliced onion;* 1 *oz sliced shallot;* 1 *oz parsley stalks;* 3 *oz mushroom trimmings;* 1 *bay leaf; the juice of half a lemon;* ½ *pint white wine;* 10 *white peppercorns* (*to be added only* 10 *minutes before straining the stock*); ¼ *teaspoon salt.* Cooking time: 25-30 minutes.

Line the saucepan with the herbs and flavouring ingredients. Place the fish bones and trimmings on top, season and moisten with the white wine and 4 pints water. Start by boiling briskly, skim, then simmer gently. Strain.

All recipes are for 8 persons unless otherwise stated.

Velouté pour Potages de Poissons * *Velouté for Fish Soups*

This is the basis of fish cream soups and is made by simmering fish stock with a white *roux* and seasoning such as peppercorns, bay leaf or thyme. The flavour is greatly improved if some mushroom peel is added.

To make 3½ pints: 2 oz butter; 3 oz flour; 3½-4 pints fish stock. Cooking time: 20 minutes.

Make white *roux* with the butter and flour. Moisten with the fish stock, season and cook gently for 20 minutes and strain. For fish soups the flour may be replaced by 2 oz rice flour.

Potage Cardinal

2 pints Fish velouté; ¾ pint Béchamel; 1-2 tablespoons tomato purée; 3 oz Crayfish or Lobster butter; diced lobster or crayfish flesh.

Mix the *velouté*, the *Béchamel* and *tomato purée.* Cook for 30 minutes, season, add butter and garnish with diced lobster or crayfish.

▣ **Dieppoise**

3 pints thick Fish velouté; 2 egg yolks; 4 tablespoons cream; Garnish: 1 oz diced carrots; 1 oz cooked rice; 15 poached mussels and their cooking liquor; 2 oz shrimps or prawns.

Cook the vegetables. Mix the *velouté* and the mussel cooking liquor, bring to the boil and thicken with egg yolks and cream. Garnish.

▣ **aux Huîtres** * *Oyster*

3 pints Fish velouté; 2 oz mushrooms (optional); 16 oysters (2 per person); 2 egg yolks; 2 fl oz cream. Cooking time: 45 minutes.

Make the fish stock and then the *velouté* from the bones of whiting, pike or soles—or use whole, economical fish such as coalfish, whiting or burbot. Open and beard the oysters; place the beards in the soup. Stiffen the oysters in their own juice, add juice to soup and do not allow it to boil again. Slice the mushrooms and cook till tender in their own juice with a pinch of salt, a little lemon juice and butter. Add this juice to the soup, strain it, and thicken with eggs and cream. Season well and add mushrooms and oysters as garnish.

▣ **Jacqueline**

A light, very well seasoned Fish *velouté* thickened with egg yolks and cream, with a garnish of freshly cooked peas, diced carrot and rice.

Potage Régence

3½ pints Fish velouté; 1 lb whiting; ¼ pint fresh cream.

Clean and trim the whiting and cook them in the *velouté*. Drain, skin and rub the flesh through a sieve. Strain the *velouté* and combine with the fish *purée*. Season well, add cream and garnish with *croûtons*.

Soup de Poisson * *Fish Soup*

For each person: ¼ lb sea fish (e.g. whiting); 1 or 2 onions; 1 tomato; 1 clove of garlic; 1 level teaspoon flour; pinch saffron; 2-3 oz pasta (macaroni); 1¾ pints water; salt, pepper, paprika; a piece of orange rind (optional); 1 bay leaf.

Put 1¾ pints of water per person in a large casserole or *marmite*, add the cleaned chopped fish, onion, garlic, tomato, salt and pepper and blend in the flour. Simmer slowly for 45 minutes. Sieve soup and return to the casserole, add the saffron mixed with a little cold water, the cooked *pasta*, correct the seasoning and serve very hot.

Velouté de Poisson * *Rich Fish Velouté*

2½ pints fish stock; 2 oz butter; 3 oz flour; ¼ lb chopped mushrooms; 2 egg yolks; ¼ pint cream.

Make a white *roux*, blend in the stock, add the mushrooms and cook for 20 minutes. Thicken with egg yolks and cream.

FRENCH REGIONAL AND PEASANT SOUPS

The recipes which follow are for soups served in the provincial towns and country regions of France. They are fairly simple to prepare, economical and substantial.

Panade * *Bread Panada*

The recipe below is for Bread panada which is used to thicken soups. It is made from bread which has been soaked in milk or water, squeezed dry and then mixed with seasonings and egg yolks and dried thoroughly over heat. There is also another type of panada which is described in the chapter on Basic Preparations, and is used for binding forcemeats and *pâtés*.

1 lb stale bread; 2 eggs; ½ pint milk; ½ pint water. Cooking time: 15-20 minutes.

Place the water and stale bread in a saucepan. Add salt and pepper and place over low heat so that the bread can swell slowly and absorb most of the water. When it has come to the boil, crush and whisk the bread to make a smooth *purée*. Beat the whole eggs and milk in a bowl for a long time. Pour into the very hot soup and continue to whisk over heat. Boil up once more. Remove from heat and add butter and seasoning. Add milk if required.

Potée Auvergnate

This is made like *Soupe aux Choux* but using half a pickled pig's head, more cabbage than other vegetables and some lentils. Cooking time: about 3 hours.

Potée Vosgienne

Made in exactly the same way as *Soupe aux Choux*, only replacing the pickled pork by the same quantity of ham.

Soupe aux Choux * *Cabbage Soup*

2 lb pickled pork; ½ lb bacon; 1 boiling sausage; ¾ lb carrots; 6 oz turnips; 3 leeks; 1½ lb potatoes; 2½ lb white cabbage. Cooking time: about 2 hours.

Wash the pickled pork well and, if very salt, soak for a short time. Put pork and bacon in stock pot, add six pints cold water, bring to the boil, skim, add carrots, turnip and leeks, but do not add salt. Cook slowly for 1 hour, add the quartered cabbage from which the stalk and largest ribs have been removed and about 30 minutes later add 5 or 6 large potatoes and the sausage. Cook for a further 25-30 minutes and serve. The meat can be served with the vegetables and makes an excellent main dish for a family meal.

⊡ à la Comtoise

3 oz cornflour; ¾ pint milk; 1½ pints water; 2 oz butter; slices of bread. Cooking time: 25 minutes.

Mix cornflour with a little cold water, bring rest of slightly salted water to boil and mix with the cornflour stirring constantly. Cook slowly for 20 minutes, then add the boiling milk, season well, add butter and pour whole over small slices of French bread. Allow to stand for 5 minutes before serving.

⊡ Fermière

¼ lb carrot; ¼ lb turnip; the white of two leeks; 2 oz celery; ¼ lb potatoes; ¼ lb onion; 6 oz cabbage; 4-5 pints stock; ¼ lb butter. Cooking time: 1 hour.

Finely shred vegetables and sweat in butter. Add stock, season, and cook slowly till all the vegetables are tender. At the completion of cooking time some haricot beans which have been cooked separately can be added. Serve with *croûtons.*

⊡ Maraîchère

¼ lb onion; ½ lb leeks; ¼ lb turnips; ¼ lb celeriac; ½ lb curly kale; ½ lb potatoes; 1 lettuce; 1 small handful each of spinach and sorrel; 2 oz butter; 1 pint milk; 2 oz crescent noodles or vermicelli; 4 pints water. Cooking time: 1 hour.

Dice onions, leeks, turnips, celeriac and cabbage, add butter, cover and sweat. Add diced potatoes, cover with water, season and simmer without lid until everything is half cooked. Chop sorrel, spinach and lettuce finely, add to soup with noodles or *vermicelli* and boiling milk. Season well and serve with chopped chervil or chives sprinkled on top.

⊡ à l'Oignon au Fromage ou 'Gratinée' * *French Onion*

2 lb onions; ¼ lb butter; 1 clove garlic; 4 pints water; 3 oz gruyère cheese; 1½ oz flour. Cooking time: 15 minutes.

Slice onion thinly, slowly fry a light gold in the butter with the crushed garlic, dust with flour, fry flour golden and add water. Add salt and pepper and simmer until onions are tender, remove fat. Place small slices of bread and the cheese cut in thin small slices in a soup tureen or individual soup bowls. Pour the boiling hot soup on top, cover, and allow to stand 5-6 minutes before serving. This soup can also be served *au gratin* in fireproof bowls, in this case use less water so that the soup is a little thicker.

Soupe à l'Oseille * *Sorrel Soup*

$\frac{1}{2}$ *lb sorrel;* $1\frac{1}{2}$ *lb potatoes;* $1\frac{1}{2}$ *oz butter; the white of* 1 *leek;* 4 *pints bouillon or stock;* 2 *oz cream.* Cooking time: 1 hour.

Slice the leeks and potatoes and sweat in butter for ten minutes. Add the stock and cook slowly until tender. Chop the sorrel, save a little for garnish and stew in its own juice. Then add to the soup. Skim, season and add the cream to the soup and garnish with the very finely chopped remaining sorrel.

⊡ à la Paysanne

$\frac{3}{4}$ *lb carrots;* $\frac{1}{4}$ *lb turnips;* $\frac{1}{2}$ *lb leeks;* 1 *lb potatoes;* 2 *oz butter;* 4 *pints water.* Cooking time: 1 hour.

Cut carrots, turnips and leeks in small, thin slices, add butter and simmer gently. Add the potatoes after cutting them in thin half-slices, add water and cook slowly for about 1 hour. Season well, add a small piece of butter and pour over thin slices of bread toasted in the oven, or if preferred, left untoasted. Serve at once. Since this soup is not strained the vegetables must be cut very small and thin. Sprinkle a few chopped chervil leaves on top.

⊡ au Pistou

For 6 persons: $\frac{1}{2}$ *lb French beans;* $\frac{1}{2}$ *lb potatoes;* 2 *oz haricot beans;* $\frac{1}{2}$ *lb vermicelli;* $\frac{1}{2}$ *lb tomatoes;* 2 *cloves of garlic;* 2 *tablespoons tomato purée;* 2 *egg yolks;* 3 *tablespoons olive oil; sage; thyme; basil; grated cheese.* Cooking time: $1\frac{1}{4}$ hours.

Cut the French beans in small pieces and place with the sliced potatoes and the peeled, chopped tomatoes in water with salt and pepper and a few freshly shelled haricot beans. When the vegetables are almost ready, add the *vermicelli* and finish cooking slowly. Make a garlic sauce, a variation of garlic mayonnaise, as follows: pound the garlic with the herbs, gradually mix in very thick tomato *purée* and the egg yolks and combine with olive oil. Place this mixture in the soup tureen and pour the soup on gradually so as not to cook the egg yolks. Sprinkle with grated cheese. The flavour of garlic and basil should predominate.

(*Speciality of Provence*)

⊡ au Potiron * *Pumpkin*

1 *lb pumpkin;* 1 *pint milk;* 1 *oz butter.* Cooking time: 45 minutes.

Cut the pumpkin into small pieces and cook in salted water. Rub through a fine sieve with the liquor, then add the heated milk in order to give the soup a creamy consistency. Season and add a little sugar. Put some fairly thick slices of bread in the soup and simmer gently for 6 minutes. Remove from heat, add butter and pour into a soup tureen.

⊡ Savoyarde

$\frac{1}{4}$ *lb fat, mildly salted bacon;* 1 *head celery;* 2 *leeks:* 2 *turnips;* 2 *onions;* 3 *large potatoes;* 2 *oz butter; grated cheese;* 1 *pint milk;* 3 *pints water.* Cooking time: about 1 hour.

Shred celery, leeks and onions, and chop the bacon finely. Fry bacon in butter, add shredded vegetables, stew lightly then add finely sliced potatoes. Add the water and bring to the boil. Simmer for 45 minutes, add hot milk. Season and serve with *croûtons* and cheese.

Soupe Thourin

2½ *lb onions;* ¼ *lb lard;* 6 *egg yolks;* 4 *pints water*. Cooking time: 30 minutes.

Slice onions thinly and slowly fry pale yellow in the lard. Add cold water, salt and pepper and allow to boil for 10 minutes. Mix the egg yolks well with a few spoonfuls of stock, thicken soup with them but do not allow to boil again. Serve with thin slices of bread browned in the oven.

FOREIGN SPECIALITIES

Aran Scallop Soup

For 6 *persons:* 6 *scallops;* 4 *peeled, deseeded, diced tomatoes;* 2 *oz lean bacon;* 2 *oz red marrow;* 1¼ *lb sliced potatoes;* 2 *oz butter;* 1½ *pints fish stock; salt, pepper, mace; a small bunch of parsley stalks and a little thyme; chopped parsley;* 1-2 *tablespoons crushed rusks or browned breadcrumbs;* ¼ *pint cream*. Cooking time: 45-50 minutes.

Gently heat the diced bacon in half the butter and add the sliced potatoes. Blanch the scallops. Add the fish stock and scallop liquor to the potatoes, add the herbs, season lightly and cook over low heat. Add the diced scallops and marrow to the soup. Cook for another 15 minutes. Add the diced tomatoes and boil again. Remove the herbs, bring the soup to the desired consistency by adding crushed rusks and add the remainder of the butter and the cream. Sprinkle with mace and chopped parsley. (*Ireland*)

Batwinja (ou Botwinja) * *Cold Russian Soup*

For 6 *persons:* 6 *oz sorrel;* 6 *oz spinach;* ¼ *lb tops of young beetroot;* 6 *oz cucumber;* 2 *pints Kvass* (*a type of light beer with a very low alcoholic content*) *or if unobtainable, dry white wine;* 1 *heaped tablespoon chopped chervil, tarragon, fennel tops and parsley;* 1 *tablespoon chopped dill;* 2 *oz bouillon fat;* 1 *bay leaf*. Cooking time: 25 minutes.

Chop sorrel, spinach and beet tops very finely and cook in their own juice with a pinch of salt. Cool, pass through a hair sieve with the liquid, stir in the Kvass and season with salt and a pinch of sugar. Cut the peeled and deseeded cucumber in short, thin strips and place in soup together with the chopped herbs. Serve the cold soup in soup plates. Place two ice cubes on each and serve at once. Usually a small piece of salmon, or sturgeon without skin and bones, is served on the side, and a little grated horseradish mixed with vinegar. (*Russia*)

Beef-tea

For 1 *cup*. Cooking time: 3 hours.

Coarsely chop some raw and very lean top-side or rump steak. Put into a wide-necked bottle with a pinch of salt and 2 tablespoons of water. Cork the bottle and put it into a pan of cold water so that it is immersed up to the beginning of the neck. Allow the contents of the bottle to boil as if it were in a *bain-marie*. In this way a cup of very strong broth is obtained which is poured through a fine-meshed strainer. Beef-tea may be prescribed for invalids and convalescents. (*Great Britain*)

Borschtch Malorussiski * *Ukranian Beetroot Soup*

For 8 *persons:* 1¼ *lb beetroot;* ¾ *lb white cabbage;* 2 *carrots;* 1 *parsley root;* 1 *stick celery;* 2 *leeks;* ½ *lb bacon;* 1¼ *lb brisket beef;* 2 *tablespoons tomato purée;* ½ *pint sour cream;* 1 *smoked sausage.* Cooking time: 2½-3 hours.

Cut ⅔ of beetroot and other vegetables into strips and toss for a little while in *bouillon* fat. Add 4½-5 pints of water, season lightly, add the beef, the bacon, the tomato *purée*, bay leaf and some peppercorns and simmer together till the meat and bacon are soft. Grate the remainder of the beetroot, strain the juice through a cloth and add a few drops of vinegar. Remove meat and bacon, slice, and put in soup tureen. Add the beetroot juice to the soup at the last moment, pour over the meat and vegetables and sprinkle chopped dill on top. Serve with a sauce-boat of thick sour cream, from which everyone pours a little into the soup. For special occasions a browned duck is boiled in the soup from the beginning.

Chicken Broth

For 6 *persons:* 1 *small chicken;* ¾ *lb carrots;* ½ *lb turnips;* 1 *large stick celery; the white of two leeks;* ¼ *lb rice.* Cooking time: 1¼ hours.

Blanch chicken for three minutes and place in stock pot and add 4 pints water. When the water boils add vegetables cut in small dice, season, and cook slowly. If a boiling fowl is used the cooking time will be 2-3 hours; remove vegetables as soon as they are tender. Add rice 20 minutes before the chicken is ready. Before serving, skin chicken and cut into attractive pieces, add vegetables and serve with the well-seasoned broth. Sprinkle with chopped parsley just before serving. (*Great Britain*)

Chicken Gumbo Creole

For 6 *persons:* 1 *young chicken;* 1 *carrot;* ¼ *lb turnip;* 4-5 *pints stock;* 2 *green peppers;* 2 *sticks celery;* 2 *medium-sized onions; the white of* 2 *leeks;* ¼ *lb bacon;* 2 *oz butter;* 3 *oz rice;* 6 *medium-sized tomatoes;* ½ *lb okra.* Cooking time: 1 hour.

Bone chicken and make stock with meat and carcase, carrot and turnip. When cooked, dice breast of chicken, sweat in butter with diced ham, chopped onions, leeks, celery and peppers. Add 4 pints stock and cook for 40 minutes. Then add tomatoes. Cut okra in small *bâtons* and cook. Boil the rice separately and add to soup with okra. Season and serve. (*United States*)

Gazpacho Andaluz

For 6 *persons:* 12 *caraway seeds;* 4 *cloves garlic;* ¼ *lb fresh breadcrumbs,* ¾ *lb tomatoes;* 1 *red capsicum, skinned, deseeded and cut into fine julienne;* 1 *small cucumber; peeled and diced;* ½ *pint oil;* ½ *pint Mayonnaise;* 2½ *pints water; vinegar.* Cooking time: 20 minutes.

Peel and deseed the tomatoes; reserving three. Soak the crumbs and squeeze dry. Pound the caraway seeds and garlic together, incorporate the crumbs and tomatoes, season with pepper, add 1 pint of water and the oil and allow to stand for 1 hour. Mix well, add the rest of the water and Mayonnaise and other ingredients. Now mix in 3 or 4 tablespoons of vinegar, season with salt and chill well before serving. There are several types of Gazpacho—this is the most popular one. (*Spain*)

Magyar Gulyas Leves * *Hungarian Goulash Soup*

For 8 *persons:* 1 *lb lean shoulder beef;* 1 *lb potatoes;* ¼ *lb onions;* 2 *oz lard;* 3 *tomatoes;* 2 *green peppers;* ½ *oz paprika; caraway seeds; marjoram;* ½ *lb Noodle dough.* Cooking time: about 2 hours.

Fry the onions pale yellow in the lard, add the meat cut in small cubes, the paprika, a little salt, marjoram and crushed caraway seeds and cook for 20 minutes in their own juice. Cut the tomatoes in small pieces, dice the peppers and add to the soup. From time to time add a tablespoon of water till the meat is three-quarters cooked. Now add the diced potatoes and about 4 pints water; simmer until everything is cooked. Roll the Noodle dough out thinly and dry slightly. Tear it into small pieces by hand, cook in plenty of salt water, drain, rinse and add to the hot soup. *(Hungary)*

Mille Fanti * *Italian Bread Soup*

For 6 *persons:* ¼ *lb fresh breadcrumbs passed through a coarse sieve;* 2 *oz grated Parmesan cheese;* 3 *eggs;* 2½ *pints strong bouillon.* Cooking time: 10 minutes.

Stir the bread thoroughly with the cheese and beaten eggs and season with salt, pepper and grated nutmeg. Boil up *bouillon* and whisk into bread mixture, cover, and simmer slowly for another 7-8 minutes. Do not boil. When serving stir well once more with the whisk in order to prevent lumps from forming. *(Italy).*

Minestra di Trippa alla Milanese * *Milanese Tripe Soup*

For 10 *persons:* 5½ *lb tripe;* ½ *lb celery;* ½ *lb carrots;* 1 *cabbage;* ¼ *lb parsley;* 2 *oz oil;* 1 *onion;* 1¼ *lb potatoes;* ½ *lb leeks;* 6 *oz haricot beans;* ½ *lb smoked lean bacon;* ¼ *lb skinned tomatoes;* 1 *clove garlic.* Cooking time: 3 hours for beef tripe; 2 hours for veal tripe.

Cut up the tripe into chunks, add plenty of water, bring to the boil, add the salt and continue cooking. Fry the onion in oil until golden coloured, add all the vegetables and sweat for 20 minutes. Add 5 pints water and then the cooked tripe. Boil for a few moments, serve with grated Parmesan cheese. *(Italy)*

Minestrone alla Milanese

For 8-10 *persons:* ¼ *lb fat bacon;* ¼ *lb lean bacon;* 1 *large onion;* 2 *carrots;* 1 *small turnip; the white of* 2 *leeks;* ¼ *lb white cabbage or curly kale;* 2 *potatoes;* ½ *lb fresh tomatoes;* 2 *oz shelled peas;* ¼ *lb French beans;* 1 *large clove garlic;* 2 *oz spaghetti or rice;* ¼ *lb grated cheese.* Cooking time: 1 hour.

Place diced fat bacon in a saucepan, add diced bacon and fry pale yellow with the thinly sliced onion. Thinly slice all vegetables except beans, peas and tomatoes, add to soup with 1 pinch each of basil and thyme and half a bay leaf and fry until the vegetables at the bottom of the pan start to turn yellow. Add 3½ pints water, the peeled deseeded and diced tomatoes, the peas, sliced beans and rice or broken *spaghetti*, season and cook slowly for 45 minutes. Crush garlic into soup and serve with chopped chervil sprinkled on top. Grated cheese is served separately. *(Italy)*

Mulligatawny

For 6 persons: 3½ pints brown stock; 2 oz butter; 2 oz flour; 1 tablespoon tomato purée; 2 medium-sized onions; 1 large cooking apple; ½ oz curry powder; 1 level tablespoon chutney; 1 oz boiled rice; 3 tablespoons cream; seasoning. Cooking time: 2-2½ hours.

Fry the chopped onions gently in butter, mix in curry powder, cook for a few minutes. Mix in flour to make a *roux*, blend in the tomato *purée*. Moisten with stock then add the chopped apples and chutney. Bring to the boil and skim, simmer 40 minutes, strain, season and stir in the cream. Garnish with the rice boiled separately. (*India*)

Olla Podrida * *Spanish Pot-au-Feu*

For 6 persons: ¾ lb brisket; ¾ lb shoulder of mutton; ½ lb raw ham; ½ lb bacon; 1 pig's ear; 1 pig's trotter; 1 small young chicken; 1 partridge (when in season); 2 chorizos (Spanish garlic sausage); ¼ lb carrots; the white of 3 leeks; 1 onion; ¼ lb white cabbage; 1 lettuce; 3 potatoes; ½ lb chick peas (garbanzos) which are absolutely essential; 3 cloves of garlic; 1 bouquet garni. Cooking time: 3-4 hours.

Soak the chick peas overnight, 24 hours if possible. Put all the meat in a large saucepan except the chicken and partridge with plenty of cold water. Bring to the boil, skim, add the crushed garlic, a little salt, the herbs and the chick peas and cook slowly for 2 hours. After 2 hours add the chicken, the browned partridge and the *chorizos*. Simmer for another 30 minutes and add all the vegetables, except the potatoes, cut in thick slices. The potatoes, also sliced are added after a further 25 minutes. Each piece of meat is removed when it is tender and kept warm in a little stock. Season the soup as soon as it is ready. The meat and vegetables are arranged on a large dish and the unstrained soup is served in a tureen. (*Spain*)

Oxtail Soup

For 6-8 persons: 2¼ lb oxtail; 2 onions; 2 carrots; piece turnip; 2 oz beef dripping; 2 oz flour; 1 tablespoon tomato paste; marjoram; rosemary; basil; sage; 1 small bay leaf; thyme; ¼ pint sherry; 5 pints stock. Cooking time: about 4 hours.

Cut oxtail into 2-inch pieces, blanch for 3 minutes, drain well, and brown thoroughly in the dripping together with 1 carrot and 1 onion both coarsely diced. Dust with flour, brown this lightly, and add tomato paste and stock or water and stir well. Cook the soup slowly for 3-4 hours with the seasoning and herbs. In the meantime cut the remaining carrots, the turnip and the onion in small dice and cook in butter in their own juice. Strain the soup, add the sherry and garnish with the oxtail meat cut in biggish cubes and the diced vegetables. (*Great Britain*)

Schtschi Russki * *Russian Cabbage Soup*

For 4 persons: 2 oz onions; 2 oz carrots; 2 oz leeks; 2 oz celery; 1¼ lb cabbage; 1 quart beef stock (preferably beef and pork stock); ¾ lb boiled beef; 1 bay leaf; 6 peppercorns; 1 oz stock pot fat; ¼ pint sour cream. Cooking time: 40 minutes.

Gently stew the vegetables except the cabbage in the fat. Coarsely chop and blanch the cabbage, add to the other vegetables with the bay leaf, peppercorns and salt; moisten with the stock and simmer. Cut the beef into small cubes, place in the soup bowl, add the soup and serve with the sour cream in a sauce-boat. (*Russia*)

Scotch Mutton Broth

For 6 *persons:* 1 *lb shoulder or neck of mutton;* $\frac{1}{4}$ *lb carrots;* $\frac{1}{4}$ *lb turnips;* $\frac{1}{4}$ *lb celery;* 1 *leek;* 1 *onion;* 2 *oz pearl barley;* 2 *oz dried peas; seasoning; chopped parsley.* Cooking time: 2 hours.

Soak the peas and barley overnight and place the meat and onion in about $3\frac{1}{2}$ pints water. When it boils skim, salt, add barley and parsley and cook slowly for 1 hour. Cut vegetables in small dice and add to the soup. Cook slowly until everything is cooked. Remove meat, discard bones, dice meat and replace in soup. Season, remove surplus fat and serve very hot, well peppered and sprinkled with chopped parsley. (*Great Britain*)

Straciatella alla Romana * *Consommé with Eggs*

For 3 *persons:* 2 *eggs;* 1 *tablespoon breadcrumbs;* 2 *tablespoons grated Parmesan; the zest of* 1 *lemon;* $1\frac{1}{2}$ *pints bouillon.*

Beat the ingredients. Combine this mixture with the hot *bouillon* and bring to the boil, stirring all the time. As soon as the mixture thickens the soup is ready. (*Italy*)

Vichysoisse

For 8 *persons: white of* 4 *leeks;* 2 *oz butter;* 1 *onion;* $\frac{3}{4}$ *lb potatoes;* 2 *pints chicken bouillon;* $\frac{1}{2}$ *pint fresh cream;* 1 *tablespoon chopped spring onion.* Cooking time: 40 minutes.

Melt the butter and sweat the finely chopped onion and leeks, without allowing them to brown. Add the sliced potatoes and finally the *bouillon*, season and cook slowly for 35-40 minutes. Pass through a very fine sieve, leave to get quite cold, stirring occasionally, adjust the seasoning and add the cream. Serve chilled sprinkled with chopped spring onions. (*North America*)

Waterzooi de Poulet à la Gantoise * *Chicken Soup*

1 *tender chicken or cockerel weighing about* 2 *lb;* 2 *leeks;* 2 *carrots;* 1 *small onion;* 2 *sticks celery;* 1 *small bay leaf;* 1 *sprig thyme;* 6 *peppercorns;* 1 *small clove garlic;* 3 *potatoes;* 2 *oz butter;* 2 *oz flour;* $2\frac{1}{2}$-3 *pints water.* Cooking time: 1 hour.

Put the drawn and washed chicken and giblets in water, bring to the boil and skim well. Add a carrot, the green part of the leeks, the onion, bay leaf, thyme, peppercorns and a little salt and cook slowly. Cut the remaining vegetables into *julienne* and cook in 1 oz butter and a little water. When the chicken is cooked make a white *roux* of the remaining butter and the flour, pour on the strained chicken stock and cook slowly, season well and strain; if the soup is too thick add a little stock. Skin and cut up the chicken, place it with the *julienne* and 3 freshly boiled potatoes (quartered lengthwise) in the soup tureen and pour the soup on top. (*Belgium*)

Zuppa alla Pavese * *Consommé with Egg and Bread*

For 1 *person.*

Fry a slice of bread in oil or buttter, place in ovenproof soup bowl, break a raw egg over the bread, season and sprinkle with Parmesan. Add a ladleful of good *Consommé*, place in a hot oven, 425° F or Gas Mark 7, until the egg is set, then serve. (*Italy*)

There are hundreds of ways of preparing eggs and one could easily serve egg dishes for a whole year without once repeating oneself. It is essential to success that eggs should be as fresh as possible and cooked with due regard for their delicate flavour, texture and great sensitivity to heat.

Eggs are very valuable in cookery because of their versatility. They are used to thicken soups and sauces, to bind ingredients together, as a means of incorporating air into mixtures and to coat food for frying. They are also served on their own and cooked in a great variety of ways all of which are explained in the recipe section. Egg dishes are usually quick to prepare and are invaluable when time is short or unexpected guests arrive. In addition to all these virtues eggs are economical and nutritious as they are rich in valuable protein, vitamins, fat and mineral salts.

The types of eggs eaten include hen, duck, goose, plover, quail, turkey, etc.

The relative freshness of an egg may be determined by placing the eggs in a large bowl of cold water, the ones that float are unusable. Another test is to break the eggs on to a plate; the truly fresh egg has a high rounded yolk and a thick translucent white which keeps its shape round the yolk.

To whisk egg whites always use whites that are at least 24 hours old otherwise they will be difficult to whip. Other essentials to success are that all utensils to be used should be absolutely free of any grease and are cold; also there should be no speck of yolk in with the whites. If there is, remove it with a piece of shell. An unlined copper bowl and thin balloon whisk are the perfect utensils for whisking egg whites. To test if the egg whites are really stiff, the mixture should stand in a stiff snowy peak at the end of the whisk when it is lifted out of the bowl. Use whisked egg whites immediately, for if they are left to stand they soon lose bulk. The incorporation of whisked egg whites into other mixtures must be done very carefully. Always add the whisked egg whites to the other mixture, for example, a sauce for *soufflé*, because this is usually heavier. Then using a large cold metal spoon or spatula fold the egg whites quickly and firmly through the mixture, turning the bowl with the free hand. Take care that this cutting and folding action is not overdone or the egg whites will lose their bulk.

An egg will cook and set at a temperature much lower than boiling point, therefore sauces, soups, or other mixtures to which eggs have been added should be cooked slowly and kept below boiling point. If too high a temperature is reached, the egg sets quickly and unevenly in small hard lumps, and a curdled appearance results.

When using several eggs it is wiser to break them separately into a basin otherwise one stale one may spoil the rest. It is a good idea to plunge hardboiled eggs into cold water as soon as they are cooked to prevent a dark ring forming at the junction of the white and yolk.

Eggs should be stored pointed end down in a cool place away from strong smelling foods as these can taint the eggs. They may be stored in a refrigerator but remember to take them out and allow to reach room temperature some time before using them.

HOT EGG DISHES

LES ŒUFS POCHÉS * *POACHED EGGS*

To ensure poached eggs are a good shape they must be perfectly fresh. Put an appropriate amount of water in a flat casserole (*sautoir*) and add ⅓ oz salt and 1 tablespoon vinegar per 4 pints water. As soon as the water boils, break one egg after another into it. Not too many eggs should be poached at a time since they should not be allowed to touch. As soon as the water boils again the pan should be drawn aside sufficiently to keep it at boiling point without bubbling. Poaching takes 3 minutes, the time required for the white to become hard enough to surround the soft yolk. Only when the eggs are to be used for cold dishes, are they poached for 4 minutes. When they are ready they should be removed from the hot water immediately and placed in cold, slightly salted water to prevent them from cooking further. They can therefore be prepared in advance and need only be placed in hot, not boiling, water to heat them up again.

▣ à l'Anglaise

For 4 persons: 8 eggs; 8 croûtons; 1 oz grated cheese; 2 oz butter.

Place poached eggs on *croûtons* and arrange in a baking dish. Sprinkle a little grated cheese on each egg, pour melted butter on top and put in a hot oven or under the grill for 2 minutes. Serve with a bunch of watercress in the centre.

▣ Archiduc

For 4 persons: 8 eggs; 8 fried croûtons; 1 small truffle; ½ lb chicken livers; ½ pint sauce Hongroise; brandy.

Sauté the chicken livers and sliced truffle, add brandy and reduce. Pile this mixture on the *croûtons*, place the egg on top and coat with the sauce.

▣ Argenteuil

For 4 persons: 8 eggs; 8 tartlet cases; 32 white asparagus tips; ½ pint sauce Crème; ¼ pint white asparagus purée.

Pile the tartlets with the asparagus tips, place the poached egg on top, then coat with *sauce Crème* mixed with asparagus *purée*.

▣ à l'Aurore

For 4 persons: 8 eggs; 8 croûtons; ½ pint sauce Aurore; sieved hardboiled egg yolk.

Arrange poached eggs on fried *croûtons*, coat with the sauce and sprinkle the chopped egg yolk on top. (*See illustration p.* 288).

▣ au Bacon

For each person: 2 eggs; 2 slices bacon. Cooking time: 3 minutes.

Drain the eggs well on a cloth and serve on thin slices of well grilled bacon. Pour bacon fat or melted butter on top.

Œufs Pochés à la Beaugency

For 4 persons: 8 *eggs;* 8 *artichoke bottoms;* ½ *pint sauce Béarnaise;* 8 *slices of poached ox or beef marrow.*

Heat large artichoke bottoms in butter, place an egg on each, coat lightly with *Béarnaise*, and place a slice of marrow on each. (*See illustration p.* 284).

▣ Bonvalet

For 4 *persons:* 8 *eggs;* 8 *round croûtons, hollowed out and fried in butter;* ½ *pint chicken Velouté;* ¼ *pint sauce Béarnaise with tomato;* 8 *slices truffle.*

Place the poached eggs in the hollow of the *croûtons*, coat with the chicken *Velouté*. Surround with a ring of *Béarnaise* and decorate with truffle slices.

▣ à la Bourguignonne

For 4 *persons:* 8 *eggs;* 1 *pint red wine;* ¼ *lb mushrooms;* 8 *croûtons;* 1 *oz butter;* 1 *teaspoon flour;* 1 *teaspoon chopped shallot.*

Reduce wine by half together with shallots and thyme. Strain, remove from heat and thicken with the flour which has been kneaded with half the butter, stirring with a whisk till smooth. Add the poached sliced mushrooms, boil up once and add the remainder of the butter. Place the eggs on the fried *croûtons* and cover with the sauce.

▣ Budapest

For 6 *persons:* 6 *eggs;* ¾ *lb boiled spinach;* ½ *pint sauce Vin Blanc;* ¼ *pint Demi-glace mixed with a little purée;* 6 *large mushroom caps;* 1 *oz butter;* 1 *oz grated cheese; paprika.*

Drain and dry spinach well, toss in butter and season with salt, pepper and nutmeg. Place spinach in a buttered baking dish, and arrange the poached eggs in a ring on top. Coat eggs with rather thick *sauce Vin Blanc* seasoned with paprika. Place mushrooms in the centre of the ring, and cover with *Demi-glace*. Sprinkle eggs and mushrooms with grated cheese. Pour a little melted butter on top, and brown in a hot oven. (*See illustration p.* 286).

▣ Cardinal

For 4 *persons:* 8 *poached eggs;* 8 *croûtons;* ½ *pint sauce Cardinal;* 8 *truffle slices;* 8 *thin lobster slices.*

Place eggs on *croûtons*, with a slice of lobster on top, coat with *sauce Cardinal* and garnish with a small round truffle slice.

▣ à la Chantilly

For 4 *persons:* 8 *eggs;* 1 *lb freshly cooked green peas;* 8 *baked tartlet cases;* 1 *oz butter;* ½ *pint sauce Mousseline.*

Pass the peas through a sieve, mix with butter and season well. Place *purée* in the hot tartlet cases, put a poached egg in each and coat with *sauce Mousseline.*

Oeufs Pochés à la Chartres

For 4 persons: 8 eggs; 8 fried croûtons; ½ pint thickened Veal Gravy, flavoured with tarragon; blanched tarragon leaves.

Place the eggs on the *croûtons,* coat with the gravy and decorate with 2 crossed blanched tarragon leaves.

▣ Chasseur

For 4 persons: 8 eggs; 8 baked tartlet cases; ½ lb chicken livers; ½ pint sauce Chasseur; chopped parsley.

Sauté the livers in butter to cook them completely. Fill the tartlets with sliced chicken livers. Place the eggs on top and coat with sauce. Sprinkle with chopped parsley.

▣ Comtesse

For 4 persons: 8 eggs; 8 baked tartlet cases; ¾ lb asparagus purée; ½ pine sauce Allemande; chopped truffle.

Fill the tartlets with asparagus *purée.* Place the eggs on top and coat with *sauce Allemande,* sprinkle with chopped truffle.

▣ Daumont

For 4 persons: 8 eggs; 8 baked tartlet cases; 6 oz poultry meat; ⅛ pint chicken Velouté; 1 tablespoon cream; ½ pint sauce Nantua; 8 truffle slices.

Make a *purée* with the poultry meat and bind with the *Velouté* and cream then heat and season. Fill tartlet cases with this *purée,* place an egg in each, coat with *sauce Nantua* and put a truffle slice on top.

▣ à la Florentine

For 4 persons: 8 eggs; 1 lb spinach; 1 pint sauce Mornay; 1 oz grated cheese; 2 oz butter; seasoning.

Cook young leaf spinach, cool, squeeze out moisture, simmer in butter, season with salt, pepper and grated nutmeg and place in the bottom of a baking dish. Place the drained eggs on it, coat evenly with the *sauce Mornay,* sprinkle with grated cheese and melted butter and brown in very hot oven, 425° F, or Gas Mark 7.

▣ Grand-Duc

For 4 persons: 8 eggs; 8 Puff pastry tartlets; 6 oz asparagus; ½ pint sauce Mornay; 8 small truffle slices; 1 oz butter.

Chop asparagus tips, boil, drain and toss in butter. Then divide between the tartlet cases, place a poached egg on top of each, then a truffle slice, coat with *sauce Mornay* and glaze quickly in a very hot oven.

Oeufs Pochés à la Hollandaise

For 4 persons: 8 eggs; 8 baked Puff pastry tartlets; ½ lb boiled salmon; 2 tablespoons cream; ½ pint sauce Hollandaise.

Make salmon into a *purée*, mix with the cream and a little *sauce Hollandaise* and season well. Fill tartlets with the *purée*, place an egg in each and pour a little *Hollandaise* over each.

▣ à la Hussarde

For 4 persons: 8 eggs; 8 half tomatoes, deseeded and grilled; 2 chopped onions sautéed in butter; ¼ lb diced ham; ⅛ pint Demi-glace; ½ pint Velouté well seasoned with cayenne pepper.

Bind the onions and ham with the *Demi-glace* and place in the bottom of the tomato halves. Place the eggs on top and coat with *Velouté*.

▣ à l'Indienne

For 4 persons: 8 eggs; ¼ lb rice; ½ pint Curry sauce.

Boil the rice in plenty of salt water until it is soft. This will take about 17 minutes. Drain, rinse with boiling water and dry in a cool oven. Arrange eggs in a ring on a round dish, coat with sauce and serve rice in a heap in the centre.

▣ à la Joinville

For 4 persons: 8 poached eggs; 8 croûtons; ½ pint sauce Nantua; 8 prawns.

Placed poached eggs on *croûtons*, coat with sauce and decorate each with one prawn or two shrimp tails. (*See illustration p.* 286).

▣ à la Massena

For 4 persons: 8 eggs; 8 cooked artichoke bottoms; ¼ pint sauce Béarnaise; ½ pint sauce Tomate; 8 slices of poached ox or beef marrow.

Heat artichoke bottoms and cover with a very little *sauce Béarnaise* and place a poached egg on each. Coat with thick Tomato sauce, place a slice of ox or beef marrow on top and sprinkle with a pinch of chopped parsley.

▣ Mignon

For 4 persons: 8 eggs; 8 cooked artichoke bottoms; ½ lb peas; 16 shrimp tails; 2 oz butter; ½ pint sauce Nantua; 8 truffle slices.

Heat the peas and shrimps with butter and place them in the artichoke bottoms. Place the eggs on top and coat with Shrimp sauce. Place a truffle slice on each egg.

Oeufs Pochés à la Miss Helyett

For 4 persons: 8 eggs; 8 tomatoes; 16 boiled, peeled shrimps; ¼ lb sliced, cooked mushrooms; ½ pint sauce Nantua; 8 truffle slices.

Hollow out the tomatoes, season them and brush with melted butter; cook them in a hot oven, 400° F or Gas Mark 6. Drain the tomatoes and fill with the shrimps and mushrooms bound with a little *sauce Nantua*. Place an egg on each tomato and coat with the remainder of the sauce. Place a truffle slice on each egg.

▣ à la Monseigneur

For 4 persons: 8 eggs; ½ lb cooked fish; 8 baked Short pastry tartlet cases; ½ pint Béchamel; 1 oz butter.

Make a *purée* of fish leftovers such as cod, haddock, whiting, bind with a little *Béchamel* and butter and season well. Distribute *purée* among tartlets, place a poached egg in each and coat with slightly buttered, well-seasoned *Béchamel*.

▣ à la Mornay

For 4 persons: 8 eggs; 8 round croûtons; ½ pint Béchamel; 2 oz grated cheese; 1 tablespoon white breadcrumbs; 1 oz butter.

Place the well-drained eggs on *croûtons* fried in butter. Coat with the well-seasoned *Béchamel* which has been mixed with a little of the cheese, sprinkle breadcrumbs and cheese on top, dot with butter and brown quickly either in a very hot oven or under the grill.

▣ à la Nantua

For 4 persons: 8 eggs; 8 croûtons; ½ pint sauce Nantua; 8 small crayfish tails or 8 crayfish claws.

Place eggs on *croûtons*, coat with sauce, and place crayfish tail or claw on top.

▣ à l'Orientale

For 8 persons: 8 eggs; 8 artichoke bottoms; 6 oz minced cooked chicken; ½ pint sauce Suprême; ¼ pint sauce Crème mixed with a little curry powder; 1 tablespoon tomato purée; 2 fillets of sole; ¼ poached red pepper; 4 slices truffle; 1 green pepper.

Heat the artichoke bottoms in butter and fill with the minced chicken meat bound together with 2 tablespoons *sauce Suprême*. Arrange the artichoke bottoms in a dish and place a poached egg on top of each. Coat 3 of the eggs with curry sauce and the other 3 with the *sauce Suprême* which has been mixed with the tomato *purée*. Decorate the curried eggs with small round pieces of red pepper and the other eggs with a round of truffle. Garnish the centre with fillets of sole and the green pepper, cut in strips, rolled in flour and deep fried in very hot fat. (*See illustration p.* 285).

▣ à la Périgourdine

For 4 persons: 8 eggs; 8 croûtons; sauce Périgourdine; 8 truffle slices.

Place eggs on *croûtons*, cover with Truffle sauce and place a thin truffle slice on each egg. (*See illustration p.* 285).

Oeufs Pochés à la Phileas Gilbert

For 4 persons: 8 eggs; 8 large croûtons; ½ pint sauce Suprême; ¼ pint sauce Béarnaise.

Place eggs on *croûtons* and coat lightly with *sauce Suprême.* Using a forcing bag and fluted tube, pipe a circle of *Béarnaise* around each egg on the *croûton.*

▣ à la Polonaise

For 4 persons: 8 eggs; ½ lb minced lamb; ½ pint Demi-glace; 2 oz butter; 1 tablespoon white breadcrumbs.

Mince leftover mutton and bind with a little *Demi-glace.* Place mince in a baking dish, arrange eggs on it, and coat lightly with *Demi-glace.* Brown the breadcrumbs in butter and pour over eggs.

▣ à la Régina

For 4 persons: 8 eggs; 8 baked tartlet cases; ½ lb salpicon of poached fillet of sole; shrimp tails and mushrooms; ⅛ pint sauce Nantua; ½ pint sauce Normande; 1 oz truffle cut in julienne.

Bind the sole *salpicon*, shrimps and mushrooms with the *sauce Nantua* and fill the tartlets with it. Place the eggs, coated with *sauce Normande* on top. Sprinkle the truffle *julienne* over the eggs.

▣ à la Reine

For 4 persons: 8 eggs; 8 baked Puff pastry tartlet cases; 6 oz chicken; ½ pint sauce Suprême; 1 tablespoon cream.

Purée or mince boiled or roast poultry leftovers, bind with a little *sauce Suprême* or cream and fill tartlets with mixture. Place a poached egg in each tartlet, coat with sauce and sprinkle a little chopped truffle on top. (*See illustration p.* 287).

▣ à la Rossini

For 4 persons: 8 eggs; 8 baked Puff pastry tartlets; 8 very small slices foie gras; ½ pint sauce Madère; 8 thin truffle slices.

Heat *foie gras* gently in a little butter and place in the tartlets and place egg on top. Coat with *sauce Madère* and put a truffle slice on each egg.

▣ à la Saint-Hubert

For 4 persons: 8 eggs; 8 fried, heart-shaped croûtons; 6 oz game; ½ pint sauce Poivrade.

Mince the roast game, bind with a little sauce and place in a baking dish. Arrange eggs on top, coat with remaining sauce and garnish with heart-shaped *croutons.*

▣ à la Villeroi

For 4 persons: 8 eggs; ½ pint sauce Villeroi; ½ lb very fine breadcrumbs; ½ pint sauce Tomate.

Coat the eggs completely with *sauce Villeroi* and allow to set slightly. Breadcrumb them, fry them in deep fat for 2-3 minutes and drain. Serve with fried parsley and *sauce Tomate* separately.

LES ŒUFS MOLLETS * *MEDIUM BOILED EGGS*

All the recipes for poached eggs can also be made using medium boiled eggs.

LES ŒUFS MOULÉS * *MOULDED EGGS*

Moulded eggs are another variation of poached eggs. They are cooked in small moulds and turned out before serving. Special poached egg moulds, *baba* moulds or *cocottes* are used, which must be very thickly lined with soft, but not liquid butter. After buttering, chopped ham, truffles, tongue or herbs may be sprinkled in the mould before the egg is broken into it. The moulds are placed in a water-bath and cooked gently for 2-3 minutes before being put in the oven to finish cooking without boiling. They take 8-10 minutes to cook. Here too the yolk must remain soft and the white must be only just hard enough to make it possible to turn the eggs out of the moulds. They are best left to stand for 1-2 minutes so they leave the mould more easily. If necessary, run the tip of a knife round the edge of the mould before turning out. Another way of making these eggs is to mix lightly scrambled eggs with raw beaten egg, put in buttered moulds and poach until the outside has set but the inside is still soft.

▣ à la Napolitaine

For 4 *persons:* 7 *eggs;* 5 *oz grated Parmesan;* ½ *pint Demi-glace flavoured with tomato.*

Very lightly scramble 5 eggs with 3 oz of the Parmesan; remove from heat and add the two raw eggs. Place the mixture in well-buttered, fluted *brioche* moulds. Complete the cooking by putting the moulds in a water-bath. You could use a *sauté* pan with a little water in it. The water should never boil or the eggs will become tough and hard. Turn out on a buttered ovenproof dish. Sprinkle the rest of the Parmesan on top, coat with the sauce and glaze in a very hot oven, 425° F or Gas Mark 7, or under the grill.

▣ à la Ninette

For 4 *persons:* 7 *eggs;* 6 *croûtons;* ¼ *lb butter and* 2 *egg yolks for sauce Mousseline;* 2 *oz shrimp tails.* Cooking time in water-bath: 4-5 minutes.

Make lightly scrambled eggs with 6 eggs and the shrimp tails. Remove from heat and combine with beaten raw eggs. Fill into well-buttered moulds, poach very gently in water-bath and make sure that the egg remains soft. Turn out on *croûtons* and coat with *sauce Mousseline.*

▣ Pain Moulés à la Fermière

For 4 *persons:* 1 *lb cream cheese;* ¼ *lb butter;* ¼ *lb boiled ham;* ¼ *pint cream;* 10 *eggs;* 1 *pint sauce Crème.* Cooking time: 30 minutes.

Squeeze cream cheese out well in a cloth, place in a bowl and stir very thoroughly to make it smooth. Combine with the soft butter, the ham cut in tiny dice and the whole eggs; gradually add the cream and season. Place mixture in a well-buttered mould and poach in a moderate oven in a water-bath. Before turning out leave to stand for a little while and coat with the *sauce Crème.*

LES ŒUFS BROUILLÉS * *SCRAMBLED EGGS*

For 8 eggs: Put 1 oz butter in a bowl and place this in a water-bath of boiling water. When the butter has melted, break the eggs in the bowl, season and add about 3 tablespoons double cream. Stir briskly with a whisk or wooden spoon until the mixture coheres but is still soft and creamy. Good scrambled eggs should not be hard, if however, this does happen remove the pan from heat and stir in 1-2 egg yolks and a little butter.

▣ aux Champignons * *with Mushrooms*

For 4 persons: 8 eggs; ¼ lb mushrooms; 1 oz butter; 2 fl oz cream.
Cooking time: 8-10 minutes.

Clean and wash mushrooms thoroughly, slice thinly, fry light brown in the butter and mix with the scrambled eggs.

▣ à la Chasseur

For 4 persons: 8 eggs; 2 fl oz cream; ¼ lb chicken livers; 2 oz mushrooms; 2 oz butter.

Dice mushrooms and livers coarsely. First brown mushrooms in the butter, then add livers and fry till cooked. Season, arrange in centre of scrambled eggs and sprinkle chopped parsley on top.

▣ à la Clamart

For 4 persons: 8 eggs; ¼ lb peas prepared à la Française; 2 fl oz cream; ¼ pint sauce Crème.

Add the peas and cream to the scrambled eggs, serve surrounded with *sauce Crème*.

▣ aux Crevettes * *with Shrimps*

For 4 persons: 8 eggs; 3 oz shrimp tails; 2 oz butter.

Sauté shrimp tails in butter and serve mixed with scrambled eggs.

▣ aux Croûtons

For 4 persons: 8 eggs; 3 slices white bread cut in small cubes; 2 oz butter.

Fry cubed bread in the butter till brown and crisp and mix with scrambled eggs at last moment.

▣ aux Ecrevisses * *with Crayfish*

Cut crayfish tails in pieces, toss briefly in butter and mix with scrambled eggs. A little Crayfish sauce may be poured round if desired.

▣ aux Fonds d'Artichauts * *with Artichoke Bottoms*

For 4 persons: 8 eggs; 2 large, chopped, cooked artichoke bottoms; 1 oz butter.

Cut artichoke bottoms in small dice, toss in the butter, season and mix with the scrambled eggs.

Œufs Brouillés à la Forestière

For 4 persons: 8 eggs; 2 oz butter; 2 oz diced bacon; ¼ lb morels or mushrooms.

Blanch diced bacon, fry and mix with scrambled eggs. Peel and wash mushrooms thoroughly, drain, cut in pieces, *sauté* in the butter and serve in the middle of the scrambled eggs. Sprinkle chopped parsley on top.

▣ au Fromage * *with Cheese*

For 4 persons: 8 eggs; 2 oz grated gruyère cheese.

Make the scrambled eggs in the usual way and fold in the cheese.

▣ à la Georgette

For 4 persons: 8 eggs; 3 oz crayfish tails; 4 fairly large potatoes of regular, round shape. Cooking time of potatoes: 40-50 minutes.

Bake potatoes in the oven. When they are cooked cut off a lid, scoop out, mash part of scooped-out potato with butter, season and replace. Make scrambled eggs and add crayfish tails and fill up remaining space in potatoes with them.

▣ à la Marivaux

For 4 persons: 8 eggs; 1 oz chopped truffle; 3 oz mushrooms; meat glaze; 1½ oz butter.

Cook the mushrooms in butter. Mix the truffles with the scrambled eggs and place in a dish. Garnish with the mushrooms. Surround with a ring of meat glaze.

▣ à la Montpensier

For 4 persons: 5-6 eggs; 2 tablespoons peeled, deseeded, diced tomatoes, cooked in butter; ½ lb calf's kidney; 2 oz butter; 2 fl oz sauce Madère.

Mix eggs with the diced tomatoes and arrange in a deep dish. Slice kidney thinly and fry quickly in butter; it should still be rosy. Bind with *sauce Madère* and pile in the middle of the scrambled eggs.

▣ à la Normande

For 4 persons: 8 eggs; 8 poached oysters; ½ pint sauce Normande.

Place the scrambled eggs in a dish. Garnish with the oysters, bound with *sauce Normande.*

▣ aux Pointes d'Asperges * *with Asparagus Tips*

For 4 persons: 8 eggs; ½ lb asparagus tips; 2 oz butter.

Cut asparagus tips in small pieces, boil, toss in butter and season. Serve up scrambled eggs with the asparagus tips arranged in the centre.

Œufs Brouillés à la Portugaise

For 4 persons: 8 eggs; ½ lb tomatoes; 1 oz butter; 1 tablespoon oil.

Peel, deseed and dice tomatoes and simmer in the oil with the butter until they are fairly dry. Mix scrambled eggs with two-thirds of tomatoes, serve, place remainder of tomatoes in centre and sprinkle chopped parsley on top.

⊡ Reine Margot

For 4 persons: 8 eggs; 1½ oz Almond butter; 8 baked tartlet cases; ¼ pint Béchamel completed with Pistachio butter.

Mix the Almond butter with the scrambled eggs and fill the tartlet cases. Surround with a ring of *Béchamel* with Pistachio butter.

⊡ aux Truffes * *with Truffles*

For 4 persons: 8 eggs; 4 slices truffle; chopped truffle; 1 oz butter.

Mix the finely diced truffle, except for the slices, with the scrambled eggs, place truffle slices on top and glaze with a little melted butter.

⊡ Yvette

For 4 persons: 8 eggs; ¼ lb asparagus tips; 3 oz crayfish tails; 8 small, Puff pastry vol-au-vent cases; 8 truffle slices.

Dice the asparagus tips and crayfish tails and mix them with the eggs. Place the scrambled eggs in the *vol-au-vent* cases with a truffle slice on each.

LES ŒUFS SUR LE PLAT * *FRENCH FRIED EGGS*

There are special dishes for making *œufs sur le plat.* They are usually small shallow copper pans with handles or small shallow fire-proof dishes with ears. First melt a little butter in the dish, heat it and break in the eggs. Then put the dish immediately into a hot oven, 400° F or Gas Mark 6, for 4-5 minutes until the eggs are just set. When serving sprinkle a little salt and pepper on the egg whites and a little melted butter on the yolks.

⊡ aux Anchois * *with Anchovy*

For 4 persons: 8 eggs; 12 anchovy fillets; 2 oz butter.

Melt the butter in the egg dishes, dice anchovy fillets and sprinkle on the bottom of the dish. Break eggs into the dishes, season lightly and cook in a hot oven, 400° F or Gas Mark 6, for 4-5 minutes until the eggs are just set.

⊡ au Bacon * *with Bacon*

For 4 persons: 8 eggs; 8 rashers bacon; 1 oz butter.

Fry bacon rashers, and place in the bottom of a buttered egg dish, add the eggs and cook in a hot oven.

Oeufs sur le Plat à la Bercy

8 *eggs;* 8 *chipolata sausages;* 1 *oz butter;* ¼ *pint sauce Tomate.* Cooking time of sausages: 4-5 minutes.

Cook eggs *sur le plat* and garnish with the fried sausages. Pour *sauce Tomate* round them in a ring.

◘ au Beurre Noir * *with Black Butter*

For 4 *persons:* 8 *eggs;* 2 *oz butter; vinegar.*

Cook the eggs *sur le plat.* Meanwhile heat some butter and allow it to become brown. Then add a dash of vinegar and pour over the eggs.

◘ à la Chartres

For 4 *persons:* 8 *eggs;* 3 *oz Veal gravy; pinch chopped tarragon;* 2 *blanched tarragon leaves.*

Pour the Veal gravy into the bottom of a baking dish together with the chopped tarragon. Place the eggs on top and cook in a hot oven for 4-5 minutes. Garnish the egg yolks with 2 crossed tarragon leaves.

◘ à la Forestière * *with Cooked Ham*

For 4 *persons:* 8 *eggs;* 3 *oz morels;* 2 *oz streaky bacon;* 2 *oz butter.*

Dice the blanched bacon and slice the morels. Cook them slowly in butter and garnish the bottom of a buttered fire-proof dish with them. Break the eggs on top and cook first of all on top of the cooker and then in a hot oven.

◘ au Jambon

For 4 *persons:* 8 *eggs;* 2 *oz butter;* 4 *small slices ham.*

Fry ham for 2-3 minutes, place in egg dish and then proceed as for *Oeufs sur le Plat.*

◘ Jockey-Club

For 4 *persons:* 8 *eggs;* 8 *slices of toast;* 3 *oz foie gras purée;* ½ *lb calf's kidney; half a truffle, diced;* ¼ *pint Demi-glace.*

Cook the eggs *sur le plat,* cut them out with a round cutter and place them on toast spread with *foie gras purée.* Arrange in a ring. *Sauté* the sliced kidney and diced truffle in butter, bind with *Demi-glace* and place in the middle of the ring.

◘ à la Meyerbeer

For 4 *persons:* 8 *eggs;* 4 *lambs' kidneys;* 2 *oz butter;* ¼ *pint sauce Périgueux.* Cooking time of kidneys: 5-10 minutes.

Skin the kidneys, halve and grill them. Garnish the eggs cooked *sur le plat* with the kidneys and pour a little Truffle sauce round them.

Œufs sur le Plat à la Mirabeau

For 4 persons: 8 *eggs;* 1 *oz Anchovy butter;* 8 *anchovy fillets in oil, which have been soaked in water;* 8 *stoned olives; tarragon leaves.* Cooking time: 2-3 minutes.

Butter egg dish with the Anchovy butter, break in eggs and cook *sur le plat.* Do not add salt. When serving place an anchovy fillet round each egg yolk and decorate with 2 blanched crossed tarragon leaves. Garnish with the blanched olives.

⊡ à la Mireille

For 4 persons: 8 *eggs;* ¼ *lb poultry livers;* 4 *small tomatoes;* 2 *oz butter;* ¼ *pint sauce Périgueux.* Cooking time of livers: 4-7 minutes.

Coarsely dice the livers and *sauté* them. Halve and grill the tomatoes. Cook the eggs *sur le plat* and garnish with the tomatoes. Place a small spoonful of liver on each and coat thinly with *sauce Périgueux.*

⊡ à la Mistral

For 4 persons: 8 *eggs;* 2 *tomatoes;* 4 *stoned olives;* 2 *oz butter.*

Halve and cook the tomatoes in butter. Cook the eggs *sur le plat* and garnish with tomato chopped with an olive.

⊡ à la Montmorency

For 4 persons: 8 *eggs;* ½ *lb asparagus;* 1 *bunch of asparagus tips;* 4 *sliced artichoke bottoms sautéed in butter;* 2 *fl oz thick cream;* 2 *oz butter.*

Garnish the bottom of the dish with the asparagus, bound with the cream and the butter. Break the eggs on top and cook *sur le plat.* Garnish with sliced artichokes and the asparagus tips glazed with butter.

⊡ à la Nantua

For 4 persons: 8 *eggs;* 6 *oz salpicon of crayfish tails;* 16 *crayfish tails;* 8 *truffle slices;* 2 *fl oz sauce Nantua;* 1 *oz butter.*

Butter the bottom of a dish and place the *salpicon* on it. Break the eggs on top and cook *sur le plat.* Garnish with the crayfish tails. Place a truffle slice on each egg yolk. Surround with a ring of *sauce Nantua.*

⊡ à la Portugaise

For 4 persons: 8 *eggs;* ½ *lb diced tomatoes;* 2 *oz butter;* ¼ *pint sauce Tomate.*

Cook the eggs and cook the tomatoes in butter. Garnish the dish with tomatoes, sprinkle with chopped parsley and surround with a ring of *sauce Tomate.*

⊡ à la Savoyarde

For 4 persons: 8 *eggs;* ½ *lb potatoes;* ¼ *lb butter;* 2 *oz grated cheese;* 2 *fl oz cream.*

Cut the potatoes into thin, round slices, *sauté* them and line the bottom of the dish with them. Break the eggs on top and sprinkle with the cheese. Pour cream on top and cook *sur le plat.*

Œufs sur le Plat à la Victoria

For 4 persons: 8 eggs; 6 oz lobster and truffle salpicon; ½ pint sauce Homard; 1 oz butter.

Cook the eggs. Garnish with the *salpicon* bound with half the *sauce Homard.* Surround with a ring of the remaining sauce.

LES ŒUFS EN COCOTTE * *EGGS IN A COCOTTE*

These eggs are simply a variation of poached eggs, except that they are placed in a small butter dish, known as a *cocotte*, of fire-proof china or earthenware, and poached in cream, *bouillon* or other liquid. Heat the poaching liquid, allowing 1 tablespoon for each egg and pour into the heated *cocotte*, break in the egg and put the *cocotte* in a water-bath allowing the water to come half-way up each *cocotte*. Heat for 2-3 minutes with the water at simmering point. Cover and complete the cooking in a moderate oven, 375° F or Gas Mark 5. The total cooking time should take about 8 minutes. The white should be set while the yolk is still soft. Each *cocotte* is wiped dry and served on a napkin. The water-bath may consist of a *sauté* pan with a lid or a roasting tin covered with a baking sheet.

▣ à la Bergère

For 6 persons: 6 eggs; 2 oz finely minced, cooked lamb; 2 oz finely minced mushrooms; 2 oz butter; 2 tablespoons Demi-glace; 2 tablespoons meat glaze. Cooking time: 6-8 minutes.

Cook the mushrooms in butter then add the lamb and bind with *Demi-glace*. Butter the *cocottes* and place a little of the meat mixture in the bottom of each. Break an egg into the middle and poach carefully in a water-bath for 3 minutes. Cover and complete the cooking in a moderate oven, 375° F or Gas Mark 5. The total cooking time should take about 8 minutes. The white should be set while the yolk is still soft. Serve with a little melted meat glaze over the top.

▣ au Chambertin

For 4 persons: 8 eggs; ½ pint Chambertin.

Garnish the bottoms of the *cocotte* with boiling Chambertin, break the eggs into the middle and cook for 2 minutes in a water-bath. Cook 3 minutes in a hot oven, 400° F Gas Mark 6, to glaze them.

▣ à la Colbert

For 6 persons: 6 eggs; 4 oz Fine forcemeat mixed with a few chopped herbs; 2 oz beurre Colbert. Cooking time: 6-8 minutes.

Butter the *cocottes* and line with forcemeat. Break the eggs into the middle, poach 3 minutes in a water-bath on top of the cooker, then complete the cooking in the oven. Pour a little *beurre Colbert* over the egg yolk and serve each *cocotte* on a napkin.

▲ Œufs Mollets Casino, p. 302

A selection of Cold Hardboiled Eggs, pp. 300-301 ▼

▲ Œufs Mollets en Gelée au Jambon de Parme, p. 302

Œufs Pochés en Gelée à la Colinette, p. 303 ▼

▲ Œufs Pochés à la Tartare, p. 305

Œufs Pochés Carmen, p. 303 ▼

▲ Œufs Pochés en Gelée à la Jeannette, p. 303

Œufs Pochés à la Beaugency, p. 269 ▼

▲ *Œufs Pochés à l'Orientale, p. 272*

Œufs Pochés à la Périgourdine, p. 272 ▼

▲ *Œufs Pochés Budapest, p. 269*

Œufs Pochés à la Joinville, p. 271 ▼

▲ *Omelette à l'Arlésienne*, p. 292

Œufs Pochés à la Reine, p. 273 ▼

▲ *Œufs Pochés à l'Aurore, p. 268*

Omelette Chasseur, p. 293 ▼

Oeufs en Cocotte à la Crème * *with Cream*

For 6 persons: 6 eggs; ¼ pint cream; 2 oz butter.

Butter the *cocottes*, warm the cream and pour a little in each *cocotte*. Break eggs on top, season lightly and proceed as for basic recipe.

▣ à la Diane

For 6 persons: 6 eggs; 6 oz minced cooked game; 2 fl oz Game sauce; 6 truffle slices; 2 oz butter. Cooking time: 6-8 minutes.

Line the buttered *cocottes* with minced game; pour a little sauce on top. Break the eggs into the middle and cook 3 minutes in a water-bath. Cover and finish cooking in the oven. Place a truffle slice in the middle and serve on a napkin-lined dish.

▣ à la Florentine

For 6 persons: 6 eggs; 4-6 oz spinach; 1 oz butter; ¼ pint cream; 1 oz grated cheese. Cooking time: 6-7 minutes.

Sauté the spinach in butter, then line the *cocottes* thinly with this mixture, break an egg in the centre and start to poach slowly. When the bottom has started to set top with a little cream, sprinkle with grated cheese and brown in a hot oven, 400° F or Gas Mark 6, for 3-4 minutes.

▣ à la Parisienne

For 6 persons: 6 eggs; 3 oz Fine forcemeat; 1 oz tongue; 1 oz chopped truffles or mushrooms; ¼ pint sauce Demi-glace. Cooking time: 7-8 minutes.

Mix together the forcemeat and very finely chopped tongue and truffles. Line the bottom and sides of buttered *cocottes* with this mixture. Break the eggs in the centre and poach in the water-bath for 3 minutes. Place in a hot oven for the remaining cooking time. Serve with a ring of *Demi-glace* on top of each *cocotte*. Eggs surrounded by forcemeat or mince take a little longer to poach since the heat penetrates more slowly; about 7-8 minutes altogether.

LES ŒUFS FRITS * *BRITISH FRIED EGGS*

They are often used to garnish such dishes as Chicken Marengo, Calf's Head *en Tortue*, etc.

Heat about ¼ pint of oil in a small frying pan. Break each egg singly on to a saucer and salt the white lightly. When the oil is hot and begins to send off a pale blue smoke, hold the pan at a slight angle, slide in the egg and turn it over at once with a spatula or egg slice. Press the white down lightly and baste with hot fat. When one side is brown turn the egg over so that the other side can brown too and so that the egg keeps its oval shape. The yolk must remain soft. When one egg is ready remove from pan and drain on paper. The eggs are fried singly until the desired quantity is obtained.

▣ au Bacon

For 4 persons: 8 eggs; 8 thin slices lean bacon.

Grill bacon and fry the eggs as directed for *Oeufs Frits*, arrange on a round dish, place eggs on top and sprinkle with a little of the bacon fat.

Oeufs Frits à la Bordelaise

For 4 persons: 8 eggs; 4 large tomatoes; ¼ lb boletus or mushrooms; 1 chopped shallot; 2 tablespoons oil; 1 tablespoon chopped parsley. Cooking time: about 12 minutes.

Halve tomatoes, scoop out, season, sprinkle with oil and bake in a moderate oven for 10-15 minutes; they must not fall apart. Cut boletus in very small slices, *sauté* in oil with the chopped shallot, season, mix with the chopped parsley and fill into tomato halves. Place a fried egg on each.

⊡ Cavour

For 4 persons: 8 eggs; 8 tomato halves; 3 oz rice à la Piémontaise; Veal gravy.

Scoop out the halved tomatoes and cook slowly in a little butter. Place the tomatoes on a dish garnished with rice. Place a fried egg on each tomato. Serve Veal gravy separately.

⊡ au Jambon * *with Cooked Ham*

For 4 persons: 8 eggs; 4 slices thick ham or gammon. Cooking time: 10-15 minutes, depending on thickness of the ham.

Prepare the gammon by removing the rind and snipping the fat at 1-inch intervals with a pair of scissors. Brush with oil and grill slowly, turning the meat frequently. Top with fried eggs.

⊡ à la Mexicaine

For 4 persons: 8 fried eggs; 8 tomato halves; ¼ lb Creole rice; ½ pint sauce Tomate.

Scoop out the tomatoes and cook in oil, then fill with rice. Place tomato and egg in a circle alternately, garnish with fried parsley. Serve sauce apart.

⊡ à la Pastourelle

For 4 persons: 8 eggs; 8 slices of streaky bacon; 4 lambs' kidneys; ½ lb mushrooms; 1 chopped shallot.

Sauté mushrooms in butter with chopped shallots and chopped parsley. Grill the bacon and halved kidneys. Place the bacon in a ring on a round dish with the fried eggs on top and cover the eggs with the half kidneys. Garnish the centre with mushrooms and shallots and sprinkle with chopped parsley.

⊡ à la Provençale

For 4 persons: 8 eggs; 1 large aubergine; 6 oz tomatoes.

Peel aubergine, slice fairly thickly, dip in flour and salt and fry in hot oil. Skin and cook tomatoes in oil. Arrange the fried egg in a ring round the aubergine slices on a round dish and place the cooked tomatoes in the centre.

Œufs Frits à la Saint-Benoit

For 4 persons: 8 eggs; ¾ lb Brandade of dried cod.

Serve *Brandade* in a mound and arrange fried eggs round it.

⊡ à la Sauce Tomate * *with Tomato Sauce*

For 4 persons: 8 eggs; ½ pint sauce Tomate; fried parsley.

Fry the eggs, arrange on a dish paper with fried parsley in the centre and serve the *sauce Tomate* separately.

⊡ Yorkshire

For 4 persons: 8 eggs; 8 small slices raw ham; 8 small fried heart-shaped croûtons; fried parsley; ½ pint sauce Tomate.

Fry or grill ham, arrange alternately with the eggs, garnish with the *croûtons* and place the fried parsley in the centre of the dish. Serve the *sauce Tomate* separately.

LES OMELETTES * *OMELETTES*

To make good omelettes a thick heavy pan, which is used for no other purpose, is required. The inside must never be washed, only rubbed dry, or cleaned with a little heated fat and salt. A pan with a 7-inch base is practical for household purposes and will make a 3-4 egg omelette.

Two eggs are required per person but do not try to make an omelette of more than 6 eggs at a time. Season and beat them slightly with a fork, just enough to mix the whites and yolks together. Melt some butter in a saucepan and heat the omelette pan. Pour in enough butter just to cover the bottom of the pan. When the butter begins to foam pour in the eggs. Then begin to move the pan over the heat, shaking it slightly and using a fork stir the mixture slowly, loosening it from the edges as it sets. Leave it for a moment over the heat, although the egg should still be soft. Now loosen with a fork from the side nearest the handle and fold into the middle. Now fold in the opposite side towards the middle, holding the pan at an angle and banging the handle several times with the fist to loosen the omelette. When the omelette has been rolled up hold the serving dish at an angle to the pan and let omelette slide on to it. The finished omelette must be soft and juicy inside. Brush surface with melted butter to glaze it. Omelettes may be garnished with all types of meat, poultry, vegetables, cheeses and herbs.

⊡ Agnès Sorel

For 4 persons: 8 eggs; 3½ oz raw, sliced mushrooms; 2 oz chicken purée; 16 *tiny round slices of boiled tongue; 1½ oz butter; ¼ pint Veal gravy.*

Sauté the mushrooms in butter and mix with the chicken *purée.* Prepare the omelettes and fill with the chicken mixture, serve surrounded with Veal gravy. Garnish the top with slices of tongue.

Omelette Archiduc

For 4 persons: 8 eggs; 6 oz chicken livers; 2 fl oz Demi-glace; 8 truffle slices; 2 oz butter.

Fill the prepared omelette with the chicken livers, sliced, sautéed in butter and bound with *Demi-glace*. Place on a dish, garnish the top with truffle slices. Serve with *Demi-glace*.

⊡ à l'Arlésienne

For 4 persons: 8 eggs; 1 oz butter; ¼ lb peeled, deseeded and diced tomatoes; 1 peeled, diced aubergine; 1 teaspoon chopped onions; ½ crushed clove of garlic; 2 fl oz sauce Tomate; 1 tablespoon oil.

Toss onions thoroughly in the oil, then add the diced *aubergine* and, when it has started to cook, the tomatoes and garlic. Season and simmer till almost all liquid has evaporated. Fill omelette with mixture except for a small spoonful which is placed on top. Sprinkle with chopped parsley. Serve with *sauce Tomate*. (*See illustration p.* 287).

⊡ à la Bohémienne

For 4 persons: 8 eggs; 2 oz boiled ham; 2 oz mushrooms; 1 small truffle; ¼ lb tomatoes; 2 fl oz sauce Tomate.

Peel, deseed and chop tomatoes, then cook in butter. Cut ham, mushrooms and truffle in short thin strips, mix with tomatoes and fill completed omelette with mixture, keeping a little back. Make a slit in top of omelette, fill with remainder of mixture, sprinkle with chopped parsley and serve with *sauce Tomate*.

⊡ à la Boulonnaise

For 4 persons: 8 eggs; ¼ lb mackerel roes; ¼ lb buerre Maître d'Hôtel; 1 oz butter.

Fill the prepared omelette with the roes sautéed in butter and half the Herb butter. Place on a dish. Surround with a ring of melted Herb butter.

⊡ aux Champignons * *with Mushrooms*

For 4 persons: 8 eggs; 6 oz sliced mushrooms.

Sauté the mushrooms in butter. Make the omelette in the usual way.

⊡ à la Chartres

For 4 persons: 8 eggs; 1 oz chopped tarragon; 2 oz butter; blanched tarragon leaves but save the liquid.

Mix the chopped tarragon with the eggs. Serve the omelettes garnished with the blanched leaves and a little of the blanching liquid poured over.

Omelette Chasseur

For 4 persons: 8 eggs; 2 oz butter; ¼ lb poultry livers; 2 oz mushrooms; ¼ pint sauce Demi-glace; chopped parsley.

Slice mushrooms and livers, *sauté* quickly in butter, season and bind with *Demi-glace.* Make omelette and fill with the mixture, only keeping back a small spoonful. Make a slit in the top of the omelette, fill with the remaining mushroom and liver mixture and sprinkle chopped parsley on top. (*See illustration p.* 288).

⊡ à la Chevreuse

For 4 persons: 8 eggs; ¼ lb cooked artichoke bottoms; diced asparagus and truffle; 8 truffle slices.

Combine the artichoke bottoms, asparagus and truffles with the eggs. Make the omelette, serve and decorate with truffle slices.

⊡ à la Clamart

For 4 persons: 8 eggs; 6 oz peas à la Française; 2 oz butter.

Fill the omelette with two-thirds of the peas. Serve, make a slit in the top and fill the remainder of the peas.

⊡ aux Crevettes * *with Shrimps*

For 4 persons: 8 eggs; ¼ lb peeled shrimp tails; ½ pint sauce Crevette; 1½ oz butter.

Bind 3 oz shrimp tails with half the *sauce Crevette.* Fill the prepared omelette with this garnish. Place on a dish, make a slit in the top and place the remaining shrimp tails, sautéed in butter, in the slit. Surround with a ring of *sauce Crevette.*

⊡ aux Croûtons

For 4 persons: 8 eggs; 1 oz butter; 2 oz very small white bread cubes fried in butter.

Add bread cubes to beaten eggs and cook as described.

⊡ du Curé

For 5 persons: 10 eggs; 2 large carp roes; piece of tinned tuna fish; 1 chopped shallot; 2 oz butter; ½ teaspoon each of chopped parsley and chives.

Clean carp roes, blanch for 5 minutes in salt water, drain, chop and mix with the mashed tuna fish and the shallot and briefly simmer in butter. Mix a little butter with the parsley and chives. Make omelette in the usual way, fill with tuna and roe mixture and serve on a dish on the bottom of which the Herb butter has been placed.

⊡ à la Fermière

For 4 persons: 8 eggs; ¼ lb ham; chopped parsley; 2 oz butter.

Mix the diced ham and chopped parsley with the eggs. Make the omelette and turn out flat on to a round dish.

Omelette aux Fines Herbes * *Mixed Herb Omelette*

For 4 persons: 8 eggs; 1 oz parsley; tarragon, chervil and chive; 2 oz butter.

When beating the eggs add the chopped herbs.

⊡ à la Florentine

For 4 persons: 8 eggs ; 5 oz leaf spinach; 2 oz butter.

Blanch and cook the spinach in butter then mix the spinach with the eggs, and make the omelette.

⊡ à la Forestière

For 4 persons: 8 eggs; ¼ lb sliced morels and boletus; ¼ pint Demi-glace; 2 oz lardons; 2 oz butter.

Sauté the morels and boletus in butter, then add the lardons, *sauté* briefly and bind with half the *Demi-glace*. Fill the omelette and place on a dish, serve with remaining *Demi-glace*.

⊡ au Fromage * *with Cheese*

For 4 persons: 8 eggs; 1 oz butter; 2 oz grated Parmesan or gruyère cheese.

Add cheese to beaten eggs and cook in usual way.

⊡ au Jambon * *with Cooked Ham*

For 4 persons: 8 eggs; ¼ lb cooked ham; 1 oz butter.

Dice ham finely and fry in butter for a moment before the eggs are poured on top and the omelette is made.

⊡ à la Joinville

For 4 persons: 8 eggs; 6 oz salpicon of shrimp tails, mushrooms and truffles; ¼ pint sauce Crevette; 2 oz butter.

Fill the cooked omelette with the *salpicon*, place on a dish and serve with *sauce Crevette*.

⊡ au Lard * *with Bacon*

For 4 persons: 8 eggs; 1 oz butter; ¼ lb lean bacon; 2 oz butter.

Dice bacon finely, blanch, drain and fry in the butter. Pour eggs on top and make the omelette.

⊡ à la Lyonnaise

For 4 persons: 8 eggs; 2 oz butter; 2 oz onions; parsley.

Slice onions, cook in butter till soft, add to beaten eggs with a little chopped parsley and make omelette in the usual way.

Omelette Mexicaine

For 4 persons: 8 eggs; 2 oz sliced mushrooms sautéed in butter; 1 oz chopped red peppers; ¼ lb tomatoes concassé; 2 oz butter.

Mix the mushrooms and pepper with the beaten eggs. Serve the omelette, make a slit in the top and place the tomatoes in the opening.

▣ à la Mousseline

For 4 persons: 8 eggs; ¼ pint double cream; 3 oz butter.

Separate the egg yolks from the whites. Mix the yolks with the cream and fold in the stiffly beaten whites. Heat a very large frying pan with the butter and pour in the egg mixture as for an ordinary omelette. Serve at once.

▣ à la Nantua

For 4 persons: 8 eggs; ¼ lb crayfish tails; 2 oz butter; ¼ pint sauce Nantua.

Bind half the crayfish tails with half the *sauce Nantua*. Fill the omelette with this garnish. Serve on a dish garnished with the remaining crayfish and surrounded with a ring of *sauce Nantua.*

▣ à la Normande

For 4 persons: 8 eggs; 15 poached oysters; 2 oz butter; ½ pint sauce Normande.

Fill the omelette with the poached and bearded oysters, bound with half the *sauce Normande*. Serve the omelette on a dish surrounded with a ring of the remaining sauce.

▣ à l'Oseille * *with Sorrel*

For 4 persons: 8 eggs; 2 oz sorrel; 2 oz butter.

Shred sorrel finely, simmer in butter, drain, mix with beaten egg and make the omelette.

▣ à la Parmentier

For 4 persons: 8 eggs; 1 oz butter; 6 oz diced potatoes, fried brown in butter.

Cut potatoes in very small dice, fry in butter, pour beaten eggs on top and make omelette.

▣ à la Paysanne

For 4 persons: 8 eggs; 1 oz butter; 2 oz diced lean bacon; 2 oz finely diced potatoes; 1 oz sorrel.

Fry the bacon, potatoes and sorrel in butter, add all ingredients to beaten eggs. When the omelette is cooked, turn over on to other side like a pancake, cook very briefly and arrange on a round dish and serve flat.

Omelette aux Pointes d'Asperges * *Asparagus Omelette*

For 4 persons: 8 eggs; 2 oz butter; 6 oz cooked asparagus.

Drain asparagus and cut into 1-inch pieces, reserving the tips for garnish. Toss pieces in butter, pour eggs on top and make omelette in the usual way. Make a slight incision in the middle of the omelette with the point of a knife, put the asparagus tips in it and pour a very little melted butter on top.

▣ à la Portugaise

For 4 persons: 8 eggs; 6 oz tomatoes concassé; 1 oz butter; ¼ pint sauce Tomate.

Fill finished omelette with tomatoes and surround with ring of *sauce Tomate.*

▣ à la Princesse

For 4 persons: 8 eggs; ¼ lb cooked asparagus tips; ¼ pint sauce Crème; 1 oz butter; truffle slices.

Bind the asparagus tips with half the *sauce Crème* and fill the omelette with them. Place it on a dish, garnish the top with truffle slices and serve with remaining *sauce Crème.*

▣ à la Reine

For 4 persons: 8 eggs; ¼ lb chicken purée; 2 fl oz sauce Suprême; 2 oz butter.

Fill the omelette with the chicken *purée*. Serve on a dish surrounded by *sauce Suprême.*

▣ à la Rossini

For 4 persons: 8 eggs; 3 oz cooked foie gras; 1 oz finely diced truffle; 2 oz butter; 8 truffle slices; ¼ pint Demi-glace with truffle essence.

Add the *foie gras* and diced truffle to the eggs. Make the omelette, serve and decorate the top with truffle slices and surround with a ring of *sauce Demi-glace.*

▣ à la Savoyarde

For 4 persons: 8 eggs; 2 small onions; 2 potatoes; 2 oz lean bacon; 3 oz gruyère cheese; chopped herbs; 2 oz butter.

Cut potatoes in small dice and fry in butter with the potatoes. Slice onions, dice and blanch bacon and fry them until they are all cooked. Beat eggs, season, add chopped herbs and the cheese cut in tiny dice. Pour over potatoes, fry both sides a pale brown and serve flat like a pancake.

▣ au Thon * *with Tuna Fish*

For 4 persons: 8 eggs; ¼ lb tuna fish in oil; 1½ oz butter; 1 oz Anchovy butter.

Dice the tuna and mix with the eggs. Make the omelette and serve sprinkled with melted Anchovy butter.

Omelette aux Truffes * *Truffle Omelette*

For 4 persons: 8 eggs; 1½ oz butter; 2 small truffles, finely diced; truffle slices.

Mixed the diced truffles with the eggs. Make the omelette and serve. Garnish the top with truffle slices.

▣ à la Victoria

For 4 persons: 8 eggs; 3½ oz salpicon of crawfish and truffles; ¼ pint sauce Homard.

Bind the *salpicon* with half the *sauce Homard.* Fill the omelette with it and serve it on a dish surrounded with a ring of the remaining sauce.

▣ à la Vosgienne

For 4 persons: 8 eggs; 1 oz butter; 3 oz bacon; 2 oz gruyère cheese; 1 tablespoon cream.

Cut bacon and cheese in small squares, then fry the bacon. Mix the bacon and cheese with the eggs together with the cream.

LES ŒUFS DURS CHAUDS * *HARDBOILED EGGS*

▣ à l'Aurore

For 6 persons: 10 eggs; 2 hardboiled egg yolks; ½ pint Béchamel; ¼ pint sauce Tomate.

Slice the eggs and heat in the *Béchamel* without boiling. Place in a *gratin* dish and sprinkle 2 chopped egg yolks on top. Brown under the grill and surround with a ring of *sauce Tomate.*

▣ à la Béchamel

For 6 persons: 10 eggs; ½ pint Béchamel.

Slice hardboiled eggs thinly and heat in fairly thin *Béchamel* without bringing to the boil.

▣ à la Berrichonne

For 6 persons: ¾ pint Béchamel; 10 hardboiled eggs; 3 boiled potatoes.

Slice the eggs and the potatoes while hot. Arrange the eggs and potatoes in alternate layers, and coat with the *Béchamel,* finishing with a layer of *Béchamel.*

▣ à la Boulangère

For 6 persons: 6 long bread rolls; 8 hardboiled eggs; ½ pint Béchamel; 6 oz sliced onions cooked in butter; chopped parsley.

Dice the egg whites and half the egg yolks, add the onions and bind with the *Béchamel.* Remove the bread from the inside of the rolls and fill with the egg mixture. Chop the remaining egg yolks and sprinkle them over the rolls, together with the parsley.

Œufs Durs à la Bretonne

For 6 persons: 10 *hardboiled eggs;* 2 *oz butter;* ½ *pint Béchamel;* 3 *oz onions; the white of half a leek;* 2 *oz mushrooms.*

Slice onions and leeks thinly, blanch thoroughly and simmer in butter till cooked. Slice the mushrooms very finely, cook in butter and mix mushrooms, onions and leek with fairly thin *Béchamel.* Place sliced eggs in a deep bowl and pour sauce on top.

⊡ Sauce Poulette

For 6 persons: 10 *hardboiled eggs;* 2 *oz butter; chopped parsley;* ¼ *lb mushrooms;* ½ *pint sauce Poulette;* ½ *lemon.*

Cook the finely sliced mushrooms in butter. Slice eggs and add the cooked mushrooms. Bind both with the sauce and add lemon juice and chopped parsley.

⊡ à la Tripe

For 6 persons: 10 *hardboiled eggs;* ½ *pint Béchamel;* ¼ *lb onions.*

Slice the onions and cook them in butter. Add the *Béchamel* and cook gently for 10 minutes. Place the sliced eggs in this sauce and serve piled in a dish.

LES ŒUFS FARCIS * *STUFFED EGGS*

If hardboiled eggs are to be perfect, the following points must be remembered: Do not boil longer than 8-10 minutes, according to size. If the eggs are cooked longer than necessary the white becomes tough, the yolk turns an ugly greenish colour and the whole egg gives off an unpleasant smell. The eggs must therefore be placed in boiling water, boiled briskly, and be plunged in cold water as soon as they are ready and then shelled. Cooking them in this way has the further advantage that the yolk remains in the centre so that stuffed eggs have a better appearance. It is useful to use a frying basket to boil a large number of eggs.

⊡ à l'Aurore

For 6 persons: 6 *hardboiled eggs;* 2 *oz butter;* 1 *tablespoon sauce Tomate;* 1 *tablespoon Béchamel;* ½ *pint sauce Aurore.*

Halve the eggs lengthwise, remove the yolks and pass them through a sieve. Beat the butter and combine with the *sauce Tomate*, *Béchamel* and sieved egg yolks. Fill the whites with this mixture, pour melted butter over them and place them in a hot oven for 8 minutes. Garnish the bottom of a dish with the *sauce Aurore* and place the eggs on top.

⊡ à la Chimay

For 6 persons: 9 *hardboiled gegs;* 4 *oz mushrooms;* 2 *tablespoons Béchamel;* ½ *pint sauce Mornay;* 2 *oz grated cheese;* 1 *oz butter.*

Chop the mushrooms, very finely and cook in butter. Halve the eggs lengthwise, remove the yolks and mix with the mushrooms, season and place in a piping bag fitted with a star nozzle. Pipe this mixture into the white of egg. Coat the bottom of a *gratin* dish with some *sauce Mornay.* Place halved eggs on top and coat egg with sauce, sprinkle with cheese and dot with butter. Place in a hot oven or under the grill to brown the top.

Œufs Farcis à la Hongroise

For 6 *persons:* 9 *hardboiled eggs;* $\frac{1}{4}$ *lb onions;* $\frac{1}{2}$ *lb tomatoes;* $\frac{1}{2}$ *pint sauce Crème; paprika;* 2 *oz butter.*

Chop two-thirds of the onions, cook in butter till soft, season well with paprika and cool. Halve the eggs, pass yolks through a sieve, mix with a little butter and the chopped onions and fill eggs. Slice remaining onions, simmer in butter, mix with *sauce Crème* and season very highly with paprika. Cut tomatoes in thick slices and fry carefully. Arrange eggs on tomato slices and coat with Paprika sauce.

Bouchées, Vol-au-Vent, Croustades

Pastry cases such as *bouchées*, *vol-au-vent* cases, tartlets, small pies and flan cases may all be filled with sliced, hardboiled eggs mixed with *Béchamel* and served as *hors d'oeuvre*.

Cromesquis

For 6 *persons:* 8 *hardboiled eggs;* 2 *oz cooked mushrooms;* 2 *raw egg yolks;* $\frac{1}{2}$ *pint very thick Béchamel;* 1 *pint Frying batter;* $\frac{1}{2}$ *pint sauce Tomate.* Cooking time 2-3 minutes.

Finely dice eggs and mushrooms, bind with the *Béchamel*, add the egg yolks, heat gently until the mixture thickens and season well. Cool, then shape it into croquettes the size of a pigeon's egg on a floured table, dip in batter and fry in hot, deep fat. Serve on a dish paper with fried parsley and serve *sauce Tomate*.

Cotelettes

Make a *Cromesquis* mixture as above but shape into cutlet shapes and egg and breadcrumb. Fry in butter, arrange in a ring and garnish with spinach, young peas or asparagus tips.

Rissoles

For 6 *persons:* 10 *hardboiled eggs;* 2 *raw egg yolks;* 4 *pints thick Béchamel;* $\frac{3}{4}$ *lb Puff pastry or unsweetened Short pastry.* Cooking time: 4-5 minutes.

Prepare a *Cromesquis* mixture as above and cool. Roll out dough $\frac{1}{8}$-inch thick, cut circles about 4-inches across with a round cutter and place a small spoonful of *Cromesquis* mixture in the middle of each. Moisten the edges of the pastry with egg yolk or water, fold in half and press down the sides. Fry in very hot deep fat, drain, arrange on a dish paper with fried parsley and serve as they are, without sauce.

COLD EGG DISHES

ŒUFS DURS FROIDS * *COLD HARDBOILED EGGS*

▣ à la Mayonnaise

For 6 persons: 12 hardboiled eggs; 1 pint Mayonnaise.

Slice or halve the eggs and serve on a dish, coated with *Mayonnaise.* The eggs may be placed on a bed of lettuce leaves and garnished in a variety of ways. (*See illustration p.* 281).

▣ à la Mimosa

For 6 persons: 8 hardboiled eggs; 12 oval croustades of unsweetened Short pastry (2 *8-inch flans baked blind may be used*)*; 1 lb diced, cooked, mixed vegetables; 1 pint Mayonnaise.*

Fill *croustades* or flans with the mixed vegetables bound with a little *Mayonnaise* and place half an egg on it, round side up. Coat with *Mayonnaise* and sprinkle a mixture of chopped hardboiled egg yolk and chopped herbs on top.

▣ à la Riga

For 6 persons: 18 hardboiled eggs; ¾ lb Tomato salad with tarragon; ½ pint Mayonnaise; 6 fillets of anchovy; capers.

Slice off the tip of each hardboiled egg. Then carefully remove a strip of egg white round the middle of each egg, repeat this above and below the centre of each egg so that you have 3 grooves in each egg. Cut a slice from the base of the egg so it will stand upright and remove the yolk without damaging the whites. Fill eggs with salad. Cut each strip of anchovy in four and place in the grooves channeled out of the eggs to simulate the hoops of a barrel. Coat the bottom of a dish with *Mayonnaise* and place the eggs on it. Decorate with capers.

▣ à la Toulonnaise

For 6 persons: 6 hardboiled eggs; ½ pint Mayonnaise; 8 to 10 anchovy fillets.

Halve the eggs lengthwise and place them flat side down in an *hors d'œuvre* dish. Cover with plenty of *Mayonnaise* which has been well seasoned to compensate for the relative lack of flavour of the eggs. Decorate each egg half with shreds of anchovy fillets. (*See illustration p.* 281).

LES ŒUFS FARCIS * *STUFFED EGGS*

▣ à l'Indienne

For 6 persons: 6 hardboiled eggs; 2 oz butter; ½ pint Mayonnaise; curry powder; ketchup.

Halve the eggs lengthwise. Remove the yolk and pass it through a sieve; mix it with the butter, season with salt and curry powder and put this mixture back into the half eggs. Make a sauce by mixing together the *Mayonnaise,* ketchup and some curry powder and mask the eggs with it.

Œufs Farcis à la Macédoine

For 6 persons: 6 hardboiled eggs; 1 lb Russian salad.

Halve the eggs lengthwise. Remove the yolks. Fill the whites with Russian salad and sprinkle the chopped yolks on top. (*See illustration p.* 281).

◘ à la Roscoff

For 6 persons: 6 hardboiled eggs; ½ lb macédoine of vegetables; ¾ pint Mayonnaise; ¼ lb lobster flesh; lettuce leaves.

Dice the lobster, bind with the *Mayonnaise* and add seasoning. Halve the eggs lengthwise, remove the yolks and fill the whites with the lobster salad. Coat with *Mayonnaise* and sprinkle with crumbled egg yolk. Pile up the *macédoine* of vegetables bound with *Mayonnaise* in the middle of the dish and surround with the lettuce leaves on which the stuffed eggs are placed.

◘ à la Strasbourgeoise

For 6 persons: 6 hardboiled eggs; ¼ lb foie gras purée; chopped truffle; ¾ pint chopped aspic.

Halve the eggs lengthwise. Remove the yolks, sieve them and combine with the *foie gras.* Stuff the eggs and sprinkle the chopped truffle on top. (*See illustration p.* 281).

◘ en Variétés

For 6 persons: 12 hardboiled eggs; 24 small Puff pastry tartlets; ½ lb butter; ¼ pint Mayonnaise; ¼ lb cooked duck liver; 12 very small crayfish tails; 1 teaspoon chopped herbs: parsley, chervil, tarragon, chives; ⅓ oz red or black caviar; 6 anchovy fillets; 6 slices of stuffed olive; 1 small truffle; ½ pint aspic; Madeira; chili sauce; four different spices; brandy.

Halve the eggs and cut a slice off the ends so that they will stand up. Remove the yolks without damaging the whites. Pass them through a sieve and combine with the creamed butter and the *Mayonnaise* and divide this mixture into four.

Cut the duck liver into 6 slices and trim them into medallions with a slightly smaller diameter than that of the eggs. Make a *purée* of the trimmings. Mix the *purée* with one part of the egg yolk mixture, season and add the Madeira and the four spices. Fill 6 egg halves with this mixture, using a piping bag with a plain tube. Place a liver medallion on top and decorate with a small truffle slice.

Trim 6 crayfish tails, mix them with one part of the yolk mixture and the remainder of the chopped truffles, season, add a drop of brandy and chili sauce. Check the seasoning. Fill 6 egg halves with this mixture and place a small crayfish tail on top.

Mix the chopped herbs with 1 part of the yolk mixture, season and check the seasoning. Fill 6 egg halves with this mixture and garnish with a dab of caviar.

Purée the anchovy fillets, mix with the remainder of the yolk mixture and the diced egg white trimmings. Fill the remaining egg halves with this mixture. Garnish each one with a slice of stuffed olive.

Chill the eggs for a few minutes. Glaze all the egg halves lightly with aspic. Place in tartlets of a suitable shape and size, and garnish with a ring of the stuffing used and place in rows on a rectangular dish.

Œufs Farcis à la Vert-Pré

For 6 persons: 6 hardboiled eggs; 3 oz butter; 1 large tablespoon spinach purée; a few chervil and tarragon leaves; a few watercress leaves; ½ pint Mayonnaise; 1 pint aspic.

Halve eggs lengthwise, pass yolks through a sieve and mix with the butter. Combine with herb *purée*, which has been made by squeezing all moisture from the spinach. Blanch watercress, tarragon and chervil leaves and pass them through a hair sieve. Fill egg halves with herb mixture, allow to set in refrigerator and coat with *Mayonnaise* which has also been mixed with a little of the herb *purée*. Decorate each egg with tarragon leaves, coat with half-set aspic, arrange on a dish and garnish with diced aspic.

Œufs Filés à l'Espagnole * *Spanish-style Spun Eggs*

Place 5 egg yolks and 1 whole egg in a bowl. Mix well without foaming and strain. Boil ½ lb sugar and ¼ pint water to the blow degree. This measures 37° on the saccharometer and will be at a temperature of 230° F. Draw to one side of the stove. Pour the eggs into the special funnel which has 4 or 5 spouts and is held above the pan containing the boiling syrup. Allow the egg to fall into the syrup in spirals. Cook for 2 or 3 minutes. Remove with a skimming ladle. Dip into cold water, drain on a cloth and allow to dry. Spun eggs may also be made using one or more cornets of strong paper. They are used mainly for filling *croustades* and decorating cold ham.

ŒUFS MOLLETS FROIDS * *COLD MEDIUM BOILED EGGS*

⊡ Casino

For 6 persons: 12 medium boiled eggs; ½ lb asparagus tips; ½ lb cooked breast of chicken; 6 boat-shaped Puff pastry cases; 12 slices Bayonne ham; ½ pint tomato-flavoured Mayonnaise; 1 truffle.

Fill the pastry cases with the finely sliced breast of chicken and asparagus tips. Mask 6 eggs with the tomato-flavoured *Mayonnaise* and decorate with small pieces of the white of hard-boiled egg. Place these eggs on the pastry cases and arrange them in the middle of a long dish. At each end of the dish place the rest of the eggs, garnished with slices of truffle, placed on the slices of ham. (*See illustration p.* 281).

⊡ en Gelée au Jambon de Parme * *In Aspic with Parma Ham*

For 6 persons: 6 medium boiled eggs; 6 slices of Parma ham; ½ pint aspic with port; 6 truffle slices; 1 sprig of tarragon.

Line 6 oval moulds with aspic. Decorate the bottoms with tarragon leaves and truffle slices. Place the eggs, wrapped in ham, on top. Complete with half-set aspic. Put in a cool place to set. Serve surrounded with a ring of aspic. (*See illustration p.* 282).

⊡ Okinawa

For 6 persons: 6 medium boiled eggs; 6 round tartlets, made from Half Puff pastry; 3 oz rice; 5 oz lobster flesh; 10 oz tomatoes; 1 green pepper; ½ pint Mayonnaise; ¼ pint aspic; 1 sheet gelatine; ketchup.

Cook the rice, cool it in cold water and drain. Shred the pepper very finely, cut up the lobster flesh, dice all the tomatoes except one which is kept for garnishing. Mix all these ingredients with the rice and bind with a little *Mayonnaise*; season with the ketchup and fill the tartlet cases. Stir the melted gelatine into the rest of the *Mayonnaise* and use to mask the eggs. Decorate them with a piece of tomato cut out with a pastry cutter. Glaze with aspic jelly and, when it has set, place the eggs in the tartlet cases and arrange these in the form of a star on a plate.

ŒUFS POCHÉS FROIDS * *COLD POACHED EGGS*

▣ Carmen

For 6 persons: 12 *poached or medium boiled eggs;* 1 *pint sauce Soubise;* 4 *sheets or* 1 *oz gelatine;* 1 *pint aspic;* 1 *lb green peppers.*

Soak gelatine in water and when it is soft mix with the *sauce Soubise* and coat the eggs. Decorate the top of each egg with red pepper. Place in a ring on a round dish. Make the peppers into a salad and place in the middle. Garnish with chopped aspic. (*See illustration p.* 283).

▣ à l'Estragon * *with Tarragon*

For 6 *persons:* 12 *poached eggs;* 24 *blanched tarragon leaves;* 1 *pint Tarragon aspic.*

Line *cocottes* with aspic which has been strongly flavoured with tarragon. Place 2 blanched tarragon leaves crosswise on the base, put a cold, well-trimmed poached egg on top and fill up with tarragon aspic. Turn out eggs as soon as aspic has set.

▣ à la Frou-Frou

12 *poached eggs;* ¼ *lb green asparagus tips;* ¼ *lb young green peas;* ¼ *lb French beans;* 1 *pint thick Mayonnaise;* 1 *hardboiled egg yolk.*

Make a salad of boiled, drained and cooked peas and chopped beans and asparagus tips and bind with a little *Mayonnoise*. Trim eggs well, coat with a thick *Mayonnaise* at last moment, sprinkle with chopped egg yolk and arrange vegetable salad in centre. A little aspic may be mixed with the *Mayonnaise* to stop it sliding off if the salad has to be prepared in advance. It is better, however, to coat and arrange them at the last moment.

▣ en Gelée à la Colinette

For 6 *persons:* 6 *poached eggs;* 3 *oz peeled shrimps;* ½ *pint sauce Chaudfroid;* ¼ *pint Fish aspic;* 6 *oz cooked salmon;* ¼ *pint cream;* 3 *oz smoked salmon;* 12 *truffle slices.*

Line a *savarin* mould with aspic. Decorate the bottom with shrimp tails and truffles and place the eggs, coated with *sauce Chaudfroid* combined on top. Fill up with cool aspic and leave to set in a cold place. Unmould on a round dish. In the middle place the fresh salmon decorated with smoked salmon and truffle slices. (*See illustration p.* 282).

▣ en Gelée à la Jeannette

For 6 *persons:* 6 *poached eggs;* ½ *pint sauce Chaudfroid;* 3 *oz foie gras purée;* 2 *oz butter;* 1 *pint aspic;* 6 *truffle slices.*

Coat eggs with *sauce Chaudfroid* and allow to set. Place one egg in each aspic-lined *cocotte* with a slice of truffle placed in the bottom. Mix butter and *foie gras* and pipe a border round the egg. Fill *cocotte* with cold aspic. Alow to set. Then unmould. (*See illustration p.* 284).

Oeufs Pochés à la Madrilène

For 6 persons: 6 poached eggs; 6 Puff pastry croustades; ¼ lb short julienne of green peppers; ¼ lb celeriac cut in julienne; ¼ lb peeled deseeded and diced tomatoes; 1 *pint Mayonnaise; ⅛ pint tomato purée; ½ pint aspic;* 3 *stuffed olives;* 2 *sheets or ½ oz gelatine;* 1 *chopped shallot; vinegar; olive oil.*

Marinate the celeriac, tomatoes, peppers and chopped shallot for 1 hour in the vinegar, olive oil and a little salt. Soak and melt the gelatine. Drain the vegetables and bind with ½ pint *Mayonnaise* to which has been added the melted gelatine. Fill the *croustades* with this salad. Coat the eggs with the remainder of the *Mayonnaise* mixed with the tomato *purée* and a little aspic. Let the sauce set. Garnish each egg with 3 olive rings and glaze lightly with aspic. Place the eggs on the *croustades* and serve.

⊡ à la Niçoise

For 6 persons: 6 poached eggs; ½ lb boiled French beans; ½ lb cold, boiled potatoes; ½ lb tomatoes; ½ pint Mayonnaise mixed with 1 *tablespoon tomato purée.*

Dice beans and potatoes finely. Peel tomatoes, remove seeds, dice, mix with other ingredients and season with oil, vinegar, salt and pepper. Arrange cold, well-trimmed eggs in a ring on a round glass dish, coat with *Mayonnaise* and decorate each egg with a chervil leaf. Place salad in centre at last minute.

⊡ à la Printanière

For 6 persons: 6 poached eggs; 6 tartlet cases of Puff pastry; ½ lb mixed vegetables; 2-3 *tablespoons Mayonnaise; ½ pint white sauce Chaudfroid; ½ pint red sauce Chaudfroid; ½ pint aspic; a few cooked French beans.*

Place well-trimmed cold eggs on a wire tray and coat one half of each egg with the white and the other with the red *sauce Chaudfroid.* Before the sauce has quite set, place a very thin strip of French bean across eggs so as to separate the two colours entirely. Marinate diced vegetables, bind with the *Mayonnaise,* fill tartlets with them, place an egg in each and glaze with aspic. Place a narrow ring of chopped aspic round each egg.

⊡ à la Reine

For 6 persons: 6 poached eggs; 6 Puff pastry tartlet cases; ½ lb boiled, minced poultry; 2-3 *tablespoons Mayonnaise; ½ pint chicken sauce Chaudfroid; 6 small round truffle slices; ½ pint aspic.*

Coat the well-trimmed eggs with the *sauce Chaudfroid,* decorate with a truffle slice, allow to set and glaze lightly with aspic. Bind poultry meat with the *Mayonnaise,* season well and place in tartlet cases. Place an egg in each tartlet and surround with a border of chopped aspic.

⊡ à la Russe

For 6 persons: 6 poached eggs; 6 thin, round truffle slices; Russian salad; 1 *pint aspic.*

Place *cocottes* in crushed ice. When they are quite cold fill with cold, but still liquid aspic, leave to stand for a minute and at once pour out aspic. This should leave the bottom and sides coated with a thin layer of aspic. Place a truffle slice dipped in aspic on the bottom of the *cocotte*. Place a cold, well-trimmed poached egg in each *cocotte*, fill up with cold, liquid aspic and leave it to set. Before turning out, dip *cocotte* in hot water for a moment and arrange in a ring around the salad. The salad can also be put in an aspic-lined mould and turned out in the middle of the dish. Garnish the intervening spaces with diced aspic.

Oeufs Pochés à la Tartare

For 6 persons: 6 poached eggs; 3 large tomatoes; ½ lb macédoine of vegetables; ½ pint Mayonnaise; mixed herbs; 2 *gherkins; lettuce leaves.*

Cut the tomatoes in halves, scoop them out, drain well and season the inside. Bind the vegetable *macédoine* with a little *Mayonnaise*, season and fill the tomato halves. Place one egg on each filled tomato and cover with thick *Mayonnaise*. Sprinkle with mixed herbs and chopped gherkins and arrange the tomatoes on the lettuce leaves. (*See illustration p.* 283).

Fish

The rivers, lakes and coasts of Britain abound with many different types of fish, but unfortunately we do not always make the most of this great variety or of the numerous methods by which they may be cooked. You will be interested to discover in this chapter that there are many attractive and delicious recipes which are really very simple to prepare. You will find recipes for the many different varieties of fish from the popular fish eaten in Britain to the more unusual and delicious varieties which are popular in France. Nowadays, thanks to speedier methods of transport and improved methods of freezing fish, a much wider selection is now available.

For the purpose of this chapter, fish has been classified into three sections: seafish, freshwater fish and shellfish.

Nutritionally, fish is a good source of protein, containing approximately the same amount per ounce as meat. The fat content of fish is usually considerably lower than that of beef but this depends on the type of fish. White fish such as cod, haddock, sole and whiting contain a smaller amount of fat than the flesh of the oily, darker fish such as salmon, turbot and mackerel.

Fish should be eaten as fresh as possible and when buying fish the following points should be taken into consideration. Fresh fish has firm flesh which should spring back when pressed with the finger. There should be plenty of fresh scales and the eyes should be protruding and bright. Never buy fish which has dry or flabby flesh, or that which has an unpleasant smell. If you prefer to buy fish already filleted from the fishmonger ask for the trimmings with which to make stock and sauce. When buying whole fish they must be scaled before they are gutted. There are special knives for scaling or you can use the back of a chopping knife, scraping from head to tail. Then cut off the fins and half the tail with a pair of strong scissors. Remove the gills, cut a whole in the belly and remove the guts. Large fish can be gutted by pushing the handle of a large skimming ladle through the gills and removing the guts with it.

All fish should be washed thoroughly before use and then dried with a cloth kept specially for the purpose. Fish should not be stored in the wrapping paper but in a covered container in the refrigerator or put on a plate and covered with a cloth wrung out in vinegar and water. If it is possible fish should be eaten the day it is purchased.

Fish has a fine delicate texture and should be cooked with care. It is always tender and therefore easily digested since it contains none of the tough, connective tissue found in meat and, consequently, cooks more quickly.

The various methods of cooking fish include:

BRAISING

This method is used for large fish or pieces of fish such as salmon, salmon trout, carp, turbot, sturgeon and pike. Place a layer of thinly sliced carrots, onions, and shallots which have been briefly simmered in butter on the bottom of a fish kettle or other suitable vessel. Place the fish on top and cover with thin slices of bacon. Add red or white wine or a mixture of half wine and fish stock, until the fish is half covered. Season lightly with salt and peppercorns, add a *bouquet garni,* bring the liquid to the boil and then place fish in a fairly moderate oven, 350° F or Gas Mark 3-4, cooking slowly and frequently basting with the liquor. (If necessary the bacon may be replaced with oiled or buttered paper.)

Fish for braising can also be skinned on one side and larded with thin strips of bacon, truffle, anchovy or gherkin. The stock from braised fish is always used to make the sauce to be served with it. Either it is reduced by boiling and added to the sauce or it is actually used as the sauce after thickening and beating up with butter.

POACHING

Poaching is a method of cooking with a little liquid which must be kept just on simmering point and must not boil up. Poaching is especially suitable for sole, trout, small turbot and for sliced fish such as fillets.

The fish is placed in a fire-proof baking dish or flat casserole (*sauteuse*) according to size, after it has been first buttered and sprinkled with chopped or thinly-sliced onions or shallots. After seasoning, half cover the fish with wine, mushroom stock or fish stock, or some of each, cover the dish with a sheet of buttered paper and place in a warm oven, 350° F or Gas Mark 3-4. Baste the fish from time to time with the stock, which is also used to make the sauce.

SHALLOW FRYING

This method of cooking fish is not as popular in Britain as it deserves to be. It is both quick and delicious to eat, although it does need care. It is suitable for fillets and slices of fish and for small fish weighing not more than 4-6 ounces. This is a favourite way of cooking small river trout. First dip fish in milk, then turn in flour, shake thoroughly and place in a frying pan in which butter has been heated well without browning. Fry fish golden brown on both sides and salt lightly. As soon as it is cooked, arrange on a hot dish, sprinkle with lemon juice and chopped parsley and pour the frying butter, to which a suitable quantity of freshly browned butter has been added, on top. Fish weighing more than about 6 oz are first scored lightly. Care must be taken to ensure that the fish have not cooked over too high a heat or the skin will become too brown and tough. On the other hand if the fish is cooked too slowly, the fish will become soft.

DEEP FAT FRYING

In general the best fish for deep fat frying are the flat fish, such as sole, plaice and turbot. Oil is the best fat for deep frying. Small fish weighing 4½-6 ounces may first be scored so that the heat penetrates the middle more quickly. It is important to use plenty of oil in the pan so that the fish is completely submerged. The fat should be very hot (a faint blue haze will be seen) and the fish should sizzle when immersed. Care should be taken not to put in too many fish at once, since this cools the fat too quickly. Unless the fish is to be breadcrumbed it should be immersed in slightly salted milk and coated with flour, the surplus being shaken off.

Fat used for frying fish should not be used for any other purpose since the flavour of the fish is imparted to the fat. It is also important to strain the fat after use to remove the crumbs, etc.

The fish will be cooked when it rises to the surface and is a golden-brown colour. Lift it out with a draining spoon and dry on crumpled kitchen paper, salt, and serve as soon as possible on a table napkin.

GRILLING

This method is most suitable for small fish such as herring, mackerel, trout, red mullet, eels or perch and also for slices of salmon, turbot, tunny fish, etc. If the fish has very thick flesh, it may be scored to facilitate cooking. Season the fish, turn in flour, shake off surplus and dip in oil so that it does not stick to the grill. The grill must be red hot before the fish is placed on it otherwise the fish will stick to the grill and probably break when turned. When one side is done, turn and grill the other. The heat should be regulated according to the type of fish. Small pieces of fish should be cooked under fierce heat but large thick pieces should be cooked more slowly. During grilling the fish is salted and brushed with oil from time to time so that it does not become too dry. The use of a fish grill is strongly recommended because the fish is easier to turn and there is less danger of damaging it than if it is placed directly on the grill. This too must be red hot before the fish is placed on it. As soon as the fish is done, place on a hot dish. Serve Herb butter, or some other butter mixture or a sauce separately.

Sea Fish

ALOSE * *SHAD*

This fish, found in salt water from the Baltic to the Mediterranean, is similar to the herring in appearance and may be prepared in the same manner as cod, herring, mackerel and perch.

⊡ Grillée à l'Anglaise * *Grilled*

For 6 persons: 2 lb shad; 1½ lb small peeled potatoes; ¼ lb butter. Cooking time: 30 minutes.

Score the cleaned, dried fish with regular, fairly deep incisions in the thick part of the back on both sides; brush with oil, and grill slowly for about 30 minutes. Serve with boiled potatoes and melted butter.

⊡ Oseille I * *with Sorrel*

For 7-8 persons: 3 lb shad; 4 lb cooked sorrel (see below); ¼ pint cream or ½ pint sauce Crème; ¼ lb carrots; ¼ lb onions; ½ pint white wine; 2 tablespoons oil. Cooking time: 45-50 minutes.

Place shad in a fish kettle or other suitable vessel after covering the bottom with sliced carrots and onions which have been tossed briefly in butter. Season fish, pour wine, sprinkle oil on top and marinate for 2 hours. Bring to the boil on the stove, cover and finish cooking in a moderate oven, 375° F or Gas Mark 4. Drain fish well and serve on sorrel in *sauce Crème*, reduce stock to a syrup and glaze fish with it.

⊡ Oseille II * *with Sorrel*

Steam 2 lb of sorrel with 3 thinly sliced onions which have been tossed in butter and season with salt, pepper, a little crushed garlic and a little chopped chervil. Brown shad on both sides, place in a suitable vessel with the sorrel arranged above, below and all round. Braise slowly in a warm oven, 350° F or Gas Mark 3, for 1½ hours. If possible cook the fish in a fire-proof dish so that it can be served at once.

ANCHOIS * *ANCHOVY*

Small fish of the herring family; it has a strong flavour and it is mainly smoked or packed in oil and used for garnishing different preparations or as *purées*, mixed with butter (see cold *hors d'œuvre*). Anchovy can only be fried immediately after it has been caught when it is absolutely fresh.

BAR * *BASS*

In the Mediterranean it is known under the name of *Bar* or *Loup de mer*. There are many ways of preparation. The small fish are deep fried, shallow fried, grilled or poached. Similar in shape to salmon, bar has very white flesh and a great number of bones.

▣ Grillé au Fenouil * *Grilled with Fennel*

Grill the fish, if possible, on a barbecue. Before grilling insert a branch of green fennel through the mouth into the body. Serve with White Butter sauce or *sauce Hollandaise.*

▣ Poché, Sauce Chivry * *Poached with Chivry sauce*

For 8 *persons:* 1 *bass, weighing about* 3½ *lb;* 1¼ *lb potatoes;* ¾ *pint sauce Chivry.* Cooking time: 45 minutes.

Cook the fish in fish stock and serve with *sauce Chivry* and boiled potatoes. Poached bass can be served with any of the usual fish sauces.

▣ Rôti I * *Baked*

For 8 *persons:* 1 *bass, weighing about* 3½ *lb;* 2 *tablespoons oil;* 6 *oz butter.* Cooking time: 45-50 minutes.

Score fish, toss in seasoned flour, brush with oil and place in a pan or baking tin which has been well heated and buttered so that it does not stick. Put in a hot oven, temperature 450° F or Gas Mark 6, and repeatedly baste with melted butter while it cooks. Bake golden brown and serve with Herb butter or a fish sauce. All large fish can be prepared in this way.

▣ Rôti II * *Baked*

For 10 *persons:* 1 *bass, weighing about* 5½ *lb;* 6 *oz butter;* ¼ *pint oil;* 20 *small boiled potatoes.* Cooking time: 8 minutes.

Cut the fish into steaks each weighing about 7 oz, toss in seasoned flour, brush with oil and arrange in a greased, shallow ovenproof dish. Pour the melted butter all over and bake until golden brown in a hot oven, temperature 425° F or Gas Mark 7. Remove from the oven, sprinkle with *Noisette* butter and either garnish with the boiled potatoes or serve the latter separately. (*See illustration p.* 326).

BARBUE * *BRILL*

This excellent fish is treated in the same way as turbot. Whole fish must be scaled. Cook in fish stock, garnish with parsley and lemon slices and serve with *sauce Hollandaise*. Fillets of brill are treated in the same way as fillets of sole. This fish is served at formal dinners, prepared in a number of different ways.

Barbue à l'Amiral

For 8 persons: 1 brill or 1 turbot, weighing about 3½ lb; ¾ lb Zéphyr forcemeat; ¾ pint white wine; 2 oz buerre Homard; 1 lobster, weighing about 1¼ lb; 2 pints mussels; ½ lb shrimps; 12 mushrooms; 1 truffle; 1¼ pints sauce Cardinal; ¾ pint sauce Villeroi. Cooking time: 40-50 minutes.

Slit the black skin of the fish along the middle and raise the fillets in order to remove the backbone. Fill the inside of the fish with the *Zéphyr* stuffing and replace the fillets. Cover the fish with a buttered greaseproof paper and, after adding the white wine and seasoning, bake in a moderate oven, 375° F or Gas Mark 4, basting frequently. Serve the fish on a hot dish and mask it with the *sauce Cardinal* to which has been added the reduced cooking liquor and the *beurre Homard.* The following are used to garnish the fish; slices of the lobster's tail; the mussels which have been poached, drained, dipped in the *sauce Villeroi* and fried; the turned, cooked mushrooms and slices of truffle.

▣ Farcie Denise * *Stuffed*

For 10 persons: 1 brill, weighing about 4½-5 lb; ½ lb whiting without skin or bones; 1 pint thick cream; ½ lb mushrooms; ½ pint white wine; ½ pint sauce Béchamel; 1 onion; 3 shallots; 2 egg whites; 2 oz butter. Cooking time: 1 hour.

Clean, scale and trim the brill. Make a long incision on the dark side and loosen fillets just enough to make it possible to take out the backbone carefully. Pass the whiting flesh several times through the finest blade of the mincer, mix with the two egg whites, season with salt and pepper and pass through a fine sieve. Place this forcemeat on ice in a bowl until thoroughly cooled, gradually fold in ½-¾ pint cream and test in boiling water to see if it coheres; if it breaks up when dropped into the boiling water, add more egg white. Finally, mix the forcemeat with a *purée* of mushrooms which have been passed through a fine sieve raw, cooked in butter and cooled. Stuff the fish with this mixture and replace fillets on top of it; use the remainder of forcemeat to make small *quenelles* and poach in salted water. Place the stuffed fish and sliced onions and shallots on the bottom of a fish-kettle, season and add white wine. Cover with buttered paper and place in a moderate oven, temperature 375° F or Gas Mark 4 and cook, basting frequently. Remove the fish from the fish-kettle and leave in a warm place covered with buttered paper. Strain stock, reduce, add the *Béchamel* and remaining cream, season with paprika and strain the sauce. Garnish the fish with the *quenelles*, coat lightly with the sauce and serve the rest separately.

▣ Soufflée Victoria

For 8 persons: 1 brill or turbot, weighing about 3 lb; ½ lb salmon; ¼ pint cream; 1 egg white; 1½ pints white wine; 1 small lobster; 1 truffle; 1¼ pints sauce Cardinal. Cooking time: 1 hour.

Prepare the brill in the same way as for *Barbue Farcie Denise* (*see* above), which is then seasoned and stuffed with a *Zéphyr* stuffing made with the salmon, egg white and cream. Replace the fillets and place on a buttered dish containing the white wine and seasoning and poach carefully in a hot oven, 400° F or Gas Mark 6. The fish should not be covered with the wine and a piece of buttered greaseproof paper is placed on top. Lift this paper and baste frequently. Carefully put the brill on a large hot dish, mask with some of the *sauce Cardinal* and garnish with the round slices of lobster and truffle. The rest of the sauce is served separately.

Barbue Théodora

For 7-8 persons: 1 *brill, weighing about* 3¼ *lb;* 1 *pint white wine;* 1 *lb potato croquette mixture;* ¼ *lb shrimp tails;* 2 *oz flour;* 2 *oz butter;* 1 *tablespoon concentrated tomato purée;* 1 *small onion; parsley; thyme; bay leaf.* Cooking time: 35-45 minutes.

The fish may be filleted or cooked whole; in the latter case it should not weigh more than 3¼ lb. Line a buttered dish with sliced onions, parsley stalks, a piece of bay leaf and thyme and place fish on top. Season, add white wine and a little water, cover with a piece of buttered paper and poach slowly in a moderate oven, 375° F or Gas Mark 4. Mix shrimp tails with potato mixture, shape into tiny pears on a floured board, breadcrumb and fry in deep fat at the last moment. Make a *roux* with the flour and butter, add the strained cooking liquor to make a sauce, reduce, season and strain. Keep back 5 spoons of this sauce and mix with the tomato *purée.* Serve the drained fish, coat with the white wine sauce and decorate in a lattice pattern with the red sauce, using a strong paper bag with a corner cut off. Place *croquettes* all round and serve the rest of the sauce separately.

▣ Tosca

For 6 *persons:* 1 *brill or* 1 *turbot, weighing about* 3 *lb;* ⅜ *pint white wine;* 4 *fl oz tomato purée;* 2 *oz flour;* ¼ *lb butter;* 1 *lb forcemeat for fish quenelles.* Cooking time: 30-40 minutes.

Poach the fish and prepare a white wine sauce from the butter, flour and wine. To one-third of this sauce add the tomato *purée* and season with paprika. Use a spoon to shape the fish *quenelles.* Set the fish on a dish, mask it with the rest of the white wine sauce, surround with the *quenelles,* coated with the tomato sauce. Serve very hot.

▣ Filets Chauchat

For 4 *persons:* 1 *brill, weighing about* 2 *lb;* 1 *onion; thyme; bay leaf; parsley;* ½ *pint white wine;* 1 *oz flour;* 2 *oz butter;* 2 *egg yolks;* ½ *lb potatoes, boiled in their jackets and then peeled;* 2 *oz grated Parmesan;* 1 *tablespoon breadcrumbs.* Cooking time: 15 minutes.

Remove and skin fillets. Make a fish stock with the bones, the sliced onion, a small piece of bay leaf, thyme, parsley stalks, the white wine and ½ a pint water. Place fillets in a buttered pan, add stock, cover with a piece of buttered paper and poach. When done make a *roux* with the butter and flour, reduce the stock and boil it up with the *roux.* Season, remove from heat and thicken with the egg yolks. Arrange the fillets on a dish large enough to arrange the potatoes around them. Sprinkle with a little cheese, coat well with the sauce, sprinkle again with cheese and the breadcrumbs and melted butter. Brown in a very hot oven and serve at once.

▣ Suprême Cambacérès

For 8 *persons:* 1 *brill, weighing about* 4½ *lb;* 1 *carrot;* 1 *onion;* 2 *leeks;* ¾ *lb mushrooms;* 1 *small truffle;* ½ *pint cream;* ¼ *pint Béchamel;* ½ *pint sauce aux Crevettes;* ¼ *lb shrimp tails;* ½ *pint white wine; thyme; bay leaf; parsley.* Cooking time: 15 minutes.

Carefully loosen fillets of brill along backbone and skin. Remove gills from the head, crush bones and make a concentrated stock with the white wine, water, bay leaf, thyme, onion and parsley stalks. Cut the red part of the carrot, the white of the leeks, 1 onion, 2 oz mushrooms and the truffle in *julienne*, toss lightly in butter, add the strained fish stock, season and simmer for 10 minutes. Place brill fillets in a buttered fire-proof dish and pour on stock with *julienne*. Poach the fish fillets slowly in the oven, 375° F or Gas Mark 4, remove from stock and place on a dish. Reduce the stock to a creamy sauce with the cream and the *Béchamel*, season well, and pour over the fillets without straining. Garnish with 8 large grilled mushroom heads filled with the shrimp tails bound with the *sauce aux Crevettes*.

Baudroie (Lotte de Mer) * *Burbot*

The flesh of this fish is white and firm and it is economical to use, since there is hardly any waste apart from the backbone. Since however, it gives off a lot of moisture in cooking, it should not be deep or shallow fried, but boiled or poached and served with a fairly thick sauce.

Bouillabaisse Marseillaise * *Fish Broth*

For 10 persons: 5½ lb of fish (John Dory, red mullet, conger eel, whiting); 1 lb crawfish (lobster tails are very suitable); the white of two leeks; 2 large onions; ½ lb tomatoes; 2 cloves of garlic; 3 fl oz olive oil; parsley; bay leaf; saffron; savory; fennel leaves. Cooking time: 20-25 minutes.

Clean, scale and wash fish thoroughly then cut in pieces. Slice onions and leeks thinly and fry light brown in oil; add the peeled, seeded and coarsely chopped tomatoes and the crushed garlic. As soon as the tomatoes have softened, add the crawfish and the fish except for the red mullet and whiting, add enough water barely to cover them, salt lightly, add coarsely chopped parsley, a large pinch of saffron, bay leaf, fennel and savory and the remainder of the oil and boil briskly for 8-10 minutes. The brisk boiling means that the oil binds the contents to a certain extent. To bind even further, the whiting and red mullet are now added. Cook for another 10 minutes. Pour broth into a soup tureen on to thin slices of French bread and serve the fish on a dish (with the crawfish, or crawfish tails cut in pieces) and serve both together. In Paris, *Bouillabaisse* is made very successfully from gurnard, conger eel, grey mullet, sole, dory, whiting, crawfish (or rock lobster), or Dublin Bay prawns. If one does not want to eat the broth separately, the fish is taken out, the broth is boiled down considerably and poured over the fish, garnishing the dish with small slices of white bread fried in oil.

Bourride * *Mixed Fish Dish*

This regional dish is less well known than *bouillabaisse*. It is made from conger eel, gurnard, red mullet, rock salmon, whiting and others; it is not necessary to use every one of these varieties. Cover the bottom of a casserole with sliced onions, 1 piece fennel, a *bouquet garni* and dried orange peel (this is indispensable), cut the fish in pieces and lay on top; cover with water, season with salt and pepper and boil briskly for 15 minutes. In the meantime make *sauce Aïoli*, (*see p.* 160) and mix a little of it with 2-3 egg yolks and a few spoonfuls of the fish stock. Pour a little fish stock on to some slices of French bread in a soup tureen. Remove fish with a skimming ladle and place in a serving dish, thicken the fish stock with the egg mixture over heat but without boiling and strain on to bread. Serve the fish, the thickened broth and the *sauce Aïoli* together.

CABILLAUD, AIGLEFIN, COLIN * *COD, HADDOCK, HAKE*

These three fish are members of the same family. Cod and haddock are also dried and salted. They are freely interchangeable for most recipes. They can all be cooked in fish stock and served with any desired sauce, or filleted or sliced and shallow or deep fried.

▣ à l'Anglaise * *Poached Cod or Hake*

For 5 persons: 2 lb fresh cod or hake; 2 lb potatoes; ½ lb butter; 2 lemons; parsley. Cooking time: 25 minutes.

Cook the cod in fish stock or in salt water with a dash of vinegar. Drain well, and arrange on a suitable dish. Garnish with boiled potatoes, chopped parsley and lemon. Serve with melted butter. The potatoes may also be served separately.

▣ Frit Sauce Tartare * *Deep Fried with Tartare Sauce*

Clean fish, cut into slices ¾-inch thick, egg and breadcrumb, fry in very hot deep fat and serve with fried parsley. Serve *sauce Tartare* separately.

▣ Grillé * *Grilled*

Cut the fish into slices 1½-inches thick, sprinkle with oil or melted butter and grill. Served with quarters of lemon, anchovies, or *Maître d'Hôtel butter.*

▣ Mistral

For 4 persons: 1 cod, weighing about 1½ lb; ¾ lb tomatoes; ½ lb mushrooms; 1 small clove garlic; ¼ pint white wine; ¼ pint oil; ½ oz breadcrumbs. Cooking time: 20 minutes.

Cut fish into 4 equal slices, flour and fry for 2 minutes on each side in hot oil; place in a deep baking dish. Dice peeled, seeded tomatoes coarsely and toss well in oil together with the sliced mushrooms, season with salt, pepper and crushed garlic, add white wine, boil up briefly and pour over fish. Sprinkle with breadcrumbs and a little oil, cook and brown top in oven.

Carrelets et Limandes * *Plaice, Dab and Lemon Sole*

These are all very popular flat fish and vary in quality. The dab has a grey skin while the lemon sole is dark brown with a marbled pattern. It can, if necessary, replace the sole. These fish are usually shallow or deep fried.

COLIN * *HAKE (see Cod)*

The flesh of this fish is white and flaky and is very easily digested.

▣ à l'Anglaise * *Poached*

(*See Cabillaud à l'Anglaise above; also illustration p.* 324).

Colin Parmentier

For 6 persons: 1 *lb potatoes, boiled in their jackets and sliced;* 1 *boned and skinned hake, weighing about* 1 *lb;* ¼ *lb mushrooms;* 2 *hardboiled eggs;* 1 *pint sauce aux Crevettes, or sauce Béchamel with a little tomato;* 2 *oz butter.* Cooking time: 15 minutes.

Make a ring of overlapping potato slices round a rather shallow round baking dish. Put the flaked hake (or other left-over fish) in the middle and cover with thinly sliced mushrooms sautéed in butter. Coat with sauce, sprinkle chopped, hardboiled egg yolk on top, sprinkle with butter and put in a moderate oven, 375° F or Gas Mark 4, for about 15 minutes.

◘ Filets Bercy

For 4 persons: 1 *hake, weighing about* 1½ *lb;* ¼ *pint white wine;* 2 *shallots;* ½ *oz flour;* 2 *oz butter; lemon juice; parsley;* 1 *oz breadcrumbs.* Cooking time: 8 minutes.

Fillet the fish and make stock with the bones and trimmings. Place fillets in a buttered dish and poach with the prepared stock. Toss the chopped shallots in butter, reduce with white wine and boil down to half. Strain stock and add salt, pepper, the juice of ½ lemon, the shallot mixture and chopped parsley. Bring to the boil, remove from heat, and using a whisk stir in the flour kneaded with 1 oz butter. Bring to the boil briefly, remove from heat and combine with remainder of butter. Place fillets in a buttered baking dish, pour the sauce over the fish, sprinkle with breadcrumbs and a little melted butter and brown in a hot oven or under the grill.

◘ Bretonne

For 4 persons: 1 *hake, weighing about* 1½ *lb;* ¼ *pint white wine;* 1 *carrot;* 1 *turnip; the white of* 1 *leek;* 2 *shallots; parsley; lemon;* 2 *oz butter;* ½ *oz flour; breadcrumbs.* Cooking time: 20 minutes.

Proceed in the same way as for *Filets Bercy*, but add a *julienne* of carrot, turnip and leek cooked in butter to the sauce and then brown in a hot oven.

◘ Florentine

For 4 persons: 1 *hake, weighing about* 1½ *lb;* 1½ *lb spinach;* 1 *pint sauce Mornay;* 1 *oz grated cheese;* 2 *oz butter;* ¼ *pint white wine.* Cooking time: 10 minutes.

Fillet fish, skin fillets and make a little fish stock with the bones, white wine and aromatics, i.e., onions, shallots, seasonings, *bouquet garni.* Remove stalks from spinach, boil, squeeze out all moisture, toss in butter and season with salt, pepper and grated nutmeg. Poach fillets in the fish stock, pour off stock, reduce, and add to *sauce Mornay.* Place the cooked spinach in an oval baking dish, place the well-drained fillets on top, cover entirely with *sauce Mornay*, sprinkle with grated cheese and a little melted butter and brown in the oven or under the grill.

Congre (Anguille de Mer) * *Conger Eel*

This fish is larger and coarser than the river eel. It is usually cut in chunks, cooked in stock and served with Caper sauce. It can also be larded with strips of bacon and baked in the oven, being frequently basted with butter, and served with a fish sauce and baked potatoes. Fillets, cut in longish pieces, marinated, dipped in batter and deep fried, are served with *sauce Tomate.*

DAURADE (BRÈME DE MER) * *SEA BREAM*

The sea bream is either cooked in fish stock and served with any desired fish sauce or deeply scored and grilled, being brushed with oil at frequent intervals. *Maître d'Hôtel butter* or some other *beurre composé* is one of the best accompaniments.

◘ Bercy aux Champignons

For 6 persons: 3 *sea bream, each weighing about* 1 *lb*-1¼ *lb;* ¾ *pint dry white wine;* ½ *pint water;* ½ *lb thinly sliced, poached mushrooms;* 4 *shallots; chopped parsley;* ¼ *lb butter;* 1 *oz flour; juice of* ½ *lemon.* Cooking time: 25 minutes.

Poach the fish in ¼ pint of white wine and the water and then remove it from the liquor. Strain off about ½ pint fish stock to which has been added salt, pepper, lemon and parsley. Fry the shallots in the butter and add the remainder of the dry white wine. Reduce by half and stir in the fish stock. Bring to the boil and add a mixture of the flour and melted butter. Boil for a few minutes and, after removing from the heat, add a knob of butter. Serve the fish on a long dish, decorate with the mushrooms and mask with the sauce.

◘ aux Champignons * *with Mushrooms*

For 2 persons: 1 *sea bream, weighing about* 1¼ *lb;* ¼ *pint white wine;* ½ *lb mushrooms, sliced;* 3 *shallots, chopped;* ½ *lemon;* 2 *oz butter;* 2 *oz butter;* 1 *tablespoon flour; chopped parsley.* Cooking time: 20 minutes.

Scale fish, clean inside and cut off the fins and half the tail. Sweat the shallots in a little butter, place them on the bottom of an oval baking dish and poach the mushrooms with butter and lemon juice. Put the sea bream on top, season with salt and pepper and poach with white wine and the mushroom stock. When the fish is cooked arrange it on a long dish and keep it hot. Strain the fish stock, thicken it with flour, mixed with a little butter, bring to the boil, remove from the heat, add a large lump of butter and strain. Cover the fish with this sauce, garnish with the poached sliced mushrooms and a fluted mushroom cap and sprinkle chopped parsley on the mushroom slices. Serve very hot.

◘ Rôtie * *Baked*

For 3-4 persons; 1 *sea bream, weighing about* 1 *lb;* 2 *very thin, large slices of bacon;* 2 *oz butter;* ¼ *pint cream.* Cooking time: 45 minutes.

Prepare fish, salt lightly, wrap in bacon and place in a dish in which some butter has been heated. Place the fish in a hot oven, 400° F or Gas Mark 6, and bake, basting several times. When the bacon comes away from the fish and it is a golden brown, take it out and place on serving dish. Pour off most of the fat from the pan and remove bacon. Reduce the residue with the cream, stir in a knob of butter, season lightly and pour this sauce round the fish.

Eperlans Frits * *Deep Fried Smelts*

Smelts are a very delicate small fish which require careful cleaning. Pull out the gills which will also remove the entrails, then wipe and dry gently and cook whole.

For 4 persons: 1½ *lb smelts; lemon; parsley.* Cooking time: 2-4 minutes.

Dip smelts in milk, coat with flour, shake off surplus and fry fish in very hot deep fat until they are very crisp. Serve very hot with fried parsley and lemon slices. They can also be breadcrumbed and deep fried.

Equilles ou Lançons Frits * *Deep Fried Sand Eels*

For 4 persons: 1½ lb sand eel; lemon; parsley. Cooking time: 2-4 minutes.

Treat these small, eel-like fish in the same way as smelts. They are always deep fried, but never breadcrumbed.

Friture Méditerranée * *Assorted Fried Mediterranean Fish*

This is a Mediterranean speciality for the utilisation of the various small fish which are caught in abundance. A typical assortment would be the following: red mullet, sardines, whiting, sprats, *solinettes* (a small sole which rarely exceeds 5 inches in length), anchovies, mussels, Venus shells and *julienne* or strips of John Dory.

Wash, dry, season with salt and a squeeze of lemon juice and marinate the fish for half an hour. Dip in milk, then flour and deep fry in oil. Drain well and arrange in clusters, garnishing with lemon halves and fried parsley. Allow approximately half a pound of fish per person. (*See illustration p.* 326).

HARENG * *HERRING*

These fish may be eaten fresh, salted or smoked (if they are salted and then dried in smoke, they are known as kippers), and can be served in a number of ways. They can be grilled or prepared *à la Meunière*. They may be accompanied by various fish sauces, or *sauce Moûtarde*.

▣ Grillés Diable * *Devilled and Grilled*

For 6 persons: 6 herrings, each weighing about ½ lb; mustard; breadcrumbs; oil: ½ pint sauce Ravigote. Cooking time: 10 minutes.

Score the fish, coat with mustard and sprinkle with breadcrumbs. Grill the herrings, basting them with oil, if necessary. Serve the *sauce Ravigote* separately.

▣ Grillés Maître d'Hôtel

Grill some herrings and serve with *Maître d'Hôtel* butter.

▣ Grillés, Sauce Moutarde * *Grilled with Mustard Sauce*

Cut open the belly of the herrings, clean them, bone if preferred, flour and brush with oil. Grill or fry in the pan. Serve with *sauce Moûtarde.*

▣ Meunière * *Shallow Fried*

For 6 persons: 6 herrings; 1 lemon; 2 oz butter; 1 tablespoon oil; chopped parsley. Cooking time: 10 minutes.

Trim, clean, wash, score and season the herrings, flour them and fry brown on both sides in half butter and half oil. Arrange on a long dish, sprinkle with lemon juice and chopped parsley and pour plenty of *Noisette* butter on top.

Limande * *Dab*

See under Plaice, Dab and Lemon sole.

MAQUEREAUX * *MACKEREL*

Small mackerel are usually fried while large ones are cut up into pieces which are poached in water containing salt and vinegar. They may be accompanied by a white wine sauce, by *Maître d'Hôtel* butter or, if cold, by a *sauce Vinaigrette* with mixed herbs. Alternatively the fish can be filleted and prepared according to the following recipes.

⊡ Grillés Maître d'Hôtel * *Grilled with Herb Butter*

Cooking time: small mackerel fillets of ¼ lb—10 minutes; larger mackerel fillets of about ½ lb—15 minutes.

Prepare fish; flour, oil and grill them. Serve on a hot dish sprinkled with melted Herb butter and chopped parsley. Cut open large mackerels down the back, so that the two halves are held together by the belly skin and incise the backbone in 2 places to aid cooking. Grill slowly.

⊡ Filets Meunière * *Shallows Fried Fillets*

Prepare in the same way as all fried fish. Score whole mackerel before frying. Frying time for fillets—4-5 minutes, for whole fish of ½ lb—10 minutes.

⊡ Filets Mireille

For 4 persons: 2 mackerels, each weighing about 1 *lb; ¼ lb mushrooms;* 1 *small onion;* 2 *shallots; ½ lb tomatoes.* Cooking time of fillets: 5-6 minutes.

Fillet fish, season, flour and shallow fry in very hot oil on both sides. Remove and place on a dish. Place fresh oil in the pan. Fry the chopped mushrooms, shallots, onion and a little garlic in it and pour over the fillets, together with a few drops of vinegar which have also been heated in the pan. Surround with the peeled, seeded tomatoes which have been fried in oil and sprinkle chopped parsley over all.

⊡ Vénitienne

For 4 persons: 2 mackerels, each weighing about 1 *lb; ¼ pint white wine;* 1½ *lb potatoes; ½ pint sauce Vénitienne; parsley, chervil, tarragon.* Cooking time of fillets: 5-6 minutes.

Poach fillets in white wine and pour over them the *sauce Vénitienne* to which the reduced white wine has been added. Sprinkle chopped parsley, tarragon and chervil on top and serve with boiled potatoes.

Matelote Spéciale * *Special Fish Stew*

For 6 persons: ½ lb salmon; ½ lb fillets of sole; ½ lb turbot (the weights are net of skin and bone); ¼ lb quartered and poached mushrooms; ¼ lb small onions, steamed so that they remain white; ¼ lb fish quenelles; ½ pint white wine; ¼ pint mushroom stock; 2 *oz butter;* 1 *oz flour; ¼ pint cream;* 3 *egg yolks;* 2 *chopped shallots; meat glaze;* 12 *half-moon shaped pieces of Puff pastry.* Cooking time: 5-6 minutes.

Cut the fish into pieces and poach in white wine and mushroom stock together with the chopped shallots. Remove the fish and reduce the liquor a little. Thicken with the butter and flour mixed together and bring the sauce to the right consistency by mixing in the egg yolks which have already been blended with the cream. Season to taste and take off the boil. Add the fish to the sauce and serve garnished with the mushrooms, small onions and *quenelles*. Pour over a little melted glaze and surround with the Puff pastry shapes.

MERLAN * *WHITING*

Whiting is also considered an economical fish, but its flesh is finer and more delicate than that of the herring. It can be prepared in many ways and it is very suitable for fish forcemeats.

◘ Frits * *Deep Fried*

1 *whiting per person, weighing about* ½ *lb:* Cooking time: 7-8 minutes.

Clean, wash and dry the whiting; dip in seasoned milk, turn in flour, shake off surplus, and fry till crisp in very hot deep fat. Serve with fried parsley and lemon slices. It can also be served with *sauce Rémoulade.*

◘ Bercy

For 4 *persons:* 4 *whiting, each weighing about* ½ *lb;* ¼ *pint white wine;* ¼ *pint fish stock;* 2 *shallots; parsley; lemon;* 2 *oz butter;* ½ *oz flour;* 1 *oz breadcrumbs.* Cooking time: 10-12 minutes.

Treat the whiting in exactly the same way as *Filets de Colin Bercy* (*see p.* 315). Fish stock may be replaced by light *bouillon* or water.

◘ à la Dieppoise

For 4 *persons:* 4 *whiting, each weighing about* ½ *lb;* ¼ *pint white wine;* ¼ *pint fish stock;* 2 *shallots;* 1 *oz butter;* ½ *oz flour;* ¼ *lb shrimp tails;* 1½ *pints cooked mussels.* Cooking time: 12-15 minutes.

Poach whiting in white wine with the fish stock and chopped shallots. Remove the fish, strain the cooking liquid and thicken with half the butter made into *buerre manié* with the flour. Enrich with the remaining butter and incorporate the mussels and shrimp tails. Coat with the prepared white wine sauce and sprinkle a little chopped parsley on top.

◘ Dugléré

For 6 *persons:* 6 *whiting, each weighing about* ½ *lb;* ½ *pint white wine;* 2 *onions;* 1 *lb tomatoes;* ¼ *lb butter; just under* 1 *oz flour; parsley.* Cooking time: 10-12 minutes.

Chop up the onions and tomatoes and simmer in a little butter in a frying pan until soft. Lay the fish on top and simmer for a further 10-12 minutes with the seasoning and the white wine. Remove the whiting, reduce the liquor by half and thicken with 2 oz butter blended with the flour. Serve on an oval dish and mask with sauce. Sprinkle with chopped parsley.

◘ aux Fines Herbes * *with Piquant Sauce*

For 6 *persons:* 6 *whiting, each weighing about* ½ *lb;* ¼ *pint white wine;* ½ *pint mushroom stock;* 1 *pint sauce Ravigote.* Cooking time: 10 minutes.

Poach the fish in the white wine and mushroom stock for 10 minutes. Serve on an oval dish and mask with hot *sauce Ravigote* or *Vénitienne.*

Merlan au Gratin

For 4 persons: 4 *whiting, each weighing about* ½ *lb;* 2 *shallots;* 2 *fl oz white wine;* ¼ *lb mushrooms;* 1 *tablespoon oil;* ½ *pint Demi-glace;* 1 *tablespoon tomato purée;* 2 *tablespoons breadcrumbs;* 2 *oz butter; chopped parsley.* Cooking time: 10-12 minutes.

Chop raw mushrooms; brown slightly in oil, add chopped shallots and simmer, add the white wine and boil this down to almost nothing. Add the *Demi-glace*, the tomato *purée* and chopped parsley and bring to the boil. Arrange whiting in a fire-proof dish, pour sauce on top, sprinkle with breadcrumbs and plenty of melted butter and put in a hot oven to cook the whiting and brown the top at the same time. When cooked, sprinkle lemon juice and chopped parsley on top. Fish cooked in this way must always be covered with plenty of sauce since most of the liquid is absorbed. The sauce therefore must not be too thick.

⊡ sur le Plat

For 4 persons: 4 *whiting, each weighing about* ½ *lb;* ¼ *pint white wine;* 2 *shallots; chopped herbs;* 2 *tablespoons breadcrumbs;* 2 *oz butter.* Cooking time: 10-12 minutes.

Butter a fire-proof dish, sprinkle the bottom with chopped shallots, place the scored and seasoned whiting on top, pour on white wine and sprinkle with chopped herbs. Sprinkle with the breadcrumbs and plenty of melted butter and cook and brown in a hot oven, 400° F or Gas Mark 6.

Filets de Merlan Orly * *Fillets of Whiting Orly*

Cooking time: 3-4 minutes.

Carefully fillet the required number of whiting, halve fillets lengthwise and marinate for 30 minutes with chopped parsley, salt, pepper and lemon juice. Dip in batter, fry in very hot deep fat and serve with Tomato sauce.

Quenelles de Merlans en Sauce * *Quenelles in sauce*

For 4 persons: 1½ *lb whiting forcemeat;* 1 *pint sauce Nantua or other suitable sauce.* Cooking time of *quenelles*: 7-8 minutes.

Make *quenelles* with Panada or *Mousseline* forcemeat (see *Forcemeats*) and shape with a soup spoon or fill into buttered *barquettes* and poach in slightly salted water. Drain well and serve with *Nantua*, *Joinville*, *Soubise* or other suitable sauce. The *quenelles* may also be served in a large *vol-au-vent* or in a *croustade* and may also be used to garnish large fish.

MORUE * *DRIED COD*

Dried, salt cod is still popular in southern France, Italy and other countries of the south. Since the introduction of refrigerator trucks and of deep frozen fish it has, however, lost a great deal of its former importance especially in northern and central Europe. Before use it must be soaked thoroughly for about 24 hours in several changes of water. It is mainly used in *Brandade* and *Bouillabaisse*.

▲ Vol-au-Vent de Filets de sole La Vallière, p. 340

Filetti de Sogliola Venini, p. 355 ▼

 ▲ *Filets de sole Herriot, p. 340*

Paupiettes de sole Daumont, p. 347 ▼

▲ *Filets de sole Monte-Carlo, p. 342*

Filets de sole Paillard, p. 344 ▼

▲ Colin à l'Anglaise, p. 314

Filets de sole Murat, p. 343 ▼

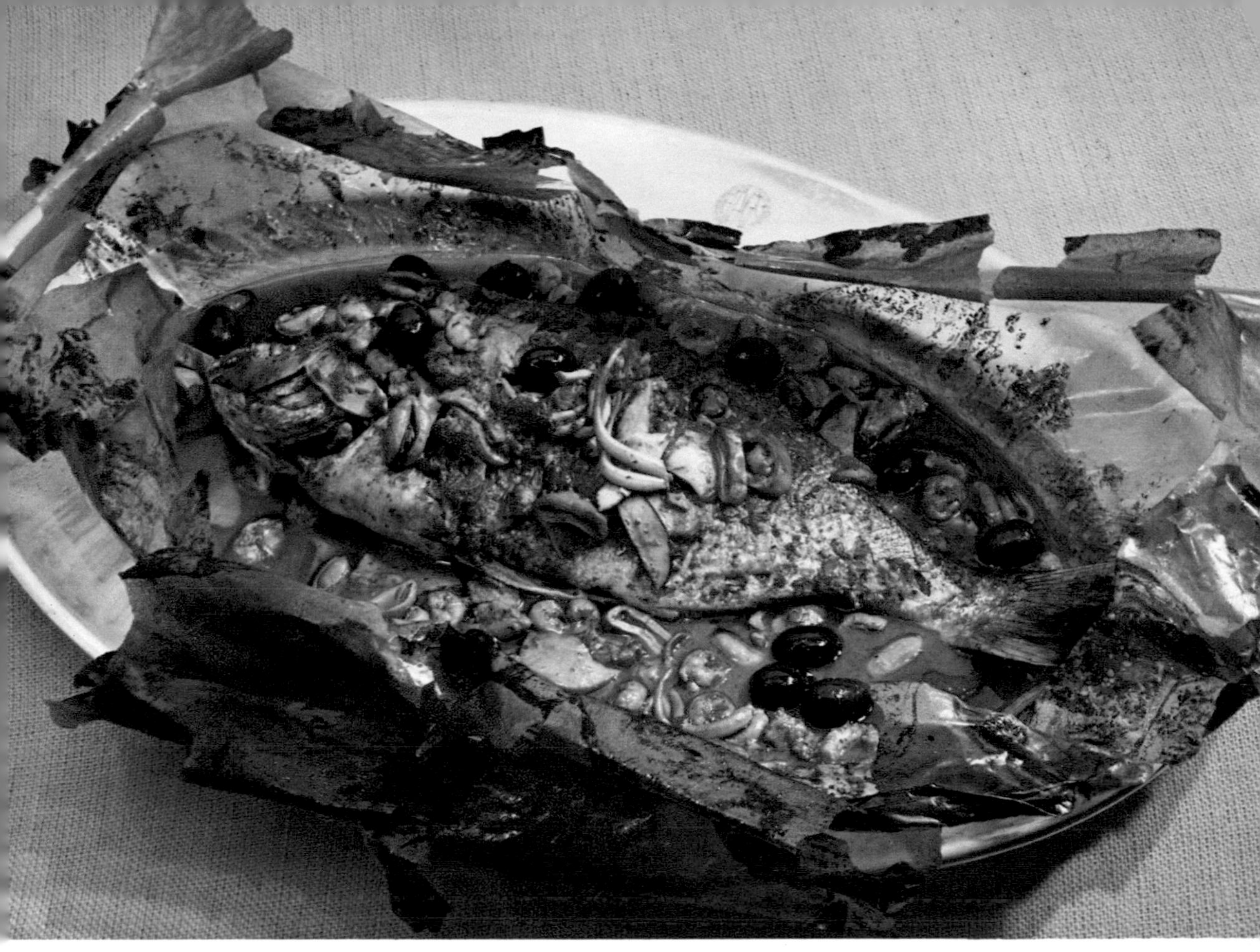

▲ Orata in Cartoccio, p. 355

Turbot Poché sauce Hollandaise, p. 350 ▼

▲ *Bar Rôti, II, p. 310*

Friture Méditerranée, p. 317 ▼

▲ Colin Froid à la Russe p. 351

Rougets Froids à la Niçoise, p. 352 ▼

 ▲ *Filets de sole Floralies, p. 352*

Timbale de sole à la Gelée, p. 353 ▼

Morue Bénédictine

For 3-4 persons: 1 lb dried cod fillets; ½ lb peeled potatoes; ¼ pint oil; 6 fl oz milk; ¼ pint cream. Total cooking time: 25 minutes.

Poach the dried cod fillets in water, then flake and mash finely in mortar with the boiled and well-drained potatoes. Stirring constantly, combine first with the oil and then with the milk and season. Finally fold in the whipped cream gently. Fill the mixture, which should be rather soft, into a buttered baking dish in a mound, sprinkle with melted butter and brown in a hot oven. It is usually filled into *barquettes* and tartlets and used as a garnish.

⊡ au Beurre Noir * *with Black Butter*

For 6 persons: 2 lb dried cod; ½ lb butter; chopped parsley; juice of 1 lemon. Cooking time: 15 minutes.

Soak the dried cod (see general notes about dried cod). Poach in water for 15 minutes, drain, serve on a dish, sprinkle with the lemon juice and parsley and pour over the black butter. (*See Black Butter, p.* 331).

⊡ à la Biscaïenne

For 3-4 persons: 1 lb dried cod fillets; 1½ lb tomatoes; 2 cloves of garlic; ¼ pint oil. Cooking time: 10 minutes.

Soak dried cod fillets, cut in pieces, dry, flour and fry brown in very hot oil. Remove from pan and in the same oil cook the peeled, seeded and quartered tomatoes. Season with salt and pepper and add the crushed garlic. Pour the finished tomatoes, which act as a sauce, over the fish and sprinkle chopped parsley on top.

⊡ aux Epinards * *with Spinach*

For 6 persons: 1 dried cod, weighing about 1½ lb; 1 lb spinach; 2 oz butter; ½ pint sauce Béchamel; 2 cloves garlic; 2 tablespoons breadcrumbs; 1 tablespoon oil. Cooking time for cod: 15-20 minutes.

Cook the chopped spinach together with the garlic in some butter until all the water has evaporated and then blend in the *sauce Béchamel*. Season and add the cooked and flaked cod. Pass through the mincer and pour into a shallow ovenproof dish. Sprinkle with breadcrumbs and brown in a hot oven, 400° F or Gas Mark 6.

⊡ à la Fermière

For 6 persons: 1½ lb dried cod fillets; 1 lb potatoes; 2 oz butter; 2 cloves garlic; parsley; ¼ pint cream; 1 oz gruyère; 1 tablespoon breadcrumbs. Cooking time: 15 minutes.

Poach the cod, bake the potatoes and mash the two together thoroughly. Add the fresh butter, garlic, chopped parsley, and cream. Put in a shallow ovenproof dish, sprinkle with cheese and breadcrumbs and brown in a hot oven, 400° F or Gas Mark 6.

Morue sautée Lyonnaise

For 6 *persons:* 1½ *lb dried cod fillets;* ¼ *lb butter;* 1 *lb boiled potatoes;* 4 *medium-sized onions; vinegar; chopped parsley.* Cooking time: 20 minutes.

Cut up the cod into pieces of the same size, toss in flour and cook in butter. Slice the onions and fry in butter until golden coloured. Add the sliced potatoes and then the prepared cod. *Sauté* in butter for a few minutes and sprinkle over a little vinegar. Serve on a hot dish with chopped parsley on top.

⊡ à la Marinière

For 2-3 *persons:* 1 *lb dried cod;* 1¾ *pints mussels;* ¼ *pint white wine;* ½ *pint milk;* ½ *oz flour;* 2 *oz butter; parsley.* Cooking time: 15-20 minutes.

Poach the well-soaked fish in plenty of water at simmering temperature, starting it in cold water and reduce the temperature at the first signs of the water boiling up. In the meantime cook the mussels (*see p.* 400), remove them from their shells and beard them. Make a sauce with milk and a little of the mussel stock (but do not salt), and butter well. Flake cod, and serve surrounded with mussels; pour on sauce and sprinkle with chopped parsley.

⊡ à la Ménagère

For 2-3 *persons:* 1 *lb dried cod;* 1 *lb potatoes;* 1 *large onion;* 1 *oz butter;* 1 *oz flour;* 1 *pint milk.* Cooking time: 15 minutes.

Cut fish into squares and soak for 24 hours, then poach in fresh water for 15 minutes. Boil the potatoes in their jackets. Toss the chopped onion in the butter, sprinkle with flour, fry the flour without letting it brown, add the milk, season and cook slowly for 15 minutes. Peel the potatoes, slice evenly, place in a fire-proof dish, with the well-drained fish on top, add the sauce and cook slowly for another 10 minutes.

⊡ Parmentier

For 6 *persons:* 1¾ *lb dried cod;* 1 *lb Duchesse potatoes;* 1 *pint sauce Mornay.* Cooking time: 15-20 minutes.

Poach the cod for 15 to 20 minutes. Separate the fish into flakes and arrange in a shallow ovenproof dish, edged with the *Duchesse* potato. Mask with the *sauce Mornay* and brown in a hot oven, 400° F or Gas Mark 6.

⊡ à la Provençale

For 6 *persons:* 1¾ *lb dried cod;* ¼ *pint olive oil;* 1 *chopped onion;* 2 *skinned and cut up tomatoes;* 1 *crushed clove garlic;* ¼ *lb black olives; salt, pepper and chopped parsley.* Cooking time: 25 minutes.

Cut up the cod into large pieces and poach these for 15 minutes. Fry the onion in the oil. Add the tomatoes, garlic and olives. Season, add the drained cod and simmer for 10 minutes. Serve with chopped parsley.

Brandade de Morue * *Brandade of Salt Cod*

For 5 persons: 1 lb very white dried cod fillets; ½ pint oil; ¼ pint milk. Cooking time: 12-15 minutes.

Poach the fish for 12-15 minutes. Do not overcook. Drain, skin, flake and place in a casserole—in which ¼ pint oil has been made seething hot—together with a clove of garlic. Pound fish with a wooden spoon to crush it and gradually combine with the remainder of oil, but add only 2 tablespoons at a time. When the fish has absorbed 6 spoonfuls of oil, add 3 tablespoons of boiling milk and continue adding oil and milk until the mixture resembles mashed potatoes in consistency. Add a little salt and plenty of pepper, arrange in a mound and garnish with triangular white bread *croûtons* fried in oil. The milk may be replaced by cream.

▣ **aux Pommes de Terre** * *with Potatoes*

For 5 persons: 1 lb soaked dried cod; ¼ lb butter; ½ lb potatoes; ¼ pint oil; ¼ pint thick sauce Béchamel; ¼ pint double cream. Cooking time: 25-30 minutes.

Poach fish for 25-30 minutes, drain, skin and flake. Place in a casserole with 1 tablespoon lemon juice and the butter; heat slowly and stir till the butter is absorbed. Mash the boiled, well-drained potatoes and stirring constantly, add first the oil, then the *Béchamel* and finally the fish. Place everything in a casserole, season, add the double cream very gradually and heat slowly.

Mulet * *Grey Mullet*

This fish is rather like bass in appearance and has a white, fatty flesh. The smaller fish are the better and may be grilled, deep or shallow fried, boiled in fish stock or served cold with *sauce Vinaigrette.* All the foregoing recipes for bass are suitable for grey mullet.

Raie * *Skate (Ray)*

A large, flat diamond-shaped fish, skate has a firm tasty flesh. Some skate exude an unpleasant smell of ammonia varying in strength during cooking. This odour has nothing to do with the freshness of the fish, but is a feature of certain individual fish. The thornback ray is the most popular of these fish.

▣ **au Beurre Noir** * *with Black Butter*

For 6 persons: 3½ lb ray; 6 oz butter; 2 tablespoons capers; 1 tablespoon vinegar; chopped parsley. Cooking time for pieces of 9-10 oz: 15 minutes.

Cut fish in pieces, simmer in fish stock, drain well and arrange on a long dish. Season with salt and pepper and sprinkle the capers and coarsely chopped parsley on top. Brown the butter in a pan, add the vinegar, reduce to half and pour over fish.

▣ **Frite** * *Deep Fried*

If obtainable, very small ray should be used. Large ones must be cut into suitable pieces. Dip in seasoned milk, flour, and fry in deep fat for 6-8 minutes. Serve with fried parsley and lemon. Tomato sauce should be served separately with the larger pieces.

Raie à la Normande

For 6 persons: 3½ lb ray; 2 tablespoons capers; ½ pint thick cream. Cooking time: 15 minutes.

Poach fish as for *Raie au Beurre Noir*, drain well, serve and sprinkle capers on top. Season cream, reduce a little, pour over fish and sprinkle a few drops of vinegar over whole.

Croûtes au Foie de Raie * *Skate Liver with Croûtons*

Ray liver is much appreciated by gourmets and it can be served as an *entrée*. First stamp out white bread *croûtons*, as for *tournedos*, and fry them brown and crisp in butter. Poach liver in slightly salted water with vinegar; drain, slice and arrange on *croûtons*. Sprinkle with lemon juice, pour on black butter and sprinkle chopped parsley on top.

ROUGETS * *RED MULLET*

The red mullet is one of the best Mediterranean fish and so delicate in flavour that it should always be prepared in the simplest way. Since it has no gall it does not need to be cleaned. In Nice it is known as the snipe of the sea. On the Côte d'Azur it is taken fresh from the water, wiped, floured and grilled, a method that is highly recommended.

▣ à la Catalane

For 6 persons: 6 small red mullet; 1 *lb tomatoes; ½ lb rice;* 1 *clove of garlic;* 2 *green peppers; fennel leaves; breadcrumbs.* Cooking time of mullet: 7-8 minutes.

Skin, quarter and seed tomatoes and simmer in oil with the crushed clove of garlic and add a little chopped parsley. Clean the red mullet, flour, and fry in oil. Make a *pilaf* with the rice and mix with the seeded, fried and thinly sliced peppers. Put half the tomatoes in an oval baking dish, place mullet on top, cover with the remaining tomatoes and surround with rice. Sprinkle breadcrumbs mixed with chopped fennel on top and brown in a hot oven.

▣ à la Egyptienne

For 6 persons: 6 red mullet, each weighing about 4-5 *oz;* 1 *lb tomatoes;* 1 *clove of garlic; ¼ pint oil; chopped parsley; breadcrumbs.*

Cook tomatoes as for *Rougets à la Catalane*, and mix with chopped parsley. Flour the mullet and fry in oil. Place half the tomatoes in the bottom of an oval baking dish, place red mullet on top, cover with the remaining tomatoes, sprinkle with breadcrumbs and chopped parsley and brown in a hot oven.

▣ au Gratin

Prepare in the same way as *Merlan au Gratin*. (*See* p. 320).

▣ Grillés Maître d'Hôtel * *Grilled with Maître d'Hôtel Butter*

Cooking time for red mullet weighing about 5-6 ounces—7-8 minutes. Prepare in the same way as *Maquereaux Maître d'Hôtel*. (*See* p. 318).

Rouget Meunière * *Shallow Fried Red Mullet*

Prepare in the same way as *Filet de Sole Meunière* (*see* p. 342).

▣ Monte-Carlo

For 6 persons: 6 red mullet, each weighing about 5-6 *oz;* ¼ *lb Anchovy butter;* 1 *lb potato sticks;* 2 *oz Maître d'Hôtel butter;* 6 *slices of white bread cut into the shape of the fish.* Cooking time: 7-8 minutes.

Grill the red mullet, toast the bread shapes and spread these with Anchovy butter. Place the grilled mullet on the toasted bread shapes and arrange the fish on a suitable serving dish. Garnish with the potato sticks and pour over a little *Maître d'Hôtel* butter.

Saint-Pierre * *John Dory*

This excellent but ugly fish is little known. It is so ugly that Saint Peter is alleged to have thrown it back in the water when fishing. The head is unusually large, so there is a great deal of waste. It is however an essential ingredient of *Bouillabaisse* and is also used to make forcemeats. The fillets can be prepared in accordance with any of the methods described so far.

Sardines et Royans * *Fresh Sardines*

These small fish are cleaned and wiped carefully, but not washed, since the flesh would become soft. There are many ways of cooking them, but they are too complicated for ordinary every-day cookery. They are therefore usually simply grilled and served with *Maître d'Hôtel* butter or shallow fried.

SOLES * *SOLE*

The true Dover sole is an excellent fish which may be prepared in a number of different ways. Absolutely fresh sole is an unequalled delicacy. Fish erroneously called sole include lemon sole, dab, grey sole, winter flounder, but they may be substituted successfully in all the following recipes.

▣ Bercy

For 5 persons: 5 *soles, each weighing about* 5-7 *oz;* 2 *shallots;* ¼ *pint white wine;* ¼ *pint fish stock;* 2 *oz butter;* 1 *oz flour; lemon juice; parsley.* Cooking time: 7-8 minutes.

Prepare in exactly the same way as *Filets de Colin Bercy.* (*See p.* 315).

▣ à la Bretonne

For 5 persons: 5 *soles, each weighing about* 6-8 *oz;* ¼ *pint white wine;* 1 *carrot;* 1 *turnip; the white of* 1 *leek;* 2 *shallots;* ½ *oz flour;* 2 *oz butter; parsley;* 2 *small tablespoons breadcrumbs.* Cooking time of soles: 7-8 minutes.

Prepare in the same way as *Filets de Colin Bretonne.* (*See* p. 315).

Sole Colbert

Per person: 1 sole, weighing 7-8 oz. Cooking time: 7-8 minutes.

Skin sole and cut off fins but do not cut off head. Clean, wash and dry and make an incision on the thick side, as though preparing to fillet, but only cut open far enough to roll fillet aside. Cut through the bones at the top and bottom so that they can be removed after cooking. Leaving fillets folded back, dip in flour, egg and breadcrumbs and deep fry in hot fat. Drain well, carefully remove bone and fill hollow with *beurre Colbert*.

▣ à la Dieppoise

For 5 persons: 5 soles, each weighing about 6-7 oz; 2 pints mussels; ¼ lb shrimp tails; ½ pint fish stock; ¼ pint white wine; 1 large shallot; 1 oz flour; 2 oz butter; chopped parsley. Cooking time of soles: 7-8 minutes.

Cook mussels with the white wine, the chopped shallot and pepper but without salt; remove from shells, beard and keep warm in a little of the stock. Poach the sole in a little of the mussel stock, cook the shrimp tails in mussel stock. Make a white *roux* with the flour and half the butter, add the fish stock and the poaching stock of the sole and cook slowly without salting, since the mussel stock is salt enough. Strain sauce, season and add the remainder of the butter. Serve sole garnished with the well-drained mussels and shrimps. Coat with the sauce, sprinkle chopped parsley on top and serve very hot.

▣ Dugléré

For 5 persons: 5 soles, each weighing about 6-7 oz; 5 large tomatoes; 2 shallots; ¼ pint white wine; ½ pint fish stock; 1 oz flour; 2 oz butter; chopped parsley. Cooking time: 7-8 minutes.

Peel, deseed and coarsely dice tomatoes. Cover a buttered baking dish with the chopped shallots and the tomatoes, place sole on top, season, cover with the white wine and fish stock and poach in the oven. When cooked, remove fish, reduce stock including the tomatoes to half, knead the butter and flour together and bind with the reduced stock. Bring to the boil once or twice, add a little chopped parsley, season and pour over the sole.

▣ à la Fécampoise

For 5 persons: 5 soles, each weighing about 6-7 oz; 2 pints mussels; ¼ lb shrimp tails; ¼ pint white wine; 1 shallot; ½ pint thick sauce Joinville without shrimps. Cooking time of sole: 7-8 minutes.

Cook the mussels with the shallot in the white wine, remove from shells and beard; keep the shrimps warm in a little mussel stock. Poach the sole in a little mussel stock and when cooked, reduce stock and add to the sauce. Do not salt. Serve sole, add well drained mussels and shrimps to sauce and cover fish with it. Sprinkle a little chopped parsley on top.

▣ à la Florentine

For 6 persons: 6 soles, each weighing about 7 oz; 2 lb spinach; 1 pint sauce Mornay; 2 oz grated cheese; ¼ pint white wine; 1½ pints fish stock. Cooking time: 8-10 minutes.

Proceed in the same way as for *Colin Florentine*. (*See p.* 315).

Sole Frite au Citron * *Deep Fried Sole with Lemon*

Per person: 1 *sole, weighing about* 6-8 *oz.* Cooking time: 5-7 minutes.

Wash the fish, dry, dip in slightly salted cold milk, then flour and shake off the surplus. Fry sole golden brown in very hot deep fat so that they are firm and crisp. Drain well on a cloth or draining paper and salt lightly on both sides with fine salt. Then throw a handful of washed and carefully dried parsley in the hot fat, remove immediately with a ladle and drain on a cloth. Serve the sole at once on a suitable dish, garnished with the fried parsley and lemon slices.

▣ **au Gratin**

Prepare in exactly the same way as *Merlan au Gratin.* (*See p.* 320). Cooking time: 7-8 minutes.

▣ **Grillée** * *Grilled*

Per person: 1 *sole, weighing about* ½ *lb.* Cooking time: 10-12 minutes.

Skin sole on both sides, cut off the fins and the head if preferred, wash and dry well. Flour (optional), dip in oil and grill, basting with oil from time to time. The grill must be very hot and lightly oiled before placing the sole underneath. Serve on a hot dish, garnished with parsley and lemon, and serve melted butter or *Maître d'Hôtel* butter at the same time.

▣ **Meunière** * *Shallow Fried*

Per person: 1 *sole, weighing about* 7 *oz.* Cooking time: 8-10 minutes.

Season and flour the sole and cook in hot butter. When cooked, pour over the remaining hot melted butter, a few drops of lemon juice and seasonings. Serve very hot.

▣ **Meunière aux Champignons** * *Fried with Mushrooms*

For 6 *persons:* 6 *soles, each weighing about* ½ *lb;* ½ *lb mushrooms.* Cooking time: 8-10 minutes.

Thinly slice the mushrooms and *sauté* them in *Noisette* butter to make a sauce which is then poured over the sole which has been cooked *à la Meunière.*

▣ **Meunière à la Provençale**

For 6 *persons:* 6 *soles, each weighing about* ½ *lb;* ¾ *lb tomatoes;* 6 *anchovy fillets;* 6 *black olives.* Cooking time: 8-10 minutes.

When the sole has been cooked *à la Meunière*, garnish with tomatoes which have been sautéed in oil, and with rolled anchovy fillets having a black olive in the centre of each. Serve with *Noisette* butter.

▣ **Mornay**

For 3 *persons:* 3 *soles, each weighing about* ½ *lb;* ¼ *pint white wine;* ½ *pint sauce Mornay;* 1 *oz grated cheese;* 1 *oz butter.* Cooking time: 10-12 minutes.

Season sole and poach in the white wine. Reduce white wine to ⅓ and add to the sauce. Arrange sole in a buttered baking dish, coat with the sauce, sprinkle cheese on top, sprinkle with melted butter and brown quickly in hot oven or under the grill.

Sole Nantua

For 6 persons: 6 soles, each weighing about ½ lb; the flesh from the tails of 12 crayfish; ¾ pint sauce Nantua. Cooking time: 10-12 minutes.

Poach the sole and arrange on a dish. Garnish with the crayfish tails and mask with the sauce.

⊡ Niçoise

For 6 persons: 6 soles, each weighing about ½ lb; ¾ lb tomatoes, which have been skinned, deseeded and sautéed in butter with a crushed clove of garlic and chopped tarragon; 6 slices of lemon without any rind or pith; 6 anchovies; 6 black olives. Cooking time: 10-12 minutes.

Grill the sole, which have been brushed with oil, and arrange on a dish. Garnish with the tomatoes, decorate with the lemon slices on which are placed the rolled anchovy fillets with a black olive in the centre of each.

⊡ sur le Plat

For 6 persons: 6 soles, each weighing about ½ lb; ½ pint white wine; 2 shallots; mixed herbs; 2 oz breadcrumbs; 2 oz butter. Cooking time: 10 minutes.

Proceed in the same way as for *Merlans sur le Plat*. (*See p.* 320).

⊡ à la Provençale

For 6 persons: 6 soles, each weighing about ½ lb; 10 tomatoes; 1 chopped onion; chopped parsley; 1 clove garlic; 2 oz breadcrumbs; 5 anchovy fillets; ¾ pint sauce Provençale. Cooking time: 10 minutes.

Poach the sole, drain them and serve on a dish. Cut 6 tomatoes in halves, remove the pips and fry. When they are half cooked, remove them in order to fill them with a stuffing made from the following ingredients: the rest of the tomatoes which have been deseeded and sautéed in butter together with the chopped onion, crushed garlic, parsley, mashed anchovy and breadcrumbs. Garnish the fish with the stuffed tomatoes, mask with the sauce and reheat in the oven.

⊡ Saint-Germain

For 3 persons: 3 soles, each weighing about ½ lb; sauce Béarnaise made with 2 egg yolks and ¼ lb butter; 2 oz melted butter; fresh white breadcrumbs; ¾ lb potatoes cut in ball shapes; frying butter. Cooking time: 8-10 minutes.

Prepare sole, dry thoroughly, season, dip in melted butter and then in the breadcrumbs and press down well with a palette knife. Either grill sole after sprinkling them liberally with melted butter or shallow fry in butter. First blanch the nut-sized potato balls, rinse, drain well and fry brown in butter. Serve sole, garnish with the potatoes and serve the *sauce Béarnaise* separately.

Sole au Vin Blanc * *Sole in White Wine Sauce*

For 6 persons: 6 soles, each weighing about ½ lb; ½ pint white wine; 1 *small thinly sliced onion; ¼ pint White Wine sauce; 6 fleurons.* Cooking time: 10 minutes.

Butter a dish and sprinkle with the sliced onions. Place the sole on top, add white wine and bake in a moderate oven, 375° F or Gas Mark 4. When cooked remove sole, strain cooking liquor and reduce by half. Add the White Wine sauce. Serve sole on a dish coated with the completed sauce and arrange *fleurons* around.

FILETS DE SOLE * *FILLETS OF SOLE*

There are innumerable recipes and garnishes for these fillets.

▣ à l'Américaine

For 6 *persons: 3 soles, each weighing about ¾ lb; ¾ lb lobster; ½ lb tomatoes;* 1 *tablespoon cognac; ½ pint white wine; 2 oz butter; parsley; cayenne; tarragon; 2 shallots.* Cooking time of sole: 8-10 minutes. Cooking time of lobster: 10 minutes.

Fillet the sole, make a fish stock with the fish bones and cook the fillets which have been folded in two in this stock. Cook the lobster exactly as for *Homard à l'Américaine.* (*See p.* 391). Reduce the fish stock to a *fumet* and add to the Lobster sauce. Strain the sauce and enrich with butter. Arrange the folded fillets in a ring so that they overlap, put lobster meat in centre and coat with sauce and sprinkle with chopped parsley.

▣ à l'Anglaise

For 6 *persons: 3 soles, each weighing about* 1 *lb; ½ lb fresh breadcrumbs;* 6 *oz butter;* 3 *oz Maître d'Hôtel butter.* Cooking time: 6-7 minutes.

Coat the fillets with egg and breadcrumbs, fry in butter and serve on a dish. Garnish with the softened *Maître d'Hôtel* butter.

▣ Atelier

For 6 *persons:* 3 *soles, each weighing about ¾ lb;* 3 *cooked lobsters, each weighing about* 10-12 *oz; 6 oz cooked mushrooms; ½ lb sweetbreads; ½ pint sauce Homard; ½ pint White Wine sauce; 12 slices truffle; ¼ pint fish stock; ¼ pint white wine.* Cooking time: 8-10 minutes.

Fold the sole fillets and poach them in the white wine and fish stock. Split the lobsters in halves and take out the flesh including that from the claws. Cut up the lobster flesh, mushrooms and sweetbreads into ½-inch cubes and make into a *salpicon* with the *sauce Homard.* Fill the half lobster shells with this *salpicon* and place on top of each 2 well drained overlapping sole fillets. Garnish with one slice of truffle and mask with the White Wine sauce blended with the reduced cooking liquor. Glaze under a hot grill.

Filets de Sole Belle Aurore

For 8 persons: 2 *soles, each weighing about* 1 *lb;* ½ *lb salmon Mousseline forcemeat;* 8 *large crayfish;* 1 *truffle;* ⅜ *pint sauce Nantua; white wine; mirepoix.* Cooking time: 10-12 minutes.

Remove fillets from the sole, stuff them with a little *Mousseline* forcemeat, fold them in two and poach them in some white wine and fish stock. Butter a small conical mould, decorate with truffle slices, fill with salmon forcemeat and poach in water-bath. Cook the crayfish in some white wine with *mirepoix* and shell the tails. Unmould the salmon *mousse* in the middle of a round dish and arrange the fillets in a rose shape with the point in the centre. Cover the fillets with the sauce and garnish with crayfish tails and truffle slices. Place a crayfish head with the claws between the fillets on two sides.

▣ Bercy

For 8 *persons:* 8 *soles, each weighing about* ½ *lb;* 2 *oz shallots;* ½ *pint white wine;* ½ *pint fish stock;* ½ *pint cream;* ¼ lb *butter; juice of half a lemon;* 2 *oz chopped parsley.* Cooking time: 12-15 minutes.

Prepare as for *Filets de Colin Bercy.* (*See p.* 315).

▣ Bombay

For 2 *persons:* 4 *fillets of sole, each weighing about* 3 *oz;* 2 *peeled bananas;* 2 *small slices pineapple;* 1 *sweet red pepper;* ¼ *lb rice;* 2 *oz butter;* ¼ *pint Curry sauce.*

Cook rice in boiling, salted water for 17 minutes; drain, cool, and dry gently with a little butter and a pinch of salt. Season and coat the fillets with flour and fry them in butter. Arrange the fillets on the rice. Cover them with the bananas, cut in slices, the pineapple, cut in small pieces, and the red pepper, cut into strips, all sautéed in butter. Serve Curry sauce at the same time.

▣ Bonne Femme

For 6 *persons:* 3 *soles, each weighing about* 1 *lb;* ¼ *pint white wine;* ½ *lb mushrooms; sauce Hollandaise, made with* 2 *egg yolks and* 6 *oz butter; parsley;* 1 *oz finely chopped shallots.* Cooking time: 8-10 minutes.

Fillet sole and arrange in an oval fire-proof dish with shallots, season and poach with the white wine and an equal quantity of fish stock (made from the bones). Slice the cooked mushrooms, reduce the fish stock almost to a glaze and add both to the *sauce Hollandaise.* Season and add a little chopped parsley. Coat fillets with the sauce, which should not be too thick, and glaze quickly at maximum heat under the grill. The grill must be red hot if the sauce is to brown without curdling.

▣ à la Bourguignonne (ou Mâconnaise)

For 3 *persons:* 3 *soles, each weighing about* ¾ *lb;* 24 *small onions;* ½ *lb mushrooms;* ½ *pint red wine;* ¼ *pint sauce Demi-glace;* 1 *tablespoon chopped shallot;* 1 *oz melted butter mixed with a little flour.* Cooking time: 10 minutes.

Poach the sole in the well-seasoned red wine. Reduce the liquor by half and thicken it with the butter and flour and the *sauce Demi-glace.* Arrange the mushrooms, which have been sautéed in butter, along one side of each fish and the glazed onions along the other side. Mask with the prepared red wine sauce.

Filets de Sole à la Cancalaise

For 6 *persons:* 3 *soles, each weighing about* 1 *lb; the flesh of* 12 *prawns;* 6 *trimmed, poached oysters;* ¾ *pint sauce Normande;* 2 *oz butter.* Cooking time: 10 minutes.

Poach the fillets in white wine and butter, drain them and arrange in the form of a crown. Fill the centre with the prawns and oysters and mask with the *sauce Normande* to which has been added the cooking liquor reduced by half.

◘ Caprice

For 6 *persons:* 12 *fillets of sole;* ½ *lb white breadcrumbs;* 6 *oz butter;* 3 *bananas; mango chutney;* 1 *lemon.* Cooking time: 6-8 minutes.

Coat fillets of sole and peeled quartered bananas with melted butter and white breadcrumbs. Place on a buttered tray and grill under a salamander or grill, occasionally sprinkling with butter. When cooked and an even golden brown, arrange on a dish with banana on top of each fillet and place a spoonful of chutney between each. Cover with *Noisette* butter, garnish with fine slices of lemon and sprinkle with chopped parsley.

◘ Cardinal

For 6 *persons:* 12 *fillets of sole;* ¾ *pint sauce Cardinal;* 6 *oz cooked lobster;* ¼ *pint white wine.* Cooking time of fillets: 8-10 minutes.

Poach fillets in white wine, take them out, reduce stock to almost nothing and add it to the sauce. Cut lobster into small cubes, mix with the sauce and coat the fillets with it.

◘ à la Carmelite

For 8 *persons:* 2 *soles, each weighing about* ¾ *lb;* 1 *lb fresh salmon;* ½ *pint mussels;* ¼ *lb shrimp tails;* ¼ *lb mushrooms;* 12-16 *small crayfish;* 2 *artichoke bottoms;* 8 *truffle slices;* ½ *pint sauce Béchamel;* 2 *fl oz thick cream;* 1 *egg;* 3 *egg yolks;* ½ *pint sauce Nantua; butter.* Cooking time: 25 minutes.

Remove the fillets from the sole, beat them lightly with a flat knife, wipe them dry and place them in a buttered *savarin* mould, alternately with thin fillets cut from a fresh, red salmon. From the remaining salmon, passed twice through the finest blade of a meat grinder, prepare a forcemeat with the thick, cold *Béchamel*, the cream, 1 egg, 3 egg yolks and seasoning. Fill up the mould with this mixture and fold the ends of the fillets over the filling. Poach in water-bath in a moderate oven, 350° F or Gas Mark 3, without allowing the water to boil. Unmould on a round dish. Fill the middle with a garnish of mussels, shrimps, mushrooms, artichoke bottoms and a few slices of truffle, all mixed with *sauce Nantua*. Decorate the mould with a few slices of truffle, and serve the rest of the sauce separately.

◘ aux Champignons * *with Mushrooms*

For 6 *persons:* 3 *soles, each weighing about* 1 *lb;* ½ *lb blanched mushrooms;* ¾ *pint sauce Champignon.* Cooking time: 8-10 minutes.

Poach the folded fillets in the liquor in which the mushrooms were blanched and then arrange them in the form of a crown. Fill the centre with the mushrooms and mask with the *sauce Champignon* to which has been added the cooking liquor reduced by half.

Filets de Sole Crevettes * *Fillet of Sole with Shrimps*

For 6 persons: 3 soles, each weighing about 1 lb; ½ lb shrimp tails; ¾ pint sauce Joinville. Cooking time: 8-10 minutes.

Fillet sole and poach in a concentrated fish stock made from the bones. Reduce stock, add to the sauce, combine with shrimp tails and coat the fillets with sauce.

◘ Herriot

For 6 persons: 3 soles, each weighing about 1 lb; 18 pike quenelles, shaped with coffee spoons; 12 small artichoke bottoms; ½ pint sauce Homard; 12 small slices of truffle; ¼ pint White Wine sauce; 2 oz butter; juice of half a lemon; ¼ pint fish stock; 2 shallots. Cooking time: 8-10 minutes.

Fillet sole, fold and place in a buttered dish sprinkled with finely chopped shallot. Add the lemon juice and fish stock, season with salt, cover with a buttered paper and poach. Drain off the cooking liquor, reduce to a near glaze, add the White Wine sauce, boil and mix in the *quenelles*. Cut the artichoke bottoms into quarters, fry in butter, season with salt and pepper. Arrange the fillets of sole overlapping each other, garnish each fillet with a slice of truffle and mask with the *sauce Homard.* Garnish the dish with the *quenelles* at one end and add the artichokes at the other. (*See illustration p.* 322).

◘ Joinville

For 6 persons: 3 soles, each weighing about ¾ lb; ½ lb flesh of whiting; ½ lb mushrooms; ½ lb shrimp tails; 1 truffle; 1 pint sauce Joinville. Cooking time for fillets: 10-12 minutes.

Prepare a fish *quenelle* filling with the flesh of the whiting. Remove the fillets from the sole, wipe them, stuff with filling, and fold in two. Poach them in well-flavoured fish stock. Prepare a garnish of the mushrooms, shrimps and a few truffle slices. With the rest of the filling, make a flat crown in the centre of a round dish. Place a buttered paper on top, and poach for about 8 minutes in a warm oven, 350° F or Gas Mark 3. Arrange the fillets like a turban on this filling. Heat and bind the garnish with *sauce Joinville* and fill it in the middle of the turban. Cover the fillets with *sauce Joinville* and place a truffle slice on each.

◘ La Vallière

For 4-6 persons: 8 fillets of sole, each weighing about 2½ oz; ¼ lb whiting forcemeat; ½ lb mushrooms; ½ lb crayfish tails; 2 quarts mussels; ¼ pint white wine; 1 small truffle; 1¾ pints sauce Nantua; 1 large pastry case (vol-au-vent). Cooking time of fillets: 10-12 minutes.

Flatten fillets with a knife, spread a layer of whiting forcemeat on each, fold them in two, and poach them with white wine and fish stock. Prepare a garnish of cooked, bearded mussels, mushrooms, shrimps and crayfish tails, bound with *sauce Nantua.* For a dinner party the mussels may be replaced by small fish *quenelles.* Fill the garnish into hot *vol-au-vent*, and arrange the fillets of sole in a ring on top, overlapping each other. Decorate with a slice of truffle, after having covered the fillets with *sauce Nantua.* Instead of using the crayfish tails with the garnish, they may be placed between the fillets of sole. Serve very hot. (*See illustration p.* 321).

Filets de Sole à la Madrilène

For 6 persons: 3 soles, each weighing about 1 lb; 1 lb tomatoes which have been skinned, deseeded and diced; 2 green peppers which have been deseeded and shredded; 12 *stuffed, blanched olives; ¼ lb butter; ¼ pint olive oil; 1 clove garlic; 1 lemon; chopped parsley.* Cooking time: 10-12 minutes.

Stew the tomatoes together with the crushed garlic in butter, then add the olives so that the latter are stewed for only a few seconds. Add a little seasoning. *Sauté* the peppers in oil until they are thoroughly cooked. Fillet the soles and cut up into small pieces. After dipping these first in seasoned milk and then in flour, *sauté* them in olive oil and a little butter until they are brown and crisp. Add the tomatoes, olives and peppers and *sauté* all the ingredients for a few seconds. Add salt and pepper and serve sprinkled with a few drops of lemon juice and some *Noisette* butter.

▣ au Malaga

For 6 persons: 3 soles, each weighing about 1 lb; 48 *Malaga grapes; ½ lb sliced mushrooms; ½ lb chopped tomatoes; 2 oz chopped shallots; ¾ pint Malaga wine; ¼ pint sauce Demi-glace; ¼ lb butter; 1 clove garlic; chopped parsley.* Cooking time: 8-10 minutes.

Fold the fillets of sole and poach together with the grapes in the Malaga. Fry the shallots in 2 oz of butter, add the mushrooms and stew until almost dry. Add the chopped tomatoes and *sauce Demi-glace* and leave to cook for a few minutes. Remove the fillets of sole and reduce the liquor by half. Next add to this liquor the mixture of mushrooms and tomatoes. Season with salt, freshly milled pepper and crushed garlic and finally whisk in the butter. Serve the fillets of sole on a dish, mask with the sauce and sprinkle liberally with chopped parsley.

▣ Marcelle

For 6 persons: 3 soles, each weighing about 1 lb; 1¾ pints cooked mussels; ¾ pint sauce Vin Blanc; ¼ pint fish stock; 1 truffle. Cooking time: 8-10 minutes.

Fold sole fillets in two and poach them for 8 to 10 minutes in the fish stock. Pass the mussels through a sieve and blend the *purée* obtained into the very hot White Wine sauce. Arrange the fillets in a round dish, mask with the sauce and sprinkle with the shredded truffle.

▣ Marguery

For 6 persons: 3 soles, each weighing about 1 lb; 6 oz shrimps; ¾ pint mussels; ¾ pint sauce Vin Blanc; 2 oz butter. Cooking time: 10-12 minutes.

Cook mussels, remove from shells and beard; heat shrimp tails in butter. Poach folded fillets of sole in white wine, reduce stock almost completely, use it to make the sauce and complete the latter with butter. Cover the bottom of an oval baking dish with a little sauce, place fillets on top and garnish with the mussels and shrimp tails. Coat entirely with sauce and glaze in a hot oven or under the grill.

Filets de Sole à la Marinère

For 6 persons: 3 soles, each weighing about 1 lb; 2 pints mussels; ½ pint Fish Velouté made with stock from the sole bones; ¼ pint white wine; 2 shallots. Cooking time: 8-10 minutes.

Cook the mussels with the white wine and the finely chopped shallots, remove from shells and beard. Poach fillets of sole with a little mussel stock without salt, add this stock to the Fish *Velouté*, reduce and enrich with a little butter and cream. Serve fillets side by side. Garnish with the mussels, coat with the sauce and sprinkle with chopped parsley.

▣ Meunière * *Shallow Fried*

For 6 persons: 3 soles, each weighing about 1 lb; ¼ lb butter; ¼ lb flour; 1 lemon; chopped parsley. Cooking time: 6-7 minutes.

Flour the fillets of sole and shallow fry them. Place them on a dish, arrange slices of lemon on top, pour over *Noisette* butter and sprinkle with chopped parsley.

▣ Messaline

For 6 persons: 3 soles, each weighing about 1 lb; ½ lb tomatoes; ¼ lb thinly sliced raw mushrooms; ½ lb shelled prawns; 3 oz butter; paprika; 1 oz tomato purée; ¼ pint dry champagne; 6 globe artichoke bottoms which have been blanched, cooked in butter and cut into quarters. Cooking time: 15 minutes.

Fold the fillets, season with salt and pepper and place them in a long dish. Spread the mushrooms evenly on top of the fish and pour the champagne over. Add the fish bones and bake in a moderate oven, 375° F or Gas Mark 4, for 10 minutes. Take out the bones. Drain the fillets. Reduce the liquor by half and mix in the tomato *purée*. Add the tomatoes which have been skinned, deseeded and cut into quarters. Boil until a creamy sauce is obtained. Remove from the heat, add butter and season with the paprika. Mask the fillets with the sauce and arrange the prawns, artichokes and chopped parsley around the fish.

▣ Monte-Carlo

For 8 persons: 4 soles, each weighing about 1 lb; ¼ pint oil; ¼ lb butter; 2 oz fillets of anchovy; garlic. Cooking time: 6-7 minutes.

Fillet the sole. Salt, flour and fry in oil. Pound the fillets of anchovy and mix with the melted butter. Pour this mixture upon the fillets of sole, decorate with some fillets of anchovy. (*See illustration p.* 323).

▣ Montrouge

For 4 persons: 2 soles, each weighing about 1 lb; ½ lb fresh mushrooms; ½ pint sauce Mornay; 1 oz butter; ¼ pint sauce Béchamel; 1 oz grated cheese. Cooking time: 10 minutes.

Trim and wash mushrooms, drain well and either pass through a sieve or pass them several times through the finest blade of the mincer. Heat the butter, add the mushroom *purée* and a little lemon juice, season lightly and simmer until the liquid has evaporated; then bind with the *Béchamel*. Poach the fillets without folding in fish stock made from the bones. Reduce stock to almost nothing and add to the *sauce Mornay*. Serve the fillets in a baking dish on the mushroom *purée*, coat with the *sauce Mornay*, sprinkle with grated cheese and brown under a hot grill. The mushroom *purée* may be replaced by artichoke, pea or other similar *purée*.

Filets de Sole Murat

For 6 persons: 3 soles, each weighing about 1 lb; 1¼ lb potatoes; 6 artichoke bottoms; 3 large firm tomatoes; parsley; ½ lb butter. Sautéing of fillets: 4-6 minutes.

Dice potatoes finely. Fry brown and crisp in lard, pour off fat and toss potatoes in butter. Dice raw artichoke bottoms and cook in butter. Halve fillets of sole lengthwise, dip in salted milk, dip in flour and fry brown and crisp in clarified butter. Toss fillets, potatoes and artichokes together, season, arrange in a deep dish, sprinkle with lemon juice and brown butter, place the thickly sliced fried tomatoes on top and sprinkle with chopped parsley. (*See illustration p.* 324).

▣ Nabuchu

For 6 persons: 3 soles, each weighing about 1 lb; ½ lb cooked noodles; ¼ lb cooked mushrooms; 2 oz whole spinach leaves; ½ pint sauce Vin Blanc; ¼ pint sauce Hollandaise; 2 oz grated Parmesan cheese; 2 oz butter; 1 lemon. Cooking time for the fillets: 8-10 minutes.

Fold the fillets and poach them in some fish stock flavoured with lemon juice. Cover the bottom of an oval, ovenproof dish with the noodles, which have been mixed with the butter, Parmesan and shredded mushrooms. Arrange the fish on top. Meanwhile stew the shredded spinach leaves in butter and add them to the *sauce Vin Blanc*. Blend in the *sauce Hollandaise* and mask the fillets with it. Sprinkle with some grated Parmesan cheese, dot with melted butter and brown quickly in the oven or under the grill.

▣ à la Normande

For 6 persons: 3 soles, each weighing about 1 lb; 12 large mussels; 6 slices of truffle: 6 very large prawns; 6 gudgeons, egged and breadcrumbed; 6 Short Crust pastry tartlets; ¼ lb shrimp tails; ½ pint Fish Velouté; ¼ pint sauce Nantua; 2 egg yolks; 3 tablespoons cream; 2 oz butter; ½ pint white wine; 2 shallots; lemon. Cooking time: 8-10 minutes.

Poach fillets in white wine with chopped shallots. Reduce the poaching liquid, mix with the *Velouté* and bind it with the egg yolks and a little cream. Remove from the heat, add a lump of butter and season with lemon juice. Bind the shrimp tails with the *sauce Nantua* and fill them into the pastry cases. Arrange the fillets on a long dish, garnish with the mussels, cover with sauce and decorate with truffle slices and prawns. Border with the pastry cases, the fried gudgeon and some fried *croûtons.*

▣ Orly

For 4 persons: 1 lb fillets of sole; chopped parsley; lemon juice; sauce Tomate; Coating batter. Cooking time: 4-5 minutes.

Halve the fillets lengthwise and macerate in lemon juice with salt, pepper, and chopped parsley. Dip in batter, deep fry in oil and serve with lemon, parsley and *sauce Tomate* served separately.

Filets de Sole à l'Ostendaise

For 6 persons: 3 *soles, each weighing about* 1 *lb;* 24 *oysters;* ¼ *lb mushrooms;* 1 *truffle;* ½ *pint white wine;* ½ *pint fish stock;* ¾ *pint sauce Normande;* ¼ *pint sauce Béchamel;* 1 *egg; breadcrumbs.* Cooking time: 15 minutes.

Fillet the soles, fold and poach them in a mixture of the white wine, fish stock and liquid from the oysters. Arrange the fillets in a crown and fill the centre with the poached and trimmed oysters. Reduce the liquor almost to glazing consistency and mix with the *sauce Normande.* Mask the fillets and oysters with this sauce. Surround with small *croquettes* made with the sole trimmings, diced mushrooms and truffle bound together with a thick *sauce Béchamel.* The *croquettes* should be coated with egg and breadcrumbs and fried at the last moment.

▣ Paillard

For 8 *persons:* 4 *soles, each weighing about* 1 *lb;* 6 *oz flesh of whiting;* ½ *pint thick cream;* 1 *egg white;* 12 *crayfish;* ½ *lb fresh mushrooms;* 2 *small truffles;* 2 *oz butter;* ½ *pint Fish Velouté;* ½ *pint white wine.* Cooking time: 7-8 minutes.

Prepare a *Mousseline* farce with the flesh of the whiting, egg white, cream and seasoning. Cook the crayfish in advance with a *mirepoix* and white wine. Peel them, remove the flesh from the shells, empty the heads, and prepare Crayfish butter with the shells. Remove the fillets from the sole and use the fish bones for the *Velouté.* Flatten and pare the fillets, wipe them dry, spread a layer of *Mousseline* forcemeat on the fillets and fold them in two. Place the pointed end of the fillets in the heads of the crayfish and fill the remaining space with forcemeat; this will keep them in place. Poach the fillets in the strained white wine, in which the crayfish have been cooked. When cooked, reduce the liquid, mix it with the *Velouté,* season well and stir in a little butter. Prepare a garnish of crayfish tails, mushrooms and truffles, bound with a little *Velouté* sauce. Arrange the fillets in shape of a fan with the crayfish heads outside, cover the fillets with sauce and place a slice of truffle on each. Garnish with the mushroom mixture and drop a little melted Crayfish butter between the fillets. (*See illustration p.* 323).

▣ Pompadour

For 8-9 persons: 2 *soles, each weighing about* 1 *lb;* 20 *oysters;* ½ *lb shrimp tails;* ½ *lb mushrooms;* 1 *truffle;* ¾ *lb whiting flesh;* 1 *tablespoon concentrated tomato purée;* 1 *pint sauce Nantua; white of two eggs;* ½ *pint double cream.* Cooking time: 40 minutes.

Make a well-seasoned *Mousseline* forcemeat with the whiting flesh, egg whites and double cream. Colour half of this filling with the tomato *purée.* Remove the fillets from the sole, wash, dry and beat them a little to break the fibres. Stuff the fillets with the pink forcemeat, roll and tie with string. Poach them in fish stock and a little lemon juice and allow them to cool in the stock. For the filling, prepare a garnish of the shrimp tails, cooked mushrooms, cut in quarters, poached bearded oysters and the truffle. Bind this garnish with a little *sauce Nantua.* Prepare this garnish in advance, because it must be cooled before being filled into the mould. Butter a timbale thickly. Drain the *paupiettes* and wipe them dry. Cut them into slices about ¼-inch thick and place them all around the bottom and the sides of the mould. Cover the sides and bottom of the mould with a layer of the white *mousseline* filling and spread it evenly about ¾-inch thick. Fill up with the garnish and the remaining *paupiette* slices and cover with the rest of the filling. Poach in a water-bath in the oven, without allowing the water to boil. Turn out on a round dish, pour over a little *sauce Nantua,* and serve the rest in a sauce-boat.

Filets de Sole Riviéra

For 6 persons: 3 soles, each weighing about 1 *lb;* 1 *carrot;* 1 *onion;* 1 *stick celery;* 1 *shallot;* 2 *mushrooms;* 1 *small truffle;* ½ *pint cream;* ½ *pint sauce Béchamel;* 12 *mussels;* 12 *peeled scampi;* ½ *pint sauce Villeroi;* 2 *fl oz Madeira.* Cooking time for fillets: 10-12 minutes.

Finely dice the carrot, onion, celery, shallot, mushrooms and truffle. Cook with a little butter in a small, tightly closed saucepan for 8-10 minutes. Add the Madeira and pour the mixture over the fillets of sole which have been folded in two in an ovenproof dish. Cover with buttered greaseproof paper and bake for 12 minutes. Take out and drain the fish. Reduce the liquor quickly and add the cream and *sauce Béchamel.* When this sauce is creamy, take it off the heat and season to taste. Arrange the fillets of sole in a long dish and cover them liberally with the unstrained sauce. Surround alternately with a ring of mussels in *sauce Villeroi* and scampi.

▣ Suchet

For 4 persons: 2 soles, each weighing about 1 *lb;* ½ *lb carrots;* 1 *oz leek;* 1 *oz celery;* 1 *small truffle;* ½ *pint sauce Vin Blanc;* 1 *lb Duchesse potato.* Cooking time: 8-10 minutes.

Cut red part of carrots, the truffle, leek and celery into *julienne* and cook slowly in butter in a covered casserole till soft. In the meantime prepare the potato mixture and, using a forcing bag and star-shaped nozzle, pipe an attractive border round the inside of an oval baking dish up to the level of the rim. Cook golden brown in oven. Poach the folded fillets of sole in a little fish stock and use the latter to make the sauce. Drain fillets and arrange inside potato ring; combine vegetables and truffle strips with sauce and coat fish with it.

▣ Suzanne

For 6 persons: 3 soles, each weighing about 1 *lb;* 12 *boat-shaped pastry cases;* 6 *oz blanched spaghetti;* 1 *pint sauce Mornay.* Cooking time: 10 minutes.

Fold the fillets and poach them in white wine and serve in the pastry cases which already contain some *spaghetti* sautéed in butter. Mask with *sauce Mornay* and brown in the oven.

▣ Sylvette

For 6 persons: 3 soles, each weighing about 1 *lb;* 2 *tablespoons fine mirepoix;* 12 *small, regular shaped tomatoes;* ½ *lb whiting forcemeat;* ½ *pint cream;* ¼ *pint Madeira;* ½ *pint sauce Béchamel.* Cooking time: 8-10 minutes.

Arrange the well-trimmed fillets in a suitable dish. Toss fine *mirepoix* in butter, reduce with Madeira, simmer for 10 minutes, pour over soles while still hot and poach them. As soon as they are cooked, pour off the stock with the *mirepoix*, boil the cream and *Béchamel* together to make a bland sauce and season well. Peel the tomatoes, cut out a lid, deseed them and salt lightly inside. Fill each tomato with whiting forcemeat using a forcing bag and round nozzle, place side by side in a suitable dish, cover with buttered paper and poach carefully in a moderate oven, so that the tomatoes remain whole. Serve the fillets on a long dish, coat with the sauce and *mirepoix* and surround with the stuffed tomatoes.

Filets de Sole Sylvie

For 6 persons: 3 *soles, each weighing about* 1 *lb;* ¼ *lb butter; breadcrumbs;* 10 *sorrel leaves;* 3 *large mushroom caps;* ½ *pint Chablis;* 2 *fl oz cream; roasted almonds;* 2 *oz prawns;* 1 *fl oz brandy;* 12 *s-shaped pieces of Puff pastry.* Cooking time: 10 minutes.

Fillet the sole and wash in running water, flatten slightly, pat dry and season with salt and pepper. Dip them in 4 oz melted butter and then coat them on one side only with fresh and very white breadcrumbs. Arrange on a dish with the coated sides uppermost. Bake in a hot oven, 425° F or Gas Mark 7, basting frequently. To make the sauce, shred the sorrel leaves (discarding the ribs), thinly slice the firm, white mushroom caps and place both ingredients with a tablespoon butter in a small thick-bottomed ovenproof dish. Cover and cook for 10 minutes; add the *Chablis* and a glass of fish stock made with the bones and trimmings of the soles. Reduce by half. Add the cream and reduce further to achieve a coating consistency. Season and mix in a tablespoon of butter away from heat. Mask the fillets with the sauce and sprinkle with the roasted, flaked almonds. Decorate each fillet with shelled prawns which have been lightly cooked in butter and brandy until moisture starts oozing out. Decorate the dish with the pastry shapes and serve the rest of the sauce separately.

⊡ Tout-Paris

For 6 persons: 3 *soles, each weighing about* 1 *lb;* ¼ *lb prawns;* 6 *truffle slices;* ½ *pint white wine; sauce Hollandaise, made from* 3 *egg yolks;* ½ *lb butter; Crayfish butter.* Cooking time: 8-10 minutes.

Poach the fillets in white wine, reduce the stock and mix with freshly made *sauce Hollandaise.* Colour half this sauce pink with Crayfish or Shrimp butter, leaving the other half as it is. Arrange folded fillets evenly along both sides of a long dish and coat one side with plain, the other with pink *Hollandaise.* Place a prawn tail on top of the white fillets and a truffle slice on the pink ones.

⊡ Villeroi

For 4 persons: 2 *soles, each weighing about* 1 *lb;* ¾ *pint sauce Villeroi.* Cooking time: 6 minutes. Frying time: 1-2 minutes.

Fillet sole, fold, poach, allow them to cool a little, dry thoroughly and coat with *sauce Villeroi* prepared with the fish stock. When the sauce has cooled a little, egg and breadcrumb the fillets twice, fry in very hot deep fat, drain and serve. Garnish with fried parsley.

⊡ au Vin Blanc et Champignons * *with White Wine and Mushrooms*

Poach mushroom caps in butter and lemon juice with a pinch of salt. Fold the fillets in two, season with salt and pepper and poach them in the mushroom stock and a little white wine. Arrange the fillets in a ring on a round dish. Cover them with White Wine sauce to which the reduced poaching liquid has been added. Garnish the centre with the mushrooms and sprinkle them with chopped parsley. Surround the fillets with *fleurons.*

Filets de Sole Walewska

For 4 persons: 2 *soles, each weighing about* 1 *lb;* 8 *truffle slices;* 6 *small crayfish tails;* ¾ *pint sauce Mornay.* Cooking time: 10-12 minutes.

Fillet sole, fold, season and poach in fish stock. Reduce stock and add to the *sauce Mornay*. Arrange fillets in an oval fire-proof dish and place a truffle slice on each. Halve the crawfish tails and arrange in a ring round fillets. Coat the whole with *sauce Mornay* and glaze in the oven or under a fierce grill.

PAUPIETTES DE SOLE

Sole fillets stuffed and rolled and served with a hot sauce.

▣ Daumont

For 6 *persons:* 3 *soles, each weighing about* 1 *lb;* ½ *lb whiting forcemeat;* 1 *pint mussels;* ½ *lb mushrooms;* ½ *bottle dry white wine;* 2 *oz Crayfish butter;* 12 *crayfish tails;* ½ *pint sauce Nantua;* 3 *oz butter;* 2 *oz flour.* Cooking time: 15 minutes.

Prepare a *Mousseline* forcemeat from the whiting. Wash, dry and gently flatten the fillets of sole. Spread the skin side of the fillets with the forcemeat, place a crayfish tail in the centre of each, and roll up from the tail end. Cook the mushrooms and mussels in the white wine. Arrange the fillets in a buttered saucepan and poach them in the mussel and mushroom liquor. Prepare a *roux* with the butter and flour and then convert into a *Velouté* with the cooking liquors. Remove from the heat, incorporate the Crayfish butter and correct seasoning. Combine the mushrooms and mussels with the *sauce Nantua*. Serve the fillets in a circle, mask with the prepared sauce and place a crayfish carapace upon each. Garnish the centre with the prepared mussels and mushrooms. (*See illustration p.* 322).

▣ Georgette

For 12 *persons:* 3 *soles, each weighing about* 1 *lb;* 12 *large, regular potatoes;* 12 *crayfish tails;* 1 *lb mushrooms;* 1 *pint sauce Nantua.* Cooking time: 7-8 minutes.

Bake potatoes in the oven, cut out a lid and scoop out the flesh except for a thin layer. Beat fillets lightly, roll up, tie, arrange in a suitable dish and poach with fish stock. Make a fine *salpicon* with the crayfish tails and poached mushrooms, bind with a few spoons of *sauce Nantua*, and put a small spoon of *salpicon* in each potato. Drain fillets of sole well and remove string, place in potatoes, coat with *sauce Nantua* and serve remainder of sauce separately. Add the poaching stock, boiled down to a glaze, to the sauce. Either replace lid on the potato or top each with a thin slice of truffle.

▣ Jacqueline

For 10-12 *persons:* 3 *soles, each weighing about* 1 *lb;* 12 *sweet apples (preferably rennet apples), all the same size;* ¾ *lb whiting forcemeat;* ¼ *lb shrimps;* ¾ *pint fish stock;* 1 *oz flour;* 2 *oz butter;* ¼ *pint cream;* 1 *tablespoon concentrated tomato purée;* 12 *prawn tails.* Cooking time of fillets: 12 minutes.

Peel apples, rub with lemon to prevent their browning and hollow out, leaving the sides about ½-inch thick. Place on a buttered baking sheet, sprinkle with butter and cook carefully in the oven; they must not brown or collapse. Wipe fillets well, flatten slightly to break up the fibres, spread with the whiting forcemeat mixed with the shrimps, roll up and tie with string. Place rolls close together in a buttered dish, pour fish stock made from the bones on top and poach. Reduce stock to half, bind with a light *roux* from 1 oz flour and 1 oz butter, add cream and tomato *purée*, cook and season well; the sauce should be pink and very creamy. Arrange apples on a round dish and alternate with a well-drained fish roll, from which the string has been removed. Coat liberally with the sauce and skewer a prawn in each roll.

THON * *TUNNY FISH*

Tunny is caught in large quantities in the Mediterranean. It is a splendid fish, reaching a weight of 100 to 450 pounds and a length of 1½ to 2 yards. The flesh is firm, fat and very delicate in flavour. Larger pieces can be braised or roasted in the same way as veal. Tunny can be prepared in many ways and is always available tinned in oil.

▣ à la Bordelaise

For 4 *persons:* 1 *lb tunny;* 1 *onion;* 2 *shallots;* 5 *tomatoes;* ¼ *pint white wine;* ¼ *pint Demi-glace;* ½ *lb mushrooms.* Cooking time: 30 minutes.

Brown the fish on both sides in equal parts of oil and butter and add the thinly sliced onions and shallots and the peeled, deseeded and quartered tomatoes. Season, add the *Demi-glace* and white wine and braise slowly. Remove the cooked fish. Reduce stock, add quartered, browned mushrooms, pour over fish and sprinkle with chopped parsley.

▣ Grillé Maître d'Hôtel * *Grilled with Herb Butter*

Per person: 6 *oz tunny fish with bones.* Cooking time per lb: 20-25 minutes.

Flour a thick slice of tunny, shake off surplus, oil and grill. Brush with oil several times while cooking. When done the bones can be removed easily. Serve and cover with *Maître d'Hôtel* butter or serve it separately.

▣ à l'Indienne * *Curried*

For 6 *persons:* 1½ *lb tunny fish;* 12 *fillets of anchovy;* ⅜ *pint white wine;* ¼ *lb mirepoix of vegetables;* ⅜ *oz curry powder;* ½ *pint Fish Velouté; thyme; bay leaf; parsley; juice of* 1 *lemon.* Cooking time: 25 minutes.

Cut the tunny fish into slices and insert the anchovy fillets into these. Marinate for an hour in the white wine containing the herbs. Fry the *mirepoix* with the curry powder and after pouring in the strained marinade, braise the tuna slices slowly. Remove the fish, skim off the fat and strain the liquor. Thicken the latter with the *Velouté*, add the lemon juice and mask the fish with this sauce. Serve with rice cooked *à l'Indienne.*

▣ Ménagère

For 4 *persons:* 1 *lb tunny;* 2 *oz butter;* 2 *oz chopped onions;* ½ *oz flour;* ¼ *pint white wine;* 3 *tablespoons tomato purée;* 1 *lemon;* ½ *lb mushrooms.* Cooking time: about 35 minutes.

Place a thick piece of tunny in cold water, bring to the boil and blanch for 5-6 minutes. Remove fish, drain well; season and brown on both sides in butter. Toss the chopped onions thoroughly in butter in a suitable casserole, sprinkle flour on top, cook for a moment, add the white wine and an equal quantity of water. Stir well and add the tomato *purée* and lemon juice. Put tunny in this sauce, cover when it comes to the boil and braise in the oven. When the fish is cooked add either the quartered mushrooms cooked in butter or diced tomatoes cooked in butter, bring to the boil once more and serve with the well-seasoned sauce.

Thon Meunière * *Shallow Fried Tunny Fish*

6 oz per person.

Cook as for *Filet de Sole Meunière*. (*See p.* 342).

▣ Orly

For 4 persons: 1 lb tunny fish; 1 lb Coating batter; ¾ pint sauce Tomate Cooking time: 8-10 minutes.

Cut up the fish into long thin slices and proceed as for *Filets de Sole Orly*. (*See p.* 343).

▣ braisé à l'Oseille * *Braised with Sorrel*

For 8 persons: 2 lb tunny; 8 anchovy fillets; 1 carrot; 1 onion; ¼ lb bacon; ⅜ pint white wine; ⅜ pint bouillon; 1 bouquet garni; 3 lb sorrel; ¼ pint cream; 4 egg yolks. Cooking time: 45-50 minutes.

Lard a piece of tunny 3-4 inches thick with soaked anchovy fillets. Place in cold, slightly salted water to which a little vinegar has been added and bring to the boil quickly. As soon as it boils, take out fish, drain well and put in a suitable braising pan, the bottom of which has been lined with carrot and onion slices and with thin bacon slices. Add the white wine and *bouillon*, pepper and the *bouquet garni*. Add very little salt, since the anchovies are salty. Cover and braise slowly in a moderate oven, 375° F or Gas Mark 4. In the meantime, cook the sorrel in its own juice, pass through a sieve and bind with the cream which has been mixed with the egg yolks. As soon as the fish is cooked, serve on the sorrel. Remove fat from stock, reduce to a syrup together with 2-3 tablespoons of *Demi-glace* and pour over the fish.

▣ à la Provençale

For 6 persons: 1½ lb tunny fish; 12 fillets of anchovy; ¼ pint oil; 1 chopped onion; 3 chopped tomatoes; 2 crushed cloves garlic; 1 bouquet garni; 1 pinch basil; ¼ pint sauce Demi-glace; ¼ pint white wine; ⅜ pint fish stock; 3 oz capers; 1 small bunch parsley, finely chopped. Cooking time: 45 minutes.

Insert the anchovy fillets into the tunny fish and marinate in oil for an hour. Next fry in the oil and, when the fish is golden brown, add the onions, tomatoes, garlic, *bouquet garni*, basil, white wine and stock and braise slowly. Remove the fish, strain the liquor, skim off the fat and reduce by half. Add the capers, the sauce *Demi-glace* and parsley. Mask the fish with the sauce.

TURBOT * *TURBOT*

Turbot is known as the prince of the sea, and rightly so, for it is a splendid fish which graces every table on special occasions. Fine large fish, suitable for serving at dinners, are carefully poached in fish stock and served with *sauce Hollandaise*, *Mousseline*, or *Fines Herbes*. For smaller meals for 4-5 persons it is best to choose the smaller turbot weighing 2-2¼ pounds. All recipes given for brill can also be used for turbot.

Turbot à l'Amiral

Prepare as for *Barbue à l'Amiral.* (*See p.* 311).

▣ Crème Gratin

For 6 persons: 1-1¼ *lb boiled turbot without bones or skin;* ¾ *pint sauce Mornay;* 1 *oz grated cheese;* 1 *lb Duchesse potatoes.* Cooking time: 6-8 minutes.

Pipe a lightly buttered round or oval dish with a high border of the potato mixture, using a forcing tube and star-shaped nozzle. Put in oven to brown slightly. Flake turbot leftovers, bind with sauce and put inside potato ring and sprinkle with grated cheese and a few breadcrumbs. Sprinkle a little butter on top and brown well in a hot oven, 400° F or Gas Mark 6. Sliced mushrooms may be mixed with the sauce. Almost all fish leftovers can be used up in this way.

▣ Edouard VII

For 4-5 *persons:* 1 *turbot, weighing about* 1½ *lb;* ¼ *bottle dry champagne;* ½ *pint fish stock;* 2 *shallots;* ½ *lb mushrooms;* 1 *lb potato croquettes;* 12 *oysters;* 12 *mussels;* ¼ *pint Béchamel;* 2 *oz Crayfish butter;* 3 *crayfish tails;* 1 *truffle.* Cooking time: 40 minutes.

Season turbot lightly and braise in the oven with the sliced shallots and mushroom peel, covering with the champagne and fish stock, basting from time to time. In the meantime prepare a garnish of very small potato *croquettes*, oysters and mussels, egg and breadcrumb and fry at the last moment. When the fish is cooked, place it on a large dish and keep warm, covered with buttered paper. Strain the stock, reduce and add to a very thick, very lightly salted *Béchamel.* Reduce sauce to required consistency. Season with a little curry powder, beat up with the Crayfish butter, strain and finally complete with the diced crayfish tails. Lightly coat the fish with the sauce and garnish the dish alternately with the prepared potatoes, oysters and mussels. Decorate the centre of the fish with truffle slices and place sautéed mushroom heads on either side. Serve the rest of the sauce separately.

▣ Frit, Sauce Tartare * *Deep Fried with Tartare Sauce*

Cut turbot into 6 ounce slices, dip in seasoned milk, flour and fry in hot, deep fat. Arrange on a dish and serve with *sauce Tartare*. Cooking time: 8-10 minutes.

▣ Poché, Sauce Hollandaise * *Poached with Hollandaise Sauce*

For 6 *persons: about* 2¼ *lb whole turbot.* Cooking time for 2¼ lb: 12-14 minutes.

Commence cooking whole turbot in cold fish stock, add a few slices of lemon, slowly bring to the boil and simmer. Large pieces require relatively less time than smaller ones. A piece weighing a pound or a little over will take about 30 minutes, one weighing about 1½-1¾ pounds takes only 40 minutes. When turbot is served whole, the head is tied up to prevent its breaking during poaching, the string being removed later. It is served on a folded napkin, white side up, and garnished with some parsley and slices of lemon. *Sauce Hollandaise* and boiled potatoes are served with it. If it is desired to have the turbot very white, we recommend starting it not in fish stock but in cold, slightly salted water with a little milk and a few slices of lemon. (*See illustration p.* 325).

Filets de Turbot * *Fillets of Turbot*

Just like brill, turbot can be filleted and served with all the sauces and garnishes indicated for fillets of sole. The fillets must be cut to a suitable size. Cooking time: 8-10 minutes.

TURBOTIN * *BABY OR CHICKEN TURBOT*

A good fish for stuffing and serving with attractive garnishings. All brill and sole preparations are suitable.

◘ Grillé * *Grilled*

For 4-5 persons: 1 *small turbot, weighing about* 1-1½ *lb.* Cooking time: 30-35 minutes.

Score turbot a few times on both sides, season and grill in the usual way. As it grills it must be brushed with oil or melted butter several times. Serve with melted butter, *Maître d'Hôtel* butter or *sauce Béarnaise* and boiled potatoes.

◘ Mirabeau

For 6-8 persons: 1 *turbot, weighing about* 4 *lb;* 1¼ *pints red wine;* 2-3 *shallots;* 1 *bouquet garni;* ¾ *pint Demi-glace;* 1 *tablespoon anchovy paste;* 16 *anchovy fillets in oil;* 2 *oz butter.* Cooking time: 50-60 minutes.

Season fish very lightly, place on the tray of the fish kettle, add red wine, the sliced shallots and the *bouquet garni* and braise slowly in the oven, basting repeatedly. When done, remove from fish kettle, strain stock, reduce, add to *Demi-glace* and boil to required thickness. Mix the sauce with the anchovy paste and enrich with the butter. Coat fish lightly with butter, decorate with a lattice of anchovy fillets and serve the rest of the sauce separately.

◘ Saint-Malo

Grill fish as above and serve surrounded with well-shaped boiled potatoes or with sliced fried potatoes. Serve with *sauce Saint-Malo.*

POISSONS DE MER FROIDS * *COLD SEA FISH*

Colin Froid à la Russe * *Cold Hake*

For 6 *persons:* 2 *lb middle piece of hake;* 6 *small jellied Russian salad timbales* (18 *oz Russian salad*)*;* 18 *small cooked prawns;* 18 *small truffle slices;* 24 *fillets of anchovy; aspic jelly;* 3 *olives.* Cooking time: 25-30 minutes.

Poach fish in salt water with a dash of vinegar and allow to cool, in the stock. Drain well and remove the skin from one side of the fish. Arrange the fish on an oval silver dish. Decorate alternately with truffle slices and prawns in a line down the centre. Glaze with aspic jelly. Arrange the *timbales* around the sides of the dish and garnish these with fillets of anchovy and a halved olive in the centre. Parsley and lemon slices are placed on one end of the dish. (*See illustration p.* 327).

Rougets Froids à la Niçoise * *Cold Red Mullet*

For 2 persons: 2 red mullet, each weighing about 6 oz; ½ pint white wine; 2 small onions; ½ lb tomatoes; 2 lemons; anchovy fillets; pitted green olives; parsley. Cooking time: 7-8 minutes.

Poach red mullet in white wine with thin rings of onions. When the fish is cold, place in a serving dish and garnish all around with overlapping tomato and lemon slices. Place a lemon basket on top of the fish, and decorate with olives, and if liked, a small anchovy fillet wrapped round, and small sprigs of parsley. Reduce the fish liquid, season with lemon juice, oil, salt and pepper, and pour it over the fish. Serve very cold. (*See illustration p.* 327).

FILETS DE SOLE FROIDS * *COLD FILLETS OF SOLE*

Port or Madeira flavoured aspic may be used to glaze these fillets, instead of the normal aspic.

▣ à la Gelée * *In Aspic*

For 8 persons: 4 soles, each weighing about 1 lb; ½ pint white wine; juice of ½ lemon; 1 pint fish aspic; 1 small truffle. Cooking time: 8-10 minutes.

Fillet fish, wash the fillets and trim to even shape. Sprinkle with lemon juice, season lightly, poach in the white wine and leave to cool under light pressure. Trim again, decorate with truffles, coat with cold, almost set aspic and allow to set. When quite cold carefully arrange on a long dish, fill spaces with chopped aspic and serve with a cold piquant sauce, such as *Mayonnaise, Ravigote*, etc.

▣ Floralies

For 10 persons: 10 soles, each weighing about ½ lb; 1½ pints fish Chaudfroid; 1½ lb macécoine of vegetables; 3 tomatoes, sliced; 4 tomatoes blanched, peeled, cut into quarters and the centres removed; 20 black olives; 1½ pints aspic; 1 gherkin; 1 lemon.

Fillet the soles, flatten with a cutlet bat and poach; put under press. Pour a thin film of aspic on the dish, allow to set and arrange the fillets attractively. Mask the cold fillets with the *Chaudfroid* sauce, place on a bed of the *macédoine*, decorate with the tomato flesh and gherkin in the form of flowers and glaze with the aspic. Surround with the sliced tomatoes and stoned olives. Place a cut lemon in the centre. (*See illustration p.* 328).

▣ à la Moscovite

For 6 persons: 3 soles, each weighing about 1 lb; 2 large cucumbers; 3 oz caviar; ¾ pint fish aspic; 1 lemon; ¾ pint Mayonnaise. Cooking time: 8-10 minutes.

Remove the fillets, trim them and roll them up tightly. Next poach them in a fish stock made from the bones and trimmings of the sole. Remove and leave to cool. Peel the cucumbers and cut them into pieces of the same length as the rolled fillets; scoop out the centre so as to leave a sort of pipe open at each end and blanch well. Drain and season lightly with salt and lemon juice. The rolled fillets are then put inside the pieces of cucumber. Decorate one end of each with a little caviar and arrange on a round dish with the aspic which has set and been diced. Serve the *Mayonnaise* separately.

Paupiettes de Sole Cicéron

For 6 persons: 3 soles, each weighing about ¾ lb; ½ lb crayfish mousse; 12 artichoke bottoms; 12 small crayfish tails; 12 half round slices of truffle; ¼ pint of fish stock; 1 lemon; olive oil; vinegar; ⅜ pint sauce Chantilly; 1½ pints fish aspic.

Fillet the sole and flatten the fillets. Roll round wooden cylinders, place close together in a buttered saucepan, season with salt, add the lemon juice and fish stock, cover and poach. Remove the cylinders and allow to cool in their cooking liquor. Season the artichoke bottoms and mascerate in oil and vinegar. When the fillets are cold, drain, dry and fill the centres with the crayfish *mousse* to which a little chopped dill has been added. Drain and dry the artichoke bottoms and place a fillet upon each. Garnish with a crayfish tail and slice of truffle, and glaze with aspic. Serve in a crystal dish and garnish with diced aspic. Serve the sauce in a sauce-boat.

Timbale de Sole à la Gelée

For 6 persons: 3 soles, each weighing about 1 lb; ½ lb of Fine forcemeat enriched with Lobster butter; 1 truffle; 1 pint fish aspic; 1 pint sauce Tartare or Chantilly. Cooking time: 8-10 minutes.

Fillet and trim the sole. Flatten slightly; spread with the forcemeat, roll up and poach in a fish stock prepared from the bones and trimmings of the sole. Allow to become cold in the cooking liquor. Line a mould with the fish aspic and decorate the base with slices of truffle dipped in a little aspic to ensure that they remain in position. Cut the fish rolls in slices ⅛-inch thick, arrange them round the sides and centre of the mould vertically, fill the centre with aspic, allow to set, then continue in this manner until the mould is full. Unmould when set and surround with cubes of aspic. Serve the sauce in a sauce-boat. (*See illustration p.* 328).

TURBOT FROID * *COLD TURBOT*

If possible, poach this fish a short time before it is served and remove from stock as soon as it has cooled. All recipes for cold salmon are suitable for cold turbot.

⊡ Farci aux Fruits de Mer * *Stuffed with Sea Food*

For 8 persons: 1 turbot, weighing about 4 lb; 1 lb Zéphyr forcemeat; ¼ lb sweet red peppers; 2 oz truffles; ½ pint fish stock; ½ pint white wine; 1¾ pints fish aspic; 1½ lb mixed sea food; 1½ pints cream flavoured with tomato ketchup; lemon. Cooking time: 40-45 minutes.

Clean the fish and rub the white side thoroughly with lemon juice. Open up the fish lengthwise on the dark side and lift out the fillets with a very sharp knife. Remove the backbone. Fill the fish with the *Zéphyr* stuffing to which has been added the finely diced red peppers and truffle. Replace the fillets and put the fish, white side uppermost, on the well-buttered grill of a special turbot pan. Pour the cold fish stock, white wine and lemon juice over the fish and add seasoning. Cover with buttered greaseproof paper and poach, covered in a moderate oven, 375° F or Gas Mark 4. Leave the fish to cool down in the liquor and, when it is completely cold, remove the head with a semicircular cut. Next split the fish lengthwise and cut each half into 5 or 6 portions which are then glazed with the aspic. Spread a thin layer of aspic on an oval dish, arrange the portions of turbot symmetrically and garnish with some cubes of aspic. Serve together with the mixed sea food and ketchup flavoured cream.

FOREIGN SPECIALITIES

Barboni auf Gradeser Art * *Red Mullet Gradese*

For 6 persons: 6 medium-sized red mullet; 4 fl oz oil; 3 small shallots; ½ pint red wine; 3 large mushrooms; 2 tablespoons tomato purée; 1½ lb boiled potatoes; chopped parsley. Cooking time: about 35 minutes.

Score red mullet, season with salt and pepper, brown quickly in hot oil, add the finely chopped shallots and reduce with the red wine. Add the tomato *purée* and sliced mushrooms and simmer, with the lid on, for about 15 minutes. Arrange the fish on a long dish, cover with the sauce, sprinkle with chopped parsley and surround with the boiled potatoes.
(*Austria*)

Bloaters

Bloaters are lightly salted and lightly smoked herrings which must be processed immediately after catching and eaten fresh. They may be brushed with butter and grilled or fried in butter in a saucepan and served for breakfast. (*Great Britain*)

Smoked Haddock

This mildly salted and lightly smoked fish is a very popular breakfast dish. Halve fish lengthwise and cut into portions. Place in milk or half milk and half water, bring to the boil and simmer for 7-10 minutes, according to thickness. Drain and serve for breakfast with melted butter. (*Great Britain*)

Smoked Haddock with Egg Sauce

For 4 persons: 1½-1½ lb smoked haddock; 1 lb potatoes; ½ pint Egg sauce. Cooking time: 7-10 minutes.

Poach fish as above, drain well, serve with Egg sauce and boiled potatoes as a luncheon dish. If the haddock is very dry, soak in a mixture of half milk and half water for a few hours before cooking and then poach in fresh milk. (*Great Britain*)

Kedgeree

For 8 persons: 2 lb fish; ½ lb rice; 4 hardboiled eggs; 1½ pints Béchamel; 1 teaspoon curry powder. Cooking time: 20-25 minutes.

Remove skin and bone from fish leftovers—leftovers of turbot, cod, haddock, etc., are very suitable—flake it and, if leftovers are cold, warm in oven at low heat. Season not too thick *Béchamel* very highly with curry powder. Boil rice in water till done but grains are still separate, rinse with hot water and drain well. Place alternate layers of rice, fish and sliced hardboiled egg, with sauce between the layers, in a deep dish until it is full; the top layer should be sauce. Serve very hot for breakfast or lunch. (*Anglo-Indian*)

Kippers

Split, fresh lightly salted and smoked herrings. They are prepared in the same way as bloaters and also served for breakfast. (*Great Britain*)

Machi Badam-Malai * *Fish with Almonds and Cream*

For 4 *persons:* 1½-2 *lb firm fish without skin or bones;* ¼ *pint yoghourt;* ¼ *pint cream;* ¼ *pint milk;* 1 *teaspoon powdered curcuma;* ½ *small teaspoon black pepper;* 1 *stick of cinnamon about* ¾*-inch long;* ½ *lb blanched, peeled almonds;* 3 *onions; salt;* ¼ *lb butter.* Cooking time: 30 minutes.

Wash fish thoroughly and cut in pieces of about 2 ounces each. Put half the butter in a shallow casserole, melt it and add the very thinly sliced onions with the cinnamon and fry light brown. Add fish, sprinkle with curcuma and pepper, salt lightly and add milk. Shake casserole and cook fish till almost cooked. Reduce liquid to almost nothing, add remainder of butter and continue to cook till the fish and onions start to fry again. Pound almonds very fine, mix with the yoghourt and cream and reduce to almost half. Pour over fish and keep hot for 15 minutes with lid on at simmering point, tossing gently 4 or 5 times during this time. When serving remove cinnamon and serve with boiled rice. (*India*)

Filetti de Sogliola Venini * *Fillets of Sole Venini*

For 10 *persons:* 10 *soles, each weighing about* ½ *lb;* 1 *quart of water;* ½ *pint white wine; half an onion;* ¼ *pint consommé;* ½ *lb butter;* 3 *tablespoons Béchamel;* ¼ *pint cream;* 30 *shelled, medium-sized scampi;* ½ *pint sauce Tomate;* 1 *liqueur glass brandy.*

Fillet the sole. Chop the bones and trimmings, put into a stewpan with the chopped onion, water and half the wine. Bring to the boil and cook vigorously for half an hour; strain and reduce to 1½ pints. Poach the fillets in the *consommé* and the rest of the wine, remove to a *gratin* dish and keep warm. Strain the cooking liquor into a saucepan, reduce to half, add 2 oz butter, bring to the boil, add the fish stock and whisk in the *Béchamel*; simmer until of a sauce consistency. Add the cream and 5 oz butter, aerate with a whisk and keep warm. Lightly fry the scampi in 1 oz butter, add the *sauce Tomate* and cook for 5 minutes; add the brandy and correct seasoning. Arrange the fillets overlapping round the edge of the dish and mask over with the sauce. Arrange the scampi in a circle in the centre of the dish and pour *sauce Tomate* in the centre. (*See illustration p.* 321). (*Italy*)

Orata in Cartoccio * *Sea-Bream in a Paper Bag*

For 10 *persons:* 1 *sea bream, weighing about* 6-7 *lb;* 10 *oz mixed shellfish;* 3 *tomatoes;* ¼ *lb butter;* 2 *fl oz oil;* 20 *olives;* ¼ *lb mushrooms;* ⅛ *pint white wine;* 1 *lemon;* ⅛ *pint brandy.* Cooking time: approximately 40 minutes.

Slash the bream along the sides to facilitate cooking. Lightly fry in a tablespoonful of oil and knob of butter. Cook in a warm oven, 335° F or Gas Mark 3, for about 20 minutes. Add the white wine and when the liquid is well reduced, add the shellfish, the tomatoes *concassés*, olives, lemon juice, salt and pepper. Remove to a hot oven, 425° F or Gas Mark 7, for 10 minutes. Butter a sheet of sulphur paper, arrange in the centre a layer of shell fish, place the bream on top, then the rest of the garnish. Brush over the edge with the beaten white of an egg and fold over to envelope the fish completely; fasten the joint securely by overlapping and pinching the edges of the paper together. Place upon an oiled dish and then into a hot oven, 425° F or Gas Mark 7, until the paper bag is blown up by the interior steam and crisp from the heat. Serve as it is. (*See illustration p.* 325). (*Italy*)

Freshwater Fish

ANGUILLE * *EEL*

Eels found in still water usually taste rather muddy, while those from the sea or from running rivers taste fresher.

▣ Grillée Tartare * *Grilled with Tartare Sauc*

For 4 persons: 1½ *lb eel;* 1 *onion;* 1 *bouquet garni;* ½ *pint white wine;* 1-2 *eggs; breadcrumbs;* ½ *pint sauce Tartare.* Cooking time: 2-3 minutes.

Cut prepared eel in pieces about 2-inches long, place in white wine with the finely chopped onion, *bouquet garni*, a few peppercorns, salt and a little water. Cook slowly keeping the eel undercooked rather than overcooked; allow to cool. Drain fish well, dry, coat with beaten egg and breadcrumbs, brush with oil and grill. Serve with fried parsley and *sauce Tartare*.

▣ Pompadour * *Fried with Béarnaise Sauce*

For 4 *persons:* 1½ *lb boiled eel;* ¾ *pint sauce Villeroi; sauce Béarnaise made with* 6 *oz butter;* 1-2 *eggs; breadcrumbs.* Cooking time: 2-3 minutes.

Boil eel as for grilled eel, when cold, dry well, coat with *sauce Villeroi*, breadcrumb and fry in deep fat. Serve with fried parsley and with *sauce Béarnaise.*

▣ au Soleil * *Deep Fried in Batter*

For 4 *persons:* 1½ *lb boiled eel;* ½ *pint Coating batter;* ½ *pint sauce Tomate.* Cooking time: 3-4 minutes.

Dip boiled, dried eel in the batter and fry in deep fat. Serve with fried parsley and *sauce Tomate.*

Matelote Bourguignonne * *Eel Casserole*

For 4 *persons:* 1½ *lb eel;* 1 *lb button onions;* ½ *lb button mushrooms;* 1 *onion;* 2 *shallots;* ½ *oz flour;* 2 *oz butter;* 2 *tablespoons brandy;* ¾ *pint red wine; croûtons.* Cooking time: 20 minutes.

Place slices of onion, shallots and garlic, a *bouquet garni* and a few peppercorns in a casserole. Put the eel, cleaned, skinned and cut into pieces about 2¼-inches, on top. Place on the heat and flame with brandy. Add enough red wine to cover the fish, season with salt, and cook for 18 to 20 minutes. Remove the pieces of eel and place them in another casserole. Add cooked mushrooms and glazed button onions. Strain the cooking liquor, reduce a little with the rest of the red wine, and bind with the flour kneaded with the butter. Boil up and darken a little with caramel, for the wine gives an ugly violet colour to the sauce. Pour the sauce which should be creamy, but not too thick, over the fish and garnish with fried *croûtons.*

La Meurette * *Mixed Fish Casserole*

For 6 *persons.*

Make this dish in exactly the same way as the previous recipe, but using 3-4 types of fish, such as eel, carp, tench and pike. *Flambé* with grape husk brandy instead of cognac and use white wine instead of red, if preferred. Cut *croûtons* in any desired shape, rub with garlic after frying and place in bottom of dish. Place fish on top and thicken sauce with *beurre manié.* The crayfish may be omitted.

Barbillon * *Young Barbel*

Per person: 1 *young barbel weighing about* 5-6 *oz.* Cooking time: 7-9 minutes. Large barbel have a cooking time of approximately 12-15 minutes per lb.

Young barbel are best fried, grilled or poached in fish stock. Serve poached barbel with *sauce Hollandaise* or *sauce aux Câpres.*

Brème * *Bream*

Per person: a piece weighing about 5-6 *oz.* Cooking time: 7-8 minutes.

A tasty fish but it has rather a lot of bones. Small bream are deep fried, larger bream may be grilled and served with *Maître d'Hôtel* butter or *beurre Anchois.*

BROCHET * *PIKE*

Found in abundance in the rivers and lakes of Britain. They are usually braised since the flesh of the larger fish is rather dry.

▣ en Blanquette * *Blanquette*

For 4 *persons:* 2 *lb pike;* 2 *oz butter;* ¾ *oz flour;* ¼ *pint white wine;* ½ *lb small mushrooms;* 16 *small onions;* 1 *bouquet garni;* ¼ *pint cream;* 2 *egg yolks.* Cooking time: 30 minutes.

Cut fish, except for head, in fairly thick slices and toss in heated butter without allowing to brown. Sprinkle with the flour, cook it for a moment, add the white wine and an equal quantity of water. Season, add the *bouquet garni*, the mushrooms, the onions and simmer slowly. When cooked, remove the *bouquet garni* and thicken with the egg yolk mixed with the cream.

▣ au Bleu * *Blue-Poached*

Use very small, freshly caught pike, prepare and treat in the same way as blue-poached trout. Cooking time: 8-10 minutes.

▣ sauce Câpres * *with Caper Sauce*

For 4 *persons:* 2 *lb pike;* 1 *onion; thyme; bay leaf; parsley;* ½ *pint sauce aux Câpres.* Cooking time: about 30 minutes.

Slowly poach pike in well seasoned fish stock, drain, serve on a napkin and carefully remove the skin. Garnish with parsley and serve with *sauce aux Câpres.* Left-overs can be served with *Mayonnaise* or any other piquant sauce.

Brochet à la Nantaise au Beurre Blanc

The famous Loire pike with white butter is a well-known Nantes speciality, which is however prepared differently in different places. Poach the pike in fish stock, skin and serve with *sauce au Beurre Blanc.* (*See p.* 157). The quality of this dish depends mainly on the butter used.

▣ Palestine

For 6 persons: 1½ *lb cooked pike, free from bones and skin;* 1½ *lb noodles;* ¼ *pint sauce Béchamel;* 2 *oz grated cheese.*

Cook the noodles, drain and fry in butter and place in a *gratin* dish. Cover with the flaked fish, mask with the *Béchamel*, sprinkle with the cheese and gratinate in a hot oven.

Côtelettes Soubise * *Pike Cutlets with Onion Purée*

For 4 *persons:* ¾ *lb pike flesh;* ½ *pint cold thick sauce Béchamel;* ¼ *pint double cream;* 4 *eggs; breadcrumbs;* ½ *pint thick onion purée (purée Soubise); butter.* Cooking time: 45-50 minutes. To poach cutlets: 7-8 minutes. To fry cutlets: 4-5 minutes.

Mince the flesh twice through the finest blade of a meat grinder. Combine with the *sauce Béchamel*, cream, 1 egg and 2 egg yolks. Season well, and rub through a sieve. Fill this forcemeat into small buttered cutlet moulds and poach in a water-bath in the oven. Allow the cutlets to cool, take them out of the moulds, and dip in flour then egg and breadcrumbs. Fry the cutlets in butter in a frying pan. Arrange in a ring on a round dish with onion *purée* in the middle. Put frills on the cutlets and serve *Maître d'Hôtel* butter at the same time.

PAIN DE BROCHET * *PIKE PASTE*

This dish may be served hot or cold and is delicious served with a green salad.

▣ sauce Fines Herbes * *with Piquant Sauce*

For 6 *persons:* ¾ *lb pike, without skin or bones;* ½ *pint very thick cold Béchamel;* ¼ *pint thick cream;* 2 *egg yolks;* 1 *egg;* ⅛ *pint white wine.*

Pass pike several times through the finest blade of the mincer, mix with the *Béchamel* and pass through a sieve. Season the mixture well, combine with the egg yolks, the whole egg and cream and press into a well-buttered cylindrical mould. Poach in the oven in a water-bath for 35-40 minutes without allowing the water to boil. For the sauce, make a fish stock from the pike bones and trimmings with white wine and the usual seasonings, strain and reduce to ¼ pint. Mix 2 oz butter with 1 oz flour in a casserole, add the reduced fish stock, ½ pint water and 2 egg yolks and stir to a smooth sauce over heat with a whisk. When it comes to the boil remove from heat, add a nut of butter and plenty of chopped mixed herbs and season well. Turn out the paste on a round dish and pour the sauce on top; a garnish of mushrooms, shrimps or mussels may be added to it.

▣ Némoura

For 6 *persons: Paste as above;* 1 *lb Croquette potatoes;* 3 *oz shrimp tails;* 1 *egg; breadcrumbs;* ¾ *pint sauce Joinville.*

Put the paste, prepared as above, in a buttered cylindrical mould or flan tin and poach. Mix the potato mixture with the finely diced shrimp tails, shape into hazelnut-sized balls, breadcrumb and deep fry at the last moment. Turn out the cooked paste on a round dish, pour a little sauce over it, garnish with the *croquettes* and serve the remainder of the sauce separately.

QUENELLES DE BROCHET * *PIKE QUENELLES*

These are excellent served with a hot sauce or vegetable *purée.*

◘ à la Lyonnaise

For 6 persons: 1 pike, weighing about 1¼ lb without skin or bones; 4 eggs; ¼ lb flour; 2 oz butter; ½ pint milk; ½ lb kidney suet. Cooking time of quenelles: 15 minutes.

First make a panada, stirring the eggs with the flour, the milk, 2 eggs and a pinch of salt over heat into a thick, homogeneous mixture of the consistency of *Choux* pastry. Pound the skinned and well dried suet finely in a mortar, remove, pound pike finely, then add suet, mix well and, pounding constantly, add 2 more eggs, salt and pepper. Pass this mixture through a sieve, mix well with the prepared panada, then make a small test *quenelle* and poach it in boiling water. If the mixture is not sufficiently coherent add another egg or a little egg white. Shape spoon-sized *quenelles* on a moistened table, poach in salt water without boiling and then simmer the well-drained *quenelles* for a short time in *sauce Nantua* with crayfish. (*See illustration p.* 362).

◘ à la Maritime

For 6 persons: 1 lb raw pike flesh; 4 eggs; 3 oz butter; ½ pint milk; ½ lb beef suet; ¼ lb flour; ½ lb small mushroom caps; ¾ lb peeled, poached scampi tails; ¾ pint sauce Vin Blanc; ¼ pint sauce Hollandaise; the juice of half a lemon; 1 teaspoon chopped mixed herbs (parsley, chevril, tarragon); 12 small Puff pastry crescents.

Make the forcemeat as for *Quenelles Lyonnaise.* Divide into two, leaving one half as it is and incorporating the mixed herbs in the other. Make the *quenelles* with a coffee spoon, poach in salted water and drain. Cook the mushroom caps till soft in butter and lemon juice with a pinch of salt. Drain and reserve the stock. Cut the scampi into 2 or 3 pieces, according to size, add to the mushrooms and keep hot with a little butter. Reduce the *sauce Vin Blanc* to a pouring consistency together with the mushroom stock, remove from heat and bind with the *sauce Hollandaise.* Without heating too much, combine the *quenelles,* mushrooms and scampi with the sauce, stirring gently all the time. Serve in a casserole and garnish with the Puff pastry *crescents.*

CARPE * *CARP*

A river or lake fish, carp is found throughout Europe.

◘ Auguste Deland

For 10 persons: 1 carp, weighing about 5½ lb with roe; 1 lb Fish forcemeat; 1½ lb perch; 1 lb gudgeons; ½ pint fish stock; 1 bottle red Burgundy; 15 fluted mushroom caps; 1 lb cèpes; ½ pint double cream; 1 large truffle; mirepoix; 1 lb butter; ½ lb carrots.

Remove the backbone from the carp and leave the roe on one side. Clean the carp with a damp cloth and stuff it with a mixture of Pike forcmeat and a few diced carrots and mushrooms cooked in butter. Cut off a triangular piece of skin from the middle of the carp and mask the flesh with a thin layer of the stuffing saved for this purpose. Imitate the scales of the fish using crescent-shaped pieces of truffle, mushrooms and tomato pulp. Protect this decoration with a thin strip of bacon fat. Butter a fish pan large enough to contain the carp;

at the bottom place the fish bones and a bed of *mirepoix* (sliced onions and carrots, stick of celery, parsley stalks, shallots and sprigs of thyme and bay leaf); sweat until juices begin to appear. Lay the carp on a grill on top of the contents of the pan and, after adding seasoning, pour in the reduced fish stock and one-third of the bottle of red wine which is then ignited. Add a few dried *cèpe* stalks. Bring to the boil, cover with a lid and bake in the oven, basting from time to time. When the carp is cooked, drain it and keep warm under a cover, wrapped in a muslin cloth. Strain the liquor, pressing the bones and aromatic vegetables, and add a little reduced red wine. Reduce by half and thicken slightly with a little butter mixed with flour. Skim off any impurities as they slowly rise to the surface and, when the right consistency is obtained, strain the sauce and finally add a knob of fresh butter.

The following garnishes should be prepared while the carp is being cooked.

1. Remove the bones from the gudgeons and fill with perch forcemeat. Roll these gudgeons in thin herb pancakes lined with stuffing, leaving the heads and tails exposed and fry at the last minute.

2. Steam the large, fluted mushroom caps and garnish with a *purée* made from the carp roe, truffle and the pieces left over from the decoration of the carp. Flat cakes of *Duchesse* potato may be coated with egg and breadcrumbs, fried, scooped out, garnished with diced *Cèpes à la Bordelaise* and served separately.

Remove the strip of bacon fat from the carp and glaze the latter with some of the reduced cooking liquor. Place it on a decorative, fish-shaped base. Arrange alternately the gudgeon pancakes and roe-filled mushrooms. Surround with fish-shaped pieces of pastry and decorate the neck of the carp with a necklace (literally: bracelet). The dish should be served very hot. Some of the sauce is piped round the dish before the garnishes are added, while the remainder is served in a sauce-boat.

(*Recipe of Jean Liban, Paris, Prosper Montagné Prize,* 1963.)

Carpe à la Bière * *Carp in Beer*

For 5 *persons:* 2½ *lb carp; carp roe;* 3 *onions;* 2 *small sticks of celery;* 2 *oz gingerbread crumbs; about* 1½ *pints light ale; bouquet garni.* Cooking time: 35 minutes.

Slice the onions, dice the celery finely and toss in butter. Place the carp on top, add the beer, season, add a *bouquet garni* and braise slowly in the oven covered with the gingerbread crumbs. Slice the carp roe, season and poach with lemon juice and butter. When the carp is cooked take it out and reduce the stock by half, remove the herbs and pass through a sieve. Season this thickish sauce, enrich with a piece of butter, pour over carp and garnish with the roes.

▣ au Bleu * *Blue-Poached*

Use small carp weighing about ¾ lb and treat in the same way as blue poached trout. Larger carp, cut in pieces of about 6 ounces, can also be used. Blue-poached carp is served with melted butter, horseradish or Horseradish cream and boiled potatoes.

▣ Chambord

For 6 *to* 8 *persons:* 1 *carp, weighing about* 4½ *lb;* 2 *lb forcemeat for Fish Quenelles;* ¼ *lb carrots;* ¼ *lb onions;* ¼ *lb celery; parsley;* ½ *bottle red Burgundy;* ¾ *pint fish stock;* 10 *carp roes;* ¼ *pint white wine;* 16 *oysters;* 3 *fl oz sauce Villeroi;* ½ *lb mushrooms;* 12 *gudgeons;* 6 *crayfish;* 2 *truffles;* 1 *egg;* ¾ *pint milk; breadcrumbs;* ¼ *lb butter.* Cooking time: 50-60 minutes.

▲ Truite de Rivière aux Amandes, p. 375

Trotelle Renato, p. 383 ▼

▲ *Filets de perche à la Meunière, p. 372*

Quenelles de brochet à la Lyonnaise, p. 359 ▼

▲ *Mouselline de saumon Chantilly, p. 373*

Truite à la Mâconnaise, p. 376 ▼

▲ Féra au Vin Blanc, p. 371

Saumon Grillée, p. 373 ▼

▲ *Saumon en Bellevue, p. 380*

Saumon Froid à la Moscovite, p. 380 ▼

▲ Truite Froide Vladimir, p. 381

Truites de Rivière Glacée Andréa, p. 381 ▼

▲ Truites de Rivière en Gelée Palace-Hôtel, p. 382

Truite Froide en Bellevue, p. 380 ▼

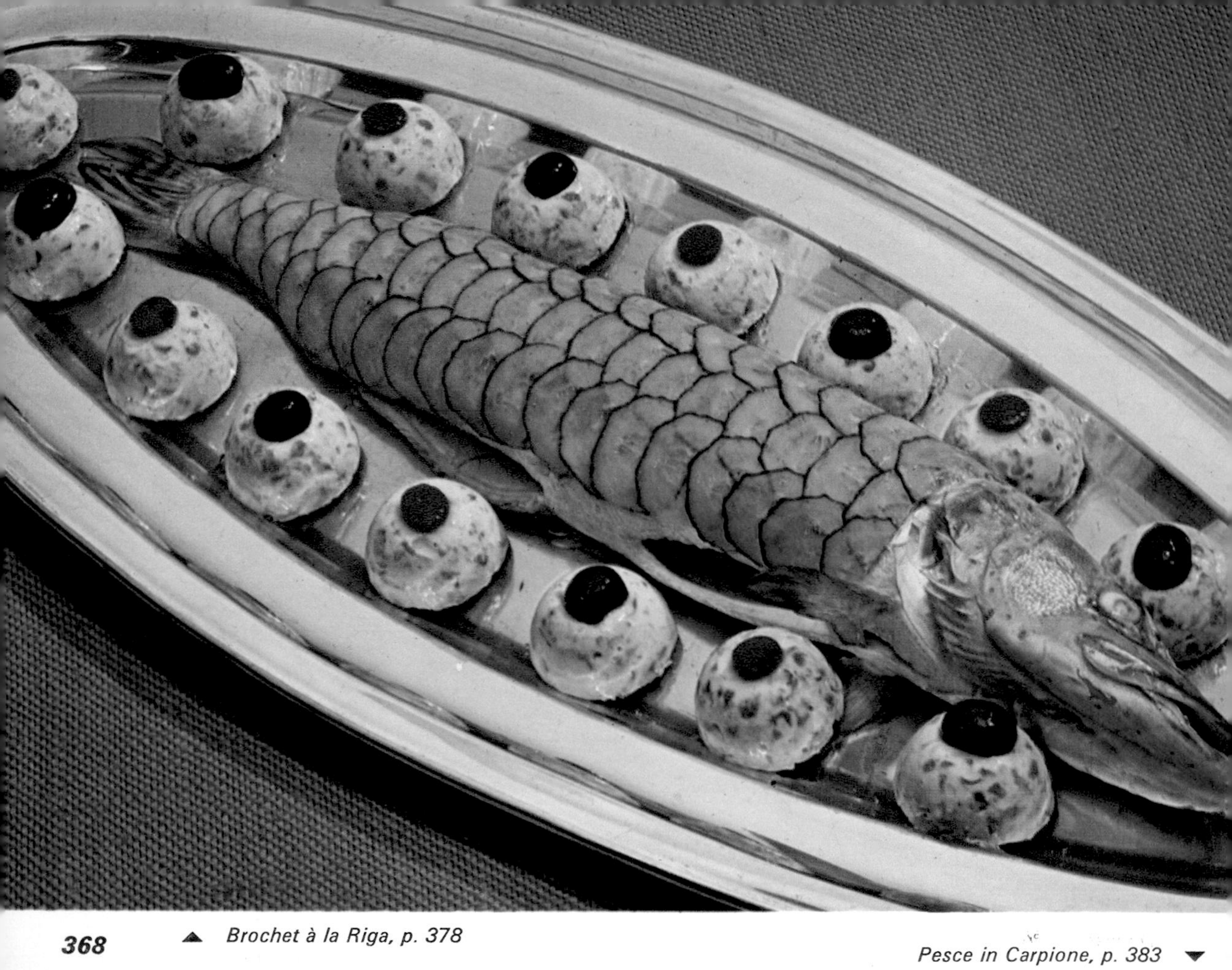

▲ *Brochet à la Riga*, p. 378

Pesce in Carpione, p. 383 ▼

Draw out the entrails of the carp through its gills and remove the skin from the middle of one side of the fish. Stuff the carp with a large portion of the *quenelles* mixture. Reserve a small quantity. Smooth off the bare flesh which is then inlaid with small slices of truffles. Season, cover up with strips of bacon fat and braise in the oven on a bed of vegetables (carrots, onions, parsley and celery). Add the red wine and fish stock. Baste frequently. Reduce the liquor which is then strained and mixed with ¼ pint *sauce Genève*. *Garnish:* 4 large Spoon-shaped *quenelles* decorated with truffles; 12 small, round truffle-flavoured *quenelles*; carp roes which are cooked in white wine, allowed to cool, thinly sliced, coated in egg and breadcrumbs and fried; oysters which are poached in their own juice, dried with a cloth, dipped first in *sauce Villeroi*, then in egg and breadcrumbs and finally fried; fluted mushroom caps which are cooked and drained; cooked crayfish with their tails in their mouths and gudgeons coated in egg and breadcrumbs and fried. The *quenelles* should be poached. Serve the carp surrounded by the various garnishes. A little of the sauce is poured over the fish and the rest is served separately.

Carpe Farcie * *Stuffed Carp*

For 10 persons: 1 carp of 6 lb; 1 lb cleaned and prepared pike flesh; 30 crayfish; 1 quart of mussels; ½ lb prawns; ½ lb mushrooms; 1 lb cooked spinach purée; 15 scallops; ½ lb rice; 1 pint Fish Velouté; 1½ lb butter; 1½ pints cream; ¼ pint Burgundy brandy; ½ bottle Chablis; ⅛ pint oil; 2 carrots and 2 onions for mirepoix; 2 cloves of garlic; 1 bouquet garni; 1 lb tomato concassé; 1 oz tomato purée; tarragon; parsley; chervil; ¼ pint milk; 1 tablespoon meat glaze; ½ lb chopped almonds; 1 dessertspoon arrowroot. Also required: butter for frying; egg and breadcrumbs for coating; 10 fish-shaped Puff pastry cases, baked and scooped out; 4 egg yolks; sauce Hollandaise made from 5 yolks of egg and 1 lb butter; ½ pint Pancake batter.

Cook the crayfish with the Chablis. Remove the flesh from the tails and claws, put 15 tails on one side and keep warm in butter. Cut the other flesh into small dice. Strain the cooking liquor and reduce to almost a glaze. (This is called a *coulis*.) Pound the *mirepoix* (made from the carrots and onions) and the crayfish shells to a fine paste in a pestle and mortar, pass through a fine seive, and put this in a cool place. Cook the mussels as for *Moules Marinière* (*p.* 400). Remove from the shells, beard them and put on one side. Allow the mussel cooking liquor to settle then decant, leaving all sediment behind. Strain carefully and keep on one side. Cut the mushrooms into dice and cook in butter, add the ½ lb of prawns and cooked mussels. Keep warm. Open the scallops, separate the flesh from the small coral tongue, egg and breadcrumb both these parts and fry in butter. Cook the ½ lb of rice as for a *risotto* (*p.* 678). Lightly roast the almonds, add ¼ pint of the *Velouté* and 4 egg yolks and cook carefully to a thick creamy consistency. Fill into the pastry cases. Season the prepared pike flesh, pound and sieve, incorporate 1 pint of the cream and put on ice to firm—this now forms the pike forcemeat. Season the spinach with salt, pepper and nutmeg, blend with ½ lb of the pike forcemeat, pack into buttered moulds and poach in a water-bath. Scale, trim, empty and wash the carp. Remove the skin from one side and the central bones and season with salt and pepper. Blend the crayfish liquor (*coulis*) and the diced flesh with the rest of the chilled pike forcemeat. Mix 1 dessertspoon of arrowroot in a little brandy, add to the forcemeat, stuff the carp with this mixture and sew up. Fry a little of the chilled *mirepoix* mixture in oil and butter and spread in a dish. Lay the fish on top and flame with brandy, moisten with the mussel liquor, and the fish stock if necessary. Add the tomatoes, tomato *purée*, garlic, tarragon stalks and *bouquet garni*. Cover with a buttered paper and cook in a cool oven, 325° F or Gas Mark 3, for one hour with frequent basting; remove and keep warm. Incorporate the Pancake batter with the chopped tarragon, chervil and parsley. With this batter make 10 small pancakes. Reduce the cooking liquor, add the other ¾ of a pint of *Velouté*, ¼ pint of the cream and the meat glaze. Check the seasoning and consistency and correct if necessary. Strain and blend in half the *sauce Hollandaise.* Take the mixture of prawns, mussels and mushrooms and bind with some of this sauce; fill into the pancakes, fold into four, mask with *sauce Hollandaise* and glaze under the grill or salamander. Shape the rice *risotto* to the form of a carp, place the fish on top and mask over with the sauce. Arrange the scallops and prawn tails alternately down the centre; decorate with a band of chopped parsley on either side. Garnish the dish with the pancakes and Puff pastry cases. Unmould the spinach mixture on a round dish and decorate with the scallop tongues.

Carpe à la Polonaise

For 5 persons: 1 carp, weighing about 2¼-2½ lb; 3 onions; parsley; thyme; bay leaf; ½ pint red wine; 1 pint light ale; 2 oz almonds; 2 oz sultanas; 2 oz gingerbread; 2 oz butter. Cooking time: 35 minutes.

Scale the freshly killed carp, remove gills and fins, cut in portion pieces. Wash and put in a buttered *sauté* dish or other suitable vessel after buttering and lining with sliced onions, thyme, bay leaf, parsley, a clove and a few pepper and coriander corns. Add the carp roe, salt lightly, add the beer and red wine, a pinch of sugar and a dash of vinegar and bring to the boil. When it boils add the grated gingerbread to bind it. As soon as the fish is cooked remove the pieces, strain the sauce, season and enrich with butter. In a saucepan heat the peeled, chopped, blanched almonds with the sultanas, a piece of butter, a dash of vinegar, a few drops of water and a pinch of sugar. Add to the sauce and pour it over the pieces of fish. Serve with boiled potatoes.

Laitances de Carpe Diplomate * *Carp Roe*

For 4 persons: 1 lb carp roe; 2 oz butter; 8 large baked Puff pastry cases; ¼ pint sauce Nantua; 8 truffle slices. Cooking time: 4-5 minutes.

Carp roes are a much esteemed delicacy. First soak well in cold water, then poach slowly in butter with a few drops of lemon juice and a pinch of salt. Slice, fill into *croustades,* coat with the sauce and decorate with a truffle slice. Serve very hot.

Quenelles de Carpe Saxonne * *Carp Quenelles*

For 6 persons: 1 carp, weighing about 4½ lb; ½ pint brown ale; ¼ lb butter; 2 oz gingerbread crumbs; chopped parsley; mixed herbs; 2 pints cream; 4 egg whites. Cooking time: 15 minutes.

Fillet the carp and make ¼ pint stock with the bones, head and herbs. Pound the flesh of the carp with the egg whites. Make a forcemeat of the flesh and the cream. Season highly and rub through a seive. Heat ¼ pint beer with the fish stock and the butter in a *sauté* pan. Make 18 small Spoon *quenelles* with the forcemeat and poach gently for 5 minutes in this beer sauce. *Purée* the gingerbread with ¼ pint beer. Thicken the sauce with this *purée* and poach the *quenelles* for another 10 minutes. Serve the *quenelles* in a bowl, coat with the sauce and sprinkle with chopped parsley. Serve plain boiled rice or boiled potatoes separately.

Esturgeon * *Sturgeon*

Sturgeon is treated in the same way as veal, which it resembles in appearance after cooking. A piece may be braised in the same way as a *fricandeau* and garnished with vegetables, but it can also be served with the usual sauces. Its flesh has no particular flavour and it is sought after mainly because of its rarity.

FÉRA * *WHITEFISH*

▣ Filets Meunière * *Shallow Fried Fillets*

For 4 persons; 4 pieces of féra, 6-7 oz each; ¼ lb butter; flour; lemon; parsley. Cooking time: 5-7 minutes.

Cut the fish with a sharp knife down the back, cut off the head and remove the bone. Wash and dry, season, dip in flour and fry both sides in a frying pan to a golden brown. Arrange the fish on a long dish and squeeze a little lemon juice on top. Garnish all along the fish with thin slices of lemon. Pour bubbling hot Brown butter on top and sprinkle with chopped parsley.

▣ au Vin Blanc * *In White Wine*

For 5 persons: 1 large féra, weighing about 2 lb or 5 small fish of 7 oz each; ½ pint white wine; ¾ pint Fish Velouté; 1 shallot; 2 oz butter; 12 fleurons; lemon juice; parsley. Cooking time: 8-10 minutes to poach the small fish, 15-18 minutes for the large one.

Clean, scale, wash and dry the *féra*. Place the chopped shallot at the bottom of a buttered dish. Season the fish, place it on top, moisten with white wine and cover with buttered paper. Poach in the oven. Drain the fish and arrange it on a long dish with the *fleurons* along the sides of the dish. Reduce the fish stock and mix with the *Velouté*. Cook for a few minutes longer, remove from the heat, whip in the butter and season with lemon juice. Cover the fish with this sauce and sprinkle chopped parsley over the fish, if liked. (*See illustration p.* 364).

Goujons et Gardons * *Gudgeon and Roach*

The former of these two fish is by far the better. They are always deep fried, i.e., dipped in seasoned milk, floured and fried in deep fat. Larger fish may also be fried in the frying pan.

Lavaret * *Lake Trout*

This very delicate white-fleshed fish is poached in fish stock or shallow fried, according to size. Its fine flavour makes any additions superfluous.

Lotte Princesse de Monaco * *Burbot*

For 12 persons: 1 burbot, weighing about 5 lb and its liver; 3 lb carrots; 1 lb mushrooms; 2 lb courgettes; 1 lemon; 1 clove garlic; 2 shallots; thyme; bay leaf; parsley; 1 bottle dry white wine; 1½ pints double cream; 2 eggs; ¼ lb white breadcrumbs; ½ pint oil; some coriander seeds; ¼ lb butter; 1 oz salt; freshly ground pepper. Cooking time: 45 minutes.

Trim the burbot well and slash lightly. Insert small slices of garlic all down the back on either side of the backbone. Tie up with string so that it does not disintegrate during cooking. Prepare part of the fennel *à la Grècque*, the *courgettes* which should be cut into 12 equal parts, seeded and blanched, and poach 12 fluted mushrooms. Lightly butter a long fire-proof dish. In it place the *julienne* of carrots, mushrooms and some of the fresh fennel, the sliced shallots and *bouquet garni*. Place the burbot on top, add the white wine, cream, salt, freshly ground pepper, cover with buttered paper and place in a moderate oven, 375° F or Gas Mark 4. When the burbot is cooked, remove it from the oven, remove the string and the backbone, which gives it the shape of a leg of mutton. Place the burbot on a serving dish. Thicken the sauce with the 2 egg yolks without straining it, leaving it rather oily. Coat the burbot with this sauce and place the poached turned mushrooms along its back. Around the edge of the dish alternate the *courgettes* stuffed with fennel and the slices of burbot liver which have been breadcrumbed and fried in butter. Serve the sauce separately in a sauce-boat.

(*Recipe by Boutines, Paris, Prosper Montagné Prize for* 1959.)

Matelote de Moselle * *Mixed Fish Casserole*

For 6 *persons:* ½ *lb eel;* ½ *lb carp;* ½ *lb pike;* ½ *lb tench;* ¼ *pint fresh cream;* 2 *egg yolks;* 6 *chopped shallots;* 2 *finely chopped cloves of garlic;* ½ *lb mushroom caps;* ½ *lb small onions;* 2 *fl oz brandy;* 1 *bouquet garni;* ¼ *lb butter;* 12 *small heart-shaped croûtons;* 1¼ *pints white wine.* Cooking time: 25-30 minutes.

Cut the scaled, cleaned and washed fish into pieces. Brown the shallots in butter. Add the eel. In the meantime poach the mushrooms with a nut of butter and lemon juice. *Flambé* the eel with brandy, add white wine and reduce. Add the other fish, the mushroom stock, garlic, *bouquet garni* and the small onions. Season and cook gently for 15-18 minutes. Remove the fish, keep hot, covered with buttered paper. Cook the stock until the small onions are soft and thicken with *beurre manié* (½ oz flour, 1 oz butter). Mix thoroughly, remove from the heat and thicken with the egg yolks and cream. Check seasoning. Add the poached mushrooms, coat the fish with the sauce and garnish with *croûtons.*

Omble Chevalier * *Char*

This fish, which has flesh the colour of that of trout but far surpasses it in flavour, might well be called the king of all fish. It tastes best when blue-poached, served only with a fine *sauce Hollandaise.*

Pauchouse

This Burgundy speciality is a sailor-style dish made with white wine. It is always made from several kinds of fish, such as eel, tench, small pike, perch, trout, young mullet, etc. After the fish have been scaled, cleaned and washed, cut them up, place in a casserole with small onions, blanched diced bacon, some cloves of garlic and a *bouquet garni.* Cover with white wine, season, boil briskly for 25 minutes, remove from heat and take out the herbs and garlic. Make a not too thick sauce from white *roux* and the stock, season well and bring fish to the boil in it for a few moments. Serve in a deep dish garnished with heart-shaped white bread *croûtons* fried in butter and rubbed with garlic. Allow 6 oz of fish per person.

Perche * *Perch*

The perch is a very tasty fish. When it is small it is best deep fried, but larger fish are shallow fried or poached and served with a sauce. (*See illustration, p.* 362).

SAUMON * *SALMON*

This large and beautiful fish is found all over Northern Europe. It is a cold water fish which lives in the sea during the winter and travels upriver during the spring months to spawn. Salmon is caught in the rivers of various European countries such as Holland, Denmark, Norway and England, although the best is considered to be from the Scottish rivers. Frozen salmon from Canada and Japan is also imported into Britain but does not compare favourably with the European salmon. On the Continent, Rhine and Loire salmon were highly esteemed but are becoming very scarce due to dams and river pollution. Salmon, being firm fleshed and a pleasing pink colour, lends itself to various preparations, particularly when served cold with elaborate garnishes and decorations. However, the principal methods of serving hot salmon are to poach the fish in *court-bouillon* and serve with a *sauce Hollandaise* or *Mousseline*, or to grill the fish and serve with *Maître d'Hôtel* butter. Smoked salmon is a delicacy which enjoys a well-deserved reputation as an *hors d'œuvre*.

Saumon Cancalaise

For 8 *persons:* 2 *pieces of salmon, each weighing about* 1 *lb;* 1 *lb whiting forcemeat;* 16 *oysters;* 16 *mushrooms;* 2 *large croûtons;* ¼ *pint sauce Villeroi;* ½ *pint sauce Nantua*. Cooking time: 40 minutes.

Stuff the centre of two middle cuts of salmon with the whiting forcemeat. Wrap each piece separately in a muslin cloth. Tie up gently and poach for 15 minutes. Drain, dress on an oval flat dish and garnish with *croûtons* fried in oil. At each end of the dish put eight oysters *Villeroi*, replaced on their shells, and arrange the mushroom caps on either side. Coat with th c *sauce Nantua*. Place the whiting *quenelles* on top. Serve very hot.

▣ Foyot

For 6 *persons:* 6 *steaks of salmon, each weighing about* 5-6 *oz;* ½ *pint sauce Foyot;* 2 *oz butter;* 1¾-2 *lb potatoes*. Cooking time: 8-10 minutes.

Season steaks, flour them and fry in butter; remove backbone. Serve fish, garnish with *Noisette* potatoes and serve *sauce Foyot* separately.

▣ Grillées * *Grilled*

Per person: 1 *salmon steak weighing about* 5-6 *oz*. Cooking time: 8-10 minutes.

Dry the steaks, oil them and place under a hot grill. First apply great heat on both sides then finish cooking slowly at moderate heat. When the backbone can be easily removed with the tip of a knife, the salmon is cooked. Serve with a pat of *Maître d'Hôtel* or Anchovy butter on a round of lemon. (*See illustration p*. 364).

Mousseline de Saumon Chantilly * *Salmon Mousse*

For 4 *persons:* ¾ *lb salmon without skin or bone;* ½ *pint thick cream;* 2 *egg whites;* ½ *lb small mushrooms;* 8 *crayfish tails; sauce Mousseline made with* 6 *oz butter;* 1 *oz Crayfish butter*. Cooking time: 12-15 minutes.

Pass the salmon twice through the finest blade of the mincer, mix with the egg whites, pass through a fine sieve and place in a container on ice to cool thoroughly. When quite cold, season highly with salt and pepper and gradually fold in the cream with a wooden spoon. Test by dropping a small piece in boiling water to see if the forcemeat coheres without being too solid. Press forcemeat into 8 buttered *baba* moulds and poach in the water-bath in the oven without letting the water bubble. Trim the mushrooms and poach in lemon juice with a little butter and a pinch of salt, letting the liquor boil away completely. Turn out the *mousselines*, drain well and arrange on a round dish. Coat with *sauce Mousseline* beaten up with Crayfish butter and garnish with a crayfish tail. Fill the centre with the mushrooms and sprinkle chopped chervil on top. (*See illustration p*. 363).

Pain de Saumon Valois * *Salmon Loaf Valois*

For 4 persons: 1 lb salmon without skin or bone; ½ pint cold, very thick sauce Béchamel; 1 egg; 3 egg yolks; approximately ¼ pint cream; ½ pint sauce Foyot. Cooking time: 30-35 minutes.

Pass the salmon twice through the finest blade of the mincer, mix well with the *Béchamel* and eggs, season with salt, pepper and a small pinch of grated nutmeg and fold in the cream. Pass this mixture through a sieve, stir well once again and place in a large buttered mould. Poach in a water-bath at moderate heat, 350° F or Gas Mark 3, without letting the water boil up. Test by inserting a needle; when it comes out hot and dry, the paste is done. Turn out on a round dish and pour *sauce Foyot* on top.

Soufflé de Saumon Diva * *Salmon Soufflé Diva*

For 6-8 persons: ½ lb boiled salmon without skin or bones; 1 lb shrimp tails; ¼ pint Béchamel; ¼ pint cream; 4 eggs; 1 large lightly baked croustade case of unsweetened Short pastry or 8 tartlet cases. Cooking time: about 10 minutes.

Bind the shrimp tails lightly with half the cream and a few spoons of *Béchamel* and cover the bottom of the *croustade* with them. On this place the following mixture and smooth the top; pound the salmon—leftovers will do—mix well with 2 oz butter, the remaining *Béchamel* and cream. Heat, stir to a paste, season, remove from heat and stir in 4 egg yolks followed by 2 stiffly beaten egg whites. Bake in the oven at moderate heat, 375° F or Gas Mark 4.

Tanches à la Lorraine* *Tench in White Wine Sauce*

For 6 persons: 6 tench of 5-6 oz; 2 medium-sized onions; 2 shallots; bay leaf; thyme; peppercorns; ½ pint Lorraine or other dry white wine; ¼ pint cream; 2 egg yolks; 2 oz butter; chopped parsley.

Scale, clean and wash tench and place in a suitable vessel on thinly sliced onions, a few peppercorns, thyme and bay leaf. Add the white wine and about ¼ pint water, salt lightly and simmer slowly for about 8 minutes. Remove tench, strain the stock and reduce to half, so that about ¼ pint of liquid is left and thicken with the two egg yolks, beat up with the butter. Place the tench on a baking dish and sprinkle with finely chopped shallots and parsley. Pour the sauce over the fish and place in a very hot oven, 425° F or Gas Mark 7, for 5 minutes and after removing it sprinkle with lemon juice.

Truite * *Trout*

Trout are among the most popular of freshwater fish. There are several varieties including the common brown or river trout and the salmon and sea trout; the latter have pink flesh and resemble salmon. They all have a very delicate and well-flavoured flesh and can be served hot or cold. It is important to note, however, that the rainbow trout, which is bred in captivity, bears no resemblance other than in name to those which live in fresh running water.

TRUITE DE RIVIÈRE * *RIVER TROUT*

These fish are found in rivers throughout Britain and Northern Europe. They are best when served with a simple dressing.

Truite de Rivière aux Amandes * *River Trout with Almonds*

For 6 persons: 6 *trout;* 1 *oz peeled almonds;* ½ *lb butter.* Cooking time: 6-8 minutes.

Dip trout in salted milk, flour and fry brown on both sides in butter. Put fresh butter in pan, fry chopped almonds light brown in it and pour them over the trout with the butter. (*See illustration p.* 361).

▣ au Bleu * *Blue-Poached*

Per person: 1 *trout weighing* 5-6 *oz.* Cooking time: 7-8 minutes.

For this recipe live trout are necessary. Kill them at the last minute before cooking. They must be cleaned quickly without scraping or wiping, because it is the film of slime that covers the trout which gives them the blue colour. Put them into well-salted boiling water, bring to the boil, and poach them until they are cooked, without allowing the water to boil. Serve on a napkin, garnish with parsley and lemon and serve melted or creamed butter or *sauce Mousseline* at the same time.

N.B. Contrary to general opinion it is absolutely *un*necessary to put vinegar in the water or to sprinkle the fish with hot vinegar before cooking it. Trout will always cook "blue," if the covering film of slime is not removed. Vinegar spoils the delicate taste of trout.

▣ à la Crème * *with Cream Sauce*

For 6 *persons:* 6 *trout, each weighing about* 6 *oz;* ¾ *pint double cream.* Cooking time: 15 minutes.

Arrange the trout in an ovenproof dish with salt, pepper, a *bouquet garni* and the juice of 1 lemon, adding only a few spoonfuls of water. Bake in a moderate oven, 375° F or Gas Mark 4, remove and then drain. Put the cooking liquor in a saucepan, stir in the cream, reduce by half and pour over the trout. Sprinkle with breadcrumbs, and brown in the oven.

▣ Glacée au Vin Rouge * *Glazed with Red Wine*

For 6 *persons:* 6 *trout, each weighing about* 6 *oz;* 1 *onion;* ¾ *pint red wine;* 1 *oz flour;* 2 *oz butter.* Cooking time: 10 minutes.

Slice onion thinly and place in a casserole. Arrange the trout on top, season, pour on red wine and poach in a hot oven, 400° F or Gas Mark 6. Pour off red wine, reduce to half, bind with the butter kneaded with the flour and pour the sauce over the trout in the baking dish. Glaze quickly in a very hot oven or under the salamander or grill and surround with heart-shaped fried white bread *croûtons.*

▣ à la Grenobloise

Prepare the trout *à la Meunière* but sprinkle with fried breadcrumbs, a tablespoonful of capers, lemon juice and chopped parsley.

Truite de Rivière à la Hussarde

For 6 *persons:* 6 *trout;* 2 *oz sieved white breadcrumbs;* ½ *lb onions;* ½ *pint milk;* 2 *oz butter;* ¼ *pint white wine;* 1 *egg.* Cooking time: 30 minutes.

Clean the trout and stuff with forcemeat made by soaking the bread in cold milk and mixing it with 4 oz onions cooked white in butter, chopped parsley, 1 egg and seasoning. Cook remaining onions white in butter and place them in the bottom of a baking dish. Place trout on top, season, add the white wine and poach. When cooked, pour off stock, reduce to half, bind with 1 oz butter mixed with ½ oz flour, boil up once, enrich with butter, and season. Pour over trout and glaze quickly in a hot oven or under the grill.

▣ à la Mâconnaise

For 6 *persons:* 6 *trout, each weighing about* 6 *oz;* 18 *small onions;* ½ *lb mushrooms:* ¾ *pint red wine;* 3 *oz butter;* ½ *oz flour.* Cooking time: about 10 minutes.

Season the prepared trout and poach in red wine. Brown the onions in butter, add some *bouillon* to cover them, add salt and a generous pinch of sugar. Simmer till they are cooked, the moisture has evaporated and the onions are glazed. *Sauté* the mushrooms, which should be as small as possible. When the trout are cooked, pour off the red wine, reduce to a little less than half, add a nut of meat glaze and bind with the flour, kneaded with a little butter. After boiling up three or four times, beat in remainder of the butter and season well. Serve trout on a long, hot dish, arrange mushrooms at one end and onions at the other and coat the fish with the sauce. (*See illustration p.* 363).

▣ à la Mantoue

For 8 *persons:* 8 *trout of* 6 *oz each;* ¾ *pint sauce Italienne; frying butter.* Cooking time: 8-10 minutes.

Fry trout as in *Truite Grenobloise*, serve and pour over *sauce Italienne*, made without ham.

▣ Meunière * *Shallow Fried*

For 6 *persons:* 6 *small trout;* ¼ *lb butter;* 1 *lemon; a little milk; flour; parsley.* Cooking time: 6-8 minutes.

Dip the trout in milk, flour and fry them in *Noisette* butter. Sprinkle with lemon juice and *Noisette* butter. Decorate the dish with half-slices of lemon and chopped parsley.

▣ à la Vauclusienne

Same method as for Shallow Fried Trout, but using oil instead of butter.

TRUITE SAUMONÉE * *SEA TROUT*

The trout and salmon belong to the same family.

▣ Castellane

For 10 *persons:* 1 *sea trout of* 4 *lb;* 2 *lb Fish forcemeat;* 4 *small fillets of sole;* ½ *bottle white wine;* 8-10 *small prawns;* ½ *lb shrimp tails;* 10 *small pastry cases;* 4 *truffle slices;* 10 *poached oysters;* ½ *lb diced stewed tomatoes;* 10 *fleurons;* 1½ *pints sauce Béchamel;* ¼ *pint cream.* Cooking time: 40-45 minutes to poach the fish.

Clean the trout through the gills, wash and drain. Stuff with the forcemeat, and remove the skin from the back, but leave the skin on head and tail. Spread a thin layer of forcemeat on back and sides of the fish. Wash and drain the fillets of sole, beat them flat with the back of a knife, and cover the forcemeat with the fillets. Stud the fillets with slices of truffle cut in half, and wrap the fish first in thin slices of fat bacon and then in oiled paper. Tie with string on the grid of a fish kettle, keeping the fish on its belly and braise it in white wine and well-seasoned fish stock. Prepare *croquettes* with the shrimp tails and thick, well-seasoned *sauce Béchamel* and coat them with egg and breadcrumbs. Fry them in hot fat. Use the rest of the forcemeat to make rather large, oval *quenelles*. As soon as the fish is cooked, remove bacon and paper, drain well, and arrange in the middle of a long hot dish. Strain the fish stock, reduce it, adding the liquid of the poached oysters and thick *Béchamel*. Finish with the cream, add the oysters and correct the seasoning. Impale the prawns in a row all along the back, and garnish with shrimp *croquettes*, *quenelles*, tartlets filled with stewed tomatoes and *fleurons*. Serve the sauce at the same time.

Truite Saumonèe Chivry

For 6-8 persons: 1 sea trout, weighing about 3½ lb; 8 baked tartlet cases; 1½ lb spinach; ¾ pint sauce Chivry; ¼ pint cream; 2 oz butter. Cooking time: about 40 minutes.

Poach trout as above, drain, serve and garnish with the tartlet cases, filled with a *purée* made from the spinach with the butter and cream. Serve the *sauce Chivry* separately.

▣ Laguipière

For 8 persons: 1 sea trout, weighing about 3½ lb; 8 crayfish; 8 scallops; 16 oysters; ¼ lb shrimps; ¼ lb mushrooms; 1 truffle; ½ pint white wine; ½ pint sauce Mornay; ½ pint sauce Nantua; parsley. Cooking time: 40-50 minutes.

Poach the trout carefully in a slow oven, 350° F or Gas Mark 3. Serve with a garnish of crayfish cooked in *court-bouillon* with white wine and of scallops filled with oysters, mushroom and shrimp *ragoût* bound with *sauce Mornay* and gratinated. Skin the exposed side of the trout and decorate with truffle slices and curly parsley. Serve with *sauce Nantua*.

▣ Montgolfier

For 6-8 persons: 1 sea trout, weighing about 3½ lb; 1 lb Fish forcemeat; ½ pint white wine; ¾ pint Fish Velouté; 8 lobster slices; 8 truffle slices; 8 large mushroom heads. Cooking time: 45-50 minutes.

Carefully clean the fish through the gills, wash, and fill with the well-seasoned forcemeat through the gill opening by means of a forcing bag. Place the fish in a fish kettle on a bed of thinly sliced carrots, onions and shallots. Add the white wine, season lightly and braise in a warm oven, basting frequently. When cooked, skin and keep warm, cover with buttered paper. Reduce fish stock, strain, add to the white wine sauce and reduce to a coating consistency. Season well and enrich with a little butter. Serve fish, coat lightly with sauce, decorate with truffle slices and garnish with the lobster slices and mushrooms. Serve the remainder of the sauce separately.

Truite Saumonée, sauce Mousseline

For 6-8 persons: 1 *sea trout weighing about* 3½ *lb;* ¾ *pint sauce Mousseline;* 2½ *lb potatoes.* Cooking time: about 40 minutes.

Place the trout on its belly in a fish kettle, add cold fish stock so that it is well covered, bring slowly to the boil. When it boils up, draw aside and simmer till cooked. Remove carefully, skin—although connoisseurs prefer to have it served in its silvery skin—and serve garnished with parsley and lemon. Serve the *sauce Mousseline* and well-shaped boiled potatoes separately.

⊡ Régence

For 8 *persons:* 1 *sea trout, weighing about* 3½ *lb;* ¾ *pint court-bouillon;* ¾ *pint Fish Velouté;* 3 *egg yolks;* 3 *oz Crayfish butter;* 8 *small fish quenelles;* ½ *lb blanched, mushroom caps;* ½ *lb peeled shrimps;* 8 *peeled crayfish.* Cooking time: 30 minutes.

Cook the trout in *court-bouillon.* Reduce ¾ pint *court-bouillon* to half, incorporate *Velouté* sauce and thicken with the egg yolks. Add the Crayfish butter. Gradually incorporate the garnish of cooked fish *quenelles,* mushrooms, shrimps and crayfish. Pour this sauce around the fish.

POISSONS D'EAU DOUCE FROIDS * *COLD FRESHWATER FISH*

BROCHET * *PIKE*

After braising or poaching this fish may be served cold with a cold sauce or decorated with aspic and a cold vegetable garnish.

⊡ à la Manon

For 10 *persons:* 1 *pike, weighing about* 4 *lb;* 10 *small cooked prawns, shell removed from the tail;* 10 *small pastry cases;* 1 *lb shrimp tails, bound with Mayonnaise;* 1 *small truffle; parsley; white asparagus tips, marinated in advance.* Cooking time: 40-45 minutes to poach the pike.

Poach the pike in fish stock and allow to cool in the stock. Drain well and skin the back, leaving the skin on head and tail. Place the pike on a long dish, keeping the fish on its belly. Impale a row of prawns all along the back. Garnish the sides with the pastry cases, filled with shrimp salad decorated with a round slice of truffle and chopped parsley. Place the asparagus tips at both ends.

⊡ à la Riga

For 6 *persons:* 1 *pike, weighing about* 4 *lb;* 1 *lb Russian salad, moulded in small timbales;* 1¾ *pints fish aspic;* 10 *black olives;* 1 *small cucumber.*

Clean the pike, cook it carefully in *court-bouillon* and cool in the stock. Remove the skin and coat a long dish with a film of aspic. When set, place the fish in the middle of the dish and decorate the fish with very thin slices of cucumber to imitate the scales of the fish. Turn out the *timbales* of Russian salad and coat with fish aspic. Place a halved black olive and a round of tomato on alternate salads. Serve with a highly seasoned *sauce Verte.* (*See illustration p.* 368).

Carpe à la Juives aux Raisins * *Carp with Sultanas*

For 8 persons: $3\frac{1}{2}$ *lb carp;* 1 *onion;* 2 *shallots;* $\frac{1}{4}$ *pint oil;* 1 *oz flour;* $\frac{3}{4}$ *pint dry white wine;* $\frac{1}{4}$ *lb sultanas;* $\frac{1}{4}$ *lb currants;* 1 *bouquet garni.* Cooking time of carp: 30 minutes.

Slice the onions and shallots and *sauté* in the oil without allowing them to colour. Dust with the flour, simmer a moment and add the wine and an equal quantity of water. Add salt, peppercorns, the *bouquet garni* and the remaining oil. Bring to the boil. Add the carp, cut in pieces of about 6 ounces—it should be well covered by the liquid—and cook slowly for 30 minutes. Soak the sultanas and currants briefly in warm water and drain. Place the fish on a long, deep dish, surround with sultanas and currants. Strain the fish stock, reduce to three-quarters the quantity and pour over everything. Put in a cold place and serve when the stock has slightly set.

SAUMON FROID * *COLD SALMON*

This excellent fish is usually presented whole or in thick steaks. It is always cooked in a *court-bouillon* never exceeding 200° F and cooled in its cooking liquor. When cooked whole it is advisable not to scale the fish as this method prevents the loss of its valuable oils. This fish is invariably skinned and glazed with aspic jelly. Its presentation is legion, according to the artistry of the cook. Tarragon, chervil, eggs, truffles, radishes, prawns and cucumbers are only some of the accompaniments used for this fish. Others include stuffed eggs, tomato cases filled with various vegetable preparations, asparagus tips, artichoke bottoms, pastry boats and tartlets of various *purées*, cucumber and lettuce. The best weight to buy is from 10 to 15 pounds.

⊡ Filets "Porte-Bonheur" * *Cold Salmon Steaks*

For 8-10 *persons:* $3\frac{1}{2}$-4 *lb salmon or sea trout; truffle slices;* 1-2 *tomatoes;* 5 *hardboiled eggs;* $\frac{1}{2}$ *pint aspic jelly;* 1 *pint Mayonnaise or sauce Chantilly or Gribiche;* 1 *bottle white wine.* Cooking time for the steaks: 6-7 minutes.

First cut off head and tail, and then cut the salmon into steaks about $\frac{3}{8}$-inch thick. Arrange the steaks in a buttered pan, and poach them in white wine and fish stock, covered with buttered paper. Allow them to cool in the stock. Poach head and tail in fish stock, and allow to cool in the stock. Drain the steaks and cut them in half with a sharp knife. Remove skin and bone and decorate each steak with truffle and peeled tomato and glaze with aspic. Drain head and tail and decorate to taste. Line a long dish with a very thin sheet of aspic. When set, place head and tail at the two ends, and the steaks on a slant along the two sides. Halve the eggs and arrange in the centre of the steaks, decorated with a lady-bird made of tomato and truffle and glazed with aspic. Serve with *Mayonnaise* or other suitable sauce.

⊡ Médaillons Majestic

For 8 *persons:* 3 *lb salmon;* $\frac{1}{2}$ *pint white wine;* $\frac{1}{4}$ *pint cream;* $\frac{1}{2}$ *lb shrimps;* $\frac{1}{2}$ *lb potatoes;* $\frac{1}{2}$ *lb celeriac;* 2 *oz walnuts;* 16 *prawns;* 1 *lemon;* $\frac{1}{2}$ *pint Mayonnaise.* Cooking time of middle pieces: about 8-10 minutes.

Cut small, well-shaped round slices of salmon out of salmon steaks and poach them in the oven with white wine, pepper and salt. Poach the trimmings at the same time. Allow to cool. Make the trimmings into a salmon *mousse* with cream. Wipe the medallions, add some shrimp tails to the *mousse* and arrange in a mound on the medallions. Coat with thick *Mayonnaise*, arrange round a salad of potatoes, celeriac and walnuts bound with the same sauce. Skewer a prawn in each medallion.

Saumon Froid à la Moscovite

For 6 persons: 2 *middle pieces of salmon, each weighing about* 1 *lb;* 16 *prawn tails;* 16 *strips anchovy fillets in oil;* 16 *small cooked tartlet cases;* ¼ *lb beetroot;* ¼ *lb chopped celeriac;* ¾ *pint Mayonnaise;* ½ *oz grated horseradish;* ½ *pint aspic; caviar.* Cooking time of middle pieces: about 8-10 minutes.

Skin the poached and cooled salmon pieces, glaze with aspic, decorate with the dried, soaked anchovy strips and the prawn tails and glaze again lightly. Arrange side by side on a long dish and garnish with tartlet cases, filled alternately with a salad of the finely diced vegetables lightly bound with *Mayonnaise* and with caviar. Serve with highly seasoned *Mayonnaise* mixed with the horseradish. All salmon trout recipes are also suitable for salmon. (*See illustration p.* 365).

▣ à la Norvégienne

For 8 *persons:* 2 *middle cuts of salmon, each weighing about* 1½ *lb;* 8 *prawns;* 8 *half hardboiled eggs glazed with aspic;* 8 *small barquettes garnished with shrimp tails bound with Mayonnaise.*

Place the cooked pieces of salmon on a long dish and decorate with the peeled prawn tails. Decorate with the eggs and *barquettes.* Serve *Mayonnaise* separately.

TRUITE FROID * *COLD TROUT*

The methods given for Cold Salmon are also applicable to Cold Trout. This fish is usually served with the head and tail intact, and the skin removed from the sides to expose the flesh.

▣ en Bellevue

For 6-8 *persons:* 1 *sea trout, weighing about* 2-2½ *lb;* 4 *tomatoes;* 1 *lb macédoine of vegetables;* ¾ *pint Mayonnaise;* 2 *hardboiled eggs;* 20 *peeled prawn tails;* 8 *artichoke bottoms;* 16 *asparagus tips;* 1¼ *pints aspic jelly; truffles.*

Poach the trout in a well-seasoned fish stock and allow to cool in the stock. Drain well. Arrange the trout on the dish on its belly. Remove the skin from the middle section. Glaze lightly with aspic jelly. Garnish with prawns and truffles. The hardboiled eggs are decorated with slices of tomatoes and truffles and the cooked asparagus tips are held in place on the artichoke bottoms with aspic. (*See illustrations, pp.* 365 *and* 367).

▣ Daubigny

For 8-10 *persons:* 1 *sea trout, weighing about* 3½-4 *lb;* 1½ *pints aspic;* 4-5 *prawns;* 1 *lb fine vegetable salad;* 4 *hardboiled eggs; caviar; truffle slices;* ¾ *pint Mayonnaise.*

Poach the trout as described above; skin when cold. Decorate the sides with truffles, glaze the whole with aspic and arrange on a long dish on a layer of aspic. Garnish alternately with small mussel shells, filled with vegetable salad, garnished with small pieces of prawn and glazed with aspic, and hardboiled eggs, halved crosswise, scooped out and filled with caviar. Fill the spaces with diced aspic and serve with light *Mayonnaise.*

Truite Froid à la D'Orsay

For 8 persons: 1 cooked sea trout, weighing about 3½ lb; 8 shrimps set in small moulds of aspic; 4 halved hardboiled eggs; 2 oz caviar; ¼ lb tomato salad; ¾ pint sauce Verte.

Arrange the trout on a thin layer of aspic poured and allowed to set on the bottom of the dish. Garnish with the shrimp aspic moulds and the hardboiled eggs, some filled with tomato salad and some with caviar. Serve the *sauce Verte* separately.

⊡ à la Russe

For 6 persons: 1 sea trout, weighing about 2½ lb; fish stock; 1 pint fish aspic; 6 tartlet cases; 1 lb Russian salad; ¾ pint Mayonnaise. Cooking time: about 40 minutes.

Carefully poach the sea trout in the fish stock and leave it to cool. Drain, skin, decorate to taste and glaze with aspic. Arrange fish on its belly and garnish with tartlet cases filled with Russian salad. Fill spaces with diced aspic. Serve with a light *Mayonnaise.*

⊡ Vladimir * *Glazed Trout Vladimir*

For 8 persons: 1 trout, weighing about 3½ lb; 8 hardboiled eggs; 2 oz spinach purée; sprig of tarragon and chervil; 2 oz concentrated tomato purée; 2 lemons; ¼ pint Mayonnaise; ¼ lb softened butter; ¾ pint sauce Verte; ¾ pint tarragon aspic; salt, pepper.

Cook trout, cool and drain, skin and arrange on a long dish. Remove a diamond shaped piece of the skin of the fish. Half the eggs lengthwise and rub the egg yolks through a sieve; combine with the softened butter. Blend in the *Mayonnaise*, and season. Divide this mixture into two; combine one half with the spinach and the other with the tomato *purée*. Fill some of the egg halves with the red and some with the spinach *purée*. Pipe the rest of the two colours of *purée* in a decoration on the fish. Garnish the trout with the half eggs placed on lemon slices, alternating the colours. Coat the whole with tarragon aspic. Border the dish with fluted half-slices of lemon. Serve the *sauce Verte* separately. (*See illustration, p.* 366).

Truite de Rivière Glacée Andréa * *Glazed River Trout*

For 4 persons: 4 trout, each weighing about 5-6 oz; ¼ pint white wine; ½ pint fish stock; 12 large pink shrimps; ¾ lb tomato mousse (purée of raw tomatoes, aspic, unsweetened whipped cream, seasoning); ½ lb shrimp mousse (prepared like tomato mousse, using shrimp purée instead); lemon; tarragon leaves; 4 pastry boats. Cooking time: 7-8 minutes to poach the fish.

Clean the trout through the gills without cutting open the stomach. Cut off fins, scale and wash the trout. Poach in white wine and fish stock flavoured with tarragon. Allow to cool in the stock. Prepare aspic with the stock, adding some gelatine and clarify with egg white. Fill the pastry boats with shrimp *mousse*, decorate each with 2 shrimp tails and 1 unshelled shrimp. Spread the tomato *mousse* on a long dish. When set, arrange the skinned trout on the *mousse*. Decorate them with blanched tarragon leaves and thinly sliced rounds of radishes, imitating flower shapes. Glaze lightly with aspic. Place the pastry boats at the two ends of the dish and garnish with finely diced aspic. (*See illustration p.* 366).

Truite de Rivière en Gelée * *River Trout in Aspic*

For 8 *persons:* 8 *trout, each weighing about* 5-6 *oz;* ¼ *pint white wine; thyme;* 1 *small onion;* 1 *piece bay leaf; tarragon;* ¾ *pint aspic.* Cooking time: 8-10 minutes.

Clean trout which are as fresh as is possible and tie up with string in a ring, mouth and tail touching. Poach carefully in the white wine with the sliced onion, the aromatics and a little water, so that they remain intact. Cool in the stock. Reduce stock to half, add the aspic and clarify. Decorate the trout with tarragon leaves dipped in aspic, carefully coat the trout with the aspic when it has almost set, arrange attractively and decorate with diced aspic.

▣ en Gelée Palace-Hôtel

For 8 *persons:* 8 *trout, each weighing about* 6 *oz; court bouillon;* 30 *crayfish tails;* ½ *lb white cooked asparagus tips;* ½ *lb cooked French beans;* ½ *lb peeled, deseeded tomatoes;* 1 *pint aspic jelly;* ¾ *pint sauce Vinaigrette; dill; vinegar.* Cooking time: 6-7 minutes.

Have the trout as fresh as possible. Loosen the two fillets, but leave them still attached to the head. Roll each fillet around a centre of potato on either side of the head, giving the appearance of a pair of lorgnettes. Poach and allow to cool in the *court bouillon.* Reserve 16 crayfish tails. Dice the remainder with the asparagus tips, French beans and tomatoes and marinate with salt, pepper, vinegar and a little olive oil. Drain the trout and place on a wire tray. Fill the openings with the vegetable salad mixture bound with a little aspic. Decorate the sides of the trout fillets with dill. Garnish the salad with crayfish tails. Glaze the whole with aspic. Serve *sauce Vinaigrette* separately. (*See illustration p.* 367).

▣ en Gelée au Vin Rouge * *in Red Wine Aspic*

Treat the trout in the same way as Trout in Aspic, substituting red wine, and when clarifying the aspic, colour slightly with caramel. Garnish the trout with hard-boiled egg white or truffles and proceed as above.

FOREIGN SPECIALITIES

Anguille au Vert * *Flemish-style Eel*

For 8 *persons:* 4½ *lb eel;* 2 *onions;* 4 *shallots;* 1 *lb fresh spinach;* ½ *lb sorrel;* 1 *small bunch each of tarragon and chevril;* 1 *bouquet garni;* ¾ *pint white wine;* ¾ *pint fish stock;* ¼ *lb butter; the juice of* 1½ *lemons;* 3 *egg yolks.* Cooking time: 15-20 minutes.

Clean and wash the eel and cut off fins. Cut in 2-inch pieces and place in a *sauté* pan in which the chopped onions and shallots have been lightly tossed in butter. Cover the eel with the onions, etc., and simmer a few minutes. Then add the finely chopped spinach, sorrel and herbs, season with salt, pepper and grated nutmeg. Fill up with the wine and the fish stock (water can be used if necessary), cover and simmer for 15 minutes. Remove from heat and thicken with the egg yolk mixed with a little of the stock and season with lemon juice. Serve the eel pieces cold with ¼ lemon per person. (*Belgium*)

Filets de Féra Lucernoise * *Fillets of Féra*

For 5 *persons:* 10 *fillets of féra, each weighing about* 3 *oz* ; ¼ *pint white wine;* ½ *lb mushrooms;* ½ *lb tomatoes;* ½ *pint Fish Velouté;* 2 *oz butter;* 10 *fleurons; thyme; marjoram; mace; sage; salt and pepper.* Cooking time: 8 minutes.

Place the fillets in a buttered pan with the sliced raw mushrooms, the tomatoes, peeled, seeded and diced on top. Mix the salt with pepper and a pinch each of thyme, sage, marjoram and mace. Season the fillets with this mixture, moisten with white wine, cover with buttered paper and poach in the oven. When the fillets are done, pour off the liquid and mix with the Velouté. Cook for a few minutes and remove from the heat. Whip in the butter, season with lemon juice and pour over the fish without straining. Garnish with *fleurons.* (*Switzerland*)

Pesce in Carpione * *Small Marinated Freshwater Fish*

For 10 *persons:* 3½ *lb of small perch, char, etc.;* 1 *carrot;* 1 *onion;* 1 *zest of lemon;* 1 *head celery;* 3 *bay leaves;* 1¾ *pints of vinegar;* 2¼ *pints of white wine; salt.* Cooking time: approximately 1 hour.

Clean the fish, flour and fry. Shred the onion, cut the celery and carrot into *julienne* and stew in oil until tender. Add the vinegar, wine and bay leaves, chop the lemon zest, add and simmer for 30 minutes. Arrange the fish in a casserole, pour over the marinade and allow to cool. (*See illustration p.* 368). (*Italy*)

Trota Salmonata alla Genovese * *Genoa Sea Trout*

For 6 *persons:* 1 *trout, weighing about* 2½ *lb;* 6 *Dublin Bay prawn croquettes;* 12 *boiled potatoes;* 1 *oz pistachios;* 1 *oz pine kernels;* 2 *egg yolks; salt and pepper;* ½ *pint oil;* 1⅛ *oz blanched parsley, chervil, tarragon and chives, rubbed through a sieve;* 1 *lemon.*

Cook the trout in *court-bouillon.* Serve on a long dish and garnish with the *croquettes* and potatoes. Serve the following sauce separately: crush the pistachios and pine kernels, add the egg yolks, salt and pepper and stir in the oil. Incorporate the lemon juice and the herb *purée.* (*Italy*)

Trotelle Renato * *Trout Renato*

For 10 *persons:* 10 *trout, each weighing about* 6 *oz;* 3 *oz capers;* 2 *bay leaves;* ¼ *pint white wine;* ¼ *pint oil;* 10 *fillets of anchovy cut into strips.*

Open and clean the trout and remove the bones. Open out flat like a book, season and place the capers and anchovy strips on top. Fold the tail towards the head. Place the oil in a *sauté* pan, put the trout in it, add the white wine and cook gently for 10 minutes. Cover in the pan with sulphurated paper. Serve the trout and keep them hot. Reduce the pan residue, season and pour over the trout. Garnish with steamed potatoes, tomatoes and lemon slices. (*See illustration p.* 361). (*Italy*)

Waterzooi de Poissons Flamande * *Mixed Fish*

For 8 *persons:* 4½ *lb fish (eel, tench, carp, pike, etc.);* ½ *lb celery;* ¼ *lb butter;* 1 *bouquet garni.* Cooking time: 20 minutes.

Cut up fish and place in a buttered casserole lined with thinly sliced celery. Cover with water, season with salt and pepper, add the *bouquet garni;* flake the butter on top. Boil up, cover and continue boiling briskly to reduce the stock. Remove herbs and lightly bind stock with 2-3 grated unsweetened rusks; the sauce must not be thick. Serve very hot with thin brown bread and butter. (*Belgium*)

Shellfish

CRABES * *CRABS*

To dress: place the crab on its back, twist off claws and remove flaps or aprons. Separate the upper from the lower shell or carapace. Remove the small twisted greenish intestines and the stomach, which is a small bag placed near the head, and the gills, fingers which lie round the big shell. Extract all the flesh. Wash and dry the shell and rub the outside with a little oil. Crack the claws and remove the meat.

▣ Coquilles à la Mornay * *in a Shell with Mornay Sauce*

Crabs are very tasty but even the biggest have very little flesh and that mainly in the claws. Boil the crabs in salt water only, 35 minutes per 2¼ pound. Empty the shell, remove the creamy parts of the body, mix with the chopped flesh from the claws and bind with *sauce Mornay*. Place in the cleaned shell, sprinkle with grated cheese and melted butter and brown in a hot oven. Arrange on a bed of curly parsley and serve hot.

▣ en Pilaf * *Pilaf*

For 6 persons: 6 medium-sized crabs; 1 pint sauce Joinville; ¾ lb Pilaf of rice.

Remove flesh from shell and bind with a little *sauce Joinville*. Press rice into a ring mould, turn out on a round dish and arrange flesh in centre.

CREVETTES * *SHRIMPS AND PRAWNS*

These shellfish are found in rivers, estuaries and rocky coastal waters. Live shrimps are thrown in boiling, very salty water, boiled for 2-3 minutes and drained at once. Shrimps are used for *hors d'œuvres*, sauces, *pilaf* and garnish. The large prawns, known in France as *bouquets*, are also used to decorate hot and cold fish dishes.

▣ Frites * *Fried*

For 6 persons: 1½ lb raw peeled shrimps; ¼ pint olive oil; ¾ lb rice; salt; cayenne; parsley.

Fry the shrimps very briskly in the hot olive oil. Drain and season with salt and cayenne. Serve with the parsley and serve Creole rice separately.

Langouste Bouquetière, p. 397 ▶

▲ *Langoustes en Bellevue, modern presentations, p. 397* ▼

▲ Ecrevisses au Court-Bouillon ou à la Nage, p. 389

Homard ou Langouste Thermidor, p. 393 ▼

▲ *Scampi Thermidor, p. 394*

Brochettes de Langoustines ou de Scampi, p. 394 ▼

Crevettes à l'Indienne * *Curried Shrimps*

For 6 persons: 1½ lb peeled shrimps; 1 onion; ½ oz curry powder; ½ pint Fish Velouté; 2 oz butter.

Lightly fry the finely chopped onion, add the curry powder and then the shrimps. Bind with the *Velouté* and bring to the boil. Serve plain boiled rice separately.

ECREVISSES * *CRAYFISH*

These are small river shellfish which are found in many streams. It is most important that they are thoroughly washed in plenty of cold water and that the black intestinal tube (central fin) is removed with the point of a small knife. This will be found in the opening under the middle phalanx of the tail. If this is not removed, the crayfish will be bitter. Live crayfish, when obtainable, should be killed by throwing them into briskly boiling water for 2-3 minutes, then pouring off this water at once. Remove the intestinal tube and cook as indicated in the recipes.

⊡ à la Bordelaise

For 4 persons: 24 crayfish; 2 tablespoons mirepoix of carrots, onions and shallots; 2 fl oz brandy; ¼ pint white wine; ¼ pint Fish Velouté; ¼ pint fish stock; meat glaze; parsley. Cooking time: 12 minutes.

Wash the fish in plenty of cold water. Toss the *mirepoix* in butter, add the crayfish and cook till they are red. Flame with the brandy, reduce with the white wine, add the *Velouté* and the fish stock and cook for another 6 minutes. Remove crayfish when cooked and keep hot in a dish. Reduce the stock and add a nut of meat glaze. Season well, enrich with butter away from heat, pour over the crayfish and sprinkle chopped parsley on top.

⊡ en Buisson

Per person: 6-8 crayfish, according to size.

Boil the crayfish for 10 minutes in a *court-bouillon* which has been heavily flavoured with white wine, allow them to become cold in the liquid and then pile them in the special utensil for this dish which has been decorated with curly parsley. Alternatively, they can be served on a napkin folded in the form of a cone.

⊡ au Court-Bouillon ou à la Nage

Per person: 6-8 crayfish according to size. Cooking time: 10-12 minutes.

Make a *court bouillon* with thinly sliced onion, carrot, shallot, *bouquet garni*, a little salt and a few peppercorns. When the vegetables are cooked add ½ pint white wine, boil up and strain. Clean crayfish, place in boiling liquor, boil till cooked and serve in a tureen in the liquor or reduce the liquor to half, add a little butter and pour over crayfish. (*See illustration p.* 387).

Ecrevisses au Gratin

For 4 persons: 24 *large crayfish;* ¾ *pint Béchamel;* 2 *oz butter;* 2 *fl oz brandy;* ¼ *pint white wine;* 1 *oz grated cheese.* Cooking time of crayfish: 12 minutes.

Boil the prepared crayfish in simple stock without wine or vinegar and pour off liquid. Remove flesh from claws and tails. Pound the shells finely, brown in butter, add water to cover them, boil up briefly, strain and put in a cold place. As soon as the butter on the surface has hardened, remove and drain it. Keep back a tablespoon of butter, heat the rest in a *sauté* pan, add the crayfish, and cook for a moment. *Flambé* with brandy, add the white wine and reduce to half. Add the not too thick *Béchamel*, boil up, season well with cayenne and if necessary add salt. Place these bound crayfish in a flat, buttered baking dish, smooth top, sprinkle with the cheese and the remainder of the melted crayfish butter and brown in the oven.

QUEUES D'ECREVISSES * *CRAYFISH TAILS*

These may be used to garnish a dish or may be prepared as a dish on their own.

⊡ à la Mode du Couvent de Chorin

For 6 *persons:* ½ *pint water;* ¼ *lb butter;* ¼ *lb flour;* 3 *or* 4 *eggs;* 36 *crayfish;* ½ *lb mushrooms;* ¼ *lb grated cheese;* ½ *pint Béchamel;* ¼ *pint fresh cream;* 2 *tablespoons fine mirepoix;* 2 *fl oz brandy;* ¼ *pint white wine;* 3 *tomatoes concassés;* 2 *fl oz olive oil.* Cooking time of crayfish: 12 minutes.

Make a *Choux* paste with ½ pint water, 2 oz butter, 4 oz flour, 3 or 4 eggs, a pinch of salt, a pinch of grated nutmeg and 2 oz grated cheese added after removing mixture from heat. Divide this paste into *noisettes* or walnut-sized pieces, drop them in boiling salted water, poach slowly and drain. *Sauté* the crayfish and the *mirepoix* in half oil and half butter. *Flambé* with brandy. Add white wine, reduce, season, add the tomatoes *concassés* and cook with the lid on. As soon as they are cooked, shell the crayfish tails and keep them hot in a little of the liquor. Pound the shells and legs with a little butter and add the crayfish liquor after reducing it. Pass through a fine sieve. Quarter the mushrooms and poach them with a pinch of salt, lemon juice and a very little butter. Add the mushroom liquor and the cream to the *Béchamel* and cook for a few minutes. Add the crayfish *purée* and a few drops of lemon juice and check the seasoning. Add the *Choux* paste *noisettes*, mushrooms and crayfish tails to this sauce and serve in a round or oval fire-proof dish. Sprinkle with grated cheese and brown in a hot oven.

⊡ en Sauce à l'Aneth * *Crayfish Tails in Dill Sauce*

For 6 *persons:* 36 *medium-sized crayfish;* 2 *tablespoons fine mirepoix;* 1 *pint fish stock;* 1 *tablespoon brandy;* ¼ *pint white wine;* ¼ *pint cream;* 2 *oz butter;* 3 *oz beurre manié;* 1¾ *oz butter;* 1¼ *oz flour;* 1 *tablespoon chopped dill;* ¾ *lb rice.* Cooking time: 10-12 minutes.

If the crayfish are live, throw them into boiling water to kill them. Remove from water after 3 minutes and drain. Toss the *mirepoix* in butter in a large frying pan, add the crayfish, and allow them to become slightly rosy. *Flambé* with brandy and reduce with white wine. Cook the white wine until almost completely reduced. Add the fish stock and boil till the crayfish are cooked. Peel the tails and remove the intestinal tract (if the crayfish were live). Strain the crayfish stock, boil for a moment, thicken with the cream and the *beurre manié*, simmer and taste. Enrich with the remainder of the butter and the dill. Incorporate the crayfish tails which have been kept hot. Serve with boiled rice tossed in butter.

Queues d'Ecrevisses en Timbales Nantua * *Crayfish in a Pastry Case*

For 6 persons: 30 *crayfish;* $\frac{1}{4}$ *lb mirepoix of carrots; onion; shallot;* 1 *sprig of thyme;* $\frac{1}{2}$ *bay leaf;* 18 *small whiting forcemeat balls;* 12 *blanched mushrooms;* $\frac{1}{2}$ *pint sauce Crème;* $\frac{1}{4}$ *lb butter;* 1 *truffle.*

Prepare a *timbale* of Puff pastry. Cut out a lid and bake blind. *Sauté* the crayfish in butter with the cooked *mirepoix* and cook for 10 minutes. Peel the tails. Pound the shells and the *mirepoix* very finely. Pass through a fine sieve, combine the resulting *purée* with the Cream sauce and heat the whole to boiling point; remove from heat and add butter. Pour this sauce over the forcemeat balls, mushrooms and crayfish tails. Mix carefully and fill the *timbale.* Decorate with the sliced truffle and put the lid on top.

HOMARD * *LOBSTER*

Lobster should always be bought live and may be killed by one of the following methods. The first, the most humane method, is to cover the live lobster with cold water or *court-bouillon* and bring gradually to boiling point, then cook 10-15 minutes to the pound. The second method is to plunge the live lobster into fast boiling water for a few minutes and then take out and prepare as indicated in the recipes. This second method is the better from the culinary point of view. Cutting up a live lobster is a good method of preparation for the following dishes. In most countries, however, it is illegal to cut up live creatures. That is why we recommend killing the lobsters by throwing them into boiling water for a few minutes. The inedible parts of the lobster are the little pouch in the head and the intestine which will appear as a thin grey or black line running down through the tail meat. These parts may be removed when the lobster has been split. The coral is recognisable by its bright red colour in the cooked lobster or greeny-black when raw.

⊡ à l' Americaine

For 4 persons: $2\frac{3}{4}$-3 *lb lobster;* 1 *lb tomatoes;* 1 *tablespoon concentrated tomato purée;* 3 *chopped shallots;* 2 *fl oz brandy;* $\frac{1}{2}$ *pint white wine;* 2 *oz butter;* 1 *tablespoon oil; meat glaze; parsley; tarragon.* Cooking time: 20 minutes.

Choose small lobsters preferably and kill by throwing them into boiling water, leaving for a few minutes and then taking them out. Remove tails, cut into slices of about $\frac{3}{4}$-inch and crush the claws with the back of a large knife so that the flesh can more easily be removed later. Cut the body in half lengthwise; remove and reserve the green coral, remove and discard the inedible parts. Heat the oil and a small piece of butter, add pieces of lobster and heat until they are a red colour. Add the chopped shallots and a minute later a small crushed clove of garlic; flame with the brandy and add the white wine and reduce. Add the peeled, seeded and coarsely chopped tomatoes and the tomato *purée*, season with salt and a pinch of cayenne and cook for 18 minutes. As soon as the lobster is cooked, remove and keep hot in a deep dish, reduce the sauce a little with a small piece of meat glaze, the chopped tarragon and the chopped parsley and bind with the green coral, mixed with a little butter. Boil up two or three times and, without straining, pour over the lobster pieces and sprinkle chopped parsley on top. Serve with Creole rice. It is more pleasant to eat if the flesh is removed from the shells before pouring sauce on top.

Homard à la Bordelaise

For 6 persons: 4 lb lobster; 6 oz butter; ¼ lb chopped shallots; 1 crushed clove of garlic; 2 fl oz brandy; ½ pint white wine; ¾ pint sauce Tomate; ½ oz chopped tarragon and chervil; ¾ pint fish stock; ¾ pint sauce Espagnole. Cooking time: 30 minutes.

Cut up the lobsters and throw them into a pan containing butter until the shell starts to colour. Add the shallot and garlic. Boil up once or twice. *Flambé* with brandy. Add the white wine, fish stock, *sauce Espagnole* and *sauce Tomate*. Cook for 20 minutes without a lid. Remove the lobster and keep hot. Reduce the liquor to half and add butter. Add the herbs. Serve the pieces on a dish and pour the sauce over them.

▣ à la Cardinal

For 6 persons: 3 lobsters, each weighing about 1¼ lb; ¾ pint sauce Cardinal; 1 truffle; ½ lb mushrooms; 1 oz grated cheese. Cooking time: 30 minutes.

Boil the lobsters, remove claws and cut body through lengthwise without damaging shell. Remove the intestine which runs all down the body and the pouch in the head and cut flesh into diagonal, not too thin slices. Remove flesh from the claws, dice, mix with the poached, diced mushrooms and bind with *sauce Cardinal*. Fill the shells with this mixture and arrange the lobster slices on top, alternately with one small truffle slice. Coat entirely with thick *sauce Cardinal* seasoned with cayenne. Sprinkle with grated cheese and glaze in a very hot oven, 450° F or Gas Mark 8. Arrange on a napkin on a long dish with curly parsley.

▣ à la Créole ou à l'Indienne * *Curried*

For 6 persons: Lobsters to the total weight of 4 lb; ¾ pint Curry sauce; ½ lb rice; 2 oz butter. Cooking time: 30 minutes.

Cook the lobsters in *court bouillon* for 20 minutes. Cut them in two, discard inedible parts and remove the meat. Slice the meat and heat lightly in butter, then simmer in the Curry sauce for 10 minutes. Arrange the meat and sauce in the centre of a border of rice *Créole.*

▣ Fra-Diavolo

For 2 persons: 1 lobster about 1¼ lb; ¾ lb tomatoes; 1 oz butter; ⅛ pint white wine; 1 tablespoon chopped parsley; 1 clove garlic; 2 tablespoons olive oil; a pinch of marjoram; ground black pepper; salt. Cooking time: 25 minutes.

Cook the lobster in fish stock. Cut in half lengthwise and remove the inedible parts. Break off the top side of the claws. Simmer the lobster for a few minutes in hot butter and white wine in a baking dish, the cut side turned down. Peel and seed the tomatoes, cut them into dice, and *sauté* them in hot oil. Add crushed garlic, chopped parsley and a pinch of marjoram, and season highly with salt and ground black pepper. Arrange the lobster on a long dish with the cut side upwards, and cover with the sautéed tomatoes. Garnish with parsley and lemon, and serve rice *Pilaf* separately.

▣ Newburg

For 4 persons: 2 lobsters, each weighing about 1¼ lb; 2 oz butter; 2 fl oz brandy; 4 fl oz Madeira; ½ pint thick cream; 2 egg yolks. Cooking time: 30 minutes.

Boil lobsters for 20 minutes, remove flesh from claws and tails, remove inedible parts and cut flesh into not too thin slices. Heat the butter, toss the flesh in it, *flambé* with brandy, add Madeira, reduce. Simmer for a few minutes in the wine, then add the cream, simmer a little longer and boil down. Season with salt and pepper, remove from heat and thicken the sauce with the egg yolks mixed with 2 spoonfuls of cream kept back for this purpose. Do not boil again. Arrange in a deep dish and serve with rice *Créole*.

Homard à la Palestine

For 6 persons: 4 lb lobster; ¾ pint white wine; 2 pints fish stock; 2 fl oz brandy; ½ pint oil; ½ lb mirepoix; ¾ pint Fish Velouté; 6 oz butter; ½ tablespoon curry powder; ¾ lb rice Pilaf.

Cut up the lobsters and *sauté* in hot oil with the *mirepoix* until the shell colours. *Flambé* with brandy. Moisten with fish stock and white wine and cover. Cook for 20 minutes. Remove the lobster. Extract the flesh and keep hot in a covered dish with a little butter. To make the sauce, crush the shells and trimmings, *sauté* them in oil and drain well. Moisten with the liquor and cook for 20 minutes. Strain through muslin, reduce to half, add the creamy parts of the lobster and pass through a sieve together with the Fish *Velouté*. Cook for a few moments, remove from heat and add butter. Check seasoning, adding a little curry powder. Cook rice *Pilaf*, mould it in a *savarin* mould, unmould on a dish and place the lobster in the middle. Coat with sauce and serve the remainder separately.

⊡ ou Langouste Thermidor * *or Rock Lobster Thermidor*

For 4 persons: 2 lobsters about 1¼ lb each; 1 *small glass white wine; ½ pint sauce Béchamel; ½ pint double cream;* 1 *oz butter; mustard powder; 2 chopped shallots;* 3 *oz grated gruyère*. Total cooking time: 30 minutes.

Cook lobster in fish stock. Cut them in half and break off the claws. Remove all the meat from the claws and the bodies, and reserve the bodies, without spoiling the shells. Cut the meat into small dice. Brown the shallots lightly in butter, and add the white wine. Reduce this to a quarter, then add the double cream and the *sauce Béchamel*. Season with salt and cayenne pepper, add chopped chervil, and reduce well, until it coats the spoon with which it has been stirred. Add the meat to the sauce and continue cooking for a minute or two. Remove from the heat, finish off with a little mustard powder and about 3 oz grated cheese. Fill the shells with this mixture, sprinkle with grated cheese and glaze at great heat in the oven or under the grill. (*See illustration p.* 387).

Langouste * *Rock Lobster* (*or Crawfish*)

This shellfish is also known as spiny lobster because of the spines on its back. All methods of preparing lobster can also be used for rock lobster. It should however be noted that rock lobster tastes best cold, while lobster tastes best hot.

⊡ Grillée à la Diable * *Grilled and Devilled*

Place a crawfish in boiling water for a few minutes to kill it and split lengthwise. Season, brush with oil, place on a hot grill and cook slowly brushing repeatedly with oil or clarified butter. If 5 minutes is allowed for killing it, another 20-25 minutes is needed to grill a rock lobster of 2¼ pounds. Arrange on a napkin, brush lightly with melted butter, garnish with curly parsley and serve with *sauce Diable*.

Langouste à la Normande

For 6 persons: 3 rock lobsters, each weighing about 1¼ lb; 2 pints mussels; ½ lb mushrooms; 1 *truffle; ¾ pint sauce Normande;* 12 *gudgeons (optional).* Cooking time of crawfish: 25 minutes.

Boil crawfish in *court-bouillon* and split lengthwise without damaging shell. Remove the flesh from the thick legs. Cut body flesh into diagonal slices and leg flesh into small pieces. Mix these pieces with the cooked, bearded mussels and the poached, quartered mushrooms and bind with *sauce Normande* made with the mussel and mushroom stock and thickened with yolk of egg. Fill shells with this mixture, cover with the body flesh, coat with thick *sauce Normande* and glaze under strong top heat. Finally place truffle slices dipped in meat glaze on top. Garnish with breadcrumbed, deep fried gudgeons, although these may be omitted.

Pilaf de Langouste ou de Homard * *Pilaf of Lobster or Rock Lobster*

For 6 persons: 1½ *lb cooked rock lobster meat;* ½ *lb rice;* 2 *onions;* 2 *oz butter; white stock;* 1 *pint sauce Cardinal.* Cooking time for the rice: 17-18 minutes.

Prepare rice *Pilaf* (*see p.* 679). Press the rice round the sides of a well-buttered *bombe* or *savarin* mould or a deep-round bowl. Fill the space in the centre of the mould with the meat of the rock lobster cut into small pieces and simmered in butter for a few minutes. Cover with rice, pack down and turn out on a round dish. Pour a little sauce around and decorate with the legs . Serve the rest of the sauce separately.

Brochettes de Langoustines * *Scampi or Dublin Bay Prawns*

For 2 persons: ½ *lb shelled and cleaned scampi, the thin black thread removed;* 2 *half lemons; Maître d'Hôtel butter; plain butter; oil.* Cooking time: 10-12 minutes.

Season the scampi or Dublin Bay prawns with salt and pepper, and fix them on skewers. First dip in flour, then in oil, and grill them on both sides. Serve with *Maître d'Hôtel* and plain butter and lemon halves. (*See illustration p.* 388).

FOREIGN SPECIALITIES

Scampi Thermidor

For 10 *persons:* 3½ *lb large, peeled scampi or Dublin Bay Prawns;* 2 *oz butter;* 3 *oz oil;* 2 *small glasses of brandy;* 20 *very thin truffle slices.*

Sauce: ½ *pint Béchamel;* 2 *oz grated cheese (Parmesan);* ¼ *pint milk;* ½ *pint cream;* 6 *oz butter;* 1½ *oz English mustard.*

Make the sauce by combining the *Béchamel,* grated cheese, milk and cream. Stir well and cook for 3 minutes until it is well bound and thick. Remove from heat and carefully stir in the butter and mustard. Pass through a sieve. Put the butter and oil in a very hot frying pan and throw in the scampi. Cook for 4 minutes, add the brandy and *flambé*. Leave on the heat for a minute. Pour the sauce over the scampi, add the truffle slices and sprinkle with grated Parmesan. Place briefly in a very hot oven, 450° F or Gas Mark 8, or under the grill. (*See illustration p.* 388). (*Italy*)

Spiedini di Scampi "Savoia Beller" * *Scampi on Skewers*

For 10 persons: 40 *scampi or Dublin Bay prawns;* 40 *medium-sized mushrooms;* 40 *slices of raw ham;* 40 *slices of Mozzarella or pieces of soft cheese* 1-*inch square and* ½-*inch thick;* ¼ *lb melted butter; crushed bay leaf and thyme; salt; pepper.* Cooking time: 12 minutes.

Shell, clean and wipe the scampi and season with salt, pepper, crushed thyme and bay leaf. Use silver or wooden skewers and impale a scampi, a piece of cheese, a slice of raw ham folded in four, and a mushroom in turn. Brush all the skewered items with melted butter and place them in a *gratin* dish. Place in the oven and cook for 10 minutes, basting from time to time with the liquor. Carefully remove the skewers and place in a ring or a round dish. Garnish the centre with a mound of rice *pilaf*. Sprinkle the scampi with lemon juice. (*Italy*)

CRUSTACÉS FROIDS * *COLD SHELLFISH*

Cocktails of shellfish * *See cold Hors d'Oeuvre*

Crabes à l'Anglaise * *Dressed Crab*

For 6 persons: 6 *medium-sized cooked crabs;* ½ *pint Mayonnaise;* ½ *oz English mustard;* 1 *hardboiled egg; chopped parsley.*

Combine the flesh and creamy parts of the crabs with the mustard-flavoured *Mayonnaise*. Fill the shells with the mixture and garnish with chopped, hardboiled eggs and parsley.

Mousse d'Ecrevisse en Pyramide * *Pyramid of Crayfish Mousse*

For 6 persons: 30 *crayfish; court bouillon;* 1 *oz butter;* ¼ *pint Fish Velouté;* ½ *pint melted aspic;* ½ *pint cream;* 3 *hardboiled eggs;* ¾ *pint Mayonnaise;* 1 *lettuce.* Cooking time of crayfish: 10 minutes.

Cook the cleaned crayfish in *court-bouillon* with white wine. Reserve 18 crayfish for the *mousse*. Pound these with the butter and the Fish *Velouté*. Add the melted aspic jelly. Pass through a fine sieve and then through muslin. Combine this mixture with the half-whipped, seasoned cream. Place in a mould lined with wax paper and chill for at least 2 hours. Fill the eggs with a stuffing of the yolks and *Mayonnaise* and decorate them. Serve the unmoulded *mousse* in the centre of a dish, arrange the rest of the crayfish, garnish with the stuffed eggs and decorate with a bunch of parsley. Serve *Mayonnaise* separately. The dish may be lined with aspic or the eggs may be placed on a bed of lettuce.

Homard à la Parisienne * *Lobster*

For 6 persons: 2 lobsters, each weighing about 1½ lb; 1 lb fine vegetable macédoine; 1¼ pints Mayonnaise; 2 good pinches gelatine; 6 cooked artichoke bottoms; 3 hardboiled eggs; 1 heart of lettuce; 1 pint white wine aspic. Cooking time: 25 minutes.

Tie the lobsters to a small board with the tail stretched out. Cook in *court-bouillon* and leave to cool in it. Extract the tail whole by making 2 incisions on either side of the shell. Cut into very regular slices, decorate with a truffle slice cut out with a pastry cutter or with a personal decoration and glaze with aspic. Extract the creamy parts and reserve them. Carefully break the claws so that the flesh can be extracted, but without detaching them from the body. Arrange the lobsters on a long oval or rectangular dish lined with aspic, the tails pointing outwards, so that the sides of the dish remain free. If possible arrange the claws pointing upwards. Glaze the shells with aspic, using a brush. Cut the lettuce into a coarse *julienne* and fill the shells with it. Arrange the lobster medallions in sequence along the lettuce, the largest nearest the head of the lobster. Bind the vegetable *macédoine* with ½ pint *Mayonnaise* and then with the melted gelatine. Fill the artichoke bottoms with *macédoine*. Decorate to taste and glaze with aspic. Halve the hardboiled eggs lengthwise, remove the yolks, chop them and combine with the remainder of the *macédoine* and the creamy parts of the lobsters. Fill the egg whites with this mixture. Decorate the eggs and brush them with aspic. Garnish the sides of the dish, alternating the artichoke bottoms, eggs and aspic cubes. Serve the remainder of the *Mayonnaise* separately and combine with a little whipped cream, if preferred.

Homard à la Russe

Same method as for *Homard à la Parisienne*, but coat the lobster slices with *Mayonnaise*.

Aspic de Homard ou de Langouste * *Lobster or Rock Lobster in Aspic*

For 6 persons: 2 cooked lobsters, each weighing about 1½ lb; 6 hardboiled eggs; 2 truffles, about 2 oz each; 3½ pints fish aspic.

Line a mould with aspic, then decorate the bottom with truffle slices alternating with slices of white of hardboiled egg. On top place fine slices of lobster tail decorated with truffle placed vertically against the side. Cover with cold but liquid aspic and put in a cold place to set. On this layer place a second row of lobster slices, cover with aspic once more and again leave to set. Continue in this way until the mould is full. Chill until the last moment. To unmould, dip the mould quickly in hot water and turn out on a round dish lined with a napkin. Shake the mould to release the aspic. Serve as it is.

Médaillons de Homard Windsor

For 8 persons: 1 lobster, weighing about 2 lb; ¼ lb celeriac; ¼ lb seeded red capsicum; ¼ lb white of hardboiled egg; ½ pint Mayonnaise; 8 Short Crust pastry tartlets baked blind; ½ pint aspic; curry powder; oil; vinegar. Cooking time of lobster: 24 minutes.

Cut the cooked lobster into 8 slices. Decorate and glaze with aspic. Cut the celeriac into small dice, blanch for a minute and rinse. After draining combine with the flesh of the lobster claws, the trimmings of the tail, the egg white and the capsicums, all finely diced. Marinate for 1 hour with oil and vinegar. Drain, bind with *Mayonnaise* and season with curry powder. Fill the tartlets with this mixture, level with the top edge. Place a lobster medallion on top. Surround the medallion with chopped aspic.

Soufflé de Homard Froid * *Soufflé of Cold Lobster*

For 6 persons: 2 lobsters, each weighing about 1¼ lb; ¼ pint Fish Velouté; 2 pints aspic; ½ pint half-whipped cream; 1 truffle; 3 fl oz brandy; salt; cayenne or paprika. Cooking time: 25 minutes.

Cook the lobsters in *court-bouillon* and let them cool in the liquor. Remove the shell, keeping the flesh intact so that 6 slices can be cut from it. Make a *purée* with the remainder of the flesh, including the claws, the creamy parts and a little Fish *Velouté*. Add the remainder of the *Velouté* and pass through a sieve. Season well with salt, brandy and cayenne. Add 1½ pints of the cold but still liquid aspic and the cream and check the seasoning. Line a *soufflé* dish with a collar of white paper sticking up one inch above the edge. Fill it with the mixture and flatten the top. Put in a cold place to set. Keep back ½ pint of aspic. Cut the truffle into 6 slices. Spread a very thin layer of aspic over the top of the *soufflé*. Place the lobster medallions on top, alternating them with the truffle slices. When set cover with another very thin layer of aspic. Put in a cold place and before serving carefully remove the white paper.

LANGOUSTE * *ROCK LOBSTER (OR CRAWFISH)*

Rock lobster is served in a variety of ways, each dish decorated with a colourful garnish.

▣ en Bellevue

For 6 persons: 1 rock lobster, weighing about 3 lb; 1½ pints aspic; 1 small truffle; 4 hardboiled eggs; 6 small timbales of Russian salad bound with aspic; 2 small tomatoes. Cooking time of rock lobster: 25 minutes.

Drop the rock lobster into boiling, salted water and cook for 25 minutes. Remove the flesh of the tail without damaging the shell. Cut the flesh in medallions. Decorate each with a small truffle motif and coat with aspic. Place the medallions on a dish and garnish with small unmoulded *timbales* of Russian salad in aspic, and the halved, stuffed hardboiled eggs placed on tomato slices. The empty shell is used as decoration. (*See illustration p.* 386).

▣ Bouquetière

For 6 persons: 1 rock lobster, weighing about 3 lb; 1½ lb vegetable macédoine; 1 pint Mayonnaise; ½ lb shrimps; 1 truffle; 1½ pints Fish aspic. Cooking time of rock lobster: 25 minutes.

Cook the rock lobster in *court-bouillon* and leave in the liquor until cold. Mix the *Mayonnaise* with the vegetable *macédoine* and ¾ pint aspic. Serve the mixture in a mound in the middle of a large dish. Remove the tail of the rock lobster and extract the flesh without damaging the shell; place the latter at the bottom of the domed *macédoine*. Cut the flesh into medallions, arrange them on top of the *macédoine* and decorate with the shrimps and the truffle slices. Decorate the top with the legs. Coat the whole with aspic. (*See illustration p.* 385).

Langouste Estoril

For 10-12 *persons:* 1 *rock lobster, weighing about* 4-5 *lb;* 10 *Portuguese oysters;* ¼ *lb tomatoes, concassé;* ¼ *lb sliced mushrooms;* ¼ *lb julienne of blanched celeriac;* 12-14 *pieces of leek, cut diagonally and cooked à la Grecque;* 5 *quartered hardboiled eggs, filled with egg yolk cream;* 10-12 *pieces of scooped out cucumber, filled with vegetable salad;* ½ *lb tomatoes concassé, marinated with tarragon vinaigrette; truffles; radishes;* 3 *pints aspic; mustard Vinaigrette dressing;* 1½ *pints sauce Vincent or Chantilly.* Cooking time: 35 minutes.

Cook the rock lobster in salted water and let it cool in the water. Remove the flesh from the tail without damaging the shell and drain the latter well. Cut the tail into medallion shapes, decorate with truffle slices and coat with aspic. Place the shell on a bread base on a long dish and overlap the medallions all down the back. Open the oysters. Fill the shells with a salad of crushed tomatoes, sliced mushrooms and celeriac *julienne* marinated in mustard *Vinaigrette.* Put an oyster on top and glaze with aspic. Decorate the egg quarters with a thin radish slice and glaze with aspic. Drain the leeks well and on each piece place a little crushed tomato, marinated in tarragon *vinaigrette.* Garnish the dish with the oysters, pieces of cucumber, eggs and leeks and serve *sauce Vincent* or *Chantilly* separately.

⊡ à la Parisienne

Same method as for *Homard à la Parisienne.*

⊡ à la Russe

Same method as for *Homard à la Russe.*

Langoustines en Bellevue

For 8 *persons:* 4 *lb Dublin Bay prawns;* ¾ *pint Mayonnaise.* Cooking time: 10-12 minutes.

Boil the prawns and cool in the stock. Drain well and hang up as they are by their tails round the rim of a high stemmed glass. Fill the glass itself with Russian salad or with curly parsley and serve the *Mayonnaise* separately.

Sea Food

HUÎTRES * *OYSTERS*

The best oysters are the English natives, the Belons and Cancales, the white and green Marennes, the Ostend oysters and the Dutch Imperials. The large Danish Limfjords, the Holsteins and the rather ugly green Portuguese are also very popular. It is usual to allow 6 oysters per person. They should be opened at the last minute, placed on crushed ice and served with lemon segments and very thin brown bread and butter.

◘ à la Florentine

For 4 persons: 24 oysters; ½ lb spinach; ¼ pint Béchamel; ¼ pint sauce Mornay; 1 oz grated cheese; 2 oz butter.

Stiffen the oysters and clean round the lower shells. Cook the spinach quickly, drain, and squeeze out moisture. Strain, dry with 1 oz butter, thicken with the *Béchamel* and season with salt, pepper and nutmeg. Place a small teaspoon of spinach in the bottom of each shell, place an oyster on top, cover with *sauce Mornay*. Sprinkle with grated cheese and melted butter, put the shells on a baking dish and quickly brown oysters in a very hot oven.

◘ Frites * *Shallow Fried*

For 4 persons: 24 oysters; ½ lb white breadcrumbs for coating; 1 egg; 1 tablespoon oil; butter for frying. Cooking time: 3-4 minutes.

Just stiffen oysters in their own juices but do not boil. When cold drain well, dry on a cloth, dip in flour, coat with egg and breadcrumbs, and fry golden brown in butter at the last moment. Season lightly with a mixture of salt and a pinch of cayenne pepper. Arrange with lemon slices and serve at once.

◘ à la Mornay

For 4 persons: 24 oysters; ½ pint Béchamel; 1 egg yolk; 1 oz grated gruyère.

Stiffen the oysters, keep the water and add to the *Béchamel* with the egg yolk and most of the cheese. Season well. Place a teaspoon of sauce in the bottom of a mussel dish or scallop shell and add 6 oysters. Cover well with sauce, sprinkle cheese on top and brown quickly in a hot oven.

Huîtres Villeroi

For 4 persons: 24 *oysters;* ½ *pint sauce Villeroi;* 2 *egg yolks;* 1 *whole egg;* 1 *tablespoon oil;* 8 *oz breadcrumbs for coating.*

Stiffen the oysters, mix the sauce with the oyster liquor and bind with the egg yolks. Coat the dried oysters with this sauce; roll in breadcrumbs. Quickly fry golden brown in butter, drain and serve hot.

MOULES * *MUSSELS*

Mussels are very tasty, but they must be absolutely fresh and the shells firmly closed. Before use wash thoroughly in frequent changes of water, scrub with a hard brush and remove any seaweed adhering to them. Allow 1 pint of mussels per person. As a precaution no mussels should be eaten between the beginning of May and September. Mussels should not be overcooked. The whole cooking process takes only 5-6 minutes.

▣ à la Fécampoise

For 6 persons: 6 *pints mussels;* 12 *oz celeriac.* Cooking time: 5-6 minutes.

Put the mussels, two finely chopped onions and shallots, 1 sprig parsley stalk, ½ bay leaf, pinch freshly ground pepper and ½ pint white wine in a saucepan and cover tightly. Cook quickly over fierce heat shaking the pan during the cooking which will take about 5-6 minutes. This will cook and open the shells. Remove the mussels, beard them and allow to cool. Pour off one quarter of the stock and reduce. Cut the celeriac in fine *julienne*, put in cold water, bring to the boil once, then drain well. Make into a salad with vinegar, oil, salt and pepper, mix with chopped herbs and place in an *hors d'œuvre* dish. Place the mussels on top and coat with a Mayonnaise which has been seasoned with mustard and slightly thinned with the cold, reduced mussel stock. Do not add salt as the mussel stock is salty enough. Sprinkle chopped herbs on top and serve very cold.

▣ à la Francillon

For 6 persons: 6 *pints large mussels;* ½ *pint white wine;* ½ *pint Mayonnaise;* ½ *lb peeled potatoes, boiled for a salad.* Cooking time: 5-6 minutes.

Wash and brush the mussels thoroughly and cook in the white wine. Remove from shells, beard, allow to cool and reduce part of the stock to a syrup. Make a thick Mayonnaise almost without salt, thin with the reduced stock, season with a little mustard and use to bind the mussels. Arrange in a *hors d'œuvre* dish and surround with slices of cooked potatoes.

▣ à la Marinière

For 6 *persons:* 6 *pints mussels;* ½ *pint white wine;* 3 *shallots; parsley;* 2 *oz butter;* ½ *pint cream.* Cooking time: 5-6 minutes.

Place the well washed and brushed mussels in a casserole with the chopped shallots, 1 sprig parsley, half a bay leaf, 1 sprig thyme and the white wine. Add a pinch of pepper but no salt and cook over high heat. As soon as the shells have opened and the liquid risen to the top, remove from heat since further cooking makes the mussels shrink and become hard. Strain the stock, add butter, cream, chopped parsley and pour over the mussels after removing from the shells. Sprinkle the chopped parsley on top.

Moules en Pilaf à l'Orientale * *Mussels with Curried Rice*

For 6 persons: 6 pints of mussels; 8 oz rice; 1 onion; 2 oz butter; ¾ pint sauce Velouté; curry powder or saffron Cooking time: 5-6 minutes.

Cook rice as Pilaf (*p.* 679) and cook mussels as above. Make *Velouté* with the decanted mussel stock and season well with curry powder or saffron. Remove mussels from shells, beard, bind with sauce and serve in the middle of the rice, which has been pressed into a ring mould and turned out on a round dish.

NOTE: When mussel stock is used to make sauce it must be left to stand for a while first so that the dark particles of shell which are still in it can settle. It is then carefully decanted and strained through a cloth.

⊡ Sauce Poulette

For 6 persons: 6 pints mussels; 1 chopped shallot; parsley; pepper; ½ pint white wine; ½ pint Fish Velouté; 2 egg yolks; 2 fl oz cream. Cooking time: 5-6 minutes.

Wash and put the mussels in a stewpan, add the wine and seasonings and bring to the boil to open the shells. Pour off the liquor into a bowl, allow to stand, decant, add to the *Velouté* and reduce to coating consistency; add the egg yolks, and the cream. Remove the mussels from the shells, beard them and add to the sauce; allow to heat through.

⊡ Villeroi

For 6 persons: 6 pints mussels; 1 pint sauce Villeroi.

Cook the mussels as above, remove from the shells, beard them, dry them and dip into the sauce. Allow to set; egg and breadcrumb twice and deep fry. Instead of serving these mussels as a separate dish, they are often used as a garnish for other fish dishes.

Oursins * *Sea Urchins*

Sea urchins may be eaten either raw or soft boiled (3 minutes in boiling water as for an egg). Use a small spoon or dip fingers of soft bread and butter into the opened sea urchin. To open a sea urchin, a circular incision just over 1-inch in diameter is made with sharp scissors round the creature's mouth. Both green and purple sea urchins are only really fresh when their spines are hard and standing perpendicular to the shell.

Snails and Frogs Legs

ESCARGOTS * *SNAILS*

There are two varieties of snail: the small grey and the Burgundy snails. Prior to cooking, snails must be starved for 3 weeks or else be covered for a day with coarse cooking salt. Wash with plenty of water containing vinegar. Blanch for 10 minutes and then cool down in cold water. Take the snails out of their shells and cut off the black ends. Boil for 3 to 4 hours in a *court-bouillon* (1 carrot, 1 onion, thyme, bay leaf, parsley, a large pinch of salt and 1¾ pints water) and drain the snails which are then ready to be served. Clean and dry the shells thoroughly.

▣ à la Bourguignonne

For 8 persons: 8 dozen prepared snails; 1 lb butter; 3 oz garlic; 1 oz chopped parsley; 3 small chopped shallots; 3 pinches pepper; ½ oz salt. Cooking time in oven: 5-6 minutes.

Mix the slightly creamed butter very thoroughly with the very finely grated garlic, the finely chopped shallots, the parsley, salt and pepper. Put the prepared snails in the cleaned shells, close the opening with the prepared butter and, if not required at once, put in a refrigerator for butter to harden. When needed put the snails on snail plates, or failing these, on a baking sheet covered with salt, opening upwards. Bake in a hot oven, 400° F or Gas Mark 6, till the butter in the shells starts to melt and serve at once.

NOTE: Reduce considerably the stock in which the snails are boiled and keep the prepared snails in it till needed. If half a small spoon of jellied stock is put in the snail shell before inserting the snail it enhances the flavour. Snails are also sold prepared and tinned in stock with the shells separate.

▣ à la Chablisienne

For 6 persons: 6 dozen snails; 1½ oz finely chopped shallots; ½ pint white wine; 2 oz meat glaze; ¾ lb Snail butter.

Reduce the white wine with the shallot and add the melted meat glaze. Fill the bottom of the shells with this liquid, add the snails and complete with Snail butter. Cook for 5-6 minutes in a hot oven.

▣ à la Dijonnaise

For 6 persons: 6 dozen snails; ½ lb butter; 6 oz ox marrow passed through a sieve; ⅓ oz salt; ground pepper and spices; 2 oz chopped shallot; 3 crushed cloves of garlic; ⅓ oz chopped truffle. Cooking time: 5-6 minutes.

Use the same cooking method as for *Escargots à la Chablisienne.* Instead of the usual Snail butter use *beurre manié* combined with the ingredients of the recipe. Cook in a hot oven.

GRENOUILLES * *FROGS' LEGS*

Frogs' legs are sold impaled on wooden skewers and latterly also frozen. When bought on skewers, care must be taken to see that they are fresh since they go bad very quickly. Allow 6-12 frogs' legs per person. Before using the feet must be cut off with scissors and the legs thoroughly washed.

▣ Cuisses à la Périgourdine * *In Batter*

For 6 persons: 3 dozen fairly large hind legs of frogs; 1 fresh truffle, weighing 1½ oz; 1 oz butter; 3 fl oz Madeira; ½ pint Coating batter; ½ pint sauce Périgueux. Cooking time: 4-5 minutes.

Poach the truffle in the Madeira containing the butter and a pinch of salt. Leave to cool. Marinate the frog legs in the cooking liquor seasoned with pepper and a little salt. Chop the truffle very finely and mix it into both the Coating batter and the marinade. Dry the legs on a cloth at the last minute, dip in the batter and fry in very hot fat. Serve in a pile with fried parsley and the sauce separately.

▣ Frites * *Fried*

For 6 persons: 3 dozen frogs' legs; juice of 1 lemon; 3 fl oz oil; salt; pepper; 1 crushed clove garlic; 1 bunch chopped parsley; ½ pint Coating batter. Cooking time: 5 minutes.

Marinate the frogs' legs with salt, pepper, chopped parsley, oil and lemon juice. Dry them with a cloth at the last minute, coat them with batter and fry in very hot fat. Serve in a pile with fried parsley.

▣ à la Poulette

For 8 persons: 4 dozen frogs' legs; 1 pint sauce Poulette; parsley. Cooking time: 6-8 minutes.

Simmer frogs' legs slowly in butter without letting them colour and then heat for a few minutes in the sauce. Serve sprinkled with chopped parsley.

▣ Sautées Fines Herbes

Fry the frogs' legs in hot butter, toss with chopped parsley and sprinkle with lemon juice.

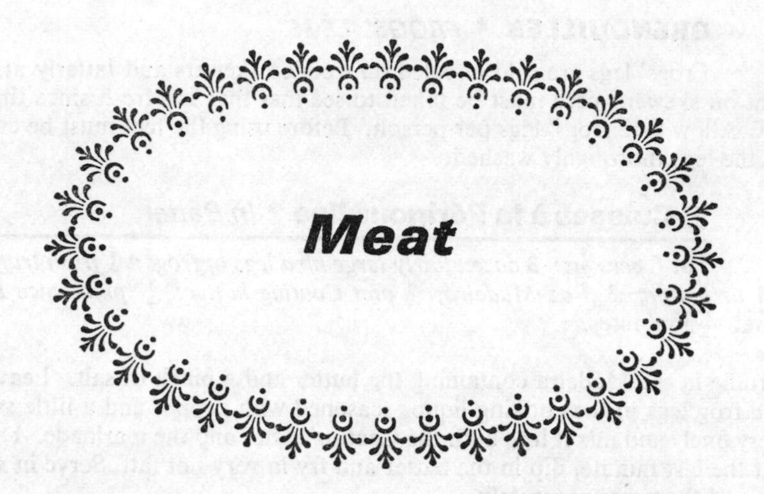

In meat cookery choosing the correct cut for each particular recipe is of vital importance. There are many different cuts of meat and the methods of cutting up the carcases of animals vary between countries and even within the counties of Britain itself. However, there is a similarity between all methods if the following points are observed.

Meat consists of bundles of muscle fibres joined together by connective tissue interspersed with globules of fat. The prime cuts of meat come from the least muscular parts of the animal so the most tender portions of meat are found on either side of the backbone—the farther the cut from the backbone, the coarser the fibres. Muscles which are more actively employed, such as leg muscles, have more and stronger connective tissue and are therefore the tougher cuts of meat which require long, slow cooking to soften the fibres.

To choose meat:

Quality in meat is difficult to determine. It depends upon the careful choosing and handling of the meat which is a skilled job. It also involves the proper breeding and feeding of the animals so that there is the correct amount of fat in proportion to the lean. Age also affects quality, the older the tastier but unfortunately the less tender.

Cuts vary in tenderness according to the age, condition of the animal and the part from which cuts are taken. When possible choose cuts from small-bodied animals as they have more tender flesh and finer fibres than large animals. Price is a poor indication of the nutritional value and flavour of meat; the lower-priced cuts are also rich in food value and flavour when properly cooked. Fresh meat has no unpleasant odour. The flesh should be firm not flabby but moist and elastic to the touch. The lean of red meat is a good colour and lightly marbled with fat; very lean meat is not tender. However good the quality of meat, sufficient time must be allowed for the meat to hang, immediately after slaughter. The time for this varies with the kind of meat. A good butcher will supply meat which has been correctly hung. Try to find a good butcher who sells good quality meat; he will advise you to select a cut which is best suited to your particular purpose.

Meat is one of our chief sources of body-building protein. It is high in nutritional value and also supplies us with the fat, minerals and vitamins essential to good health. The offal of animals such as liver, kidneys, and other internal organs of animals are even richer in iron and vitamins than the meat itself. Meat should be eaten as soon as possible after purchase, but it may be removed from its wrapping paper and stored—covered and preferably on a rack—in the refrigerator. When meat arrives from the butcher wipe with a damp cloth. Offal should be eaten the day it is bought. Chilled meat is never allowed to freeze but it is kept at a sufficiently low temperature to prevent spoilage; it does not exude its juices or lose flavour when thawed. The best known chilled meats are beef from the Argentine and lamb and mutton from New Zealand. Frozen meat is stored at a temperature slightly below freezing point and has to be defrosted *very gradually*. Thaw meat at room temperature and never try to hurry the process by thawing near a hot stove or placing it in hot water. Frozen meat should be cooked as soon as it has thawed out.

To prepare meat for cooking:

Trim the meat, bone if necessary, and remove any superfluous fat or sinews. Then weigh if the cuts are to be used for boiling, braising, roasting or steaming. The meat should be wiped with a clean damp cloth and skewered or tied into shape if the cut requires this. Meat does not normally require to be washed but salt meat and offal should always be washed.

The purpose of cooking meat is to soften connective tissue so as to render the meat tender, destroy bacteria, develop flavour and make it appetising in appearance.

MEAT ENTRÉES

Entrées are all dishes served with a sauce, irrespective of whether vegetables are included or not. Meat dishes which are braised, sautéed, steamed, deep fried, grilled or cooked *à la poêle* all come into this category. Larger pieces or joints of meat garnished with vegetables are known as *relevés*, but often served as *entrées*.

In addition, stews, blanquettes, *tournedos*, *escalopes*, sweetbreads and small garnished meat dishes are regarded as *entrées*.

BRAISING

In this method of cooking the meat is browned in fat with sliced carrot, turnip and onion. When it is browned, the fat is poured off and water or stock is added until the meat is covered. A lid is put on and the meat is cooked in the oven for 1½-4 hours, depending on the size, cut, type and quality of the meat. The garnish is added later so that the vegetables are cooked at the same time as the meat.

Lean cuts of meat such as silverside or topside should be larded. The larding bacon is cut into short thick strips, seasoned and inserted into the meat in the direction of the fibre by means of a larding tube or needle.

The most important point about braising is that the meat should be cooked slowly until it is so tender that it may be eaten without the aid of a knife. All fat should be removed from the braising liquor which is then reduced to make a sauce.

SAUTÉING

True sautéing consists of frying pieces of meat quickly in oil in a frying pan or *sauteuse*. Kidneys, *tournedos*, *escalopes*, steaks may be sautéed instead of being grilled. The characteristic of sautéing is that the meat is first browned quickly on both sides so that a crust is formed to keep in the juices; only then is cooking completed. The browning varies in duration according to the size and thickness of the piece. White meat is always floured after seasoning; this forms a thin crust which retains the juices during cooking.

COOKING À LA POÊLE

There is no English word for this method of cooking. It is only suitable for the better cuts of meat, poultry, etc. A braising pan, casserole or *sauteuse* of suitable size is first lined with thickly sliced carrots and onions, the seasoned meat such as a fillet of beef is placed on them and plenty of melted butter poured over it. Cover the dish, place in a moderate oven and cook, basting frequently. Shortly before the meat is done remove the lid in order to brown it. Remove the meat and keep hot in a covered vessel for at least 15 minutes so that the juices can concentrate inwards before carving. Meat cooked in this way has a more delicate crust than if it were roasted.

When the meat is done, the vegetables should be browned but not burnt. Pour off the fat and reduce the cooking liquor with wine to make a sauce.

GRILLING

Grilled meat is usually described as an *entrée,* although it can be served as a main dish. Grilled *Châteaubriands, entrecôtes* or ribs of beef, if served only with water-cress and Herb butter, are also a main dish. Nevertheless we repeat that all garnished grills served with a sauce are really *entrées.*

If a piece of meat is to be grilled properly and well, the grill must be spotlessly clean and very hot before the meat is placed on it, i.e., the source of heat must be warmed up before-hand, whether it is an electric, gas or charcoal grill. The meat is lightly oiled and salted on both sides, placed on the hot grill and grilled for a few minutes, and then given a half turn so as to make the popular square grill marks. As soon as beads of blood appear on the raw side, turn the meat over and grill the other side in the same way. When the blood starts to bead on the cooked side the meat is done. During grilling the meat should be neither pressed nor pierced to prevent loss of blood.

Note: As regards the terms grill, *entrée, relevé,* roast, etc., these differences only have a point at big dinners where there are a number of courses. In the case of a normal meal, only one main dish is served, which consists of meat, poultry or game.

Beef

APPROXIMATE COOKING TIMES

CUTS	TIME	TEMPERATURE
Boiled Beef	20 mins per lb+20 mins	*Boiled, Braised or Stewed Beef:* For cooking on top of the stove, the control should be set at a low simmering point.
Braised Beef	2-3 hours or until tender	
Beef à la Mode	2-3 hours or until tender	
Roast Beef	20 mins per lb+20 mins	
Fillet of Beef	18 mins per lb	
Rumpsteak (Grilled)	6-8 mins each side (medium)	*Braised or Stewed Beef:* For cooking in the oven, the temperature should be about 350° F or Gas Mark 3-4.
Tournedos (Grilled)	6-8 mins each side (medium)	
Ox Tongue	40 mins per lb	
Stewed Beef	2-3 hours or until tender	

Note: Charts on cooking times can only be looked upon as a general guide, as the finished article is influenced by a number of varying factors. The quality of meat used and the degree of cooking required being only two of these factors. These recommended times and temperatures are only approximate. For underdone or very well done meat, the cooking time should be decreased or increased according to preference, by altering the temperature.

LE BŒUF * *BEEF*

Aiguillette de Bœuf Braisée * *Braised Topside*

For 6 persons: 2½ lb topside or silverside of beef; 6 oz fat bacon; 2 oz lard; ½ lb onions; ½ lb carrots; 1 pint white wine; 1 pint Demi-glace; 1 bouquet garni. Cooking time: 2½-3 hours.

Lard the meat with lardons of fat bacon, brown well in the lard in a heavy lidded casserole together with the sliced onions and carrots. Pour off the fat, add the white wine and boil this down to half. Half-cover meat with light *Demi-glace*, add the *bouquet garni*, season, cover and braise slowly in a warm oven, 350° F or Gas Mark 3, turning several times. Remove fat from sauce, strain, and if necessary boil down slightly to obtain the desired consistency. Serve with a suitable garnish such as braised cabbage or *risotto*. (*See illustration p.* 422).

◘ à la Flamande

For 6 persons: 2½ lb topside or silverside of beef; 6 oz fat bacon; ½ lb Continental boiling sausage in one piece; ½ lb lean bacon, cut in one piece; 2 lb white cabbage; 2 lb carrots; 1 lb turnip; 30 small onions; 1½ lb potatoes; 2 fl oz white wine; 1 pint Demi-glace. Cooking time: 2½-3 hours.

Prepare and braise the meat as indicated above. Cut the washed and peeled carrots and turnips into large olive shapes, cook and glaze. Cook the white cabbage with the lean bacon and the sausage (not containing garlic), and make *Sauté* potatoes. When the white cabbage is cooked, remove and drain. Slice the braised topside, arrange on a long dish and garnish alternately with little mounds of cabbage surrounded by a slice of cooked sausage and carrots and turnips in neat clusters. Place the *Sauté* potatoes at both ends of the dish and slices of cooked lean bacon between the vegetables. Coat the meat with the sauce.

BEEFSTEAK * *FILLET STEAK OR BEEFSTEAK*

Flatten the meat slightly with a mallet but do not pound too vigorously—if it is too thin the meat may not remain pink inside. Season both sides of the meat before frying or grilling. It is usual to allow a frying time of 5-10 minutes for each side but this is a matter of personal preference and will also depend on the thickness of the steak. Place the steak in butter in a *sauté* pan and brown quickly, especially if it is thin. As soon as the beads of blood appear on the raw side, turn and fry or grill on the other side. Serve with Herb butter and Matchstick potatoes and a suitable garnish. All the recipes for *entrecôte* steak are applicable here.

◘ à Cheval * *Steak with Fried Eggs*

The term *à Cheval* in French is incorrectly applied as a description of a garnish but it is one which is commonly used. Prepare, season and *sauté* the steak as described in *Beefsteak*. Serve with two fried eggs on each steak.

Beefsteak Haché à l'Allemande * *Hamburger Steak*

For each person: 4-6 *oz minced beef;* 2 *oz chopped onions cooked in butter;* 1 *egg yolk.* Cooking time: about 10 minutes.

Mix the minced meat with the onions and egg yolk and season with salt and pepper. Shape into a fairly thick, round steak, fry in hot butter and keep inside slightly underdone. Serve with the frying butter poured on top.

BŒUF * *VARIOUS BEEF DISHES*

◘ **à la Bourguignonne**

For 6 *persons:* 2½ *lb beef (topside or silverside);* 2 *oz lard;* 1 *oz flour;* 1 *onion;* ¼ *lb lean bacon;* ½ *lb mushrooms;* 1 *tablespoon concentrated tomato purée;* 2 *cloves of garlic;* 1 *pint red wine.* Cooking time: 2½-3 hours.

Cut the beef (second quality cuts of shoulder piece or steak may be used) into fairly large cubes and brown well in the hot lard in a heavy, lidded casserole. Sprinkle with the flour, add the finely chopped cloves of garlic, fry the flour light brown, blend in the red wine and add enough water to cover the meat almost entirely. Season with salt and pepper, add a *bouquet garni* and braise in a warm oven, 350° F or Gas Mark 3. Dice the bacon, fry briefly in a frying pan, add the coarsely chopped onions, brown them and add both to the meat. Shortly before the latter is done add the tomato *purée* and the cleaned mushrooms, remove the *bouquet garni* and braise the meat for another 10-15 minutes. Remove all fat before serving.

◘ **à la Cuiller** * *Spoon Carved Braised Beef*

For 6 *persons:* 2½ *lb beef (round, topside or silverside);* ½ *lb carrots;* ½ *lb onions;* 1 *tablespoon tomato purée;* 1 *pint white wine;* ¼ *lb blanched bacon rinds;* 2 *cloves of garlic.* Cooking time: 5-7 hours.

Braise meat in the usual way, see *Aiguillette de Bœuf Braisée*, but very slowly, until it is too soft to cut with a knife. Skim fat off sauce, strain, and pour over meat; it must be very concentrated.

◘ **en Daube à la Marseillaise**

For 8 *persons:* 3½ *lb shoulder or rump steak;* ½ *lb fat bacon;* ½ *lb pork rinds;* 2 *pints wine;* ¼ *pint brandy;* ½ *lb onions;* ½ *lb carrots;* 4 *cloves of garlic;* 1 *lb tomatoes;* ½ *lb black olives;* 2 *fl oz cooking oil; peppercorns; bouquet garni.* Cooking time: 3-4 hours.

Cut the meat in large cubes. Lard each piece with a thick lardon and marinate overnight in the red or white wine, the brandy, the sliced carrots and onions, the cloves of garlic, bunch of herbs and peppercorns with the oil on top. Blanch the pork rinds well, cut up and line the bottom of a braising pan with them. Place the meat with all ingredients and the liquid on top and add the peeled, deseeded, coarsely chopped tomatoes and the stoned olives. The meat must be entirely covered with wine; add more wine if necessary. Salt very lightly, seal hermetically and cook at moderate heat, 350° F or Gas Mark 3. Remove fat before serving. A single large piece of meat can be used instead of small pieces. The method remains the same.

Bœuf à la Mode

For 6-7 persons: 3 *lb rump or topside;* 1 *calf's foot;* 2 *oz lard;* 5 *oz blanched pork rinds;* 1 *pint beef stock;* 30 *small onions;* 2 *lb new small carrots;* 1 *liqueur glass brandy;* ½ *bottle of red wine;* 6 *oz fat bacon;* 1 *oz cornflour*. Cooking time: 2½-3 hours.

Lard the beef with strips of bacon, rolled in pepper, spices, chopped parsley and garlic. Brown it in hot lard in a Dutch oven and when it is browned all over, drain off the fat. *Flambé* with the brandy, and add the red wine and the beef stock. Add salt and pepper, the calf's foot, cut in half, boned and blanched, and the blanched pork rinds. Cover and simmer in the oven for one hour. Then add the onions and the carrots, browned in lard, and continue to cook the meat slowly until it is soft. Slice the beef with a sharp knife and garnish it with the onions, carrots and the diced calf's foot. Remove the fat from the gravy, thicken it with the cornflour mixed with a little cold water, boil up, strain and pour it over the meat.

◻ Woronoff

For 6 persons: 6 *slices fillet of beef, each weighing about* ¼ *lb;* ¼ *lb Café de Paris butter;* ½ *lb fresh cucumber;* 2 *fl oz sauce Demi-glace;* 2 *fl oz dairy cream;* 2 *fl oz sour cream;* 1 *tablespoon chopped parsley*. Cooking time: 8-10 minutes.

Bœuf Woronoff is cooked in front of the guests in the dining-room; prepare and assemble all the ingredients before cooking starts. Melt the *Café de Paris* butter in a saucepan or frying pan. Add the peeled and thinly sliced cucumber, chopped parsley, *sauce Demi-glace* and both creams. Season with salt, freshly ground pepper and a pinch of sugar. Heat up the sauce almost to boiling point and poach the slightly flattened slices of beef in it, turning them over several times. When they are cooked, they must still be pink in the centre. Lay them on a dish, masked with the sauce. Serve separately roast potatoes, pickled cucumbers and slices of beetroot in vinegar.

CERVELLES DE BŒUF * *OX BRAINS*

4 *oz per person:* Cooking time: 20 minutes.

First soak the brains in cold water for at least one hour, remove the skin and veins, poach in water to which a little vinegar and salt has been added. Plunge the brains into cold water, drain well and dry, or, if necessary, allow to cool in the stock. They are served well-drained, thickly sliced and fried with *beurre noir* and capers, in *sauce Poulette* or sliced, dipped in frying batter, deep fried and served with *sauce Tomate*. Brains are also served in shells coated with *sauce Mornay* or in *sauce Italienne* and cooked *au gratin*.

◻ au Beurre Noir * *in Black Butter Sauce*

For 6 persons: 1½ *lb brains;* ¼ *lb butter;* 1 *oz capers; chopped parsley; vinegar*.

Poach the brains as described above, drain well and dry. Slice the brains if preferred, or serve on a dish sprinkled with capers and pour over them the *beurre noir*, to which a dash of vinegar has been added at the last second. Sprinkle with chopped parsley. (*See illustration p.* 471).

Cervelles de Bœuf à la Bourguignonne

For 6 persons: 1½ lb brains; ½ lb button mushrooms; 24 small onions; ½ pint sauce Vin Rouge; 12 heart shaped croûtons.

Poach the brains as described above, drain well and dry. Blanch the mushrooms briefly. Brown, but do not fully cook, the onions by rapid shallow frying and drain. Slice the brains and simmer gently with the poached mushrooms and glazed onions in the *sauce Vin Rouge*. When the onions and brains are tender (about 10 minutes), serve on a dish and garnish with the *croûtons* fried in butter.

◘ Orly

For 6 persons: 1½ lb brains; 1 pint Frying batter; chopped parsley; lemon juice; 1 pint sauce Tomate.

Poach the brains, cool and cut into thick slices. Season with salt, pepper, chopped parsley and lemon juice and leave to marinate for one hour. Dry the brains, dip them in the batter and fry in very hot fat for 5 to 6 minutes. Arrange on a serving dish with *sauce Tomate* served separately.

◘ Panées à l'Anglaise * *in Breadcrumbs*

For 6 persons: 1½ lb uncooked brains; 2 eggs; breadcrumbs; ¼ lb clarified butter. Cooking time: 8-10 minutes.

Cut the brains in half, season, dip in flour and, after coating with beaten egg and breadcrumbs, cook in the clarified butter. Serve on a dish and pour over the brains the butter used in the cooking.

◘ à la Ravigote

For 6 persons: 1½ lb poached brains; ½ pint sauce Ravigote.

Serve the brains, cut in two, in individual porcelain dishes. Mask with *sauce Ravigote*.

◘ Villeroi

For 6 persons: 1½ lb uncooked brains; ¼ lb butter; ½ pint sauce Villeroi; 2 eggs; breadcrumbs; parsley; ½ pint sauce Périgueux.

Cut the brains into slices and simmer them in butter without browning them. Next dip them in *sauce Villeroi* and leave to cool down. Fry after coating with egg and breadcrumbs. Arrange on a serving dish with fried parsley, and *sauce Périgueux* served separately.

CHÂTEAUBRIAND * *PORTERHOUSE STEAK*

A Châteaubriand, or Porterhouse steak, is a double fillet steak cut from the middle or head of the fillet, then flattened to about 1-inch in thickness. It must be wide rather than thick so that the heat can penetrate to the interior. The weight of a *châteaubriand* will be determined by the thickness of the fillet but one weighing about 12 to 14 oz is best. The *châteaubriand*, the most tender and best flavoured among the steaks, can be served with almost all the garnishes and sauces for *tournedos* and fillet steaks.

Châteaubriand Grand-Vatel

Grill and serve surrounded by *soufflé* potatoes. Serve with a sauce-boat of *sauce Béarnaise.*

⊡ Grillé * *Grilled*

For 2 persons: 1 *Châteaubriand, weighing about* 12-14 *oz.* Cooking time: 12-15 minutes.

For grilling or shallow frying, season both sides of the meat and place in hot fat. Brown both sides quickly. After browning, reduce the heat and continue to cook slowly to your personal taste. A continued fierce heat simply chars the exterior and prevents heat penetration. Thus the steak will be underdone inside with a hard tough shell on the outside. (*See illustration, p.* 425).

CONTRE-FILET * *BONED SIRLOIN*

⊡ Rôti * *Roast*

This is the boned sirloin minus fillet, bones and flank, with all tough sinews and surplus fat trimmed away. It can be wrapped in slices of bacon fat, tied securely and allowed to cook for 10-12 minutes per pound in a very hot oven, 450° F or Gas Mark 8. Then remove the bacon fat and gently colour. Alternatively, the *contre filet* may be roasted plain.

ENTRECÔTE * *SIRLOIN (OR RUMP) STEAK*

The *entrecôte*, often called the rump steak, is cut from the sirloin of top quality, well-hung beef. The upper sinew and superfluous fat is removed and the steak trimmed neatly. A steak weighing about 6-8 oz should be sufficient for 2 persons and the thinly cut "minute steak" weighing about 4 oz should be sufficient for one person. Steak should be lightly flattened with a mallet before cooking but avoid beating the meat since this will cause the meat fibres to break down resulting in the loss of tasty meat juices when cooking.

⊡ à la Béarnaise

For 4 *persons:* 4 *steaks, each weighing about* 6 *oz and cut* 1*-inch thick;* 1½ *lb potatoes;* ½ *pint sauce Béarnaise;* 2 *tablespoons meat glaze; watercress.* Cooking time: 10-15 minutes.

Prepare the potatoes according to your personal preference—either *sauté*, chips, *Château* or Straw potatoes—drain and keep warm. Grill the steaks, arrange on a serving dish, lightly coat each with half a tablespoon of meat glaze and garnish with the potatoes. Place a sprig of watercress on each steak. Serve *sauce Béarnaise* separately.

Entrecôte Bercy

For 4 persons: 4 *steaks, each weighing about* 6 *oz, cut* 1-*inch thick;* 1 *small onion or shallot;* 2 *oz butter;* 1 *teaspoon meat glaze; lemon juice; parsley; watercress.* Cooking time: 10-15 minutes.

Grill the steaks in the usual fashion. Chop the onion finely and *sauté* for 2 minutes in the butter, add the meat glaze, allow this to melt and season with lemon juice, salt and pepper. Finely chop the parsley and add to the sauce. Pour sauce into serving dish, place the grilled steaks on top and garnish each with watercress.

▣ Bordelaise

For 4 persons: 4 *steaks, each weighing about* 6 *oz;* 8-12 *slices of beef marrow;* ½ *pint sauce Bordelaise;* ¼ *pint red wine.* Cooking time: 10-15 minutes.

Fry the *entrecôtes* in the normal fashion, arrange on a serving dish and keep warm. Add the red wine to the pan residue and reduce. Add the *sauce Bordelaise* and boil up briefly. Blanch the marrow, place the slices on the meat, coat with the sauce and sprinkle a little chopped parsley on the marrow.

▣ aux Champignons * *with Mushrooms*

For 6 persons: 6 *steaks, each weighing about* 6 *oz, or* 2 *large steaks, each weighing about* 1½ *lb;* 12 *button mushrooms;* ¼ *pint mushroom stock;* 1 *pint Demi-glace;* 2 *oz butter.* Cooking time: 10-15 minutes.

Blanch the mushrooms, drain and reserve the stock. Fry the steaks and keep warm. Drain off the fat, deglaze the meat juices with the mushroom stock, add the *Demi-glace* and the mushrooms, then the butter. Place the steaks on a serving dish, decorate with the mushrooms and coat with the sauce. (*See illustration p.* 423).

▣ Forestière

For 6 persons: 6 *steaks, each weighing about* 6 *oz, or* 2 *large sirloin steaks, each weighing about* 1½ *lb;* ½ *pint veal gravy;* 2 *fl oz white wine;* ½ *lb mushrooms;* 1 *lb potatoes;* ¼ *lb bacon; parsley.*

Sauté the pieces of sirloin, place on a dish and keep warm. Dice the potatoes and *sauté* in butter. Blanch and fry the bacon and cut into dice. Slice and *sauté* the mushrooms. Garnish the steaks with alternate small mounds of potatoes, diced bacon and mushrooms. Sprinkle these with chopped parsley. Blend the meat juices in the frying pan with the white wine and veal gravy. Serve separately.

▣ Lyonnaise

For 4 persons: 4 *steaks, each weighing about* 6 *oz;* ½ *lb onions;* 2 *fl oz white wine;* 1 *oz meat glaze; parsley.* Cooking time: 10-15 minutes.

Sauté the steaks, arrange on a serving dish and keep warm. Slice the onions thinly and fry golden brown. Season with salt, pepper and a dash of vinegar, add the meat glaze and the white wine. Simmer together for a few minutes, pour over the *entrecôtes* and sprinkle with chopped parsley.

Entrecôte Maître d'Hôtel

For 4 persons: 4 *entrecôte steaks, each weighing about* 6 *oz;* ¼ *lb Maître d'Hôtel butter.*

Grill the *entrecôtes* and serve with the butter and watercress.

▣ Marchand de Vin

For 6 *persons:* 6 *entrecôtes, each weighing about* 6 *oz or* 3 *double entrecôtes;* ½ *pint red wine;* ¼ *lb shallots;* ¼ *lb butter; lemon juice; chopped parsley.* Cooking time: 10-15 minutes.

Sauté the steaks and put them on one side but keep warm. Pour off the fat from the frying pan and deglaze with the red wine, add the chopped shallots and seasoning, mix in the butter and finally the lemon juice and the chopped parsley. Pour this sauce over the steaks.

▣ Mirabeau

For 6 *persons:* 2 *steaks, each weighing about* 1 *lb;* 24 *stuffed olives;* 15 *anchovy fillets;* 1 *oz Anchovy butter; watercress.* Cooking time: 10-15 minutes.

Grill or fry the steaks on one side. Spread Anchovy butter over the uncooked side of the meat. Arrange the anchovy fillets in a neat criss-cross design across the meat. Grill the steaks and place some halved olives in the square patterns, formed by the anchovy fillets. Garnish with the rest of the olives and the watercress. (*See illustration, p.* 424).

▣ Vert-Pré * *with Watercress*

For 6 *persons:* 2 *steaks, each weighing about* 1 *lb;* ¾ *lb potatoes;* 2 *oz Maître d'Hôtel butter.* Cooking time: 10-15 minutes.

Make Straw potatoes and grill the steaks in the usual fashion. Arrange the *entrecôtes* on a serving dish, top with the *Maître d'Hôtel* butter and garnish with the Straw potatoes and watercress.

FILET DE BŒUF * *FILLET OF BEEF*

When roasting a fillet of beef whole, first remove all skin, sinews and superfluous fat. Lard carefully and roast or pot roast. Pot roasting or cooking *à la poêle* is preferable, but a suitable dish is needed which will hold the whole fillet. Large pieces of fillet are prepared in the same way as the whole. Fillet of beef, which is the best part of the animal, must be underdone. It is preferable to use a high temperature roasting method when cooking this tender cut of meat, i.e., roast the meat in a hot oven, 425° F or Gas Mark 6-7. It is better to let it rest a while after roasting so that the blood can settle. For large fillets allow 15 minutes roasting time per pound. Season the meat before cooking.

Filet de Bœuf à la Bouquetière

For 6 persons: 2 *lb fillet of beef;* 1 *lb small carrots;* ½ *lb turnips;* ½ *lb small French beans;* ½ *lb small fresh peas;* 1 *small cauliflower;* 1 *lb Château potatoes.* Cooking time: 30-45 minutes.

Season the joint and lard with strips of fat bacon. Roast or *poêlé* the fillet in a hot oven, 425° F or Gas Mark 6-7. Deglaze the meat juices with a little stock, remove fat and strain. Make *Château* potatoes and cook the cauliflower. Prepare the French beans and green peas *à l'Anglaise.* Peel, shape neatly, boil the carrots and turnips, toss in butter and season. Garnish the vegetables around the fillet in a colourful arrangement which has been transferred to a serving dish. The cauliflower may be lightly coated with *sauce Hollandaise* and the fillet masked with *déglaçage.*

▣ Brillat-Savarin

For 6 persons: 2 *lb fillet of beef;* 3 *tomatoes;* 3 *small lettuces;* 1 *lb potatoes;* ½ *pint sauce Madère; truffles.* Cooking time: 30-45 minutes.

Halve and stuff the tomatoes. Halve and braise the lettuces. Prepare *Château* potatoes. Lard the fillet with truffles, pot roast or roast in a hot oven, 425° F or Gas Mark 6-7. Pour off the fat from the roasting pan. Add the *sauce Madère* to the remaining meat juices, blend, boil up briefly. Arrange the meat on a long serving dish and garnish with the vegetables. Serve the sauce separately.

▣ Cécilia

For 6 persons: 2 *lb fillet of beef;* 6 *baked tartlet cases;* ½ *lb small carrots;* ½ *lb lean ham;* ½ *pint thick sauce Béchamel;* 3 *egg yolks;* 2 *fl oz double cream;* 1 *lb potatoes;* ½ *pint white wine;* ½ *pint Demi-glace, flavoured with tomato purée.*

Lard, season and pot roast the meat. When cooked, remove to a serving tray and keep warm. Deglaze the meat juices with white wine, boil down to half, add the *Demi-glace,* boil up briefly and strain the sauce. To make the ham *timbales,* finely mince the lean ham, fry quickly in a little butter, mix in the cold *sauce Béchamel,* cream and egg yolks, season with paprika, stir well and pass through a fine sieve. Fill the mixture into buttered *baba* moulds and poach in a water-bath. Turn out the moulds when cooked. Scoop the carrots into small balls, boil and glaze with butter. Prepare *Noisette* potatoes. Garnish the sides of the fillet alternately with the ham *timbales* and the tartlet cases filled with the glazed carrot balls. Decorate the ends of the tray with the *Noisette* potatoes. Coat the meat lightly with some of the sauce and serve the rest separately.

▣ Charlemagne

For 6 persons: 2 *lb fillet of beef;* ½ *lb duxelles mixed with* ½ *pint tomato sauce;* ½ *pint sauce Béarnaise.*

Season, lard and pot roast or roast the fillets. When cooked, slice and arrange in a porcelain dish with the *duxelles* and Tomato sauce between each slice, mask with the *sauce Béarnaise* and glaze under a fierce grill.

Filet de Bœuf Claremont

For 6 persons: 2 lb fillet of beef; 2 lb chestnuts; 1 lb carrots; 1 lb small onions; 6 slices raw ham; 2 fl oz Madeira wine; ½ pint Demi-glace.

Cut the carrots into olive shapes. Glaze the chestnuts, carrots and onions and cut ham into rounds or medallions. Pot roast the fillet after the usual preparations and add the ham trimmings. Transfer the meat when cooked to a serving dish and keep warm. Deglaze the meat juices with the Madeira, add the *Demi-glace* and boil up briefly. Skim off all fat and strain the sauce. Fry the ham medallions in butter. Alternately garnish the fillets with clusters of chestnuts, carrots and onions and place the cooked medallions in between the clusters. Coat meat lightly with the prepared sauce and serve the remainder separately.

⊡ à la Fermière

For 6 persons: 2 lb fillet of beef; 2½ lb mixed vegetables; ¼ lb fat bacon; 6 baked tartlet cases; ½ pint white wine.

Cut the vegetables into large *bâtons* and cook together with the strips of fat bacon in a little butter. Pot roast or roast the fillet. When cooked remove to a serving tray and keep warm. Deglaze the meat juices with the wine and skim away all fat. Arrange the fillet on a long dish, garnish with the pastry cases which have been filled with the vegetables. Serve the prepared sauce separately.

⊡ à la Financière

For 6 persons: 2 lb fillet of beef; Garnish: cooked cocks' combs; cocks' kidneys and sweetbreads; sautéed mushroom caps; blanched, stoned olives; truffle slices; sauce Financière.

Season, lard with strips of fat bacon and roast or pot roast the fillet. Prepare the garnish and bind with the *sauce Financière*. When cooked, remove the fillet to a serving dish and keep warm. Deglaze the meat juices with *sauce Madère*, remove excess fat and strain. Surround the fillet with small clusters of the vegetable garnish. Serve the prepared sauce separately.

⊡ Gerbe d'Or

For 6 persons: 2 lb fillet of beef; ½ pint sauce Porto; 6 bunches of asparagus tips; 1 lemon; 6 artichokes; ½ lb Duchesse potatoes; 2 oz butter; 1 hardboiled egg yolk; ¾ lb Noisette potatoes.

Pot roast the fillet with the Port Wine sauce, *sauce Porto*. Cook the artichoke bottoms in boiling, salted water till tender. Drain well. Place the artichoke bottoms on a baking tray and pipe around them a border of *Duchesse* potatoes. Bake for a few minutes in a moderate oven to allow the potato border to set. Cook the asparagus tips in the usual manner, drain well and arrange in six bundles on a baking tray. Place a strip of lemon in the centre of each, brush with melted butter, sprinkle with sieved egg yolk and reheat briefly in the oven. When the fillet is cooked, remove to a serving dish and keep warm. Remove the fat from the cooking liquor and adjust its consistency with a little *Demi-glace tomatée*. Decorate the sides of the fillet with the prepared artichokes and asparagus garnish, mask with the sauce and arrange the *Noisette* potatoes at either end of the dish.

Filet de Bœuf à la Girondine

For 6 persons: 2 lb fillet of beef; 1 lb mushrooms; 6 artichoke bottoms; ½ pint Demi-glace.

Pot roast the fillet, deglaze the pan with *Demi-glace* and strain. Cut the artichoke bottoms in quarters and simmer in butter, cut the mushrooms in fairly thick slices, *sauté* in half butter and half oil and season. Garnish the fillet alternately with mushrooms and artichoke bottoms, coat lightly with some of the prepared sauce and serve remainder separately.

◘ à la Jardinière * *with Vegetable garnish*

For 6 persons: 2 lb fillet of beef; 1 lb small carrots; ½ lb turnips; ½ lb small French beans; ½ lb small fresh peas; 1 small cauliflower; 1 lb potatoes.

Prepare this dish as for *Bouquetière*, but either cut the root vegetables in strips or cut them out with a medium-sized vegetable cutter. Divide the cauliflower into larger rosettes and coat lightly with *sauce Hollandaise*.

◘ au Madère * *with Madeira Sauce*

For 6 persons: 2 lb fillet of beef; ¾ lb mushrooms; ½ pint sauce Madère.

Lard the fillet with strips of fat bacon, season and either roast or pot roast. Transfer meat to a serving dish and keep warm. Add the *sauce Madère* to the pan drippings, boil briefly, remove fat and strain. Garnish the fillet with *sauté* mushrooms, coat lightly with some of the prepared sauce and serve the remainder separately.

◘ Moderne

For 6 persons: 2 lb fillet of beef; ½ pint Madeira wine; 6 tomatoes; ½ lb onion purée Soubise; 6 veal quenelles; 3 lettuces; 6 slices of truffle.

Deseed the tomatoes and fill with the onion *purée*. Halve and braise the lettuces. Pot roast the fillet in the usual fashion. When cooked, remove to an oval serving dish and keep warm. Deglaze the meat juices with the Madeira. Garnish the sides of the serving dish, alternately with the stuffed tomato cases and the braised lettuce halves. Arrange the veal *quenelles* at each end of the beef and decorate them with the truffle slices. Remove any fat from the prepared sauce and thicken this slightly with a little arrowroot. Serve the sauce separately.

◘ Montglas

For 6 persons: 2 lb fillet of beef; 6 escalopes of foie gras; 12 mushroom caps; 6 slices pickled ox tongue; 6 slices truffle; 2 fl oz Madeira wine; ½ pint Demi-glace.

Pot roast the fillet and deglaze the pan juices with Madeira. Skim off the fat, add the *Demi-glace* and boil up briefly. Poach the mushroom caps, remove and drain well. Fry the scallops of *foie gras* in butter. Arrange the fillet on a long dish and garnish it with alternate slices of tongue, *foie gras*, truffle and mushrooms. Serve the sauce in a sauce-boat.

Filet de Bœuf à la Napolitaine

For 6 *persons:* 2 *lb fillet of beef;* 1 *lb macaroni à la Napolitaine;* ½ *pint sauce Tomate.*

Pot roast the fillet, arrange on a long serving dish, garnish with the prepared macaroni and keep warm. Remove fat from the meat juices and blend in the *sauce Tomate.* Serve this sauce separately.

◘ à la Nivernaise

For 6 *persons:* 2 *lb fillet of beef;* 2 *lb carrots;* 1 *lb small onions;* 2 *lb Château potatoes;* ½ *pint veal stock.*

Pot roast or roast the fillet. When cooked, remove to a serving dish and keep warm. Deglaze the meat juices with the veal stock. Remove grease from the sauce and adjust the seasoning. Glaze the onions and the carrots which have been shaped like large olives. Coat the fillet lightly with the prepared sauce and serve the remainder in a sauce-boat. Garnish the fillet with alternate *bouquets* of glazed onions and carrots and place the *Château* potatoes at either end of the dish.

◘ à la Renaissance

For 6 *persons:* 2 *lb fillet of beef;* ½ *lb carrots;* ½ *lb turnips;* ½ *lb French beans;* ½ *lb young green peas;* 1 *lb Château potatoes;* ½ *pint thickened veal stock;* 12 *small baked tartlet cases.*

Roast or pot roast the fillet. Cut the carrots and turnips into neat shapes with an oval-fluted vegetable cutter and cut the French beans into squares. Cook and glaze the vegetables separately and fill each tartlet case with a decorative garnish of glazed carrots, turnips, peas and French beans. When cooked, remove the fillet to a serving dish, surround with the filled tartlet cases. Place the *Château* potatoes at both ends of the dish. Deglaze the pan juices with the veal stock, lightly coat the fillet with this sauce and serve the remainder separately.

◘ Richelieu

For 10 *persons:* 3½ *lb fillet of beef;* 10 *small tomatoes;* 5 *braised lettuces,* 10 *large mushroom caps;* ½ *lb duxelles;* 2 *oz breadcrumbs;* ¼ *pint Demi-glace;* 1 *tablespoon tomato purée;* 1½ *pints sauce Madère.* Cooking time: 40-60 minutes.

Poêlé or roast the fillet a little underdone and keep it warm for a short time before serving. Mix the *duxelles* with tomato *purée*, *Demi-glace* and enough breadcrumbs to make a smooth mixture. Scoop out the tomatoes and stuff them with this mixture. Sprinkle breadcrumbs on top, dot with butter and cook in the oven. Carve the fillet and garnish it with the stuffed tomatoes, mushrooms and braised lettuce (cut in half and folded in two). Serve *Château* potatoes and *sauce Madère* at the same time. (***See illustration p.*** 421).

Filet de Bœuf Sauté Strogonoff

For 4 persons: 1¼ *lb tail fillet;* 2 *large onions;* ¼ *pint sour cream;* ½ *pint Demi-glace;* 1 *small teaspoon mustard; the juice of* ½ *lemon;* 3 *oz butter*. Cooking time: 3-5 minutes.

Remove all skin, sinews and fat from the meat and cut in dice or short thick strips. Simmer the chopped onions in butter till almost done, add the *Demi-glace* and finish cooking. Heat the butter and add the seasoned meat, so that it browns immediately on all sides; fry at great heat so that it is still pink inside and place on a sieve to drip. Reduce the gravy with the sour cream, add the *Demi-glace* with the onions, boil up, remove from heat and season with mustard and lemon juice; add the blood which has collected. Toss the meat in the hot sauce, do not bring to the boil again and serve at once.

⊡ Wellington

For 10-12 *persons:* 1 *fillet, weighing about* 4-5 *lb;* ¾ *lb dry duxelles;* 1 *lb truffled pâté de foie gras;* 2½ *lb Puff pastry;* 1 *pint sauce Madère;* 1 *egg yolk*. Cooking time: 1-1½ hours.

Spread over the meat a generous layer of butter. Season, brown and partially cook the meat in a very hot oven, 450° F or Gas Mark 8. Allow to cool. When the joint is cold, spread the *pâté de foie gras* over the entire surface and garnish the top half with the *duxelles*. Roll out the pastry into an oblong ⅛-inch thick, place the fillet in the centre and completely enfold with the pastry. Trim the edges of the pastry and seal together. Decorate with strips of pastry, brush with beaten egg yolk, place on a baking tray, seal side down and prick lightly to allow the steam to escape. Cook in a hot oven, 425° F or Gas Mark 7, till the pastry is browned. Serve the *sauce Madère* in two sauce-boats. You may also blend the *duxelles* with a little *sauce Tomate* omitting the *pâté de foie gras*. (*See illustration p.* 421).

FILETS MIGNONS DE BŒUF * *TAIL FILLETS OF BEEF*

These are thin slices cut from the tail end of the fillet. They can be cooked like *tournedos* but more quickly. The same sauces and garnishes can be used but a vegetable garnish is preferred. They may also be cooked in butter like fillets of veal.

⊡ Saint-Hubert

First lard the slices of tail fillet with 2 or 3 strips of fat bacon and then place in a fairly weak marinade for 24 hours. Dry off as much liquid as possible and *sauté* in a little very hot oil. Serve with *sauce Poivrade* or *Chasseur* or any other suitable game sauce. You may also garnish the steaks with a *purée* of vegetables. When game is not in season, these fillets make a welcome change.

LANGUE DE BŒUF * *OX TONGUE*

Fresh tongue is always braised. Pickled tongue is usually boiled in water but it must first be soaked in cold water for 24 hours before cooking. It may also be braised after initial blanching. For a cold tongue dish, boil the pickled tongue until it is tender and allow to cool in its own cooking liquor. When cold and firm, remove from the stock and dip into the hot water. Cut off the tongue root or muscle and remove the skin. If desired, the tongue can be trimmed and skinned whilst it is still hot and then allowed to become quite cold. When set glaze with aspic. If serving hot, skin the tongue immediately after cooking and keep hot in its cooking liquor.

Langue de Bœuf à l'Alsacienne

For 6 *persons:* 1 *fresh ox tongue, weighing about* 3 *lb;* 2 *carrots;* 2 *onions;* 1 *bouquet garni;* ½ *pint wine or stock;* 2½ *lb sauerkraut;* 1½ *lb potatoes.* Cooking time: about 2 hours.

Blanch the ox tongue for about 1½ hours, trim and skin, reserve the stock. Braise on a bed of thinly sliced vegetables, bacon rinds and a *bouquet garni.* When the white wine has almost boiled away, add more stock or white wine and continue braising till tender. Cook the sauerkraut with a piece of ham *à l'Alsacienne.* Boil and mash the potatoes. Remove the braised tongue, place on a serving dish and keep warm. Strain, skim and strain again the remaining stock. Thicken slightly and reduce in volume if necessary. Garnish the tongue with sauerkraut placed on top of slices of the cooked ham, coat lightly with the prepared gravy, serve the mashed potatoes and serve the remainder of the sauce separately.

⊡ Bigarade

For 6 *persons:* 1 *pickled tongue, weighing about* 3½ *lb;* 1 *pint sauce Bigarade.* Cooking time: about 2 hours.

Blanch, trim and braise the tongue as indicated above. Serve it in a long dish, coat with a little *sauce Bigarade* combined with the cooking liquor after all fat has been skimmed off. Serve the remainder of the sauce separately.

⊡ à la Flamande

For 6 *persons:* 1 *pickled tongue, weighing about* 3½ *lb;* 1 *cabbage;* 1½ *lb turnips;* 1½ *lb carrots;* 1½ *lb potatoes.* Cooking time: about 2 hours.

Boil the tongue; prepare in the usual way. Braise the cabbage, cook the neatly shaped carrots and turnips in stock and boil the potatoes. Arrange the tongue in a serving dish. Garnish with the vegetables.

⊡ à la Limousine

For 8-10 *persons:* 1 *fresh tongue, weighing about* 4½ *lb;* 4½ *lb chestnuts;* 40-50 *small onions;* 1 *pint Demi-glace, flavoured with tomato purée;* ½ *pint white wine.*

Trim, blanch and skin the tongue and braise on sliced, browned onions and carrots with a bunch of herbs and the white wine. When the white wine has almost boiled away, add the *Demi-glace* and finish braising. Cook and glaze the chestnuts and the onions. Serve the sliced tongue, garnish with the glazed chestnuts and onions, cover lightly with sauce and serve the remainder separately.

⊡ au Madère * *with Madeira*

For 6 *persons:* 1 *fresh tongue, weighing about* 3½ *lb;* ¼ *pint Madeira wine.* Cooking time: about 2 hours.

Braise the tongue after the usual preparations and serve it on an oval dish. Skim the fat off the braising liquor, strain it and add the Madeira. Cook for a few minutes and serve this sauce separately.

▲ *Filet de Bœuf Wellington, p. 419*

Filet de Bœuf Richelieu, p. 418 ▼

 ▲ Manzo Brasato, p. 442

Aiguillette de Bœuf Braisée. p. 408

▲ *Poitrine de Bœuf Salé Belle Flamande, p. 430*

Entrecôte aux Champignons, p. 413 ▼

▲ Entrecôte Mirabeau, p. 414

Tournedos Clamart, p. 433 ▼

▲ *Châteaubriand Grillé, p. 412*

Tournedos Grillés, p. 432 ▼

▲ *Tournedos Masséna, p. 435*

Tournedos Rossini, p. 436 ▼

▲ *Filet de Bœuf Glacé en Berceau, p. 439*

Langue de Bœuf Princesse, p. 440 ▼

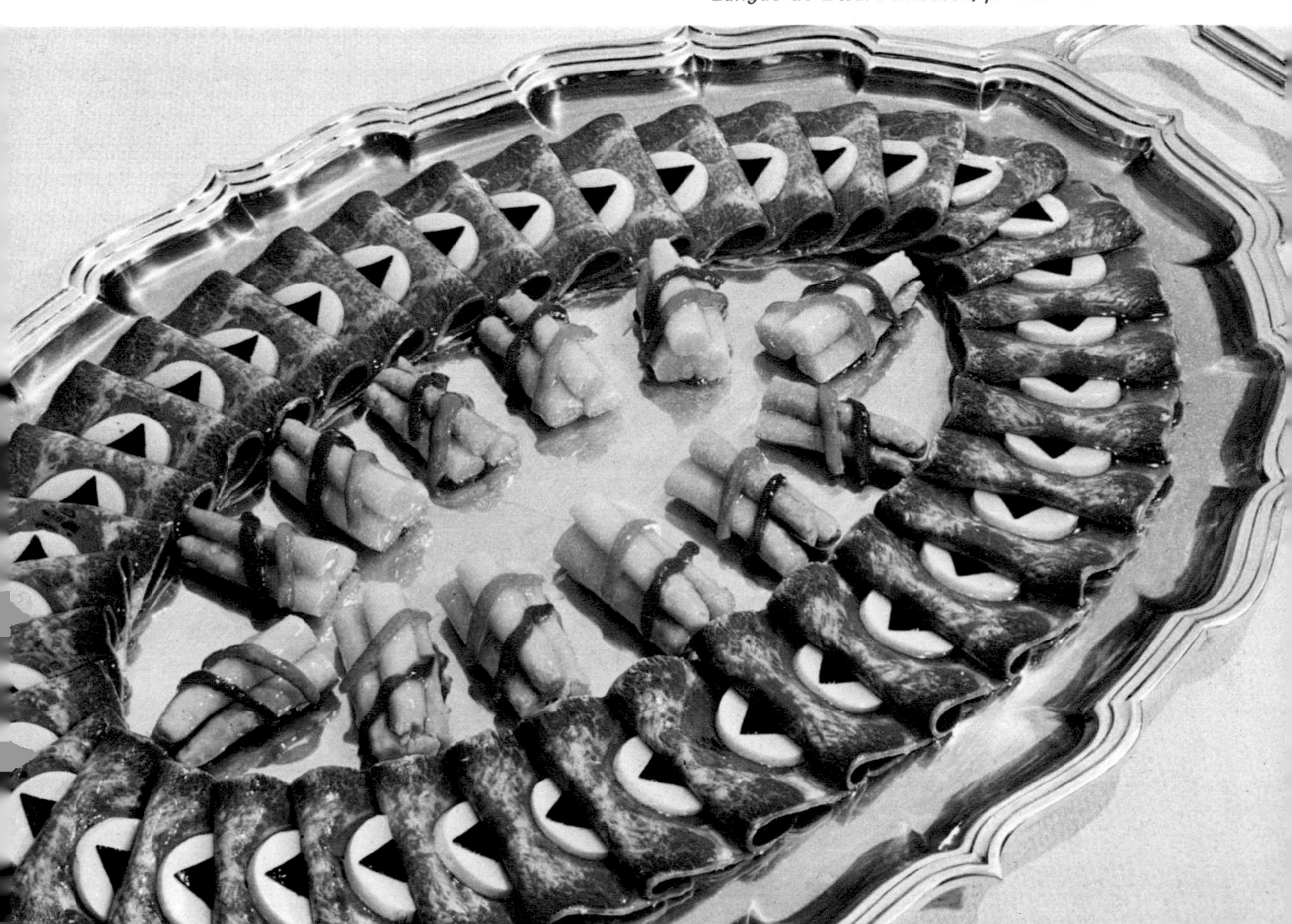

▲ *Bœuf à la Mode en Gelée, p. 438*

Langue de Bœuf Karachi, p. 440 ▼

Langue de Bœuf à la Romaine

For 8-10 *persons:* 1 *tongue, weighing about* 4½ *lb;* 1¼ *lb carrots;* 1 *lb turnip; the white of* 3 *leeks;* 1 *onion stuck with a clove;* 1 *bouquet garni;* 1 *pint sauce Romaine.* Cooking time: 3-4 hours.

Use a fresh or pickled tongue. Soak the pickled tongue for 24 hours beforehand and do not add salt to the water when cooking. Trim the tongue, blanch for 15 minutes, skin and cook with the vegetables like a *Pot-au-Feu.* When a larding needle meets with no resistance the tongue is cooked. Slice, arrange with vegetables cut in fancy shapes on a serving dish and serve the sauce separately.

◘ Saint-Germain

For 8-10 *persons:* 1 *pickled tongue, weighing about* 4½ *lb;* 2 *pints freshly shelled peas;* 3 *oz butter;* 1 *pint sauce Madère.* Cooking time: about 2-3 hours.

Boil peas quickly in salt water so that they keep their colour well, drain thoroughly, pass through a sieve, season with salt and a pinch of sugar and improve with butter. Soak, boil and skin a pickled tongue, slice—not too thinly—serve in an oval dish and coat with a little sauce. Serve the remainder of the sauce and the pea *purée* separately. The *purée* may be made from split dried peas.

PAUPIETTES OU OISEAUX SANS TÊTE * *BEEF OLIVES*

This originates from *papillotte,* meaning envelope, and nowadays means a thin slice of lean meat rolled around a forcemeat stuffing.

For 6 *persons:* 6 *thin slices of beef, each weighing about* 4 *oz, cut from the round;* ½ *lb fat bacon;* ½ *lb raw ham;* 2 *oz lard;* 2 *carrots;* 2 *onions;* ¼ *pint white wine;* 1 *lb tomatoes, or* 1 *heaped tablespoon tomato purée.* Cooking time: 2 hours.

Cut very large, thin slices, season lightly, and place 1 strip of bacon and 1 of raw ham in the centre of each. Roll up and tie; there are also special skewers for the purpose. Brown the rolls well all round in lard in a heavy lidded casserole with the sliced carrots and onions. Pour off fat, reduce with the white wine, add the chopped tomatoes, season, cover, and cook slowly till done. Remove string, strain sauce and skim off the fat. Serve with any desired vegetable.

◘ à la Milanaise

Use the same method as for Beef Olives *à la Provençale* but omit the olives and garlic in the sausage meat. Serve with macaroni *à la Milanaise.*

◘ à la Provençale

Use the same method as Beef Olives, but replace the bacon and ham by ½ lb sausage meat combined with chopped parsley and a little garlic. Add 2 stoned green olives to each beef olive as a garnish.

Paupiettes au Risotto

Same method as Beef Olives but serve with rice *à la Milanaise* or *à la Piémontaise*.

Pointe de Culotte à l'Anglaise * *Boiled Rump of Beef*

For 10 *persons:* 4½ *lb rump;* 3 *lb carrots;* 2 *lb turnips;* 6 *lb white cabbage;* 10 *leeks;* 1 *large onion.* Cooking time: approximately 1½-2 hours according to thickness.

Start the meat and all the vegetables in the same way as *Pot-au-Feu* and only season lightly. Add the white cabbage after removing outside leaves and cutting in quarters; add a little more pepper and cook, allowing 15 minutes per pound of meat. Keep the broth for soup, arrange the sliced meat on a long dish and surround with the vegetables.

Poitrine de Bœuf Salé Belle Flamande * *Salt Brisket of Beef*

For 6 *persons:* 2½ *lb boneless salt brisket;* ½ *lb carrots;* ½ *lb turnips;* 1 *heart of white cabbage;* ½ *lb French beans;* ½ *lb sliced sausage;* 1½ *lb plain boiled potatoes;* ½ *pint sauce Vincent.* Cooking time: 2½-3 hours.

Soak the meat in cold water for a minimum of 3-4 hours. Cover the beef with fresh cold water, bring to the boil, skim frequently; add the cleaned carrots, cabbage and turnips in large pieces and allow to simmer and cook slowly. When the vegetables are cooked, remove them and keep hot in a little of the cooking liquor. When the meat is cooked, cut into slices and arrange neatly on a serving dish. Cut the vegetables into pieces and garnish the dish with the addition of the plainly boiled French beans, the cabbage and the sliced sausage which have also been boiled. Pour over a little of the cooking liquor. Serve the sauce and potatoes separately. (*See illustration p.* 423).

Queue de Bœuf en Hochepot * *Oxtail Hotch Potch*

For 8 *persons:* 4½ *lb oxtail;* 2 *pig's trotters;* 1 *pig's ear;* 1 *lb carrots;* ½ *lb turnips; the white of* 6 *leeks;* 3 *lb white cabbage;* 3 *lb potatoes.* Cooking time: 3½-4 hours.

Cut up the oxtail and blanch it for 10 minutes. Place oxtail in a pot of water with the cut-up trotters and the pig's ear. Bring to the boil, season and skim thoroughly. After 3 hours add the quartered cabbage and the other vegetables and finish cooking. When everything is done, place the vegetables in the middle of the dish surrounded by the oxtail, the boned trotters, the cut-up pig's ear and usually also with some grilled chipolata sausages. Surround with a ring of steamed potatoes, or serve them separately. The *bouillon* may be served separately as soup.

ROGNONS DE BŒUF * *OX KIDNEYS*

No matter how they are prepared ox or beef kidneys are difficult to digest and they are not recommended for a person with a weak stomach. The kidneys from small younger animals such as lamb or calf are superior in flavour and quality than the larger and coarser ox or beef kidney. Ox kidneys are never grilled. They may be sautéed quickly, and cooked slowly in moist heat for at least three hours before they become tender again. The general method of the preparation remains the same for all types of kidneys. Remove the fat and the fine skin. Cut away the core and any other inedible sinews with a sharp knife. Wash in warm water and dry well. Cut into medium-sized slices.

Rognons Bercy

For 6 persons: 2 lb kidneys; 4 shallots; ¼ pint white wine; ¼ lb meat glaze; chopped parsley; 2 oz butter; juice of half a lemon.

Chop the shallots and the parsley and set aside. Remove all fat from the kidneys, prepare as indicated above and cut into ¼-inch scallops. Fry in oil and butter, drain off the fat, remove to a dish and keep warm. Add the chopped shallots, cook for a few minutes, deglaze with the wine and reduce to half. Add the lemon juice, meat glaze and parsley, bring to the boil, remove from heat, toss in the butter, mix in the kidneys and arrange on a serving dish.

◘ aux Champignons * *with Mushrooms*

For 6 persons: 2 lb kidneys; 10 oz mushrooms; ½ pint sauce Madère. Cooking time: 2-3 minutes.

Remove fat and skin from kidneys, cut them in half lengthwise, remove gristly parts and slice thinly. *Sauté* quickly in a large frying pan in hot butter so that they brown at once and do not lose any blood; they should still be a little pink inside. If the frying pan is small, fry in two instalments. Add the sliced mushrooms, sautéed in butter and the *sauce Madère*. Season with salt and pepper, serve at once in a deep dish and sprinkle with chopped parsley.

◘ Marchand de Vin

For 6 persons: 2 lb kidneys; 2 shallots; ¼ pint red wine; ¼ lb meat glaze; parsley; 2 oz butter; juice of half a lemon.

Prepare kidneys as above, *sauté* quickly and drain. Keep warm. Chop the shallots, add to the pan and cook for a few minutes. Deglaze with the wine and add the meat glaze, lemon juice and parsley. Bring to the boil, then remove from heat, blend in the butter and mix in the kidneys. Serve.

RUMPSTEAK * *RUMP STEAK*

Rump steak may be sautéed or grilled. It is served in the same way as *châteaubriands, tournedos* or *entrecôtes.* The garnishes used for the latter are equally suitable for rump steak.

◘ à l'Estouffade * *Braised*

For 6 persons: 2½ lb rump steak; 2 oz lard; ½ lb carrots; ½ lb onions; 1 pint white wine; 1 pint stock; ½ pint Demi-glace; 1 bouquet garni. Cooking time: 2-2½ hours.

Usually, rump steak is sautéed or grilled and served like an *entrecôte* or *tournedos.* If, however, it comes from an old animal, or is too tough to prepare in that way, it is best braised. Cut the meat into six large pieces of roughly equal size, brown in the hot lard, remove the meat and pour in the white wine, the *Demi-glace* and the stock. Add a bunch of herbs, season, cover and cook slowly in the oven till done. Before serving remove the bunch of herbs, skim off fat and strain the sauce.

TOURNEDOS * *TOURNEDOS*

Tournedos are obtained from the middle fillet of beef. It is denuded of all fat and sinew. They are cut 1¼-1½ inches thick, each weighing about 4 oz and are trimmed to a round shape and tied. After cooking the string must of course be removed. *Tournedos* are grilled or sautéed. When they are sautéed, the frying residue is always reduced with a liquid, wine or sauce and used in the sauce to be served with the *tournedos*. It is the custom to place *tournedos* on top of a fried, round slice of bread which is of the same diameter as the steak. These have been referred to in the following recipes as *croûtons*. *Tournedos* must always be served underdone, unless otherwise requested. (*See illustration, p.* 425).

▣ Beaugency

For 4 *persons:* 4 *tournedos;* 4 *artichoke bottoms;* ½ *lb tomatoes;* ½ *pint sauce Choron;* 4 *slices of beef marrow;* 2 *fl oz white wine;* 2 *fl oz veal stock;* 1 *shallot; butter.*

Chop the shallot and toss well in butter, add the peeled deseeded and diced tomatoes, season and lightly cook. Fill the cooked artichoke bottoms with the tomatoes, place the blanched slice of marrow on top and sprinkle with parsley. *Sauté* the *tournedos* and reduce the frying residue with the white wine and veal stock. Place the *tournedos* on *croûtons*, surround with the stock and garnish with filled artichoke bottoms. Make a ring of thick *sauce Choron* round the top of each *tournedos.*

▣ à la Bordelaise

For 6 *persons:* 6 *tournedos;* 6 *slices of poached bone marrow;* ½ *pint sauce Bordelaise; chopped parsley.*

Grill and serve the *tournedos*. Garnish with the marrow slices and parsley in the middle. Serve *sauce Bordelaise* separately.

▣ Carignan

For 6 *persons:* 6 *tournedos;* 6 *cooked artichoke bottoms;* 6 *small Anna potatoes;* ½ *lb asparagus tips;* ½ *pint sauce Madère.*

Sauté the *tournedos* and serve them on the potatoes. Coat lightly with *sauce Madère*. Garnish with the artichoke bottoms filled with asparagus tips.

▣ Cendrillon

For 4 *persons:* 4 *tournedos;* 4 *artichoke bottoms;* ¼ *pint onion purée;* 1 *oz truffle;* ¼ *pint jus lié, flavoured with tomato purée.*

Mix the onion *purée* which should be thick, with finely chopped truffle. Cook the artichoke bottoms in the usual way and fill with this onion mixture. Sprinkle with a little butter and glaze. *Sauté* the steaks, place on a dish on top of fried round slices of bread and garnish each steak alternately with the prepared artichoke bottoms. Coat lightly with the *jus lié.*

Tournedos Choron

For 4 persons: 4 tournedos; 4 croûtons; 4 artichoke bottoms; ¼ pint sauce Choron; 1 lb Noisette potatoes.

Cook the artichokes, drain well and reserve. Grill the steaks and arrange on the *croûtons* on a warm serving dish. Fill the artichokes with the *sauce Choron.* Garnish the steaks with the prepared artichokes and the *Noisette* potatoes.

▣ Clamart

For 6 persons: 6 tournedos; 6 baked tartlet cases; ¾ lb green peas; 1 lb Noisette potatoes; ¾ lb small carrots; ½ pint thickened gravy or veal stock.

Grill or fry the steaks in the usual manner. Cook the peas *à la Française.* Cook the carrots and cut into small, neat pieces. Lightly coat the steak with thickened gravy and garnish with the tartlets, filled with peas, carrot segments and the *Noisette* potatoes. (*See illustration* p. 424).

▣ Colbert

For 6 persons: 6 tournedos; 6 round chicken croquettes; 6 small eggs; 6 truffle slices.

Prepare the chicken *croquettes* and flatten into medallion shapes. Grill or fry the steaks and place them on top of the medallions of chicken. Fry the eggs, place on top of the steaks and decorate with truffle slices.

▣ Cordon Rouge

For 6 persons: 6 tournedos; 6 flat, Puff pastry cases; 3 oz pâté de foie gras; 6 truffle slices; 6 small slices of raw smoked ham; 6 small tomatoes; 12 Fondant potatoes; 1 lb spinach; ½ lb asparagus tips; ½ pint sauce Crème; butter.

Grill the tomatoes, cook the spinach and *sauté* in butter. Make the *sauce Crème* and add sautéed, sliced mushrooms to it. Season and fry the steaks, cut them open and place a small slice of *pâté de foie gras* and a slice of truffle in the opening. Wrap each *tournedos* in a thin slice of ham and place it on a hot Puff pastry case, previously filled with the mushroom *sauce Crème.* Garnish with spinach, cooked asparagus tips and grilled tomatoes. Serve very hot.

▣ à l'Estragon * *with Tarragon*

For 6 persons: 6 tournedos; ½ pint veal stock with tomato in which a few leaves of tarragon have been steeped; tarragon leaves; 2 fl oz white wine.

Fry the *tournedos*, pour off the frying butter, reduce the frying residue with white wine and boil up with the stock. Arrange the fried steaks on *croûtons,* coat with the prepared sauce and decorate each *tournedos* with 2 crossed tarragon leaves.

Tournedos Gabrielle

For 6 persons: 6 tournedos; 3 heads of lettuce; 6 small tomatoes; 6 large mushroom caps; 6 slices of truffle; ¼ pint sauce Madère; 6 croûtons.

Braise the lettuce, halve and fold and keep warm. Fry the steaks in hot butter, and arrange on the *croûtons*. Place a mushroom cap, with a slice of truffle on each *tournedos*. Garnish with grilled tomatoes and half a head of braised lettuce between each. Cover the meat and the lettuce with *sauce Madère*.

▣ Henri IV

For 6 persons: 6 tournedos; 6 croûtons; 6 artichoke bottoms; 1 lb very small Noisette potatoes; ½ pint sauce Béarnaise.

Cook the artichokes in the normal fashion. Drain well. Grill the steaks and arrange them on the *croûtons* which have been fried in butter. Garnish with the artichoke bottoms filled with *Noisette* potatoes and serve *sauce Béarnaise* separately.

▣ à la Hussarde

For 6 persons: 6 tournedos; 6 fried croûtons; 12 large mushroom caps; ¼ pint onion purée Soubise; ½ pint sauce Hussarde.

Grill the steaks and place them on *croûtons*. Garnish with the mushroom caps filled with the onion *purée*. Serve the *sauce Hussarde* separately.

▣ La Vallière

For 6 persons: 6 tournedos; 6 fried croûtons; 6 cooked artichoke bottoms; 10 oz asparagus tips; 1 lb Château potatoes; ½ pint sauce Bordelaise.

Fry the steaks and place them on *croûtons*. Coat lightly with *sauce Bordelaise*. Garnish with the artichoke bottoms filled with asparagus tips and *Château* potatoes.

▣ Maréchale

For 6 persons: 6 tournedos; 6 fried croûtons; 6 truffle slices; ¼ pint meat glaze; 6 small bunches of cooked asparagus tips; 1½ lb Noisette potatoes.

Grill or fry the steaks and place them on the *croûtons*. Coat with meat glaze and put a truffle slice on each. Garnish with the asparagus. Serve *Noisette* potatoes separately.

▣ Marie-Louise

For 6 persons: 6 tournedos; 6 cooked artichoke bottoms; ¼ pint thick onion purée mixed with finely chopped mushrooms; 2 fl oz white wine; ½ pint Demi-glace; Duchesse potatoes; frying butter.

Sauté the steaks and arrange on *croûtons*. Reduce the frying residue with the white wine and boil up with the *Demi-glace*. Fill the artichoke bottoms with mounds of the onion *purée*. Lightly coat the steaks with sauce and garnish alternately with artichoke bottoms and *Duchesse* potatoes.

Tournedos Marseillaise

For 6 persons: 6 tournedos; 6 fried croûtons; 6 olives; 6 anchovy fillets; 6 tomatoes; ½ pint sauce Provençale.

Fry the steaks and place them on *croûtons*. Place an olive surrounded by an anchovy fillet on each. Garnish with tomatoes which have been prepared *à la Provençale*. Serve the sauce separately.

▣ Mascotte

For 6 persons: 6 tournedos; 6 cooked artichoke bottoms; 1 lb Parmentier potatoes; 1 diced truffle; ½ pint sauce Périgueux; 6 fried croûtons.

Fry the steaks, place them on *croûtons* and coat with the *sauce Périgueux*. Place on each an artichoke bottom, filled with *Parmentier* potatoes and truffle.

▣ Masséna

For 6 persons: 6 tournedos; 6 fried croûtons; 6 slices of poached beef marrow; 6 cooked artichoke bottoms; ¼ pint sauce Béarnaise; ½ pint sauce Périgueux.

Fry the steaks, arrange them on *croûtons*, coat with the *sauce Périgueux* and place a slice of marrow on each. Garnish with artichoke bottoms filled with *sauce Béarnaise*. (*See illustration p.* 426).

▣ Mistral

For 6 persons: 6 tournedos; 1 lb aubergines; ½ lb tomatoes; 2 oz stoned olives; oil.

Fry the steaks in oil, place on *croûtons* and garnish the middle of the dish with *Aubergines à la Provençale* and the stoned olives.

▣ à la Moelle * *with Marrow*

For 6 persons: 6 tournedos; 6 slices poached beef marrow; 1½ pints sauce Bordelaise; 2 oz butter; parsley.

Grill the steaks and arrange them on a round dish. Coat with *sauce Bordelaise* improved with butter and place a slice of poached marrow on each. Finish with a pinch of parsley.

▣ aux Morilles * *with Morels or Mushrooms*

For 6 persons: 6 tournedos; 1 lb morels or mushrooms.

Grill the steaks and arrange them in a ring. *Sauté* the morels or mushrooms in butter and place them in the centre. Sprinkle with chopped parsley.

▣ Périgueux

For 6 persons: 6 tournedos; 6 fried croûtons; ½ pint sauce Périgueux; 6 truffle slices.

Fry the steaks, arrange them on *croûtons*, coat with the sauce and garnish with truffle slices.

Tournedos Piémontais

For 6 persons: 6 tournedos; 6 oz rice; 1 onion; 2 oz grated Parmesan cheese; 3 tomatoes; ¼ pint sauce Tomate; ½ pint thickened veal stock; frying oil.

Make a *risotto* with the rice and chopped onion, mix with the cheese and the *sauce Tomate* and arrange on a serving dish in 6 flat, round piles. Halve and fry the tomatoes, fry the steaks, arrange on the rice, place half a tomato on each and coat lightly with the stock.

⊡ à la Portugaise

For 6 persons: 6 tournedos; 6 medium-sized tomatoes; 1 lb potatoes; ¼ lb sausage meat; 2 fl oz white wine; ¼ pint sauce Tomate; breadcrumbs; butter.

Cut a lid off the tomatoes, scoop out, fill with sausage meat, sprinkle with breadcrumbs and melted butter and cook in a moderate oven, 375° F or Gas Mark 5 for about 20 minutes. Fry the steaks, arrange on the *croûtons*, garnish with the stuffed tomatoes and place Fondant potatoes in the middle. Reduce the frying residue with white wine, boil up with *sauce Tomate* and pour over meat.

⊡ Rivoli

For 6 persons: 6 tournedos; 1½ lb potatoes; ½ pint sauce Périgueux.

Prepare *Anna* potatoes and fry the steaks. Arrange the potatoes in a small round, place steaks on the potatoes. Pour *sauce Périgueux,* to which a short *julienne* of truffles has been added, on top.

⊡ Rossini

For 6 persons: 6 tournedos; 6 fried croûtons; 6 slices of foie gras; 6 slices of truffle; 2 fl oz Madeira; ½ pint Demi-glace; butter.

Fry the steaks, arrange on the *croûtons* and reduce the pan juices with Madeira. Add the *Demi-glace* and simmer till a good consistency is obtained. Decorate the steaks with a slice of *foie gras,* which has been quickly fried in butter, and a slice of truffle. Pour the prepared sauce around the *tournedos* and serve remainder separately. (*See illustration, p.* 426).

TRIPES * *TRIPE*

Tripe is the lining of the stomach from the ox, the sheep or the pig. Ox or beef tripe is the one most commonly used and it makes a very nourishing and easily digested dish. There are three kinds of tripe:

The rumen	—Paunch or *plain* tripe
The reticulum	—Fore stomach or *honeycomb*
The obomasum	—*Rennet* bag or true stomach

The first two give the white or cream-coloured tripe, whilst the last provides the red or black tripe. It is to be remembered that dressed tripe sold in Britain is, in effect, cold cooked (or part-cooked) tripe whose preparation is a specialised job undertaken by the tripe dressers. Long-cooking methods, such as in *Tripes à la Mode de Caen,* were designed for cleaned tripe not subjected to modern dressing methods used in this country. Precooked fresh tripe as sold in the butcher's shop, requires further cooking since it is only part cooked.

Tripes à la Mode de Caen

6 lb raw or undressed tripe; ½ lb fresh beef suet; 2 calf's feet; 4 carrots; 4 onions; the white part of 3 leeks; 2 pints strong cider or 3 fl oz brandy plus 2 pints water; 1 bouquet garni; 1 muslin bag containing 8 peppercorns and 4 cloves. Cooking time: about 10 hours with undressed tripe.

Soak the tripe for several hours in water, changing this frequently. Blanch, refresh and cut into 1½-inch squares. Line an earthenware or other fire-proof casserole dish, large enough to hold all the ingredients, with half the tripe. Blanch and bone the calf's feet. Cut into medium-sized pieces and add to the casserole. On top of this place the carrots and onions quartered lengthwise, the sliced leeks, the *bouquet garni,* the muslin bag and the remainder of the tripe on top. Add a little salt, then cover with the suet cut in slices, the cider and enough water to cover everything. Seal the pot hermetically with a paste of flour and water, bring to the boil over a gentle heat and finish cooking in a cool oven, 325° F or Gas Mark 2. When everything is cooked, remove the *bouquet garni,* muslin bag and vegetables, skim off all fat and serve very hot in the cooking vessel.

NOTE: With British dressed tripe the recipe must be adapted to a much shorter cooking time: about 3-4 hours.

◘ Frites, Sauce Rémoulade * *Fried, with Rémoulade Sauce*

For 6 persons: ½ pint sauce Rémoulade; 2 lb cooked tripe; 2 eggs; 1 teaspoon dry mustard; ¼ lb dried breadcrumbs; parsley sprigs.

Cut the tripe into 2-inch squares. Beat the eggs and mustard together, dip the tripe into this mixture and then into the breadcrumbs; deep fry. Arrange on a serving dish and garnish with fried parsley. Serve the sauce in a sauce-boat.

◘ à la Lyonnaise

For 6 persons: 2 lb cooked tripe cut into julienne; 1 lb of shredded onions cooked in butter; chopped parsley; ¼ lb lard; vinegar.

Cut the tripe into *julienne* and fry in burning hot lard, season, add the onions, toss well together. Arrange piled up in a serving dish. Deglaze the pan with vinegar and pour over the tripe. Sprinkle with chopped parsley.

◘ à la Niçoise

For 6 persons: 2 lb cooked tripe; ½ lb onions; ½ lb tomato concassé; ¾ pint stock; 1 bouquet garni; 1 large crushed clove of garlic; chopped parsley.

Cut the tripe into long strips and chop the onions. Fry the onions, add the garlic and shredded tripe, cook together for several minutes. Add the tomatoes and stock, season, add the *bouquet garni,* cover and simmer for approximately three-quarters of an hour or until tender. Arrange in a serving dish and sprinkle with chopped parsley.

◘ à la Poulette

For 6 persons: 2 lb cooked tripe; 1½ pints sauce Poulette; chopped parsley.

Cut the tripe into *julienne* and simmer together with the sauce for thirty minutes. Arrange in a serving dish and sprinkle with chopped parsley.

LE BŒUF FROID * *COLD BEEF*

Beefsteak Tartare

For each person: 6 oz prime beef, preferably fillet; 1 egg yolk; 2 anchovy fillets in oil; chopped onions, capers, etc.

Remove sinews from meat, chop very fine with a knife or mince the meat and season with salt and pepper. Shape into a flat circle with a hollow in the middle. Serve, place the raw yolk of egg in the middle and garnish with rolled anchovy fillets, finely chopped onions, capers, gherkins cut in fans, and slices of tomato or beetroot. The chopped onions and capers can also be put in scooped-out half tomatoes. Serve with Tomato sauce and ketchup if required. The egg white may be mixed with the meat if desired.

Bœuf Fumé * *Smoked Beef*

Smoked beef is bought ready made. A speciality of Hamburg, this should be served thinly sliced with brown bread and butter.

Bœuf à la Mode en Gelée * *Cold Braised Beef in Aspic*

For 8 persons: 2½ lb rump; 2 calf's feet; ½ lb bacon rinds; 2 oz fat; 30 small onions; 2 lb young, round carrots; 3 fl oz brandy; 1 pint white wine; 6 oz larding bacon. Cooking time: 2½-3 hours.

Prepare the meat in the same way as for beef *à la Mode*. As soon as it is cooked and tender, allow to cool, drain well and reserve the stock. Line the bottom of a flat, round mould or an ordinary salad bowl with a thin layer of aspic. When it is half set arrange alternately in this aspic the tiny onions and carrots in a neat design. Allow to set completely. Place the meat and remaining vegetables on top. Remove fat from the cold stock, strain and season well and pour over meat until the mould is full or everything is covered. If there is not enough stock add a little aspic. Let it set in the refrigerator, hold the dish in warm water for a moment and then turn out on a round dish. The calf's foot may be mixed with the vegetables if it is first cut in very thin strips; otherwise it sets too hard. (*See illustration p.* 428)

Bœuf Séché * *Dried Beef*

In Switzerland and Italy pieces of beef, which have been pickled for several days, are hung in cold, dry air and left out in the mountain air for several months, especially in the Grisons, Valais and Valtelina. The meat, *bundner fleisch*, as it is called in Switzerland, becomes hard and is cut into very thin slices with a special cutter. It is eaten as *hors d'œuvre* and as cold meat. Allow about 3 oz per person.

Cœur de Bœuf à la Tyrolienne * *Ox Heart in Aspic*

For 5-6 persons: 1 ox heart; 2 oz lard; 2 carrots; 2 onions; ½ pint sauce Rémoulade; 1 tablespoon grated horseradish; gelatine; stock; 1 bouquet garni. Cooking time: about 2 hours.

A simple but tasty dish. Brown the heart in the lard in a frying pan and place on a bed of sliced carrots and onions in a heavy, lidded casserole. Season, cover with stock. Add a *bouquet garni* and cover. Braise slowly in the oven till tender and allow to cool in the stock. Remove when cold and set aside. Degrease the stock, boil till clear, skim well, clarify with egg white and gelatine (1 oz per pint of stock). Cut the cooled heart in round slices, arrange on an oval dish, glaze with the aspic and surround with diced aspic made with the remainder of the jelly. Mix the sauce *Rémoulade* with the grated horseradish and serve separately.

FILET DE BŒUF GLACÉ * *FILLET OF BEEF IN ASPIC*

Aspic flavoured with Port or Madeira may be used for coating this dish, although the best choice is a meat-flavoured aspic.

▣ en Berceau

For 10 *persons:* 3 *lb fillet of beef;* ¼ *lb pickled ox tongue;* ¼ *lb gherkins;* 20 *truffle slices;* ¾ *lb purée of foie gras;* ½ *lb butter;* 2 *pints aspic jelly flavoured with Port.*

Roast the fillet the preceding evening, keeping it underdone. Line a long loaf tin with aspic jelly. Decorate the bottom of the mould first with slices of truffle and then with a *julienne* of ox tongue and gherkins. Cover the *julienne*, with a little half-set jelly, to keep it in its place. Slice the fillet and replace the slices, spreading a *purée* made of the *pâté* of *foie gras* and creamed butter between the slices. Place it carefully in the mould, and fill up with half-set aspic jelly. Allow to set on ice or in the refrigerator. Turn out on a long dish, cut a few slices off, and garnish these with aspic jelly. You may also decorate the bottom of the loaf tin with a design of cooked egg white and truffle. (*See illustration p.* 427).

▣ Rothschild

For 6 *persons:* 2 *lb fillet;* ½ *lb purée of foie gras; truffle slices;* 1 *pint aspic flavoured with Port.*

Pot roast the fillet, keeping it slightly underdone. Let it cool. Cut into slices ¼-inch thick and spread these with a *purée* of *foie gras*. Arrange on a long dish, overlapping the slices, with a truffle slice on each. Coat with half-set aspic jelly. Allow to set.

▣ à la Russe

For 6 *persons:* 2 *lb fillet;* 6 *tomatoes; Russian salad;* ½ *pint sauce Tartare;* 1 *pint aspic flavoured with Port.*

Roast or pot roast the fillet. Let it cool. Cut into slices, glaze each with aspic and reform the fillet. Halve and deseed the tomatoes and fill each half with some Russian salad. Arrange on an oval serving dish and garnish with the tomatoes. Serve *sauce Tartare* separately.

▣ Vigneronne

For 12 *persons:* 1 *fillet, weighing about* 5 *lb;* 2 *lb foie gras mousse;* 4 *lb Pie pastry or pâté à pâté;* 2 *bunches white grapes;* 2 *bunches black grapes;* 1½ *pints aspic flavoured with Port.*

Quickly brown the fillet all over. Let it cool. Cover with *foie gras mousse*. Roll out the pastry into a rectangle ¼-inch thick. Wrap the meat in it, seal the edges of the pastry carefully and place on a baking tray sealed side down. Cover the top of the pastry with buttered greaseproof paper or baking foil, otherwise the pastry will burn. If necessary remove this a quarter of an hour before the cooking time is completed. Bake for 1-1¼ hours in a hot oven, 425° F or Gas Mark 7. Let it cool. Slice three-quarters of it into slices ⅜-inch thick. Glaze the slices with cold aspic. Arrange on a long serving dish. Decorate with the grapes, divided into tiny bunches and glazed with aspic.

LANGUE DE BŒUF * *TONGUE*

The tongue is skinned after it is cooked and has been allowed to cool. Clear aspic is to be preferred although Port or Madeira-flavoured aspic may be used.

▣ à l'Ecarlate

For 8-10 *persons:* 1 *pickled ox tongue, weighing about* 4½ *lb;* 2½ *oz gelatine.*

Skin the boiled, pickled tongue and place in a press to set. When cold, coat with the gelatine, dissolved in a little water coloured with caramel and a few drops of carmine, and let it set.

▣ Karachi

For 8-10 *persons:* 1 *pickled tongue, weighing about* 4½ *lb;* 3 *hardboiled eggs;* 8-10 *small, peeled tomatoes;* 8-10 *small, baked tartlet cases;* 4 *hardboiled egg yolks;* 3 *oz butter;* 1 *banana;* 2 *oz rice;* 1 *red pepper;* 1 *large shallot;* ¼ *pint Mayonnaise;* 1 *sheet gelatine;* 5-6 *chopped, roasted almonds; tomato ketchup; curry powder;* 2¼ *pints aspic.*

Line a square silver serving dish with a thin layer of aspic and on it place the thinly sliced tongue, either around the edges of the dish in overlapping slices or diagonally across it. Slice the hardboiled eggs and place a half slice on each exposed section of the tongue. Glaze the garnished tongue slices with aspic. Boil the rice, drain when cooked, mix with the finely diced banana, the deseeded, very finely diced red pepper and the chopped shallot. Bind this mixture with the *Mayonnaise* which has been well seasoned with curry powder, flavoured with tomato ketchup and thickened with melted gelatine. Fill the tartlet cases with mounds of this mixture and scatter the chopped, roasted almonds on top. Cut tops off the tomatoes and reserve these. Scoop out the flesh and fill with a creamy mixture made from the blended hardboiled egg yolks and the butter and seasoned with chopped chervil, pepper and salt. Use a piping bag and a star-shaped nozzle. Decorate with a tomato star cut from the lid and glaze with aspic. Garnish the dish with an imaginative arrangement of the tomatoes and tartlets and finish off with diced aspic. (*See illustration p.* 428).

▣ Princesse

For 6 *persons:* 1 *pickled tongue, weighing about* 3 *lb;* 12 *small bundles of cooked asparagus;* 1 *pint aspic.*

Cut the pickled, boiled, pressed, skinned, cold tongue in thin slices. Line a dish with aspic and when set place the sliced tongue on it in an extended semi-circle. Glaze very lightly with aspic. Arrange the bundles of asparagus tips in the centre after marinating with oil, lemon juice, salt and pepper and draining thoroughly. Glaze asparagus with aspic and place some accurately cut aspic cubes behind the tongue. (*See illustration p.* 427).

FOREIGN SPECIALITIES

Beefsteak Pie

For 6 *persons:* 1½ *lb beefsteak (shoulder or topside);* ½ *pint water or brown stock;* ¾ *lb Puff pastry;* ½ *oz flour; eggwash; salt; pepper. Optional:* 6 *oz chopped and sweated onions;* ½ *teaspoon chopped parsley.* Cooking time: 2-2½ hours.

Cut the meat into thin slices (or into 1-inch cubes, if preferred) and dredge with the sifted flour. Place in pie dish. Season with salt and pepper and stir in the stock. Some cooks brown the steak by rapid shallow frying before dredging in flour. Traditionally, this is a plainly flavoured pie, but, if desired, sweated onion and chopped parsley may be stirred in at this stage. Roll out the Puff pastry ¼-inch thick. Eggwash the rim of the pie dish and build it up with a ½-inch strip of the Puff pastry. Brush the strip of paste with eggwash and cover the entire pie dish with the remaining paste, crimp and seal edges and cut off the surplus pastry. Eggwash the surface and allow the pie to rest in a cool place for at least thirty minutes. Bake the pie in a hot oven, 400° F or Gas Mark 6, for approximately fifteen minutes to allow the pastry to set and lightly colour. Then lower the temperature of the oven to 325° F or Gas Mark 2. During the cooking process which will be about two hours, cover the Puff pastry with greaseproof paper if it shows signs of over-colouring. Wipe the dish clean and surround with paper pie frill or table napkin.

Beefsteak and Kidney Pie

As above, replacing ½ lb of steak with ½ lb of ox kidney, cut in slices.

Beefsteak, Mushroom and Kidney Pie

As above with the addition of ¼ lb sliced mushrooms.

Beefsteak and Oyster Pie

As for Beefsteak Pie with the addition of 4-6 oysters per person.

Bitok Nowgorodski

For 6 persons: 1½ *lb tail of fillet of beef;* ¼ *lb white bread cut in cubes;* ¼ *lb butter;* ½ *lb chopped onion;* 2 *onions;* ½ *pint sauce Madère; breadcrumbs;* 1½ *lb Sauté potatoes.*

Remove the crust from the bread and cut into cubes. Soak these in milk and squeeze out well. Mince the fillet of beef finely and combine with the soaked bread, the chopped onion, half the butter and seasonings. Mix well. Make into thick cakes of about 2 oz and roll them in breadcrumbs. *Sauté* them in butter. Arrange on a dish with deep-fried onion rings. Serve the sauce and the potatoes separately. ***(Russia)***

Carbonades de Bœuf à la Flamande * *Beef Stew with Beer*

For 6 persons: 2-2¼ *lb topside of beef;* 1 *lb onions;* 2 *oz lard;* 1 *pint light ale;* ½ *pint Demi-glace;* 1 *bouquet garni;* 1½ *lb boiled potatoes.* Cooking time: 1½-2 hours.

Slice the onions and cut beef into thin slices (or into 1-inch cubes). Brown the meat on both sides in lard. Remove, and fry the onions lightly in the lard. Place a layer of sautéed onions in a suitable pot, place the meat on top, cover with the remainder of the onions, season, moisten with the beer and *Demi-glace* and add the *bouquet garni.* Cover and cook gently till the meat is tender. Remove the *bouquet garni* and skim off the fat. Serve the potatoes separately. ***(Belgium)***

Choesels à la Bruxelloise * *Belgian Offal Stew*

For 6 persons: 1 *ox tail;* 1 *large onion;* 1 *pint stock;* 3 *lb breast of mutton;* 4 *sheep's trotters split in halves;* 1 *large bouquet garni;* 3 *cloves;* 12 *peppercorns;* 6 *ox sweetbreads;* 2 *calfs' sweetbreads;* 3 *lb breast of veal;* ½ *lb ox kidney cut into slices;* ½ *pint beer or Madeira;* ½ *lb mushrooms.*

Cut the tail into sections, chop the onion and fry the onions and ox tail together in butter. Moisten with the stock and simmer for forty-five minutes. Cut the mutton into two inch squares, add to the ox tail with the *bouquet garni*, cloves, peppercorns and sheep trotters; cover with a lid and simmer for another thirty minutes. Cut the veal into two inch squares and put it with the sweetbreads and ox kidney. Place in the pot with other meats. Cook for about another two hours. Now add the diced, raw mushrooms, the beer or Madeira, cook for a further fifteen minutes. Season with cayenne. Serve hot with boiled potatoes.

Fondue Bourguignonne

For 6 persons: 2 *lb sirloin or rump of beef; selection of cold sauces* (*Mayonnaise, Aurora, Mustard, Curry, Rémoulade, Vinaigrette or ketchup*); 1 *pint oil.*

Cut the raw meat into cubes of about ¾-inch. Put the boiling oil in a small fireproof dish in the centre of the table over a spirit lamp or electric hotplate. Impale a piece of beef on a wooden skewer or fork. Dip the meat into the hot oil for a few moments. Remove it from the skewer or fork and dip into one of the sauces arranged in a ring on a separate plate. Do not use the dinner fork for dipping the meat in the oil, as this can mean painful burns on the lips. (Allegedly from Burgundy—derived from Burgundian peasants' *al fresco* meals—and developed in Switzerland and other countries).

Manzo Brasato * *Italian Braised Beef*

For 10 persons: 4½ *lb rump of beef;* ¼ *lb streaky bacon;* 1 *pint red wine;* ¼ *pint oil; sage and rosemary;* 2 *oz tomato purée;* 2 *carrots;* 1 *stick celery;* 2 *onions;* 1 *pint brown stock;* 10 *small braised onions;* 10 *small steamed potatoes;* 1 *oz beurre manié* (*optional*).

Lard the meat with the streaky bacon and roll it lengthwise around the whole carrots and the celery. Marinate in red wine, oil and the spices for two days. Remove the meat and reserve the marinade. Dry the meat and then brown it in some oil in a covered heavy casserole or roasting pan, add the chopped onions, some *julienne* of carrots and celery and cook for a few minutes. Moisten with the marinade, reduce by half, add the stock and tomato *purée*, cover and continue cooking slowly in the oven, turning the meat two or three times. When tender, remove the meat to a serving dish and keep warm. Pass the vegetables and cooking liquor through a sieve. Skim off excess fat and thicken a little if necessary with *beurre manié*. Garnish the serving dish with steamed potatoes and small braised onions and serve the sauce separately. (*See illustration p.* 422).

Marha Gulyas * *Hungarian Goulash*

For 5 persons: 2 *lb lean beef* (1 *lb of this may be replaced by heart and ox liver*); 1 *lb onions;* ¼ *teaspoon crushed caraway seeds;* 1 *generous pinch marjoram;* 1 *large crushed clove of garlic;* ½ *teaspoon paprika;* ½ *lb tomatoes;* 1 *lb potatoes;* ½ *lb Noodle dough;* 2 *green peppers;* 2 *oz lard.* Cooking time: 2½-3 hours.

Slice the onions thinly and fry golden brown in the lard. Add the meat, heart and liver, cut in biggish cubes, brown well. Season with the marjoram, caraway seeds, garlic, salt, paprika and a pinch of pepper. Add the chopped tomatoes and deseeded peppers cut in strips and cook until the meat absorbs the moisture. Thirty minutes before cooking is completed add the coarsely diced potatoes and cook together till done, adding a little water if necessary. Add *csipetke* at the last moment before serving.

Csipetke: Roll out the Noodle dough thinly and allow to dry, tear into very small pieces by hand. Poach in boiling salted water, drain well, and add to the hot goulash.

Mititei * *Roumanian Beef Sausages*

For 6 persons: 1½ lb raw minced beef; 3 cloves of garlic; ¼ pint boiling stock; 1 coffeespoon bicarbonate of soda. Cooking time: 5-6 minutes.

Season the meat with salt, pepper, thyme, allspice and crushed chopped garlic. Pour the boiling stock over the meat and mix it together quickly. Add a coffeespoon of bicarbonate of soda and work this into the paste. Divide into twenty-four pieces, roll into sausages three inches long, brush with oil and grill. Serve very hot with preserved green capsicums and vinegar.

Perisoares Cu Verdatore * *Meat Balls with Herbs*

1¼ lb raw minced beef; ¾ lb lean minced pork; 2 onions; 2 oz spinach; 1 oz chopped herbs (parsley, chervil, dill, tarragon); ¼ lb butter; ½ pint Demi-glace; ¼ pint sour cream. Cooking time: 12-15 minutes.

Chop the onions and cook in butter. Chop the spinach and mix well with the chopped herbs. Combine the meat with the chopped onions and season. Shape into walnut-sized balls and roll in the chopped herbs and spinach. Heat the butter and simmer the meat balls in it without letting them brown. Moisten with the *Demi-glace* and cook for a few more minutes. Serve the sour cream separately. (*Rumania*)

Pressed Beef

This is pickled brisket of beef, boiled till cooked and pressed into a rectangular mould and cooled. When cold it is glazed with aspic, thinly sliced and served garnished with curly parsley. Pressed beef is usually accompanied by salad and appropriate dressing. (*Great Britain*)

Stewed Steak and Carrots

For 6 persons: 1½-2 lb shoulder steak; 2 oz flour; 2 oz lard; 1 tablespoon tomato purée; 2-2½ pints brown stock or water; 1 bouquet garni; ½ lb mirepoix; ½ lb carrots; ½ lb turnips; ½ lb button onions; ¼ lb shelled peas.

Cut the meat into 1-inch cubes and fry it quickly in the hot lard in a fire-proof casserole, add the *mirepoix* and continue frying. Sprinkle the flour on top of meat and place in a hot oven, 400° F or Gas Mark 6, for five minutes. Transfer to the top of the stove, stir in the tomato *purée* and then the stock and bring to the boil. Add the seasoning and the *bouquet garni* and simmer gently. Thirty minutes before cooking is completed, remove the *bouquet garni* and add the vegetables. (The vegetables may be cut in *bâtons* or olive shapes.) Cook the peas separately and sprinkle over the meat when serving. Carrots, turnips and button onions can also be cooked separately and added after the meat has been cooked.

(*Great Britain*)

Wiener Rostbraten * *Viennese Braised Entrecôte*

For 6 persons: 6 entrecôte steaks, each weighing about ½ lb; ½ lb onions; ½ teaspoon paprika; ½ pint brown stock; ½ pint sour cream; 1½ lb boiled potatoes. Cooking time: 1½-2 hours.

Brown the steaks in lard. Slice the onions and brown in lard. Place half the onions in a suitable pot, place the steaks on top and cover with the remainder of the onions. Season with salt and paprika. Moisten with the stock and braise gently in the oven with the lid on. When cooked and tender, remove the meat, and reduce cooking liquid. Add the sour cream, simmer and pour over the meat without straining. Serve the potatoes separately. (*Austria*)

Veal

Veal is the flesh of immature calves and in Britain may be one of these two types—"slink" veal or "fed" veal. "Slink" veal is white, clear and soft with little or no flavour since it comes from the very young milk-fed animal. It is therefore cheaper and is usually boned and used for stews and casseroles. "Fed" veal is the meat of an older animal and is pale pink or off-white in colour with a fine texture and puffy connective tissue. Most of this veal comes from Holland (this variety is highly esteemed) and various parts of the Continent. Any mottling or blue or brown tints indicate stale meat and should not be purchased.

Veal is less easily digested than some other meats and should be thoroughly cooked to render it more tender. It also has a delicate flavour and must be well seasoned during cooking so that it is not insipid. The bones and trimmings of veal are very gelatinous and are useful for stocks and glazes.

APPROXIMATE COOKING TIMES

CUTS	TIME	TEMPERATURE
Cushion of Veal	15-20 mins per lb+15 mins	These cuts are cooked in a moderate oven, 375° F or Gas Mark 4-5 For underdone or very well done meat, shorten or lengthen the cooking time as desired.
Saddle of Veal	15-20 mins per lb+15 mins	
Filet Mignon	25-30 mins per lb	
Knuckle	$1\frac{3}{4}$-2 hours	
Cutlets	7-10 mins each side	
Escalopes	3-4 mins each side	
Escalopes in Breadcrumbs	3-4 mins each side	
Liver in Slices	2 mins each side (thin) 3 mins each side (thick)	
Sweetbread	blanching: 5 mins braising: 30-40 mins	
Brains	poaching: 8-10 mins	
Stewed veal	$1\frac{3}{4}$-2 hours	
Blanquette	2 hours	
Breast, Stuffed	20 mins per lb, with bone 30 mins per lb, boned *both* plus 15 mins	

LE VEAU * *VEAL*

Blanquette de Veau * *White Veal Stew*

For 5 persons: 2 *lb veal, shoulder or breast;* 1 *large onion;* 1 *bouquet garni;* 20 *small onions;* ½ *lb raw mushrooms;* 2 *oz butter;* 2 *pints white stock;* 2 *oz flour;* ¼ *pint cream;* 2 *egg yolks; the juice of* ½ *lemon.* Cooking time: 1½ hours.

Cut the meat in 2 oz pieces, blanch and refresh. Place meat in a pot with the stock and the onion stuck with cloves, the *bouquet garni* and a little salt and cook slowly. Cook the small onions in butter without letting them brown, poach the mushrooms with lemon juice and butter. When the meat is done, remove with a fork and put in a clean casserole. Make a white *roux* with the flour and butter and make into a *Velouté* with the strained veal stock and allow to simmer till cooked. Remove from heat and thicken with the egg yolks mixed with the cream. Flavour with lemon juice and season well. Add the garnish of onions and mushrooms to the meat and strain sauce over. Sprinkle with chopped parsley.

Carré de Veau Belle Jardinière * *Loin of Veal*

2 loin or best end of neck cutlets per person. Season the prepared loin or best end of neck and roast till cooked a golden brown colour. Prepare a garnish of turned, root vegetables, French beans, peas, cauliflower and mushrooms. Cut the loin or best end into cutlets, garnish with the vegetables and coat the cutlets with clear veal sauce (*Jus lié*). (*See illustration p.* 462).

Cervelle de Veau * *Calf's Brains*

For each person allow ¼ *lb calf's brains.* Cooking time: 20 minutes.

Poach the calf's brains in the same way as Ox Brains. After poaching cut into thick slices and place on a dish, season, and pour on dark Brown butter in which parsley leaves have been fried and a dash of vinegar added at the last moment.

CŒUR DE VEAU * *CALF'S HEART*

Much smaller and very much more tender than ox or lamb's hearts. It may be braised, roasted or stewed and should be cooked with care.

▣ Farci à l'Anglaise * *Stuffed*

For 4 persons: 1 *calf's heart, weighing about* 1½ *lb;* 1 *medium-sized, chopped onion;* 2 *oz suet;* ¼ *lb white bread soaked in milk and squeezed out;* 1 *egg;* ½ *tablespoon chopped parsley;* 1 *generous pinch each of marjoram, thyme and sage;* ¼ *lb streaky bacon;* 2 *oz butter.* Cooking time: 2 hours.

Wash the heart and prepare in the usual way by removing the arteries, veins and gristle. Soak the heart well to draw out the blood. Make a forcemeat with the chopped onion, which is cooked in butter and allowed to cool, finely chopped suet, the soaked bread, the herbs and the egg. Season with salt and pepper. Fill the heart with this forcemeat, wrap it in thin bacon slices, tie it and brown on all sides in a suitable pan. Half cover with good stock. Cover with a lid and braise slowly in a warm oven, 350° F or Gas Mark 3-4, till done. Remove bacon, slice the heart thinly with a sharp knife, pour the gravy, slightly thickened with cornflour on top and serve with boiled potatoes.

Cœur de Veau Sauté * *Shallow Fried Calf's Heart*

For 6 persons: 2 *calves' hearts, each weighing about* 1 *lb.* Cooking time: 8-10 minutes.

Cut the hearts into thin slices, season, flour and fry over moderate heat in butter. All garnishes for calves' livers are suitable. The heart should not be cooked in sauce as this method of cooking will toughen the flesh unless it is braised for a lengthy period.

CÔTES DE VEAU * *VEAL CUTLETS*

Veal cutlets or chops may be grilled but it is more usual to *sauté* them. Remember that veal cooks much quicker than lamb or pork.

▣ à l'Anglaise * *Breadcrumbed*

For each person: 1 *veal cutlet, weighing about* 6 *oz.*

Although veal cutlets are sometimes grilled, they are best fried in a *sauté* pan. They may be garnished with all the finer vegetables. Remember that veal, like pork, is always served well done.

▣ Bonne Femme

For 6 *persons:* 6 *veal cutlets, each weighing about* 6 *oz;* 30 *small onions;* 1 *lb new potatoes;* ½ *lb lean bacon;* 3 *oz butter;* ¼ *pint thickened veal gravy.* Cooking time: 15-18 minutes.

Fry the cutlets in butter, add the glazed onions, small new potatoes cooked in butter and short, browned strips of bacon. Add the thickened veal gravy, cover the *sauté* pan and simmer together for a few more minutes.

▣ Chenonceaux

For 6 *persons:* 6 *veal cutlets, each weighing about* 6 *oz;* 12 *slices of pickled ox tongue;* 2 *oz shredded almonds;* ¼ *lb butter;* 1½ *lb Macaire potatoes;* ½ *pint sauce Madère.* Cooking time: 15 minutes.

Season and fry the cutlets in butter. Heat the tongue in the butter left in the pan. Top each cutlet with two slices of tongue, mask over with the sauce, sprinkle with the almonds. Serve the potatoes separately. (*See illustration p.* 466).

▣ en Cocotte à la Crème * *With Cream Sauce*

For 4 *persons:* 4 *veal cutlets, each weighing about* 6 *oz;* ⅓ *pint cream;* 1 *lb Fondant potatoes.* Cooking time: 18 minutes.

Season and flour the cutlets and fry them in butter on both sides without browning them too much. When cooked add the cream, a little salt and ground pepper and simmer for five minutes in the fire-proof casserole in which they were fried. Serve in the casserole garnished with the *Fondant* potatoes.

Côtes de Veau en Cocotte à la Ménagère

For 6 *persons:* 6 *veal cutlets, each weighing about* 6 *oz;* 30 *small glazed onions;* ¾ *lb olive-shaped carrots;* ¾ *lb potatoes;* ¼ *pint white wine.* Cooking time: 30-40 minutes.

Prepare the olive-shaped carrots and potatoes. First *sauté* the cutlets and then put them in a casserole with the potatoes, carrots and onions. Add the white wine, put the lid on and simmer till cooked.

▣ aux Fines Herbes * *With Mixed Herbs*

For 6 *persons:* 6 *veal cutlets, each weighing about* 6 *oz;* 2 *tablespoons finely chopped herbs (parsley, chervil, tarragon);* ¼ *pint white wine;* ¼ *lb butter; meat glaze.* Cooking time: 12-15 minutes.

Season the cutlets, flour them and fry in butter. When cooked, remove from the pan and transfer to a serving dish. Keep warm. Reduce the pan residue with white wine and boil down to half. Add 1 small spoon liquid meat glaze, remove from heat, add the herbs and a piece of butter, bind by tossing in the pan and pour over the cutlets.

▣ Foyot

For 6 *persons:* 3 *double veal cutlets, each weighing about* ¾ *lb;* ½ *lb onions;* ½ *lb white breadcrumbs;* ¼ *lb grated gruyère;* ½ *pint white wine;* ⅓ *pint veal stock;* ¼ *lb butter.* Cooking time: 1 hour.

Chop the onions and stew in butter. Place a layer of the onions on the bottom of an oven-proof dish. On top of this place the cutlets which have been lightly fried on both sides in a little butter. Add another layer of the onions, sprinkle this with some breadcrumbs mixed with the grated cheese. Add the remaining onions and again sprinkle with the breadcrumb-cheese mixture. Moisten with the wine and veal stock. Sprinkle with melted butter, cover and bake in a cool oven, 325° F or Gas Mark 2. Baste frequently with butter.

▣ Maintenon

For 6 *persons:* 6 *veal cutlets, each weighing about* 6 *oz;* ¼ *lb ham;* ¼ *lb mushrooms;* 1 *small truffle;* 2 *tablespoons thick Béchamel;* 1 *egg yolk;* 1 *oz grated Parmesan;* ¼ *pint white wine;* ⅓ *pint Demi-glace with tomato.* Cooking time: 15 minutes.

Poach the mushrooms and, with the truffle and ham, chop up finely. Bind lightly with the *Béchamel*, thickened with egg yolk and seasoned. Fry the seasoned cutlets on both sides in the usual way. Dry one side and arrange a mound of the prepared mixture on it. Sprinkle with grated cheese and butter and brown in the oven. Reduce the pan residue with white wine by half, add the *Demi-glace* and boil for a few minutes. Place the cutlets on a serving dish and pour the sauce around the cutlets.

▣ à la Milanaise

For 6 *persons:* 6 *veal cutlets, each weighing about* 6 *oz;* 1 *egg; white bread-crumbs; grated cheese;* ½ *pint sauce Tomate;* 1 *lb macaroni or spaghetti;* 2 *oz butter; oil.* Cooking time: 12-15 minutes.

Dip the well-trimmed cutlets in seasoned beaten egg mixed with a small spoon of oil, dip in the breadcrumbs mixed with cheese and press them well. Fry till golden brown in half oil and half butter and serve with macaroni *Milanaise* or *spaghetti Milanaise* and *sauce Tomate.* (*See illustration p.* 464).

Côtes de Veau Mireille

For 6 persons: 6 veal cutlets, each weighing about 6 *oz;* 1 *aubergine;* 1 *lb tomatoes;* ½ *pint white wine; butter; oil; garlic;* ¼ *pint veal stock.* Cooking time: 12 minutes.

Fry cutlets in butter. While they are cooking, peel an *aubergine*, slice it, flour the slices and fry them in oil. Remove them and *sauté* the peeled, deseeded and quartered tomatoes in the oil. Season and add chopped parsley and a little crushed garlic. Serve the cutlets, place 2 slices of *aubergine* on each and the tomatoes on top of them. Reduce the pan residue of the cutlets with wine, boil up with a little stock and pour round the cutlets.

▣ en Papillote * *In Paper Bags*

For 6 persons: 6 veal cutlets, each weighing about 6 *oz;* ¾ *lb duxelles;* 12 *thin slices of cooked ham;* ½ *pint sauce Madère;* 6 *sheets of greaseproof paper.* Cooking time: 20-30 minutes.

Fry the cutlets in butter. Cut 6 heart-shaped pieces of greaseproof paper 1½ times the length of the cutlets. Place some *duxelles* in the centre of the paper, then a slice of ham, then the cutlet, then another slice of ham, then more *duxelles*. Fold the paper over, then overlap the joint by small folds, until the contents are completely sealed. Bake in a hot oven, 400° F or Gas Mark 6. Serve immediately with the sauce separately in a sauce-boat. Aluminium foil may be substituted for greaseproof paper.

▣ à la Paysanne

For 6 *persons: 6 veal cutlets, each weighing about* 6 *oz;* 1 *lb carrots;* ½ *lb turnips;* 2 *stalks of celery;* ½ *lb French beans;* ½ *pint veal stock;* 1 *onion.* Cooking time: 25-35 minutes.

Slice the carrots, turnips, celery and onions very thinly and cook in butter in a covered braising pan. Season, flour and brown the cutlets in butter on both sides, place on the vegetables, add stock, cover with lid and simmer till done. When serving add some sliced French beans which have been cooked separately.

▣ à la Provençale

For 6 *persons:* 6 *veal cutlets, each weighing about* 6 *oz;* 1 *large shallot;* 1 *clove of garlic; chopped parsley; a walnut-sized lump of meat glaze;* 2¾ *lb tomatoes; oil.* Cooking time: 40 minutes.

Sauté the cutlets on both sides in oil and when cooked place in a casserole and keep warm. Sweat the chopped shallot briefly in the oil, add the peeled, deseeded and diced tomatoes, season with salt, pepper and crushed garlic, boil up, add the meat glaze and the chopped parsley. Pour tomato mixture over the cutlets and simmer for 35-40 minutes, according to thickness.

▣ Vert-Pré * *with Watercress*

For 6 *persons:* 6 *veal cutlets, each weighing about* 6 *oz;* 1 *lb potatoes;* ¼ *lb Maître d'Hôtel butter; watercress.* Cooking time: 12 minutes.

Coat seasoned cutlets with butter and grill. Place *Maître d'Hôtel* butter on top of grilled cutlets and garnish with watercress and Straw potatoes. (*See illustration p.* 463).

Délices Landais

For 6 persons: 1½ lb fillet of veal; 6 oz purée of foie gras; 12 thick slices of aubergine; 12 *small potatoes;* 6 *croquettes of sweet corn; ¼ lb butter; fresh breadcrumbs.* Cooking time: 8 minutes.

Cut the fillet into 24 thin slices, spread with the *purée* of *foie gras* and sandwich together to form twelve sandwiches. Flour, eggwash, coat with breadcrumbs and fry in butter. Fry the *aubergines* in a separate pan. Poach the peeled tomatoes in a little butter. Place each sandwich of veal on a slice of *aubergine*, arrange a tomato on each and garnish with *croquettes* of sweet corn. Serve brown (*Noisette*) butter separately.

ESCALOPES DE VEAU * *VEAL ESCALOPES*

These average about 4 oz each in weight and are cut from the cushion, leg or fillet. They should be beaten with a moistened cutlet bat to no more than ⅛-inch in thickness.

▣ à l'Anglaise * *Breadcrumbed*

For 6 persons: 6 *veal escalopes, each weighing about* 4 *oz;* 6 *slices of ham;* 1 *egg; white breadcrumbs; butter.* Cooking time: 8-10 minutes.

Cut the *escalopes* from the cushion, flatten well, trim, season, eggwash and coat with breadcrumbs. Fry golden brown in butter on both sides. Garnish alternately with the grilled or fried slices of ham and pour brown butter on top.

▣ à l'Arlésienne

For 6 persons: 6 *veal escalopes, each weighing about* 4 *oz;* 6 *round croûtons;* 2 *small aubergines;* 4 *tomatoes;* 5 *oz stoned green olives;* 2 *fl oz white wine; ¼ pint Demi-glace;* 1 *teaspoon tomato purée;* 1 *clove of garlic;* 1 *oz butter;* 2 *tablespoons olive oil.* Cooking time: 8-10 minutes.

Season and flour the *escalopes* and fry them in half oil and half butter. Place the *escalopes* on *croûtons* on a round dish. Peel and slice the *aubergines*, and fry them in the pan, adding crushed garlic and, after a while, 2 peeled, deseeded and quartered tomatoes. Simmer for a few minutes, add the white wine, reduce by half and add the *Demi-glace*, the tomato *purée* and the blanched olives. Cook for a few minutes longer and arrange this garnish around the *escalopes*. Place a quartered peeled, deseeded and sautéed tomato and a stoned olive on each *escalope*, and sprinkle with chopped parsley.

▣ Chasseur

For 6 persons: 6 *veal escalopes, each weighing about* 4 *oz; ½ lb raw mushrooms;* 1 *shallot; ¼ pint white wine;* 1 *teaspoon tomato purée; ¼ pint Demi-glace; chopped parsley.* Cooking time: 8-10 minutes.

Season and flour the *escalopes* and fry them in half oil and half butter. Remove them and keep warm in a serving dish. Sweat the chopped shallot in the saucepan, add the sliced mushrooms and brown them quickly. Add the white wine, reduce to half, boil up with the *Demi-glace* and tomato *purée* and remove from heat. Add a walnut of butter and a little chopped parsley and pour over the *escalopes*.

Escalopes de Veau Jurassienne

For 6 persons: 12 *veal escalopes, each weighing about* 2 *oz;* ¼ *lb butter;* ½ *lb mushrooms;* 2 *fl oz brandy;* ¼ *pint of cream;* 2 *fl oz Port wine;* 1 *oz beurre manié;* 6 *thin slices of ham;* 6 *thin slices gruyère cheese.*

Fry the *escalopes* in butter, add the sliced mushrooms, cook lightly, drain off the butter and flambé with the brandy. Remove the *escalopes* and keep warm. To make the sauce, add the cream to the mushrooms. Add the Port wine, boil and lightly bind with the *beurre manié*. Butter a porcelain dish, place six *escalopes* in the centre, then the *gruyère* and ham cut to the same size with a cutter. Place the other *escalopes* on top, bake in a hot oven, 400° F or Gas Mark 6, for just sufficient time to heat the cheese, coat with the prepared sauce, sprinkle with chopped parsley and garnish with two Puff pastry crescents.

▣ à la Portugaise

For 6 persons: 6 *veal escalopes, each weighing about* 4 *oz;* 1½ *lb tomatoes;* 1 *shallot;* ¼ *pint white wine;* ¼ *pint Demi-glace; chopped parsley;* 1½ *lb Château potatoes.* Cooking time: 8-10 minutes.

Season and flour the *escalopes* and fry them in butter. Remove and keep warm on a serving dish. Sweat the chopped shallot briefly in the butter. Add the peeled, deseeded and diced tomatoes. Add the white wine and *Demi-glace* and reduce by half. Season, add chopped parsley and pour over the *escalopes*. Garnish the centre of the dish with the *Château* potatoes.

▣ à la Viennoise I * *Wiener Schnitzel I*

For 6 persons: 6 *veal escalopes, each weighing about* 4 *oz;* 1 *peeled sliced lemon;* 3 *hardboiled eggs;* 6 *stoned olives;* 6 *anchovy fillets;* 2 *oz chopped parsley;* 1 *oz capers;* 1 *lemon;* 1 *egg beaten with a little milk;* ½ *lb breadcrumbs;* 2 *fl oz oil;* 3 *oz butter;* 1½ *lb Sauté potatoes.* Cooking time: 8-10 minutes.

Season, eggwash and breadcrumb the *escalopes*. Separate the whites of the hardboiled eggs from the yolks and pass both through a sieve. Cut the anchovy fillets into two lengthwise and halve the lemon. Butter a large oval dish, garnish with a few capers at the edge of the dish, surround the sides of the dish with a band of sieved egg yolks, surround this with a band of sieved egg white, then with finely chopped parsley and lastly with the anchovy fillets thus presenting a pattern of alternate colours. Fry the *escalopes* in oil and arrange these in the centre of the dish with a slice of lemon on each. Squeeze over the juice of the other half lemon, brown the butter and pour over. Serve with the *Sauté* potatoes separately.

▣ à la Viennoise II * *Wiener Schnitzel II*

For 6 persons: 6 *veal escalopes, each weighing about* 4 *oz;* 1 *egg; breadcrumbs;* 3 *oz lard;* 6 *slices of peeled lemon; watercress.* Cooking time: 8-10 minutes.

Cut *escalopes* fairly thick from the cushion. Flatten them with a wooden mallet, until they are quite thin. Season with salt and pepper, dip in beaten egg and coat with breadcrumbs. Fry the *escalopes* in plenty of hot lard, until they are brown, crisp and dry. Arrange on a long dish with the watercress, and place a slice of lemon on each *escalope*. Serve lettuce salad at the same time. (*See illustration p.* 468).

Escalopes de Veau Zingara

For 6 *persons:* 6 *veal escalopes, each weighing about* 4 *oz;* 4 *oz each of pickled ox tongue, cooked ham and mushrooms;* 2 *oz truffle;* ½ *pint Demi-glace flavoured with tomato;* 2 *fl oz Madeira.* Cooking time: 8-10 minutes.

Season and flour the *escalopes*. Fry them in butter until golden all over. Reduce the pan residue with the Madeira, add the *Demi-glace*, and allow to cook gently until well boiled down. Cut the ox tongue, ham, mushrooms and truffle into *julienne*, and heat up in butter. Bind this mixture with the sauce and place a spoonful on each *escalope*. (*See illustration p.* 467).

FILET DE VEAU * *FILLET OF VEAL*

This joint corresponds to the fillet of beef in its composition and method of preparation. In Britain the fillet of veal is often the boned top of the leg which may be roasted, stuffed or sliced into *escalopes*. In France, and elsewhere on the Continent, the fillet of the veal is located under the saddle on either side of the backbone. The preparation and cooking time of both the British and French cuts remain the same. Trim the fillet free of all fat, sinew and skin. Roast in a moderate oven, 375° F or Gas Mark 4-5, allowing 30 minutes per pound. Garnish to taste.

▣ en Croûte * *in a Pastry Case*

For 6 *persons:* 1 *veal fillet, weighing about* 2½ *lb;* ¾ *lb mushrooms;* ½ *lb purée of foie gras;* ½ *pint sauce Madère;* 2 *lb Puff pastry;* 1 *egg yolk.* Cooking time: 1¼ hours.

Slice the mushrooms and cook in butter. Trim and season the meat. Roll out the pastry into a rectangle. The length and width of the Puff pastry will depend upon the length and width of the fillet. Place the fillet in the centre, spread with the *purée* of *foie gras*, then the cooked mushrooms and seal within the pastry shell. The pastry edges should overlap slightly to form a flat seam. Seal the pastry edges well, turn over, cut a few slits in the pastry to allow for the escape of steam and decorate the surface with designs made from the leftover pastry, cut to your own taste and skill. Brush over with beaten egg yolk and place on a slightly oiled baking tray, seam side down. Bake in a moderate oven, 375° F or Gas Mark 4-5. Do not allow the Puff pastry to brown too quickly. If necessary, cover the top with buttered greaseproof paper or cooking foil and remove towards the end to allow the pastry to brown evenly. (*See illustration p.* 463).

▣ Mignon

Proceed as for *Filet Mignon* of beef or pork.

MÉDAILLONS DE FILET DE VEAU * *MEDALLIONS OF VEAL FILLET*

These are small rounds cut from the fillet and resemble *tournedos* in shape.

▣ à l'Armagnac

For 6 *persons:* 1 *veal fillet, weighing about* 2 *lb;* 5 *oz butter;* 2 *fl oz Armagnac;* ½ *pint cream;* 1 *oz meat glaze; juice of* 1 *lemon;* 1½ *lb morels or mushrooms;* 2 *shallots;* 6 *round butter-fried bread croûtons.*

Trim and prepare the fillet in the usual way. Cut into six medallions, season and fry in some of the butter. Drain, place upon the *croûtons* on a serving dish, arrange in a circle and keep warm. Flambé (flame) the cooking pan with the Armagnac, deglaze with the cream, add the meat glaze and simmer for a short while. Remove the pan from the heat and finish the sauce with the remainder of the butter and the lemon juice. Strain. Chop the shallots finely and fry with the morels till cooked. Coat the medallions with the prepared sauce and garnish the centre with the morels.

Médaillons de Filet de Veau aux Champignons * *Medallions of Veal with Mushrooms*

For 6 persons: 12 medallions of veal fillet, each weighing about 3 oz; 12 mushroom caps; 3 oz butter; 1½ lb potatoes; ½ pint veal gravy.

Peel the potatoes, shape *en olives* and fry in butter. Flute and poach the mushrooms. Fry the medallions, arrange tastefully on a serving dish, place a mushroom upon each, mask with the thickened veal gravy and garnish with the potatoes. (*See illustration p. 468*).

FOIE DE VEAU * *CALF'S LIVER*

This is considered the finest variety of animal liver since it is the most tender and has a very mild flavour. It may be cooked either by sautéeing, frying or by grilling. Avoid over-cooking calf's liver otherwise it becomes hard and dry.

⊡ à l'Anglaise

For 6 persons: 12 slices of calf's liver, each weighing about 2 oz; 12 slices streaky bacon; 2 oz butter; chopped parsley. Cooking time: 8-10 minutes.

Season and flour the liver. Fry quickly in butter. Garnish alternately with crispy grilled bacon and sprinkle with chopped parsley. Pour frying butter and bacon fat on top.

⊡ Bercy

For 6 persons: 12 slices of calf's liver, each weighing about 2 oz; 2 oz butter; 6 oz Bercy butter. Cooking time: 8-10 minutes.

Season, flour and fry the liver in butter, garnish with a small pat of *Bercy* butter and sprinkle with chopped parsley.

⊡ à la Bourgeoise

For 6 persons: 2 lb calf's liver; ½ lb streaky bacon; ¼ pint white wine 1 pint brown stock; 24 small onions; 1 lb young round carrots; 1 tablespoon tomato purée; 2 oz lard. Cooking time: 1¾-2 hours.

Skin a half or whole liver thoroughly and lard with thick lardons as for *Beef à la Mode*. Brown all sides in a suitable vessel, pour off fat and reserve this. Add the white wine and brown stock, season, cover with lid and braise for 1 hour. Fry the carrots and onions lightly in the poured-off fat, add to the meat, add the tomato *purée*, recover with a lid and cook together till tender. Finally pour off the stock, reduce by half in a separate saucepan, thicken slightly with cornflour and strain over meat and vegetables.

Foie de Veau en Brochettes * *Calf's Liver on Skewers*

For 6 *persons:* 24 *pieces of calf's liver,* 1½*-inches square and* ¼*-inch thick;* 24 *pieces of streaky bacon,* 1½*-inches square and* ⅛*-inch thick;* ½ *pint of Demi-glace.*

Lightly fry the seasoned liver. Blanch and cool the bacon. Skewer the bacon and liver alternately, eggwash and breadcrumb and grill. Garnish with watercress and Straw potatoes on a serving dish. Serve with the *Demi-glace* or with *Maître d'Hôtel* butter.

◻ à la Piémontaise

For 6 *persons:* 1½ *lb calf's liver;* ¼ *pint white wine;* ¼ *pint Demi-glace;* 6 *oz rice for risotto.* Cooking time: 2-3 minutes.

Skin the liver, cut in very small, thin slices, flour them, shake off surplus and *sauté* quickly in hot butter in a frying pan large enough for all to brown at once; they must remain pink inside. As soon as they are brown place on a sieve to drain. Reduce the frying residue with white wine by half, add the *Demi-glace*, boil up for a few minutes and season well. Toss the drained liver slices in the hot sauce but do not boil. Make a *risotto* garnished with tomato *concassé*, press into a ring mould, turn out on to a serving dish and arrange liver in the centre.

Fricandeau à l'Oseille * *Cushion of Veal with Sorrel*

For 6 *persons:* 2 *lb cushion or rump of veal;* ¼ *lb streaky bacon;* 2 *carrots;* 2 *onions;* 2 *oz butter;* 2 *lb sorrel.* Cooking time: 1½ hours.

The cushion of veal is cut in thick slices of about 2-inches and these are individually larded, or it may be prepared as a whole. Skin, slice and lard the meat, place on a bed of sliced onions and carrots, season, baste with melted butter and brown lightly in a moderate oven, 375° F or Gas Mark 4. Add sufficient good stock to half cover the meat and continue to cook slowly, uncovered, adding a little more stock from time to time. Baste the meat frequently so that it will be nicely glazed. When serving pour the thickened, reduced gravy, from which the fat has been skimmed, over the meat and serve with sorrel *purée.* The sorrel can be replaced by mushroom *purée* or other fine vegetable.

Fricassée de Veau * *Veal Stew*

The *fricassée* is not unlike the *blanquette* and is in fact a variant of it. The meat, ingredients and the cooking time remain constant. The difference lies in the initial method of cooking. Instead of blanching and boiling the meat, stiffen it in butter, i.e. toss it without allowing the flesh to brown. Then dredge with flour, stir, add water or light stock, season, add a *bouquet garni* and cook slowly till tender but not too soft. The further preparation is the same as for *blanquette. Fricassées* and *blanquettes* can be garnished with all the better vegetables, such as young carrots, fresh garden peas, asparagus and celeriac. Sometimes the sauce is slightly coloured with tomato *purée.* These dishes are usually served with buttered rice.

Grenadins de Veau * *Braised Veal Medallions*

These are thick medallions cut from the boned and trimmed loin of veal, larded with fat bacon strips, fried in butter and gently braised for about 15 minutes. Arrange on butter-fried *croûtons* and serve with usual veal garnishes.

Jarret de Veau à la Milanaise * *Milanese Knuckle of Veal*

For 6 persons: 6 pieces of knuckle of veal with the bone, each weighing about ¾ lb; 3 oz butter; mirepoix (carrot, onion, celery); ¾ pint Demi-glace; ¼ pint brown stock; ½ lb green peas; 6 oz rice; 4 tomatoes. Cooking time: 1½ hours.

Ask the butcher to saw the veal knuckle into slices right through the bone. Flour the pieces, and brown both sides well in butter or lard in an ovenproof and lidded casserole dish, adding the *mirepoix*. Next add the *Demi-glace* and brown stock and braise in the oven with the cover on until tender. Garnish the meat with buttered peas, *risotto*, pressed in small moulds and turned out, and sautéed tomatoes. Strain the sauce, skim and season, and serve separately.

NOTE: This is a French recipe. The Italian equivalent "Osso Bucco" is found under the section "Foreign Specialities". (*See illustration p.* 465).

LANGUE DE VEAU * *CALF'S TONGUE*

Calf's tongue must be cooked and skinned with care as it is very delicate.

◘ Dussolier

For 6 persons: 1 large calf's tongue; 2 onions; 2 carrots; 3 shallots; 4 oz gherkins; 1 lb potatoes; 2 fl oz white wine; 1 pint Demi-glace flavoured with tomato; 2 oz butter. Cooking time: 1½ hours.

Put the tongue into a pan of cold water. Bring to the boil and simmer for 15 minutes. Remove the white skin and the root muscle and transfer whole to a fire-proof casserole. Fry the tongue together with the onions, carrots and shallots which are cut into small, regular dice. Moisten with the white wine, reduce it by half, add the *Demi-glace*, season, cover with a lid and braise gently in the oven. When cooked, remove the tongue and keep warm. Skim off the fat from the sauce and add the diced gherkins and chopped herbs. Border a long dish with a ribbon of Duchess potatoes and brown in the oven. Cut the tongue in slices and arrange it in the centre of this border. Cover with the unstrained sauce.

◘ Grillée * *Grilled*

For 6 persons: 1 calf's tongue, weighing about 3 lb; 1 pint sauce Diable.

Cook the tongue in salted water, remove skin, and cut partially but not completely lengthwise, leaving the slices attached at the thick end. Open these outwards, secure with two skewers to prevent the slices from curling, brush with mustard and dip into breadcrumbs. Sprinkle with melted butter and grill, constantly brushing with melted butter. Arrange on a dish, remove skewers, garnish with watercress and serve the *sauce Diable* in a sauce-boat.

◘ à la Romaine

Prepare in the same way as Calf's Tongue *Dussolier* but omitting vegetables and gherkins and replacing the *Demi-glace* by *sauce Romaine*.

LONGUE DE VEAU * *LOIN OF VEAL*

This cut corresponds to the sirloin of beef and may be braised or roasted. Any vegetable garnish is suitable for this dish.

For 6 persons: 1 loin of veal, weighing about 2½ lb; 2 carrots; 2 onions; ½ pint white stock. Cooking time: 1½-2 hours.

Slice the onions and the carrots. In a large heavy frying pan, fry the meat to a light brown colour, remove and fry the sliced vegetables. Place the meat in a large covered braising pan and moisten with the stock. Season, replace the lid and braise in a warm oven, 350° F or Gas Mark 3. When cooked, arrange the drained meat on a serving dish. Skim off all fat from the braising liquor, correct the seasoning, reduce this slightly, strain and pour over the meat. Garnish the dish with any of the following garnishes—*Paysanne, Bouquetière, Financière, Flamande* or *Maraîchère.*

◘ à la Bordelaise

For 6 persons: 1 loin of veal, weighing about 2½ lb; 2 carrots; 2 onions; ½ pint stock; 1¼ lb of boletus mushrooms. Cooking time: 1½-2 hours.

Proceed as above. Arrange on a serving dish and garnish with the mushrooms which have been fried in butter.

◘ du Presbytère

For 25-30 persons: 12 lb boned and trimmed loin of veal with fillets; 1¼ lb each fat and lean pork; ¼ lb Bayonne ham; 4 calves' sweetbreads; ¼ lb uncooked, pickled ox tongue; 2 pints of cream; 3 oz truffles; 4 green capsicums; ¾ pint white wine; mirepoix (turnips, celery, onions); 30 cooked artichokes; 1½ lb mushrooms. Cooking time: 2 hours.

Prepare a forcemeat with the fillets, the pork and ½ pint of the cream. With a sharp knife cut deep pockets into the thick lean part of the loin on the inside of the joint, season and fill these cavities with the forcemeat. Spread the loin with the remaining forcemeat, in preparation for the joint being rolled. Peel the capsicums, deseed and cut into fine *julienne.* Cut the Bayonne ham also into fine *julienne*, mix and sprinkle these over the forcemeat. Pat with a palette knife to secure the *julienne* in position. Stiffen the sweetbreads in butter and allow them to cool. Lard the sweetbreads with small lardons of pickled ox tongue and 2 oz of the truffle. Arrange the sweetbreads end to end upon the forcemeat, roll the loin up tightly, tie with string, and braise on top of the *mirepoix*. Remove meat and keep warm. Deglaze the pan with the white wine and veal stock, reduce to half, add 1 pint of cream, cook to a light sauce consistency, correct seasoning, strain and add 1 oz of chopped truffle. Keep hot. Heat the cooked artichokes in butter. Chop the mushrooms finely, toss in butter in a saucepan, add ½ pint cream; reduce to a thick consistency and fill into the artichoke bottoms. Prepare 30 small *Macaire* potatoes, stuff with a *purée* of spinach and garnish with some finely diced Bayonne ham. Arrange the loin on a serving tray, garnish with the prepared artichokes and potatoes, lightly mask with some of the sauce and serve the rest in a sauce-boat.

Noisettes de Veau Sautées * *Shallow Fried Veal Loin Cutlets*

For 6 persons: 6 veal noisettes or boned loin of veal cutlets, each weighing about 5 oz; ¼ lb butter; ¼ pint white wine; 2 oz flour; 12 leaves of sage. Cooking time: about 20 minutes.

Season, flour and fry the *noisettes* of veal in some of the butter and transfer to a heated casserole. Moisten with the wine, place two sage leaves upon each steak, cover with a lid and simmer for 15 minutes. Remove the cutlets to a dish and garnish with the *Château* or *Paysanne* potatoes. Toss the rest of the butter into the cooking liquor and strain over the veal. (*See illustration p.* 469).

NOIX DE VEAU * *CUSHION OF VEAL*

The cushion is used for cutting into *escalopes*, veal olives, and *grenadins*. It is also popular cooked whole, especially when there are a large number of persons to be served. In this case it should be skinned, larded, and braised. It may also be roasted, but braising is better.

▣ à l'Ancienne

For 15 *persons:* 4½ *lb cushion of veal;* 2 *carrots;* 2 *onions;* 1 *lb Fine Forcemeat quenelles;* ⅛ *lb sliced mushrooms;* 30 *cocks' combs and* 30 *chicken livers;* ⅛ *pint sauce Suprême;* ½ *lb bacon.* Cooking time: 3 hours.

Lard a small, prime cushion of veal. Place in a *cocotte* with the sliced vegetables and moisten with very little stock. Braise very slowly in a warm oven, 350° F or Gas Mark 3. Prepare a garnish of Fine Forcemeat quenelles, sautéed mushrooms, cocks' combs and chicken livers, all bound with the *sauce Suprême.* Let the veal cool slightly. Using a small sharp knife, make a round incision about ⅝-inch from the edge—do not cut right through to the bottom—and remove a large cylinder of meat to form a hollow which is then filled with the garnish. Make a lid with a slice cut from the top of the meat which has been removed so that the veal appears to be intact. Arrange decoratively on a large dish. Skim all the fat from the cooking liquid, strain and pour over the veal. Slice the remains of the inner cylinder and place around the meat.

▣ Braisée à la Breban

For 6 *persons:* 2½ *lb cushion of veal;* ¼ *lb streaky bacon;* 2 *carrots;* 2 *onions;* ¼ *pint white wine; veal stock;* 1 *lb noodles;* 6 *slices cooked pickled ox tongue;* 2 *sweet red peppers;* 2 *oz grated cheese;* 1 *pint sauce Soubise;* ¼ *lb mushrooms;* 6 *fluted mushroom caps; butter.* Cooking time: 1½-2 hours.

Lard the cushion of veal, brown it in butter, and braise it on a layer of sliced carrots and onions in white wine and stock. Poach the noodles in boiling salted water. Drain and *sauté* them in butter. Season the noodles with salt and pepper, add the red peppers which have been cut in strips and simmered in butter, and finally add the grated cheese. Mix the *sauce Soubise* with the sliced mushrooms sautéed in butter, and heat the tongue slices in a little veal gravy. Serve the veal in a round dish, and arrange the noodles in a border. Place slices of tongue around the border of the dish and garnish them with a fluted mushroom cap. Serve the *sauce Soubise* at the same time.

▣ Braisée à la Gendarme

For 12 *persons:* 1 *cushion of veal, weighing about* 4-5 *lb;* 10 *oz lardons, cut from fresh belly pork;* ½ *lb cooked lean ham;* 1 *small truffle, cut into short bâtons;* 2 *lb Duchess potatoes;* 1¼ *lb turned, glazed carrots;* 1 *lb turned, glazed turnips;* 1 *lb peas;* 1 *pint sauce Soubise;* 12 *slices truffle;* 12 *small, Short pastry tartlet cases.* Cooking time: 1¾ hours.

Trim the cushion of veal and lard with the pork lardons, strips of ham and truffle. Tie up, fry in butter, then braise the veal slowly in its own juices with frequent basting. Prepare potato *croustades* with the Duchess potatoes. Eggwash and bake these cases then fill them with *bouquets* of carrots, turnips and peas. Fill the tartlet cases with the *sauce Soubise* and place a slice of truffle on each. When cooked, remove the meat. Slice and arrange the veal upon a long dish, garnish with the prepared potato and tartlet cases. Skim and strain the cooking liquid and serve in a sauce-boat.

Noix de Veau Judic

For 6 persons: 2½ lb cushion of veal; 6 braised heads of lettuce; 6 Duchess potatoes; 3 oz bacon fat; ½ pint sauce Madère. Cooking time: 60-70 minutes.

Lard the cushion of veal with small strips of fat bacon, and roast it slowly in butter in the oven in a casserole, with frequent basting. When cooked, cut the veal in slices and arrange the meat on a long dish. Garnish with the Duchess potatoes and braised heads of lettuce, cut in half and folded in two, and covered with a little *sauce Madère*. Serve the rest of the sauce in a sauce-boat. For special dinner parties complete the garnish with cocks' combs and slices of truffle.

⊡ à la Nivernaise

For 6 persons: 2½ lb cushion of veal; 2 pints brown stock; 1 lb small new carrots; 1 lb turnips, shaped like large olives; 30 small onions; 2 lb small new potatoes; ¼ lb fat bacon; ¼ lb butter. Cooking time: 70-75 minutes.

Lard the meat and braise it slowly in brown stock. Prepare, cook and glaze the carrots, onions and turnips. Boil the new potatoes, skin, and toss them in butter. When cooked, remove the meat, drain and keep warm. Thicken the veal gravy with potato flour and strain. Slice the veal, arrange the meat on a long dish, and garnish with all the cooked vegetables except the potatoes. Cover the meat with a little gravy, and serve the rest of the gravy and the potatoes separately. You may also garnish the dish with sautéed tomatoes and French beans, cooked in butter, in place of the glazed carrots. (*See illustration p.* 461).

⊡ Orloff

For 6 persons: a cushion of veal, weighing about 2½ lb; 1 pint onion purée; 4 oz duxelles; 1 pint sauce Béchamel; 2 egg yolks; 2 oz grated gruyère cheese. Cooking time: 1½-2 hours.

Braise the veal in a casserole, remove when cooked and allow to cool a little. Mix the onion *purée* and the *duxelles* together. Bind the *Béchamel* with the yolks. Slice the braised cushion and spread each slice of veal with the onion preparation and shape back to its original form, sandwiching each slice together. Place in a *gratin* dish, coat with *Béchamel*, sprinkle with the *gruyère* and a few dried breadcrumbs. Sprinkle with melted butter and gratinate in a very hot oven, 450° F or Gas Mark 8. Boil, skim and strain the braising liquor and serve separately in a sauce-boat.

Noix de Veau Reine Margot

For 6 persons: 2½ lb cushion of veal; ¼ lb lean bacon; ¼ lb fat bacon; ¼ pint white wine; 1 pint thickened veal gravy; 1 lb Duchess potatoes; 1 lb peas; 6 medallions of cooked pickled ox tongue.

Lard the cushion with the fat bacon and braise with the wine and gravy. Mould the Duchess potatoes into the form of small *dariole* moulds, eggwash and breadcrumb, mark with a round cutter for the lid and deep fry. Remove lid and scoop out the potatoes, leaving a shell of ¼-inch thick. Prepare the peas *à la Paysanne* with the addition of the diced lean bacon. Heat the tongue medallions in a little butter. Boil, skim and strain the braising liquor. Slice the veal and arrange on a long dish. Fill the potato cases with the peas, using the medallions of tongue as lids, then garnish around the veal. Serve the sauce in sauce-boats.

Pains de Foie de Veau à la Française * *Calf's Liver Loaf*

This dish can be made in individual or large moulds and is equally delicious hot or cold.

For 6 persons: 1 lb calf's liver; ¼ pint thick Béchamel; 2 fl oz double cream; 2 egg yolks; ½ pint Demi-glace. Cooking time: 18-20 minutes.

Remove all sinews from the liver, pass it through the finest blade of the mincer to form a *purée*, mix well with the cold *Béchamel* and cream, season with salt, pepper and fold in the egg yolks. Pass this mixture through a fine sieve. Place in buttered *baba* moulds and poach in the oven in a water-bath, making sure that the water does not boil. When cooked, a needle stuck into the centre will come out dry and hot. Let the moulds rest for a few minutes, then turn out and coat with the *Demi-glace*. Serve the liver loaves with any desired vegetable *purée*.

PAUPIETTES DE VEAU * *VEAL OLIVES*

▣ en Brochettes * *on Skewers*

For 6 persons: 12 very small thin veal escalopes, each weighing about 2 oz; 12 thin rashers of bacon; 1 lb French beans; 1 lb potatoes; 6 small tomatoes; butter. Cooking time: 10-12 minutes.

Season and roll up very thin *escalopes* and wrap up each in a thin rasher of bacon. Fix them on skewers, brush with oil or clarified butter and grill them on both sides. Arrange the *paupiettes* on French beans tossed in butter.

▣ aux Champignons * *with Mushrooms*

For 6 persons: 6 escalopes of veal, each weighing about 4 oz; ½ lb sausage meat; 1 carrot; 1 onion; 1 bouquet garni; ½ pint veal stock; 1 teaspoon concentrated tomato purée; ¾ lb mushrooms. Cooking time: 1¼ hours.

Flatten the *escalopes*, trim them, spread with the sausage meat, roll up and tie. Brown well, place on a bed of fried, sliced carrot and onion in a casserole, add the veal stock and tomato *purée*, season, cover with lid and cook slowly in the oven till cooked. Remove the string from the *paupiettes* and pour over the stock which has been strained and thickened with cornflour. Garnish with quartered, sautéed mushrooms.

Paupiettes de Veau à la Grecque

For 6 persons: 6 thin veal escalopes; 6 small, thin slices of raw ham; ¼ lb chopped onions; 3 oz breadcrumbs; chopped parsley; 1 onion; 1 carrot; ½ pint veal stock; ½ lb rice. Cooking time: about 1½ hours.

Flatten the *escalopes,* season and spread with the chopped onions, cooked in butter and mixed with breadcrumbs and chopped parsley. Place a thin slice of raw ham on each, roll up the *escalopes* and tie with string at both ends. Brown them lightly in butter with round slices of onion and carrot. Moisten with the veal stock and braise in the oven basting frequently. Arrange the *paupiettes* on a mound of *Riz à la Grecque* (see Rice) and cover with the gravy, well skimmed and lightly thickened with cornflour.

⊡ Marie-Louise

For 6 persons: 6 veal escalopes; ½ lb lean veal; 4 oz Milk panada; 1 egg white; 3 fl oz thick cream; 6 cooked artichoke bottoms; 4 oz mushroom purée; 3 oz onion purée; ½ pint veal stock.

Pass the lean veal several times through the finest blade of the mincer and mix it with the panada, the egg white, cream and requisite seasoning to make forcemeat. Pass through a sieve and mix thoroughly. Flatten the *escalopes* slightly, cover with the forcemeat, roll up, tie and braise with the stock in the usual way. Remove the *escalopes* when cooked and keep warm. Thicken the stock slightly and strain it. Mix the onion and mushroom *purées* and fill the artichoke bottoms with this mixture after cooking them in butter. Arrange the veal olives on the artichoke bottoms, coat lightly with the prepared sauce and serve the rest separately.

⊡ Richelieu

For 6 persons: 6 veal escalopes, each weighing about 4 oz; ½ lb sausage meat; 1 onion; 1 carrot; 3 large, firm, halved, braised heads of lettuce; 6 large mushroom caps; 3 large tomatoes; duxelles; breadcrumbs; 2 fl oz Madeira; ½ pint light Demi-glace; 1 lb Château potatoes. Cooking time: 75 minutes.

Spread the *escalopes* with the sausage meat, roll up, tie, brown and place in a casserole on a bed of fried carrot and onion slices. Reduce with the Madeira, add the *Demi-glace* and braise slowly till done. Halve and scoop out the tomatoes and fill with the *duxelles,* fill mushroom caps with same mixture, sprinkle with breadcrumbs and cook in the oven. Dress the veal olives on the tomatoes, garnish with the mushrooms, lettuce and *Château* potatoes and pour the strained braising gravy on top.

Pieds de Veau à la Rouennaise * *Calf's Feet Rouennaise*

For 6 persons: 3 calf's feet; 1 lb fine sausage meat; 3 oz chopped onion; 1 tablespoon chopped parsley; 1 egg; 12 small pieces pig's caul; oil; 1 pint sauce Rouennaise. Cooking time: 8-12 minutes.

Calf's feet used for making aspic can be used for this recipe. Completely bone the feet and cut in half crosswise. They are already split lengthwise. Cook the chopped onion in butter. Make forcemeat with the onion, parsley, egg and sausage meat and season well. Take a square piece of pig's caul, put a little forcemeat in the middle, place a piece of calf's foot on top, cover with forcemeat, wrap in the caul and coat with beaten egg and white breadcrumbs. Sprinkle with oil and grill at high heat or bake in oven. Serve with the *sauce Rouennaise.*

▲ *Noix de Veau à la Nivernaise, p. 458*

Selle de Veau Braisée, p. 479 ▼

▲ Carré de Veau Belle Jardinière, p. 446

Rognonnade de Veau, p. 478 ▼

▲ Côtes de Veau Vert-Pré, p. 449

Filet de Veau en Croûte, p. 452 ▼

 ▲ *Saltimbocca alla Romana,* *p. 483*

Côtes de Veau à la Milanaise, *p. 448* ▼

▲ *Involtini alla Morandi, p. 482*

Jarret de Veau à la Milanaise, p. 455 ▼

▲ *Tendrons de Veau à la Paysanne, p. 479*

Côtes de Veau Chenonceaux, p. 447 ▼

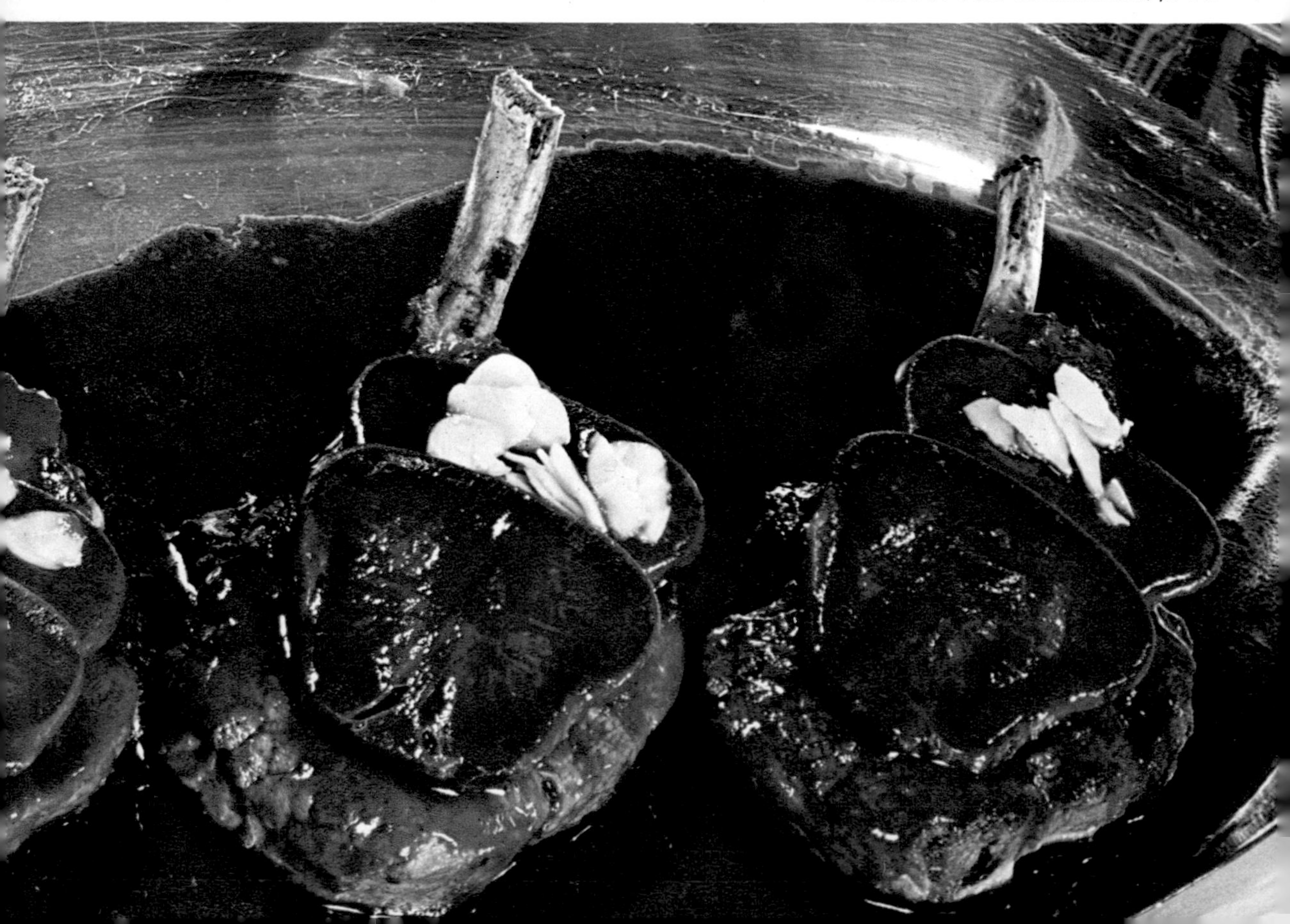

▲ Sauté de Veau Marengo, p. 479

Escalopes de Veau Zingara, p. 452 ▼

▲ Escalopes de Ris de Veau Graziella, p. 476

Ris de Veau Braisés Comtesse, p. 474 ▼

▲ *Cervelles de Veau au Beurre Noir, p. 410*

Rognons de Veau à la Bordelaise, p. 477 ▼

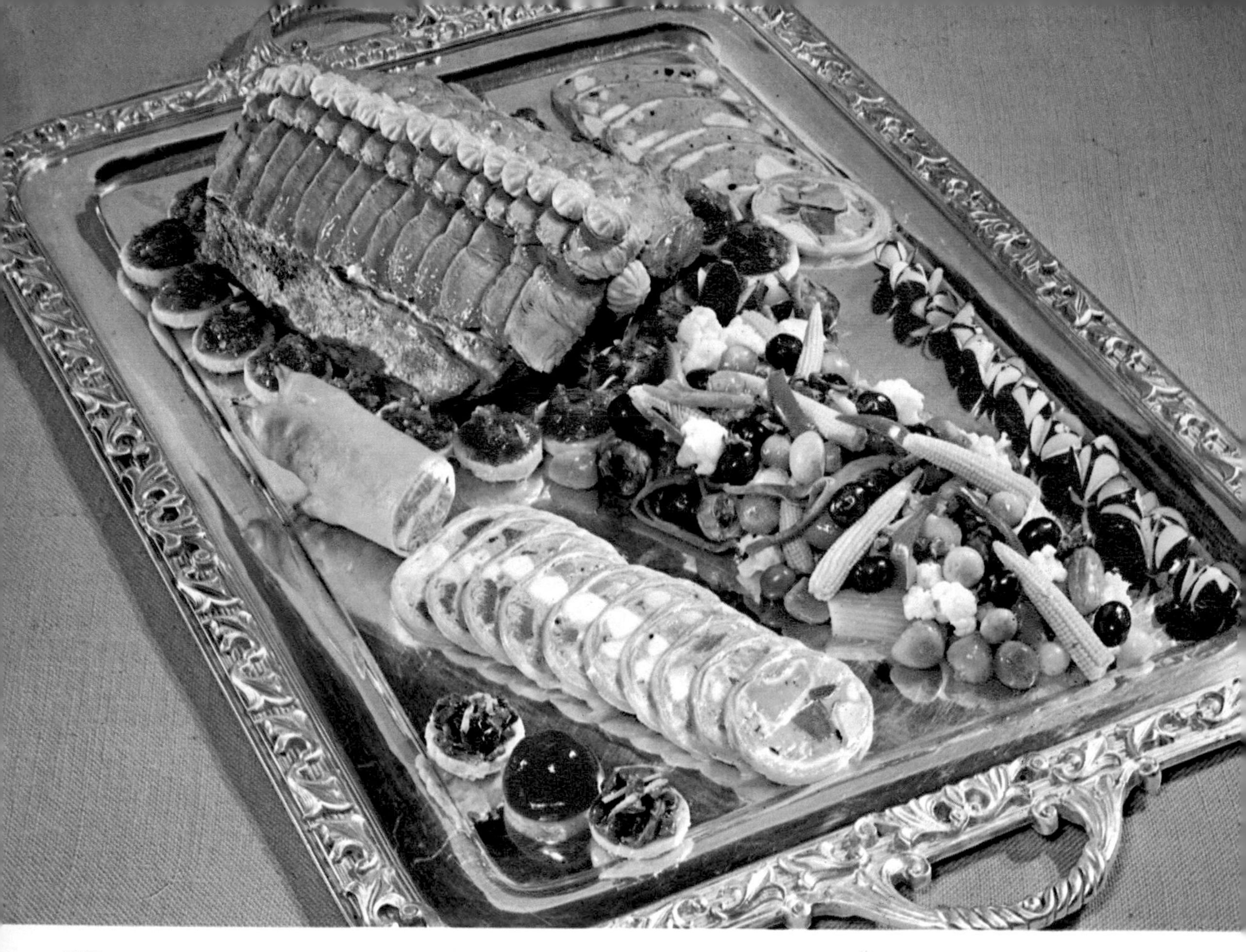

▲ *Two presentations of Cold Saddle of Veal, p. 481* ▼

POITRINE DE VEAU * *BREAST OF VEAL*

This cut is usually boned, rolled and roasted or braised. It must be absolutely fresh.

▣ Farcie * *Stuffed*

For 6 persons: 2½ *lb breast of veal;* 1 *lb sausage meat;* 1 *large chopped onion;* 1 *teaspoon chopped herbs;* 1 *egg;* 2 *carrots;* 2 *onions;* 1 *oz lard;* 1 *pint stock.* Cooking time: about 2 hours.

Remove the flat bones from the breast and cut open from end to end in the middle of the thick side, so as to form a pocket. Mix the sausage meat with the herbs, the cold onions previously cooked in butter, and 1 egg. Season the mixture, place in opening and sew it up. Grease a braising pan with the lard, place the meat on a bed of sliced onions and carrots, salt lightly, brush the meat with a little melted butter and place it in the oven. When well browned, add the stock, cover and finish cooking at moderate heat, 375° F or Gas Mark 4, basting from time to time. When cooked remove from pan, carve with a sharp knife, remove fat from stock, thicken it slightly with cornflour and pour it over meat. Serve with any desired vegetable garnish.

▣ Napolitaine

For 6 persons: 2 *lb breast of veal;* 1 *lb minced veal;* 4 *oz bread cubes;* ¾ *lb uncooked spinach;* 2 *eggs;* 2 *large tomatoes;* 1 *pint veal gravy.* Cooking time: 1½-2 hours.

Remove the flat bones from the breast. Cut it open lengthwise from end to end in the middle of the thick side, so as to form a pocket. Cut the bread into small squares, soak in milk and squeeze out excess moisture. Peel, deseed and cut the tomatoes into eighths. Prepare the stuffing with the veal which has been minced with the finest blade of the mincing machine, mix with the soaked bread cubes, the eggs, the uncooked spinach cut in strips, the tomatoes and season with salt and pepper. Fill into the breast pocket and sew the opening together. Place the stuffed veal breast in a braising pan in a hot oven, 400° F or Gas Mark 6, with a little lard on top and baste from time to time. When the veal is a good brown colour, pour off the lard, add the veal gravy, cover the pan with the lid and braise at moderate heat, 375° F or Gas Mark 4, until done. Remove the meat and allow it to rest for a while before carving. Strain the gravy and thicken with a little arrowroot or potato flour. Carve the veal into good sized slices, and garnish with buttered carrots and *Dauphine* potatoes.

RIS DE VEAU * *CALVES' SWEETBREADS*

Sweetbreads are considered a delicacy which may constitute a main dish by themselves or they may be used as a garnish or as *entrées*. They should be fresh, tender and white, with no trace of blood and the best varieties come from young calves or lambs which have been fed entirely on a milk diet. Sweetbreads may be larded with fat bacon or studded with pieces of truffle, ham or tongue. They are highly perishable being offal and thus should be cooked and eaten as quickly as possible after purchase.

Preparation

Soak in cold water overnight, cover with fresh cold water and bring to the boil, simmer for 5 minutes and refresh under cold water, trim away any irrelevant matter such as cartilage, tubes and tougher membrane. If being used for *escalopes*, place the prepared sweetbreads on a tray with another on top. Compress the trays by placing a weight on top. Methods of preparation include poaching, braising, grilling, shallow frying and as *escalopes*.

Ris de Veau Braisés Clamart

For 6 persons: 2½ lb veal sweetbreads; 4 oz fat bacon; 2 onions; 2 carrots; 3 oz butter; 1½ lb freshly shelled green peas. Cooking time: 35-45 minutes.

Soak the sweetbreads till they are very white, then blanch for 3-4 minutes, just long enough to stiffen the outside. Remove all gristly parts but do not skin. Place between 2 boards or trays under a weight for a few hours in order to crush the fibres and prevent contraction during cooking. Lard the sweetbreads, place them in a buttered casserole dish on a bed of sliced, sautéed onions and carrots. Season lightly, sprinkle with melted butter, half fill with strong veal stock (sufficient to cover the vegetables at least) and braise, covered with a lid in a moderate oven, 375° F or Gas Mark 4, until well browned. Baste several times to glaze them. When cooked, remove and keep warm on a serving dish. Skim the fat from the stock, thicken lightly with cornflour, boil, strain and pour over sweetbreads. Garnish with boiled peas tossed in butter.

◻ Braisés Comtesse

For 6 persons: 2½ lb veal sweetbreads; 6 braised lettuces; 12 small oval veal quenelles; 1 small truffle. Cooking time: 35-45 minutes.

Prepare and braise the sweetbreads as indicated. Garnish with little braised half-lettuces and veal panada *quenelles*. Place a truffle on top of the *quenelles*. Remove the fat from the braising liquid, thicken with a little cornflour and pour over the sweetbreads. (*See illustration p.* 470).

◻ Demidoff

For 6 persons: 2½ lb veal sweetbreads; ¼ lb fat bacon; ¼ pint veal stock; ½ lb carrots; 2 small onions; 3 sticks celery; 3 oz butter; 2 fl oz Madeira; 3-4 tablespoons veal stock; 1 small truffle. Cooking time: 35-40 minutes.

Prepare and braise the sweetbreads as for *Braisés Clamart* but only until half cooked. Cut vegetables into thin, half-moon shaped slices, simmer them in a casserole with butter and as soon as they start to colour reduce with the Madeira. Add to this a few tablespoons of stock, boil up, season, and add the truffle, cut in half-moon slices. Add the whole to the half-cooked sweetbreads and cook all together till done. Serve the sweetbreads surrounded with this garnish, including the reduced stock.

◻ à la Financière

For 6 persons: 2½ lb veal sweetbreads; 6 oz cooked small veal quenelles; 5 oz small mushroom caps; 3 oz stoned, blanched olives; 2 cocks' combs; 2 cocks' livers; 12 small truffle slices; ½ pint sauce Madère.

Prepare and braise the sweetbreads in the usual way. Remove the sweetbreads to a serving dish and keep warm. Strain the braising liquor, skim off fat and reduce considerably. Add the *sauce Madère* and the previously heated garnish, mix well, heat thoroughly and arrange round the sweetbreads before serving.

◻ Grand-Mère

For 6 persons: 2½ lb veal sweetbreads; ¼ lb fat bacon; ¼ lb pickled tongue; ½ lb carrot; ¼ lb turnip; 1 medium-sized onion; ½ lb raw mushrooms; ¼ pint white wine; 2 oz butter.

Press the blanched and cooled sweetbreads lightly and lard with bacon and tongue. Cut the carrots, turnips, onion and mushrooms into dice about ¼-inch thick and simmer in butter till almost cooked. Brown the sweetbreads in butter and place in a fire-proof casserole on top of the vegetables. Pour the butter out of the pan in which the sweetbreads were browned, reduce the residue with white wine and pour over the sweetbreads with a little stock till they are half covered. Season with salt and pepper, cover the casserole and braise at moderate heat, 375° F or Gas Mark 4, for 30-35 minutes. When cooked remove the sweetbreads, slice diagonally, dress slices in serving casserole so that they overlap and pour the vegetables and a little reduced stock on top. Cover with lid and serve very hot.

Ris de Veau à la Jardinière

For 6 persons: 2½ lb sweetbreads; ¼ lb fat bacon; 1 onion; 1 carrot; ½ pint veal stock; 4 oz each French beans, peas, small new carrots and turnips; 3 oz butter. Cooking time: 45 minutes.

Soak the sweetbreads in cold water for several hours. Blanch, refresh and trim them of all nerves, stringy and non-edible parts. Do not remove the outer skin. Place them under a weight for an hour or so to prevent the meat from shrinking when cooking. Lard the sweetbreads with thin lardons of fat bacon and braise on a layer of carrots and onion cut in thick slices, moistened with the stock. Remove the sweetbreads when cooked and arrange on a warmed serving dish. Garnish with the vegetables, seasoned and tossed in butter. Remove the fat from the braising liquor, reduce, thicken with a little cornflour, strain and pour over the sweetbreads.

⊡ à la Toulousaine * *Escalopes of Calves' Sweetbreads*

Made in the same way as veal sweetbreads *à la Financière*, except that they are braised white and the garnish is bound only with veal *Velouté* thickened with cream and egg yolk. Sweetbreads can be served with many garnishes, for example, spinach *purée*, mushrooms, morels, boletus, French beans, green pea *purée*, glazed onions, glazed chestnuts and chestnut *purée*.

ESCALOPES DE RIS DE VEAU

⊡ à la Crème * *in Cream Sauce*

For 6 persons: 2½ lb veal sweetbreads; 3 oz butter; ¼ pint cream; ½ lb mushrooms; brandy; juice of ½ lemon. Cooking time: 12-15 minutes.

Poach the sweetbreads for 7-8 minutes, cool, trim and slice about ½-inch thick. Season and flour the slices and fry them in butter on both sides till cooked. Remove, serve in a dish and keep warm. Reduce the pan residue with cream to a thick sauce, season with salt and pepper, a dash of brandy and a little lemon juice. Add the sliced, previously poached mushrooms, boil up again and pour over the sweetbreads.

⊡ à la Florentine

For 6 persons: 2½ lb veal sweetbreads; 2 lb leaf spinach; ¼ lb butter; 1 pint sauce Mornay; 2 oz grated cheese. Cooking time: about 10 minutes.

Blanch sweetbreads for 7-8 minutes, cool, cut in thick slices, season and flour them and fry in hot butter on both sides. *Sauté* the boiled, well drained spinach in butter, season with salt, pepper and grated nutmeg and put in a fire-proof dish. Arrange sweetbreads on it, coat with *sauce Mornay*, sprinkle with the grated cheese and butter and brown in a hot oven or under the grill.

Escalopes de Ris de Veau Graziella

For 6 persons: 2½ lb veal sweetbreads; 2 medium-sized tomatoes; ¼ pint onion purée; 4 large poached, fluted mushroom caps; 4 croûtons; 2 oz butter; 1 lb Noisette potatoes; ¼ pint sauce Madère. Cooking time: about 10 minutes.

Blanch the sweetbreads and, when cool, trim and cut them into thick slices. Season, flour, and fry them on both sides in butter until golden all over. Place them on *croûtons* and garnish them with grilled half tomatoes, stuffed with thick onion *purée*, and place a fluted mushroom cap on each. Cover with *sauce Madère* and serve the potatoes separately. (*See illustration p.* 470).

⊡ Jérôme

For 6 persons: 6 veal sweetbreads; 1 egg; ½ lb breadcrumbs; ¼ lb butter; 1¼ lb morels or mushrooms in Cream sauce; 1 lb Straw potatoes; ¼ pint sauce Béchamel; 2 egg yolks; 4 oz grated cheese. Cooking time: about 10 minutes.

Blanch, refresh and cut each sweetbread through the centre thus producing 12 medallions. Trim each to the same size, season, flour, egg and breadcrumb. Fry the sweetbreads golden brown in butter, remove and keep warm. Bring the *Béchamel* to the boil, bind with the yolks, remove from heat, stir in the cheese, add a little paprika, cover and allow to cool. When cold, mould the *Béchamel* mixture into 12 medallions, egg and breadcrumb these twice and deep fry. Place the cheese *croquettes* on a round dish then a veal medallion upon each. Serve the morels in a separate dish.

⊡ Maréchale

For 6 persons: 2½ lb veal sweetbreads; 1 egg; white breadcrumbs; 3 oz butter; 2 bundles green asparagus tips; 2 truffle slices.

Break off the woody parts of the asparagus stalks, cut off heads about 2-inches long and tie in bundles. Cut remainder into ½-inch pieces, boil together in salt water and drain well. Blanch the sweetbreads for 7 minutes cool, trim and cut in 12 equal slices. Season, dip in flour and beaten egg, breadcrumb them and press down breadcrumbs. Fry slices brown on both sides in butter. Arrange in a ring on a round dish and place a truffle slice on each. Toss the chopped asparagus in butter, season, and place in the centre. Place asparagus bundles on top, season lightly with salt and pour a little melted butter over them.

ROGNONS DE VEAU * *CALVES' KIDNEYS*

Calves' kidneys when purchased should be encased in firm white veal suet. The flesh should be a light rosy brown colour, firm and sweet smelling. They may be first soaked in cold, salted water and then blanched briefly. Veal kidneys are particularly tender and should be cooked for as short a time as possible, otherwise overcooking will toughen this delicate meat and make it unpalatable. The centre should remain slightly pink. If it is to be grilled leave a thin layer of fat over the whole kidney and cut in two lengthwise. This rich, bland fat is excellent when grilled. For other preparations the kidney is denuded of all fat, the internal nerves and membranes are removed and it is cut into ¼-inch slices.

Rognons de Veau à la Berrichonne

For 6 persons: 2 lb veal kidneys; ½ lb mushrooms; 24 small onions; 5 oz streaky bacon; ½ pint sauce Bordelaise without ox marrow. Cooking time of kidneys: 2-3 minutes.

Cut bacon into large dice, blanch, fry and remove from pan. Quarter the mushrooms and *sauté* in the same fat, browning them slightly. Glaze the onions in the usual way. Slice the kidneys thinly and *sauté* them, leaving them very pink inside. Mix with the bacon, mushrooms and onions. Boil up the pan residue with the sauce, toss the other ingredients in the hot sauce (do not boil), place in a deep dish or *timbale* and sprinkle with chopped parsley.

▣ à la Bordelaise

For 6 persons: 2 lb veal kidneys; 2 lb boletus or mushrooms; ¼ pint red wine; ½ pint sauce Bordelaise; 6-12 slices blanched ox marrow; parsley. Cooking time: 2-3 minutes.

Sauté the kidneys (see above), keeping the insides very pink. Slice the boletus or mushrooms, *sauté* them in half butter and half oil in a separate frying pan, mix with the kidneys and place in a deep dish. Put the red wine into the pan in which the kidneys were sautéed and reduce almost completely. Add the *sauce Bordelaise*, boil up briefly and pour over the kidneys. Place the hot, blanched marrow on top. (*See illustration p.* 471).

▣ Grand-Mère

For 6 persons: 2 lb veal kidney; 1 lb carrot; ½ lb turnip; ½ lb onions; ½ lb French beans; 3 oz butter; ¼ pint veal stock. Cooking time of kidneys: 7-8 minutes.

Cut the carrots, white turnips and onions into matchsticks, blanch for a few minutes, drain and simmer in butter. Add the sliced, boiled French beans and when all the vegetables are tender place them in the bottom of a fire-proof casserole. Leave a little fat round the kidneys, halve them lengthwise, and remove white inside parts. Season, flour and fry them like a veal cutlet but make sure that they are still pink inside. Place them on top of the cooked vegetables. Reduce the pan residue with stock, remove from heat, toss with a piece of butter and pour over the kidneys.

▣ Montpensier

For 6 persons: 2 lb veal kidneys; ¾ lb asparagus tips; 6 slices of truffle; 2 fl oz Madeira or sherry; 2 oz meat glaze; parsley; 5 oz butter. Cooking time: 5-6 minutes.

Cut the kidneys into thick round slices, season and fry in about 3 oz of the butter. Remove to a serving dish and keep warm. Deglaze the pan with the Madeira, add the meat glaze, allow this to melt and blend in the remaining 2 oz of the butter and some chopped parsley. Arrange the kidneys in a circle, overlapping each other, mask over with the sauce, place a truffle slice on top of each. Cook the asparagus tips in the usual fashion, toss gently in melted butter for a few minutes and with these garnish the centre of the dish.

Rognons de Veau Sautés * *Shallow Fried Kidneys*

For 6 persons: 2 lb veal kidneys.

Prepare and *sauté* the kidneys in the same way as ox kidneys. Slice thinly, fry in butter in a very hot pan for 2-3 minutes and then toss in *sauce Madère* or *Demi-glace*. Do not allow the kidneys to boil in the sauce as this will toughen the meat.

Rognonnade de Veau * *Roast Loin of Veal with Kidney*

Roll a loin of veal with the kidneys inside and tie securely. Roast and braise in the usual manner. (*See illustration p.* 462).

SAUTÉ DE VEAU * *BRAISED VEAL SLICES*

Pieces of veal, usually cut from the neck, shoulder or knuckle, cooked as a stew or casserole.

⊡ Bourguignonne

For 6 persons: 2½ *lb boned shoulder of veal;* 20 *small onions;* ½ *lb mushrooms;* 1 *bottle red wine;* 1 *bouquet garni;* 1 *heaped tablespoon flour;* 3 *oz butter; a little pure fat.* Cooking time: 1½-2 hours.

Remove sinews and cut into 1-inch cubes. Brown well in the fat, pour the excess fat off, add red wine and enough stock to cover everything. Season, add a *bouquet garni*, cover and braise slowly in a warm oven, 350° F or Gas Mark 3, till tender. Glaze the onions in butter. If the mushrooms are big halve them and brown them in butter. When the meat is tender, take out the *bouquet garni*, bind with the flour which has been kneaded with a little butter, improve the colour with a little caramel, add onions and mushrooms, braise a few minutes longer and serve sprinkled with chopped parsley and garnished with fried, heartshaped *croûtons*.

⊡ Chasseur

For 6 persons: 2½ *lb boned shoulder of veal;* ½ *lb mushrooms;* 1 *lb potatoes;* 2 *oz flour;* 24 *small onions;* ¼ *pint white wine;* 2 *pints brown stock;* 2 *oz fat;* 1 *tablespoon tomato purée.* Cooking time: 1½-2 hours.

Remove sinews and cut meat into 1-inch cubes. Brown well in half butter and half oil, sprinkle with the flour and lightly brown this a little. Mix in the tomato *purée* and moisten with the white wine and enough stock to cover the meat. Season lightly, cover and allow to simmer in a warm oven, 350° F or Gas Mark 3. After cooking for an hour add the small onions and sliced mushrooms and mix with the meat. Place on top the peeled potatoes which have been cut *en olives* with butter and let it finish cooking in the oven.

⊡ à l'Indienne * *Curried*

For 6 persons: 2½ *lb lean veal;* 1½ *oz curry powder;* ¼ *lb onion;* ½ *pint Béchamel;* 1 *bouquet garni;* ½ *lb plainly boiled rice;* 1¾ *pints stock.* Cooking time: 1½-2 hours.

Lightly brown the chopped onions in butter and add the veal which has been cut into ½-inch cubes. Continue to fry for a short time then add the curry powder. Cook together for 5 minutes, moisten with the stock, add the *bouquet garni* and simmer until tender. Separate the meat from the cooking liquor, drain and keep warm. Add the *Béchamel* to the cooking liquor, reduce and strain the sauce back over the meat; toss together. Arrange in a porcelain serving dish and serve the rice separately.

Sauté de Veau Marengo

For 6 persons: 2½ *lb shoulder of veal;* 2 *oz flour;* 1 *clove of garlic;* ¼ *pint white wine;* 1 *pint stock;* ½ *lb tomatoes;* 24 *small onions;* ½ *lb mushrooms;* 1 *bouquet garni;* 6 *heart-shaped croûtons, fried in oil.* Cooking time: 1½-2 hours.

Cut up the meat into pieces of about 2 oz, brown well in half butter and half oil, sprinkle with the flour, brown this a little and add the crushed garlic. Reduce with white wine. Barely cover with stock, season, add the herbs, cover and braise in a warm oven, 350° F or Gas Mark 3. When the veal is almost cooked, take out the meat with a fork and place in a clean casserole and strain the sauce over it. Add the peeled, deseeded and diced tomatoes lightly tossed in oil, the glazed onions and the cleaned, raw mushrooms and finish braising together. Serve with chopped parsley and the *croûtons*. (*See illustration p.* 467).

⊡ Mireille

For 6 persons: 2½ *lb shoulder of veal;* 1 *crushed clove of garlic;* 2 *fl oz white wine;* 2 *oz tomato purée;* 1½ *lb fresh tomatoes;* ½ *lb mushrooms;* 1 *bouquet garni; salt and pepper;* 1 *lb fried, diced croûtons;* 12 *stoned olives;* 2 *aubergines.* Cooking time: 1½-2 hours.

Dice the meat into 1-inch cubes. Peel, quarter and gently stew the tomatoes in butter and proceed in the same method as for Veal *Marengo* but garnish with the stoned olives and *aubergines* which have been peeled, cut into ¼-inch slices, floured and deep fried.

Selle de Veau Braisée * *Braised Saddle of Veal*

For 14-15 *persons:* 1 *medium-sized saddle of veal.* Cooking time: 3 hours.

The saddle consists of the entire back of the animal. Remove the kidneys and cook separately about half an hour before the saddle is completely braised. The saddle should be skinned and trimmed, larded with a layer of fat, the flaps of trimmed flank folded under the *filets mignons*, tied up and the whole braised slowly. Braise in a warm oven, 350° F or Gas Mark 3, or at moderate heat, 375° F or Gas Mark 4-5. The saddle should be basted frequently to keep the joint moist. When cooked, it can be served with a garnish of young vegetables, for example, *Orloff, Judic, Paysanne,* and *Bouquetière*. It is also excellent cold, garnished with small mounds of vegetable salad or with marinated asparagus tips. (*See illustration p.* 461).

Tendrons de Veau à la Paysanne * *Breast of Veal*

For 6 persons: 3½ *lb breast of veal;* 2 *carrots;* 2 *onions;* 1 *bouquet garni;* 2 *oz fat;* 2 *pints veal gravy;* 2 *oz butter. Garnish:* ½ *lb small onions;* ¾ *lb carrots;* ¾ *lb turnips;* 2 *sticks celery.* Cooking time: 2 hours.

Cut veal into strips between the ribs leaving meat on the bones. Place the *mirepoix* in a deep dish. The breast of veal should be fried lightly in hot fat and placed on top of the vegetables and then half covered with the veal gravy. Season and braise in the oven, basting very frequently. When tender remove the meat to a serving dish. For the garnish, thinly slice the onions, carrots, turnips and celery and cook them till glazed with a little melted butter. Remove the fat from the braising liquor, strain over meat and sprinkle the garnish around the meat. (*See illustration p.* 466).

TÊTE DE VEAU * *CALF'S HEAD*

When boiling a calf's head it is essential to ensure that the flesh remains as white as possible. Bone the head, place in a bowl of cold water and allow it to soak for several hours. Change the water frequently. Cover with lemon-acidulated cold water and bring to the boil, skim, continue boiling for 5 minutes then place under cold running water until quite cold.

Trim the head carefully free of all mucus, skin and hair, and cut into 2-inch square pieces; trim the tongue and the ears. Prepare a *blanc* as follows: Take 1 gallon of water, add 1 oz of salt, the juice of one lemon and bring to the boil. Blend 2 oz of flour with some cold water and whisk into the boiling water. Add an onion stuck with a clove, 1 carrot, a *bouquet garni* and twelve white peppercorns.

Add the calf's head to the *blanc*, cover the calf's head with a piece of muslin but cook without a lid, since the liquid rises in the same way as boiling milk. Bring to the boil and simmer until tender—about 2 hours. Boil the tongue with the head. The head must be tender but still firm. Allow to cool in the cooking liquor to prevent discoloration.

To serve, remove the head, wash in tepid water and heat in white veal stock. Arrange in a serving dish, garnish with the sliced tongue, sliced brain (which should have been poached separately) and fresh parsley. Serve with a sauce-boat of *sauce Ravigote.*

▣ Normande

For 6 persons: 2½ lb cooked calf's head; ½ lb mushrooms; 12 small heart-shaped croûtons, fried in butter; 1 pint sauce Velouté made with veal stock.

Cut the mushrooms into scallops and cook in the sauce. Add the calf's head, cut into 1-inch cubes; heat gently together. Arrange in a serving dish and garnish with the *croûtons.*

▣ en Tortue * *with Turtle Flavour*

For 6 persons: 2½ lb calf's head; 12 mushroom caps; 12 small veal force-meat quenelles; 12 stoned olives; 6 very small gherkins; 1 pint Demi-glace tomatée; 6 French-fried eggs; 6 heart-shaped fried croûtons; 6 truffle slices; 2 fl oz Madeira; 1 teaspoon turtle herbs.

Infuse turtle herbs in the hot Madeira and strain through a cloth. Heat the poached mushrooms, veal *quenelles*, truffle slices, blanched olives and gherkins in the Madeira. Add the hot, well drained calf's head cut in squares and bind with *Demi-glace*. Arrange everything on an oval serving dish, garnish with the eggs and *croûtons* and serve very hot.

NOTE: Turtle herbs may be bought but one can make the infusion with a pinch each of marjoram, rosemary, basil and a very little sage. Pour a little hot *bouillon* (here Madeira) on top, covering and allowing to simmer. Do not allow to boil. Strain infusion through a cloth.

▣ Vinaigrette

For 6 persons: 6 oz boned calf's head per person; 1 small cooked veal tongue; 1 poached veal brains; parsley; 2 hardboiled eggs; 1 pint sauce Vinaigrette; 1 hors d'œuvre dish containing chopped onions, chopped parsley and capers.

Serve the pieces of calf's head with slices of tongue and brains and garnish with the parsley. Serve separately in a sauce-boat, *sauce Vinaigrette* which has been enriched with chopped hardboiled egg and a little of the cooking liquor. Also serve separately the *hors d'œuvre* dish containing the chopped herbs.

LE VEAU FROID * *COLD VEAL*

CÔTES DE VEAU * *VEAL CUTLETS*

The chops are cooked and then coated in a delicately flavoured aspic when cold.

▣ en Bellevue

For 6 *persons:* 6 *veal cutlets, each weighing about* 6 *oz;* 2 *lb small new carrots;* 24 *small onions;* 3 *small tomatoes;* 1 *quart aspic jelly; chervil.* Cooking time: 40-45 minutes.

Cook to a golden brown the trimmed and seasoned cutlets in a pan. Cook the onions and carrots in butter so that everything is cooked at the same time. Place the cutlets in a dish and garnish with the carrots and onions. Decorate each cutlet with half a tomato and chervil. Skim off the fat from the jelly, clarify if necessary and allow it to cool. Glaze the cutlets and vegetables with the aspic. Serve cold.

▣ Molière

For 6 *persons:* 6 *veal cutlets;* 3 *medium-sized tomatoes;* 1½ *lb cauliflower;* 6 *slices of truffle;* 1 *slice of cooked, pickled ox tongue;* 1 *hardboiled egg;* ¼ *pint Mayonnaise;* 1 *pint aspic.*

Lightly fry the veal cutlets in butter and put under a weight to cool. Cut the cauliflower into sprigs and cook to a firm texture in salted water. Set aside to become cold. Prepare some small discs of tongue, truffle and egg white for decorating cutlets. Peel and halve the tomatoes, deseed them and marinate for a short period. Fill with sprigs of cauliflower and mask with *sauce Mayonnaise* and place a disc of tongue topped with truffle on each. Decorate the cutlets with the prepared garnish and glaze with aspic. Coat a round dish with a thin film aspic and when set, arrange the cutlets, bones to the centre, with a sprig of parsley and surround with the tomatoes. (*See illustration p.* 469).

Noix de Veau Glacée Grand-Mère * *Veal in Aspic*

For 12 *persons:* 4½ *lb cushion of veal;* ½ *lb larding bacon;* 2 *oz butter;* ½ *pint white wine;* 2 *pints veal stock;* ½ *pint strong aspic;* 2 *lb carrots;* 1 *lb turnips;* ½ *lb onions;* ½ *lb French beans.* Cooking time: 1¾ hours.

Brown the larded cushion well in butter, pour off all the butter, add white wine and stock, cover and braise. After 1 hour add the carrots, turnips and onions, cut like large, thick matches and browned in butter. Cook together till done. Slice beans diagonally and cook separately, adding them at the last moment. Place the veal with the vegetables, aspic and braising liquor which has been strained and reduced slightly in a deep serving dish and leave to stand till quite cold. Wash off the fat on the surface quickly with a little hot water and serve veal as it is, in the aspic.

Selle de Veau Froide * *Cold Saddle of Veal*

Saddle of veal is excellent cold, garnished with small *timbales* of vegetable salad or with marinated green asparagus heads or tips. Roast or braise the joint and allow to become cold. Remove meat from the bone and cut into slices. Reform joint, and glaze with aspic. Decorate to taste. (*See illustrations p.* 472).

FOREIGN SPECIALITIES

Involtini alla Morandi * *Veal Olives*

For 10 *persons:* 20 *thin escalopes of veal, each weighing about* 1 *oz;* 20 *slices of uncooked lean ham;* ¼ *lb gruyère cheese;* 20 *truffle slices;* 10 *lettuces;* 1 *lb of Riz à la Grecque;* ½ *pint Marsala.*

Flatten the *escalopes*, place in the centre a slice each of ham, truffle and cheese, roll into *paupiettes* (veal olives) and fry in butter until golden brown. Moisten with the Marsala previously reduced to half, add a spoonful of veal stock, cover and simmer for 10 minutes. Dress and garnish with the *Laitues braisés* (Braised lettuce) and *Riz à la Grecque* (Greek style rice). Strain the sauce over the meat. (*See illustration p.* 465). (*Italy*)

Mixed Grill

For 6 *persons:* 6 *small lamb cutlets;* 6 *slices of veal liver, each weighing about* 3 *oz;* 3 *lambs' kidneys, sliced lengthwise;* 6 *small pork sausages;* 6 *slices lean bacon;* 6 *large mushrooms;* 6 *small tomatoes.* Cooking time: 6-8 minutes.

Grill each piece and arrange on a serving dish. Garnish with mushrooms, grilled tomatoes and some watercress. Serve separately fried or Straw potatoes and *Maître d'Hôtel* butter. (*Great Britain*)

Osso Buco alla Milanese * *Braised Knuckle of Veal*

For 10 *persons:* 10 *pieces of knuckle of veal, sawn through and including the bone, each weighing about* 7 *oz;* 2 *oz butter;* 2 *fl oz cooking oil;* 2 *oz carrot;* 2 *oz celery;* 2 *oz onion; grated zest of* ½ *a lemon;* 2 *oz tomato purée;* 1 *quart stock;* 2 *oz flour;* ½ *pint white wine;* 1 *clove of garlic.* Cooking time: 1½ hours.

Flour the veal and lightly colour in the oil and butter. Add the *mirepoix* and continue frying till lightly browned. Moisten with the wine, add the tomato *purée*, season and reduce; add the stock and simmer until tender. Now add the lemon zest, garlic and chopped parsley. If desired, lightly thicken the cooking liquor with a little arrowroot. Dress and serve with a plain or saffron savoury rice. (*Italy*)

Piccata à la Milanaise * *Original Italian Recipe*

For 10 *persons:* 20 *veal escalopes, each weighing about* 2 *oz;* 2 *fl oz cooking oil;* ¼ *lb butter;* 1 *oz chopped parsley;* 4 *fl oz white wine.* Cooking time: 5-10 minutes.

Flatten, season and flour *escalopes*, colour quickly in the oil and 1 oz of the butter. Add the wine and gently simmer. Arrange the *escalopes* on a serving dish with the cooking liquor. Coat with *Noisette* butter and sprinkle with the chopped parsley. (*Italy*)

Piccata à la Milanaise * *French Method*

For 10 *persons:* 30 *small escalopes of veal, each weighing about* 1 *oz;* 3 *eggs;* ¼ *pint oil;* 1 *oz grated Parmesan cheese; a little flour.*

Break and beat the eggs, season with salt, pepper and the cheese. Flatten and flour the *escalopes*, dip in the egg and shallow fry in the oil to a golden colour. Dress upon *Risotto alla Milanese* or on *spaghetti au Beurre.* (*Italy*)

Saltimbocca alla Romana

For 10 persons: 2¼ *lb top loin fillet of veal;* 10 *slices of uncooked, lean ham;* 10 *sage leaves;* ¼ *lb butter;* 2 *fl oz oil;* ⅛ *pint white wine.*

Cut the fillet into 20 thin steaks, flatten with a cutlet bat, place a slice of ham and a sage leaf in the centre of each *escalope*. Sandwich together with another *escalope* and skewer with cocktail sticks. Season, flour and quickly fry in the oil. Remove the meat to a dish, remove the cocktail sticks and dress overlapping each other. Add the butter to the pan, then the wine, boil to blend together and strain over the meat. (*See illustration p.* 464).

(*Italy*)

Scaloppine al Marsala * *Escalopes with Marsala*

For 10 *persons:* 20 *escalopes of veal, each weighing about* 2 *oz;* 2 *oz flour;* ¼ *pint Marsala;* ¼ *lb butter;* 2 *fl oz cooking oil.*

Flatten the *escalopes*, season, flour and fry quickly in the oil and butter. Remove the *escalopes*, when cooked, to a dish. Reduce the cooking liquor mixed with the Marsala by half, season and strain over the meat. The reduced gravy may also be thickened with a little flour and butter (*beurre manié*) if necessary. (*Italy*)

Scaloppine alla Valdostana

For 10 *persons:* 10 *veal escalopes, each weighing about* 3 *oz;* 1 *beaten egg;* ½ *lb sliced boletus or mushrooms;* ½ *lb gruyère cheese;* ¼ *pint oil;* 5 *oz butter;* 10 *stuffed aubergines;* 10 *stuffed tomatoes;* 10 *Fondant potatoes.*

Flatten the *escalopes*, season, flour and eggwash. Colour quickly in the oil. Arrange the *escalopes* in a porcelain dish, place the *boletus* on the *escalopes* with a slice of cheese and cook in hot oven, 425° F or Gas Mark 7, until the cheese melts. Garnish with the vegetables and pour over this some *Noisette* butter. (*Italy*)

Mutton and Lamb

Lamb is from the animal when it is less than a year old, after that it is sold as mutton. Lamb is seasonable from March till September, but in the prime when 6-12 weeks old, from May till July. It is on the market from the end of December to March but is then scarce and expensive. Chilled and frozen lamb is available all the year round. Lamb is nearly always of good quality and has a fine delicate, flavour. Choose lamb which has fine, firm-grained flesh, is light pink in colour and has brittle, creamy-white fat. In a young animal the cut bones are moist and red and the leg joint rather jagged.

Mutton is usually sold in larger joints than lamb and it is just as tasty and digestible as long as it does not come from too old an animal. It is seasonable all the year round. *Southdown* mutton is famed for its high quality and so also is the French *Pré-Salé* (from sheep being reared on salt marshes or near the sea). When choosing mutton it should be a dark red colour with firm flesh and creamy fat. Small boned mutton is generally sweeter and finer in texture than large boned.

Mutton and lamb cuts for grilling are—cutlets, chops and kidneys; for roasting—leg, saddle and shoulder; for stewing and making pies—scrag, shoulder, rough cuts, pluck and feet. Although lamb can be prepared in exactly the same way as mutton, there are many dishes for which only lamb is suitable. For example, there are far more ways of preparing lamb than mutton cutlets.

APPROXIMATE COOKING TIMES

CUTS	TIME	TEMPERATURE
Roast Shoulder (Mutton)	20 mins per lb+20 mins	These cuts are cooked in a moderate oven, 375° F or Gas Mark 4-5.
Braised Shoulder (Mutton)	30 mins per lb	
Leg of Lamb	20 mins per lb+10 mins	
Leg of Mutton	15 mins per lb+20 mins	
Rack or Best-End of Mutton	15 mins per lb+20 mins	
Cutlets of Mutton	6-8 mins each side	
Cutlets of Lamb	10 mins each side	
Rack or Best-End of Lamb	20 mins per lb+20 mins	
Saddle of Mutton	30 mins per lb	
Stewed Mutton	1½-2 hours	

LE MOUTON * *MUTTON*

Baron de Mouton * *Baron of Mutton*

This joint comprises the two legs and the saddle and is always roasted. It is served with thin gravy which in certain circumstances may be lightly thickened with arrowroot. The usual garnishes are *Bouquetière, Floriste, Portugaise, Provençale* and *Richelieu.*

Carré de Mouton * *Loin of Mutton*

This is the six middle cutlets roasted in a piece. Skin, vertebrae and sinews are removed, the surplus fat is trimmed away, the bones trimmed and scraped, thus representing six unsevered cutlets. These joints are roasted and served with the same garnishes as applicable to the Baron.

Cervelles de Mouton * *Sheep's Brains*

Same preparation as for ox-brain and calf's brains and the same garnishes.

CÔTELETTES DE MOUTON * *MUTTON CUTLETS*

Loin chops are cut from the loin of the animal; chump chops from the broad end of the loin, and cutlets from the best end of neck.

⊡ à l'Anglaise * *Breadcrumbed*

Per person: 1 *cutlet, weighing about* 6 *oz.* Cooking time: 8 minutes.

Season and flour the cutlets, dip them in beaten egg to which a drop of oil has been added and turn in white breadcrumbs. Fry a nice brown on both sides in butter, keeping them slightly underdone, and serve with any desired vegetable garnish.

⊡ Champvallon

For 6 persons: 6 thick mutton cutlets, cut from the neck end; 3 lb potatoes; ½ lb. onions; 2 oz butter; stock. Cooking time: about 2 hours.

Season the cutlets and brown them on both sides. Place them in a sufficiently large oval baking dish and cover with sliced potatoes, mixed with sliced onions. Season and fill right up with stock. Place in a moderate oven, 375° F or Gas Mark 4-5, without covering and cook slowly. The cutlets should be very soft and the potatoes should have a slight crust.

⊡ aux Choux de Bruxelles * *with Brussels Sprouts*

For 6 persons: 6 cutlets; 2 lb Brussels sprouts; butter.

Fry the cutlets in butter, arrange in a ring on a round dish and arrange the sprouts, tossed in butter, in the centre.

Côtelettes au Cresson * *Cutlets with Watercress*

Per person: 1 *cutlet, weighing about* 6 *oz.* Cooking time: 8 minutes.

Have the cutlets cut rather thick, trim them and trim the bone. Lightly oil or grease both sides, season and place on hot grill. Cook on both sides, but keep them underdone. Arrange them on a hot dish, put paper frills on the bones and garnish with watercress.

▣ Montglas

For 6 *persons:* 6 *cutlets, each weighing about* 6 *oz;* 1 *lb duxelles; dried breadcrumbs;* 2 *oz melted butter;* ½ *pint Demi-glace.*

Fry the cutlets on one side only, spread the *duxelles* on the cooked side dome fashion, place on a buttered tray, sprinkle with the crumbs and melted butter and cook in a very hot oven, 450° F or Gas Mark 8 until both cooked and gratinated. Arrange in a circle overlapping each other and pour the sauce round the cutlets.

▣ Sévillane

For 6 *persons:* 6 *cutlets;* 2 *lb tomatoes;* 6 *oz green olives;* ¾ *pint Demi-glace;* 1 *small clove garlic; butter; oil.* Cooking time: 8 minutes.

Peel and quarter the tomatoes, seed them, season and *sauté* in oil to which a little crushed garlic has been added. Blanch the stoned olives, simmer them with a little *Demi-glace* and mix with the tomatoes. Fry the cutlets, arrange them on a round dish, fill the middle with the tomato and olive mixture and sprinkle chopped parsley on the latter. Serve *Demi-glace* strongly flavoured with tomato separately.

Daube de Mouton à la Provençale * *Mutton Stew*

For 8 *persons:* 3½ *lb shoulder of mutton;* 4 *sheep's trotters;* 5 *oz fat bacon;* 5 *oz lean bacon;* 3 *bacon rinds;* 1½ *lb tomatoes;* 2 *carrots;* 2 *onions;* 1 *bottle red wine; bouquet garni;* ½ *pint oil.* Cooking time: 4-5 hours.

Bone the shoulder, cut in squares of about 2 oz, lard each piece with fat bacon and marinate for 24 hours with the red wine, oil, sliced onions, carrots and *bouquet garni.* Place the meat in a pie *terrine*, add a little chopped onion, a crushed clove of garlic, diced lean bacon, the thoroughly blanched and boned sheep's trotters, the blanched rinds and the bunch of herbs. Season, strain marinade on top, add the quartered tomatoes, place lid on *terrine* and seal hermetically. Cook in a moderate oven, 375° F or Gas Mark 4, and skim off fat before serving.

ÉPAULE DE MOUTON * *SHOULDER OF MUTTON*

This is an excellent joint for roasting and may be divided into two or three pieces if it is a large shoulder.

▣ Boulangère

For 10 *persons:* 1 *shoulder, weighing about* 4 *lb;* 4 *lb potatoes:* 3 *onions;* 1 *pint of roast gravy or stock.* Cooking time: 30 minutes per lb.

Half roast the shoulder, remove, arrange the sliced potatoes and shredded onions in the dish. Season, add the stock, replace the shoulder and finish cooking in a warm oven, 350° F or Gas Mark 3. Serve with the potatoes under the meat.

Épaule de Mouton Ménagère

For 10 *persons:* 1 *shoulder of mutton, weighing about* 4 *lb;* 1 *large chopped onion;* 2 *tablespoons chopped herbs;* 3 *carrots;* 20 *small onions;* 2½ *lb potatoes;* 1 *clove garlic;* 1 *lb sausage meat.* Cooking time: 30 minutes per lb.

Mix the sausage meat with the herbs, the chopped onion cooked in butter and seasoning, spread on the shoulder, roll up and tie. Brown the shoulder in fat, add the garlic, the quartered carrots and the onions, brown them slightly and add stock so that the meat is half covered. Cover and braise in a warm oven, 350° F or Gas Mark 3. After 2 hours quarter the potatoes, brown them in fat and add to shoulder. When everything is cooked, remove string from shoulder, slice, arrange and garnish with the potatoes, carrots, onions, and pour gravy on top after skimming off the fat.

◘ aux Navets * *with Turnips*

For 10 *persons:* 1 *shoulder, weighing about* 4 *lb;* 5 *lb turnips;* 40 *small onions.* Cooking time: 2-2¼ hours.

Braise the shoulder. Cut the turnips into *bâtons*, toss them in butter and simmer till done with a little gravy from the shoulder. Cook the onions in butter and glaze them. Slice the shoulder, garnish with turnips and onions and pour the gravy on top after skimming off fat and thickening slightly with cornflour.

Épigrammes de Mouton Saint-Germain

For 6 *persons: about* 3½ *lb breast of mutton;* 1 *bouquet garni;* 2 *eggs; dried breadcrumbs;* 1 *carrot; piece of celery;* 1 *onion;* 1 *lb of green pea purée;* ½ *pint sauce Béarnaise.* Cooking time: 2 hours.

Cover the breast of mutton with plenty of water, bring to the boil and skim. Add the *bouquet garni*, an onion stuck with a clove, carrot and celery stalk and simmer till tender. Remove meat and pull out all the bones. Place meat on a tray, cover with another tray and place a heavy weight on top and allow to become cold. Cut and trim into heart or cutlet shapes, egg and breadcrumb, grill or deep fry. Garnish with green pea *purée*. Serve the sauce in a sauce-boat, separately.

Filet de Mouton * *Boned Loin*

This is the saddle split in half lengthwise, boned, rolled and tied then roasted or braised. Garnishes as applicable to the leg and shoulder are usual.

Filets Mignons de Mouton * *Mutton Fillets*

These are the two long tender fillets which lie along the underneath part of the saddle against the backbone. They can be prepared and served in the same way as *tournedos*. They may also be marinated and treated as Roedeer flesh to which there is a great similarity.

Fressure de Mouton * *Sheep's Pluck*

The pluck includes the offal such as lights (lungs), liver and heart. Dice the lungs coarsely if you intend using them and slice the heart. Brown in good fat, dust with flour, brown it lightly, season and add 2 quartered lemons and 1 *bouquet garni*. Add water or red wine and a crushed clove of garlic and braise for 1½ hours. At the last moment add the sliced, floured liver (fried underdone), and do not boil again or the liver will become hard. Quartered, fried potatoes can be added to this *ragoût* as to others. Serve sprinkled with chopped parsley.

GIGOT DE MOUTON * *LEG OF MUTTON*

The leg is usually divided into two; the shank, which is used for boiling and stewing, and the fillet, which may be roasted or sliced and grilled.

▣ à l'Anglaise * *Boiled*

For 10-12 *persons:* 1 *leg of mutton, weighing about* 5 *lb;* 1 *lb carrots;* 2 *small heads of cabbage;* 1 *lb French beans;* 2 *lb potatoes;* 2 *oz capers*. Cooking time: 1½-1¾ hours.

Trim the leg. Put it in a large pot of boiling, salted water. Cook slowly skimming regularly. Cook carrots and turnips, shaped like small *Château* potatoes, and the cabbage tied with string in the same water. Cook the French beans and the potatoes separately. When the meat is done, prepare *sauce aux Câpres* with the stock. Serve the leg of mutton garnished with the vegetables and hand round the boiled potatoes and the *sauce aux Câpres*.

▣ Boulangère

For 10 *persons:* 1 *leg of mutton, weighing about* 5 *lb;* 4 *lb potatoes;* 4 *large onions;* ¼ *lb butter*. Cooking time: 2-2½ hours.

Trim off excess fat from the leg, season, and roast it in a fairly large baking dish in a moderate oven, 375° F or Gas Mark 4. After half an hour, place thinly sliced onions and potatoes in the roasting pan under the meat. Finish cooking, basting frequently with the dripping and the butter. Mutton is usually preferred well done in Britain. In France the cooking time is shorter since the meat is preferred rather underdone. As it is almost impossible to obtain a gravy from the meat, since the potatoes absorb all the juice, make a little gravy with the bones and trimmings. (*See illustration p.* 490).

▣ Bretonne

For 6 *persons:* 1 *leg of mutton, weighing about* 3 *lb;* 3 *cloves of garlic;* 1 *lb haricot beans;* ½ *pint sauce Tomate;* ¼ *lb onions; parsley*. Cooking time: 1½ hours.

Rub the joint all over with the peeled garlic cloves. Roast the leg as above. Chop the onions and brown in part of the poured-off roasting fat. Add the *sauce Tomate*, boil up briefly, add the boiled, well-drained haricot or *flageolet* beans, season, add the remainder of the roasting fat and toss carefully. Remove the beans by straining, sprinkle with a little chopped parsley and serve in a separate vegetable dish. Skim off the fat from the sauce, strain again and serve separately.

▲ *Noisettes de Mouton, p. 494*

Carré d'Agneau Persillé, p. 497 

Selle d'Agneau à la Française, p. 501

Gigot de Mouton Boulangère, p. 488 ▼

▲ Côtelettes d'Agneau Montmorency, p. 498

Mutton Chops, p. 505 ▼

▲ *Côtelettes d'Agneau Saint-Michel, p. 499*

Côtelettes d'Agneau Cyrano, p. 497 ▼

Gigot de Mouton Soubise * *Mutton with Onion Sauce*

For 12 persons: 1 *leg of mutton, weighing about 5 lb;* 2 *onions;* 2 *carrots;* 1 *pint stock;* 3 *oz tomato purée;* 1 *oz cornflour;* 1 *lb onion purée.* Cooking time: 2¼-2½ hours.

Trim off excess fat from the leg. Melt some butter in a Dutch oven and brown the leg of mutton together with the sliced onions and carrots. Pour over the stock, season, cover with the lid and bake in a moderate oven, 375° F or Gas Mark 4. Remove the leg of mutton, strain off the gravy into a saucepan. Replace the leg of mutton in the Dutch oven and roast for 15 minutes to give it a good brown colour. Meanwhile make the sauce. Skim off the fat from gravy, reduce by half and thicken with tomato *purée* and the cornflour, previously mixed with some cold water. Serve the *purée Soubise* and the sauce separately.

Haricot de Mouton * *Mutton Stew*

Same method of preparation as for *Navarin* of mutton (*see below*), but with the addition, a few minutes before completion of cooking, of half a pound of cooked white haricot beans or *flageolets.*

LANGUE DE MOUTON * *SHEEP'S TONGUE*

Use the same proportions and proceed in the same way as for Calves Tongues (*p.* 455).

◘ à la Purée de Marrons * *with Chestnut Purée*

For 4 *persons:* 6 *sheep's tongues;* 2 *onions;* 2 *carrots;* 1 *bouquet garni;* 2 *lb chestnuts.* Cooking time: 1¼-1½ hours.

Blanch tongues thoroughly, cool and skin them and braise in the same way as calf's tongue. When cooked slice thinly lengthwise, dress on chestnut *purée* and pour the slightly thickened, strained gravy on top. Almost all recipes for lambs' tongues are also suitable for sheep's tongues.

Navarin * *Stew*

For 6 *persons:* 2½ *lb shoulder, breast or neck of mutton;* 24 *small onions;* ½ *lb carrots;* ½ *lb turnips;* 1 *lb small new potatoes;* 2 *tablespoons tomato purée;* 1 *oz flour;* 1 *bouquet garni;* 1 *clove of garlic.* Cooking time: 2½ hours.

Trim off excess fat from meat, cut into 2-inch cubes and brown in fat in a fire-proof casserole. Pour off most of the fat, sprinkle the meat with the flour, fry it a light brown and add the crushed garlic. Add water so that the meat is just covered, season, add the *bouquet garni* and the tomato *purée* cover and braise slowly for 1½ hours. Then add the onions, the carrots and turnips cut in *bâtons* and braise slowly for another 45 minutes. Remove fat from sauce, add new potatoes in season, otherwise turned old ones and continue to braise slowly on top of the stove so that everything is cooked together. If necessary skim off fat again and serve sprinkled with chopped parsley.

NOISETTES DE MOUTON * *BONED MUTTON CHOPS*

Noisettes or boned mutton chops are slices cut from the boned saddle, weighing about 2 oz. They are trimmed and the superfluous fat is cut off. They are sautéed or grilled, often placed on *croûtons* of the same shape and served with garnishes like *tournedos*. (*See illustration p.* 489).

⊡ Capucine

For 6 persons: 12 *noisettes, each weighing about* 2 *oz;* 12 *large heads of mushrooms;* 6 *oz duxelles;* ¼ *pint thick Béchamel; butter;* 12 *croûtons.* Cooking time: 4-5 minutes.

Bind the *duxelles* with the *Béchamel*, season, complete with a little butter and fill the large mushroom heads with this mixture after grilling them. *Sauté* the *noisettes* in butter, dress them on *croûtons* and garnish with the filled mushroom heads.

⊡ Giralda

For 6 persons: 12 *noisettes, each weighing about* 2 *oz;* 3 *red capsicums;* ¼ *pint Frying batter;* ½ *lb risotto;* ½ *lb raw ham;* 2 *fl oz Marsala;* ½ *pint Demi-glace;* 24 *stoned, blanched green olives.* Cooking time: 4-5 minutes.

Cut the ham into small dice, fry and mix with the *risotto.* Form into twelve small heart shaped bases and arrange on a buttered dish. Peel, deseed and cut the capsicums into quarters, lightly flour, dip into Frying batter, *Pâte à Frire*, and deep fry. Fry the *noisettes* and arrange upon the rice cases. Deglaze the pan with the Marsala, add the *Demi-glace*, boil, skim and add the olives. Mask the *noisettes* with sauce and garnish with the capiscums.

Pieds et Paquets à la Marseillaise * *Stuffed Tripe with Sheep's Trotters*

For 6 persons: 6 *sheep's trotters;* 6 *pieces tripe,* 6*-inches square;* ½ *lb tripe;* ¼ *lb lean bacon;* ¼ *lb green or unsmoked bacon;* 2 *cloves garlic;* 1 *bunch of parsley;* ¼ *lb chopped fresh pork;* 1 *bouquet garni;* 1 *onion;* 2 *shallots;* 2 *carrots;* ½ *pint white wine;* ½ *pint water;* ½ *lb tomatoes.* Cooking time: 7-8 hours.

Make a forcemeat by mincing together the tripe, the ½ lb of lean and green bacon, parsley and 1 clove of garlic and season lightly with salt and pepper. Divide this forcemeat into six, place on the squares of tripe, roll up and tie at each end. Fry the fresh pork in a stewpan and add the sliced shallots, sliced onion and sliced carrots. Add the tomatoes and the other clove of crushed garlic, arrange in a large earthenware fire-proof dish the tripe on top of the vegetables, then the sheep's trotters which have been previously boned, flambéd and blanched. Moisten with the wine and water, season and add the *bouquet garni.* Cover, seal hermetically with a flour and water paste and cook in a slow oven, 325° F or Gas Mark 2, for approximately seven hours. Remove the *bouquet garni* and cut the strings from the tripe, carefully skim away all fat. Place the tripe and feet in a casserole, add cooking liquor and the vegetables and serve boiling hot.

Poitrine de Mouton Tartare * *Breast of Mutton with Tartare Sauce*

For 6 persons: 3 *lb breast of mutton;* 3½ *pints stock;* 1 *onion;* 1 *carrot;* 1 *bouquet garni; English mustard; breadcrumbs;* ¾ *pint sauce Tartare.* Cooking time: 1½ hours.

Boil the mutton till cooked in stock. Bone it and cool under slight pressure. Cut in pieces spread with English mustard paste and dip in breadcrumbs. Brush with oil or fat and grill. Cut into pieces and serve with *sauce Tartare.* Breast of mutton can also be used for *épigrammes* of lamb.

ROGNONS DE MOUTON * *KIDNEYS*

The skin of these kidneys, which are slippery but firm when fresh, should be removed before frying or grilling.

⊡ **en Brochettes Vert-Pré** * *on Skewers*

For 6 persons: 12 *sheep's kidneys;* 2 *lb potatoes;* ¼ *lb beurre Maître d'Hôtel; watercress.* Cooking time: 3-4 minutes.

Slit kidneys open on round side but do not cut right through. Skin them and keep them open by means of a wooden or silver skewer. Brush with butter, season, cook on a very hot grill but keep slightly underdone. Serve with watercress and Straw potatoes and *buerre Maître d'Hôtel.*

⊡ **Chasseur**

For 6 persons: 12 *kidneys;* ½ *lb mushrooms;* 1 *chopped shallot;* 2 *oz butter;* ½ *pint white wine;* ½ *pint Demi-glace;* 6 *heart-shaped butter-fried bread croûtons; chopped parsley.* Cooking time: 3-4 minutes.

Skin and cut the kidneys in half. Remove fat and nerves. Cut into scallops, fry quickly in hot butter, arrange heaped up on a serving dish. Keep warm. Add the shallots to the pan, cook, deglaze with the wine and reduce to half, add the *Demi-glace* and sliced cooked mushrooms. Boil and skim, remove from the heat. Add the butter and pour over the kidneys, garnish with the *croûtons* and sprinkle with parsley.

⊡ **au Madère** * *with Madeira*

For 6 persons: 12 *kidneys;* ½ *lb mushrooms, cut into quarters;* 1 *chopped shallot;* 2 *oz butter;* ½ *pint Demi-glace;* 6 *butter-fried bread croûtons; chopped parsley;* 3 *fl oz Madeira wine.* Cooking time: 3-4 minutes.

Use the same method as for kidneys *Chasseur.*

⊡ **Sautés Berrichonne**

For 6 persons: 12 *kidneys;* ½ *lb mushrooms;* ¼ *lb lean bacon;* ½ *pint sauce Bordelaise.*

Dice the bacon and fry in butter, add the sliced, raw mushrooms and cook them slowly. Add the sliced, sautéed kidneys. Mix in the sauce and serve sprinkled with chopped parsley.

Rognons de Mouton Turbigo

For 6 persons: 12 sheep's kidneys; 12 small pork sausages (chipolatas); ½ lb mushrooms; ¼ pint white wine; ½ pint Demi-glace; 18 small onions or 6 oz medium-size onions; 2 oz butter. Cooking time: 5-6 minutes.

Cut the kidneys in half, remove the skin, season and *sauté* them in butter. Garnish them with grilled chipolata sausages and sautéed mushrooms. Reduce the pan residue with the white wine and the chopped sautéed onions and add the *Demi-glace.* Boil this sauce for a few minutes, season with cayenne pepper and pour it over the kidneys and garnish. Sprinkle a pinch of chopped parsley on top.

SELLE DE MOUTON * *SADDLE OF MUTTON*

This joint is the two loins of mutton joined together by the backbone. It is generally roasted, never braised. All garnishes applicable to the Baron of Mutton are suitable, for example: *Bouquetière, Jardinière* and *Provençale.* A saddle weighing about 4½ lb would be required for six persons.

⊡ à l'Arménienne

For 6 persons: 1 saddle, weighing about 4½ lb; ½ lb rice; ¼ lb red capsicums cut into small dice; 1 lb aubergine; 1 lb tomatoes concassé; 1 oz chopped onions; dried breadcrumbs; chopped parsley; crushed and chopped garlic; olive oil; ½ pint mutton stock; pinch saffron. Cooking time: about 2 hours.

Prepare a *risotto* with rice, capsicums, saffron and the mutton stock. Prepare the *aubergine à la Provençale.* Roast the saddle in a moderate oven, 375° F or Gas Mark 4. Bone, slice and reform on the bone. Mix the breadcrumbs with plenty of chopped parsley and garlic. Spread a layer of this mixture over the saddle, sprinkle with oil and brown quickly in a very hot oven. Garnish with the *aubergine.* Serve the *risotto* separately.

⊡ Charolaise

For 6 persons: 1 saddle, weighing about 4½ lb; 4 braised small white cabbages, cut in halves; 1¼ lb chestnuts cooked in stock; 1½ lb plain boiled and buttered potatoes; ½ pint sauce Madère. Cooking time: about 2 hours.

Roast the saddle in a moderate oven, 375° F or Gas Mark 4, and arrange on a serving dish. Garnish with the cabbages and chesnuts. Deglaze the pan with a little gravy, skim off all fat, add the *sauce Madère*, skim, strain and serve in a sauce-boat. Arrange the potatoes in a separate dish.

⊡ Roseberry

For 6 persons: 1 saddle, weighing about 4½ lb; 6 stuffed tomatoes; 6 Puff pastry bouchées or patty cases; ¼ lb morel mushrooms in Cream sauce; 1½ lb Sauté new potatoes; 1 lb buttered fresh garden peas; ½ pint sauce Béarnaise. Cooking time: 2¼ hours.

Roast the saddle in the normal fashion (see above) and arrange on a large serving dish. Garnish with the tomatoes, peas and patty cases filled with the mushrooms. Serve the sauce and potatoes separately.

L'AGNEAU * *LAMB*

Baron d'Agneau à la Cybèle * *Baron of Lamb*

This is in reality the hind half of the lamb, that is, the two legs and saddle cut to the first floating rib and naturally is cut from small or milk lambs, such as the celebrated South Down or, in France, Pauillac. To carve when cooked, the legs are cut into thick slices, then the saddle is carved and reformed and then the legs, so that the whole joint resumes its original shape. For a meal sufficient for 18 to 20 persons, prepare a Baron of Lamb. Season with salt and a little spice, wrap in caul and roast either in a moderate oven, 375° F or Gas Mark 4, or on a spit allowing approximately 7 minutes per pound of weight, with frequent basting from its own fat, and an extra half hour for the joint as a whole. This will give a well done joint. Pour into the dripping pan a ½ pint of Sauternes and a coffee-spoonful of lemon juice and baste with this sauce for the last period of cooking. Slice and reform the lamb and dress in the centre of a long oval dish. Garnish each end with a pyramid of cauliflower masked with *sauce Hollandaise*. Garnish the sides of the dish with alternate artichoke bottoms filled with *Soubise* or creamed onion *purée*, small clusters of buttered new carrots and *croquettes* of Dauphine potatoes. Dress the shank bones with paper frills. Prepare the gravy from the dripping tray or pan and serve in a sauce-boat.

Blanquette d'Agneau * *Lamb Stew*

Use the same proportions and proceed in the same way as for *Blanquette* of veal, but make the sauce more highly seasoned.

Carré d'Agneau Persillé * *Loin*

For 4-5 persons: 1 piece of loin of lamb, weighing about 4 lb; salt; pepper; mustard; fresh breadcrumbs; chopped parsley; 6 bunches of asparagus; 6 tomatoes. Cooking time: 20 minutes per pound, plus another 20 minutes for the joint as a whole.

The loin consists of the cutlets of half the back without the saddle. The spine bone is chopped off and cutlets trimmed. Season the loin with salt and pepper, and set it to roast. Ten minutes before it has finished cooking remove from oven and brush face with mustard. Sprinkle with the breadcrumbs mixed with chopped parsley and return to oven to finish roasting. Garnish with the grilled tomatoes and bunches of watercress or asparagus tips. (*See illustration p.* 489).

CÔTELETTES D'AGNEAU * *LAMB CUTLETS OR CHOPS*

Lamb chops are cut in the same way as mutton chops. The flesh should be pale pink and the fat white and creamy.

▣ Cyrano

For 6 persons: 12 loin chops; 12 small artichoke bottoms; 12 small round slices foie gras; 12 small truffle slices; ½ pint Châteaubriand or sauce Colbert. Cooking time: 5-6 minutes.

Fry the chops in butter and arrange on the artichoke bottoms. Cover each cutlet with a small slice of fried *foie gras*, garnish with a truffle slice and coat lightly with *sauce Châteaubriand* or *sauce Colbert*.

Sauce Châteaubriand: Reduce white wine with chopped shallot and a pinch each of powdered thyme and bay leaf and strain. Add ½ pint veal stock, boil down to a third, remove from heat, beat up with ¼ lb Herb butter and season. (*See illustration p.* 492).

Côtelettes d'Agneau Madelon

For 6 persons: 12 *cutlets, each weighing about* 3 *oz;* ½ *lb minced chicken;* ¼ *lb mushrooms;* 1-2 *tablespoons thick Béchamel; egg; breadcrumbs;* 2 *oz butter;* ½ *pint sauce Madère.* Cooking time: 20-30 minutes.

Brown the cutlets on one side only. Pile on top a mound of finely minced chicken and mushrooms (this is a good way of using up chicken or veal leftovers) bound with the well seasoned *Béchamel.* Breadcrumb and place on a greased baking dish, sprinkle with melted butter and cook in a moderate oven, 375° F or Gas Mark 4.

◘ Maintenon

For 6 *persons:* 12 *cutlets.*

Prepare in the same way as veal cutlets of the same name.

◘ Marie-Louise

For 6 *persons:* 12 *cutlets; egg; breadcrumbs;* 6 *artichoke bottoms;* ½ *lb cultivated mushrooms;* 4 *oz thick onion purée;* 1 *tablespoon thick Béchamel;* 2 *oz butter;* ½ *pint thickened veal stock (jus lié).* Cooking time: 10-12 minutes.

Make a *purée* of the raw mushrooms and cook and bind with the *Béchamel.* Add the onion *purée*, season and mix well; the *purée* should be thick. Season and breadcrumb the cutlets and fry them in clarified butter. Dress in a ring on a round dish and garnish with the artichoke bottoms filled with the *purée.* Serve the sauce separately.

◘ Montmorency

For 6 *persons:* 12 *lamb cutlets;* 6 *artichoke bottoms;* 6 *small pastry cases;* 1 *bunch green asparagus tips or* ½ *lb French beans; eggwash and breadcrumbs;* ¼ *lb butter;* 1 *lb Noisette potatoes.* Cooking time: 10-12 minutes.

Flatten the cutlets lightly, and trim the bones. Season, dip in egg and breadcrumb and fry a golden brown in butter in a frying pan. When cooked put a paper frill on each bone. If liked arrange the cutlets on a long dish, overlapping each other. Garnish with artichoke bottoms, filled with cream asparagus tips or buttered French beans, and pastry cases filled with very small Noisette potatoes. Serve thickened gravy flavoured with tomato, separately. (*See illustration p.* 491).

◘ Nelson

For 6 *persons:* 12 *lamb cutlets, each weighing about* 3 *oz;* 1 *pint thick onion purée; egg; breadcrumbs; butter; cream.* Cooking time: 10-15 minutes.

Brown the trimmed cutlets in butter on one side only, let them cool a little and then spread the browned side thickly with onion *purée.* Dip in flour, egg and breadcrumbs and fry in butter till done. Thin the remainder of the onion *purée* with cream, boil up, season and serve separately. *Sauce Madère* can be served instead.

Côtelettes d'Agneau Rose Pompon

For 6 persons: 12 lamb cutlets; 1 lb Mousseline stuffing; 1 pint sauce Suprème; ½ lb cooked peas; ½ lb cooked carrots, cut up to resemble peas; 12 slices truffle. Cooking time: 15-20 minutes.

Fry the chops in butter and leave to cool. Cover each chop with a layer of *Mousseline* stuffing. Place a slice of truffle on top of each and decorate with a double row of carrots and peas. Cover with a piece of buttered greaseproof paper. Place in a hot oven, 425° F or Gas Mark 7, for 8-10 minutes just before serving. Arrange on a round dish with the *sauce Suprème* and peas and carrots in the centre. Serve very hot.

▣ Saint-Michel

For 6 persons: 12 lamb cutlets; 6 Puff pastry tartlet cases; ½ pint sauce Soubise; 12 artichoke bottoms cut into quarters; 2 oz butter. Cooking time: 15-20 minutes.

Fry the cutlets in butter. Fill the tartlet cases with *sauce Soubise.* Fry the artichoke bottoms in butter. Arrange the cutlets overlapping, garnish with the tartlets. Serve the artichokes separately. (*See illustration p.* 492).

▣ Sévigné

For 6 persons: 12 lamb cutlets; ½ lb poached mushrooms; 4 large, poached artichoke bottoms; ¼ pint thick Velouté; 2 eggs; eggwash and breadcrumbs; 2 oz butter. Cooking time: 8-10 minutes.

Make a *salpicon* from the poached, diced mushrooms and the poached, diced artichoke bottoms. Place the mixture in a saucepan, add the *Velouté* to bind the vegetables, and over low heat add 2 egg yolks to thicken the mixture. Cook slowly till thick. Fry the cutlets on one side only, cover this side with *salpicon* heaped in a mound, brush the surface with a beaten egg and breadcrumbs. Place in a fire-proof dish containing some very hot butter, sprinkle with more hot butter and cook until golden brown in the oven. Pour buttered meat glaze round cutlets when serving or serve separately in a sauce-boat about ¼ pint of *sauce Colbert.*

▣ Villeroi

For 6 persons: 12 cutlets; 1 pint sauce Villeroi; 1 egg; breadcrumbs; ½ pint sauce Périgueux. Cooking time: 4-5 minutes.

Fry the cutlets in butter and let them cool. Dip in lukewarm *sauce Villeroi,* for better coating, and let it cool. Breadcrumb carefully and fry a nice brown in hot oil or clarified butter. Serve with *sauce Périgueux* and fine vegetables.

Fressure d'Agneau * *Lamb's Pluck*

Of infinitely better texture and taste than mutton pluck, the same methods of preparation are applicable to both.

Gigot d'Agneau * *Leg of Lamb*

Proceed as for Leg of Mutton.

Noisettes d'Agneau Salvatore * *Boned Lamb Chops*

For 6 persons: 12 noisettes, each weighing about 2 oz; 12 small artichoke bottoms; 12 fresh figs; ¼ lb rice; 1 small ginger root; 1 lb Straw potatoes; 1½ lb haricot beans; ½ pint sauce Béarnaise; ½ pint stock; 2 oz butter.

Prepare a *risotto* with the rice and stock and the ginger cut into small dice. Allow *risotto* to cool. Open the figs by the stalk end and fill with the *risotto*, moisten with a little seasoned stock and warm through. Heat the artichoke bottoms in butter, dress in a circle on a round dish and fill with *sauce Béarnaise*. Place a fried Noisette upon each artichoke and surmount with a fig. Garnish the centre with the Straw potatoes. Serve the cooked, buttered haricot beans in a separate dish.

RIS D'AGNEAU * *SWEETBREADS*

Although so much smaller than calf's sweetbreads, lamb's sweetbreads take longer to cook, quite apart from the fact that they are prepared in a different way. After soaking, they are blanched for 6-8 minutes and then cooked in floured water in the same way as calf's head. (*See p.* 480). Lamb's sweetbreads are mainly used with mushrooms and *quenelles*, for garnishes, Puff paste patties and tartlets, and only rarely served in the same way as calf's sweetbreads.

⊡ Chartreuse

For 6 persons: ¼ lb carrots; ¼ lb turnips cut into julienne; 1 lb Fine forcemeat with Panada; 6 oz cooked scallops of mushrooms; ¼ lb diced truffle; ¼ lb diced cock's combs and kidneys; ¼ lb diced white braised lamb's sweetbreads; 10 oz chicken Quenelle forcemeat; slices of truffle; 2 pints sauce Velouté.

Cook to a firm texture the *bâtons* of carrots and turnips, drain and dry. Butter a charlotte mould and arrange the *julienne* of vegetables in alternate layers slantwise on the bottom of the mould. Now spread over the decoration a layer of the veal and panada forcemeat. Bind the mushrooms, truffle, cock's combs and kidneys and sweetbreads with 1 pint of the *sauce Velouté* and fill into the prepared mould to within ¼-inch of the top, now completely seal this preparation within the mould with the rest of the veal forcemeat, place in a *bain-marie* (water bath) and poach in a cool oven, 325° F or Gas Mark 2, until set (35-40 minutes). Butter twelve small boat shaped moulds and place a slice of truffle in the bottom of each, fill with the chicken *Quenelle* forcemeat and poach until set, about 10-15 minutes. Remove from the oven and allow to cool slightly. Remove the charlotte mould from the oven and allow to cool and set for five minutes. Unmould upon a round dish and surround with the *quenelles*. Serve the rest of the sauce in a sauce-boat.

Rognons d'Agneau * *Kidneys*

Kidneys: 3 per person. Cooking time: 8-10 minutes each. *Brains: 1 per person.* Poaching time: 7-8 minutes.

Prepare in the same way as sheep's kidneys and brains. (*See p.* 495).

SAUTÉ D'AGNEAU * *SAUTÉ OF LAMB*

Lamb stew made with neck, scrag or breast meat. Lamb does not require as much cooking time as mutton.

Sauté d'Agneau Créole * *Curried Lamb*

For 6 persons: 1 *shoulder or neck of lamb, weighing about* 3 *lb;* 2 *oz lard;* ½ *lb chopped onions;* 2 *oz flour;* 2 *oz grated coconut;* 1 *bouquet garni;* 4 *small coffeespoons curry powder;* 2 *pints stock;* ½ *lb rice.* Cooking time: 1½-2 hours.

Cut the lamb into large cubes and place in a large fire-proof casserole in which the lard has been previously melted. Brown the meat in the lard together with the onions. Sprinkle with flour, brown it, add the curry powder, stir well, add stock, season, add the *bouquet garni* and braise slowly in a moderate oven, 375° F or Gas Mark 4, with the lid on. After 50 minutes remove the *bouquet garni*, add the coconut and continue to braise until the meat is done. Remove all fat and serve with boiled, very dry rice.

▣ aux Petits Pois * *with Green Peas*

For 6 persons: 1 *shoulder of lamb, weighing about* 3 *lb;* 2 *oz flour;* 2 *oz lard;* 1 *tablespoon tomato purée;* 2 *pints stock;* ½ *pint shelled green peas;* 12 *small onions or* ½ *lb medium-sized onions;* 1 *bouquet garni.* Cooking time: 1½-2 hours.

Cut the shoulder into large pieces after trimming off the excess fat and brown them quickly in the fat in a large fire-proof casserole. Dust with flour, brown the meat slightly and add sufficient stock to half cover the meat. Season, add the tomato *purée*, the *bouquet garni*, and the slightly browned onions. Cover this stew with a lid and braise in a moderate oven, 375° F or Gas Mark 4, for about 1½ hours. Remove the *bouquet garni*, skim off the fat and towards the end of the cooking add the peas which have been cooked separately.

▣ au Riz * *with Rice*

For 6 persons: 1 *shoulder of lamb, weighing about* 3 *lb;* 2 *chopped onions;* 1 *bouquet garni;* 1 *clove of garlic;* 2 *oz flour;* 2 *pints stock;* 6 *oz rice.* Cooking time: 1½-2 hours.

Cut up the shoulder as above and brown together with the onions. Add the crushed garlic and the flour, brown them, add the stock, season, add the *bouquet garni* and braise for about an hour in a moderate oven, 375° F or Gas Mark 4, till meat is almost cooked. Skim off fat, remove the *bouquet garni*, and add the rice after sweating it slightly in butter. Braise slowly for another 20 minutes. The rice should absorb the liquid without making the stew too dry.

NOTE: It is better to cook the rice separately till almost done and then add it to the stew.

SELLE D'AGNEAU * *SADDLE OF LAMB*

The back of the lamb from the best end of neck to the end of the loin. This, although too large for most requirements, makes an excellent roast.

▣ à la Française

For 6 persons: 1 *saddle of lamb, weighing about* 3½ *lb;* 1½ *lb Duchess potatoes;* 1½ *lb buttered peas.* Cooking time: 2-2½ hours.

Roast the saddle in a warm oven, 350° F or Gas Mark 3, bone it and slice the meat and reform back on the bone. Prepare a roast gravy from the pan juices. Shape the potatoes into cigar roll shape, egg and breadcrumb and bend into *croissant* or horseshoe shapes and deep fry at the last moment. Arrange the saddle on an oval dish, surround with the potatoes, the prongs toward the saddle and fill the cavities with the peas. You may also use potato *croquettes* as a garnish. (*See p.* 669). Serve the gravy in a sauce-boat. (***See illustration p.*** 490).

Selle d'Agneau au Safran * *Lamb with Saffron*

For 6 persons: 1 *saddle of lamb, weighing about* 3½ *lb;* 3 *pints mutton stock;* ¼ *lb diced lamb fat;* 1 *onion;* 1 *carrot;* 1 *clove of garlic; the zest of half a lemon;* 1 *small bay leaf;* 10 *crushed peppercorns;* ½ *pint cream;* 1 *oz butter and* ¾ *oz flour made into beurre manié;* 1 *large spoonful of mint leaves.* Cooking time: 2-2½ hours.

Line the base of a deep earthenware roasting dish with the sliced carrots, sliced onion, zest, bay leaf, peppercorns, crushed garlic and a small pinch of saffron. Place in the centre a roasting grid, arrange the seasoned saddle on the grid, moisten the vegetables and herbs with the stock, being careful not to touch the lamb with the stock. Cook in a warm oven, 350° F or Gas Mark 3. As the stock evaporates, keep the vegetables moistened with fresh stock. When the saddle is cooked, remove and keep warm. Strain off the cooking liquor, skim off all the fat and reduce to ¼ pint season and add the cream and another small pinch of saffron. Bring to the boil and thicken with the *beurre-manié* (flour and butter) and strain. Poach 6 figs in a little lemon and orange juice, ¾ lemon juice to ¼ orange juice. Bone, slice and reform the saddle. Arrange on an oval dish and sprinkle with the mint leaves. Serve the figs and sauce separately.

▣ à la Syrienne

For 6 persons: 1 *saddle of lamb, weighing about* 3½ *lb;* ¾ *lb rice;* 1 *onion chopped; stock;* 1 *large red pepper;* 1 *courgette;* 1 *large piece preserved ginger;* 1 *pint sauce aux Tomates;* 3 *aubergines;* 2 *oz butter;* ½ *lb breadcrumbs; chopped parsley;* 1 *clove of garlic, crushed.* Cooking time: 2-2½ hours.

Trim the saddle of lamb, tie it with string, season, roast in a warm oven, 350° F or Gas Mark 3, and keep warm in the oven. Deseed the red pepper, peel the *courgette,* cut them into small dice and half stew in butter. Cut the piece of ginger into short, thin *julienne.* Prepare a *risotto* with the rice, chopped onion, the stock, and add the red pepper, the *courgette* and the ginger. Season and cook quickly. Deglaze the roasting pan juices with a tablespoon of stock, cook with the Tomato sauce and season well. Cut the *aubergine* in round slices, dip them in flour, fry in deep fat until they are crunchy. Salt lightly. Mix the breadcrumbs with plenty of chopped parsley and the finely chopped garlic. Slice the saddle, reform on the bone, brush with melted butter and cover evenly with a layer of the prepared breadcrumb mixture. Pour over this some melted butter and place the joint in a warm oven to form a crust. Serve on a long dish and garnish with the *risotto,* which has been pressed into small buttered *dariole* moulds and turned out. Serve the sauce and the fried *aubergines* separately.

▣ aux Tomates à la Provençale * *with Tomatoes*

For 6 persons: 1 *saddle, weighing about* 3½ *lb;* ¼ *pint olive oil;* 12 *small tomatoes prepared à la Provençale;* 1 *lb French beans;* 2 *oz butter; garlic;* ½ *pint roast gravy.* Cooking time: 2-2½ hours.

Prepare a brown stock with lamb bones and trimmings for the roast gravy and flavour with garlic. Prepare, season and roast the saddle in a moderate oven, 375° F or Gas Mark 4, with the olive oil. Bone it and slice and reform on the bone, place on an oval dish and garnish alternately with tomatoes and clusters of beans tossed in butter. Prepare the gravy from the pan juices and the prepared brown stock and serve in a sauceboat.

Selle d'Agneau Froide à la Strasbourgeoise * *Cold Saddle of Lamb*

For 8-10 *persons:* 1 *saddle of lamb;* 3 *truffles;* 1 *lb foie gras;* ½ *pint Port;* 1 *pint aspic.* Cooking time: 2½ hours.

Bone the saddle carefully without damaging the skin, season the meat and stuff with the seasoned raw truffled goose liver. Fold down sides of saddle, restore to original shape, tie, wrap in a pig's caul and tie again; place in a suitable fire-proof dish and brown. Pour off fat, half fill with Port and aspic and braise slowly in a warm oven, 350° F or Gas Mark 3, till done—about 2 hours. When done, remove string, put saddle in a suitable dish and cover with aspic. Keep in a cool place till the next day, carefully remove fat from the top of the aspic and serve the saddle as it is.

FOREIGN SPECIALITIES

Agneau Pascal à l'Israélite

1 *small carcase of lamb (without head);* 1 *lamb's heart and liver, finely chopped;* 2 *lb rice;* 2 *large onions;* 8 *cloves of garlic;* 1 *lb finely chopped fine herbs;* ½ *pint oil.* Cooking time: 3-4 hours.

Put the rice to cook in one gallon of mutton stock along with the chopped heart and liver. Stew the chopped onions in the oil, add the finely chopped garlic and herbs and blend into the cooked rice. Fill the abdominal cavity of the carcase, sew up and roast for a mininum of 3-4 hours, depending on taste and the size of the carcase. Serve with a hot *purée* of fresh tomatoes.

⊡ à la Russe

1 *small carcase of lamb;* 3 *lb lean veal;* 3 *lb lean pork;* 3 *lb fat pork; salt; pepper; mace;* 1 *quart aspic.*

Mince the meats together, cut the heart, liver and lungs of the lamb into small slices or scallops and mix into the forcemeat with the seasoning. Remove the feet and head from the carcase. Now fill the lamb with the forcemeat, wrap and sew up in muslin and poach until tender with the head and feet. Allow to become quite cold. Unwrap, replace head and feet, glaze with the aspic jelly which has been formed from the mutton stock and serve with Russian cheese, butter and coloured eggs.

Barany Paprikas

For 6 *persons:* 1 *boned shoulder of lamb, weighing about* 2½-3 *lb;* ¼ *lb bacon;* 1 *large onion;* 2 *cloves of garlic;* 2 *large green peppers;* 2 *tablespoons tomato purée;* ½ *pint sour cream; paprika;* ½ *lb rice or Tarhonya.* Cooking time: 2-2½ hours.

In a large casserole dice the bacon and fry light brown with the chopped onion. Season, add the lamb, cut into walnut-sized cubes, and the crushed garlic. Brown slightly and dust with half a teaspoon of paprika; sweat it for a moment. Deseed the peppers, cut in wide strips, and add to the meat with the tomato *purée* thinned with ½ pint water. Simmer slowly till the meat is almost done, the water has evaporated and everything is floating in fat. Add the sour cream, cook till done and serve with very dry boiled rice or Tarhonya. ***(Hungary)***

Broiled Rack of Baby Lamb

For 6 persons: 1 best end of milk or baby lamb; ½ pint Mint sauce; 6-12 kidneys. Cooking time: 12-15 minutes per 1¼ lb.

Split the best end. Score the skin diagonally with a sharp knife, salt lightly and rub with oil or butter. Grill slowly. Grill the kidneys separately in their fat, dish up together and garnish with watercress. Serve with roast potatoes and Mint sauce. *(North America)*

Costolette d'Agnello Corpora

For 6 persons: 12 lamb cutlets; 3 eggs; ¼ lb grated Parmesan; 6 oz butter; ¾ lb baby marrow or courgettes; ¾ lb asparagus tips; breadcrumbs. Cooking time: 40 minutes.

Mix the cheese with the breadcrumbs. Beat the eggs with salt and pepper. Peel and thickly slice the marrow. Flour, egg and breadcrumb both the cutlets and marrow. Cook the asparagus in salted boiling water. Shallow fry the cutlets and marrows in butter and arrange overlapping alternately in a circle. Place the asparagus in the centre and pour over them Noisette butter and sprinkle with grated cheese.

Ghiveci de Miel

For 6 persons: 3 lb boned lamb, without waste or trimming: ½ lb green pepper; ½ lb aubergines; ½ lb courgettes (marrow); ½ lb French beans; ½ lb onions; ½ lb tomatoes; ¼ lb gumbo; ¼ pint oil. Cooking time: 1½-2 hours.

Dice the meat coarsely, brown it slightly in oil with the chopped onions and put it aside. Cut the peeled *aubergines* and *courgettes* in 1-inch dice, the deseeded peppers in wide strips, break the beans into small pieces and brown all the vegetables with the exception of the tomatoes in oil with the gumbo. Put meat and vegetables in layers, with the quartered tomatoes, in a pan with a well-fitting lid. Season with salt, pepper and a pinch of paprika, cover and cook in a moderate oven, 375° F or Gas Mark 4, without adding any liquid. Serve this very tasty dish in the pan in which it was cooked. *(Rumania)*

Irish Stew

For 6 persons: 3 lb scrag end neck of mutton; 2 lb potatoes; 1 lb onions. Cooking time: 2-2½ hours.

Cut up meat and slice onions and potatoes rather thickly. Place a layer of onions on the bottom of a thick casserole, followed by alternate layers of meat, potatoes and onions, finishing with potatoes. Salt lightly, pepper well and fill up to the top with water. Cover, bring to the boil, skim, then continue boiling slowly till done. The potatoes should bind the stew. Serve sprinkled with plenty of chopped parsley. *(Ireland)*

Keuftés

For 6 persons: 1½ lb minced mutton; ¼ lb fresh breadcrumbs; 2 eggs; 2 cloves garlic, crushed; pinch cinnamon. Cooking time: 8 minutes.

Soak the crumbs in water and squeeze dry. Blend meat, bread, seasonings (including salt) and eggs together, divide into 18 pieces; roll into sausages 1-inch in diameter on a wet table. Fry in oil or mutton fat. Serve very hot. *(Turkey)*

Khare Massale Ka Korma

For 6 persons: 2½ *lb lamb, without waste or trimmings;* 2 *oz butter;* 1 *small teaspoon powdered curcuma;* 1 *large pinch powdered ginger;* 3 *cloves;* 3 *seeds cardamon;* 1 *piece ginger* ½ *inch long;* 1 *clove garlic;* 2 *medium-sized onions;* 1 *pinch cayenne pepper; salt.* Cooking time: 50 minutes.

Cut meat in 1-inch cubes. Heat the butter in a casserole with a well-fitting lid and brown the meat in it. Add the spices, which should not be too finely crushed, and fry very slowly for a further 10 minutes. Then add the thinly sliced onion, crushed garlic, salt and cayenne, cover with the lid and simmer very slowly in its own juice for 35 minutes, shaking thoroughly 4 or 5 times, so that the meat does not stick. Do not remove lid in order to avoid loss of flavour. Serve dry, without sauce. Dry boiled rice can be served with it. *(India)*

Le Mechoui

Place the seasoned carcase of lamb on a spit and roast over a wood fire, basting often with butter. When well cooked, place on a dish in the middle of the table where everyone can tear off with his hands the part he desires. *(North Africa)*

Mutton Chops

For 6 persons: 6 *mutton or lamb chops, each weighing about* 6-7 *oz.* Cooking time: 12-15 minutes.

Chops are cut from the loin, never less than 1-inch thick. Turn in the ends and fasten with a small wooden skewer. Chops are almost always grilled and served with watercress and Straw potatoes. (*See illustration p.* 491). *(Great Britain)*

Pilau-I-Rarah

For 6 persons: 3 *lb boned lamb without waste or trimmings;* 8 *small, dried apricots;* 1 *large red pepper;* 2 *oz peeled pistachio nuts;* 2 *medium-sized onions;* ½ *teaspoon each of ground curcuma, coriander, ground cloves and crushed caraway seeds;* ½ *pint sour milk;* 2 *oz butter.* Cooking time: 1¼ hours.

Slice the onions, sweat them in butter, add the meat cut in 1-inch cubes and brown slightly. Add the pistachios, halved apricots, deseeded, coarsely sliced pepper, all the spices and salt. Brown for a moment, shake up well, add the sour milk and an equal quantity of water and simmer slowly till done with the lid on. Place in a deep dish and serve with dry boiled rice. *(Afghanistan)*

Roast Leg of Mutton, Roast Potatoes, Mint Sauce

For 15 persons: 1 *leg of mutton, weighing about* 6 *lb;* 2 *lb roast potatoes;* ¾ *pint Mint sauce.* Cooking time: 2½-3 hours.

Loosen the pelvic bone and trim and clean the knuckle end. Place the joint on a bed of quartered onions, season and roast in a moderate oven, 375° F or Gas Mark 4, until it is well cooked. Deglaze the pan with 1 pint of roast gravy, allow to rest, skim away all fat, simmer gently for 5 minutes and strain. Serve the joint arranged on a large serving dish, with the roast potatoes and Mint sauce placed in separate containers. *(Great Britain)*

Schaschlik Po Tatarski

For 6 persons: 1 *leg of lamb without bones, weighing about* 2 *lb;* ½ *lb fat bacon;* ½ *lb raw ham;* 10 *oz rice.* Cooking time: 10-12 minutes.

Cut meat in walnut-sized cubes and the bacon and ham in small, thick square slices, impale alternately on skewers, brush with oil or butter and grill till brown and juicy. Cook the rice in salt water so that the grains are still separate, drain well and dry off in the oven. Dress skewers on the rice; the juice from the meat should mix with it. (*Russia*)

LE CHEVREAU * *KID*

Kid is prepared in exactly the same way as lamb.

Pork

Almost every part of the pig, that encyclopaedic animal, as Grimond de la Reynière called it, can be used in the kitchen.

Pork is the fresh meat from the pig; salted and cured pig meat is called either bacon or ham. Pork used to be very much a seasonal meat but nowadays it is perfectly safe to buy it at any time of the year, although you may prefer to serve pork in cool or cold weather. Pork is a close-grained meat and some people find it indigestible. It takes longer to cook than other meats and should not be served underdone.

To determine the quality of pork ensure that the flesh is firm and smooth, and in the young animal that it is fine and pink. There should be a good layer of firm, white outside fat and a thin elastic skin. Since pork is a fatty meat it is often served with a piquant sauce.

HAM AND BACON

Bacon is salted and cured meat from a particular species of pig bred for that purpose—curing is done by dry salting or brining. The bacon may then be smoked or left unsmoked (*green* bacon).

Ham is the hind leg of the pig cut off and cured separately, very much more slowly than bacon or gammon. Hams are cured traditionally in many different ways but they all include salting and smoking. There are several kinds of ham of which York is probably the best known variety. French hams include those of Bayonne and Rheims and the small tasty "Paris hams".

Prime bacon and ham should have a smooth thin rind. The lean should adhere to the bone and the fat should be firm, pinky-white and free from black specks or yellow streaks. Both meats should have a pleasant smell and the lean be finely grained. Stale bacon is dark and dry.

APPROXIMATE COOKING TIMES

CUTS	TIME	TEMPERATURE
Best End Fillet	30 mins per lb	These cooking times are for a moderate oven, 375° F or Gas Mark 4-5. They may be varied according to taste.
Roast Pork (leg, loin, fillet)	30 mins per lb	
Cutlets	7-10 mins each side	
Grilled Sausages	10 mins	
Chipolatas	4-5 mins	
Shoulder	30 mins per lb	
Ham in one Piece	15-20 mins per lb	

LE PORC * *PORK*

Andouillettes à la Lyonnaise * *Pork Sausages*

For 6 persons: 2 lb sausages; 3 large onions; 1 tablespoon vinegar; oil and butter. Cooking time: 10-12 minutes.

Shred and stew the onions in butter. Cut the sausages into approximately ½-inch thick slices and fry in equal quantities of oil and butter. Add the onions and fry all together. Sprinkle with vinegar and chopped parsley and arrange piled up in a mound on a dish. Serve with a dish of mashed potatoes.

BOUDIN * *BLACK PUDDING*

Sausage made from pig's blood, rather like black pudding, and cooked in pig's caul.

⊡ à la Flamande

For 6 persons: ¾ pint pig's blood; 1 lb pork flank; ¼ pint cream; ½ lb onions; ¼ lb brown sugar; 3 oz sultanas; 3 oz currants; salt; 1 small pinch of mixed spice and pepper. Cooking time: 20 minutes.

Cut the pork flank into small dice, chop the onions, fry together and put away to get cold. Rinse the fruits in tepid water, drain and dry. Mix all ingredients together including the warm blood, fill into sausage skins. Tie with string and poach. As soon as the sausages float, plunge into cold water. Allow to become cold and dry. When required for use, cut with a sharp knife and fry or grill. Serve with a hot *purée* of apples.

⊡ aux Pommes Reinette * *with Rennet Apples*

For 6 persons: 2½ lb black pudding; 6 large cooking apples; ¼ lb butter. Cooking time: 10 minutes.

Peel, core, slice and stew the apples in butter. Prick the sausages with a fork or skewer before grilling or alternatively remove the skin and roll in dried breadcrumbs before grilling. Serve a base of apples with the sausages on top.

CARRÉ DE PORC * *PORK LOIN*

This is the whole or part of the ribs which have not been separated from each other. The joint, which includes all the cutlets, is chined so that it can be carved more easily when cooked. This joint is excellent when roasted and may be garnished with various vegetables. Pork should aways be well cooked. Cold pork is considered just as good as hot pork and is more digestible.

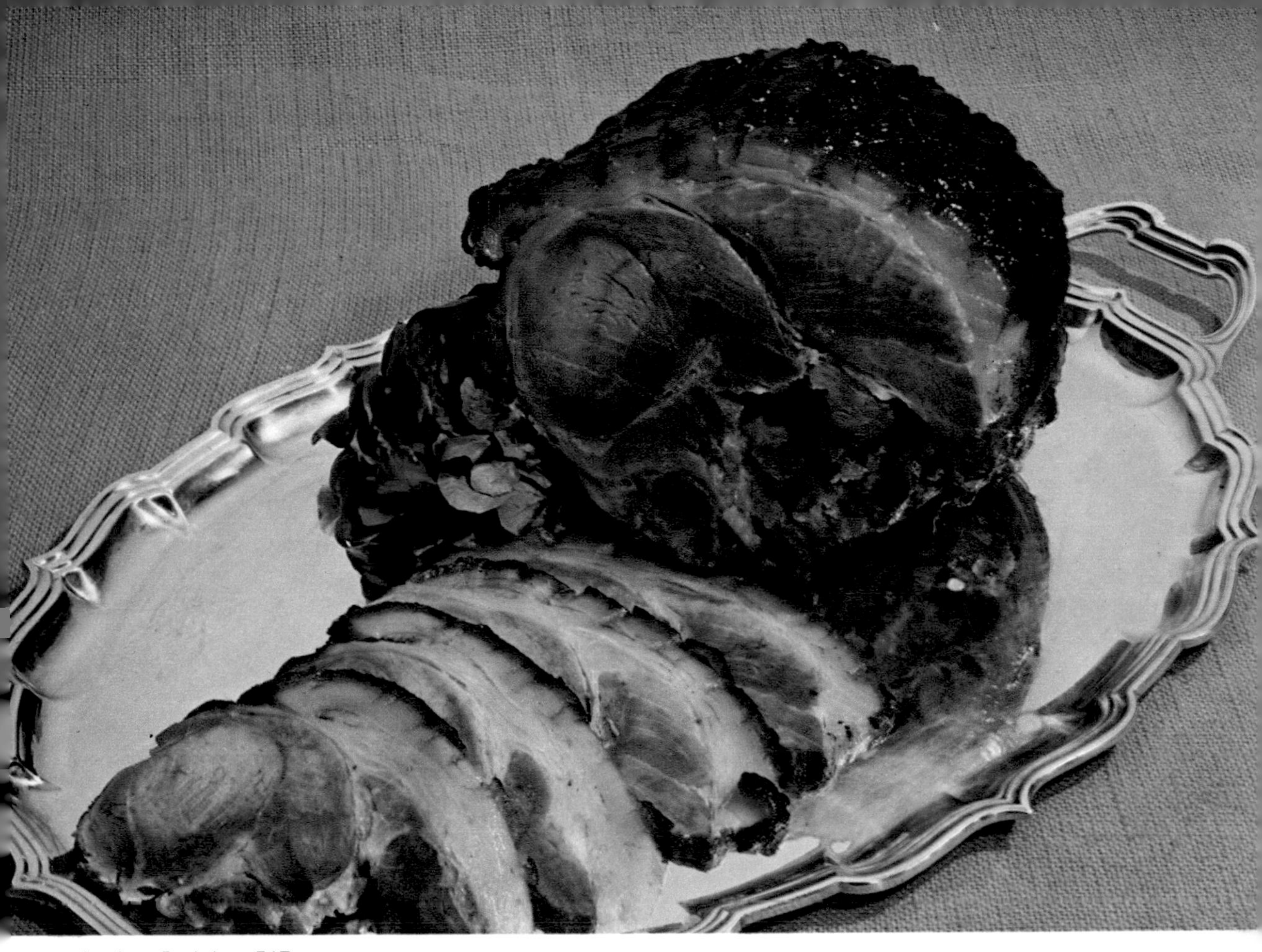

▲ *Jambon Braisé, p. 517*

Jambon à la Gelée, p. 523 ▼

▲ Carré de Porc Belle Fermière, p. 513

Côtes de Porc Bonne-Femme, p. 514 ▼

▲ Médaillons de Jambon Cézanne, p. 519

Côtes de Porc à la Normande, p. 515 ▼

 ▲ Mousse de Jambon, p. 525

Médaillons de Jambon Polignac, p. 525 ▼

Carré de Porc Belle Fermière

For 6 persons: 3 *lb pickled loin of pork;* 2 *lb Pie pastry;* 2 *lb red cabbage;* 1 *lb carrots;* 2 *lb spinach;* 2 *lb French beans;* 1 *lb turnips;* ½ *lb bacon;* 6 *small tomatoes;* 1 *pint sauce Madère*. Cooking time: 1 hour 40 minutes.

Simmer the boned loin in salted water with a carrot, an onion stuck with a clove, and a *bouquet garni* for 40 minutes and allow it to cool in the stock. Roll the pastry out thinly, making an oblong shape. Place the well drained loin in the middle of the Pie pastry, turn up the pastry at the two sides, and then at the two ends, and place it upside down on a baking sheet. Decorate with small patterns cut out from the remaining scraps of pastry, brush with beaten egg and bake in a moderate oven, 375° F or Gas Mark 4, for about 1 hour until it is nicely browned. Cut off a few slices and arrange the loin on a long, rectangular serving dish. Garnish with tomatoes, plainly cooked spinach which has been seasoned, buttered and rolled up in thin slices of fried bacon, small balls of braised red cabbage and glazed carrots and turnips which have been cut into neat *bâtons*. French beans, sautéed in butter, and *sauce Madère* are served separately. (*See illustration p.* 510).

Cayettes de Porc

For 6 persons: 1 *lb lean pork without bones;* 6 *oz pig's liver;* ¾ *lb fresh fat bacon; chopped herbs; pig's caul.* Cooking time: 45 minutes.

Chop meat, liver and bacon coarsely or pass them through the coarse blade of the mincer. Mix with the chopped herbs, season with salt and spices and divide into 3-4 oz portions. This should make about 10 portions. Wrap each in a pig's caul, arrange in a suitable fire-proof dish, add a bay leaf and about ¼ pint of water and cook in a hot oven, 400° F or Gas Mark 6. Serve with any desired vegetable *purée*. *Cayettes* are most popular when eaten cold.

Cervelles de Porc * *Pork Brains*

1 *brain per person.* Cooking time: 8 minutes.

Prepare in the same way as Calf's or Sheep's Brains.

Choucroute Garnie * *Sauerkraut*

For 6 persons: ¼ *lb bacon rinds;* ¾ *lb continental boiling sausage;* 2½ *lb sauerkraut;* ½ *lb streaky bacon;* ¼ *lb lard or goose fat;* 2 *onions each stuck with a clove;* 2 *carrots;* 1 *bouquet garni;* 1½ *lb pickled spare ribs of pork;* 6 *Frankfurter sausages;* ½ *bottle white wine.*

Wash the *sauerkraut*, and squeeze it well by hand to drain off the excess moisture. Line the bottom and the sides of a casserole with some bacon rinds. Place the *sauerkraut* in the casserole and in the middle place the blanched streaky bacon, the boiling sausage, the meat which is to be served with the *sauerkraut* (spare ribs, goose or ham), the carrots, onions and herbs. Cover with the rest of the *sauerkraut*, and add the white wine and a little water or stock. Now add the lard or goose fat, but no salt. Cover with a greased paper, place the lid on top and braise in a slow oven, 325° F or Gas Mark 2. When the *sauerkraut* is done, remove the onions and herbs. Place it in the middle of a dish and garnish with the meat, cut in slices, the bacon, sausage and carrots, all sliced, and the Frankfurters. Serve boiled potatoes at the same time.

COCHON DE LAIT * *SUCKING PIG*

Sucking pigs are roasted whole and sometimes also served stuffed. It needs an oven which is easy to regulate so that it is well done inside and has a nice brown crust outside. It is best to lay the pig on a wire tray. The legs are kept apart by a wooden skewer fastened through the two hind feet. It is best to wrap ears and tail in greased paper to prevent them burning. During roasting, brush constantly with butter or oil and cover with greased paper, which is changed several times. The bubbles in the skin caused by the fat are pricked with a needle. Roasting time: 1½-2 hours according to size, allowing an extra 15 minutes for every pound of stuffing. The sucking pig is first shown whole and then carved in the kitchen. It is best to use poultry shears for the bones. Serve with the gravy from which the fat has been skimmed.

▣ Farci

For 12-14 *persons*: 1 *sucking pig, weighing about* 8 to 9 *lbs;* 2 *lb lean pork;* 1 *lb fat pork; the sucking pig's liver;* ½ *lb white breadcrumbs;* 4 *eggs;* 2 *fl oz brandy;* 1 *oz salt;* 1 *coffeespoon each of thyme, basil and rosemary;* ¼ *lb chopped chives;* ½ *lb chopped mushrooms;* 1 *bouquet garni.*

Take and place the pork, fat pork and liver in a saucepan and season. Add spices and barely cover with stock. Simmer until tender. Drain meat and reduce cooking liquor to a glaze. Mince the meats very finely, add glaze and the breadcrumbs which have been previously soaked in milk and squeezed well to remove excess moisture. Bind with the raw eggs, add chives and mushrooms and blend into a smooth forcemeat. Fill the sucking pig with the forcemeat, sew up, place upon a trivet or grill in the roasting tray with the hind feet tucked underneath and the head resting on the front feet. Brush with pork fat or butter and roast in a moderate oven, 375° F or Gas Mark 4, with frequent basting, for about 2½-3 hours depending on the size of the pig. Serve with gravy, salad and Apple sauce.

CÔTES DE PORC * *PORK CHOPS*

These are cut from the pork loin and should be pale with creamy, pink flesh.

▣ Bonne-Femme

Same procedure as for veal cutlets of the same name. (*See illustration p.* 510).

▣ à la Charcutière

For 6 *persons:* 6 *pork chops, each weighing about* 6 *oz;* 2 *oz lard;* 2 *chopped shallots;* 2 *fl oz wine vinegar;* ½ *pint Demi-glace;* 4 *gherkins.* Cooking time: 10 minutes.

Trim the cutlets. Season, fry in hot lard, remove and keep warm on a serving dish. Pour some of the fat out of the pan, sweat the shallots briefly in the remainder, add the vinegar and reduce to almost nothing. Add the *Demi-glace* and the thinly sliced gherkins, boil up for a moment, season well and pour over cutlets.

Côtes de Porc aux Choux de Bruxelles * *Pork Chops with Brussels Sprouts*

For 6 *persons:* 6 *pork chops;* 1 *egg; breadcrumbs;* 1 *lb Brussels sprouts;* 2 *oz butter;* 2 *oz lard.* Cooking time: 10-15 minutes.

Trim and discard excess fat from the cutlets, exposing the upper part of the bone, season, breadcrumb and fry over moderately low heat until golden brown on each side. Transfer the chops to a serving dish and keep warm. Boil the sprouts quickly, drain well, *sauté* in Noisette butter, season with salt and pepper and garnish cutlets with them.

⊡ à la Normande

For 6 *persons:* 6 *pork chops;* 2 *oz butter;* ½ *pint cream; the juice of* 1 *lemon;* 2½ *lb rennet or cooking apples.*

Cut off excess fat. Season pork chops and fry them in butter. Cook slowly until pork is well done. Transfer the chops to a serving dish and keep warm. Reduce the pan residue with cream, season with lemon juice and pour over the chops. Serve with warm Apple sauce. The chops can also be garnished with apples, peeled, cored, cut in eighths and cooked in butter. (*See illustration* p. 511).

⊡ en Papillote

Same procedure as for veal chops or cutlets of the same name.

⊡ à la Piémontaise

For 6 *persons:* 6 *pork chops;* ¾ *lb rice;* 1½ *pints stock;* 2 *tablespoons tomato purée;* 3 *oz Parmesan cheese, grated;* ½ *pint gravy flavoured with tomato purée.* Cooking time: 10-15 minutes.

Make a *risotto* with the rice, stock and tomato *purée* and when finished stir in the grated cheese and some butter. Fry the cutlets, dish them up, pour a little of the gravy over them and garnish with *risotto.* Loin of pork can be treated in the same way as pork chops, whether breadcrumbed or not.

⊡ aux Pommes * *with Apples*

For 6 *persons:* 6 *pork chops, each weighing about* 6 *oz;* 3 *rennet or cooking apples;* ½ *pint veal gravy;* 3 *oz butter.* Cooking time: 10-12 minutes.

Trim off excess fat, season and fry the pork chops in butter; place on a serving dish and keep warm. Deglaze the pan juices with the veal gravy, simmer for a few minutes and strain and keep warm. Peel the apples, cut in half, remove the cores and cut into slices whilst retaining their shape. Place upon a baking tray, brush with butter and cook to a firm texture in a hot oven, 400° F or Gas Mark 6, dress each half apple on a cutlet and brown under the grill. Pour the prepared sauce over the cutlets.

Côtes de Porc Sauce Robert

For 6 persons: 6 pork chops, each weighing about 6 *oz;* ½ *pint sauce Robert;* 1½ *lb Noisette potatoes*. Cooking time: 10-15 minutes.

Prepare the pork chops in the usual way and fry carefully in butter. When cooked, arrange neatly on a serving dish and mask with the *sauce Robert*. Serve the Noisette potatoes in a separate dish.

Filet de Porc * *Pork Fillet*

Cooking time: 30 minutes per pound.

This cut is best appreciated when roasted and is treated in the same way as loin of pork. Pork must always be cooked right through, otherwise it may be harmful. It is served with fresh cooked vegetables, various types of potatoes and gravy. Particularly suitable garnishes are white cabbage, red cabbage, *sauerkraut*, lentils, haricot beans and celeriac, macaroni, noodles or rice.

FILET MIGNON DE PORC * *CUT FROM FILLET*

Small pieces cut from the fillet and cooked as for pork chops.

▣ à l'Arlonaise

For 6 *persons:* 2 *pork fillets, each weighing about* 1 *lb;* ½ *lb coarse julienne of vegetables* (*carrots, turnips, leeks and celery*); ½ *pint light beer;* ½ *pint Demi-glace;* 1 *oz sugar;* 2 *tablespoons vinegar;* 3 *oz butter*. Cooking time: 1 hour.

Stew the vegetables in butter. Pot roast (*pôelé*) the seasoned fillets in a Dutch oven, remove when cooked and keep warm. Caramelise the sugar with the cooking butter, deglaze with the vinegar and beer, reduce, add the *Demi-glace* and simmer a short while then add the *julienne* of vegetables. Arrange the fillets on a long oval dish and coat with sauce and sprinkle with chopped parsley. Serve with a dish of plain boiled or mashed potatoes.

▣ au Calvados * *with Apple Brandy*

For 6 persons: 2 *pork fillets, each weighing about* 1 *lb; a pinch of ground caraway seeds;* 2 *tablespoons of Calvados;* ½ *pint cream;* 2 *oz meat glaze;* 3 *oz butter*. Cooking time: 5-6 minutes.

Cut the fillets into *escalopes*, each weighing about 2 oz. Flatten the *escalopes* fairly thinly with a cutlet bat, season with salt and the ground caraway seeds. Fry in butter and remove to a serving dish. Deglaze and flambé with the apple brandy. Add the cream and meat glaze and simmer to the right consistency. Arrange the fillets in a circle overlapping each other and mask with the sauce. Serve with a dish of buttered noodles.

Foie de Porc * *Pork Liver*

For 6 persons: 6 slices, each weighing about 5 oz. Cooking time: 8-10 minutes.

It is prepared in the same way as calves' liver; however, pig's liver is chiefly used in the making of *pâtés*.

JAMBON * *HAM*

The leg or neck of bacon boiled until tender then coated in breadcrumbs.

▣ Bouilli * *Boiled*

Soak the ham for twenty-four hours. Put into a large pan and cover with fresh cold water. Bring slowly to the boil, reduce heat and continue simmering very gently. Allow 20 minutes cooking time per pound, except for Prague hams, which only require 15 minutes. If the ham is to be served cold, leave it in the liquor, remove when cold and skin. You may roll the ham in fine toasted breadcrumbs for easier carving. To serve hot, remove the ham from the liquor, strip off the rind and remove any excess fat. Proceed according to recipe directions.

▣ Braisé * *Braised*

Prepare the ham and simmer till cooked. Drain, skin and cut away surplus fat. Place in a shallow braising pan, score the surface, moisten with wine, champagne or sherry and sprinkle with soft brown sugar. Bake to glaze in a hot oven, 400° F or Gas Mark 6, with frequent basting until a shiny golden colour. Remove ham and skim off all the fat from the braising liquor. Add *sauce Demi-glace*, and reduce to a light consistency. When serving hot accompany with various garnishes, such as spinach, peas, *macédoine*, mushrooms and truffles. (*See illustration p.* 509).

▣ en Croûte * *in a Pastry Case*

For 18-20 *persons:* 1 *boned ham, weighing about* 12 *lb;* 4 *lb plain flour;* 1 *lb lard;* 4 *eggs;* 1 *oz salt;* 1 *pint water.* Cooking time: 5-6 hours.

Cook the ham in the normal way, see *Jambon Bouilli*, but cease simmering 1 hour before cooking would be complete. Drain and leave to cool slightly. Make *Pâte à Pâté* or Pie pastry with the flour, lard, eggs, salt and water and allow it to rest for at least 1 hour. Skin the ham and remove any excess fat. When the ham has cooled sufficiently, envelope it in the pastry which has been rolled out thinly. Moisten the edges of the pastry and draw them together to enclose the ham securely. Place on a baking tray sealed side downwards. Brush with beaten egg and cut out a small hole at the top of the pastry to allow the steam to escape during cooking. Bake for about 1-1½ hours in a moderate oven, 375° F or Gas Mark 4, being careful not to burn the crust. The crust should be brown and dry, but not too dark. Before baking you may also decorate the pastry with leaves or other designs made from the dough trimmings.

To serve: Remove an oblong piece of crust from the full length of the ham. Carve in thin slices.

Jambon en Croûte au Champagne * *Ham in a Pastry Case with Champagne*

For 18-20 *persons:* 1 *boned, cooked ham, weighing about* 12 *lb;* 1 *bottle champagne;* 5 *lb Pâte à Pâte or Pie pastry;* 1 *quart Demi-glace;* 1 *sliced truffle;* 1 *lb blanched sliced mushrooms.* Cooking time: 1 hour.

Cook the boned ham in the normal way but cease simmering 1 hour before cooking would be completed. Remove, drain and skin the ham, cutting off any excess fat. Braise in the champagne and allow to cool in the braising liquor. Drain and envelope in the pastry—which has been rolled out thinly—glazed side downwards. Bake in a moderate oven, 375° F or Gas Mark 4, for about an hour. Bring the braising liquor to the boil, add the *Demi-glace*, skim off all the fat, reduce to a light consistency, add the mushrooms and truffles and cook together for a few minutes.

To serve: Remove an oblong piece of crust from the full length of the ham so as to be able to remove the ham with ease. Arrange on a serving dish and serve the sauce separately in a sauce-boat.

▣ Marguerite

For 12-15 *persons:* 1 *ham, weighing about* 7 *lb, braised in Port wine;* 1 *lb Duchess potatoes;* 2 *lb purée of spinach;* ½ *pint thick Béchamel;* 2 *egg yolks.*

Braise the ham as before using Port in place of the sherry or the champagne. Mix the spinach *purée* with the *Béchamel* and the egg yolks; season to taste. Butter the required number of *baba* moulds to give one per person. Fill the moulds (one-third full) with the *Duchesse* potatoes and on top of this place a layer of the spinach *purée*, filling the mould with another layer of the *Duchesse* potatoes. Place the moulds in a *bain-marie* (water-bath) and poach for 12-15 minutes. Let them rest for a few moments before turning out. Carve the ham and dress on a suitable silver dish, coat with the reduced sauce from the braising and decorate with the *timbales* of potato and spinach. Extra sauce should be served in a sauce-boat.

▣ Port-Maillot

For 12-15 *persons:* 1 *ham, weighing about* 7 *lb;* 1 *lb each of carrots and turnips;* 1 *lb peas;* 12-15 *lettuce halves;* 1 *lb French beans;* 1 *quart thickened veal gravy.*

Follow the usual procedure for cooking the ham, see *Jambon Braisé*, but braise with sherry. Remove the ham and keep warm. Use the skimmed and reduced braising liquor to make the veal gravy. Prepare the vegetables to be used as a garnish. Cut the carrots and turnips *en olives* and simmer till tender in stock. Boil the peas and when cooked, toss in butter. Braise the lettuce halves. Cook the French beans and toss in butter. Slice the ham, arrange neatly down the centre of a long serving dish and garnish with clusters of the prepared vegetables. Serve the sauce separately.

▣ Saint-Germain

For 12-15 *persons:* 1 *ham, weighing about* 7 *lb;* 2 *lb dried split peas;* 4 *lettuces, shredded;* 2 *leeks, sliced;* 2 *onions, sliced;* 2 *carrots, sliced; small bunch of chervil;* 2 *oz butter.*

Braise the ham in the usual fashion with sherry. Soak the peas overnight and drain. Prepare and wash the vegetables. In a large saucepan, gently cook all the vegetables till cooked. Pass through a sieve and complete the *purée* with a pinch of sugar and the butter. Carve the ham and arrange on a suitable serving dish, coat with the reduced sauce from the braising. Serve the pea *purée* separately. *N.B.* The pea *purée* can also be piped into hollowed out tomatoes or into pastry cases and used as a garnish.

Jambon à la Strasbourgeoise

For 12-15 persons: 1 ham, weighing about 7 lb; 15 Strasbourg sausages; 4 lb sauerkraut; 4 lb small potatoes.

Braise or boil the ham in the usual fashion. Boil the potatoes. Cook the *sauerkraut* with the bacon rind taken from the skinned ham, an onion and a carrot. When cooked, serve down the centre of a suitable serving dish. Arrange slices of cooked ham on top and decorate with the cooked sausages and potatoes.

MÉDAILLONS DE JAMBON * *HAM MEDALLIONS*

Small rounds of ham decorated with ham, truffle or mushroom *mousse*, glazed in aspic and arranged in an attractive design.

▣ Cézanne

For 6 persons: 12 slices of cooked ham; 6 oz Puff pastry; ¼ lb cooked ham trimmings; ½ lb boletus mushrooms; 1 oz chopped onions; ½ lb cooked leaf spinach; 1 oz chopped parsley; ½ pint sauce Mornay; 1 oz grated cheese; ½ lb braised celery; 12 slices blanched beef marrow; 1½ pints sauce Bordelaise; 3 oz butter. Cooking time: 15 minutes.

Cut out medallions from the ham slices and reserve the trimmings. The medallions should be approximately 3 inches in diameter and weigh 1½ oz each. Roll out the Puff pastry to ⅛-inch thick, stamp with a 4-inch round cutter, prick and bake. Cut the mushrooms into small dice. Stew the onions in a little butter, add the parsley and mushrooms and simmer together; add the chopped ham trimmings and bind with a little *sauce Mornay*. Spread the Puff pastry bases with this mixture and surmount with the medallions of ham previously heated in butter. Prepare twelve small balls of spinach and place in the centre of each medallion of ham. Coat with a little of the *sauce Mornay*, sprinkle with the cheese and melted butter, gratinate under the grill. Place on a suitable serving dish, decorate with sections of celery with a slice of beef marrow upon each and lightly coated with the *sauce Bordelaise*. (*See illustration p.* 511).

▣ à la Piémontaise

For 6 persons: 12 slices of boiled ham, each weighing about 2 oz; 6 oz veal forcemeat; 6 oz rice; 2 tablespoons tomato purée; 2 oz Parmesan; ½ pint thickened veal stock flavoured with tomato; ¼ pint white wine. Cooking time: 8 minutes.

Trim slices in a round shape and sandwich together in pairs with forcemeat in between. Arrange in a buttered fire-proof dish and add white wine. Cover with buttered paper and poach in a moderate oven, 375° F or Gas Mark 4. Make *risotto* with tomato *purée* and mix with the finely diced ham trimmings and grated cheese. Arrange medallions on a bed of *risotto* and coat with the veal stock to which the boiled down poaching liquor has been added.

PIEDS DE PORC * *PIGS TROTTERS*

Singe and clean very carefully. Split in two lengthwise. Boil in lightly salted water for 2 to 2½ hours, with a *bouquet garni*, carrots and onions stuck with cloves. These are served plain, or with sauce, or are coated in breadcrumbs and grilled.

⊡ Cendrillon

For 6 persons: 6 *cooked pig's trotters;* 1 *quart sauce Périgueux.*

Place in a deep earthenware dish, cover with the sauce, and cook for about 20 minutes in a hot oven, 400° F or Gas Mark 6, basting occasionally. Serve with various *purées* of vegetables.

⊡ Panés

For 6 persons: 6 *cooked pig's trotters; flour;* 1 *egg; breadcrumbs.*

Cut the trotters in half lengthwise, dust with flour and coat with beaten egg and breadcrumbs in the usual way. Spoon over with melted butter and grill slowly.

⊡ Saint-Ménéhould

Tie well-cleaned half trotters together and cook in a stock of water, white wine, carrots and onions, *bouquet garni*, and a little salt. Remove, take out the small bones and leave till next day between two boards under a weight. Season with mustard and coarse pepper, brush with melted butter, breadcrumb with as many crumbs as they will absorb, press them down and grill or fry. Serve with mashed potatoes or a *purée* of green peas or sweet chestnuts.

Ragoût de Porc * *Stew*

For 6 persons: 1 *shoulder of pork weighing about* 2 *lb;* 24 *small onions;* ½ *lb carrots;* ½ *lb turnips;* 1 *lb potatoes;* 2 *oz tomato purée;* 2 *oz flour;* 1 *bouquet garni;* 1 *clove garlic.* Cooking time: 1¾ hours.

Same preparation as *Navarin* of Mutton.

Rognons de Porc * *Kidneys*

1 *kidney per person.* All recipes for *Rognons de Veau* (*see p.* 476) may be used successfully here.

SAUCISSES DE PORC * *PORK SAUSAGES*

⊡ Grillées aux Choux * *Grilled with Cabbage*

For 6 persons: 12 *pork sausages;* 2 *lb cabbage.* Cooking time: 8-10 minutes.

Prick sausages with a fork, place in a fire-proof baking dish, moisten with two tablespoons boiling water and bake in a hot oven, 400° F or Gas Mark 6, till sausages are evenly browned. Arrange them on a dish containing boiled, coarsely chopped cabbage which has been tossed in the remaining sausage fat.

Saucisses au Vin Blanc * *Sausages with White Wine Sauce*

For 6 persons: 12 *pork sausages;* 2 *fl oz white wine;* ½ *pint Demi-glace.* Cooking time: 15 minutes.

Prick the sausages all over with a fork, place in a roasting pan, add the white wine and put in a hot oven, 400° F or Gas Mark 6, for 15 minutes. Reduce the white wine, with the *Demi-glace*, skim off fat and pour over sausages. Garnish with vegetable *purée* or mashed potatoes to taste.

LE PORC FROID * *COLD PORK*

Charcuterie

The various preparations vary from country to country. In any event, any dish of *charcuterie* must include raw and cooked ham, various sausages and salami. *Charcuterie* items are frequently served as *hors d'œuvre,* accompanied with various raw vegetable salads.

CORNETS DE JAMBON * *HAM CORNETS*

Thin slices of ham stuffed with savoury mixtures and rolled into cone shapes. They are usually arranged radiating in a circle and garnished with olives, etc.

▣ Astor

For 10 *persons:* 10 *thin slices of cooked ham;* 2 *lb of Waldorf salad lightly bound with aspic;* ¼ *pint whipped cream;* 2 *oz grated horseradish;* 1 *or* 2 *sheets of gelatine;* 1 *quart aspic.*

To prepare the cornets, trim the slices of ham into triangular shapes with bases 3-inches wide. Dip these pieces in half-set aspic, roll them round the little finger in the shapes of cornets and introduce them into moulds. Any ham protruding beyond the end of the moulds should be cut off. Blend the cream with the grated horseradish and bind with the melted gelatine. Fill this mixture into the cornets with a piping bag and star tube. Glaze with aspic and keep in the refrigerator till set. Meanwhile, line a *bombe* mould with aspic, fill with the Waldorf salad and allow to set. Glaze a round dish with a thin film of aspic and when set unmould the salad in the centre, surround with the cornets of ham and garnish with finely diced aspic.

▣ Lucullus

For 10 *persons:* 10 *thin slices ham;* 10 *oz buttered foie gras mousse;* 2 *lb macédoine of vegetables;* 2½ *pints aspic;* ½ *pint aspic Mayonnaise* (*Mayonnaise Collée*).

Prepare the cornets as indicated above. Using a savoy bag, fill the cornets with the buttered and truffled *foie gras mousse* and top with a slice of truffle. Remove the cornets from their moulds and coat them thinly with another layer of aspic. Keep in a cool place to set. Meanwhile prepare a Russian salad bound together with the *Mayonnaise Collée* and pour it into a shallow mould. Leave to set on ice and when it is very firm, turn out of the mould. Arrange the ham rolls on this base and glaze them with the half-set aspic and surround the dish with chopped-up aspic.

Côtes de Porc en Gelée * *Pork Chops in Aspic*

For 6 persons: 1 *loin of pork, weighing about* 2½ *lb;* 2 *calf's feet;* 1 *hard-boiled egg;* 1 *raw egg white;* 3 *gherkins;* 3 *fl oz vinegar;* 2 *carrots;* 1 *bouquet garni;* 2 *onions.* Cooking time: 1½ hours.

First clean and split the calf's feet and blanch them thoroughly. Then simmer them for 3 hours with the carrots, onions and a *bouquet garni.* Remove the chine bone from the loin. After straining the liquid in which the feet have been cooked, add to it the feet, chopped chine bone, the pork loin and the vinegar; continue to simmer. When cooked, remove the meat and leave it to cool down. Skim off all fat from the stock and clarify with the egg white beaten up in some water. Strain through a cloth. Cut the joint up and trim the chops. Coat some chop moulds with aspic and decorate them with a few slices of hardboiled egg, cooked carrots and gherkins. Place a chop in each mould, fill up with aspic and leave to set in a cool place. Instead of the chop moulds, it is also possible to use a fairly deep round dish into which aspic is poured to cover the base and allowed to set. The chops are then arranged on the aspic and decorated. More aspic is poured to fill the dish. The liquor should be highly seasoned and sufficiently concentrated to solidify so that the chops can be turned out on to another dish where they are garnished with parsley. *Sauté* potatoes are usually served with this dish.

Fromage de Tête de Porc * *Pig's Head Cheese*

Boil half a cleaned pig's head in slightly salted water with root vegetables and a few peppercorns until it is soft. Bone fully, chop meat coarsely, mix with chopped onion, chopped herbs, crushed garlic and pepper, place in a bowl and add enough stock. after skimming off fat, to cover the meat. Turn out when set. The cheese will keep for several days in its own aspic if kept in a cool place. It can be served with *Vinaigrette.* Boiling time of pig's head: 3-4 hours.

JAMBON * *HAM*

▣ à l'Alsacienne

For 6 persons: 12 *slices cooked ham;* 6 *slices foie gras;* 2 *pints aspic flavoured with Port wine;* 1 *small truffle.*

Line a round mould with the aspic and decorate the bottom and sides with slices of truffle. Fill alternatively with ham and *foie gras* and complete with setting aspic. Place in a 'fridge to set. Unmould and garnish with aspic *croûtons.* These are made by cutting jellied aspic into cubes.

▣ à l'Andalouse

For 6 persons: 1 *cooked ham, weighing about* 3½ *lb;* 12 *fried croustades;* 1 *red pepper;* 4 *Spun eggs;* 1 *small truffle;* 1½ *pints aspic.*

Trim the boiled ham, cut out a piece from the middle to hold the decoration, slice it thinly, replace in original position, decorate with sliced red pepper and truffle and glaze with aspic. Place ham on a large silver dish and garnish with small baked tartlet cases of unsweetened Short pastry filled with Spun eggs and diced aspic.

Jambon à la Gelée * *Cold Boiled Ham*

For 20 *persons:* 1 *ham, weighing about* 10-12 *lb;* 1 *quart aspic jelly, flavoured with Madeira;* 1 *truffle.*

Remove the rind and excess fat from a cold, cooked ham. Trim knuckle. Cut off a slice from base so that it lies flat on the dish. Next, cut the top of the ham into very thin slices, slipping a long sharp knife into the meat, until it touches the bone. Replace these slices in correct order on the bone. When the ham has been put together again, glaze it with half-set aspic. Decorate the top with a pattern of truffle, blanched leek, cooked carrots, tomatoes, blanched tarragon leaves and hardboiled egg white. Dip each part in aspic before decorating the ham. Cover again with half-set aspic, and allow to set before serving. Cold ham is usually accompanied by a mixed salad. (*See illustration p.* 509).

⊡ en Gelée * *in Aspic*

When preparing ham in this way, let the joint cool down in the liquor in which it was cooked.

⊡ Glacé à la Cambacérès

Remove rind from a cold, cooked ham, except for a small piece round the knuckle and score this piece in an attractive design. Remove surplus fat and the brown smoke crust, and cut flat underneath so that it rests steadily on the dish. Using a sharp knife, cut into thin slices. Spread each slice thinly with well-seasoned *foie gras purée* mixed with butter and replace slices in original position with truffle slices in between. Decorate tastefully and glaze with sherry-flavoured aspic.

⊡ à la Marie-Anne

Cut thin slices from the best part of the ham and then stamp out shapes from each slice, with an oval cutter. Trim the rest of the ham to a good shape and glaze with half-set aspic. Take the trimmings and waste parts of the ham and an equal weight of *foie gras* and prepare a *mousse* with these ingredients. Dress this *mousse* on the ham to resemble the original shape. Rebuild the ham with the overlapping shaped slices of ham, decorate with truffle, glaze the whole with aspic. Dress and garnish with finely diced aspic and aspic *croûtons*.

⊡ Monselet

Cut the top part of the ham into thin slices, stamp out with a round cutter and sandwich each two slices together with a thick layer of buttered *foie gras purée*, decorate with truffle and glaze with aspic. Build up the top of the ham to a dome shape with a vegetable salad such as a Russian salad bound with thick *Mayonnaise* sauce. Arrange the medallions of ham in a neat pattern so as to completely cover the salad. Cut some truffled aspic into very fine dice and arrange round the edges of the medallions. Arrange the garnished ham on a large oval dish previously covered with a thin film of aspic. Garnish with stuffed tomatoes and small *croustades* filled with vegetable salad. Serve well chilled.

Jambon à la Rothschild

For 6 *persons:* 12 *slices York ham;* ½ *lb purée of foie gras blended with* 2 *oz butter;* 24 *slices truffle;* 1 *pint aspic flavoured with Port.*

Spread the slices of ham with the *foie gras purée*, dress on an oval dish overlapping each other, decorate with the truffle, glaze with the Port aspic, and allow to set.

⊡ à la Villandry

For 18-20 *persons:* 1 *lb Puff pastry;* 2¼ *lb vegetable salad;* 1 *cooked rolled fillet of smoked pork, weighing about* 1½ *lb;* 1½ *lb cold, cooked ham;* 40 *cold, cooked asparagus tips;* ½ *lb toasted, finely chopped hazelnuts;* 40 *small pineapple wedges;* 6 *small tomato cases;* 6 *cooked, marinated round bases of celeriac, shaped as artichoke bottoms;* 1 *lb cooked pickled ox tongue;* ¼ *lb softened butter;* 3 *quarts aspic;* 40 *small truffle slices;* 12 *poached mushroom caps.*

Roll out a piece of Puff pastry, to ⅛-inch thick, cut to the shape of a small ham, measuring approximately 9 inches by 6-inches. Place on a baking tray, prick well and bake. Allow to cool. Cover a large oblong silver serving tray with a thin layer of aspic and allow this to set. Pour a little aspic into the bottoms of some small moulds, let it set and decorate with the truffle and a small medallion of tongue, cut out from the sliced ox tongue. Finish filling the moulds with aspic and put to set. Cut the ham into 40 thin slices and stamp out medallions with a round cutter. Make a ham *purée* from the finely minced ham trimmings, the softened butter and a little mixed spice. Spread the medallions of ham with this mixture and sandwich together; roll the edges in the chopped hazelnuts. Decorate each medallion with two pineapple wedges and coat with aspic to glaze. Slice the pork fillet thinly and roll the asparagus tips in 40 of these slices. Glaze these asparagus rolls with aspic. Place the Puff pastry base in the centre of the aspic-coated tray, heap the vegetable salad on the base and with a palette knife, shape to the form of a ham. Cover the vegetable salad completely with the remaining slices of pork fillet in a neat pattern. Place a row of fluted mushrooms down the centre and glaze with aspic. Allow to set. Fill the peeled and deseeded tomato cases with some of the remaining vegetable salad and invert the stuffed tomatoes on the medallions of celeriac and glaze with aspic. Allow to set.

To decorate: Arrange in an artistic pattern around the tray, the tomatoes, medallions of ham, asparagus rolls and small moulds of tongue. This dish is suitable for serving at a cold buffet. (*See illustration p.* 169).

MÉDAILLONS DE JAMBON * *MEDALLIONS OF HAM*

⊡ à la Hongroise

For 6 *persons:* 12 *slices cooked York ham;* 12 *slices truffle;* ½ *lb ham mousse seasoned with paprika;* 3 *pints aspic.*

Stamp out medallions of ham with a round cutter, spread six slices with some of the ham *mousse* and sandwich together with the remaining six. Place a slice of truffle on top of each and glaze with aspic. Line a small *timbale* or *dariole* mould with aspic, fill with the rest of the *mousse* and put away to set. Pour a thin film of aspic on a round dish and when set unmould the *mousse* and dress in the centre of the dish and surround with finely diced aspic. Arrange the medallions around the *mousse*.

Médaillons de Jambon Polignac

For 6 persons: 12 slices cold baked ham; ½ lb purée of foie gras; 2 oz softened butter; 2 truffles; 3 pints Madeira-flavoured aspic; 2 lb Russian salad.

Cut out medallions from the ham slices. Blend the *foie gras* with the softened butter, season and flavour with Madeira. Sandwich the ham medallions with this paste. As soon as the cream has set decorate with a round truffle slice and glaze with the Madeira aspic. Coat a large round tray with aspic and allow to set. When set, arrange a mound of Russian salad, bound with lightly gelatined Mayonnaise, in the centre of the tray. Garnish with slices of truffle on small medallions of ham made from the ham trimmings. Coat with aspic and chill until set. Arrange the ham medallions round the mound of Russian salad in a circle. Make aspic *croûtons* with the remaining aspic. (*See illustration p.* 512).

MOUSSE DE JAMBON POUR BUFFET FROID * *HAM MOUSSE*

Finely-minced ham mixed with aspic and seasoning and set in a mould. It is usually served with a green salad. (*See illustration p.* 512).

For 12 persons: 2 lb cold, baked, lean York ham; 12 small slices ham; ½ lb purée of foie gras; 1 quart sherry-flavoured aspic; ½ pint rose-coloured sauce Chaudfroid; 1 quart white sauce Chaudfroid; ½ pint cream; Vinaigrette salad dressing; 2 yellow and 2 red capsicums; 12 tomato cases; 2 peeled whole tomatoes; a small piece of cucumber; ½ lb celeraic or celery.

Make a ham *mousse* by mincing and pounding the York ham with the rose *sauce Chaudfroid*, coloured by the addition of two teaspoons of tomato *purée*, sieve, blend in the cream and half a pint of half-set aspic. Pour it into a large oval mould. Chill until mixture sets. Glaze a large oval serving dish with a thin layer of aspic. When the *mousse* is firm, unmould and carve it into the shape of a small ham. Coat with the white *sauce Chaudfroid*. Allow to set. Trim the ham slices into pear-shaped pieces and cover with a dome-shaped mound of *foie gras*. Chill. Coat with white *sauce Chaudfroid* and chill again. Trim away any droplets of sauce. Skin and deseed the capsicums, cut into *julienne* and retain a little for decorative purposes. Cut the celeriac into short *julienne*. Soak the *julienne* of capsicums and celeriac in the *Vinaigrette*. Fill the twelve deseeded tomato cases with the marinated *julienne* of capsicums and celeriac. Quarter the remaining two tomatoes, deseed and retain the flesh for decorative purposes. Brush the shank end of the ham *mousse* with a little meat glaze to represent the rind. Now decorate the ham and the pear-shaped ham slices with the reserved *julienne* of capsicum, tomato flesh and cucumber peel. Glaze with aspic and chill.

To Assemble: Place the prepared ham in the centre of the aspic-coated serving tray and surround with the pear-shaped ham slices. Garnish with the filled tomato cases, interposed between the slices of ham. This is a suitable presentation dish for a cold buffet.

◘ en Damier

For 10-12 persons: 2¼ lb lean, cooked ham; ½ pint rose-coloured sauce Chaudfroid (coloured by the addition of two teaspoonfuls tomato purée); ½ pint double cream; 1½ pints sherry-flavoured aspic; truffle slices; hardboiled egg whites; 12 small baked tartlet shells; Russian salad.

Prepare a ham *mousse* as indicated above and season with paprika. Line a shallow, square dish with aspic, coating the bottom and sides completely. Chill till half-set. Cover the bottom with a chessboard pattern of small squares of truffle and hardboiled egg white and decorate the side with egg white crescents. Cover with another thin layer of aspic. Chill until firm. Mix the *mousse* with about ¼ pint cold but still liquid sherry-flavoured aspic, place in the dish and let it set before topping up with aspic. When fully set, unmould on a silver dish, surround with the tartlet cases of unsweetened Short pastry filled with some Russian salad and complete with aspic cut in fancy shapes.

Jambon à la Hongroise

For 8 persons: 1 lb finely puréed ham; ¼ lb butter; ¼ pint double cream; ¼ pint thick Béchamel; 2 teaspoonfuls tomato purée; paprika; Port-flavoured aspic.

Mix ham well with cold, unsalted *Béchamel*, butter and tomato *purée*, season with paprika and pass through a fine sieve. Complete with the cream and season well. Line a *charlotte* mould, sides and bottom with Port-flavoured aspic, decorate with truffle and egg white slices and fill with the *mousse*. Fill up with aspic and put in refrigerator to set. Turn out on a round dish and decorate with aspic. The mixture can also be filled into small moulds lined with aspic and used as garnish or *hors d'œuvre*.

Pâté de Foie * *Pork Liver Paste*

For 10-12 persons: 2 lb pig's liver; 1 lb pork fat; 2 lb green or unsmoked bacon; 2 lb each chopped onions and shallots; 1 oz butter; 1 tablespoon flour; 3 eggs. Cooking time: 1¼-1½ hours.

Pass the liver, pork fat and unsmoked bacon twice through the fine blade of the mincer, pass through a sieve, season with salt, pepper and spices and mix in the cold shallots and onions cooked in butter. Work in the flour and the eggs and fill into a ovenproof round dish lined with thinly-sliced bacon and cover with more bacon rashers. The mixture can also be wrapped in a pig's caul. Poach in a cool oven, 325° F or Gas Mark 2-3, in a water-bath. The liver paste is done when a needle stuck in it comes out hot. Let it cool, turn out and leave in bacon or caul until needed as a protection from contact with the air.

Rillettes de Tours * *Pork Sausages*

1 lb belly of pork; 1 lb breast of goose; 1 bouquet garni; 1 sprig of savory; 2 sage leaves. Cooking time: 3-4 hours.

Cut the goose and pork into large cubes, place in an earthenware casserole, ¾ cover with water, season with salt and pepper, add the herbs, cover with a lid and simmer until the water has evaporated. Continue cooking gently until the meat begins to brown but is still moist. Remove the meat to a shallow earthenware dish, remove the herbs and any bones, and mash the meat well with a fork; allow to cool. When it begins to set, give another good stir and fill into small china pots or crocks. This will keep some time in a refrigerator.

FOREIGN SPECIALITIES

Butifara à la Catalane

For 6-8 persons: 2 lb streaky pork; 2 fl oz white wine; crushed cinnamon; cloves and wild marjoram; salt; pepper. Cooking time: 1 hour.

Pass the pork through the mincer twice, mix with the white wine and work thoroughly with the spices. When well mixed, fill into intestines in the same way as Black Pudding and tie off after 4-5 inches, making a string of several sausages. Hang the sausages in the open for 2 days to dry, place in a casserole with cold, slightly salted water, bring slowly to the boil and keep at simmering temperature for 1 hour. Remove and let them get quite cold in the open. The sausages are served as *hors d'œuvre*. They only keep for a few days, especially in summer. *(Spain)*

Chorizos

For 6-8 persons: 1½ *lb lean and* ½ *lb fat pork;* 2 *teaspoons salt;* 3 *teaspoons ground allspice;* ½ *teaspoon hot Spanish pepper.*

Pass the meat through the coarse blade of the mincer, season with salt, allspice and pepper, cover and keep very cold for 48 hours. Fill into pig's intestines in batches of about 2½ oz, tie off, dry 48 hours and smoke lightly. *Chorizos* are eaten cold as *hors d'œuvre* or used hot in national specialities such as *olla podrida* and *puchero.* (*Spain*)

Chow Sub Gum Mein

For 3 *persons:* ½ *lb lean pork;* 1 *green pepper;* ½ *tin red peppers;* 1 *stalk celery;* 6 *water chestnuts;* 12 *small mushroom heads;* 1 *tin bamboo shoots;* ½ *pint stock;* 3 *tablespoons soya sauce;* 1 *tablespoon cornflour;* 6 *oz Chinese noodles.* Cooking time: about 25 minutes.

Cut the pork into thin slices and fry in hot fat till cooked. Slice and chop the pepper and celery and add all the vegetables with the exception of the red peppers. Add stock, soya sauce, salt and pepper and boil together until the vegetables are cooked. Mix the cornflour with a little water and use to thicken the stock. Boil noodles for only 5 minutes, drain, fry in fat and divide among 3 small bowls. Pour Chow Mein on top, sprinkle with coarsely-chopped red peppers and serve very hot. (*China*)

Médaillons de Porc Puszta

For 6 *persons:* 12 *medallions of pork fillet, each weighing about* 2 *oz;* 2 *red and* 2 *green capsicums;* ¼ *lb cooked, lean meat;* 2 *onions;* 4 *large tomates concassé;* 2 *fl oz white wine;* ½ *pint cream; saffron; paprika; garlic salt;* 3 *oz butter.* Cooking time: 8-10 minutes.

Season the pork medallions with the garlic salt and shallow fry in butter, remove and keep hot. Finely chop the onions, cut the lean cold meat into strips, deseed the capsicums and cut into *julienne.* Add the strips of meat, the capsicums and the onions and when half cooked, add the tomatoes and a pinch of saffron. Deglaze with the white wine, add the cream and simmer till reduced. Arrange the medallions on a suitable dish and coat with the sauce. Sprinkle with paprika. Serve with Tarhonya blended with chopped chutney. (*Hungary*)

New England Baked Pork and Beans

1 *lb haricot beans;* ½ *lb fat bacon;* 2 *oz chopped onions;* 2 *tablespoons brown sugar;* 1 *tablespoon mustard powder;* 2 *small bay leaves;* 1 *tablespoon apple vinegar;* 1 *small chopped clove of garlic;* 2 *tablespoons molasses.* Cooking time: 6-7 hours.

Soak beans overnight, then boil for 30 minutes. Dice the bacon and fry golden brown. Add beans to bacon, add remainder of ingredients, mix and put in earthenware fire-proof pot; the liquid should just reach the top. Put in a warm oven, 350° F or Gas Mark 3, and bake very slowly. Add a little water or stock if needed to prevent the beans from becoming too dry. (*North America*)

Oxford Sausages

½ lb each of fat and lean pork; 1 *lb lean veal;* 1 *lb suet;* ½ *lb white breadcrumbs; peel of* ½ *lemon;* ½ *teaspoon marjoram;* ½ *teaspoon chopped herbs;* ¾ *oz salt; pepper;* 6 *leaves of sage;* 1 *large pinch grated nutmeg.* Cooking time: 12-15 minutes, according to size.

Mince pork, veal and suet finely and mix well with the breadcrumbs, finely chopped lemon peel, finely chopped sage leaves and all the spices. Add a few tablespoons of water and mix. Fill into well-cleaned pig's intestines, tie off into sausages 4-5 inches long and cut off. Blanch briefly then prick with a fork and fry brown in butter. Serve garnished with mashed potatoes and the frying butter poured on top. The sausages are improved if butter is added to the mixture at the end. (*Great Britain*)

Poultry

Poultry in the narrower sense means chicken, but in general, geese, ducks, turkeys, pigeons, and guinea fowl are included in the same category. In other words all birds reared domestically for human consumption may be considered as poultry. When choosing young poultry, certain considerations—indications of the freshness and quality of the bird—should be borne in mind. The legs will be smooth, the feet should be supple and the beak and breastbone pliable. A good test is to press the tip of the breastbone—in a young bird this should bend easily. Fresh birds have firm pleasant smelling flesh and clear prominent eyes. Poultry, like meat, is hung by the poulterer after killing to tenderise the flesh.

APPROXIMATE COOKING TIMES

POULTRY	TIME	REMARKS
Boiling Fowl, 3½-5 lb	1-2 hours	Depending on age
Roasting Chicken, 2-4½ lb	20 mins per lb+20 mins over	Roast in a moderate oven, 375° F or Gas Mark 4-5
Small Roasting or Spring Chicken, 2-3 lb	1 hour whole or 20-30 mins jointed	
Chicken, shallow fried	10-15 mins on either side	Jointed
Pigeons	25-30 mins	Roast in a moderate oven, 375° F or Gas Mark 4-5
Guinea Fowl, 1½-2¾ lb	30-45 mins per lb	Bard, roast or braise
Ducklings, 1½-2 lb	15-20 mins per lb	Roast
Goose, 10 lb	20-25 mins per lb	Roast in an oven, 350° F or Gas Mark 3-4
Turkey, 8-25 lb	Small, 20-25 mins per lb Large, 12-15 mins per lb	Roast in an oven, 350° F or Gas Mark 3-4

LES POULETS * *CHICKEN*

DRAWING A CHICKEN

Singe the bird, clean and draw it by making an incision down the length of the neck. Pull out the windpipe and crop, chop off the neck close to the body, pulling the skin to one side, and leaving a good flap to fold over the back. Turn the bird on its back and enlarge the vent opening. Remove the remaining organs carefully and gently through this opening, using two fingers. These consist of the gizzard, intestines, heart and liver which has the gall bladder attached to it. Take great care that the gall bladder is not broken. If broken it would impart a bitter flavour to any part of the bird it touched. Now remove the lungs, small red spongy masses lying between the ribs in the hollows of the backbone, and take out the kidneys. Open and clean the gizzard together with the heart, neck and liver and wash thoroughly in cold water. These are the giblets. Wipe the bird with a damp cloth.

BONING A CHICKEN

The practice of boning poultry is quite common in French cookery. If you have never attempted it before it does require both a great deal of time and patience.

Place the drawn bird breast down on the table and make an incision down the back of the bird from neck to tail. Cut the skin arcund the lower leg joint, crack the joint and pull off the feet together with the sinews. Using a small, sharp knife and keeping the cutting edge against the bone, scrape and cut the flesh gently from the carcase bones down one side of the bird. It will help if you pull the flesh away from the carcase with your fingers as you cut. It is most important that you do not pierce the skin. Remove the leg bones by making a cut at the thigh and drumstick joint and push the ends of the bones through. Scrape away the flesh with the knife turning the bone round as you do this.

JOINTING A RAW CHICKEN OR COCKEREL FOR SAUTÉING

Slit the skin round the junction of leg and body and remove the legs. Cut off the wings together with a piece of breast close to the joint. Cut the breast from the back and cut it in half lengthwise through the bone. It may now be cut in half crosswise too, if it is large. The back should be trimmed and cut in half, according to size. The legs can be cut at the joint. Pieces which are to be sautéed should be slightly floured first. (*See Illustrated Culinary Techniques*)

CARVING A COOKED CHICKEN

In principle, the method is the same as for a raw one. The legs are removed by pressing them outwards and downwards and then cutting them off with the point of a carving knife. If the legs are large they may be cut in two. The wings may be removed by cutting down through the joints together with a portion of breast. The breast is then cut into several thin slices lengthwise, making sure each slice has a piece of skin attached. Small chickens may be simply divided into 4 pieces—the two legs and the halved breast and wings without the back. It is more convenient when entertaining to carve the bird in the kitchen, and arrange the pieces on a hot dish. (*See Illustrated Culinary Techniques*)

Note: Let the bird rest for 15 minutes at moderate heat before carving it so that the meat, expanded by heat can contract back to a firmer texture and is therefore easier to carve.

BALLOTTINES * *STUFFED DRUMSTICKS*

This is one of the ways in which a surplus of chicken legs may be utilised. They are boned, flattened with a cutlet bat and stuffed with various forcemeats. The skin, which must be left fairly long is sewn together with cotton and then they are braised and served with their cooking liquor. If these preparations are to be poached then it is unnecessary to sew into shape. It is better to tie in muslin. If one retains the knuckle bone in the leg and chops the leg bone at an angle, this provides a good representation of a bird's head and beak, thus one may form the leg into a very good representation of a small bird. The appellation of cygnet is often used to preface this method.

◘ Régence

For 8-10 *persons: 6 drumsticks of chicken*; 1 *lb Quenelle forcemeat with Panada;* 1 *truffle;* ½ *lb pickled tongue;* ½ *lb mushrooms;* ¼ *lb pitted olives,* 6 *artichoke bottoms;* 1½ *pints sauce Suprême.* Cooking time: about 35-40 minutes.

Stuff the drumsticks with the *Quenelle* forcemeat, strips of red tongue and the truffle cut in quarters. Wrap in foil and poach in rich stock made with chicken and veal bones. Make a *sauce Suprême* with this stock. Cook the mushrooms, and blanch the olives. Cut the artichoke bottoms into quarters and *sauté* them lightly in butter. Arrange the drumsticks on a dish, garnish with mushrooms, olives and artichoke bottoms and cover with a little sauce. Serve the rest of the sauce in a sauce-boat. Serve hot. The *ballotine* may also be served with *sauce Madère* instead of *sauce Suprême.* (*See illustration p.* 549).

Boudin de Volaille * *Chicken Forcemeat Roll*

◘ Marigny

For 6 *persons: Forcemeat and salpicon as below;* ¾ *pint Onion sauce;* 12 *small tartlets of unsweetened Short pastry;* 2 *lb young green peas;* 2 *lettuces.* Cooking time of sausage: 20-25 minutes.

Make forcemeat as below and coat with light, buttered *sauce Soubise.* Garnish with tartlets filled with *Petits Pois à la Française*, made with the green peas and the lettuce.

◘ Richelieu

For 6 *persons:* 1 *lb Quenelle forcemeat;* ¼ *lb boiled chicken without waste;* 6 *oz mushrooms;* 1 *small truffle;* ½ *pint sauce Périgueux;* 1 *egg white; breadcrumbs; parsley.* Cooking time: 20-25 minutes.

Make a *salpicon* of chicken, mushrooms and truffle. Cut greaseproof paper or foil into rectangles about 6×4 inches, brush with butter and flour. Place some forcemeat lengthwise on the paper, leaving edges free. Form a hollow in the forcemeat lengthwise with a finger and fill with *salpicon.* Cover with forcemeat, shape into a sausage with a moistened palette knife, roll up paper, tie up ends and poach for 15 minutes in boiling salt water. Drain well, remove from paper, egg and breadcrumb, deep fry a golden brown and sprinkle with chopped parsley. Serve the *sauce Périgueux* separately.

Coq au Chambertin * *Capon in Wine*

For 6 persons: 1 *capon, weighing about* 4 *lb;* ½ *lb small onions;* ¾ *lb mushrooms;* 2 *shallots;* 1 *bottle Chambertin;* ¼ *pint cream;* 2 *oz butter;* 1 *tablespoon olive oil.* Cooking time: 30-40 minutes.

Cut the raw capon into 12 pieces. Season and *sauté* in butter and oil. As soon as the pieces are browned on both sides, add the onions and the mushrooms cut in quarters. Transfer to another dish. Cover and cook in a hot oven, 400° F or Gas Mark 6, until tender. Meanwhile, cook the chopped shallots in the pan in which the capon was sautéed, but do not allow to brown. Moisten with the Chambertin, and reduce to half. Add the cream and simmer for a few minutes until the sauce is creamy. Arrange the capon on a hot dish, season the sauce and pour it over the capon. Sprinkle with chopped parsley. (*See illustration p.* 552).

Coq en Pâte * *Capon in Pastry*

For 8 persons: 1 *capon, weighing about* 4 *lb;* ¾ *lb foie gras;* 1 *oz truffle;* ¼ *pint champagne;* 2 *lb Short pastry;* 1 *egg yolk.* Cooking time: 1½-2 hours.

1. Draw and singe the capon, but do not remove either the neck or the head. If preferred bone the breast by removing the breastbone. Marinate the *foie gras* stuck with small pieces of truffle in dry champagne, and season with salt and paprika. Stuff the bird with the *foie gras.* Roll the pastry out about ¼-inch thick and large enough to cover the capon completely. Place the capon in the middle of the dough, pull it up in the shape of the capon, and press it down well, on all sides. The neck and the head skewered to keep them in place, should also be well covered. Imitate the feathers, tail and wings with pastry. Brush with beaten egg yolk, and bake in a hot oven, 400° F or Gas Mark 6. After 30 minutes, place a greased, paper on top to protect the crust from getting too brown. When serving, detach the upper part of the crust and slice the breast. Serve with *sauce Périgueux* to which the champagne used for the marinade has been added.

2. Draw and singe the capon, remove the breastbone, head and neck. Stuff it with the *foie gras*, truss and roast for 40 minutes. Allow to cool, and wrap in Puff pastry. Brush with egg again, and bake in a hot oven for 40 minutes, covered after 30 minutes with a sheet of greased paper. The head may be cooked separately and the eyes imitated with hardboiled egg white and truffle. Arrange the capon on a hot dish, and garnish with a small bunch of watercress. To serve, detach the upper part of the crust, and slice the breast. The second way of preparing the capon is by far the better.

Coq au Riesling * *Capon in White Wine*

For 6 persons: 1 *capon, weighing about* 4 *lb;* ¾ *lb mushroom caps;* ½ *bottle Riesling;* 2 *oz butter;* ½ *pint cream;* 2 *shallots; a small piece of meat glaze;* ¾ *lb cooked noodles.* Cooking time: 35-40 minutes.

Cut the raw capon into 6 or 12 pieces. Season the pieces and brown them in hot butter on both sides. Add the mushrooms and cook with the lid on in a moderate oven, 375° For Gas Mark 4-5. Remove the breast pieces first, because they are cooked sooner than the legs. Arrange capon and mushrooms in a dish and keep them hot. Fry the chopped shallots lightly in the butter, add the Riesling and reduce by half. Add the cooked noodles tossed in butter, or serve them separately.

CÔTELETTES DE VOLAILLE * *CHICKEN CUTLETS*

This name is given to a mixture made with *Quenelle* Forcemeat which is usually filled into a cutlet shaped mould and poached in salted water. Cutlets may also be made of a *croquette* forcemeat. This is made of cold cooked minced chicken flesh from the wings, legs or other parts of the chicken which is seasoned and bound together with *Béchamel.* The mixture is shaped by hand on a floured board into a cutlet shape, then egged, breadcrumbed and shallow fried in butter.

▣ Archiduc

For 6 *persons:* 1 *lb Quenelle forcemeat;* 2 *oz lean boiled ham;* 2 *oz poached mushrooms;* 1 *small truffle;* ½ *lb mushrooms;* ½ *pint sauce Périgueux.* Cooking time: 6 minutes.

Make *salpicon* with the ham, poached mushrooms and truffle. Line cutlet moulds thickly with the forcemeat, place a walnut of *salpicon* in centre, cover with forcemeat, smooth and poach in lightly salted water. Drain well, serve in a ring, coat with *sauce Périgueux* and arrange the mushrooms, sautéed in butter in the centre.

NOTE: In the case of all these cutlets and *quenelles,* it is not the forcemeat which gives the chicken flavour, but the sauce, made of concentrated stock obtained by boiling the raw bones. The forcemeat can therefore also be made with veal and the sauce from stock made from the giblets.

▣ Vicomtesse

For 6 *persons:* 1 *lb Quenelle forcemeat;* 1 *lb green asparagus tips;* 1 *truffle;* ¾ *pint sauce Suprême.* Cooking time: 6-8 minutes.

Fill small, buttered cutlet moulds with chicken forcemeat, smooth, poach in salt water. Drain and arrange in a ring on a round dish so that they overlap. Place a truffle slice on each cutlet and coat with sauce. Prepare asparagus tips in usual way, toss in butter and serve in centre of cutlets. A piece of cooked macaroni may be impaled into the end of each cutlet and decorated with a small cutlet frill.

Curry de Volaille I * *Chicken Curry I*

For 4 *persons:* 1 *chicken, weighing about* 3½ *lb;* 2 *chopped onions;* 1 *tablespoon of curry powder;* ¼ *pint cream;* ¼ *pint of coconut milk;* ¼ *pint of chicken stock;* 1 *bouquet garni.* Cooking time: 30-40 minutes.

Joint the chicken, colour in oil with the onions, add the curry powder and lightly fry together; then add the coconut milk and stock, cover and simmer until tender with the *bouquet garni.* Serve the chicken in a porcelain dish. Reduce the cooking liquor, add the cream and simmer to a sauce consistency; strain over the chicken and serve with plain boiled Patna rice.

Curry de Volaille II * *Chicken Curry II*

For 4 *persons:* 1 *chicken, weighing about* 3½ *lb;* 2 *chopped onions;* 2 *large peeled, cored and chopped apples;* 1 *teaspoon curry powder;* 1 *tablespoon tomato purée;* 2 *oz butter;* 1 *oz flour;* ½ *lb rice;* 1 *pint chicken stock.* Cooking time: 35 minutes.

Joint the chicken, season and lightly fry in the butter, add the onions and then the apple.

Brown together, sprinkle with the flour and curry powder. Add the tomato, moisten with the stock, mix well, season with salt, cover and simmer until tender; bone the chicken and cut meat in pieces, place in a casserole. Reduce sauce to a pouring consistency, pour over the chicken. Serve with plain boiled rice. Serve the curry with mango chutney, prawn puffs, bombay duck, poppadums, sultanas swollen in tepid water and fried in butter, chopped hardboiled eggs, chopped tomatoes, chopped capsicums, diced pineapple, diced dessert apple, sliced banana, fried onion rings and saffron *risotto.*

Fricassée de Volaille * *Chicken Fricassée*

For 6 *persons:* 1 *chicken, weighing about* 3½-4 *lb;* 2 *oz butter;* 1½ *oz flour;* 25 *small onions;* 1 *carrot;* ½ *lb mushrooms;* 2 *egg yolks;* ¼ *pint cream.* Cooking time: 40 minutes.

Carve the raw bird and toss in butter without letting it brown. Dust with flour, shake, cook for a moment, half cover with *bouillon* or water and stir. Add the carrot, *bouquet garni* and the onions, season, bring to the boil, and simmer till done. Remove *bouquet garni* and carrot. Add the separately poached mushrooms with their stock, boil up once more, remove from heat and thicken with egg yolks mixed with cream. Arrange in a deep dish garnished with heart-shaped *croûtons.*

Pain de Volaille Chaud * *Hot Chicken Loaf*

For 6-8 *persons:* 1 *lb chicken without skin or bones;* ½ *pint thick, cold sauce Béchamel;* ¼ *pint cream;* 2 *eggs;* 2 *egg yolks;* ⅜ *pint sauce Suprême.* Cooking time, according to size: 12-35 minutes.

Pound meat finely or pass several times through the finest blade of the mincer. Season with salt, pepper and *pâté* seasoning, mix with cold *Béchamel* and pass through a sieve. Combine with the beaten eggs and egg yolks and finally gently fold in the cream. Fill into a buttered *timbale* and poach in a moderate oven, 375° F or Gas Mark 4, in a water-bath, covered with buttered paper. Cooking time for small moulds: 10-12 minutes. After turning out, coat with *sauce Sûpreme* or other white sauce.

Pilaf de Volaille à l'Orientale * *Chicken Pilaf*

For 6 *persons:* 1 *chicken, weighing about* 3½ *lb;* 3 *oz onions;* ½ *lb tomatoes;* ½ *lb rice;* 2 *green peppers;* 1 *pinch saffron;* 1¼ *pints bouillon;* 2 *oz butter.* Cooking time: 30-35 minutes.

Cut raw chicken in 12 slices and fry light brown in butter with chopped onion. Add rice, simmer it for a moment and add *bouillon.* Add pepper cut in strips and peeled, quartered and deseeded tomatoes, season with salt, pepper and saffron and cook in a moderate oven. The finished dish should be moist but not like a soup. Serve in a deep dish.

NOTE: The chicken can be prepared separately like a *ragoût.* It is then arranged inside a ring of *pilaf* rice. (*See illustration p.* 548).

POULARDE * *CHICKEN AND BOILING FOWL*

Strictly speaking, the French word *poularde* indicates a special type of female bird which has been caponised to increase its size and make it become fat. However, as this type of chicken might be difficult to obtain, a large roasting chicken of 5½-9 months old may be substituted. In some of the recipes, boiling fowl has been specified. Nowadays boiling fowl are not always the rather tough elderly creatures which have finished laying. They weigh between 3-4 lb and may be poached, steamed or casseroled. The older, tough, boiling fowl should really only be used for soups, stocks and forcemeats.

◘ à l'Andalouse

For 6 persons: 1 boiling fowl, weighing about 4 lb; ½ lb diced tomato flesh; 3 red capsicums skinned, deseeded, stuffed with rice à la Grecque and braised; 1¼ pints of sauce Suprême; 2 peeled aubergines thickly sliced and fried in oil; ¼ lb of red capsicum butter. Cooking time: 1½ hours.

Poach the fowl, serve upon an oval dish. Blend the butter into the sauce and mask the chicken. Garnish the slices of *aubergine* with the tomato plant and arrange round the chicken in conjunction with the capsicums. Serve the surplus sauce in a sauce-boat. (*See illustration p.* 551).

◘ à l'Anglaise

For 6 persons: 1 boiling fowl, weighing about 4 lb; 1 lb each of carrot and turnip balls cooked in salted water; 12 slices pickled ox tongue; 1 lb plain boiled peas; 1 pint sauce Béchamel prepared with one-third of strong chicken stock. Cooking time: 1½ hours.

Poach the chicken in chicken stock. Serve on an oval dish; mask with the sauce, garnish with the tongue rolled into cones and alternate small heaps of the vegetables.

◘ à la Châtelaine

For 6 persons: 1 chicken, weighing about 4 lb; 1 lb chestnuts cooked in strong chicken stock; 1 lb onion purée; 6 cooked artichoke bottoms. Cooking time: 1-1½ hours.

Pot roast the chicken, remove and serve upon an oval dish. Deglaze the pan with chicken stock, skim away all fat, reduce to 1 pint, thicken with arrowroot, strain, mask over the chicken. Scoop out the artichoke bottoms and fill with onion *purée* and arrange around the dish alternately with the chestnuts. Serve the surplus sauce in a sauce-boat.

◘ Chivry

For 6 persons: 1 boiling fowl, weighing about 4 lb; 2 lb of macédoine of fresh vegetables tossed in butter; ¾ pint sauce Chivry. Cooking time: 1-1½ hours.

Poach the chicken, serve, mask with the sauce, garnish with the *macédoine*. Serve the surplus sauce in a sauce-boat.

Poularde Demi-Deuil

For 6 persons: 1 *boiling fowl, weighing about* 3½ *lb;* ½ *lb mushrooms;* 1 *pint sauce Suprême;* 2 *oz truffle.* Cooking time: 1-1½ hours.

Remove the breastbone from the bird then place a few thin truffle slices under the skin. Truss and poach in rich white stock. Prepare the *sauce Suprême* with a part of the stock and add a few small, very thin slices of truffle. Before serving, remove the skin of the chicken, cover with a little sauce, and serve the remaining sauce separately. The chicken may be garnished with mushroom caps, poached in butter and lemon juice, drained and decorated with a small round slice of truffle.

⊡ Demidoff

For 6 persons: 1 *chicken, weighing about* 4 *lb;* ½ *lb diced carrots;* ½ *lb diced turnips;* ½ *lb diced celery, steamed in a little butter;* 10 *small sliced onions;* 1 *diced truffle;* ¾ *pint thick reduced chicken stock.* Cooking time: 1-1½ hours.

Precook the chicken with some fat for three-quarters of the normal time in a covered fireproof dish. Then, place in a casserole with all the vegetables including the sliced onion. Finish cooking in a moderate oven and at the last minute add the truffle and chicken stock. Serve in the casserole.

⊡ à l'Estouffade

For 6 persons: 1 *chicken, weighing about* 4 *lb;* 5 *thin slices of ham;* 1 *lb onions, carrots, and celeriac, sliced and tossed in butter;* ½ *pint veal stock.* Cooking time: 1-1½ hours.

Roast the chicken till half cooked. Line the bottom and sides of a lidded *terrine* with the ham, put the chicken in it, surround it with the vegetables and add the veal stock reduced to half. Cover and seal with strip of dough. Put in a hot oven, 425° F or Gas Mark 7. Serve like this.

⊡ à l'Estragon * *with Tarragon*

For 6 persons: 1 *boiling fowl, weighing about* 4 *lb; a little chopped tarragon;* 1 *bouquet garni and* 1 *bundle of tarragon stalks;* 1 *oz arrowroot; blanched and cooled tarragon leaves.* Cooking time: 1½ hours.

Poach the chicken with the *bouquet garni* and tarragon and seasoning. Serve the chicken on an oval dish. Reduce the cooking liquor to 1 pint, thicken with the arrowroot, strain. Brush the chicken with the sauce and decorate with the tarragon leaves. Add the chopped tarragon to the sauce and serve in a sauce-boat with the chicken.

⊡ à la Financière

For 6 persons: 1 *chicken, weighing about* 3 *lb;* ¾ *pint chicken stock;* ¾ *pint sauce Madère; garnish Financière composed of* 12 *cooked mushroom caps,* 12 *small veal quenelles,* 1 *small sliced truffle,* 12 *stoned, blanched olives,* 6 *cocks' combs,* 6 *cocks' kidneys.* Cooking time: 1-1½ hours.

Braise the chicken until tender and brown in the stock. When cooked, remove the chicken and reduce the cooking liquor. Add the *sauce Madère*, boil up once and strain. Serve the chicken surrounded with the garnish and cover with a little sauce. Serve the rest of the sauce separately.

Poularde au Gros Sel * *Chicken with Coarse Salt*

For 6 persons: 1 *chicken, weighing about* 3 *lb;* 12 *carrots cut into olive shape;* 12 *small onions.* Cooking time: 1-1½ hours.

Poach the chicken with the vegetables in white stock. Serve, garnished with clusters of the carrots and onions. Serve with the cooking liquor and coarse salt.

▣ **aux Huitres** * *with Oysters*

For 6 *persons:* 1 *chicken, weighing about* 4 *lb;* 24 *poached, bearded oysters;* ¼ *pint cream; buerre manié* (1½ *oz butter,* 1 *oz flour*). Cooking time: 1-1½ hours.

Poach the chicken in white stock. Make the sauce with the reduced poaching liquor and cream. Thicken with *beurre manié*. Add the oysters and coat the chicken with the sauce.

▣ **à l'Infante**

For 6 *persons:* 1 *chicken, weighing about* 4 *lb;* ¼ *lb each diced carrots and turnips;* ¼ *lb green peas;* ½ *oz truffle;* ½ *lb rice;* 1 *oz grated cheese;* 2 *pints white stock;* ¾ *pint sauce Suprême.* Cooking time: 1-1½ hours.

Poach chicken in stock and make a well-thickened Cream sauce with some of this stock. Boil carrots, turnips and peas separately in water, drain thoroughly and add to sauce together with diced truffle. Cook rice as for *risotto* and add grated cheese to it. Skin and carve the chicken and coat with the sauce, including vegetables. Fill rice into greased *baba* moulds, turn out and arrange round chicken.

▣ **Louisiane**

For 6 *persons:* 1 *chicken, weighing* 3-4 *lb;* 12 *small maize croquettes;* 3 *bananas;* 2 *pints brown chicken stock;* 1 *oz cornflour.* Cooking time: 1-1½ hours.

Braise the chicken with the brown stock. Remove and serve on a dish. Garnish with the maize *croquettes* and the sliced bananas sautéed in butter. Reduce the stock to 1 pint, thicken it with the cornflour and strain it through a cloth. Coat the chicken lightly with the sauce and serve the remainder separately.

▣ **Marie-Louise**

For 6 *persons:* 1 *chicken, weighing about* 4 *lb;* 6 *cooked artichoke bottoms;* 4 *braised half lettuces;* ½ *lb mushroom purée;* ¼ *lb onion purée;* 1 *pint sauce Allemande.* Cooking time: 1-1½ hours.

Poach the chicken, serve and coat with the sauce. Garnish with the artichoke bottoms filled with the mixed mushroom and onion *purée* and arrange the lettuce halves around the chicken.

Poularde Masséna

For 6 persons: 1 chicken, weighing about 4 lb; 1 *lb tomatoes;* ½ *lb olives;* 1½ *lb boletus or mushrooms; 2 shallots; a trace of garlic;* ¼ *pint Madeira;* ½ *pint Demi; glace; 2 oz butter;* ⅛ *pint oil.* Cooking time: 1-1½ hours.

Brown the chicken. Add the Madeira and braise until tender. Stone and blanch the olives. Simmer with a tablespoonful of sauce, clean and slice the boletus or mushrooms, season them and *sauté* in oil with the chopped shallots. Peel, quarter, deseed and season the tomatoes and *sauté* with the garlic. Carve the chicken, garnish with tomatoes, olives and mushrooms, coat lightly with sauce and serve the remainder separately.

▣ Monte-Carlo

For 8 persons: 1 chicken, weighing about 4 lb; 1 lb veal Quenelle forcemeat; 1 *pint sauce Suprême; 4 tablespoons tomato purée.* Cooking time: 1-1½ hours.

Divide forcemeat in 2 parts, colour one part pink with 2 tablespoons tomato *purée*. Make *quenelles* with the forcemeat using a soup spoon and poach them. Poach the chicken and make Cream sauce with the stock, colour half of this with 2 tablespoons tomato *purée* too. After carving, replace chicken in original shape, coat one side with pink and the other with white sauce. Arrange pink *quenelles* on the white side and white *quenelles* on the pink.

▣ Montmorency

For 6 persons: 1 chicken, weighing about 4 lb; 6 blanched, cooked artichoke bottoms; 1 lb vegetable macédoine; 6 bunches green asparagus tips; 1 pint sauce Madère; 1 *small truffle cut into matchsticks.* Cooking time: 1-1½ hours.

Lard the chicken with truffle and braise with the *sauce Madère*. Serve and garnish with the artichoke bottoms filled with vegetable *macédoine* alternating with the asparagus bunches. Skim the fat off the cooking liquor and serve it separately.

▣ Printanière

For 6 persons: 1 chicken, weighing about 4 lb; 1 lb carrots; ½ *lb turnips; 1 lb young green peas;* ½ *lb French beans; 1 lb small new potatoes; 1 oz flour;* 1½ *oz butter; 6 oz spinach purée; blanched chervil, tarragon and watercress.* Cooking time: 1-1½ hours.

Poach the chicken in white wine with all the vegetables. Make a sauce with the reduced cooking liquor, the flour and butter, add the very finely chopped herbs. Carve the chicken, coat with the sauce and garnish with the vegetables.

▣ au Risotto * *with Risotto*

For 6 persons: 1 chicken, weighing about 3 lb; 6 oz tomato risotto; 6 oz blanched mushrooms and ham; 1 pint sauce Madère; 2 oz Parmesan. Cooking time: 1-1½ hours.

Poêlé the chicken, reduce pan residue with the sauce, thicken lightly with cornflour, skim and strain. Mix tomato *risotto,* ham, mushrooms and cheese. Pack into thickly buttered *baba* moulds. Coat chicken lightly with the sauce and serve remainder separately.

Poularde au Riz Sauce Suprême * *Chicken with Rice and Sauce Suprême*

For 6 persons: 1 *boiling fowl, weighing about* 4 *lb;* 2 *carrots;* 1 *onion stuck with a clove; the white of* 2 *leeks;* 1 *bouquet garni;* 1 *pint sauce Suprême;* ½ *lb rice.* Cooking time: 1½-2½ hours, according to age.

Blanch chicken for 3-4 minutes, cool in cold water and place in a casserole with a little cold water, a little salt, the vegetables and the *bouquet garni.* Cover and cook the chicken in a warm oven, 350° F or Gas Mark 3, until tender then skim the fat off the stock and use it to make the sauce. Sweat the rice with a little butter, add twice the quantity of chicken broth, season and cook slowly till tender and dry. Skin chicken, carve it, serve on rice, coat lightly with sauce and serve the remainder separately.

▣ Sainte-Hélène

For 8 *persons:* 1 *chicken, weighing about* 4 *lb;* ½ *lb foie gras;* 6 *truffles;* ½ *lb mushroom caps;* ¼ *lb raw ham (thick slice);* ½ *lb Quenelle forcemeat;* ¾ *pint Demi-glace;* 2 *tablespoons brandy;* 2 *tablespoons Madeira;* 2 *oz butter.* Cooking time: 1-1½ hours.

Place chicken in hot *bouillon* for a moment, remove skin from breast and keep it. Lard the breast with ham and truffle slices, replace skin, truss and bard breast with thin bacon slices. Braise the chicken, reduce pan residue with brandy and Madeira and add *Demi-glace.* Remove barding bacon and skin to show larding and serve. Garnish with fluted, poached mushroom caps, floured medallions of *foie gras* fried in butter with a truffle slice on each and with decorated spoon-shaped *quenelles* of forcemeat. Coat everything lightly with sauce and serve remainder separately.

▣ Soufflée Sauce Suprême * *Soufflé with Sauce Suprême*

For 10 *persons:* 1 *boiling fowl, weighing about* 4 *lb; Mousseline forcemeat;* 3 *truffles;* 2 *oz sliced lean ham;* 1 *egg white;* 1¼ *pints sauce Suprême.* Cooking time: about 1½ hours.

Slowly poach chicken with about 2½ pints white stock. In the meantime make a sauce with the chicken stock thickened with *beurre manié.* Skin the chicken, cut out the breasts with breastbone, remove breasts and keep warm, covered with a little stock and buttered paper. Fill hollow thus made with the forcemeat and smooth into original shape. Brush with lightly beaten egg white, decorate with thinly sliced truffle and ham. Cover with buttered paper, place in a shallow dish into which a little of the stock has been poured and place in moderate oven to cook the forcemeat. Remove paper, arrange chicken on a long dish and garnish with the breasts, cut in thin, diagonal slices with a truffle slice on each. Coat breast slices lightly with sauce and serve remainder separately.

▣ Suprême à l'Espagnole

For 6 *persons:* 1 *chicken, weighing about* 4 *lb;* ½ *lb Patna rice;* ¼ *lb chopped onions;* ¼ *lb sliced mushrooms;* ¼ *lb concassé tomatoes;* 2 *oz each of skinned, deseeded, red and green capsicums cut into a short fine julienne;* ¼ *lb peas;* ¼ *lb butter;* ⅛ *pint oil;* 1 *crushed clove of garlic;* 1 *pint chicken stock; small pinch of saffron and curry powder;* ¾ *pint thickened veal gravy.*

Roast the chicken. Soak the rice for 30 minutes. In the meantime, stew the onions in half the butter, add the mushrooms, tomatoes, capsicums, peas, garlic, seasonings and oil, and stew gently together for 15 minutes. Add the boiling stock, cover with greaseproof paper and a tightly fitting lid and cook in a hot oven, 400° F or Gas Mark 6, for 15 minutes. Remove from the oven and stand upon the table, remove lid and paper and add small pieces of the remaining butter on the surface of the rice; allow to rest for 5 minutes then gently fork to separate the grains. Remove the breasts from the chicken and slice slantwise and arrange upon an oval dish. Deglaze the pan with the thickened gravy, boil and skim. Lightly mask the chicken, garnish with the rice. Serve the rest of the sauce in a sauceboat. (*See illustration p.* 547).

Poularde Truffée

For 6 *persons:* 1 *fowl, weighing about* 4 *lb;* ½ *lb raw chicken livers;* ½ *lb fat belly bacon;* ½ *lb raw truffles;* ¼ *lb fat bacon;* 2 *oz butter.* Cooking time: 1¼-1½ hours.

Remove the breastbone from the chicken. Keep back about 12 slices of truffle. Chop raw livers and raw bacon, or pass through mincer, mix well, season with salt and pepper and combine with the brushed, washed, peeled and coarsely diced truffles; the peel may also be used if very finely chopped. Stuff chicken with this mixture. After trussing, bard with thin slices of fat bacon and keep in a very cool place for 48 hours, hanging so that the air can circulate round it if possible. Roast on the spit or in the oven, basting repeatedly. Serve only with gravy from the pan residue.

Poulets de Grain * *Frying or Small Roasting Chickens*

Frying chickens may be large spring chickens, cockerels or pullets and are available all the year round. They are tender and may be fried, roasted, sautéed or used for casseroles and *fricassées*. Spring chickens and pullets are nowadays usually a product of broiler farms, and are killed when they are about 3 months old.

⊡ en Cocotte * *Casseroled*

Truss the chicken and brown it in an open casserole dish. Put a lid on and finish cooking in the oven. At the last minute, add a little gravy, garnish and serve in its dish. Any garnish for *sauté* chicken can be used for spring chicken. The roasting time is 25-30 minutes jointed or 1 hour whole.

⊡ en Cocotte Bonne Femme

For 4 *persons:* 1 *spring chicken, weighing* 1¾-2 *lb;* 12 *small onions;* 12 *squares of belly bacon;* ½ *lb small raw mushroom caps;* 2 *oz butter;* ¼ *pint veal stock.* Cooking time: ¾-1 hour.

Truss and season the bird and brown all over in hot butter in a casserole. Add the onions and the blanched, lightly-browned bacon strips, cover, put in a moderate oven, 375° For Gas Mark 4-5. Add mushrooms after 15 minutes and finish cooking together, still with the lid on. Finally remove trussing string, carve if desired, add gravy, cover and put back in hot oven for a few minutes. Serve in the casserole with the lid on. Almost all garnishes for sautéed chicken can be used for *Poulet de Grain en Cocotte.*

Poulet de Grain en Cocotte à la Paysanne

For 4 persons: 1 *spring chicken, weighing* 1¾-2 *lb;* ⅛ *pint white wine;* ¼ *pint Demi-glace;* ½ *lb potatoes;* ½ *lb carrots;* ¼ *lb turnips;* 8 *small onions;* ¼ *lb squares of belly bacon.* Cooking time of chicken: ¾-1 hour.

Cut carrots, turnips and potato into olives or other fancy shapes and simmer separately in butter till half cooked. Dice the bacon, blanch and brown. Fry the onions till half cooked and glaze. Brown the chicken all over in butter in a fire-proof casserole, add all the vegetables, season, cover and finish cooking in a warm oven, 350° F or Gas Mark 3. Reduce with the white wine, add the rather thin *Demi-glace*, cover and put back in hot oven for a few more minutes to brown. Serve in the casserole.

⊡ en Cocotte du Père Lathuile

For 4 persons: 1 *spring chicken, weighing about* 1¼-2 *lb;* ½ *lb carrots;* ¼ *lb turnips;* ½ *lb potatoes;* 4 *artichoke bottoms;* ¼ *lb onion rings;* ⅛ *pint white wine;* ¼ *pint veal stock;* 2 *oz butter*. Cooking time: 1-1¼ hours.

Quarter the raw artichoke bottoms, cut all vegetables into small olive shapes and blanch unless they are very young. Brown the chicken in hot butter in a fire-proof dish, season, toss the vegetables in butter and add them to the chicken, cover and cook in a cool oven, 325° F or Gas Mark 2-3, for 1-1¼ hours. Reduce with the white wine, add the concentrated veal stock, and serve with deep fried onion rings.

⊡ Crapaudine

For 3-4 persons: 1 *spring chicken, weighing about* 2½-2¾ *lb;* ¼ *lb butter; breadcrumbs;* 1 *oz Maître d'Hôtel butter*. Cooking time: 25-30 minutes.

Draw and singe the chicken. Chop off the feet above the joint. Cut the breast through the thickest part, starting at the point of the breast and stopping at the wings, so that it is not completely cut through. Flatten the chicken with a heavy knife, this will give it the shape of a toad about to jump. Fix it on a skewer to keep it open. Cook it in butter in a hot oven for about 30 minutes. Coat with butter and breadcrumbs, and grill. Arrange on a hot dish, cover with *beurre Maître d'Hôtel* and garnish with a bunch of watercress and Straw potatoes. The chicken may also be garnished with grilled tomatoes and asparagus tips.

⊡ à la Diable * *Devilled*

For 2 persons: 1 *spring chicken, weighing about* 1½ *lb;* ½ *pint sauce Diable;* 4 *rashers of bacon;* 2 *oz made mustard; breadcrumbs; watercress; Straw potatoes.* Cooking time: 30-40 minutes.

Cut chicken in half lengthwise and trim away the vertebrae, spread flat, beat with a cutlet bat, season and part roast for 20 minutes in a hot oven, 425° F or Gas Mark 7. Mix breadcrumbs, and mustard, sprinkle over chicken, remove and finish upon the grill; dot with butter and grill to finish cooking. Garnish with grilled rashers of bacon, watercress and Straw potatoes. Serve with sauce-boat of *sauce Diable*. (*See illustration p.* 546).

Poulet de Grain Grand-mère

For 2 persons: 1 spring chicken, weighing about $1\frac{1}{2}$ lb when cleaned; $\frac{1}{4}$ lb chopped fat bacon; 1 small chopped onion; 4 chicken livers; salt, pepper, spice; $\frac{1}{4}$ lb bread-crumbs; chopped parsley; $\frac{1}{4}$ pint thickened veal gravy. Cooking time: 30-40 minutes.

Fry the bacon and onion together, add the coarsely chopped livers, fry together, then add the crumbs and parsley. Truss the chicken and stuff with the prepared mixture and roast in a casserole in a hot oven, 400° F or Gas Mark 6. Deglaze the casserole with the veal gravy, boil and skim. Add the chicken, allow to boil and serve.

⊡ Grillé à l'Américaine

For 2-3 persons: 1 chicken, weighing about $1\frac{1}{2}$ lb when cleaned; $\frac{1}{4}$ lb butter; fresh breadcrumbs; 6 rashers of bacon; 6 tomatoes; watercress; 6 mushrooms; 2 oz beurre Noisette; Straw potatoes. Cooking time: 30-40 minutes.

Proceed in the same manner as for *Poulet de Grain à la Crapaudine*. Serve and garnish with bacon, tomatoes, mushrooms, Straw potatoes and watercress. Pour over the *beurre Noisette* at the last moment.

⊡ Jaqueline

For 4 persons: 1 spring chicken, weighing 2-$2\frac{1}{2}$ lb; 2 oz butter; $\frac{1}{8}$ pint Madeira or Port; 3 large apples (rennet of possible); $\frac{1}{4}$ pint double cream; lemon juice; $\frac{1}{4}$ pint concentrated veal stock; almonds. Cooking time: 30 minutes.

Cut bird in to 6 parts—the legs, wings, breast and trimmed back. Brown the pieces very lightly in butter, season and reduce with Madeira or Port. Add the veal stock, cover and simmer slowly till tender. In the meantime peel and core the apples, slice them thickly and cook them in the oven in butter without stirring, so that they remain intact. Serve chicken on a round dish and surround with apple slices. Reduce the cooking stock to a thick sauce with the cream, remove from heat and beat up with some flakes of butter. Add a good tablespoon roasted chopped almonds and pour over bird. Sprinkle the apples with a few drops of lemon juice.

POULETS SAUTÉS * *SAUTÉED SPRING OR YOUNG ROASTING CHICKEN*

Any type of young chicken is suitable for this method of cooking including spring chickens, cockerels, pullets and broilers. This is the general method for *sauté* chicken to be used in the following recipes.

Heat in the pan, 4 oz clarified butter or 2 oz of each of oil and butter. Season the jointed chicken with salt and pepper and brown quickly on all sides, place in a baking tin, cover and continue cooking in a hot oven, 400° F or Gas Mark 6. This will take about 20-30 minutes. When tender, remove the white flesh and keep warm and covered. The legs, back, etc., will take longer so return these to the oven for another 7-8 minutes, then remove from the pan. Deglaze the pan with white wine, chicken stock, mushroom essence, etc. Reduce to half and add the necessary sauce according to individual recipes, add chicken meats and simmer gently until all the ingredients are heated through. For the white preparations, just lightly fry the chicken without colouring in the butter and then continue as for individual recipes.

Poulet Sauté Archiduc

For 6 persons: 1 *chicken, weighing about* 3 *lb;* $\frac{1}{4}$ *pint white Port;* $\frac{1}{8}$ *pint brandy;* $\frac{1}{4}$ *pint sauce Béchamel;* $\frac{1}{4}$ *pint double cream;* 3 *bundles cooked green asparagus tips.* Cooking time: 40 minutes.

Cut up bird and season, toss in butter without letting it colour. Cover and cook in a hot oven, 400° F or Gas Mark 6, until chicken is tender. Remove the breast and wings which will be cooked first—they must remain very juicy—then the other pieces, and keep everything hot. Reduce the pan residue with the brandy and Port. Add the *Béchamel* and the cream, reduce to coating consistency stirring constantly with the spatula, remove from heat, season and enrich with a little butter. Chop asparagus tips and toss in butter. Serve, pour sauce on top of chicken and garnish with asparagus tips. (*See illustration p.* 553).

⊡ à l'Arlésienne

For 4 persons: 1 *chicken, weighing about* 3 *lb;* $\frac{1}{4}$ *pint white wine;* 1 *crushed clove of garlic;* $\frac{1}{2}$ *pint tomato-flavoured Demi-glace;* 2 *onions and* 2 *aubergines, both sliced and fried in oil;* 3 *diced tomatoes tossed in butter.* Cooking time: 40 minutes.

Sauté the chicken as above and reduce with the white wine. Add the garlic, reduce, add the *Demi-glace*. Combine them and simmer for 3-4 minutes. Serve, pour on sauce and garnish with the onions, *aubergines* and tomatoes.

⊡ Bercy

For 4 persons: 1 *jointed chicken, weighing about* 3 *lb;* 1 *small tablespoon chopped shallots;* $\frac{1}{2}$ *lb chopped raw mushrooms;* $\frac{1}{4}$ *pint white wine; a walnut-sized lump of meat glaze;* $\frac{1}{4}$ *lb butter; lemon juice; parsley.* Cooking time: 40 minutes.

Sauté chicken in 2 oz butter as above. Meanwhile sweat the chopped shallots in the frying butter, reduce with white wine and reduce to half. Add the meat glaze, the mushrooms and a few drops of lemon juice. Boil together slowly for 5 minutes, season, remove from heat and add remaining butter. Pour sauce over meat and sprinkle with chopped parsley.

⊡ à la Bordelaise

For 4 persons: 1 *chicken, weighing about* 3 *lb;* 4 *artichoke bottoms;* $1\frac{1}{2}$ *lb cèpes or mushrooms;* $\frac{1}{2}$ *lb onion rings;* $\frac{1}{4}$ *pint strong veal stock or Demi-glace;* 2 *oz butter;* 2 *oz oil.* Cooking time: 40-50 minutes.

Joint chicken, brown on both sides in half butter and half oil, season, cover and cook in a moderate oven. In the case of all sautéed poultry the more tender breast and wings should be removed first, as they are cooked before the legs and back and must be very juicy. Slice and *sauté* the mushrooms and artichokes separately in butter, when the chicken is tender, arrange it on a plate surrounded by small heaps of artichokes and mushrooms. Reduce pan residue with the veal stock, to half and pour over meat. Arrange deep fried onion rings on top. All brown sautéed poultry is prepared in this way.

Poulet Sauté à la Bourguignonne

For 4 persons: 1 chicken, weighing about 3 lb; ¼ pint light Demi-glace; 4 artichoke bottoms; a small bunch of parsley; 1 lb of sliced cèpes or mushrooms; 2 tablespoons of oil; 2 large Spanish onions cut into rings; 2 oz butter; ¼ pint chicken stock. Cooking time: 35-40 minutes.

Sauté the chicken, deglaze the pan with the chicken stock, add the *Demi-glace*, boil and strain. Cut the artichokes into four and fry in butter. Slice the *cèpes* or mushrooms and fry in oil. Dip onion rings in milk then flour and deep fry. Deep fry the parsley. Serve the chicken, garnish with small heaps of *cèpes* and artichokes, arrange the onion rings over the chicken and four clusters of fried parsley.

⊡ Champeaux

For 4 persons: 1 jointed chicken, weighing about 3 lb; 24 small onions; 1 lb potatoes; ¼ pint white wine; veal stock; 2 oz butter. Cooking time: 35-40 minutes.

Sauté chicken in butter. Cook and glaze the onions and prepare the potatoes as for *Pommes Noisette*. Deglaze pan residue with white wine, reduce to half, boil up with veal stock, remove from heat and add a large piece of butter. Serve chicken, coat with sauce and garnish with the onions and potatoes.

⊡ Chasseur

For 4 persons: 1 *jointed chicken, weighing about 3 lb; ½ pint sauce Chasseur; ½ lb mushroom caps; ¼ pint white wine; oil; butter.* Cooking time: 35-40 minutes.

Sauté the chicken in half oil and half butter, grill mushrooms and prepare heart-shaped *croûtons*. Remove chicken from *sauté* pan when cooked and deglaze pan residue with white wine. Reduce to half, add sauce and pour over chicken. Garnish with mushrooms and *croûtons* and sprinkle chopped parsley on meat.

⊡ à l'Estragon * *with Tarragon*

For 4 persons: 1 chicken, weighing about 3 lb; 2 tablespoons oil; 1 pint white wine; 2 oz butter; ¼ pint Demi-glace flavoured with tarragon; tarragon leaves. Cooking time: 35-40 minutes.

Sauté the jointed chicken in the oil and butter, deglaze with the wine, boil with the *Demi-glace* and strain. Serve chicken and coat with the sauce, arrange the blanched tarragon leaves over the chicken.

⊡ Fermière

For 4 persons: 1 chicken, weighing about 3 lb; ½ lb carrots; ¼ lb turnips; 1 lb potatoes; ½ lb French beans; 1 lb green peas; ¼ lb belly bacon; ¼ lb butter; ¼ pint of veal stock or Demi-glace; ½ pint white wine. Cooking time: 35-40 minutes.

Sauté chicken, cut potatoes, carrots and turnips into small olives, simmer in butter, slice beans, boil them and boil the peas; toss the two latter lightly in butter. Garnish chicken with the vegetables in alternate colours and between each arrange a small mound of the bacon, cut in very small slices and fried. Deglaze pan residue with *Demi-glace* or with stock, reduce, add a nut of butter and pour over meat.

▲ *Suprêmes de volaille Maryland, p. 560*

Dinde Rôtie, p. 564 ▼

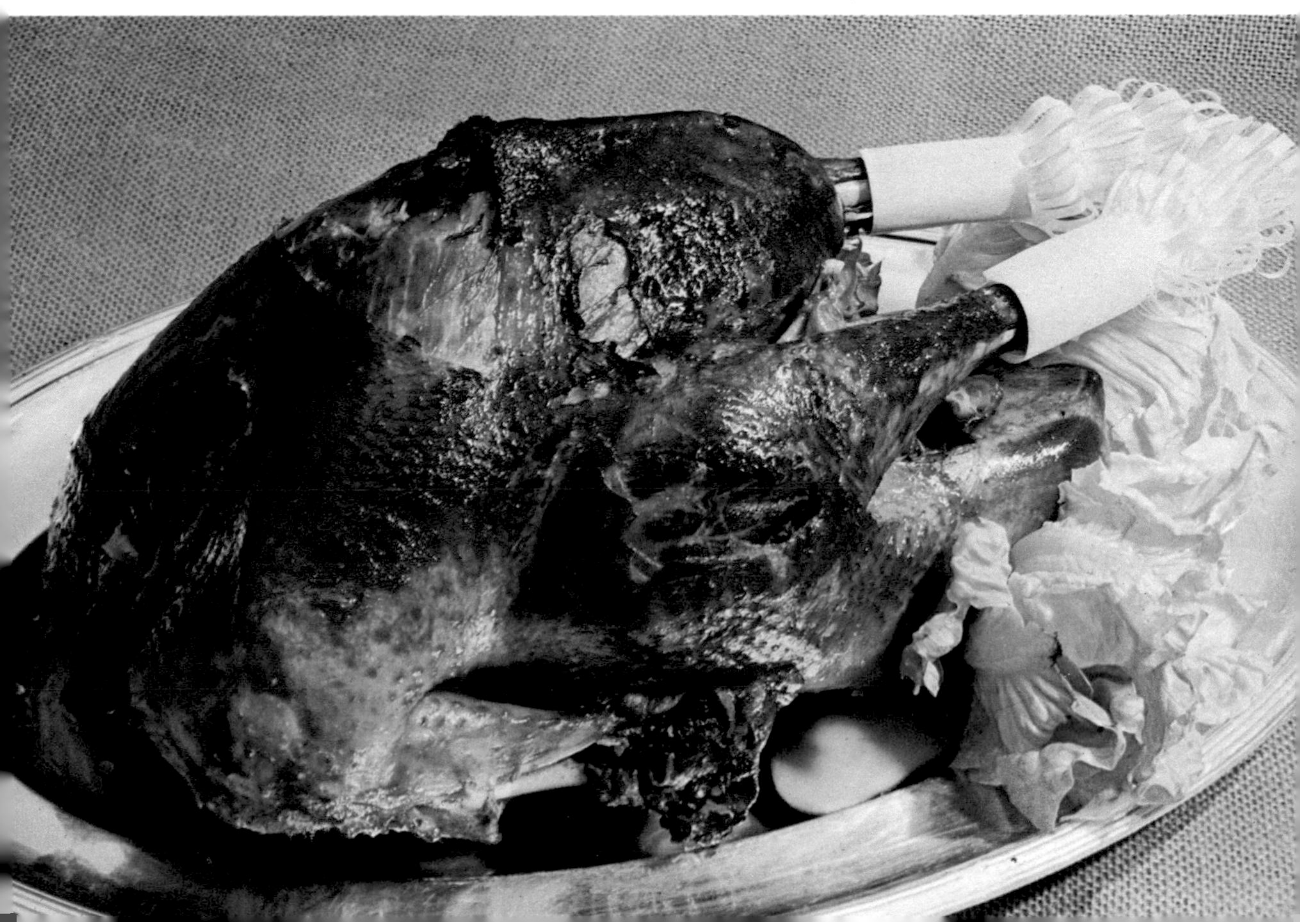

▲ Poulet de grain à la Diable, p. 541

Suprême de dindonneau à la Saxe, p. 565 ▼

▲ *Suprême de poularde à l'Espagnole, p. 539*

Poulet Sauté Stanley, p. 559 ▼

▲ *Poulet Sauté Forestière, p. 557*

Pilaf de volaille à l'Orientale, p. 534 ▼

▲ *Ballotines de volaille Régence, p. 531*

Suprêmes de volaille Sandeman, p. 560 ▼

▲ Poulet Sauté à la Portugaise, p. 558

Quenelles de volaille Isabelle, p. 559 ▼

▲ Poularde à l'Andalouse, p. 535

Canard à la Niçoise, p. 562 ▼

▲ Pigeonneaux aux Petits Pois, p. 569

Coq au Chambertin, p. 532 ▼

▲ *Poulet Sauté Archiduc, p. 543*

Poularde en Chaudfroid p. 573 ▼

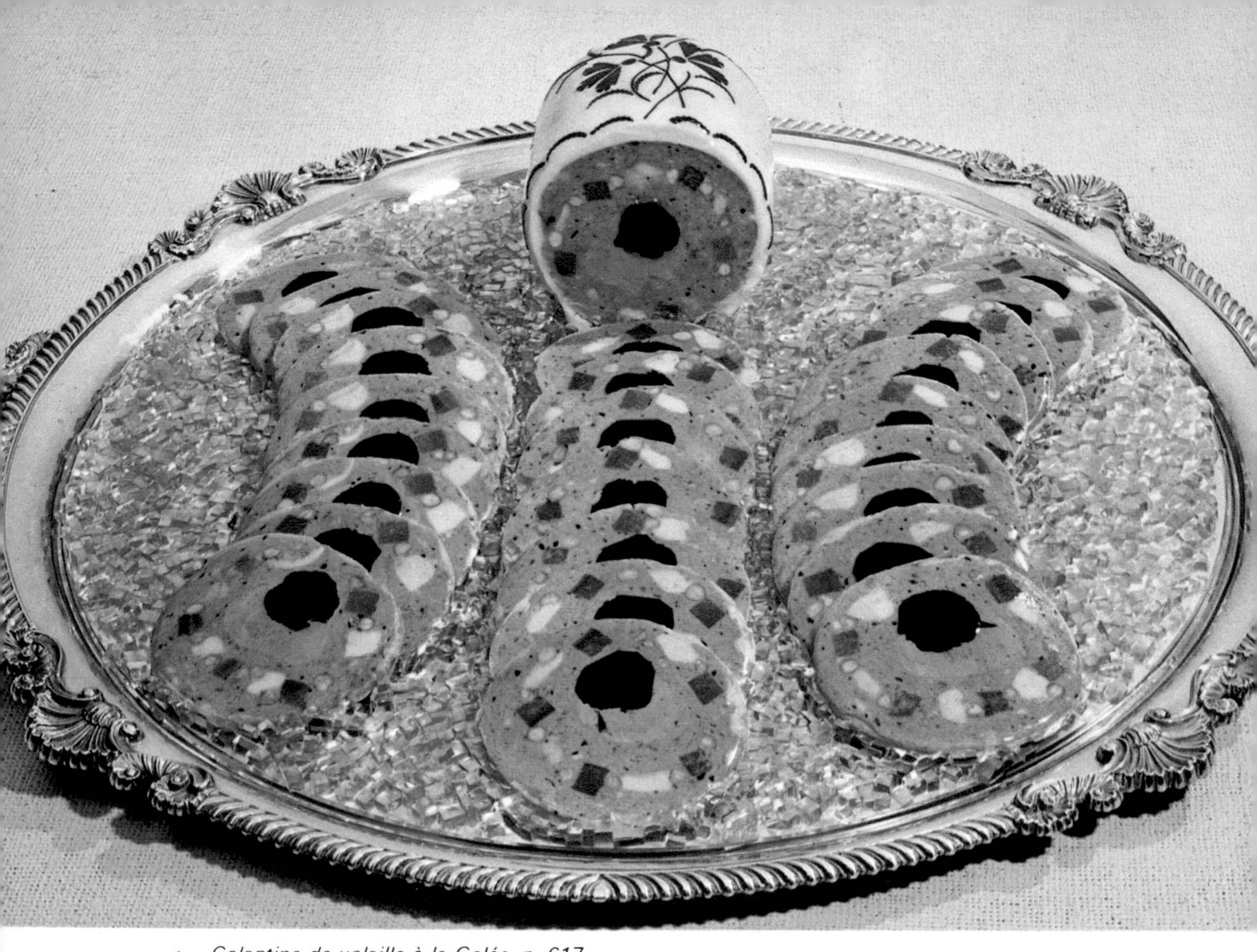

▲ *Galantine de volaille à la Gelée, p. 617*

Poularde Arlequin, p. 572 ▼

▲ *Poularde Lambertye, p. 574*

Dodine de canard Charles Vaucher, p. 576 ▼

556 ▲ *Aspic de Volaille et Jambon Mercédès, p. 572*

Suprêmes de dindonneau Mercure, p. 577 ▼

Poulet Sauté Forestière

For 4 persons: 1 *chicken, weighing about* 3 *lb;* 6 *oz morels or mushrooms;* 1 *lb sautéed potatoes;* 2 *oz butter;* ¼ *pint white wine;* ½ *pint Demi-glace.* Cooking time: 1¼ hours.

Sauté morels or mushrooms in butter, drain and save the liquid, since they give off a great deal. *Sauté* chicken with the morels in the usual way. Remove and keep hot. Deglaze pan residue with white wine, reduce to half, add a nut of butter, add *Demi-glace* and liquid from morels or mushrooms, reduce to required thickness, season, pour over chicken and garnish with sautéed potatoes. (*See illustration p.* 548).

▣ à la Grecque

For 6 *persons:* 1 *chicken, weighing about* 4 *lb;* ¼ *pint white wine;* 6 *oranges;* 1 *lb courgettes;* 1 *lemon; a walnut-sized lump of meat glaze;* 2 *oz butter;* 3 *tablespoons oil.* Cooking time: 1 hour.

Sauté chicken in half butter and half oil. Simmer the peeled, quartered courgettes in butter and cut 5 oranges into segments removing the white skin and pips. Deglaze pan residue with white wine, reduce to half, add the juice of 1 orange, ½ lemon and the meat glaze. Boil up, remove from heat, add a large lump of butter and season well with cayenne pepper. Arrange on a hot dish, pour sauce on top and garnish with courgettes and orange segments.

NOTE: We emphasise again that all sautéed poultry must be cooked dry, i.e., only in butter, without liquid and with the lid on. That is the characteristic of this method. If it were cooked in a sauce or a liquid it would become a *ragoût.*

▣ Hongroise

For 4 *persons:* 1 *chicken, weighing about* 3 *lb;* 3 *oz onions;* ½ *lb rice;* ½ *lb fresh tomatoes;* 1 *small spoon concentrated tomato purée;* 1½ *pints bouillon;* 2 *oz butter;* 1 *teaspoon paprika.* Cooking time: 45-60 minutes.

Cut up chicken as for sautéing, season, quickly fry until brown in butter and put aside Put another piece of butter in the pan, sweat the chopped onions in it, add the rice and fry it for a moment. Add the *bouillon,* the diced tomato and the tomato *purée* and the paprika and, as soon as everything starts to boil, the pieces of chicken. Cover and simmer slowly for about 25 minutes, if necessary add a little water. By this time the rice should have absorbed the liquid and the meat should be tender. Serve, very hot, in a deep bowl.

▣ à l'Indienne * *with Curry Sauce*

For 4 *persons:* 1 *chicken, weighing about* 3 *lb;* ½ *lb rice;* 3 *oz onions;* 1 *heaped teaspoon curry powder;* ¼ *pint thick sauce Béchamel;* 1 *oz grated coconut;* 2 *oz butter.* Cooking time: 45-60 minutes.

Cut up chicken, fry lightly in butter, brown onion slightly at the same time, season, dust with curry powder and fill right up with *bouillon.* Simmer everything for 25 minutes or until the meat is cooked. Place it in a clean casserole, add the *Béchamel* to the stock, reduce to required thickness, strain and add the coconut. Pour over the meat and boil for a few minutes. Serve in the sauce with *Riz à la Créole.*

Poulet Sauté Louisette

For 4 persons: a jointed chicken, weighing 3-3½ *lb;* ¼ *lb diced raw ham;* 1 *carrot;* 1 *onion diced;* 1 *chopped shallot;* ¼ *pint white wine;* 4 *diced mushrooms;* ¼ *pint tomato flavoured sauce Demi-glace;* 2 *oz butter;* ½ *lb Riz à la Pilaf.* Total cooking time: approximately 1 hour.

Sauté the chicken. Thoroughly brown the ham, carrot and onion in butter. Add the shallot, the white wine and then the mushrooms and simmer for 10 minutes. Thicken with the *Demi-glace* and remove from the heat and add the butter. Pour this sauce over the cooked chicken and serve surrounded by rice.

▣ Marengo

For 6 persons: 1 *chicken, weighing about* 3 *lb;* ¼ *pint white wine;* 2 *peeled, deseeded and crushed tomatoes;* 1 *tablespoon tomato paste;* 1 *crushed clove of garlic;* 10 *small onions;* ½ *pint of stock;* ¼ *lb quartered mushrooms;* 6 *fried croûtons; chopped parsley;* 2 *fl oz oil;* 1 *oz butter; bouquet garni.* Cooking time: 1 hour.

Rub the chicken with salt and pepper, dip in flour and *sauté* to brown in oil and butter. Add chicken stock, peeled onions and tomatoes and paste, garlic and *bouquet garni*, cover and simmer for 40 minutes or until chicken is tender. *Sauté* the mushrooms in butter, add the wine and pour this into the chicken mixture. Five minutes before cooking is completed, garnish with *croûtons* and chopped parsley and serve with boiled rice. This dish may also be garnished with cooked crayfish and fried eggs.

▣ Mireille

For 4 persons: 1 *chicken, weighing about* 3 *lb;* 1 *lb aubergines;* 1½ *lb tomatoes;* ¼ *pint white wine;* ¼ *pint Tomato sauce; oil; butter; flour; parsley; garlic.* Cooking time: 35-40 minutes.

Season the chicken, flour and *sauté* in oil. Meanwhile slice and flour *aubergines* then deep fry in oil and peel and quarter tomatoes; *sauté* in butter. Pour oil out of pan, reduce pan residue with white wine, add a pinch of chopped garlic and the rather thin Tomato sauce. Boil up several times, season and pour over meat. Sprinkle chopped parsley on top. Garnish alternatively with the *aubergines* and tomatoes.

▣ à la Portugaise

For 4 persons: 1 *chicken, weighing about* 3 *lb;* ¼ *pint white wine;* ¾ *lb tomatoes;* 4 *small tomatoes;* ¼ *lb duxelles;* 1 *small onion;* ¼ *lb mushrooms;* 1 *clove garlic;* 2 *oz butter;* 1 *tablespoon olive oil.* Cooking time: 35-40 minutes.

Joint, season and *sauté* the chicken. Meanwhile brown the chopped onion slightly in butter, add the peeled, deseeded and diced tomatoes. Season, and simmer for a few minutes. Now add the mushrooms, cut in quarters and crushed garlic, chopped parsley and white wine. Simmer for a few minutes longer, and pour over the cooked chicken. Garnish with four small tomatoes stuffed with *duxelles* (*see Vegetables*) and cooked in the oven. (*See illustration p.* 550).

Poulet Sauté Stanley

For 6 persons: 1 chicken, weighing about 3 lb, cut in pieces; 1 teaspoon curry powder; ½ lb onions, sliced; a pinch of cayenne; 6 oz mushrooms; 4 slices of truffle; 2 oz butter; juice of half a lemon; ½ pint cream. Cooking time: 1 hour.

Cook the chicken and onions together in the butter for about 15 minutes, add the curry powder and cook 3-4 minutes. Mix well, now add the sliced mushrooms. Cook a further few minutes, add the cream, cayenne and lemon juice, cover and cook in a moderate oven, 375° F or Gas Mark 4, for 50 minutes or until chicken is tender. Serve and garnish with the slices of truffle. (*See illustration p.* 547).

QUENELLES DE VOLAILLE * *CHICKEN QUENELLES*

▣ Isabelle

For 6 persons: 1¼ lb chicken flesh forcemeat with Egg panada; croûtons; 2 oz butter; 2 oz flour; ½ pint chicken stock; 2 fl oz double cream; salt; pepper; 1 teaspoon meat glaze; 2 oz chopped cooked tongue; 1 small truffle, finely chopped. Cooking time: 10-15 minutes.

Make forcemeat of minced raw chicken and Egg panada and pass through a fine sieve. Shape this forcemeat into *quenelles* either with a tablespoon, by rolling on a floured table or by filling into small, buttered *barquette* moulds. Poach for 10-15 minutes in a deep pan containing 3-4 inches slightly salted, barely simmering water or chicken stock. Never allow the liquid to boil. Remove from water, drain and arrange on small *croûtons* of the same size and shape as *quenelles*. Meanwhile make a *sauce Suprême*, melt butter in saucepan, remove from heat, blend in flour stir and cook 1 minute. Add stock and cook 2 minutes or until thickened. Blend in cream, salt, pepper, and meat extract. Heat and sprinkle with finely diced truffle and tongue. (*See illustration p.* 550).

▣ à l'Estragon * *in Tarragon Sauce*

For 6 persons: 1¼ lb chicken forcemeat with Egg panada; ¾ pint tarragon-flavoured sauce Suprême; 12 medium-sized cooked mushroom caps; tarragon leaves. Cooking time: 8-15 minutes according to size of *quenelles.*

Make *quenelles* as above, coat each one with tarragon-flavoured *sauce Suprême*, decorate with two blanched, crossed tarragon leaves and garnish dish with a ring of mushrooms.

SUPRÊMES DE VOLAILLE * *BREASTS OF CHICKEN*

The section of chicken known as the *suprême* can vary according to the size of the bird. In a large bird it is usually the breast without the bone, whereas in a small spring chicken it is the breast removed together with the wing. If the *suprême* is large it is usually cut into 3 or 4 pieces, flattened slightly and trimmed to an oval shape, unless it is to be stuffed. *Suprême* may be cooked in a number of ways including poaching and coating in egg and breadcrumbs for grilling and sautéing. It is important to remember that *suprêmes* cook very quickly.

Suprêmes de Volaille à la Crème de Noisette * *Breasts of Chicken with Hazelnut Cream Sauce*

For 6 persons: 6 suprêmes of chicken; 2 tablespoons of Port wine; 1 pint cream; 36 marble-sized apple balls of cooking apples; 3 oz hazelnuts; ¼ lb butter; 1 oz meat glaze; ½ lb Riz à la Pilaf. Cooking time of *suprêmes*: 10-15 minutes.

Season, flour and fry the *suprêmes* in butter. When tender remove from pan, deglaze with the Port wine, add the cream and meat glaze and simmer together. Put the nuts in a very hot oven for a few minutes to loosen the skins but take care that they do not burn. Rub off the skins and pass through a very fine sieve, blend into the sauce and keep hot, but do not allow to boil. Fry the apples in butter. Serve the *suprêmes*, mask with Hazelnut sauce, and garnish with the apples. Serve the rice separately.

▣ Maryland

For 4 persons: 4 suprêmes of chicken; 1 small tin of sweet corn; 2-3 tablespoons thick sauce Béchamel; 2 eggs; white breadcrumbs; 4 small tomatoes; 4 very small bananas; 4 rashers of bacon; parsley; Horseradish sauce; flour. Cooking time of *suprêmes:* 10-15 minutes.

Flatten the *suprêmes* slightly and dip them in flour, beaten eggs and white breadcrumbs. Drain the sweet corn well, bind with thick *sauce Béchamel*, add an egg yolk, and season with salt and pepper. When the mixture is cold, shape into small flat *croquettes*, dip in beaten egg and coat with breadcrumbs. Skin and half the bananas and *sauté* them in butter. Grill the tomatoes. Fry the chicken pieces in a bath of deep oil until they are golden all over and arrange them on a long dish. Garnish with the corn fritters, bananas, fried bacon and grilled tomatoes. Serve the Horseradish sauce at the same time. *Horseradish sauce*: Whip ¼ pint of cream, add 2 tablespoons of grated horseradish, and season with paprika, a pinch of sugar and a few drops of vinegar. (*See illustration p.* 545).

▣ Sandeman

For 6 persons: 6 suprêmes of chicken; 2 red capsicums cut into julienne and stewed in butter or 1 canned pimento; ¾ pint cream; 2 fl oz whisky; 1½ oz meat glaze; 1 glass sherry; ¼ lb butter; ½ lb Riz à la Pilaf. Cooking time: 10 minutes.

Skin and half the *suprêmes* then season and fry in butter. Remove, flame the pan with the whisky, add the cream, sherry and meat glaze and simmer together for about 5 minutes. Add the capsicums and a squeeze of lemon juice. Serve the chicken, mask with the sauce. Serve the rice separately. (*See illustration p.* 549).

Zéphyrs à la Crème * *Zéphyrs in Cream Sauce*

For 6 persons: 1¼-1¾ lb chicken Zéphyr forcemeat; ¾ pint sauce Suprême; ¼ pint cream; 2 tablespoons whipped cream; paprika. Cooking time: 12-15 minutes.

Fill buttered beaker or *baba* moulds with forcemeat and poach very slowly in water-bath. Turn out and coat with *sauce Suprême* heated with cream till very creamy and completed with whipped cream and plenty of paprika. Possible garnishes are mushrooms, asparagus tips, quartered artichoke bottoms, all tossed in butter.

CANARD * *DUCK*

There are many kinds of edible ducks, in England the large white Aylsbury is considered the best and in France, the Rouen and Nantes are preferred. Ducks are available all the year round but are at their best in the summer. If a duck is required for roasting choose one from 6-10 months old.

When choosing, remember that fresh prime ducklings and ducks should have fine pink flesh, pliable feet, a plump breast and the liver should be pale in colour. Young birds should be free from hair and the windpipe of a young bird should yield when pressed with the fingers. If the windpipe is hard and the neck long and lanky, the bird is old. Domesticated ducks are always well cooked, whereas the wild species are often served underdone.

◘ Bigarade

For 6 persons: 1 duck, weighing about 5 lb; juice of 4 oranges (bitter if possible) and half a lemon; 1 oz castor sugar; zest of 2 oranges cut in fine julienne and well blanched; 2 fl oz vinegar; 2 oranges cut into thin slices; ¼ pint veal stock; ¼ pint sauce Demi-glace. Cooking time: 1-1¼ hours.

Roast the duck in a moderate oven, 375° F or Gas Mark 5. Caramelise the sugar by cooking it in a very small saucepan until it is dissolved and slightly browned, but be careful it does not burn. Add the vinegar, the fat-free cooking juices, the veal stock and *Demi-glace*, the orange and lemon juice and the zest. Simmer for 5 minutes. Slice the duck into long thin slices, arrange upon a dish and garnish with the slices of orange. Serve surplus sauce in a sauce-boat.

◘ Braisé aux Chipolatas * *Braised with Chipolatas*

For 6 persons: 1 duck, weighing about 5 lb; 6 oz raw mushrooms; 12 button onions, peeled; ½ lb braised chestnuts; 12 grilled chipolata sausages; ¾ pint sauce Demi-glace. Cooking time: 1-1½ hours.

Brown the duck in a very hot oven for 15 minutes, pour off some of the fat and fry the onions in this fat. When these are brown, drain off the fat, add the *Demi-glace*, pour over the duck and simmer in a moderate oven, 375° F, or Gas Mark 4-5, for 35-40 minutes; then add the mushrooms and chipolatas and cook for about 10 minutes and garnish the duck. Skim the sauce, correct seasoning and pour over the duck. Serve garnished with the chestnuts and serve the rest of the sauce in a sauce-boat.

◘ Braisé aux Petits Pois * *Braised with Peas*

For 6 persons: 1 duck, weighing about 5 lb; ¼ pint brown stock; 2 lb shelled peas; ¾ pint Demi-glace; 24 button onions; bouquet garni; ½ lb lardons of bacon. Cooking time: 1½ hours.

Brown the duck on all sides in butter, remove and fry the lardons and button onions until they begin to colour. Drain off the fat, add the stock, sauce, seasonings, and *bouquet garni*. Replace the duck, cover and braise over low heat or in a moderate oven, 375° F or Gas Mark 4-5. Serve with sauce in sauce-boat, and boiled peas.

Canard en Compôte * *Stewed Duck*

For 6 persons: 1 *duck, weighing about* 4 *lb;* 24 *small onions;* 24 *small chunks diced lean bacon;* ½ *lb uncooked mushrooms;* 1 *bouquet garni;* 1 *glass white wine;* ½ *pint sauce Demi-glace.* Cooking time: 1-1½ hours.

Brown the duck in butter and then remove it from the pan. Fry onions and bacon in the same butter. Skim off the fat, add the white wine and *Demi-glace*, then replace the duck in the pan with the *bouquet garni*. Cover and cook slowly for 40 minutes. Again skim off the fat, add the mushrooms and simmer until completely cooked.

⊡ aux Navets * *Braised with Turnips*

For 6 *persons:* 1 *duck, weighing about* 4 *lb;* ¼ *pint white wine;* ¾ *pint sauce Demi-glace;* 1 *bouquet garni;* 1 *lb turnips trimmed into olive shapes, sautéed in butter, and glazed with a pinch of sugar;* 20 *small onions cooked in butter.* Cooking time: 1¼ hours.

Brown the duck in butter and remove it from the pan. Skim off the fat and stir in the white wine. Reduce and mix in the *Demi-glace* before replacing the duck. Put a lid on the pan and cook for 50 minutes. Next, add the turnips and onions and finish cooking until tender. Serve the duck on a dish surrounded by the turnips and onions.

⊡ à la Niçoise

For 4-5 *persons:* 1 *duckling, weighing about* 3 *lb;* 2 *lb tomatoes;* ½ *lb olives;* ¼ *pint white wine;* 1 *glass brandy;* 1 *clove of garlic;* 1 *bouquet garni*; ¼ *pint bouillon;* 2 *oz butter.* Cooking time: 55-60 minutes.

Brown duck well and add the crushed garlic, the peeled, quartered and seeded tomatoes, the stoned, blanched olives and the *bouquet garni*. Season, add the white wine, brandy and *bouillon* and braise till done. Serve with the garnish. (*See illustration p.* 551).

⊡ aux Olives * *with Olives*

Proceed in the same way as for *Canard aux Navets*, leaving out the onions and replacing the turnips with ½ lb stoned and blanched olives.

⊡ à l'Orange * *with Orange*

For 4-5 *persons:* 1 *duckling, weighing about* 3-3½ *lb;* 8 *oranges;* 1 *pint Demi-glace;* ½ *lemon;* 2 *lumps of sugar; a few drops of vinegar.* Cooking time: 50 minutes.

Brown the duck, pour off the fat, and cook, covered, in a hot oven, 400° F or Gas Mark 6, and moistened with *Demi-glace*. When it is cooked, skim off the fat and strain the sauce. Add the juice of two oranges, the juice of half a lemon, the sugar burnt to caramel and dissolved in a few drops of vinegar, and the rind of three oranges, cut into *julienne* and blanched for three minutes in boiling water. Arrange the duck on a long dish, cover with sauce, and garnish with orange segments without seeds or skin. Serve the rest of the sauce in a sauce-boat. The orange segments may be filled in half oranges, scooped out and serrated.

Canard Rôti * *Roast Duck*

For 4 persons: 1 *duckling, weighing about* 3 *lb; salt; pepper;* 1 *oz butter.* Cooking time: underdone 35-40 minutes; well done about 1-1½ hours.

Season and roast the duck in a moderate oven, 375° F or Gas Mark 4-5. Roast without butter if the duck is very fat. When it is cooked, pour out the fat from the pan and reduce with good gravy. Strain, skim off the remaining fat and serve the gravy in a sauce-boat.

▣ à la Rouennaise

For 4-5 persons: 1 *duckling, weighing about* 3 *lb;* 1 *small shallot;* ¼ *pint red wine.* Cooking time: 25-30 minutes

Roast the duck in a very hot oven, 425° F or Gas Mark 7, for 15 minutes. It must be underdone. Remove legs and finish roasting them. Cut breast in thin, long slices and put them on a hot dish over the bottom of which finely chopped shallot has been sprinkled. Season with salt and pepper and pour the blood of the carcase, pressed out with the red wine, over it. Put dish in a very hot oven for 1-2 minutes, arrange carved legs and wings at either end and serve at once.

▣ Rouennaise à la Presse * *Pressed Rouen Duck*

Take a large Rouen duck (these are ducks that are smothered) and roast very underdone, i.e., at most 18-20 minutes. Remove legs, which must be used for something else. Cut breast in long, thin slices and put them side by side on a dish that is barely lukewarm. Put the carcase, which should be quite bloody, in the duck press together with a large glass of red wine. Mix the juice collected in this way with a dash of brandy and pour over slices of duck after seasoning them with salt and pepper. Place dish on a hotplate to heat and thicken the juice. Great care must be taken to see that it does not boil, otherwise it will curdle. Serve at once. This method was invented by the "Great Fréderic" of the Tour d'Argent restaurant in Paris, who prepared the duck in the presence of the guests. It can only be served where there is a duck press and tastes good only when served and eaten at once.

▣ à la Valencienne

For 4-5 persons: 1 *ducking, weighing about* 3 *lb;* ½ *lb rice;* 2 *tablespoons tomato purée;* ½ *pint rather thin Demi-glace;* 1 *pint white stock;* 2 *oz green peas;* 1 *oz grated Parmesan;* 2 *oz each of cooked tongue, boiled ham and mushrooms;* 1 *small truffle.* Cooking time: 1-1½ hours.

Brown the duck, add the *Demi-glace* and braise slowly until tender. Twenty minutes before it is completely cooked sweat the rice in butter, add stock and tomato *purée* and prepare in the same way as *risotto*. Just before serving add the peas (cooked separately) and the grated cheese. Cut breast of duckling into long thin slices, carve legs and back and serve on a bed of rice. Skim fat off sauce, boil it up once with the truffle, tongue, ham and mushrooms cut in *julienne* and pour over duckling.

Caneton à la d'Orsay

For 6 persons: 1 duck, weighing about 5 lb; 1½ pints Demi-glace; ¼ lb fat bacon; 6 tomatoes; 6 oz calves' liver; ½ lb onion purée; 1 shallot; ½ lb cooked peas; sprig of thyme; 1 glass sherry; 1 bay leaf; 6 deep tartlet cases (croustades); a few parsley stalks. Cooking time: 1¼-1½ hours.

Lightly fry together the cubed fat bacon and liver, shallot and herbs, then pound and sieve. Stuff the duck with the liver mixture, truss, brown in a casserole in the oven, add the sherry and *Demi-glace*. Cover and simmer in a moderate oven until tender. Drain off the sauce, skim away all fat and strain. Empty the tomatoes and fill with onion *purée*. Toss the peas in butter and fill into the *croustades*. Serve the duck, mask with sauce, arrange garnishes round the duck. Serve the rest of the sauce in a sauce-boat.

Civet de Canard * *Jugged Duck*

For 6 persons: 1 duck, weighing about 5 lb; ¾ pint Chambertin; ½ lb button onions; ½ pint cream; ½ lb mushrooms; 2 oz butter; 2 chopped shallots; 2 fl oz oil. Cooking time: 1¼-1½ hours.

Joint the bird and fry in oil and butter, add the onions and mushrooms, cover and finish cooking in a warm oven, 350° F or Gas Mark 3. Drain off the liquor into a saucepan, add the wine and chopped shallots, reduce to half its volume, and add the cream. Dress the duck, mask over with the sauce, sprinkle with chopped parsley and serve. Serve the surplus in a sauce-boat.

DINDES * *TURKEY*

Turkey is now available all the year round. The hen bird is preferred to the cock, but it is usually more expensive. Turkeys are best from 7 months to a year old, after which age they become tough. The flesh of turkeys is fine and delicate but inclined to be dry. Roasting is the most popular method of cooking when they are usually stuffed. It is important to use plenty of fat when cooking turkey in order to keep the flesh moist. The most famous English turkeys are those from Norfolk. (*See illustration p.* 545).

▣ Truffée * *Truffled*

For 10-12 persons: 1 turkey, weighing about 14 lb; 1 lb raw poultry livers; 1 lb lard; ¾ lb truffles which have been scrubbed and peeled; salt and pepper. Cooking time: 3-4 hours.

Proceed in the same way as for Truffled Chicken.

DINDONNEAU * *YOUNG TURKEY*

▣ à l'Américaine

For 12 persons: 1 turkey, weighing about 14 lb; 2 eggs; ½ lb breadcrumbs soaked in milk and squeezed dry; 2 egg yolks; ½ finely chopped beef suet; salt, pepper, ground sage to taste; ¼ lb chopped onion stewed in butter; 1 pint Cranberry sauce; 2 oz chopped parsley.

Mix the suet, breadcrumbs, onions, herbs, eggs and seasoning together. Stuff the prepared cleaned turkey with this mixture, truss, roast at 350° F or Gas Mark 4 for approximately 3½ to 4 hours. Serve with the gravy made from the pan residue and the Cranberry sauce. Garnish with grilled bacon, chipolatas, watercress and Game chips.

Dindonneau Farci aux Marrons * *with Chestnut Stuffing*

For 12 persons: 1 turkey, weighing about 14 lb; 1½ lb soft breadcrumbs; 2 lb chestnuts; salt and pepper; 2 lb sausage meat; 2 fl oz cognac. Cooking time: 3½-4 hours.

Make an incision on the convex side of chestnuts, cover with water and bring to boiling point. Draw pan aside and remove chestnuts one at a time from the water and peel off shells and skins while nuts are hot. Cook in chicken stock for ½ hour or until nuts are just soft. Drain and chop, add to remaining ingredients and mix well. Stuff the turkey with the forcemeat, truss and roast in a warm oven, 325° F Gas Mark 2-3. Serve with gravy and watercress.

▣ Foies et Champignons au Riz * *Turkey Livers and Mushrooms with Rice*

For 6 persons: 1½ lb turkey livers; 2 chopped shallots; ½ lb mushrooms; ¼ lb butter; ½ pint of Demi-glace; 1 lb rice; 1 glass sherry; 1½ pints turkey stock. Cooking time: 20-30 minutes.

Cut the mushrooms in quarters and fry in 2 oz of butter, remove, add the shallots, and the diced livers. Fry quickly, place in a basin, deglaze the pan with sherry, add the *Demi-glace*, boil and strain. Cook the rice with the stock as a *risotto* and press into a large *savarin* mould, unmould upon a round dish or form a ring of rice on the serving plate. Mix the livers, mushrooms and sauce together and fill the centre of the rice mould. Sprinkle with chopped parsley.

Suprême à la Saxe * *Garnished Turkey Breast*

For 6 persons: 6 thick slices of roast turkey; 2 oz julienne of black olives; 6 slices of continental sausage, each weighing 1½ oz; 1 lb of Duchess potatoes made into 18 potato croquettes; ¾ lb mushrooms; ½ pint of turkey jus lié; ½ lb each of red and green capsicums or tinned pimento. Cooking time for turkey breast: 50-55 minutes.

Heat the sausage slices in butter and serve upon a slice of turkey. Skin the capsicums, remove seeds and cut into fine strips and stew in butter. Fry the mushrooms in butter. Mask the turkey with the thickened gravy, garnish with the mushrooms and capsicums mixed together and sprinkle with the olive strips. Serve with the *Croquette* potatoes and thickened gravy separately. (*See illustration p.* 546).

▣ Tamerlan

For 10 persons: 1 turkey, weighing about 14 lb; 3 tins of tangerine segments (or mandarin oranges); ¼ lb butter; 10 small artichoke bottoms; ¼ pint cold sauce Béchamel; 1½ oz truffle; 1 white of egg; ¾ lb chestnut purée; ¾ pint cream; 1 carrot; 1 pint Demi-glace; 1 onion; juice of 5 tangerines; 1 glass sherry. Cooking time: 1 hour.

Slice the carrot and onion, spread in a pan, lay the breast of turkey upon them, cover with slices of fat bacon and pot roast. Mince the thighs and liver of the turkey finely, then pound and sieve. Season with spiced salt, beat in the white of egg, *Béchamel* and lastly the cream. Dice the truffle and mix into the liver *mousse* mixture, fill into an oval buttered mould and poach in a water-bath. When the turkey is cooked, remove and deglaze the pan with the tangerine juice, skim away all fat, add the *Demi-glace*, bring to the boil and strain. Heat the tangerine segments in butter. Heat the hollowed-out artichoke bottoms in butter and fill with the chestnut *purée*. Serve the liver *mousse* in the centre of the dish. Cut each breast into 10 slices, re-form and arrange on each side of the *mousse*; mask over with the sauce. Garnish with the tangerine and artichoke bottoms. Serve the surplus sauce in a sauce-boat and a dish of *pommes Marie*.

OIES * *GOOSE*

The rules for the general choice of poultry may be followed for geese. Up to 6 months old, both the male and the female are known as "green geese" or goslings; geese are really only tasty when they are under a year old. Geese are in their prime in Britain from September to February.

The goose provides us with the jewel of the kitchen the "fat liver" or *foie gras* which is very highly esteemed by gourmets. Goose flesh is extremely fatty and will exude a great deal of this fat when roasted. This may be reserved and used to cook vegetables and *sauerkraut*.

▣ à l'Allemande

For 10 *persons:* 1 *goose, weighing about* 8 *lb;* ½ *pint white wine;* 3 *lb peeled and cored cooking apples;* ¾ *pint of Demi-glace.* Cooking time: 2-3 hours.

Slice half the apples and fill into the goose, truss and fry until completely browned all over. Drain off the fat, add the wine and *Demi-glace*, cover with lid and finish cooking in a warm oven, 350° F or Gas Mark 3-4. Slice the rest of the apples, moisten slightly with water, cover and simmer to a pulp. When goose is cooked, skim away all fat from the pan residue, add wine and mask over the goose. Serve a sauce-boat of Wine sauce and Apple sauce separately.

▣ à l'Alsacienne

For 10 *persons:* 1 *goose, weighing about* 8 *lb;* 4 *lb of sauerkraut;* 2 *lb sausage meat;* 2 *lb lean bacon.* Cooking time: 2-3 hours.

Stuff the goose with the sausage meat, truss and roast in a casserole. Braise the *sauerkraut* with the bacon until part cooked then bury the goose in the *sauerkraut* and complete cooking.

▣ à l'Anglaise

For 10 *persons:* 1 *goose, weighing about* 8 *lb;* 2 *eggs;* 1¾ *lb onions;* 1 *pint Apple sauce;* 1½ *lb fresh breadcrumbs;* 1 *pint stock;* 2 *oz butter; watercress;* 1 *oz sage; milk, salt and pepper.* Cooking time: 2-3 hours.

Sauté the chopped onions in butter, mix into the breadcrumbs previously moistened with milk and squeezed dry. Add the chopped sage, butter and eggs, mix well with salt, pepper and ½ teaspoonful mace and stuff the goose. Truss, season and roast in a moderate oven, 350° F or Gas Mark 4-5 for 2-3 hours. When cooked skim away all fat. Blend flour with stock and add to the turnkey pan residue, stir and cook until thickened, add salt and pepper, boil and strain. Serve the goose, garnish with watercress; serve the Apple sauce and gravy in sauce-boats.

▣ aux Chipolatas * *with Chipolata Sausages*

For 8-10 *persons:* 1 *goose, weighing* 8 *lb;* 20 *cooked chestnuts;* ½ *pint white wine;* 20 *button onions (glazed);* 1 *pint Demi-glace;* 20 *chipolata sausages;* 20 *small, turned glazed carrots.* Cooking time: 2-3 hours.

Fry or roast the goose in a very hot oven until browned all over, drain off the fat, add the wine and *Demi-glace* and cook in a moderate oven, 375° F or Gas Mark 4, until tender. Remove the bird to a deep dish. Skim away all fat from the sauce, strain, add the garnishes and simmer for 5 minutes. Garnish round the bird and mask the sauce. Serve the surplus sauce in a sauce-boat.

Oies à la Lyonnaise

For 8-10 *persons:* 1 *goose, weighing* 8 *lb;* 20 *small onions:* 20 *peeled sweet chestnuts;* ½ *lb raw mushrooms;* ¼ *lb chipolata sausages;* ¼ *pint white wine;* ¾ *pint Demi-glace.* Cooking time: 2-3 hours.

Truss goose, place in a very hot oven, 450° F or Gas Mark 8, for 20-25 minutes to brown. Pour off fat. Add white wine, *Demi-glace*, and the onions previously browned in butter. Cover, season and braise in a moderate oven, 375° F or Gas Mark 4, for 1¼ hours. After 30 minutes add the chestnuts, the washed mushrooms and grilled sausages. Braise slowly till everything is cooked. Serve goose surrounded by garnish, skim fat from sauce, strain it and serve it separately.

⊡ à la Mecklembourgeoise

For 10 *persons:* 1 *goose, weighing about* 8 *lb;* 4 *lb red cabbage;* 2½ *lb of cooking apples;* 1 *lb chestnuts;* 2 *oz sultanas and currants;* 1 *pint stock made from giblets;* 1 *oz arrowroot.* Cooking time: 2-3 hours.

Peel, quarter and core the apples, part cook in a little butter. Swell the dried fruit in boiling water, drain and dry, mix with the apples and stuff the goose, truss and roast in a casserole or baking tin in a moderate oven, 375° F or Gas Mark 4-5, for 2-3 hours. Cut the cabbage into small quarters, blanch and braise with the chestnuts in 1 oz butter and a little stock. When goose is cooked, deglaze the pan with remaining stock, skim away all fat, blend with a little arrowroot, boil and strain. Carve the goose and arrange in the centre of the dish, mask with the gravy. Garnish the dish with the apples and cabbage.

⊡ Ragoût aux Marrons * *Stewed with Sweet Chestnuts*

Treat the goose as a stew but instead of potatoes add peeled chestnuts, which must remain whole. Braise slowly and skim fat off sauce thoroughly before serving.

Cassoulet de Castelnaudary

For 6-8 *persons:* 1 *lb dried white beans* (*haricot*)*;* 2 *pints boiling water;* 2 *medium-sized onions;* 2 *whole cloves;* 1 *carrot, cut in half;* 1 *small clove garlic, crushed;* 1 *stalk parsley;* 1 *stick celery;* 2 *oz finely diced salt pork;* 4 *oz garlic sausage;* 2 *teaspoons salt;* 2 *tablespoons goose or duck drippings;* ¾ *lb cubed lean pork;* ¾ *lb cubed lean lamb;* 4 *shallots, chopped;* ½ *lb diced deseeded tomatoes;* ¼ *pint sauce Tomate, or tomato purée;* 1 *tablespoon chopped parsley;* ¼ *pint dry white wine;* ½ *teaspoon black pepper;* 1-2½ *lb sliced roast goose or duck;* 8 *oz soft breadcrumbs;* 2 *oz butter, melted.*

Wash the beans, add the boiling water, cover and boil 2 minutes. Draw pan aside and leave to soak for 1 hour. Stud 1 onion with the cloves and add to the beans. Add carrot, garlic, parsley, celery, salt pork, sausage and salt. Bring to boiling point, uncovered. Skim, cover and simmer 30 minutes; remove the sausage and put on one side. Cover the pan and continue to simmer the beans 30 minutes longer. Melt the goose drippings in a frying pan, add pork and lamb and *sauté* for 10-15 minutes until the meats have been browned. Transfer the drained meat to the bean mixture. Chop the remaining onion and shallots and add to the fat, cook and stir for 5 minutes until onion is lightly browned. Add the tomatoes, sauce and chopped parsley and wine. Stir and cook 5 minutes then add to bean mixture, cover and simmer 1 hour or until beans are tender; add more boiling water. Remove and discard the whole onion, carrot, parsley stalk and celery. Add black pepper and additional salt if necessary. Fill a casserole with alternate layers of beans, sliced goose or duck, and the garlic sausage making sure there is a layer of beans at the top and bottom of the casserole. Mix the breadcrumbs and the melted butter and sprinkle over the beans. Bake in a moderate oven for 30-40 minutes, until the crumbs are brown. Serve in the casserole.

Confit d'Oie * *Potted Goose*

Cut goose in 4 pieces, cover with salt and leave for 24 hours. Dry very thoroughly and poach slowly in melted goose fat. Do not let the fat become too hot, otherwise the goose would be fried and not poached. It is cooked when no blood runs out after it is pricked. Remove from fat with a spoon, remove bones as far as possible and put pieces in earthenware or china pot. Decant goose fat and pour over pieces of goose so that they are fully covered. If the fat, when cold, does not cover the goose properly, top up with cooled, clarified lard. This preserve will keep for some time in a cool place. It is advisable to use small pots, as once a pot is opened it must be used quickly or it will go bad.

PIGEONNEAUX OU PIGEONS * *PIGEONS*

The only pigeons used for food in Britain are wood pigeons. Bordeaux, a popular variety from the Continent, are in season from March-October. Young pigeons of any kind of about a month old are called squabs. As with most types of game, pigeons are best eaten when young. The age can be determined as for general poultry but an additional pointer is the colour of the flesh. In the young bird this will be a pale colour but an old bird will have dark red, almost purple flesh. Pigeons are not usually hung.

▣ sur Canapés * *on Fried Croûtons*

For 6 persons: 3 young pigeons; 3 strips fat pork; 6 croûtons of bread fried in butter; ¼ pint white wine; ¼ lb foie gras purée; ¼ pint chicken stock; 2 tablespoons brandy; 2 oz butter; salt and pepper; 1 oz melted butter. Cooking time: 25-30 minutes.

Brush skins of pigeons with melted butter, then put in a roasting tin or casserole and put the strip of fat bacon over the breast of the pigeons. Roast the pigeons in butter, in a hot oven, 400° F or Gas Mark 6, basting well. After 15 minutes remove the bacon to brown the breast. When cooked remove and cut in half and remove the interior bones. Fry the pigeon livers, mince and sieve and blend into the *foie gras*. Spread this *purée* upon the *croûtons*. Skim fat from roasting tin drippings, add the brandy and wine, and reduce to half, add the stock, boil and strain. Arrange the pigeons upon the *croûtons*, garnish the centre of the dish with watercress. Serve the gravy in a sauce-boat.

▣ en Compôte * *Stewed*

For 4 persons: 2 plump young pigeons; 20 small onions; 20 pieces diced bacon; ½ lb mushrooms; 2 oz butter; ¼ pint white wine; ½ pint Demi-glace. Cooking time: 45-60 minutes.

Draw, singe and truss the pigeons and brown them slowly in butter. As soon as they are brown, remove from pan, put in onions and bacon, dice and fry light brown. Add the white wine and *Demi-glace* and replace pigeons in pan; they must be covered by liquid. Season, add *bouquet garni*, cover and braise slowly in a warm oven for 30 minutes. Remove herbs, skim fat off sauce, add the well-cleaned raw mushrooms, cook another 15 minutes and serve either in a *cocotte* or in a deep dish. Allow half a large pigeon per person.

Pigeonneaux en Crapaudine * *Spatchcocked Pigeon*

Use very young pigeons and prepare in the same way as *Poulet en Crapaudine.*

▣ **Farcis à l'Anglaise** * *Stuffed*

For 6 persons: 3 young pigeons; 3 chopped onions; 2 yolks of egg; ¼ lb finely chopped beef suet; ¼ lb fresh breadcrumbs, moistened with good stock; thyme; sage; 2 oz chopped parsley; salt and pepper; ¼ lb butter; ½ pint game stock. Cooking time: 20-35 minutes.

Stew the onions in butter, add the suet, breadcrumbs, seasoning, herbs and egg yolks and mix well together. Stuff the pigeons, truss and roast with some butter in a casserole for 20-35 minutes. Remove, cut in half and serve overlapping. Deglaze the pan with the stock, skim off the fat, boil, strain. Garnish the birds with watercress, and serve the gravy in a sauceboat.

▣ **aux Navets** * *with Turnips*

For 6 persons: 3 pigeons; ½ pint Demi-glace; 12 small onions; 3 small white turnips; 2 oz butter; 2 tablespoons tomato purée; 1 tablespoon oil. Cooking time: 40-60 minutes.

Brown the pigeons in oil and half the butter in a casserole or saucepan. Add tomato *purée* and *Demi-glace*, cut turnips and onions into the shape of large olives and brown in hot fat; add to the pigeons. Cover and simmer until pigeons and vegetables are cooked. Skim fat off gravy, adjust seasonings and serve in a deep dish sprinkled with parsley.

▣ **aux Petits Pois** * *with Peas*

For 4 persons: 2 young pigeons; 12 small onions; 12 pieces diced bacon; ¼ pint white wine; Demi-glace; ¾ lb young green peas. Cooking time: 45-60 minutes.

Prepare pigeons as *en Compôte* and instead of mushrooms, add peas after 20 minutes. If tinned peas are used, add only 5 minutes before pigeons are ready. Frozen peas, which cook more quickly than fresh ones, should be added 20 minutes before the end. (*See illustration p.* 552).

PINTADES * *GUINEA FOWL*

Guinea fowl has rather a dry flesh so it is always barded with bacon and then roasted, braised or casseroled. During cooking it must be basted frequently and kept rather underdone. Young guinea fowl may also be sautéed like chicken.

Pintades Limousine

For 6 persons: 2 guinea fowl; ½ lb belly bacon; 2 lb white cabbage; 3 carrots; 3 turnips; 1 lb sweet chestnuts; 2 tablespoons tomato purée; ¼ pint white wine; ¾ pint Demi-glace. Cooking time: 50-60 minutes.

Bard guinea fowl and brown them in butter. Add white wine, tomato *purée* and *Demi-glace* then cover and braise in a moderate oven. Braise cabbage with the bacon, boil carrots and turnips separately. Heavily butter small *bombe* moulds and line with alternate rows of cold, sliced carrots and turnips. Braise chestnuts with a little thin *Demi-glace*. Drain cabbage thoroughly, squeeze dry, chop coarsely, mix with finely diced bacon and press down hard in *bombe* moulds. Skim fat from guinea fowl braising residue, and carve guinea fowl. Arrange it in the middle of a long dish and coat lightly with sauce. Serve chestnuts at the sides and cabbage moulds at one end.

▣ à la Modane

For 6 persons: 2 guinea fowl; 2 tablespoons tomato purée; ¼ pint white wine; ¾ pint Demi-glace; ½ lb ravioli with spinach; 2 oz butter; 2 oz grated cheese. Cooking time: 50-60 minutes.

Brown barded guinea fowl in butter, reduce with white wine, add the tomato *purée* and rather thin *Demi-glace*, cover and braise in the oven. Boil ravioli in lightly salted water (approximately 25 minutes), pour water off and drain. When fowl are cooked, strain the sauce, skim off fat and use half to bind ravioli with grated cheese. Carve guinea fowl, coat with a little sauce and serve ravioli and the remainder of the sauce separately.

▣ Sautés à l'Africaine

For 6 persons: *2 young guinea fowl; ¼ lb onions; 1 oz flour; 1½ oz butter; ¼ pint white wine; 1 teaspoon concentrated tomato paste; ½ lb sweet potatoes; 4 bananas.* Cooking time: 30 minutes.

Joint the guinea fowl as for sautéed chicken, season with salt and pepper, brown in butter. Dust with flour, brown it slightly, add the white wine, tomato paste and ½ pint water, cover and braise for thirty minutes. Peel and slice the sweet potatoes, cover and cook in butter until tender, peel the bananas, cut them in thick diagonal slices and fry them in butter. Skim fat off sauce, and reduce it. Pour over the guinea fowl and garnish alternately with bananas and sweet potatoes.

POULTRY GIBLETS

The giblets include the liver, gizzard and heart and also the winglets, neck, head and feet. The livers of ducks and geese are kept apart because of their value in so many culinary preparations. It is important that all giblets be thoroughly washed and cleaned before use.

Abatis aux Navets * *Giblets with Turnips*

For 5 persons: 2 lb poultry giblets; 2 oz butter; 1 oz flour; 1 lb turnips; 12 small onions. Total cooking time: 1½ hours.

The giblets include the stomach, neck, heart, liver, head and feet; the two latter can be omitted. This dish can be made from chicken, goose, duck or turkey giblets. Cut giblets up as necessary, brown in butter, dust with flour and brown this, too, slightly. Add a small crushed clove of garlic and 1 tablespoon tomato *purée,* half cover with *bouillon* or water. Season, add *bouquet garni* and the slightly browned small onions, cover and cook slowly. After 30 minutes add the peeled, quartered and browned turnips and finish cooking together. Skim off fat before serving.

Abatis au Riz * *Giblets with Rice*

For 5 persons: 2 lb giblets; parsley; 2 large chopped onions; 1 bouquet garni; 7 oz rice; 1½ oz butter; 1½ pints bouillon or water. Total cooking time: 1½ hours.

Cut up giblets in small dice, brown in butter and add the onion. When brown, add *bouillon* or water and herbs and cook slowly; 1 hour for chicken and duck giblets and 1½ hours for goose or turkey giblets. Sweat rice in butter and add to giblets. Cover and cook slowly for another 25-30 minutes. The rice must be almost dry at the end. Sprinkle with chopped parsley.

LA VOLAILLE FROIDE * *COLD POULTRY*

Cold poultry dishes play an important part in cookery, providing ample testing ground for the imagination and ability of the cook. For it is in this field that one must pay attention to detail, both in the taste of the finished result and the appearance of the food. Do not forget that aspic is not only a decoration, it is also meant to be eaten. The obvious advantage in serving cold dishes is that they can be prepared in advance but this does not mean that they should be made days beforehand and kept in a cold place. The flavour and appearance of such dishes would suffer greatly as a result.

Apsic de Volaille * *Chicken in Aspic*

For 6 persons: 1 poached and tender chicken weighing 3-3½ lb; 1 truffle; 1½-2 quarts aspic.

Remove the skin of the chicken, and cut the breast into thin slices. Cut these slices into round medallions about 2 inches in diameter. Decorate each medallion with a small round slice of truffle dipped in aspic. Line a *savarin* (ring) mould with aspic jelly. Place the medallions on the bottom and on the sides of the mould, overlapping slightly, with the truffles on the outside. Place the mould in crushed ice and pour in a little half-set aspic. Now, place a second and third layer of small pieces of boned fowl in the mould, so that they are not visible when unmoulded and fill up completely with half-set aspic. Allow to set, and unmould on to a round dish. Garnish to taste. This is the principle of all aspics. The medallions may be coated with *foie gras purée* or a *mousse* of ham or chicken. They may also be covered with *sauce Chaudfroid* and decorated before they are placed into the mould. Covered with *sauce Chaudfroid*, the dish is called a *Chaudfroid* of chicken.

Aspic de Volaille et Jambon Mercédès * *with Ham*

For 8 persons: 3 pints chicken aspic; a little white pepper; 1 *chicken, weighing about* 3 *lb, poached and boned;* ½ *pint whipped double cream; baked ham slices;* 1 *or* 2 *truffles or large black olives; salt to taste; aspic triangles;* 2 *hardboiled eggs.*

Coat the inside of a 3 pint mould with liquid aspic and chill on ice until set. Cut chicken in cross-wise slices about ¼-inch thick. Trim an equal number of ham slices to the same size. Set aside. Reserve trimmings, cut some of the remaining chicken into small pieces and add the remaining diced ham—you should have 1 pound altogether; mince finely, add to chicken aspic with some salt and pepper, chill until mixture begins to set; fold in whipped cream. Decorate the centre part of the bottom of the mould with truffles and hardboiled egg whites cut in petal shapes. Using a piping bag, pipe the *mousse* on enough ham and chicken slices to surround the egg and truffle decoration, and place them *mousse* side up, alternating ham and chicken slices. Chill until set. Pour in a layer of aspic and chill. Arrange alternating chicken and ham slices topped with aspic around the sides of the mould. Finish filling mould with half set aspic. Chill until firm, then unmould and garnish with aspic triangles. (*See illustration p.* 556).

POULARDE * *CHICKEN*

⊡ Arlequin * *Harlequin Chaudfroid*

For 6 *persons:* 1 *poached chicken, weighing about* 3 *lb;* ½ *lb foie gras mousse;* ½ *lb tongue mousse;* ¾ *pint white sauce Chaudfroid;* ¾ *pint tomato flavoured sauce Chaudfroid;* 1 *sliced truffle;* 6 *slices of tongue; cubed aspic;* 6 *baked tartlet shells.*

The tongue *mousse* is prepared in the same way as *Mousse de Jambon en Damier* (see p. 182). The *foie gras mousse* is prepared in the same way as *Mousse de Foie Gras Alexandra* (see p. 182). Slice away the meat from the sides of the chicken. Remove the bone from the sides of the chicken using poultry shears, but leave the wings and legs intact. The chicken will now have hollow sides. Mix together the two types of *mousse* and fill the interior sides of the chicken with this, then replace the slices of meat to reform the chicken shape. Coat one side of the chicken with the white *sauce Chaudfroid* and the other with the tomato flavoured sauce. Decorate the pink side with the truffle and the white side with slices of tongue, use the rest of *mousse* to fill the tartlet shells and coat 3 with the pink *Chaudfroid* and 3 with the white. Decorate the dish with the tartlets. (*See illustration p.* 554).

⊡ Astor

For 8 *persons:* 1 *chicken, weighing about* 4½-5 *lb;* 1½ *lb Waldorf salad;* 8 *tartlet cases, baked blind;* 3 *bananas;* 10 *round slices of apple,* 2 *inches in diameter and* ⅜-*inch thick, lightly stewed;* 10 *segments of mandarin oranges;* ¼ *pint Cumberland sauce;* 8 *skinned walnut halves;* 3 *pints aspic;* 16 *cherry halves; blanched, shredded rind of* 1 *orange.*

Roast the chicken until golden brown and leave to cool. Lifting off the white meat on either side, remove the breastbone. Fill the inside of the bird with the *salade Waldorf* to which has been added some partially set aspic, and smooth it off into a dome. Leave to set in a cool place. Next arrange the walnut halves along the middle of the bird and decorate both sides with the cherry halves. Thoroughly glaze the chicken with the aspic. Now cut each chicken breast into 5 thin slices, which should be trimmed into oval shapes and placed on the apple rings. Top each with a mandarin segment and glaze with aspic. Dice the bananas and mix the pieces with the Cumberland sauce and a little half-set aspic. Fill the tartlet cases with this mixture and sprinkle over the shredded orange rinds. Pour some aspic over the bottom of an oblong dish and leave to set. Place the chicken in the middle and garnish with the prepared slices of breast and the tartlets. Surround with cubes of aspic.

Poularde Césarine

For 10-12 persons: 1 *chicken, weighing* 3-3½ *lb;* 1 *lb lean cooked ham;* 1 *pint cream;* ¼ *lb butter;* ¼ *pint Madeira; stufled olives; green peas;* 2 *pints aspic.*

Roast the chicken until it is tender and brown. Allow to cool. Pour out the fat from the pan and reduce residue with Madeira. Drain and mix with the aspic. Prepare ham *mousse* by pounding the ham with the butter and half the cream. Pass through a wire sieve, and season with paprika. Add about ¼ pint of half-set aspic and the rest of the cream, whipped, and mix carefully. Remove the breast fillets in one slice and cut away the breastbone of the chicken. Fill with the prepared *mousse* and shape it into the form of the breast. Cut the two fillets in thin slices and place them on top of the *mousse.* Leave a little space free in the middle for the decoration. Decorate with slices of stuffed olives and green peas; the decoration may also be cooked carrots and turnips cut into small balls about the size of a pea. Glaze the whole chicken with aspic, place it in the middle of a round dish and allow to cool for at least two hours. Garnish with vegetable salad in aspic moulded in small *timbales* and small cornets filled with *foie gras* cream. The garnish may also be omitted and replaced by diced aspic.

▣ en Chaudfroid

For 8 *persons:* 1 *chicken, weighing* 4-4½ *lb;* 2 *pints white sauce Chaudfroid;* 1½ *quarts aspic;* 1 *truffle;* 1 *small tomato or sweet red pepper.*

Poach the chicken in rich white stock, and allow to cool, in the stock. Prepare *sauce Chaudfroid* with one half of the stock and aspic jelly with the other half. Remove the skin from the chicken, detach the breast and the legs, and remove the bones. Cut the two breast halves into thin slices about 2½ inches long. Trim these slices into an oval shape, and coat them with half-set *sauce Chaudfroid.* The meat of the legs may be prepared in the same way, but it is usually reserved for other purposes. When the *sauce Chaudfroid* is set, decorate each oval of meat with two truffle stars and a very thin strip of tomato or red pepper. Glaze with half-set aspic jelly. When the aspic is quite set, arrange the meat on a round or oval dish and garnish with diced aspic. To make a brown *Chaudfroid* of fowl, the chicken is braised in rich brown stock and the sauce and aspic are prepared with this stock, and flavoured with Madeira. (*See illustration p.* 553).

▣ Chaudfroid Rosemonde

For 5 *persons:* 1 *chicken, weighing about* 3¼ *lb;* 2½ *pints Port-flavoured aspic;* 1½ *pints tomato mousse; truffle.*

Poach the chicken, let it cool, carve and bone it. Make aspic with the poaching stock. Place pieces of chicken on a wire tray and coat all over with cold, but still liquid aspic. When set, neatly trim off the drops of aspic round the lower edge, decorate each piece with a truffle or other pattern and glaze with cold, but still liquid aspic. Put a layer of tomato *mousse* in a deep dish or on a round, deep platter, let it set and cover it with a thin layer of aspic. Arrange chicken attractively on top and garnish with diced aspic. *Tomato mousse:* Make a *purée* of fresh tomatoes, drain off water on a cloth, season with salt, pepper and a pinch of sugar, mix with an equal quantity of aspic and when the mixture begins to thicken, gently fold in half the quantity of stiffly whipped cream. Decorate with truffle slices and glaze with aspic all over. Line an oval dish with a sheet of aspic, place chicken on top and garnish with some tartlets filled with the mixed vegetables bound with *Mayonnaise,* glazed with aspic and decorated with chopped aspic.

Poularde en Gelée à l'Estragon * *in Tarragon Aspic*

For 5 persons: 1 chicken, weighing about 3¼ lb; 2½ pints tarragon-flavoured aspic.

Usually a roast chicken is used, but it can also be poached. In the latter case it must be skinned. Carve the chicken in the usual way, which is much easier with cold birds than with hot, replace in original shape and place in a china casserole or other suitable dish. Fill up the casserole with tarragon-flavoured aspic so that the chicken is fully covered; the aspic should be cold but still liquid. It may also be flavoured with Port, Madeira or other good wine.

⊡ Lambertye

For 10-12 persons: 1 chicken, weighing 4-4½ lb; 1 spring chicken, weighing about 2¼ lb; 6 oz foie gras; 2 oz butter; ¼ pint double cream; 2 truffles; 2½ pints white sauce Chaudfroid; 2 pints aspic; 2 calf's feet; 2 blanched bacon rinds.

Poach the two chickens in good veal stock in which the bacon rinds and calf's feet have first been boiled. Remove small chicken first. Cut off the meat, *purée* it, mix with double cream, soft butter, and *foie gras;* pass through a sieve, season well and mix with 2-3 tablespoons *sauce Chaudfroid.* The double cream may be replaced by ½ pint whipped cream. Skin the fowl, remove breasts and bone, slice breasts diagonally, coat slices with *sauce Chaudfroid,* decorate with truffles and trim when sauce has set. Fill hollow of breast with chicken and *foie gras mousse,* smooth in shape of breast and replace breast slices in original position. Glaze the large chicken, including legs with *Chaudfroid,* then with aspic. When it has set trim off aspic which has collected underneath. Line a large oval dish with a sheet of aspic, serve chicken on it and garnish with chopped aspic. (*See illustration p.* 555).

⊡ Lucullus

For 10-12 persons: 1 chicken, weighing about 4 lb; 1 spring chicken, weighing about 2 lb; ¾ lb foie gras; 2 pints cream; 1½ pints brown sauce Chaudfroid; 2½ pints aspic; 2-3 truffles.

Prepare as for *Poularde Lambertye,* but coat with brown *sauce Chaudfroid* flavoured with Port. Fill with chicken *mousse* and serve breast slices on *mousse* with small slices of *foie gras* in between. Make rest of *foie gras* into very small aspics in *baba* moulds decorated with a round truffle slice. Line a large oval or square dish with a sheet of aspic, serve chicken on it and decorate with turned out *foie gras,* aspics and chopped aspic.

⊡ à la Muguette

For 10 persons: 1 chicken, weighing about 4 lb; 1 lb cooked, lean ham; 4 oz foie gras; 1 truffle; ½ pint cream; ¼ lb butter; 1 hardboiled egg; 1 quart white sauce Chaudfroid; ¼ pint tomato purée; 2½ pints aspic; a few tarragon leaves. Cooking time: 50-60 minutes.

Poêlé the chicken in butter and allow to cool. Remove the breast fillets and the breastbone. Fill with a *mousse* made of ham and *foie gras* rubbed through a sieve, mixed with creamed butter, aspic, whipped cream, well seasoned with salt and paprika, and shaped to reform the breast. Entirely cover the chicken with *sauce Chaudfroid* mixed with a little tomato *purée*. When set, decorate with a lily-of-the-valley decoration, using blanched tarragon leaves and slices of hardboiled egg white. The flower pot may be imitated with a piece of cooked carrot or skinned tomato. Cut the breast fillets in slices, coat with *sauce Chaudfroid*, decorate with a lily-of-the-valley pattern, and glaze with aspic. Serve the chicken on one end of a long dish and the breast of fillets at the other end. Garnish with diced aspic.

CANARD ET CANETON * *DUCK AND DUCKLING*

Many of the recommended methods of preparing chicken can also be used in the preparation of other types of poultry, but wherever the recipe involves the use of *sauce Chaudfroid*, brown *chaudfroid* should be used.

▣ à la Dino

For 6 persons: a plump roasted duckling; 2 truffles; 1 lb foie gras; 3 oz butter; Madeira; 1¾ pints liquid aspic; chopped aspic; 1¾ pints sauce Chaudfroid.

Poach the truffles and *foie gras* in Madeira or Port. Make brown *sauce Chaudfroid* from the carcase and trimmings, strain and let it cool. Cut the breast in long thin slices and cover each one with *foie gras purée*, using a forcing bag and plain nozzle. Make this *purée* from the sieved *foie gras* and 3 oz butter, seasoning, and a little of the *foie gras* stock. Coat slices with *sauce Chaudfroid* on the point of setting and decorate with a truffle slice. Arrange slices in a long deep dish, cover entirely with setting aspic and surround with a ring of chopped aspic mixed with chopped truffle peel.

▣ Glacé Marivaux * *Glazed*

For 6 persons: 1 duck, weighing about 6 lb; ¼ lb butter; 1 lb cooked macédoine of vegetables bound with ½ pint Mayonnaise; 1 quart duck aspic; salt; pepper; lettuce; ½ lb foie gras.

Roast the duck, keeping the flesh slightly underdone so it is a rose colour. Cool, remove the breasts and cut into long thin slices (*aiguillettes*). Mask with aspic. Remove the breast bone and fill the cavity with the *macédoine* of vegetables. Arrange the *aiguillettes* of duck to cover the *macédoine*, and mask over with the aspic. Mix the *foie gras* and butter and fill into 6 small moulds (duck-shaped if possible). Allow to set, unmould, imitate the eyes with truffle dots and mask with aspic. Cover the bottom of the dish with aspic, arrange duck in the centre, garnish round with the small moulds and lettuce.

▣ Glacé Montmorency

For 6 persons: 1 duck, weighing about 6 lb; 1½ lb of mousse prepared from the liver, duck trimmings and foie gras; 1 pint brown sauce Chaudfroid; 1½ pints of duck aspic flavoured with Port wine; 1 lb cherries cooked in red wine, stoned and glazed with aspic. Cooking time: 45 minutes.

Roast the duckling keeping it slightly underdone, cool, remove the breast and cut into long thin slices. Remove the breast bone from the duck and fill the cavity with the *mousse* and reform. Mask the fillets of duck with the *Chaudfroid*, decorate with truffles and arrange along the breast; mask the whole with aspic. Serve upon a dish covered with a layer of aspic, garnish with the cherries and chopped aspic.

Canard à la Néva

For 6 persons: 1 duck, weighing about 6 lb; ¾ lb Gratin forcemeat; ¼ lb truffles; 1½ pints Chaudfroid; 1½ pints aspic; 1 glass Madeira.

Draw and singe duck, fill with Gratin forcemeat mixed with diced truffles, truss and poach for 1½ hours in aspic enriched wuth Madeira. When tender drain well and make brown *sauce Chaudfroid* with the stock. Coat duck with it, decorate with truffles, glaze with aspic, arrange on a dish lined with a sheet of aspic and garnish with aspic.

◘ au Porto * *with Port*

For 6 persons: 1 duck, weighing about 6 lb; 1 oz flour; 2 oz butter; 1 tablespoon tomato purée; ¼ pint Port; about 2½ pints mild-flavoured aspic.

Roast a duck the evening before, keeping it underdone. Pour off fat, reduce residue with Port. Chop the giblets coarsely, brown them, dust with flour, add tomato *purée* and half the aspic, season lightly, simmer mixture for 2 hours and skim off fat from time to time. When this mixture is cooked remove it from pan, boil up with sauce, strain and let it cool. Slice breast of duck lengthwise, place on a wire tray and coat with the sauce when it is on the point of setting. When quite set decorate with truffles. Arrange the decorated duck breasts on a large, fairly deep dish and coat with light aspic on the point of setting to give a final glaze.

Dodine de Canard Charles Vaucher

For 15 persons: 2 ducks, each weighing about 4 lb; 3 lb fresh, lean shoulder of pork without bones; ½ bottle white wine; liqueur glass brandy; 1 truffle; pâté seasoning; salt; a pinch each of thyme, sage, sweet basil and rosemary. Garnish: ½ lb foie gras; chopped truffle; stuffed olives; aspic.

Split the ducks the whole length of the back as for Galantine. Remove all the bones except for the drumsticks. Be careful not to pierce the skin. Remove all the duck meat from skin and bones. Marinate it together with the pork, cut in cubes, in white wine and brandy and all the herbs and spices for 24 hours. Pass through the mincer two or three times, mix well and add the truffle cut into small dice. Stuff the ducks with this filling and sew up the opening, giving the ducks their original shape. Braise them very slowly, about 1½ hours, in good brown stock made with the bones and be careful that the skin of the ducks does not burst. Allow to cool. Cut half each duck into thin slices and decorate body and sides with slices of stuffed olives and a dot of hardboiled egg white. Arrange on a dish and glaze with aspic. Garnish with the *foie gras*, rubbed through a wire sieve, seasoned, shaped into small balls, rolled in chopped truffle, and glazed with aspic. (*See illustration p.* 555).

Suprêmes de Caneton aux Oranges en Gelée * *Breasts of Duckling with Orange in Aspic*

For 6 persons: 2 oz gelatine; 2 crushed egg shells; ½ pint orange juice; 1 lb sliced cooked cold duck; 1½ pints stock from duck carcases; 6 slices truffle; salt; black pepper; 2 cooked sliced carrots; 3-4 mushrooms poached and sliced; 1 tablespoon vinegar; 12 orange segments; 2 teaspoons fresh chopped tarragon; watercress; 2 stiffly beaten egg whites.

Soften gelatine in orange juice and set aside. Place stock, seasonings, vinegar, tarragon, egg whites and shells in a large saucepan. Bring to boiling point, stirring constantly. Remove from heat, add gelatine and allow to stand 10 minutes. Strain through a fine sieve. Pour 1 pint of the gelatine mixture into a 4-5 pint oiled mould and chill until set. Keep the remaining aspic at room temperature until the aspic in the mould is set. Then chill this remaining aspic until it almost reaches the point of setting. Arrange the sliced duck, truffles, carrots, mushrooms and orange segments in an attractive pattern over the aspic in the mould. Cover with the almost set remaining aspic. Chill until aspic is firm and you are ready to serve. Unmould and garnish with watercress.

Suprêmes de Dindonneau Mercure * *Breasts of Turkey Mercury*

For 6 persons: 6 suprêmes of turkey about ¼-inch thick, each weighing about 5 oz; ¼ pint white wine; 1 lb of macédoine of vegetables; 6 slices truffle; ¼ pint of Mayonnaise; 1 skinned tomato; ¼ pint semi-liquid aspic; 1 hardboiled egg; ¼ pint of turkey consommé; 6 tartlet cases; 2 lb butter.

Cream the butter till white and soft then chill. Mix the *macédoine*, *Mayonnaise* and aspic together and fill into a conical mould; allow to set. Stew the *suprêmes* gently in butter keeping tightly covered; add the white wine, simmer for 15 minutes, add the turkey *consommé* and simmer a further 15 minutes. Allow to cool in the cooking liquor, remove, trim to shape, garnish with a slice of truffle, tomato and egg and glaze with aspic. Cover the serving platter with a thin film of aspic and allow to set. From the chilled butter model the legs and forelegs of two horses on the serving platter (*see illustration p.* 556), leaving an oval space in the centre. Place the moulded *macédoine* in the centre and surround with the breasts of turkey point upwards and leaning against the *macédoine*. Garnish with tartlet cases filled with vegetable *macédoine* decorated with tomato, truffle, and small triangles of cooked breast of turkey. Keep in the refrigerator until required. (*See illustration p.* 556).

PIGEON * *PIGEON*

▣ **Foyot**

Draw a pigeon, singe it, cut it open down the back and completely bone it without damaging the skin. Keep back breasts and pass the remainder of the meat, with an equal quantity of veal and liver trimmings, or a little tinned liver if necessary, several times through the mincer. Add 1 egg and season well. Spread pigeon skin with a little forcemeat, place breasts, some pieces of truffle and strips of *foie gras* on it, cover with remaining forcemeat and roll up like a galantine. Wrap in a cloth, tie up, place in a casserole, cover with aspic, bring to the boil and poach for 45 minutes. Drain, cool under slight pressure, remove cloth, coat with brown *sauce Chaudfroid* flavoured with Port, decorate with truffle slices and glaze with aspic and garnish like a galantine.

▣ **Médaillons à la Gelée** * *Medallions in Aspic*

Prepare pigeons as for *Pigeonneaux Foyot* but do not coat with sauce. Cut in ¾-inch slices, coat each slice with brown *sauce Chaudfroid*, decorate with pistachio halves, hardboiled egg white and truffles and glaze with aspic. Serve a salad of potatoes, apples and walnuts bound with *Mayonnaise* in a mound in the middle of a round dish and arrange medallions in a ring round it.

FOREIGN SPECIALITIES

Anglo-Indian Chicken Curry

For 6 persons: 1 *young chicken, weighing* 3-3½ *lb;* 2 *oz grated coconut;* 2 *oz butter;* 2 *medium-sized onions;* 1 *small teaspoon powdered turmeric;* 1 *small tablespoon coriander;* 2 *small dried chilis;* 1 *large pinch powdered ginger;* 1 *clove garlic; juice of* 1 *lemon;* 2 *hardboiled eggs;* 3 *almonds;* ½ *lb rice;* 1 *medium-sized onion;* 5 *peppercorns;* 2 *grains cardamon;* 1 *inch cinnamon stick;* 1 *oz butter; chicken stock;* 1 *small bay leaf.* Cooking time: 1 hour.

Pound the chilis, coriander, garlic, almonds, turmeric and ginger to paste in a mortar. Slice the onions and fry to a light brown in butter. Add the curry paste, fry for a minute and add the chicken cut in pieces. Allow the chicken to brown very lightly and be careful that it does not burn. Pour on enough coconut milk to cover the pieces, season with salt and lemon juice, mix well, cover, and cook gently for about 30 minutes. When the chicken is tender the sauce should be well reduced. Arrange in a dish, cover with hardboiled eggs cut in quarters and fried onion rings. Serve rice and chupatties at the same time.

Indian Rice: Cook the rice for a few minutes gently in butter together with a chopped onion, without allowing it to brown. Add peppercorns, cardamon, cinnamon, bay leaf and salt. Cover with double the amount of chicken stock, put a lid on and cook for 17 minutes. When the rice is ready, the grains will have absorbed all the liquid and be tender. Remove the spices before serving.

Coconut Milk: Grate the coconut and mix it with a cup full of lukewarm water. Cover, and allow to stand for 10 minutes. Press the liquid out through a clean cloth, and repeat twice, until the required amount of coconut milk is ready.

Chupatties: 7 oz flour; 1 tablespoon oil; a scant ¼ oz yeast; 1 pinch salt. Mix all the ingredients with a little lukewarm water to a rather soft dough. Allow to rest for 4 hours. Roll out this dough into very thin rounds about the size of a saucer. Bake these on both sides on a hotplate until golden brown or use a chupatty iron if available. Serve the chupatties with curry. *(India)*

Arroz a la Valenciana * *Chicken with Spanish Rice*

For 6 persons: 1 *chicken, weighing about* 2¼ *lb;* ½ *lb fillet of pork;* 12 *frogs' legs;* 1 *small rock lobster (crawfish);* 3 *cooked artichoke bottoms;* ½ *lb green peas;* ½ *lb rice;* 1 *large onion;* 1 *clove of garlic;* 1 *pinch of saffron.* Cooking time: about 1 hour.

Joint chicken as for sautéed chicken, slice fillet of pork thickly, and brown both briefly in oil. Put in a large casserole with the chopped onion and crushed garlic, fill up with *bouillon* or water, season, add saffron and simmer for 30 minutes. Then add the cut-up rock lobster, the peas, the quartered artichoke bottoms and the frogs' legs, simmer till everything is cooked. Add rice about 15 minutes before cooking time is completed. If necessary add a little extra liquid for serving. It should not be too dry. *(Spain)*

Berliner Hühnerfrikassee * *Chicken Fricassee Berlin*

For 6-8 persons: 1 *roasting chicken, weighing* 3¼-4 *lb;* 1 *small calf's tongue;* 10 *Puff pastry crescents;* ¼ *lb calf's sweetbreads;* 6 *oz mushroom or* ½ *lb morels;* 10 *crayfish;* ¼ *lb Quenelle forcemeat;* 1 *oz capers;* 1 *lemon;* 1 *glass white wine;* 2 *oz butter;* 1 *oz flour;* 1 *carrot;* 1 *onion, stuck with a clove;* 1 *bouquet garni.* Cooking time of chicken: 1½-2½ hours according to age.

Cook chicken in water with the carrot, onion, herbs and peppercorns. Skin and carve it and keep it warm in a little chicken broth. Boil the crayfish then shell. Scrub shells and remove gall bladder from flesh. Make forcemeat with soaked white bread, eggs, chopped herbs, finely grated onions, salt, pepper and nutmeg and fill some crayfish shells with it and poach in salt water; make Crayfish butter with the rest of the shells. Poach calf's tongue and sweetbreads. Make *quenelles* of forcemeat with a teaspoon, poach in salt water and cook the mushrooms (or morels when in season). Make White *Roux* with the butter and flour, add chicken *bouillon*, stir, add a little lemon peel, some soaked anchovies and reduce. Remove from heat and quickly stir in an egg yolk mixed with lemon juice and white wine, reheat but do not boil. Cut calf's tongue and sweetbreads in pieces, add mushrooms and *quenelles*, heat with a little chicken broth, drain well and bind with the well-seasoned sauce. Place well-drained chicken pieces in a deep dish, cover with plenty of sauce, garnish with crayfish flesh and shells and Puff pastry crescents, sprinkle with Crayfish butter and scatter capers on top.

Boboc de Rata Cu Castraveti * *Duck with Pickled Cucumbers*

For 4 persons: 1 duckling, weighing about 3½ lb; 2 medium-sized onions; 1 lb pickled cucumbers; ⅝ pint Demi-glace; 1 tablespoon tomato purée; 1 oz butter; ¼ pint sour cream. Cooking time: about 50-60 minutes.

Joint duck in 4 pieces, brown in butter or lard and brown chopped onions at the same time. Add rather thin *Demi-glace* and tomato *purée*, season, cover, and braise slowly. Peel cucumbers, quarter lengthwise, seed them, cut in regular pieces and flute them slightly. After 15 minutes add cucumbers to duck and braise till everything is soft. If the sauce becomes too thick, add a little *bouillon* or water. Arrange in a deep dish and serve sour cream separately. (*Rumania*)

Chicken à la King

For 6 persons: 1¼ lb poached chicken breast without skin; 3 green peppers; ½ lb raw mushrooms; ½ pint cream; 2 oz butter; 1 small truffle (optional); 3 egg yolks; 1 glass dry sherry; paprika. Cooking time: 20-30 minutes.

Cut peppers in thin slices, simmer them for a few minutes in butter, add sliced mushrooms, season and cook together till tender. Add the cream. Reduce a little, add the chicken breasts cut in thin diagonal slices, heat and season with paprika. Mix egg yolk with the sherry and add to rest of mixture away from heat; it must not boil again. Serve with *Riz à la Créole*.

There are many variations on this popular American dish, but binding with sherry and egg yolk is compulsory in all of them. (*North America*)

Chicken Pie

For 5 persons: 1 young chicken, weighing about 2½ lb; 6 oz mushrooms; 6 rashers of bacon; ½ lb potatoes; 2 hardboiled eggs; 1 lb Puff pastry; 2 oz butter; ¼ pint chicken stock. Cooking time: 40-45 minutes.

Cut the chicken in pieces. *Sauté* in butter until half cooked, but not browned, and allow to cool. Line the edge of a pie dish with Puff pastry. Place the chicken, the raw mushrooms cut in quarters or thick slices and the diced potatoes inside, and cover with chopped onion, the hardboiled eggs cut into thick slices and the rashers of bacon. Season with salt and pepper, and pour over some chicken stock. Cover with Puff pastry, decorate with leaves or other motifs of Puff pastry, brush with egg, and make a hole in the middle of the cover to allow the steam to escape. Bake in a hot oven, 425° F or Gas Mark 7, and as soon as the crust begins to brown, reduce the heat and cover with a sheet of buttered paper. (*Great Britain*)

Kuriny Koteletki Pojarski * *Chicken Cutlets Pojarski*

For 8-10 persons: 1 lb raw chicken meat; ¼ pint cream; ¼ lb white bread without crust; 2 egg yolks; 6 oz butter; 1 egg; white breadcrumbs. Cooking time: 10 minutes.

Soak the white bread in cream but do not squeeze it out. Chop the chicken very fine, adding a little cream, then add the bread, 2½ oz of butter, the egg yolk, salt, pepper and a pinch of nutmeg and continue chopping and mixing until the mixture binds well. Divide this mixture into 8 large or 16 small pieces and shape them first into balls, and then, using a palette knife, into cutlet shapes on a floured table. Egg and breadcrumb. Fry cutlets in butter so that they are golden brown and not dry. Serve sprinkled with lemon juice and Noisette butter and with a vegetable garnish to taste. (*Russia*)

Stuffed Pigeons

For 4 persons: 2 young, very plump pigeons; 2 medium-sized chopped onions; 2 oz suet; ¼ lb white bread without crust; 1 egg; 1 teaspoon parsley; 2 rashers bacon fat; 1 large pinch each thyme and sage. Cooking time: about 30-40 minutes.

Chop the onions, brown them slightly in butter, let them cool and mix well with the soaked, squeezed-out bread, the finely chopped suet, parsley, thyme and sage, season with salt and pepper and mix with the egg. Fill with the stuffing, sew up opening, cover with pieces of fat bacon. Roast the pigeons in a hot oven—after 15 minutes remove the fat bacon so that the pigeon will brown. Serve, reduce pan residue with a little gravy and pour over pigeons. Chickens, geese and turkeys can be filled with the same stuffing and roasted. (*Great Britain*)

Wiener Backhendl * *Viennese Fried Chicken*

For 6 persons: 3 cockerels, each weighing about 1¼ lb; 2 eggs; white breadcrumbs; lemon; parsley. Cooking time: 12-15 minutes.

Draw and singe the chicken, wash well and cut each one in 4 pieces—2 legs and 2 breast pieces. Season and egg and breadcrumb the chicken joints and livers. Fry golden brown in hot deep fat, adding livers only when the joints are almost ready. Drain well, season lightly with fine salt, serve on a paper napkin and garnish with parsley and lemon slices. Serve with green salad. (*Austria*)

Foie Gras

This delicacy is made of the livers of either geese or ducks. The birds are specially bred and fed on selected foodstuffs so that the livers become abnormally enlarged. The finest and most expensive is *foie gras entier* which consists of whole livers of large size. Less expensive is the *foie gras au naturel* which is sold as two or three smaller livers. *Foie gras* is sold in *terrines* and cans, hermetically sealed and flavoured with spices and truffles.

French *foie gras* comes from the Toulouse and Alsace region but good *foie gras* is also exported by Germany, Czechoslovakia and Hungary.

Goose liver is of a fairly firm texture, whilst duck liver is more tender and liable to break up during cooking. As *foie gras* is such a delicacy and therefore expensive it must be cooked very carefully, either in a *terrine*, a pastry crust or casserole. It can also be sliced, floured and *sautéed* in butter and served hot.

COLD FOIE GRAS

For cold dishes *foie gras* should always be poached in a good wine, which is added to the aspic before clarifying. It is usually cooked with truffles, whose aroma harmonises perfectly with *foie gras*. Since, however, truffles do not take nearly as long to cook as *foie gras*, they should be added 15-20 minutes after the *foie gras* has been started. The best known of the recipes is *Foie Gras* in Aspic which follows below.

Aspic de Foie Gras * *Foie Gras in Aspic*

For 6 persons: 1 whole, cooked foie gras or goose liver; semi-liquid chicken aspic; 6 slices truffles; melba toast; watercress or parsley.

Place whole cooked *foie gras* on a chilled serving tray. Cover the *foie gras* with several layers of aspic, chilling after each layer is applied. On each side of the *foie gras* place 3 truffle slices, mask again with several layers of aspic, chilling after each layer. Chill until ready to serve. Slice and serve on melba toast garnished with watercress. (*See illustration p.* 594).

Carolines au Foie Gras * *Eclairs with Foie Gras Purée*

½ pint Choux pastry; ½ lb foie gras purée. Cooking time: 10-12 minutes.

Pipe out small *éclairs* with a ¼-inch round tube about 1½ inches long, eggwash and bake in a hot oven, 425° F or Gas Mark 7. When cooked slit open immediately, cool and fill with the *foie gras*. These small *éclairs* may be dipped in a white or coffee coloured *sauce Chaudfroid*, or served plain.

Foie Gras en Croûte * *Foie Gras in a Crust*

For 5-6 persons: 1-1¼ *lb fresh foie gras;* 2 *peeled raw truffles;* 1-1¼ *lb flour;* 6 *oz lard;* ¼ *pint Madeira or other good wine.* Cooking time: 50 minutes.

Season the *foie gras* and marinate with the truffles in Madeira for 24 hours in a covered container. Make a stiffish dough with the flour, lard and lukewarm water and let it rest for several hours. Roll out into 2 large rounds, ¼-inch thick, place the drained *foie gras* and truffles on one, moisten the edge, cover with the other and press down firmly. Leave a small hole for the steam in the centre and bake in a hot oven, 425° F or Gas Mark 7. If the *foie gras* is to be eaten hot, cut off the upper part of the crust, coat lightly with *Demi-glace* enriched with the reduced marinade and serve the rest separately. The crust is not eaten.

MÉDAILLONS DE FOIE GRAS

⊡ Marie-Thérèse

For 6 persons: 1-1¼ *lb poached foie gras;* 1 *pint aspic;* 1½ *pints white sauce Chaudfroid;* 2 *tablespoons very red tomato purée;* 1 *small truffle.*

The *foie gras* should be poached, underdone, in dry champagne and kept pink inside. Cut the *foie gras* into 10 medallions with a round cutter. Prepare *mousse* with the remains of the *foie gras.* Coat each medallion with a thick layer of *mousse* and cover with *Chaudfroid.* Decorate the medallions with round slices of truffle, and glaze with aspic. Shape the remaining *mousse* into very small balls and cover with *Chaudfroid,* to which red tomato *purée* has been added, to make them look like cherries. Glaze with aspic. Arrange the medallions in a circle on a round dish, and garnish with the *foie gras* balls and chopped aspic.

⊡ Tosca

For 6 persons: 6 *tartlets of Flaky pastry;* 1 *lb cold foie gras poached in Madeira;* 6 *round, cored slices of cooking apple;* 1½ *oz grilled, pounded and sieved hazelnuts;* 6 *round truffle slices;* ¼ *pint fresh cream;* 1½ *pints aspic with Madeira.*

Poach the apple slices carefully and let them cool. Cut 6 round medallions about ½-inch thick and 2-inches across out of the *foie gras.* Rub the remainder through a fine sieve. Make this into a *purée* with the half-whipped cream and a little cold aspic. Season with salt, paprika and a little of the poaching Madeira; add the hazelnuts. Three-quarters fill the tartlets with *mousse* and put them in a cold place. Put the apple slices on the medallions with a truffle slice in the centre. Glaze with aspic. Put the medallions on the tartlets and surround with chopped aspic.

Mousse de Foie Gras en Forme au Alexandra

For 8 persons: ¾ *lb poached cold foie gras;* 2 *oz butter;* ¼ *pint double cream;* 1 *large truffle; paprika; pâté seasoning;* 1¼ *quarts Madeira aspic.*

Line a *timbale* or decorative mould with Madeira aspic, and decorate with slices of truffle cut with a round cutter. Pass the *foie gras* through a fine sieve and cream the butter. Mix the butter with the *foie gras,* beating vigorously, add about ¼ pint half-set aspic and the half whipped cream. Season with salt, paprika and *pâté* seasoning, add the rest of the truffle cut in dice, and fill the mould with the *mousse.* Seal with half-set aspic and allow to set on ice or in the refrigerator. Unmould on to a cold round dish, and garnish with aspic.

Pâté de Foie Gras à la Strasbourgeoise or Croûte de Foie Gras

For 12-15 persons: 1 *large foie gras, weighing about* 1¼ *lb;* ¾ *lb unsmoked bacon;* ¼ *lb lean pork;* ¼ *lb calf's liver;* ¼ *lb lean veal;* 3-4 *truffles;* 1 *liqueur glass brandy;* 1 *small glass Madeira;* 2-2½ *lb Pie pastry; salt; pepper; pâté seasoning;* 1 *bay leaf; thyme.* Cooking time: 1 hour.

The evening before marinate a large *foie gras* in brandy, Madeira, *pâté* seasoning, salt, pepper and bay leaf, together with 3 or 4 brushed and peeled truffles. Cover to avoid loss of aroma. The next day, prepare the following stuffing; dice the bacon and melt it in a frying pan without allowing it to colour. Remove it from the pan and *sauté* the pork, calf's liver and veal, all cut into small pieces, rapidly in the fat, just enough to stiffen, but not to colour them. Allow to cool, including the bacon. Pass two or three times through a mincing machine, season with *pâté* seasoning, salt, pepper and a pinch each of powdered thyme and bay leaf. Rub through a fine sieve, add the brandy and Madeira used to marinate the liver and mix well. Line a deep round or oval mould with ½ of an inch thick Pie pastry. Spread some of the stuffing on the bottom and the sides of the mould. Place the *foie gras,* larded with large pieces of raw truffle, upright in the middle of the pie. Press down and trim off if necessary. Place a layer of stuffing on top so that the liver is completely surrounded by stuffing. Close with a dough lid, in which a hole is pierced to allow the steam to escape. Decorate with leaves and rosettes of dough and brush with egg yolk. To prevent the fat from escaping through the hole, insert a small tube of paper. Brush with egg and bake in a hot oven, 400° F or Gas Mark 6. Test with a needle. If it is warm at the end of 30 seconds the pie is ready. Allow pie to become completely cold and pour Madeira aspic through the hole.

Terrine de Foie Gras

Cooking time: 20 minutes for a *foie gras* weighing 1 pound and 35 minutes for one weighing 2 pounds.

Line an earthenware dish with some finely minced veal forcemeat and arrange the *foie gras* inside. Make some holes in the *foie gras* and fill these with cloves of quartered truffles. Cover over with some more finely minced veal forcemeat, put a lid on the dish and bake in a *bain-marie.* On no account should the water in the *bain-marie* boil.

Truffes en Surprise

For 6 *persons:* 1 *lb foie gras poached in sherry;* 6 *oz of finely chopped, cooked truffles;* ¼ *lb butter;* ¾ *pint sherry-flavoured aspic.*

Make *purée* with *foie gras* and softened butter, cook it a little, make it into walnut-sized balls and roll in chopped truffle or finely chopped truffle peel so that they are well-coated. Dip in half-set aspic, chill and arrange in a pyramid. They are also used to garnish cold meat, poultry, and game dishes.

HOT FOIE GRAS

One of the most popular ways of serving *foie gras* hot is to slice and flour it and then *sauté* in butter or goose fat. It may be served accompanied with Apple sauce or truffles.

Escalopes de Foie Gras Lucullus

For 6 persons: 1 *raw foie gras, weighing about* 1¼ *lb;* 1 *glass of sherry;* 12 *slices truffle;* 12 *round butter fried croûtons of* 2*-inch diameter;* ½ *pint sauce Demi-glace;* ¼ *lb butter; flour*. Cooking time: about 10 minutes.

The *foie gras* can be cooked sliced as well as whole. Cut it in diagonal, fairly thick slices, season and marinate in Madeira with raw truffle slices for 2 hours. Wipe, flour and fry in butter like calf's liver. Reduce the stock with wine from the marinade, add a little light *Demi-glace*, add truffle slices. Boil slowly for a few minutes and pour over *foie gras* arranged on *croûtons.*

Foie Gras à la Périgourdine

For 6 persons: 1 *foie gras weighing about* 1¼ *lb;* ½ *pint of sauce Périgueux.*

Poach the *foie gras* in sherry for about 10 minutes. Make the Truffle sauce with sliced or quartered truffles. Cover the *foie gras* with sauce and garnish with truffles. The *foie gras* can also be stuck with quartered truffles before it is cooked.

Friands au Foie Gras

For 6 persons: ½ *lb Puff pastry;* ½ *lb purée of foie gras or* ½ *lb of foie gras puréed with butter;* 1 *yolk of egg*. Cooking time: 12-15 minutes.

Roll out Puff pastry thinly, cut in triangles and put a small piece of poached *foie gras* or buttered *purée* in the middle. Slightly moisten sides, fold so as to enclose filling, score top lightly with a knife, brush with egg yolk and bake in a hot oven for 15 minutes.

Surprise du Périgord

For 6 persons: 6 *well-shaped truffles of the same size;* 1 *tablespoonful of cream;* 6 *oz raw foie gras;* 1 *small glass Madeira;* 1 *egg white;* ½ *pint of sauce Périgueux.* Cooking time: 15 minutes.

Cook peeled truffles of equal size in Madeira. Cut a lid off the top, scoop out deeply and fill with a *mousse* of the pounded *foie gras*, egg white, cream, salt and spices, and the Madeira in which the truffles were cooked. Replace lid, wrap in buttered paper and poach in the Madeira. Remove paper and serve covered with *sauce Périgueux* made with the scooped-out truffle pieces and reduced Madeira.

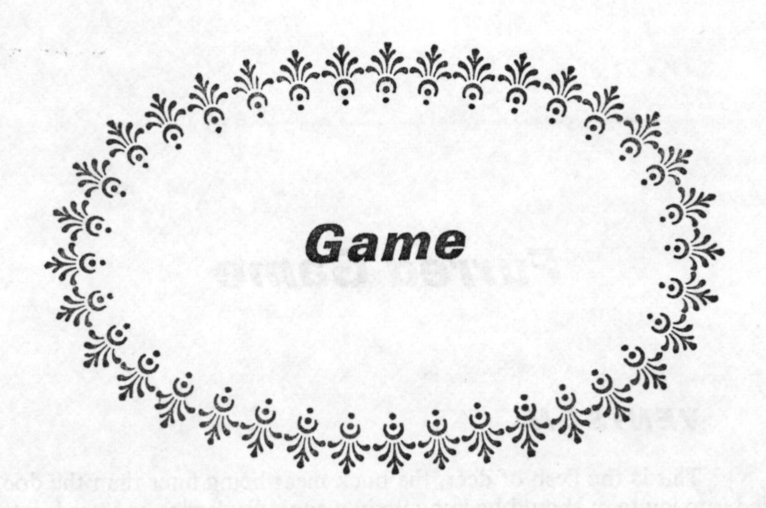

Game

Game is the term usually applied in cookery to all wild birds and animals which are hunted primarily for sport and whose highly flavoured flesh may be cooked and eaten. Many of them are protected by specific Game Laws and are available only in certain seasons. From August till February, generally speaking, is the season in which it is permitted to hunt game. However, nowadays game is imported and some varieties of game are available all the year round. If you cook a great deal of game—and for this you will require an appreciation of the strong and assertive taste of game flesh—it is advisable to find out the prime season for each particular variety of game. When preparing game remember that the flesh is usually very lean and it is almost essential to lard it.

We distinguish between furred and feathered game.

APPROXIMATE COOKING TIMES

GAME	COOKING TIMES	
Roast Saddle of Hare	About 40 mins	These game are roasted in a moderate oven, 375° F or Gas Mark 4-5, or if the flesh is not very tender they are braised in a warm oven, 350° F or Gas Mark 3. To prevent dryness, it is recommended that they are barded with fat bacon or basted frequently with butter.
Jugged Hare	$1\frac{3}{4}$-2 hours	
Roast Leg or Saddle of Venison	12-15 mins per lb	
Roast Pheasant	$\frac{3}{4}$-1 hour	
Wild Duck (Roasted)	20-45 mins according to size and weight	
Partridge (Young)	20-25 mins	
Partridge	20-30 mins	
Thrush	10-15 mins	
Quail	12-15 mins	
Hazelhen	20-30 mins	
Black Game (Roasted)	$\frac{3}{4}$-1 hour	
Rabbit (Roasted)	45 mins	
Jugged or Stewed Rabbit	$1\frac{1}{2}$-$1\frac{3}{4}$ hours	

Furred Game

VENISON

This is the flesh of deer, the buck meat being finer than the doe. As soon as it is divided into joints, it should be hung up in a cool, dry larder or stored in the refrigerator at a temperature which will keep it merely chilled. If it has to be kept for any length of time in the larder, sprinkle lightly with ground ginger and pepper to keep off flies. Examine, wipe and re-pepper every day. In cold weather keep it a fortnight before cooking but if the weather is close a few days will be long enough. Venison should be served in season. A good test for venison is to run a fine skewer into the haunch close to the bone, then remove. If it comes out clean with only a gamey smell, it is in perfect condition. If there is the slightest musty smell, cook at once.

The choice animal has a certain amount of fat round the haunches especially if young but as venison is a rather dry meat, it is advisable to marinate it before cooking. (*See section on* Marinades p. 113).

There are three kinds of venison available in Great Britain—the red deer, roebuck and fallow deer. The flesh of the latter is the finest. The haunch, liver and kidneys are highly prized in the roebuck and fallow deer, but the haunch is the best part of the red deer.

Civet de Chevreuil * *Jugged Venison*

For 6 *persons:* 4 *lb venison* (*shoulder, breast or best end of the neck*); 1¼ *pints red wine marinade;* 6 *oz rashers of lean bacon which have been blanched and fried;* ½ *lb raw mushrooms;* 18 *small onions fried in butter;* ¼ *pint blood;* ¼ *pint cream;* 2 *fl oz brandy;* 2 *oz flour.* Cooking time: 1½ hours.

Marinate for 48 hours, drain and dry the venison. Start frying in hot fat, flour and then brown again in the pan. Next pour the brandy over the meat and set it alight and then add marinade. If necessary, add water so that the meat is completely covered, put a lid on and boil for an hour. Remove the pieces of venison, strain the cooking liquor and then put both in a casserole dish. Add the bacon, onions and mushrooms and finish cooking. Skim off the fat and thicken with the blood and cream. Serve with boiled *spaghetti.*

CÔTELETTES DE CHEVREUIL * *VENISON CUTLETS*

These cutlets should be marinated in red wine and oil for at least 24 hours in order to tenderise them.

▣ Bélisaire

For 6 *persons:* 12 *venison cutlets;* 3 *lb celeriac;* ¾ *pint sauce Poivrade; the juice and peel of* 1 *orange; frying oil.* Cooking time: 7-10 minutes.

Season cutlets, fry in oil, when cooked wipe them, arrange in a ring and fill centre with celeriac *purée*. Complete the *sauce Poivrade* with orange juice and blanched *julienne* of orange peel and coat cutlets with this sauce.

Côtelettes de Chevreuil Châtelaine

For 6 persons: 12 *venison cutlets;* 12 *very small baked tartlet cases;* 1 *lb mushrooms;* ½ *pint sauce Béchamel;* 2 *fl oz cream; frying oil; about* ½ *pint sauce Venaison.*

Make a *purée* of mushrooms with the *Béchamel*, season and enrich with the cream. Season cutlets, fry them and coat with *sauce Venaison*. Garnish with tartlets filled with mushroom *purée*.

⊡ aux Mandarines * *with Mandarin Oranges*

For 6 persons: 12 *venison cutlets, each weighing about* 3 *oz;* 1 *dessertspoon brandy; the juice of* 1 *tin mandarin oranges;* ¾ *pint sauce Venaison.* Cooking time: 7-10 minutes.

Season the cutlets and *sauté* them in butter. Deglaze with the brandy and ⅔ of the mandarin juice. Moisten with the *sauce Venaison* and cook for a few minutes. Heat the mandarin segments, after draining them in the remainder of the mandarin juice. Drain again and pour the juice into the sauce. Serve the cutlets in a ring. Coat with sauce and garnish the middle with the mandarin segments. (*See illustration p.* 591).

⊡ Nesselrode

For 6 persons: 12 *venison cutlets, each weighing about* 3 *oz;* 2 *lb sweet chestnuts;* ¾ *pint sauce Poivrade; frying oil.* Cooking time: 7-10 minutes.

Season cutlets and *sauté* quickly in hot oil. Drain, serve in a ring on a round dish, coat with *sauce Poivrade* and serve chestnut *pureé* in a mound in the centre.

⊡ à la Slave

For 6 persons: 12 *venison cutlets;* 1½ *lb cucumber;* 1 *lb boletus or mushrooms;* ½ *pint sauce Poivrade; oil; butter.* Cooking time of cutlets: 7-10 minutes.

Sauté the cutlets, arrange each on a thick slice of braised cucumber and coat with *sauce Poivrade*. Garnish with boletus or mushrooms sautéed in oil.

GIGUE DE CHEVREUIL * *HAUNCH OR LEG OF VENISON*

Remove all sinews from the haunch and lard upper surface with fine lardons. It can be pickled in a raw marinade for 4 days or in a cooked one for 24 hours, but on the whole this is not recommended since the haunch of a young animal is very tender in itself. The roasting time is 10-15 minutes per lb in a moderate oven, 350° F or Gas Mark 4. The haunch like the saddle is always slightly underdone. Possible garnishes are *purée* of chestnuts, celeriac or lentils, red cabbage and mashed potatoes; possible sauces are *Poivrade, Grand Veneur* and *Venaison.*

Gigue de Chevreuil aux Girolles

For 8 persons: 1 haunch of venison of 4½ lb; ½ lb fat bacon; 4 oz butter; 2 lb mushrooms (skirret if possible); 2 oz chopped onions; 2 oz diced lean bacon; 1 oz chopped parsley; 1½ lb potato Croquettes; ¾ pint sauce Poivrade. Cooking time: 50 minutes.

Lard, season and roast the haunch in a moderate oven, 350° F or Gas Mark 4. Brown the onions and diced bacon. Add the mushrooms and fry golden brown; complete with chopped parsley. Serve the haunch with the mushrooms. Serve the *Croquettes* and the sauce separately.

▣ Marie-Stuart

For 8 persons: 1 haunch of venison of 4½ lb; 1½ lb chestnuts; ½ lb Gratin forcemeat; 3 egg yolks; ¾ pint sauce Poivrade. Cooking time: 50 minutes.

Lard the haunch and roast it in a moderate oven, 350° F or Gas Mark 4. Garnish with *croquettes* made out of the chestnut *purée* combined with the *Gratin* forcemeat, cooked with the egg yolks, cooled, shaped into pears, breadcrumbed and deep-fried. Serve *sauce Poivrade* separately.

Médaillons de Chevreuil aux Cerises * *Medallions with Cherries*

These are round slices cut from the fillet as for beef *médaillons.* Meat from an older animal will require to be marinated for about 24 hours.

For 6 persons: 12 venison medallions, 3 oz each; 1 lb stoned cherries; ¼ pint red wine; a small piece of cinnamon; 3 oz butter; 1½ lb potato Croquettes; a little arrowroot; ½ pint sauce Poivrade; salade Waldorf. Cooking time: 10-12 minutes.

Season the medallions and fry quickly in butter, remove and arrange in a circle. Cook the cherries in the wine with the cinnamon, drain, reduce the juice and thicken with the arrowroot; mix with the cherries and serve in the centre of the circle. Lightly mask the meat with a little sauce. Serve the sauce in a sauce-boat and the salad and potatoes separately. (*See illustration p.* 591).

NOISETTES DE CHEVREUIL * *VENISON STEAKS*

These are cut either from the loin fillet or from the haunch or saddle. They are cut fairly thick averaging 2½ to 3½ oz each.

▣ Duxelles * *Mushroom Stuffed*

For 6 persons: 6 large noisettes of venison, 3½ oz each; 4 oz butter; 8 oz thick duxelles; 1-2 eggs; 8 oz white breadcrumbs. Garnish: 2 oz veal forcemeat quenelles; 2 oz lamb's sweetbreads; 2 oz mushrooms; 12 stoned, blanched olives; 2 oz cocks' combs and kidneys (optional); about ½ pint sauce Venaison. Cooking time of *noisettes*: 10 minutes in all.

Season the *noisettes* and fry in butter over high heat so that they are very underone. Cool slightly, cut open but not through and fill with thick *duxelles*, using a forcing bag. Press down slightly, flour, egg and breadcrumbs and fry golden brown on both sides in clarified butter. Serve in a ring on a round dish and fill the centre with *Financière* garnish which consists of *quenelles*, olives, diced sweetbreads and mushrooms, heated and bound with *sauce Venaison.*

▲ *Civet de lièvre, p. 600*

Râble de lièvre Diane, p. 603 ▼

▲ *Médaillons de cerf Madame Lacroix, p. 606* .

Selle de chevreuil aux Cèpes et Girolles, p. 598 ▼

▲ Côtelettes de chevreuil aux Mandarines, p. 587.

Médaillons de chevreuil aux Cerises, p. 588 ▼

▲ Perdreaux Titania, p. 614

Perdreaux sur Canapés, p. 613 ▼

▲ *Faisan en Cocotte, p. 609*

Faisan Glacé Marie-Jeanne, p. 615 ▼

▲ Pâté de Lièvre, p. 622

Aspic de Foie Gras, p. 581 ▼

▲ Pâté de veau et jambon, p. 620

Selle de chevreuil Grand-Duché, p. 23 ▼

▲ Game Pâtés, pp. 621-622

Poultry Pâtés, p. 620 ▼

Noisettes de Chevreuil Magenta

For 8 *persons:* 16 *noisettes of venison, about* 2 *oz each;* 2¼ *lb potatoes;* 1¾ *pints sauce Soubise;* ½ *pint sauce Roman; frying oil and butter.* Cooking time: 7-10 minutes.

Cut round *noisettes* out of the filleted saddle like small *tournedos*; the nut of a well-hung young haunch is also suitable. Season *noisettes*, fry in half oil and half butter so that they are juicy, place on small fried bases of *Duchesse* potato mixture and coat lightly with *sauce Roman*. Serve the *sauce Soubise* separately.

Sauté de Chevreuil à la Forestière * *Stewed Venison*

Shoulder, neck and breast are the best cuts of venison for stewing or casseroling. They should be cut into small pieces and marinated before cooking.

For 6 *persons:* 2¼ *lb venison without bones (shoulder, neck, breast);* 2 *oz flour;* ½ *pint white wine;* 1 *teaspoon concentrated tomato purée;* 7 *juniper berries;* 1 *bouquet garni;* ¼ *pint oil;* 2 *oz butter;* 1¼ *lb mushrooms;* 2 *shallots.* Cooking time: 1½-2 hours.

Cut meat in suitable pieces and marinate in white wine for a few hours. Dry well, flour and brown in hot oil at great heat and add enough *bouillon* or water for the meat to be just covered. Stir well, add salt, pepper, crushed juniper berries, tomato *purée* and *bouquet garni*, cover and braise slowly in a warm oven, 325° F or Gas Mark 3, until cooked. Then transfer it to a clean casserole, strain sauce over it, add mushrooms, which have been thickly sliced, and *sautéed* in half oil and half butter with chopped shallots. Boil everything together for a little longer. Before serving skim fat off sauce and garnish with heart-shaped *croûtons* of white bread fried in butter.

SELLE DE CHEVREUIL * *SADDLE OF VENISON*

The best cut of venison is the saddle, which is freed from sinews, trimmed and larded. For formal dinners it is usual to use only the saddle. Saddle should be rather underdone, as in a warm temperature the inside of the joint continues to cook. The saddle of a young animal should never be marinated, otherwise the flavour suffers. For roasting allow approximately 10-15 minutes per lb.

For 8-10 *persons:* 1 *saddle of venison, weighing about* 4½-5 *lb;* 10 *medium-sized firm apples;* 5 *oz fat bacon; redcurrant jelly;* 2 *oz butter;* 1 *pint sauce Poivrade.* Cooking time: 50-60 minutes.

Trim the saddle and remove skin and sinews from the top. Lard with strips of fat bacon, season and roast in a hot oven, 400° F or Gas Mark 6. Baste frequently. Peel the apples, trim to a round shape, scoop them out with a vegetable cutter, and poach them carefully in water with a little lemon juice. Drain well, and fill with redcurrant jelly. Arrange the saddle on a long dish and garnish with apples. Boil up the pan residue with sauce and serve in a sauce-boat.

Selle de Chevreuil à l'Allemande

For 8 persons: 1 saddle, weighing about 4 lb; 2 lb red cabbage; 4 oz diced apples; 1½ lb potatoes; 1 onion; pork or goose fat; 2 fl oz vinegar; a little brown sugar; 1 pint of sour cream; juice of half a lemon. Cooking time: 50 minutes.

Trim, bone and lard the saddle, chop the bones finely and roast underdone to a rose colour in a hot oven, 400° F or Gas Mark 6. Remove the saddle, deglaze the pan with a little stock, add the cream and lemon juice, simmer until it becomes a sauce consistency and strain. Cut the cabbage into fine slices and braise with the fat, chopped onion and apple, sugar, vinegar and a little stock. Serve the saddle, coat with a little sauce and serve the rest in a sauce-boat. Serve the cabbage and a dish of mashed potatoes separately.

⊡ Belle-Créole

For 8 persons: 1 saddle, weighing about 4 lb; 4 oz lardons of fat bacon; 4 bananas; 2 slices of pineapple cut into small dice; 2 oz redcurrant jelly; a small glass of white wine and pineapple juice; ½ pint sauce Poivrade. Cooking time: about 50-60 minutes.

Lard the saddle and roast. Remove the saddle, deglaze the pan with the wine and juice. Cook the diced pineapple, add the juice to the *sauce Poivrade* with the redcurrant jelly, boil and strain and garnish with diced pineapple. Skin and cut the bananas into halves lengthwise, egg and breadcrumb and fry in butter. Serve the saddle, garnish with the bananas. Serve the sauce in a sauce-boat.

⊡ aux Cèpes et Girolles * *with Mushrooms*

For 6 persons: 1 saddle of venison, weighing about 3½ lb; 1 lb boletus; 1 lb skirret mushrooms; 4 oz butter; 2 oz chopped onions; 1 oz chopped parsley; 1 lb potatoes; ½ pint cream; ½ pint brown stock; ¼ pint Demi-glace; ½ lb lardons of fat bacon. Cooking time: 40 minutes.

Lard the saddle, season it and roast in a hot oven, 400° F or Gas Mark 6. Baste several times with butter. Drain. Add the brown stock to the pan residue and reduce. Add the cream and the *Demi-glace*. Allow to cook until it has reached the desired consistency and check the seasoning. Strain. *Sauté* the boletus and skirret mushrooms separately with the chopped onions which have been browned first in butter. Season and add chopped parsley. Serve the saddle. Garnish the sides with two kinds of mushrooms. Serve the sauce and the potatoes separately. If possible, serve ring potatoes, potato *Croquettes* or *purée* or *Château* potatoes. (*See illustration p.* 590).

⊡ Metternich

For 10 persons: 1 saddle of venison, weighing about 5½ lb; 2¼ lb chestnuts; 10 apples; 1½ lb red cabbage; ½ lb redcurrant jelly; 1 pint sauce Grand Veneur; frying butter. Cooking time: 60 minutes.

Lard saddle in the usual way, season and roast in a hot oven. Garnish with braised chestnuts, very dry red cabbage and the peeled scooped out apples, carefully poached and filled with redcurrant jelly. Coat saddle very lightly with the reduced pan residue and serve sauce separately.

Selle de Chevreuil Windsor

For 8-10 *persons:* 1 *saddle of venison, weighing about* 4½ *lb;* ½ *lb larding bacon;* 4-5 *sticks of celery;* 2½ *lb sweet chestnuts;* 1 *pint sauce Poivrade;* 1 *tablespoon grated horseradish;* ¼ *pint cream; butter*. Cooking time: 50 minutes.

Remove sinews from saddle, lard it and roast in a hot oven. Garnish with braised celery and whole braised chestnuts. Coat very lightly with *sauce Poivrade* boiled up with the pan residue. Complete the remainder of the sauce with grated horseradish and cream and serve separately.

WILD BOAR

This is not one of the tastiest varieties of game and only the legs and saddle are generally used, provided that they have been thoroughly marinaded beforehand. The young animal up to a year old, *le marcassin*, weighing 55-56 pounds is much tastier. The cutlets, particularly appreciated by connoisseurs, can be prepared in the same way as venison cutlets. The best part of the wild boar is the head, which, when stuffed, is one of the most splendid of cold dishes.

CÔTELETTES DE MARCASSIN * *WILD BOAR CUTLETS*

These should be marinated in wine and oil for 24 hours before cooking.

▣ aux Cerises * *with Cherries*

For 6 *persons:* 12 *cutlets, each weighing about* 3 *oz;* 1 *lb stoned sour cherries;* ¼ *pint red wine;* 1 *pinch powdered cinnamon;* ½ *oz potato flour or cornflour;* 4 *oz butter;* 1 *lb potato Croquette balls;* ½ *pint sauce Poivrade*. Cooking time: 6-7 minutes.

Poach the cherries in red wine with a pinch of cinnamon and very little sugar. Drain and reduce the liquor. Thicken with the potato flour or cornflour and add the cherries. Season the cutlets and *sauté* them in butter. Serve them in a ring and place the cherries in the centre. Serve the *sauce Poivrade* and the potato *Croquettes* separately.

▣ Saint Mark

For 6 *persons:* 12 *cutlets of young boar, each weighing about* 3 *oz;* ¾ *pint game stock;* 1 *carrot;* 1 *onion; thyme;* 1 *small bay leaf; parsley;* 6 *oz larding bacon;* ¼ *pint oil;* 2 *oz butter;* ½ *pint Cranberry sauce;* 2 *lb chestnut purée;* ¼ *lb pickled tongue*. Cooking time: 45 minutes.

Prepare a braise of sliced onions and carrots, parsley, thyme, bay leaf, and game stock. Trim cutlets neatly, and lard each one with 2-3 lardons, brown in oil and butter with the sliced tongue and place on top of the braise. Cook in a moderate oven, 375° F or Gas Mark 4. When they are cooked, remove to a round plate. Deglaze the pan with Cranberry sauce and reduce; serve this sauce apart. The chestnut *purée* is made into *croquettes* and served piled up in the centre of the dish.

Jambons de Marcassin * *Haunches or Hams*

This is cut from the leg as for pork and should be well hung before cooking. It is not necessary to marinate it. They are generally braised and served with various garnishes, the most appropriate being a *purée* of turnips, celery or chestnuts. The sauce is prepared from the well-skimmed cooking liquor and finished as a *sauce Poivrade.*

⊡ à la Vernon

The haunch may be marinated or simply well hung. The marinade will make it more tender and slightly transform the very marked gamey smell. Roast for 25 minutes per 2 lb or braise for 4-5 hours. Serve with turnip *purée* on one side and chestnut *purée* on the other, and *sauce Vernon* separately.

For the sauce Vernon: 2 *oz sugar;* ¼ *pint vinegar;* 1 *oz each of currants and sultanas;* 1½ *oz pine kernels;* 1 *pint Demi-glace;* ½ *pint cooking liquor;* 2 *oz chocolate.*

Lightly caramelise the sugar, add the vinegar and reduce to a syrup, add *Demi-glace* and stock, simmer until the right consistency and strain. Soak the fruits in tepid water, shred and grill the pine kernels. Melt the chocolate, stir into the sauce with the garnish.

HARE

Hares and leverets are in season from August to March. Young hares may be recognised by the fact that it is easy to press in the ribs, to loosen the skin between the ears, to tear the ears lengthwise and to break the legs. The carcase should be full and plump. Young animals should be used for roasting and casseroling, whereas older hares may be utilised for *civets* and *terrines.*

Civet de Lièvre * *Jugged Hare*

For 8 *persons:* 1 *hare, weighing about* 4½-5 *lb;* ½ *lb mushrooms;* 6 *oz lean bacon;* 1½ *pints red wine;* 20 *small onions; bouquet garni;* 2 *fl oz brandy.* Cooking time: 1½-2 hours.

Cut hare into pieces and marinate 48 hours in the red wine. Wipe the pieces dry, brown over high heat in fat, sprinkle with a little flour, let it brown, flambé with brandy and add the red wine marinade. Mix well. Add as much water as red wine, add 1 tablespoon tomato *purée,* 1 crushed clove of garlic, *bouquet garni,* salt and pepper, cover and braise for 20 minutes. Add browned onions and diced bacon, simmer for 45 minutes, add raw, washed mushrooms and finish cooking together. When cooked, mix the hare's blood, which is an essential ingredient, with a few spoonfuls of sauce and the same quantity of cream, stir into sauce, boil up again, once only, season, remove *bouquet garni* and put in a deep dish. Garnish with fried mushrooms and bacon and serve with boiled *spaghetti.* (*See illustration p.* 589).

Civet de Lièvre à l'Allemande

For 6 persons: 2½ lb weight of fore-legs of hare; ½ lb quartered mushrooms, lightly fried in butter; ½ lb bacon strips, lightly fried; ½ lb button onions, glazed brown; ½ bottle red wine; 1¼ pints Demi-glace; ¼ pint blood.

Fry the hare, add the wine, reduce to half, add the sauce and simmer until tender. Serve the meat in a casserole. Thicken the sauce with the blood, season well with the freshly ground pepper. Garnish the hare with the mushrooms, bacon strips and button onions strain over the sauce and heat without allowing to boil. Serve with a dish of buttered *spätzle* and stewed apples.

▣ aux Marrons * *Jugged with Chestnuts*

The same ingredients as above, but replacing the mushrooms by 1 lb sweet chestnuts. Score peel, cook in oven till almost tender, peel and add to jugged hare.

▣ à la Solognaise

For 8 persons: 1 *hare, weighing about* 4-5 *lb;* 2 *onions;* ½ *bottle red wine;* 3 *shallots;* 6 *oz streaky bacon;* ½ *lb mushrooms;* 1 *clove garlic;* 32 *button onions glazed in butter;* 1 *bunch of chervil and parsley;* 16 *heart-shaped butter-fried croûtons;* 1 *glass of brandy.*

Put the heart, liver, kidney and blood into a basin. Cut up the hare. Take all the trimmings, neck, head, etc., fry with a shredded onion, add the other onion stuck with two cloves and the bunch of herbs. Cover with good stock, boil, skim and simmer. Take the heart, liver and kidneys, lightly flour, lightly fry, add half the wine and stock and simmer. In the meantime fry the hare, put in a casserole, add 2 chopped shallots to the pan with the crushed chopped garlic and the streaky bacon cut into dice, fry and flambé with half of the brandy. Add the rest of the wine, pour over the hare and moisten to two-thirds full with the hare stock made with the trimmings. Bring to the boil, cover with lid and cook in a moderate oven, 350° F or Gas Mark 4. Finely chop together one shallot, the parsley, chervil, heart, liver and kidneys, add the blood and the rest of the brandy. Add the mushrooms to the hare 10 minutes before serving then add the blood mixture. Allow to thicken the sauce and serve with the *croûtons.*

Côtelettes de Lièvre Pojarski * *Cutlets*

For 6 persons: 1 *lb lean hare meat without sinews;* 1 *small onion;* 2 *oz butter;* 2 *oz white bread without crust; Pepper sauce;* 1 *egg;* 1 *tablespoon water;* 1 *teaspoon oil;* 8 *oz white breadcrumbs.* Frying time: 10-12 minutes.

Sweat finely chopped onion and let it cool. Chop the hare meat finely with the soaked and squeezed out bread, the butter and onion, season with salt and pepper and mix well. Shape into small cutlets on a floured board, coat with egg beaten with oil and water and dip in breadcrumbs, press down well. Fry a golden brown slowly on both sides in butter and serve with *sauce Poivrade* mixed with a few spoonfuls of cream.

LEVRAUT * *LEVERET*

◻ à la Forestière * *Sautéed Leveret with Mushrooms*

For 6 persons: 1 *young hare, weighing about* 3½ *lb;* 1 *lb field mushrooms fried in butter;* 1 *oz flour;* ¼ *pint white wine;* 1 *clove of garlic;* 1 *bouquet garni.* Cooking time: 1 hour.

Joint the hare and fry in butter, sprinkle with the flour, and brown. Add the wine, barely cover with water; add seasoning, *bouquet garni* and chopped garlic, bring to the boil. Then simmer for ¾ hour in a moderate oven; add the mushrooms and bacon, simmer another 10 to 15 minutes. Serve and sprinkle with chopped parsley.

◻ farci Magnac-Laval * *Stuffed*

For 15 persons: 1 *hare, weighing about* 8-9 *lb;* 1 *lb foie gras;* 1 *lb pork fillet;* 1 *lb fat pork;* 10 *chicken livers; slices of fat bacon;* 15 *small firm mushrooms;* 2 *stalks celeriac;* 2 *lb apples;* 2 *lb prunes;* 1 *oz skinned pistachio nuts;* 1 *oz salt;* ½ *level teaspoonful ground black pepper;* ½ *level teaspoon of each of the following herbs mixed together: thyme, wild thyme, marjoram, rosemary and savory;* 1 *bottle red burgundy;* 1 *glass brandy;* 2 *quarts game stock;* 4 *oz breadcrumbs;* 15 *small pastry tartlet cases;* 2 *carrots;* 2 *onions;* 3 *eggs;* 1 *bread croûton cut to the length of the hare,* ½*-inch thick and* 4*-inches wide and slightly hollowed out along the centre.* Cooking time: approximately 2½ hours.

Bone the hare completely, except for the head and paws. Dip the ears and paws into boiling water and remove the skin. Cut away a little flesh from the bone cavities of the legs. Keep the liver and heart for the forcemeat and the blood for the sauce. Prepare a forcemeat with 5 chicken livers and 2 ounces of the pork fat, lightly fried with a chopped shallot and a little brandy. Finely mince the pork fillets, 5 chicken livers, the liver and heart of the hare, the flesh trimmings of the hare, the stalks of the mushrooms, some shallots and parsley, pound and sieve. Add half the minced pork fat, herbs, salt, pepper, brandy and eggs; blend well and mix in the pistachios. Lay the hare upon the table and fill with some of the forcemeat, not forgetting to fill the bone cavities in the legs; cut the *foie gras* into slices and arrange upon the forcemeat. Now cover over with the rest of the forcemeat, sew up to reform the animal, wrap in the bards of fat bacon, arrange the head and legs, and tie into position. Place in a tray in a cool oven, 325° F or Gas Mark 3, to set the shape. Butter a long braising pan, line with the sliced carrots and onions and chopped hare bones, place the hare on top, moisten with the wine and game stock and cook in a moderate oven, 375° F or Gas Mark 4, for 2 hours. In the meantime cook the prunes, the celeriac and apples. Stone two-thirds of the prunes, pound the other third in a mortar and pass through a fine sieve. With this pulp, stuff the stoned prunes and heat in the oven. Sieve the celeriac and add a little butter. Sieve the cooked apples. Take the rest of the pork fat, mix with the breadcrumbs, parsley, chervil, shallot, and heat in the oven. Fry the mushrooms in butter and fill with the above forcemeat. Fill the *purée* of celeriac into the tartlet cases. Fry the bread *croûton* in butter and spread with the chicken liver forcemeat. Remove the string and bards of bacon fat from the hare and place upon the *croûton*; garnish round the dish with the mushrooms and tartlets. Reduce the cooking liquor to 1½ pints, skim, thicken with the hare blood, strain. Serve the prunes in a separate dish. Brush the hare with a little sauce. Serve the sauce and apple *purée* in sauce-boats.

Levraut à la Royale

For 8-10 persons: 1 hare, weighing about 4½ lb; 2 large onions; 2 carrots; 10 shallots; ½ lb sliced bacon or bacon rinds; 6 cloves garlic; 1 bouquet garni; 1¼ pints red wine; ¼ pint wine vinegar; peppercorns; hare's blood; butter. Cooking time: 2 hours.

Draw a whole, skinned hare and keep the blood, heart, liver and lungs. Line a dish that is only just big enough with bacon rashers or rinds, cover them with sliced carrots, onions and shallots, garlic and *bouquet garni.* Place hare on top and let it brown a little in a hot oven. Cover with wine and vinegar, season, cover and braise very slowly in the oven for 2 hours. In the meantime chop the remaining shallots and garlic very fine, almost to a *purée,* with the lungs, liver and heart. Remove the hare, which should be very tender, carefully from the pan, strain the stock and thicken with the hare's blood mixed with the *purée.* Cook at very low heat till sauce looks like a thick cream, then pass through a sieve once again, pressing it through with a pestle. Arrange hare on a long, hot dish and pour well seasoned sauce over it.

RÂBLE DE LIÈVRE * *SADDLE OF HARE*

The back includes the saddle and loin from the first ribs to the legs. Usually only the saddle which is the best part, is used; it is well skinned and larded with bacon. The saddle can be marinated for 48 hours in red or white wine, but nowadays that is usually only done with older hares which are braised instead of being roasted.

⊡ à l'Allemande

For 6 persons: 2 saddles of hare, each weighing about 1½ lb; 6 oz fat bacon; 2 oz butter; 6 oz dried hare meat; ½ pint red wine; 3 tablespoons Demi-glace; ½ pint fresh cream; 3 lb red cabbage; 1 lb apples. Cooking time: 30 minutes.

Lard the saddles with thin lardons and roast them in a hot oven, 400° F or Gas Mark 6, basting frequently. Remove and keep them at moderate heat. Add red wine and reduce by three-quarters, add the *Demi-glace* and the cream and cook for another moment. Serve the saddles on a dish, coat lightly with sauce, and sprinkle with a *julienne* of dried meat browned in butter. Serve the remainder of the sauce, the red cabbage and some potato fritters separately. Overlap slices of peeled apple, cooked in butter in the oven, on top of the red cabbage.

⊡ Bergère

For 6 persons: 2 saddles, each weighing about 1¼-1½ lb; 2 lb mushrooms; 1 lb potatoes; 3 oz fat bacon; 2 oz butter; ½ pint white wine. Cooking time: 30 minutes.

Lard the saddle and if preferred marinate in white wine. Wipe, dry and roast in butter in a hot oven, 425° F or Gas Mark 7, so that it is still underdone. Reduce pan residue with white wine, boil down to half and enrich with butter and chopped parsley. Pour some sauce over saddle and garnish with Straw potatoes and sautéed mushrooms. Serve remainder of sauce separately.

⊡ Diane

For 6 persons: 2 saddles of hare, each weighing about 1½ lb; 1 pint sauce Diane; 1½ lb chestnut purée; 4 oz fat bacon; 2 oz butter. Cooking time: 30 minutes.

Lard the saddles, roast in a hot oven, 425° F or Gas Mark 7, keep underdone. Serve the saddles and garnish with fried, sliced bacon. Serve separately with mashed chestnuts and *sauce Diane.* (*See illustration p.* 589).

Râble de Lièvre Saint-Hubert

For 6 persons: 2 saddles of hare, each weighing about 1½ lb; 1¼ lb small mushrooms; 4 oz fat bacon; 1 lb thick Apple sauce; 2 chopped shallots; ¾ pint Game sauce; 4 oz butter; 1 oz chopped parsley. Cooking time: 30 minutes.

Lard the saddles and roast in a hot oven. Keep underdone. Fry the shallots and mushrooms in butter and toss in the parsley. Serve the saddle and garnish with the mushrooms. Serve the *sauce Poivrade* and Apple sauce in sauce-boats.

◘ Sauce Chevreuil Aigre-Douce * *with Sweet Sour Game Sauce*

For 6 persons: 2 saddles of hare, each weighing about 1½ lb; ½ pint sauce Venaison; ¼ pint cream; 1 chopped shallot; ¾ pint white wine; cayenne, sugar, salt and pepper. Cooking time: 30 minutes.

Marinate the saddle for 24 hours, then roast. Remove, deglaze the pan with a ¼ pint of marinade. Strain into a clean pan, add the sauce and the rest of the marinade. Reduce to a sauce consistency, add the cream, simmer together with the shallot. Heighten the taste with cayenne and sugar, correct consistency, strain. Arrange saddle and serve the sauce in a sauce-boat.

RABBITS

Rabbits and hares are best eaten from September to March. Choose rabbits in the same way as hares. When freshly killed, the flesh is moist and of a slightly bluish tinge. We distinguish between wild rabbits and tame rabbits. Wild rabbits are prepared in the same way as hare, jugged, in cutlets, as *pâtés* and pies, and, like the tame rabbit, can also be stewed. Since they are smaller, rabbits are easier to stuff and braise than hares. Both wild and tame rabbits may be eaten, the flesh of the former is stronger in flavour. Rabbits like fowls should be cooked while very fresh; hanging for one day is sufficient but hares, to be tender, should be well hung. Rabbits should be paunched as soon as they are killed but do not skin either hare or rabbit until just before cooking as otherwise the flesh will become dry.

Lapin Farci à l'Ardennaise * *Stuffed Rabbit with Ham*

For 8-10 *persons: 1 rabbit, weighing about 4½* lb; *1 lb sausage meat; 4 oz boiled lean ham; 2 chopped onions cooked in butter; 1 crushed clove of garlic; pâté seasoning; 1 large pinch each powdered thyme and bay leaf; chopped parsley; 1 large onion; 1 carrot; 2 oz lard; ¾ pint white wine.* Cooking time: 2 hours.

Mix the sausage meat with the chopped onions, garlic, herbs, chopped parsley, coarsely chopped ham and chopped rabbit liver. Season, mix well and stuff rabbit through slit along belly. Sew up opening, bend rabbit in a ring, put in a suitable casserole and heat in lard in moderate oven, 375° F or Gas Mark 5, together with sliced onion and carrot. Season, add white wine, cover and braise slowly in a warm oven, 325° F or Gas Mark 3, for 2 hours. Skim fat off stock, strain it and serve with rabbit. Rabbits are also served hot or cold in *pâtés* (p. 621) and taste excellent in this form.

Lapin Farci Ménagère * *Rabbit Stuffed with Forcemeat*

For 6 persons: 1 *rabbit, weighing about* 4-4½ *lb;* 12 *oz sausage meat;* 4 *oz white bread without crust;* 4 *oz lard;* 3 *large onions;* 1 *clove garlic;* 1 *carrot; thyme; bay leaf; parsley;* ¼ *pint white wine;* ½ *pint bouillon.* Cooking time: 1½ hours.

Draw the rabbit and keep the blood, liver, heart and lungs. Except for the blood chop everything finely with an onion, mix thoroughly with the soaked and squeezed-out bread, sausage meat, chopped parsley, crushed garlic, powdered thyme and bay leaf and season well. Stuff rabbit with the forcemeat, sew up and brown it in a braising pan in hot lard, together with the sliced carrot and onions. Season, add white wine and *bouillon,* cover and braise in a warm oven, 325° F or Gas Mark 3 until cooked. Skim fat off sauce, strain it and thicken with the blood. Red wine may be used instead of white.

▣ Garenne Jeanneton

For 8 persons: 2 *wild rabbits, each weighing about* 3 *lb;* ½ *lb tomatoes;* 2 *chopped shallots; a trace of garlic;* ¼ *pint white wine;* 1 *bouquet garni with plenty of thyme;* 2 *oz butter;* 2 *fl oz oil.* Cooking time: 1½ hours.

Prepare rabbits, cut them in pieces, brown them over a hot flame in butter with a little oil. Add the garlic, the chopped shallots and the peeled, seeded and coarsely chopped tomatoes and simmer for 5 minutes. Season with salt and pepper, add the white wine, an equal quantity of water and the *bouquet garni,* cover and cook slowly in a warm oven, 325° F or Gas Mark 2-3. When cooked, put pieces in a clean casserole, strain sauce, pour it over meat and sprinkle with chopped parsley. Surround with deep fried onion rings and garnish with fried, heart-shaped white bread *croûtons.*

▣ Gibelotte * *Rabbit Stew*

For 6 persons: 1 *drawn rabbit, weighing about* 4 *lb;* 2 *oz lard;* 1½ *oz flour;* 6 *oz lean bacon;* 2 *cloves of garlic;* 2 *shallots;* ¾ *pint red wine;* 20 *small onions;* 1 *lb new potatoes.* Cooking time: 1½ hours.

Cut up rabbit, brown it, sprinkle with flour and add half the crushed garlic and the chopped shallots. Season, add red wine and an equal quantity of water, braise in a warm oven, 325° F or Gas Mark 3. After 20 minutes add the diced bacon and the onions, both browned in butter. After another 20 minutes add new potatoes, substitute well-shaped old ones when not in season and complete braising together. Add a few drops of caramel to improve the colour, if necessary.

▣ Sauté Chasseur

For 6 persons: 1 *rabbit, weighing about* 4 *lb;* 2 *oz lard;* 1 *oz flour;* 3 *shallots;* 2 *oz tomato puree;* ½ *lb mushrooms;* 1 *pint white wine;* 1 *bouquet garni.* Cooking time: 1½ hours.

Sauté the cut-up rabbit in a casserole containing the sizzling hot lard. Brown well, sprinkle with flour, add the chopped shallots and when the flour has browned moisten with one-third white wine and two-thirds water. Add salt, pepper, *bouquet garni* and tomato *purée.* Cook over low heat for one hour, then add raw quartered or whole mushrooms, according to taste. Remove fat and serve sprinkled with chopped parsley.

RED DEER AND FALLOW DEER

The haunch, loin and saddle are the best parts of these animals. Here are 2 recipes which are specially recommended.

Médaillons de Cerf Madame Lacroix * *Medallions of Stag*

These are cut from the fillets as for beef *médaillons.*

For 6 persons: 6 medallions cut from the filleted saddle each weighing about 4-5 *oz;* ½ *lb rice;* 1 *pint bouillon;* 2 *tablespoons chopped mustard pickles;* 2 *oz chopped onion;* 2 *tablespoons redcurrant jelly;* ½ *pint sauce Poivrade;* ¼ *pint cream;* 2 *pieces of candied ginger;* 1 *pint olive oil;* 1 *lettuce.* Cooking time: 7-8 minutes.

Marinate the medallions in oil for 30 minutes. Prepare a *risotto* with the onion, rice and stock, add the finely diced ginger. Wipe dry and season the medallions and *sauté* them in butter. Reduce the pan residue with the cream, add the *sauce Poivrade* and redcurrant jelly. Cook for a few minutes and strain. Add the mustard pickles to the sauce. Press the *risotto* into a domed mould and turn out into the middle of a round dish. Place the medallions round it in a ring and coat them lightly with the sauce. Serve the remainder of the sauce and lettuce salad separately. (*See illustration p.* 590).

Steak de Daim à la Sibérienne * *Fallow Steak*

If the meat comes from an older animal it should be left to soak in a raw marinade for 24 hours.

For 6 *persons:* 6 *steaks cut from the saddle, each weighing about* 4-5 *oz each;* ¼ *pint brown game stock;* ½ *pint sour cream; the juice of half a lemon;* 8 *oz coarse julienne of peeled preserved cucumbers.* Cooking time: 7-8 minutes.

Season the steaks and *sauté* them in butter. Arrange them on a dish. Deglaze the pan residue and reduce with the brown stock, boil down to half and add the sour cream. Cook for a few minutes and add the diced cucumbers after blanching them and the lemon juice. Coat the steaks with the sauce and serve potato *purée* separately.

Feathered Game

It is more difficult to judge the age and condition of feathered game than poultry, because it is frequently sold unplucked. However, you can generally tell by the feel of the breastbone whether it is fit for roasting or not. When young, the end bends easily; when old it is quite firm when pressed. All young birds have soft, even feathers, smooth pliable legs, supple toes and short spurs. Hens are more juicy and tender than male birds but the latter have a stronger flavour. Ducks and other water-fowl should have supple moist feet. Young grouse are distinguished by the short spur and V-shaped quill feathers. Young partridges are famed for yellow legs, dark bill and the whiteness of the breast when the feathers are lifted.

For the flesh to become tender, game (with a few exceptions) requires to hang longer than poultry. Never wash game but wipe the birds inside and outside with a damp cloth. Many types of game birds require to be larded before cooking as the flesh tends to be dry.

BÉCASSES ET BÉCASSINES * *WOODCOCK AND SNIPE*

Snipe and woodcock taste best underdone and served on a *croûton* spread with the intestine or trail. If you prefer the birds fully cooked: a woodcock should be roasted for 20-25 minutes, and snipe for 10-12 minutes. Do not draw, just remove the stomach. Snipe and woodcock must be well hung, but must not be on the point of decomposition. Bard before roasting by wrapping in a thin slice of bacon.

▣ Sautée au Champagne * *Sautéed in Champagne*

For 2 persons: 1 *woodcock;* 2 *oz butter;* ¼ *pint dry champagne*. Cooking time: 10-15 minutes.

Cut woodcock in 5 pieces and *sauté* quickly in butter. As soon as both sides are stiff, season, draw to one side of stove, cover and let it stand there for 6-7 minutes. Remove, reduce pan residue with champagne, add the crushed entrails, boil up quickly, season and strain over woodcock.

▣ Souvaroff

For 6 persons: 3 *woodcock;* 6 *oz foie gras;* 8 *oz truffles;* ½ *pint Madeira;* ¼ *pint strong game stock;* 2 *oz butter*. Cooking time of woodcocks: 20-25 minutes.

Divide *foie gras* into 3, impale a quarter of a truffle in each, marinate in Madeira with the remaining truffles. Heat until the *foie gras* becomes firm, then cool. Draw the woodcock (i.e. remove, intestines) fill each woodcock with a piece of truffled *foie gras*, truss and brown quickly in a *cocotte* or small casserole. Surround with quartered truffles, add Madeira from marinade and game stock, cover, seal hermetically with dough and put in a hot oven, 425° F or Gas Mark 7, for 18-20 minutes. Serve in the sealed casserole only removing the seal at the table.

Bécassine Flambée * *Flambéed Snipe*

1 *snipe per person.* Roasting time: 10-12 minutes.

Roast barded snipe in a very hot oven, 450° F or Gas Mark 8, remove, cut in 4 (2 legs and 2 breasts) and keep hot for 2-3 minutes. During this time reduce the pan residue together with a small glass of champagne or good white wine, add crushed intestines, press out blood from finely chopped back and mix with juice. Season and pour over snipe. Pour a generous dash of brandy on top, light it and serve at once.

Salmis de Bécassines Vatel

For 6 persons: 6 snipe; 2 chopped shallots; ¼ pint Madeira; ¼ pint champagne; 2 oz butter; ½ pint Demi-glace; ½ lb mushrooms; 2 small truffles. Cooking time: 10-12 minutes.

Roast snipe so that they are still underdone. Sweat shallots in butter, add champagne and Madeira, a pinch each of powdered thyme and bay leaf, reduce to a quarter, add *Demi-glace*, simmer slowly in a warm oven, 325° F or Gas Mark 3 for 45 minutes and skim off fat. Half roast snipe lengthwise, skin them, pound the back coarsely, add to sauce, boil up once and press through a tammy cloth or *chinois*. In the meantime keep the snipe warm with a dash of Madeira, but do not heat too much. Add sautéed mushrooms and truffle slices to sauce, heat it without boiling, pour over snipes and garnish with heart-shaped *croûtons* fried in butter, spread with *Gratin* forcemeat.

CAILLES * *QUAILS*

Wild quail is protected by law so that it is not readily available. However, quail are now being reared and imported. If hung, the bird will keep for several days. They can be roasted like snipe or drawn from neck end according to taste but you must remove the gizzard.

▣ Bonne-Maman

For 6 persons: 6 quails; ½ lb carrots; 4 oz celery; 4 oz onions; 2 oz butter; ¼ pint veal stock. Cooking time: 10 minutes.

Cut celery, onions, and the red of the carrot only in fine *julienne* and simmer slowly in butter until almost tender. Season quails, just stiffen in butter, place on *julienne*, add stock, cover, simmer for 10-12 minutes and serve as it is.

NOTE: Quail prepared in this way can also be served cold. In that case, use very gelatinous stock for poaching.

▣ à la Judic

6 quails; ¼ pint strong game stock or veal stock; small glass Port; 1 lb potatoes; 3 lettuces. Cooking time: 12 minutes.

Poach quails in the stock with Port, drain, serve on small round, flat potato *croquettes* and garnish with halved, braised, folded lettuces. Reduce stock, thicken slightly with cornflour and coat quails lightly with it.

▣ à la Turque

6 quails; ½ lb rice; 2 oz grated Parmesan; 2 oz butter; 4 oz onions; ½ pint light Tomato sauce, made from fresh tomatoes if possible. Cooking time: 12 minutes.

Make *risotto*, cook 5-6 minutes, brown quails quickly in butter, add them to *risotto* and finish the cooking together. Put rice in a deep dish, place quails on top and cover with Tomato sauce to which the pan residue of the quails, reduced with a few drops of stock, has been added.

COQ DE BRUYÈRE * *BLACK COCK OR GAME*

Belonging to the grouse species, the male is known as "black cock" or "heath cock" and females as "grey hen" or "brown hen". The thighs of black game are considered the choicest morsels. These birds may be barded, roasted for 35-40 minutes and served with with redcurrant jelly and Bread sauce.

FAISANS * *PHEASANT*

Often called the "King of Game Birds". It is the most popular and has a delicious flavour which is not too gamey if hung for a minimum period. The hen bird is preferred since it has more flavour and is less dry.

▣ en Casserole * *Casseroled*

For 5 persons: 1 pheasant, weighing about 3½ lb; 1 glass brandy; ½ pint game stock; 4 oz butter. Cooking time: 1-1¼ hours.

Truss the pheasant, brown in a casserole with the butter, cover with lid and cook. Drain off the fat, deglaze the pan with the brandy and stock, reboil and serve.

▣ en Chartreuse

For 6 persons: 1 pheasant, weighing about 3½ lb; 4½ lb white cabbage; 1½ lb carrots; 1 lb turnips; 2 oz string beans and 2 oz peas cooked in salted water; 1 garlic sausage; ½ lb lean bacon; 2 oz lard; 2 sliced onions; ¼ pint Demi-glace; 1 clove of garlic; 1 bouquet garni. Cooking time: 2 hours.

Remove main stem of the cabbage, blanch, refresh and braise with the onions, ½ pound carrots, the sausage, bacon, lard, garlic and *bouquet garni.* Fry the pheasant to a golden colour and place on the cabbage and continue cooking. Cut the turnips and the remaining carrots into ½-inch long batons and cook in salted water, drain and cool. Butter a charlotte mould and on the base arrange a circle of carrots, then of string beans, then of turnips, then of peas and so on until the base is covered. When the cabbage is cooked, drain, line the prepared mould with the larger leaves, fill the centre with the rest of the cabbage, press down well and keep hot. Take the cooking liquor, add ¼ pint of *Demi-glace*, skim well and reduce to less than half a pint, strain. Cut the pheasant, sausage and bacon into thin slices. Unmould the cabbage in the centre of the dish, pour round a little of the sauce and then arrange the meats round the dish. Serve with boiled potatoes and surplus sauce in sauce-boat.

▣ en Cocotte

For 5 persons: 1 pheasant, weighing about 2¾ lb; 15 small onions; 15 raw mushrooms; 2 oz butter; glass Madeira. Cooking time: 50 minutes.

Truss the pheasant, bard with bacon and brown well in a fire-proof casserole. Remove bacon after 15 minutes, add browned onions and raw mushrooms, cover and finish cooking together. At the last moment add Madeira and reduce. Remove the trussing thread and serve covered in the casserole. In the case of all pheasant dishes, the bird must be underdone since it becomes dry otherwise. (*See illustration p.* 593).

Faisans à la Crème * *Sautéed Pheasant in Cream Sauce*

For 8 persons: 2 *young pheasants, each weighing about* 2¼ *lb;* 2 *oz butter;* 1 *lb mushrooms;* ¾ *pint cream; a walnut-sized lump of meat glaze.* Cooking time: about 25 minutes.

Cut up pheasant as for sautéed chicken, season and *sauté* quickly over high heat so that it is still underdone. Reduce pan residue with cream, boil to a thick sauce with the meat glaze and season well. Coat pheasant with sauce and garnish with sautéed mushrooms. Serve at once so that the meat has no time to dry out. Sautéed pheasant can be garnished to taste, but salmis and roasting are the best ways of preparing pheasant.

▣ Demidoff

For 5 persons: 1 *pheasant, weighing about* 2¾-3¼ *lb;* ½ *lb carrots;* ½ *lb celery;* 2 *truffles;* ¼ *pint Madeira.* Cooking time: 40-60 minutes.

Brown pheasant in butter in a fire-proof casserole, add carrots cut in thin half-moon shapes and thinly sliced celery, cover the casserole and cook. Five minutes before it is removed from the oven, add the truffles cut in half-moons and the Madeira; cover, finish cooking and serve in casserole.

▣ à la Financière

For 6-8 persons: 1 *pheasant, weighing about* 3¼ *lb;* 1¾ *lb garnish Financière;* ¾ *pint sauce Madère.* Cooking time: 45-60 minutes.

Cook the pheasant in butter *en Cocotte.* Arrange on a dish and surround with the garnish *Financière.*

▣ en Salmis

For 4-5 persons: 1 *pheasant, weighing about* 2¾ *lb;* 1 *small onion;* 1 *shallot;* ½ *clove garlic;* 1 *small glass white wine;* ½ *pint Demi-glace;* 1 *small glass red wine;* 1 *small bouquet garni;* ½ *lb mushrooms;* 1 *small glass Madeira.* Cooking time: 45 minutes.

Bard the pheasant and roast it underdone. In the meantime fry the chopped onion light brown in oil, add the chopped shallot and a little afterwards the crushed garlic, a pinch of thyme and bay leaf and 3 parsley stalks. Add the red and white wine, boil away to almost nothing, add the *Demi-glace* and simmer slowly. Carve the pheasant into the legs, 2 wings, and 2 breasts, cutting breast in 5-6 slices and the legs in 2. Keep these pieces lukewarm in Madeira. Pound the bones almost to a *purée,* add them to the prepared sauce, boil up only once more and then press through a sieve in order to extract the maximum of flavour. Pour the hot sauce over the meat, add the sautéed mushrooms, heat, but do not boil again to prevent the meat from becoming hard. Arrange pieces on top of each other, pour sauce with mushrooms over it and garnish with grilled, heart-shaped white bread *croûtons.* Sliced truffles may be used instead of mushrooms.

▣ Vallée d'Auge

For 5 persons: 1 *pheasant, weighing about* 2¾-3¼ *lb;* 2 *oz butter;* ¼ *pint cream;* 1½ *lb apples; lemon.* Cooking time: 45-60 minutes, according to size.

Roast pheasant in a casserole. Five minutes before it is cooked, pour cream over it and finish cooking, adding a few drops of lemon juice. Serve in a casserole and serve hot unsweetened Apple sauce separately. The apples can also be peeled, quartered, cored and added when the pheasant is half cooked.

GELINOTTE * *HAZELHEN (OR HAZELGROUSE)*

This is found in France, but is mainly imported from Russia and Scandinavia. Hazelhens have a slightly resinous flavour, since they live on the buds of fir trees. This taste can be eliminated by soaking the birds in milk for about 2 hours before cooking.

▣ Rôties à la Russe * *Roast*

For 6 persons: 3 hazelhen; 2 oz clarified butter; juice of ½ lemon; ½ pint veal stock; ½ pint Sour Cream sauce; cold milk. Cooking time: 20-30 minutes according to size.

Pluck, singe and draw the hazelhen. Macerate in cold milk for 2 to 3 hours. This removes the harsh fir-cone taste. Dry inside and out; season with table salt and pepper, truss and bard. Place in a casserole with a few crushed juniper berries, sprinkle with a little lemon juice and the warm, clarified butter. Cook in a hot oven. Remove the hazelhen and drain off the fat in which a large slice of bread is fried. Place the latter on a dish and serve the hazelhen on top. Stir the veal stock into the meat juices, boil for a moment and pour it over the hazelhen. Serve the Sour Cream sauce separately.

GRIVES * *THRUSH*

Thrushes are usually drawn, roasted and served on *croûtons*. The song thrush has the most delicate flavour.

▣ Bonne Femme

For 6 persons: 6 thrushes; ½ lb lean bacon; 4 oz white bread without crust; white wine or brandy; 2 oz butter. Cooking time: 10 minutes.

Season thrushes, brown them in butter, add diced bacon and diced fried bread, add a dash of brandy or white wine, cover dish, put in hot oven for 8-10 minutes and serve at once.

▣ en Cocotte

For 6 persons: 12 thrushes; 1 bouquet garni; 4 juniper berries; ⅛ pint white wine; a little brandy; 4 oz butter; 6 shredded shallots; ¾ lb mushrooms; 12 bards of fat bacon; 12 butter fried bread croûtons; 4 oz lardons. Cooking time: 15 minutes.

Remove the gizzards, then wrap the birds in the bards of bacon fat and fry in goose fat in a casserole. Remove the birds, pour away the fat, add some butter, then the shallots, lardons, mushrooms, juniper berries and *bouquet garni.* Fry a little, add the thrushes, flame with the brandy, add the heated wine, cover and cook in a moderate oven, 350° F or Gas Mark 4 for 12 minutes. Now toss in 2 oz of butter. Serve upon the *croûtons*, garnish with Straw potatoes and mushrooms. Strain sauce and serve in a sauce-boat.

▣ au Cognac * *with Brandy*

For 6 persons: 6 thrushes; 1 lb peeled and deseeded grapes; 1 glass brandy; ½ pint game stock; 2 oz butter. Cooking time: 15 minutes.

Roast the thrushes in butter in a *cocotte* for 6 minutes, serve in a silver *tymbal* with 12 grapes per person, moisten with the grape juice and brandy. Deglaze the cooking pan with the stock, strain over the birds, cover and heat in a hot oven, 400° F or Gas Mark 6, for 10 minutes.

Grives au Gratin

6 thrushes; ½ lb Gratin forcemeat; 6 oz mushrooms; ⅛ pint Madeira; 2 oz butter; breadcrumbs. Cooking time: 8 minutes.

Bone the birds, fill with a nut of forcemeat, truss, and brown in butter. Add Madeira and simmer for 8 minutes. Line a fire-proof baking dish with a layer of *Gratin* forcemeat, place birds on top, pour on a little *Demi-glace* mixed with chopped fried mushrooms and the cooking Madeira, sprinkle with breadcrumbs and brown in hot oven.

GROUSE * *GROUSE*

Many gourmets consider grouse the finest game bird. They may be eaten without hanging and are often roasted but older birds may be braised. Bard, roast for 25 minutes according to size and serve with Bread sauce and Game Chips. Grouse is prepared in the same way as hazelhen.

MAUVIETTES * *LARKS*

There are many varieties of this bird; the meadow lark is that used for the table since its flesh is the most tender.

▣ à la Bonne-Maman

For 6 persons: 18 larks; ½ lb carrots; 4 oz onions; 4 oz celery; 2 oz butter; ½ pint veal stock. Cooking time: 8-10 minutes.

Prepare larks in the same way as *Cailles Bonne-Maman*, allowing for the fact that they only need 8 minutes to cook.

▣ Mère Moinet

For 6 persons: 18 larks; 2 lb apples; 2 oz butter; ¼ pint double cream. Cooking time: 8-10 minutes.

Make thick Apple sauce with cooking apples and put it in a hot, deep dish. Roast larks in butter in hot oven, 400° F or Gas Mark 6, press them into Apple sauce, cover each bird with a little cream and serve the remainder separately.

▣ à la Milanaise

For 6 persons: 18 larks; ½ lb macaroni; ½ pint Tomato sauce; 2 oz butter. Cooking time: 8-10 minutes.

Roast larks in a hot oven and serve on macaroni *à la Milanaise*. Serve Tomato sauce, mixed with the reduced pan residue, separately.

Ortolans et Becfigues * *Ortolands and Figpeckers*

These birds are specially fattened in the South of France. They are highly esteemed and are considered best when roasted in their own fat. The same recipes as for larks may be used.

PERDREAUX * *PARTRIDGES*

There are several kinds. The usual one found in Britain is the "grey" or common partridge which is at its best when young. Another variety is the French or "red-legged" partridge which is prime when mature. It is easy to recognise the older birds by the horse-shoe shaped mark in the breast plummage. Partridges are roasted or braised according to age. All the recipes for pheasant are applicable.

▣ à l'Allemande

For 4 persons: 2 large partridges; 1 carrot; 1 onion; 1 bouquet garni; 2 thin bacon slices: ¾ pint bouillon; ¼ pint sour cream. Cooking time: 1½-2 hours.

Bard partridges, brown well in butter, place on browned onion and carrot slices, season, add *bouillon* and *bouquet garni,* cover and braise slowly in a moderate oven, 375° F or Gas Mark 4, till tender. Remove, take off bacon, reduce stock with the sour cream, season well and strain. Carve the partridges, coat with a little sauce and serve the remainder of the sauce, *Sauerkraut* and mashed potatoes are served separately.

▣ Camélia

For 4 persons: 3 young partridges; 1 oz flour; ¾ pint cream; 2 oz butter; 4 oz currants; 2 tablespoons brandy; 8 croûtons. Cooking time: 35-40 minutes.

Cut each partridge in 4, season, flour and brown quickly in butter over high heat. Flambé with the brandy, reduce with cream, season, cover and simmer slowly for 15-20 minutes. Add the cleaned currants after soaking them in water, simmer slowly for another 5 minutes and garnish with fried *croûtons.*

▣ sur Canapés * *with Fried Bread Croûtons*

For 6 persons: 3 partridges; 4 oz foie gras; 1 truffle; 3 bards of fat bacon; chopped parsley; 6 croûtons; ⅛ pint champagne. Cooking time: 30 minutes.

Truss, season and bard the partridges and cook in butter in a casserole. After 15 minutes, sprinkle with the champagne and complete the cooking. Fry the *croûtons,* remove and fry the partridge livers. Chop the livers and truffle, mix with the *foie gras* and parsley and spread upon the *croûtons.* Arrange the partridges on the *croûtons.* Pour the juices over and garnish with the vegetables of your choice. (*See illustration p.* 592).

▣ aux Choux * *with Cabbage*

For 6 persons: 3 partridges; 3 lb cabbage or savoy; 12 oz garlic sausage; 6 oz lean bacon; 2 oz lard; 2 carrots; 2 onions; ½ pint Demi-glace; 1 bouquet garni. Cooking time: approximately 2 hours.

Truss and fry the partridges to brown them, and blanch the cabbage. Place the cabbage in a stewpan, bury the partridges in this, add the sausage, the blanched bacon, carrots, onions and *bouquet garni;* barely cover with fat stock, bring to the boil, cover with lid and simmer in the oven until the partridges are tender. If young birds they will cook in one hour, when they must be removed. The braising of the other ingredients must continue until tender. Drain off the stock, skim off all fat, add the *Demi-glace* and reduce to half a pint and strain. Serve the cabbage in the centre of the dish, carve the birds and arrange on top. Slice the other ingredients and arrange round dish, lightly mask with the sauce. Serve the rest in a sauce-boat.

Perdreaux Titania

For 4 persons: 2 partridges; 2 bacon rashers; 5 oranges; ½ lb grapes; 2 oz butter. Cooking time: 30-40 minutes.

Tie thin slices of bacon round partridges, arrange in a *cocotte* or casserole, surround with quarters of skinned, seeded oranges and skinned, seeded grapes, baste with game stock mixed with the juice of 1 orange. Cover and bake covered in a hot oven, 400° F or Gas Mark 6, serve very hot. (*See illustration p.* 592).

⊡ en Salmis

½ partridge per person. Cooking time: 20-30 minutes.

Prepare in the same way with the same ingredients as Pheasant Salmis. It takes at least 2 or 3 partridges to make really good salmis.

⊡ à la Vigneronne

For 6 persons: 3 young partridges; 6 slices fat bacon; 6 butter fried croûtons; 1 lb grapes, skinned and deseeded; 3 oz butter; ½ pint white wine; ½ pint partridge stock. Cooking time: 25-30 minutes.

Truss the partridges, lay the fat bacon over the breasts, tie in position with fine twine and roast in a casserole. Drain off the fat, deglaze with the wine, reduce to half, add the stock, boil and simmer for 15 minutes, strain. Cut the partridges in half, remove the small bones, serve upon the *croûtons*; cut the fat bacon into strips and arrange criss-cross over the birds. Gently heat the grapes and garnish the dish. Serve the gravy in a sauce-boat.

LE GIBIER FROID * *COLD GAME BIRD DISHES*

Chaudfroid de Bécasses au Porto * *Chaudfroid of Woodcock, with Port*

For 6 persons: 3 woodcock; ¾ pint Brown Chaudfroid sauce; ¾ pint Port flavoured aspic; 2 truffles. Cooking time: 15-20 minutes.

Roast woodcock underdone and let them cool. Cut each into 6 pieces (2 legs, 2 wings and 2 breasts), chop up carcases, boil them with the *sauce Chaudfroid*, add crushed entrails and pass the whole through a sieve. Coat the individual pieces with cold, but still liquid sauce, let it set, decorate with a truffle slice and arrange in a deep dish. Finally cover completely with cold but still liquid aspic and cool well before serving.

Salmis de Bécasses à la Charbonnière

For 6 persons: 3 woodcock; 3 shallots; ¼ pint Madeira; ¼ pint champagne; ½ pint Demi-glace; 2 truffles; ¾ pint aspic. Cooking time: 20-25 minutes.

Prepare the salmis as for the hot dish, but omitting mushrooms. Serve pieces in a deep, fireproof dish (*plat russe*), coat entirely with the cold, but still liquid sauce, when it starts to set sprinkle with fine strips of truffle and cover completely with aspic.

Cailles en Chaudfroid * *Chaudfroid of Quails*

For 6 *persons:* 6 *quails;* 6 *oz foie gras;* ¾ *pint of brown sauce Chaudfroid;* 1 *pint aspic flavoured with Port.* Cooking time: 10-15 minutes.

Truss and roast the quails, cool, cut in halves lengthwise, remove bones from the interiors, stuff with the *foie gras*; mask with sauce, decorate and glaze with aspic. Arrange upon a film of aspic on a dish with a border of finely diced aspic.

Ballotine de Faisan en Mosaïque * *Mosaic Ballotine of Pheasant*

For 12-15 *persons:* 1 *pheasant, weighing about* 3-3½ *lb;* 5 *oz fat bacon;* 5 *oz cooked ham;* 5 *oz foie gras;* 2 *oz truffle;* 5 *oz pickled ox tongue;* 1 *oz pistachios;* 1 *liqueur glass brandy;* 4-4½ *pints aspic jelly. Filling:* 5 *oz veal;* 5 *oz lean pork;* 4 *oz unsmoked bacon;* 2 *oz foie gras;* 1 *egg;* 1 *liqueur glass brandy;* 1 *large thin slice of fat bacon.*

Pluck the bird without damaging the skin, singe and draw. Bone it exactly as for Galantine of fowl keeping the skin intact. Remove the sinews from the legs and cut the breast fillets into strips. Marinate all flesh together with 3 oz fat bacon, ⅓ of the tongue and ham, 1 truffle, all cut into short thin strips, the *foie gras*, left whole, as well as salt, pepper and a pinch of spices, cover; leave 24 hours. Cut the remaining tongue, ham, bacon and truffle into very long thin strips, to decorate the *ballotine.* Pass the veal, pork, unsmoked bacon, the 2 oz *foie gras* and the legs of the pheasant twice through the finest blade of the mincer. Add the egg and the brandy, season to taste, and rub this mixture through a sieve. Mix with the marinated lardons of pheasant, bacon, ham, tongue, truffle and the shelled pistachios. Stuff the remaining truffles into the *foie gras.* Method of preparing the ballotine: Place a clean napkin on the table and cover with a large thin slice of bacon. Spread the skin of the pheasant on top. Roll the filling—with the *foie gras* in the middle—on a slightly moistened marble slab with moistened hands into the shape of a large sausage. Press the long strips of tongue, bacon, ham, etc. evenly along the length of the surface. Place this decorated side in the centre of the pheasant skin, and decorate the other side in the same way. Cover the *ballotine* with the skin, and then with the bacon and roll it carefully in the napkin. Tie the two ends and tie two pieces of string round the middle to keep it in shape. Poach the *ballotine* in good game stock (20 minutes for each pound), to which the browned bones of the pheasant have been added. Once cooked the *ballotine* is left in the stock until nearly cold. Then take the *ballotine* out of the napkin and re-wrap as tightly as possible; tie securely. Place it between two small boards, put a weight of about ½ pound on top and allow to cool. Unwrap the *ballotine* and cut off a few slices. Line a long dish with a sheet of aspic and glaze the *ballotine* with aspic. Place it at one end of the dish, and the slices at the other end. Garnish with aspic.

NOTE: If the skin of the pheasant is damaged or in poor condition, the *ballotine* may be simply rolled in the bacon before it is wrapped in the napkin.

Faisan Glacé Marie-Jeanne

For 8 *persons:* 1 *pheasant, weighing about* 3-3½ *lb;* 1 *lb foie gras;* ½ *lb chestnuts;* 4 *oz peeled walnuts;* 4 *oz cashew nuts;* ½ *pint Demi-glace;* ¼ *pint cream;* 2 *truffles;* 2½-3 *pints game aspic;* ½ *pint Madeira.* Cooking time: 1-1¼ hours.

Braise the pheasant the previous evening and allow to cool. Prepare the *sauce Chaudfroid* with the pan juice, *Demi-glace* and game aspic. Remove the fat from this sauce. Poach the *foie gras* for 20 minutes in Madeira, without allowing it to boil. Prepare a *mousse* with the *foie gras*, the cooked chestnuts, rubbed through a sieve, 15 pounded walnut kernels, thick cream and a little aspic. Check the seasoning. Remove the breast and the breastbone from the pheasant. Stuff with the *mousse*, and reshape the breast. Cut the breast fillets into thin strips, and replace them on top of the *mousse*. Cover lightly with the prepared sauce, and decorate the middle of the top with the remaining half-peeled walnut kernels and both sides with slices of truffle. Glaze with aspic. Line 8 small *baba* moulds with the remaining *mousse*, seal with aspic and allow to set. Line 8 other small moulds with aspic, decorate with a dot of truffle and half-grilled cashew nuts. Fill them with the rest of the pheasant sauce and place on ice to set. Arrange the pheasant on a large oval dish and garnish with the small *foie gras mousses*, the sauce aspics, and peeled halved green grapes. (*See illustration p.* 593).

Chaudfroid de Grives * *Chaudfroid of Thrushes*

6 *thrushes;* ½ *lb poached foie gras;* ¾ *pint brown sauce Chaudfroid flavoured with juniper;* ¾ *pint aspic.* Cooking time: 8-10 minutes.

Roast the thrushes, let them cool, halve and fill each half with well-seasoned *foie gras purée.* Coat each half with brown *sauce Chaudfroid* to which a few crushed juniper berries have been added during cooking. Serve birds symmetrically on a round dish lined with aspic and glaze.

Grives Glacées Modernes

For 6 persons: 6 *thrushes;* 6 *oz foie gras;* ¼ *pint game sauce Chaudfroid;* 1 *pint aspic.* Cooking time: 25 minutes.

Bone the thrushes, stuff with the *foie gras*, roll and tie in small pieces of muslin and braise with the bones and trimmings; allow to cool. Strain the cooking liquor, skim off the fat and reduce to a near glaze and add to the *Chaudfroid.* Unwrap the birds, trim if necessary, wipe dry and mask with the sauce, then glaze with some of the aspic. Cut the rest of the aspic into small dice, fill into small porcelain dishes and place a thrush upon each.

Mauviettes en Buisson Glacées en Cerises * *Pyramid of Larks in Chaudfroid*

For 6 persons: 12 *larks;* 6 *oz Gratin forcemeat;* 6 *oz foie gras;* 1 *truffle;* 1 *hardboiled egg;* ½ *pint of sherry;* 1 *pint game stock;* 3 *oz Brown Roux;* 1½ *pints aspic.* Cooking time: 30 minutes.

Bone the larks, lay upon pieces of muslin, stuff with the forcemeat and *foie gras*, pull the skin to the centre, then the muslin; tie into small balls with string, place in a buttered shallow baking tin, add the sherry, stock and lark bones and braise; allow to cool in the stock. Add the *Roux* to the cooking liquor, bring to the boil, set with a little aspic, colour to a light cherry red, skim, strain and cool. Unwrap the larks, dry with a cloth and mask with the sauce; glaze with aspic. Scald and skin the heads, glaze with brown aspic, imitate the eyes with egg white and truffle. Serve in a pyramid upon a bed of rice, arrange heads round the base with chopped aspic.

Perdreaux à l'Alsacienne * *Partridge*

For 6 persons: 3 *young partridges;* ½ *lb foie gras;* 1 *large truffle;* ½ *pint brown sauce Chaudfroid with Madeira;* 1¼ *pints game aspic;* 2 *oz butter.* Cooking time: 30-40 minutes.

Cut *foie gras* in 3 pieces, impale each with truffles, season, stiffen in Madeira and stuff partridges with them after carefully removing breastbone. Sew up, pour butter on top and cook *en cocotte*. Reduce pan residue together with *sauce Chaudfroid*, boil up, skim off fat and strain. When cold, coat the partridges with cold but still liquid sauce, let it set, decorate with truffle, hardboiled egg white, etc., to taste and glaze with aspic. Line an oval dish with a thin sheet of aspic, place partridges on it and garnish with chopped aspic.

These dishes are all part of the cold table. They take considerable time to make but are delicious for cold buffet parties or special occasions. The preparation of Pie pastry or *Pâte à Pâté* is described in the chapters entitled "Pastry and Basic Mixtures"—see page 724. The quantities given there are sufficient for a pie for six persons. The recipes for the various forcemeats can be found in the "Basic Ingredients and Preparations" chapter.

GALANTINES * *GALANTINES*

This is a preparation made by completely boning the items of poultry or game. The carcase usually of poultry is stuffed with the desired forcemeat and rolled into a thick sausage shape. It is then wrapped in a cloth and cooked in stock. The *galantine* is pressed when cold and subsequently glazed.

▣ de Volaille à la Gelée * *Jellied Galantine of Chicken*

For 12 persons: 1 boiling fowl, weighing about 4 lb; ½ lb cooked lean ham; ¼ lb fat bacon; ¼ lb pickled tongue; 2 truffles; a few peeled green pistachios; 1½ lb Galantine forcemeat; 2 fl oz Madeira; 1 liqueur glass brandy; salt and spices. Cooking time: 1¼ hours.

Split the chicken the whole length of the back. Loosen the carcase being careful not to pierce the skin. Start at the back and carefully cut away the skin from the meat. Remove the carcase and finish the removal of the breast and leg bones. The skin should be removed in one piece. Make a good stock with the bones. Cut the breast pieces, the ham, bacon and tongue into strips about the length of a little finger, and marinate with Madeira, brandy and spices. Use the meat of the legs when preparing the Galantine forcemeat and the Madeira and brandy used for the marinade should be added to the stuffing. Spread the skin out with the inside up on a large clean cloth or several thicknesses of cheese cloth which has been buttered generously. Spread half the stuffing on the skin and cover with the pieces of breast, ham, tongue, bacon, the truffles cut into quarters and the pistachios, alternating the colours. Cover with the remaining stuffing, turn up the edges of the skin and close firmly to cover the filling. Stitch the skin together with fine thread along the edge of the roll and at the ends. Now, roll the galantine up in the napkin like a sausage and tie the ends and the middle with string. Make sure that it has a smooth and regular surface. Place the galantine in a large saucepan, cover with the prepared stock and bring the stock to the boil. Poach the galantine in the chicken stock. When it is cooked, cool it between two boards with a weight of 2-3 pounds on top. This pressure gives more cohesion to the meat and permits easier cutting. Prepare aspic jelly with the stock. The next day slice the galantine or a part of it, and arrange it on a round or oval dish. Garnish with nicely diced, not chopped, aspic. The galantine may also be coated with Chaudfroid sauce, decorated with truffle, and glazed with aspic. (*See illustration p.* 554).

PÂTÉ * *PÂTÉS OR PIES*

In Britain the term *pâté* is understood to mean a preparation of meat, fish or poultry which is finely ground and mixed with spices and flavourings. It is served as a first course either alone or as part of a mixed *hors d'œuvre*. *Pâté* baked in an earthenware dish is called a *terrine*, or it may be baked in a pastry crust, *pâté en croûte*. The latter, often simply called a "pie", will only keep for a short period whereas a *terrine* which is also the name of the special dish in which the forcemeat is baked, has the advantage that it can be kept for several months, since it is usually sealed with a good layer of clarified butter or pork fat. A well seasoned forcemeat is required to make a successful *pâté* and fish *pâtés* in particular should be highly seasoned otherwise they will taste insipid.

Pâtés may be baked in almost any kind of baking dish—apart from the *terrine*—from a *soufflé* dish, a casserole, or an earthenware pot. Cover the meat mixture with aluminium foil and the dish with a heavy lid. It is not absolutely necessary to seal hermetically, that is, with a thick flour and water paste. The inside of the baking dish is usually lined with sheets of pork fat. (*See Illustrated Culinary Techniques*).

How to line a Pâté Mould

The *Pâté* or Pie dough must rest for at least 2 hours first. Take two-thirds of the dough, roll out a square about ¼-inch thick, trim and line the buttered pie mould with it in such a way that the dough projects ½-inch beyond the edge all round. Press it tightly against the sides and into the corners with the fingers or with a piece of dough. Fill with the forcemeat, coat the edges with egg, place the prepared lid on top and press down well with the aid of special pincers. Leave a round hole in the centre about ¾-inch across for the steam to escape. Cut off the superfluous dough, brush the top with egg, place a ring round the opening and in this place a roll of paper to act as "chimney". Decorate the top to taste with trimmings of dough, brush with egg again and bake in a preheated moderate oven, 375° F or Gas Mark 4. The baking time depends on the size and contents of the pastry and the heat must be carefully regulated. Pies which take a long time to bake are covered with greased paper after browning to stop the top becoming too dark. The pie is ready when the liquid appearing in the opening is clear and no longer contains any drops of blood. There are various kinds of pie moulds—round, oval, square and rectangular, with straight or ribbed sides.

FISH PÂTÉS

All fish *pâtés* must be highly seasoned, otherwise they taste insipid. They require less time for baking than *pâtés* of meat or poultry.

Pâté de Filets de Sole * *Pâté of Fillets of Sole*

For 8-10 *persons:* 3 *soles, each weighing about* 14 *oz;* 1 *lb Fish forcemeat;* 1 *truffle; about* 1 *lb Pie pastry.* Cooking time: 55-60 minutes.

Fillet the soles, flatten the fillets, spread with truffled Fish forcemeat, roll up, poach in fish stock and leave to cool. Line a square mould with Pie pastry, fill with layers of forcemeat and sole, ending with forcemeat, cover with pastry, prepare the mould according to previous instructions and bake in a moderate oven, 375° F or Gas Mark 4-5. Serve hot or cold.

⊡ de Filets de Truite * *Fillets of Trout*

For 8-10 *persons:* 4 *trout, each weighing about* 6 *oz;* 1 *lb Fish forcemeat;* 1-1¼ *lb Pie pastry.* Cooking time: 45-50 minutes.

Prepare in the same way as Salmon *Pâté* (see below) but using skinned and boned fillets of trout. Serve hot with light Shrimp sauce.

⊡ de Saumon * *Salmon*

For 8-10 *persons:* 1 *lb salmon, without skin or bone;* 1 *lb Fish forcemeat;* ½ *lb Pie pastry.* Cooking time: 40-45 minutes.

Season the salmon, place it between 2 layers of forcemeat in a mould lined with Pie pastry and bake in a moderate oven, 375° F or Gas Mark 4-5. When the juice rising in the chimney is clear, the *pâté* is cooked. To serve, unmould on a serving tray and slice.

⊡ de Truite * *Trout*

For 10 *persons:* 1 *lb trout fillets, skinned and boned;* 1 *lb Fish forcemeat;* 1 *chopped shallot;* 1 *lb Pie pastry;* ¼ *pint oil;* 1 *tablespoonful brandy;* 1 *bouquet garni; about* 1½ *pints fish-flavoured aspic.* Cooking time: 45 minutes.

Cut the fillets into scallops or round slices and marinate in the oil, brandy, shallot and seasoning. Line a rectangular mould with the pastry, fill the bottom with half of the forcemeat, arrange on top the trout scallops and complete filling with the rest of the forcemeat. Cover with pastry, pinch up the edges, eggwash, decorate and bake at 375° F or Gas Mark 4-5 for about 45 minutes. Allow to become cold, then fill with the almost set aspic.

MEAT PÂTÉS

⊡ Pantins * *Family Pie*

For 12 *persons:* 1 *lb Fine forcemeat;* ½ *lb topside of veal;* 2 *oz lean boiled ham;* 1½ *lb Pie pastry;* ¼ *pint brandy; about* ½ *oz salt; seasonings.* Cooking time: 1¼-1½ hours.

These *pâtés* are made without a mould. Roll out the dough rather thickly in an oval, the ends rather thinner than the middle. Spread half the forcemeat on the dough, leaving the edges free, place ham and veal on top, spread with forcemeat again and moisten the edges all round with water. Fold up the two sides towards the centre, then fold over two ends and press down well. Place on a baking sheet upside down, put a chimney in the centre, brush with egg twice so that the dough will cohere well and bake in a moderate oven, 375° F or Gas Mark 4-5. These small pies are easy to make, but they are apt to come apart, so that the juice runs out.

Pâté de Veau et Jambon * *Veal and Ham Pie*

For 10 persons: 1 *lb Pâté forcemeat;* ½ *lb topside of veal, in one piece and free of all skin and sinews, spiced, salted and macerated in brandy;* ½ *lb thinly sliced, cooked ham;* 1 *lb Pie pastry;* 1 *pint sherry-flavoured aspic.* Cooking time: 1½ hours.

Line a fairly deep rectangular mould with pastry, spread half the forcemeat over the bottom, then cover with half of the ham, place the nut of veal in the centre, cover with the rest of the ham then with the forcemeat. Cover with pastry, pinch up the edges, egg wash, decorate and bake, 375° F or Gas Mark 4-5, for about 1½ hours. Allow to become cold and pour almost set aspic into the chimney. (*See illustration p.* 595).

POULTRY PÂTÉS

See illustration, p. 596

▣ de Canard d'Amiens * *Amiens Duck Pie*

For 6-8 *persons:* 1 *duck, weighing about* 3¼ *lb;* 10 *oz Gratin forcemeat;* 5 *oz fat bacon;* 2¼ *Pie pastry.* Cooking time: 1½ hours.

In Amiens they have a speciality consisting of one or two unboned ducks cooked in a pastry crust. Lard the duck with bacon, do not bone but stuff with very good *Gratin* forcemeat (*see* p. 116). Put in the oven for a short time to stiffen the duck but do not brown it. Remove and when the duck is quite cold, place it on a square of Pie pastry, cover with a second piece, press down well and fold the ends. Decorate to taste with strips of Pie pastry, brush with egg and bake in a moderate oven, protecting it with greased paper against becoming too brown. This *pâté* is not filled with aspic.

▣ de Pigeons Virgile * *Virgil Pigeon Pie*

For 10 *persons:* 2 *large pigeons;* ¾ *lb Gratin forcemeat;* 1 *lb Fine, truffled forcemeat;* 1½ *lb Pie pastry; about* 1 *pint aspic.* Cooking time: 1½ hours.

Bone fully the very tender young pigeons and stuff with *Gratin* forcemeat as for galantine. Reform as far as possible into the orginal shape. Line an oval mould with Pie pastry, partly fill with the truffled forcemeat, place pigeons on top, fill with forcemeat, and sprinkle with a pinch each of powdered thyme and bay leaf. Cover with pastry, decorate, brush with egg and do not forget chimney. Bake in a moderate oven, allow to cool and pour aspic through the chimney.

▣ de Poulet * *Chicken*

For 12 *persons:* 1 *lb Fine forcemeat;* ½ *lb chicken flesh;* 3 *oz sliced ham;* 1½ *lb Pie pastry;* ¼ *pint brandy;* 1 *pint Madeira aspic;* 1 *truffle; salt, seasoning.* Cooking time: about 1¼ hours.

Season the finely sliced chicken and marinate in brandy. Line a rectangular mould with Pie pastry. Fill the mould first with a layer of forcemeat, then with half the sliced ham and truffle (if used). Add the chicken and remaining ham, truffle and forcemeat. Close with a lid of pastry and cook as above. When completely cooled, fill with the aspic.

GAME PÂTÉS

All these *pâtés* are eaten cold. When they are quite cold the filling contracts, leaving a hollow which must be filled with strong aspic. Pour cold but still liquid aspic into the pastry through the chimney, using a funnel. Cool the *pâté* well so that the aspic sets hard enough for cutting. (*See illustration p.* 596).

⊡ de Bécasses * *Woodcock*

For 12 *persons:* 4 *woodcocks;* ¼ *lb chicken livers;* 1½ *lb Fine forcemeat;* ¼ *lb raw foie gras;* 1 *pint aspic;* 2 *lb Pie pastry.* Cooking time: about 1½ hours.

Bone the woodcocks, leave the breast meat on the skins; remove the legs and bone them. Remove the gizzards from the intestines. Fry the chicken livers, then the intestines; pound and sieve. Add to this about ½ lb of the pork forcemeat and the minced flesh of the legs; season with spiced salt. Fill this forcemeat into the woodcock skins and reform into the original shape of the birds. Cut the *foie gras* into small cubes and mix them into the rest of the pork forcemeat with a little sherry. Line the pie mould with the Pie pastry, then the bottom and sides with the forcemeat. Arrange the woodcocks in the middle, seal over with the rest of the forcemeat and cover with the remaining dough. Pinch up the edges, crimp, egg wash, decorate, egg wash again, then bake at 400° F or Gas Mark 6 for 15 minutes, then at 375° F or Gas Mark 4-5, for the remainder of the cooking time.

⊡ de Faisan ou de Perdreau * *Pheasant or Partridge*

For 6 *persons:* ½ *lb Fine forcemeat;* ½ *lb pheasant or partridge meat;* 3 *oz fat bacon; the poultry livers;* 4 *fl oz Madeira;* 1 *lb Pie pastry; seasoning; salt; pepper.* Cooking time: 55-60 minutes.

Remove sinews from meat, marinate with Madeira and season well. Remove sinews from legs, pound and mix with the forcemeat and the livers. Pass through a sieve. Then proceed as for other *pâtés*.

⊡ de Grives * *Thrush*

For 6 *persons:* 12 *thrushes;* 6 *oz Fine forcemeat;* ¼ *lb foie gras;* 1 *truffle;* 1 *lb Pie pastry; salt; pepper; seasoning.* Cooking time: 40-50 minutes.

Bone the birds completely and stuff each with a small piece of truffle and *foie gras* and roll up into a ball. *Sauté* the livers quickly, pass them through a sieve and mix with forcemeat. Season well. Make the pastry in the usual way, pressing the birds between two layers of forcemeat.

⊡ de Lapin * *Rabbit*

For 12-15 *persons:* 1 *lb Fine forcemeat;* 1 *lb rabbit meat;* 6 *oz fat bacon;* 1 *lb Pie pastry;* ¼ *pint brandy;* 1 *pint Madeira aspic;* 1 *chopped shallot; salt; seasoning.* Cooking time: about 1½ hours.

Remove sinews from rabbit meat and marinate with salt, shallot and brandy or Madeira. Line the mould with pastry and fill with alternate layers of forcemeat, rabbit and bacon slices, ending with forcemeat, and proceed in the usual way. Cool, and fill with aspic. The total weight of the forcemeat should be the same as the weight of a rabbit before boning.

Pâté de Lièvre * *Hare Pie*

For 12 *persons:* 1 *lb Fine forcemeat;* 1 *lb hare meat; the hare's liver;* 2 *tablespoons hare's blood;* ¼ *pint brandy;* 1¾ *lb Pie pastry;* 6 *oz fat bacon;* 1 *chopped shallot;* 1 *pint aspic; seasoning.* Cooking time: about 1½ hours.

Make in the same way as Rabbit pie, but add the finely chopped liver and the blood to the forcemeat and season highly. (*See illustration p.* 594).

⊡ **de Mauviettes** * *Lark*

For 10 *persons:* 10 *larks;* ½ *lb Gratin forcemeat;* ¼ *lb of truffled foie gras;* 1¼ *lb Fine forcemeat;* 2 *lb Pie pastry;* 1 *pint lark-flavoured aspic;* 1 *tablespoon of sherry; spiced salt.* Cooking time: 1½ hours.

Bone the larks from the back and marinate overnight with the spiced salt and sherry. Make the aspic from a stock prepared with the lark bones and trimmings. Fry the livers and intestines in a little butter, pound, sieve and mix into the *Gratin* forcemeat. Spread out the boned larks, place a ball of *Gratin* forcemeat in the centre, then a cube of the *foie gras* and pull the edges together to completely enclose the forcemeat. Mix the rest of the *Gratin* forcemeat with the Fine forcemeat. Roll out ⅓ of the pastry into a square and cover with a layer of the forcemeat. Arrange the larks on the forcemeat and then cover over with the rest of the forcemeat. Egg wash the edges, cover with the rest of the pastry, seal and trim the edges. Egg wash, decorate with pastry designs and bake in a moderate oven, 375° F or Gas Mark 4-5, for about 1¼ hours. When cold fill with the almost set aspic.

⊡ **Piroschkis I** * *Small Russian Pies*

For 6 *persons:* ½ *lb unsweetened Brioche dough;* 6 *oz lean bacon cut into small dice;* 3 *oz chopped onion;* 1 *oz butter; a pinch of ground cumin;* 1 *yolk of egg.* Cooking time: 10-12 minutes.

Fry the onions and bacon in the butter, season with salt, pepper and cumin; cool. Roll out the dough ¼-inch thick by 2 inches in diameter, water wash the edge; put a nut-sized piece of the mixture in the centre of each, cover with another piece of dough and egg wash. Prove by leaving in a warm place, until doubled in size and bake in a very hot oven, 450° F or Gas Mark 8.

⊡ **Piroschkis II**

For 6 *persons:* 6 *oz cream cheese;* ½ *lb Puff pastry;* 1 *egg;* 2 *oz butter;* 1 *tablespoon of sour cream;* 1 *yolk of egg.*

Cream the cheese and butter, egg and cream together. Proceed with the pastry as above. Fill with mixture in centre, cover, egg wash and bake in a very hot oven, 450° F or Gas Mark 8. They may also be filled with a mixture of chopped bacon fat, onions and white cabbage stewed together.

TERRINES * *TERRINES*

Since *terrines* are made in the same way as *pâtés en croûte*, there is no need to describe their preparation again. The difference is that they are not cooked in a pastry crust but in fire-proof dishes—*terrines*—of china or earthenware. Whatever dish is selected it must have a tight fitting cover. The sides and bottom of a *terrine* are usually lined with thin bacon rashers and after the forcemeat and garnish have been filled in, they are covered with more bacon. A sprig of thyme and a small bay leaf may be placed on top, then the lid, and finally the *terrine* is sealed with a thick flour and water paste. It is also possible to cover the mixture with aluminium foil and then with a heavy lid.

To cook the *terrine*, place it on a roasting tin, pour in about 1½ inches of water and put it in a hot oven, where the water should boil gently. To test if the *terrine* is done, remove lid after 45-50 minutes. If the fat appearing on the surface is quite clear, the *terrine* is ready. To cool, remove the lid, place a small board on the meat and put a 2-pound weight on it to press it down. All *terrines* are made in this way. If the *terrine* is to be filled up with aspic it must be quite cold and the aspic must be cold but still liquid. It is best to make the aspic from the bones and trimmings of the poultry, game, etc., contained in the *terrine*.

How to Keep Terrines for Several Months

Terrines intended for consumption within 8-10 months should be filled with liquid lard instead of aspic and kept in a cold place. If, however, the *terrines* are to be kept longer, turn them out, remove fat, bacon and any gravy, dry well and keep only the edible part. Clean the *terrine*, wipe out thoroughly, replace meat and pour in liquid lard till the meat is entirely covered and protected from the air. As soon as the lard has set, place a piece of tinfoil on top, cover the *terrine* with a lid and stick strips of paper round the joint to make it airtight. The *terrines* should be stored in a room that is cold but not damp.

⊡ d'Anguilles au Vert à la Brabançonne * *Brabant Terrine of Eels with Herbs*

For 6 persons: 2¼ *lb small eels;* ½ *bottle light beer or white wine;* 1 *large handful chiffonade of very fresh sorrel, parsley, chives, burnet, sage, tarragon and chervil;* 2-3 *egg yolks;* 2 *oz butter; juice of* 1 *lemon;* 1 *small coffeespoon potato flour.* Cooking time: 20 minutes.

Skin the eel, cut in 2-inch pieces and stiffen in butter. Add the herbs, cook them for a moment and add just enough beer to cover everything. Season with salt, pepper, bay leaf and thyme and cook slowly till done. In the meantime make a thickening of 3 egg yolks mixed with the lemon juice, potato flour and a little water. Thicken the stock with this, boil up once only, pour into *terrine* at once and eat hot or cold.

⊡ de Bécassines * *Snipe*

For 10 *persons:* 3 *snipes;* 10 *oz calf's liver;* ¾ *lb lean pork;* ¾ *lb green, back bacon;* 2 *oz ham;* 1 *thin rasher of bacon; salt; pepper; seasoning.* Cooking time: 2-2½ hours.

Pluck, singe, draw and clean the snipe and bone them completely. Cut into four sections, season, and lard with bacon and ham. Brown the entrails (without stomach) with a little minced bacon, add diced calf's liver—it must be underdone inside—and allow to cool. Mince the bacon with the pork, add the liver and entrails, mince these too, season well and pass through a sieve. Line *terrine* with bacon, put half the forcemeat in the bottom, arrange pieces of snipe on top, cover with remainder of forcemeat and finish off with bacon. Close *terrine*, place in waterbath and cook in oven. Prick with a needle and if it comes out hot, or if the juice is quite clear, the *terrine* is ready. Remove it, drain off the juice and cool under slight pressure. Add aspic, cover and put in a cool place.

Terrine de Foie de Porc * *Pig's Liver Terrine*

For 10 *persons:* 1 *lb pig's liver;* ½ *lb lean veal;* ½ *lb unsmoked or green bacon;* ½ *lb white bread without crust;* 1 *large cooked onion;* 3 *eggs;* 1 *teaspoon chopped parsley; salt; pepper;* ½ *teaspoon dried thyme;* ¼ *teaspoon dried marjoram; brandy.* Cooking time: about 1½ hours.

Soak the bread in milk and when softened squeeze out the excess moisture. Skin the liver. Pass through the finest blade of the mincer together with the veal, the green bacon, the prepared bread and the cold, chopped onion. Place in a mixing bowl, beat in the three eggs, one at a time, and blend in the herbs and spices. Mix well and treat in the same way as other *terrines*. Do not place under a weight until 30 minutes after removing from the water bath in the oven.

⊡ Ménagère * *Family*

For 8-10 *persons:* ¾ *lb rabbit meat;* ¾ *lb lean veal or pork;* ½ *lb unsmoked or green bacon; salt; pepper; chopped parsley; bay leaf; thyme and spices;* 1 *onion, chopped;* 1 *shallot, chopped; Madeira;* ¼ *pint white wine; sherry-flavoured aspic.* Cooking time: about 1½ hours.

These family *terrines* may be made from any meat available, such as veal, rabbit, chicken and game. Cut the rabbit meat, veal or pork and bacon into fairly large *julienne*—about the size of a finger. Stiffen the meat in a frying pan but do not cook it. Then marinate these in a *terrine* mould preferably the evening before—with the seasonings, herbs and spices, the chopped onion and shallot. Pour a dash of Madeira and the white wine over everything and cover. Next day—or after several hours—put the covered *terrine* in a water bath in the oven and poach for the specified time. Remove when cooked and allow the meat to become quite cold. Cover with liquid aspic. This simple *terrine* may be served as soon as the aspic has set.

There are so many home-grown and foreign vegetables that it is only possible to give recipes for the most important ones. Nevertheless the selection should be large enough to satisfy the most spoilt of gourmets.

By vegetables we mean all plants or parts of plants used in the kitchen; the only ones excluded are cereals, spices and aromatic herbs. Vegetables can be classified as follows:

GREEN AND LEAFY VEGETABLES	cabbage and spinach family.
LEGUMINOUS GREEN VEGETABLES	French and runner beans, peas.
SALAD VEGETABLES	lettuce, celery, chicory, endive.
BULBS, ROOTS AND TUBERS	artichokes (Jerusalem), beetroots, carrots, onions, potatoes and parsnips.
SEEDS	cereals and pulses.
GOURDS AND FRUITS	aubergines, cucumber, marrow, pumpkins, squash and tomatoes.

Many fresh vegetables have a short season which restricts the time in which they are available. Yet it is better to buy vegetables when they are in season not only from the economical point of view but also because really fresh vegetables are more nutritious and will have the finest flavour. The preparation of vegetables includes blanching, refreshing, cooking in salted water and braising. Also included are the methods of preparation for the various *purées* and the dried vegetables. (*See illustration p.* 632).

BLANCHING

Blanching in reality can mean two different operations. The first means the complete cooking of certain vegetables such as French beans and spinach to conserve their natural green colour. Real blanching is the opposite of the first for it is the means by which sharp, sour or too pungent natural flavours are removed from vegetables such as celery or cabbage. This method is the one mostly cited in the Vegetable chapter. It consists of washing, peeling and preparing vegetables, covering with slightly salted cold water and bringing to the boil and then straining away the water. They are often refreshed in cold running water.

VEGETABLES FOR BRAISING

It is unwise to refresh blanched vegetables except when they are to be braised, for otherwise much of their flavour would be lost. The method is, after blanching, for them to be completely cooled in cold running water for their easy manipulation and removal of unwanted flavours.

ENGLISH METHOD OF COOKING VEGETABLES

Cooking *à l'anglaise* is the accepted term used in Continental European countries for this simple method. Cook the vegetables in plain salted water, drain, dry and dress. Serve accompanied by dishes containing pats of butter or with melted butter.

BRAISING

Blanch and refresh the vegetables, drain and fold if necessary. Line the cooking vessel with thin slices of fat bacon, sometimes also with thickly sliced carrots and onions, arrange the vegetables on top and allow to sweat together. Then moisten with the *degraissée* (stock pot skimmings), cover and braise in a warm oven, 350° F or Gas Mark 3.

VEGETABLE PUREÉS

This consists of passing cooked vegetables through a fine sieve, then drying them upon the stove to remove excessive moisture and finishing them with butter and/or cream or milk.

DRIED VEGETABLES

Wash and cover the vegetables with cold water and allow to soak until fully swollen before cooking. Bring to the boil, skim, add a *bouquet garni*, an onion stuck with a clove, a carrot and a piece of bacon bone or rind and simmer until tender. Do not add salt to these vegetables until they are practically cooked otherwise they will remain hard.

ARTICHAUTS • *ARTICHOKES*

Only the leaves of the artichoke are eaten, usually dipped in melted butter. There are a number of artichokes—the globe, which is the most popular; the Jerusalem, which is a native of Canada; and the chinese or *Crosnes*, which is cultivated in France.

Artichauts Entiers Cuits * *Whole Cooked Artichokes*

For 6 persons: 6 large Globe artichokes; ½ pint Vinaigrette dressing. Cooking time according to size and quality: 45 minutes or longer.

Cut off the stems and the tops of the artichokes. Trim off the tips of the leaves, and wash well. Pare the bottoms evenly and rub them over with lemon juice. Cook in salted, boiling water until the leaves in the middle can be pulled out easily. Cool a little, and drain well. Remove the inside leaves and the choke with the help of a teaspoon, and put a little parsley in the opening. Serve *sauce Vinaigrette* in a sauce-boat. Hot artichokes can also be served with *sauce Hollandaise, Mousseline* or *Bâtarde*. (*See illustration p.* 629).

Fonds d'Artichauts * *Artichoke Bottoms*

The artichokes must be raw when the bottoms are prepared, for if they were cooked one would tear part of it off. Cut off the leaves close to the bottom with a sharp knife and trim bottom like a potato. Immediately rub each bottom with lemon juice and place in water and lemon juice in order to keep them white. Mix a little flour with plenty of cold water, salt lightly, place bottoms in mixture, slowly bring to the boil and cook until the choke, which has been left on the bottom, is easily detached. They are now ready for further processing. To keep them for several days remove the choke, put in an earthenware bowl, pour strained stock on top and put in a cold place.

▣ Argenteuil

For 6 persons: 6 large artichoke bottoms; 1 lb asparagus tips; ½ pint Cream sauce; 1 oz butter.

After cooking the bottoms simmer them a little in butter and arrange in a ring on a round dish. Fill the middle with asparagus tips lightly bound with Cream sauce and sprinkle with chopped parsley. The asparagus tips can also be placed inside the artichoke bottoms.

▣ Clamart

For 4 persons: 8 small artichokes; 8 small round new carrots; ¾ lb shelled peas; 2 oz butter; 1 tablespoon flour. Cooking time: 30 minutes.

Cut off the leaves of the artichokes on a level with the bottoms. Trim and cook in salted water. Do not allow to get too soft. Remove the small leaves from the inside and the choke and drain. Simmer the peas and the carrots in butter with a pinch of salt; cook each vegetable separately. Bind the peas with the 2 ounces butter mixed with the flour. Fill the artichoke bottoms with the peas and place a carrot in the middle. Arrange in a baking dish and place in the oven for a few minutes.

▣ Colbert

For 6 persons: 6 artichokes; 1 egg; white breadcrumbs; sauce Colbert.

Prepare and cook the artichokes as for *Fonds d'Artichauts.* Season and flour the prepared bottoms, dip in beaten egg, breadcrumb and fry golden brown in butter. Serve with a small spoonful of *sauce Colbert* (p. 146) on each bottom.

▣ Farcis * *Stuffed*

For 6 persons: 6 large artichokes; ¾ lb cooked meat. Cooking time: about 45 minutes.

Cut off leaves ½-inch above bottom, trim, boil in the usual way, and fill with any desired minced meat, mushrooms or other *purée*, brown and serve with a suitable sauce.

Artichauts Farcis aux Champignons * *Mushroom Stuffed Artichokes*

For 6 persons: 6 large cooked artichoke bottoms; ½ lb of mushroom purée; 2 tablespoonfuls of Béchamel; 1 oz grated Parmesan; 1 egg; 1 oz butter. Cooking time: 10 minutes.

Place the cooked artichoke bottoms on a buttered dish. Bring the mushroom *purée*, *Béchamel* and yolk of egg to boiling point, remove from the heat and fold in the whipped egg white. Fill into the artichokes, sprinkle with the cheese and melted butter and bake in a moderate oven, 375° F or Gas Mark 5. (This dish is also called *Agnès Sorel.*)

▣ à la Printanière

For 6 persons: 1½ lb small tender artichokes; ¼ pint white wine; ¼ pint veal stock; ½ lb carrots; ½ lb young turnips; 6-8 small new potatoes; 2 tomatoes; 1 oz butter; chervil. Cooking time: 35-40 minutes.

Quarter the artichokes lengthwise, parboil and drain. Place in a fire-proof casserole and add the white wine and the veal stock. Round the edge place a few young carrots, young quartered turnips, the potatoes, the peeled, quartered and deseeded tomatoes, the butter and some chopped chervil. Season with salt and pepper, cover, simmer and serve in the casserole.

▣ Quartiers d'Artichauts * *Quartered*

For 4 persons: 6 small artichokes; ½ pint Vinaigrette sauce. Cooking time: 25-30 mins.

Trim the artichokes and cut them in quarters. Remove some of the middle leaves and the choke. Trim the base, rub with lemon juice, and place the quarters in acidulated water as soon as they are done. Drain and cook in boiling salted water. Drain again, arrange on a dish, and serve with a sauce-boat of *sauce Vinaigrette.*

ASPERGES * *ASPARAGUS*

The most famous asparagus are those from Argenteuil. These are distinguished by a violet tip, but good asparagus is to be found elsewhere too. The thin green asparagus is also very popular; only that part of the stalk is used that can be easily broken off. It is used as a vegetable but even more as a garnish. Usually one allows ¾ lb of raw untrimmed asparagus per person. It must be peeled, tied in a bundle and cut straight at the ends.

▣ en Branches

For 6 persons: 4-5 lb asparagus; 1 pint sauce. Cooking time: about 20 minutes.

Peel and wash the asparagus. Tie into bundles, and cut the hard ends straight, trimming to an even length. Cook in salted, boiling water, but do not allow the water to boil too fast or the tips may get damaged. Drain well. Arrange on a napkin, an asparagus grill or in a baking dish and remove the string. Serve *sauce Hollandaise*, *Mousseline* or *Bâtarde* or plain melted butter in a sauce-boat at the same time.

▲ *Artichauts Entiers Cuits, p. 620*

Poireaux en Branches, p. 656 ▼

630 ▲ *Melanzane Ripiene alla Toscana, p. 661*

Melanzane Carlton, p. 661 ▼

▲ *Poivrons Farcis au Gras, p. 657*

Legumi alla Mediterranea, p. 660 ▼

▲ Zucchine Ripiene alla Milanese, p. 662

A selection of vegetables, p. 625 ▼

▲ *Aubergines à la Provençale, p. 638*

Tomates Farcies Duchesse, p. 659 ▼

▲ *Céleris en Branches Braisés, p. 640*

Cèpes Sautés à l'Italienne, p. 672 ▼

▲ *Ratatouille Niçoise, p. 658*

Cardons à la Moelle, p. 638 ▼

▲ A selection of potatoes, pp. 663-671

Patate Ripiene al Forno, p. 671 ▼

Asperges à la Milanaise

For 6 persons: 5 lb asparagus; 4 oz butter; ¼ lb grated cheese.

Cook the asparagus in the usual way and drain well. Arrange in overlapping rows in a baking dish, so that all the tips are visible. Sprinkle with grated cheese and drop a little melted butter on top. Brown in a hot oven, 400° F or Gas Mark 6. When serving pour over them plenty of browned butter.

◘ à la Polonaise

For 6 persons: 5 lb asparagus; 2 hardboiled eggs; ¼ lb butter; 2 oz breadcrumbs; chopped parsley. Cooking time: 25-30 minutes.

Cook the asparagus and arrange them in a large baking dish the same way as *à la Milanaise*. Cover the tips with chopped hardboiled egg and chopped parsley. Melt the butter in a frying pan and fry the breadcrumbs a light brown in the butter. Pour all this over the tips and serve immediately.

Pointes d'Asperges à la Crème * *Asparagus Tips in Cream Sauce*

For 6 persons: 4½ lb asparagus; ½ pint Béchamel; 4 fl oz cream; 1-2 egg yolks.

After peeling oreak off wooden part of stalk and cut tender parts in 2-inch pieces. Boil in salt water, drain and simmer for a few moments in light *Béchamel* mixed with a little cream. Season well and at the last moment remove from heat and thicken with 1-2 egg yolks mixed with a few spoons of cream. Serve in a vegetable dish. Boiled asparagus cut in small pieces can also be mixed with young green peas; it can also be sautéed in butter and sprinkled with chopped parsley.

AUBERGINES * *EGGPLANT*

Originally from India, this plant has been cultivated in France since the seventeenth century. The long purple variety is most often used in cooking.

◘ Farcies à la Boston

For 6 persons: 3 large aubergines; ¼ pint Béchamel; 1 egg yolk; ¼ pint thick cream; 4 oz grated gruyère cheese; ½ pint oil. Cooking time: 8-10 minutes.

Halve *aubergines* lengthwise and cut the flesh crosswise several times with a knife without damaging the skin. Cook in oil in the oven till the flesh can easily be scooped out, leaving the skin whole. Chop the *aubergine* flesh, thicken with *Béchamel* and egg yolk, season well and mix with half the grated cheese. Fill skins with this mixture, place in a shallow oval fire-proof dish, sprinkle with the remainder of the grated cheese and brown in a hot oven, 400° F or Gas Mark 6. When serving pour hot, slightly salted cream on top.

Aubergines Meunière * *Shallow Fried Eggplant*

For 6 *persons:* 3 *aubergines;* ¼ *lb butter; salt; lemon juice; chopped parsley.* Cooking time: 4-5 minutes.

Cut aubergines into ½-inch slices lengthwise, sprinkle with salt, leave to sweat a little and wipe off moisture. Flour each slice, shake off surplus and fry in butter. Serve sprinkled with lemon juice, chopped parsley and Brown butter.

▣ à la Piemontaise

For 6 *persons:* 3 *large aubergines;* 1 *medium-sized onion;* ¼ *lb rice;* 3 *tomatoes;* 2 *oz grated cheese;* 1 *pinch saffron;* 2 *oz butter; oil.* Cooking time: about 20 minutes.

Peel the *aubergines* and cut them in half lengthwise. Scoop out carefully, leaving just a little flesh on all sides. Cook in oil in the oven without allowing them to get too soft. Fry the chopped onions lightly in butter and add the chopped *aubergine* flesh and the rice. Cook for a minute or two and moisten with twice as much stock as the volume of the rice. Season and add the tomatoes, peeled, deseeded and cut into dice, and the saffron. Cook until the rice is nearly done, and fill into the *aubergines.* Sprinkle generously with grated Parmesan cheese, drop a little melted butter on top and gratinate in a very hot oven.

▣ à la Provençale

For 6 *persons:* 2¼ *lb aubergines;* 2¼ *lb tomatoes;* 3 *small cloves of garlic; olive oil; chopped parsley.* Cooking time: 15 minutes.

Cut *aubergines* lengthwise, score flesh with a knife. Fry in oil and scoop out flesh, leaving an outer casing. Fry tomatoes (blanched, deseeded and diced) in oil and add garlic; to this, add chopped flesh of *aubergine.* Season and add chopped parsley. Fill casing with this mixture. Place in buttered *gratin* dish and cook in hot oven, 400°F or Gas Mark 6, for 5-10 minutes to heat through. A cordon of Tomato sauce is placed round the *aubergines.* (*See illustration p.* 633).

CARDONS * *CARDOONS*

Cardoons can be used in a similar way to celery. After the green leaves have been removed string the stalks lengthwise, rub them with lemon juice and boil in floured water with plenty of lemon juice to keep them from darkening.

▣ à la Moelle * *with Beef Marrow*

For 6 *persons:* 2 *lb cardoons;* 2 *onions;* 1 *pint fat bouillon;* ½ *pint Demi-glace;* 12 *good slices beef marrow;* 2 *carrots.*

First blanch the stalks for 5 minutes, cool them, remove prickles, strings and inside skin and cut in 3-inch pieces. Rub these with lemon juice, throw into well-floured water at once, bring to boil and simmer for about 2 hours. Cool, drain, place on a seasoned bed of sliced onions and carrots, add just enough *bouillon* to cover the pieces, cover with greased paper and braise very slowly in the oven with the lid on. Drain, place blanched slices of marrow on top, pour on *Demi-glace* and sprinkle with chopped parsley. The total cooking time is very long, it may be as much as 4 hours. (*See illustration p.* 635).

Cardons au Parmesan

For 6 persons: 3 cardoons; ½ pint veal gravy; 4 oz grated Parmesan.

Prepare and cook the cardoons, simmering for two hours as indicated above. They will be three-quarters cooked. Drain and arrange in a baking dish, pour the veal gravy on top and simmer slowly for another 10-15 minutes to complete the cooking. Sprinkle with the grated Parmesan and serve at once.

CAROTTES * *CARROTS*

New carrots are best cooked whole in salted water but they may be cut in halves or in quarters. Old carrots are scraped, cut into strips, or made into olive shapes or diced. They are blanched in salted water before cooking.

▣ Chantilly

For 6 persons: 2½ lb new round carrots; 1 lb peas; 2 oz butter; ¼ pint sauce Béchamel; ½ pint cream. Cooking time of carrots: 20-30 minutes.

Use new carrots if possible and clean them. If old carrots are used, cut them into thin slices. Cook in salted water and drain. Put them into a saucepan, cover with cream and *Béchamel* sauce, season and cook until creamy. Cook the peas in boiling, salted water and drain well. Toss them in butter and season with salt and a pinch of sugar. Arrange the carrots in a round dish and surround them with the peas.

▣ à la Crème * *in Cream Sauce*

For 6 persons: 2½ lb new carrots; ½ pint cream; 1½ oz butter. Cooking time: 20-40 minutes according to quality.

Take small round carrots if possible, clean them and cook in salt water. Drain, simmer in butter for a few minutes, add cream, season and cook till sauce is thick.

▣ Glacées * *Glazed*

For 6 persons: 2½ lb new carrots; 2 oz butter; salt; 1 oz sugar. Cooking time: about 20 minutes.

Put the small, cleaned carrots in enough *bouillon* to cover them completely, add salt, sugar and a nut of butter and cook slowly till they are done and the liquid has evaporated, leaving only a syrupy juice. Toss the carrots in this to give them a glazed surface. Cut large carrots in pieces or fancy shapes and treat in the same way.

▣ Panachées * *Mixed*

For 6 persons: 1½ lb carrots; 1½ lb potatoes; 2 oz butter; parsley. Cooking time: 25-30 minutes.

Clean long carrots, slice them thinly and boil in salt water till almost soft. Mix with small round potato slices and cook together till both are done. Drain, season, toss gently in plenty of butter to keep the potato slices whole if possible. Serve sprinkled with chopped parsley.

Carottes Vichy

For 6 persons: 2½ lb carrots; 2 oz butter; 2 oz castor sugar; chopped parsley. Cooking time: approximately 25 minutes.

Thinly slice the carrots, add butter and sugar, cover with water (correctly Vichy water, but plain water may be used). Season with a little salt and allow to boil steadily until the carrots are cooked and all the liquid evaporated. The butter will form a glaze on the surface. Serve sprinkled with chopped parsley.

CELERIS * *CELERY*

This vegetable may be eaten raw, with salt, Mayonnaise or *Vinaigrette* dressing, or cooked and served as a garnish with a main dish.

⊡ en Branches, braisés * *Braised*

For 6 persons: 3 large sticks of celery; 1 carrot; 1 onion; 1 pint rather fat bouillon; ½ pint Demi-glace. Cooking time: about 1½ hours.

Remove damaged outside stalks of celery, trim root, wash thoroughly inside and out and blanch in salt water for about 15 minutes. Cool, halve lengthwise, fold, and place in a braising pan on a bed of sliced carrot and onion. Pour on just enough fat, lightly salted *bouillon* to cover the celery, cover with greased paper, put on lid and cook slowly in the oven, 325° F or Gas Mark 2, till done. Drain well, if the pieces are too large halve again lengthwise and coat with *Demi-glace* mixed with the *bouillon* after skimming off fat and boiling down considerably. Sprinkle chopped parsley on top. Blanched beef marrow may be placed on the celery; coat with *Demi-glace* or *sauce Madère*. (*See illustration p.* 634).

⊡ à la Ménagère

For 6 persons: 3 large sticks of celery; 2 onions; 2 carrots; ½ lb tomatoes; 1¾ pints bouillon. Cooking time: about 1 hour.

Clean and blanch celery and cut in 2-inch pieces. Brown the thickly sliced onions and carrots slightly, place celery on top; add peeled, deseeded and quartered tomatoes. Season, add *bouillon*, cover and cook in the oven till done. Well blanched celery can also be placed round a piece of veal which is to be braised. It tastes excellent when cooked in the gravy.

⊡ à la Milanaise

For 6 persons: 3 large sticks of celery; 2 oz grated cheese; 2 oz butter; chopped parsley. Cooking time: 25 minutes.

Clean and peel celery and cut into *bâtons* 1½ ins by ¼ in. Cook them in boiling salted water. Do not allow to get too soft. Drain well. Arrange in a buttered baking dish. Sprinkle with grated cheese and drop a little butter on top. Brown lightly in a hot oven, 400° F or Gas Mark 6. Pour Brown butter on top, and sprinkle with chopped parsley.

Céleris au Parmesan

For 6 persons: 3 sticks of celery; 1-2 carrots and onions; 1 pint bouillon; ½ pint strong veal stock; 3 oz grated Parmesan cheese. Cooking time: about 1 hour.

Prepare celery as described, but do not cook quite so soft. Arrange the folded, well drained sticks in a baking dish, pour stock on top and simmer slowly for another 10-15 minutes. Sprinkle with grated Parmesan and serve at once.

CELERI-RAVE * *CELERIAC*

This is the root of the celery plant and may be used in the same manner as celery.

▣ en Beignets * *Fritters*

For 6 persons: 2½ lb celeriac; flour; 2 eggs; breadcrumbs; ½ pint sauce Tomate.

Peel the celeriac, cut in slices about ½-inch thick and boil in salt water without letting it get too soft. Drain, and if the slices are large, halve or quarter them. Flour and breadcrumb and deep fry in clarified butter or hot fat. Serve with light Tomato sauce.

▣ à l'Italienne

For 6 persons: 3 lb celeriac; 2 oz butter; 1 pint Italian sauce; parsley. Cooking time: 25-30 minutes.

Peel the celeriac and cut it into quarters or eighths, according to size. Blanch in salted, boiling water until nearly cooked. Drain and simmer for a while in butter until ready. Arrange in a vegetable dish, cover with *sauce Italienne* and sprinkle chopped parsley on top.

Le Cerfeuil Bulbeux * *Turnip-rooted Chervil*

These small roots have a very delicate, sweetish flavour. Peel them, blanch thoroughly in salt water and simmer till done in butter or concentrated stock. They can also be dipped in batter and deep fried, used for soup or served as garnish with game.

Chicorée à la Crème * *Endive Purée in Cream Sauce*

For 6 persons: 6½ lb endive; 2 pints bouillon; ½ pint Béchamel; ¼ pint cream; 2 oz butter; 1 oz flour. Cooking time: about 1½ hours.

Blanch the green part of the endive thoroughly (which takes rather a long time), pour off water, cool, drain, squeeze out well and chop finely or pass through the mincer. Make a light *roux* with flour, butter, mix with the endive *purée*, add *bouillon*, stir, cover and braise in a warm oven, 350° F or Gas Mark 3, for at least one hour. Transfer to a clean casserole since the endives tend to stick. Mix with *Béchamel* and a little cream, season well, simmer a little longer and garnish with fried white bread *croûtons*.

Pain de Chicorée à la Crème * *Endive Loaf with Cream Sauce*

Prepare *purée* (*see* p. 641), remove from heat and mix with three whole beaten eggs per 2¼ pounds of *purée.* Place in a buttered, rather shallow beaker mould and poach in a water-bath for 25-30 minutes. Let it rest for a few minutes, turn out on a round dish and pour light *Béchamel* or hot cream, seasoned with salt and pepper, on top.

CHOUX * *CABBAGE*

The important members of this rather large group of vegetables are: white cabbage, used principally in the preparation of *sauerkraut*, red cabbage as vegetable and *hors d'œuvre*, green cabbage braised, as a garnish and plainly boiled, spring and Savoy cabbages plainly boiled, and cauliflower, *broccoli*, Brussels sprouts, and *kohlrabi.*

▣ à l'Anglaise * *Boiled*

For 6 persons: 3 lb white cabbage or curlykale; 3 oz butter. Cooking time: about ½ hour.

Quarter the cabbage and remove stalk. Cook in salt water till quite soft, squeeze out all moisture between 2 plates, cut in squares or rectangles, place in a vegetable dish, salt lightly and pepper and pour plenty of melted butter on top.

▣ Braisés * *Braised*

For 6 persons: 4 lb white cabbage; 2 carrots; 2 onions; ¼ lb fat bacon; 1 ham bone or ham trimmings. Cooking time: 1½-2 hours.

Remove damaged leaves from cabbage, quarter, cut out stalk, blanch thoroughly and drain well. Line the bottom of a casserole with bacon rashers, put the cabbage, carrots, onions and ham bone in centre, just cover with fat *bouillon*, salt lightly, pepper, cover with greased paper, put on lid and braise in a warm oven, 350° F or Gas Mark 3, for at least 1 hour; in principle all the liquid should be boiled away.

▣ Farcis, Entiers * *Stuffed, Whole White*

For 6 persons: 4½ lb white cabbage; 1 lb sausage meat; 5 oz white bread; 1 chopped onion; 1 clove of garlic; 1 egg; chopped parsley; 1 large thin rasher of fat bacon. Cooking time: 1¾ hours.

Remove any damaged outer leaves, scoop out the middle and keep for other use and blanch cabbage for 10 minutes. Drain very thoroughly and stuff with a mixture of the sausage meat, white bread soaked in milk and squeezed out, chopped onion cooked in butter, chopped parsley, crushed garlic, 1 egg, salt and pepper. Wrap this stuffing in bacon. Tie up the stuffed cabbage and braise slowly in a casserole with good stock till done. Before serving remove string.

▣ Farci, Vert * *Stuffed, Green*

For 6 persons: 4 lb green cabbage; 1 lb sausage meat; 1 rasher fat bacon; ¼ lb breadcrumbs; 1 onion; 1 egg.

Proceed in the same way as above.

Choux au Gratin

For 6 persons: 4 lb white cabbage; ¾ pint Béchamel; 2 oz grated cheese. Cooking time: ¾ hour.

Quarter the white cabbage, cut out stalk and boil in slightly salted water till done. Cool, drain, squeeze out well, chop finely, bind with a little *Béchamel* and season. Remove from heat, stir in a little grated cheese, put in a baking dish, coat with *Béchamel*, sprinkle with grated cheese and brown in a hot oven, 400° F or Gas Mark 6.

Choucroute Garnie * *Sauerkraut, Garnished*

For 6 persons: 6 oz bacon rinds; ½ lb boiling sausage; 2½ lb sauerkraut; ½ lb streaky bacon; 3 oz lard or goose fat; 2 onions each stuck with a clove; 2 carrots; a bouquet garni; 1½ lb pickled spare ribs of pork, goose or ham; 6 Frankfurter sausages; ½ bottle white wine. Cooking time: 2-2½ hours.

Wash the *sauerkraut*, and squeeze it well by hand. Line the bottom and the sides of a casserole with some bacon rinds. Place about half the *sauerkraut* in the casserole and in the middle place the blanched bacon, the boiling sausage, the meat which is to be served with the *sauerkraut* (spare ribs, goose or ham), the carrots, onions and herbs. Cover with the rest of the *sauerkraut*, and add the white wine and a little water or stock. Now add the lard or goose fat, but no salt. Cover with a greased paper, place the lid on top, and braise in a slow oven. When the *sauerkraut* is done, remove the onions and herbs. Place the *sauerkraut* in the middle of a dish, and garnish with the meat, cut in slices, the bacon, sausage and carrots, all sliced, and the Frankfurters. Serve boiled potatoes at the same time.

Dolmas * *Stuffed Cabbage Leaves*

For 6 persons: 1 white cabbage; 1 lb cooked mutton; 3 oz chopped onions; 2 oz soaked, squeezed out white bread; 2 oz rice; oil; mutton broth; tomato purée or fresh tomatoes; 1 carrot; 1 large onion. Cooking time: 1-1¼ hours.

Dolmas are prepared from vine leaves; but other green leaf vegetables may also be used. Blanch medium-sized cabbage leaves until they are soft enough to roll up, cool in cold water, drain, spread side by side on a table and cut out thick ribs. Mince the mutton, mix well with a little dry boiled rice, chopped onions cooked in oil, white bread, chopped parsley, salt and paprika and put a little of this mixture on each cabbage leaf. Wrap the filling tightly in the leaves, compress slightly with a cloth to give them all the same round shape and place in a dish generously greased with oil on sliced carrot and onion. Put in a hot oven to brown slightly. Fill up with mutton broth, add a little tomato *purée* or peeled, deseeded and chopped tomatoes, cover with oiled paper, put on lid and cook in oven at moderate heat, 375° F or Gas Mark 4, till done. Serve rolls with peeled deseeded lemon slices laid on top and the greatly boiled down stock (flavoured with lemon juice) poured over them. (*Turkish*).

CHOU ROUGE * *RED CABBAGE*

This may be braised or eaten raw as an *hors d'œuvre.* It is very often cut into strips and pickled.

Chou Rouge à la Flamande

For 8 *persons:* 4 *lb red cabbage;* 10 *oz apples;* ½ *lb lard;* 1 *tablespoon vinegar;* 1 *tablespoon Demerara sugar.* Cooking time: 2-3 hours.

Remove damaged leaves, quarter the cabbage, cut out stalk and cut in *julienne*. Place in a thickly greased casserole and season with salt, pepper and a pinch of cinnamon, and the vinegar. Simmer slowly for 1-2 hours. Add the peeled, cored and quartered apples, distribute them well, add the sugar, cover and braise till tender. Serve in a casserole or vegetable dish.

◻ à la Limousine

For 6 *persons:* 3 *lb red cabbage cut into julienne;* 1 *lb of shelled chestnuts;* 2 *oz of lard;* ½ *pint of stock.* Cooking time: 2 hours.

Grease a braising pan with the lard, add the cabbage, chestnuts, stock and seasoning, cover and braise in the oven at 350° F or Gas Mark 4.

◻ au Vin Rouge * *with Red Wine*

For 8 *persons:* 3¼ *lb red cabbage;* 3 *oz onions;* ½ *lb lean bacon;* 1 *oz lard;* 2 *oz flour;* 1 *pint red wine.* Cooking time: about 2 hours.

Remove damaged leaves from cabbage, quarter it, cut out stalk, and shred the leaves finely. Sweat the chopped onions and diced bacon in the lard, sprinkle with flour and fry light brown. Add red cabbage, stir thoroughly, season with salt and pepper, cover and braise in the oven for 30 minutes. Boil up wine, add it to the cabbage, finish cooking together, season and serve in a vegetable dish.

Choux Brocolis * *Broccoli*

This greenish or bluish member of the cabbage family has some resemblance to cauliflower in appearance. Boil in salt water without letting it get too soft, drain well and serve with *sauce Vinaigrette* or as for Cauliflower *à la Polonaise*.

CHOUX DE BRUXELLES * *BRUSSELS SPROUTS*

These are cabbage buds which are removed from the leaf axil before they are allowed to grow. They are in season from October to March.

◻ à l'Anglaise * *Boiled*

For 6 *persons:* 2 *lb of prepared sprouts;* 2 *oz butter.* Cooking time: approx. 20 minutes.

Cook in boiling salted water, drain well, dress and place some small pieces of butter on top.

◻ à la Crème * *in Cream Sauce*

For 6 *persons:* 2½ *lb Brussels sprouts;* 1 *pint sauce Crème.* Cooking time: about 20 minutes.

Prepare and cook the Brussels sprouts in the usual way, in boiling salted water. Arrange neatly on a vegetable serving dish. Serve the sauce separately in a sauce-boat.

Chou de Bruxelles au Gratin

For 6 persons: 2 *lb of plainly cooked Brussels sprouts;* 1 *pint Béchamel;* ½ *oz butter;* 2 *oz grated cheese.* Cooking time: approx. 30 minutes.

Lightly bind the Brussels sprouts with two-thirds of the sauce, arrange in a porcelain dish, mask over with the rest of the sauce, sprinkle with the cheese and melted butter, and gratinate in hot oven, 400° F or Gas Mark 6.

▣ à la Milanaise

Prepare in the same way as cauliflower *à la Milanaise.*

▣ à la Polonaise

Proceed in the same way as for cauliflower *à la Polonaise.*

▣ Sautés

Allow ½ *lb sprouts per person.* Cooking time in boiling salted water: 20-25 minutes.

Drain well and brown lightly in butter in a *sauté* pan.

CHOU-FLEURS * *CAULIFLOWER*

Remove outer green leaves, cut stalk straight at bottom and hollow it out slightly. Boil in plenty of salt water and drain well. Serve with *sauce Hollandaise*, *Mousseline* or *Crème.*

▣ à l'Anglaise * *Boiled*

For 6 persons: 1 *large cauliflower;* ¼ *lb of melted butter.* Cooking time: approx. 25 minutes.

Trim away all the main stem and outside leaves, leaving only a single covering of the young interior leaves, then cut away the centre of the main stalk to facilitate its cooking, wash well in salted water. Cook carefully in boiling salted water, drain and arrange in a serving dish. Serve with butter in a sauce-boat.

▣ à la Crème * *in Cream Sauce*

As above, but serve with a large sauce-boat of *sauce Crème.*

▣ au Gratin

For 6 persons: 3 *lb cauliflower;* ¾ *pint sauce Mornay*; 1 *oz grated cheese;* 1 *oz butter.* Cooking time: about 20 minutes.

Boil cauliflower, drain well and, if it is very loose restore the shape by pressing it into a *bombe* mould. Cover the bottom of a baking dish with 1-2 spoonfuls of sauce, sprinkle it with grated cheese, and put unmoulded cauliflower on top, round side up. Coat all over with *sauce Mornay*, sprinkle with grated cheese and melted butter and brown in a hot oven, 400° F or Gas Mark 6.

Chou-Fleurs à la Milanaise

For 6 persons: 3 *lb cauliflower;* 2 *oz grated Parmesan;* $\frac{1}{4}$ *lb of butter.* Cooking time: approximately 20 minutes.

Cut the cauliflower into large flowerets and cook in salted water. Drain, arrange in a buttered porcelain dish, sprinkle with the cheese and half of the butter and gratinate in a very hot oven, 450° F or Gas Mark 8. Then pour over two ounces of *Noisette* butter, that is, melted butter which has been lightly browned until it smells and looks nutty.

⊡ à la Polonaise

For 6 persons: $3\frac{1}{2}$-4 *lb cauliflower;* 2 *hardboiled eggs;* 2 *oz breadcrumbs;* 4 *oz butter; chopped parsley.* Cooking time: about 20 minutes.

Cut off the stalk, remove the leaves, and cook the cauliflower in salted boiling water. Drain well. Turn out on to a round shallow dish. Cover with chopped hardboiled egg and chopped parsley. Brown the breadcrumbs in a frying pan with plenty of butter. Pour this butter over the cauliflower and serve immediately.

Choux-Raves * *Kohlrabi*

This vegetable, which resembles a green capped turnip, with lateral leaves growing from the root, is prepared in the same manner as turnips and celeriac. A good method with young *kohlrabi* is to place on them a layer of coarse salt and bake in the oven. Slice off the top, replace and arrange neatly in a vegetable serving dish. Serve with melted butter.

CŒURS DE PALMIERS * *YOUNG PALM SHOOTS*

Tender young palm shoots are boiled in salt water after having been completely skinned. In Europe they are only available in tins. A $2\frac{1}{4}$ pound tin contains 4 to 6 shoots according to size. They are prepared in the same way as asparagus, either hot with various sauces or cold with oil and vinegar.

⊡ au Gratin

For 6 persons: $1\frac{1}{2}$ *lb palm shoots;* $\frac{1}{2}$ *pint Italian sauce;* 1 *oz Parmesan cheese; toasted breadcrumbs;* 2 *oz butter.* Cooking time: 12-15 minutes.

Split the shoots in two and cut up into pieces 3 ins long. Warm them up in their own liquor and then drain. Arrange in a shallow ovenproof dish. Mask with the *sauce Italienne*, sprinkle with the grated Parmesan cheese and breadcrumbs. Splash with melted butter. Brown in a hot oven, 425° F or Gas Mark 7.

⊡ Hollandaise ou Mousseline

For 6 persons: $1\frac{1}{2}$ *lb palm shoots;* $\frac{1}{2}$ *to* $\frac{3}{4}$ *pint Hollandaise or Mousseline sauce.*

Warm up the shoots in their own liquor, drain and then cut in half lengthwise and crosswise. Serve garnished with a bunch of parsley. Serve the *sauce Hollandaise* or *Mousseline* separately.

Cœurs de Palmiers à la Milanaise

For 6 persons: 1½ *lb palm shoots;* 2 *oz Parmesan cheese;* ¼ *lb butter.* Cooking time: 8-10 minutes.

Split the shoots and cut in halves. Warm them up in their own liquor. Drain well and arrange in a shallow ovenproof dish. Sprinkle with grated Parmesan cheese and pour over plenty of *Noisette* butter. Lightly brown in a hot oven, 400° F or Gas Mark 6, or under a salamander.

▣ Orly

For 6 *persons:* 1½ *lb palm shoots;* ⅜ *pint Coating batter;* ½ *pint sauce Tomate; parsley.* Cooking time: 4-5 minutes.

Dry well and split each shoot into 4 pieces. Dip them in Coating batter and fry in hot fat. Dish up on a paper napkin with fried parsley and serve the *sauce Tomate* separately.

COURGETTES * *BABY MARROWS*

This tasty vegetable is very popular in France. Allow about a half pound per person. All the recipes for eggplant are suitable for this vegetable.

▣ Farcies * *Stuffed*

For 4 persons: 2 *marrows;* ¾ *lb duxelles;* 1 *clove garlic; chopped parsley;* 2 *oz breadcrumbs;* ½ *pint sauce Tomate; oil.* Cooking time: 25-30 minutes.

Cut the marrows in half lengthwise and remove seeds. Make small cuts with a knife all around the edge, about ¼-inch thick, and a few in the middle. Sprinkle with salt and allow to steep for 15 minutes. Wipe off the salt and fry in hot oil. Drain and scoop out being careful not to damage the skins. Chop the flesh and mix it with chopped parsley, a little crushed garlic and add an equal amount of *duxelles.* Season well, and stuff the skins with this filling. Sprinkle with breadcrumbs, a little oil on top, and brown in a very hot oven, 425° F or Gas Mark 7. Serve a sauce-boat of *sauce Tomate* at the same time.

▣ Farcies à l'Orientale

For 6 *persons:* 6 *courgettes;* ½ *lb rice;* ¼ *lb cooked mutton;* 1 *medium-sized onion;* 1 *sweet green pepper;* 4 *tomatoes;* 1 *clove garlic; bouillon; grated cheese; breadcrumbs; olive oil.* Cooking time: 25 minutes.

Chop the onion and fry lightly in oil. Add the green pepper, cut into very small dice, and the rice, and allow to cook for a minute or so. Moisten with twice as much stock as the volume of the rice, and add crushed garlic, peeled and deseeded tomatoes cut into quarters, salt and pepper. Cook the rice for not more than about 12-14 minutes, keeping it a little liquid. Cut the *courgettes* in half lengthwise, remove the seeds, and cook the *courgettes* in a little oil in the oven. Scoop them out carefully so as not to damage the skin, and chop the flesh. Mix the flesh and the minced mutton with the rice. Stuff the *courgettes* with this mixture, sprinkle with grated cheese and breadcrumbs, and drop a little oil on top. Brown in a very hot oven, 425° F or Gas Mark 7.

Courgettes Frites * *Deep Fried Marrows*

For 6 persons: 3 lb courgettes. Cooking time: 4-5 minutes.

Peel the *courgettes*, slice lengthwise, sprinkle with a little salt and leave to stand for 20 minutes to extract moisture. Wipe, dip in Coating batter and dry in deep fat.

▣ Meunière * *Shallow Fried*

Prepare *courgettes* as above, then wipe, flour, fry on both sides in butter and serve very hot sprinkled with chopped parsley and with Brown butter poured on top.

▣ à la Vauclusienne

For 4 persons: 2 courgettes or aubergines; 1 lb tomatoes; ¼ pint olive oil; 1 clove garlic; chopped parsley; breadcrumbs. Cooking time: 15-20 minutes.

Peel and quarter the *aubergines* lengthwise. Steep in salt for 15 minutes. Wipe off the salt, roll in flour and fry in hot oil. Arrange the *aubergines* side by side in rows in a baking dish. Peel and deseed the tomatoes. Cut them into large dice, and cook them in hot oil, adding crushed garlic, chopped parsley, salt and pepper. Cover each *aubergine* with a layer of tomatoes. Sprinkle with breadcrumbs, drop a little oil on top and finish cooking in a hot oven, 425° F or Gas Mark 7, until nice and brown on top.

CROSNES * *CHINESE ARTICHOKES*

These artichokes originated from China and were first cultivated at Crosnes in France, hence their name. They may be prepared as for Jerusalem artichokes.

▣ aux Fines Herbs * *with Herbs*

For 6 persons: 2½ lb Chinese artichokes; ¼ lb butter; 1 tablespoon chopped herbs. Cooking time: 25-30 minutes.

Clean, boil and drain the Chinese artichokes, *sauté* them in hot butter, season and toss with the chopped herbs.

▣ au Velouté * *in Velouté Sauce*

For 6 persons: 2½ lb Chinese artichokes; ½ pint veal Velouté. Cooking time: about 20 minutes.

Prepare and boil the Chinese artichokes, drain well and bind with strong, well-seasoned *Velouté*. After blanching they can also be cooked with a piece of veal.

ENDIVES * *CHICORY OR BELGIAN ENDIVE*

The white, bleached heads called endive in France and the United States are known as chicory or Belgian endive in Britain. The best method of cooking is as follows. Remove any damaged outer leaves, place in a flat casserole with nothing but salt, pepper, the juice of 1 lemon and just enough water to cover the chicory. Cover with buttered greaseproof paper, put on lid and cook slowly in oven till done. When cooked in this way the bitter flavour—which is appreciated by connoisseurs—vanishes almost entirely.

Endives Braisés * *Braised Chicory*

For 6 persons: 2 lb chicory; 2 oz butter; 1 lemon; ¼ pint Demi-glace. Cooking time: 1¼ hours.

Remove any damaged outer leaves and simmer for 15 minutes in salted water. Remove, drain well and place in a flat casserole. Season with pepper, the juice of 1 lemon and pour over enough *Demi-glace* to cover the chicory. Cover with buttered greaseproof paper, replace the lid and cook slowly in a cool oven, 325° F or Gas Mark 2, till done.

▣ à la Flamande

For 5 persons: 2 lb chicory; 2 oz butter; 1 lemon; ½ pint Demi-glace. Cooking time: 1 hour.

Prepare chicory as above, see *Braisés*. Place in a fire-proof dish with butter, lemon juice and salt and only very little water. Cook in the oven till all the moisture has evaporated and the butter begins to brown. Serve with *Demi-glace* poured over it. The *Demi-glace* can also be replaced by slightly browned butter or *Noisette* butter.

▣ au Gratin

For 5 persons: 2 lb chicory; 1 lb potatoes; 2 chopped onions; ½ pint bouillon; breadcrumbs; butter. Cooking time: 1½-2 hours.

Cut chicory into small pieces, boil in salt water with lemon juice till almost done and drain. Boil potatoes in their jackets for 5 minutes, peel and slice thickly, fry onions golden brown in butter. Fill a deep baking dish with layers of potato and chicory (both seasoned) with onions in between, pour in a little stock, sprinkle with plenty of breadcrumbs and melted butter and put in a moderate oven, 375° F or Gas Mark 4, to cook and brown.

▣ Gratinées au Jambon * *au Gratin with Ham*

For 6 persons: 6 large heads of chicory; 6 thin slices of boiled ham; ½ pint sauce Mornay; 2 oz grated gruyère cheese. Cooking time: 1 hour.

Boil chicory in slightly salted water with a little lemon juice, changing the water twice to remove the bitter flavour. Drain well, wrap each head in a slice of ham of suitable size and put in an oval baking dish in the bottom of which 1 tablespoon of sauce has been placed. Coat each roll entirely with *sauce Mornay*, sprinkle with grated cheese and brown in a hot oven, 400° F or Gas Mark 6.

▣ Meunière * *Shallow Fried*

For 6 persons: 2 lb of chicory; 3 oz butter; juice of one lemon. Cooking time: 1½ hours.

Prepare in the same manner as for *à la Flamande*, replacing the *Demi-glace* sauce with *Noisette* butter.

Endives Soufflé

For 6 persons: 2 lb of cooked purée of chicory; 3 eggs; ½ pint of thick Béchamel. Cooking time: 25 minutes.

Heat the *purée* and *Béchamel* together, stir in the yolks, then fold in the whipped whites of egg, fill into a buttered *soufflé* mould, place in a tray of water and cook in a moderate oven, 375° F or Gas Mark 4-5.

ÉPINARDS * *SPINACH*

Spinach and other green vegetables are usually cooked in boiling salted water but many people object to this method of cooking because of the considerable loss of valuable vitamins and minerals. Spinach may, therefore, be cooked at great heat in its own juice with just a pinch of salt without losing colour. It must not be cooled in water, but just drained and pressed by hand.

▣ en Branches à l'Anglaise * *Boiled*

For 6 persons: 4½ lb young spinach; ¼ lb butter. Cooking time: 8-12 minutes.

Remove stalks from spinach, wash several times, drain very thoroughly and boil briskly in salt water. Drain, cool, squeeze out well and just before serving heat in hot butter. Salt lightly, stir with a fork to loosen it and place in a vegetable dish.

▣ en Purée à la Crème * *Creamed, Spinach Purée*

For 4 persons: 2 lb spinach; ½ pint thick sauce Béchamel; ¼ pint thick cream; 2 oz butter. Cooking time: 7-8 minutes to cook the spinach.

Wash the spinach several times, and remove the stalks. Cook the leaves in boiling salted water. Do not cover while cooking. Drain, cool in running water, drain again and press with the hands. Chop finely or pass through the finest blade of the mincer or through a wire sieve. Dry the *purée* with butter on the heat for a minute or two, season with salt, pepper and grated nutmeg and mix with the *sauce Béchamel.* Cook for a few minutes over low heat. Just before serving, add a little thick cream.

▣ en Pain * *Spinach Loaf*

For 6-8 persons: 4 lb spinach; ½ pint thick Béchamel; 2 oz butter; 3 eggs; ¼ pint cream. Poaching time: about 30 minutes.

Wash spinach thoroughly, boil, drain well, cool, squeeze out and pass through a sieve. Bind with the *Béchamel*, season well, remove from heat and bind with 3 beaten eggs or 5 egg yolks. Place in a well-buttered beaker or *bombe* mould, poach in a water-bath in the oven at moderate heat, 375° F or Gas Mark 4, and let it rest for a few minutes before turning out on a round dish. Pour hot cream or *sauce Velouté* on top when serving.

Fenouil * *Fennel*

This excellent vegetable, which smells and tastes slightly of aniseed, resembles celery in appearance, but is much shorter. Trim the root end, cut off tops, wash and blanch well. It is best braised with *bouillon* on sliced carrots and onions and bacon trimmings. It is also excellent as *hors d'œuvre* when prepared *à la Grecque* (see *Hors d'Oeuvre*). All the recipes for celery and cardoons are applicable here.

Fèves * *Broad Beans*

Only use young beans and do not shell till the last moment as they are inclined to lose their flavour if exposed to the air. When skinned cook for a few minutes only in a very little boiling salted water. The addition of a little winter or summer savory brings out the full flavour of the beans. Drain well and serve tossed in butter, in Cream sauce or as *purée*.

Gombos * *Gumbo or Okra*

An exotic vegetable which is also available tinned. There are two kinds, the long and the round. Cut both ends smooth, but do not cut open, blanch in salt water, simmer in butter or cream and season well.

HARICOTS BLANCS * *HARICOT BEANS*

This term covers all white beans, that is butter beans and the smaller haricot beans.

⊡ à la Bretonne

For 6 persons: 2½ *lb freshly shelled or* 1 *lb dried haricot beans;* ¼ *lb onions;* ½ *pint thin sauce Tomate.* Cooking time of fresh beans: 30-40 minutes; of dried beans 1-2 hours.

Put fresh beans in boiling salt water, soak the dried ones for 2 hours first and start them in cold water. Sweat the chopped onion well in butter or lard, add the rather thin *sauce Tomate*, put in the drained beans and boil slowly for a few minutes. Sprinkle with chopped parsley and use as garnish with roast leg of lamb.

⊡ à la Crème * *in Cream Sauce*

For 6 persons: 1 *lb dried haricot beans;* 1 *onion;* 2 *carrots;* 1 *bouquet garni;* ½ *pint light Béchamel;* ½ *pint cream.* Cooking time of beans: about 2 hours.

Cook as indicated above. Bind the boiled, drained beans with the *Béchamel* and cream and boil up briefly. Season well.

Haricots Flageolets * *Flageolets*

This is a dwarf or pea bean which is shelled before cooking. Both fresh and dried flageolets are prepared in the same way as haricot beans, either in *sauce Crème* or *à la Bretonne* or used with French beans (see below).

Haricots Rouges au Vin * *Kidney Beans in Wine*

For 6 persons: 1 *lb dried red kidney beans;* ¾ *oz flour;* ½ *pint red wine;* 1 *chopped onion;* ¼ *lb lean bacon.* Cooking time: about 2 hours.

Soak the beans and cook till done. Sweat the chopped onion in butter, add the diced bacon, brown it slightly, dust with flour and pour on red wine. Boil for 10 minutes, simmer beans in it for a few minutes and season well.

HARICOTS VERTS * *FRENCH BEANS*

These should be picked when young, that is, as soon as the peas are formed within the shell so that they will not become stringy and tough.

▣ à la Crème * *in Cream Sauce*

For 5 persons: 2 lb French beans; 2 oz butter; ½ pint thick cream. Cooking time: 20 minutes.

Cook beans in salt water, drain, toss in hot butter, pour the cream or thin *Béchamel* on top and boil till thick.

▣ Maître d'Hôtel

6 *oz French beans per person.* Cooking time: 15-20 minutes.

Boil beans briskly in salt water, if they are very large cut them in long thin strips. Drain well, bind with light *Béchamel* and serve sprinkled with chopped parsley.

▣ à la Paysanne

For 6 persons: 1½ lb French beans; 1½ lb potatoes; 3 oz butter. Cooking time: 25 minutes.

Boil the beans together with the peeled, quartered potatoes, drain and *sauté* quickly in very dark brown butter.

▣ à la Portugaise

For 6 persons: 2 lb French beans; ½ lb tomatoes; ¼ lb unsmoked bacon; ½ pint bouillon. Cooking time: about 30 minutes.

Dice the bacon finely, put it in a casserole with the cut or broken beans and the peeled, deseeded and coarsely chopped tomatoes, add *bouillon*, season with salt and pepper, bring to the boil, cover and cook in a warm oven, 350° F or Gas Mark 3-4. Although the beans lose some of their distinctive green colour they taste delicious. Serve sprinkled with chopped parsley.

LAITUES * *LETTUCE*

A salad vegetable, lettuce has been growing from time immemorial, throughout Europe and Asia, both in its wild and cultivated states.

▣ Braisées au Madère * *Braised with Madeira Sauce*

For 6 persons: 6 large firm heads of lettuce; 1 onion; 1 carrot; ¼ lb fat bacon; veal stock or bouillon; ½ pint sauce Madère. Cooking time: ¾-1 hour.

Scrape the stem of the lettuces. Do not cut the stem off, so that the leaves remain attached. Wash carefully in running water, drain, and blanch for 15 minutes in salted water. Cool in cold water and press out the remaining moisture by hand. Cut in half lengthwise. Fold each half in two by turning down the ends of the leaves under each half. Arrange in a *sautoir* on slices of onion and carrots and the fat bacon. Add a little veal stock or *bouillon*, season, and cover with a buttered greaseproof paper. Put the lid on, and braise in a warm oven, 350° F or Gas Mark 3-4. Drain well, arrange in a vegetable dish or *plat russe* and cover with *sauce Madère*.

Laitues Chevalière

For 6 persons: 6 heads of lettuce; 1 carrot; 1 onion; ¼ lb bacon; 3 slices of ham; 1 pint bouillon; ½ pint sauce Madère. Cooking times: about 45 minutes.

Blanch the lettuces, drain, cool, squeeze out well, halve and braise slowly on sliced carrots, onions and bacon in fat broth, covered with buttered greaseproof paper. When cooked, drain well and arrange in a ring, alternating with slices of fried ham of the same size. Pour *sauce Madère* on top.

LENTILLES * *LENTILS*

A pulse which originated in Central Asia, where it has been cultivated for centuries. It has a higher protein content than any other vegetable.

⊡ à la Lorraine

For 6 persons: 1 lb lentils; 1 large onion; ¼ lb lean bacon; 1 clove of garlic; 1 bouquet garni; 1 carrot; 1 oz butter; ¾ oz flour. Cooking time of lentils: 1-2 hours, according to quality.

Soak the lentils and boil them. They should not be soft enough to fall apart. Remove lentils. Sweat a chopped onion in butter with diced bacon, add a little lentil stock and the lentils, boil up, add crushed garlic and thicken slightly with kneaded butter or *beurre manié* made from the ounce of butter and the flour. Lentils, like dried beans, are best boiled with a carrot, an onion and a *bouquet garni.*

Maïs en Epis * *Corn on the Cob*

Only use very young cobs which are still milky, remove outer leaves, boil in salted water for 20 minutes and leave in the hot water for a little longer. Do not overcook, otherwise the cobs turn hard and yellow. Skewer, place on a dish and serve with hot butter. Young cobs can also be baked in the oven. They are also served with butter.

MARRONS * *CHESTNUTS*

These have a very high nutritional value and may be eaten raw, boiled, steamed or grilled. They are used in various preparations of sweets and pastries in addition to being used as a vegetable.

⊡ Braisés * *Braised*

The following is one method recommended for peeling chestnuts. First cut all round them with a sharp knife, then immerse them in hot deep fat, in a wire basket if possible. The fat should not be hot enough to fry them immediately. When they are half done, the peel comes open of its own accord so that it can be removed easily. Drain well on a coarse cloth and peel without damaging them. Braise carefully in good stock or light Brown sauce. When stuffing a goose or a turkey use the same method, but leave chestnuts in the the fat till they are fully cooked.

⊡ Purée

Peel the chestnuts and boil them till soft in salt water or light *bouillon* with a small piece of celeriac. They should be simmered gently for about 40 minutes. Drain, pass through a sieve and stir to a smooth, well seasoned *purée* with a little of the stock, milk, cream and a little butter.

NAVETS * *TURNIPS*

A bulbous, fleshy root vegetable, turnips are usually served with fatty meat as they have the property of absorbing large quantities of fat.

◘ à la Crème * *in Cream Sauce*

For 6 persons: 3 *lb turnips;* 1 *oz butter;* ½ *pint Béchamel;* 1 *pint cream.* Cooking time: 30-40 minutes.

Quarter the young turnips, or slice and shape *en olives*, boil in salt water and drain. Toss lightly in butter, cover with the *Béchamel* and cream, cook for a few minutes and season.

◘ Farcis * *Stuffed*

For 6 *persons:* 2 *lb round turnips;* 1 *lb minced meat;* 1 *pint bouillon; breadcrumbs.* Cooking time: about 40 minutes.

Use small round turnips with a violet coloured skin; scoop out the middle part of each with a vegetable scoop, blanch in salt water for 8-10 minutes and drain well. Fill with any desired seasoned minced meat. Put in a suitable fire-proof dish, half fill with *bouillon*, sprinkle each stuffed turnip with breadcrumbs, cook in a fairly hot oven, 400° F or Gas Mark 6, and brown. Use mainly as garnish.

◘ Glacés * *Glazed*

For 6 *persons:* 3 *lb turnips;* 2 *oz butter;* 1 *oz sugar*. Cooking time: 20-30 minutes.

Cut the peeled turnips into large olives and place them in a casserole with butter, sugar, a little salt and just enough water to cover them. Boil without a lid till the liquid has evaporated completely and the turnips are covered with a shiny surface.

◘ en Ragoût * *Stewed*

For 6 *persons:* 3 *lb turnips;* 6 *oz onions;* 1 *oz flour;* 2 *oz lard or good fat;* 1½ *pints bouillon.* Cooking time: 45-60 minutes.

Prepare turnips as for *Navets Glacés*, brown in the fat, sprinkle with flour, add chopped browned onions, simmer everything for a few minutes, fill up with *bouillon* or water, season with salt and cook till done without a lid. At the end they should have the appearance of being bound by a thick sauce.

OIGNONS * *ONIONS*

A bulb vegetable with a strong, pungent smell, onions are used a great deal in cooking for their flavour and texture and are excellent served with braised or stewed meats.

◘ Farcis * *Stuffed*

Use large Spanish onions and treat in the same way as for *Navets Farcis.*

Oignons Frits * *Deep Fried Onions*

Slice large onions across and separate the rings. Sprinkle a little fine salt on them, turn in flour, shake off the surplus flour and first blanch in hot oil. At the end of 4-5 minutes, remove and drain the onion which should be soft and colourless. Then dip in hot oil or deep fat a second time to make them golden brown and crisp. These are usually served as a garnish.

⊡ Glacés * *Glazed*

Prepare small onions in the same way as *Carottes Glacées*, after having first blanched them.

⊡ Purée Soubise

For 4 persons: ½ lb onions; 2 oz rice; ½ pint bouillon; ½ pint thick Béchamel; 1 oz butter. Cooking time: 45-60 minutes.

Slice the onions, blanch them briefly and sweat them in butter. Add the rice and the *bouillon*, season, cover and cook for about 40 minutes in a warm oven, 350° F or Gas Mark 3, till done. Pass through a sieve, stir to a thick *purée* with the *Béchamel* and do not boil again. Served with egg dishes, meat, etc., as is indicated in many recipes.

OSEILLE * *SORREL*

This vegetable can be cooked in any of the ways suitable to spinach and a mixture of spinach and sorrel is often used since the sharp flavour of sorrel is a rather acquired taste. It makes a fine accompaniment to veal dishes as well as combining well with many poached or baked egg dishes. It is also used as a garnish for certain soups but for this must first be cut in *julienne* and sautéed in butter for a few minutes.

⊡ comme Légume ou Garniture * *as a Vegetable or Garnish*

For 4 persons: 1 lb sorrel; 1 oz butter; ¾ oz flour; ¼ pint Béchamel; 2 egg yolks. Cooking time: about 2 hours.

Thoroughly wash and drain the sorrel, boil in salt water, drain and pass through a sieve. Make a *roux* with the flour and butter, mix with *purée*, cover and braise slowly in a cool oven, 325° F or Gas Mark 2. Bind with very thick *Béchamel*, put in a clean casserole, bind with 1-2 egg yolks mixed with a little milk or cream and boil up briefly, stirring thoroughly.

⊡ Fondue * *Melted*

Shred washed sorrel finely, melt only in a little butter, without water, with salt and pepper, and serve as it is. If it is too acid add a little cream. Cooked in this way, sorrel may be used in omelettes or certain soups.

POIREAUX * *LEEKS*

Probably a variety of cultivated oriental garlic, leeks are mainly used in the stock pot but may also be prepared as an accompaniment for a main dish.

Poireax Braisés * *Braised Leeks*

For 5 persons: 3 lb leeks; 1 pint bouillon; 1 carrot; 1 onion; some bacon trimmings; ½ pint gravy. Cooking time: about 1½ hours.

Cut off green part, score white lightly, wash very thoroughly, drain and blanch for 10 minutes. Line a *sauté* pan with sliced carrot and onion and bacon trimmings, place leeks on top, cover with *bouillon*, place a piece of greased paper on top, cover and braise till done in a moderate oven, 375° F or Gas Mark 4. Drain well and serve covered with strong, slightly thickened gravy.

⊡ en Branches * *Boiled*

For 5 persons: 3 lb leeks; ½ pint sauce Crème, Hollandaise or Mousseline. Cooking time: 30-40 minutes.

Prepare leeks as above, tie in bundles and boil in salt water for 30 minutes changing the water twice to get rid of the strong flavour. Drain well and serve with one of the above sauces in the same way as asparagus. (*See illustration p. 629*).

PETITS POIS * *PEAS*

Eaten "green" before they reach full maturity, these are fresh garden peas.

⊡ à l'Anglaise

For 5-6 persons: 1½ pints freshly shelled peas; 2 oz butter; salt; sugar. Cooking time: 15-20 minutes.

Throw young green peas into boiling salt water, do not boil too briskly or the skin will crack; drain, dry thoroughly in a casserole and season with salt and a pinch of sugar. Put in a vegetable dish with a sizeable knob of butter on top.

⊡ à la Francaise

For 5 persons: 1½ pints freshly shelled peas; 12 small button onions; 2 oz butter; bunch parsley and chervil; 1 small lettuce. Cooking time: 20-30 minutes, according to size and quality of the peas.

Put peas in a *sauté* pan with butter, washed and shredded lettuce, the onions and possibly a small spoon of flour and stir. Fill up pan with water, season with salt and a pinch of sugar, add herbs and boil briskly. When everything is done the ingredients should be bound to a certain extent and should be the thickness of single cream. The peas and onions should be tender. The flour and butter can be omitted and kneaded butter or *beurre manié* be used at the end for binding.

⊡ aux Laitues * *with Lettuce*

The same method and quantities as for *Petits Pois à la Française*, but add 3 firm quartered lettuces and when done arrange these on the cooked peas.

Petit Pois Ménagère

For 6 persons: 1½ pints freshly shelled peas; 3 oz lean bacon; 12 small button onions; 1 medium-sized chopped onion; ¾ oz flour; 1½ oz butter; salt; sugar. Cooking time: 20-30 minutes.

Dice and blanch the bacon, toss it in the butter; add the chopped onion, brown slightly and sprinkle with flour. After a few moments add enough water to cover the peas and boil up. Add the peas and onions and only salt lightly because of the bacon. Boil briskly at good heat and toss slightly before serving.

◘ à la Menthe * *with Mint*

For 5 persons: 1½ pints shelled peas; 1 small bunch mint; 2 oz butter. Cooking time: 15-18 minutes.

Put peas in lightly salted boiling water with the mint, boil briskly, drain well, simmer for a few minutes with butter, salt and a pinch of pepper, toss and put a few leaves of mint on top.

◘ à la Paysanne

For 6-7 persons: 1 pint shelled peas; 12 small button onions; 12 small carrots; 12 very small new potatoes; 2 lettuces. Cooking time: 20-30 minutes.

Prepare in the same way as *Petits Pois à la Française*, using all the ingredients, but quarter the lettuces instead of shredding, and serve everything together.

POIVRONS * *PEPPERS*

There are two varieties; red and green peppers. They are eaten raw, marinated in oil and vinegar, or stuffed with meat and baked in the oven. They are also added to risottos and salads to give colour and flavour.

◘ Farcis au Gras * *Stuffed with Meat*

For 5 persons: 5 peppers; 1 lb sausage meat; chopped parsley; 1 egg; 2 tablespoons oil; garlic; ½ pint Tomato sauce. Cooking time: 1-1½ hours.

Cut out stalks of peppers, remove seeds carefully through hole, wash out well and stuff with the sausage meat mixed with chopped parsley, crushed garlic, 1 tablespoon oil, 1 egg, salt and pepper. Place upright in an oiled *sauté* pan, add a little *bouillon*, sprinkle the tops with breadcrumbs and a little oil or butter and cook slowly in a moderate oven, 375° F or Gas Mark 4. Pour Tomato sauce round them when serving. (*See illustration p.* 631).

◘ Farcis au Riz * *Stuffed with Rice*

For 5 persons: 5 peppers; ¼ lb rice; 5 tomatoes; 1 tablespoon oil; a little bouillon. Cooking time: about 1½ hours.

Parboil the rice and mix with the peeled, deseeded, chopped tomatoes, salt, pepper, oil and chopped parsley. Cut out stalks of peppers, remove seeds through hole, wash out well and fill with the rice. Place upright in a *sauté* pan, add a little *bouillon*, cover with oiled paper, put on lid and cook slowly in a moderate oven, 375° F or Gas Mark 4-5.

Ratatouille Niçoise

For 6 persons: *1 lb tomatoes concassé; 1½ lb courgettes or marrows; 1½ lb aubergines; 2 red capsicums; 2 cloves of garlic; 1 bouquet garni; 2 sliced onions; 3 fl oz of oil.*

Halve the marrows or *courgettes* and the *aubergines* and cut into slices, ⅛-inch thick. Crush and chop the garlic. Peel, remove seeds carefully and cut the capsicums into strips. Lightly fry the onions in the oil, add the tomatoes, then the marrows, *aubergines*, capsicums, garlic, *bouquet garni*, salt and pepper, cover with lid, bring to the boil, remove the lid and cook until all the liquid has evaporated. (*See illustration p.* 635).

SALSIFIS * *SALSIFY*

This is a white, skinned vegetable rather like the parsnip. Another variety, *scorzonera*, has a black skin and is considered the better of the two.

⊡ Frits * *Deep Fried*

For 6 persons: *2 lb salsify; 1 pint Frying batter; lemon juice; parsley; vinegar.* Cooking time: 50-60 minutes.

Scrape salsify carefully and throw them into acidulated water. Then cut them into pieces about 3 inches long. Cook in floured water like cardoons. Wash off the flour with hot water, drain and marinate with chopped parsley and lemon juice. Shortly before serving dip in Frying batter or *Pâte à Frire*, and fry a golden brown in very hot fat. Drain, arrange on a napkin and garnish with fried parsley.

⊡ Sautés au Beurre * *Sautéed in Butter*

For 6 persons: *2 lb salsify; 3 oz butter; chopped parsley.* Cooking time: about 45 minutes.

Boil the salsify in water seasoned with salt, vinegar and herbs with the addition of a little flour. Drain well, then *sauté* in a very hot butter. Sprinkle with chopped parsley.

⊡ au Velouté * *in Velouté Sauce*

For 6 persons: *2 lb salsify; 1 pint veal Velouté.* Cooking time: about 45 minutes.

Prepare and boil salsify as above, rinse and drain. Heat for a few moments in *Velouté* or light cream sauce.

TOMATES * *TOMATOES*

These originated in South America but are now cultivated throughout Europe and America. There are many varieties ranging from red to yellow, round to oval. Tomatoes are used for salads or for cooking. They may be stewed, stuffed and baked or grilled.

Tomates Algérienne

For 6 persons: 9 medium-sized tomatoes; 1 lb aubergines; 2 cloves of garlic; oil; chopped parsley. Cooking time: 4-5 minutes.

Halve and scoop out the tomatoes, sprinkle them with oil and cook in the oven or in a frying pan without letting them lose their shape. Peel and thickly slice the *aubergines*, sprinkle with salt to extract moisture, wipe and fry in oil. Drain, chop finely, season, add crushed garlic, fill tomatoes with mixture and sprinkle with chopped parsley without browning.

▣ Farcies * *Stuffed with Meat*

For 6 persons: 6 large tomatoes; ½ lb cooked meat (beef, veal or mutton); 3 oz chopped onions; 1 oz lard; 1 oz grated cheese; 2 oz bread; breadcrumbs; chopped parsley; 1 small clove of garlic. Cooking time: 15-18 minutes.

Mince the meat. Brown the onions lightly in lard. Mix the minced meat with chopped parsley, crushed garlic, salt, pepper and the bread, soaked in water and pressed out. If the mixture is not smooth enough, add a little cold Tomato sauce. Cut the tomatoes in half, and scoop out the middle lightly. Stuff with the mince. Sprinkle with grated cheese and breadcrumbs and drop a little oil on top. Place in a hot oven to cook and gratinate the tomatoes. Serve with chopped parsley on top.

▣ Farcies Duchesse * *Stuffed with Duchesse Potatoes*

For 6 persons: 6 tomatoes; 1 lb Duchess potatoes; 2 oz grated cheese. Cooking time: 10 minutes.

Cut the tomatoes in halves; empty, season and fill with the *Pommes de terre Duchesse*, sprinkle with the cheese and melted butter, cook in a very hot oven, 450° F or Gas Mark 8. (*See illustration p.* 633).

▣ au Maigre * *Stuffed*

For 6 persons: 9 medium-sized tomatoes; 1 lb duxelles; breadcrumbs; oil. Cooking time in oven: 7-8 minutes.

Halve the tomatoes, scoop them out and deseed them, salt lightly and fill with the *duxelles* in a mound. Arrange on a slightly oiled baking sheet, sprinkle with breadcrumbs and a little oil and cook and brown in a very hot oven, 450° F or Gas Mark 8.

▣ à la Mode d'Avignon

For 6 persons: 3 aubergines; 2 lb tomatoes; 2 cloves of garlic; 4 oz breadcrumbs; 4 fl oz oil. Cooking time: 45 minutes.

Peel the *aubergines*, slice lengthwise about ½-inch thick, sprinkle with fine salt to extract moisture; wipe, flour and fry slowly in oil. Peel the tomatoes, deseed them, chop rather fine, cook till soft in oil, season and add crushed garlic. Add a few breadcrumbs as thickening. Arrange *aubergines* in a baking dish, put tomatoes on top, sprinkle with breadcrumbs and oil, and brown in a hot oven.

Tomates Mireille

For 6 persons: 2 lb aubergines; 2 lb tomatoes; 1 large clove of garlic; oil; parsley. Cooking time: about 20 minutes.

Peel and slice the *aubergines*, sprinkle with salt to extract moisture and wipe. Flour and *sauté* in oil. Peel, quarter and deseed the tomatoes and *sauté* them in a different pan. Season each vegetable, mix them, add a little crushed garlic and chopped parsley, toss well and serve in a vegetable dish.

⊡ à la Piemontaise

For 6 persons: ½ lb rice; 6 tomatoes; 2 oz grated cheese; breadcrumbs; oil. Cooking time of tomatoes: 6-8 minutes.

Make ***risotto*** with the rice and mix with the grated cheese. Halve and scoop out the tomatoes, fill with a mound of rice, arrange on a baking sheet, sprinkle with more grated cheese, breadcrumbs and oil and cook and brown in a hot oven.

⊡ à la Portugaise

For 6 persons: 3 lb tomatoes; 2 shallots; 2 cloves of garlic; oil; a walnut-size piece of meat glaze. Cooking time: about 15 minutes.

Quarter the tomatoes with or without peeling them, deseed and *sauté* in a frying pan in hot oil on a hot fire. When cooked add chopped shallots and crushed garlic, season with salt and pepper, add the meat glaze and simmer slowly for another five minutes. Serve sprinkled with chopped parsley.

Topinambours * *Jerusalem Artichokes*

Jerusalem artichokes should be very well washed in several waters, before being cooked. They may be cooked with their skins on or they may be scraped or peeled very thinly and put at once into water which has been acidulated with a little vinegar. This prevents them from blackening. Peel carefully, blanch briefly, simmer carefully in butter and season. The larger roots can be sliced, blanched, dipped in batter and deep fried; they can be served in Cream sauce, *puréed* or sliced, boiled and made into salad.

FOREIGN SPECIALITIES

Legumi alla Mediterranea * *Mediterranean Vegetable Dish*

For 10 persons: 4 aubergines; 4 small marrows; 8 tomatoes; 2 oz cooked rice or risotto; ¼ lb cooked peas; ¼ pint oil. Cooking time: 20 minutes.

Cut four tomatoes into thick slices. Cut the other tomatoes in halves, and empty. Mix the rice, peas and a few breadcrumbs together. Chop all together finely. Fill into tomato halves. Cut deep incisions along the *aubergines* and marrows and insert the slices of tomatoes. Arrange the *aubergines* and marrows on separate oiled dishes and sprinkle with oil and seasoning, cook the *aubergines* in a 375° F or Gas Mark 5 oven for 20 minutes, the marrows for 10 minutes, and the tomatoes for 5 minutes. Dress alternately upon a long oval porcelain dish and garnish with the tomatoes. (*See illustration p.* 631).

Melanzane Carlton * *Eggplant Carlton*

For 10 persons: 10 *medium-sized aubergines;* 6 *oz gruyère cut into small dice;* 2 *tomatoes, roughly concasséd;* ½ *pint oil.*

Cut the *aubergines* in half lengthwise, remove and chop the flesh, season with salt and pepper, and mix with the cheese and tomatoes, fill back into the shells, place on an oiled dish, sprinkle with oil and cook in a hot oven, 425° F or Gas Mark 7. (*See illustration p.* 630). (*Italy*)

▣ Ripiene alla Siciliana * *Eggplant Sicilian*

For 10 *persons: aubergines, each weighing about* 6-8 *oz;* 1 *medium onion;* 6 *large concasséd tomatoes;* 3 *oz pine kernels;* 3 *oz grated Parmesan;* ½ *pint of oil.* Cooking time: 30 minutes.

Cut the *aubergines* into halves lengthwise, cut round the edges with a sharp knife, criss-cross the flesh, place on an oiled dish, sprinkle with oil and cook in a fast oven, or otherwise shallow fry in oil, then remove the flesh from the skins and chop coarsely. Stew the chopped onion in a little oil, add the tomatoes and cook. Mix in the *aubergine* flesh, simmer together for 2 minutes, mix in the pine kernels and fill the skins. Arrange in a porcelain dish, sprinkle with the cheese, and gratinate in a very hot oven, 450° F or Gas Mark 8. (*Italy*)

▣ Ripiene alla Toscana * *Eggplant Tuscan*

For 10 *persons:* 10 *medium-sized aubergines;* 2 *concasséd tomatoes;* 1 *chopped onion;* 6 *oz of mozarella or soft curd cheese;* ½ *pint of oil; salt and pepper.* Cooking time: about 20 minutes.

Cut the *aubergines* into halves lengthwise and remove flesh. Reserve 10 skins. Divide the flesh into two halves. Chop one half and mix with the tomato, a few breadcrumbs, salt and pepper and fill into the ten skins; arrange a slice of the cheese upon each. Stew the onion in a little oil, add the remaining chopped flesh and fry together, then complete filling the skins with this prepared mixture, cover the surface with the rest of the cheese cut into thin slices, dress in a porcelain dish and cook in a moderate oven, 375° F or Gas Mark 4. (*See illustration p.* 630). (*Italy*)

Parmigiana di Melanzane * *Eggplant au Gratin*

For 10 *persons:* 10 *medium-sized aubergines;* ½ *pint of strong stock and* ½ *pint of Tomato sauce blended together;* ¼ *lb of gruyère;* ¼ *lb grated Parmesan;* 2 *oz butter; a little crumbled basil.* Cooking time: 30 minutes.

Peel and cut the *aubergines* into halves lengthwise, dress 10 halves in a buttered porcelain dish and cover with thin slices of *gruyère*, arrange a second layer of *aubergines* on top. Cut the rest of the *gruyère* into dice, mix with the sauce, season, add the basil and pour over the vegetables. Sprinkle with the Parmesan, place in a water-bath and cook in a warm oven until tender, remove and gratinate under the grill. (*Italy*)

Zucchine Ripiene alla Milanese * *Milan Courgettes*

For 10 persons: 5 small marrows, each weighing about ½ lb; 1 chopped onion; 2 oz butter; ¾ pint Béchamel; 6 oz pounded and coarsely-sieved bitter almond macaroons; 2 oz grated Parmesan.

Cut the marrows into two, lengthwise, remove seeds and cook in salted water for about 6 minutes, refresh in cold running water. Drain, dry and remove the interior flesh and chop. Fry the onion in butter, add the chopped flesh, simmer together for 3 minutes, add the *Béchamel*, simmer, then mix in the macaroon powder. Blend well and allow to cool. Place this preparation in a piping bag with a star tube and pipe into the marrow shells, sprinkle with Parmesan and melted butter and gratinate in a very hot oven, 475° F or Gas Mark 9. (*See illustration p.* 632). (*Italy*)

Potatoes

POMMES DE TERRE * *POTATOES*

There are countless ways of preparing potatoes, and it is no doubt the most common and popular of all vegetables. Allow about ½ lb potatoes per person. (*See illustration p.* 636).

⊡ Allumettes * *Matchstick*

For 5 persons: 2 lb potatoes. Cooking time: 6-7 minutes.

Fry like Straw potatoes, but do not cut as finely—about the size of a match.

⊡ Anna

For 6 persons: 2½ lb potatoes; 6 oz butter. Cooking time: 40-45 minutes.

Cut out cylinders of potato from peeled potatoes with a large apple corer and slice them very thinly and evenly. Dry slices well, salt and pepper, and place in a round well-buttered tin or Anna mould. Arrange bottom layer decoratively with the slices overlapping, then fill evenly with layers of potato slices until the mould is well filled. Pour slightly browned butter over the top and bake in a hot oven like a cake. When the potatoes are done, press them down lightly and turn out carefully on a round dish. Before serving glaze lightly by brushing with butter. The potato slices can also be placed in a smaller *sauteuse*. They turn out particularly well and evenly if the mould or *sauteuse* is placed inside a second dish filled with hot fat before being put in the oven.

⊡ à la Badoise

For 5-6 persons: 2 lb potatoes; 2 eggs; 2 oz butter; 2 oz grated cheese. Cooking time: about 20 minutes.

Peel, boil and thoroughly drain potatoes, pass through a sieve and mix with butter, 2 egg yolks and grated cheese; season well. Finally gently fold in the stiffly beaten egg white and place the potatoes in a mound in a buttered baking dish. Using a forcing bag and fluted nozzle use some potato that has been kept back to decorate attractively and bake in the oven at moderate heat like a *soufflé*.

⊡ Boulangère

For 6 persons: 2½ lb potatoes; ½ lb onions; good fat or lard; 2 pints bouillon. Cooking time: 35-40 minutes.

Cut peeled potatoes in thick round slices, mix with sliced onions, season and put in well-greased baking dish. Cover with *bouillon* and cook in hot oven till the *bouillon* has evaporated and the potatoes start to roast. Usually potatoes are put round mutton for roasting with *bouillon*. The potatoes and onions can simply be quartered.

Pommes de Terre Château

For 5 persons: 2 lb potatoes; 3 oz butter; chopped parsley. Cooking time: 20-30 minutes.

Cut peeled potatoes into the shape of large olives or cloves of garlic, put on in cold water, bring to the boil, cool immediately in cold water and dry thoroughly. Put them in hot butter in a *sauté* pan, salt lightly and bake them a nice colour in the oven, tossing them from time to time. Sprinkle with chopped parsley when serving.

◘ Chips * *Game Chips*

5½-6 *oz per person.* Cooking time: 4-5 minutes.

Trim peeled potatoes in shape of a cork or cut them out with a large apple corer. Cut into very thin rounds with a special slicer, wash and dry them on a cloth. Cook them, not too many at a time, in hot fat, using a frying basket shaking them all the time. When they are a golden brown and crisp, drain, salt well and serve them on a napkin, or as a garnish for roast fowl or game birds.

◘ en Couronne * *Potato Crowns*

For 6 persons: 1½ lb Duchess potato mixture; ¾ lb Choux pastry. Cooking time: 5-6 minutes.

Blend the Duchess potato mixture with the *Choux* pastry and season according to taste. Using a Savoy bag with a star pipe, arrange the mixture on buttered greaseproof paper in the shape of small rings. Dip them in hot frying fat, holding the paper on one side until all the rings have slipped off into the fat. When golden brown, remove and drain. (*See Illustrated Culinary Techniques.*)

◘ à la Crème * *Creamed Potatoes*

For 6 persons: 2½ lb potatoes; ¾ pint cream; 1 oz butter. Cooking time: about 30 minutes.

Boil potatoes in their jackets, peel, slice thinly and put in a *sauté* pan. Season with salt, pepper and nutmeg, add butter and cream. Cook slowly till thick, add butter and pour on a little more cream when serving.

◘ Dauphine

For 6 persons: 1½ lb potatoes; 2 oz butter; 3 egg yolks; ½ lb Choux pastry; nutmeg. Cooking time: 6 minutes.

Prepare a mixture as for *pommes Duchesse* and blend with *Choux* pastry, made without sugar. Season with grated nutmeg. Shape into small balls, or fill the mixture into a piping bag with a large plain tube, and drop it into not too hot fat, cutting it off with a knife into pieces about the length of a little finger. Increase the heat gradually, until the potatoes are a golden brown. Dry well and season with fine salt.

Pommes de Terre Duchesse * *Duchess Potatoes*

For 6-8 persons: 2½ lb potatoes; ¼ lb butter; 4 egg yolks. Cooking time: 30 minutes.

Cook the peeled potatoes in salted water as for *purée*. When they are cooked, dry the potatoes thoroughly and pass them through a sieve. Dry the *purée* with the butter, season and add the egg yolks. Remove from the heat. The potatoes will be stiff and easy to handle. Sprinkle flour on a pastry board or on the table, and shape the *purée* into flat round cakes, *brioches*, or buns. Place them on a buttered baking sheet, brush with egg, and bake in a hot oven. If you are decorating the edges of a baking dish, keep the mixture softer. Use three eggs and a few drops of milk. Shape the rosettes, etc., with a piping bag and a fluted tube.

▣ Fondantes

For 5 persons: 2 lb potatoes; 6 oz butter; ½ pint light bouillon. Cooking time: about 30 minutes.

Shape potatoes as for Château potatoes, but bigger, and blanch for 5 minutes. Drain, dry thoroughly and put in a *sauté* pan in hot butter. Salt lightly, cover and roast till done, but do not let them get too brown. Cook the potatoes over moderate heat shaking from time to time so that they will brown evenly. As soon as they are done add the *bouillon*, leave to stand and do not serve until the potatoes have absorbed both butter and *bouillon*. The addition of the *bouillon* makes them softer.

▣ au Four * *Baked*

2 medium-sized potatoes per person. Cooking time: 30-35 minutes.

Choose good floury potatoes of equal size. Wash and bake them in their jackets on a baking sheet covered with coarse salt. Cut off the top lengthwise, and scoop out the pulp taking care not to damage the skin. Crush the pulp with a fork, mix it with a small piece of butter, and season with salt and pepper. Replace the lid on top and serve very hot. The potatoes may also be opened by a small cut in the middle of the top, pressed open by hand and a small piece of butter put in the opening.

▣ Frites dites Pont-Neuf * *French Fried or Pont-Neuf*

6 oz per person. Cooking time: 7-8 minutes.

Peel large potatoes and trim the sides as for *Pommes Frites*. Cut them into even, oblong strips barely ½-inch thick. Wash and dry well. Put them in hot, but not too hot fat, and cook them for 5-6 minutes. They will now be cooked but still colourless. This is called blanching. Take them out of the fat and drain. Just before serving, plunge them into very hot fat, until crisp and a golden brown. It is best to use a frying basket so that they may be taken out of the fat quickly. Spread them on a cloth to drain. Salt well. Serve as a garnish for a roast or grilled meat.

▣ Gaufrettes * *Waffles*

6 oz peeled potatoes per person. Cooking time: 5-6 minutes.

Trim the potatoes, giving them either a square or cylindrical shape. Cut them into thin wafers with a special knife, and wash them thoroughly in running water. Drain and dry on a cloth. Fry a few at a time in very hot fat. It is best to use a frying basket, and to shake it all the time, to prevent the wafers from sticking together and the fat from overflowing. Drain well in the basket and dry on a clean cloth. Salt well and serve.

Pommes de Terre à la Hongroise

For 3-4 persons: 1 *lb potatoes;* ¼ *lb onions;* ½ *pint bouillon;* 2 *oz butter;* 2 *tablespoons tomato purée; paprika.* Cooking time: 20 minutes.

Slice the onions and fry golden brown. Add the peeled, sliced potatoes and the tomato *purée*, just cover with *bouillon*, add a little salt and plenty of paprika, cover and cook in a moderate oven, 375° F or Gas Mark 4-5, till done. Serve sprinkled with chopped parsley.

▣ au Lard * *with Bacon*

For 6 persons: 2½ *lb potatoes;* 6 *oz lean bacon;* 18 *small onions;* ¾ *oz flour;* 2 *oz butter;* 1 *tablespoon tomato purée;* ½ *pint bouillon.* Cooking time: 35-40 minutes.

Fry onions pale brown in butter, add diced bacon and when this is browned sprinkle with flour and brown this too. Add *bouillon* and tomato *purée* and cook for 20 minutes. Add small new potatoes or old ones shaped like Château potatoes, cook together till done and serve sprinkled with chopped parsley.

▣ à la Lyonnaise

For 6 persons: 2½ *lb potatoes;* ½ *lb onions; about* ¼ *lb butter; parsley.* Cooking time: 30-40 minutes.

Boil potatoes in their jackets, peel, slice and fry an even brown in the frying pan in hot butter. Slice onions thinly and fry golden brown at the same time in another pan. Mix the two carefully, season, fry together for a few minutes and serve sprinkled with parsley.

▣ Macaire

For 5 persons: 2 *lb potatoes;* 6 *oz butter.* Cooking time in oven: 40-50 minutes.

Choose nice large potatoes, wash and bake in the oven in their jackets. When done cut them open, scoop out the flesh with a spoon, crush coarsely with a fork mixing in a piece of butter at the same time and season with salt and pepper. Heat butter in a frying pan, put in potato mixture evenly, and press spreading it down a little. First brown one side like a pancake and then turn and brown the other side. Serve whole or cut in quarters. The potatoes can also be fried in small *crêpe* pans.

▣ Maître d'Hôtel

For 6 persons: 2½ *lb potatoes;* 1 *pint milk; salt and pepper;* 1 *oz butter.* Cooking time: 30 minutes.

Boil potatoes in their jackets. Peel and slice into a *sauté* pan. Cover with boiling milk and season. Reduce the milk until it is a thick coating residue. Serve with chopped parsley sprinkled over.

▣ Marie

For 6 persons: 2½ *lb potatoes;* ¾ *pint bouillon;* ¼ *pint milk.* Cooking time: 15-20 minutes.

Peel, slice and cook in *bouillon* with butter. When cooked, add boiling milk.

Pommes de Terre Mont d'Or

For 5 persons: 2 lb potatoes; 3 oz butter; 3 eggs; ¼ lb gruyère cheese. Cooking time: about 25 minutes.

Quarter the peeled potatoes, boil in salt water, drain well and rub through a sieve. Season with salt, pepper and nutmeg, mix with beaten eggs, butter and 3 ounces cheese cut in small thin slices and fill into a buttered baking dish in an irregular pile like a mountain. Sprinkle with grated cheese and brown in a hot oven, 400° F or Gas Mark 6.

▣ Ninon

For 6 persons: 2 lb Duchess potatoes; 2 tablespoons thick tomato purée; ¼ lb boiled ham; 1 egg. Baking time: 5-6 minutes.

Blend the potato mixture with tomato *purée* and finely chopped ham. Shape into small oval cakes, place on a greased baking sheet, brush with egg and bake golden brown in a hot oven, 425° F or Gas Mark 7.

▣ Noisette * *Nut-shaped*

For 6 persons: 2½ lb potatoes shaped with a special round spoon; ½ lb butter. Cooking time: 20 minutes.

Blanch the potatoes for 2 minutes, drain and season. Cook in butter until they are golden brown and soft.

▣ à la Normande

For 3-4 persons: 1 lb peeled raw potatoes; the white of 2 leeks; 1 medium-sized onion; ¼ lb lean bacon; ¼ pint cream; 2 oz butter; bouillon. Cooking time: 25-30 minutes.

Brown the sliced onions and leeks lightly in butter, add the blanched, diced bacon and brown this too. Add the thinly sliced potatoes, cover with *bouillon* or if necessary water, season and boil briskly till done. Add the cream at the last moment and serve covered with chopped parsley.

▣ Pailles * *Straw Potatoes*

6 oz peeled potatoes per person. Cooking time: 4-5 minutes.

Cut the potatoes into very thin strips (*julienne*). Wash and dry well. Cook them like Waffle potatoes. Because potatoes always retain moisture, which will make the fat rise and overflow, use a frying basket so that they may be quickly removed. Keep them very crisp, dry well, and salt before serving.

▣ à la Paysanne

For 6-8 persons: 2½ lb peeled potatoes; ½ lb lean bacon cut into small strips (lardons); 12 small onions; 1½ pints bouillon; 1 oz butter; 1 tablespoon flour; chopped parsley. Cooking time: 30 minutes.

Brown the onions and lardons in butter. Sprinkle with flour and allow to brown lightly. Moisten with *bouillon*, mix well, and add the potatoes cut into quarters or eighths, according to size. Season, cover and cook slowly until the potatoes are ready. Serve with chopped parsley sprinkled on top.

Pommes de Terre Persillées * *Parsley Potatoes*

For 5 persons: 2 lb potatoes; 2 oz butter; ½ pint bouillon; chopped parsley. Cooking time: about 20 minutes.

Shape potatoes as for Château potatoes, put in a *sauté* pan in hot butter, brown slightly, season with salt and pepper and half cover with *bouillon.* Add chopped parsley, cover with buttered paper and cook in the oven. Serve sprinkled with freshly-chopped parsley which may be boiled, drained and buttered.

▣ Pont-Neuf

These are simply chips. Cut almost double the thickness of *Pommes Frites*, they were formerly grooved on one side to look like a bridge.

▣ à la Savoyarde

For 6 persons: 2½ lb potatoes; 6 oz onions; ¼ lb gruyère cheese; 3 oz butter; about ½ pint bouillon. Cooking time: 35-40 minutes.

Slice the onions and sweat them in butter. Mix the raw sliced potatoes and cheese cut in small thin slices, season and place in an oval baking dish. Half cover with *bouillon* and cook and brown in a moderate oven, 375° F or Gas Mark 4-5.

▣ Soufflées

For 4 persons: 1½ lb potatoes. Cooking time: 6-7 minutes.

Peel large potatoes, trim, and cut them evenly in slices ⅛-inch thick. Dry the slices and blanch them in not too hot fat for 4-5 minutes, stirring constantly and keeping temperature even. Take them out of the fat as soon as they rise to the surface and begin to puff up. Drain. Just before serving, dip them once more into very hot fat, using a frying basket, so that they will puff up again and become crisp and dry. Drain and salt well. Serve them piled up on a napkin.

NOTE: *Soufflé* potatoes may be blanched early in the morning. Placed in very hot fat, they will puff up again several hours later. The best fat for the frying of *soufflé* potatoes is beef suet. Dutch potatoes with yellow flesh and the Magnum Bonum variety are the best for *soufflé* potatoes. New potatoes should not be used for *soufflé* or French Fried potatoes before the month of September.

▣ Suzette

For 6 persons: 3 lb potatoes; 2 oz butter; 2 tablespoons cream; 2 egg yolks. Cooking time: 40-50 minutes.

Peel the potatoes, trim each one the size and shape of an egg. Cut a small piece off one end, that they may stand up. Place on a tray and bake in the oven. When cooked, scoop out inside carefully, leaving a shell of potato. With a fork mash the pulp and add butter, cream and egg yolks. Mix well and season. Fill potato shells with this mixture. Brush with melted butter and put back in a hot oven, 425° F or Gas Mark 7, to glaze.

Pommes de Terre à la Vapeur * *Steamed, New Potatoes*

This method requires a steamer. Use small potatoes if possible, put them in the upper, perforated part, season lightly with salt, cover with a damp cloth, put on the lid and put upper part of pan on the lower after half filling it with water. For large kitchens there are special steam ovens with drawers in which large quantities of potatoes can be steamed at a time. Steaming is the best way of preparing plain potatoes.

▣ Voisin

For 6 persons: 2½ lb potatoes; 3 oz grated cheese; ½ lb butter. Cooking time: 35-40 minutes.

Prepare in the same way as Anna potatoes, but with grated cheese between the various layers.

▣ Yvette

For 3 persons: 1 lb potatoes; 6 oz butter. Cooking time: 25-30 minutes.

Cut the raw, peeled potatoes in *julienne*, wash thoroughly, drain well and put in a frying pan in which the butter has been made very hot. Season with salt and pepper, toss the potatoes in butter and fry first on one side and then on the other like a pancake. When one side is golden brown press down slightly before turning. Serve like a pancake. Brush with melted butter before serving.

LES CROQUETTES * *POTATO CROQUETTES*

For 4-5 persons: 2 lb potatoes; 2 oz butter; 3 egg yolks; 1 egg white; breadcrumbs. Cooking time: 3-4 minutes.

Prepare a mixture as for *Pommes Duchesse* and allow to cool. Divide into pieces of about two ounces. Sprinkle flour on a pastry board, and shape the pieces into balls, pears or corks. Roll in beaten egg and then in breadcrumbs. Fry in hot deep fat just before serving.

▣ aux Amandes * *with Almond*

Mixture as for Potato Croquettes: thinly sliced almonds. Cooking time: 3-4 minutes.

Use the same mixture as for *Pommes Duchesse* and shape into small balls. Dip into beaten egg and coat with almonds, cut into very thin shavings. Fry in very hot deep fat just before serving. Drain and salt well.

▣ aux Raisins * *with Currants*

For 4-5 persons: 1¾ lb potatoes; 4 egg yolks; 2 oz butter; 2 oz currants; 6 oz chopped almonds; 1 egg. Cooking time: 2-3 minutes.

Prepare potato mixture as for ordinary Potato *Croquettes* and mix in the soaked and well-dried currants. Make into round, slightly flattened cakes, dip in beaten eggs and chopped almonds and fry in deep fat. These *croquettes* are served mainly with game.

Gnocchi de Pommes de Terre * *Boiled Potato Dumplings*

For 4 *persons:* 1½ *lb potatoes;* 1 *oz butter;* 3 *oz flour;* 6 *oz grated gruyère cheese;* 2 *eggs.* Cooking time of dumplings: 10-12 minutes.

Boil and drain the potatoes and rub them through a sieve. Mix with a nut of butter, the eggs, flour and 2 ounces grated cheese and make into balls the size of a large hazelnut on a floured table. Flatten them slightly and poach at simmering temperature in salt water. Drain well and place in a buttered baking dish with grated cheese between the layers, sprinkle the top with grated cheese and melted butter and brown in a hot oven, 425° F or Gas Mark 7.

Gratin Dauphinois

For 6 *persons:* 2½ *lb potatoes;* 1 *egg;* 1 *oz butter;* ½ *pint milk;* 3 *oz gruyère cheese; garlic.* Cooking time: 40-50 minutes.

Rub a baking dish generously with garlic, butter it thickly and fill with raw, peeled potatoes cut in thin round slices, seasoned with salt, pepper and nutmeg. Beat the egg, mix with cold milk, pour over potatoes so that they are fully covered and bake in a moderate oven. Cut cheese in small thin slices and mix with potatoes; it can, however, be omitted.

Knepfes au Fromage * *Potato Dumplings with Cheese*

For 4 *persons:* 1½ *lb potatoes;* 1 *egg;* 2 *oz flour;* 2 *oz grated cheese.* Cooking time: 10-12 minutes.

Boil the potatoes until cooked, drain well and rub through a sieve. Mix with the flour and beaten egg, season and shape into small balls on a floured table. Poach in salt water and drain well. After draining fry the balls golden brown in butter and serve sprinkled with grated cheese.

Nids de Pommes Pailles * *Potato Nests*

These are made with the aid of two frying baskets which are hinged together. Dip baskets in deep fat, then line the larger basket evenly with raw Straw potatoes, press down smaller basket and put in hot fat to fry. As soon as the nest is brown and crisp remove the baskets from fat and carefully take out the nest.

Purée de Pommes Mousseline * *Mashed Potatoes*

For 3-4 *persons:* 1½ *lb potatoes;* 3 *oz butter; about* 1 *pint milk.*

Cut the peeled potatoes in quarters and cook in salted water. Drain and dry well. Pass through a wire sieve. Mix over low heat with the butter, and stir in hot milk, a little at a time. When the *purée* is soft enough, whip with a whisk to make it light and foamy. Serve immediately.

Soufflé de Pommes de Terre * *Potato Soufflé*

For 3 *persons:* ¾ *lb potatoes;* 1 *oz butter;* 4-5 *tablespoons cream;* 3 *eggs.* Cooking time: 20-25 minutes.

Peel, boil, drain, and *purée* the potatoes and dry with the butter in a casserole. Season with salt and pepper and stir to a thick *purée* with the cream. Remove from heat, combine with 3 egg yolks and then gently fold in the stiffly beaten egg whites. Place in a buttered *soufflé* dish, put in a moderate oven, 375° F or Gas Mark 5, and bake like any other *soufflé.*

Subrics de Pommes de Terre * *Potato Pancakes*

For 6 persons: 2 lb potatoes; 3 oz flour; 1 clove of garlic; 2 eggs; chopped parsley; 3 oz butter. Cooking time: 7-8 minutes.

Grate the potatoes, squeeze out moisture in a cloth and mix this pulp with flour, crushed garlic, 2 eggs and chopped parsley; season with salt and pepper. Make butter, oil or lard very hot in a frying pan, put in spoonfuls of the mixture, fry on both sides like small pancakes and serve very hot.

FOREIGN SPECIALITIES

Patate Ripiene al Forno * *Baked, Stuffed Potatoes*

For 10 persons: 10 potatoes each weighing about 5 oz; ¼ pint cream; ¼ pint milk; 2 oz grated Parmesan; 2 oz butter. Cooking time: approx. 50 minutes.

Scrub and wash the potatoes first then cook in their jackets till almost done. Remove the caps from the potatoes lengthwise, empty them leaving a shell of about ¼-inch thick, season with coarse salt and put in a moderate oven. In the meantime, mince the potato flesh, mix in the cream, milk and a little salt, fill back into the potato shells, sprinkle with the cheese and butter and return to oven to finish cooking and gratinating. (*See illustration p.* 636).

⊡ Roesti * *Sauté*

Cook potatoes in their jackets, peel and cut into thin slices, fry in butter in an omelette pan, cover with a lid and continue cooking until the bottom side is golden. Turn out upon the lid, slide back into the pan and colour the other side. Arrange on a round dish. It is usual to serve these with *escalopes of veal* in cream.

Mushrooms

Mushrooms are a delicious vegetable and a fine adjunct to many meat and fish dishes. There are several hundred edible varieties but these are known only to experts. Some mushrooms are inedible because they are bitter but only very few are really poisonous. The vast majority of fungi are edible, but without extensive knowledge of the different varieties it is better to leave them alone. Various tests with onions, silver spoons and other objects are supposed to reveal the presence of poison by discolouring in the pot. Do not believe it. Only experts know the difference between edible and poisonous fungi.

All mushrooms that are not absolutely fresh should be rejected. When they are black, sticky or worm eaten, do not hesitate to throw them away. Use only cultivated mushrooms and those that have been rigorously controlled.

CÈPES * *BOLETUS*

A genus of fungi which grows wild especially under oak, chestnut and beech trees and is recognised by its bronze coloured cap, white underparts, and thick white stem. It may be substituted for mushrooms but should be avoided by people with weak digestion.

▣ à la Bordelaise

¼ lb for each person; olive oil; chopped shallots; butter; breadcrumbs; chopped parsley. Cooking time: 10-15 minutes.

Trim the stem, wash well and cut the boletus into rather thick slices. For each person reserve 1 ounce of stem and chop coarsely. *Sauté* the boletus in a frying pan in very hot oil and butter until they are browned. Then add the chopped shallots, chopped stems, salt and pepper and continue sautéing for a few minutes longer. Then add a few breadcrumbs to absorb the superfluous oil and serve in a vegetable dish sprinkled with chopped parsley.

▣ à la Provençale

Cook in the same way as for *à la Bordelaise* but replace shallots by crushed garlic and fry in oil only. Finish with a squeeze of lemon.

▣ Sautés à l'Italienne

For 6 persons: 3½ lb cèpes (boletus edulis); 6 cloves of garlic; ½ pint oil (preferably olive oil); ¼ lb parsley. Cooking time: about 8 minutes.

Skin the *cèpes*, wash quickly in running water and cut them into very thin slices. Meanwhile, fry 5 cloves of garlic in the oil until they are first transparent and then golden coloured, after which they should be discarded. *Sauté* the *cèpes* in this oil for 2 minutes. Drain them and then repeat the process with fresh oil and garlic and, after replacing the garlic by some chopped parsley, cook for another 2 minutes. Sprinkle the rest of the chopped parsley on top. (*See illustration p.* 634).

CHAMPIGNONS DE COUCHE * *CULTIVATED MUSHROOMS*

Cut off the ends of the stalks, wash mushrooms thoroughly in several changes of water, drain and for ½ lb of mushrooms use the juice of half a lemon and 1 ounce of butter. Put everything in a casserole and cook briskly for 5 minutes. If they are not to be used at once, put them in a small bowl so that they are entirely covered with juice and cover with buttered paper to prevent them from becoming dark.

◻ à la Crème * *in Cream Sauce*

For 6 persons: 3 lb very small cultivated button mushrooms; 2 oz butter; ½ pint sauce Béchamel; ½ pint thick cream; lemon juice. Cooking time: 10-12 minutes.

Shorten the stems, but do not peel the mushrooms. Wash and rub them with lemon juice and salt, and wash them again. Drain well. Simmer them for a few minutes in a *sautoir*, with butter, with the lid on and seasoned with salt and pepper. Then cover with half *sauce Béchamel* and half cream, and cook them with the lid off until they are done. At the last minute, add a few drops of lemon juice.

◻ Farcis * *Stuffed*

For 6 persons: 12 very large cultivated mushrooms; ¾ lb duxelles; breadcrumbs; oil. Cooking time: 10-12 minutes.

Wash very large mushroom caps without peeling them and hollow them out a little. The stems may be used for preparing the *duxelles.* Salt lightly and stuff them with *duxelles.* Sprinkle with breadcrumbs, drop a little oil on top, and cook in a very hot oven, 450° F or Gas Mark 8, until well browned on top.

◻ Grillés * *Grilled*

For 6 persons: 12 very large cultivated mushrooms; 3 tablespoons oil; 3 oz Escargot or Maître d'Hôtel butter. Cooking time: 10-12 minutes.

Separate the stalks from the heads (they may be used for making *duxelles*), hollow out, but do not peel. Sprinkle with oil and grill in a hot oven. Season with salt, and stuff either with *Escargot* or *Maître d'Hôtel* butter and serve at once.

◻ au Porto * *in Port Wine Sauce*

For 6 persons: 3½ lb small mushroom caps; ½ pint Port wine; 2 oz butter; ½ pint cream. Cooking time: 12-15 minutes.

Brown the mushrooms in butter. Add the Port and seasoning and reduce the liquor by three-quarters of its original quantity. Mix in the cream and simmer until the mushrooms are completely cooked.

Croquettes de Champignons * *Mushroom Croquettes*

For 6 persons: 1½ lb mushroom purée; ½ pint very thick sauce Béchamel; 2 oz butter; 3 egg yolks; 2 eggs; flour; white breadcrumbs. Cooking time: 2-3 minutes.

Mix the *purée* with the butter and the juice of half a lemon and reduce until all excess liquid has evaporated. Blend with the *sauce Béchamel* over heat but do not allow to boil, then, taking the mixture off the heat, stir in the egg yolks. Leave to cool down completely. Divide the mass into pieces weighing 1 ounce and roll these on a floured table into small sausages. Coat with egg and breadcrumbs and fry in very hot fat. These *croquettes* are used principally as a garnish.

Purée de Champignons * *Mushroom Purée*

For 6 persons: 2½ *lb large white cultivated mushrooms;* 2 *oz butter; lemon juice;* ½ *pint very thick Béchamel.* Cooking time: 8-10 minutes.

Clean, thoroughly wash and drain the mushrooms, pass them quickly through a well-galvanised metal sieve and cook them in hot butter with the juice of half a lemon in a *sauté* pan, stirring constantly, until the moisture has evaporated completely. Season with salt and pepper, bind with very thick *Béchamel* and do not bring to the boil again. Use the mushroom *purée* as a garnish, to fill tartlets, *barquettes,* artichoke bottoms, etc.

Soufflé de Champignons * *Mushroom Soufflé*

For 6 persons: 1 *lb mushroom purée;* ¼ *pint sauce Béchamel;* 2 *oz butter;* 3 *eggs.* Cooking time: 18-20 minutes.

Mix the *purée* with the butter and the juice of a lemon and reduce until all the excess liquid has evaporated. Blend in the *sauce Béchamel* and season. Remove from heat, stir in the egg yolks and then fold in the stiffly whisked egg whites. Pour the mixture into a buttered *soufflé* dish and bake in a hot oven, 425° F or Gas Mark 7.

Girolles or Chanterelles

These edible fungi are prepared with butter, cream or *à la Provençale,* etc.

Morilles * *Morels*

½ *lb per person; butter; parsley.* Cooking time: 10-15 minutes.

Trim the stems and wash the morels several times in plenty of salt water, to remove earth and grit sticking to them. Melt a little butter in a large *sautoir* and simmer the morels in butter until they are cooked in their own juice. Drain well and *sauté* in butter until lightly browned. Season with salt and pepper and serve in a vegetable dish sprinkled with chopped parsley. The liquid may be used for sauces and gravies. The morels may also be simmered until the liquid has evaporated completely and then sautéed in butter.

⊡ à la Crème * *in Cream Sauce*

Cook morels till all moisture has evaporated and then boil up briefly with a little very creamy *Béchamel* and a few spoons of cream.

⊡ aux Fines Herbes * *with Fine Herbs*

For 6 persons: 2½ *lb morels;* 3 *oz butter; chopped parsley.* Cooking time: about 15 minutes.

Cut morels in half or quarter, according to size, first cutting off the end of the stalk. Wash very thoroughly, as they contain a lot of sand, and drain well. Put in a casserole with a nut of butter, season with salt and pepper and boil briskly until they are done and all the moisture has evaporated. Heat butter in a frying pan, *sauté* the morels in it with chopped parsley and serve at once. They make a very good garnish for meat and poultry.

Morilles à la Sévillane

For 4-5 persons: 2 lb cooked morels; ¼ raw diced ham; 2 *oz butter; ¼ pint dry sherry; ¾ pint cream.* Cooking time: 8-10 minutes.

Lightly brown the ham in the butter. Add the morels and, after seasoning, *sauté* them together with the ham. Pour in the sherry and reduce the liquor to three-quarters of its original quantity. Stir in the cream and simmer until the sauce is smoothly blended.

⊡ à la Villeneuve

For 4-5 persons: 1½ *lb cooked quartered morels:* 1 *oz butter; ½ pint sauce Béchamel*; ½ *pint cream; 6 bouchée cases.* Cooking time: 6-8 minutes.

Proceed in the same way as for Morels in Cream sauce. Fill the *bouchée* cases with the morels and serve very hot.

LES TRUFFES * *TRUFFLES*

Truffles are used principally as a garnish and for decorative purposes. It is exceptional for them to be served as vegetables. Then, the most simple preparation is indicated because of their own inimitable flavour and aroma.

⊡ en Serviette au Porto * *in a Napkin with Port Wine*

Although truffles are not an everyday pleasure, everybody should know the best way of cooking them. Here is one of the best recipes: Soak 1 pound of truffles, brush well in order to remove all soil, wash throughly and drain. Make a fine *mirepoix* of onion, carrot and lean bacon, toss it well in butter, add unpeeled truffles and pour on ½ pint of Port, Madeira or champagne. Season with salt and pepper, cover and if possible cook in a warm oven. Remove truffles, drain them and arrange them on a napkin. Boil the stock down to a quarter, add a nut of meat glaze, remove from heat and beat up 2 ounces of butter and serve this sauce separately.

Pasta and Cereals

Under this heading we are concerned with the various bland wheat flour preparations known collectively as pastas and specifically as noodles, macaroni, *spaghetti* and *lasagne* and the like. We have also included a small section at the end of this chapter, listing a few unusual and delicious cereal preparations. Although rice is a completely distinct and separate cereal product differing in taste, appearance, method of preparation and nutritional value, it is included in this section because it performs a similar role to pasta in the menu. As part of our staple diet, rice is appreciated as a main dish in itself—like pasta—and it, too, combines well with fish, meat, poultry and eggs.

In this chapter you will find the basic recipes for pasta and rice dishes served as accompaniments and garnishes. There are various recipes for individual rice and pasta dishes to be found in the chapter on *Entrées*, especially among the Foreign Specialities section. Pastas may be served in many ways, either accompanied by savoury sauces or stuffed with meat fillings and they should be served as soon as they are cooked. Grated dry cheese such as Parmesan and *gruyère*, should be served at the same time.

PÂTE * *PASTA DOUGH*

The following are a selection of basic dough mixtures from which will be made the desired pasta shapes.

Pâte à Cannelloni et à Lasagne * *Cannelloni and Lasagne Dough*

For 8-10 *persons:* 1¼ *lb bread flour;* 3 *eggs;* 2 *tablespoons olive oil; pinch salt;* 2 *fl oz water.*

Make a well in the flour. Mix the eggs, oil, water and salt together, pour into the well and work into a smooth dough, wrap up and rest for an hour. Cut into 4 oz pieces and roll out each piece to the thickness of a sheet of paper. Cut into squares or oblongs for *cannelloni* and into ¼-inch or ⅜-inch wide strips for *lasagne*.

Pâte à Nouilles Fraîches * *Noodle Dough*

½ lb sifted bread flour; 2 whole eggs; pinch of salt. Cooking time: 8-10 minutes in boiling salted water.

Fresh home-made noodles are better than those bought ready-made. They are very easy to make. Make a firm dough with the flour, a pinch of salt and the eggs and let it rest for at least 2 hours wrapped in a cloth. Divide into 3 pieces and roll these out as thinly as possible with a rolling pin on a floured board. Let it dry a short time, fold several times and cut in very thin long strips. If they are not to be used at once, dry completely and store in a tin with a well-fitting lid.

Pâte à Nouilles Vertes * *Green Noodles*

For 10 persons: 1½ lb bread flour; 4 eggs; 4 fl oz oil; 2 fl oz water; 1 lb spinach purée.

Knead all the ingredients together—the flour, eggs, water, oil and spinach. Mix well to form a stiff dough. Divide the dough into three equal parts and roll out one piece at a time. Roll out the pasta as finely as possible. Allow it to dry out. Cut into very thin strips of about 8-10 inches wide. Use as needed.

Pâte à Ravioli et à Tortellini * *Ravioli and Tortellini Dough*

Same dough as for *Cannelloni.* The technique of making *ravioli* is shown in the *Illustrated Culinary Techniques.*

Nouilles à l'Alsacienne

For 4 persons: ½ lb sifted bread flour; 2 eggs; 2 oz butter; pinch salt; 3 oz grated cheese. Cooking time: 8-10 minutes.

Prepare the dough and noodles as for *Nouilles Fraîches.* Reserve a few of the raw noodles and cut into fine dice, place in an omelette pan with some butter and cook with constant tossing until crisp and golden. Boil the rest of the noodles, drain, rinse in hot water, drain and fry in butter, toss in the cheese. Arrange on a serving dish and sprinkle with the golden diced noodles. These small crisp pieces of noodles give a pleasant slant to this dish.

Panier en Pâte à Nouilles * *Noodle Basket*

The attractive appearance of these baskets leads one to imagine that they are difficult to make. On the contrary, they are not only simple to produce, but, as an additional benefit, may be made several days before they are required and will usually serve several times. Cut a thick slice of stale bread about 1 inch thick, trim it to a round or oval shape. Pierce an uneven number of holes round the edge, 15, 17, 19, for example—the number to be determined by the desired size of the basket. Implant in these holes at an angle of approximately 90 degrees, even lengths of macaroni. This provides the cage for the basket. Roll out a quantity of Noodle dough into thin lengths, dust with rice flour, roll into coils and cut into narrow bands. Now weave the long strips in and out of the pieces of macaroni until the basket is complete. Prepare a plait to finish the top of the basket. It can now be eggwashed and baked in a very slow oven to dry and stop distortion. If you have a deep cauldron of fat, you can deep fry these baskets. Simpler still is to leave them in a dry room to harden. Once they are dry they can be decorated in a number of ways.

LE RIZ * *RICE*

The success of rice preparations depends essentially on the type of grain chosen in the context of the dish. Thus for *pilafs* it is better to use Patna rice, whilst for *risottas* Italian rice is preferable. It is advisable always to wash the rice thoroughly before cooking to keep the grains firm and separate. American Carolina rice is generally factory treated and is excellent for savoury dishes. The grains are boiled in an abundance of salted water and are refreshed by washing thoroughly in cold running water. Untreated Carolina rice is undoubtedly the wisest choice for the preparation of sweet rice dishes.

Rice is not always appreciated as it should be since it is only rarely cooked really well. It is often too soft and therefore soggy, so that it is attractive neither to the eye nor to the palate. In Europe nearly all the rice sold is polished. This is of lesser value than the unpolished variety because important vitamins are lost in the polishing process.

Risotto * *Savoury Rice*

For 6 persons: 1 *onion;* 3 *oz butter;* 2 *lb rice;* 2 *quarts chicken stock.* Cooking time: 30 minutes.

Chop the onion finely and stew in the butter; add the rice, cook dry until the rice becomes a definite opaque colour, add the boiling stock all at once, and simmer gently for 15-17 minutes, with an occasional stir. When cooked, remove from the heat and blend in gently the butter and grated Parmesan using a spatula. (Other recipes for *risottos* will be found in the chapter on *Entrées*.)

Riz au Blanc * *Plain White Rice*

For 6 persons: 10 *oz Carolina rice;* ¼ *lb butter.*

Boil the rice in 3 quarts salted water, drain, wash in tepid water, drain again and let dry in a serviette to drain off the excess moisture. Arrange in a mound and pour over the melted butter.

▣ à la Créole

For 6 persons: 10 *oz Carolina rice;* 5 *oz butter;* 1 *pint water.* Cooking time: 18 minutes.

Place the rice in a casserole with half the butter, add the water, season with salt, cover and cook in a warm oven, 350° F or Gas Mark 3 for approximately 18 minutes or until the grains are tender and have absorbed all the liquid. Remove the lid, add the butter in small pieces, allow to stand for a further 5 minutes and separate the grains with a fork.

▣ au Curry * *Curried Rice*

For 6 persons: 10 *oz Patna rice;* ¼ *lb butter;* 1 *oz curry powder;* 1¾ *pints white stock;* 1 *onion.* Cooking time: 18 minutes.

Lightly colour the finely chopped onion in 2 oz of the butter, add the rice and curry powder, cook gently together, add the stock, bring to the boil, cover and cook in a warm oven, 350° F or Gas Mark 3, until tender and the rice has absorbed all the liquid. Remove the lid, add the butter in small pieces, allow to stand for 5 minutes and separate the grains with a fork.

Riz au Gras * *Rice Cooked in Stock*

For 6 persons: 10 *oz Patna rice;* $1\frac{3}{4}$ *pints fatty stock;* 2 *oz butter*. Cooking time: 16-18 minutes.

Sweat the rice slightly in the hot butter, cover with the boiling stock, salt lightly and simmer until cooked.

⊡ à l'Indienne

For 6 persons: 10 *oz Patna rice.* Cooking time: 16-18 minutes.

Cook the rice in at least 3 pints of boiling salted water, drain and wash in tepid water, thoroughly drain again, spread over a napkin or clean cloth placed on a baking sheet and dry in a cool oven. Fluff up the grains with a fork; they must separate easily.

⊡ Pilaf

For 6 persons: 10 *oz Patna rice;* 1 *pint chicken stock;* 1 *onion;* 2 *oz butter.* Cooking time: 20 minutes.

Stew the finely chopped onion in the butter, but do not let it brown. Add the rice, cook together till the rice is opaque, add half the boiling stock, stir well, then add the rest of the stock. Cover with a buttered paper and lid and cook in a hot oven, 400° F or Gas Mark 6, for about 18 minutes. Remove the lid and paper, add some small pieces of butter, let it stand for 5 minutes and separate the grains with a fork.

⊡ à la Portugaise

For 6 persons: 10 *oz Patna rice;* 1 *onion;* 2 *oz butter;* $\frac{1}{2}$ *lb tomatoes concassé;* 2 *red capsicums;* $\frac{1}{4}$ *lb butter;* 1 *pint stock.* Cooking time: 18 minutes.

Skin, deseed and cut the capsicums into fine dice. Chop the onions finely and stew in the butter, add the rice, stew until opaque, add the tomatoes, capsicums and half the stock. Stir to the boil, add the rest of the stock, cover with a buttered paper lid, cook in a hot oven, 400° F or Gas Mark 6. Remove lid and paper, add the rest of the butter in small pieces, let rest and separate the grains with a fork.

LES SEMOULES ET MAIS * *VARIOUS CEREAL DISHES*

Le Couscous

For 5 persons: $\frac{3}{4}$ *lb coarse wheat semolina;* 1 *pint water to swell the semolina;* 2 *quarts water to provide steam to cook Couscous.*

Put the semolina in a wide mouthed basin. Lightly salt the pint of water, add a little to the semolina and rub through the hands to form small grains. Continue in this manner until the whole pint of water has been absorbed. The appearance is that of small shot.

Pour this semolina into a special strainer (*keskes*), fit it tightly on a tall stewpan containing the 2 quarts of water, cover with a tight fitting lid, bring to the boil, and allow to cook in the steam until the semolina is cooked and swollen. If not using a *keskes*, it is necessary to make sure that the holes in the strainer are small enough to prevent the small grains of semolina from falling into the water. Now return the *Couscous* to the original basin and break back into small grains with a fork, return to the *keskes*, place over the boiling water, cover tightly and cook for another half hour. Now add 2 oz of butter and fork into the *Couscous*. This preparation replaces bread and is eaten with meat, hardboiled eggs and dried fruit such as raisins. Apart from serving with meat it accompanies the Arab equivalent of the French *Pot-au-Feu*, or *Marga*, prepared from chicken, mutton, artichokes, capsicums, baby marrows, onions, carrots, turnips, broad beans, peas, dried peas and various peppers. Here the *Couscous* is prepared in the steam of the cooking ingredients, which impregnates the semolina with its aroma and flavours. The broth is served separately, being highly seasoned with cayenne or an equally hot pepper.

The meats are arranged on a serving dish; garnished with the vegetables in clusters and served with the *Couscous*. As the *Couscous* takes nearly as long as the meats to cook, the vegetables are only added according to their required cooking time.

Gnocchi à la Romaine

¼ lb semolina; 1 pint milk; ¼ lb grated Gruyère cheese; 1 oz breadcrumbs; 1 oz melted butter. Cooking time: 20 minutes.

Cook the semolina in the milk until it resembles a fairly thick dough. Add the salt and pepper, remove from fire and mix with 3 oz of grated cheese. Pour this mixture into a buttered and floured baking sheet about 1-inch thick, and flatten it slightly. Allow to cool. Cut into half moons with a cutter, place these half moons on an oval baking dish, sprinkle them with breadcrumbs and the rest of the grated cheese, and pour melted butter on top. Brown them in a very hot oven, 450° F or Gas Mark 8.

Kaché de Sarrasin * *Buckwheat Semolina Paste*

1 lb buckwheat semolina; 1¾ pints stock or water.

Mix the stock or water into the buckwheat to obtain a thick paste, season with salt and pepper, fill into a high straight-sided stewpan, cover tightly and cook in a hot oven, 400° F or Gas Mark 6, for an hour. Turn out, remove the surrounding crust. The interior is used in the preparation of *Coulibiac*.

Kaché de Semoule * *Semolina Paste*

½ lb semolina; 1 egg; 3½ pints consommé. Cooking time: 20 minutes.

Beat the egg and mix into the semolina, kneading lightly. Spread the mixture on a tray and dry in a cool oven or hotplate. Force through a coarse strainer into the gently boiling *consommé*, stir constantly and cook till thick, then drain. This is used in *Coulibiac* and other specialities of the Russian kitchen.

Polenta à la Gênoise

For 6 persons: ¼ *lb maize semolina;* ⅜ *pint water; salt;* 2 *oz grated cheese;* 2 *oz butter.* Cooking time: 1 hour.

Sprinkle the maize semolina slowly into boiling water, salt lightly and cook till thick, stirring constantly. Fold in the grated cheese and fill this mixture into a well buttered beaker or *bombe* mould. Put in a warm place for 25 minutes. Turn out on a round dish and pour melted butter on top. When cold it may cut into slices and served in place of bread.

Polenta Sautée * *Shallow Fried Polenta*

For 6 *persons:* ½ *lb maize semolina;* 1¾ *pints water; salt;* ¼ *lb butter;* 2 *oz grated Parmesan.* Cooking time: about 1 hour.

Sprinkle the maize semolina into boiling water, salt lightly and cook till thick, stirring constantly. Mix with grated cheese and an oz of butter and spread the thick smooth mixture on a moistened baking sheet. When cold, cut in squares or diamonds and fry golden brown in butter in a frying pan.

Salads

The popularity of the salad has grown in recent years. It is appreciated not only as a main dish in itself, but also when served with cold meat or as an accompaniment to a grilled meat or fish in place of the ordinary vegetables.

A good salad should look attractive and be composed of the best quality fresh vegetables. Salads may be served in individual salad plates or in a large glass or wooden salad bowl. Before assembling a salad, all the ingredients must be cleaned thoroughly by washing under cold running water; they should then be steeped in salted water for 5 minutes. After washing and steeping, the vegetables should be dried thoroughly without bruising in a salad basket or in clean tea towels.

There are two types of salad: *green* salads, made up with green vegetables such as lettuce, endive or chicory, are the simplest and are served with grills accompanied by a *Vinaigrette* dressing; *composite* or mixed salads often consist of mixed vegetables bound together with *Mayonnaise* and are served with cold meat.

ASSAISONNEMENTS * *SALAD DRESSINGS*

When preparing *Vinaigrette* dressing it is advisable to use the finest olive oil and white wine vinegar although good quality ground nut oil (*huile d'arachide*) can be used. The correct proportion for a dressing is *three* tablespoons of oil to *one* tablespoon of vinegar. This basic salad dressing can be flavoured with French mustard, garlic, herbs, freshly ground pepper, salt or sugar. Always add the dressing to the salad at the last minute as otherwise the vegetables will become slimy.

⊡ à la Crème * *Cream*

1 *pint cream; pepper; salt; juice of one lemon.*

Mix together. This dressing is used especially with the cos or romain lettuce.

⊡ à l'Huile * *Oil or Vinaigrette*

$\frac{3}{4}$ *pint oil;* $\frac{1}{2}$ *oz salt;* $\frac{1}{4}$ *pint vinegar; fresh black pepper.*

Mix together.

⊡ au Lard * *Bacon fat*

This dressing is used in particular with dandelion, wild chicory, cabbage and lamb's lettuce. Using streaky bacon, render the fat which is then mixed with boiling hot vinegar, salt and pepper.

Assaisonnement à la Mayonnaise * *Mayonnaise*

4 egg yolks; 1 pint oil; salt; pepper; 1 small tablespoon vinegar.

Mix egg yolks well in a bowl with salt, pepper and half the vinegar. Stir in oil with a whisk, first in a very thin flow, and then a dash at a time. Stir vigorously all the time; the direction does not matter. As soon as the *mayonnaise* starts to thicken, add the remainder of the vinegar and continue to stir until all the oil has been used and the sauce is thick and smooth. Lemon juice may be used instead of vinegar. Always keep the oil at room temperature, if it is too cold the *mayonnaise* will curdle. Finally stir a tablespoon of boiling water into the *mayonnaise.*

NOTE: Curdled *mayonnaise* may be restored by placing a spoon of boiling water in a clean bowl and stirring in the *mayonnaise* drop by drop, stirring constantly. Do not add any more egg yolk. Used with various cooked vegetables.

▣ **à l'Oeuf** * *Egg*

Blend the yolks of hardboiled eggs with mustard, oil, vinegar, salt and pepper and finally add the chopped whites of the eggs.

SALADES * *SALADS*

▣ **Aida**

2 *heads of curly chicory;* 4 *peeled and sliced tomatoes;* 4 *raw, sliced globe artichoke bottoms;* ½ *green capsicum cut into fine strips; a little Vinaigrette; coarsely sieved hardboiled eggs.*

Peel, chop and slice finely all the ingredients. Mix with *Vinaigrette* and sprinkle with the egg.

▣ **Américaine**

Equal quantities of peeled, sliced tomato; cooked, sliced potatoes; celery cut into fine strips.

Season with a salad dressing of oil and vinegar. Arrange and garnish with onion rings and slices of hardboiled eggs.

▣ **Andalouse**

Celeriac; ½ *lb large Spanish onions;* 2 *sweet peppers;* 1 *lb tomatoes;* 2 *oz rice; olives; tomato jelly.*

Peel the celeriac, cut in *julienne,* blanch briefly and drain. Coarsely chop the onions and simmer in butter without browning. Peel peppers, seed and cut in strips, boil rice and let it cool. Peel, seed and finely dice the tomatoes. Bind everything with a well-seasoned *Mayonnaise* made with lemon juice instead of vinegar, mixed with a little gelatine. Add some black and green stoned olives. Fill salad into a *bombe* mould, let it set and turn out on a round glass dish. Garnish with tomato jelly and stoned olives. Tomato jelly: Bind tomato *purée* lightly with gelatine and season with pepper and a pinch of salt. Pour into a moistened baking sheet and allow to set.

Salade Argenteuil

For 6 persons: 1 lb finely diced vegetables; 10 oz cooked green asparagus tips or white asparagus heads; 2 hardboiled eggs; ½ pint Mayonnaise.

Bind vegetables with well-seasoned Mayonnaise, serve in a mound and decorate with asparagus tips and sliced hardboiled eggs.

▣ d'Artichauts à la Grecque

See *Cold Hors d'Oeuvre, p.* 191. (*See illustration p.* 685).

▣ Béatrix

For 6 persons: 2 lb French beans; ½ lb tomatoes; 2 hardboiled eggs; a little cress; oil; vinegar.

Mix cooked French beans with *Vinaigrette* salad dressing and garnish with a ring of tomato slices. Put a tiny bunch of cress on each slice and sprinkle with chopped yolk of hardboiled egg.

▣ Beaucaire

For 6 persons: ¼ lb celeriac; ¼ lb celery; ½ lb boiled potatoes; ½ lb tomatoes; 6 oz boiled beetroot; 12 walnuts; 1 truffle; ¼ lb ham; Mayonnaise.

Cut celeriac in coarse *julienne*, blanch, drain and mix with the thinly sliced celery, *julienne* of ham, finely diced potato and beetroot and bind with thick, well-seasoned *Mayonnaise.* Serve salad in a mound in a salad bowl, decorate with tomato slices, chopped truffle and sliced beetroot and put a small celery heart or lettuce in the middle. (*See illustration p.* 685).

▣ Belle-Hélène

For 6-8 persons: 1 lb celeriac; 3 oz beetroot; 3 oz peeled walnuts; 2 hardboiled eggs; 1 egg yolk; ½ pint olive oil; a little vinegar; a few truffle slices; chervil.

Cut the celeriac into a very fine *julienne*, and blanch it for a minute or two in order to make it tender. Drain, and dry on a cloth. Make a *Mayonnaise* with two hardboiled egg yolks, one raw egg yolk, oil, a few drops of vinegar, salt and pepper, and add chopped chervil. Mix the celeriac and a few coarsely chopped walnut kernels with this dressing. Arrange in a mound in a salad bowl. Decorate with a ring of beetroot slices, cut out with a round fluted fancy cutter, and in the middle truffle slices and half walnut kernels. (*See illustration p.* 686).

▣ Camerata

For 6 persons: ¼ lb celeriac; ½ lb chicory; ½ lb boiled potatoes; 6 oz boiled French beans; 3 cooked artichoke bottoms; ¼ lb raw cultivated mushrooms; ¼ lb boiled beetroot; ½ lb tomatoes; ½ pint Mayonnaise.

Cut celeriac in coarse *julienne* and blanch, slice other ingredients thinly except for tomatoes and beetroot. Mix everything, bind with well-seasoned *Mayonnaise*, place in salad bowl and decorate with a ring of round tomato and beetroot slices.

▲ *Salade Beaucaire, p. 684*

Salade d'artichauts à la Grecque, p. 684 ▼

▲ Salade Belle-Hélène, p. 684

Salade Tonello, p. 692 ▼

▲ *French cheeses, p. 693*

Swiss cheeses, p. 693 ▼

▲ Italian cheeses, p. 693

Dutch and Danish cheeses, p. 693 ▼

Salade Carmen

For 8 persons: 1 lb celeriac; 2 large apples; ½ lb French endives; ¼ lb tomatoes; ½ pint Mayonnaise; 2 hardboiled eggs; 1 small truffle.

Cook the celeriac, but do not let it get too soft. Peel and cut it into *julienne*, and mix it with one of the apples cut in the same way, and chicory sliced thinly. Bind this salad with thick, well-seasoned *Mayonnaise*. Arrange this salad piled up into a dome in a salad bowl, and decorate with a ring of thin slices of apple rubbed with lemon to keep them white, a ring of thin slices of hardboiled eggs and a ring of peeled, sliced tomatoes. Cut the truffle into rounds, halve them, and place them on the apple slices.

▣ Lorette

For 6 persons: 1 lb lamb's lettuce; 4 oz celery; ½ lb boiled beetroot; oil; vinegar.

Cut celery and beetroot in coarse *julienne* or slice thinly, and mix with the washed and prepared lamb's lettuce. Season with salt pepper, oil and vinegar only.

▣ Macédoine

For 6 persons: ½ lb carrots; 3 oz turnips; ¼ lb French beans; ¼ lb green peas; 2 artichoke bottoms; ⅓ lb potatoes; ⅓ pint Mayonnaise; 2 hardboiled eggs; ½ lb beetroot.

Finely dice all ingredients except beetroot and eggs; boil, drain and cool. Bind these with well-seasoned *Mayonnaise* and serve decorated with round slices of boiled beetroot and sliced hardboiled egg.

▣ Marguerite

For 8 persons: ¾ lb cauliflower; ¾ lb potatoes boiled in their jackets; ½ lb small French beans; ½ lb asparagus tips; 1 pint Mayonnaise; 3 hardboiled eggs.

Cook all the vegetables separately, allow to cool, and drain well. Peel the potatoes and cut them into thin slices. Cut all the other vegetables into small dice, and marinate these and the potatoes. Place the potatoes in a salad bowl and pile all the other vegetables on top. Cover completely with plenty of *Mayonnaise*. In the centre make a daisy with the white of hardboiled egg, cut into thin slices and shaped like leaves. Cut the remaining egg white first into slices and then cut out with a round fluted cutter, to imitate small daisies. Place the small daisies in a circle all around the salad bowl. Mash the egg yolk and mix it with a little butter or *Mayonnaise*, and use it to imitate the yellow centre of the daisy.

▣ Mercédès

For 4-5 persons: 4 endives (only the white heart); ½ lb cooked beetroots; ½ lb celery; 2 large oranges; 2 hardboiled eggs; 2 lemons; ½ pint olive oil; salt; pepper; mustard; chopped herbs.

Chop the eggs and mix them with the oil, lemon juice, salt, pepper, chopped herbs and mustard. Break the endives into small pieces with your fingers and place in the salad bowl, and toss the salad with the dressing. Wipe the edge of the salad bowl. Garnish with small piles of celery and beetroots cut into *julienne*, and place segments of oranges in the middle. Each guest helps himself, taking some of the garnish as well as the endives.

Salade Mimosa

For 6 persons: 2 lb mixed vegetables cut in very small dice (carrots, turnips, potatoes and French beans, green peas and dwarf beans); 1 pint Mayonnaise; 4 hardboiled eggs; 1 small truffle; parsley.

Method I: Cook all the vegetables separately, cool and drain well. Bind each type of vegetable separately with well seasoned *Mayonnaise* and correct the seasoning. Arrange all the vegetables separately in a dome in a salad bowl forming sections changing the colours as far as possible. Garnish each section individually with hardboiled chopped egg white and egg yoke, truffle and parsley evenly sprinkled on top.

Method II: Season lettuce salad with French dressing, and arrange it in the salad bowl. Sprinkle with hardboiled egg yolk rubbed through a coarse wire sieve.

NOTE: In France a small crust of bread rubbed with garlic is usually mixed with green salads. This is called a *chapon.* It imparts a very good taste to all green salads, but should be taken out before serving the salad.

▣ Mousmé

Use one tomato per person. Remove the top section from some ripe but firm tomatoes to act as lids, or halve large tomatoes. Scoop out, season and marinate for 2 hours. Clean and wash 1 pound very small Chinese artichokes, boil for 6-7 minutes in slightly salted water with lemon juice and marinate with salt, pepper, oil and vinegar. Drain tomatoes and fill with a small spoon of finely diced celery bound with a sharp sauce or dressing and garnish neatly with Chinese artichokes placed side by side. Arrange on lettuce leaves on a round dish and serve very cold.

▣ Muguette

Make in the same way as Marguerite salad but decorate with small posies of lilies-of-the-valley made of blanched tarragon leaves and cut-out egg white. Almost all salads except green salads can be decorated in this way.

▣ Niçoise

For 6 persons: 1 lb string beans; 1 lb potatoes; 4-5 tomatoes; 3 hardboiled eggs; 6 anchovy fillets; 12 green, pitted olives; ½ pint Vinaigrette dressing.

Peel potatoes cooked in their jackets and cut them into small dice. Cut the beans in squares, cook them in salted, boiling water, cool and drain. Mix the vegetables, season these with *Vinaigrette* dressing and pile the salad up in a salad bowl. Decorate with peeled tomatoes, cut in slices or quarters, anchovy fillets, hardboiled eggs cut in quarters, pitted olives and, if liked, neat chunks of tunny fish, preserved in oil.

▣ Orloff

For 6 persons: ½ lb celery; 4 cooked artichoke bottoms; ¼ lb ham; ¼ lb chicken breast; ¼ lb cooked spaghetti; ¼ lb raw cultivated mushrooms; 2 truffles; 6 poached mushroom caps; 2 tomatoes; ½ pint tomato-flavoured Mayonnaise.

Cut ingredients in fine *julienne*, chop *spaghetti* and bind with well-seasoned *Mayonnaise.* Serve in a mound in a salad bowl and decorate with truffle and tomato slices and white, fluted mushroom caps.

Salade Parisienne

For 8-10 persons: 1½ *lb mixed vegetables (carrots, string beans, turnips, peas, dwarf beans, etc.);* ¼ *lb tomatoes;* ½ *lb cooked crawfish meat;* 2 *hardboiled eggs;* 1 *pint Mayonnaise;* 4-5 *large lettuce hearts.*

Mix the vegetables with the crawfish meat cut into dice. Bind with *Mayonnaise* and season well. Arrange in a dome in a salad bowl, and decorate with slices of peeled tomatoes, hard-boiled eggs and half lettuce hearts.

▣ Rachel

For 6 *persons:* 6 *cooked artichoke bottoms, not too soft;* 10 *oz asparagus tips;* 10 *oz raw cultivated mushrooms; brandy; Port.*

Slice mushrooms and artichoke bottoms thinly, cut asparagus into small pieces except for heads, bundle heads and boil briefly so they are not too soft. Marinate each ingredient separately with salt, pepper, a dash of brandy, oil and a little Port. Dress in small bunches and place asparagus heads in centre.

▣ Richelieu

Cut out carrots, some turnips and potatoes with a very small olive-shaped vegetable cutter, cut French beans in squares, and boil them and some green peas and very small cauliflower rosettes separately. Decorate a *bombe* mould with the carrots and turnips, some round potato slices and French beans. Mix the remaining vegetables with well-seasoned *Mayonnaise* mixed with a little melted gelatine, fill mould with them and close with a thin layer of cold but still liquid aspic. Cool well, leave to set and turn out on a round glass dish.

▣ de Riz Derby

For 6 *persons:* ½ *lb Carolina rice;* 10 *oz cooked green peas;* 6 *oz poached mushrooms;* ¼ *lb cooked ham;* 18-20 *walnuts;* ½ *pint Vinaigrette dressing;* ¼ *pint Mayonnaise.*

Cook the rice in salted, boiling water. Drain, cool, and dry on a cloth; the grains must be absolutely dry and separate easily. Mix with the peas, mushrooms cut into slices and the ham cut into strips. Marinate with the *Vinaigrette* and bind with the *Mayonnaise*. Garnish with walnuts halves.

▣ Russe

For 10-12 *persons:* 1 *lb cooked mixed vegetables;* ¼ *lb ham or red pickled tongue;* ½ *lb cooked crawfish or lobster meat;* 1 *oz capers;* 2 *oz gherkins;* 2 *oz anchovy fillets;* 2 *oz caviar;* ¼ *lb cooked beetroot;* 1 *truffle;* 1 *tomato;* 2 *hardboiled eggs;* 1 *pint Mayonnaise.*

Cut all the ingredients into small dice, with exception of the tomato, truffle, hardboiled eggs and beetroot. Bind with well-seasoned *Mayonnaise,* and arrange in a dome in a salad bowl. Decorate the top with slices of beetroot, hardboiled eggs and tomato. Make a well in the middle and fill it with caviar. It is wrong to call all salads of mixed vegetables "Russian salads". The true Russian salad is made of dried mushrooms, soaked and cooked potatoes, cabbage, leeks, all cut into dice, fish, meat, pitted olives, pickled cucumbers and chopped olives, seasoned with chopped dill and *Vinaigrette* dressing.

Salade Tonello

For 6 persons: 1 lb cold, cooked diced potatoes; 1 lb sliced, cold, cooked green beans; 3-4 fl oz Vinaigrette dressing; salt; freshly ground black pepper; clove of garlic; 3 tomatoes, quartered; 3 hardboiled eggs, quartered; 6 oz tin tuna fish; pitted ripe olives; 6-12 anchovy fillets.

Toss the potatoes and beans with the *Vinaigrette* dressing and season with salt and pepper. Rub the inside of a salad bowl with the cut clove of garlic. Place potatoes and beans in the bowl. Decorate the salad with quartered tomatoes interspersed with quartered hardboiled eggs, pieces of tuna fish, olives and anchovy fillets. (*See illustration p.* 686).

◘ Waldorf

For 6 persons: 10 oz celeriac; 3 oz hazelnuts; 10 oz rennet or cooking apples; ½ pint Mayonnaise.

Cut celeriac into small dice or *julienne*, blanch, drain and re-fresh. Cut apples in small dice or *julienne*, mix both together, season with lemon juice and salt and allow to mascerate at least one hour. Bind with the *Mayonnaise*, serve and sprinkle with sliced nuts.

Salade de Fruits de Mer * *Sea Food Salad*

6 oz mussels; 6 oz shrimps or prawns; 6 oz scampi or Dublin Bay prawns; 6 oz winkles; ½ lb mushrooms; 1 lemon; vinegar; olive oil; paprika; chopped parsley, chervil and tarragon.

Cook the mussels and remove the beards, shell the shrimp and *scampi*, cook the winkles and poach the mushrooms. Cut the *scampi* into small pieces and either halve or quarter the mushrooms according to their size. Mix these with the mussels, the shrimps and the winkles. Season all with salt, pepper, vinegar, and olive oil and allow to marinate for at least 2 hours. Before serving, add the chopped herbs, combine all thoroughly and correct the seasoning. Serve very cold.

Cheese

Cheese may be made from several varieties of milk, the most common being cows', goats', and ewes' milk. All cheese is made by making milk clot as in junket making. The coagulation or clotting takcs place by the addition of rennet. The resulting curd (separated fat milk protein) is strained and pressed to remove some of the liquid. This results in a soft cheese. The curd may be heated to make it firmer and help to squeeze out more liquid (whey). The curd is then strained, mixed, blended, salted and pressed. High pressure produces a hard cheese.

The next process in cheese-making is ripening which is accomplished by exposing the cheese to the air. The ripening is a fermentative process brought about by certain bacteria in the air. The ripening of cheese may also be achieved by the introduction of various cultivated moulds. Chemical changes take place and the particular flavour imparted to the cheese varies with the bacteria or mould which has been introduced to it. Other factors which can alter the flavour of a cheese include the breed of cow, the type of pasture and varying climatical conditions.

Mild cheeses are those which have not been allowed to mature for any length of time. Strong cheeses have a longer maturing period. Cheese reaches a definite peak of maturity; and after this has passed it begins to deteriorate.

The nutritive value of cheese is appreciated when it is understood that it takes approximately 8 pints of milk to make 1 lb cheese. Cheese is thus a highly concentrated food and an excellent source of protein (and one of the cheapest available at that). It is also a rich source of calcium and some vitamins.

To store cheese wrap loosely in a polythene bag or foil and put in a cool place or in the refrigerator. Remove from the refrigerator one hour before use to allow it to reach room temperature. If cheese is purchased in a box or wrapper keep it in this. Grated cheese can be stored in a glass jar loosely covered, in a cool dry place or in the refrigerator.

Cheese is used in cookery for *mousses*, cocktail savouries, sauces and egg dishes, but it must be remembered that in cooked dishes the cheese should be added towards the end of the cooking time so that it does not become overheated. Over-cooking will make the cheese hard, stringy and indigestible.

There are hundreds of varieties of cheese, (*See illustrations pp.* 687 *and* 688). France alone has more than 300 different kinds of cheese.

Bleu cheese is a blue, French cheese which is available in different varieties designated by the name of the district where it was made.

Brie cheese is made of whole milk and innoculated with a mould which makes the cheese soften as it matures, until it becomes liquid. It is circular and when ready should be soft enough to yield to pressure when pressed in any part; after this it deteriorates quickly. It is sold packed in straw.

Camembert is a whole milk soft cheese which is innoculated with *Penicillium album* which gives it a runny texture when the cheese is mature. It must be really ripe when ready and should yield to the pressure of the fingers. Store at room temperature.

Carré de l'est. This is a soft cheese sold in wooden boxes; test as for Camembert.

Coulommiers. This is a rich, double cream cheese and is prepared from fresh milk enriched with cream. It should be eaten fresh and not allowed to mature.

Demi-sel. This is a cottage cheese made in Normandy from whole milk. It is slightly salted and sold in foil-wrapped squares.

Double crème is a mild and very rich cheese made from milk which has been enriched with extra cream. Rennet is used to make it clot and when the curd has been drained and pressed, more cream is worked in. It is then moulded and wrapped.

Monsieur cheese. This is similar in flavour to *Camembert* and is made in Normandy.

Neufchatel. A small, loaf-shaped ripe cheese with a red skin which is dark yellow inside.

Petit Suisse is a very creamy, unsalted cheese made from milk to which extra cream has been added. It is small and cylindrical in shape. The best petit-suisse is the Gervais.

Pont L'Evèque is a semi-hard fermented cheese, packed in wooden boxes. It is firmer than *Camembert* but also has a pale, wrinkled crust.

Port du Salut—a delicious, semi-hard whole milk cheese with a mild flavour.

Roquefort—a blue-veined cheese made from ewes' milk and innoculated with the same culture as Stilton. It is matured in limestone caves. True *Roquefort* is fairly scarce and expensive. It is considered in France to be "the king of cheeses".

Tomme. There are several varieties of this cheese which is reminiscent of *Port Salut* but whiter. The outside is covered closely with grape pips taken from the vine press.

Cheese is manufactured all over the world and some of the best cheeses come from Germany. *Tilsiter* is a semi-hard German cheese. Some other better known German cheeses include *Steinbuscher*, *Limburger* and *Romadour*. *Limburger* is a semi-hard whole milk cheese with a pungent smell which is flavoured with herbs.

Holland is justly proud of its excellent cheeses which include the famous *Edam*, made from cows' milk, renneted and coloured at the same time. It is round like a ball, bright red outside and orange-yellow inside. *Gouda* is similar in taste and texture to *Edam*, but of a different shape, being flat and much larger and weighing about 20 lb. *Baby Gouda* and *Baby Edam* are smaller versions which weigh only about 1 lb.

Italy, too, has many excellent cheeses which deserve special mention. *Romano* cheese, once made only in Latium, is now made in Southern Italy and Sicily from cows' and goats' milk. There are three distinctive kinds—*Pecorino Romano*, made of sheep's milk, *Vacchino Romano*, made of cows' milk and *Caprino Romano*, made of goats' milk. When allowed to mature for five to eight months, they make an excellent table cheese; if matured for a longer period, a year or more, they become sharp and hard and are only suitable for grating. *Bel Paese* is a delicate soft cheese and *Mozzarella* and *Scamorze* are soft, only slightly ripened fresh cheeses, *Mozzarella* being the cheese par excellence for *pizzas*.

An excellent English cheese is *Cheshire* cheese mistakenly known as *Chester* cheese on the Continent. It is not as easy to imitate as are many other English cheeses, since the milk from which it is made has a slightly salty flavour, due to the nature of the grazing in Cheshire. The oldest and one of the best of English cheeses is undoubtedly *Cheddar*, a cutting cheese from semi-hard, to part crumbly or flaky, based upon its maturing period whose colour varies from pale yellow to ochre.

Four other excellent English cheeses are *Gloucester*, *Wensleydale*, *Leicester* and *Lancashire*. *Gloucester* is a semi-hard, cartwheel in shape. *Wensleydale* is a cylindrical double cream cheese, similar in shape and texture to *Stilton*, otherwise a loosely packed curd. *Leicester* is a rich reddish ochre coloured semi-hard cheese, greatly esteemed for its clean, sharp taste. *Lancashire*, a white cheese, semi-hard, slightly crumbly, with a distinctive sharp taste, the best of all our cheeses for toasting or grilling or for Welsh Rarebit. *Caerphilly*, the famous Welsh cheese is of the soft cream type, ideal for those who appreciate the creamy slightly sour taste of the freshly made dairy cheeses. *Dunlop* is the famous Scottish cheese, pure white in colour, unless unnaturally coloured, cheddar type in texture, but differing slightly in flavour because of the northern pasturages. *Dorset Vinney* and *Stilton* develop blue veins in their maturities and blue-veined *Cheshire* is also obtainable. *Stilton* and *Wensleydale* traditionally were made only from summer milk and thus were seasonal.

Three-quarters of all American cheeses are of the English Cheddar type, whether they call themselves American Stone, Yankee or Wisconsin cheese.

Good cheese is also made in Austria, Belgium, Sweden, Norway, Hungary and Greece, but they are too numerous to be mentioned here. Gourmets do not consider a meal complete if it does not include at least one or two types of cheese.

Cheese on the Menu

Whether to eat cheese before or after the dessert is a matter of national taste. In France, cheese is always eaten before the dessert; in Germany, England and some other countries it is always eaten at the end of the meal. By way of a change it is possible to have a meal consisting entirely of cheese, bread and butter, accompanied, of course by a suitable drink. This brings us to the question of what to drink with cheese. In France this is no problem, a fruity red wine is preferred with almost all cheeses, *rosé* is drunk with only a few, such as Reblochon or Saint-Nectaire. The dry Alsatian wines go with Mûnster, and really any wine goes with goat's cheese. In England a glass of burgundy, or even claret, is preferred with cheese. At lunchtime, beer or stout is occasionally drunk with English cheeses such as Cheddar or Cheshire. In the Scandinavian countries the usual drink with the strong, especially the strongly smelling cheeses is beer and a small glass of spirits, mainly Akvakit, Vodka, distilled grain brandy, Allasch, Kummel, etc.

Cheese in Cooking

Cheese is not only eaten as such, it is also grated and used for many kinds of dishes. The main cheeses for grating are *gruyère* and Parmesan. There are many cheese dishes and pastries. Cheese pastries can be served with aperitifs or cocktails, and to replace or supplement a cheese platter. When serving cheese dishes, national customs should be observed. Many of these dishes are served in France as a hot *hors d'œuvre*, whereas in Great Britain they are served as a savoury at the end of the meal, instead of cheese. Hot and cold cheese dishes and pastries are an agreeable addition to our menus and should be used to a greater extent than they have been in the past. A cheese *soufflé* instead of a dessert is always particularly popular at a stag dinner.

It has been the custom in England to round off a meal by serving a small savoury. This is not common in France and few French menus include savouries in their composition. This section is new and has been created specially for the British and American editions. Formerly served after the sweet course, the savoury very often replaces this, appealing especially to those people who are not very fond of sweets and puddings. It may also act as a substitute for the cheese course blending well, as does cheese, with Port. The savoury may take the form of buttered toast (*canapés*), buttered biscuits, *tartelettes, barquettes* and small puff pastry cases, *bouchées*. Traditionally the filling should contain as much cheese as possible but it is quite normal to find savouries of creamed and flaked fish and fish roes since there is an ample supply of fresh fish in Britain. They should certainly be spicy, with a refreshing tang and be served very hot. Savoury ingredients are never presented on their own. They are served on fried or toasted bread or in pastry cases or, when impaled on a skewer, placed on a bed of fried or toasted bread.

Many after-dinner savouries resemble cocktail savouries and *hors d'œuvre* and you can refer to these sections for additional recipes. The following selection of savouries has been classified according to pastry containers, such as *barquettes*, but it is as well to remember that the fillings are interchangeable.

BARQUETTES

These are oval tartlet shells of Short Crust pastry which are filled with various savoury compositions. The uncooked pastry may be filled and then set in the oven to bake or they may be baked blind and then filled.

◘ Cadogan

Per person: 1 *tablespoon ham purée;* 1 *tablespoon cheese sauce;* 1 *dessertspoon grated Lancashire cheese;* 1 *finely diced gherkin;* 1 *barquette.* Cooking time: 2-3 minutes.

Heat the ham and gherkin together, fill into the pastry boat and mask with the cheese sauce. Sprinkle with cheese and gratinate in a very hot oven, 450° F or Gas Mark 8, for a few moments.

Barquettes Devonshire

Per person: 1 *oz cooked lobster;* 1 *tablespoon cheese sauce; a dash of mustard;* 1 *teaspoon grated cheese; a dash of Worcester sauce;* 1 *barquette.* Cooking time: 5 minutes.

Dice the lobster and heat in the sauce with the mustard and Worcester sauce. Fill into the pastry boat, sprinkle with the cheese and gratinate in a hot oven, 400° F or Gas Mark 6.

▣ Reform Club

Per person: 1 *mushroom; a small piece of cooked ham;* 1 *oz smoked haddock fillet;* 1 *tablespoon Cheese Soufflé mixture;* 1 *dessertspoon grated cheese;* 1 *barquette.* Cooking time: about 10 minutes.

Cook the haddock and mushroom in butter, cut in small dice with the ham and blend into the *soufflé* mixture. Fill into the pastry boat, shape with a knife, sprinkle with the grated cheese and bake until browned in a hot oven, 400° F or Gas Mark 6.

BOUCHÉES

These Puff pastry cases are baked blind and filled with various tasty preparations. You will find several recipes for Puff pastry *bouchées* in the *Entrées* section. The method of preparation is described on page 199.

▣ Avondale * *Avondale Puffs*

Per person: 1 *oz smoked haddock;* 1 *mushroom;* 1 *tablespoon oyster sauce;* 1 *poached, bearded oyster;* 1 *Puff pastry case.*

Poach the haddock and mushroom in butter, cut into small dice and blend into the oyster sauce. Fill this mixture into the pastry case and place the oyster on top. Sprinkle with cayenne.

▣ Helford * *Helford Puffs*

Per person: 6 *oysters;* 1 *tablespoon sauce Homard;* 1 *Puff pastry case; paprika.*

Stiffen the oysters by heating for a few moments in their own juice. Remove beards. Remove the oysters, reduce the juice to half and add the sauce *Homard.* Return the oysters to the pan, reheat and serve in a pastry case. Sprinkle with paprika.

CANAPÉS

This is now understood to mean a small platform or base of fried or toasted bread or pastry used as the foundation of a savoury or *hors d'œuvre* but it was originally a slice of crustless bread. The *canapé* may be cut into rectangular or oval shapes of varying size and thickness. They are spread with the desired filling, garnished to taste and cooked under the grill or heated in the oven.

Canapés Baron

Per person: 1 *large grilled mushroom;* 2 *small slices of grilled streaky bacon;* 1 *slice of poached beef marrow; cayenne pepper.*

Arrange the mushroom upon the toast, then the bacon and lastly garnish with the marrow. Sprinkle with the cayenne.

▣ Derby

Per person: 1 *oz ham purée;* 1 *tablespoon sauce Béchamel;* 1 *half walnut; cayenne.*

Heat the ham and sauce together, arrange piled up on a round piece of toast and sprinkle with cayenne. Heat the walnut in the oven and place on top.

▣ Diana

Per person: 1 *chicken liver;* 1 *tablespoon sauce Diable;* 1 *small grilled mushroom.*

Dice the liver and fry quickly in butter. Drain, mix with the sauce and pile upon the toast. Place the mushroom on top.

▣ Guard's Club

Per person: 1 *slice of gammon,* $\frac{1}{8}$ *inch thick* × 1 *inch square;* 1 *teaspoon chopped chutney;* 1 *small grilled mushroom; cayenne.*

Spread the piece of gammon with a little mustard, brush with melted butter and grill. Heat the chutney. Place the gammon on a square of toast, then the chutney and lastly the mushroom. Sprinkle with cayenne.

▣ Hollandais

Per person: 1 *oz smoked haddock fillet;* 3 *slices of hardboiled egg;* 1 *tablespoon sauce Béchamel.*

Cook the haddock in butter, beat together with the sauce and serve piled upon a round of toast. Place the overlapping slices of egg on top and sprinkle with cayenne.

▣ Ivanhoe

Per person: 1 *oz smoked finnan haddock;* 1 *tablespoon Cream sauce;* 1 *half pickled walnut; cayenne pepper.*

Cook the haddock in butter, chop, season with cayenne and mix in the sauce. Heat thoroughly. Heat the walnut in butter. Pile up the mixture upon a round piece of toast and place the heated walnut in the centre.

Canapés Montrose

Per person: 1 *tablespoon of puréed venison; a little mushroom ketchup and claret;* 1 *teaspoon chopped chutney;* ½ *pickled walnut; cayenne pepper; grated cheese.*

Heat the venison *purée* and chutney together, mix to a thick *purée* with the ketchup, claret and cayenne and pile on the toast in a dome shape. Place the walnut half in the centre, sprinkle with cheese and gratinate in a hot oven, 400° F or Gas Mark 6, or under the grill.

▣ St. James'

Per person: 1 *large mushroom;* 1 *tablespoon cheese sauce; a little grated cheese and chopped chives; a small slice of foie gras.* Cooking time: 3-4 minutes.

Peel and remove the stalk from the mushroom. Chop the stalk and stew it in butter, cook and mix with *foie gras* and chives. Lightly cook the mushroom cap and fill it with the prepared mixture. Place on a round of toast, mask with the sauce, sprinkle with the cheese and brown in a hot oven, 400° F or Gas Mark 6, for a few minutes.

▣ Windsor

Per person: 1 *tablespoon ham purée;* 1 *mushroom; cayenne.*

Spread toast with the *purée* of ham, place a grilled mushroom on top and sprinkle with cayenne.

CHEESE SAVOURIES

The following are a selection of miscellaneous cheese savouries which are normally served on a table napkin. The serving of Melba toast as an accompaniment is optional.

▣ Cheddar Pearls

Per person: 1 *tablespoon Choux pastry;* 1 *dessertspoon grated Cheddar cheese.*

Blend the *Choux* pastry and the grated cheese together. Place in a piping bag with ⅛-inch plain tube and pipe a long line, then cut into ⅛-inch long pieces into a deep pan of oil. Fry to a golden colour, drain well, season with cayenne and serve on a table napkin.

▣ Croque-Monsieur

Per person: 2 *thin slices bread;* 2 *thin slices gruyère cheese;* 1 *thin slice ham.*

Place the *gruyère* on one slice of bread. Cover with the slice of ham, the remaining slice of cheese, then the bread and press together. Cut out a round with a pastry cutter and fry until crisp in clarified butter.

▣ Croquettes Stilton * *Stilton Corks*

For 8 *persons:* 6 *oz Stilton cheese;* 2 *oz breadcrumbs;* 1 *oz chopped parsley and chives;* 2 *fl oz Port wine; beaten egg; breadcrumbs.*

Cream the cheese, breadcrumbs, Port and herbs together. Shape the mixture into 8 small *croquettes,* egg and breadcrumb. Deep fry and serve these on a table napkin.

Savoury Fried Cheese

Per person: 1 small wedge of Camembert cheese; beaten egg; breadcrumbs.

Egg and breadcrumb the cheese twice and deep fry. Serve with toast.

⊡ Lancashire Titbit

Per person: 2 *thin square pieces of Lancashire cheese;* 1 *teaspoon chopped chutney; made mustard; toast.*

Spread one side of the cheese with mustard and grill. Place the grilled side down of one piece of cheese on a piece of toast, spread with the chutney, place the grilled side of the other piece of cheese on the chutney, spread the surface with a little more mustard and grill.

TARTLETTES * *TARTLETS*

These are small tartlets or shaped pastry cases which are filled with savoury fillings.

⊡ Berkeley

Per person: 1 *tablespoon purée of chicken, creamed with a little sauce Béchamel; half a chicken liver;* 1 *mushroom;* 1 *dessertspoon sauce Diable;* 1 *tartlet.*

Dice the liver and mushroom, fry quickly in butter and bind with the *sauce Diable*. Pipe a border of chicken *purée* round the tartlet and fill the centre with the liver mixture. Decorate with half a stoned olive in the centre.

⊡ Boodles

Per person: 6 *oysters;* 2 *tablespoons cream; cayenne;* 1 *tartlet.*

Stiffen the oysters in their own juice and remove the beards. Reduce the cream and oyster juice to a thick sauce consistency in a separate saucepan. Toss in the oysters and fill into a tartlet case. Sprinkle with cayenne pepper.

⊡ Calcutta

Per person: 1 *tablespoon cooked shrimps;* 1 *tablespoon Curry sauce;* 1 *teaspoon chopped chutney; sieved hardboiled egg yolk;* 1 *tartlet.*

Heat the shrimps in the Curry sauce, fill into a tartlet case and place heated chutney in the centre. Sprinkle with egg yolk.

⊡ Chester Oyster

Use the same ingredients and method as Tartlet Boodle, but sprinkle with grated Cheshire cheese and gratinate.

Tartlettes Devilled Wensleydale

For 8 persons: 24 small Short pastry tartlets; ½ lb Wensleydale cheese; 4 fl oz sauce Béchamel; 2 egg whites; ¼ pint cream; cayenne. Cooking time: 10-15 minutes.

Grate the cheese and beat into the sauce and cool a little. Whip the whites of egg and cream separately, blend together and then fold gently into the cheese mixture. Fill into the tartlets and bake in a hot oven, 400° F or Gas Mark 6.

▣ Dorset Delight

Per person: 1 tablespoon chicken purée; 1 teaspoon foie gras purée; 1 tablespoon sauce Béchamel; 1 plover's egg; 1 tartlet.

Heat the chicken, *foie gras* and *Béchamel* together and fill into the tartlet case. Egg and breadcrumb the plover's egg, deep fry and place in centre of the tartlet.

▣ Florentine

Per person: 4 oysters; 1 tablespoon leaf spinach, tossed in Noisette butter; 1 tartlet case.

Stiffen the oysters in their own juice. Fill the tartlet with the leaf spinach, arrange the oysters on top and pour over *Noisette* butter. Sprinkle with chopped chives.

▣ Rajah

Per person: 1 oz prawns; 1 tablespoon Curry sauce; 1 mushroom; 1 tartlet.

Dice the prawns and heat in the sauce. Cook the mushroom in butter and fill this mixture into a tartlet case. Place the mushroom on top and sprinkle with cayenne.

▣ Ramequins Chester * *Cheshire Custard Tartlets*

For 8-12 persons: 24 small Puff pastry tartlets; ½ pint milk; ¼ pint cream; 4 eggs; ½ lb finely diced Cheshire (or Cheddar) cheese; salt and pepper; mace. Cooking time: 10-15 minutes.

Mix together the milk, slightly beaten eggs, cream and seasoning. Place a little cheese in each tartlet, then ¾ fill with the custard and bake in a moderate oven, 375° F or Gas Mark 4-5. Serve immediately.

▣ Richmond Cheese Cakes

For 8-12 persons: 24 small Puff pastry tartlets; ½ pint milk; 5 oz breadcrumbs; 4 eggs; 6 oz grated Cheddar cheese; salt; cayenne. Cooking time: about 10 minutes.

Boil the milk, add the breadcrumbs and work the mixture to a thick consistency. Cool, season, add 4 ounces of the grated cheese and 4 egg yolks and mix well. Fold in three whipped egg whites, fill into the tartlet cases. Sprinkle on top the remaining 2 ounces of grated cheese. Bake in a hot oven, 400° F or Gas Mark 6.

TOAST

Savouries and savoury fillings may be served on *croûtes* or rounds of toasted bread. They are normally simpler in composition than a *canapé* but in Britain there is little distinction drawn between the "toast" and the "*canapé*" on the average menu.

▣ Anchovy

Spread slices of toast with Anchovy butter and cover with fillets of anchovy. Cut into rounds, oblongs, squares or diamonds and brush with melted butter. Heat gently. Sprinkle with a little cayenne.

▣ Bloater

Fillet and skin the bloaters, carefully remove all small bones and place on a buttered tray. Brush with melted butter, sprinkle with cayenne and heat for 5 minutes in a hot oven, 400° F or Gas Mark 6. Arrange on the toast.

▣ Captain's

Per person: 1 *small thin slice of gammon rasher,* 1½ × 1½ *inches; a little made mustard;* 1 *slice of cooked lobster; dash of Worcester sauce;* 1 *stoned olive, wrapped in an anchovy fillet.*

Grill the gammon and place on a square piece of toast. Heat the lobster in the mustard and Worcester sauce and place on top of the gammon. Heat the olive in butter and place in the centre.

▣ Findon

Per person: 1 *square piece of smoked fillet of haddock,* 1-*inch square; a little Mustard butter;* 1 *rasher streaky bacon.*

Spread the square haddock fillet with the butter, wrap in the bacon and grill. Serve on toast.

▣ Fisherman's Snack

Per person: 1 *tablespoon mashed smoked cod's roe;* ½ *rasher streaky bacon; cayenne; a little lemon juice;* 2 *anchovy fillets; oblong piece of toast.*

Heat the roe, season with cayenne and lemon juice and spread thickly on toast which has been buttered with Mustard butter. Lay the anchovy fillets on top, then the piece of bacon. Heat in a hot oven, 400° F or Gas Mark 6.

▣ Friars

Per person: 1 *small rasher of bacon;* 1 *tablespoon grated Lancashire cheese; a dash of Worcester sauce;* 6 *rings of pickled onion; grated cheese.*

Cut the bacon into fine dice, fry in butter and season with the Worcester sauce. Mix in the tablespoon of cheese until you have a firm paste. Spread the paste thickly on toast, decorate with a row of overlapping onion rings, sprinkle with the grated cheese and gratinate in a hot oven, 400 °F or Gas Mark 6, or under the grill.

Haddock Toast

Skin and bone the haddock, cut into squares of about 1 inch. Place in a buttered dish, lightly moisten with milk, cover and cook in a hot oven, 400° F or Gas Mark 6. Serve on toast and sprinkle with black pepper.

◘ Kipper

The same preparation as for Bloater on Toast substituting kipper.

◘ Marrow

Per person: 4 thick slices of beef marrow; cayenne.

Blanch the marrow in well salted water, remove, drain and arrange on a round of toast. Sprinkle with chopped parsley and cayenne. Heat for a few minutes in a hot oven.

◘ Mushrooms

Per person: 1 *large mushroom; bacon fat; cayenne.*

Grill the mushroom in the bacon fat, sprinkle with cayenne and serve on a round of buttered toast.

◘ Perthshire

Per person: ½ *slice of smoked salmon; a little Anchovy butter; lemon juice; oblong piece of toast.*

Butter the toast with the Anchovy butter, lay the salmon on top, brush with melted butter and cook lightly on a hot oven. Remove, brush with more melted butter and sprinkle with cayenne.

◘ Sardines

Per person: 1 *large skinned sardine; a piece of buttered toast of the same shape and size; squeeze of lemon juice; cayenne.*

Season the sardine with cayenne and heat in butter. Serve on the toast and sprinkle with the lemon juice.

◘ Scotch Woodcock

Per person: 1 *tablespoon scrambled egg;* 2 *anchovy fillets, cut into fine strips; a few capers.*

Pile the scrambled egg on a square piece of toast and arrange the fillets of anchovy on top in a trellis pattern. Fill each cavity with a caper. Reheat gently.

◘ Soft Roes

Per person: 1 *large soft herring roe; cayenne.*

Curl the herring roe, poach in butter and arrange on a round of buttered toast. Sprinkle with cayenne.

Yarmouth Toast

Per person: 1 *large grilled mushroom;* 1 *soft, curled herring roe poached in butter; chopped parsley; paprika.*

Arrange the mushroom on a small round of toast and top with the soft roe. Sprinkle with the parsley, pour over the cooking butter and sprinkle with paprika.

OYSTERS AND OTHERS

In this section you will find a few of the classic savoury titbits, such as Devils on Horseback, which do not fit into any of the specific categories already noted.

Angels on Horseback

3 *oysters per person.*

Open and lightly stiffen the oysters by heating for a few moments in their own juice. Beard and wrap each oyster in a small piece of streaky bacon, place on a skewer and grill in a fierce heat. Serve on an oblong piece of toast.

Devilled Oysters

6 *oysters per person.*

Stiffen the oysters by heating for a few minutes in their own juice and remove beards. Season with mustard and Worcester sauce, egg and breadcrumb. Deep fry and serve on a table napkin. Serve with toast.

Devils on Horseback

Per person: 1 *chicken liver;* 3 *pieces streaky bacon; an oblong piece of toast or biscuit.*

Divide the liver into three pieces and fry quickly in butter. Wrap the sautéed liver pieces in the bacon, place on skewer and grill. Serve on the toast and sprinkle with cayenne.

Marrow Bones

Saw the ends of beef marrow bones flat and then saw them into about 5-inch lengths. Make a stiff dough with flour and water, place a cap of dough over the marrow end of the bones, stand upright in a pan, surround with water and steam for one hour. Serve with fingers of toast in table napkins, accompanied by the special long spoon designed for this savoury.

Oyster Fritters

4 *oysters per person.*

Stiffen the oysters by heating for a few moments in their own juice. Beard them, season with cayenne, lemon juice and chopped parsley, dip into Frying batter and deep fry. Serve in a folded table napkin.

Palatinate Titbit

3 *per person: butter; beaten egg; breadcrumbs; a purée of hardboiled egg yolks creamed with a little anchovy, sauce Béchamel, mustard and cayenne.*

Roll the butter into small marble-sized balls. Egg and breadcrumb twice, deep fry, remove caps and drain. Fill with the egg mixture, replace caps and serve in a table napkin.

The term *sandwiches* originated from the eating habits of the Earl of Sandwich, who, reluctant to leave the gaming table for lunch, insisted on bringing his roast beef to the table with him between two slices of bread. He was not the inventor of this dish, however, but he did carve a place for himself in gastronomical history by lending his name to this savoury snack.

Basically, there are three types of sandwiches: *French* sandwiches, which are usually made with rolls (*petits pains*) or crusty bread and filled with some kind of meat; *American* sandwiches, which are sometimes two or three layers of different fillings separated by thin slices of bread; *hors d'œuvre* sandwiches, which are made with crustless bread, buttered and garnished as desired, then cut into fancy shapes. These are also known as open sandwiches.

Sandwiches prepared ahead of time—or left-overs—should be wrapped in a damp cloth, tinfoil or greaseproof paper to prevent their drying and curling at the edges. Fillings should not overlap the edge of the bread as this gives an untidy appearance. The recipes below indicate some of the various garnishes and butters which may be used and the variety of shapes into which the bread may be cut.

SANDWICHES * *SANDWICHES*

▣ aux Anchois * *Anchovy*

Spread with Anchovy butter, fill with well-drained anchovy fillets in oil and sprinkle chopped hardboiled egg on top. Cut in small triangles.

▣ au Caviar * *Caviar*

Spread with slightly salted butter. Spread one piece of bread with a thin layer of caviar, sprinkle with a few drops of lemon juice, cover with second slice of bread and cut diagonally into four triangles. Usually brown or rye bread is used.

▣ à la Crème Olga

Pass 6 egg yolks through a sieve, mix with 2 oz butter, salt, pepper and 2 small dessertspoons oil and spread bread with the mixture. Sprinkle chopped egg yolk on top and cut in squares.

Sandwiches aux Ecrevisses * *Crayfish Sandwiches*

Butter the bread, fill with chopped crayfish tails and cut in triangles.

▣ **de Foie Gras**

Pass *foie gras pâté* or *purée* through a fine sieve, combine with ⅓ the quantity of creamed butter and mix with 1 spoon of roasted, crushed and ground hazelnuts. Spread this cream on the bread and cut in triangles.

▣ **de Gibier** * *Game*

Spread with Almond butter, fill with thinly sliced or chopped game and cut in triangles.

▣ **au Gruyère, ou Cheshire** * *Cheese*

Spread with butter or Mustard butter, cover with very thin cheese slices and cut in triangles. Soft cheese such as Camembert and Brie are best passed through a sieve and mixed with ⅓ the weight of butter, seasoned with a pinch of cayenne pepper and spread on the bread.

▣ **au Jambon** * *Ham*

Spread with Mustard butter, fill with very thin slices of ham and cut across the middle once to make a sandwich of 1½-3 inches.

▣ **au Laitue** * *Lettuce*

Spread bread with Mustard butter, fill with finely shredded, slightly salted lettuce and cut once diagonally.

▣ **au Poivrons** * *Pepper*

Grill the peppers, skin them, remove seeds and white skin and chop fine. Spread bread with Cress butter, sprinkle with chopped peppers and cut in rectangles.

▣ **aux Radis** * *Radish*

Spread with butter, fill with thinly sliced radishes and salt lightly. Cut in rectangles.

▣ **aux Rillettes**

No butter is used. Spread the *Rillettes* (*see* p. 526), press the slices of bread firmly together and cut up into oblongs.

Sandwiches au Saumon * *Smoked Salmon Sandwiches*

Spread with unsalted butter or with Horseradish butter, fill with very thin slices of smoked salmon, fold in half and cut in triangles.

⊡ **au Thon** * *Tunny*

Spread with butter, fill thinly with tunny preserved in oil crushed finely with a fork; cut in rectangles.

⊡ **à la Tomate** * *Tomato*

Spread with Horseradish butter, fill with thin slices of skinned tomatoes from which seeds and liquid have been removed and cut the sandwiches in triangles.

⊡ **de Veau** * *Veal*

Spread with Horseradish or plain butter, fill with thin slices of cold roast veal and cut in rectangles.

⊡ **de Volaille** * *Chicken and Poultry*

Spread with Mustard or Horseradish butter, cover with thinly sliced or chopped poultry meat and cut in rectangles.

To critics who mocked him for eating too much fruit, George Bernard Shaw the well-known writer, who was much known for his irascible character as for his wit, made the following reply: "Look here, when you bury a piece of meat, it rots: when you bury a fruit it comes up a tree!"

There is a great deal of truth in this joking remark. G. B. Shaw lived to become an old man, and if this was not due to his becoming a vegetarian, the regular consumption of fresh fruit may well be responsible for the fact that he enjoyed excellent health until he died.

Fruit plays an important part in nutrition since it is a rich source of vitamins, especially vitamin C, and also mineral elements. It gives bulk to the diet in the form of cellulose. Candied, *glacé*, and dried fruits contain no vitamin C but are often a source of iron. For maximum benefit, fruit should be eaten fresh and uncooked, when it may be served on its own to round off a meal or as part of a prepared dessert.

Choose fruits at the peak of their season when they will be superior in quality and also relatively inexpensive. If fruit is purchased in an under-ripe condition, store at room temperature in a dark place and do not allow the fruit to touch each other. It is most important when preparing fresh fruits to wash them thoroughly in gently flowing water and dry at once. Fruit should be stored in a cool place—preferably in a single layer rather than piled up—and inspected regularly to see that it is not going bad. To store soft fruit in the refrigerator, place it in a single layer in a plastic box with a lid. (*See illustration p.* 758).

Compôtes de Fruits * *Stewed Fruit*

The fruit to be cooked should not be too ripe. It is cut either in halves or quarters, according to the size and type of fruit, and stewed in a vanilla flavoured Stock syrup of about 180° (Saccharometer reading). Some fruit such as pears, cherries, or prunes may be cooked in a syrup containing red wine and flavoured with cinnamon instead of vanilla. Once the fruits are cooked, the liquor should be reduced and, in some cases, it should be thickened with some apricot *purée*, redcurrant jelly or a little starch. In principle, however, it is the liquor in which the fruit has been stewed which is the essential ingredient.

Sirop Vanille * *Stock Syrup*

1 lb loaf sugar; 2 pints water; vanilla pod.

Dissolve the sugar slowly in the water, bring to the boil and cook until the syrup acquires a density of 18°, when tested with the saccharometer (see *Sugar Boiling*, p. 726). Remove the pan from the heat, cool and strain through muslin. Use as required.

Compôte d'Abricots * *Stewed Apricots*

Cut the apricots in half and put in a Stock syrup of about 18° (Saccharometer reading). Simmer for 7 to 8 minutes, then drain the apricots and reduce the syrup to approximately half its volume. Serve the apricots on a dish, pour the syrup over them and garnish with halves of the kernels extracted from the stones.

▣ d'Ananas * *Pineapples*

Peel the pineapple, cut in half lengthwise, remove the core and cut each half into thin slices. Stew in a Stock syrup and leave to cool. Arrange the pineapple in a circle inside a fruit dish and pour over it the reduced liquor which has been flavoured with Kirsch or rum. With tinned fruit, the same procedure is followed but the juice from the tin is used to make the syrup.

▣ de Bananes * *Bananas*

Skin the bananas which may be used whole, split lengthwise or cut diagonally in fairly thick slices. Simmer them in a rum flavoured Stock syrup which is then reduced and thickened with apricot *purée.*

▣ de Cerises * *Cherries*

Stew the stoned cherries in Stock syrup, drain the cherries, reduce the syrup which should be thickened with a little redcurrant jelly before being poured over the fruit. It is also possible to mix in a little arrowroot and flavour with Kirsch. Cherries may also be stewed in red wine flavoured with cinnamon.

▣ de Figues * *Figs*

Soak figs in water overnight. Stew whole figs gently in a vanilla Stock syrup. Drain with care, reduce the syrup and flavour with a little Kirsch.

▣ de Fraises * *Strawberries*

Simmer the strawberries in a vanilla flavoured Stock syrup. Place them in a fruit dish, reduce the syrup and thicken with a little redcurrant jelly.

▣ de Framboises * *Raspberries*

Bring the Stock syrup to the boil and pour over the raspberries which should then be covered. Drain them and place in a fruit dish. Reduce the syrup, thicken with a little starch and pour over the raspberries.

▣ de Pêches * *Peaches*

Treat in the same way as apricots. Only remove the skin after cooking.

Compôte de Poires * *Stewed Pears*

According to the size of the pears, they are left whole or cut in halves or quarters. Sprinkle with a little lemon juice and simmer in vanilla Stock syrup. Pears can also be stewed in sweetened red wine and flavoured with cinnamon.

▣ **de Pommes** * *Apples*

If the apples are to be served whole, small ones must be selected. They are then peeled and cored, sprinkled with lemon juice and simmered in vanilla Stock syrup. Apples may also be cut into quarters before they are stewed. Care must be exercised to cook gently and not too long to prevent the apples from breaking up.

▣ **de Prunes** * *Plums*

All plums may be stewed but some of the larger varieties must be cut in halves.

▣ **de Pruneaux** * *Prunes*

Soak the prunes in water or wine the night before. Simmer in syrup containing a little treacle, ½ lemon, ½ cinnamon stick and the water or wine in which the fruit has soaked.

▣ **de Rhubarbe** * *Rhubarb*

Remove the skin, cut the stalks of rhubarb into pieces 2 inches long and place in a very small quantity of Stock syrup. Since rhubarb contains a lot of moisture, it turns easily into *purée* when it starts to boil; it is preferable to cover the fruit with grease-proof paper and bake in the oven. Drain carefully, reduce the syrup and pour it over the fruit.

Macédoine * *Fruit Salad*

A variety of fruits may be used and they are generally simmered separately one after the other in the same syrup. However, while several fruits may sometimes be stewed together, certain other fruits have to be stewed separately as they would give their colour to the other fruit. Finally all the fruits are added together and the slightly thickened syrup is poured over them.

PASTRY AND BASIC MIXTURES

Flour, the foundation of pastry, bread and cakes, is one of the most common ingredients in daily use, and the numerous varieties of flour and their special properties have been fully described in the Basic Culinary Preparations (*see p.* 101). In this the Pastry and Basic Mixtures Chapter and in the following chapters dealing with Sweets and Puddings, Large Cakes and Pastries and Small Cakes and Pastries, *plain* flour must be used at all times but the correct type of flour should be chosen to achieve the best results. For example, fine pastry flours such as Vienna or Hungarian should be chosen for fancy bread and rich light pastries and cakes.

Perfect pastry needs fine flour and good quality fat and, of course, a light touch and careful baking. Once you have chosen the correct flour make sure that it is quite fresh, dry and free from lumps. The lumps will be removed from the flour by a careful sieving. The fat used and indicated in the recipes is butter, but if this proves too expensive, a mixture of lard and butter may be employed quite successfully. Fresh butter is best for Puff pastry since excess saltiness can spoil the pastry. Working in a cool room, using a marble slab, having cool hands—all these points help to make good pastry. Before starting the actual processes of mixing and rolling, assemble all the ingredients and utensils and remember that these too should be as cool as possible.

PÂTE À BISCUIT * *SPONGE CAKE MIXTURES*

There are two main types of sponge cakes in French baking, those classified as *Pâte à Génoise* and those classified as *Pâte à Biscuit*. They are both similar but they differ in that *Pâté à Biscuit* is made with separated eggs and has a firmer, slightly less fluffy texture. Most cooks agree that it is easier to make than *Génoise*, and it can often be substituted in recipes which call for *Génoise*.

$\frac{1}{4}$ *lb sugar;* 3 *oz flour;* 2 *oz butter;* 4 *eggs.* Cooking time: 20 minutes.

Put the sugar into a basin with the egg yolks and beat well until they become pale and frothy. Next add the sifted flour which is folded in lightly together with the stiffly whisked egg whites. As soon as these ingredients are well blended, quickly add the melted butter. When mixing the ingredients take the same precautions as for *Génoise* sponge. Pour immediately into a greased and floured cake tin. Bake in a moderate oven, 320° F-350° F, or Gas Mark 3-4.

Pâte à Biscuit à Boudoir * *Boudoir Sponge Fingers*

For about 3 *dozen sponge fingers:* ½ *lb sugar;* 11 *oz flour;* 4 *eggs;* 1 *tablespoon honey;* ¼ *oz cream of tartar.*

Whisk the whole eggs, sugar and honey together. Flavour with orange flower water and when the mixture is stiff and firm fold in the cream of tartar sieved with the flour. For baking see *Biscuits à la Cuiller*.

⊡ **à la Cuiller** * *Sponge Fingers*

For about 1 *dozen sponge fingers:* 3 *oz sugar;* 3 *oz flour;* 3 *eggs; vanilla.* Cooking time: 6 minutes.

Thoroughly mix the sugar and egg yolks, lightly fold in the sifted flour and stiffly whisked egg whites. Do not try to obtain a perfectly blended mixture, as excessive handling causes the mixture to liquify and the sponge fingers, when baked, tend to be flat and cracked. Pipe the mixture through a ½-inch plain tube on to greaseproof paper, dredge with castor sugar and bake in a hot oven, 400° F or Gas Mark 6.

⊡ **Fin au Beurre** * *Butter Sponge*

¼ *lb sugar;* 3 *oz flour;* 2 *oz butter;* 4 *eggs.* Cooking time: 20 minutes.

Put the sugar in a basin with the egg yolks and beat well until they become pale and frothy. Next add the sifted flour which is folded in lightly together with the stiffly whisked egg whites. As soon as these ingredients are well blended, quickly add the melted butter. When mixing the ingredients take the same precautions as for *Génoise* sponge. Pour immediately into a greased and floured cake tin. Bake in a moderate oven, 320° F-350° F or Gas Mark 4.

⊡ **de Savoie** * *Simple Sponge*

½ *lb castor sugar;* 3 *oz flour;* 3 *oz cornflour;* 7 *egg yolks;* 7 *egg whites; vanilla.* Cooking time: 30 minutes.

Prepare in the same way as for Sponge Fingers. Mix the flour and cornflour together and fold in lightly alternatively with the stiffly whisked egg whites. Baking requires considerable care. Place in a buttered and floured cake tin. Bake in a warm oven, 325° F or Gas Mark 3.

PÂTE BRISÉE * *SHORT CRUST PASTRY*

When making Short Crust pastry, *Pâte Brisée*, Puff pastry, and *Pâte Feuilletée*, the following points should be observed. Sieve together the flour, salt and baking powder. For mixing use freshly drawn tap water, as this is cooler and more aerated than water which has been standing. Add water gradually to avoid making the pastry over-moist. The uniform distribution of fat throughout the flour is essential whatever method is used to add it. If the fat is not distributed evenly and incorporated thoroughly the resultant dough has a streaky appearance and the finished pastry will be tough and hard. Try not to rub off the pieces of dough which normally cling to the finger tips back into the mixture. This will only make it rough.

The rolling out of pastry must be performed with care so that the pastry is not stretched. Over-stretched pastry dough will shrink during cooking. The board and rolling pin should be dusted lightly with flour and the dough rolled with short, quick, light, forward strokes. Always roll in one direction—forward—and keep both hands on the rolling pin. Uneven rolling will make the pastry of uneven thickness. Any excess flour should always be brushed off the pastry with a pastry brush.

A hot oven is necessary for most pastries especially puff pastries so that the entrapped air is quickly heated allowing the water and gluten, which have become incorporated in the mixing process, to be converted quickly into steam. The pastry will then rise. As baking continues in this hot atmosphere the steam will evaporate and the fat (being of a viscous nature) is absorbed in the flour leaving a crisp golden pastry. Pastry cooked in too cool an oven will be tough, greasy and heavy. On the other hand, if the oven is too hot the surface of the pastry will set too quickly, forming a thin crust and resulting in hard, tight pastry.

Do not bake Puff pastry at the same time as any food which is steaming in the oven or it will not be crisp or light. If possible pastry should be cooked on its own in the oven and the door must be open and closed gently. Pastry should be cooled on a wire rack in a warm kitchen.

Pâte Brisée Fines pour Tartes et Tartelettes * *Sweet Pastry for Tarts and Flans*

½ lb flour; ½ lb butter; ½ oz sugar; a pinch salt; about 7 fl oz water.

Sieve the flour on to a marble slab or baking board, rub in the butter finely, make a well in the centre, put in the remaining ingredients and mix everything quickly and carefully with the fingertips so that the dough does not become elastic. Wrap in polythene or a cloth and allow to rest for two hours in a cool place. It can be made the evening before, since resting for a longer period means that the paste will become firmer and lose any elasticity it may have acquired from too much handling. The above quantity is enough for 2 large fruit flans for 8 persons each or 30 small tartlets.

▣ Sucrée ou Pâte Sèche * *Rich Sweet Shortcrust*

This crisp, short, sweet pastry is used for flans, tarts and as a basis for many other fine pastries. It is rather more difficult to make than other short pastries as it has a dry, crumbly texture. The main points to remember are that the ingredients must be blended together carefully using only the finger-tips and that the pastry must be handled lightly and carefully.

¼ lb flour; 2 *oz butter;* 2 *oz sugar; pinch table salt;* 1 *whole egg or* 2 *egg yolks.*

Heap the sifted flour on a board or marble slab. Make a well in the flour, pour in the sugar, then make a well in the sugar to receive the salt, butter and egg. First blend the sugar and butter with the egg with the finger tips of one hand, then draw in the flour until the paste is thoroughly mixed and forms a smooth, firm ball. Care should be taken not to overwork the paste or it will become oily and sticky. Make this paste 2 or 3 hours in advance and leave in a cool place. In summer, when the butter is soft, the whole egg is replaced by two egg yolks; in this way a firmer paste is obtained. This paste is used for lining flans—tartlets and small *petit four* cases. Baking temperature is generally 350° F or Gas Mark 3-4, but this is really governed by the filling.

PÂTE À CHOUX * *CHOUX PASTRY*

Choux pastry may be used for both sweet and savoury dishes and may be either fried or baked. The following is a general method for making *Choux* pastry. Sieve the flour on to a sheet of greaseproof paper. Put the fat, water, salt (and sugar if used) into a saucepan and bring to the boil. When it is rapidly boiling, shoot in all the flour at once and stir over the heat with a wooden spoon until the mixture leaves the sides of the pan. Allow the mixture to cool slightly and then gradually add in the beaten eggs. Beat thoroughly until the mixture is smooth and shiny. You may not need all the eggs specified or you may need a little more. The pastry should be soft enough to pipe.

4½ *oz flour;* 3½ *oz butter;* ½ *oz sugar;* $\frac{1}{16}$ *oz (or a pinch) salt;* 9 *fl oz water;* 4 *eggs.*

Put the cold or warm water in a saucepan with the butter, salt and sugar and bring to the boil. Tip in all the sieved flour at once and mix quickly. Cook over low heat, stirring all the time until the mixture leaves the side of the pan. Remove from heat, cool slightly and add the beaten eggs gradually beating well between each addition. The paste should be of a medium consistency suitable for piping, and smooth and shiny looking. A little less or more egg may be necessary to obtain the correct consistency. For some uses, such as *hors d'œuvre*, make the pastry without sugar.

⊡ à Beignets Soufflés * *Soufflé Fritter Mixture*

½ *lb flour;* 3 *oz butter;* 1 *oz sugar; pinch salt;* ¾ *pint water;* 7 *or* 8 *eggs.*

Proceed in the same way as for *Choux* pastry. Mould between two spoons and fry in hot deep fat. When coloured and crisp, drain and roll in castor sugar.

⊡ pour Gnocchi

Make the paste as above, but using only 2 oz butter and no sugar, and season instead with pepper and grated nutmeg.

PÂTE FEUILLETÉE * *PUFF PASTRY*

Puff pastry is a crisp light pastry consisting of paper-thin layers of dough. It is used for all dishes that require a very light pastry such as *bouchées*, sweet pastries and *vol-au-vent* cases. It was formerly held that the basic Puff pastry dough should not be worked too much, but this directive is not in accord with the modern understanding of the reasons for the "lift" in Puff pastry. Contrary to popular belief the trapping of air during folding has no significant effect on the lift. Briefly it is caused by the change of water into steam in the gluten while in the oven and the consequent expansion which lifts the leaves of pastry that are insulated one from the other, by the melting butter. It is therefore necessary to mix the dough well to obtain the maximum gluten hydration. The rest period of 15 minutes mentioned in the recipe below will get rid of any excess elasticity.

9 *oz flour;* 8-9 *oz butter; about* ¼ *pint water;* ⅛ *oz salt.*

Put sieved flour on a table or marble slab. If available, a marble slab is better since it is more smooth and a better conductor of heat. Make a well in the middle, put in the salt and water and gradually incorporate the flour and water together using the finger tips. The dough should be firm, yet slightly sticky. Knead the dough for 20 minutes to develop the gluten content, it should be smooth and satiny. Let the dough rest for at least 15 minutes. The consistency of butter for Puff pastry is important; it should have the same consistency as the dough itself, that is firm rather than soft, but do not use butter which has come straight out of the refrigerator. Then roll the dough into a square, pulling out the sides slightly so that they are thinner than the middle. Put the block of butter in the middle, fold the four corners over it so that the dough is three times as long as it is wide. Use as little flour as possible for dusting and always brush it off again before folding. The dough should be about ½ inch thick at this stage. Now fold in one end towards the middle and fold the other end over it, press the edges together. This is the first turn. The dough must be rolled slowly and carefully at first so that the butter is not squeezed out. With the sealed ends towards you roll away from you. Fold in three again and turn the paste round so that the open edge faces you and roll again. This completes the second turn. Cover with polythene or a cloth and let the pastry rest in a cool place, or in a refrigerator for 15-20 minutes and give it 4 more turns, letting it rest for 15 minutes after every second turn. The total is therefore 6 turns with 2 rests in between. (*See Illustrated Culinary Techniques*).

NOTE: The amount of water depends on the quality of the flour, i.e. its capacity for absorption.

Pâte Demi-Feuilletée * *Half-Puff or Rough Puff Pastry*

In "*grande cuisine*" the Half-Puff pastry is obtained from the trimmings of the Puff pastry. These are rolled into a ball and given only one turn. However, in the domestic kitchen it may be made from the following recipe.

7 oz flour; 7 oz butter; ⅛ oz salt; juice of half a lemon; water.

Sieve the flour and heap on a marble slab or board and make a well in the centre. Chop the butter into pieces the size of a walnut and add to the flour together with the lemon juice, salt and enough water to make a light only roughly mixed paste. Wrap in a cloth or foil and leave to rest for ten minutes in a cool place. Roll the paste into a strip of about one inch thick, fold in three as for Puff pastry and turn round. With the open ends towards you, roll out to a thickness of ½ inch, fold in three and leave in a cool place for 15 minutes. Give the dough 2-3 turns as for Puff pastry and let it rest and chill a short while before using. This pastry is used for Three Kings Cake, apple turnover, pies, cheese straws, etc.

▣ Feuilletée Rapide * *Quick Puff Pastry*

1 *lb flour;* 1 *lb butter; pinch of salt; juice of* 1 *lemon; approximately ½ pint water.*

Prepare in the same way as for Puff pastry but use butter which has been creamed and chilled. Then proceed as follows. Knead the dough lightly then give 4 half turns one after the other and use straight away. A good pastry is obtainable, but it is more likely to break when baked.

▣ Feuilletée Russe * *Russian Puff Pastry*

1 *lb flour;* 1 *lb butter; pinch of salt;* 2 *eggs; juice of* 1 *lemon; a little water.*

Using half the flour, place it on the marble slab, make a hollow in the middle and add the salt, eggs and lemon juice and knead thoroughly for some time until it has an elastic consistency and leaves the hands without sticking as for *Brioche* dough. When the paste is suitably smooth, wrap it up in a cloth and keep it in a cold place for 3 hours. Cream together the butter and the rest of the flour with as little water as possible (water is unnecessary if the butter is soft enough). Next roll out the first piece of paste and place the flour and butter mixture in the middle of it. Leave to stand for 30 minutes and then give 2 half turns and a further 2 after a rest. Use in the same way as ordinary Puff pastry.

Pâte à Galette des Rois * *Twelfth Night Cake made with Puff Pastry*

This cake is made with scraps of Puff pastry. Roll the scraps into a ball, without handling them too much, give a half turn so that the scraps become well amalgamated, and when the paste is smooth, it is shaped into a crown, decorated with slices of lemon, egg washed and baked slowly for 30 minutes, in a warm oven, 325° F or Gas Mark 3.

PÂTE À FRIRE ET PÂTE À CRÊPES * *PANCAKE AND COATING BATTERS*

There is a wide range of dishes, both sweet and savoury, to be made from batter mixtures ranging from a simple pancake to the rich yeast batter. This is a branch of cookery where it is especially important to understand the basic principles for success.

Batter is basically a mixture of flour, liquid, fat and eggs. The secret of success depends upon a smooth batter which has been well-beaten and a high temperature for cooking. The following is a general method of making a batter. Sieve the flour, salt and sugar into a basin. Make a deep well in the centre of the flour, drop the unbeaten eggs into the well and about 1 tablespoon of the liquid and begin to mix with a wooden spoon. Gradually mix in the flour and up to half the total liquid quantity. If the batter is kept rather thick at this stage of mixing there is less risk of lumps forming. When the batter is thick and smooth, an egg whisk takes the place of the wooden spoon and the mixture is beaten for at least 10 minutes. The melted, lukewarm butter or oil are now stirred in. The basin is covered and left for at least 2 hours in a cool place. The purpose of this rest is to allow the starch grains in the flour to soften and swell so that they will cook quickly over the high heat and a light crisp batter will result.

Some recipes, such as the recipe for Rich Pancake batter, require stiffly whisked egg whites and these are folded in after the resting period and immediately before cooking. When making pancakes choose a frying pan suited to the desired size of pancakes—fairly small if possible. The pan itself should be perfectly clean and have a smooth level surface.

Pâte à frire is a special batter used for food which is to be cooked in deep fat. Although the method of making this batter is the same as that used for pancakes, the consistency should be slightly thicker and the recipe contains yeast. The purpose of this batter is to form a light crisp coating for various foods, the most popular of which are fritters. The use of yeast in this batter is important as it gives a particularly crisp light result. The rules of yeast cookery which are explained in a later section apply also to yeast batter. The addition of oil also helps to give crispness. Food to be coated may be cooked or uncooked but it should be dry so that the batter will adhere to the surface. Use the curve of a fork or flat whisk to dip the food in the batter. Then lift it out and plunge immediately into the hot fat. When the food is cooked (and the time taken for this will depend upon whether cooked food is used) it should look crisp and golden brown. Then drain well and serve very hot.

⊡ à Crêpes * *Plain Pancake Batter*

4½ oz flour; 1 oz vanilla sugar; 1 oz melted butter; 1 pinch salt; 2 eggs; 7½ fl oz cold milk; brandy or rum (enough for 12 small pancakes).

Put the sieved flour and salt in a bowl, make a well in the centre and break in the eggs. Add sugar and a small amount of milk and mix to a smooth batter with a consistency like thick cream, using an egg whisk. Gradually beat in the rest of the milk, it may be necessary to add a little extra milk. Finally gently fold in the butter. Let the batter stand for 2-3 hours before use. If desired, use single cream instead of milk and leave out the butter. Do not use more sugar than stated in the recipe, otherwise the pancakes will brown too much and too quickly when fried.

Pâte à Crêpes Fine * *Rich Pancake Batter*

¼ *lb flour;* 1 *whole egg and* 1 *egg yolk;* 1 *oz castor sugar; pinch salt;* 1 *pint cold milk;* 1 *oz melted butter;* 1 *whisked egg white; orange flower water, or rum or Cognac.*

Make as for Plain Pancake batter but lightly fold in the stiffly whisked egg whites at the last moment when you are ready to use the batter. Use for *Crêpes Suzette*, etc.

⊡ à Croustades Frites * *Batter for Deep Fried Croustades*

3 *oz flour;* 1 *egg; pinch of salt; approximately* ¼ *pint milk and water (mixed).*

Prepare a fairly thick Pancake batter (*Pâte à Crêpes*). This may be used for *Delices de Manon.*

⊡ à Frire * *Basic Coating Batter*

7 *oz flour; a pinch salt;* 2 *fl oz olive oil;* ½ *pint lukewarm water;* 2 *egg whites;* ¼ *oz yeast.*

Warm the flour in a bowl and make a well in the centre. Dissolve the yeast in the lukewarm water. Add the oil, salt, water and yeast then mix quickly by hand gradually incorporating the flour, until the batter becomes smooth and just coats the fingers. Use more or less water according to the quality of flour. Mix batter lightly so that it does not become elastic, it is best to add all the water at the beginning in order to avoid unnecessary mixing. Cover with a plate and allow to stand in a warm place for 3-4 hours. The yeast will rise and bubble. Just before using gently fold in 2 stiffly beaten egg whites.

PÂTE À GÉNOISE * *BASIC GÉNOISE SPONGE MIXTURE*

Génoise pastry is a rich sponge mixture containing almost equal quantities of fat, eggs and sugar. It should be rich, yet delicate and light. The very best ingredients should be chosen for a *Génoise* sponge. This means castor sugar, fresh eggs, cake flour and unsalted butter.

First of all, prepare the baking tins since the mixture must be baked as soon as mixing is completed. The tins may be lined with buttered floured greaseproof paper.

The method is rather like that of a whisked sponge. Whole eggs and sugar are whisked together in a bowl over a pan of hot, but not boiling, water. (It is important that the bowl does not touch the water.) Whisking is continued until the mixture is thick and doubled in volume. Then the bowl is removed from the saucepan and whisking is continued until the mixture is very thick, firm and cool. Flavourings, if used, may be added at this stage and the flour sifted over the mixture. Quickly cut and fold the flour in with a metal spoon, or spatula and add the melted butter which should have been melted in a *bain-marie* or double boiler so that it is just melted and barely lukewarm. The cutting and folding action should be done with sharp, even strokes turning the bowl around with the free hand. As soon as the mixture is even and there are no more dry "pockets" of flour, through the mixture or at the bottom of the bowl stop folding immediately. If the mixture is over-worked it turns green and is completely spoiled. Fill at once into the prepared tin and bake immediately in a preheated oven.

3 *oz flour;* ¼ *lb sugar;* 3 *oz butter;* 4 *whole eggs; flavouring to taste.* Cooking time: 25-35 minutes.

Put the sugar and eggs in a basin over a pan of hot water but check that the basin is not actually in contact with the water. Whisk up these ingredients until they have doubled their volume and are slightly warm. Remove from the heat and continue to whisk until the mixture is cool and thick. Then, using a spatula, fold in the sifted flour and finally the melted butter, the butter should be just melted but not hot otherwise the sponge would not have the same pleasant flavour. To keep the sponge light, it should be mixed very quickly and lightly; over-mixing will make the sponge heavy. Pour into a *Génoise* flan ring or cake tin which has been greased. Bake in a moderate oven, 350° F or Gas Mark 4, then turn out on to a cooling wire.

Pâte à Génoise au Caramel * *with Caramel*

Use the same proportions as for an ordinary *Génoise* sponge. Caramelise 3 tablespoonfuls of the sugar. Pour this on an oiled marble slab and, when it is cold, grind it and mix it with the sugar. Now follow the recipe for basic *Génoise* sponge.

▣ Pralinée * *with Praline*

Follow the same method as for *Génoise*, replacing 1 oz of the flour by 1 oz of powdered praline. Bake in a cooler oven, 330° F-340° F or Gas Mark 3.

PÂTE LEVÉE * *YEAST DOUGHS*

This section includes bread, pastries and batters incorporating the use of yeast as a raising agent. An understanding of the natural properties and correct handling of yeast is necessary to ensure the best results from your yeast cookery. Please consult the notes on yeast in "Basic Ingredients" (*p.* 103). It is best to use a hard wheat flour for yeast mixtures. For yeast breads and pastries all utensils should be warmed to blood heat. This is most important since a cold atmosphere retards the action of the yeast. Blood heat is considered the best temperature for yeast being neither too cold to retard the action nor too hot to kill the yeast.

The rich doughs used for *Croissants* and *Brioches* and indeed the whole mixing and making processes of these doughs differs considerably from the way in which English bread is made. First of all, sieve the flour on to the board and divide it into four portions with a knife. Crumble the yeast with the lukewarm water and mix until smooth and the yeast has dissolved. Pour this into one of the four portions of the flour gradually mixing them together. Reserve the remaining three sections. You may find you need a little extra warm water to make a smooth soft dough. Cut a cross on top and place the dough in a pan of warm water—it should be blood heat, which means you could comfortably bear your hand in it. Leave this on one side. As the dough develops it gradually rises in the pan. The dough is called "the ferment" at this stage. In the meantime draw together the remaining three portions of flour, make a well in the centre, break in the eggs and mix together to make a fairly firm paste.

The next stage is the beating process whereby the dough is lifted up with the fingers and with a flick of the wrist thrown down again. You will find the dough sticks to the fingers at this point but do not be discouraged. Continue this beating process until you find it no longer adheres to the fingers but becomes a fine elastic dough. Now work in the softened butter, sugar and salt and continue beating for 5-6 minutes.

Remove the yeast dough from the pan by putting the hand, fingers spread out in the pan, underneath it and drain on a clean muslin cloth for a minute or two. It is important that you remove this yeast dough from the pan when it is ready, that is, when it has doubled in volume and the top is rather like a cauliflower. If necessary it can always be left covered in muslin until you have finished beating the bulk of the dough. When both doughs are ready mix them together without kneading or beating.

The next stage is to put the dough into a large floured bowl, cover with a floured cloth and leave it in a cool place or refrigerator to chill. The chilling takes about 12 hours so it is advisable to make the dough the day before it is needed. Before being left to rest overnight the dough should be folded over again to make it firmer. The next day the dough may be shaped, proved and baked in a very hot oven, 425° F or Gas Mark 7.

Pâte Levée à Biscottes Grillées * *Rusk Bread Dough*

1 *lb flour;* ¼ *oz salt;* 1 *oz butter;* 1 *tablespoon cold milk;* 1 *egg.*

For the ferment: ½ *pint warm milk* (100° *F or* 38° *C*); ½ *oz yeast;* ¼ *lb flour.*

First of all prepare the ferment, mix the yeast with the warm milk in a large bowl using the fingers and add the quarter pound of sifted flour, sprinkle a little flour over the top. This process which is known as "sponging" accelerates the activity of the yeast. Cover the basin with a cloth and put in a warm place until the mixture is double in bulk. Meanwhile, in a warm bowl sift the one pound of flour with salt, and rub in the butter, then stir in 1 tablespoon cold milk mixed with the egg. Mix this with the fermented dough and put to prove 1 hour, covered and in a warm place. Then press the dough down with the knuckles and leave for a further 30 minutes. Mould the dough into shape and place in warmed, greased oblong tins. Prove until well-risen, this will take about 15-20 minutes and then bake in a very hot oven, 425° F or Gas Mark 7, for about 35 minutes. Next day cut into neat slices and toast carefully and not too quickly in an oven or under the grill.

⊡ à Brioche * *Brioche Dough*

9 *oz flour;* 9 *oz butter;* ½ *oz sugar;* ⅛ *oz salt;* ¼ *oz yeast;* 3 *small eggs;* 4 *fl oz water* (*approximately*).

Put one quarter of the flour on a table or marble slab, make a well in the middle and put in the yeast, which has been dissolved in the lukewarm water. Mix the water, yeast and flour into a soft dough, adding more lukewarm water if necessary. Roll the dough into a ball, cut a cross in the top and place this ferment in a casserole or wide, shallow saucepan, containing a little lukewarm water, until it has doubled in volume. In the meantime mix the remainder of the flour with the eggs and knead until the dough is elastic and leaves the hands without sticking. Now add the butter, which must be rather soft, the salt and the sugar and knead together for another 5-6 minutes. Drain the ferment, which should have doubled in volume, and combine the two carefully without kneading, place the dough in a floured bowl, cover with polythene or a damp cloth, to prevent a skin from forming and keep in a cool place till needed. Usually the dough is made about 5 to 6 o'clock in the evening so that by 8 or 9 o'clock the next morning it will have doubled in volume once more. It is folded over again before being left to rest overnight. This makes the dough firmer, so that it can be given the desired shape, according to individual recipes.

NOTE. If the recipe is considered too expensive the amount of butter can, if necessary, be reduced to 3½ oz.

⊡ à Coulibiac * *Coulibiac Dough*

For 8-10 *persons:* ¾ *lb flour;* ¼ *lb butter; pinch of salt;* ½ *oz yeast;* 2 *eggs.*

Coulibiac is made either with *Brioche* dough prepared with the above ingredients or it may be made with Puff pastry. Keep the *Brioche* dough firm so that it can be rolled out. The full method of preparation of this dish may be found in the fish section.

Pâte Levée à Croissants de Boulanger * *Croissant Dough*

For 15 portions: 5 oz flour; 2 oz butter; pinch salt; ¼ oz yeast; 4 fl oz water or milk. Cooking time: 7-8 minutes.

Make a ferment with a quarter of the flour, the yeast and some of the water, place in a saucepan of warm water and leave until risen (*see general notes p.* 719). Meanwhile mix the rest of the flour with the salt, rub in half the butter and add a little warm water and milk. When the yeast ferment has risen, blend into the mixture. The dough should not be too soft. Put it in a basin, cover with a cloth and leave in a warm place to rise for 5-6 hours. Then put the dough on a marble slab, knead well and flatten out with the fist. Spread the remainder of the butter on the dough and roll it by giving first three half turns and then a quarter of an hour later, another two half turns, following the same method as for Puff pastry. To shape the *croissants*, roll out the dough into a fairly thin strip and cut into triangular pieces with the sides about 3 inches long. Roll up tightly and curl each piece into a crescent shape on a baking sheet, leave to rise in a warm place for about 20-30 minutes, until double in bulk. Brush over lightly with egg wash and bake in a very hot oven, 425° F or Gas Mark 7, for 15-20 minutes.

▣ à Kugelhopf * *Kugelhopf Cake Dough*

½ lb flour; 2 oz butter; 1 oz castor sugar; ½ oz yeast; ¼ lb Muscatel raisins; pinch salt; 2 eggs; 7½ fl oz milk; 3 oz blanched and split or shredded almonds (optional). Cooking time: 40-45 minutes.

Cream the yeast with 1 teaspoon sugar. Add a little lukewarm milk. Sift flour and salt into a warm mixing bowl. Make a well in the centre of the flour. Pour in the yeast, sprinkle some flour over, cover and stand in a warm place for 15 minutes or until the yeast cracks through the flour. Beat in the eggs, one at a time, then add the warm milk, melted butter, and remaining sugar and beat by hand until the dough is soft and elastic. This will probably take about 10-15 minutes. It may be necessary to add a little more milk in order to obtain the correct soft consistency. Lastly add the raisins to the dough. Butter a fluted mould or special *Kugelhopf* mould, and dust with some castor sugar and the almonds if used. Put the dough in the prepared tin and leave to rise to double its original volume in a warm place (the dough should have risen to almost fill the tin). Stand the tin on a thick baking sheet and bake in a moderate oven, 375° F or Gas Mark 5. Cool the cakes in the tins for 5 minutes then turn them out on to cooling racks.

▣ à Pain Brioche * *Plain Brioche Dough (for Bread)*

½ lb flour; 3 oz butter; pinch of salt; ¼ oz yeast; 1 *egg; ¼ pint water.* Cooking time: about 20 minutes if baked in a tin.

Prepare this dough like a *Brioche* dough, keeping it soft. Make the day before, transfer to a cylindrical mould with a lid or simply make little rolls on a baking sheet. Leave to rise in a warm place, brush with egg and bake in a hot oven, 375°-400° F or Gas Mark 5-6.

▣ à Pain de Mie ou Pain Anglais * *Bread Dough or English Loaf*

1 *lb flour; ¾ oz yeast; ½ oz salt; ½ pint warm milk.* Cooking time: 1 hour altogether.

Prepare a dough by mixing together a quarter of the flour and the yeast which has been dissolved in a little warm milk. This mixture should be very soft. Sieve the rest of the flour over the top of the yeast dough and leave in a warm place until the yeast rises and cracks through the flour. Mix everything together thoroughly in the bowl and gradually add the remaining warm milk and salt. Beat the dough until it is smooth, glossy and soft, then place the dough immediately into special hermetically sealed tins. If these are not available use an ordinary bread tin and place a lid and a weight on top. The tin should only be half full. Bake in a very hot oven, 425° F or Gas Mark 7. Do not open the tin to see if the bread is ready for at least 45 minutes after putting it in the oven.

Pâte Levée à Petits Pains au Lait * *Milk Rolls*

For about 24 *rolls:* 7 *oz flour;* 2½ *oz butter;* ½ *oz sugar; good pinch salt;* ¼ *oz yeast;* 7 *fl oz milk.* Cooking time: 6-8 minutes.

Make a ferment with a quarter of the flour, the yeast and enough warm milk to make a smooth soft ball of dough. Mark a cross on the top and put it to rise in a saucepan of warm water, as described in the general notes (p. 719). Meanwhile rub the butter into the rest of the flour, add the salt and moisten with the remaining warm milk. Beat this dough as for *Brioche* until it becomes a fine elastic dough. Incorporate the yeast ferment and leave in a warm place for 3-4 hours. When the dough is well risen, knead it thoroughly on a marble slab, then shape into pieces the size of a pigeon's egg. Roll these pieces, into longish, slightly pointed rolls on a floured marble slab and place on a baking sheet. Let them rise in a warm place until double their size. This will take about 20-30 minutes. Brush with beaten egg and bake in a hot oven, 400° F or Gas Mark 6. These rolls are cut open lengthwise and used for French sandwiches.

⊡ à Savarin et à Babas * *Savarin and Baba Dough*

¼ *lb flour;* 1 *oz butter;* ¼ *oz yeast;* 1 *oz sugar; pinch salt;* 2 *eggs;* 3-4 *fl oz lukewarm milk.* Cooking time: 20 minutes.

Cream the yeast with 1 teaspoonful sugar. Add a little warm milk. Sift flour and salt into a warm mixing bowl. Make a well in the centre of the flour. Pour in the yeast, sprinkle some flour over. Cover and stand in a warm place for 15 minutes or until the yeast cracks through the flour. Add beaten eggs, warm milk, melted butter and remaining sugar and beat well with the hand for 10-15 minutes. The dough should be of a soft consistency. Two-thirds fill a well-greased *savarin* mould with the dough. Allow to prove until the dough rises just above the level of the mould. Bake in a hot oven, 400° F or Gas Mark 6.

Babas are made with the same dough as *savarin*, but, for the proportions given above, cleaned, dried fruit is added, about 2 oz currants and 1 oz sultanas. Prepared in *dariole* moulds and baked as *savarin.*

NOTE. This method of preparing the dough allows *savarins* and *babas* to be made within two hours and gives perfect results. Details of the syrup in which *babas* and *savarins* are soaked are given in the section on Creams and Custards.

⊡ à Pizza * *Pizza Dough*

For 6 *persons:* 14 *oz flour;* ¾ *oz yeast;* ¾ *oz salt;* 7 *fl oz milk and water;* ½ *oz lard or butter; pepper;* 8 *fl oz olive oil to sprinkle on the pizza.*

Sift the flour and salt into a warm bowl. Dissolve the yeast in the warm water and milk. Make a well in the flour and pour in the yeast mixture; beat thoroughly then work in the softened fat. Cover with a cloth and allow to stand one hour in a warm place. When it begins to rise divide the dough into 6 pieces, mould into balls and allow to stand for a further

15 minutes. Then flatten gently with a rolling pin, pull out each gently with the fingers into a circle about ¼-inch thick. This must be done with the fingers to ensure that the dough remains light and supple. Place the circles on a well greased baking sheet. Arrange the ingredients as indicated in the particular *Pizza* recipe. When completed, moisten the *Pizza* with the oil, and bake in the oven at 375° F or Gas Mark 4-5, for 8-10 minutes. (*For recipes see p.* 238.)

Pâte Levée à Viennois (Weiner Krapfen) * *Viennese Fritter Dough*

9 oz flour; 3 oz butter; ½ oz sugar; pinch salt; ¼ oz yeast; 2 eggs; about ½ pint warm milk.

Blend the milk and yeast together. Follow the same method as for *Brioche* dough, keeping the dough fairly firm so that it can be rolled out after it has been left to stand. Cook as for *Beignet soufflés.*

PÂTE DIVERSES * *ASSORTED PASTRY RECIPES*

In this section you will find a selection of miscellaneous basic pastry recipes which cannot be classified according to the categories of pastry mixtures mentioned in this chapter. The marzipan paste in *Pâte d'Amandes Fondante* may be used for a multitude of *petits fours* and sweetmeats, such as marzipan fruits. Marzipan should be handled as little as possible otherwise the heat of your hands will "oil" it and, in this condition, it will not mould smoothly.

Pâte d'Amandes Fondante * *Fondant Almond Paste*

7 oz almonds; 1½ lb castor sugar; 1 vanilla pod; 2 liqueur glasses of cold water; 1 tablespoon glucose.

Blanch the almonds, wash them in cold water, drain them and then grind them very finely in a mortar while gradually adding the two liqueur glasses of cold water. The addition of water to the almonds prevents them from becoming oily. However, the water must be added very, very gradually, otherwise it would impede the grinding process. Bring the sugar to the crack (*see Sugar Boiling p.* 726) and when it is cooked, remove from the heat and stir into the ground almonds with a spatula. Mix thoroughly until a sandy texture is achieved. At this moment, return the mixture to the mortar and grind again until it is almost cold. Now place on a marble slab and knead with the hand until the mixture is quite malleable, and has a consistency of a short paste. Wrap in a damp cloth and keep in a covered basin in a cool place until the paste is required for use. Almond paste is an ingredient of a large number of *petits fours.*

Recipe 2: ½ lb dried, blanched almonds reduced to a very fine powder in a mortar and then mixed by hand on the table with 7 oz Fondant icing and a little powdered vanilla. In this way a similar paste is obtained, although it is not so white and smooth, but it is made more rapidly and can be used for the same purposes.

▣ à Berrichons * *Macaroon Paste*

¼ lb ground almonds; ¼ lb vanilla sugar; 2 oz flour; 4 whisked egg whites.

Cooking time: 7-8 minutes.

Whisk the egg whites until stiff and firm then fold in the almonds, sugar and sifted flour. Use a Savoy bag to pipe the mixture on a greased and floured baking sheet either in a round shape like little macaroons or in elongated fingers like *Langues de Chat.* Bake in a hot oven, 400° F or Gas Mark 6. These biscuits may be used to make good quality *petits fours.*

Pâte à Frolle Dite Napolitaine * *Neapolitan Almond Paste*

½ lb flour; 5 oz blanched almonds; 5 oz butter; 5 oz castor sugar; 2 small eggs; pinch salt; zest of 1 *lemon.*

Grind the almonds finely, gradually adding the sugar so as to prevent them becoming oily. Add a whole egg. Make a well in the flour and pour in the mixture, adding the butter, the second egg, salt and lemon or orange zest. Vigorously knead this paste which must be firm and easy to roll out. Leave for 1 hour before use. It is generally used for the preparation of *petits fours* and the lining of small tartlets and *barquettes*.

Pâte à Galette des Rois * *Twelfth Night Cake Mixture*

½ lb flour; 6 oz butter; pinch of salt; ¼ pint water.

Place the sifted flour on a marble slab, make a well in the centre and put in the salt, water and well creamed butter. Mix these ingredients lightly and quickly. When the paste is fairly well mixed, roll it into a ball and wrap it up in a cloth or foil. Let it stand for at least an hour in a cool place. Then give it four half turns as for Puff pastry, allowing it to rest after the second half turn. This paste is used after four half turns instead of six.

Pâte à Pain d'Epices * *French Spice Bread*

1 *lb sifted flour;* 1 *lb honey; ¼ lb castor sugar;* 1 *oz chopped candied orange peel;* 1 *oz chopped candied lemon peel; pinch (⅛ oz approximately) bicarbonate of soda;* 2 *tablespoons water; pinch cinnamon; pinch ground cloves; zest of* 1 *orange and* 1 *lemon.*

Put the flour in a basin, add the sieved spices and pour in the melted but not too hot honey. Add the sugar, peel and bicarbonate dissolved in the water. Mix all the ingredients first with a wooden spoon and then by hand, pulling the dough and folding it back upon itself until it is of an even consistency. Leave to stand for 4 to 5 days covered with a cloth. Then roll out the dough to a thickness of about 1 inch and place on a greased baking tray. Bake in a moderate oven, 350° F or Gas Mark 3-4, for 30 minutes.

Pâte à Pâtés pour Croustades et Timbales * *Pie Pastry*

9 oz flour; 3 oz butter; 1½ oz lard; 2 fl oz olive oil; ½ oz salt; 1 egg yolk; 7½ fl oz cold water.

Sieve the flour and salt on to a board, make a well in the centre and put in all the ingredients. Mix the ingredients in the centre together and gradually incorporate the flour, then knead well. The dough should be pushed backwards and forwards again and again with the ball of the hand so as to give it plenty of body, develop the gluten in the flour and make it strong enough to hold the filling later and not be softened by the moisture. The paste will begin to feel more rubbery and elastic. The quantities given are sufficient for a pie for 6 persons.

NOTE: The pastry can be made with 5 oz of lard only and a little warm water; this improves its baking qualities but the flavour is different.

LES MASSES À MERINGUÉS * *BASIC MERINGUE MIXTURES*

Meringue is a light airy confection made by whisking egg white, sugar and air, plus salt and flavouring. Only fresh, perfect egg whites should be chosen for making meringue, and it is a good idea to break each egg one by one into a small bowl first and then transfer it to a larger bowl for whisking. This initial separation will ensure that if one of the eggs should be bad it will not spoil the rest. The egg white must be separated very carefully from the yolk, as it is important that no egg yolk gets into the white. The bowl and all utensils used for whisking egg whites must be absolutely free from grease. When beating, add a little sugar which is subtracted from the total quantity, as this helps the mixture to beat more smoothly. Only use very fine castor sugar; coarse sugar does not dissolve easily in egg white.

◘ aux Amandes ou Japonais I * *Almond Meringue*

For 6 persons: 5 egg whites; 7 oz castor sugar; 6 oz ground almonds; vanilla or other flavouring.

Use the same method as for Swiss meringue, but mix the ground, dried almonds with the sugar before adding the latter to the stiffly whisked egg whites.

◘ aux Amandes ou Japonaise II

For 6 persons: 10 *egg whites;* 14 *oz castor sugar;* 7 *oz ground almonds;* 4 *oz flour;* 2 *oz melted butter.*

Whisk the egg whites with 2 oz sugar until stiff and firm and then, with a spatula, fold in the ground almonds and flour and finally the melted butter. Pipe into rounds or ovals on a greased and floured baking tray. Bake for approximately 15 minutes in a warm oven, 350° F or Gas Mark 4.

◘ Cuite * *Cooked Meringue*

4 *egg whites;* 8 *oz vanilla flavoured icing sugar.*

Whisk the egg whites and icing sugar over a very gentle heat until the mixture is firm enough to form a thick trail. Although it should be warm, it must not be cooked. Bake in a very cool oven, 225° F or Gas Mark ½-1. This meringue is used for making featherlight *petits fours, rochers* and imitation mushrooms, etc.

◘ aux Fraises * *Fruit Meringue*

5 *egg whites;* 8 *oz sugar;* 8 *oz strawberry purée;* 2 *oz glucose.*

Boil the sugar with the glucose to the small crack degree or 280° F: stir in the strawberry *purée*, which will reduce the temperature of the sugar, and bring back to the small ball degree or 245° F. Pour on to the stiffly whisked egg whites, stirring with a spatula, and add a few drops of cochineal. This meringue may be made with all sorts of fruit *purées*. It is used as a filling for *petits fours*, cakes and ice cream *soufflés*. Allow to dry out in a very cool oven for 2 hours. Oven temperature: must not exceed 225° F or Gas Mark ½-1.

Masse à Meringue Italienne * *Italian Meringue*

3 egg whites; 8 oz loaf sugar; vanilla.

Boil the sugar to the soft ball degree or 245° F. Pour it over the stiffly whisked egg whites and continue to whisk at the same time. Leave to cool down and cover with a damp cloth. This meringue is used on various cakes and desserts.

▣ Suisse * *Swiss*

4 egg whites; 8 oz vanilla flavoured castor sugar.

Whisk the egg whites until they are stiff. Then whisk in half the sugar. Stop whisking and sprinkle in the rest of the sugar and fold this in quickly and carefully with a spatula or metal spoon. This meringue is used to make shells or bases which are filled with ice cream or Chantilly cream.

LA CUISSON DU SUCRE * *SUGAR BOILING*

It is not difficult to make candies, fondants, ices, fruits and spun sugar confections providing you have the proper utensils. The following special equipment will be invaluable for this type of work.

A large aluminium saucepan with a smooth interior, or if possible, an untinned copper sugar boiler is preferable.

A broad spatula.

A sugar "thermometer" or saccharometer which measures the density, not the temperature, of a syrup.

A basin of hot water containing a soft brush.

The basic method of sugar boiling which is included in the preparation of many sweets depends on the fact that when sugar and water are boiled together, first of all the sugar dissolves and then the two form a syrup. Once the mixture becomes a syrup and heat is applied, it continues to cook through various stages of density due to the evaporation of the water. It eventually becomes pure sugar once more and turns to caramel. The numerous varieties of confectionery are made by stopping the boiling at certain variable temperatures which results in the different densities of sugar syrup.

General Method

Place the sugar, preferably castor or lump sugar, in the boiler and add the liquid. Heat until the sugar has completely dissolved stirring with a wooden spoon or spatula, but being careful not to splash the syrup up the sides of the pan. Immediately the sugar has dissolved, add the liquid glucose, cream of tartar, lemon juice or whatever is called for in the recipe to prevent the sugar from crystallising or graining.

Remove the spoon and on no account stir again. Now boil rapidly until the desired density is reached. While the syrup is cooking crystals will form on the sides of the pan; these are wiped off with a brush dipped in hot water. This prevents all the sugar from crystallising.

It is important to remember to dip the saccharometer (or thermometer) in hot water before putting it in the boiling hot syrup and to take the temperature at eye level. When the syrup reaches the right density or temperature, boiling must not be allowed to continue.

Remove the pan from the heat and dip it in a bowl of cold water for a moment to prevent further boiling. The various degrees of sugar boiling correspond to the following density degrees on the saccharometer. A special sugar boiling thermometer may be used for measuring the temperature of liquids at very high temperatures, so the equivalent fahrenheit temperatures have also been listed.

Sugar is ready for testing as soon as the boiling process produces many small bubbles which are very close together. This means that all the water has evaporated and the sugar has started to cook. It is most important at this stage, to watch the liquid very carefully so that the boiling can be stopped when the required stage or degree is reached.

THREAD	215-220° F	or a reading of 25 degrees on the saccharometer
LARGE THREAD/PEARL	225-230° F	” ” ” ” 30 ” ” ” ”
BLOW/SOUFFLÉ	230° F	” ” ” ” 37-38 ” ” ” ”
SOFT/SMALL BALL	240° F	” ” ” ” 39 ” ” ” ”
HARD BALL	260° F	” ” ” ” 40 ” ” ” ”
SOFT/SMALL CRACK	280° F	
HARD/LARGE CRACK	310° F	
CARAMEL	380-390° F	

From the small crack degree onwards the syrup is too stiff to allow the saccharometer to be used, although the latter is graduated up to 44 degrees.

The various degrees of sugar boiling are named and described below, they follow each other naturally during the boiling. It is advisable to dip the fingers into cold water before testing.

THREAD (215-220° F)

Take a little syrup between the thumb and forefinger and stretch them apart; a thin thread is formed which does not break when stretched.

LARGE THREAD/PEARL (225-230° F)

A few moments later the same test will produce a much stronger thread.

BLOW OR SOUFFLÉ (230° F)

Dip a skimmer in the syrup, remove and blow through it immediately and small bubbles should appear which float off the skimmer and burst in the air.

SOFT/SMALL BALL (240° F)

Dipping a piece of wood first in water and then in the boiling syrup, a small soft globule adheres to the tip.

HARD/LARGE BALL (260° F)

When the test is repeated a few moments later, a firmer ball is obtained—rather like a jelly sweet or gum drop.

SOFT/SMALL CRACK (280° F)

Dipping some of the syrup in water, it becomes brittle but still sticks to the teeth when bitten.

HARD/LARGE CRACK (310° F)

A few minutes later the syrup becomes even more brittle—it breaks cleanly like glass and no longer sticks to the teeth.

If sugar is boiled beyond these degrees, during which it remains colourless, the syrup will turn yellow, then brown and the sugar is said to caramelise.

CARAMEL FOR COLOURING PURPOSES

Boil the sugar until the caramel becomes dark brown and gives off a pungent smoke. Remove from the heat and pour in slowly and carefully, about a quarter of a pint of cold water. This will make the sugar rise up and release a great deal of smoke. Reboil until the burnt sugar dissolves completely and a thin syrup forms. Strain through a cloth, pour into a bottle and cork. Keep the caramel syrup sufficiently fluid to pour easily.

SPUN SUGAR

Follow the directions for sugar boiling and boil the sugar to the hard/large crack (310° F) and leave to cool until it becomes very thick. Holding a fork in the right hand, dip it lightly into the syrup taking up only a very small amount of syrup, then lift it out at arm's length, as high as possible, and move it to and fro rapidly above an oiled spatula (or rolling pin) so that the thin silky threads of the sugar are caught over the handle of the spatula. Dip the fork in the syrup again and repeat until the syrup is too cool. Reheat with a little water and continue. Remove the spun sugar very carefully from the spatula and use as required. It may be used as decoration or additional decoration for *gâteaux*, and cold sweets like ices and *soufflés*.

THE SACCHAROMETER

This small instrument which should have a place in every kitchen is used for measuring the density not the temperature of a syrup. It resembles a thermometer in appearance and is constructed in such a way that the various degrees of sugar can be read off on it. The saccharometer is unaffected by heat and is used for measuring syrups for water ices, confectionery, candied fruits, etc.

For measuring use a tall, narrow container and pour in enough syrup to make it possible to put in the saccharometer so it will float and not touch the bottom. If the reading is 25°, for example, and a syrup of 28° is required more sugar must be added; if however it measures only 20° or 22° further reducing by boiling is required.

LES CRÈMES, GLACES ET APPAREILS DIVERS * *CREAMS, ICINGS AND FILLINGS*

Here is a selection of the most popular and frequently used icings and fillings. The basis of many cream fillings are eggs and butter and for good results these should be as fresh as possible. There are three distinct forms of icing—*water* icing, *royal* icing and *fondant icing*.

Chocolat Granulé * *Chocolate Vermicelli*

Melt some chocolate over a double boiler, allow to cool slightly. Then force it through a sieve with a pestle, allowing it to fall on sheet of greaseproof paper where it resembles thick vermicelli. Leave it to dry in the open air and then separate by hand.

CRÈME * *CUSTARD CREAMS*

▣ aux Amandes I * *Almond Custard Cream*

7 oz almonds; 7 oz sugar; 2 oz butter; 4 egg yolks; 1 fl oz rum.

Grind the almonds finely with the sugar. Add the egg yolks, butter and finally the rum. Mix thoroughly with a spatula.

▣ aux Amandes II

7 oz Almond paste; 3 oz vanilla sugar; 2 oz butter; 4 egg yolks; 1 fl oz Kirsch.

Cream the Almond paste with the sugar. Stir in the egg yolks, butter and finally the Kirsch. If the mixture is too thick, add a few drops of water. This custard is used as a filling for various *gâteaux* and notably *Gâteau Pithiviers.*

▣ Anglaise * *Vanilla*

4 oz castor sugar; 4 egg yolks; ½ pint milk; vanilla pod; zest of lemon or other flavouring.

Infuse the vanilla or lemon zest in boiling milk. Cream the sugar and the egg yolks together with a wooden spoon and then slowly stir in the boiling milk. Place over low heat to thicken the custard, stirring all the while, and making sure the custard never boils which would curdle it. Continue until the custard thickens and begins to coat the wooden spoon. Pass through a conical sieve and stir until cool. For a coffee flavoured custard, stir in one or two teaspoonfuls of coffee powder or essence. For a chocolate flavoured custard, blend one level tablespoonful of cocoa with a little of the half pint of cold milk. Add this chocolate mixture to the creamed egg yolks and sugar and then add the boiling milk in the usual way. To prevent the custard from curdling, it is possible to add a small spoonful of starch to the egg yolks. Hot custard cream may be served with hot desserts. Cold, it is served with cold desserts and is used for making butter creams.

▣ Anglaise Collée * *Thick Vanilla*

Prepare the Custard cream in the usual way. While mixing the ingredients, add two sheets or ⅓ oz of gelatine which have previously been soaked. Pass through a sieve and stir until cool. This custard is suitable during hot weather as an accompaniment for cold desserts as it is of a thicker consistency. Custard creams may be flavoured with liqueurs or brandies. For the proportions given above, add a little Kirsch, rum, Cognac, Cointreau, Curaçao, which is stirred in when the custard is cold. In this case do not use lemon zest or vanilla.

CRÈME AU BEURRE * *BUTTER CREAM*

There are numerous butter creams. The best known recipes are those of butter creams made with Custard cream, syrup, meringue or vanilla. All these butter creams follow in alphabetical order.

▣ aux Avelines * *Hazelnut*

Use the same method as for Vanilla butter cream, adding 1½ oz hazelnuts which have been lightly roasted, ground and sifted.

Crème au Beurre au Chocolat * *Chocolate Butter Cream*

Use the same method as for Vanilla butter cream, and when it is ready, add 1½ oz slightly bitter chocolate melted with a little water.

⊡ à la Crème Anglaise * *Made with Custard Cream*

1 *lb butter;* 1 *pint cold, unflavoured Custard cream.*

Cream the butter in a basin until it is soft and fluffy. Gradually add the Custard cream, beating it up at the same time. Add flavouring.

⊡ aux Liqueurs * *Liqueur*

While mixing the butter and Custard cream, add the selected liqueur or spirit in the proportion of 1 fluid oz to 8 oz butter. The traditional flavourings are Kirsch, Curaçao, Benedictine, Cointreau, Grand-Marnier, apricot brandy and cherry brandy.

⊡ au Moka * *Coffee*

Make in the same way as Vanilla butter cream, adding coffee powder or essence to the Custard cream. Use more or less coffee according to taste.

⊡ au Moka ou Pralinée * *Coffee or Chocolate Praline*

Add to Chocolate or Coffee butter cream 2 oz ground and sifted praline.

⊡ Mousseline au Sirop * *Mousseline Syrup*

8 *oz syrup at a density of* 28°; 6 *yolks;* 8 *oz butter; flavouring.*

Whisk the egg yolks and pour over them the boiling syrup, beating all the time until the mixture cools down; it should be light and frothy. Soften the butter slightly in a basin and beat it to make it smooth and creamy. Gradually mix all ingredients together while still warm. Add the vanilla or lemon zest or coffee when the syrup is being boiled. Liqueurs, however, should be added at the last minute. Use about 2 fluid oz liqueur for the proportions given above.

⊡ aux Noix * *Walnut*

Use the same method as for Vanilla butter cream, adding 2 oz ground walnuts.

⊡ aux Pistaches * *Pistachio*

Make in the same way as Vanilla butter cream, adding 2 oz skinned and finely ground green pistachio nuts.

⊡ Pralinée * *Praline*

The same method is followed as for Vanilla butter cream, but 2 oz ground and sifted praline is added. 1 fluid oz Kirsch may also be added according to taste.

Crème au Beurre à la Vanille * *Vanilla Butter Cream*

1 lb butter; 1 pint to 1¼ pints Custard cream strongly flavoured with vanilla.

Beat the butter until it is light and fluffy. Gradually add the Custard cream. This butter cream should be used before it cools down too much as otherwise it may curdle while being utilised as a filling or decoration for various cakes.

CRÈME CHANTILLY * *WHIPPED CREAM FILLINGS*

▣ **Fouettée** * *Whipped*

This is simply whipped fresh double cream to which is added 2-3 oz of vanilla sugar for each pint of cream. Leave ¾ pint fresh cream for several hours in a cool place and then whip it until it becomes fairly stiff. Do not whip for too long or the cream will turn into butter.

▣ **Frangipane**

4 oz sugar; 4 oz flour; 2 eggs; 3 egg yolks; 1¼ pints milk; 1 vanilla pod; pinch salt; 1 oz broken up macaroons; 1 oz butter.

Blend together the eggs, egg yolks, sugar and flour in a saucepan. Gradually add the boiling milk in which the vanilla bean has been infused. Thicken over heat while stirring all the time until the mixture reaches the consistency of a smooth cream. Boil for 2 minutes and then pour into a basin. Next add the pieces of macaroon and butter. Place knobs of butter on top to prevent a skin forming on the surface.

▣ **Pâtissière** * *Pastry Cream or Confectioners' Custard*

5 oz sugar; 2 oz flour; 4 egg yolks; ¾ pint milk; 1 vanilla pod.

Infuse the vanilla bean in the boiling milk. Beat up the egg yolks and sugar with a small whisk and when they become pale, add the sifted flour. Strain the boiling milk which contains the vanilla and blend into the other ingredients. The custard must be stirred with a whisk while it is being brought to the boil and cooked for a short time while it thickens.

▣ **à Saint-Honoré et Choux à la Crème**

The same ingredients are used as for Confectioners' custard with the addition of 6 egg whites. Whisk the egg whites until stiff. Add the custard while still boiling and mix thoroughly with the whisk. In warm weather, 2 sheets of soaked gelatine may be added to the custard while it is still hot.

FONDANT * *FONDANT ICING*

Boil the sugar to the blow degree (a density of 37-38°) and pour it immediately on to a marble slab brushed with cold water where it is left to spread and cool down. When it is almost cold, scrape up mixture, turning it towards the centre with a spatula to make it compact and perfectly white and knead firmly with the palm of the hand until it is smooth. Cover with a cloth rung out in cold water and leave for 30 minutes. Cut it up into small pieces and store in an airtight stoneware or glass jar with a lid. When the fondant is required slightly warm it by putting it in the top of a double boiler over a pan filled as full as possible with cold water. Place over low heat and heat until the water reaches about 175° F—it must not boil on any account. Remove pan from heat and stir fondant gently with wooden spoon until it is pourable. Then colour and flavour to taste and stir well. If the fondant is too thick, add a little warm syrup. The fondant will not be glossy if it is heated too much. If, on the other hand, the fondant is too cold it will remain too thick and be difficult to use. The temperature of the fondant itself should not exceed 120° F.

Fondant au Café, Chocolat etc. * *Flavoured Fondant*

Carefully melt the chocolate and add the Fondant together with a little syrup if necessary. Thoroughly mix so as to obtain a perfect blend. It is preferable to use bitter chocolate to avoid making the Fondant too sweet. Coffee fondant is made with coffee powder or essence which is blended first with a little syrup. The Fondant may similarly be flavoured with orange or lemon juice.

⊡ à Fourrer les Gaufres * *Waffles*

7 oz Fondant; 7 oz butter (or peanut butter); 3 oz icing sugar strongly flavoured with vanilla.

Melt the Fondant icing and gradually work in the butter and icing sugar on a marble slab and mix by hand.

⊡ au Kirsch

Gently heat the required quantity of Fondant in a double saucepan or *bain-marie*. Add one or two tablespoonfuls of Kirsch, mix well and test for taste; the Fondant should have a pronounced flavour of Kirsch. According to the type of cake to be iced the Fondant can be flavoured with rum, Cognac, whisky, Cointreau, Grand-Marnier, Bénédictine, etc.

Ganache * *Chocolate Cream Filling*

Ganache is an easily made mixture of *couverture* and cream. A cheaper variety can be made using a mixture of milk and cream, or by using milk alone. The *couverture* may be either plain or milk. Because plain *couverture* imparts a pronounced flavour of chocolate, an additional flavour is not generally used. *Ganache* made from milk *couverture* may be flavoured with an addition such as rum, Kirsch or coffee. The consistency of *ganache* may be adjusted by decreasing or increasing the proportion of chocolate, an increase is advised in hot weather. A further increase will cause the *ganache* to set quite firm and it may then be used for chocolate centres.

Ganache is normally used for spreading and piping. It is prepared by beating the mixture until it is light and workable. If it should curdle or separate during beating, it should be warmed; or a little warm chocolate may be run in. Properly prepared *ganache* should be soft when used; it will, however, set quickly making it suitable for dipping into Fondant icing or chocolate.

½ pint cream; ¼ pint milk; 12 *oz good quality chocolate.*

Boil the cream with the milk remove from heat and add the chocolate in small pieces. Mix thoroughly with a fork or a whisk and leave to cool down. Before use, beat the *ganache* to make it frothy.

GLÂCE * *ICING*

⊡ à l'Eau * *Water*

4 oz sieved icing sugar with very little cold water. Add the water to the sugar very slowly to form the correct coating consistency; warm it slightly and use to ice cakes and *petits fours*. Flavouring should be introduced when the water is being added to the sugar. If the icing becomes too liquid when it is warmed up, add some icing sugar. This type of icing is harder and less glossy than Fondant icing.

⊡ Royale * *Royal*

$2\frac{1}{2}$ *egg whites; 1 lb icing sugar (approx).*

Take a basin and a wooden spoon, making certain that they are free from grease. Add about one-third of the sugar with the egg whites and beat well. The remaining sugar is added in portions, beating well with each addition. If a machine is used, mix with a beater on middle speed. The use of a whisk or a beater at high speed will produce a light fluffy icing, useless for decorative purposes. Royal icing must be kept covered with a damp cloth.

⊡ Royale pour Décors * *Royal Icing for Decorating Purposes*

Make some Royal icing and add a few drops of lemon juice, beating thoroughly with a small wooden spoon. This icing is used for writing names on cakes or for decorations.

⊡ Royale Pralinée ou Pralin à la Condé * *Praline Royal Icing*

Make Royal icing, adding finely chopped almonds. The quantity of almonds varies according to the use to which the icing is to be put.

SAUCES CHAUDES POUR ENTREMETS * *HOT DESSERT SAUCES*

Sauce à l'Abricot * *Apricot*

Cook some apricot jam with a little water and sugar. Pass through a fine meshed sieve and flavour with Kirsch, Cognac or rum.

⊡ aux Amandes * *Almond*

Prepare a Custard cream, but, while mixing it, add 2 oz finely ground almonds per $1\frac{3}{4}$ pints milk.

⊡ à l'Ananas * *Pineapple*

Peel and core the pineapple. Mash it and cook it with sugar, vanilla and a little water. Thicken with a little arrowroot (1 oz per pint approx). Add a little diced pineapple which has been cooked in its own juice. Bring to the boil to cook the starch. Alternatively you may also slightly thicken a little tinned pineapple juice and flavour with Kirsch. Add chunks of tinned pineapple.

Sauce Brandy * *Brandy Hard Sauce*

Cream 8 oz butter with 5 oz icing sugar until the mixture is light and fluffy. Next gradually add 4 fl oz of Cognac and a few drops of lemon juice. This is the special sauce for Christmas pudding.

▣ au Caramel * *Caramel*

Boil the sugar until it turns into a light caramel and then blend it with a little boiling milk. Add a suitable amount for flavouring purposes with some hot Custard cream.

▣ aux Cerises * *Cherry*

1 *lb Morello cherries;* 12 *oz sugar; lemon zest;* ¾ *pint red wine;* 1 *small vanilla pod;* 1 *cinammon stick; cornflour*. Cooking time: 25 minutes.

Stone the cherries and grind a few kernels. The latter should be cooked with the cherries, sugar, vanilla pod, cinnamon stick, lemon zest, and red wine. When the cherries are cooked, remove the lemon zest, vanilla and cinnamon and pass through a piece of muslin or fine meshed sieve. Recook and thicken with a little cornflour or arrowroot.

▣ au Chocolat * *Chocolate*

Blend 3 oz cocoa with a little water and mix into ¾ pint Custard cream. Boil for 2-3 minutes and sieve before use. You may also melt some good quality chocolate in a double saucepan or *bain-marie*. Add some fresh cream until a thick sauce is obtained.

▣ au Citron * *Lemon*

Prepare some Custard cream, add a generous quantity of finely shredded blanched lemon zest and finally some fresh cream and lemon juice.

▣ à l'Orange * *Orange*

Use the same method as for Cold Orange sauce.

▣ au Pralin * *Praline*

Use the same method as for Cold Praline sauce.

Sirops Liés * *Thickened Syrups*

The juice of stewed fruit is very suitable for these syrups. Cook the juice and thicken with a little cornflour or arrowroot. Flavour with spirit or liqueur according to taste.

SAUCES FROIDES POUR ENTREMETS * *COLD DESSERT SAUCES*

Sauce à l'Abricot * *Apricot Sauce*

8 oz ripe, stoned apricots or 4 oz soaked, dried apricots; ¾ pint syrup at a density of 28°; 1 vanilla pod. Cooking time: 20 minutes.

Sieve the apricots and add the syrup and vanilla. Cook until the sauce coats the spoon and then remove from heat. Take out the vanilla pod and stir until the sauce is completely cold. Instead of vanilla, Kirsch, rum or Cognac may be used to flavour the sauce.

◻ à l'Anglaise * *Custard Cream*

Use the same method as for *Crème Anglaise*, but make it a little thinner. This sauce can be flavoured not only with Kirsch, Cognac, rum, Curaçao, cherry brandy, but also with vanilla, lemon or orange. It is possible to add a few tablespoonfuls of not too stiffly whipped cream to the sauce in order to make it lighter.

◻ aux Cerises * *Cherry*

1 lb ripe Morello cherries; 14 oz sugar; zest of 1 lemon; cinnamon; starch. Cooking time: 15 minutes.

Stone the cherries and cook them with a little lemon zest and cinnamon, then sieve them. Thicken slightly with a little cornflour blended with water. Stir, bring to boiling point to cook starch, and stir whilst cooling to prevent the formation of a skin on the surface.

◻ au Chocolat * *Chocolate*

¾ pint of still hot Crème Anglaise; 2 oz of slightly bitter melted chocolate.

Blend chocolate into sauce, stir occasionally until completely cold, then blend in 2 oz of unsweetened whipped cream.

◻ aux Fraises * *Strawberry*

8 oz very ripe strawberries; ½ pint cold syrup at a density of 28°.

Thoroughly wash and drain the strawberries and pass them through a sieve. Blend in the syrup to obtain a thick but liquid sauce. The syrup may be flavoured with a little vanilla.

◻ aux Framboises * *Raspberry*

Use the same method as for Strawberry sauce. Alternatively, the raspberries may be sieved, mixed with a little castor sugar and blended with enough white wine to achieve the desired consistency.

◻ aux Groseilles * *Redcurrant*

Cook redcurrant jelly with a little water, thicken it with starch, boil for a few minutes, sieve and stir until completely cold. Flavour with a little Kirsch.

Sauce à l'Orange * *Orange Sauce*

Pass some orange marmalade through a sieve and mix this with the same quantity of apricot jam. Flavour with Curaçao and add fine shreds of blanched orange zest.

⊡ au Pralin * *Praline*

Add to ¾ pint Custard cream a little vanilla sugar and 2 oz finely ground and sifted praline.

Sauce Mousseline * *Foamy Sauce*

3 *egg yolks;* 4 *oz sugar;* ¾ *pint cream.* Cooking time: 10 minutes.

Boil the sugar with a little water to the soft ball degree. Add this syrup to the egg yolks, stirring all the time. Beat up until cold and then fold in the half-whipped cream.

⊡ au Chocolat * *Chocolate*

Follow the same method as above, but, before beating up the mixture to cool it down, add 3 oz melted chocolate to the cream. Then fold in half-whipped cream.

⊡ aux Framboises * *Raspberry*

Prepare the sauce with 4 egg yolks instead of 3. As soon as it is cold, add 4 oz *purée* made of fresh raspberries and then the half-whipped cream.

⊡ au Grand-Marnier

Add about 1 fluid oz Grand-Marnier for the proportions indicated.

Sabayon * *Sabayon Sauce*

4 *egg yolks;* 4 *fl oz castor sugar;* 7 *fl oz white wine.*

Whisk the egg yolks and sugar in a double saucepan or *bain-marie* until they are light and fluffy. Gradually mix in the white wine. Place over heat and, whisking all the time, allow the custard to thicken and become very frothy. When the right consistency is reached and without letting it come to the boil, remove the saucepan from the heat. At this moment add flavouring and serve immediately while the custard is still frothy, as it collapses very quickly. If, however, the *sabayon* must be made in advance, half a teaspoonful of cornflour should be added to the egg yolks. *Sabayon* is more of a sauce than a cream which is served hot or cold, with various puddings. It may be made with Port, sherry, Marsala (this is the *Italian Zabaglione*) or with champagne flavoured with rum, Cognac, Kirsch.

⊡ Glacé * *Iced*

Use the same ingredients as above with two additional egg yolks. When the *Sabayon* has thickened, place it on ice and whisk it until completely cold. Finally flavour with Maraschino, Kirsch, Cointreau or any other spirit or liqueur. In the summer, it is advisable to add one or two sheets of gelatine which have been soaked in water. Iced *sabayon* can also be served in glasses as a dessert together with sponge fingers.

Sabayon Frappé à la Vigneronne

6 egg yolks; 2 whole eggs; 5 oz sugar; ¼ pint Marsala; ½ pint whipped cream; 4 sheets gelatine.

Use Marsala to make the *Sabayon*, adding the gelatine which has been soaked in water. Place on ice and whisk until completely cold, then carefully fold in the whipped cream. Serve in glasses.

Hot Sweets and Puddings

In the past, no dinner party was complete without an elaborate course of fruit; fruit was called "dessert". Nowadays all forms of pudding, including ice cream as well as fruit are sometimes classified as dessert. They may be a combination of ice cream and fruit or sauce, fresh or cooked fruit, sweet pastries, yeast mixtures or *gâteaux*. At a formal dinner, fresh fruit can follow a hot or cold pudding, pastry or a savoury.

When choosing a dessert consider the other courses of the meal. If these are substantial you will choose a rather light dish; if the meal is light, prepare a rich or substantial dessert.

BEIGNETS * *FRITTERS*

Fruit is often steeped in a brandy or liqueur before being coated in batter for fritters.

▣ d'Abricots * *Apricot*

For 6 *persons:* 1 *lb fully ripe apricots; vanilla sugar; Coating batter.* Cooking time: 4-5 minutes.

Peel the apricots, halve them, sprinkle with vanilla sugar and leave them to marinate. Drain the fruit and lightly dust with flour before dipping it in the batter and fry in very hot fat.

▣ d'Ananas * *Pineapple*

For 6 *persons:* 12 *half slices of pineapple;* 1 *fl oz Kirsch; vanilla sugar; Coating batter.* Cooking time: 4-5 minutes.

Soak the pineapple slices in Kirsch and sugar for 1 hour. Drain and dry and dust with flour. Dip in the batter and fry in very hot fat. Drain on soft kitchen paper and sprinkle with vanilla sugar.

▣ Florida

For 6 *persons:* 18 *macaroons;* $1\frac{1}{2}$ *pints concentrated apricot jam;* 1 *egg;* 2 *small tablespoons water;* $\frac{1}{2}$ *lb white breadcrumbs; Kirsch.* Cooking time: 2-3 minutes.

Scoop out small, soft macaroons slightly, fill with thick apricot jam, put together in pairs, soak lightly in Kirsch-flavoured sugar syrup and drain. Breadcrumb and fry in very hot deep fat. Dust with icing sugar and serve immediately.

Beignets d'Oranges * *Orange Fritters*

For 6 persons: 18 segments of large, seedless oranges; 2 fl oz Grand-Marnier; castor sugar; Coating batter. Cooking time: 3-4 minutes.

Soak the orange segments in Grand-Marnier and sugar for 2 hours. Dry them on a cloth, dust with flour, dip in batter and fry in very hot fat. Serve with a Grand-Marnier flavoured Apricot sauce.

▣ aux Pommes * *Apple Fritters*

For 6 persons: 1½ lb cooking apples; 3 oz sugar; rum; vanilla sugar; Coating batter. Cooking time: 4-5 minutes.

Peel cooking apples, cut in not too thin slices, cut out the core, dredge with sugar, sprinkle with rum or Kirsch and macerate for 1 hour. Wipe, dip in batter, fry in deep fat, drain and serve dusted with vanilla sugar. (*See illustrations p.* 753).

▣ aux Pommes en Surprise * *Apple Fritter Surprise*

For 8 persons: 4 apples; ½ pint Confectioners' custard; 3 macaroons; Coating batter. Cooking time: 3-4 minutes.

Cut peeled, not too ripe, apples in half, core them and cook carefully in Stock syrup, not letting them get too soft, and without damaging them. When cool drain thoroughly, fill the hollow with Confectioners' custard mixed with crushed macaroons, dip carefully in batter and fry in clean, hot deep fat.

▣ Soufflés * *Soufflé Fritters*

½ lb Choux pastry; vanilla sugar; custard or jam.

Put small balls of *Choux* pastry in moderately hot deep fat and gradually raise the temperature until the fritters have risen well and are golden brown. Drain, serve well dredged with icing sugar and serve with Custard. The inside can also be filled with jam with the help of a forcing bag and small nozzle.

Bugnes

For this Lyons speciality make a medium firm dough with 1 lb flour, 2 oz butter, 1 oz sugar, 4 eggs and 1 tablespoon brandy, roll into a ball and let it rest for 2 hours. Cut into strips 1-inch wide and 4-inches long, tie into a knot without pressing them down, fry in deep fat for 4-5 minutes, drain and dust with icing sugar.

Casse-Museau * *Apple Dumplings*

For 4 persons: 4-6 apples; ½ lb Short Crust pastry; sugar; butter. Cooking time: 20 minutes.

Peel and core whole apples, roll out Short pastry ⅛-inch thick. Cut the dough in squares, place an apple in the middle of each, fill the hole with a little butter and sugar, wrap dough round apple and brush with egg. Decorate top with a piece of pastry cut out with a small crimp cutter and bake apples in a hot oven, 400° F or Gas Mark 6, for 20 minutes. They can also be wrapped in Puff pastry.

Charlotte aux Pommes * *Apple Charlotte*

For 6 persons: 1 *sandwich loaf;* 4 *oz butter; apple purée; rum; Apricot sauce.* Cooking time: 45 minutes.

Cut from a sandwich loaf a dozen small, triangular pieces of bread which are dipped in melted butter and laid, overlapping each other, to cover completely the bottom of a charlotte mould. Next cut some strips of bread 2 fingers in width and the height of the mould and dip these too in the butter. Arrange them closely round the side of the mould, overlapping each other. Fill the mould with the Apple Marmalade Filling.

Filling: 2 *lb peeled, cored, sliced cooking-apples;* 2 *oz thick apricot jam;* 4 *oz demerara sugar;* 4 *oz butter; grated zest of half a lemon;* 2 *cloves.*

Melt the butter and sugar, add the apples, zest and cloves, cover and cook. Stir in the jam and evaporate the moisture to form a firm *purée,* allow to cool before filling mould. This *purée* can be flavoured with vanilla and rum. Put the mould in a hot oven for 45 minutes. The slices of bread round the mould must be golden brown and fairly crisp so as to support the weight of the charlotte when it is turned out of the mould. A not too thick, hot, rum-flavoured Apricot sauce is served with this dessert.

Although the true charlotte is that described above, a simpler method is to use a fairly shallow, square mould and line it completely with little strips of bread dipped in butter and packed closely together without actually overlapping. Fill to the brim with a reduced apple *purée* and bake in a very hot oven, 425° F or Gas Mark 7. Serve with an Apricot sauce or a rum-flavoured Custard sauce.

Clafoutis Limousin * *Cherry Flan*

For 8 *persons:* 1½ *lb black cherries;* 4 *oz sugar;* 2 *oz flour;* ½ *pint milk;* 3 *whole eggs; vanilla; pinch of salt.* Cooking time: 1 hour.

Mix flour with the sugar and the salt and gradually beat well with the eggs, vanilla and milk and pass through a strainer. Stone the cherries, put them in a round baking dish and pour the mixture on top. Sprinkle with sugar and bake in a fairly hot oven, 375° F or Gas Mark 4-5.

Crème Frite * *Cream Fritters*

For 8 *persons:* 4 *oz sugar;* 3 *oz rice flour;* 3 *eggs;* ½ *pint milk; vanilla or zest of orange or lemon.* Cooking time: 3-4 minutes.

Mix the eggs with the sugar, add the flour and combine with hot milk and the desired flavouring. Stir to a very thick cream on the stove and spread on a greased and floured baking sheet about 1-inch thick. When cold cut in fingers, flour and dip in beaten egg, breadcrumb and fry in very hot deep fat. Serve dredged with icing sugar.

CRÊPES * *PANCAKES*

Thin rich pancakes which are usually stuffed with fruit or jam or served with a fruit or liqueur sauce or cream.

Crêpes Bretonnes

For 6 persons: ¼ lb flour; ¼ lb buckwheat flour; 1 pinch of ground cinnamon; 3 fl oz rum; ¾ pint milk; 2 oz Noisette butter; brown sugar. Cooking time: 4-5 minutes.

Mix the two types of flour with a pinch of salt, cinnamon, rum and enough milk to obtain a fairly thin batter. Cook the pancakes in the normal way. Before removing them from the pan sprinkle with a little brown sugar and *Noisette* butter. Fold and serve very hot.

▣ à la Confiture * *with Jam*

Make thin pancakes in the usual way, spread thinly with redcurrant jelly or any desired jam, roll up, dust with icing sugar, arrange on a hot dish and serve at once.

▣ Fines

Heat the frying pan—preferably use a very small one—or the special small pancake pans, butter and cover with a paper-thin layer of Pancake batter. When one side is brown, turn at once and fry the other side till that is brown too. Dust with icing sugar, fold, place on a hot dish and serve at once.

▣ Georgette

For 6 persons: ¾ pint Plain Pancake batter; 4-6 oz finely crushed pineapple or thin slices of pineapple; 2 fl oz Maraschino; icing sugar. Cooking time: 3-4 minutes.

Macerate the pineapple with sugar and Maraschino. Pour a thin layer of batter over the entire surface of a small heated and greased frying pan. Quickly spread a layer of pineapple over this and pour over another thin layer of batter. Cook the pancakes on both sides. Then serve sprinkled with sugar.

▣ Mentschikoff

For 6 persons: 12 small pancakes; ½ pint very thick apple purée mixed with 3 oz finely diced pineapple; castor sugar; ½ pint aniseed-flavoured Sabayon. Cooking time: 3-4 minutes.

Fill the pancakes with the apple *purée*, roll up or fold into four, sprinkle them with sugar and mark them quickly with a heated skewer. Serve the *Sabayon* separately.

▣ du Palais

For 6 persons: 12 small pancakes; ½ pint whipped cream; 1 oz ground and softened hazelnut praline; ½ pint Chocolate sauce. Cooking time: 3-4 minutes.

Mix the whipped cream with the praline and place a tablespoonful in the centre of each pancake while it is still hot, and cover by folding both sides of the pancake towards the middle. Serve on hot plates immediately and pour the Chocolate sauce over each pancake.

▣ Soufflées * *Soufflé*

Cooking time: about 10 minutes.

Make 12-15 thin pancakes and a small amount of Coffee or other *soufflé* mixture. Put a spoonful of the *soufflé* mixture on each pancake, fold both sides over it, place on a buttered baking sheet and bake in a moderate oven, 375° F or Gas Mark 4-5.

Crêpes Suzette

2 oz butter; 2 oz icing sugar; the zest of 2 oranges (best rubbed off on to cube sugar and crushed); Curaçao or brandy.

Stir the butter, sugar, zest of orange and a little Curaçao or brandy to a cream. Make pancakes as above, spread immediately with a little of the cream, fold, dress on a hot dish and dust with icing sugar. The pancakes may be flambéed with brandy at table. (*See Illustrated Culinary Techniques.*)

CROQUETTES * *CROQUETTES*

Finely chopped or *puréed* fruit or nuts bound with thick sauce, shaped into balls or corks, coated in egg and breadcrumbs and deep fried.

⊡ de Marrons * *Chestnut*

1 lb chestnuts; 2 oz butter; 3 oz sugar; 3 egg yolks; ¾ pint milk; vanilla.

Peel and skin the chestnuts (p. 875), boil in vanilla-flavoured milk, drain and sieve. Stir the *purée* on the stove with icing sugar, butter and egg yolks, dry off and let it cool. Shape into small balls, dip in flour, beaten egg and white breadcrumbs and fry in very hot deep fat. Serve Apricot sauce with rum separately.

⊡ de Riz * *Rice*

For 6 persons: 3 oz carolina rice; 2 oz sugar; 3 egg yolks; ½ pint milk; vanilla. Cooking time: 25-30 minutes.

Blanch the rice briefly and cook rather soft in the milk with the vanilla. Add the sugar and egg yolks and stir on the stove till the mixture leaves the sides of the pan. Let the mixture cool completely, divide into egg-sized pieces, shape into *croquettes* rather like corks on a floured table, dip in beaten egg and white breadcrumbs and fry golden brown and crisp in deep fat. Serve with Custard or Apricot sauce.

⊡ de Riz au Chocolat * *Chocolate Rice*

Prepare the mixture as above with ½ oz less sugar and 2 oz grated chocolate instead. Serve with a Vanilla Custard cream.

⊡ de Semoule * *Semolina*

For 6 persons: 3 oz semolina; 3 oz sugar; vanilla; ¾ pint milk; 1 oz butter; 4 egg yolks. Cooking time: 3-4 minutes.

Boil the milk with the vanilla and a pinch of salt. Sprinkle the semolina into the milk, stir and cook for about 10 minutes. When the semolina is cooked and thickened, add the sugar, butter and egg yolks and continue in the same way as for Rice *croquettes*. Serve together with a rum or Kirsch-flavoured Apricot sauce.

CROÛTES * *CROÛTES OR CRUSTS*

Slices of stale bread or sponge mixture sprinkled with liqueur, crisped in the oven and used as the base for fruit and cream preparations.

Croûtes aux Abricots * *Apricot Croûtes or Crusts*

For 6 persons: 6 slices of Savarin; 12 stewed apricot halves; 12 red cherries; 2 oz butter; ½ pint Kirsch-flavoured Apricot sauce. Cooking time: 5-6 minutes.

Bake the *Savarin* at least one day in advance in a loaf tin. Cut into slices ⅜-inch thick and lightly fry on both sides in butter. Put two apricot halves on each slice with the hollow side uppermost in which a cherry is placed. Cover with a hot, Kirsch-flavoured Apricot sauce.

▣ à l'Ananas * *Pineapple*

For 6 persons: 6 slices of Savarin as above; 6 slices of pineapple poached in Kirsch-flavoured syrup; 6 red cherries; 2 oz butter; ½ pint Kirsch-flavoured Apricot sauce. Cooking time: 5-6 minutes.

Lightly fry the slices of *Savarin* in butter. Place on each slice a cored slice of pineapple with a cherry in the centre. Cover with hot Apricot sauce. (*See illustration on p.* 758).

▣ aux Fruits * *Fruit*

Bake a *Savarin*, do not soak it in Stock syrup, but cut it in diagonal ½-inch slices. Place them on a baking sheet, dust with icing sugar, and bake on both sides. Serve the slices in a ring overlapping them, and fill the centre with hot, mixed, stewed fruit, including some candied fruit, with thick apricot *purée* flavoured with rum or a liqueur. Several different kinds of fruit or a single kind may be used. The *Savarin* itself can also be decorated with candied fruit.

▣ à la Parisienne

Serve *croûtes* as above and arrange half pineapple slices, heated with apricot jam and Kirsch, on top. Fill the centre with well-drained stewed pears, cover with Confectioners' custard, sprinkle with chopped almonds, dust with icing sugar and put in a very hot oven for 2 minutes to brown.

OMELETTE * *OMELETTE*

Sweet omelettes are usually served with a filling of fruit or jam. A fruit or brandy sauce is usually poured over just before serving.

▣ à la Confiture * *Jam*

For 5 persons: 8-10 eggs; 1 oz sugar; pinch of salt; 3-4 tablespoons jam; 1 oz butter; 1 oz castor sugar. Cooking time: 3-4 minutes.

Beat the eggs as for plain omelette together with the sugar and a pinch of salt. Melt the butter and prepare the omelette in the usual way, keeping it very light and spongy. Before rolling the omelette in the frying pan, pour in a few spoonfuls of warmed jam. Place the omelette on a long dish and sprinkle generously with castor sugar. With a red hot skewer make a criss-cross pattern on top to caramelise the sugar.

▣ Martinique

For 5 persons: 8 eggs; 1 oz sugar; 3 bananas; 1 oz butter; sugar for dredging; about 2 fl oz rum.

Cook the bananas in butter until they are soft. Make the omelette as above, fill with banana, dredge with sugar, pour rum on top, light the rum only when the omelette is brought to the table and baste with burning rum.

⊡ au Rhum * *with Rum*

For 5 persons: 8 *eggs;* 1 *oz sugar; pinch of salt;* 2 *fl oz rum;* 1-2 *oz sugar for dredging;* $\frac{1}{2}$ *oz butter.*

Lightly beat the eggs with the salt and 1 oz sugar, strain, and make omelette in the usual way, keeping it very fluffy. Slide it on to a shallow oval baking dish, dredge with sugar, pour the warmed rum on top, light and baste omelette with it till the rum ceases to burn. Serve at once. These omelettes can also be made with brandy, Kirsch, *framboise*, etc.

⊡ Stéphanie

Prepare a *soufflé* omelette and fill it with about 9 oz small, sweet strawberries. Sprinkle with sugar and serve at once.

OMELETTE SOUFFLÉE * *SOUFFLÉ OMELETTE*

Sweet omelettes may also be made with separated eggs. They are then usually cooked in the oven and not on top of the stove. These are known as *soufflé* omelettes. The same care taken in *soufflé* making should be employed for this type of omelette.

For 4 persons: 3 *egg yolks;* 5 *egg whites;* 4 *oz icing sugar; vanilla or lemon zest;* 2 *oz butter.* Cooking time: about 8 minutes.

Beat up the yolks with the sugar and vanilla, until light in colour. Lightly fold in the whisked egg whites. Pour the mixture into long greased baking dish. Smooth the surface with a knife dipped in water and make a well in the centre. Dredge with icing sugar. Bake in a hot oven, 425° F or Gas Mark 7. Dust with icing sugar and *serve immediately.*

⊡ au Citron ou à l'Orange * *Orange or Lemon*

Rub some lumps of sugar on orange or lemon peel, crush and make the same mixture as *soufflé* omelette without vanilla.

⊡ au Rhum, Kirsch, Grand-Marnier * *Rum or Kirsch*

Use the same method as for Vanilla *Soufflé* omelette, but add the liqueur or spirit to the egg yolks and sugar before folding in the whites.

Omelette Soufflé Néron

For 4 persons: 1 *round base of Génoise sponge;* $\frac{3}{4}$ *pint Kirsch-flavoured Parfait;* 4 *fl oz Kirsch-flavoured syrup; Italian meringue mixture made with* 4 *egg whites and* 9 *oz sugar;* 1 *very small round meringue with the centre scooped out;* 1 *tablespoon Kirsch; castor sugar.* Cooking time 3-4 minutes.

Place the *Génoise* sponge at the bottom of a round dish and lightly sprinkle with the Kirsch-flavoured syrup. Place the *Parfait* on top of the sponge and seal completely with the Italian meringue mixture. The surface should be dome-shaped, smoothed and decorated quickly with a piping bag containing meringue. Dust with sugar. Brown in a hot oven, 425° F or Gas Mark 6 or 7. Top with the small meringue with its hollow uppermost to receive the warmed Kirsch which is ignited. Serve at once.

Omelette Soufflé Norvégienne ou en Surprise * *Norwegian Surprise Omelette or Baked Alaska*

This sweet must be prepared at the last moment and the ice-cream must be really firm, otherwise the whole sweet will become soggy and collapse.

This is a delicious sweet with ice cream in the centre. Prepare ice cream of the desired flavour—vanilla, strawberry, chocolate, and keep it in the freezer until serving. Place a layer of sponge cake on the bottom of a long ovenproof dish. This sponge should be soaked very slightly with a cold syrup flavoured with Kirsch, brandy or other spirit. The aim of this sponge is to form an insulation between the dish and the ice cream. Now, cover the ice cream with another very thin layer of sponge and coat it fairly thickly and completely with ordinary meringue (4 whites and ½ lb vanilla-flavoured sugar). Smooth the surface and decorate quickly with meringue, using a piping bag and a fluted tube; candied fruit may also be used for decorating. Dredge with icing sugar, and place quickly in a very hot oven, 425° F or Gas Mark 7, to brown and crust the surface before the ice cream has had time to melt. When serving a little warmed Kirsch or rum may be poured around the omelette and set alight. It is essential to serve this dish the moment it is ready. (*See illustration p.* 754).

PANNEQUETS * *LARGE PANCAKES*

Fry the pancakes in a large pan, fill with jam or a cream, roll up, cut diagonally into fairly large slices and dust with icing sugar. These pancakes can also be savoury and made without sugar, filled with meat or minced poultry and served with a suitable sauce.

⊡ à l'Anglaise * *with Lemon*

Prepare in the same way as above, sprinkle with sugar and serve with lemon juice squeezed over.

⊡ à la Confiture * *Caramelised with Sugar and Jam*

Make small, thin pancakes, put one level dessertspoon of any desired jam in the middle, roll up, cut off both ends diagonally, dredge with icing sugar and put in a very hot oven to caramelise the sugar.

⊡ Meringués à la Crème * *with Cream and Meringue*

Make small, thin pancakes, leaving them rather pale. Brush thinly with apricot jam, put 1 tablespoon of Confectioners' custard in the middle and fold up the ends to form a rectangle. Serve on a fire-proof dish, pipe an attractive decoration of meringue mixture on top. Dust with sugar and put in a cool oven, 325° F or Gas Mark 2, for a few minutes to dry the meringue.

Pudding Cabinet ou Diplomate Chaud * *Cabinet Pudding*

For 4 persons: 4 oz sponge fingers; 2 oz sugar; 2 whole eggs; 2 oz mixed currants and candied fruit; ½ pint milk; ½ pint Custard sauce or Jam sauce; vanilla and rum. Cooking time: ¾-1 hour.

Beat the eggs and sugar in a bowl. Boil the milk with a vanilla pod and add to the eggs and sugar. Stir with a fork while pouring in the milk, then let this cream rest, skimming the foam off the top. In the meantime butter a straight-sided *soufflé* dish or pudding basin, sprinkle it with sugar, then fill with the sponge fingers broken in pieces; *Génoise*, left over *Brioche* or any type of sponge may be used instead. Arrange the sponge in alternate layers with the currants and finely candied fruit soaked in rum. The basin should be filled right up. Now pour in the egg cream mixture, very slowly so that the sponge can absorb it, until the basin is full. Allow to stand for 15 minutes. Place it in a water-bath and poach in the oven for $\frac{3}{4}$ hour. The pudding is ready when the blade of a small knife inserted into the pudding comes out dry. Turn out pudding 5 minutes after removing it from oven and serve with Custard or Jam sauce.

Pudding de Cerises * *Cherry Pudding*

For 8 persons: 3 oz butter; 3 oz sugar; 3 oz stale bread; 1 lb cherries; 3 egg yolks; 5 stiffly beaten egg whites; vanilla; Kirsch. Cooking time: 35-40 minutes.

Soak the bread, squeeze it out, rub it through a sieve and mix well with the soft butter. Add the vanilla sugar and the egg yolks, one by one, and the stoned cherries which have been poached in red wine with 5 oz sugar, thoroughly drained and cooled, and lastly the beaten egg whites. Fill into a buttered mould sprinkled with breadcrumbs and cook in a water-bath in a moderate oven, 350° F or Gas Mark 4. As sauce serve the poaching liquor of the cherries, bound with a little apricot jam and flavoured with Kirsch.

SOUFFLÉ SAXON * *SAXON PUDDING*

For *soufflé* puddings, use the following recipe for Saxon pudding as a basis.

For 6 persons: 3 oz sugar; 3 oz flour; 3 oz butter; $\frac{1}{2}$ pint milk; 4 egg yolks; 3 egg whites; vanilla; pinch salt. Cooking time: 35-40 minutes.

Stir the butter in a bowl, mix with the flour and slowly thin with the warm milk in which a vanilla pod has been steeped. Mix well, put in a saucepan and stir on the heat till the mixture leaves the spoon. Remove from the heat and stir in the sugar, salt and egg yolks until a thickish cream results; fold the stiffly beaten egg whites very gently into it. Butter a tall mould or *soufflé* dish thoroughly, sprinkle with sugar and three-quarters fill it with mixture. Poach the pudding in a water-bath in the oven, keeping the water at simmering point only, otherwise the pudding would rise too much and collapse correspondingly later. After the surface begins to brown protect it with a piece of greased paper. In baking the pudding should rise about $1\frac{1}{2}$ inches above the edge of the mould. When cooked let it stand for a few minutes to regain its normal size, turn out on a round dish and cover with Custard or *Zabaglione*. A slight collapse after baking is normal and has no connection with the excessive swelling caused by the boiling water. Bake in a moderate oven, 350° F or Gas Mark 4.

⊡ au Chocolate * *Chocolate*

Follow the same method as for a Saxon pudding, but add $2\frac{1}{2}$ oz chocolate to the milk and use $\frac{3}{4}$ oz less sugar, to allow for the sugar in the chocolate; 1 more egg white should also be used.

⊡ au Citron * *Lemon*

Follow the same method as for Saxon pudding, using grated lemon zest instead of vanilla. Serve with a lemon-flavoured Custard sauce.

Soufflé Saxon Fleur de Marie

For 6 persons: 3 oz sugar; 3 oz semolina; 3 oz butter; 4 egg yolks; 3 egg whites; ½ pint milk; vanilla; 1 pinch salt. Cooking time: 15-20 minutes.

Boil up the milk with the vanilla, sprinkle in the semolina, boil for a little and as soon as it thickens add butter, yolks and sugar and, away from heat, the stiffly beaten egg whites. Pour into a straight-sided ovenproof dish, *soufflé* dish or cylindrical mould with some caramel in the bottom and cook in a water-bath in a moderate oven, 350° F or Gas Mark 4. Serve with caramel-flavoured Custard.

▣ au Grand-Marnier

For 6 persons: 3 oz sugar; 3 oz sifted flour; 3 oz butter; ½ pint milk; 4 eggs; grated zest of half an orange; 2 oz macaroons; ⅛ pint Grand-Marnier. Cooking time: 30-35 minutes.

Cut up the macaroons into large pieces and soak them in Grand-Marnier. Prepare the pudding mixture as for Saxon pudding, having infused the orange zest in the milk. Amalgamate both mixtures and bake. Serve with a Grand-Marnier flavoured Custard cream.

▣ aux Marrons * *Chestnut*

For 8 persons: 1 lb chestnuts; 2 oz butter; 3 oz sugar; 4 egg yolks; 3 egg whites; vanilla; pinch of salt. Cooking time: 25-30 minutes.

Boil the peeled chestnuts in vanilla-flavoured milk. When tender, drain and strain. Dry the *purée* in a saucepan with sugar and butter for 6-7 minutes at low heat, stirring constantly. Remove from heat, fold in the egg yolks followed by the stiffly beaten egg whites. Fill into a buttered mould sprinkled with flour, bake in a moderate oven, 350° F or Gas Mark 4, in a water-bath and serve with Custard or Apricot sauce with rum.

▣ Mousseline

For 6-8 persons: 2 oz butter; 3 oz sugar; 5 egg yolks; 4 egg whites. Cooking time: 15-20 minutes.

Beat the butter to a cream with the sugar and the desired flavour—vanilla, orange or lemon peel, fold in the yolk of egg and cook at moderate heat like a custard, but do not on any account let it boil. As soon as the mixture coats the spoon, remove from the heat and gently fold in the stiffly beaten egg whites. Fill a buttered mould sprinkled with sugar not more than half to three-quarters with the mixture, since the pudding rises considerably. Bake in a water-bath in a moderate oven, 350° F or Gas Mark 4. Serve with *Zabaglione*.

▣ Néron

For 6 persons: 3 oz sugar; 3 oz sifted flour; 3 oz butter; ½ pint milk; 4 eggs; 3 oz candied fruits; 2 fl oz Curaçao; 2 fl oz Cognac. Cooking time: 30-35 minutes.

Finely dice the candied fruit and soak in Curaçao. Prepare a Saxon pudding and mix in the candied fruit. Bake in a plain, deep mould with a central funnel. Turn out on a round dish. Pour into the central hole the slightly warmed Cognac which is then ignited when the pudding is brought to the table. Serve separately a *Sabayon* sauce flavoured with Curaçao.

Soufflé Saxon au Riz * *Rice Soufflé Pudding*

For 6 *persons:* 5 *oz rice;* 4 *oz sugar;* 3 *oz butter;* 4 *egg yolks;* 5 *egg whites;* 1½ *pints vanilla-flavoured milk.* Cooking time: 50 minutes.

Blanch the rice for 3 minutes. Drain, rinse with boiling water and cook in the vanilla-flavoured milk for 30 minutes. Stir in quickly the butter, the egg yolks and sugar and last of all the stiffly whisked egg whites. Fill into a buttered and sugared mould. Cook 15-20 minutes in a water-bath in a moderate oven. Serve with vanilla Custard sauce.

▣ Royal

Line the bottom and sides of a charlotte mould or a shallow tin with some thin slices of apricot jam Swiss roll. Fill with Saxon pudding mixture and bake in a *bain-marie* in the oven. Turn out on a round dish and top with a crown made with cooked *Choux* pastry. Serve an Apricot sauce separately, flavoured with Madeira or Muscatel wine. (*See illustration p.* 755).

▣ Rubané * *Layered or Rainbow*

Follow the same method as for Saxon pudding, but divide the mixture into two parts before folding in the stiffly whisked egg whites; to one part add 2 oz chocolate which has been melted in a little milk; rather more of the egg whites should now be added to the chocolate mixture than to the vanilla one, so that they are both equally light. Fill a greased mould sprinkled with sugar with alternate layers of the two mixtures. Bake and serve with a vanilla-flavoured Custard.

▣ Sans-Souci

Proceed in the same way as for Saxon pudding, but add 5 ounces peeled, cored, finely diced cooking apples cooked in butter. Serve with Custard.

Rissoles de Fruits * *Jam Turnovers*

For 8 *persons:* 1 *lb Puff pastry;* 6 *oz thick jam.* Cooking time: 3-5 minutes.

Roll out Puff pastry ⅛-inch thick and cut out rounds about 3 inches across with a crimp cutter. Moisten the edge, fill the middle with a little thick jam, fold like Apple turnovers, press edge down firmly and fry in deep fat.

Riz Condé * *Rice Condé*

For 5 *persons:* 5 *oz rice;* 3 *oz vanilla sugar;* ¾ *pint milk;* 3 *egg yolks.*

This is usually served as part of other sweets but it can also be served separately. Blanch rice for 3 minutes, drain, rinse and boil for 25 minutes in vanilla-flavoured milk. Gently stir in sugar, a walnut of butter and the egg yolks and continue cooking at low heat till the rice is creamy and binds well, but it must not boil.

SOUFFLÉ À LA VANILLE I * *VANILLA SOUFFLÉ PUDDING*

For sweet *soufflés*, use the following recipe for Vanilla *soufflé* as a basis.

For 4-5 persons: 3 oz sugar; 1 oz flour; 1 oz butter; 7 fl oz milk; 5 egg yolks; 4 stiffly beaten egg whites; vanilla pod. Cooking time: 20-25 minutes.

Melt the butter, add the flour and sugar, immediately add the hot milk in which vanilla has been steeped. Stir over heat until the mixture thickens and comes to the boil, and draw aside; add the egg yolks, then carefully fold in the egg whites. Three-quarters fill a buttered and sugared *soufflé* dish with the mixture, put in a moderate oven, 375° F or Gas Mark 5. Serve immediately it is cooked. A good method of stopping the *soufflé* from collapsing too quickly is first to put it in a shallow water-bath for 10-12 minutes and then to bake it dry till done.

⊡ à la Vanille II

For 8 persons: $\frac{3}{4}$ pint milk; 2 oz flour; 4 oz sugar; 4 egg yolks; 6 large egg whites; vanilla pod. Cooking time: 17-20 minutes.

Make mixture in the same way as Confectioners' custard and then very gently fold in the stiffly beaten egg whites. Fill into a buttered and sugared *soufflé* dish and bake in a moderate oven. This method is suitable for larger quantities; also it does not collapse so quickly. (*See illustration p.* 753).

⊡ Amandine * *Almond*

Make in the same way as Hazelnut *soufflé*, but with peeled, freshly-ground almonds in the milk.

⊡ au Café * *Coffee*

Make in the same way as Vanilla *soufflé*, but adding a little instant coffee powder or essence to the milk instead of vanilla.

⊡ Cécilia

For 8 persons: 3 pints milk; 2 oz flour; 4 oz sugar; 4 egg yolks; 6 egg whites; 4 sponge fingers; 3 oz hazelnuts; Chartreuse. Cooking time: 18-20 minutes.

Make in the same way as Hazelnut *soufflé*, but with the inclusion of layers of coarsely-chopped sponge fingers soaked in Chartreuse.

⊡ aux Cerises * *Cherry*

For 6 persons: 1$\frac{3}{4}$ lb black cherries; 4 oz stale brown bread; 6 oz sugar; a pinch cinnamon; 5 eggs; grated lemon. Cooking time: 20-25 minutes.

Beat the sugar with the egg yolks, lemon and cinnamon. Add the sifted breadcrumbs, the cherries which have been stoned and boiled in syrup and fold in the stiffly whisked egg whites. Pour the mixture into a *soufflé* or *timbale* mould which must be not more than three-quarters full and bake in a moderate oven, 375° F or Gas Mark 5. Sprinkle with sugar before serving.

Soufflé au Chocolat * *Chocolate Soufflé Pudding*

Follow the same method as for a Vanilla *soufflé*, but add 2½ oz chocolate to the milk and use ¾ oz less sugar, to allow for the sugar in the chocolate; 1 more egg white should also be used.

⊡ **au Citron ou à l'Orange** * *Lemon or Orange*

Proceed in the same way as for a Vanilla *soufflé*, but flavour the milk with lemon, clementine or orange zest, which should not be cooked, however, as it would make the *soufflé* taste bitter.

⊡ **Elvire**

For 6 *persons:* ¾ *pint milk;* 2 *oz flour;* 4 *oz sugar;* 4 *egg yolks;* 6 *egg whites;* 6 *macaroons; orange zest; Curaçao.* Cooking time: 18-20 minutes.

Proceed in the same way as for Orange *soufflé*, but include in the middle a layer of macaroons well soaked in Curaçao.

⊡ **aux Fruits**

This can be made with all soft fruit, such as strawberries, apricots, peaches, raspberries. The method is different from that for cream *soufflés*. Example:

For 4-5 *persons:* 8 *oz strawberries;* 6 *oz sugar;* 3 *egg whites; vanilla.* Cooking time: 18-20 minutes.

Sieve the strawberries and mix them with sugar boiled to the crack. Allow to boil up several times, pour over the stiffly beaten egg whites and combine gently. Bake in the same way as any other *soufflé* and serve with stewed strawberries flavoured with Kirsch.

⊡ **au Grand-Marnier**

For 6 *persons:* 3 *oz sugar;* 2 *oz flour;* ½ *oz butter;* ½ *pint milk; grated zest of* 1 *small orange;* ⅛ *pint Grand-Marnier;* 4 *broken large macaroons;* 4 *egg yolks;* 5 *large egg whites.* Cooking time: 18-20 minutes.

Soak the large pieces of macaroons in half of the Grand-Marnier. Add to the mixture the orange zest and the other half of the Grand-Marnier together with the egg yolks. Proceed in the same way as for *Soufflé Elvire* adding layers of the macaroons when filling the *timbale* mould or *soufflé* case.

⊡ **Jacqueline**

Make the mixture in the usual way but firmer and with two additional egg yolks. Before folding in the egg whites combine with 3 oz strawberry *purée*, made with wild strawberries if possible. Bake in the usual way and serve together with a bowl of strawberries marinated in sugar and Kirsch.

⊡ **Noisettine** * *Hazelnut*

Make in the same way as Vanilla *soufflé*, but with the addition of 3 oz lightly roasted, finely ground hazelnuts steeped in the milk.

Soufflé aux Pommes * *Apple Soufflé Pudding*

Mix 9 oz thickly concentrated, heavily sweetened apple *purée* with 3 egg yolks and 2 stiffly beaten egg whites. Bake in the same way as any other *soufflé*. A few spoonfuls of *Frangipane* or Confectioners' custard may be mixed with the apple *purée* to bind it.

▣ Prince Nicolaï

Use the same method as for Orange *soufflé*, adding 3½ oz wild strawberries which have been soaked in 1 fluid oz Grand-Marnier. Serve together with stewed strawberries flavoured with Grand-Marnier.

▣ Rothschild

Vanilla *soufflé* mixture mixed with diced fruit macerated in brandy. When the *soufflé* is just a minute or two from being ready garnish the top with a ring of strawberries rolled in sugar and put in the oven for another moment.

Subrics de Semoule * *Semolina Fritters*

For 6 persons: 3 oz semolina; 3 oz sugar; ¾ pint milk; 1½ oz butter; 2 egg yolks.

Boil the semolina in vanilla-flavoured milk until it is rather thick, add sugar and butter, remove from heat and combine with the egg yolks. Heat butter with a little oil in a frying pan, put in spoonfuls of the mixture, fry golden brown on both sides and serve with red currant or quince jelly.

Tôt-Fait

For 6 persons: 3 oz flour; 3 oz icing sugar; 3 eggs; 2 egg whites; 3 oz butter; ¾ pint milk; vanilla. Cooking time: about 45 minutes.

Mix the sifted flour with the sugar and add milk. Mix with 3 beaten egg yolks and the melted butter, fold in the stiffly beaten egg whites and flavour to taste. Place in a buttered charlotte mould or *moule à manqué* and bake in a moderate oven, 350° F or Gas Mark 4.

HOT FRUIT SWEETS

Abricots Colbert

For 6 persons: 24 choice apricot halves; 3 oz Rice Condé; 2 oz glacé cherries; 1 piece of angelica; ½ pint Kirsch-flavoured Apricot sauce. Cooking time: 4-5 minutes.

Poach the apricot halves without letting them become too soft. Drain them, dry them on a cloth and put them together in pairs, filling their centres with a tablespoon of Rice *Condé* containing chopped *glacé* cherries. Flour the apricots, dip them in egg and cover with breadcrumbs. Fry in extremely hot fat, just before serving pile up on a napkin and sprinkle with castor sugar. Serve an Apricot sauce separately.

Abricot Condé * *Apricot Condé*

For 6 persons: 6 large apricots or peaches; 5 oz rice; 1 pint milk; vanilla; ¼ lb sugar; 2 tablespoons thick cream; 2 egg yolks; 1½ oz butter; ½ pint Apricot sauce.

Dip the peaches for a few seconds in boiling hot water and peel them. Cut them in half and poach in vanilla-flavoured syrup. Blanch the rice, drain and cook it in milk flavoured with vanilla. Remove from the heat, add sugar and butter and bind with the egg yolks mixed with the cream. Take out the vanilla pod. Make a base of the rice on a round dish, and smooth top and sides. Arrange the well-drained fruit on top and decorate with candied cherries and angelica. Cover with very hot Apricot sauce, flavoured with Kirsch, Maraschino or as desired.

Ananas Condé * *Pineapple Condé*

Put some Rice *Condé* round the edge of a dish and cover with thin pineapple slices. Decorate and pour rum-flavoured Apricot sauce over the dessert.

Ananas Marina

For 6 persons: 1 base of Génoise sponge ¾ inch thick and about 6 inches in diameter; 12 thin half slices of pineapple; 2 fl oz Kirsch-flavoured syrup; ½ lb stewed cherries of which the liquor has been much reduced and thickened with starch; 1 fl oz Cognac; flaked pistachio nuts; ½ pint hot Sabayon sauce flavoured with Grand-Marnier.

Poach the pineapple slices in water containing sugar and cognac. Sprinkle the *Génoise* sponge with the hot Kirsch-flavoured syrup and place it in a hot round dish. Arrange the slices of pineapple on the sponge overlapping each other in the form of a crown. Put the stewed cherries in the middle and sprinkle over the pistachio nuts. Serve a *Sabayon* sauce separately.

BANANES * *BANANAS*

▣ Condé

Place the halved bananas, or any other fruit, poached in Stock syrup, on a ring or base of Rice *Condé*, decorate with candied fruit and coat with Apricot sauce with rum.

▣ Flambées Martinique

For 6 persons: 6 skinned bananas, split lengthwise; juice of 1 orange; 2 oz butter; 3 oz sugar; ½ pint Apricot sauce; flaked, roasted almonds; 2 fl oz rum. Cooking time: 6-8 minutes.

Melt the sugar and butter in a copper pan over a high flame until it begins to caramelise. Add the orange juice to dissolve the sugar and then the Apricot sauce. Cook for a few seconds, add the banana halves and simmer them in the sauce for 3-4 minutes. Sprinkle with rum and ignite. As soon as the flame goes out, serve the bananas on hot plates. Cover with the sauce and sprinkle with the flaked almonds.

▲ Soufflé à la Vanille, p. 749

Beignets aux Pommes, p. 739 ▼

 ▲ Omelette Soufflée Norvégienne, p. 745

Charlotte Royale, p. 776 ▼

▲ *Soufflé Saxon Royal, p. 748*

Babas and Savarin au Rhum, pp. 825, 828 ▼

▲ *Zabaione Gritti, p. 798*

Gâteau Saint-Honoré, p. 821 ▼

▲ *Gâteau Pithiviers, p. 821*

Abricots Condé, p. 787 ▼

▲ Baskets of summer fruit, p. 709

Croûte à l'Ananas, p. 743 ▼

▲ *Fruits Rafraichis au Champagne, p. 792*

Poires à la Floretta, p. 796 ▼

▲ *Tarte aux Pommes Grillagée, p. 848*

Tarte aux Oranges, p. 848 ▼

▲ *Tarte aux Fraises, p. 847*

Tarte aux Pommes Meringuée, p. 848 ▼

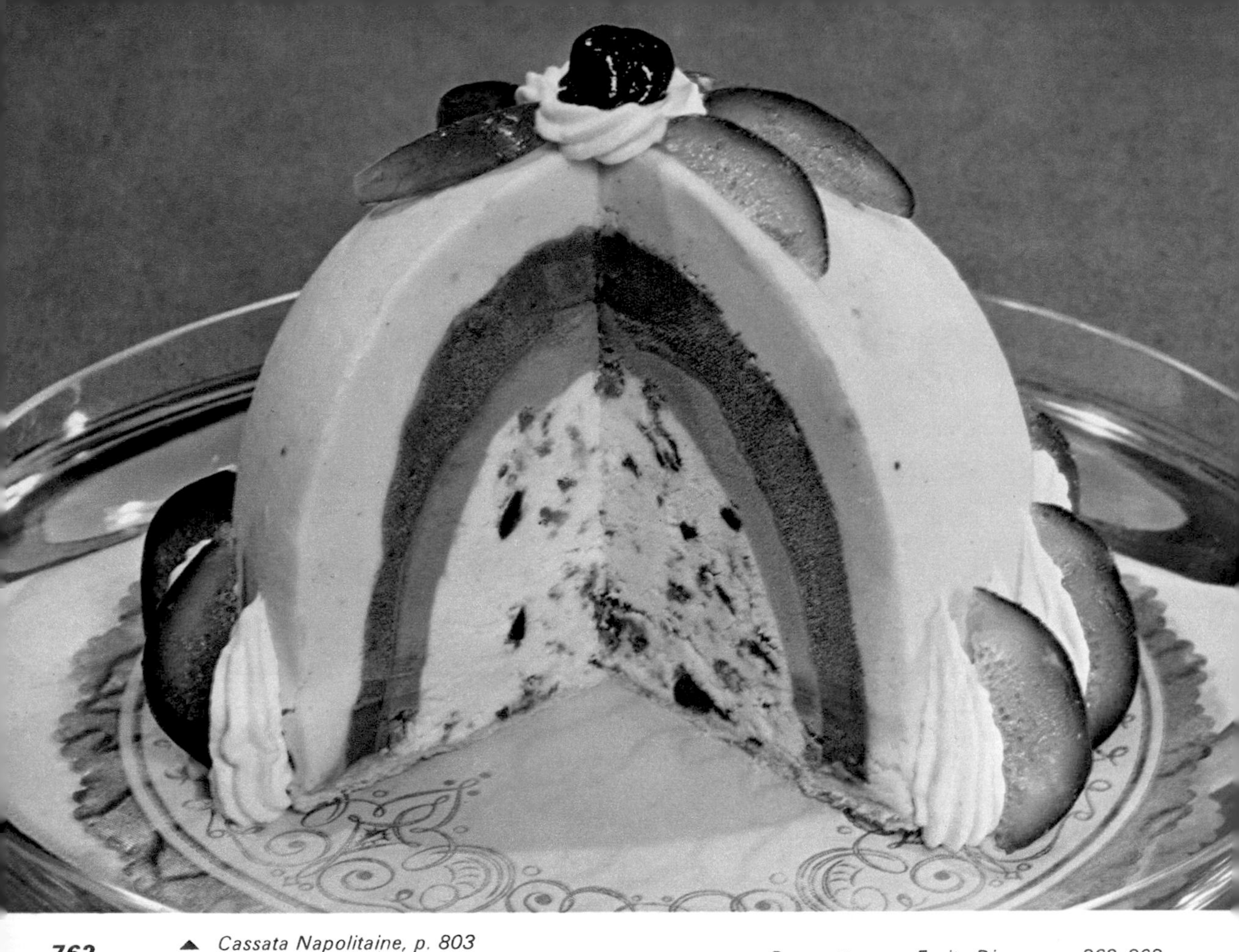

▲ Cassata Napolitaine, p. 803

Barquettes aux Fruits Divers, pp. 862-863 ▼

▲ Citrons Givrés, p. 790

Parfait au Moka, p. 805 ▼

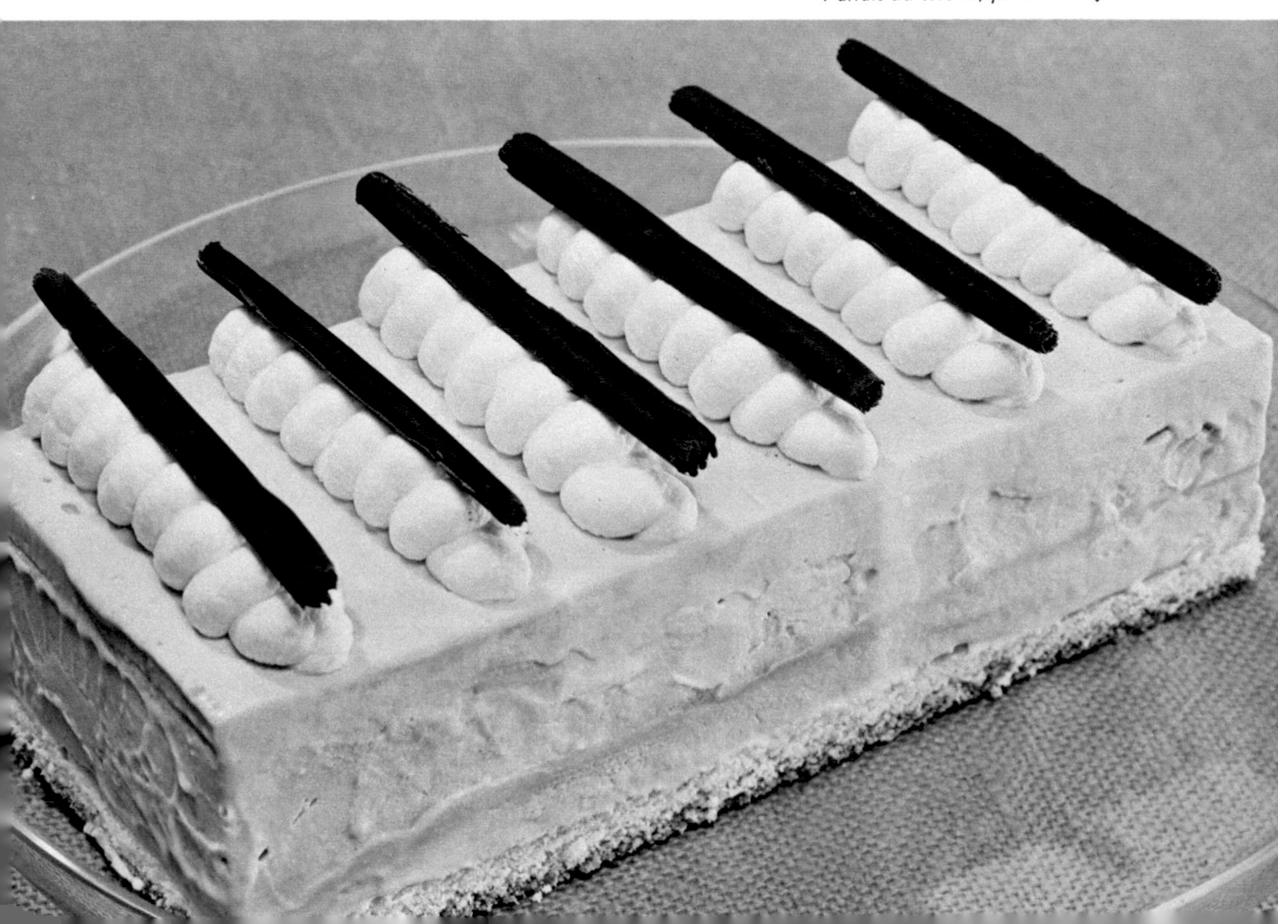

▲ Bombe Diane, p. 807

Ice Cream Cake, p. 812 ▼

Bananes Soufflés * *Soufflé Bananas*

For 6 persons: 8 choice bananas; 3 oz vanilla sugar; ½ oz butter; 2 eggs; 1 fl oz rum. Cooking time: 6-8 minutes.

Carefully slit the skin of six of the bananas along three quarters of their length and remove the flesh without damaging the skins. Completely skin the other two bananas. Pass the flesh through a sieve and cook to make a thick *purée*, adding the butter and sugar. Flavour the *purée* with rum and, after removing from the heat, mix in the egg yolks and fold through the very stiffly whisked egg whites. Use a Savoy bag fitted with a plain pipe to fill the banana skins with this mixture. Sprinkle with sugar and bake in a moderate oven.

Cerises Flambées * *Flambéed Cherries*

Stone 1 lb cherries and poach them in 1½ pints red wine with a piece of cinnamon. Drain them, strain the wine, reduce to a quarter and mix with a little potato flour or cornflour and bring to the boil. Pour it over the cherries arranged in a silver *timbale* or in small, individual *cocottes*, pour 1 spoonful warmed Kirsch on top and *flambé* at table. A little red jelly may be added to the red wine.

Cerises Victoria

Place a round slice of *Brioche* in the middle of a *cocotte* and soak it with a little Kirsch. Prepare cherries as above, place them in *cocottes* (without red wine) and cover with slightly sweetened, warmed strawberry *purée*, flavoured with a few drops of lemon juice.

Douillons à la Normande * *Normandy Apple Dumplings*

For 6 persons: 6 apples; 2 oz butter; 2 oz sugar; ½ lb Sweet pastry. Cooking time: 15 minutes.

Peel and core the apples. Put a little butter and sugar in the centres and wrap up in a piece of pastry. Top with a small piece of pastry cut out with a fluted pastry cutter. Decorate with lines, brush with egg and bake in a hot oven, 400° F or Gas Mark 6.

PÊCHES * *PEACHES*

▣ Condé * *Condé*

Make in the same way as apricots of the same name, but skin them first.

▣ Flambées I * *Flambéed*

For 6 persons: 6 peaches; 1 glass Kirsch; icing sugar. Cooking time: 6-8 minutes.

Poach the peaches in a vanilla syrup. Peel them and serve in a metal container. Sprinkle icing sugar on top, and pour a little of the hot syrup over them, then the hot Kirsch and light at the table.

▣ Flambées II

For 6 persons: 6 peaches; 8 oz strawberry purée; 1 glass Kirsch. Cooking time: 6-8 minutes.

Poach the peaches as above. Serve upon a bed of sweet, hot strawberry *purée*. Add the hot Kirsch and light at the table.

Pêches Montréal

For 6 persons: 12 peach halves; 12 soft macaroons; 1 fl oz Bénédictine; 2 fl oz Kirsch; castor sugar. Cooking time: 4-6 minutes.

Poach the peaches in syrup. Drain them, dry on a cloth and place one on each macaroon which has been soaked in Bénédictine. Sprinkle with sugar, moisten with warmed Kirsch and ignite when serving.

▣ Pralinées * *Praline*

Poach halved, peeled peaches in Stock syrup, drain well and serve each half on a round sponge base. Coat with *Pralin à la Condé* mixed with a very little flour, dust with icing sugar and put in a moderate oven for 3 minutes in order to brown the peaches slightly. Serve the reduced Stock syrup, bound with a little apricot jam, separately.

POIRES * *PEARS*

▣ Flambées * *Flambéed*

Make in the same way as *Pêches Flambées*, but bind the syrup with a little apricot jam.

▣ à l'Impériale

For 6 persons: 6 pears; 6 oz Rice Condé; ¼ lb candied fruit; ¾ pint cold Apricot sauce flavoured with Kirsch.

Prepare the rice with half the usual amount of gelatine. Fill it into a *savarin* mould and allow to cool. Poach the peeled and halved pears in vanilla-flavoured syrup and cool. Unmould the rice on to a round dish or a glass bowl and arrange the pears either on top or around the rice. Cover with cold Apricot sauce and decorate either with half cherries or with leaves of angelica. Serve chilled, with a little cold Apricot sauce in a sauce-boat.

▣ Marie-Anne

Bake a *Génoise* sponge in a sandwich tin and when it is cooked, remove the centre with a large biscuit cutter. Place it on a round dish and fill the centre with Rice *Condé*, leaving a sufficient border free to stand a whole small or half a large pear. Decorate the rice with simple meringue mixture without touching the pears and put the dish in a hot oven for a few minutes in order to dry the meringue. Decorate the spaces between the pears with candied cherries and angelica and coat the pears themselves with the reduced Stock syrup in which they were poached, bound with apricot jam.

▣ Schouvaloff

For 6 persons: 12 small pear halves; 1 thin, round Génoise sponge; 12 oz ordinary meringue mixture; ¼ pint reduced apricot jam; redcurrant jelly; halved pistachio nuts. Cooking time: about 10 minutes.

Poach the pears in a Stock syrup. Drain and dry them on a cloth. Spread the jam all over the sponge and place the pears on top with their stalk ends pointing towards the centre. Cover over with meringue, smooth with a knife and pipe a criss-cross pattern with some more of the meringue. Dust with sugar and put in a hot oven to brown the meringue. In the spaces between the criss-cross lines, drop a spot of redcurrant jelly and place half a pistachio nut on top. Serve separately a thickened Kirsch-flavoured syrup (optional).

POMMES * *APPLES*

◘ Bonne Femme

For 4 persons: 6-8 cooking apples; sugar; butter. Cooking time: 20-25 minutes.

Core dessert apples with a corer without peeling them. Then score the peel all round the centre with a knife. Place in a baking dish with a nut of butter and a teaspoon of sugar in the hole of each apple. Pour ½ inch water or white wine into the dish and bake in a moderate oven, 375° F or Gas Mark 5, until apples are tender. Serve either hot or cold.

◘ à la Bulgare

For 6 persons: 6 apples; ½ pint Confectioners' custard; 1 oz almonds; 1 oz roasted and chopped hazelnuts; 2 oz chopped muscatels; ½ pint red wine; 3 oz sugar; 3 oz redcurrant jelly; 6 tartlet cases made with Sweet pastry and baked blind. Cooking time: 10-12 minutes.

Peel and core the apples and poach them slowly in a syrup composed of red wine, sugar and a little water, taking care not to let them break up. Drain them and fill the centre of each apple with some Confectioners' custard which contains the chopped almonds, hazelnuts and muscatels. Place the stuffed apples in the tartlet cases and cover with a thin coating of the syrup which has been reduced, thickened with a little starch boiled and mixed with redcurrant jelly.

◘ Châteaubriand

Prepare peeled apples as above and make sure that they do not collapse. Put apples on small, round *croûtons* fried in butter and coat with redcurrant jelly thickened with a little cornflour.

◘ Condé

Make in the same way as Apricot Condé.

◘ Manon

For 8 persons: 16 apple quarters poached in sugar syrup; 1 lb thick apple purée; 16 small macaroons; ½ pint Apricot sauce with rum.

Serve the apple quarters on the apple *purée* and place the macaroons in between. Coat with Apricot sauce and serve very hot.

Pommes Mariette

For 6 persons: 6 apples; ½ lb chestnut purée, sweetened and flavoured with rum; ½ pint rum-flavoured Apricot sauce; 1 oz flaked, roasted almomds. Cooking time: 10-12 minutes.

Core and peel the apples and poach them in a Stock syrup without letting them break up. Drain them carefully and arrange on a round dish. Fill the centre with some chestnut *purée* using a Savoy bag fitted with a plain nozzle. Cover over with an Apricot sauce and sprinkle the almonds on top.

▣ Pralinées

For 8 *persons:* Carefully poach 8 well-shaped peeled apple halves in vanilla-flavoured Stock syrup, drain, and serve on thickly concentrated apple *purée* in a baking dish. Coat them with *Pralin à la Condé*, consisting of an egg white, 4 oz sugar, 2 oz finely chopped almonds and, a pinch of cornflour, dust with icing sugar and put in a hot oven for a few moments to dry the icing.

FOREIGN SPECIALITIES

Aloo Halva * *Potato and Nut Halva*

For 6 persons: 1 lb peeled potatoes; 2 oz fine semolina; 4 oz butter; 1 oz chopped almonds; 1 oz chopped pistachio nuts; 1 oz chironjes (small Indian nuts); 1 teaspoon ground cardomom seeds; 1 oz flaked pistachio nuts. For the syrup: ½ pint water; ½ lb sugar; 8 cloves; 1 small piece of cinnamon; ½ vanilla bean; 12 whole cardamom seeds. Cooking time: about 30 minutes.

To make the syrup, cook the sugar, vanilla and spices in the water for 10 minutes. Strain and keep on one side. Cook the potatoes with a very little salt as for mashed potatoes and pass them through a metal sieve. Melt the butter in a frying pan and fry the *chironjes* for a moment. Add the mashed potatoes and stir in one quarter of the syrup. Pour the semolina on top. Stir over heat while mixing in thoroughly the chopped almonds and pistachio nuts and then the syrup a little at a time and cook in the same way as a *Choux* pastry. When the semolina has swollen and come off the sides of the pan like a smooth *purée*, the halva is ready. Serve on a round dish like a cake, decorate the middle with gold leaves and sprinkle with flaked pistachio nuts and ground cardamom seeds. Serve very hot. (*India*)

Bayrische Dampfnudeln * *Bavarian Noodles*

For 6 persons: 14 oz flour; ¾ oz yeast; 2 oz sugar; 2 eggs; zest of 1 lemon; 1 oz melted butter; ¾ pint milk; 1¼ pints vanilla Custard sauce or white wine Sabayon. Cooking time: 30 minutes.

Prepare a *Brioche* dough containing very little butter. Divide it into pieces about the size of small apricots and leave to rise in a warm place. Pour into a shallow pan ½ pint hot milk with ¾ oz sugar and ¾ oz butter. Place in this liquid the pieces of dough well spaced out so that they can expand without joining up. Cover with a cloth and cook over a gentle heat until the milk has completely evaporated. Serve with the caramelised side uppermost and cover with sauce. (*Germany*)

Crêpes au Slivowitz * *Pancakes with Slivovitz*

For 6 persons: ¼ pint milk; ¾ oz butter; ¾ oz cornflour; 4 to 5 eggs; 5 oz sloe jelly; 30 soaked prunes; 4 oz butter; 3 cloves; zest of ¼ lemon; 1 piece of cinnamon; ground cinnamon; 5 oz sugar; ¼ pint sour cream; 2 fl oz cognac; 4 fl oz Slivovitz. Cooking time: 10 minutes.

Prepare a rather thin *Choux* pastry with ¼ pint milk, ¾ ounce butter, ¾ oz cornflour and 4 to 5 eggs. Make 12 thin pancakes, spread them lightly with sloe jelly, roll them up loosely and keep them hot on a dish. Prepare a syrup with ¾ pint water, 4 oz sugar, the zest of a lemon, cinnamon and cloves. Poach the prunes for 10 minutes in the syrup. Drain and stone them. Strain the syrup, reduce it and flavour with 2 oz cognac and 2 oz Slivovitz. The final preparation takes place in the presence of the guests. Melt ¾ oz butter in a copper pan placed over a spirit stove. Put the pancakes in the pan and add the prunes and a little syrup. Bring the syrup to the boil, pour the rest of the Slivovitz over the pancakes and ignite. Serve the pancakes immediately on hot plates. Cover each pancake with a tablespoonful of syrup and a teaspoonful of sour cream and sprinkle it with sugar mixed with ground cinnamon. (*Yugoslavia*)

Mahallebi * *Turkish Creamed Rice*

For 6 persons: 2 oz rice; 5 oz rice flour; 1 pint fresh cream; ½ lb castor sugar; rose water. Cooking time: 1 hour.

Simmer the rice in ½ pint water until it is well cooked, and strain off the water through a cloth into a bowl. As soon as this liquor is cold, mix it with the rice flour, add the cream and sugar and cook slowly, stirring all the time. When the mixture thickens, remove from the heat and leave to cool while still stirring. Pour into small glass cups, sprinkle with sugar and add a few drops of rose water. (*Turkey*)

Apple Pie

For 6 persons: 14 oz Puff pastry; 1¼ lb peeled apples; 4 oz sugar; a little zest of lemon. Cooking time: 25-30 minutes.

Core the apples, slice them thinly, place in a pie dish, sprinkle with sugar and zest of lemon and only add a few drops of water. Brush the edge of the pie dish with water and place a strip of pastry round this edge. Cover with a Puff pastry lid rolled out ¼-inch thick, trim the edges, decorate with leaves of pastry, and brush with egg. Place in a hot oven, 425° F or Gas Mark 7, for 15 minutes then reduce the heat to 350° F or Gas Mark 4, for remaining time. If necessary protect the top with greased paper. (*Great Britain*)

Blackberry and Apple Pie

For 6 persons: 1 lb Sweet Short pastry; 1¼ lb of peeled, cored, thickly sliced apples; ¾ lb blackberries; 6 oz sugar; juice of half a lemon; 1 or 2 tablespoons water. Cooking time: 40 minutes.

Proceed as for Apple pie.

Gooseberry Pie

For 6 persons: 14 *oz Puff pastry;* $1\frac{1}{2}$ *lb cleaned green gooseberries;* $\frac{1}{2}$ *lb sugar.* Cooking time: 25-30 minutes.

Make in the same way as Apple pie. *(Great Britain)*

Mince Pie

For 10-12 persons: 5 *oz suet;* 10 *oz apples;* 3 *oz roast fillet of beef;* 5 *oz each sultanas and currants; the zest of a lemon;* $\frac{1}{2}$ *lb castor sugar;* 1 *pinch each of cinnamon, mace, powdered ginger and powdered clove;* $\frac{1}{4}$ *pint brandy and* $\frac{1}{4}$ *pint Madeira.*

Chop suet fairly fine, mix with the peeled, seeded and chopped apples, the cold, finely diced beef, currants, sultanas and sugar, season with lemon zest, cinnamon, cloves, mace and ginger and mix well. Place in jars, fill up with brandy or half brandy and half Madeira, sprinkle with sugar, tie up jars with cellophane and store in a cool place; the mince should be made at least 2-3 weeks before it is required. At Christmas, line tartlet tins with Puff pastry, fill with a spoonful of the above mixture, cover with a Puff pastry lid moistened at the edge, press down well and bake for about 20 minutes in a hot oven. Serve hot, dredged with icing sugar. *(Great Britain)*

Rhubarb Pie

For 6 persons: 14 *oz Puff pastry;* 2 *lb rhubarb;* 7 *oz sugar.* Cooking time: 25-30 minutes.

Peel the rhubarb, cut in small pieces and make in the same way as Apple pie. *(Great Britain)*

Baked Custard Pudding

For 6 persons: $1\frac{3}{4}$ *pints milk;* 5 *oz sugar;* 6 *eggs; lemon zest.* Cooking time: 25-30 minutes.

Infuse the lemon zest in the hot milk and strain it on to the beaten eggs and sugar, stirring all the time. Pour into a pie dish and bake in a warm oven in a *bain-marie.* *(Great Britain)*

Bread and Butter Pudding

For 6 persons: 6-8 *slices sandwich loaf without crust;* 2 *oz butter;* 2 *oz currants;* 1 *pint milk;* 4 *eggs; vanilla or zest of lemon;* 3 *oz sugar.* Cooking time: 25-30 minutes.

Spread bread thickly with butter, cut slices in half and arrange in a pie dish so that they overlap. Sprinkle with currants and pour on the beaten eggs mixed with sugar, flavouring and milk and strained; the bread should soak this up before the pudding is baked in a moderate oven, 375° F or Gas Mark 4-5. Serve dredged with sugar. *(Great Britain)*

Plum or Christmas Pudding

For 12 persons: ½ lb suet; ½ lb breadcrumbs; ¼ lb flour; ½ lb raisins; 2 oz sultanas; 2 oz chopped prunes; 2 oz chopped candied orange peel; 2 oz chopped candied lemon peel; 4 oz grated apple; 4 oz brown sugar; 3 eggs; the juice and grated rind of ½ lemon and ½ orange; pinch salt; 1 level teaspoon mixed spice; 2 fl oz brandy; 2 fl oz sherry. Cooking time: 6-8 hours.

Skin and chop the suet and put into a large mixing bowl. Mix in all the ingredients gradually, adding the Cognac and Madeira last of all. Mix very thoroughly. The mixture should be of a stiff dropping consistency but if it is too stiff you could add a little milk. Cover and leave to stand for 24-48 hours. Fill buttered pudding basins with this mixture, cover with buttered greaseproof paper and a cloth tied down firmly. Place the puddings in boiling water to come half-way up the sides of basins and boil slowly but steadily. Alternatively put the puddings in a steamer and steam for the same length of time. Replenish the pan with boiling water when necessary. When serving the pudding pour Cognac over it and set it alight when about to serve. Serve accompanied by Brandy sauce, or Custard sauce flavoured with rum. The pudding may be half cooked and kept for several months. The cooking time is completed before serving the pudding. *(Great Britain)*

Roly Poly Pudding

For 6 persons: ½ lb flour; 4 oz suet; pinch of salt; 1 oz sugar; a little water; jam. Cooking time: 2 hours.

Chop suet finely, work into a fairly firm dough with the flour, sugar, salt and a little cold water and leave to stand for at least 1 hour in a cool place. Roll out into a rectangle about ⅛-inch thick, brush thinly with jam, roll up and tie in a cloth like a *galantine*; the cloth should be greased and floured first. Place in boiling water and boil slowly for 2 hours. Unwrap, slice and serve with hot fruit sauce poured over it. *(Great Britain)*

Tapioca Pudding

For 6 persons: 1¼ pints milk; 4 oz sugar; 4 oz tapioca; 2 oz butter; 4 eggs; zest of lemon or almond essence. Cooking time: about 30 minutes.

Pour tapioca into boiling milk, boil for 10 minutes, flavour with lemon or almonds, mix with sugar and butter and, away from the heat, with the beaten eggs. Pour into a lightly buttered pie dish and bake in a warm oven. *(Great Britain)*

Rasgollah * *Curdled Milk Rolls*

For the syrup: ½ lb sugar; 20 cardomom seeds; 10 cloves; 1 small piece of cinnamon; 2 or 3 shreds of saffron; 2 tablespoons rose water. For the curdled milk: 5 pints milk; 3 or 4 lemons. Cooking time: 15 minutes.

Cook the sugar and the spices in half a pint of water for 10 minutes and then add the rose water. Do not strain this syrup. Bring the milk to the boil and curdle it with the lemon juice. Cover and leave to stand for 5 minutes and then drain through a muslin cloth. While the curds are still warm, beat them up to make them smooth. Divide into 18 pieces which are then shaped like little sausages 2¾ inches long. Arrange on a dish and pour the hot syrup over them. They may also be served with a cold syrup. *(India)*

Salzburger Nockerl * *Salzburg Dumplings*

For 6 persons: 3 oz butter; 6 oz sugar; 10 egg yolks; 10 egg whites; 1½ oz flour; ½ pint milk; sugar for dredging. Cooking time: 6-7 minutes.

Beat the butter to a foam with half the sugar and the egg yolks, fold in the very stiffly beaten egg whites mixed with the rest of the sugar and carefully stir in the flour. Put the mixture in a baking dish with the hot milk, put in a hot oven, 400° F or Gas Mark 6, and bake until light brown. Cut out large dumplings with a tablespoon and dredge with sugar. The mixture can also be baked in butter instead of milk. *(Austria)*

Wiener Krapfen * *Vienna Fritters*

Roll out Viennese fritter dough ⅛-inch thick and cut out rounds about 2 inches across. Moisten the edges lightly with water, put a teaspoon of apricot or other jam in the middle, cover with a second round, press down edges, place on a floured cloth to rise and leave to prove for 30 minutes. Put in deep fat, not too many at a time, and fry for 2 minutes with the lid on. Remove lid, turn fritters with a knife, fry another 4 minutes, drain well and dust with icing sugar. Serve hot or cold. *(Austria)*

Cold Sweets

BAVAROIS À LA CRÈME * *BAVARIAN CREAM* (*Basic Recipe*)

This is the basic recipe which may be flavoured and decorated in a great many different ways. Basically this mixture is a Custard cream thickened with gelatine and enriched with whipped cream.

For 6 *persons:* 3 *egg yolks;* 4 *oz sugar;* ½ *pint milk;* ½ *oz gelatine;* ¾ *pint whipped cream;* ⅛ pint water.

Beat up the egg yolks with the sugar until pale in colour and slowly pour the boiling milk over them. Mix until smooth, replace on the heat and thicken without letting the mixture boil. As soon as the custard cream coats the spatula, remove from the heat and strain. Dissolve gelatine in water and heat to slightly above blood heat. Stir into custard cream, continue stirring, when the gelatine is mixed, strain and leave to cool. Just before the custard sets, fold in the whipped cream. Pour into a mould with a central funnel which has been moistened with cold water and surround it with crushed ice or else leave in the refrigerator. To turn out of the mould, dip in hot water for a second.

▣ au Café * *Coffee*

Use the basic mixture. Flavour the milk strongly with coffee essence or soluble coffee powder.

▣ Cerisette * *Cherry*

For 6 persons: Bavarian cream; 2 fl oz Kirsch; 4 oz cherries in spirit.

Flavour the basic Bavarian cream with Kirsch and add the stoned cherries cut in halves.

▣ au Chocolat * *Chocolate*

Make as basic Bavarian cream, but use 1 oz sugar less and melt 4½ oz chocolate in the milk.

▣ Diplomate

Make the basic cream in the usual way and fill into the mould in alternate layers with 3 oz finely diced fruit macerated in Kirsch and 3 oz crushed sponge fingers lightly soaked in Kirsch.

Bavarois aux Fraises * *Strawberry Bavarian Cream*

For 8 persons: $\frac{1}{2}$ lb wild strawberries; 6 oz icing sugar; $\frac{1}{2}$ lemon; $\frac{1}{3}$-$\frac{1}{2}$ oz gelatine; $\frac{1}{2}$ pint whipped cream; $\frac{1}{8}$ pint water.

Sieve the strawberries through a hair sieve and mix with the sugar and the juice of half a lemon. Soak the gelatine and dissolve in water to just above blood heat mix with the *purée* and stir well and let the *purée* cool. As soon as it starts to set fold in the whipped cream and fill into a mould in the usual way.

⊡ aux Framboises * *Raspberry*

Proceed in the same way as for Fruit Bavarian cream. Decorate with raspberries and Chantilly cream.

⊡ aux Fruits * *Mixed Fruit*

For 6 persons: $\frac{1}{2}$ lb fresh fruit purée; 4 oz icing sugar; juice of $\frac{1}{2}$ lemon; $\frac{1}{2}$ oz gelatine; $\frac{3}{4}$ pint whipped cream; $\frac{1}{8}$ pint water.

Sieve some full-flavoured fruit. Mix the *purée* in a basin with the sugar and lemon juice. Dissolve the gelatine in water and mix well into the *purée*. Leave to stand until the mixture is half set before folding in the whipped cream and pouring into the mould as described above.

⊡ Nesselrode * *Chestnut*

Mix fresh chestnut *purée* with the basic mixture and use 1-2 sheets gelatine more than usual. When turning out decorate with a ring of glazed chestnuts.

⊡ à l'Orange * *Orange*

For 8 persons: $\frac{1}{4}$ lb sugar; 3 egg yolks; $\frac{1}{2}$ pint milk; the zest of 1 orange; juice of $\frac{1}{2}$ orange; $\frac{1}{2}$ oz gelatine; $\frac{1}{2}$ pint cream. Garnish: $\frac{1}{4}$ pint cream; a few orange slices; a very few red, stoned cherries.

Flavour hot milk with the zest of orange. Beat the egg yolks with the sugar and orange juice until white and foamy. Mix gently with the strained milk and cook very slowly over heat or in a water-bath. Allow to thicken without letting it boil, stirring with a spatula all the time. As soon as it begins to thicken, remove from the heat and add the gelatine, previously dissolved as above. Add to the orange cream, strain and allow to cool, stirring from time to time. Before it has set, add the whipped cream, mixing it in lightly. Pour the cream into a charlotte or ring mould, wetted with cold water, and place the mould in crushed ice or in the refrigerator. Unmould on a round dish, and decorate with whipped cream, using a piping bag and a fluted tube, slices of orange and cherries.

⊡ Praliné

Make in the same way as basic Bavarian cream and fold in 2 oz crushed, sifted praline together with the whipped cream.

Bavaroise Rubané * *Layered Bavarian Cream*

Proceed in the same way as for basic Bavarian cream. Divide the mixture into four parts, flavouring them respectively with vanilla, chocolate, pistachio and coffee. Pour each flavour into the mould separately. Care should be taken to ensure that the layers do not mix. A similar effect may be obtained using other Bavarian cream mixtures.

▣ à la Vanille * *Vanilla*

For 6 persons: 3 *egg yolks;* 4 *oz sugar;* ½ *pint milk; vanilla;* ½ *oz gelatine;* ½ *pint whipped cream.*

Beat the egg yolks and sugar to a foam and gradually add the milk, in which a vanilla pod has been steeped. Stir over heat till it thickens. Remove at once, add gelatine, and when it has melted, pour the cream into a bowl through a conical strainer. Let it cool and as soon as the cream starts to set, gently fold in the stiffly whipped cream. Fill into a cylinder mould wetted with cold water. Put in crushed ice or a refrigerator to set and turn out on a round dish.

BLANC-MANGER * *BLANCMANGE*

A very white jelly made by infusing almond milk with water and gelatine. It may be flavoured with a liqueur before it sets.

For 8 persons: 4 *oz almonds;* 3 *oz sugar;* ½ *oz gelatine;* ½ *pint whipped cream; vanilla; Kirsch or orange juice.*

Grind the almonds finely and gradually combine them with ½ pint cold water. Squeeze the almonds through a cloth to extract the liquid (almond milk). Dissolve the sugar in the cold almond milk, add the soaked, and melted gelatine and as soon as it starts to set fold in the whipped cream. Flavour to taste. Fill into a cylinder mould in the same way as Bavarian cream and when set turn out on a round dish.

▣ aux Avelines * *Hazelnut*

Proceed in the same way as above, but use fresh hazelnuts.

▣ au Chocolat * *Chocolate*

Proceed in the same way as for ordinary Blancmange, using ½ oz less sugar and adding 2 oz chocolate melted in a *bain-marie* or double boiler.

▣ aux Framboises * *Raspberry*

For 6 persons: 8 *oz blanched sweet almonds;* 3½ *oz sugar;* ½ *oz gelatine;* 4½ *oz raspberry purée;* ¾ *pint whipped cream.*

Proceed in the same way as for ordinary Blancmange, but mix in the raspberry *purée* before folding in the whipped cream. Blancmange can also be made with strawberry, apricot, peach *purée* or orange juice.

▣ aux Liqueurs * *Liqueur*

Prepare the Blancmange in the usual way and flavour with 2 fl oz Kirsch, Maraschino, Cointreau, Curaçao, etc.

CHARLOTTE * CHARLOTTE

A cold charlotte consists of a sweet made by lining a round mould or tin with sponge fingers or strips of sponge cake, then filled with a rich cream, flavoured to taste.

⊡ au Chocolat Pralinée * *Chocolate and Praline*

For 6 *persons:* 12 *sponge fingers;* 3 *egg yolks;* 3 *oz sugar;* 3 *oz plain chocolate;* ½ *pint milk;* ½ *oz gelatine;* 2 *oz praline;* ¾ *pint whipped cream.*

Line the sides of a charlotte mould with sponge fingers. Fill with a Chocolate Bavarian cream to which praline has been added. Leave to set in a cold place and turn out on to a round dish. Decorate with Chantilly cream and a few candied fruits. A chilled Custard cream can also be served separately.

⊡ au Chocolat Princière * *Chocolate Princess*

For 6 *persons:* 12 *sponge fingers; Strawberry Bavarian cream;* 3 *oz wild strawberries;* 3 *oz chocolate vermicelli;* 3 *tablespoons sieved strawberry jam;* ¼ *pint Chantilly cream; a few small cultivated strawberries.*

Line the sides of the charlotte mould with the sponge fingers; fill with the Strawberry Bavarian cream mixture containing the wild strawberries. Leave to set in a cold place. After turning the charlotte out of its mould, cover the top and sides with strawberry jam and coat with chocolate vermicelli. Serve on a round dish and, using a Savoy bag fitted with a plain pipe, decorate with Chantilly cream round the edge; on each blob of cream place a cultivated strawberry.

⊡ Malakoff

For 6 *persons:* 12 *sponge fingers;* 4 *oz almonds;* 4 *oz sugar;* 4 *oz butter;* ¼ *pint whipped cream; vanilla;* 1 *fl oz Kirsch.*

Line the mould as for Charlotte *Russe* apart from the bottom which is only covered with a round of greaseproof paper. Finely grind the almonds, gradually adding the sugar and powdered vanilla and mix in the slightly softened butter; all these ingredients are pounded in the mortar with the pestle until they become creamy and pale in colour. Add a liqueur glass of Kirsch, put the mixture in a basin and fold in the whipped cream. Pour into the mould lined with sponge fingers and then surround it with crushed ice. When the charlotte is quite firm, trim the sponge fingers to the same height as the cream and turn out on to a dish. Peel off the greaseproof paper and decorate the top with a vanilla-flavoured, sweetened whipped cream, using a Savoy bag fitted with a star pipe. The cream should not have been fully whipped.

⊡ Royale

For 6-8 *persons: Sponge mixture:* 5 *oz butter;* 4 *oz sugar;* 10 *egg yolks;* 10 *egg whites;* 5 *oz flour;* 5 *oz strained and reduced apricot jam;* 2 *oz redcurrant jelly;* ¼ *pint white wine jelly;* ½ *lb Coffee fondant. Custard:* ¾ *pint milk;* 2 *egg yolks;* 3 *oz sugar;* 1 *teaspoon cornflour or arrowroot;* ¼ *oz gelatine;* 2 *oz chopped candied fruit;* 1 *fl oz Maraschino;* ½ *pint whipped cream.* Cooking time: 6-8 minutes.

Cream the butter with 2 oz sugar and incorporate the egg yolks one at a time. Whisk the egg whites with 2 oz sugar until very stiff, mix in the flour and carefully amalgamate the two mixtures. Spread thinly on a greased floured baking sheet and bake in a hot oven, 425°

F or Gas Mark 7, ensuring that the sponge does not dry up. When it has cooled down, sandwich together five layers of the sponge alternatively with apricot jam and redcurrant jelly. Cut up into strips 1-inch wide and line a dome-shaped mould with them.

For the custard: Macerate the candied fruits in the Maraschino. Mix the egg yolks, sugar, starch and milk together and cook until it coats the back of a spoon and finally add the gelatine which has been dissolved in water. When the custard begins to set, fold in the whipped cream and candied fruit. Fill the lined mould with this mixture and leave to set in a cool place. Turn out the charlotte on to a round jam sponge sandwich of the same diameter as the charlotte itself. The same sponge mixture is used to make heart-shaped *petits fours* which are brushed with apricot *purée* and iced with Coffee fondant icing. Coat the charlotte with apricot jelly, glaze with white wine jelly and arrange *petits fours* all round. (*See illustration on p.* 754).

Charlotte Russe

For 6-8 *persons:* 12 *to* 15 *sponge fingers;* 4 *oz sugar;* 3 *egg yolks;* ½ *pint milk;* ¼ *oz gelatine; vanilla;* ¾ *pint whipped cream.*

Take some very dry sponge fingers for lining the charlotte mould. First, for the bottom, cut some fingers into thin, triangular pieces and place these upside down with their tips meeting at the centre and packed closely together. Trim the sides and one end of the other sponge fingers so that they will fit more compactly round the sides of the mould; these, too, should be arranged with the upper surface against the side of the mould. It does not matter at all if all the fingers are not of the same height, because they will be trimmed to the height of the cream before the charlotte is turned out of the mould. The inside is filled with a Vanilla or other flavoured Bavarian cream which contains rather less gelatine than usual. Leave to set in a cool place. Turn out just before serving and decorate with Chantilly cream.

Profiteroles * *Profiteroles with Chocolate Sauce*

½ *lb Choux pastry;* ¾ *pint vanilla-flavoured whipped cream or Confectioners' custard;* ¾ *pint thick Chocolate sauce.*

Pipe tiny round *eclairs* and bake in a hot oven, 400° F or Gas Mark 6, for 15-20 minutes until they are crisp and dry inside. Split open immediately they are baked. Cool and fill with whipped cream, coat with hot Chocolate sauce and serve at once.

Chocolate sauce. Melt 6 oz plain chocolate with a little water, stir till smooth, add a small piece of fresh butter and pour over the *profiteroles.*

LES CRÈMES * *VARIOUS CREAM SWEETS*

These are all cold sweets; some are cooked, others are simply a combination of whipped cream and fruit *purée.*

⊡ Hindoue

4 *oz sugar;* 2 *oz ground almonds;* 3 *egg whites;* ½ *pint whipped cream; vanilla;* ½ *pineapple.* Cooking time: about 35 minutes.

Thinly slice peeled fresh or tinned pineapple, poach in vanilla Stock syrup and drain on a cloth. Butter a *savarin* ring, sprinkle with sugar and line with overlapping pineapple slices. Stiffly beat the egg whites, fold in vanilla sugar and very dry ground almonds, fill into the mould and poach in a water-bath in a moderate oven. When cold, turn out, fill centre with whipped cream and coat the edge with Apricot sauce with Kirsch.

Crème à l'Orange Arlequin * *Orange Harlequin Cream*

For 6 persons: ½ pint orange juice; ½ pint white wine; ½ pint water; 3 oz sugar; 6 egg yolks; ½ oz cornflour; ½ oz gelatine; ½ pint whipped cream; ¼ pint white wine jelly; Chocolate royal icing; skinned pistachio nuts.

Beat up the egg yolks with the sugar until pale in colour and add the orange juice, white wine, cornflour and water. Thicken over heat as for a Custard cream and, as soon as it coats the spoon, stir in the gelatine which has first been dissolved in a little water. Leave to cool and, when the mixture begins to set, fold in the whipped cream. Pour into a glass dish and leave to set completely in a cool place. Decorate with Chocolate royal icing and pistachio nuts and cover with partially set jelly.

▣ Printania

Mix vanilla-flavoured whipped cream with a little strawberry *purée* and serve in glasses. Garnish with strawberries macerated in sugar and Kirsch.

▣ à la Vigneronne

For 6 persons: ½ pint white wine; ½ pint water; juice and grated zest of 1 lemon; 5 oz sugar; 6 egg yolks; ½ oz cornflour; ½ oz gelatine; ½ pint whipped cream; ¼ pint white wine jelly; 2½ oz sieved apricot jam; melted bars of chocolate; wafer biscuits shaped like vine leaves. Cooking time: 10 minutes.

Mix together the egg yolks, sugar, cornflour and lemon juice. Boil the white wine with water and lemon zest. Pass through a conical strainer and gradually pour over the egg yolks; stirring all the time. Cook in the same way as a Custard cream, being careful it does not boil, until it coats a spatula. Add the gelatine which has first been dissolved in water. Leave to cool, stirring occasionally. When the custard begins to set, fold in the whipped cream. Immediately pour into Champagne glasses and fill to just below the brim and leave to cool in a cold place to help the Custard cream to set. Using a piping bag fitted with a fine tube, pipe a bunch of grapes composed of little rings of chocolate which is left to harden. Fill in the rings with cold, reduced apricot jam and cover with half-set white wine jelly. Serve with the wafer biscuits.

▣ au Xérès * *Sherry*

For 6 persons: 3 *egg yolks;* 2 *oz sugar; ½ oz cornflour; ½ pint milk; ¼ oz gelatine; ¼ pint sherry; ½ pint whipped cream;* 2 *egg whites whisked with ¾ oz sugar until stiff.* Cooking time: 5 minutes.

Beat up the egg yolks with the sugar and cornflour until pale in colour. Gradually add the hot milk and thicken over heat as for Custard cream, and add the gelatine which has first been dissolved in cold water. Leave to cool, stirring occasionally. When completely cold, stir in the sherry, fold in the whipped cream and then the egg whites. Pour into Champagne glasses and decorate.

CRÈMES RENVERSÉES OU MOULÉES * *MOULDED CREAM SWEETS*

These are basically Custard creams which are poached in a water-bath in the oven, and when they are cold they may be decorated with whipped cream. Care should be taken to cook the cream in a water-bath in the oven so that there is no danger of the mixture reaching boiling point which would tend to curdle it.

Renversée à la Vanille * *Basic Vanilla Moulded Cream*

For 5-6 persons: 2 *eggs;* 4 *egg yolks;* ¾ *pint milk;* 4 *oz sugar; vanilla.* Cooking time: about 30 minutes.

Beat up in a basin the egg yolks and sugar and stir in the boiling milk in which the vanilla has been infused. Leave to stand for a few minutes, remove the froth and strain. Pour into a slightly oiled or greased mould and bake in a warm oven, 325° F or Gas Mark 3, in a water-bath without letting it boil. Allow the custard to become completely cold before turning it out of the mould.

⊡ Beau-Rivage

For 6 *persons:* 2 *eggs;* 4 *egg yolks;* ¾ *pint milk;* 1 *oz sugar; vanilla;* ½ *pint Chantilly cream;* 6 *Almond wafer cornets; Chocolate fondant; angelica; glacé cherries.* Cooking time: 20-25 minutes.

Prepare the Custard cream with ⅓ ordinary sugar and ⅓ caramelised sugar. Poach in a greased *savarin* mould sprinkled with sugar. Leave until cold and turn out on to a round dish. Fill the centre with Chantilly cream and decorate with the cherries. Ice the cornets with Chocolate fondant, fill them with Chantilly cream and decorate with leaves made of angelica. Arrange the cornets round the dessert.

⊡ au Café * *Coffee*

Prepare the basic mixture without vanilla, but add instead a heaped teaspoonful of coffee powder or essence to the warm milk.

⊡ au Caramel * *Caramel*

4 *oz sugar;* ¾ *pint milk;* 2 *eggs;* 4 *egg yolks; vanilla pod.* Cooking time: 35 minutes.

Steep the vanilla in hot milk. Mix the sugar with the eggs and egg yolks and gradually thin with the milk; strain. Line a tall mould with light caramel, fill with mixture and poach in a warm oven, 325° F or Gas Mark 3, in a water-bath without letting the water boil.

⊡ au Chocolat * *Chocolate*

For 6 *persons:* 3 *eggs;* 4 *egg yolks;* 3 *oz sugar;* 2 *oz chocolate;* ¾ *pint milk.* Cooking time: about 30 minutes.

Proceed in the same way as for Basic Vanilla mould, but first melt the chocolate in the milk.

⊡ Royale

Proceed in the same way as for Basic Vanilla mould with praline and when cold turn out on a round dish. Fill the centre with vanilla-flavoured whipped cream mixed with strawberries and decorate with wild strawberries.

PETITS POTS DE CRÈME * *INDIVIDUAL CREAM POTS*

The same method as Caramel cream, but fill into small fire-proof *cocottes* and poach in a water-bath. Since this cream is not turned out omit the egg yolks, and of course the caramel. Cooking time: about 20 minutes.

⊡ aux Amandes * *Almond*

Proceed in the same way as above and add $1\frac{1}{2}$-$2\frac{3}{4}$ oz blanched almonds finely ground with a little Kirsch.

⊡ au Café * *Coffee*

Add to the milk a teaspoonful of coffee powder or essence.

⊡ Caracas

1 *egg;* 3 *egg yolks;* 2 *oz sugar;* 2 *oz chocolate;* $\frac{3}{4}$ *pint milk;* $\frac{1}{2}$ *pint Chantilly cream;* 1 *tablespoon rum;* 3 *glacé cherries; chocolate vermicelli.* Cooking time: 18-20 minutes.

Proceed in the same way as explained above melting the chocolate in the hot milk in a double boiler. Bake in a water-bath in individual tiny earthenware pots. When completely cold, decorate with a whirl of Chantilly cream flavoured with rum. Sprinkle with chocolate vermicelli and place half a *glacé* cherry in the middle.

⊡ au Chocolat * *Chocolate*

Prepare this cream using only $2\frac{1}{2}$ oz sugar and 2 oz chocolate dissolved in the hot milk. Decorate with Chantilly cream.

⊡ Pralinée * *Praline*

Proceed in the same way as above, using $\frac{3}{4}$ oz less sugar and adding $1\frac{3}{4}$ oz ground and sifted praline. When cold, each pot of cream can be decorated with a whirl of Chantilly cream and sprinkled with a little praline.

Flameri de Semoule * *Semolina Flummery*

For 6 persons: 7 fl oz white wine; $\frac{1}{2}$ *pint water;* $4\frac{1}{2}$ *oz semolina;* $4\frac{1}{2}$ *oz sugar;* 3 *egg whites;* 2 *egg yolks; vanilla.* Cooking time: 35 minutes.

Boil the water and white wine together, sprinkle the semolina into this liquid and cook until thick. Add the sugar and vanilla. Remove from the heat and rapidly stir in 2 egg yolks and then fold in the 3 stiffly whisked egg whites. Pour the mixture into a funnel mould, which has been greased and sprinkled with sugar, and bake slowly in a *bain-marie* in a warm oven. Leave to cool and turn out of the mould on to a cold dish. Pour some Kirsch-flavoured Redcurrant sauce round the flummery and serve some more separately.

Frou-Frou aux Marrons * *Frou-Frou of Chestnuts*

For 4-5 persons: 3½ oz rice; 3½ oz sugar; 4 oz candied fruit; ½ oz gelatine; 4 yolks of eggs; 1 pint milk; ¾ pint whipped cream; 8-10 small Almond cornets; a little chestnut purée.

Make *Riz à l'Impératrice* and when it begins to stiffen fold in about ½ pint whipped cream. Fill the rice into a *savarin* mould and allow to set. Turn out on to a round dish, and garnish the middle with whipped cream. Fill the cornets about two-thirds full with chestnut *purée* mixed with a little whipped cream and fill them up with whipped cream, using a piping bag and a star tube. Arrange these cornets all around the whipped cream in the middle of the rice.

Himalaya ou Vacherin Meringué * *Meringue Vacherin*

For 8 persons: 8 egg whites; 14 oz sugar; 1 pint whipped cream; candied fruit.

Beat the whites stiffly and fold in the sugar. Mark out 6 circles on a greased and floured baking sheet. Pipe around these with meringue and fill two circles with lattice work. Bake in a very cool oven, 200-225° F or Gas Mark ½, without allowing the *vacherin* to colour too much. When baked, having a lattice work circle as the base, stick the circles on top of each other with remaining meringue making sure there are no gaps between the circles, smooth with a palette knife and decorate with a star tube. Replace in a cool oven, 325° F or Gas Mark 2, and bake until quite dry. Fill the centre of the cold *vacherin* with sweetened whipped cream. Place the remaining circle with lattice work on top and garnish with a star tube with whipped cream and decorate with candied fruit. According to season, crushed glazed chestnuts or wild strawberries may be mixed with the whipped cream.

Île Flottante Pralinée * *Floating Island*

For 4 persons: 2 oz ground roasted almonds or 3 oz coarsely ground pink praline; 4 oz sugar; 4 egg whites; vanilla.

Whisk the egg whites until very stiff and mix in the sugar, vanilla, praline or almonds. Pour this mixture into a charlotte mould which has been buttered and sugared or coated with caramel. Bake in a very cool oven, 225° F or Gas Mark ½, in a *bain-marie* for about 20 minutes. Leave to cool slightly and turn out on to a fruit dish containing a chilled Custard cream. The Floating Island may be sprinkled with coarsely chopped pistachio nuts.

Marquise Alice

For 6 persons: Praline Bavarian cream mixture; 8 sponge fingers; 2 fl oz Kirsch or Anisette; ¾ pint firm Chantilly cream; ¼ pint redcurrant jelly.

Prepare the Praline Bavarian cream and pour half of it into a shallow, round mould. Place on top of the sponge fingers which have been soaked in the Kirsch or Anisette and cover with the rest of the Bavarian cream. Leave in a cold place to set. Turn out on to a round dish and cover over with Chantilly cream. Using a paper bag filled with redcurrant jelly, decorate the top with parallel lines which are then drawn with the blade of a small knife as for a Mexican cake.

MERINGUES CHANTILLY * *CREAM MERINGUE SWEETS*

These are sweets made with various types of meringue mixture to which are added whipped cream and flavourings. (*See Meringues, p.* 725.) These meringues should be made fairly small and baked slowly until they are dry. However they should not be over-baked as they can become too dry or brittle.

For 6 persons: Swiss meringue mixture; ¾ pint Chantilly cream.

Using a Savoy bag fitted with a large, plain nozzle pipe meringue shells on a greased and floured baking sheet leaving a space between each. Sprinkle generously with castor sugar and brush away excess sugar. Bake the meringues in the oven at the lowest setting with the door open, until they are completely dry but not coloured. When they are cold, sandwich them together in pairs with some Chantilly cream, arrange them on end on a dish and decorate with Chantilly cream.

▣ Colette

For 6 persons: 5 egg whites; 10 oz sugar; 1 teaspoon coffee powder or essence; 2-3 oz warmed couverture or plain chocolate; 3 glacé cherries; ¾ pint Chantilly cream; 2 fl oz Kirsch.

Prepare a meringue mixture with the egg whites mixed with the sugar and coffee. Pipe the mixture in a spiral 2½-inches in diameter and ½-inch thick. Dry slowly in a very cool oven. When cold, brush the inside surface with a little chocolate and leave to set. Sandwich the meringues together in pairs with Chantilly cream flavoured with Kirsch. Decorate with a whirl of Chantilly cream and place half a *glacé* cherry on top.

▣ Fraisalia * *with Wild Strawberries*

For 6 persons: 12 meringues; ½ lb wild strawberries; 2 fl oz Kirsch; ¾ pint Chantilly cream.

Cover the meringues first with a layer of wild strawberries, cut up and soaked in Kirsch and then Chantilly cream. Decorate with a few whole strawberries.

▣ Mayaguana * *with Pineapple*

5 egg whites; 10 oz sugar; ¾ pint whipped cream; ½ lb finely diced, cooked pineapple; 2 fl oz cherry brandy; 2 oz chocolate cigarettes or chocolate shavings.

Prepare a meringue mixture and pipe it in squares 2½×2½ inches and leave to dry. Soak the pineapple in the cherry brandy and a little sugar and mix in ⅓ of the whipped cream and sandwich the meringues together with this mixture. Decorate with a whirl of Chantilly cream and sprinkle with chocolate.

Mon Rêve * *My Dream*

For 6 persons: 4 oz best chocolate; ¼ pint Stock syrup; ¾ pint whipped cream; 1¾ oz ground and sifted praline; 6 Snow Eggs; 1 fl oz Kirsch; ½ pint Custard cream. Cooking time: 5-6 minutes.

Melt the chocolate in the syrup. As soon as it is cold, fold in the whipped cream and praline. Pile up in a fruit dish in the shape of a smooth dome. Cover with the Snow Eggs and pour a Kirsch-flavoured Custard cream over.

Mousse au Chocolat * *Chocolate Mousse*

For 6 persons:

Melt ½ lb chocolate with 3 tablespoons milk, add 1½ oz icing sugar, cool slightly and briskly stir in 4 egg yolks. Let it stand for a few minutes then, gently fold in 4 stiffly beaten egg whites, pour into a glass dish and chill well before serving.

Mousse aux Fraises * *Strawberry Mousse*

For 8 persons: 1 lb strawberries; 4 egg whites; 5 oz icing sugar; ¾ pint whipped cream.

Pass the strawberries through a hair sieve, combine with the stiffly beaten egg whites and the sugar and fill into a glass dish. Garnish with small strawberries and whipped cream.

Mousse aux Framboises * *Raspberry Mousse*

For 6 persons.

Pass 1 lb raspberries through a hair sieve and mix with ½ lb icing sugar. Add the juice of ½ a lemon and ¾ oz melted gelatine, let it set and gently fold in ½ pint stiffly whipped cream. Fill into ice *coupés* or a glass dish and when set decorate with whole raspberries. Serve with sponge fingers.

Oeufs à la Neige * *Snow Eggs*

For 4 persons: 3 egg whites; 6 oz vanilla sugar; 3 egg yolks; vanilla pod; ½ pint milk. Total cooking time: 20 minutes in all.

Stiffly beat egg whites and fold in the sugar. Very slowly heat the milk with a vanilla pod and drop moulded tablespoonfuls of the meringue into it; poach them without boiling and turn over with a fork after 2 minutes. When the eggs are fairly firm to the touch, drain them on a cloth. Use the milk to make custard with the egg yolks, allow to cool. Then pour in a dish and place the eggs on top. Serve cold. They may also be made as above but poached in water and served as above but covered with melted chocolate. Snow eggs poached in water have a better appearance than those poached in milk.

Oeufs à la Religieuse * *Snow Eggs with Chocolate Sauce*

4 egg whites; ½ lb sugar; 2 egg yolks; 5 oz chocolate; ½ pint milk; almonds.

Stiffly beat the egg whites and fold in 4½ oz sugar. Make Snow eggs as above, drain well and let them cool. Make custard with chocolate, the 2 egg yolks, 3½ oz sugar and poaching milk and cool. Coat the Snow eggs with cold sauce and sprinkle with coarsely chopped roasted almonds or praline.

RIZ * *RICE*

Dessert rice may be flavoured with fruit peel, cinnamon or liqueur. Carolina is the most suitable type of rice for puddings and sweets.

▣ à l'Impératrice

For 6 persons: 3 *oz Carolina rice;* 3 *oz sugar;* 3 *oz candied fruit;* 3 *egg yolks;* ¾ *pint milk;* ½ *pint whipped cream;* 2 *oz redcurrant jelly;* ½ *oz gelatine;* 1 *fl oz Kirsch; vanilla.* Cooking time: 25 minutes.

Boil the rice in water for 2 minutes, drain it and finish cooking in ½ pint milk containing ½ a vanilla pod. Prepare a Custard cream with the egg yolks, sugar and the rest of the milk When the custard has thickened, remove from the heat and add the gelatine which has first been melted in 2 tablespoons hot water. Pass through a fine strainer. When the rice is cooked, remove it from the heat and add the Custard cream and leave the mixture until it starts to set. Then fold in the whipped cream and finely diced candied fruit which has been macerated in the Kirsch for 1 hour. Cover the bottom of a funnel mould or pudding basin with redcurrant jelly and when this has set, pour in the mixture and leave to set in a cold place.

▣ à la Mandarine * *Mandarin Orange*

For 6 persons: 3 *oz Carolina rice;* 3 *oz sugar;* 3 *egg yolks;* ¾ *pint milk;* ½ *pint whipped cream;* ½ *oz gelatine;* 5 *tangerine oranges;* 1 *fl oz Curaçao.*

Prepare the rice as for *Riz à l'Impératrice*, but flavour the Custard cream with tangerine zest. Pour the mixture into a dome-shaped mould and leave to set in a cold place. When the pudding is turned out of the mould, decorate with tangerine segments macerated in sugar and Curaçao. For the decoration, tinned Japanese mandarin orange segments may be used.

▣ Singapour

For 6 persons: 3 *oz Carolina rice;* 3 *oz sugar;* 3 *egg yolks;* ¾ *pint milk;* ½ *pint whipped cream;* ½ *oz gelatine;* ½ *lb diced pineapple;* 2 *fl oz Maraschino;* ½ *pint Apricot sauce.*

Prepare the rice as indicated above and mix in the pineapple which has been poached and macerated in Maraschino. Pour into a mould. Turn out on to a round dish and serve with a cold Apricot sauce flavoured with the Maraschino used to soak the pineapple.

Tartelettes Bettina * *Chocolate Tartlets*

For 6 persons: chocolate; ½ *pint milk;* 2 *egg yolks;* 2 *oz sugar;* ½ *oz cornflour;* ½ *oz gelatine;* 2 *oz chopped candied fruit;* 2 *fl oz Maraschino;* ½ *pint whipped cream;* 6 *Florentine biscuits.* Cooking time: 30 minutes.

Melt the chocolate and use to line (to a thickness of ⅓ of an inch) some silver ice cream cups or small foil tartlet cases. Allow the chocolate to harden and then, after trimming the edges, carefully remove from the moulds. Fill the chocolate cases with a custard prepared as follows: macerate the candied fruit in the Maraschino. Make a Custard cream with the egg yolks, milk, sugar and cornflour and add the gelatine which has first been soaked in water or melted in 2 tablespoons hot water. When the custard begins to set, fold in the whipped cream and the candied fruit. Fill the chocolate cases straight away and cover them up with a Florentine biscuit of the same diameter as the chocolate case to serve as a lid.

Preparation of the Florentine biscuits: ½ *lb butter;* 12 *oz sugar;* 4 *oz honey;* 1 *lb flaked almonds;* 4 *oz chopped candied orange peel;* 4 *oz glucose;* ¼ *pint whipped cream; chocolate; glacé cherries.* Cooking time: 20 minutes.

Place the ingredients in a saucepan and heat together stirring constantly. Put small spoonfuls of the mixture on a greased baking sheet and bake in a hot oven, 425° F or Gas Mark 7, for about 10 minutes. Take out of the oven and cut out each biscuit with a round pastry cutter. Place half a *glacé* cherry in the middle of each biscuit and replace in the oven to finish baking. Remove the biscuits with a knife from the baking sheet while they are still hot. As soon as they are cool, coat the base of each with melted chocolate. Leave to harden and add a second layer of chocolate which is then marked in wavy lines with a fork or scraper.

LES GELÉES * *JELLIES*

Always use the finest quality gelatine which is sold in thin leaves. Allow ¾-1 ounce of gelatine to set 1 pint of liquid and 1½-2 ounces to set 1 quart, according to the density of the liquid to be set. Wash the leaf gelatine, place it in cold water until it is soft and then dissolve it in the warm liquid indicated in the recipe. The following points may be useful if you are using gelatine or making jellies for the first time.

Measure the gelatine carefully, just a little too much can spoil a recipe. If a recipe suggests the use of ¾ ounce of gelatine to 1 pint of liquid increase the amount of gelatine to 1 ounce in hot weather unless a refrigerator is available. Never stir boiling water into any dry gelatine. When dissolving gelatine in milk do not allow the milk to come to the boil, or else it will curdle. Allow a jelly from 2-4 hours to set if you have no refrigerator. Do not stir in any fruit, nuts or other solid ingredients until the jelly shows signs of congealing, otherwise the ingredient added will not be evenly distributed throughout. Make sure that gelatine is absolutely dissolved before using it. Always stir the gelatine into the mixture it is required to set until the setting point is reached.

To prepare moulds for jelly

Rinse the mould, first with boiling water, then with cold. Copper moulds should be cleaned thoroughly, dried and then rubbed with a piece of tissue paper dipped in oil. Turn the mould upside down on a plate to allow surplus oil to drain away.

Gelée de Base * *Basic Jelly Recipe*

6 *oz sugar;* 1 *oz gelatine;* 3 *fl oz white wine; juice of* 1 *lemon; zest of* ½ *lemon;* 1 *egg white;* ¾ *pint water.* Cooking time: 20 minutes.

Soak the gelatine in cold water and dissolve it in ¾ pint of hot water. Add the sugar, lemon juice and zest and bring to the boil. Cover, remove from the heat and leave to stand for 10 minutes. Beat the egg white with the white wine and gradually whisk in the syrup. Continue to stir over heat until the jelly forms a crust, then simmer for 10 minutes. Cover over again, remove from the heat and leave to stand for a few minutes. Strain through a cloth which has been wetted with cold water and if the jelly is not completely clear, strain a second time.

Gelée aux Fruits * *Fruit Jelly*

For 6 persons: ¾ pint jelly (see basic recipe); ½ pint strained fruit juice.

For fruit jellies the most suitable fruits are red ones such as: raspberries, strawberries, cherries, redcurrants, blackberries. The fruit should be very ripe. Pass through a sieve, adding 4-7 fl oz water for every 1 lb fruit and strain. Mix the filtered juice with the cold jelly, pour into a mould and leave to set in a cold place. To turn the jelly out of its mould, dip the latter for an instant in hot water and let the jelly slide out on to a round dish. For a lighter jelly, mix ¾ pint jelly with ¾ pint of fruit juice and serve either in sundae glasses or in a cut glass fruit bowl.

▣ au Kirsch

5 oz sugar; ½ oz gelatine; ¾ pint water; 1 small piece vanilla; 2 fl oz Kirsch.

Make Stock syrup with sugar, water and vanilla. Boil slowly for 2-3 minutes and add the soaked, and melted gelatine, strained through a cloth. As soon as the jelly is cold but still liquid flavour it with Kirsch. Used mainly as a garnish for cold sweets.

▣ Macédoine de Fruits * *Mixed Fruit*

Use fruit in season, such as strawberries, raspberries, red-, white- and blackcurrants, stoned cherries, peeled, quartered peaches or apricots, but use ripe fruit. Put in a glass or silver dish and pour cold Kirsch or champagne jelly, made with only half the usual quantity of gelatine, on top. Serve very cold.

▣ à l'Orange * *Orange*

Halve 12 ripe oranges, scoop out the flesh with a spoon and remove white skin. Place in a copper pan, crush slightly, allow to boil up once and immediately squeeze the juice out through cloth. Mix with the same weight of sugar, add 2-3 lumps of sugar rubbed on the peel, allow to boil up and skim. When the syrup ceases to foam remove from heat and when almost cold add ½ oz soaked, melted and strained gelatine and 1 tablespoon Curaçao. Before it sets pour into half orange skins or small glass dishes.

▣ au Vin * *Wine*

For 6 persons: ¾ pint of jelly; ¼ pint good quality wine.

Mix the wine with the cold jelly while the latter is still liquid. Pour into a mould and leave to set in a cold place. For wine jellies, good quality, full-bodied wines should be used: *Château Yquem*, champagne, sherry, Madeira, Port, Marsala, etc. To obtain a lighter jelly, use ½ pint wine and serve in sundae glasses.

Moscovite aux Fraises * *Strawberry Whip*

For 4-5 persons.

Mix ½ pint of liquid Kirsch jelly with ½ pound strawberries passed through a fine sieve. Put the bowl on ice and beat quickly like egg whites. As soon as the mixture becomes foamy and starts to bind fill into a mould wetted with cold water and leave to set on ice or in a refrigerator. Turn out on a round dish and serve with slightly sweetened strawberry *purée.*

COLD FRUIT SWEETS

ABRICOTS * *APRICOTS*

These are rather like small peaches in appearance and are one of the most popular fruits used in cooking.

▣ Bourdaloue

For 6 persons: Génoise sponge mixture; 12 apricots; 1 pint Frangipane cream; 3 fl oz whipped cream; 3 macaroons; candied cherries; angelica; 7 fl oz Apricot and Kirsch sauce.

Cook the *Génoise* cake in a buttered *savarin* mould. Leave to cool and turn out on to a round dish. Place halved apricots poached in Stock syrup on top, overlapping each other. Decorate with cherries and angelica and cover with Apricot sauce. Mix the Frangipane cream with the whipped cream, place in the middle of the *Génoise* and sprinkle with crushed macaroons.

▣ Condé

For 6 persons: 12 *apricots;* 5 *oz rice;* 1 *pint milk;* 4-5 *oz sugar;* 3 *egg yolks;* 1½ *oz butter; glacé cherries; angelica;* ½ *pint Apricot and Kirsch sauce.* Cooking time for rice: 25-30 minutes.

Poach the halved apricots in syrup. Cook rice in the milk until thick then beat in yolks, sugar and butter. Pour into serving dish or wetted mould and leave to cool. Arrange the apricots on the rice, decorate with *glacé* cherries and leaves of angelica. Cover with syrup. (*See illustration p.* 757).

▣ Monte-Cristo

For 6 persons: 12 *apricots;* 1½ *pints Apricot ice;* ½ *pint raspberry purée;* 1½ *oz almonds, roasted and shredded.*

Poach the apricots whole in vanilla syrup, peel and leave to cool in the syrup. Garnish the bottom of a *timbale* mould with the ice, drain and place apricots on top and cover with raspberry *purée*. Sprinkle with roasted almonds.

▣ Négus

For 6 persons: 12 *apricots;* 1½ *pints Chocolate ice;* 7 *fl oz Apricot and Kirsch sauce;* 7 *fl oz Chantilly cream.*

Halve and poach the apricots in vanilla syrup and leave to cool. Garnish the bottom of a *timbale* mould with Chocolate ice. Drain the apricots and place on the ice. Cover with Apricot sauce and decorate with Chantilly.

ANANAS * *PINEAPPLE*

When ripe, the leaves at the top of this fruit may be pulled out easily.

Ananas Edouard VII * *Pineapple Edward VII*

For 6-8 persons: 1 pineapple; 1 pint Vanilla ice; 6 oz stoned cherries poached in syrup; 2 tablespoons Kirsch; 7 fl oz Apricot sauce; 3 fl oz Chantilly cream.

To prepare the pineapple without damaging the green leaves: remove the top of a fresh pineapple, then remove a slice from the bottom to form a firm base. Insert a small sharp knife into the flesh ½-inch from the outside edge and holding the blade firm, turn it round to loosen the flesh, do not widen the opening. Repeat this at the top end of the pineapple until the central flesh part has loosened all round and may be removed in one piece. The pineapple should now be hollow. Divide the flesh lengthwise and remove the tough central core. Cut the flesh of half the pineapple into dice, mix with the well drained cherries, sprinkle with half the Kirsch and leave to soak. Cut the other half into slices and steep in the remaining Kirsch, place the base of the pineapple on a well chilled round dish. Mix Vanilla ice with cherries and diced pineapple and fill the shell. Decorate with Chantilly cream. Place the pineapple slices round the base of the pineapple overlapping each other and cover with a little iced Apricot sauce. Replace the green leafy top part of the pineapple.

⊡ Princesse

For 6 persons: 6 round pieces of sponge cake; 12 half slices raw pineapple; 2 fl oz Maraschino; 1 pint Strawberry ice; 7 fl oz Chantilly cream; a few small strawberries.

Steep pineapple with sugar and Maraschino. Place two slices on each piece of sponge. Put some Strawberry ice in the centre and decorate with Chantilly cream forced through a forcing bag with round nozzle. Place the small strawberries on top.

⊡ en Surprise

For 6-8 persons: 1 pineapple; 1 pint Pineapple ice; 2 fl oz Kirsch.

Cut the fresh pineapple as for *Ananas Edward VII.* Fill with Pineapple ice mixed with small pieces of pineapple steeped in Kirsch.

AVOCATS * *AVOCADO PEARS*

An exotic type of pear, the avocado's flesh is soft and nutty. It is served either as an *hors d'œuvre* or as a dessert.

⊡ à la Libanaise

For 6 persons: 3 avocado pears; 1 pint Vanilla ice; ½ pint whipped cream; 2 oz pistachio nuts; 2 fl oz Cointreau.

Cut the avocados in two lengthwise and remove the stones. Pour a little Cointreau into each fruit and leave to saturate in the cold. Pound the pistachio into a paste with a few drops of water and put in any of the remaining Cointreau. Mix this paste with the whipped cream until firm. Place the halves of avocado pears on pounded ice on a circular dish with the pointed ends towards the centre. Put a little Vanilla ice in the cavities and using a fluted nozzle decorate with the whipped cream and pistachio paste.

Avocats à la Tel Aviv

For 6 persons: 3 avocado pears; 2 Jaffa oranges; 2 bananas; 1 fl oz brandy; 1 teaspoon Curaçao; 7 oz thick Apricot sauce; shredded almonds.

Cut the avocados in two lengthwise and remove the stones and flesh without damaging the skin. Peel the oranges, remove all the pith and divide into segments; cut bananas and avocados into dice. Steep with sugar, brandy and Curaçao; chill. Bind with the iced Apricot sauce, fill avocado shells with this mixture and sprinkle with almonds.

BANANES * *BANANAS*

This fruit, which comes from tropical countries, may be used for both sweet and savoury cookery.

◘ Copacabana

For 6 persons: 6 bananas; 1 pint Vanilla ice; ½ pint Chocolate sauce; 2 fl oz rum; 1½ oz shredded pistachios.

Peel the bananas, divide into two, and poach in a rum syrup. Leave to cool in the syrup. Place the Vanilla ice at the bottom of the dish and arrange the drained bananas on the ice. Cover with Chocolate sauce and sprinkle with almonds.

◘ à l'Orientale

For 6 persons: 1 pint Almond ice; 1 oz Custard flavoured with rose water; 3 oz Chantilly cream; 2 lemons; roasted and shredded almonds.

Peel and cut bananas into thick slices and poach in strongly-flavoured lemon syrup, cool, drain and serve upon a bed of Almond ice. Coat with the Custard sauce, decorate with the cream and sprinkle with the almonds.

CERISES * *CHERRIES*

There are many varieties of cherry and their uses are numerous. *Morello* cherries are bottled as "cocktail" cherries and are also made into liqueurs and brandies.

◘ à la Dijonnaise

For 6 persons: 1½ lb stoned cherries; 2 fl oz Cassis; 1 fl oz Kirsch; sponge fingers.

Poach the cherries in syrup with the Cassis. Leave to cool, place in a deep bowl embedded in a container packed with ice and pour the Kirsch over the cherries. Serve with sponge fingers.

◘ Van Dyck

For 6 persons: 1½ lb stoned cherries; 1 pint Vanilla ice; ½ pint Custard; 1 tablespoon Arack (a liqueur).

Poach the cherries in Stock syrup. Leave to cool. Drain and place in a dish on the Vanilla ice. Cover with Custard flavoured with the Arack.

Cerises à la Viennoise

For 6 persons: 1 lb stoned cherries; 3 oz blackcurrant jelly; 2 egg yolks; 1 whole egg; arrowroot; ½ pint milk; ¼ lb sugar; 3 oz Chantilly cream; 1 oz pistachios. Cooking time: 25 minutes.

Poach the cherries in Stock syrup and drain. Reduce the syrup, bind with a little arrowroot and the currant jelly. Pour over cherries and leave to cool. Caramelise 1½ ounces sugar. Prepare a thick Custard Mould mixture (*Crème Beau-Rivage*) with the egg, the yolks, milk, sugar and caramel and poach in a mould. Leave to cool and turn out on to a round dish. Place cherries in the middle and sprinkle with finely shredded pistachios. Decorate the edge with Chantilly cream.

Citrons Givrés * *Frosted Lemons*

For 6 persons: 6 lemons; 1 pint Lemon ice; angelica.

Slice the top of the lemons off horizontally. Remove pulp and prepare the Lemon ice cream with the juice. Fill the lemon skins with this and replace the top. Place in a 'fridge for half an hour. Brush lightly with water and leave them to frost over. Remove from 'fridge, decorate with angelica and serve immediately. (*See illustration p.* 763).

FRAISES * *STRAWBERRIES*

These soft fruits are used as desserts, garnishes and as flavourings. They are especially good served frosted.

⊡ Astoria

¾ lb large strawberries; ¼ lb pineapple; ¾ pint Vanilla ice; ¼ pint raspberry purée; 1 fl oz Kirsch; icing sugar; 3 crushed macaroons.

Cut the strawberries and pineapple into small pieces and steep in the Kirsch and icing sugar. Place in champagne glasses with a little Vanilla ice on top and cover with raspberry *purée*. Sprinkle with crushed macaroons.

⊡ en Barquettes à la Congolaise * *in Chocolate Cases*

For 6 persons: 6 large barquettes of Short pastry; 2 oz melted chocolate; 1 banana; ¼ lb large strawberries; 18 very small strawberries; a little gelatine; ½ pint whipped cream; 2 fl oz rum; 2 oz icing sugar.

Prepare a cream as for *Fraises en Timbale Princesse* with a *purée* of the large strawberries, 1½ oz icing sugar, the gelatine and 7 oz whipped cream. Add the banana cut in dice soaked in rum and a little sugar. Brush the inside of the *barquettes* with melted chocolate and leave to solidify. Fill the *barquettes* with cream, dome shape and decorate each with whipped cream and three small strawberries.

⊡ Cardinal

For 4 persons: ½ lb strawberries; 6 oz raspberries; ¼ lb icing sugar; a teaspoon of lemon juice; almonds.

Cool some large firm strawberries on ice, then *purée* the raspberries and combine them with icing sugar and lemon juice. Allow the sugar to melt in the cold, keeping the *purée* on ice. Divide the strawberries between 4 iced glasses, coat with raspberry *purée* and sprinkle with fresh splintered almonds. Peaches or pears may also be prepared in this way, but they should be cooked in syrup first, cut in half and chilled. Add the raspberry *purée* at the last moment.

Fraises Cécile

For 6 persons: about 1 lb strawberries; 1 pint Vanilla ice cream; 4 oz honey; 3 oz fresh apricot purée; 2 fl oz apricot brandy; 1 fl oz Kirsch.

Heat the honey slightly, mix with the apricot *purée* and leave to cool completely. Incorporate apricot brandy and Kirsch. Put Vanilla ice in the bottom of a bowl embedded in a receptacle filled with crushed ice. Place the strawberries on top and cover with honeyed apricot *purée.*

▣ Melba

For 6 persons: about 1 lb large strawberries; 1 pint Vanilla ice cream; ½ pint slightly sweetened raspberry purée.

Arrange the strawberries on the Vanilla ice in an iced bowl or individual glasses and cover with raspberry *purée.*

▣ Romanoff * *with Orange*

For 6 persons: about 1 lb strawberries; 1 orange; 2 fl oz Curaçao; ½ pint Chantilly cream.

Steep the strawberries in the orange juice and Curaçao. Place in an iced bowl and decorate with Chantilly cream piped through a forcing bag with fluted nozzle.

▣ en Timbale Princesse

For 6 persons: 1 lb strawberries; ¼ lb castor sugar; juice of half a lemon; ¼ oz gelatine; 1 pint whipped cream; 1½ oz grated chocolate.

Sieve half the strawberries, add the sugar, lemon juice and the gelatine which has been melted in a *bain-marie* with a little water. Stir well and as soon as the mixture thickens, incorporate half the whipped cream and the remainder of the strawberries cut up. Pour into a Charlotte mould and place in 'fridge. Turn out on a round dish, decorate with a large Chantilly cream rosette and small rosettes all around. This dish may be decorated with a crown made of *Choux* pastry placed on the large rosette and sprinkled with the grated chocolate.

FRAMBOISES * *RASPBERRIES*

These soft fruits are very popular for tarts and jam making, although they have a great number of small seeds.

▣ à la Gourmande * *in Melon*

For 6-8 persons: 1 ripe cantaloupe; 1 lb raspberries; 2 fl oz Kirsch; ¼ lb sugar.

Cut out a circle round the stem of the melon. Using a spoon, scoop out the melon without damaging the rind. Mix the melon cut up into dice with the raspberries. Steep in Kirsch and sugar and fill the melon with this mixture. Replace the top and place in 'fridge for 2 hours before serving.

Framboises Ninette

For 6 persons: 1 lb raspberries; icing sugar; 14 oz Orange ice cream; Zabaglione flavoured with Curaçao and orange; shredded pistachio nuts.

Cover raspberries lightly with icing sugar and place on the Orange ice cream. Cover with *Zabaglione* flavoured with orange, and Curaçao, and sprinkle with shredded pistachio nuts.

Fruits Rafraîchis * *Fruit Salad in Champagne*

Peel and cut fruit in season in slices, leaving small berries such as strawberries, raspberries, whole. Chill well and decorate with the same fruit used for the salad. Pour a little very cold thick syrup over the fruit and place the glass bowl in a second bowl filled with crushed ice. Add a large glass of dry champagne and serve immediately. Fruit salad may also be flavoured with Grand-Marnier, Bénédictine, Cointreau, Kirsch, Maraschino. (*See illustration p.* 759).

LICHIS * *LYCHEES*

An Oriental fruit, the lychee has sweet white flesh with a large stone. It is sold with its hard outer husk which is easily removed.

⊡ Stromboli

For 6 persons: 1 lb tinned lychees; 18 oz Vanilla ice cream; 9 oz Apricot sauce flavoured with whisky; 1 fl oz whisky; 2 oz roasted and shredded almonds.

Heat the lychees in their juice in a saucepan and set alight with the whisky. Place a spoonful of Vanilla ice on each plate and a spoonful of lychees. Cover with a little Apricot sauce and sprinkle with the roasted and shredded almonds.

MANDARINES * *TANGERINES*

⊡ Côte d'Azur

For 6 persons: 12 tangerines; ½ lb pineapple; ¼ lb tangerine sections; ¼ lb peaches; 2 oz stoned cherries; 1 fl oz Curaçao; 3 oz sugar.

Cut all fruit, except the whole tangerines, into dice and steep in sugar and Curaçao. Cut the tangerines to form baskets, empty the pulp and prepare the Tangerine ice cream with juice. Keep the shells cool. To serve, put a spoonful of fruit *macédoine* in each basket and cover with the Tangerine ice cream. Serve immediately.

⊡ Givrées * *Frosted*

8 persons: 8 large tangerines, if possible with stalk and leaves; 1½ pints Tangerine water ice.

Make a circular opening at the stalk end of the tangerines. Reserve the piece cut off and empty the fruit neatly, without damaging the peel. Make a Tangerine water ice with the squeezed out juice and that of a few more tangerines. Fill the ice into the peel, and replace the round piece that was cut off. Put the fruit into a deep freezer or the freezing compartment of the refrigerator for a short time. Brush with cold water and allow the tangerines to frost until time to serve them. Do not put them into the deep freezer too early because the ice would become too hard.

MELON * *MELON*

A melon is ripe when the ends can be pressed in slightly and you can smell the juice. It should be heavy to the feel.

▣ Majestic

For 6-8 persons: 1 cantaloupe; 1 lb small strawberries; 1 fl oz Kirsch; ½ lb icing sugar; 7 oz Chantilly cream; 1½ oz chocolate cigarettes.

Cut out a circle of rind round the stem. Remove the pulp with a spoon without damaging the rind. Prepare a Melon ice cream with the pulp. Soak the strawberries with sugar in the Kirsch, leave on ice. Place melon on crushed ice and fill with the Melon ice cream. Place strawberries on top and decorate with Chantilly. Sprinkle with the chocolate cigarettes and sprinkle with icing sugar.

▣ Glacé à l'Orientale * *Iced with Pineapple and Bananas*

For 8 persons: 1 melon; 10 oz diced pineapple; 5 diced bananas; ¼ lb icing sugar; 2 fl oz Kirsch.

Remove melon pulp as above without damaging the rind. Cut into small pieces and mix with pineapple and bananas. Leave to soak in sugar and Kirsch. Fill the melon with this mixture, put back the top and keep in 'fridge for 2 hours before serving.

ORANGES * *ORANGES*

There are many varieties of oranges; those available in Britain come mostly from Spain, Israel and California. Seville oranges are bitter and are used for making jam and marmalade.

▣ Ilona

For 6 persons: 6 large oranges; 10 oz Chocolate ice; 2 oz crystallised ginger; 3 oz Apricot sauce; 6 oz Chantilly cream; 2 oz finely ground praline.

Remove a circle of rind round the stem of each orange. Remove pulp without damaging rind. Cut the sections into dice and bind with a little Apricot sauce. Mix the cut-up ginger with the Chocolate ice and half fill the orange skins. Place a spoonful of diced orange on top and decorate with a little Chantilly. Sprinkle praline over the top. If there are not enough segments, some may be added.

▣ à la Reine * *with Strawberries and Cream*

For 6 persons: 6 large oranges; ½ lb wild strawberries; 2 fl oz Kirsch; 3 oz sugar; ½ pint Chantilly cream.

Prepare and empty oranges as above. Cut the fruit into dice, mix with the strawberries and steep with sugar and Kirsch. Leave in 'fridge. Fill orange skins with mixture and decorate with Chantilly cream.

Oranges Riviéra

For 12 persons: 1 large orange made of orange-coloured blown sugar; top, stem and leaves in Almond paste and blown sugar; 12 oranges; 1 large and 12 small lotus flowers in Almond meringue paste; about 2 pints Orange ice cream.

Cut off tops of oranges, empty and remove juice to make the Orange ice cream. Clean the skins and tops and decorate with the Almond paste stems and leaves coloured green. Place the blown sugar orange on a large lotus flower and fill with *petits fours.* Arrange the oranges filled with the ice cream all round, each on a small lotus flower, and put tops back on oranges. (*See illustration p.* 28)

⊡ à la Sévillane

For 6 persons: 6 large oranges; 1 banana; 1 slice pineapple; 2 peaches; 5 oz stoned cherries; 3 oz sugar; 2 fl oz peach brandy; 3 fl oz Kirsch jelly.

Empty the oranges as above. Prepare a *salpicon* of fruit with the pulp, the banana, the pineapple, peaches and cherries and leave to steep in sugar and peach brandy. Fill the orange skins with this *salpicon* and glaze with half-set jelly.

⊡ en Surprise * *with Orange Ice and Meringue*

For 6 persons: 6 large oranges; 10 oz Orange ice; 8 oz Italian meringue mixture.

Remove top of oranges horizontally about three-quarters of the way up and remove pulp without damaging the skin. Prepare an Orange ice with this pulp. Place the oranges on crushed ice and fill with the ice cream. Cover with Italian meringue mixture using a forcing bag with round nozzle, sprinkle with sugar and place in a very hot oven, 425° F or Gas Mark 7 so that the meringue colours quickly. Serve at once.

PAMPLEMOUSSE * *GRAPEFRUIT*

This citrus fruit is larger than the orange and paler and sweeter than the lemon. It is usually served at the beginning of a meal.

⊡ à la Californienne * *Californian Grapefruit*

For 6 persons: 3 grapefruit; 3 large oranges; half a melon; 2 oz shredded walnuts; $\frac{1}{4}$ *lb sugar; 1 tablespoon Curaçao; 1 tablespoon Maraschino.*

Cut grapefruit in two horizontally and remove pulp. Cut in segments together with the oranges and melon. Steep in sugar, Curaçao and Maraschino. Leave to cool. Clean the rind and fill this with *macédoine.* Sprinkle with shredded walnuts.

⊡ Florida

For 6 persons: 3 grapefruit; 2 large oranges; 5 oz stoned cherries; 5 oz small strawberries; 2 fl oz sherry; $\frac{1}{4}$ *lb sugar; 2 oz shredded almonds.*

Prepare the grapefruit as above. Cut the pulp up and mix with orange pieces, cherries and strawberries steeped in sugar and the sherry. Leave to cool and fill the fruit with the mixture. Sprinkle with flaked almonds and serve very cold.

PÊCHES * *PEACHES*

Peaches make delicious jams and preserves and are used in tarts and flans. There is also an excellent peach brandy.

◘ Cardinal

For 6 persons: 6 well-shaped peaches; 10 *oz raspberries;* ¼ *lb icing sugar; juice of half a lemon;* 2 *oz shredded white almonds.*

Poach the peaches in vanilla-flavoured syrup and leave to cool. When cold, peel, put into an iced bowl and cover with raspberry *purée*. Sprinkle shredded almonds on top. Pears may also be prepared in the same way.

◘ Dame Blanche

For 6 persons: 6 peaches; 12 *slices pineapple;* 14 *oz Vanilla ice cream;* 2 *fl oz Maraschino;* 1 *fl oz Kirsch;* ½ *pint Chantilly cream.*

Poach the peaches in vanilla-flavoured syrup, leave to cool and peel. Steep pineapple in sugar, Maraschino and Kirsch. Place a layer of Vanilla ice at the bottom of an iced bowl then the pineapple slices. Place the peaches on top and between each peach decorate with Chantilly cream.

◘ Flambées à la Bénédictine * *Flambéd*

For 6 persons served at table: 12 *half peaches;* 6 *slices Pistachio ice cream Parfait;* 6 *oz Apricot sauce;* 2 *fl oz Bénédictine;* 1 *fl oz brandy;* 2 *oz shredded white almonds.*

Poach the peaches in vanilla-flavoured syrup. Place a heat resistant dish on the stove, pour in the Apricot sauce and 2 or 3 spoonfuls of syrup. Let mixture boil for a few moments. Heat the peaches in the sauce and light with Bénédictine and brandy. Place quickly a slice of ice cream *Parfait* on cold plates, put hot peaches on top, cover with a little sauce and sprinkle the almonds on top.

◘ Germaine

For 6 persons: 6 peaches; 14 *oz Vanilla ice cream;* 3 *macaroons;* 2 *fl oz Grand-Marnier;* 3 *oz thick Custard;* 3 *oz strawberry purée;* 3 *oz whipped cream;* 1 *oz chopped pistachio nuts.*

Crush the macaroons and dip in the Grand-Marnier. Mix with Vanilla ice. Poach fruit in vanilla-flavoured syrup, leave to cool and peel. Decorate an iced bowl with the ice and peaches on top. Cover with a sauce consisting of Custard, strawberry *purée* and whipped cream. Sprinkle with pistachio nuts.

◘ Melba

For 8 *persons:* 8 *medium-sized peaches;* 1½ *pints Vanilla ice cream;* ½ *lb raspberries;* 3 *oz icing sugar.*

Poach the peaches in vanilla-flavoured syrup without allowing them to get too soft. Cool in the syrup. Remove the skin and the kernel without damaging the fruit. Put the Vanilla ice cream in a bowl or individual glasses and arrange the well drained peaches on top. Cover them with very cold raspberry *purée*, made of the raspberries rubbed through a sieve and mixed with the icing sugar. For this dessert, created by *Maître Escoffier*, pears, strawberries or other fruit may also be used.

Pêches Sobieski

For 6 persons: 6 peaches; 14 oz Raspberry ice cream; 6 oz redcurrant jelly; 6 oz Chantilly cream flavoured with aniseed.

Poach and peel the peaches. Place on the ice and cover with the sieved jelly. Decorate generously with aniseed-flavoured Chantilly cream.

POIRES * *PEARS*

Pears are very popular and are used for making tarts, *compôtes* and jellies, as well as being eaten fresh.

▣ à la Floretta

For 6 persons: 2 oz semolina; ½ pint milk; 3 oz vanilla-flavoured sugar; a little gelatine; ½ pint whipped cream; 4 whole pears; and a compôte of quartered pears; pistachio nuts.

Cook semolina in milk; add vanilla-flavoured sugar and the gelatine melted in a *bain-marie* and leave to cool. When the mixture begins to set, mix in the whipped cream and pour into a mould previously rinsed with cold water. Place on ice. Meanwhile make a *compôte* of 4 whole pears cut into quarters and cooked in syrup of sugar, red Bordeaux, a little red-currant jelly flavoured with a little cinnamon. Cook the quartered pears in sugar syrup and reduce the syrup. When the semolina mould is set turn out on a round dish. The pears must be well chilled. When used for decorating, cover with respective sauces and place the white pears round the edge. Decorate with pistachio nuts cut in half. (*See illustration p.* 759).

▣ Géraldine

For 6 persons: 6 pears; 14 oz Chocolate ice cream; 6 oz vanilla-flavoured Custard; about ¼ pint whipped cream; 5 oz Almond paste; 1 tablespoon honey; 1 oz roasted and chopped nuts.

Peel and poach the pears in vanilla-flavoured syrup. When cool, drain and remove core. Mix Almond paste and honey until soft enough to fill the pears through a forcing bag with a round nozzle. Place the Chocolate ice cream in a bowl, place pears on top and cover with Custard mixed with whipped cream. Sprinkle chopped nuts on top.

▣ Hélène

For 6 persons: 6 pears; 14 oz Vanilla ice cream; 7 oz hot Chocolate sauce.

Peel and poach the pears and leave to cool. Place on Vanilla ice cream and serve with hot Chocolate sauce. It is customary to sprinkle candied violets in the ice cream.

▣ Joinville

For 8 persons: 4 pears; Caramel cream; ¾ pint vanilla-flavoured whipped cream; ½ pint Apricot sauce with Kirsch.

Halve the pears, poach them in Stock syrup and let them cool in it. Make Caramel cream in a mould and when it is cold turn it out on a round dish. Fill the centre with well-drained pears and decorate generously with whipped cream. Serve the sauce separately.

Poires à la Martiniquaise

For 6 persons: 3 pears; 6 oval-shaped slices Génoise sponge; 7 oz Almond ice cream; 7 oz Chocolate sauce; ½ pint Chantilly cream; 2 fl oz rum; 1½ oz shredded pistachio nuts.

Peel, core and poach the half pears in vanilla-flavoured syrup. Hollow out the sponge slices a little and pour in a little of the syrup strongly flavoured with rum. Fill with a little Almond ice and place half a pear, well drained, on top. Cover with a very thick cold Chocolate sauce and the shredded pistachio nuts. Decorate with Chantilly cream through a forcing bag with a fluted nozzle.

POMMES * *APPLES*

There are two kinds of apple—cooking and eating apples. A great variety of desserts can be made with apples, in addition, there is cider and apple brandy (Calvados).

▣ Brissac

For 6 persons: 6 apples; 1 round Génoise sponge; 2 fl oz Grand-Marnier; 2 oz redcurrant jelly; ½ pint Zabaglione flavoured with Grand-Marnier; angelica.

Poach apples in a vanilla-flavoured syrup and leave to cool. Place on the *Génoise*, sprinkle with a little syrup flavoured with Grand-Marnier. Cover the apples with the jelly and put two diamond shaped pieces of angelica into each apple. With this, serve the *Zabaglione* flavoured with Grand-Marnier.

▣ Mariette

For 6 persons: 6 apples; 7 oz vanilla-flavoured purée of chestnuts; ½ pint rum-flavoured Apricot sauce; 2 or 3 tablespoons whipped cream.

Peel the apples, remove the core and poach in vanilla-flavoured syrup. Leave to cool in the syrup. Mix the chestnut *purée* with the whipped cream. Drain the apples, and fill the centres with the chestnut *purée* and cover with Apricot sauce.

▣ Mistral

For 6 persons: 6 apples; 7 fl oz purée of wild strawberries; 2 oz freshly chopped almonds; 6 fl oz Chantilly cream; Kirsch.

Peel the apples, remove the core and poach in Kirsch-flavoured syrup. Cool well, cover with strawberry *purée* and sprinkle chopped almonds on top. Serve the Chantilly cream separately.

FOREIGN SPECIALITIES

Chocolate Rum Pie

For 8 persons: 1 flan baked "blind"; 1 pint milk; 4 egg yolks; 4 whites whipped; ½ oz arrowroot; 2 fl oz rum; 3 oz chocolate; vanilla; 3 oz sugar; ¼ oz gelatine; ½ pint Chantilly cream; 2 oz chocolate cigarettes.

Prepare a Custard with the yolks, milk, sugar, vanilla, starch and chocolate and add melted gelatine. Leave to cool stirring constantly and, before the Custard begins to set, flavour with rum and add well beaten whites of egg. Pour this mixture into the flan crust, cover with Chantilly and smooth the surface. Sprinkle with broken up chocolate cigarettes. (*America*)

Eton Mess

For 6 persons: 1 lb strawberries; 3 oz sugar; 1 pint whipped cream.

Squash the strawberries slightly with a fork and add whipped cream and sugar. Put into a salad bowl. Serve with sponge fingers. *(Great Britain)*

Gooseberry Fool

For 6 persons: 1 lb gooseberries; 5 oz sugar; 1 pint whipped cream.

Poach the gooseberries with 1 oz sugar and leave to cool. Drain and sieve. Add the rest of the sugar and if the *purée* is not sweet enough add more sugar. Incorporate whipped cream and serve in individual dishes. *(Great Britain)*

Rote Grütze * *Redcurrant and Raspberry Purée*

For 6 persons: 1½ lb redcurrants; ¾ lb raspberries; about ½ lb sugar; 3 oz cornflour; 7 oz Custard or fresh cream. Cooking time: 5-6 minutes.

Put the fruit in a saucepan with a little water and cook. Pass through a sieve. Measure the *purée* and add enough water to make 2¼ pints. Boil again and add sugar. Mix the starch with a little water and pour into the *purée* stirring well. Boil for a few seconds to cook the starch. Pour into individual dishes and leave to cool. Serve with vanilla-flavoured Custard or fresh cream. For a lighter sweet, add only 2 oz cornflour. *(Germany)*

Royal Gooseberry Trifle

For 6 persons: 14 oz gooseberries; 3 oz sugar; 8 sponge fingers; 2 or 3 macaroons; 2 fl oz sherry or Madeira; 6 fl oz thick Custard; 6 fl oz Chantilly cream.

Prepare the Gooseberry fool as above, add sugar and cool. Break sponge fingers into two and dip in the sherry. Put the *purée* in a bowl and cover with the sponge fingers. Pour well chilled Custard on top and then the Chantilly cream. Sprinkle with crushed macaroons. Redcurrant jelly can also be used to decorate this dish. *(Great Britain)*

Zabaione Gritti

For 6 persons: 12 yolks of egg; 3 fl oz Marsala; 5 oz sugar; 3 fl oz whipped cream; 3 candied cherries; 3 oz chocolate cigarettes. Cooking time: 15-16 minutes.

Beat egg yolks, Marsala and sugar together. Put in a double saucepan and beat until mixture thickens. Continue stirring as it cools. Pour into dishes and place in the 'fridge. Beat the cream and 2 oz sugar, and use this to decorate the sweet, place half a cherry on top and broken chocolate cigarettes all round. (*See illustration p.* 756). *(Italy)*

Ices

There are 2 methods of making ice cream. The best method is to use the special ice cream churn or bucket. This consists of a cylindrical container fitted with paddles held in place with a metal clamp and geared to a handle which is turned manually. This cylinder is fitted into a wooden bucket and the space between the two is filled with crushed ice and freezing salt, obtainable from the fishmonger.

The second method is to use the freezing compartment of your refrigerator. If you make ice cream this way you must set the dial of the refrigerator at the coldest point and every 20 minutes take the ice cream out and whisk it. Alternatively there is also a device on the market now, which is electrically driven and fits into the freezing compartment of most modern refrigerators. This churns the ice cream as it is freezing and so produces a smooth ice cream.

When using the ice cream churn, the mixture to be frozen must be cold. Fill the inner container to a depth of two-thirds as the cream will increase in bulk during freezing.

Adjust the paddles and cover in place and make sure each part is properly connected together before you pack the broken ice and freezing or rock salt into the outer pail. Leave to stand 3-4 minutes then turn the handle slowly and regularly at first until the mixture offers resistance which means it is beginning to freeze. This usually takes about 20 minutes depending on the quantity.

Now remove the handle and paddle equipment. Scrape the ice cream mixture down into the container. Cover with the lid and cover the hole in the lid with a cork or plug of soft paper. Pour off the brine in the pail, repack with ice and salt, using salt and ice in the proportion of 1: 4. Cover with sheets of newspaper (2 or 3 thicknesses) or a blanket, then with ice. Stand in a cool place for at least one hour to ripen, replenishing ice and salt when necessary. This method makes the very best ice cream, with a smooth texture, no large unpleasant splinters of ice, and a full flavour.

Ice creams always contain a high proportion of sweetening and flavouring because these seem to lose their strength during the process of freezing. Colouring, of course, must always be used sparingly as pastel shades are the most acceptable. Other important factors to note are that as far as possible all utensils and ingredients should be chilled before use. Sugar must always be thoroughly dissolved before starting to freeze ice-cream mixtures.

Ice Moulds

Ice moulds are usually made of tin. They may be tall or flat and oval. There are many different sizes and the most attractive moulds are made of copper lined with tin. In addition there are special *bombe* moulds. These have tightly-fitting lids and a screw at the base which is loosened after freezing to allow unmoulding.

To mould ice cream

Collect a chilled mould, a bucket of broken ice, freezing salt, butter, muslin and greaseproof paper. As soon as the ice cream to be used is frozen and stiff in the can or tray, remove it and pack it down well into a mould taking care that no air spaces are left in the mould. Fill to overflowing. Cover with buttered greaseproof paper and seal round the edge with a strip of muslin dipped in melted butter. Pack in ice and salt (4 parts ice to 1 of salt). Cover with layers of newspaper and leave for 2-3 hours.

Alternatively place the mould in the freezing compartment of the refrigerator or for family meals the simplest method of all is to mould the ice cream, perhaps using a variety of flavours, in the freezing tray of your refrigerator.

To unmould

Remove the mould from the bucket or refrigerator and take off the paper. Wipe the mould thoroughly—otherwise the salt might get into the ice cream and spoil it. Dip for a moment in cold water to loosen the ice and then turn quickly on to a chilled serving dish and unscrew the mould. Decorate as indicated in individual recipes.

Frozen ice may be divided into 2 *categories—Cream* ice which is made with milk, yolk of egg and sugar, such as Vanilla ice cream, and, *fruit* ice, which is made with sugar syrup, fruit pulp and sometimes a little cream.

GLACE À LA CRÈME * *BASIC ICE CREAM RECIPE*

For 6 persons: 5 *oz sugar;* 6 *yolks of egg;* 1½ *pints milk; for Vanilla ice cream add half a vanilla pod to the milk.*

Beat together the yolks and sugar until the mixture becomes pale. Very gradually blend in the boiling milk and cook on the stove, stirring continuously. Do not allow to come to the boil. Cook until the mixture coats the back of a spoon. Rub through a fine sieve. Stir occasionally until quite cold. Freeze in the freezer. A richer ice is obtained by increasing the proportion of egg yolks and sugar which can be up to 7-16 yolks and 7 oz-1 lb sugar for 2 pints of milk. A smoother texture is obtained by adding whipped cream to the mixture in the proportion of 10 per cent. The average proportions given in this basic recipe being always the same, we shall not repeat these for each recipe.

▣ aux Amandes * *Almond*

Pound 2 oz blanched almonds with a little water. Infuse in boiling milk for 20 minutes. Rub through a fine conical sieve and prepare as for the Basic ice cream recipe.

▣ aux Avelines * *Hazelnut*

Roast the hazelnuts slightly and proceed as for Almond ice cream.

▣ au Café * *Coffee*

Proceed as for Basic recipe, but use approximately 1 pint milk and 1 tablespoonful of instant coffee to make the cream.

▣ au Caramel * *Caramel*

Make the same mixture as for Basic recipe but without vanilla. Boil 2 oz sugar to fairly brown caramel, dissolve in a little water and add to ice cream mixture.

Glace au Chocolat * *Chocolate Ice Cream*

Proceed as for Basic ice cream recipe, but use 1¾ oz less sugar and add 3½ oz chocolate to the milk.

▣ aux Marrons * *Chestnut*

Prepare the Basic recipe, and when set, mix in 7 fluid oz well chilled chestnut *purée* and 2 oz whipped cream.

▣ Nelusko * *Chocolate and Nut*

Make Chocolate ice with only 2½ oz chocolate and mix with 2½ oz pounded and sieved praline.

▣ aux Pistaches * *Pistachio Nut*

Pound 2 oz finely crushed pistachio nuts with a little water and infuse for 20 minutes in the boiling milk. Proceed as above.

▣ Pralinée * *Praline*

Proceed as for Basic recipe with only 3½ oz sugar and add 4½ oz pounded and sieved praline to the mixture.

FRUIT ICES

These are delicious and refreshing ices. When making fruit ices you will find that a saccharometer is indispensable. Fruit ices are made from fruit, sugar and water. They can be frozen in the refrigerator, but no matter how much they are beaten, they will not be as light as those frozen in the freezing churn where they are beaten continually. A fruit ice is left to mellow like ice cream and may be used as part of a more elaborate ice cream dish or served in small glasses.

GLACE AUX FRUITS * *BASIC FRUIT ICE RECIPE*

Rub the fruit through a fine sieve to form a *purée*. Prepare a Stock syrup with a density of 32° and leave to cool. Add an equal quantity of sieved *purée* and some lemon juice, the amount will depend upon the acidity of the fruit used. The whole mixture must register a standard density (generally 18° to 19°) on the saccharometer. Add more cold water or syrup to bring mixture to the required density. Pour into freezer. It is also possible to pound the fruit with 7 to 10 oz sugar per lb fruit, rub through a sieve and add as much water as necessary to bring to the right density of 18°. Ices made with red fruit are better if 20 per cent fresh cream is added. The ices are frozen when cold.

▣ aux Abricots * *Apricot*

Pass 1 lb fruit through a hair sieve and mix with 1 pint Stock sugar syrup. Add a little lemon juice and boil until the reading on the saccharometer is 19°.

Glace à l'Ananas * *Pineapple Ice*

Pass pineapple flesh through a hair sieve and boil with Stock sugar syrup until the saccharometer reading is 21°.

▣ aux Bananes * *Banana*

For 6 persons: 14 oz peeled bananas; 14 fl oz Stock sugar syrup at 32°; 1 fl oz Maraschino; lemon juice.

Mash the bananas with 2 fl oz syrup and flavour with Maraschino, leaving mixture to steep for one hour. Sieve the *purée*, and add lemon juice and syrup. The saccharometer reading should be 20°.

▣ au Citron * *Lemon*

For 6 persons: ¾ pint Stock sugar syrup; zest of 2 lemons; the juice of 5 lemons.

Infuse the zest of the lemons for 2 hours in cold syrup. Add the juice of the lemons and sieve, boil to a density of 21°.

▣ aux Fraises * *Strawberry*

For 6 persons: 1 lb strawberry purée; 16 oz Stock sugar syrup; the juice of 1 orange and 1 lemon.

Dilute the *purée* with the syrup and add the fruit juices. Boil to a density of 18°.

▣ aux Framboises * *Raspberry*

Make in the same way as a Strawberry ice.

▣ aux Mandarines * *Tangerine*

Make in the same way as Lemon ice; i.e. reduce Stock sugar syrup of 32° with orange or tangerine juice. Boil to a density of 21°.

▣ au Melon * *Melon*

For 6 persons: 1 lb fresh melon; 16 fl oz Stock sugar syrup; juice of ½ a lemon and 1 orange.

Sieve the melon flesh and add the syrup and fruit juices. Boil to a density of 21°.

▣ à l'Orange * *Orange*

For 6 persons: ¾ pint Stock sugar syrup; zest of 2 oranges; juice of 3 oranges and a lemon.

Proceed in the same way as for Lemon ice.

▣ aux Pêches * *Peach*

Proceed in the same way as for Apricot ice.

Glace aux Poires * *Pear Ice*

For 8 persons: 1 lb pear purée; juice of ½ lemon; 14 fl oz Stock sugar syrup.

Pass soft raw pears through a hair sieve; only boil in sugar syrup first if they are very hard. Mix the *purée* with syrup and lemon juice. Boil to a density of 22°.

MIXED ICE CREAM DISHES

The following recipes involve the use of a number of other ingredients such as *meringue* and cake, as well as the various ice creams, which prevents them from being pure ice-cream dishes in the sense of being composed solely of ice-cream.

Assiette Martiniquaise

Arrange Orange water ice on a round glass plate. Cover with slices of bananas macerated in sugar and rum, and garnish with whipped cream.

Assiette Tentation

Arrange Pistachio ice cream in an elongated shape on a glass plate, and scatter roasted, stripped almonds on top. Place half a peach poached in syrup on one side and garnish with whipped cream.

Boule de Neige * *Snow Ball*

For 6 persons: 1 pint Vanilla ice; ½ lb candied fruit; ½ pint Chantilly cream; 2 fl oz Kirsch; crystallised violets.

Cut the candied fruit into dice and steep for 1 hour in the Kirsch. Mix into Vanilla ice which is still soft. Fill a round shaped mould with the ice and freeze for about 45 minutes. Turn out, and decorate by piping stars of Chantilly cream close together. Put crystallised violets on tips and leave in freezer long enough for the cream to set. Serve with a *Zabaglione* flavoured with Kirsch.

Cassata Napolitaine

For 8 persons: ½ pint each Vanilla, Raspberry and Pistachio ice cream; 3 egg whites; 5 oz sugar; 5 oz diced candied fruit; 2 fl oz rum; ¾ pint whipped cream. Time: 2-3 hours.

Macerate the diced fruit in rum. Boil the sugar to the ball stage with a little water, and mix it with the stiffly beaten egg whites, beating all the time. Allow to cool and mix in the candied fruit and the whipped cream. Surround a *bombe* mould with crushed ice. When it is quite cold, fill the sides in even layers with Vanilla, Raspberry and Pistachio ice cream. Fill the centre with the cream and fruit mixture, smooth the top and freeze. Unmould on to a round dish and decorate with whipped cream and candied fruit. (*See illustration p.* 762).

Cassata Sicilienne

For 8 persons: ½ pint each Vanilla and Orange ice cream; 4 egg whites; 7 oz sugar; ¾ pint whipped cream; 2 oz candied cherries; 2 oz candied orange peel, diced and blanched; 5-6 large dry macaroons; 2 fl oz brandy. Freezing time: 2-3 hours.

Macerate the cherries, cut into quarters, the macaroons broken into small pieces and the orange peel in brandy. Boil the sugar to the ball stage with a little water, and pour it hot over the stiffly beaten egg whites, beating all the time. Allow to cool and mix in the candied fruit, the macaroons and the whipped cream. Line a cold *bombe* mould in even layers with Vanilla and Orange ice cream, fill the centre with the cream mixture, smooth the top and freeze.

Comtesse Marie

For 8 persons: 1 pint Vanilla ice cream; 1 pint Strawberry mousse.

Line a special square mould, *Countess Marie* mould or use a deep square cake tin, with Vanilla ice cream and fill the inside with Strawberry mousse. Close hermetically and freeze for 1 hour. After having been unmoulded the ice may be garnished with whipped cream, mixed with a little strawberry *purée* and replaced in the freezer to stiffen the garnish.

Madeleine

For 6 persons: 1¼ pints Vanilla ice cream; 8 fl oz whipped cream; 4 oz candied fruit; 2 tablespoons Kirsch.

Macerate the finely diced candied fruit in Kirsch. Make a rather soft Vanilla ice cream, add the cream and fruit. Fill a madeleine or shell mould with this mixture and freeze.

Marie-Thérèse

For 6 persons: ½ pint Chocolate ice; 14 fl oz Chantilly cream; 5 sponge fingers; 2 fl oz Kirsch; candied pineapple.

Line a square mould with Chocolate ice and put Chantilly cream mixed with sponge fingers soaked in Kirsch inside. Decorate with candied pineapple.

Plombières

For 6 persons: 1½ pints Vanilla ice cream; 6 oz finely diced candied fruit; 2 tablespoons Kirsch; 2 tablespoons apricot jam or a few macaroons.

Macerate the candied fruit in the Kirsch. Then mix with Vanilla ice cream. Using a shallow mould or tin, spread alternate layers of the ice cream and apricot jam. Macaroon biscuits which have been soaked in Kirsch may be substituted for the jam.

Meringues Glacées * *Iced Meringues*

For 6 persons: 12 meringue shells; ¾ pint Vanilla ice cream; 8 fl oz whipped cream.

Fill meringue shells in pairs with Vanilla ice, and garnish with whipped cream.

Profiteroles Glacées au Chocolat * *Iced Profiteroles*

For 6 persons: 12 medium-sized Choux pastry buns; 14 fluid oz Vanilla ice; 7 fl oz Chantilly cream; chopped pistachios; ½ pint hot Chocolate sauce.

Fill the *Choux* pastry buns with Vanilla ice. Decorate with Chantilly cream and sprinkle the pistachio nuts on top. Serve with hot Chocolate sauce.

ICE CREAM PARFAITS

Parfaits are light frozen ices which are packed in a tall mould. They have no outside coating as do *Bombes Glacés* (*see p.* 806), i.e., they consist of just one type of ice.

The basic mixture described below is usually used, flavoured with rum, Kirsch, or brandy, coffee or chocolate or praline. The mixture is filled directly into the mould and chilled. *Parfaits* should only be sufficiently chilled so that they hold their shape when turned out.

PARFAIT * *BASIC PARFAIT MIXTURE*

For 8 persons: 7 fl oz Stock syrup at 32° *saccharometer reading; 8 egg yolks; ¾ pint whipped cream; flavouring.*

Blend the egg yolks into the cold syrup. Beat up the mixture in a *bain-marie* over a gentle heat in the same way as for a *Génoise* sponge, until it thickens. When it has well risen, remove the mixture from the *bain-marie* and place on ice, continuing to beat until it is completely cold. Add the flavouring and whipped cream, pour into a mould and freeze for 2 hours.

▣ **au Chocolat** * *Chocolate*

As above but add 3 oz slightly melted bitter chocolate to the syrup.

▣ **au Kirsch, Rhum, Cognac, Bénédictine**

Add 3 fluid oz liqueur to the mixture before adding whipped cream.

▣ **au Moka**

Use the Basic recipe but add 1 tablespoon of soluble coffee to the syrup. Put the mixture into a square *parfait* mould or deep rectangular cake tin. Put a slice of *Génoise* sponge cake, cut to fit the tin exactly, on top of the ice cream. When frozen, turn out the mould and decorate with lines of cream and chocolate cigarettes. (*See illustration p.* 763.)

▣ **du Père Noël** * *Father Christmas*

For 6 persons: 1½ pints Chocolate parfait; about 14 oz Almond meringue mixture; 5 oz chopped almonds; 6 Christmas trees and 6 Bambis in Almond paste; 6 small Sweet pastry stars; 6 glacé cherries; ½ pint Chantilly cream; a little melted chocolate.

Spread the meringue out on a buttered sheet of paper in the shape of fairly large triangles and sprinkle with chopped almonds. Cook in a hot oven, 400° F or Gas Mark 6, and when cooked wrap at once round metal cornets. Leave to cool. Remove the cornets and fill with Chantilly cream. Cut the *parfait* into six round slices. Place one slice on a cake plate and put cornet on top. Fix a star at the top of the cornet and a little chocolate and decorate with a Xmas tree, a bambi, Chantilly and red cherry.

Parfait aux Pistaches * *Pistachio Nut Parfait*

Pound 2 oz green pistachio nuts, with 2 or 3 tablespoons water and a few drops of Kirsch into a fine paste. Follow the Basic *parfait* recipe after beating egg yolks with the syrup and before adding the whipped cream, mix this into the mixture.

▣ Praliné * *Praline*

Add 2 oz sieved pralines to the mixture with the whipped cream.

▣ à la Vanille * *Vanilla*

Prepare the *parfait* with a strongly-flavoured vanilla Stock syrup.

ICE CREAM BOMBES

Bombes consist of two types of ice cream, one which is used to line the mould and the other, generally a rich cream ice, is used to fill the mould.

How to line a bombe mould

The bottom and sides of the chilled mould are coated with a thin layer of frozen ice. This coating is usually a plain ice cream or fruit ice according to the type of *bombe* being prepared. The easiest way to smooth the coating ice is to use the back of a spoon. The space is then filled with the frozen Basic *Bombe* mixture, flavoured according to each recipe. Smooth the top and cover with a sheet of greaseproof paper, close the mould and if it is to be packed in ice and salt, seal the cracks and seams with melted butter.

After freezing, dip the mould in cold water for a minute. Then let the *bombe* slide out on to a round chilled serving dish. Decorate to taste and serve at once.

BOMBE GLACÉE * *BASIC BOMBE MIXTURE*

Basic Bombe Mixture: 8 egg yolks; ½ pint cold Stock syrup at 28°; ¾ pint whipped cream; flavouring.

Combine the two ingredients in a double boiler or use a pan in a water-bath and beat first hot and then cold like *Génoise* sponge. Gently fold in cream and flavouring.

▣ Cardinal

Coat the mould with Raspberry ice and fill with iced Kirsch *mousse*.

▣ Dame Blanche

Coat with Vanilla ice and fill with the Basic *bombe* mixture flavoured with almonds.

▣ Diable Rouge * *Red Devil*

Coat the chilled *bombe* mould with Strawberry ice mixed with a little cream. Fill with Curaçao *Bombe* mixture combined with a fine *julienne* of candied orange peel.

Bombe Diane

Line mould with Pistachio ice cream and fill with a *parfait* mixture flavoured with chocolate. Turn out pipe with whipped cream and decorate with chopped pistachio nuts, chocolate cigarettes, *glacé* cherries and deer shapes cut out of wafer-thin Almond paste which has been baked. (*See illustration p.* 764).

▣ Fanchonnette

Coat with Orange ice and fill with Basic *bombe* mixture with praline. Decorate with liqueur chocolates when serving.

▣ Javanaise

Coat the mould with Coffee ice mixed with a little double cream, fill with iced Banana *mousse*, flavoured with rum and mixed with some coffee liqueur chocolates.

▣ Mac-Mahon

Line the mould with Orange ice. Fill with Basic *bombe* mixture, flavoured with Curaçao to which crystallised segments of orange are added. Decorate with Chantilly, *glacé* cherries and angelica.

▣ Marinette

Coat with Vanilla ice and use a Raspberry *mousse* as the filling.

▣ Marocaine

Coat with Chocolate ice and fill with rum Basic *bombe* mixture with chopped dates.

▣ Paul

Coat with Praline ice. Fill centre with vanilla-flavoured whipped cream with 2 oz chocolate vermicelli in the centre; these must not be mixed with the cream.

▣ Prince Nicolaï

Soak about 2 oz diced candied pineapple in Cointreau. Line the mould with Chocolate ice. Fill with Basic *bombe* mixture flavoured with Kirsch to which candied pineapple has been added. When the *bombe* has been turned out, decorate with Chantilly cream and little triangles of candied pineapple. A *Choux* pastry decoration may be placed on top.

▣ Romaine

Line the mould with Praline ice and fill with Basic *bombe* mixture flavoured with Strega (*an Italian liqueur*).

▣ Singapour

Coat with Strawberry ice and fill with iced Pineapple *mousse* mixed with diced pineapple.

Bombe Vanderbilt

Soak wild strawberries in Grand-Marnier. Line the mould with Orange ice and fill with Kirsch-flavoured Basic *bombe* mixture mixed with the wild strawberries. Decorate with Chantilly, wild strawberries and crystallised violets.

NEAPOLITAIN ICE CREAM

These ices are made in rectangular moulds, and consist of layers of ice cream and water ices in varying flavours and colours packed alternately in the mould. They are frozen in the usual way, either in a bucket of ice and salt or in the refrigerator and then unmoulded. When the ice cream is ready to be served it is cut in slices and may be served decorated with fruit and cream.

How to use Ice Cream Gâteaux Moulds

Ice cream *gâteaux* moulds are generally rectangular in form, fitted with two covers. You could use a rectangular loose-bottomed cake tin and fix foil securely over the top of the tin. The mixture lining the mould is generally different from that in the main part. After filling, the moulds are placed in the freezer. To turn out, dip the mould for a moment in hot water, wipe quickly and turn out. Then cut the ice cream *gâteau* with a knife dipped in hot water into regular rectangles about 1½ inches thick, decorate and put back in freezer until ready to serve.

BISCUIT GLACÉ CLASSIQUE * *CLASSICAL ICE CREAM GÂTEAUX*

For 8 persons: 6 egg yolks; 7 oz sugar; 4 oz Italian meringue; 1 pint whipped cream; flavouring.

Mix yolks and sugar and heat in a double saucepan like a *Génoise* mixture. Continue beating on ice until cold. Add the Italian meringue and incorporate the whipped cream and flavouring.

BISCUIT GLACÉ MODERNE * *MODERN ICE CREAM GÂTEAUX*

For 6-8 persons: 5 egg yolks; 7 oz sugar; 1 pint whipped cream; flavouring.

Cook sugar in a little water. Blend the eggs with boiling syrup, beating and whipping until cold. Add the flavouring and whipped cream. Ice cream *gâteaux* can also be made with a *bombe* mixture.

▣ à la Bénédictine

Strawberry ice cream; Violet-flavoured ice cream; Basic bombe mixture; 1 fl oz Bénédictine; ¼ lb sponge fingers; cream and pistachio nuts for decoration.

Break up sponge fingers into small pieces, pour Bénédictine over them and mix with the Basic *bombe* mixture. Place a layer of strawberry mixture in the mould first, then the Bénédictine and finally the violet mixture. Place in an ice bucket or refrigerator. After turning out, cut the ice in rectangles, decorate with Chantilly cream and sprinkle with chopped pistachio.

Biscuit Glacé Moderne Délice

Fill mould with first a Kirsch and then chocolate Ice cream *gâteaux* mixture using Modern recipe, with 3 oz melted chocolate, alternating the colours. After turning cut into rectangles and decorate each portion with Chantilly cream and a little grated chocolate.

Fanchonnette

Fill base first with vanilla, then pistachio, and finally praline vanilla Ice cream *gâteaux* mixtures. Decorate with Chantilly cream and half a *glacé* cherry.

▣ Lyrique

Alternate layers of vanilla Ice cream *gâteaux* mixture mixed with diced candied fruit which has been steeped in Cointreau and Strawberry *mousse* mixture. After turning out, sprinkle chocolate flakes and decorate with gold *paillettes.*

▣ Napolitain * *Neapolitan*

One layer vanilla, one strawberry and one praline Ice cream *gâteaux* mixtures.

▣ Reine des Fées

To a Basic *bombe* vanilla mixture, add 3 oz candied pineapple cut in dice, steeped in 1 fluid oz Grand-Marnier and 3 oz diced *Génoise* mixture. Fill the mould with this mixture and freeze. After turning out and before cutting the portions, sprinkle with finely chopped pistachio nuts and dust lightly with icing sugar.

▣ Sylvia

Vanilla Ice cream *gâteaux* mixture with roasted and pounded nuts added and top layers, with an Apricot *mousse* mixture mixed with sponge fingers flavoured with Kirsch in the centre.

ICE CREAM MOUSSE

These ices are not frozen in the freezer before being moulded but are put immediately into the mould and frozen in the mould either in the salt and ice bucket or in the refrigerator or even the deep-freeze cabinet.

MOUSSE GLACÉE CLASSIQUE * *CLASSICAL ICE CREAM MOUSSE*

For 8 persons: ½ pint thick Custard (made with 6 egg yolks, 7 fl oz milk and 6 oz sugar); 1 pint whipped cream; flavouring.

Flavour the chilled Custard and add whipped cream. Pour mixture into a mould and freeze. Vanilla *mousse* is made with a custard with strong vanilla flavouring.

MOUSSE GLACÉE MODERNE * *MODERN ICE CREAM MOUSSE*

For 8 persons: 6 to 7 oz sugar; 5 egg yolks; 3 egg whites; 1 pint whipped cream; flavouring.

Mix egg yolks with sugar. Place in double saucepan and heat slowly whipping all the time as for *Génoise* sponge. When the mixture thickens remove from heat and continue beating until quite cold. Add flavouring, stiffly beaten egg whites, and whipped cream. Pour into a Charlotte mould and freeze.

▣ au Café * *Coffee*

Prepare the Coffee *mousse* as above adding a tablespoonful of soluble coffee to the egg yolks.

▣ à la Favorite

For 8 persons: ½ pint Crème Anglaise; ½ lb raspberries; 3 oz icing sugar; ¾ pint whipped cream; 8 meringue shells; 2 tablespoons Maraschino.

Mix the *Crème Anglaise* with the sugar and Maraschino and combine with the coarsely crumbled meringue. Fill into a *bombe* mould and freeze for 2 hours. Turn out on cold round dish and coat with raspberry *purée* mixed with the icing sugar.

▣ aux Fruits * *Fruit*

For 8 persons: ½ pint cold syrup at a density of 35° *on the saccharometer; ½ pint fruit purée; 1 pint whipped cream.*

Mix the cold syrup with fruit *purée* and add whipped cream. Pour the mixture into a mould and freeze. Fruit *mousse* is made with various fruit such as apricots, strawberries, bananas, raspberries, peaches.

▣ au Grand-Marnier, Kirsch, Marasquin, Rhum

Follow the Modern recipe for the *mousse* adding half the liqueur to the egg yolks when beating up and the other half before adding the stiffly beaten whites of egg.

ICE CREAM SOUFFLÉS

How to use an Ice Cream Soufflé Mould

Large ice cream *soufflés* are served in *soufflé* dishes, surrounded by white paper about 1¼ to 1½ inches deeper than the dish and tied with string. The dish is filled to overflowing giving the illusion of a *soufflé* when the paper frill is removed. The mixture is poured into the dish and then put in the freezer. When serving, sprinkle first with cocoa then with a little icing sugar and remove paper band. Small *soufflés* are set in small porcelain dishes and surrounded with paper like the larger ones.

SOUFFLÉS GLACÉS * *BASIC ICE CREAM SOUFFLÉ*

For 8 persons: 5 whites of egg; ½ lb sugar; ½ pint fruit purée; 14 fl oz whipped cream.

Whisk whites of eggs stiffly and add sugar cooked to the *soufflé* degree whisking continuously. Leave to cool, add fruit *purée* and incorporate whipped cream.

Soufflé Glacé aux Amandes * *Almond Ice Cream Soufflé*

5 oz sugar; 5 egg yolks; 3 egg whites; 3 oz shelled almonds; 1 pint whipped cream; 1 tablespoon Kirsch.

Mix egg yolks with sugar. Place in double saucepan and whisk as for *Génoise* sponge mixture. When the mixture thickens remove from the heat and whisk on ice until completely cold. Add the almonds pounded into fine paste with a little water, the Kirsch, the stiffly beaten egg whites and incorporate the whipped cream. Pour into a mould and place in freezer. Before removing the paper band, sprinkle with pounded and sieved almond pralines and a little icing sugar.

▣ à la Bénédictine, Cointreau, Chartreuse

Prepare these ice cream *soufflés* with Basic ice cream mixture and 2½ tablespoons liqueur. Add half the liqueur when beating the egg yolks. Break up 3 oz sponge fingers into small pieces or cut 3 oz *Génoise* cake into dice and steep with remainder of the liqueur. Mix with mixture and with whipped cream. The same method can be used for the *Soufflé au Grand-Marnier.*

▣ au Chocolat * *Chocolate*

Prepare an ice cream *soufflé* with the Basic ice cream mixture and add 3 oz cold melted chocolate before adding the whipped cream.

▣ au Grand-Marnier

For 8 persons: ½ pint thick Custard; 1 pint cream; ½ oz gelatine; 3 fl oz Grand-Marnier; icing sugar; cocoa.

Fasten some stiff white paper around a *soufflé* dish. This paper should project about 2½ inches above the edge of the dish. Make Custard in the usual way. When it is cold add the cream, Grand-Marnier and the soaked and melted gelatine. Beat this mixture vigorously with a whisk, until it is very foamy and begins to solidify. Fill it immediately into the *soufflé* dish. The mixture should be about 2 inches higher than the dish, being kept up by the strip of paper. Place it in a freezer and freeze for 2-3 hours. When about to serve, dredge the top of the *soufflé* generously with cocoa and then with a little icing sugar, this will give the dessert the illusion of a hot *soufflé*. Remove the paper carefully and serve the *soufflé*.

▣ aux Pistaches * *Pistachio nut*

As for Almond ice cream *soufflé* replacing the almonds with pistachio nuts.

▣ Tortoni

Prepare an ice cream *soufflé* with the Basic ice cream mixture, flavour with Kirsch and add 3 oz praline almonds crushed and sieved. Using a piping bag with a small plain round nozzle, pipe Chantilly cream in a spiral on the *soufflé* and put in the freezer to harden the cream. When serving, sprinkle roasted and crushed nuts on the cream and a little icing sugar.

Petits Soufflés Glacés * *Small Apricot Soufflés*

For 8 persons: 8 *oz soufflé syrup* (230° F)*;* 8 *fl oz apricot purée cooked in vanilla-flavoured Stock syrup;* 1 *tablespoon Kirsch;* 5 *egg whites;* ¾ *pint whipped cream.*

Beat the whites until stiff. Pour the boiling sugar syrup cooked to the *soufflé* degree over them, beating until cool. Allow them to become cold. Add the apricot *purée* and Kirsch and incorporate the stiffly beaten whipped cream. Surround porcelain or silver dishes with a paper band. Pour mixture into the dishes and place in freezer. Before removing the paper, sprinkle cocoa and a little icing sugar on the top.

Petits Soufflés Glacés Yolande

For 8 *persons:* 8 *oz soufflé syrup* (230° F)*;* 8 *oz raspberry purée;* 3 *oz pineapple cut in dice and steeped in* 1 *tablespoon Curaçao;* 5 *egg whites;* ¾ *pint whipped cream.*

Prepare as above, before adding the whipped cream, add pineapple cut in dice and steeped in Curaçao and place in a freezer.

ICE CREAM CAKES

Place a slice of *Génoise* sponge about ¼-inch thick in a square or round mould and add some liqueur-flavoured syrup. Now add one or more layers of different flavoured ice cream mixtures, a second slice of *Génoise* and so on. Put in freezer. After turning out, decorate with Chantilly cream, candied fruit etc. (*See illustration p.* 764.)

⊡ Dolorès

Place a slice of Almond *Génoise* sponge in a square mould and soak with Kirsch syrup. Add a Vanilla *bombe* mixture with diced candied fruit steeped in Kirsch, and cover with another slice of cake and freeze. After turning out cover with grated chocolate and some finely chopped pistachio nuts. Serve with Chantilly cream.

⊡ à la Jamaïque

Place a slice of *Génoise* cake in a square mould and soak with Curaçao syrup. Fill with *Bombe* mixture mixed with diced pineapple steeped in sugar and Curaçao. Cover with a slice of *Génoise* steeped in Curaçao syrup. Freeze and, after turning out, decorate with roasted and shredded almonds. Before serving, cut like a cake and sprinkle with icing sugar.

⊡ à la Japonaise

Place a slice of *Génoise* cake steeped in a little tangerine syrup in a round mould and fill with a *Bombe* mixture flavoured with tea mixed with some sponge fingers soaked in tangerine liqueur. After turning out decorate with roasted almonds cut into small pieces, Chantilly cream and pieces of candied peaches. Put the cake back into the freezer to harden the Chantilly.

⊡ à la Reine

Line a round mould with a thin slice of *Génoise* cake steeped in Kirsch syrup. Fill with an Almond *bombe* mixture and a layer of Strawberry *bombe* mixture, then another slice of *Génoise*. After turning out, cover with Apricot sauce and place crushed macaroons around and on top and a light dusting of icing sugar.

ICE CREAM COUPES OR SUNDAES

Les Coupes Glacées * *Ice Cream Coupes or Sundaes*

Sundaes usually consist of some kind of ice, garnished with whipped cream and fruit, and are served in special silver or glass cups called *coupes*.

▣ Alexandra

Fill the glass or ice-cup half full of fruit soaked in Kirsch. Fill with Strawberry ice and decorate with strawberries.

▣ à l'Ananas * *Pineapple*

Fill the glass or ice-cup with diced pineapple pieces soaked in Kirsch and put some Pineapple ice on top. Decorate with Chantilly cream and crystallised pineapple.

▣ à la Créole

Half fill the glass with a *salpicon* of pineapple and bananas soaked in Kirsch and place a ball-scoop of Lemon ice on top. Decorate with Chantilly cream.

▣ Frou-Frou

Half fill the glass with Vanilla ice and cover with a *salpicon* of peaches soaked in Curaçao. Decorate with Chantilly cream and place a *glacé* cherry in the middle.

▣ Jacques

Macerate chopped candied fruit with rum, and place a spoonful in the bottom of each glass. Top with Lemon ice mixed with a little cream. Sprinkle with rum.

▣ Marcelle

Fill *coupe* with Raspberry ice, cover with wild strawberries soaked in Curaçao and coat with thick, sweetened, vanilla-flavoured cream.

▣ Marguerite

Put a little strawberry ice in the *coupe* and a half peach, poached in syrup on top, and decorate with vanilla-flavoured whipped cream. Surround with wild strawberries.

▣ à la Mexicaine

Half fill the glasses with fresh pineapple cut in dice and soaked in Curaçao and cover with Tangerine ice.

▣ Ninon

Fill *coupe* with Praline ice, make a small hollow in the centre, fill it with seedless redcurrant jam and decorate with a ring of vanilla-flavoured whipped cream.

Coupe Glacé Romanoff

Fill the glasses with Vanilla ice cream, small strawberries soaked in orange juice and Curaçao and fill with Chantilly.

⊡ Sylvia

Half fill glasses with diced bananas soaked in orange juice and Kirsch. Cover this with Hazelnut ice cream and decorate with Chantilly cream.

⊡ à la Tsarine

Fill the glasses with Lemon ice and chopped cherries. Fill up with Chantilly cream piped through a forcing bag with a star tube.

⊡ Tutti-Frutti

Fill the glasses with layers of Strawberry ice cream, Lemon ice and Pineapple ice and a *salpicon* of fruit soaked in Kirsch between the layers.

⊡ Vanderbilt

Half fill the glasses with Orange ice cream and arrange on top wild strawberries soaked in Grand-Marnier. Pour a little Champagne in the glasses just before serving.

⊡ Viennoise * *Coffee*

Place a ball of Coffee ice cream into the *coupe*. Garnish with stars of whipped cream and put a chocolate drop on each star.

⊡ Walewska

Half fill the glasses with Vanilla ice cream and arrange on top of fresh peaches sliced and soaked in Kirsch. Decorate with Chantilly cream and top with a strawberry.

SORBETS OR WATER ICES

A *sorbet* is a very light, half-frozen ice which used to be served after the *entrée* and before the roast in very formal meals in order to refresh the palate. Nowadays it is served as a light ice or as a refreshment at cold buffets, dances, etc. Sorbets are made on a basis of wine, liqueurs or fruit juice. Weak Stock syrup is flavoured and added and finally mixed with meringue mixture. They are best when churn frozen.

⊡ au Citron * *Lemon*

For 6 *persons:* 1 *pint Stock syrup at* 22°; 5 *or* 6 *lemons; Italian meringue made with one egg white.*

Allow the zest of 2 lemons to infuse in hot syrup and leave to cool. Add the juice of the lemons and measure the density of the syrup, it should register 17° on the saccharometer. Strain and freeze. Finally stir in the meringue.

Sorbet aux Fruits * *Mixed Fruit Sorbet*

For 6 persons: ¾ *pint Stock syrup at* 22°; ¾ *pint fruit juice—pineapple, strawberry, cherry, peach; Italian meringue mixture made with* 1 *egg white; juice of* 1 *lemon.*

Mix the syrup with the fruit juices and the lemon juice, it should have a density of 15°. Freeze and mix with the Italian meringue.

◘ aux Liqueurs * *Liqueur*

Prepare a syrup which should register 18° on the saccharometer when lemon juice is added and the mixture is chilled. Pour into the freezer. Add meringue, when sorbet is almost set add 2 fluid oz of chosen liqueur for each pint of syrup. Fill into sorbet cups and add a little liqueur. Liqueur sherbets are made with Kirsch, rum, brandy, Maraschino, Cointreau, Curaçao.

◘ à l'Orange * *Orange*

As for Lemon sorbet but add the juice of a lemon to the juice of 5 oranges.

◘ au Vin * *Wine*

For 6 persons: 14 *oz Stock syrup at* 22°; 7 *fl oz wine; juice of one lemon; Italian meringue made with* 2 *oz sugar and* 1 *egg white.*

Mix cold syrup with the wine and lemon juice; the mixture must have a density of 16° by syrup saccharometer. Add water if too thick and add castor sugar in the opposite case. Freeze. When almost frozen, add meringue, mix well and serve in ice sorbet cups three quarters filled. Pour a spoonful of the wine into each cup. Wine sherbets are made with wines such as Sauternes, Rhine wines, sherry, Port, Madeira, etc.

Punch à la Romaine * *Roman Punch Sherbet*

A derivation of sorbet. Use 20° syrup infused in a closed container with the zest and juice of 1 lemon and 2 oranges. Reduce to 16° with Champagne or white wine. Freeze and combine with Italian meringue mixture made with 2 egg whites and 4 oz sugar. Sprinkle with a few drops of rum when serving.

Les Granités * *Granulated Sherbet*

Granités are made with very light syrup and fruit juice. They should still be granular in texture after freezing. The mixture should have a density of 12-14°.

Les Marquises

These are made with fruit juice; pineapple, orange, tangerine or with Kirsch mixed with 18° syrup. When they are frozen ½ pint of whipped cream for every 1¾ pints of mixture is added. They are served principally as sweets and for cold buffet parties.

Les Spooms * *Wine Sherbet*

Spooms are *sorbets* made with wine only, preferably white wine or Champagne and containing double the amount of meringue mixture.

Gâteaux and Pastries

Fine pastries and cakes, both large and small, of good quality and finish, are an essential part of most menus. Because they are attractive they appeal to the eye and then to the palate, and so take part in the aesthetic enjoyment of a meal. No cookery book of this nature could be considered complete without a reasonably comprehensive section on this subject. The whole field of *pâtisserie*, however, is vast and this section cannot be considered complete. Only a selection is given based on the accepted basic mixtures. Before approaching these mixtures, however, some important considerations must be studied and borne in mind.

Preparation

Making fine pastries and sweets is far more difficult than making other dishes. In the kitchen one can, by and large, manage without a pair of scales. In the case of *pâtisserie*, however, this is impossible. If failure is to be avoided, the weighing of ingredients must be accurate; there can be no question of guesswork. Occasionally in the text a weight is qualified by the word "approximately" applied generally to moistening materials such as milk and water; this is necessary because of the variable absorption property of flour.

On the pages that follow, therefore, much detail is given so that, assuming one has a basic knowledge of the subject, success is assured if the recipes are carefully followed. Amongst those given there are many that appear for the first time in this book.

Fresh ingredients are all important to ensure the delicate flavour of many cakes and *gâteaux*. This means fresh sweet butter and perfectly fresh eggs. *Plain* flour is recommended for the cakes and pastries in this section. The oven should be preheated for 15 minutes before use. Use only melted butter for greasing tins, and brush on with a pastry brush; dust with flour, then tip the tin upside down to remove surplus flour.

Baking

Cakes are baked when the heat penetrates to the centre and then up to the centre of the crown, which, because it is the point at which steam escapes, is the last part of the cake to bake. Each cake has a precise baking temperature and time, but so much depends on the following factors: the size, the thickness, the quality, and the density. A large cake will obviously take longer to bake because the heat cannot penetrate so quickly. More time and a lower baking temperature is therefore necessary. As the quality of the mix becomes richer the cake generally becomes more dense. Baking temperatures must therefore be reduced and baking time extended. Cakes rich in sugar such as ginger, honey cakes and macaroons, must be baked in a cool oven or the sugar will caramelise and burn. Meringues should not take on a colour in the oven and are not really baked but dried. Therefore, the oven temperature must be low.

Most modern ovens are fitted either with a thermometer or a heat regulating device. The temperature of domestic ovens will vary according to the level at which the cake is placed in the oven; it is important to use the thermal figures and baking times as a guide only. Generally speaking cakes and pastries should be baked more or less in the centre of the oven.

When removing the cake from the tin, the usual procedure is to allow the cake to settle for a few minutes after it has been removed from the oven. Then, run a thin palette knife round the edge between the cake and the tin, reverse the two and give a short, sharp downward jerk to dislodge the cake from the tin. Allow the cake to become absolutely cold before attempting to cut or ice it.

Icing a Cake

Use a piping bag for filling meringues, *éclairs* and cakes where practical. You may find it helpful to put the piping bag in a jug or jar and drape the edges over the edge of the jug, this will allow you both hands free for filling the bag with the mixture.

Vanilla sugar is often called for in the following recipes; the simplest method of making this is to keep a vanilla pod or bean in your jar of castor sugar. (*See Spice section p.* 126.)

Storage

Almost all types of baked products including home-made bread will freeze perfectly. Cake layers, bread and biscuits should be carefully wrapped in aluminium foil or other suitable covering.

CAKES MADE WITH SPONGE MIXTURES

This section comprises *gâteaux* and cakes made with *Pâte à Biscuit.* (*See general notes on p.* 712.)

Gâteau Chocolatine * *Chocolate Cake*

For 6-8 persons: 1 *round Génoise base;* 4 *eggs;* 4 *oz sugar;* 2½ *oz butter;* 3½ *oz flour. Butter cream:* 4½ *oz butter;* 5 *oz thick chocolate Custard;* 3½ *oz roasted nibbed almonds.* Cooking time: about 30 minutes.

Make up the *Génoise* as for Swiss roll, place into a lined 8-inch cake tin and bake in a moderate oven, 350° F or Gas Mark 4. When cool, slice in two and spread with the butter cream made by beating the butter and chocolate Custard together. Coat top and sides with the butter cream. Roll the sides of the cake in roasted almonds. Decorate the top with a piped Chocolate butter cream design.

⊡ Hongrois * *Hungarian*

For 6 *persons:* 3 *eggs;* 4 *oz Almond paste;* 1½ *oz sugar;* 3 *oz crushed nougat;* 1½ *oz flour;* 2 *oz melted butter;* 10 *oz Chocolate butter cream;* 6 *oz chocolate shavings.* Cooking time: about 30 minutes.

Mix the egg yolks and Almond paste. Fold in the whipped whites, sugar, flour, crushed nougat and the melted butter. Place into a greased, lined 8-9-inch flan ring or cake tin. Bake in a moderate oven, 375° F or Gas Mark 4, allow to cool, sandwich and coat with the Chocolate butter cream and mask with chocolate shavings. Lightly dust with icing sugar and place a red *glacé* cherry in the centre. (*See illustration p.* 835.)

Gâteau Java * *Orange Cake*

For 6 persons: 4½ oz sugar; 1¾ oz flour; 1¾ oz cornflour; 4 egg yolks; 3 stiffly whipped whites; the zest of an orange; 1¾ oz candied orange peel; 10 oz orange marmalade; 7 oz Orange fondant; 4 candied orange slices. Cooking time: about 40-50 minutes.

Whip the egg yolks and sugar stiffly and fold in the stiffly whipped egg whites. Add the finely chopped orange peel and the flour and cornflour that have been sieved together. Bake in a tin about 8 inches square in a moderate oven, 375° F or Gas Mark 4. When baked and cold, slice and spread with marmalade. Coat with Orange fondant and decorate with the candied orange slices.

⊡ Mexicain

For 6 persons: 4½ oz sugar; 3¼ oz flour; 2¾ oz butter; 4 eggs; 1 egg yolk; 1¼ oz cocoa; apricot jam; Chocolate fondant; Royal icing. Cooking time: about 35-40 minutes.

Whip the sugar and the five yolks to a stiff foam. Fold in the stiffly whipped egg whites and at the same time the flour and the cocoa which have been sieved together. Finally, fold in the melted butter and pour into a ring or sandwich tin about 10 inches in diameter. The tin should be greased and dusted lightly with flour. Bake in a moderate oven, 375° F or Gas Mark 4. When baked and cold, slice through the cake twice and sandwich with Chocolate butter cream. Half fill a small greaseproof paper piping bag fitted with a small plain nozzle with Royal icing. Mask the cake with well-boiled apricot jam and then with prepared Chocolate fondant. Before the fondant has time to set, pipe parallel lines of Royal icing across the top very quickly. Pass the point of a knife lightly over the top, first in one direction and then in the opposite direction to create a feathered effect. (The bag of Royal icing must be prepared before the *gâteau* is coated with fondant.) (*See illustration p.* 832).

⊡ Moka * *Coffee*

For 6–8 persons: Génoise base; 4 oz icing sugar; 4 eggs; 3½ oz flour; 2½ oz butter. Cooking time: about 30 minutes.

Whip the egg yolks and sugar to a stiff foam. Add the flour and about ⅓ of the stiffly-whipped egg whites. Fold in the rest of the whites and the melted butter and place into a greased and lightly floured tin about 8-inch square. Bake in a moderate oven, 375° F or Gas Mark 4. When the cake is baked and cold, slice into two or three layers and spread with Coffee butter cream (see Yule Log). Mask the top and sides of the *gâteau* with the cream and mask the sides with roasted nibbed almonds. Decorate the top with butter cream in the form of parallel lines of stars. (*See illustration p.* 832). Alternatively, the *gâteau* can be coated with well-boiled apricot jam and Coffee fondant, the name "Mocha" piped in the centre with a fine tube. Finish with a border of piped fondant and decorate with chocolate coffee beans. (*See illustration p.* 833).

⊡ Mousseline aux Noisettes * *Hazelnut*

For 6-8 persons: 4½ oz icing sugar; 1¾ oz flour; 1¾ oz cornflour; 4 egg yolks; 3 stiffly whipped egg whites; 1½ oz roasted, finely ground hazelnuts. Cooking time: about 40 minutes.

Whip the egg yolks and sugar until stiff. Gently fold in the egg whites, flour, cornflour and hazelnuts which have been sieved together. Place into a greased and floured sandwich tin about 8 inches in diameter and bake in a moderate oven, 375° F or Gas Mark 4. When cold, dust the top and sides with icing sugar. Serve for tea or with ices.

Biscuit Roulé * *Swiss Roll*

For 6-8 persons: 3 oz sugar; 3 oz flour; 1 oz butter; 3 large eggs; 1 egg yolk. Cooking time: 6-8 minutes.

Separate the eggs and whip the sugar with the yolks until thick. Fold in the stiffly whipped whites with, at the same time, the flour and the melted butter. Spread carefully on a paper-lined baking sheet about 16 inches × 12 inches. Cook in a hot oven, 400 ° F or Gas Mark 6. After baking, turn out on to a dry cloth and remove the paper. When cool, spread with jam or butter cream and roll up. Dredge with icing sugar and cut into slices. If the roll is cream filled, refrigerate before cutting. Instead of dredging with sugar, the roll may be coated with white, rum-flavoured fondant; alternatively other coloured and flavoured fondants can be used. Swiss roll is used as a basis for many sweets and cakes.

Biscuit de Savoie * *Savoy Sponge*

For 8 persons.

Clean the savoy mould or a 7-inch deep cake tin thoroughly and brush carefully and evenly with butter or cooking fat. Dust first with castor sugar and then with cornflour. Three-quarters fill with the sponge mixture as for Swiss roll and carefully bake at a temperature and for a time that will depend entirely on the size of the sponge. A medium-size sponge will take about 50 minutes in a moderate oven, 375° F or Gas Mark 4-5.

Buche de Noël * *Chocolate Yule Log*

For 6-8 persons: Mixture as for Swiss roll. For the Coffee butter cream: 4½ oz butter; 5 oz coffee-flavoured Custard (Crème Anglaise): Chocolate butter cream: 4½ oz butter; 5 oz chocolate Custard (Crème Anglaise); icing sugar; blanched chopped almonds.

Make a Swiss roll exactly as above. When cool, spread with Coffee butter cream made by beating the coffee Custard with 4½ ounces butter until light. Cut off both ends a little on the slant. Make up the Chocolate butter cream in exactly the same way as for Coffee butter cream, using the chocolate Custard. Place in a savoy bag fitted with a star tube and pipe lines close together along the length of the roll until it is covered. Sprinkle with chopped pistachio nuts to imitate moss with a little sieved icing sugar to imitate snow. A plaque with "Merry Christmas" piped on, and an imitation fir leaf completes the decoration. Chocolate fondant can be used to coat the roll instead of Chocolate butter cream. (*See illustration p.* 838).

CAKES MADE WITH CHOUX PASTRY

This section includes various types of *éclairs* and also larger *gâteaux* which combine *Choux* pastry and Short Crust pastry. (*See general notes on p.* 715).

Choux à la Crème * *Cream Buns*

Pipe *Choux* pastry (as for Coffee *Eclairs*) into buns about the size of a small apricot, on a baking sheet, using a plain tube. Bake at 450° F or Gas Mark 8, until crisp and dry. When cold, cut open and fill with vanilla flavoured-whipped dairy cream and dredge with icing sugar. Place in paper cases.

Eclairs au Café * *Coffee Eclairs (Basic Recipe)*

Makes about 1 *dozen: Choux pastry:* 4½ *oz flour;* 3½ *oz butter;* 9 *fl oz water;* ½ *oz sugar; pinch salt;* 4 *eggs (approximately).* Cooking time: 15-18 minutes.

Prepare *Choux* pastry as directed on p. 715. Using a savoy bag with a plain tube, pipe the *Choux* pastry in very straight fingers about 3 inches long on to a lightly greased baking sheet. Brush each with beaten egg and bake in a very hot oven, 425° F or Gas Mark 7, until crisp and dry. Cut open with scissors or a sharp knife at the side near the top. Fill with coffee Confectioners' custard. Coat the tops with Coffee fondant. (*See illustration p.* 841).

Eclairs au Chocolat * *Chocolate Eclairs*

Proceed as above but fill with chocolate-flavoured Confectioners' custard or vanilla-flavoured whipped dairy cream. Coat the tops with Chocolate fondant.

Favoris

9 *oz flour;* 4½ *oz butter;* ½ *oz sugar; pinch of salt;* 1½ *fl oz water.* Cooking time: about 15 minutes according to size.

Choux pastry as above. Make the sweet Short Crust pastry, roll out and cut out small oval biscuits. Pipe a figure "8" on each with *Choux* pastry, using a savoy bag with a small plain tube. Bake at 400° F or Gas Mark 6. When cold, fill the openings with vanilla-flavoured Confectioner's custard and place half a candied or *glacé* cherry in the centre.

Madelon

Pipe *Choux* pastry (as above) into "S" shapes using a savoy bag with a plain tube, on to a lightly-greased baking sheet. Brush with egg and sprinkle with sugar nibs or use crushed lump sugar. Bake at 425° F or Gas Mark 7, for about 15 minutes. When cold, cut open and fill with redcurrant jelly.

Paris-Brest

For 8 *persons: Choux pastry (see Basic Recipe);* 1 *pint Confectioners' custard, well-flavoured with ground praline;* 1 *oz chopped almonds.* Cooking time: about 30 minutes.

Pipe a ring of *Choux* pastry, about two fingers wide, on to an ungreased baking sheet. Brush with egg, sprinkle with chopped almonds and then lightly with sugar. Bake in a hot oven, 400° F or Gas Mark 6, until the ring is dry and crisp. When cold, cut it open and fill with the praline Confectioners' custard and dust with icing sugar.

Rognons

Choux pastry (see Basic Recipe). Cooking time about 25-30 minutes.

Using a plain tube, pipe out kidney shapes on a lightly greased baking sheet and bake in a hot oven, 425° F or Gas Mark 7, until they are dry and crisp. When cold, split them open and fill with coffee-flavoured whipped dairy cream. Coat the tops with Coffee fondant.

Saint-Honoré

For 6-7 persons: 9 oz Sweet pastry or Puff pastry; Choux pastry (see Basic Recipe); 1¼ *pints St. Honoré cream; whipped dairy cream.* Cooking time: 25-30 minutes.

Roll out pastry—either Sweet or Puff—to about ¼-inch in thickness and make a round base. Place on a baking sheet and prick well with a fork. Brush the edge with egg and pipe a ring of *Choux* pastry on top, not too close to the edge. Brush this with egg and bake at 400° F or Gas Mark 6. Pipe about 15 small cream buns on to another baking sheet about the size of a walnut, brush with egg and bake at 425° F or Gas Mark 7, until dry and crisp. Boil 6 oz sugar with 2 oz water to the "crack" degree (270-280° F). Impale the buns one by one on a fork and dip into the sugar and place immediately around the edge of the cooked base. Fill the middle with *St. Honoré* cream and decorate with whipped cream and candied cherries. (*See illustration p.* 756).

CAKES MADE WITH PUFF PASTRY

This section contains some of the simpler recipes based upon the use of Puff pastry such as apple turnovers as well as the more elaborate and well-known *gâteaux* such as *Mille-Feuille*. This is a delicious confection of layers of Puff pastry filled with fresh cream and strawberries. (*See general notes on p.* 715).

Gâteau d'Amandes dit Pithiviers * *Almond Gâteau*

For 5 *persons:* 1½ *lb Puff pastry;* 9 *oz Almond custard cream;* 1 *egg. Almond cream:* 4½ *oz ground almonds;* 2½ *oz sugar;* 2 *oz butter;* 2 *egg yolks;* 1 *oz rum or brandy*. Cooking time: 20-30 minutes.

Cut out two large circular bases of Puff pastry, one about ⅛-inch thick and one about ¼-inch. Place the thin base on to the baking sheet and brush the edge lightly with water. Fill the centre generously with Almond custard cream, cover with the thicker Puff pastry circle and press down the edges firmly. Make a scallop design on the edge with the back of a knife. Eggwash the top and score curved lines on the top with the point of a sharp knife, starting from the centre and radiating to the edge in such a way that a flower design is formed. Bake in a hot oven, 400° F or Gas Mark 6. Five minutes before the cake is baked, dredge with icing sugar and return to the oven so that the sugar will caramelise to give a nice glazed appearance. Protect with greased paper if necessary.

To make Almond cream:

Mix the ground almonds with the sugar and beat with the rest of the ingredients to make a rather soft mixture. Alternatively, marzipan can be used instead of ground almonds. In this case use 7 oz of marzipan, deleting almonds and sugar. Mix all ingredients thoroughly. (*See illustration p.* 757).

⊡ d'Artois

For 8 *persons:* 14 *oz Puff pastry;* ¾ *pint Confectioners' custard;* 1 *egg.* Cooking time 20-25 minutes.

Roll out Puff pastry to about ⅛-inch thick. Cut a strip about 10 inches long and about 4 inches wide. Moisten the edges lightly and deposit Confectioners' custard or jam in the centre. Cut another strip slightly wider and place on top. Seal and trim the edges. Egg wash and score the top with parallel lines at right-angles to the long edges. Bake in a hot oven, 400° F or Gas Mark 6. Serve whole or cut into slices.

Gâteau Champigny

For 8 persons: 1¾ *lb Puff pastry;* ½ *lb thick apricot jam;* 1 *egg.* Cooking time: 25-30 minutes.

Make in exactly the same way as for Almond Gâteau, but fill instead with apricot jam and make in a square shape. Dust with icing sugar as soon as baked.

▣ Hollandais

For 8 persons: 9 *oz Puff pastry or Puff pastry trimmings;* ¼ *lb sugar;* ¼ *lb butter;* ¼ *lb ground almonds;* 2 *eggs; zest of* 1 *lemon;* 1¾ *oz flour; apricot jam; icing sugar; Kirsch.* Cooking time: 25 minutes.

Line a flan ring with Puff pastry trimmings, prick the base and trim off the pastry at the top of the ring. Cream the butter and sugar and add the zest of lemon, then the ground almonds. Beat in the eggs and fold in the flour. Place this mixture into the prepared ring and smooth level. Roll out the remaining Puff pastry thinly, cut in strips, and arrange them in trellis pattern on the top and press down at the edges. Bake in a moderate oven, 375° F or Gas Mark 5. After baking, brush lightly with well boiled apricot *purée*, then glaze with Kirsch-flavoured water icing.

▣ Mille-Feuille

For 8 persons: 1 *lb Puff pastry;* 10 *oz jam;* ½ *lb apricot jam;* ½ *pint vanilla-flavoured whipped cream;* 6 *oz wild strawberries.* Cooking time: 7-8 minutes.

Roll out Puff pastry ⅛-inch thick and cut out 5 or 6 circles about 10 inches in diameter. Cut out the centres of each with a cutter 3-4 inches in diameter. Cut out another circle, this time slightly larger and without removing the centre. Prick all of them and after allowing them to rest for 30 minutes bake at 425° F or Gas Mark 7. When cold, sandwich the rings with the jam and trim so that the outside is round then brush with well boiled apricot jam. Place the whole on to the base also brushed with apricot jam. Decorate the outside with small Puff pastry decorations (baked separately) candied fruits, almonds, etc., and shortly before serving, fill centre with whipped cream mixed with strawberries.

▣ Niçois

For 10 persons: 14 *oz Puff pastry;* 2 *lb Almond paste;* 3½ *oz diced candied orange peel;* 3½ *fl oz white Curaçao; zest of* 1 *orange;* 3½ *oz Royal icing;* 1¾ *oz flaked almonds; a segment of candied oranges;* 1 *glacé cherry.* Cooking time: 45 minutes.

Line a flan ring with half the Puff pastry. Fill with the Almond paste, moistened with Curaçao mixed with candied peel and zest. Cover with the rest of the Puff pastry and trim by passing the rolling pin round the edge of the ring. Spread the top with Royal icing and sprinkle with the flaked almonds. Place the orange segment in the centre and the *glacé* cherry. Allow to rest before baking, having pricked the *gâteau* thoroughly to allow the escape of steam. Bake in a hot oven, 400° F or Gas Mark 6. (*See illustration p.* 831).

Chausson aux Pommes * *Apple Turnovers*

For 6 persons: ¾ lb Puff pastry; ¾ lb apples; 3 oz sugar; 1 oz butter; 1 egg; 1 fl oz brandy. Cooking time: 10-12 minutes.

Peel and slice the apples and cook them in butter without allowing them to get too soft. Add the sugar and brandy and allow to cool. Roll out Puff pastry ⅛-inch thick and cut out large circles using a 4-inch plain or fluted cutter. Brush lightly with water and place a spoonful of apple in the centre of each. Fold over and seal edges firmly. Brush with egg and make a few holes in the centre with the point of a knife. Bake in a hot oven, 400° F or Gas Mark 6. Shortly before they are baked, dust with icing sugar and return to the oven to caramelise the sugar on top.

CAKES MADE WITH GÉNOISE MIXTURE

Cakes made with *Génoise* should be removed from the baking tin as soon as they are cooked to prevent them from becoming damp and heavy. In addition to the recipes in this section there are of course many other ways of decorating and flavouring a Basic *Génoise* sponge and you may suit these to your own taste and the special occasion for which you are catering. (*See general notes on p.* 718).

Gâteau d'Anniversaire * *Birthday Cake*

For 8 *persons: 5½ oz icing sugar; 5½ oz flour; 3½ oz butter; 5 eggs. Butter cream: 5½ oz butter; 5 oz Custard; Kirsch.* Cooking time: 25-30 minutes.

There is no special recipe for this cake. It may be made of *Génoise* or sponge, baked and then sandwiched with Kirsch-flavoured Butter cream. The ingredients given above are made up by first separating the eggs and whipping the yolks with the sugar. The stiffly whipped whites are then folded in together with the flour. Lastly the melted butter is carefully stirred in. Alternatively, the sugar and egg may be whipped to a stiff sponge and then the flour and melted butter is folded in. Bake in a moderate oven, 375° F or Gas Mark 4-5. The decoration is the most important part. Coat the cake, for example, with pink Fondant and pipe "Happy Birthday" or the person's name with chocolate coloured Royal icing or piping chocolate. Pipe a border and decorate with candles in holders fixing them with royal icing. Complete the cake with modelled marzipan roses or roses made with pulled sugar. Add any other suitable decoration.

⊡ Caraque

For 8 *persons: 5 oz plain chocolate; ½ lb sugar; 6 oz flour; 2 fl oz strong black coffee; 4 eggs; 1 tablespoon Crème de Menthe; Fondant icing; 1 oz chocolate.* Cooking time: 30 minutes.

Have all ingredients at room temperature. Grease and line a 9-inch round cake tin. Cut a circle of waxed paper 2 inches in diameter. Melt the 5 oz of chocolate in a double boiler and use a little of it to spread on the waxed paper circle. Chill. Beat the eggs in a mixing bowl over a pan of hot water and gradually beat in the sugar, continue beating until the mixture has doubled in volume and will hold its shape when the beater is withdrawn. Carefully fold in the sifted flour, using a spatula or metal spoon. Fold the cooled melted chocolate and coffee into the mixture. Pour into the prepared tin and bake in a moderate oven, 375° F or Gas Mark 4. Cool the cake in the tin for 10 minutes and then turn out and cool on a wire tray. Add the Crème de Menthe to the half-melted fondant. Pour the icing on top of the cake but do not allow it to run down the sides of the cake. Allow the icing to set, melt the remaining 1 oz of chocolate mix with the remaining Fondant icing and using a piping bag and fine tube decorate the top of the cake. Remove the chocolate from the waxed paper and place in the centre of the cake. *(See illustration p. 837)*.

Gâteau Cluny

For 6 persons: 4½ *oz sugar;* 3½ *oz flour;* 3½ *oz butter;* 4 *eggs. Butter cream:* 3½ *oz butter;* ¼ *pint vanilla Custard;* 1¾ *oz ground pistachio nuts;* 5 *oz apricot purée;* 3½ *oz roasted chopped hazelnuts;* ½ *fl oz Bénédictine;* 5 *oz Fondant.* Cooking time: 35-40 minutes.

Prepare the *Génoise* as for Birthday Cake and bake in a greased and floured tin about 7-inch square. Place in a moderate oven, 350° F-375° F or Gas Mark 4-5. When cold cut in 2 and sandwich with the Butter cream made with the butter, Custard and pistachio nuts flavoured with Bénédictine. Mask top and sides of base with well boiled apricot jam (*purée*) and coat the top with Bénédictine-flavoured Fondant. Coat the sides with roasted hazelnuts. Place a star design with piping chocolate on top. This is piped on paper first, and removed carefully with a palette knife when set.

◘ Damier * *Chessboard*

For 8 persons: 4½ *oz sugar;* 3½ *oz flour;* 3½ *oz butter;* 4 *eggs;* 2 *oz roasted ground hazelnuts. Praline butter cream:* 4½ *oz butter;* ¼ *pint thick Custard;* 2 *oz praline.* 5 *oz roasted chopped almonds;* 6 *oz strained apricot jam cooked to jelly; plain white Fondant; Chocolate fondant; Royal icing.*

Prepare as for Birthday Cake mixture and add the hazelnuts. Bake in a greased and floured square tin and allow to cool. When cold, turn out, slice and sandwich with Praline butter cream. Place the cake in the refrigerator to allow the butter cream to set. Coat top and sides very thinly with apricot *purée* and coat the sides with roasted, chopped almonds. Fill a paper bag with Royal icing and trace regular squares on top, imitating a chessboard. Fill half the squares with plain Fondant and the other half with Chocolate fondant. Finally, finish the decoration with a border of butter cream around the edge, using a piping bag and star tube.

◘ Lutétia * *Chestnut*

For 6-8 persons: 1 *round Génoise sponge;* 7 *oz peeled and skinned chestnuts;* 5 *oz butter;* 3½ *oz icing sugar;* 1 *egg white;* ½ *liqueur glass rum; Chocolate fondant; marzipan; Royal icing.*

Bake *Génoise* sponge in a greased and floured round tin as for Birthday Cake. Prepare Italian meringue with the egg white and sugar, and allow to cool. Rub the cooked and well-drained chestnuts through a wire sieve and mix the *purée* with the Italian meringue as soon as it is cold. Finally, add softened butter and rum. Slice base into three layers and sandwich them with the chestnut cream. Place in the refrigerator to allow the cream to set. Coat entirely with Chocolate fondant. Decorate with Royal icing, using a very fine tube, and with chestnuts made out of marzipan. *(See illustration p. 836)*.

Gâteau Mascotte

For 8 persons: 4½ oz sugar; 3½ oz flour; 3½ oz butter; 4 eggs. Praline butter cream: 4½ oz roasted, nibbed almonds; 4½ oz butter; ¼ pint Custard; 2 oz ground and sieved nougat.

Bake the *Génoise* mixture in a round tin in a moderate oven, 350° F or Gas Mark 4. Allow to cool. Slice twice and layer with Praline butter cream. Coat top and sides thinly with butter cream, and sprinkle roasted nibbed almonds on top and sides. Dredge lightly with icing sugar. *Praline butter cream*: Cream the butter, and gradually whisk in the barely lukewarm custard. Finally, add the ground and sieved nougat. (*See illustration p.* 833).

▣ Praliné * *Praline*

For 8 persons: 4½ oz icing sugar; 3½ oz flour; 3½ oz butter; 4 eggs; 7 oz Praline butter cream; 7½ oz apricot jam; 3½ oz roasted chopped almonds. Cooking time: 30-35 minutes.

Make *Génoise* mixture and bake in a greased and floured round tin in a moderate oven, 375° F or Gas Mark 4-5. When cold, cut across once, sandwich with Praline butter cream and replace. Coat top and sides with concentrated apricot jam and sprinkle with almonds. Dust lightly with icing sugar.

Génoise Glacée * *Iced Génoise Sponge*

For 6-8 persons: 4½ oz sugar; 3½ oz flour; 3½ oz butter; 4 eggs. Butter cream: 4½ oz butter; ½ pint vanilla Custard. Icing: 7 oz rum-flavoured Fondant. Candied fruit; blanched almonds. Cooking time: 30-35 minutes.

Prepare *Génoise* mixture and bake it in greased and floured round tin, then bake in a moderate oven, 375° F or Gas Mark 4-5. Allow to cool in the tin and turn out on to a cooling wire. Slice twice and sandwich with Vanilla butter cream. Coat top and sides with lukewarm rum-flavoured Fondant. Decorate with candied fruit and split almonds.

CAKES MADE WITH YEAST MIXTURES

Some of the cakes in this section are often served as sweets or puddings; these include Rum *Baba* and the *savarins*. (*See general notes on p.* 719).

Baba au Rhum * *Rum Baba*

For 4 persons: 4½ oz flour; 1¾ oz butter; ¼ oz yeast; ¼ oz sugar; ⅛ oz salt; 1½ oz each of cleaned currants and sultanas; 3½ fl oz lukewarm milk. Cooking time about: 35 minutes.

Make *Baba* dough as indicated (see p. 722) and half fill a deep, well greased cake tin with it. Let it rise at moderate heat, start baking in a hot oven, 425° F or Gas Mark 7, and reduce heat as soon as the cake starts to brown on top. When ready remove from tin and soak at once in hot rum-flavoured Stock syrup. Take out and drain on a wire tray. Decorate with whipped dairy cream.

Brioche en Couronne * *Brioche Ring*

For 6 persons: 11-12 *oz Brioche dough* (*see recipe, p.* 720). Cooking time: 15-18 minutes.

Roll the dough out to a ball and flatten lightly. Make an opening in the centre with a finger dipped in flour and continue enlarging with a little flour until the opening is big enough to put a fist in. Now, make the dough into a complete ring shape, place on a greased baking sheet and allow to rise for about 15 minutes. Brush with egg and cut top and sides of the crown with a pair of scissors dipped in water. Bake in a hot oven, 425° F-450° F or Gas Mark 7-8.

▣ Mousseline

For 6 persons: 4½ *oz flour;* 3½-4½ *oz butter;* ¼ *oz sugar;* 1/16 *oz salt;* ¼ *oz yeast;* 1 *egg.* Cooking time: 30-35 minutes.

Make *Brioche* dough (see p. 720), place it on a floured marble slab and shape into a ball with both hands without pressing too hard. Butter a wide beaker mould or round 5-6-inch wide bread tin, put dough in it and set in a warm place to rise. As soon as it has doubled in volume, brush with egg and tie a sheet of white paper round the edge so that it stands up 2 inches above it. Put in a hot oven, 425° F or Gas Mark 7, and, as soon as the top begins to crown, cover with greased paper to stop it from becoming too dark. To see if the cake is ready stick a thin larding or other needle into the centre. If it comes out hot and dry the bake is done. This applies to all cakes.

▣ à Tête

For 6 *persons:* 4½ *oz flour;* 4½ *oz butter;* ⅓ *oz sugar;* 1 *pinch of salt; lukewarm milk;* ¼ *oz yeast;* 1 *large egg.* Cooking time: 30-35 minutes.

Prepare *Brioche* dough (*see recipe, p.* 720), and divide into pieces weighing about 3 oz. Place the dough in lightly-buttered, crimp-edged *brioche* tins. Make a depression in the centre with a finger dipped in flour. Roll out the remaining dough into balls and make them into the shape of a pear. Set these knobs as upright as possible on top of the bigger pieces with the point stuck in the centre. The tins ought not to be more than half-full. Allow to rise until the dough has doubled its volume. Brush carefully with egg and make four or five snips below the knob with scissors. Cover with a sheet of greased paper, to prevent the *brioches* browning too much. Bake in a very hot oven, 425° F or Gas Mark 7. (*See illustration p.* 830).

Couronne aux Amandes * *Almond Ring*

½ *lb Twelfth Night Cake mixture* (*see p.* 724); 2 *oz almond filling;* 1 *oz roasted flaked almonds.* Cooking time: about 20 minutes.

Divide the mixture into 3 equal parts and roll out into identical rectangles. Spread each with almond filling made from Almond paste softened to spreading consistency with egg. Roll up each rectangle to form three almond-filled ropes. Plait them and form into a ring. Bake in a hot oven, 400°F or Gas Mark 6. Brush immediately with apricot *purée* and sprinkle with roasted almonds. (*See illustration p.* 829.)

Gâteau des Rois de Bordeaux * *Bordeaux Three Kings' Cake*

For 10 *persons:* 9 *oz flour;* 4½ *oz butter;* 3½ *oz sugar;* ½ *oz yeast;* ¼ *oz salt;* 2 *eggs; a little water.* Cooking time: 20-25 minutes.

Prepare a *Brioche* dough (see p. 720). When ready make the dough into a round ball, then with the fingers, enlarge into a ring shape. Put on to a baking sheet to rise. Before baking, brush with sweetened orange-flower water and decorate with very thin slices of lemon peel and sprinkle with sugar nibs. Bake in a hot oven, 400° F or Gas Mark 6.

Kugelhopf

For 6 *persons:* 9 *oz flour;* 3 *oz butter;* 1 *oz sugar;* ½ *oz yeast;* 2 *oz chopped almonds;* 2 *oz sultanas; pinch of salt;* 2 *eggs;* ¼ *pint milk.* Cooking time: 35-40 minutes.

Make a ferment by blending the lukewarm milk into the yeast. Put 2 oz flour on a table or marble slab, make a well in the centre and pour in the yeast and milk. Mix this into a soft dough. Cut a cross in the top and place in a casserole containing a little lukewarm water until it has doubled in volume. As it rises it will float on the water. Then add the rest of the ingredients except sultanas. Make into a medium-firm dough, adding more milk if necessary. Finally, add the sultanas. Grease and flour a special *kugelhopf* mould and place blanched almonds in the cavities. Fill half full only and allow to rise. Bake in a moderate oven, 375° F or Gas Mark 4-5. After baking, turn out and dredge with icing sugar. (*See illustration p.* 829).

Manon

For 6 *persons:* 9 *oz Savarin dough;* ½ *pint Confectioners' custard;* ½ *pint chocolate Confectioners' custard;* 8 *oz apricot jam;* 7 *oz almonds.* Cooking time: 15-20 minutes.

Fill a metal *timbale* mould one-third fill of dough, let it rise and bake in a hot oven, 425° F or Gas Mark 7. When the cake has cooled somewhat cut it across into 5 equal slices, soak lightly with neat Kirsch and replace the slices, coating them alternately with Chocolate and Vanilla cream but leaving the top free. Brush the whole cake with thickly concentrated, strained, apricot jam; sprinkle finely roasted chopped almonds on top and dust with icing sugar.

Marignan

For 6 *persons:* 9 *oz Savarin dough; Italian meringue mixture from* 2 *egg whites or* ½ *pint St. Honoré cream.* Cooking time: 15-20 minutes.

Put the *Savarin* dough into a flat cake tin, oval if possible, let it rise, bake in a hot oven, 425° F or Gas Mark 7, soak with Stock syrup flavoured with Kirsch, rum or brandy, drain and turn upside down. Cut off a slice, about ½-inch thick across the top, in such a way that when the ends are lifted, they resemble the lids of a basket. Lift both ends and fill with meringue mixture, *St. Honoré* cream or possibly vanilla-flavoured whipped cream. Put a thin slice of angelica in the middle like a handle and glaze the top of the lids with strained apricot jam.

SAVARIN * *SAVARIN CAKE*

A yeast cake baked in a ring mould and soaked in flavoured syrup when cold. It may be decorated with fruit and cream. (*See Savarin dough, p.* 722).

▣ Chantilly * *with Fresh Cream*

For 6 persons: 1 *Savarin; ½ pint vanilla-flavoured whipped cream; Kirsch-flavoured Stock syrup.*

After baking, soak the *Savarin* with the Kirsch syrup, drain, cool and place on a round serving dish. Pile a mound of vanilla-flavoured whipped cream in the middle and also garnish with it. When in season mix some wild strawberries with the cream. Serve cold.

▣ Montmorency * *with Cherries*

For 6 persons: 9 *oz Savarin dough;* 1¼ *lb stoned cherries; Kirsch-flavoured Stock syrup.*

Bake *Savarin* in the usual way, soak with the syrup and place on a round, fairly deep serving dish. Fill the middle with stewed cherries thickened with a little cornflour and flavoured with Kirsch. Serve lukewarm.

▣ au Rhum * *with Rum*

For 4 persons: 4½ *oz flour;* 2 *oz butter;* ¼ *oz yeast;* ½ *oz sugar;* 2 *eggs; pinch of salt; milk as required; Savarin syrup; rum; small piece vanilla pod and cinnamon; slice of lemon peel.* Cooking time: 15-20 minutes.

Prepare *Savarin* dough (see doughs p. 722). Fill a buttered *savarin* mould half full of dough and allow to rise. When it has risen well, bake in a hot oven, 425° F or Gas Mark 7. Boil sugar and water with lemon peel, vanilla pod and cinnamon to a syrup with a density of 25° when measured with the saccharometer. Strain the syrup and flavour it with a little lemon juice and rum. Place the *Savarins* in the hot syrup until they are fully soaked. Shortly before serving, pour a few drops of rum on each *savarin.* Serve hot or cold. Fill the centre with whipped cream and decorate with candied cherries and angelica. if the *Savarin* is to be served cold.

ASSORTED GÂTEAUX AND CAKES

This section includes a variety of cakes and *gâteaux* which cannot be classified according to foregoing sections. Indeed there is a recipe for *Turinois,* a chocolate and chestnut cake, which does not require any baking at all!

Gâteau Alcazar

For 6 persons: 4½ *oz ground almonds;* 4½ *oz sugar;* 2¼ *oz butter;* 3 *eggs; vanilla. Filling:* 3½ *oz ground almonds;* 3½ *oz sugar. Short pastry; apricot jam; pistachios.* Cooking time: 40-45 minutes.

Mix the ground almonds with the sugar. Add 2 yolks of egg and one whole egg, flavour with vanilla, and whip to a foam. Fold in two stiffly-beaten egg whites and finally the luke-warm butter. Grease a *moulé à manque* or use a deep sandich wtin and line with Short pastry, prick the base, and press edges off with a rolling pin. Spread a little apricot jam on

▲ Kugelhopf, p. 827

Couronne aux Amandes, p. 826 ▼

▲ *Gâteau Lémania, p. 852*

Brioches à Tête, p. 826 ▼

▲ *Small cakes made with puff pastry, pp. 823, 855-856*

Gâteau Niçois, p. 822 ▼

▲ *Gâteau Moka, p. 818*

Gâteau Mexicain, p. 818 ▼

▲ Gâteau Mascotte, p. 825

Gâteau Moka, p. 818 ▼

▲ Zuger Kirschtorte, p. 854

Gâteau Caravelle, p. 850 ▼

▲ Gâteau Hongrois, p. 817

Schwarzwälder Kirschtorte, p. 853 ▼

▲ *Gâteau Zigomar, p. 854*

Gâteau Lutétia, p. 824 ▼

▲ *Dobos Torta, p. 851*

Gâteau Caraque, p. 823 ▼

▲ *Bûche de Noël, p. 819*

Le Croquembouche, p. 878 ▶
Frankfurter Kranz, p. 851 ▼

▲ *A selection of small cakes,* *pp. 857-861* ▼

▲ *Bretzels Fondants, p. 858*

A selection of small cakes, pp. 857-861 ▼

▲ *Plain and almond petits fours, pp. 866-870*

Iced petit fours, p. 870 ▼

▼ Confectionery, pp. 872-876 ▼

the bottom and fill with the almond mixture. Bake in a moderate oven, 375° F or Gas Mark 4-5. Meanwhile prepare Almond paste with pounded or finely ground almonds, mixed with sugar and egg white, added little by little. This should make a fairly soft paste. Take the cake out of the tin and pipe a criss-cross pattern on top with the Almond paste, using a piping bag and a star tube. Place the cake in a hot oven for a few minutes to brown the surface. Brush immediately with very thick, hot strained apricot jam, and place half a very green blanched pistachio in each square.

Gâteau Fédora

For 8 persons: 5½ oz icing sugar; 3½ oz ground almonds; 2 whole eggs; 3 egg yolks; 3 stiffly beaten egg whites; 1 fl oz Kirsch; 2½ oz flour; 3½ oz melted butter; 3½ oz candied cherries; 6 oz cherries in brandy; 8 oz apricot jam; ½ pint Kirsch fondant; chopped roasted almonds. Cooking time: 40-45 minutes.

Soak the candied cherries in Kirsch. Whip the icing sugar, almonds, 2 whole eggs and Kirsch to a foam, then gently fold in the stiffly-beaten egg whites and the flour and lastly fold in the butter. Fill the mixture into a round, buttered, floured cake tin alternately with the cherries which have been soaked in Kirsch and bake in a moderate oven, 375° F or Gas Mark 4-5. When cold, cut across and fill with a fine *salpicon* of cherries in brandy, bound with jam to taste. Brush cake thinly with apricot jam and coat with Kirsch fondant. Coat 12 brandy cherries with left-over fondant: they must be drained and well dried first. Decorate the middle of the cake with a St. Andrew's Cross of roasted chopped almonds and the edge with brandy cherries.

▣ Guayaquil

For 8 persons: 3½ oz ground almonds; 3½ oz sugar; ½ oz flour; 5 egg whites; 1½ oz butter. Butter cream: 4½ oz butter; 5 oz thick Custard; 2 oz ground and sifted nougat. Chocolate cigarettes: 7 oz plain chocolate or couverture. 5 oz vermicelli. Cooking time: about 15 minutes.

Beat the egg whites stiffly, lightly fold in the flour and ground almonds, and finally the melted, barely lukewarm butter. Spread this mixture in three round bases about ⅛-inch thick and about 6 inches in diameter on a greased and floured baking sheet. Bake in a moderate to warm oven, 325° F-350° F or Gas Mark 3-4. Remove the rounds from the baking sheet, trim and place them on a flat surface to cool. Fill with layers of Praline butter cream, and coat sides with the same cream. Roll in chocolate vermicelli to coat the sides. Cover the top with Praline butter cream. Then place chocolate cigarettes tightly packed, against one another on top. Put two strips of paper on a slant on top, dredge with icing sugar, and lift off the strips of paper carefully. Chocolate cigarettes: Melt chocolate or *couverture* in a basin over a pan of water and mix well with a spatula. Do not beat because the *couverture* may produce bubbles and will become dull. Mix constantly until barely lukewarm (blood-heat) so that the *couverture* is not streaky or grey, when it gets cold. Spread on a marble slab and cool until the *couverture* no longer sticks to the finger when tested. Now, hold a large knife upright vertically on the chocolate, and holding with both hands, pull it along the top of the *couverture*. The top will now become loose and form thin cigarette-shaped layers. If it gets too cold the *couverture* will break up and may be melted again.

Gâteaux Napolitain

For 8 persons: 9 oz flour; 5½ oz ground almonds; 5½ oz butter; 5½ oz icing sugar; 2 small eggs; 1 pinch salt; the zest of a lemon. Cooking time: 7-8 minutes.

Make Neapolitan almond pastry and roll out ⅛-inch thick. Cut out 8 discs, using a round cutter about 6½ inches across and cut out the centres with a round cutter; the rings should be about the width of 2 fingers. Also cut out 2 slightly larger discs and do not cut out the centre. Put rings and circles on a baking sheet, prick lightly and bake in a hot oven, 400° F or Gas Mark 6. When cold, sandwich the rings with thickly reduced, strained apricot jam. Fasten to one of the bases with jam, brush with jam all round and decorate with candied fruit or piped icing. Pile a mound of Confectioners' custard or vanilla-flavoured whipped cream in the middle, put the remaining circle on top, brush with jam and decorate in the same way as the sides. The height of the cake can be changed by varying the number of rings used.

▣ aux Noisettes * *Nut Cake*

For 8 persons: 4½ oz butter; 10½ oz sugar; 5 eggs; 4½ oz each ground almonds and walnuts; 2¾ oz sifted flour; 1 fl oz Kirsch. Cooking time: 30-35 minutes.

Whip the butter and sugar to a foam and add the whole eggs one by one. Add the Kirsch, ground almonds and walnuts and finally fold in the flour. Fill into a round, buttered and floured cake tin after covering the bottom with a circle of greased paper and bake in a moderate oven, 350° F or Gas Mark 3-4. Do not turn out until quite cold and dust with icing sugar.

Turinois * *Unbaked Chocolate Chestnut Cake*

For 8 persons: 1 lb chestnuts; 3½ oz butter; 3½ oz grated chocolate; 3½ oz vanilla sugar.

Peel and cook the chestnuts (see p. 875), drain them well and rub through a sieve. While still hot, mix thoroughly with the butter, sugar and grated chocolate till very smooth. Fill this mixture into a lined cake tin, square if possible. Press down smoothly and put in a refrigerator for several hours to cool. When set, turn out and slice with a knife dipped in hot water.

TARTS AND FLANS

These are usually made of Short Crust pastry, but Flaky pastry is sometimes used for apple and rhubarb tarts. Flans are composed of fruit with Custard cream, Confectioner's cream or fresh cream. They are more elaborate than tarts which use only fruit.

Lining a Flan Ring—Tarts and flans should be baked in a ring and not in a round tin; the latter are often too thin and bend in heat; it is also difficult to take out the flan without breaking it. Rings have the advantage that after baking they can be easily removed without danger of damaging the flan. When lining the ring, proceed as follows. Place the ring on a thick baking sheet. Roll out Sweet pastry about 1½-inch thick and in the shape of a rough circle. Roll the pastry round a rolling pin, unroll over the greased ring, line it and press it down well into the corners. Roll the rolling pin over the edge of the ring to cut off superfluous pastry. Roll these trimmings into a thin sausage shape, moisten with a little water, fasten to the inside edge of the lined ring and pinch all round. Prick the bottom several times with a fork. If the pastry case is to be baked without filling, line with a large circle of paper and fill with dried peas or crusts. This is called "baking blind".

Tarte aux Abricots * *Apricot Tart*

For 8 persons: 1 lb Sweet pastry or Puff pastry; 2½ lb fresh apricots; ¼ lb icing sugar; strained apricot jam. Cooking time: 25-30 minutes.

Line a flan ring with the pastry, prick, dust bottom lightly with icing sugar and fill with halved, stoned apricots, lightly flattened and overlapping slightly. Bake in a moderate oven, 375° F or Gas Mark 5. When cooked glaze at once with thick, hot apricot jam.

▣ à l'Ananas * *Pineapple*

For 10-12 persons: 10 oz butter; 10 oz sugar; 8 egg yolks; 8 whites of egg; 8 oz flour; 10 oz chopped pineapple; 12 oz Sweet pastry; 3½ oz apricot jam; 7 oz Fondant; crystallised pineapple. Cooking time: 30 minutes.

Line flan rings with Sweet pastry as for Apricot tart and fill with the following mixture: Beat the butter with half the sugar, add egg yolks one by one. Beat the whites stiffly with remainder of the sugar. Mix these two together with the flour, pineapple and jam and bake in a moderate oven, 375° F or Gas Mark 5. Mask with apricot *purée* and spread with pale yellow fondant. Decorate with pieces of pineapple.

▣ aux Cerises * *Cherry*

For 8 persons: 1 lb Sweet pastry; 2 lb stoned cherries; ¼ lb icing sugar; ½ lb redcurrant jelly. Cooking time: 25-30 minutes.

Put a flan ring on a baking sheet, line it with the pastry, pinch the edge, prick the bottom several times and dust lightly with icing sugar. Place the cherries closely together with the hole (left by stoning) facing down and bake in a moderately hot oven, 375° F or Gas Mark 4-5. After 10 minutes reduce the heat slightly. When cooked, dust heavily with vanilla-flavoured icing sugar or, better still, glaze with strained redcurrant jelly. This flan can also be made from tinned cherries.

▣ aux Fraises * *Strawberry*

For 8 persons: 1 lb Sweet pastry; 2 lb strawberries; ½ lb redcurrant jelly. Cooking time: 20-25 minutes.

Line a ring with Sweet pastry and then place another ring of pastry about ¾-inch wide on the edge. Flute the edge of the flan. Bake blind, i.e. line with paper, and fill with dried peas or broken rice, which can be used again and again, and bake in a moderate oven, 375° F or Gas Mark 5. Remove paper and peas and when cold fill with strawberries of the same size. Mask with redcurrant jelly. Do not fill too early, otherwise the fruit juice will soak the pastry. Most fruit tarts are baked with the filling; it is only in case of soft fruit such as strawberries, raspberries, blackberries, etc., that they are baked blind. (*See illustration p.* 761).

NOTE: To stop the bottom of the tart becoming soaked when soft fruit is used, sprinkle fine, stale cake or rusk crumbs on the bottom before filling; they will absorb the moisture.

Tarte aux Oranges * *Orange Tart*

For 8 persons: 1 lb Sweet or Puff pastry; 2 lb orange segments; apricot jam; orange and crystallised cherries. Cooking time: 25-30 minutes.

Make a Puff pastry case, or line a flan ring with Sweet pastry, bake blind in a moderate oven, 375° F or Gas Mark 5. When the pastry is cool, put in the orange segments from which pith, pips and skin have been removed. Glaze with a covering of hot apricot *purée*. Decorate with pieces of orange and crystallised cherries. Never decorate this tart in advance because the pastry will become soft. (*See illustration p.* 760).

⊡ aux Poires * *Pear*

For 8 persons: 1 lb Sweet pastry; 1 lb thick apple purée; 4 pears; red wine; sugar; 3½ oz redcurrant jelly. Cooking time: 25 minutes.

Line a ring with Sweet pastry and flute the edge. Prick the base with a fork and fill with apple *purée* and bake in a moderate oven, 375° F or Gas Mark 4. Meanwhile, peel the pears, cut them in half and scoop out the core. Poach them in sweetened red wine. Drain well and arrange them on top of the apple *purée*, pressing them down a little. Coat generously with strained redcurrant jelly.

⊡ aux Pommes à l'Anglaise * *English Apple*

For 6-8 persons: 1 lb Sweet pastry; 1 lb thick apple purée; 3 large cooking apples; ¼ lb apricot jam. Cooking time: 25-30 minutes.

Line a greased ring with Sweet pastry, keeping the rim a little thicker than the sides and base. Pinch it with a pastry cutter and make a design all around the edge. Fill with cold apple *purée* and smooth the top. Cover completely with thin slices of apples cut in half moons and overlapping one another. Bake in a hot oven, 400° F or Gas Mark 6. When baked, spread a thin layer of apricot jam on top or dredge with icing sugar.

⊡ aux Pommes Grillagée * *Trellised Apple*

For 6 persons: 1 lb Sweet pastry; 1 lb thick, cold apple purée; 1 egg; ¼ lb redcurrant jelly. Cooking time: 25 minutes.

Line a plain ring and trim off the pastry at the edge. Fill up to the top with lightly sweetened apple *purée*. Cut the remaining Sweet pastry into strips and arrange them in a trellis on top. Press down well at the edges. Brush with egg on top and bake in a hot oven, 400° F or Gas Mark 6. After baking, brush the top with redcurrant jelly. Serve cold, decorated with whipped cream if desired. (*See illustration p.* 760).

⊡ aux Pommes Meringuée * *Apple Meringue*

For 8 persons: 1 lb Short pastry; 1 lb thick apple purée. Meringue: *2 egg whites; 3½ oz icing sugar; 3 oz redcurrant jelly; 3 oz apricot jam.* Cooking time: 25 minutes for the tart, 3-4 minutes to brown the meringue.

Line the greased flan ring with Short pastry, prick the base, and press edges off with a rolling pin. Fill with apple *purée* and bake in a moderately hot oven, 375° F or Gas Mark 5. Coat fairly thickly with meringue and smooth top and sides. Pipe a diamond pattern and on top, pipe a scallop border. Dredge with icing sugar and place the tart in a hot oven, 400° F or Gas Mark 6, to crisp the meringue and to brown it lightly. Finally fill the cavities alternately with redcurrant jelly and apricot jam. (*See illustration p.* 761).

Tarte aux Quetsches * *Plum Tart*

For 8 persons: *1 lb Short pastry; 2 lb plums; 3 oz icing sugar; 7 oz red-currant jelly.* Cooking time: 20-25 minutes.

Line the ring with Short pastry, fill with halved, stoned and slightly flattened plums and overlap them slightly. Bake in a moderate oven, 350° F or Gas Mark 4, and mask with red-currant jelly when cooked.

▣ aux Reines-Claudes * *Greengage*

Make in the same way as Plum tart, but mask with apricot jam to blend with their colour.

▣ à la Rhubarbe * *Rhubarb*

For 8 persons: *1 lb Short or Sweet pastry; 2 lb rhubarb; 5 oz icing sugar; 7 oz apricot jam.* Cooking time: 30-35 minutes.

Peel the rhubarb, cut in 1-inch pieces and macerate with the sugar for 1 hour. Drain very thoroughly before filling the tart, bake in a moderate oven, 375° F or Gas Mark 4, and mask with apricot jam.

FLAN * *SPECIAL FLANS*

▣ à l'Andalouse * *Orange*

For 8 persons: *1 lb Short pastry; 1¼ pints of orange Confectioners' custard; 7 oz Orange fondant; 2 pieces of candied orange peel.* Cooking time: 25 minutes.

Line the ring with Short pastry, prick it and fill with Confectioners' custard heavily flavoured with orange. Bake in a moderately hot oven, 375° F or Gas Mark 5, and spread with Orange fondant when cold. Decorate with pieces of candied orange peel.

▣ à la Frangipane * *Frangipan*

For 8 persons: *1 lb Short pastry; 1½ lb Frangipan cream; 2 oz ground almonds.* Cooking time: 25 minutes.

Fill the pastry-lined flan ring with Frangipan cream mixed with ground almonds. Do not fix a roll of pastry round the edge but cover with a lattice of crimp-edged strips of pastry. Bake in a moderate oven, 375° F or Gas Mark 4.

▣ au Lait * *Plain Custard*

For 8 persons: *1 lb Short pastry; 2 eggs; 3½ oz sugar; 2 oz flour; ½ pint cold milk.* Cooking time: 25-30 minutes.

Line ring in the usual way, fill with a mixture of the beaten eggs, flour, sugar and milk poured through a strainer. Bake in a moderate oven, 350° F or Gas Mark 4.

Flan au Lait à l'Alsacienne * *Alsatian Custard Flan*

For 8 persons: 1 lb Short pastry; 4 eggs; $3\frac{1}{2}$ oz sugar; vanilla; $\frac{1}{2}$ pint milk; 10 oz apples; 1 oz butter. Cooking time: 30-35 minutes.

Slice the peeled apples, simmer in butter and cool. Line the flan ring in the usual way, cover the bottom with apples, add vanilla-flavoured custard mixture and bake in a moderate oven, 350° F or Gas Mark 3-4.

FOREIGN SPECIALITIES

Apfelstrudel * *Apple Strudel*

For 10 persons: $\frac{1}{2}$ lb strong bread flour (rich in gluten); $\frac{3}{4}$ oz butter or lard; $\frac{1}{2}$ small egg; pinch salt; $\frac{1}{8}$-$\frac{1}{4}$ pint water as required; $1\frac{3}{4}$-2 lb apples; 3 oz cinnamon sugar; 3 oz sultanas; 3 oz toasted white breadcrumbs; 3 oz butter. Cooking time: about 35 minutes.

Beat the egg and add about half the water, mix with the flour to make a soft dough, adding more water if necessary. Beat thoroughly on a floured board until it leaves the hands clean and is of an elastic consistency. Shape into a ball, brush with oil, cover and let it rest for 45 minutes. Now put a large cloth on a table so that it hangs down over the edge, dredge heavily with flour, brush the ball of dough with oil once more and roll into a thick wide strip with the rolling pin. Brush the fingers with oil, catch hold of the middle of the dough from underneath and pull it outwards all round the table in turn until it reaches the edges of the table and the thicker edges hang slightly over it. The dough must be paper thin, smooth and transparent without holes. Peel, core and thinly slice the apples and spread them over the dough, leaving a long edge of about 6 inches free. Distribute them evenly, sprinkle with plenty of cinnamon sugar, the sultanas, breadcrumbs and finally with plenty of melted butter. After filling, cut off thick edges of dough and with the help of the raised cloth, roll the whole into a long sausage shape. Place it on a baking sheet; if it is too long, shape it into a horseshoe. Brush well with butter and bake golden brown at 375° F or Gas Mark 5. Dust with icing sugar, cut into strips two fingers wide and serve hot or cold. *(Austria)*

Caravelle * *Caravelle Sponge Gâteau*

For 10 persons: 5 eggs; $\frac{1}{4}$ lb sugar; 3 oz flour; 1 oz cocoa; 2 oz melted butter; $\frac{3}{4}$ lb Chocolate butter cream; 5 oz plain chocolate or couverture; 2 oz chocolate vermicelli.

Prepare a *Génoise* base. When cold, sandwich with two layers of butter cream, mask sides with the same cream and roll the sides in the chocolate vermicelli. Coat the top with butter cream. Melt the chocolate and pour on to a sheet of rice paper; when cold cut out in the shape of the flan. Heat a knife and divide the chocolate disc into 16 equal parts. Place these triangles on top, each one slightly tilted. Pipe a little cream under each to maintain the tilt. Pipe a whirl of cream in the centre. (*See illustration p.* 834). *(Switzerland)*

Cramique * *Belgian Fruit Loaf*

For 6 persons: 9 oz flour; 2 oz butter; 2 egg yolks; $\frac{1}{3}$ oz yeast; 1 oz icing sugar; $1\frac{1}{2}$ oz currants; $1\frac{1}{2}$ oz sultanas; 4 fl oz milk. Cooking time: 40 minutes.

Put the yeast in the middle of 2 oz flour, pour warm milk on top, stir into a very soft dough with the fingers and cover with the remaining flour. Put in a warm place and when the flour rises add the egg yolks, sugar, a pinch of salt and liquid butter and beat by hand till the dough no longer sticks to the fingers. Put in a warm place to rise for 1 hour, then mix with currants and sultanas. Half fill a buttered tin with the mixture, let it rise, brush the top with milk and bake in a hot oven, 400° F or Gas Mark 6. *(Belgium)*

Dobos Torta * *Hungarian Torte*

For 8 persons: 10 *eggs;* 14 *oz sugar;* 7 *oz flour;* ½ *oz vanilla sugar; zest of lemon; juice of lemon;* 10 *oz Chocolate butter cream.* Cooking time: 8-10 minutes.

Beat the yolks with half the sugar, the vanilla sugar, a few drops of lemon juice and a tablespoon of water. Beat the 10 whites into a snow with 2 oz sugar and a little lemon zest. Carefully mix whites and yolks and flour together. Grease the baking trays and stencil out 6 circles about ¼-inch thick and 6 inches in diameter. Bake at once in a moderate oven, 375° F or Gas Mark 5. The discs must be crisp and of equal size. When baked trim each round and place five together with the butter cream between each and as a coating round the sides. Prepare the sixth one for the top as follows: make a pale caramel with 5 oz sugar and the juice of half a lemon, stirring continuously. Pour this hot caramel on to the disc and cut with a greased knife into 8 or 10 pieces. Pipe whirls of butter cream from the centre to the edge. Arrange the segments on the top, slightly tilted. (*See illustration p.* 837).
(*See Illustrated Culinary Techniques*). *(Hungary)*

Dresdner Stollen * *Fermented Fruit Loaf*

For 10-12 *persons:* 1 *lb flour;* 1¼-1½ *oz yeast;* 3½ *oz sugar;* 7 *oz soft butter;* 2 *eggs;* 2 *egg yolks; zest of half a lemon;* 1 *pinch each grated nutmeg, mace and cloves;* 2 *oz sultanas;* 2 *oz currants;* 1 *oz each finely chopped candied orange and lemon peel; a little lukewarm milk; butter for brushing; icing sugar;* ¼ *oz salt;* 5 *ground bitter almonds;* 1¾ *oz ground sweet almonds.* Cooking time: 45-60 minutes.

Make a ferment with 4½ oz flour, 1¼ oz yeast and a little lukewarm milk. Place the remaining sifted flour on to a pastry board and make a well. Put the ferment, eggs, egg yolks, zest of lemon, spices, sugar and soft butter in it and knead into a firm dough. Work in the sultanas, currants and finely diced candied peel, mix well once more, let the dough rise again and work through again. Shape into a high, narrow, longish loaf, indent one side slightly by hand, let it rise once more and bake in a moderate oven, 375° F or Gas Mark 5. As soon as it is cooked, brush with plenty of hot, melted butter and dust twice generously with icing sugar. Do not eat for 48 hours. Wrapped in cellophane, these loaves will keep fresh for several weeks. *(Germany)*

Frankfurter Kranz * *Frankfurt Ring*

5 *oz sugar;* ¼ *lb butter;* 4 *eggs;* 3 *oz flour;* 3 *oz cornflour; a little baking powder;* 1 *lemon. For decoration:* 12 *oz Vanilla butter cream;* 7 *oz praline;* 10 *glacé cherries;* 20 *pistachio nuts.* Cooking time: 40 minutes.

Cream the sugar and soft butter well. Beat in the eggs one at a time. Add the sieved flour, cornflour and baking powder together with the lemon zest. Place this mixture into a tall, circular *savarin* mould and bake in a moderate oven, 350° F or Gas Mark 4. Leave to cool. Slice into four and sprinkle with rum, Kirsch or Grand-Marnier. Sandwich all together with butter cream. Cover with butter cream and sprinkle with crushed praline. Decorate with butter cream whirls and place the half cherries and pistachio nuts on top.
(*See illustration p.* 838). *(Germany)*

Gâteau Lémania

Pastry: 2 *fl oz milk;* ¼ *oz yeast; sugar;* ¼ *lb flour;* 1 *oz butter. For* 6 *oz Hollandaise filling:* 1½ *oz sugar;* 1½ *oz butter;* 1½ *oz blanched almonds;* 1 *oz flour;* 1 *egg; lemon zest.* 3 *oz fresh cherries, stones removed; a few glacé cherries cut in halves; icing sugar*. Cooking time: 30 minutes.

Prepare Pastry as for *Croissant* dough (see p. 721). To make the Hollandaise mixture beat together the butter and half the sugar, pound the almonds and remaining sugar. Combine these two mixtures with the egg and lemon zest and add the flour.

Line a flan ring with the pastry; half fill with *Hollandaise* mixture. Add the stoned cherries, and cover with remainder of *Hollandaise* mixture. Bake in a hot oven, 400° F or Gas Mark 6. When baked, turn cakes over to flatten them. Leave to cool. Place three strips of paper on top. Dust with icing sugar and carefully remove the strips. Finish with *glacé* cherries. (*See illustration p.* 830). (*Switzerland*)

Linzer Torte

7 *oz flour; pinch cinnamon;* 7 *oz butter;* 7 *oz icing sugar;* 7 *egg yolks;* 7 *oz blanched ground almonds;* 3 *oz unstrained redcurrant jam; the zest of a quarter lemon.* Cooking time: 45 minutes.

Cream the butter and mix with the icing sugar. Beat in 4 raw eggs and add 3 hardboiled egg yolks passed through a sieve, the zest, almonds and flour. Fill into a round greased and floured sandwich tin and bake in a moderate oven, 375° F or Gas Mark 5. When cold, sandwich with jam and dust with icing sugar. (*Austria*)

Moques

9 *oz flour;* 5 *oz butter;* 3 *oz brown sugar;* ½ *oz baking powder;* 1 *egg; a pinch of powdered cinnamon and aniseed.* Cooking time: about 10 minutes.

Mix all the ingredients into a paste, without working it too much and make into a long roll. Keep in a cool place till next day, then cut into slices ¼-inch thick, brush with egg and bake in a hot oven, 400° F or Gas Mark 6. (*Belgium*)

Panettone

For 8-10 *persons:* 21 *oz flour;* 7 *oz butter;* 5 *oz sugar;* ½ *oz salt;* 10 *egg yolks;* 5 *oz sultanas;* 3 *oz candied citron; zest of* 1 *lemon;* 1½ *oz yeast.* Cooking time: 35-40 minutes.

Spread the flour in a circle, make a well in the centre and put in the salt, sugar, 7 egg yolks, 6 oz butter and the yeast. Mix these ingredients together in the centre with a little warm water, then gradually incorporate the flour very slowly. Then beat the dough until it becomes elastic and leaves the hands, spread in a layer, sprinkle with a little castor sugar, add the 2 yolks of egg and the rest of the softened butter, sprinkle with sultanas and diced peel and blend the dough together for a few minutes. Mould the dough into two or three round pieces; leave on a table covered with a cloth for about 15 minutes. Then mould the pieces and put into deep hoops, 7 inches diameter, 6 inches deep, lined with oiled paper bands or roll into a ball and put in a buttered, floured baking tin. Leave to rise. Brush with the remaining egg yolk mixed with a little castor sugar, cut the top crossways, sprinkle with a little granulated sugar and bake in a hot oven, 375° F-400° F or Gas Mark 5-6. (*Italy*)

Plumcake

For 8 persons: 4 oz sultanas; 4 oz currants; 2 oz each chopped, candied orange and lemon peel; 4 oz sugar; 4 oz butter; 3 eggs; 5 oz flour; 1 oz ground almonds; the zest of ½ lemon and ½ orange; 1 large pinch each cinnamon, clove and mace powder; 1 fl oz rum; ½ teaspoon baking powder. Cooking time: 45-60 minutes.

Steep sultanas and currants in water and blanch candied peel. Drain well and macerate with rum, grated lemon and orange rind and spices. Cream the butter and sugar, add the beaten yolks and 2 oz flour and 1 oz ground almonds. Fold in the stiffly whisked whites and at the same time the rest of the flour, mixed with baking powder and sieved, as well as the macerated fruits with their liquor. Fill in to a greased, rectangular tin, lined with greased paper; the paper should be about an inch higher than the edges of the tin. Plum cake may also be baked in round cake tins. Bake in a warm oven, 350° F or Gas Mark 3-4. *(Great Britain)*

Sachertorte

For 6 persons: 5 oz vanilla-flavoured chocolate; 5 oz sugar; 5 oz flour; 6 eggs; 3 oz apricot jam; 7 oz Chocolate fondant. Cooking time: about 30 minutes.

Break the chocolate and melt in a *bain marie*. Beat up the yolks of egg with the sugar and mix with the melted, slightly warm chocolate. Carefully add the stiffly beaten whites and the flour. Pour into a paper-lined *torte* ring or sandwich tins. Bake in a warm oven, 350° F or Gas Mark 3. When cold, turn out, brush with apricot *purée* and coat with Chocolate fondant. This cake is always served with whipped dairy cream. *(Austria)*

Schwarzwälder Kirschtorte * *Black Forest Cherry Cake*

For 12-14 persons: 8 yolks of egg; 1 egg; 7 oz sugar; 3 oz sponge cake crumbs; 3 oz ground almonds; 1½ oz cocoa; 2 oz flour; 8 whites of egg; 14 oz Morello cherries, stoned; 1½ pints dairy cream; 1 oz Kirsch; a little chocolate; cornflour or arrowroot. Cooking time: about 25 minutes.

Beat yolks of egg and egg with the sugar and a tablespoon of warm water. Add the crumbs and ground almonds and then the stiffly beaten whites, followed by the sieved flour and cocoa. Pour into a round sandwich tin, greased and floured, 10 inches in diameter. Bake in a moderate oven, 375° F or Gas Mark 5. When baked and cold, slice into three. Put the cold cherries cooked and bound together with cornflour on one of these layers, then another layer on top and cover with Kirsch-flavoured whipped dairy cream. Put on the third slice. Cover with the same cream. Decorate the edge and sides with chocolate shavings. Pipe rosettes of cream inside the top edge. Place chocolate shavings in the centre. Dust with icing sugar, and arrange the cherries. (*See illustration p.* 835). *(Germany)*

Scones

1 lb flour; ¾ oz baking powder; 3 oz butter; 2 oz sugar; pinch of salt; ½ pint cold milk; pinch of nutmeg; 2 oz sultanas (if desired). Cooking time: about 15 minutes.

Rub the butter finely into the sieved flour, baking powder, salt and nutmeg. Add the sugar and sultanas and mix to a soft moist dough with the milk. Knead very lightly. Divide into rounds, flatten to about 6 inches diameter and $\frac{3}{4}$-inch thick. Mark into four and arrange on a floured baking sheet. Wash with egg. Bake at 425° F or Gas Mark 7.

For Tea Scones, the dough is rolled to about $\frac{1}{2}$-inch thick and small scones are cut out with a plain $2\frac{1}{2}$-inch cutter. These are also egg washed. Bake at 450° F or Gas Mark 7-8. Cooking time: 10-15 minutes. *(Great Britain)*

Tresse Suisse * *Swiss Plait*

For 8 persons: 21 *oz flour;* 5 *oz butter;* $\frac{1}{2}$ *pint milk;* 2 *eggs;* $\frac{1}{4}$ *oz salt and* 1 *oz yeast; sugar to taste.* Cooking time: 30-35 minutes.

Make a medium-firm dough with the flour, the yeast dissolved in lukewarm milk, eggs, salt and sugar and put in a warm place to rise. When well risen, work in the soft butter by hand. Cut the dough into two equal parts and roll out to about 10 inches in length. Plait the two strands into a tail as wide as possible and somewhat pointed at the end. Allow to rise for 30 minutes, brush with egg and bake in a hot oven, 425° F or Gas Mark 7.

(Switzerland)

Weggli * *Milk Rolls*

1 *lb flour;* 3 *oz butter;* $\frac{1}{2}$ *pint cold milk;* 1 *oz yeast;* $\frac{1}{4}$ *oz salt.* Cooking time: 12-15 minutes.

Mix the yeast in the milk, stir in a little flour and leave overnight. Add rest of flour, butter, pinch of salt and if necessary a little more milk to make a firm dough. Mould into small oval shapes and leave to rise for an hour in a warm place. Brush the top with milk, slit carefully with a sharp blade and bake in a very hot oven, 450° F or Gas Mark 8.

(Switzerland)

Zigomar

For 10 *persons:* 5 *egg yolks;* 3 *egg whites;* 3 *oz sugar;* 2 *oz couverture or chocolate;* $1\frac{1}{2}$ *oz flour;* 8 *oz Pistachio butter cream;* 3 *oz Chocolate butter cream;* 5 *oz couverture or chocolate.* Cooking time: 30 minutes.

Whip the egg yolks and sugar together. Add the *couverture* which has been melted and mixed with a little warm water. Fold in the stiffly whipped whites and the flour. Bake in a well-greased and floured sandwich tin in a moderate oven, 375° F or Gas Mark 5. When cold, slice into three and sandwich with Pistachio butter cream. Cover thinly with Chocolate butter cream. Cool and cover with melted *couverture.* Decorate with a border and a large Z. (*See illustration p.* 836). *(Switzerland)*

Zuger Kirschtorte

For 10 *persons:* 1 *lb round Génoise base; Japanese meringue mixture, made of* 4 *egg whites;* 4 *oz sugar;* 8 *oz ground almonds;* 1 *oz flour.* 7 *oz Butter cream;* 2 *oz roasted almonds;* 1 *oz icing sugar.*

Pipe meringue mixture into two circular spiral bases on to greased and floured baking sheets, using a savoy bag and plain pipe. Bake for 15 minutes at 350° F or Gas Mark 3-4. Dip the *Génoise* base in Kirsch syrup (one-third Kirsch) and drain on a wire tray. Place the *Génoise* between the two baked meringue circles, sandwich together with Butter cream. Cool, then spread the sides with Butter cream, roll in roasted almonds and dust the top with icing sugar, decorating with a few almonds coloured green in the centre.
(*See illustration p.* 834). *(Switzerland)*

Small Cakes and Pastries

SMALL CAKES MADE WITH PUFF PASTRY

These cakes may be made with Puff pastry trimmings left over from a previous batch of pastry.

Bâtons Glacés

Roll out some Puff pastry in an oblong ⅛-inch thick and spread a thin layer of Royal icing on top. Use a pastry wheel to cut up into small oblong pieces and moisten the wheel frequently with water so that the icing does not stick to it. Put the *bâtons* on a baking sheet, leave the icing to dry and bake in the oven at 375° F or Gas Mark 5. (*See illustration p.* 831).

Condé

Cut ⅛-inch thick Puff pastry into strips 3-4 inches wide. Brush with Royal icing mixed with plenty of finely chopped or ground almonds. Cut pieces about 2 inches wide with a knife dipped in hot water and place them on a baking sheet. Bake 12 minutes. To prevent top from caramelising bake low down in a moderate oven, 375° F or Gas Mark 5.

Cornets Feuilletés à la Crème * *Cream Horns*

Roll out Puff pastry or Puff pastry trimmings 1/12 inch thick and cut into strips 2 inches wide and 7-8 inches long. Wrap these strips round moistened cream horn tins, overlapping the edges slightly. Place on a baking sheet, brush with egg and bake 10-12 minutes in a hot oven, 400° F or Gas Mark 6. Remove from tins while still hot and when cold fill with whipped cream or Confectioners' custard to taste.

NOTE: They can also be served hot, filled with scrambled egg or various minced mixtures or cold as *hors d'œuvre* filled with fine *purées*, caviar, etc. The pastry must then be unsweetened.

Couques ou Langues de Bœuf * *Ox Tongues or Puff Pastry Ovals*

Roll out Puff pastry ⅛ inch thick and cut out biscuits about 2 inches across with a crimped cutter. Sprinkle a little castor sugar on a marble slab and lengthen the rounds into an oval by rolling over them once. Place on a baking sheet, sugared side up, and bake 7-8 minutes in a hot oven, 400° F or Gas Mark 6. (*See illustration p.* 831).

Fers à Cheval * *Horse Shoes*

Roll out Puff pastry into strips about 6 inches wide, ⅛-inch thick and as long as necessary. Cut into triangles. Spoon or pipe a little apricot jam in the centre and fold up from the base so that the jam cannot come out when baking. Brush with egg, sprinkle with sugar and place in the shape of a horse shoe on a baking sheet. Bake in a hot oven, 400° F or Gas Mark 6 for 10-15 minutes. (*See illustration p.* 831).

Mille-Feuilles

Roll out Puff pastry very thinly, cut strips 3-4 inches long, prick and bake at 400° F or Gas Mark 6. Place 3 strips on top of one another, filling with *Bourdaloue* cream with ground almonds, press down slightly, dust top heavily with icing sugar and cut carefully into 1½-inch strips with a saw-edged knife.

Palmiers Glacés

Roll Puff pastry into a square dusting with castor sugar instead of flour. Roll in both directions to flatten it, fold over on itself so that the two ends join in the centre, then fold over as if closing an open book. This gives a strip four layers thick. Cut into ¼-inch slices and place, cut side down, on a greased baking sheet a little distance from each other. Bake at 400° F or Gas Mark 6, for 10-12 minutes, turning them over after a few minutes so that the sugar underneath does not caramelise. Puff pastry trimmings may be used to make *Palmiers*. (*See illustration p.* 831, *and Illustrated Culinary Techniques*).

Puits d'Amour * *Sweet Vol-au-Vents*

Cut out some round pieces of Puff pastry with a fluted pastry cutter about 1½ inches in diameter. Place these on a moistened baking sheet and brush them with water. Cover with smaller circles of Puff pastry from which the centres have been removed so as to form a crown. Brush the tops with egg and bake at 425° F or Gas Mark 6-7 for 8 to 10 minutes. The result is a type of *vol-au-vent* which may be filled with a little redcurrant jelly.

Sacristains

Roll out 4 oz of scrap Puff pastry into a strip the width of a hand and ⅛-inch thick. Brush with beaten egg, sprinkle with finely chopped almonds and dust with icing sugar. Cut up into fingers and, taking an end in each hand, twist them like corkscrews; next place them on a baking sheet and bake at 400° F or Gas Mark 6, for 5 minutes.

Viennois * *Viennese Puffs*

Roll out Puff pastry thinly and cut into 3-inch squares. Fill the middle with a small mound of Almond cream, Confectioners' custard or jam, fold the 4 corners over it, brush with egg, sprinkle with chopped almonds, dust with sugar and bake at 400° F or Gas Mark 6 for 10 minutes.

VARIOUS SMALL CAKES AND BISCUITS

This section includes a variety of plain sponge fingers which are served with ices and sweets and also used as a basis for *charlotte* puddings. There are also recipes for small iced cakes. biscuits and meringues.

Abricotines

Fill *Savarin* dough into very small, scalloped *barquette* moulds and put a small piece of candied apricot in the middle. Let it rise, bake at 400° F or Gas Mark 6. Soak with rum-flavoured Stock syrup and glaze with reduced, strained apricot jam.

Baguettes Flamandes

For 18 *fingers:* 4½ *oz sugar;* 4½ *oz flour;* 2 *oz chopped almonds;* 1 *egg;* 1 *egg yolk; vanilla.* Cooking time: 8 minutes.

Whip sugar, egg and egg yolk to a foam, fold in flour and vanilla and pipe pieces 1-inch wide and 3-4 inches long on to a greased and floured baking sheet using a plain pipe. Sprinkle with chopped almonds and bake in a moderate oven, 375° F or Gas Mark 5.

Biscuits à la Cuiller * *Sponge Fingers*

For the mixture (see *under Sponge Cake*, p. 713). Fill the mixture into a large savoy bag with a plain tube and pipe very straight fingers about 4 inches long on to a greased and floured baking sheet. Dust heavily with icing sugar and tilt baking sheet to shake off superfluous sugar. Bake until very dry at 375° F or Gas Mark 5 for 15-18 minutes, otherwise they quickly become soft. They can be made in advance and kept in a tin with a tight-fitting lid.

Biscuits de Reims * *Champagne Fingers*

For 18 *fingers:* 5½ *oz icing sugar;* 5½ *oz flour; pinch sodium bicarbonate; pinch cream of tartar;* 3 *eggs; vanilla.* Cooking time: 15 minutes.

Whip the eggs and sugar to a stiff sponge as for *Génoise*, add the sodium bicarbonate and cream of tartar; gently fold in the sifted flour and vanilla. Butter special moulds, known as Rheims sponge moulds, pipe mixture into them with a plain pipe and bake in a moderately hot oven, 375° F or Gas Mark 5. These sponges will keep fresh for some time.

Bouchées au Chocolat * *Chocolate Fingers*

Using a savoy bag and plain tube, pipe biscuits of Sponge Finger mixture the size of a macaroon and bake at 400° F or Gas Mark 6, for about 10 minutes without dusting with sugar. When cold, scoop out slightly, fill in pairs with Confectioners' custard or vanilla-flavoured whipped cream, coat with Chocolate fondant and put half a blanched almond on top.

Bretzels Fondants * *Fine Pretzels*

4½ oz flour; 2½ oz butter; ¾ oz sugar; 1 pinch crushed aniseed; 1 egg; 1 pinch salt. Cooking time: 7-8 minutes.

Mix all the ingredients into a paste and divide into pieces the size of a pigeon's egg. Roll each piece on a marble slab into 3-inch lengths with tapering ends. Shape into the form of a loose knot and secure ends with egg yolk. Brush with egg yolk, sprinkle with nibbed sugar and bake in a hot oven, 400° F or Gas Mark 6. Coat with chocolate or vanilla *Glacé* icing. (*See illustration p.* 841).

Caraques

Make small round bases of *Sablé* pastry and bake at 400° F or Gas Mark 6, and allow to cool. Sandwich with vanilla *Ganache* cream. Coat with Pistachio fondant, and place a tiny chocolate button in the centre. (*See illustration p.* 840).

Citrons

Cut out small round bases of *Sablé* paste (see p. 861), bake at 400° F or Gas Mark 6, and allow to cool. Pipe *Lemon* or *Citron* on top with chocolate *Glacé* icing.

Craquelins

4½ oz flour; 2¾ oz butter; ½ oz sugar; pinch of salt; 1 egg yolk; a little milk. Cooking time: 4-5 minutes.

Mix the ingredients on the marble slab without overworking the paste. Leave to stand and then roll out to a thickness of $\frac{1}{10}$ inch. Cut out into small squares, brush with egg yolk, trace lines on top with the tip of a knife and bake in a very hot oven, 450° F or Gas Mark 8. Dust with icing sugar.

Croquets de Bordeaux

4½ oz flour; 1¾ oz butter; 1¾ oz sugar; 2½ oz unblanched almonds; 1 egg; ½ teaspoon baking powder; vanilla; salt. Cooking time: 15-18 minutes.

Mix all ingredients together and when really well mixed, chop coarsely, to cut up the almonds. Roll the mixture into a large sausage-shape, place on a baking sheet, flatten lightly by hand, but keep it fairly rounded. Brush with egg yolk, score along the whole length with a knife and bake at 375° F or Gas Mark 5. It should rise slightly. After baking, cut into slices the thickness of a finger.

GALETTES * *BISCUITS*

⊡ Bretonnes

¼ lb flour; 2 oz butter; 2 oz currants; 1½ oz sugar; 1 egg; 1 pinch salt; 1 pinch cinnamon. Cooking time: 7-8 minutes.

Make paste as for *Nantes* biscuits, mould round balls the size of an egg and flatten slightly by hand. Brush with egg, score with a knife and sprinkle a few currants (as well as those in the dough) on each biscuit and bake at 400° F or Gas Mark 6. Other flavours can be used instead of cinnamon.

Galettes Nantaises * *Nantes Biscuits*

¼ lb flour; 2 oz butter; 2 oz sugar; 1½ oz ground almonds; 2 egg yolks; pinch salt. Cooking time: 7-8 minutes.

Mix all the ingredients into a smooth paste and allow to rest for 1 hour in a cool place. Roll out ⅛ inch thick, cut out small, round biscuits with a crimp cutter, place on a greased baking sheet, brush with egg and score crosswise with a fork. Sprinkle a pinch of ground almond in the middle, dust with icing sugar and bake at 400° F or Gas Mark 6.

▣ à l'Orange * *Orange*

3½ oz chopped almonds; 3½ oz icing sugar; 3½ oz finely chopped preserved orange peel; 2½ oz butter; 1 oz flour; 1 tablespoon milk; a few drops of carmine if liked. Cooking time: 5-6 minutes.

Cream the butter slightly, then stir for a few minutes with the sugar and add the almonds, chopped orange peel, sifted flour and milk. Place walnut-sized bulbs of the mixture on a greased baking sheet, flatten slightly with a moistened fork and bake in a hot oven, 400° F or Gas Mark 6. Do not remove from baking sheet till quite cold, since the biscuits are very fragile.

▣ Suisses * *Almond*

4½ oz flour; 4½ oz ground almonds; 4 oz sugar; 1½ oz butter; 1 egg; 3 egg yolks; vanilla; salt. Cooking time: 8-10 minutes.

Beat the almonds, sugar and egg yolks to a foam. Make a well in the flour, put the mixture in it together with the egg, vanilla and salt and work into a firm paste. Allow to rest for 1 hour, then roll out ⅛ inch thick. Cut out round biscuits, brush with egg, sprinkle with chopped almonds, dust with icing sugar and bake at 400° F or Gas Mark 6. Instead of chopped almonds a half almond may be placed on top.

Japonais

Make very small round bases of Japanese meringue mixed with ground hazelnuts and bake at 350° F or Gas Mark 4. Sandwich two bases with Praline butter cream, and coat top and sides thinly with the same cream. Roll top and sides in crushed, very dry meringue and pipe a dot of pink Fondant in the centre of the top. Place in paper cases. (*See illustration p.* 840).

Madeleines de Commercy

2 oz sugar; 2 oz flour; 2 eggs; vanilla; 1 oz butter. Cooking time: 10-15 minutes.

Whip eggs and sugar to a foam in a bowl. With a spatula, fold in first the flour, then the cool, melted butter and the vanilla. Lighly butter scalloped *madeleine* (shell) moulds and flour them, fill and bake in a hot oven, 400° F or Gas Mark 6.

Magali

Fill some pastry cases made of Milanese paste with *Ganache*. Coat the tops with warm Chocolate fondant and decorate the edges with ground, roasted almonds.

Marignan

Half-fill buttered *barquette* (boat-shaped) moulds with *Savarin* dough. Let it rise, bake at 425° F or Gas Mark 7, and while still hot soak with rum-flavoured Stock syrup. Cut a thin slice off the top, raise it at one side and pipe in a filling of vanilla-flavoured Italian meringue mixture, vanilla-flavoured whipped cream or any desired cream, using a fluted pipe.

Meringues Chantilly * *Meringues*

Fill a savoy bag fitted with a large plain pipe with Swiss meringue mixture and pipe ovals the size of half an egg on greased, floured baking sheets. They must not be too close together. Dust generously with icing sugar and after 1 minute tilt baking sheet to remove superfluous sugar. Dry rather than bake the meringue for 15-20 minutes at 250° F or Gas Mark 1 or, better still, in a hot cupboard. Remove them carefully from the baking sheet and scoop out or press in the soft inside. Replace on the baking sheet hollowed side up and return to cool oven till they are quite dry. They can be made a considerable time ahead provided they are kept in a tin with a close fitting lid.

Parfaits au Chocolat

Make small round bases of *Sablé* (Sand) paste and bake at 400° F or Gas Mark 6 and allow to cool. Sandwich two bases with Chocolate butter cream and leave to set. Coat top with *couverture* or melted chocolate and place half a very small blanched almond in the centre. (*See illustration p.* 840).

Pavés Moka * *Iced Moka Cakes*

Slice *Génoise* sponge about 1-inch thick and sandwich with Mocha butter cream. Place in the refrigerator to set the cream. Cut the cake into regular squares of about 1½ inches. Coat with Mocha fondant, decorate as desired and serve in paper cases. (*See illustration p.* 840).

Pomponettes au Kirsch

Butter small *dariole* moulds, place a deseeded raisin in the bottom of each, half-fill with *Savarin* dough, let it rise and bake at 400° F or Gas Mark 6, for 6-7 minutes. Soak with Kirsch-flavoured Stock syrup, drain and coat lightly with Kirsch fondant.

Réligieuses

Line tartlet moulds with Short pastry and bake blind for 10 minutes in a hot oven, 400° F or Gas Mark 6. For each tartlet bake a *Choux* pastry cream bun big enough to fit into the tartlet and 1 very tiny one as for *Gâteaux St Honoré*. Fill all the buns with Confectioners' custard and coat the large ones with Chocolate and the small ones with Coffee fondant. Have a little Coffee butter cream ready. Put a little Confectioners' custard into the bottom of each tartlet, put the larger cream bun on it and pipe a ring of Coffee butter cream round it with a star pipe. Place the smaller cream bun on top, also surround with butter cream and pipe a rosette of Coffee butter cream on top. (*See illustration p.* 841.)

Rochers aux Amandes * *Almond Rocks*

4 egg whites; 9 oz icing sugar; 4 oz finely shredded almonds; vanilla. Cooking time: 15-20 minutes.

Make Italian meringue mixture and add the almonds and vanilla powder. Place small piles of the mixture on a greased and floured baking sheet shaping them with a tablespoon to resemble rocks. Bake in a warm oven, 325° F or Gas Mark 3, until the outside is crusted but the inside remains soft. They can also be flavoured with chocolate, coffee or strawberries.

SABLÉS * *SABLE PASTE*

Sablé paste must not be over-mixed, especially in warm weather. The paste should be kept in a refrigerator or in a very cool place. The paste is baked in a hot oven, 400°-425° F or Gas Mark 6-7. Currants, roasted hazelnuts or even candied fruits may be added to *Sablé* paste. Moreover it can easily be flavoured with chocolate when making dominoes, chocolate *sablés*, etc.

4½ oz flour; 3 oz butter; 2 oz sugar; 2 hardboiled egg yolks passed through a sieve; pinch of salt; the zest of 1 lemon. Cooking time: 7-8 minutes.

Make a well in the flour, put in the other ingredients, mix and allow to rest for 2 hours. Roll out ⅛ inch thick and cut out small triangular cakes. Place on a greased baking sheet and bake without brushing with egg in a hot oven, 400° F or Gas Mark 6. If no triangular cutter is available, use a round one and cut circles into four wedges.

⊡ de Trouville

4½ oz flour; 3½ oz butter; 1¾ oz ground almonds; 2½ oz sugar; 2 egg yolks; 1 pinch salt; the zest of 1 lemon. Cooking time: 7-8 minutes.

Make paste as above but with raw egg yolks, cut out with a large, round cutter and cut each piece in 4. Brush with egg, score in squares with a knife and bake in a moderately hot oven, 375° F-400° F or Gas Mark 5-6.

Souvaroff

4½ oz flour; 3½ oz butter; 2 oz sugar; 1 pinch salt. Cooking time: 6-7 minutes.

Make a well in the flour, put in the melted butter, sugar and salt and mix lightly with the finger tips, so that the dough does not become sandy. Do not add water or egg. Allow to rest for 1 hour, then roll out ⅛ inch thick, cut out oval or oblong biscuits and bake at 400° F or Gas Mark 6. When cold, sandwich in pairs with redcurrant jelly and dust with icing sugar. (*See illustration p.* 840).

TARTLETS AND BARQUETTES

These are small Sweet or Short Crust pastry cases.

Tartelettes aux Abricots * *Apricot Tartlets*

Poach the apricot halves in a Stock syrup and leave them to cool. Line some tartlet tins with Sweet pastry (see p. 714) and bake blind at 375° F or Gas Mark 4. Thoroughly drain the apricots, put one in each pastry case and brush with apricot *purée*. Surround each apricot half with chopped roasted almonds.

Tartlettes aux Cerises * *Cherry Tartlets*

Stone the cherries and poach them in a syrup, flavoured with lemon zest. When they have been cooked, reduce the liquor and thicken it slightly with cornflour. Line some tartlet tins with Sweet pastry and bake blind at 375° F or Gas Mark 4. When cold, fill with the cherries which have cooled down and sprinkle with finely chopped pistachio nuts. The fruit can also be covered with an Almond meringue mixture which is dusted with icing sugar; in this case, the tartlets are returned to the oven for 5 minutes so that the tops become golden and crisp. (*See illustration p.* 762).

⊡ de Linz * *Jam*

Line very small tartlet moulds thinly with Sweet pastry (see p. 714). Fill the mould with a little raspberry jam and cover criss-cross with two crimp-edged dough strips. Bake at 375° F or Gas Mark 4 until crisp and golden, glaze with raspberry jelly and cool. Serve in paper cases. (*See illustration p.* 840).

⊡ aux Pêches * *Peach*

Line some moulds with Neapolitan Almond paste (see p. 724) and bake blind at 375° F or Gas Mark 4. As soon as they are cold, brush the insides with *couverture* or melted chocolate and leave to harden. Next, place a small spoonful of Frangipan cream at the bottom and place on top half a peach which has been poached in a Stock syrup, cooled and drained. Brush each peach with apricot *purée*, surround with chopped pistachio nuts and top with half a *glacé* cherry.

⊡ aux Pêches à la Napolitaine * *Neapolitan Peach*

Line tartlet moulds with Neapolitan Almond pastry (*see p.* 724) and bake blind in a moderate oven, 375° F or Gas Mark 4 for 5-6 minutes. When cold, fill with a half peach, cooked in Stock syrup, cooled and drained; mask with a little strained apricot jam and put half a blanched almond in the middle.

BARQUETTES * *BOAT-SHAPED PASTRY CASES*

These small pastry cases are in the shape of small boats.

⊡ aux Fraises * *Strawberry Boats*

Neatly line boat-shaped moulds with Sweet pastry and bake blind at 375° F or Gas Mark 4. When cold, fill with well shaped strawberries, lightly dusted with icing sugar and mask with redcurrant jelly.

⊡ aux Fruits Divers * *Mixed Fruit*

Line some boat-shaped tartlet moulds with Rich Sweet pastry and bake blind. When cold, brush the inside with *couverture* or melted chocolate and leave to harden. Place a layer of Frangipan cream or Confectioners' custard and place the fruit on top (grapes, mandarine segments, pineapple triangles, cherries, grapefruit). Lightly brush the fruit with apricot *purée* (optional) and surround with flaked roasted almonds. (*See illustration p.* 762).

Barquettes aux Oranges * *Orange Boats*

Line some boat-shaped tartlet moulds with some Sweet pastry and bake blind at 375° F or Gas Mark 4. Place a layer of Curaçao-flavoured Confectioners' custard in each tartlet case and fill with 5 or 6 prepared segments of large, seedless Jaffa oranges, round sides uppermost. Coat with a Curaçao-flavoured Wine jelly.

⊡ aux Pommes * *Apple*

Peel and core some russet apples and dip them in lemon juice. Cut each apple into 6 to 8 segments shaped like half-moons and poach them in a Stock syrup. Also prepare a reduced apple *purée*. Line some boat-shaped tartlet moulds with Sweet pastry and bake blind at 350° F or Gas Mark 4. When they are cold, place some of the apple *purée* in each, thickened with a little apricot jam. Place on top 5 or 6 pieces of apple with the round sides uppermost and coat with Kirsch flavoured apricot jam.

Conversations

Line tartlet moulds with Puff pastry, prick, fill up with Confectioners' custard, cover all of them with a single, thinly rolled out piece of Puff pastry and run the rolling pin over it to cut the dough off smoothly. Brush thinly with Royal icing, make a cross on the top with two strips of Short pastry and bake in a moderate oven, 375° F or Gas Mark 4 for 25 minutes. (*See illustration p.* 840).

Exquis

3½ oz ground almonds; 3½ oz melted sugar; 1½ oz flour; half an egg white; a little vanilla; 5½ oz melted chocolate; 3 tablespoons double cream; 1½ oz butter.

Mix the ingredients into a paste, roll out and use to line small, buttered, floured tartlet moulds. Bake at 375° F or Gas Mark 4. In the meantime, make Butter cream with the melted chocolate, stirred smooth with the double cream and the butter. After baking carefully remove tartlets from moulds, fill smoothly with Butter cream, coat with Chocolate fondant and put half a very green pistachio in the middle.

Florette

Line deep scalloped, tartlet moulds with Sweet pastry, put a little thick apple *purée* in the bottom and fill up with the following mixture: Beat two egg whites stiffly and gently fold in 3 oz icing sugar, a little vanilla, 2½ oz ground almonds and a dash of Kirsch. Sprinkle with coarsely chopped almonds, dust with icing sugar and bake at 375° F or Gas Mark 4 for 15 minutes.

Frascati

Line 12 small tartlet moulds with Sweet pastry and fill with the following mixture: Beat 3½ oz ground almonds, 3½ oz sugar, 1 egg and 1 egg yolk to a foam, add a good dash of Kirsch and 3½ oz chopped, candied fruit and bake for 10 minutes at 375° F or Gas Mark 5. Cover with chocolate Italian meringue mixture, then dry meringue in a moderate oven for a few minutes without browning.

Lisette

Line boat-shaped moulds with Sweet pastry and fill with a mixture of 2 oz ground almonds, 2 oz sugar, 1 oz chopped, candied peel and 2 stiffly beaten egg whites. Decorate with a slice of candied orange peel, bake for 10 minutes at 400° F or Gas Mark 6 and dust with icing sugar.

Mirlitons

Line small, deep, tartlet tins with Puff pastry or Half puff pastry. Put a little apricot jam in the bottom and fill with the following mixture. Whip 2 eggs to a foam mix with 3½ oz sugar and with 3 macaroons pounded to a powder and a little vanilla. Decorate with 3 almond halves like a clover leaf, dust with icing sugar and bake for 15 minutes in a moderately hot oven, 375° F or Gas Mark 4. Ensure that the baking sheet is in a position in the oven where it will get more heat below than on top.

Nancéens

2 *oz ground almonds;* ¼ *lb vanilla sugar;* 2 *egg whites; Short pastry.* Cooking time 12-15 minutes.

Stir the ground almonds thoroughly in a saucepan with the sugar and 1 egg white, and heat slowly on the stove, stirring constantly with a wooden spoon, until it is too hot to hold a finger over. Remove from heat and fold in 1 stiffly beaten egg white. Line boat-shaped moulds with Sweet or Short pastry, fill with the mixture—not too full—decorate with 2 halved blanched almonds, dust with icing sugar and bake at 350 °F or Gas Mark 4.

Saint-André

Line boat-shaped moulds with Short pastry and fill with very thick cold apple *purée*. Brush with Royal icing, garnish with 2 narrow, crossed strips of Short pastry and bake for 10 minutes in a hot oven, 400° F or Gas Mark 6.

WAFFLES, WAFERS AND CIGARETTES

Cigarettes * *Waffle and Cigarette Paste*

2 *egg whites;* 3½ *oz vanilla icing sugar;* 1½ *oz butter;* 1½ *oz flour.* Cooking time: 3-4 minutes.

Whip egg whites very stiff and using a metal spoon, gently fold in the sugar followed by the sifted flour and the melted, barely lukewarm butter. Test the consistency by baking 2 wafers on a greased and floured baking sheet. If they are too fragile, add a pinch of flour, if they are too firm, add a little melted butter. Bake in a moderate oven, 375° F or Gas Mark 4.

Gaufres * *Plain Waffles*

9 *oz flour;* 5½ *oz vanilla sugar;* 3 *eggs;* 3½ *oz melted butter;* 17 *fl oz cold milk; salt.* Cooking time: 4-5 minutes.

Whisk all the ingredients except the butter in a bowl until a smooth batter is obtained. Lastly add the butter, cook the mixture in a very hot, well-greased waffle iron and serve dusted with icing sugar.

Gaufres Bruxelloises * *Brussels Waffles*

9 *oz sifted flour;* 2 *oz butter;* 1½ *oz sugar;* ¼ *oz yeast;* 2 *eggs;* 1 *pinch salt; milk.* Cooking time: 4-5 minutes.

Mix the yeast in a little lukewarm milk, put it in the middle of the flour, add eggs, sugar, salt and more milk if necessary. Finally add the melted butter and leave to rise for 2 hours. When the dough has doubled in volume, cook using a well-greased waffle iron and dust with icing sugar when served.

⊡ à la Canelle * *Cinnamon*

9 *oz sifted flour;* 4 *oz sugar;* 3 *oz butter;* 2 *eggs;* ¼ *oz ground cinnamon; pinch of salt; a good pinch of baking powder.* Cooking time: 4-5 minutes.

Cream the butter and sugar, add the eggs one at a time, the salt, cinnamon and finally the flour and baking powder. Leave to stand for an hour before cooking the waffles in a well-greased iron.

⊡ Sultane

12 *oz flour;* 9 *oz sugar;* 5½ *oz butter;* 6 *egg yolks;* 6 *stiffly beaten egg whites;* 17 *fl oz milk.* Cooking time: 2-3 minutes.

Mix all the ingredients thoroughly and fold in the stiffly beaten egg whites last. Bake very thin in a special iron and fill in pairs with the special waffle filling (*see recipe p.* 732).

Oublies ou Plaisirs * *Rolled Wafers and Cornets*

9 *oz flour;* 6½ *oz sugar;* 1½ *oz butter;* 2 *eggs; half water, half milk.*

Make a Plain Waffle batter, but make them very thin, cook and roll up at once.

⊡ aux Amandes

4 *oz Almond paste;* 3 *oz icing sugar;* 1 *oz sifted flour;* 3-4 *egg whites; a little grated lemon zest; about* 3 *oz fresh cream.* Cooking time: 6-7 minutes.

Mix the Almond paste, sugar, flour, lemon zest and egg whites and stir in the cream to obtain a smooth mixture. Spread on a greased baking sheet and bake for 2 minutes at 350° F or Gas Mark 3-4. Take out of the oven and allow to cool. Bake again, cut up. Place the pieces on a rolling pin or shape into tiles or leaves, etc. Wafers need to be cooked twice to achieve a pleasing colour.

Petit Fours

Petit fours are the name given to a large variety of tiny cakes, biscuits, pastries, and glazed and marzipan fruits. Iced *petits fours* are usually *Génoise* cut into squares or other fancy shapes and coated with Fondant icing. *Petit fours* are usually served at the end of a meal accompanied by coffee and liqueurs.

In this chapter you will find recipes for the following varieties of *petit fours*:
the Plain Wafer and Cigarette *petit fours*;
Macaroon and Almond *petit fours*;
Iced *petit fours* based on *Génoise* sponge mixtures;
Petit fours based on *Choux* pastry;
Various *petit fours*, for example, meringues, small tartlets and glazed fruits.

SIMPLE PETIT FOURS

These preparations are used mainly for decorating larger pieces, such as *bombes* and *gâteaux*.

Cigarettes Russes pour Glaces * *Russian Cigarettes for Ice Cream*

Spread Cigarette paste fairly thinly in oblongs, the size of a cigarette paper, on a greased and floured baking sheet and bake 5-6 minutes, 375° F or Gas Mark 4. Remove from sheet, turn over and immediately roll round a pencil on a table. Remove the pencil.

Cornets * *Cornets*

2 *oz vanilla-flavoured icing sugar;* 1 *oz flour;* 1 *oz melted butter;* 1 *oz ground almonds;* 1 *egg white*. Cooking time: 4-5 minutes.

Beat the sugar and egg white till slightly foamy, add the sifted flour, the almonds, and, last of all, the melted butter. Spread small thin rounds of this soft paste on to a slightly greased baking sheet and bake in a moderate oven, 375° F or Gas Mark 4-5. Remove from baking sheet at once, twist into small cornets by hand and place in cornet-shaped tin moulds to cool without being damaged. They may then be dipped in *couverture* or melted chocolate. (*See illustration p.* 842).

Langues-de-Chats * *Cats' Tongues*

2 oz butter; 2 oz vanilla sugar; 2 oz flour; 2 egg whites. Cooking time: 4-5 minutes.

Beat the butter till slightly creamy, add the sugar and then, very gradually, the unbeaten egg whites. When everything is well mixed, fold in the sifted flour. Using a small plain tube, pipe on to a greased and floured baking sheet in the shape of pencils the length of a little finger, not too close together. Bake in a hot oven, 400° F or Gas Mark 6, and remove from baking sheet before they are cold.

Milanais

4 oz flour; 1½ oz ground almonds; 1½ oz butter; 1 egg; 1 pinch of salt; the zest of half a lemon or orange. Cooking time: 5-10 minutes, according to thickness.

Make in the same way as for Sweet pastry and allow to rest for 2 hours in a cool place. Cut out into different shapes, place on a greased baking sheet, decorate with half almonds, candied cherries, etc., and bake in a hot oven, 400° F or Gas Mark 6.

Palais de Dame

2 oz butter; 2 oz sugar; 2½ oz flour; 1½ oz currants; 1 egg; 1 dash of rum. Cooking time: 5-6 minutes.

Cream the butter and sugar vigorously for 3-4 minutes. Add the egg, continue beating and finally add the currants, flour and rum. Pipe the mixture like macaroons on to a greased and floured baking sheet, and bake in a hot oven at 400° F or Gas Mark 5-6.

Tuiles d'Amandes * *Almond Wafers*

2 egg whites; 3½ oz sugar; 1½ oz flour; 1½ oz butter; 1½ oz finely sliced almonds. Cooking time: 4-5 minutes.

Make the mixture in the same way as Cornets. Place small piles on a greased baking sheet, spread slightly with a fork, dust with icing sugar and bake in a moderate oven, 375° F or Gas Mark 5. Remove from the baking sheet at once and press round a rolling pin to curl them.

Tuiles Dentelles * *Lace Wafers*

2½ oz vanilla sugar; 2½ oz very thin sliced almonds; 2½ oz butter; 1½ oz flour. Cooking time: 4-5 minutes.

Cream the butter and sugar and fold in first the almonds, then the flour. Place out as above and bake at 375° F or Gas Mark 5. These wafers are very fragile and should be handled with care.

MACAROON AND ALMOND PETIT FOURS

These sweetmeats contain almonds—sweet and bitter—and sometimes almond milk.

Macarons d'Amiens * *Amiens Macaroons*

5 oz freshly-blanched almonds; 5 oz icing sugar; 1 egg white; 1 oz apricot jam; vanilla. Cooking time: about 18 minutes.

Grind the almonds very finely or grate them and then pound thoroughly. Add the sugar and egg white slowly, a little at a time. Flavour with vanilla and mix in the apricot jam. The paste should be fairly firm. Allow the finished paste to rest for 12 hours before rolling and cutting. Then make a rope of the paste and cut into small pieces, place white paper on double baking sheets to protect the underside from excessive heat. Bake in a warm oven, 325-350° F or Gas Mark 3. This paste will become too hard if it is left to rest for longer than 12 hours.

⊡ au Chocolat * *Chocolate*

4½ oz ground almonds; 7 oz sugar; 2 oz melted chocolate; 2 egg whites. Cooking time: 7-8 minutes.

Make in the same way as *Nancy* macaroons with a slightly firmer paste. Shape into macaroons by hand, flatten slightly, place on a sheet of paper on a baking sheet, moisten lightly with water and bake at 325-350° F or Gas Mark 3.

⊡ de Nancy

3½ oz finely-ground almonds; 7 oz sugar; vanilla; 2 egg whites. Cooking time: 12-15 minutes.

Work the almonds into a soft paste with the sugar, gradually adding the egg whites and the vanilla; it should not, however, be runny. Pipe the mixture into rounds on white paper using a large plain tube. Sprinkle with a little water, dust with icing sugar and bake for 12-15 minutes in a warm oven, 325°-350° F or Gas Mark 3. In order to remove the macaroons from the paper, place them on a moistened baking sheet for a few minutes, paper side down.

⊡ à l'Orange * *Orange*

2 oz ground almonds; 2½ oz sugar; ½ oz flour; 2 egg whites; the zest of 1 orange; orange-flavoured Fondant icing. Cooking time: 6-7 minutes.

Stiffly beat the egg whites and gently fold in the almonds, sugar, flour and zest. Pipe as for *Macarons de Nancy*. When cold, sandwich together in pairs with thick marmalade and coat with Fondant flavoured with orange or Curaçao.

Bâtons Vanillés

¼ lb almonds; 3 oz sugar; vanilla; a little flour; a little water; Royal icing. Cooking time: 7-8 minutes.

Grind the almonds and sugar together moistening with water to obtain a smooth paste. Roll out on a marble slab lightly dusted with icing sugar until about ⅛ inch thick. Spread with a thin layer of Royal icing, cut into strips ¾ inch wide and 2 to 3 inches long. Put these strips on baking trays and bake at 325-350° F or Gas Mark 3. These strips can be flavoured with chocolate or coffee.

Calissons d'Aix

9 oz almonds; 10 oz sugar; water; orange flower water; Royal icing. Cooking time: 15 minutes.

Grind the almonds with 1 oz sugar and a little water. Make Stock syrup with a density of 24° (measured with the saccharometer) with 9 oz sugar and about ½ pint water. Mix with the almonds, flavour with orange flower water and brown at low heat in a saucepan, stirring constantly, until a thick mixture which can be spread is formed. Spread on to large, rectangular pieces of rice paper, allow to dry, coat thinly with Royal icing. Using a small, oval cutter dipped in hot water each time, cut out biscuits, place them on a baking sheet and bake in a cool oven, 325° F or Gas Mark 2.

Cyrano

5½ oz ground almonds; 5½ oz sugar; 1 egg white; 1 tablespoon rum; 1 oz flour; Royal icing. Cooking time: 8-10 minutes.

Mix the ground almonds with sugar and egg white, add the rum and flour; the whole should result in a soft paste. Butter tiny *barquette* moulds, fill with the mixture, sprinkle with finely chopped almonds and smooth. Cover with a thin layer of Royal icing and bake in a cool oven, 325° F or Gas Mark 2 so that the top does not caramelise. To turn out, first run the tip of a knife round the case and turn them out carefully.

Eugenia

The same mixture as above, but replace almonds by blanched, lightly roasted, ground hazelnuts. Shape into small balls, coat with hot chocolate Fondant and immediately roll in chocolate vermicelli.

Negritas

¼ lb ground almonds; ¼ lb sugar; 1½ oz chocolate; 5 egg whites; Chocolate butter cream; chocolate Fondant. Cooking time: about 10 minutes.

Mix the almonds with the egg whites and add the sugar and melted chocolate. Fold in the stiffly whipped egg whites and spread about ½ inch thick on to a paper lined baking sheet. Bake in a warm oven, 325-350° F or Gas Mark 3. Turn over at once and remove the paper. Cut the piece in half and sandwich with Chocolate butter cream. Coat the top with chocolate Fondant and when set, cut into small squares.

Patiences

¼ lb ground almonds; 7 oz icing sugar; 3 egg whites; vanilla. Cooking time: 6-7 minutes.

Mix the ground almonds and 2 egg whites thoroughly in a saucepan, then heat slightly and combine with the sugar and the last egg white. Using a small plain tube, pipe like macaroons on to a waxed baking sheet. Allow to dry overnight and bake next day in a warm oven at 350° F or Gas Mark 4.

Senoritas

3 oz almonds; ¼ lb vanilla sugar; 3 stiffly beaten egg whites. Cooking time: 5-7 minutes.

Mix the ground almonds, sugar and a few drops of water into a soft paste and fold in the stiffly beaten egg whites. Fill into oval, crimped paper cases, place half a blanched almond on top, dust with icing sugar and bake in a warm oven, 350° F or Gas Mark 4.

ICED PETITS FOURS MADE WITH GÉNOISE MIXTURE

(*See illustration p.* 842.)

Aiglons * *Eaglets*

Cut out thin round bases of *Génoise* sponge about 1¼ inches in diameter. Decorate the top with a cone of Coffee butter cream, using a piping bag and round tube. As soon as the cream is set, dip into Kirsch fondant. Spread *couverture* or melted chocolate very thinly on a piece of stiff white paper and detach from the paper when cold. Cut the *couverture* into diamond shapes with a hot knife, and stick three of them into each Eaglet.

Chocolatines

Bake *Génoise* mixture on a baking sheet the preceding evening, cut in small squares, sandwich with Butter cream, spread cream thinly over top and sides and sprinkle with finely chopped roasted almonds. Pipe a star of Chocolate butter cream in the centre with a star pipe.

Gitanes * *Gipsies*

Cut out *Génoise* as above and pipe on an oval of Strawberry butter cream with a plain pipe. Put in refrigerator to set, dip into Fondant of a different colour, cut open with a knife dipped in hot water and slightly press the edges apart.

Martinique

Cut *Génoise* in small squares and garnish top with Coffee butter cream mixed with a little marzipan and rum. Let it set, dip into Coffee fondant flavoured with rum and decorate with a chocolate coffee bean.

Oranges * *Orange and Chocolate*

Sandwich a *Génoise* with orange marmalade. Spread the top with a thin layer of Orange butter cream and put in refrigerator to set. Cut into small crescent shapes with a round cutter. Dip into Chocolate fondant and decorate the tops with a small slice of candied orange.

Pavés

Sandwich a square of *Génoise* with coffee and Kirsch butter cream and put in refrigerator to set. Cut into squares of about 1 inch. Dip in coffee and Kirsch Fondant and decorate with a little piece of *glacé* cherry or a coffee bean.

Simone

Cover very thin pieces of *Génoise* with a layer of glazed chestnut *purée* and pipe an oval of Italian meringue mixture on top with a large plain pipe. Sprinkle very finely-shredded roasted almonds on top diagonally and put in a moderate oven for 3 minutes to dry the meringue mixture.

ALMOND PETITS FOURS WITH AND WITHOUT BUTTER CREAM

All *petits fours* filled or covered with butter cream must be put in the refrigerator to set before they are iced. Lukewarm fondant sets on the butter cream on top of *petits fours* as soon as it is cold. A very good method of coating is to sprinkle a little castor sugar on top of the butter cream, because the fondant immediately adheres to the sugar.

Berrichons * *Berrichon Paste*

¼ lb ground almonds; ¼ lb vanilla sugar; 1½ oz flour; 4 stiffly beaten egg whites. Cooking time: 7-8 minutes.

Gently fold the almonds, sugar and flour into the stiffly beaten egg whites. Pipe this mixture on to greased and floured baking sheets with a plain pipe in the shape of macaroons or fingers and bake in a hot oven, 400° F or Gas Mark 6. These excellent *petits fours* are used for many purposes.

Caprices

Garnish round *Berrichons* with very thick apple *purée*, brush with apricot *purée* and sprinkle with chopped roasted almonds.

Clémence

Bake *Berrichon* paste in the shape of small bars, when cold, coat with Coffee fondant and put half a roasted almond in the centre.

Colombine

Bake small round bases of *Berrichon* paste and allow to cool. Pipe Kirsch butter cream in a dome on top and place a piece of candied cherry in the centre. When set, coat lightly with Kirsch fondant so that the cherry is visible through the icing.

Suédois

Pipe a garnish of Chocolate butter cream on to *Berrichon* paste with a star pipe. Coat with Chocolate fondant and place half a pistachio on top.

PETITS FOURS MADE WITH CHOUX PASTRY

Caroline

This is the name of tiny *éclairs* of *Choux* pastry, no bigger than the little finger. They are baked at 425° F or Gas Mark 7. One end is pierced, and the filling—Confectioners' custard or whipped cream—is piped in with a very small, plain tube. Carolines are iced in the same way as large *éclairs* and served in oval paper cases.

Nini

Make oval buns of *Choux* pastry, and bake at 425° F or Gas Mark 7, until crisp and dry. Fill with Confectioners' custard mixed with finely chopped candied fruit. Complete with Kirsch-flavoured white Fondant and place a small piece of candied cherry on top.

Tyroliens

Pipe small cream buns, the size of walnuts, from *Choux* pastry. Scatter chopped almonds on top, and bake at 425° F or Gas Mark 7. Fill with Almond butter cream and dredge with icing sugar. All these *petits fours* are served in paper cases.

Victoires

Bake small oval cream puffs at 425° F or Gas Mark 7. Fill with Kirsch-flavoured butter cream containing chopped *glacé* cherries soaked in Kirsch. Finish with a Grand-Marnier fondant and place a tiny piece of angelica on top.

VARIOUS PETIT FOURS

(*See illustration p.* 843.)

Ananas * *Pineapple*

Using a small oval cutter, cut out pieces of *Génoise* sponge, sandwiched with Pineapple butter cream. Pipe an oval on top with the same cream. When the cream is set, dip into Pineapple-flavoured fondant. Decorate with little dots of Royal icing mixed with cocoa and at one end place a small piece of angelica.

Cerises Marquises ou Déguisées * *Disguised Cherries*

Drain brandied cherries and dry a little. Dip them in white or pink Fondant and put them on a marble slab dredged with icing sugar to set.

Cerisettes

Make tartlet cases with Short pastry. When baked and cold, fill with Kirsch butter cream. Place half a *glacé* cherry steeped in Kirsch in the middle. Coat with Kirsch fondant, decorate by piping two lines of chocolate across the top.

Citrons * *Lemons*

Make some tartlet cases with Short pastry. When baked and cold, fill with Lemon butter cream. Leave to set. Coat with Lemon fondant, decorate with chocolate and a small piece of *glacé* cherry.

Dattes Farcies * *Stuffed Dates*

Make a slit on one side of the date and remove the stone. Stuff with an olive-shaped piece of marzipan or Fondant Almond paste which is larger than the stone; it should stick out slightly. Dip in sugar boiled to the crack and place on an oiled surface to harden the sugar. Serve in small paper cases.

Doigts de Dame au Chocolat * *Chocolate Ladies' Fingers*

Prepare Italian meringue and at the same time as mixing in the hot sugar, add 1½ ounces each cocoa powder and sieved icing sugar. Pipe the mixture on a greased and floured baking sheet in sticks about the size of the little finger. Bake at 250° F or Gas Mark 1 with the door open for 10-12 minutes. Remove from the baking sheet while still hot.

Doigts de Dames au Café * *Coffee Ladies' Fingers*

Make Italian meringue, but use strong coffee instead of water for boiling the sugar. Add 1½ oz sieved icing sugar, and bake in the same way as for Chocolate Ladies' Fingers.

Esplanades

Make small square tartlets of Short pastry. When baked and cold, fill with candied apricots steeped in Cointreau. Coat with Cointreau fondant, place a small piece of candied apricot on top and some pistachio nuts in each corner.

Marrons Déguisés * *Disguised Chestnuts*

Cook 1 lb of peeled and skinned chestnuts in a light vanilla Stock syrup. Drain well and pass through a wire sieve. Mix with 10 oz sugar boiled to the crack stage (this will measure 310° F, using a thermometer) and stir until this mixture is cold. Divide this paste into small balls and shape them into small chestnuts with hands dusted with icing sugar. Dip each chestnut separately in *couverture* or melted chocolate and allow to cool on an oiled marble slab.

Meringuettes * *Tiny Meringues*

Bake very small meringue shells until crisp and dry in a cool oven, 250° F or Gas Mark 1. Sandwich them together in pairs with Butter cream of any desired flavour.

Noix * *Nuts*

Line tartlet tins with Short pastry and bake blind. When cold, fill with Butter cream, mixed with finely chopped, lightly roasted almonds or hazlenuts. Coat with Fondant and decorate with a caramelised nut.

Noix Farcies * *Stuffed Nuts*

Sandwich two walnut halves together with a ball of marzipan or Fondant Almond paste and dip in sugar boiled to the crack (310° F). Cool on a wire tray.

Paula

Pipe small rounds of *Langues-de-Chat* (Cat's Tongues) mixture and bake at 400° F or Gas Mark 6, for 5-8 minutes. Trim and allow to cool. Sandwich the bases in pairs with Mocha butter cream and dredge tops with icing sugar.

Sarah

Pipe Coffee butter cream in a conical shape on very small bases of Meringue. Allow to set in the refrigerator and coat with Coffee fondant.

Truffes en Surprise * *Surprise Truffles*

Shape Parisian *Nougat* into small balls by hand. Dip in *couverture* or melted chocolate, allow to drain and roll in chocolate vermicelli.

There is a popular, but completely erroneous myth, that the making of sweets, candies and other confectionery can be tackled only by experts and that the highest point to which the average cook can aspire is to produce a quantity of sticky fudge or toffee. Admittedly success in sweet making requires practice, skill and patience as well as attention to detail, but, to be fair, these principles apply to the entire range of culinary know-how. One must practise before acquiring the skill to boil an egg properly. Skill in sweet making is an acquired—but perfectly obtainable—art. Of course, proper equipment for the job is vital to your success and you will find the following list of equipment indispensable. (*See illustration*, *p.* 843).

Equipment

The following equipment will be necessary in addition to the basic equipment required for Sugar Boiling:

Setting-tins—choose small rectangular tins with straight sides and about 1¼ inches deep, a marble slab, pastry brush, broad spatula for fondant-making, wooden spoons for beating and stirring, cellophane or waxed paper for wrapping, hair sieve, double boiler, rolling pin, scissors, caramel bars and cutters, dipping forks for coating bon-bons and chocolates, rubber moulds for shaping chocolates, fondants, jellies, funnel and plug (this is for filling tiny moulds with hot liquids), marzipan moulds, crystallizing tray, 10 inches broad and 14 inches long, and starch tray—required when moulding fondants, etc., in starch.

Amandes Salées * *Salted Almonds*

Dry freshly blanched almonds well with a cloth, beat egg white lightly, moisten the almonds with it, place them on a thick, baking tray, sprinkle with fine salt, Shake up a little and place them in a cool oven, 325° F or Gas Mark 2. As soon as they start to colour shake them well. They should only be pale yellow. Treat hazelnuts and quartered walnuts in the same way. Roast the hazelnuts slightly first so that the skin can be rubbed off.

Brésiliennes

3 *oz ground almonds;* ¼ *lb icing sugar;* ¼ *lb chocolate; a little milk;* 1 *dash of rum; a little coffee essence.*

Mix the almonds, sugar, grated chocolate, rum, coffee essence and milk into a pliable paste. Shape into hazelnut-sized balls by hand. Roll the balls in grated chocolate or chocolate vermicelli and cool well for several hours.

Caramels au Lait * *Milk Caramels*

9 oz icing sugar; 2¾ oz glucose or honey; 1¾ oz butter or coconut oil.

Put the sugar and honey in a sugar boiler that is not tinned inside, mix, bring to the boil but take care that the syrup does not boil over. Stir from time to time to prevent it sticking and continue brushing the sides of the pan with a brush dipped in cold water to prevent graining. Add the butter or coconut oil, boil to the ball degree. This will measure a density of 39-40° when tested with the saccharometer. Pour on to an oiled marble slab surrounded by 4 oiled metal bars to prevent the mixture from running off. Do not cut into pieces until almost cold.

Caramels à la Vanille * *Vanilla Caramels*

Make in the same way as Milk caramels, adding a vanilla pod.

Cerises au Caramel * *Cherry Caramels*

Drain brandy cherries well and dry them. With a fork, dip them into sugar, boiled to the crack degree (300-310° F), and place on a marble slab to cool.

Mandarines Glacées * *Glazed Tangerines*

Cut in slices and treat exactly the same as Glazed Orange Slices.

Marquisettes

½ lb ground almonds; ¼ lb icing sugar; ½ lb grated chocolate; 1-2 *egg yolks.*

Thoroughly mix the almonds with the sugar, chocolate and 1-2 egg yolks to make a firm paste. Make into hazelnut-sized balls, roll in grated chocolate and dry in the air for 2 hours or longer.

Marrons Glacés * *Glazed Chestnuts*

Carefully peel 4 lb specially selected chestnuts. Put the peeled chestnuts in a colander with large holes and place this in a pan of cold water mixed with a little flour. Put the pan on the heat, bring slowly to simmering point but do not let them boil. Simmer for 20 minutes. Remove chestnuts and place them immediately in fresh, boiling hot water without giving them time to cool and simmer for another hour until they can easily be pierced by a needle. Remove the chestnuts from the water one by one, skin carefully so that they do not break and put them in a sugar boiler with boiling hot vanilla Stock syrup which should have a density of 20° when tested with the saccharometer. The syrup must be kept constantly at simmering point but must never boil. Do not cover the pan so that the sugar is constantly becoming thicker as a result of evaporation; this may take up to 24 hours. As soon as a thin crust forms on the surface of the syrup, the chestnuts are finished. At this stage the sugar should have a density of 34-36°. Carefully remove the chestnuts and put on a wire tray to dry.

Noisettes Masquées * *Masked Hazelnuts*

Roast hazelnuts and rub off the skin by hand. When cold, dip in melted *couverture* or chocolate.

Noisettines

3 oz ground, roasted hazelnuts; ⅛ fl oz of rum; 3 oz castor sugar; ¼ lb chocolate.

Mix the nuts, sugar, rum and a few drops of water into a firm paste and make into hazelnut-sized balls. Melt the chocolate, dip the balls in it, coat all over, put on a wire tray to drain and keep in a cool place for several hours.

Noix Chocolatées * *Chocolate Nuts*

5 oz walnuts; 5 oz icing sugar; 5 oz chocolate.

Blanch the walnuts and pound them to a firm paste with sugar and a little water and shape into walnut-sized balls. Melt the chocolate slowly and carefully with a little water, dip the balls in the mixture when almost cold and roll in cocoa.

Nougat Parisien dit Nougat Brun * *Paris or Brown Nougat*

9 oz sugar; 8 oz chopped, well dried almonds; a few drops of lemon juice.

Melt the sugar to a pale yellow caramel without water in an ungalvanised sugar boiler, add a few drops of lemon juice, then add the almonds, sifted to remove very fine particles and dust. Mix well at the side of the stove and keep the mixture in a warm place until needed in order to keep it soft.

Oranges Glacées en Tranches * *Glazed Orange Slices*

Carefully peel the oranges—it is best to use the seedless ones—remove all white pith. Cut into slices and place upright on a sieve without allowing the slices to touch. Dry a little in gentle heat. Boil sugar to the crack (300-310° F). Dip in the slices and place on an oiled marble slab to set.

Truffettes de Chambéry * *Chambery Truffles*

Mix ½ lb, pounded, sifted nougat thoroughly with ½ lb melted chocolate, ½ lb Fondant and 6 oz best butter. Divide this creamy mixture into very small pieces, put in a cold place for 1 hour, shape quickly into small balls, roll in cocoa powder mixed with castor sugar or in grated chocolate and put in a cool place till required.

THE ART OF SUGAR CONFECTIONERY

A Basket of Roses in Pulled Sugar

To make a basket of pulled sugar, a wooden board the shape of a basket and about 1 inch thick is needed. Drill holes at regular intervals all round the edge in which wooden or metal rods may be stuck. The number of holes must be an odd number if a regular weave is to be obtained, either 15, 17 or 19 at most. The rods or spokes should be 3-4 inches long. They must fit in firmly, but be easily detachable and the holes must therefore be made sufficiently deep. Before use, boards and rods are greased carefully with oil. About 14 oz of pulled sugar is needed for the basket and the handle. The sugar is boiled to the small crack (280°F), but not quite as much as for Orange Glazed slices or other candied or caramelised fruit. (*See illustration p.* 844).

How to Pull Sugar

When the sugar is boiled to the desired degree, remove it from the heat and wait till it has stopped boiling and there are no more bubbles. Now, pour it on a marble slab, lightly oiled, and allow to cool for a minute or so. With the help of a palette or a broad knife, start bringing the sides of the sugar towards the centre until it begins to become very thick. Grasp it with oiled hands (it will still be very hot), and pull it out and fold it together, and continue doing this until the sugar is very white, velvety and as malleable as a firm dough. If desired the sugar may be coloured a pale green or pink.

How to Weave the Basket

Do not make more pulled sugar than necessary as it cannot be kept in reserve. The help of a second person is almost indispensable for quick and good sugar pulling. It is best to wrap the pulled sugar around the handle of a skimmer or oiled rolling pin and keep it warm above the stove at low heat. One person now holds the skimmer or rolling pin, the second person takes hold of the sugar and begins to pull it between thumb and index finger, shaping it into a flat long, ribbon of even width and thickness. The ribbon is now woven in and out between the oiled rods, starting at the base and working up to the top. It is even better if one person pulls and stretches the sugar to the shape of a ribbon or cord and the other person weaves it. As soon as the top is reached, two even lengths of sugar about as thick as a pencil are twisted together to finish off the top part. For this twist the sugar may be re-boiled and coloured. As soon as the sugar is quite hard pull the rods out carefully and place the basket on an oiled, marble slab.

Handle and Rods

The rods or spokes are usually made of pulled sugar of a different colour from the weave—for contrast—and are inserted after the wooden rods have been pulled out. They are shaped round by hand and must be all of the same height and quite straight. As soon as they are cold and hard, slide them into the woven sugar basket. To make the handle, twist two round lengths of sugar about as thick as a pencil together evenly. It may also be made in two colours. It is then curved; the distance between the two ends must correspond to the width of the basket. It is nearly always necessary to bend the handle over some source of heat. When it is finished, place it on a marble slab to get cold. To fix the handle on the basket, warm the two ends lightly and press them carefully on to the two sides of the basket.

It is better to cook the sugar in two separate halves or to boil new sugar for handle and rods, otherwise the sugar will get too cold to work. This also makes it possible to use two different colours.

Finally make the base of the basket. Re-boil the remaining sugar to light caramel and pour it on an oiled, marble slab. Use an oiled flan hoop as mould for the base and lift it off when the sugar starts to harden. Now place the basket on top and before the caramel is quite hard pass a palette knife underneath the base to loosen it, otherwise it may be difficult to remove it from the marble slab.

How to Make Sugar Roses and Other Flowers

Boil 7 oz sugar or more, to make the roses, according to the size of the basket. It may be coloured red, pink or a pale yellow for tea-roses. This colour is made by a mixture of carmine and yellow. Leaves must be a good, natural green. The sugar is boiled in the same way as for pulled sugar and worked by hand till it is smooth. To be able to make roses, the sugar must be kept warm over some source of very low heat all the time. They are made petal by petal and the best idea is to have a natural rose near by to study and to copy it. To make the petals, the sugar is pulled out very thin between the thumb and the index finger and shaped on the inner part of the thumb; this will give the petals the curved shape. The bud is made of three small petals shaped by hand. As one works outwards on the rose each petal must be made a little larger than the last. Instead of a bud, a small ball of sugar may be made for the centre. To fix the petals together the bases of the petals must be heated over a flame for a second or two and then stuck on to the bud or centre ball and pressed tight. To make leaves and stems, boiled sugar must be coloured green with vegetable colouring. The sugar can be easily pulled into the shape of a leaf. It may now be pressed into a metal mould greased lightly with oil to take the imprint of veins, or they may be marked with a knife. The leaves are fixed on to the stems by holding the ends over a flame for a moment.

The last thing to do is to make the ribbon which should be a different colour to the handle. The bows are made separately and fixed with boiled sugar on each side of the basket. Finally, the roses and leaves are arranged artistically and fixed in position.

Pulled sugar work is a highly skilled operation needing a great deal of experience. To those who would aspire to be specialists in this field, long periods of practice are necessary, preferably under the supervision of an acknowledged craftsman.

Le Croquembouche

For this *gâteau,* special moulds can be bought in different sizes. For a smallish cake a charlotte mould may be used. It must be inverted and oiled lightly on the outside. First of all bake very small buns of *Choux* pastry crisp and dry. Allow to cool and fill with Confectioners' custard or other cream. Meanwhile boil 10 oz sugar, ½ glass water and a tablespoon glucose, to a pale caramel and keep it warm. Dip the buns in the caramel one by one with a confectioner's fork and stick them all around the mould close to one another row by row with the round side turned outwards. To give the pyramid the right form make the last rows smaller, finishing with two or three buns. The *croquembouche* may be placed on a base of Parisian *Nougat* pressed into a lightly oiled cake hoop with the flat side up. Finally an *aigrette* of spun sugar or some ornament made of *nougat* is placed on top of the *croquembouche. Le croquembouche* is one of the oldest French desserts. It may also be made with Glazed Orange Slices; it is rather difficult to make evenly. (*See illustration p.* 839).

Piece Montée * *Tier Cake (Wedding, Birthday or Celebration Cake)*

For 18 *persons:* 9 *oz ground almonds;* 14 *oz sugar;* 2 *eggs;* 9 *egg yolks;* 12 *egg whites;* 9 *oz flour; red jam; zest of orange; apricot jam; Fondant.* Cooking time for the cakes: 25-45 minutes according to size.

For this cake, 8 or 10 plain round cake tins of different sizes are required, but 4 or 5, graduated in size, are sufficient to make an attractive cake. There should be a difference of about 1½ inches in diameter between each tin, i.e., if the largest is 10 inches in diameter, the next one must be about 8½ inches, and so on. After the tins have been greased and floured they are filled with the following mixture: Beat the finely ground almonds to a foam with 4½ oz sugar and 2 eggs. Add the remaining sugar, 9 yolks and the zest of orange, and continue beating the mixture until quite white and very foamy. Fold in the stiffly beaten egg whites and the flour at the same time. Bake in a moderate oven, 375° F or Gas Mark 4-5. Remove the smallest cakes from the oven first and allow all cakes to cool. Place the cakes one on top of the other with red jam or jelly in between. Coat the whole cake very thinly with strained apricot jam cooked to jelly and coat carefully with Fondant, flavoured to taste. As soon as the Fondant has set, decorate with candied fruit or with Royal icing, using a paper bag. Each layer may also be iced separately, one layer white, one pink and so on, and then placed one on top of the other. For a wedding or a christening cake, the icing should be all white and some sort of symbol in sugar, a bridal couple, cradle, etc., placed on top. These ornaments can be bought ready made.

Wines

The praise of wine has been sung since Noah or Bacchus planted the first vine and pressed out the first juice. Poets, sacred or profane, pagans, Jews or Christians, even one Muslim, Omar Khayyam, have sung its excellence and its virtues.

In France, wine has been treasured for more than two thousand years, and the wine has repaid this affection, for although great vintages exist elsewhere, there is no other country where such a great variety can be found.

But if wine is something wonderful in itself, nothing is more important than the right dish to bring out its full value.

It would be as ridiculous, and sad, to imagine a superb dinner accompanied by water as to drink a sumptuous and venerable bottle together with a plate of macaroni. In the same way, everyone of us would be aghast at the thought, for example, of Chambertin with a chocolate cake, of Sauternes with beef *en daube*.

These extreme examples show the need for care—harmonising fully the flavour of the wine and the food. According to personal taste one will seek out a wine which will be the best accompaniment to a certain dish, or pick the dish which will best bring out the chosen wine. That is not to say that there may not be some charm in certain discords, as in music. But dissonance is a form of art which must not be confused with a false note or squawk.

That is why, during our saunter among the wines of France we are adding to our description of each region a few bars of harmony, of counterpoint, for food and wine.

In addition to describing the wines of France, we have also described in this chapter the wines of other European countries and those of the wine-producing countries outside Europe. Since wines the world over fall into the same general categories—red, white, *rosé*, fortified, still, sparkling, etc.—the advice on serving wines, though using chiefly French examples, can be applied to the wines of the other countries as well.

ADVICE ON WINE

Glasses

Just as music needs a room with good acoustics if we are to hear it at its best, so the aroma of a wine must be able to benefit by that olfactory sounding box, the glass. Pouring a great wine into a small glass is like putting a full symphony orchestra on the stage of an intimate theatre. A wine glass must be capacious; it must never be filled up. The finer the crystal, the more intimate will be the contact between lips and liquid.

There are several types of glasses and each French wine-growing region has taken pains to create the shapes best suited to bring out the special qualities of its wines. We do not intend to describe them all here, but will confine ourselves to those intended for Bordeaux, Burgundy and Champagne.

A Bordeaux glass should not be too full-bellied; its curve should have a harmonious line, the top of the bowl slightly narrowed for red wine in order to hold the bouquet captive for a moment. A Burgundy glass, on the other hand, should have long sides (without however becoming too much like a tankard). This is explained by the fact that the aroma of Bordeaux, more vegetable in character, gives the impression of rising in a sheaf, while that of Burgundy, more animal by nature, seems to spread in the round.

For Champagne, a coupe should never be used, in spite of the elegance of the shape. It rather foolishly lets the subtle scent of the wine escape. A flute is better, but the ideal is the tulip-style glass, so called because of its resemblance to the barely opened calyx of this flower.

The temperature of wines

How many sins are committed in this matter, the worst being white wine which has been iced, ruined by the cold, and lukewarm red wine, where the bottle has been put in a corner of the fireplace, when it hasn't been placed in hot water!

Somewhere, between these two equally annoying extremes lies a happy, sensible medium.

It would be bold indeed—not to say arbitrary—to lay down a temperature for each wine. The laws of relativity must be applied. A wine served at 70° F will seem almost lukewarm if served in a room where the temperature is 65° and almost cold if served in a room at 80°.

Without being too definite, one can safely say that a dry white wine should give an impression of pleasant coolness when drunk, but not of cold, let alone of being iced. It should be served at cellar temperature, which is usually 50-55°. Champagne can be served colder, at about 45°. The great rich white wines are those which will take the lowest temperature, i.e., 40-45°.

Important note: the wine cooler should not be crammed full of ice, but filled with very cold water, or water made cold by means of pieces of ice. When the wine is cool enough, remove it from the cooler.

Light red wines of the type drunk young, such as Beaujolais and Loire wines, are served cool. Though cellar temperature may be felt to be rather cold, it should not be forgotten that at table they will quickly rise to some 60°.

It is generally said that red wines should be served "*chambré*", i.e., at room temperature. True enough, but this does not mean the temperature of the dining-room (which is usually about 70°). It means bringing up the wine from the cellar and letting it take on the temperature of the coolest room in the house.

As a general rule red wines, especially old ones, must be brought up in advance so that they can rest and so that any sediment can settle on the bottom of the bottle. If the bottle has to be fetched at the last moment, a wine-cradle will be used. This is frequently used without rhyme or reason, especially in restaurants wishing to impress. Its only purpose is to keep the bottle in the horizontal position it has held in its rack so that the sediment remains undisturbed on the lower side. A bottle that has been standing upright must therefore not be placed in a cradle; this would mean mixing the sediment with the wine, which is precisely what one is trying to avoid. The bottle must be slid gently from the rack into the cradle without turning it and carried carefully upstairs.

We shall go into the problem of sediment in the section on decanting. As regards temperature, red Burgundies should be brought to the table at about 60°; they develop their full bouquet at about 65°.

Red Bordeaux is served at 65°; it reaches its full aroma at about 70°. But it must never be served at this temperature.

Decanting

This is the operation of separating the wine from the sediment or lees. Decanting has its supporters and its opponents. The opponents say that wine is too sensitive, that it suffers trauma, that it is best to pour it from its bottle at the table, carefully, until the sediment becomes apparent.

For the supporters of decanting, there are two cases where it should be practised; for separating old wine from the sediment and for oxydising certain young wines.

The older a wine, the more necessary is it to beware of the aeration brought about by decanting and to postpone this operation to the last moment before the wine is to be drunk.

For young wines which one wants to mature artificially by oxydation (and also for some wines which have remained "hard" or "aggressive," which do not mellow), decanting should be done beforehand, sometimes several hours before.

Let us briefly recall the method. Hold the bottle by the bottom, not the neck, in the right hand; hold the decanter in the left hand in front of a bright light and pour the wine from the bottle into the decanter as gently as possible, without gurgling. Stop pouring as soon as the first threads of the sediment are seen floating towards the bottle neck.

Allowing wine to settle

Wine is a living thing; travelling tires it. Do not forget to let it rest in the cellar for several days—several weeks in the case of venerable bottles—before drinking it. In the same way, if you buy a good wine from a merchant, it is best to let it settle for a few days before drinking it. Once the bottle is in your cellar, it is usually considered proper to bring it up in the morning for dinner, and the night before for next day's luncheon.

The order of wines during a meal

In principle, the first wine served with a meal is a dry white wine. This is followed by red, from the youngest to the oldest, from the lightest to the most full-bodied. Sweet white wine is served with dessert.

Exceptions are possible. In Bordeaux, for example, Sauternes is served with *foie gras* (at the beginning of the meal, of course). In this case it must be followed by a dry white wine with sufficient body, or a generous red wine.

There are also exceptions to the rule of an order of increasing age. One must not serve a light year after a full-bodied one because it is older. For instance, one would not serve a 1956 after a 1959; one would unhesitatingly do the reverse.

The same applies to the order of registered brands. In theory one would serve a Pomerol or Saint-Emilion after a Graves or a Médoc. Burgundy follows Bordeaux and Côtes-du-Rhône follows Burgundy. Nevertheless, we might have a very rich, very generous Pomerol, which might harm the subtlety of a Volnay. In this case, with all due respect to the purists, a man of taste would not hesitate, he would serve the Volnay, Burgundy though it is, before the Pomerol, although it comes from the Gironde.

In conclusion, let us point out that the drinking of wine, if it is a matter of knowledge and even more of experience, is above all a question of taste, in both senses of the word.

The Wines of France

In France, vines have the good fortune to be exposed to three different climates, Mediterranean, oceanic and continental, a geology with a great variety of soils, a place where the Greeks landed early and where religion led to the settlement of viticulturist monks from the time of the Middle Ages.

The limits of viticulture follow a line which starts a little above Nantes, north of the Loire, follows the southern limits of Brittany, Normandy and Picardy, passes a little to the west of Paris and reaches the Belgian frontier just north of Champagne. Vines cover an area of about 3,705,000 acres, of which 617,500 acres are vineyards with an official description of origin. The size of the harvest varies from one year to the next. The 1962 harvest (A.O.C. wines), was one of the biggest and amounted to 27,742,000 bushels, whereas the 1957 harvest only amounted to 9,793,750 bushels.

Les Appelations d'Origine Controlée

Another element of good fortune for the vines and wines of France, the most recent and by no means the least important, is due to a legal spirit inherited from the Romans combined with a countryman's and craftsman's pleasure in a good job well done. This is the unique legislation concerning registered brands (*Appelations d'Origine Contrôlée*) thanks to which the consumer knows exactly what he is drinking.

The categories are as follows:

Local wines (*les vins de pays*)*:* The label on the bottle must bear the words "local wine from the district of . . ." The minimum alcoholic content is 9.5 degrees. These are the regional wines, often very pleasant, which one usually drinks locally during one's holidays.

Blended wines (*les vins de coupage*)*:* The alcoholic content must also be at least 9.5 degrees. They are sold under the label and responsibility of the dealer who has obtained them by mixing and combining wines of different origins (and not only French). They are divided into "ordinary table wines" ("*vins de consommation courante*") and "choice wines without description of origin" ("*vins de marque sans appellation d'origine*"), the latter being of higher quality than the former.

Wines bearing a registered brand "controlled appelation" (*les vins d'appellation d'origine contrôlée, A.O.C.*). These wines may be recognised by their labels, which must bear the words "*appellation contrôlée*" (e.g., *Appellation Margaux contrôlée*); there is a single exception, namely, Champagne. These wines are subject to very strict rules of production and vinification, and to a geographical limitation of the area where the vine grows.

Regional wines of superior quality (*Vins délimités de qualité supérieure—V.D.Q.S.*)*:* These are the regional wines which are not covered by the law on the official description of origin and for which this category, subject to similar regulations, was subsequently created.

Our study will only deal with wines of guaranteed origin (A.O.C. and V.D.Q.S.), region by region, since blended wines, whatever their quality, have no specific origin.

BORDEAUX

The town of Bordeaux has given its name to a very important group of vineyards, all lying in the Department of Gironde and flanking the banks of the rivers Garonne and Dordogne and their common estuary, the Gironde. Bordeaux offers wine-lovers a very complete range, from light red wines to the most full-bodied, from dry white wines to the very sweet.

Médoc

This covers an area 50 miles long and 4-8 miles wide on the left bank of the Garonne. The most famous wines come from the southern part, Haut-Médoc, where one finds the celebrated place names of Margaux, Saint-Julien, Pauillac, Saint-Estèphe, Listrac and Moulis.

Haut-Médoc wines from good years will age almost indefinitely. In principle, these wines should not be drunk when young. When they have matured they have an incomparable bouquet, ranging in savour so some say, from flowers to truffles, a solid backbone combined with a full-flavoured body. When aged they may reach the peak of perfection.

Graves

The vineyard encircles the town of Bordeaux to the north and extends along the left bank of the Garonne towards the south as far as the Sauternes district.

The red wines resemble those of Médoc, but are perhaps more vigorous; they also age extremely well. The white wines are dry, especially those harvested in the north; they have a typical bouquet and aroma and a great deal of elegance. There are also very popular sweet white Graves, especially from the south of the district.

Saint-Emilion

This district lies north-east of Bordeaux, near the town of Libourne, on the right bank of the Dordogne. Apart from the district of Saint-Emilion proper, there are the neighbouring districts of Saint-Georges-Saint-Emilion, Lussac-Saint-Emilion, Montagne-Saint-Emilion, Parsue-Saint-Emilion, Puisseguin-Saint-Emilion, Parsac-Saint-Emilion and Sables-Saint-Emilion.

The wines are red, generous and full-bodied, with more roundness than on the Côtes, and more vigorous than Graves. They too will mature, but will not keep for as long as Médoc and Graves.

Pomerol

The vines of Pomerol also grow at the gates of Libourne, on the right bank of the Dordogne, and produce a rich, mellow and fragrant red wine.

We should make a note of the neighbouring districts of Néac-de-Pomerol and Lalande-de-Pomerol.

The great sweet white wines

Bordeaux has the privilege of producing those sumptuous sweet white wines, clad in gold, honey-scented. The grapes are harvested almost one by one in successive pickings when they have reached an over-ripeness as the result of which they are almost candied (known as "*pourriture noble*" or noble rot, thanks to the action of a beneficent fungus).

The most famous region producing these wines is Sauternes-Barsac, on the left bank of the Garonne, to which should be added Cérons and, on the right bank of the river, opposite, Loupiac and Sainte-Croix-du-Mont.

Other districts

Among red wines, there are the rich wines of Côtes-de-Fronsac and Canon-Fronsac, those of Bourgeais and Blayais (which may also be white).

Among white wines we have the Entre-Deux-Mers, Graves de Vayres and Sainte-Foy-Bordeaux.

The first Côtes de Bordeaux, on the right bank of the Garonne, produce popular red and white wines, as do the Côtes de Bordeaux-Saint-Macaire.

The whole of this region produces Bordeaux, Bordeaux *supérieur* (red and white) and *clairet* or *rosé* Bordeaux.

Bordeaux and the dishes to accompany them

Haut-Médoc, Moulis, Listrac, Saint-Estèphe	Red meat; grilled meat; feathered game; furred game if not high (wines of sound years; *gruyère*-type cheeses.
Margaux, Saint-Julien, Pauillac	Lamb; white meat; poultry; roast or grilled; truffles; fresh game birds; *foie gras; gruyère*-type cheeses.
Red Graves	As for Médoc; grilled meat; fresh game; *gruyére*-type cheeses.
Dry white Graves first Côtes de Bordeaux (dry)	Oysters; shellfish; fish and shellfish grilled or in a mildly seasoned sauce; caviar.
Mellow white Graves	*Apéritif*; *foie gras*; dessert.
Saint-Emilion and Pomerol	Red meat; grilled meat or meat in a sauce (duck or chicken cooked with Saint-Emilion), furred or feathered game (Pomerol or Saint-Emilion of a good year); lampreys in red wine; cheese; *foie gras.*
Sauternes-Barsac and sweet white wines	*Apéritif*; *foie gras*; fresh duck liver; fish in fine sauces; desserts (if not too sweet). Some people drink them with roast chicken, Roquefort and ices.

BURGUNDY

The wine-growing area of Burgundy spreads, from north to south, over four departments—Yonne, with Chablis; the Côte-d'Or, divided between the slopes of Nuits and of Beaune; Saône-et-Loire, which includes the Chalons slopes, the Mâcon area and the north of Beaujolais; and Rhône, which include almost the whole of Beaujolais.

Chablis

This is the most northerly vineyard of Burgundy. It only produces dry, fresh, elegant and scented white wines, of a beautiful pale gold with greenish lights. The Appelation covers the Grand Cru Chablis, first growth Chablis, Chablis and little Chablis.

The department of Yonne produces a red wine, Yrancy Burgundy, which is excellent in good years.

Côte de Nuits

The Côte-de-Nuits starts south of Dijon; it covers a line of rather exposed slopes. From north to south, there are the famous parishes of Gevrey-Chambertin, Morey-Saint-Denis, Chambolle-Musigny, Vougeot, Flagey-Echezeaux, Vosne-Romanée, Nuits-Saint-Georges, with their "climats"—the Burgundian name for a place entered in the regional register—some of which, e.g., Chambertin, have the right to be registered as brands.

It produces almost entirely full-bodied red wines, rich and with a full fragrance, sometimes verging on that of game; they mature well.

Côte de Beaune

The Côte-de-Beaune follows on the Côte-de-Nuits with the parishes of Aloxe-Corton, Pernand-Vergelesse, Chassagne-Montrachet, Puligny-Montrachet, Meursault, Savigny, Beaune, Pommard, Volnay, Santenay. The characteristic of the Côte-de-Beaune is that it produces both red and white wine.

The red wines are lighter than those of Nuits, more flexible, with a floral or fruity aroma, a great deal of subtlety and elegance. They also mature well.

The white wines are among the greatest of Burgundy and of France. They are dry but mellow, with a very full-blown bouquet, a typical flavour of almond or hazel-nut. The most illustrious name is Montrachet with the finest wines coming from Chassagne-Montrachet and Bâtard-Montrachet. Meursault and Corton-Charlemagne are also worthy of special mention.

Châlons

The town of Chalons-sur-Saône has given its name to this region. Adjacent to the Côte-de-Beaune and with very similar wines, the white wine of Rully and the red wine of Mercurey, when well made, are much appreciated by gourmets. Further south, the white of Montagny and the red of Givry are not without merit.

Mâcon

This region gets its name from the town of Mâcon. Under the Appelation of Mâcon it produces very agreeable red, *rosé* and white wines.

But the ornament of Mâcon is Pouilly-Fuissé and its two brothers, Pouilly-Loché and Pouilly-Vinzelles. These are dry, fragrant, vigorous and rather full-bodied white wines.

Beaujolais

The actual capital is Villefranche-sur-Saône, but the name is taken from that of the old capital, Beaujeu. Starting in Saône-et-Loire with the parishes of Leynes, Saint-Amour and Romanèche-Thorins, the region extends into the department of Rhône, as far north of the city of Lyons.

Beaujolais, Beaujolais Supérieur and Beaujolais-Villages are, above all, wines to drink cool. They should be tender, fragrant and smooth.

Apart from the ordinary Beaujolais, there are the parishes, nine in number—Brouilly, Chénas, Chiroubles, Côte-de-Brouilly, Fleurie, Juliénas, Morgon, Moulin-à-Vent, Saint-Amour. Each has its own characteristics, but by and large they are best drunk when young. Some of the Fleurie, Morgon and above all Moulin-à-Vent wines may mature, but never as long as a Burgundy from the Côte-d'Or.

Burgundies and the dishes to accompany them

Côte-de-Nuits and some Cortons (good years)	Roast or grilled red meat; stewed meat or meat in a sauce (especially a wine sauce); chicken (Chambertin); hung furred or feathered game; pies and *terrines*, especially of game; all cheeses.
Côte-de-Beaune (red), Mercurey, also Givry, Morgon, Fleurie, Moulin-à-Vent; some red Mâcons	White grilled or roast meat (red meat for the more full-bodied ones); meat in a sauce, especially if made with Beaune wine; fresh or lightly hung game; soft cheeses if not too ripe; *gruyère*-type and pressed cheeses.
Beaujolais, Beaujolais-Villages and light vintages; Rosé from Marsannay	May accompany a whole meal (even oysters); perfect with cold meat.
Vintage Beaujolais; red Mâcon	Charturic (sausages and pork butchers' products) hot and cold (regional, especially from Lyons); grilled or roast meat; dishes in a sauce; cheese.
Chablis, Pouilly-Fuissé (or Loché or Vinzelles), Rully and also Montagny, Mâcon and white Beaujolais	Oysters, shellfish, grilled fish and crustaceans, *pauchouse*, especially for the first three. Cold meat, goat cheese, especially for the latter three.
Meursault, Corton-Charlemagne	Fish and shellfish in a sauce (preferably made with the same wine); smoked fish (salmon, trout, eel); *terrines*; *foie gras*.
Montrachet, Chevalier-Montrachet Puligny-Montrachet, etc.	Oysters; caviar; shellfish and fish, grilled or in a sauce (same wine); *foie gras*.

CHAMPAGNE

Champagne is unlike any other wine. Often imitated, never equalled, it remains unique and irreplaceable.

It is made in accordance with many very strict rules by means of lengthy and delicate operations and manipulations. The main rule is development of the sparkle by a natural method, that is in the form of a secondary fermentation of the wine which must take place in the bottle. This is the "Champenoise" method developed by Dom Pérignon and since improved by the shippers of Rheims and Epernay.

There is another important matter in connection with Champagne—*Blanc de Blancs* and *Blanc de Noirs*. Except in relation to Champagne, these two terms are quite meaningless since Champagne is the only region where white wine is made from black grapes. "*Blanc de Blancs*" therefore means white wine made from white grapes (Pinot Chardonnay) while "*Blanc de Noirs*" means white wine made from black grapes (black Pinot). Incidentally most Champagne, unless the opposite is stated specifically, consists of a mixture of the two.

Brands (*vins de marques*) and growths (*vins de crus*):

Although there are named growths in Champagne, they do not in general have the importance that the named growth has in Bordeaux or Burgundy, as each famous manufacturer blends the various growths. Each one having his own secret proportions.

The main vineyards of Champagne are: the hills of Rheims—Verzenay, Verzy, Mailly, Sillery, Louvois, Beaumont; between the hills and the Marne valley—Bouzy, Ambonnay; the Marne valley—Ay, Cumières, Hautvillers, Mareuil, Dizy; the Blancs slopes (favourable soil for the Blanc de Blancs)—Cramant, Avize, Oger, Mesnil, Vertus.

Vintage and non-vintage: Champagne may bear the date of a given year, in which case it is a vintage Champagne. Only the good years are used for vintage Champagne, which must be at least 3 years in bottle. Non-vintage Champagne is a blend of different years and must be at least 1 year in bottle.

Still Champagne

These are the red and white wines harvested in the Champagne region and which have remained "still," that is, not subjected to "champagnisation."

The white wines are fresh, dry and pleasantly fruity in character. They are mainly harvested on the Blancs slopes. The very elegant Mesnil and the more full-bodied Cramantare well known.

The red wines, of which the most esteemed are those of Bouzy and Cumières, are delicate, fruity and delicious; they are usually drunk young, but in exceptional years (especially 1959) they are heavier in character and may be left to mature.

Champagne and the dishes to accompany it

It is said that Champagne is the wine for all occasions. Nevertheless, it should not be turned into a maid of all work. It is undeniably a wine for special occasions. It is the perfect accompaniment for the whole of a fine supper, from start to finish.

Blanc de Blancs (extra dry)	Perfect as an *apéritif*; fish and crustaceans, grilled or cooked with Champagne; caviar; smoked salmon.
Other Champagnes (extra dry)	Luncheons, light meals, for the whole of a meal other than fish. A *Blanc de Noirs* of a rich year is best with meat (especially red meat and game); *foie gras*. If you insist on serving Champagne with the dessert choose a medium dry.
Still white Champagnes	Oysters, shellfish, crustaceans and grilled fish, in a sauce or boiled (same wine).
Still red Champagnes	White meat, roast, grilled or in a sauce (same wine); fine cold meats.

ALSACE

The Alsatian vineyards are to be found on the eastern slopes of the Vosges, between Strasbourg in the north and Mulhouse in the south.

The peculiarity of Alsatian wines (compared with other French wines, at least) is that they bear the name of the grape from which they are made instead of the names of the vineyards or parishes. The best known varieties are:

Chasselas and Sylvaner, which give light, fresh and fruity wines.

Grey Pinot (wrongly known as Tokay in Alsace), which yields strong and heady wines.

Muscat, famous for its fruity bouquet.

Riesling, which yields first class wines, elegant, fragrant, dry and thoroughbred.

Traminer and Gewürztraminer, oily wines sometimes almost resembling liqueurs, with a strong fragrance, wines of the first order.

There are also Zwicker and Edelzwicker, which are blends, often very agreeable ones, of several variety of grape.

Alsatian wines and the dishes to accompany them

Chasselas, Sylvaner, Zwicker, Edelzwicker	*Apéritif*; cold meat; *sauerkraut*; shellfish; fish.
Riesling or grey Pinot	Oysters; shellfish and fish, grilled or in a sauce (same wine); fresh salmon; white meat (chicken cooked in Riesling); Münster cheese (grey Pinot).
Traminer, Gewürztraminer or Muscat	*Foie gras*; smoked salmon; desserts (if not too sweet).

FRANCHE-COMTÉ

Between Burgundy and Switzerland the old province of Franche-Comté produces well-known wines, harvested on the last foot-hills of the Juras.

The most original is the *vin jaune* ("yellow wine") with a nutty flavour which is the result of a special wine-making process, and the most famous of these is Château-Chalon.

The region has another speciality, the *vins de paille* ("straw wines"), made from grapes dried on straw.

The other wines of Franche-Comté or Jura are the red, white, *rosé* and yellow Arbois and the wines of Etoile and Côtes-du-Jura.

Jura wines and the dishes to accompany them

Yellow wines	Will stand up (especially the Château-Chalon) to "difficult" dishes (duck with orange) with a strong flavour. Shellfish, crustaceans, also game and cheese.
Red wines	All kinds of meat.
White wines	Fish and shellfish.
Rosé wines	Cold meat. Throughout a whole meal.

THE LOIRE VALLEY

The name of the Loire valley (*Val de Loire*) groups together the wines harvested on the slopes along the Loire and its tributaries. If one travels down the river from its source to its mouth one finds Pouilly-sur-Loire, Sancerre-Quincy-Reuilly, Touraine, Saumur and Anjou, Muscadet.

The wines of Pouilly-sur-Loire, on the right bank of the river, of Sancerre on the left bank and those of Quincy and Reuilly share, with the variations caused by different soils, the fruity bouquet, the delicacy and the elegance of the Sauvignon vine, from which they are all made; they are dry and fresh.

The Touraine wines must be divided into red and white.

The best known of the white wines, Vouvray, is always thoroughbred and fragrant. It may be dry, medium-dry or sweet; treated by the "Champenoise" method it yields a most agreeable sparkling wine for an *apéritif* (extra dry) or dessert (medium dry). Let us also mention Montlouis, the neighbour of Vouvray (on the other bank) and the wines of Touraine accompanied by the name of the parish of origin.

Among red wines there are the well-known, violet-scented Chinon wines and Bourgeuil and Saint-Nicolas-de-Bourgueil, with a raspberry flavour (also registered as Touraine, accompanied by the name of the parish of origin).

Samur: Dry white wines, thoroughbred, which take fermentation well. The red wine of Saumur-Champigny, cousin of those of Chinon and Bourgueil—very fruity. Dry *rosés.*

Anjou: The white wines of Anjou are famous. Dry or sweet, they all have a remarkable scent or aroma. The different regions are Côteaux du Layon and the famous Bonnezeaux and Quarts-de-Chaume, which can mature magnificently. Côteaux de la Loire has drier, crisper wines, with the famous growths of Roche-aux-Moines and Coulée-de-Serrant, of very great quality; Côteaux de l'Aubance. The dry and sweet *rosés* are also well-known (*rosés* Cabernet).

Muscadet: This very dry, fresh and smooth wine, sometimes slightly sparkling (on lees) is harvested in the department of Loire-Atlantique. There are two regions—Sèvre-et-Maine and Côteaux de la Loire.

Loire wines and the dishes to accompany them

Pouilly-Fumé, Sancerre, Quincy, Reuilly, dry Vouvray, Montlouis, Saumur, dry Anjou, Muscadet	Oysters, shellfish; grilled or boiled crustaceans; fresh water fish (fresh salmon) or salt water fish (not fat), grilled, cooked in fish stock or in a sauce (same wine); regional pork specialities (Vouvray *rillettes* and *rillons, andouillette*); local goat cheeses (Chavignol and Sancerre),
Sweet Anjou and Vouvray	Dessert or *apéritif* (especially mature wines); *foie gras.*
Sparkling Saumur and Vouvray	*Apéritif,* lunch, light meals (extra dry); dessert (medium dry).
Chinon, Bourgueil, Saumur-Champigny	White meat, grilled or roast, in a sauce, (chicken cooked in wine, the same wine for the sauce and to drink); fish cooked with red wine (eel matelote); local cheeses.

CÔTES du RHÔNE

The vineyards of the Côtes du Rhône form terraces on both banks of the river over a distance of 125 miles, from the south of Lyons to the Rhône delta. The wines are different according to whether they were harvested in the north or in the south. They are therefore divided into two groups:

Northern Côtes-du-Rhône: Elegant, fragrant, heady red wines: Côtes-Rôties; Cornas; Hermitage; Crozes-Hermitage; Saint-Joseph. Dry, fragrant and aromatic white wines: Condrieu; Château-Grillet; Hermitage; Crozes-Hermitage; Saint-Péray; Saint-Joseph.

Southern Côtes-du-Rhône: Châteauneuf-du-Pape, a strong, full-bodied, luscious red wine. The generous red wines of Gigondas. The very dry, aromatic *rosé* wines of Tavel, Lirac, Chusclan.

Rhône wines and the dishes to accompany them

Northern Côtes-du-Rhône (red)	Red meat; grills; game; cheese.
Northern Côtes-du-Rhône (white)	Shellfish, crustaceans, grilled fish, fish in a sauce, smoked fish.
Châteauneuf-du-Pape and southern Côtes-du-Rhône (red)	Red meat; grills; furred game, even when well hung; cheese even when very ripe.
Tavel, Chusclan	Cold meat; entrées.

MEDITERRANEAN WINES

From Nice to Narbonne, vines have been cultivated for more than two thousand years. The vines swollen with the Mediterranean sun. The red wines are generous, full-bodied; the white wines dry, also full-bodied; the *rosé* wines, dry and true to type. There are also liqueur wines, very rich and keeping the fruity aroma of the Muscat grapes from which they are made.

Comté de Nince: Bellet wines (red and white). Provence: Cassis, Bandol and the V.D.Q.S., Côtes-de-Provence (red, *rosé*, white). Languedoc: V.D.Q.S. Costières-du-Gard (*rosé*), Corbieres and Miervois (red), A.O.C. Fitou (red); and the Muscats of Frontignan, Lunel, Mireval, Saint-Jean-Minervois.

Mediterranean wines and the dishes to accompany them

White wines	Shellfish and crustaceans; *bouillabaisse;* fish soup; *bourride*; grilled Mediterranean fish.
Rosé wines	*Pizza; paella; pissaladière;* all meat, fish and vegetables cooked in the local style.
Red wines	Red meat; grills with herbs; cheese.
Muscat	*Aperitif* and above all, dessert.

THE CATALAN COAST

These are the wines of Roussillon and the coast between Argelès and Cerbère. These are generous and full-bodied wines, of which the best-known and most elegant are Banyuls and Banyuls *grand cru*, which can compete on equal terms with the analogous wines of Spain and Portugal. Côtes-d'Agly, Rivesaltes and Muscat de Rivesaltes are also worth mentioning.

As regards the dishes to accompany them, these wines are often badly used and served as an *apéritif*, which is not their proper place.

A Banyuls *grand cru* goes perfectly with *foie gras*, fresh duck liver and local dishes (such as rock lobster stew). Like Port, it is a perfect drink at the end of a meal, with cheese or after dessert; it certainly increases a feeling of euphoria by several degrees. We also recommend it with melon.

VARIOUS WINES

Outside the major wine-growing regions in France there are many excellent wines of merit, which have their devotees. Most of them are drunk locally.

In the south-east, in the Garonne basin minus Bordeaux, there are a number of vineyards. Special mention should be given to Monbazillac, which produces a sweet white wine, similar to Sauternes, fragrant and aromatic.

Among the *appellations contrôlées* (officially named) wines you will discover Bergerac (red and white), Montravel (white), Madiran (red), Jurançon (white); Blanquette de Limoux is an excellent white wine which is sparkling by nature, like Gaillac, which also yields very fine still white wines. Among the V.D.Q.S. we have Cahors, Fronton, Rosé du Bearn, Irouléguy, Tursan, etc.

In the centre, the Côtes d'Auvergne and Forez (V.D.Q.S.) yield delicate red wines; let us also mention the wines of the Orléans region (*gris meunier*), and among the A.O.C., the Côteauex-du-Loir and Jasnières are not without merit.

In the south-east, in the Drôme area, there is the Clairette-de-Die, deliciously fruity, and, further south, the Muscat de Beaune-de-Venise. To the east of Champagne we have the Côtes-de-Toul.

Finally, the wines of Savoy, light, fragrant, very pleasant and fresh, sometimes having a slight sparkle merit the attention of the connoisseur: among the A.O.C. there are Crépy and Seyssel and among the V.D.Q.S., there are Abymes, Apremont, Marestel, Montmélian, etc., and the wines of Bugey.

What to eat with them? Naturally the regional products and specialities. These are perfect holiday wines. Monbazillac goes perfectly with fish in a fine sauce, *foie gras* and desserts that are not too sweet.

QUALITY OF THE FRENCH WINE VINTAGES

based on 20, from 1920 to 1962

This 58th edition of ratings based on 20 has been worked out as the result of many wine tastings.

This classification has a purely relative value. It is given by way of indication and the marks only apply to the whole of the year's successful wines. It in no way prejudges possible failures of an individual character and due to an œnological fault. In the same way they do not, in mediocre years, exclude very honorable wines, even brilliant successes, due to special circumstances.

R.V.F.

	Red Bordeaux	White Bordeaux	Red Burgundy	White Burgundy	Beaujolais	Alsace	Côtes du-Rhône	Loire Region	Champagne
1962	14	13	14	15	16	15	13	13	Vintages: 1945, 1947, 1949, 1952, 1953, 1955, 1957, 1959. Non-Vintage: Individual blend by each shipper.
1961	18	17	18	17	18	17	15	16	
1960	12	11	7	11	8	13	13	10	
1959	17	16	16	17	16	18	9	18	
1958	11	12	10	12	11	12	14	12	
1957	14	15	14	14	13	13	16	12	
1956	9	10	9	9	10	9	12	9	
1955	16	16	16	14	16	15	15	15	
1954	10	10	10	11	10		13		
1953	17	16	16	16	18	16	14	17	
1952	15	15	16	15	16	15	16	14	
1951	9	7	8	7		9	9		
1950	15	14	11	16		12	14	12	
1949	17	16	17	12		17	16	16	
1948	15	14	12	11			7	11	
1947	18	18	16	18		19	18	20	
1946	11	9	10	10			14		
1945	20	20	19	14			17	17	
1943	13	16	12	15			15	16	
1942	12	16	12	15			13	12	
1937	14	17	13	15			15	13	
1934	17	16	15	15			15	13	
1933	10	9	17	15			15	14	
1929	18	18	18	18			18	15	
1928	19	16	17	16			15	14	
1926	15	13	12	12			12	12	
1924	16	15	11	11			15	13	
1923	11	12	19	15			16	15	
1921	14	19	13	16			13	18	
1920	16	14	10	11			12	8	

Table established by "*Revue des Vins de France*".

The years which are not included are those where the wines can no longer be tasted. The years 1922, 1925, 1927, 1930, 1931, 1932, 1933, 1936, 1938, 1939, 1940, 1941, 1944, have been excluded because they were too mediocre. In fact, they do not have even a historical interest.

FRANÇOIS-M. D'ATHIS,
Secretary General of the
"*Revue du vin de France*"

▲ *Harvesting grapes in Swiss Vineyards* ▼

A village wine press

A selection of wines at the Lucas Carton Restaurant, Paris

896

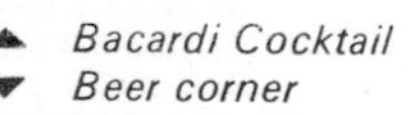

▲ *Bacardi Cocktail*
▼ *Beer corner*

The decoration and presentation of cocktails ▼

SWISS WINES

The major Swiss vineyards are situated in the sunny valleys of the Rhône, the Rhine and the Ticino, and on the sheltered and wide-spread banks of the Lakes of Bienne, Constance, Geneva, Lugano, Maggiore, Morat, Neuchâtel and Zürich. All these regions, with mild climates, are favourable for the ripening of grapes. The range of the wines of these different regions is very great and varies from one region to the next; it varies from dry and pearly white wines to the sweetest, from sparkling *rosés* and light red wines to the most full-bodied and smoothest.

The cultivation of the vine, the stock and the nature of the wines changes from one canton to the next. For this reason we distinguish between three groups of vineyards—those of French Switzerland, those of eastern Switzerland and those of southern Switzerland.

The vineyards of French Switzerland alone cover more than two-thirds of the area under vines. Soil and climate are particularly favourable to the Chasselas and Fendant (white stock) and the Pinot and Gamay (red stock). In eastern Switzerland the red stock is the commonest, particularly the black Pinot. The white stocks of Riesling and Sylvaner yield a wine that is much appreciated. South of the Alps, in Ticino and in the Grisons valley of Mesocco, the old vines, native varieties, yield the Nostrano, a wine scented with the aroma of the region. All the vineyards are now being planted with Merlot, a new stock originating in Bordeaux, which gives a smooth and velvety wine.

JUGOSLAV WINES

Jugoslavia offers a vast range of wines made from various stocks, some said to be directly descended from those of Roman times.

The major wine-growing region is found in Slovenia. White Burgundy, Traminer, Rheinriesling, Sauvignon and Furmint are grown there, white wines of remarkable quality, some dry, some sweet. The Gutedel stock produces an excellent table grape.

The red wines of Dalmatia and Brazza are tanned, very deep in colour and have a high alcohol content. Refosco and the Istrian Picolit are mellow and fragrant red wines.

GERMAN WINES

The German Federal Republic is the most northerly wine-growing country. Thanks to the exceptional climate of some regions the wines reach an absolutely remarkable quality.

The Rhineland produces white wines of the first quality (Riesling, Traminer, Gutedel and Mueller-Thurgau stock). The German red wines come from the same region. The Rhenish wines or hocks such as Ungstein, Deidesheimer, Kallstadt, Forst, Wachenheim, are perfumed, elegant and very agreeable to drink. The red wine of Bad Duerkheim is very well known. The wines of Hardt are very good little wines of everyday quality.

The wine-growing regions of Moselle, Saar and Ruwer produce only white wines. These growths have a world-wide reputation thanks to their elegant and fruity bouquet and their agreeable freshness.

The wines of Rheinhessen are fruity and characteristic, some are predominantly sweet in taste (Niersteiner, Oppenheimer). Many of the exported German wines are labelled Liebfrauenmilch. This is a sign of quality and of recognition of a product coming from

Rheinhessen. Liebfrauenmilch does not describe either a region or the product of any given producer. The red wine of Ingelheim has a high reputation.

The wine-growing region of Nahe produces thoroughbred wines with a generous bouquet. These wines come from the purest Riesling stock.

The wines of the Rheingau and middle Rhine are, with a few exceptions, harmonious and well-balanced Rieslings. Let us take note of the red wine of Assmannshausen.

The wine-growing regions of Baden produce white wines for everyday consumption and wines of great quality around the Kaiserstuhl. The surroundings of Buehl produce both red and white wine. Wuerttemberg is a region of red, fruity, thoroughbred and strong wines.

Franconia, with its capital Wuerzburg, produces a very well-known white wine known as Steinwein, bottled in bottles the shape of a goatskin bottle, hence the name Bocksbeutel. These wines have a flavour characteristic of the soil. Klingenberg is a much-appreciated red wine (Burgundy stock).

The Ahr region is famous for its red wines. We find little local wines there, agreeable, sweet and smooth. The stock is of Burgundy and Portuguese origin. The latter yields very light wines.

Thanks to selected grapes and the care of preparation, the wines of the Rhineland, Moselle-Saar-Ruwer, Rheinhessen, the middle Rhine and the Rheingau are of international standing and exceptional quality.

AUSTRIAN WINES

Among the wine-growing regions, lower Austria and the Burgenland should have first mention.

In lower Austria, the white stocks of Rheinriesling, Mueller-Thurgau, Neuburger, Gruener Weltliner, yield full-bodied, fruity wines. These stocks coming from white Burgundies are also cultivated in the Burgenland. The red Weltliner stocks yield an aromatic wine.

Ruster-Ansbruch, from the region of the lake of Neusidedel, is made from selected, half-dried grapes. It is a wine of pronounced character, closely resembling Tokay.

In the Vienna region, the growths coming from the Klosterneuburg domain are soft, with a fine bouquet and of great value. The stocks come from Burgundy.

The fruity wines of Sievering, Nussberg and Kallenberg are also much appreciated.

The Sudbahn region (south of Vienna) yields white wines of notable quality, produce of Riesling, Sylvaner and Traminer Muscat stocks. Rotgipfler is the product of a red vine from Burgundy. Styria produces wines of medium to good quality, products of Rheinriesling, Gutedel, Traminer and Furmint.

SPANISH WINES

Sherry, the wine of Jerez (or Xéres), has a world-wide reputation. However, the production of red wine is even greater. The major wine-growing regions are Levante, La Mancha, Rioja and Aragon. The red wines of Levante, Murcia and Alicante are the most famous and are the produce of Monastrell and Garnacha stocks. The red wines of La Mancha resemble Beaujolais, but are stronger. Those of Rioja are full-bodied and smooth and are reminiscent of Bordeaux. The sweet wines of the Ebro region (Aragon) are excellent, but are not yet exported.

HUNGARIAN WINES

The wines of Tokay are world-famous and come from the upper Tisza valley. White wine accounts for 70 per cent of all wine production. The main stocks, apart from Welschriesling (not to be confused with German Riesling or Rheinriesling), are green Sylvaner and grey Pinot. The other 30 per cent consist of red and *rosé* wine.

The Tokay wines of world-wide reputation have been produced for centuries on the southern slopes of the Carpathians, in the southern part of Hegyalja, the more distant surroundings of the town of Tokay. The stocks are Furmint and Muscat.

The manufacture of this wine is unusual in as much as the grapes are harvested as late as possible, that is when they look like dried currants. So the *marc* resembles a cake of dried raisins and is in no way comparable with ordinary *marc*.

A honey-like liquid remains at the bottom of the vat with the appearance and density of syrup. This liquid is known as essence of Tokay and has a sugar content of 40-60 per cent. This essence only ferments slowly and with difficulty and the alcohol content does not exceed 6-8 per cent even after several years of fermentation. Essence of Tokay is only produced in small quantities. After partial fermentation, this essence is mixed with the must in order to make a drink of great quality. The natural sweetness may be increased by adding up to 5 or 6 vats of essence to the must content of a cask (130 litres). A vat weighs some 12 to 13 kilos. One talks of a one-vat, two-vat, etc., wine, depending on the number of vats added to the cask. The label indicates the number of vats added, which makes it possible to recognise the sugar content. This wine keeps unusually well.

ITALIAN WINES

". . . no other plant is as interesting. It speaks to those who understand its language, is demanding or confiding; sometimes it sulks and denies itself, but in the end it again shows itself generous. One must always be close to it, never stop studying it. Sometimes it must be treated gently, sometimes artfully, sometimes even roughly, but it must always be served, always be loved and often satisfied. One year it is prodigal, the next miserly. It has charming caprices and diabolical perversities, but it is the Italiana plant honoured since time immemorial, the plant which yields the wine for our rites and our festivals, for our health, our lively youth and our smiling old age." Thus Arturo Marescalchi praised this "divine" plant, linked with the actual history of mankind.

The large variety of vineyards, systems of cultivation, nature and position of the various regions, gives Italy a number of qualities of wine and Piedmont, Tuscany, Venetia, Apulia and Sicily are the regions where production is highest.

Piedmont

Piedmont has a single type of dry white wine, Cortese, a wine for meatless *hors d'œuvre* and fish. The fresh and fragrant Moscato, with a white and persistent sparkle, is suitable with desserts. Using the "Champenoise" method, the same vineyard produces the medium dry, fresh and young Asti Spumante, which is exported all over the world. This region also has the red wines Barbara, Dolcetto, Grignolino, Bonarda, Nebbiolo *secco* and Freisa *secco*, the sparkling Brachetto and Freisa Amabile suitable for whole meals and desserts.

The Piedmontese growths also yield some great classical wines to drink with roasts and game, such as the thoroughbred Barolo, the elegant Barbaresco, the full-bodied Gattinara, the savourous Ghemme and the gentle Carema, all products of the Nebbiolo grape.

Liguria

Liguria does not have a large wine production. Its best known wines are the slightly bitter and fragrant red Rossese, a good accompaniment to an elegant meal; the white Vermentino, delicately perfumed, served with fish; and, near La Spezia, Cinqueterre served with fish if it is dry or with desserts if it is sweet; in the latter case it is known as Sciacchetrà. Mention should also be made of the white wines of Coronata and the Polcevera valley; they are served with fish and also with whole meals.

Lombardy

The great prestige wines of Lombardy are harvested in Valtellina. Grumello, Sassella and Inferno, suitable for ageing, they become superb in their maturity. They are drunk with roasts and game. Excellent red and *rosé* wines, light and fragrant, are produced on the banks of Lake Garda (Moniga). The very distinguished Lugana is the perfect accompaniment to Italian *hors d'œuvre*. The left bank of the Po, in the province of Pavia, yields an excellent Moscato, sparkling, with a gentle and delicate perfume, and the Pinots and Italian Rieslings to serve with fish.

Venetia

The three Venetias offer excellent red and white wines; the tender Terlano and the fruity Traminer, the fine Lago di Caldaro, Santa Maddalena and Termeno of the province of Bolzano; the fragrant Mezzocorona, Marzemino and Teroldego, of solid structure, from the province of Trento, all red wines of superior quality. The region of Gorizia yields excellent white wines, especially at Padua, Treviso and Conegliano. They include the famous Prosecco, dry, medium dry or sparkling, and the delicious sparkling Cartizze, which is drunk with dessert or between meals. Udine has its lemon yellow Tocai and its diuretic Verduzzo, which is a beautiful golden yellow. Among the red wines, the Merlot and Cabernet growths, which are very wide-spread, yield good products suitable for ageing. Verona is famous for its white Soave with *hors d'œuvre* and fish and for its Bardolino, Valpolicella and Valpantena, which are savoury and dry, and served throughout the meal.

Emilia-Romagna

Emilia is the district of light wines, produced in the plain, such as the nervy, sparkling and perfumed Lambrusco which blends harmoniously with pork, sausages and the "*zampone*" of Modena. Romagna is proud of its white Albana and the red Sangiovese, suitable for moderate ageing.

Tuscany

Tuscany is rightly celebrated for its Chianti Classico from the Siena vineyards, its gentle and harmonious Brunello di Montalcino and its Vino Nobile di Montepulciano, a superb trio to drink with roasts, after suitable maturing in cask. Florence offers the delicate white Pomino and the red Carmignano and Nipozzano, warm and even more thoroughbred then the classical Chianti itself.

Umbria

The green region of Umbria excels by its dry and soft Orvieto, dear to Pinturicchio, suitable with fish soups and thick soups, while the Marches, in the province of Ancona, offer the Verdicchio of the typical straw colour, a wine particularly suitable with fish.

Lazio (Latium)

In Latium the wines "*dei Castelli Romani*" (of the Roman castles), Frascati, Velletri and Marino, are at least as well known as Rome and they are drunk with meals, at room temperature or chilled (50-55° F); at Sperlonga they serve Cecubo, another good wine, already known in ancient times.

Abruzzi e Molise

In the Abruzzi, the vineyards of Sangiovese and Montepulciano yield other good wines to be drunk with meals.

Campagna

The region of Campagna, provides Aglia which blends harmoniously with the smoked sausage of the Irpinia region. Other good red and white wines are found at Solopaca—Asprino, of a delicate light green shade, very refreshing, to be drunk during the year; the historic white and red Falerno; in the province of Naples there is the famous Capri *bianco* and the delicate wine of Ischia, which goes well with fish and especially with deep fried dishes. The golden yellow Lacrima Christi and Gragnano with its aroma of faded violets are also appreciated. Vesuvius also offers a good range of wines, both red and white.

Apulia

In the beautiful region of Apulia, where the olive tree is often wedded to the twisted vine, and where the plain runs into the green hills, red, blended wines predominate, while the historic hamlets of Alberobello and Locorotondo produce an excellent white wine for meals and fish, the very famous Castel del Monte with a delicate aroma of candied fruit and the golden Malvasia, a dry and vigorous wine to serve with tasty fish soups, and the exquisite Aleatico, with desserts.

Calabria

The strong earth of Calabria offers a good wine, Cirò, bright in colour and with a full-bodied aroma, suitable for long ageing. Its alcohol content may be as high as 15%; it is served with piquant cheeses or desserts and it is served at room temperature. The hills of Reggio di Calabria yield the Greco di Gerace, a sweet dessert wine. This region has two other wines, Savuto and Pellaro, which after long ageing are particularly suitable as an accompaniment to roasts and braised dishes.

Sicily

The southern part of Italy also has a fairly considerable wine production. In Sicily, on the slopes of Etna, at a height of between 1,300 and 3,300 feet, excellent red and white wines are obtained. In the province of Syracuse an elegant dessert wine is found, obtained from a blend known as Pollio. White, red and *rosé* Ciclopi, Val di Lupo, exquisite with fish, Corvo di Casteldaccia, capable of rivalling the best Chablis of the year, are growths from the Catania region. In the western part of the island lies Marsala, a town which became famous in the second half of the eighteenth century, thanks to Sir John Woodhouse, who had an inquiring spirit and who made the whole world acquainted with the full-bodied wine of this region, called Marsala; it is capable of rivalling the Madeira, Port and Sherry.

Sardinia

In Sardinia, the site of an ancient civilisation, the vine has been cultivated since ancient times. The best-known wine of this region is the thoroughbred Vernaccia with a strong perfume and dry aroma, which can be aged for over 30 years. Oliena, of a bright red colour and strawberry scented, celebrated by Gabriele d'Annunzio, is the wine to take with a meal. The blonde Malvasia di Cagliari, dry and a little acidulated, with the typical scent of a flowering almond, goes well with rock lobster. The delicate golden Nasco, moss-scented, accompanies desserts. The red Monica is as delicate and thoroughbred as a Malaga. Girò, savorous thanks to its high alcohol content, is recommended for convalescents.

This brings us to the end of our short promenade across the vineyards of this country, known since the remotest times of antiquity under the famous name of Oenotria, which offers us wines of a very rich variety, appreciated down the ages and up to our times.

STEFANO ZACCONE
Maestro dell'ordine naz. assaggiatori di vino

PORTUGUESE WINES

The wines of Porto have a world-wide reputation and are produced from red stock. The white wines are less well known abroad but of very great quality. The wine of Minho (Minho verde) has an elegant and fruity bouquet. The wines produced from the Alvarinho and Azal growths are fresh, sparkling and similar to Moselle. The white wines of Dâo are fresh and light. Moscatel de Setubal is a characteristic sweet wine, coming from the south of Lisbon. North of Lisbon, a slightly acid wine, Bucelas, is harvested.

Wines from the New World

When introducing wines from the New World, we in Europe do make comparisons between their products and our own. An important fact to remember however, is that the wine producing countries of the New World are European in descent and culture. Their populations include the descendants of many *vignerons* from Europe. The skills, patient efficiency and desire to excel have travelled with them.

Soil and climatic conditions are different, but ancient acquaintance with viticulture has enabled these pioneers to seek out the best districts and climatic conditions for growing vines. They have been able to choose their sites and root stocks; naturally they met with many vicissitudes. In the majority of cases the early difficulties of wine production have been overcome and South Africa, Australia and America have now evolved vines which are evincing characters of their own, quite separate from those of Europe. This separateness will undoubtedly produce great wines in their own rights in the course of further and constant refinement, but they will not be the bulk wines of general purchase, any more than the great wines of France and Germany are. Because of their limited quantity, these growths are only for the connoisseurs and the discriminating few with sufficient wealth to indulge these undoubted luxuries of an ancient craft.

It is more to the point, if comparisons must be made, to compare the *Vins des Familles*, the great bulk productions, the *vins ordinaires* of health-giving, pleasant, stimulating properties which are in general use in the wine consuming countries, where the partaking of wine as the national drink is as old as their ancient civilisations.

One must go to the Midi with its Mediterranean climate and its close proximity to Algeria, from where wine is imported in tankers to be blended with the native product.

These are the wines consumed by a great many of the ordinary people of France, apart from local wines.

It would be folly to attempt a comparison between these *ordinaires*, the local wines of France, with the great wines of such famous communes as Burgundy, Bordeaux, Macon, Chablis, Rhône and Loire.

So also it would be just as odious were we to compare the bulk productions from the New World with the great growths of Europe.

The comparison is between the *ordinaires* of both, new and old. All are health giving and stimulating.

SOUTH AFRICAN WINE

The South African wine producing areas are within the temperate zones and enjoy a similar climate to the countries bordering the Mediterranean. As in Europe, there are small climatic differences which affect the quality, quantity and bouquet of the wines produced. The Cape and Stellenbosch areas have a distinctly insular climate which makes for greater variety of wines. Further inland, but still within the coastal belt, are situated the famous Paarl and Malmesbury districts.

The districts situated farther inland like Worcester, Tulbagh, Robertson, become more and more Continental in their climatic conditions.

These varying climatic and soil differences make for subtle yet marked differences in production.

During the vintage season, rainfall is at its minimum, allowing the grapes to ripen in ideal conditions without fungus diseases, where the term "*pourriture noble*" is unknown. Consequently every year is a more or less vintage year. A bad year is as rare as the true vintage years in Europe.

As a result of such favourable conditions, they lend themselves more readily to sweet wines as well as more full bodied and fortified dry wines.

In recent years much of the wine growing areas have been planted with the best vines, resulting in wines of real quality. This is the policy of the South African Government. The necessary improvements in vinification and cellar manipulation are progressing hand in hand.

The world famous Constantia district, though reduced in area through urbanisation, still produces the best quality light-bodied, red table wines from the Cabarnet Sauvignon, Schiras, Malbec and Cinsaut vines.

Stellenbosch and Paarl also produce excellent red table wines from the same sort of vines.

It is Cape policy to increase constantly the percentage of such vines as Sauvignon, Pinot, Gamay and Malbec and to eliminate those of mediocre quality.

White wine production is at a disadvantage because of the constant sunny climate which produces grapes of high sugar content and low in fixed acids. They are high in alcohol content, 11 to 12 per cent, but without much bouquet, similar to some of the white Burgundies. Grape types are Riesling, Sauvignon Blanc, Semillon, Clairette Blanche and Fransdruif or Spanish Palermino. The Paarl district is considered to produce the best wines of this type with really outstanding growths from the Stellenbosch and Tullagh districts.

Paarl and Stellenbosch also produce wines of excellent port character, both vintage and tawny, Cinsaut, Schiras and Teinturier being the vine species.

The Cape also produces a good sweet red wine comparable to Red Muscat de Frontignac, from the red Muscadel variety.

The inland districts of Worcester, Robinson, Montagu and Bonnievale likewise produce very good muscat wines of robust character, slightly lacking finesse and bouquet, whilst others of less robust character, principally from the Montagu and Bonnievale areas, produce wines of fine and delicate bouquet. There is also another variety of white from the same district which yields a wine of delicate flavour and excellent quality.

South Africa is justly proud of its sherries. Here soil is the determining factor. The lighter types of alluvial soils produce a light-bodied, delicate sherry, whilst the residual soils of granite and shale boast those of the robust type. The grape varieties being Steindruif, Fransdruif, Groendruif and to a lesser extent Pedro Ximines.

All sherries must conform to the exact formula of production. According to what is desired in the finished wine they must mature for the minimum period of two years up to ten in wooden casks of approximately 110 gallons.

The natural *flor* or mould which so characterises Spanish sherries is likewise indigenous to South Africa which ensures the production of excellent Finos, Olorosos and Brown sherries.

With the abundance of sweet grapes available the purest form of wine spirit is distilled. Brandy is only distilled from selected wines made to a rigidly controlled fixed prescription.

There is little doubt that South Africa with its short three-hundred years of viticulture and viniculture is producing wines of excellent quality, red and white table wines, sherries, ports and brandies, and is determined that her wines shall reach the highest levels of perfection.

AMERICAN WINE

When America was first discovered by the Norsemen a thousand years ago they named the new country Vinland, because of its profusion of wild grape vines. When, in turn, America was colonised by England and Holland, these early pioneers were also amazed at the prolific growths of the native vines.

Wine making was commenced but the results were disappointing. Thereafter European vines were imported but with despairing results for they sickened and died; it was to take more than two centuries to discover the reason. A few stalwarts, however, continued with the native vines and by cultivation they have been greatly improved, but the resultant wine does not suit the European palate. The State of New York, the biggest wine producing area outside of California, still grows a preponderance of the native vines and their derivatives under cultivation and produce wines of more than average quality.

American viticulture vis-a-vis European had been both *villain and saviour*. American root stocks were imported into France in the latter half of the nineteenth century for experimental purposes; in consequence of which both oidium and phylloxera were unwittingly introduced in the American stock, which attacked the European vines with disastrous results. As American stocks were generally immune to these diseases, great quantities of immune varieties were exported to Europe to redress the balance. However, the resultant wine was poor in quality. So grafting and hybrids have had to be cultivated to restore quality, and these combined researches in both France and America are achieving such good results that New York State is growing an increasing number of disease free hybrids with a resultant improvement in quality.

In California, with a Mediterranean climate, the vine has found conditions similar to Europe and, was first introduced there by the Spaniards in the sixteenth century. Since then, Californian wine production has improved in quality and increased in productivity, until today, this western State produces at least 90 per cent of all the wines of America.

Unfortunately for America, its viticulture has suffered a chequered history. After long years of careful siting and the choice of vines, its *vignerons* were dismayed and many went out of business during the period of prohibition. Famous vineyards were destroyed or given over to other varieties, and the experience, loyalties and expertise of its viticulturists disrupted and dispersed. With the repeal of this menacing law, viticulture had to hoist itself up again by its shoe-strings. This long up-hill struggle is still continuing and with help from the oenological branches of university research, great progress is being made.

American wine production is still small in comparison with that of France. So too is its pattern of production, for more than 80 per cent of its wines are of the fortified type such as sherry, ports and Vermouths, which the hot sun, irrigation and rich soils of California produce in abundance.

The higher and more temperate vineyards produce the red and white table wines, many of them of excellent quality.

Much grape juice is sent to the eastern States from which a great deal of champagne type and sparkling wines are made.

In fact, the American wine industry is very much alive with its attendant vast possibilities of growth. In the course of time, great growths comparable to those of Europe will surely be produced, with this reservation that, like those of Europe, they will be in short supply.

AUSTRALIAN WINE

Australia, the only continent entirely in the southern hemisphere, stretches from the rain forests of the tropical north to snow covered mountains in the south.

In such a great land mass there must be great variations in soil and climate, ranging from rich alluvial to granite, shale and calcareous, from hot to temperate climate. A small population in relationship to area has enabled the viticulturist more or less to choose the sites of his vineyards at will and this choice is far wider than that in Europe.

Good rainfall during the dormant period coupled with a dry, sunny atmosphere during the vintage time, must and does produce wines of excellent quality and great variety.

The transfer of the vine stocks of Europe to the new climatic conditions of Australia has produced wines with a different palate and bouquet, differed and intriguing, thereby establishing themselves in their own rights as wines of purity, quality and character.

The variety of choice of vines can best be exemplified by the weight of crop. The shy bearers from areas of average rainfall yield up to 3 tons per acre, the "*cépages d'abondance*" from the river valleys average 15 tons per acre. These crops may be either delicate red and white table wines or the robust and full-bodied table wines; sherries, ports and herbal wines such as vermouth.

The history of Australian wines has been one of continual progress from the day in 1788 when Captain Arthur Phillip planted the first vine, to the present day. Free of violent atmospheric changes and deadly pests, the vines have progressed and proliferated over this newly discovered continent. A great name in Australian viticulture—Gregory Blaxland—who was awarded the Silver Medal in London in 1822 and the Gold Medal in 1827 for his red wines, pointed clearly to the potentialities of Australian wine culture. Other great *vignerons* followed, men of experience and enthusiasm, who were well acquainted with the great vineyards and *vignerons* of Europe, knew their land was a land of promise and planted accordingly.

With an established oenological research department, constant revision of cellar manipulation and great storage cellars, wines of purity and quality are constant.

There are five great wine producing States: New South Wales; Victoria; South Australia; Western Australia and Queensland.

Queensland the youngest of the States and youngest and smallest of the wine producers whose first wines were not planted until 1899 produces principally red and white table and dessert wines.

Western Australia next to Queensland in volume of production, specialises in red and white table wines as well as a variety of others.

New South Wales. The oldest State where the first vines were planted produces a great variety of wines including red and white table wines, dry fortified white and red wines, sparkling, sherries, ports, vermouths, muscats and brandy.

Victoria has a similar production to New South Wales.

South Australia. The largest wine producing State in Australia which produces 75 per cent of the total quantity. South Australia has good rainfall during the dormant period, a sparkling climate and the summer sun tempered by the waters of the St. Vincent Gulf. Here celebrated vineyards extend for mile upon mile on the undulating hills. Here grow the Rieslings, Cabernet, Pinots, Shiraz, Tokay, Verdelho, Malbec, Grenache, Carignan and Mataro vines, producing every variety of wine.

Cocktails

Cocktails are not drunk a great deal in this country, most people preferring the rather stereotyped gin and tonic, or gin and bitter lemon. Indeed many people are apt to look askance when presented with a strange mixture from a jug at a cocktail party. However it is a pleasant change to mix the occasional cocktail and the most popular are listed below.

The basic ingredients for all cocktails are spirits, vermouths, liqueurs, and fruit juice in various proportions. Apart from the liquid ingredients you will need a cocktail shaker, a tall jug for mixing and a spoon, a nutmeg grater and fruit squeezer, an ice pick, an ice crusher, drinking straws, Angostura bitters, red curaçao, orange bitters, Worcester sauce, tabasco, cloves, cocktail onions and olives. You will also need a salt and pepper shaker.

Except for sours and flips which are special kinds of mixtures, all the cocktails listed below are in alphabetical order.

MIXING COCKTAILS

Cocktails are either shaken or stirred. The procedures indicated in the recipes which follow by the words "stir and strain" or "shake and strain" are as follows:

Stir and strain: put ice into the mixing glass, pour in the necessary ingredients, stir with the mixing spoon until chilled, then strain into the required glass.

Shake and strain: put ice into the cocktail shaker, pour in the necessary ingredients, shake shortly and sharply (unless otherwise instructed). Strain into the required glass.

Glasses: unless otherwise stated the normal 2 oz or 3 oz cocktail glass should be used.

Alaska

Cocktail shaker:
$\frac{1}{3}$ yellow Chartreuse
$\frac{2}{3}$ gin

Shake and strain and serve in a cocktail glass.

Alexander

Cocktail shaker:
1 teaspoon fresh cream
$\frac{1}{3}$ Crème de Cacao
$\frac{2}{3}$ brandy

Shake and strain and serve in a double cocktail glass.

Americano

A tumbler:
$\frac{1}{3}$ Campari bitter
$\frac{2}{3}$ Italian vermouth
Zest of lemon

Put the above ingredients in a tumbler with some ice, top up with a little soda water.

Barbotage

Cocktail shaker:
1 coffeespoon of grenadine
$\frac{1}{2}$ lemon juice
$\frac{1}{2}$ orange juice

Shake and strain and pour into a double cocktail glass and fill up with champagne.

Bellini

A champagne glass or tumbler:
$\frac{1}{6}$ fresh peach juice

Fill up the glass with dry champagne.

To make the peach juice, take ripe peaches, remove the stones and pass them through a sieve till only the skin remains. Add the juice of 2 lemons, bottle and place in the refrigerator. (Will keep two days.)

Black Velvet

Gently pour equal parts of stout and champagne into a tumbler.

Bloody Mary

A small tumbler:
Some pieces of ice
1 dash of lemon juice
2 dashes of Worcester sauce
1 glass of vodka

Fill up with tomato juice and stir well.

Bourbon Collins

Use bourbon instead of gin.

Bourbon Old-Fashioned

Crush a quarter of a lump of sugar soaked in angostura in a half-tumbler. Fill with ice, add a glass of bourbon whisky and decorate with oranges, cherries, or zest of lemon.

Brandy Egg Nog

Cocktail shaker:
1 coffeespoon of sugar
1 egg yolk
1 glass of brandy

Fill up with milk. Shake and strain and serve in a large tumbler and dust with with grated nutmeg.

Brandy Fizz

Cocktail shaker:
1 coffeespoon sugar
The juice of half a lemon
1 glass of brandy

Shake and strain and serve in a tumbler and fill up with soda.

Brandy Old-Fashioned

Use brandy instead of the bourbon.

Bronx

Cocktail shaker:
2 dashes of orange juice
$\frac{1}{6}$ dry vermouth
$\frac{1}{6}$ Italian vermouth
$\frac{2}{3}$ gin

Shake and strain and serve in a cocktail glass.

Cardinal

Cocktail shaker:
$\frac{1}{6}$ Campari bitter
$\frac{1}{3}$ dry vermouth
$\frac{1}{2}$ gin
Shake and strain and serve in a cocktail glass. Add lemon zest.

Champagne Cocktail

A champagne glass:
A quarter of a lump of sugar
A dash of Angostura
A dash of brandy
Fill the glass with champagne.
Press and add the zest of an orange.

Cuba

A tumbler full of ice:
1 glass of Bacardi rum
Fill up with Coca Cola. Decorate with a slice of lemon.

Daiquiri

Cocktail shaker:
1 coffeespoon of sugarcane syrup
The juice of half a lemon
1 glass of white rum
Shake and strain and serve in a cocktail glass.

Daisy Gin

Cocktail shaker:
A dash of grenadine
The juice of half a lemon
1 measure of gin
Shake and strain and serve in a double cocktail glass filled with finely crushed ice.

Dubonnet Cocktail

A mixing jug:
$\frac{2}{3}$ Dubonnet
$\frac{1}{3}$ gin
Stir and strain and serve in a cocktail glass.

Gin Fizz

Cocktail shaker:
1 coffeespoon of sugar
The juice of half a lemon
1 glass of gin
Shake and strain and serve in a tumbler with soda.

Golden Fizz

Cocktail shaker:
1 egg yolk
1 coffeespoon of sugar
The juice of half a lemon
1 glass of gin
Shake and strain and serve in a tumbler and add soda water.

Gritti

Cocktail shaker:
$\frac{1}{6}$ dry Martini
$\frac{1}{3}$ Campari bitter
$\frac{1}{2}$ dry vermouth
Shake and strain and serve in a double cocktail glass. Add a dash of soda water and the zest of one orange.

Honeymoon

Cocktail shaker:
The juice of $1\frac{1}{2}$ lemons
1 coffeespoon of honey
1 glass of rum
A little egg white
Shake and strain and serve in a double cocktail glass.

Manhattan

A few drops of Angostura
$\frac{1}{5}$ Italian vermouth
$\frac{4}{5}$ bourbon, rye or blended whisky
Stir and strain and serve in a cocktail glass and add a cherry.

Dry Martini

A mixing jug:
$\frac{1}{5}$ dry vermouth
$\frac{4}{5}$ gin
Stir and strain and serve in a cocktail glass.

Negroni

Cocktail shaker:
$\frac{1}{3}$ Campari bitter
$\frac{1}{3}$ gin
$\frac{1}{3}$ red vermouth
$\frac{1}{2}$ slice of orange
Shake and strain and serve in a cocktail glass with a zest of lemon.

Orange Blossom

Cocktail shaker:
The juice of half an orange
$\frac{1}{2}$ glass of gin
Shake and strain and serve in a double cocktail glass.

Paradise

1 coffeespoon of orange juice
$\frac{1}{3}$ apricot brandy
$\frac{2}{3}$ gin
Shake and strain and serve in a cocktail glass.

Pimm's No. 1

A $\frac{1}{2}$-pint tankard:
Put 3 or 4 lumps of ice in the tankard
1 measure of Pimm's
Fill with lemonade. Decorate with half a slice of orange, 2 cherries and a twist of 1 lemon.
Cucumber peel and a bunch of fresh mint can also be added.

Pink Lady

Cocktail shaker:
1 dash of grenadine
The juice of half a lemon
1 glass of gin
Shake and strain and serve in a double cocktail glass.

Rum Fizz

Cocktail shaker:
1 coffeespoon of sugar
The juice of half a lemon
1 glass of rum
Shake and strain and serve in a tumbler and fill up with soda.

Rose Cocktail

A mixing jug:
$\frac{2}{3}$ dry vermouth
$\frac{1}{6}$ Kirsch
$\frac{1}{6}$ red currant syrup
Stir and strain and serve in a cocktail glass and add a cherry.

Scotch Old-Fashioned

Replace the bourbon by Scotch.

Side-Car

Cocktail shaker:
1 coffeespoon of lemon juice
$\frac{1}{3}$ Cointreau
$\frac{2}{3}$ brandy
Shake and strain and serve in a cocktail glass.

Silver Fizz

Cocktail shaker:
The white of an egg
1 coffeespoon of sugar
The juice of half a lemon
1 glass of gin
Shake and strain and serve in a tumbler and add soda water.

Singapore Sling

Cocktail shaker:
The juice of half a lemon
$\frac{1}{2}$ glass of gin
$\frac{1}{2}$ glass of cherry brandy
Shake and strain and serve in a tumbler and add soda water.

Tom Collins

A large glass or tumbler:
Some pieces of ice
1 coffeespoon of sugar
The juice of half a lemon
1 glass of gin

Add soda water and stir.

White Lady

Cocktail shaker:
1 coffeespoon of lemon juice
$\frac{1}{3}$ Cointreau
$\frac{2}{3}$ gin

Shake and strain and serve in a cocktail glass.

FLIPS

Brandy Flip

Cocktail shaker:
1 coffeespoon of sugar
1 egg yolk
1 glass of brandy

Shake and strain and serve in a double cocktail glass. Dust with grated nutmeg.

Port Flip

Cocktail shaker:
1 coffeespoon of sugar
1 egg yolk
1 glass of port
A few drops of brandy

Shake and strain and serve in a double cocktail glass. Dust with grated nutmeg.

Planter's Punch

A large tumbler full of ice:
2 dashes of Angostura.
The juice of half a lemon
1 measure of golden rum

Fill with soda, decorate with half a slice of pineapple or add a dash of pineapple juice.

Sherry Flip

Cocktail shaker:
1 coffeespoon of sugar
1 egg yolk
1 glass of sherry
A few drops of brandy

Shake and strain and serve in a double cocktail glass. Dust with grated nutmeg.

SOURS

Armagnac Sour

Cocktail shaker:
1 coffeespoon of sugar
The juice of half a lemon
1 glass of Armagnac

Shake and strain and serve in a double cocktail glass.

Bourbon Sour

Use bourbon instead of Armagnac

Brandy Sour

Use brandy instead of Armagnac

Gin Sour

Use gin instead of Armagnac

Rye Sour

Use rye whisky instead of Armagnac

Whiskey Sour

Cocktail shaker:
1 teaspoon of sugar
The juice of half a lemon
1 glass of whiskey

Shake and strain and serve in a double cocktail glass.

We are indebted to:

THE RESTAURANT LUCAS CARTON, PARIS

THE HOTEL CARLTON SENATO, MILAN · THE GRAND HOTEL DES BAINS, VENICE-LIDO

THE HOTEL-GRITTI-PALACE, VENICE · THE CONFISERIE KRANZLER, FRANKFURT

MESSRS. LACROIX, Pâtés and Delicatessen manufactores, FRANKFURT

MANUEL & CIE, Delicatessen merchant and Pastry shop, LAUSANNE

THE RESTAURANT MÖWENPICK, ZURICH

THE PARKHOTEL, FRANKFURT

THE PIZZERIA "A SANTA LUCIA", MILAN

who contributed the various dishes illustrated in this book

BÉARD INC., MONTREUX · CHRISTOFLE, PARIS, LONDON AND NEW YORK

DOMINICI, VENICE · MAPPIN AND WEBB, PARIS AND LONDON

STEIGER, LAUSANNE AND BERN

whose silverware was kindly placed at our disposal

COPELAND . RICHARD GINORI, VENICE, PARIS AND NEW YORK

MEISSEN . PRIMAVERA, ATELIER D'ART "AU PRINTEMPS" IN PARIS

THE CRYSTAL FACTORIES BACCARAT, SAINT-LOUIS, VAL-SAINT-LAMBERT, FRANCE

THE ART GLASS FACTORIES VENINI, VENICE

for the loan of crockery, chinaware and glass

MR. JESURUM, napery/lace-work, VENICE

THE HOTEL GRITTI-PALACE IN VENICE · PRIMAVERA, ATELIER D'ART "AU PRINTEMPS" IN PARIS

THE GALLERY ZÉBERLI, Antique-shop, LAUSANNE

in whose premises the interior photographs were taken

MR. MARC LEYVRAZ, viticulturist and wine-merchant at RIVAZ

for pictures of his cellars

MR. JEAN FROEHLICH, LA CHAUX-DE-FONDS . MR. ERIC MULLER-GRUNITZ, ASCHAFFENBURG

MR. JACQUES PRIMOIS, PARIS, photographers

Index

NOTE ON SUB-HEADINGS: Sub-headings (under names of ingredients) are arranged basically in two groups: (1) those which put the ingredient into a particular context, e.g. *Onions: soups*, (2) those which consist of actual recipe titles referring to chapters where the ingredient is being dealt with at length, e.g. *Onions: oignons frits*. The sub-headings in each of these groups are arranged in the order of the book—i.e. page number order—and not in alphabetical order. This has been done mainly to ensure consistency with the many entries in the index where the sub-headings follow the order of the text—entries which perform in fact the function of a detailed contents list for the chapters concerned (see *Meat*). This has been made a feature of the index since in a work of this type a "bird's-eye view" or "map" of a chapter is of great assistance, obviating as it does the necessity of scanning many pages of text. For examples of the above principles please refer to the entries under *Apples* and *Sauces*.

Page numbers in **bold type** refer to illustrations.

The Chef's
Supplement

Cooking and Nutrition

It is not enough to prepare tasty dishes, as a healthy body largely depends on the proper and balanced supply of the nutrients which are the important parts of all foods.

Proteins, carbohydrates (sugars and starches), fats, minerals and vitamins all have an important role to play in the body and the value of a diet must be expressed in terms of required daily amount of these nutrients.

DAILY REQUIREMENTS

Historically the necessary daily energy requirements have dominated nutrition, and people are still classified into groups depending on their sex, age, type of work, etc.

Today it is realised that good health is controlled more by a correct balance of protective and protein foods rather than by the total calorie intake. This does not imply that energy is unimportant, merely that Calorie intake should take second place when planning balanced meals.

PROTECTIVE FOODS

The protective foods are those which supply the vitamins and minerals required for the normal functioning of body processes. Important nutrients include: calcium, iron, sodium, iodine, vitamins A.D.C.B. complex. Foods relatively rich in these nutrients include dairy produce, eggs, meat, fish, green vegetables, tomatoes, carrots, fruits, whole cereals and offal. Many of these commodities have multiple roles as, in addition, they supply proteins and calories.

PROTEIN FOODS

Protein foods supply the materials required to build body tissues. A normal adult man would require 1 g. of protein per day for every kilogram of body weight. Thus a man weighing 11 stones (70 kilos) would require approximately 2½ oz. (70 g) and a woman weighing 8 stones 11 pounds (56 kilos) would need 2 oz. (56 g). During adolescence, pregnancy and child weaning the values would be increased to deal with these special growth conditions.

Foods supplying proteins can be graded according to their value in a diet. High on the list are milk, eggs, meat and fish while at the lower end of the grading there would be cereals, pulses and nuts.

From all the facts it appears that animal foods are better promoters of growth than vegetable produce, but there are exceptions to this which should be fully exploited when planning vegetarian diets. But in general all diets should include at least a proportion of animal foods, with children and adolescents receiving proportionately more than the adults. Of the 70 g of protein, required daily by a normal male adult, approximately 37 g should be obtained from animal sources. Again many protein foods are also suppliers of vitamins, minerals and calories.

ENERGY FOODS

The fats, carbohydrates (sugars and starches) and to a lesser extent protein are the suppliers of Calories to the body which are required to move muscles, maintain body temperature, etc. A normal man doing moderately active work would require approximately 3,000 calories a day, a normal woman would find 2,500 adequate.

Fat foods are a particularly valuable source as weight for weight they produce a little more than twice the calories that carbohydrate and protein foods supply. Fat also has a satiety value, lying in the stomach for longer periods of time. As few people would enjoy a very high fat diet, the proper balance of fat, carbohydrate and protein foods must be maintained. It has been suggested that in a diet, fat should supply approximately 25 per cent of the calories, protein 11 per cent, and the balance being supplied by the carbohydrates.

When foods are calculated in terms of Calories per 3½ oz (100 g) of food as per tables the cook is able to see at a glance the weight of a particular foodstuff supplying the necessary calories. High calorie foods include: Fats and oils, cereals, flour, pastry, bread, bakery products, sugar and honey, potatoes and starches.

The figures in the table refer to averages for the various foodstuffs which vary somewhat according to quality and season. The figures give the percentages of the edible part of the raw foodstuff. The "waste" column covers the edible waste—bones, skin, sinews, fish bones, peel, etc. K Cal stands for the number of calories per 3½ oz food. The signs ++ indicate a high vitamin content, + a considerable vitamin content and . an insignificant or unknown vitamin content.

This section on nutrition is, by its very nature, merely an outline, and caterers interested in nutritional needs are well advised to attend one of the specialised courses devoted to nutritional studies. However, one can state that cooks should always attempt to ensure that the protective and protein (especially animal) foods are well represented in all diets and menus.

NUTRITION CHART

Food	Protein %	Fat %	Carbohydrate %	K cal 3½ oz (100g)	Waste %	Vitamins A	B_1	B_2	C	D	E
1. Meat and Offal											
Duck, oven-ready . . .	18.0	4.0	—	111	13.5	.	.	.	+	.	.
Goose, oven-ready . .	11.0	34.5	—	366	22.2	.	.	.	+	.	.
Chicken, oven-ready . .	17.0	4.0	—	107	15.5	.	++	.	+	.	.
Rabbit	19.0	7.0	—	142	13.0	.	++	.	.	.	.
Venison, haunch . .	18.1	3.4	0.5	109	12.5	.	.	.	.	.	.
Offal, average	15.9	4.8	1.0	114	9.5	++	+	++	++	+	.
Veal, average	16.1	6.9	0.2	131	18.7	.	.	.	.	.	.
Beef, medium fat, average	16.7	6.6	0.3	131	16.0	.	.	.	.	.	.
Pork, fat average . . .	11.0	20.1	0.2	233	31.4	.	+	.	.	+	.
Bacon, smoked and salted	9.0	72.8	—	714	—	.	.	.	.	+	.
Calves' brains	8.5	8.1	—	110	5.7	.	.	+	+	.	.
2. Fish											
Eel	9.3	20.9	—	233	24.0	Fish meat, average					
Eel, smoked	13.2	22.4	0.2	263	24.0	.	.	+	.	.	.
Buckling	13.7	9.9	—	148	37.0						
Herring, fresh . . .	8.3	3.5	—	67	33.5	Fish roe, average					
Herring, salt	14.0	11.4	0.9	167	31.7	.	++	++	+	.	.
Cod	8.3	0.1	—	35	54.0						
Carp	7.5	4.4	—	72	55.0	Fish, liver, average					
Plaice	11.1	0.5	—	50	37.1	++	+	+	.	++	.

Food	Protein %	Fat %	Carbo-hydrate %	K cal 3½ oz. (100g)	Waste %	Vitamins A	B1	B2	C	D	E
3. Egg and Egg Products											
Hen's egg	12.3	10.7	0.5	152	12.7	++	.	+	.	++	+
Egg yolk	16.1	31.7	0.3	362	—	++	.	+	.	++	+
Egg white	12.8	0.3	0.7	58	—	.	.	+	.	.	.
Dried whole egg	43.2	40.9	2.0	566	—	.	.	.	.	.	.
Dried egg yolk	35.1	53.2	1.0	643	—	.	.	.	.	.	.
Dried egg white	73.4	0.3	4.0	320	—	.	.	.	.	.	.
4. Milk and Milk Products											
Cow's milk, 3.6% fat content	3.4	3.6	4.8	67	—	+	.	+	+	+	.
Skim milk	3.7	0.1	4.8	36	—	.	.	+	+	.	.
Buttermilk	3.7	0.5	3.7	35	—	.	.	.	.	.	.
Condensed milk	8.0	9.3	10.9	164	—	+	.	+	.	+	.
Whipped cream	2.7	30.0	3.0	302	—	+	.	.	.	.	.
Cheese: whole fat	25.6	26.6	2.1	361	5.9	+	.	+	.	+	+
half fat	36.2	9.9	3.0	253	4.2	.	.	.	.	.	.
lean	37.2	2.6	3.8	192	4.8	.	.	.	.	.	.
Cream cheese (curds)	17.6	0.1	4.1	90	—	.	.	.	.	.	.
5. Fats and Oils											
Butter, average	0.9	80.0	0.9	751	—	++	.	.	.	++	.
Cocoa butter	—	99.8	—	928	—	.	.	.	.	++	+
Margarine	0.5	80.0	0.4	748	—	++	.	.	.	.	.
Vegetable oil	—	99.5	—	925	—	.	.	.	.	.	+
Beef suet	0.5	99.2	—	925	—	.	.	.	.	.	.
Lard	0.3	99.4	—	926	—	.	.	.	.	.	+
6. Cereals, Flour and Pasta											
Semolina	9.4	1.0	74.6	354	—	.	+	+	.	.	.
Oatflakes	14.4	6.8	66.5	395	—	.	+	+	.	.	.
Rice	7.9	0.5	77.8	356	—	.	+	+	.	.	.
Potato flour	0.9	0.1	80.7	335	—	.	.	.	.	.	.
Rye flour	5.9	0.6	75.7	340	—	.	.	.	.	.	.
Wheat flour	11.6	0.9	71.5	349	—	.	.	.	.	.	.
Egg noodles	10.2	2.2	74.1	366	—	.	.	.	.	.	.
Macaroni	9.6	1.0	75.9	360	—	.	.	.	.	.	.
7. Bread and Bakery Products											
Rye wholemeal bread	7.4	1.1	50.4	247	—	.	+	+	.	.	.
Wheat flour (white)	8.2	1.2	48.6	244	—	.	+	.	.	.	.
Crispbread	11.4	1.8	78.6	386	—	.	+	+	.	.	.
Rolls	9.5	1.4	58.3	291	—	.	+	.	.	.	.
Rusks	9.9	5.2	78.2	410	—	.	.	.	.	.	.
8. Sugar, Honey											
Beet sugar	—	—	99.8	409	—	.	.	.	.	.	.
Bee honey	0.4	—	81.0	334	—	.	.	.	.	.	.
9. Potatoes											
Potatoes (peeled)	2.0	0.2	20.9	96	—	+	+	.	++	.	+

Food	Fruit acid	Protein %	Fat %	Carbo-hydrate %	K cal 3½ oz (100g)	Waste %	Vitamins A	B1	B2	C	D	E
10. Vegetables, Mushrooms												
Cauliflower		1.5	0.2	2.8	20	38.0	·	+	·	++	·	·
Mushrooms		2.6	0.1	1.9	19	46.0	·	·	·	·	++	·
Green peas		2.6	0.2	5.0	33	60.0	+	+	+	++	·	·
French beans		2.5	0.2	6.1	37	4.0	+	·	+	+	·	·
Cucumbers		0.6	0.2	1.0	8	27.5	·	·	·	+	·	·
Carrots		0.5	0.1	3.9	19	52.0	++	+	·	·	·	·
Lettuce		1.3	0.1	1.5	12	33.0	++	·	+	+	·	++
Pot herbs		3.7	0.8	8.0	56	2.5	++	·	+	+	·	+
Marrow		0.8	6.1	4.5	23	30.5	·	·	·	+	·	·
Leeks		2.0	0.3	4.5	29	17.8	+	·	·	+	·	·
Green peppers (whole)		10.0	8.0	21.8	205	36.4	·	·	·	++	·	·
Chanterelles		2.1	0.3	3.0	24	20.0	·	·	·	·	++	·
Radish		1.4	0.1	6.1	32	27.8	·	+	·	++	·	·
Brussels sprouts		4.7	0.4	5.9	47	11.4	+	+	·	++	·	·
Beetroot		1.0	0.1	5.4	27	21.0	·	+	+	·	·	·
Red Cabbage		1.3	0.2	3.8	23	21.0	·	+	+	++	·	·
Sauerkraut		1.4	0.3	2.8	26	—	·	·	·	++	·	·
Celeriac		0.9	0.2	5.4	28	38.3	·	·	·	·	·	·
Asparagus		1.3	0.1	1.6	13	33.0	·	·	·	·	·	·
Spinach		1.8	0.2	1.6	16	20.0	++	·	+	++	·	·
Boletus		4.3	0.3	4.2	38	20.0	·	·	·	·	++	·
Tomatoes		0.9	0.2	3.4	21	15.0	+	·	·	++	·	·
White cabbage		1.2	0.2	3.2	20	23.0	·	·	+	++	·	·
Onions		1.2	0.1	8.9	42	53.0	·	·	·	·	·	·
11. Pulses												
Beans		23.7	2.0	56.1	346	—	·	+	·	·	·	
Peas		23.4	1.9	52.7	330	—	·	+	·	·	·	·
Lentils		26.0	1.9	52.8	341	—	·	+	+	·	·	·
12. Fruit	Fruit acid											
Apples	0.64	0.4	—	13.0	58	2.7	·	·	·	+	·	·
Oranges	0.96	0.6	—	9.0	43	29.0	·	·	·	++	·	·
Apricots	1.2	0.9	—	10.5	51	5.4	+	·	+	+	·	·
Bananas	0.3	0.9	—	15.5	68	12.0	·	·	·	+	·	·
Pears	0.26	0.4	—	13.0	56	4.3	·	·	·	·	·	·
Strawberries	1.8	1.3	—	7.6	43	2.4	·	·	·	++	·	·
Hips	3.3	4.1	—	24.6	129	—	++	·	·	++	·	·
Hazelnuts	—	8.7	31.3	3.6	341	50.0	·	+	·	+	·	+
Redcurrants	2.4	1.3	—	7.4	44	1.6	+	·	·	++	·	·
Cherries, sweet	0.6	0.8	—	15.1	68	4.5	+	·	·	+	·	·
Plums	0.9	0.8	—	15.7	71	5.8	·	+	·	+	·	·
Sultana	—	1.6	1.2	66.2	295	—	·	·	·	·	·	·
Gooseberries	1.9	0.9	—	8.6	45	—	·	+	·	++	·	·
Walnuts	—	6.7	23.5	5.2	267	60.0	·	+	·	++	·	+
Lemons	5.9	0.6	—	2.3	32	35.7	·	+	+	++	·	·
Dried fruit	—	1.9	0.9	60.3	269	5.6	·	·	·	·	·	·
13. Cocoa and Cocoa Products												
Cocoa powder (average)		18.0	14.0	51.0	413	—	·	·	·	·	·	·
Chocolate		6.9	26.0	62.0	525	—	·	·	·	·	·	·

A Short Outline on Food Freezing

The object of any food preserving technique is to take food at its point of maximum palatability and nutritive value and keep it at this stage instead of allowing it to undergo natural changes which make it unfit for human consumption.

Natural deterioration is caused by the growth and metabolism of bacteria and other micro-organisms together with the action of enzymes on the foods concerned.

One method of retarding microbial growth and at the same time slow down enzymic reactions would be to remove the "liquid" state of water by simply turning it into ice. This is the aim of food freezing processes.

As most foods have relatively high moisture contents, (almost two-thirds of the raw weight) most freeze solidly at temperatures between 32°F and 23°F (0°C to −5°C).

The success of any freezing method will depend on the speed with which water may be turned into ice. Ordinary freezing, for example in the ice-box of a domestic refrigerator, is very slow, taking three hours or more, so that large pointed ice crystals are formed which damage the cells of food especially fruit and vegetables. On thawing, the foods tend to lose their texture as well as many valuable nutrients and flavouring compounds which are lost to the drip fluid.

For this reason it is imperative that foods be frozen as quickly as possible. Manufacturers call this process Quick Freezing.

Ideally Quick Freezing is that process where the temperature of the food drops through the zone of the maximum ice crystal formation (32°F to 23°F) in 30 minutes or less. In practice a time of 2 hours is accepted as normal.

These relatively short times ensure that only small ice crystals are formed which are not so damaging to the food tissues.

By further reducing the temperature of the food to 0°F (−18°C) the manufacturer ensures that minimum bacterial and enzymic reactions occur so prolonging the storage life of the commodities.

Many authorities state that the nutritive value of such products is often superior to fresh market produce. This claim is difficult to substantiate, but certainly quick frozen foods are usually of top quality and peak freshness when frozen. Much research has been undertaken into food varieties and as a result of breeding it has become possible to grow certain varieties of fruit and vegetables which are outstandingly suitable for quick freezing.

Currently, foods can be frozen by a variety of processes, the choice of method being largely dependent on the foods involved, their sizes and the methods of packaging.

Freezing in Air

There are two types of air systems for food freezing—still air and forced air. Still air freezing is relatively slow and has largely been superseded by the second method of moving very cold air at high speeds over the foods (Blast Freezing). As dehydration of the commodities is a hazard most foods are protected by packaging.

Indirect Content

Foods, like water, may be frozen by being placed in contact with a metal surface which is cooled by a refrigerant. The foremost equipment in the field is the Multi-plate Freezer (Birdseye and Hall). The apparatus consists of a series of hollow horizontal plates between which the foods may be placed (usually packaged). The plates which circulate a freezing brine or evaporating ammonia solution may be raised or lowered hydraulically to make firm contact with the packages.

Direct Immersion Freezing

Direct immersion of a food particle in a liquid refrigerant offers the most rapid method of food freezing. Food particles or packages can be frozen in liquid baths, in sprays and in fog systems.

Individual fruits and vegetables can be frozen in a matter of minutes without the product accumulating surface frost.

Flo Freezing

Flo-Freezing, one of the newer methods of freezing is used principally for small food particles like peas. The particles are passed over a stream of freezing air which reduces the internal temperature of the food to 5°F in 13 minutes. The product is again without surface frost.

The packaging of all frozen foods require particular care, as it is of decisive importance for the success and quality of the finished articles. For example a package which is air-tight, waterproof, and which protects the food from contamination by outside odours and micro-organisms will have a good storage life.

But even the best quality in quick-frozen foods can only be retained if the products are kept uninterruptedly at a temperature of not more than 0°F (−18°C) from the producer right down to the consumer.

Thawed foods should never be frozen again as the food may have deteriorated during thawing, and also this process of re-freezing allows large ice crystals to form which will destroy textures.

Today with such a variety of manufacturers producing frozen items, the caterer is well advised to choose carefully and pick a commodity to suit his individual needs, bearing in mind the advantages of such products in terms of labour, cost, storage facilities, etc. He should also consider whether the products are up to the standards expected in his catering unit and whether the frozen food supplier is dependable or not.

Current trends seem to indicate that the caterer is well pleased with many of the products on the market and if the American situation is to be compared with the British scene, there will be a vast expansion in the range of quick frozen foods over the next decade.

Gas in the Kitchen

One of the most essential tools for work in the kitchen is heat. Just as a sculptor has to use different chisels for the various parts of a sculpture to achieve the completeness of its final form, a chef needs different degrees of heat to produce successfully the variety of dishes that go to make up a complete menu.

The demand for a source of heat that can be easily regulated and is always ready for use and immediately effective is met in a positively ideal manner by gas, a well-tried, high-quality form of energy.

In the past gas was exclusively produced by the dry distillation of coal, but nowadays increasing use is made of natural gas and liquified gas. Natural gas is obtained from natural, subterranean sources, while liquified gas is a by-product obtained in the course of refining crude petroleum oil. Liquified gas is filled into steel cylinders and thus makes it possible to use appliances in areas which have no mains supply of town gas or natural gas.

The amount of heat in gas is expressed in terms of its calorific value. The types of gas in public supply have roughly the following calorific values:

Town gas	3,800 kcal./m³	(450 B.T.U. per cu. ft.)
Natural gas	8,500 kcal./m³	(950 B.T.U. per cu. ft.)
Bottled (liquified) gas	11,000 kcal./kg.	(19,800 B.T.U. per lb.)

As the gas is under pressure in the pipes, no additional energy is required to convey it; the pressure in the pipes serves to supply it to the burners. This means, too, that where gas is used there is no need to lay in a fuel supply—thus no storage space or delivery facilities are required for this purpose.

The flow of gas to a burner can be varied infinitely over a very wide range; this makes it possible to regulate the amount of heat very accurately. Gas is smokeless and does not form any soot or leave a residue when burning correctly nor does its use give rise to any unpleasant smell.

A variety of gas appliances corresponding to the functions to be performed is available for the modern kitchen. The most important and universal appliance is the gas cooker; this modern household appliance is the focal point in the kitchen. It may take the form of an integral cooker complete with the thermostat, grill and automatic ignition, or it may be in two parts, the hob and oven being designed as separate built-in units for the modern fitted kitchen. These modern appliances, together with an efficient, adequate hot water supply provided by modern gas water heaters, make the housewife's work very much easier.

GAS IN THE PROFESSIONAL KITCHEN

In professional kitchens gas cookers are equipped with open type boiling burners or solid-tops. One special open-top type is the stock pot stove which is only about 20 inches high and particularly suitable for cooking with large saucepans. It is also intended for use when there is an unexpectedly heavy work load and to supplement available cooker capacity. While its performance is high, it takes up relatively little space. The open burners on a gas range are chiefly used for lightly fried foods or for fast boiling. They are covered by radial hotplate grids which serve as pan supports; the distance between these and the burners is important for satisfactory operation. The solid boiling top on a gas range makes it possible to cook a large number of small dishes. It consists of a heat-resisting steel plate measuring approximately 36 in by 36 in. It can, of course, be used as a hot plate if the heat is reduced accordingly.

Gas cookers are generally about 34 inches high. A large range may have up to 14 boiling burners and 6 roasting ovens.

Cooking ranges are often constructed on the unit principle to suit a customer's wishes. Thus a range specially designed, as regards its size and fittings, for the functions it is to perform can be assembled on site and subsequently added to if necessary.

The specific features of gas ranges are as follows. They have a large number of independent burners, each of which is heated separately and capable of infinitely fine control; they offer freedom of choice in construction and in the siting of the various functional units; each burner is always ready for instant use at full capacity; they are very clean in operation. Economical operation is achieved by low heat retention in the range, minimal loss of heat by radiation and the possibility of using only the unit required at any given time.

The use of special separate appliances starts at the point where large quantities require to be cooked and would be too inconvenient and unwieldy on an all-purpose gas range. This development, together with the desire for the rationalisation of kitchen operation and the demand for the easing of the physical strain on kitchen staff, has given rise to such equipment as gas-heated boiling pans, quick boilers, tilting pans for boiling and frying, and vegetable steamers; each type being designed for a specific function.

Gas-heated boiling pans are either single or double and can be rectangular shape. The lids are designed to provide a steam-tight seal and are fitted with back balance gear. Standard boiling pans are only suitable for liquids and for steaming on perforated racks. The common type of general-purpose boiling pan is the type with a liner or having a double water jacket. This arrangement prevents food from burning.

Steaming ovens generally consist of a single steaming compartment containing perforated or wire trays for the food; one model is designed so that individual compartments can be swung out independently to give easy access to the contents.

Steamers are suitable for root vegetables, sweet and savoury puddings and some fish dishes. Different foods may be cooked together in the steamer without any intermingling of flavours.

Tilting boilers are double pans heated by means of a steam jacket operated at low pressure; their capacity varies between 1 and 13 gallons. They are used for fairly small quantities of cocoa, milk, milk puddings, etc., and for special individual dishes. A tilting boiler unit consists of a table with tilting pans arranged above it. Each pan can be heated independently by steam raised in a gas-heated steam generator under the table. The operational efficiency of gas-heated tilting frying pans makes them indispensable for any fair-sized catering establishment. The quick fryer is a similar, somewhat smaller item of equipment. It has special advantages in use and is particularly popular on account of its high performance at peak periods.

Gas grills and rotating spits, fish fryers and hot closets are other appliances which are especially suitable for large kitchens, being conducive to efficiency and economy in kitchen operation. Gas-heated tiered pastry ovens installed in addition to the ovens incorporated in the gas range are valuable adjuncts to kitchens where pastry-making is a major activity.

Washing-up facilities are of particular importance for a well-run kitchen. In small kitchens a sink with a hot and cold water supply and waste pipe is sufficient. Larger kitchens may be equipped with an efficient gas-heated dish-washing machine. In these machines the crockery, arranged on racks, is sprayed by strong jets of warm washing solution, and rinsed in hot water. The crockery is heated by the rinsing water, which is at a temperature of 190°F; as a result, it quickly dries off of its own accord at the end of the process.

An important matter for any kitchen is hot water supply. A wide range of efficient gas appliances is available for heating water. In the first place, there are instantaneous water heaters which heat the water as it runs through the appliances and supply about 1, 2, 3 or 3½ gallons per minute, depending on their size, the water temperature being raised between 90°F and 150°F.

Storage heaters are valuable for larger kitchens. They provide hot water in amounts corresponding to their capacity at the desired, thermostatically controlled temperature. The stored hot water is available for use in the kitchen as required. Instantaneous and storage gas water heaters are supplied either for connection to a chimney or for venting through an outside wall without the need of a chimney.

The amount of hot water used naturally depends on the size of the kitchen. In large kitchens a consumption of about ½ a gallon per meal is to be expected; smaller kitchens will require up to 1 gallon per meal. The total gas consumption in a large-scale kitchen with a complete gas installation varies between 10½ and 17½ cubic feet per meal.

Proper planning of a kitchen is of major importance for efficient operation. The layout must be planned in such a way as to reduce the distances covered to a minimum and to achieve maximum separation of the different sections, with due regard to the logical sequence of individual operations. The use of gas guarantees economy as well as the satisfactory working of the kitchen from the point of view of quick, high-quality service for patrons. Gas of uniformly good quality is available as required; it is always ready for instant use, with great flexibility of control. Thus, with a series of other advantages, gas offers the best prospects of both customer and caterer being satisfied with the activities of the kitchen brigade.

Electricity in the Kitchen

In the planning of the electrical services to a kitchen, domestic or commercial, it is essential that the designs of all circuits are related to the statutory requirements of the Institute of Electrical Engineers Regulations for the Electrical Equipment of Buildings 1966 (14th Edition). In the larger kitchen the load demands will need to be balanced in relation to the electrical phases available. It is preferable that wherever possible all circuits are brought to a master board with clear definition of each line to the piece of equipment it serves.

The total furnishing and subsequent operation of a successful new catering establishment or extension to present business must take into account the realistic demands that all the components; labour, raw materials, space and equipment be carefully chosen if quality service presentation operating with maximum efficiency and profit is to result.

Labour good or bad, must without doubt be the highest cost ingredient in the shortest supply. It follows therefore that to make the greatest use of experienced staff there will need to be initial capital expenditure for the purchase of labour saving devices, such as food preparation machinery including slicers, mixers, peelers and chippers; and mechanised dishwashing and cleaning equipment. Even in the smallest commercial establishment hand wash up should give way to machine operation.

Raw Materials To offset not only labour costs, but the great waste which occurs in local preparation, or losses due to stock deterioration great contributions to cost and portioning control economics are being made by the increasing use of "convenience foods". This means a range of food prepared and portioned away from the local kitchen to enable standard routine handling for supply direct to the cooking or service areas. Such food may be frozen, dried, canned, or in a raw condition (when it will be supplied in any of the new hygienic wrappings). In many cases refrigeration by the use of Cold Stores, Service Cabinets and deep freezes, will be needed to a much greater degree.

Space In taking a new look at the kitchen it is obvious that the increased use of these convenienced foods enables more food to be stocked in smaller areas. The employment of new multi-purpose cooking units (such as bratt pans) and fresh thoughts on layout positioning for cooking, preparation and service can result in very considerable savings of space. Not only will high rentals be reduced but space thus saved can usually be turned to advantage by an increase in dining seat capacity to give a higher revenue.

The refrigerator is particularly important in a modern household. There are many sizes and models. It is almost always covered with enamelled sheet metal inside and out, double-walled and heat insulated. The door is made air-tight with rubber and there is usually an automatic light which goes on when the door is opened. Depending on the size of the refrigerator, the inside is fitted with a number of compartments and metal or glass shelves to hold food. At the top, either to one side or in the middle, there is freezing unit, consisting of a pipe wound several times around a metal box, the freezing compartment, in which ice cubes can be made. Most refrigerators have a special deep-freeze compartment at the top, for freezing food or storing deep-frozen foodstuffs, and which is also useful for making ice dishes. Most refrigerators also have a drawer at the bottom for keeping vegetables, salads and fruit. The inside temperature of the refrigerator on the average varies between 34° and 46°F; there is a thermostat for maintaining the temperature when the door is opened, for of course warm air streams in every time, which has to be cooled off.

No strong smelling food should ever be placed in the refrigerator unwrapped. Fish and strong cheeses are best packed in cellophane bags, raw meat is best wrapped in sandwich paper, so that the air can circulate around it. For cooked food and left-overs there are square and rectangular containers with lids which can easily be placed side by side or on top of each other and take up little room.

The following rules generally apply when storing perishable food:

Meat, poultry and game, raw	3-4 days	best kept under the freezing unit
Fish, raw	1-2 days	immediately under the freezing unit
Milk, raw, in closed container	2-3 days	central compartment
Cream, in closed container	3-4 days	central compartment
Butter, well packed	2-3 weeks	
Root vegetables	1 week	vegetable compartment
Salads	1 week	vegetable compartment
Soft fruit, according to ripeness	1-2 days	lowest compartment
Eggs	2-3 weeks	egg compartment
Leftovers, according to kind	1-4 days	

Deep-frozen meat, fish, vegetables and fruit in their original package can be kept for several months if the refrigerator has a deep-freeze compartment. Opened tins should be emptied into glass containers and used as soon as possible.

Equipment must be designed to give maximum efficiency, and be simple to operate, easy to clean and maintain. A modern food mixer for instance, seeks not only to reproduce the best results of the original hand movements but to improve aeration to such a degree that the greater employment of mechanized methods will lead to improved standards of quality throughout the kitchen. Automatic energy regulators now give a close control to the new high speed, lower loaded, boiling plates, fitted to ranges designed to give greatly improved efficiency in operation.

In its fast rate of cooking the micro-wave oven opens new fields of opportunity, and the re-circulating oven makes an equally valuable contribution as a more orthodox speedier alternative to the conventional cooking oven.

This age of movement is personified in the ceaseless action of the conveyor belt attended by mobile heated and refrigerated service units centrally sited to satisfy a mass demand for individually plated meals. Alternatively the sophisticated vending unit, a far cry from the earlier automatic prototype, stands silently by to give a constant service throughout the 24 hours of the day.

Presentation This must be the point at which all the arts employed by the caterer are met to satisfy the customer. The importance of a good background, imaginative lighting, comfortable heating, attractive furnishing, adequate air conditioning allied to a well prepared meal cannot be over emphasised. If these considerations are overlooked then the operation will not succeed.

Reflecting social and economic changes with the life of the community, the catering service will be continually presented in a variety of exciting new techniques.

The kitchen which makes the greatest use of electrical equipment will be the best equipped to meet these foregoing demands and will provide a clean, fresh and attractive environment to attract and hold quality kitchen staff.

ELECTRICITY IN THE DOMESTIC KITCHEN

Electricity is accepted by modern housewives because of its labour-saving qualities and the freedom it gives. Not only is it the perfect choice for cooking because of its cleanliness and ease of control, but it can provide constant hot water year in and year out without any attention or servicing. It can provide heat when it's wanted, where it's wanted; and the electric motor has revolutionised the whole idea of "work" in the kitchen and around the house. Because electricity may be controlled automatically, today's housewife is able to leave much of her work to be carried out efficiently and easily in her absence.

Cooking

The pleasing modern design of electric cookers is attractive and practical. The cookers are easy to keep clean and most important, due to there being no products of combustion, the kitchen itself stays very much cleaner. Being fully aware of the limited space in many modern kitchens, electric cooker manufacturers have designed family cookers that are only 18 inches wide, in addition to the normal size standard cookers. There are also double-width cookers with two full-size ovens for the large country house. An interesting development is the present trend towards built-in cooking units in which the oven and boiling-rings may be mounted independently at the most convenient height.

There is a wide choice of styling, revolving round the position of the grill which may be at waist or eye level or in the oven. Some eye-level grills incorporate rotary spits and may even be enclosed to form a second oven. Some standard cookers include two ovens as well as an eye-level grill.

All ovens are thermostatically controlled and most now offer automatic time-control to enable the oven to be switched on and off and a meal to be cooked in the housewife's absence.

Boiling rings on electric cookers are usually radiant and are very fast indeed; the controls are infinitely variable from a gentle simmer to a fast boil and some rings incorporate a pan thermostat which controls the temperature of the pan's contents to a nicety—a great advantage when using a deep-fat frier. Some rings may be switched to heat the centre only, for use with small pans.

Small table-cookers make electric cooking even more flexible and electric grills, rotating spits, plate-warmers, coffee-percolators, kettles and toasters all make day-to-day living, as well as entertaining, a real pleasure.

Refrigeration

The hygienic and labour-saving advantages of a refrigerator are paramount in the modern kitchen. Housewives, whether they go out to work or not, find that shopping-time can be cut to a minimum by wise use of refrigerated storage for perishable foods and they appreciate the reassuring knowledge that the family's food is being kept in perfect condition, whatever the temperature. All new refrigerators use a system known as 'star-marking' which indicates how long packets of commercially-frozen food may be stored in the frozen food storage compartment.

1 star ★	1 week
2 stars ★★	1 month
3 stars ★★★	3 months

Refrigerators need the minimum of attention, and most new models have automatic or semi-automatic defrosting devices which discourage unnecessary build-up of ice.

An extension of refrigeration into the field of home freezing is introducing this very simple and natural method of food preservation into the home. Home-freezers ranging upwards from 3 cubic feet in capacity are available in two main types—a chest type with a counter-balanced lid, and an upright, front-opening type which is more suitable where space is limited. Both types offer facilities for freezing and storing one's own home-grown produce and cooked food. Originally used only by country-dwellers, home-freezers are now rapidly gaining popularity among townspeople as the advantages of preserving cooked foods such as bread, cakes, meat and poultry dishes are appreciated. The housewife who also goes out to work, the hostess who likes to entertain, the bachelor-girl, the mother of a growing family—all these and many others find the home-freezer helps planning and preparation and saves valuable time.

Other Domestic Appliances

The electric motor has revolutionised work in the modern kitchen. Hygienic waste-disposal is simply effected by electric grinders plumbed in to the sink unit and electric dish-washers cope with the unpleasant routine chore of washing-up far more efficiently than it can be done by hand.

A number of smaller items also prove themselves invaluable in the kitchen, among which the electric food mixer/blender holds pride of place. Most mixers have attachments which make them very versatile; these include mincers, slicers, shredders, graters, can-openers, vegetable peelers, etc. Carving knives, knife-sharpeners, can-openers may also be obtained as separate items.

Menus

In the following selection of menus prepared for formal luncheon or dinner banquets it will be noticed that the main dishes are of a relatively uncomplicated nature. This is a sound basic principle as the greater the numbers for which one is catering, the less opportunity is there for detailed presentation of elaborate dishes. When drawing up a menu involving service for a large number of people, it is a good idea to use the concept of simplicity of food as a guiding light. It will be noticed, further, that the menu itself ranges usually from 4–5 courses, no matter how formal the occasion, the only exception being the menu for the occasion of the state visit to France of King George VI and Queen Elizabeth. Here the composition of the menu follows more classical lines being composed of seven courses in an approved sequence.

Note, too, the selection of an appropriate wine to fit in with each course. It is just as important to the over-all success of a meal to choose the right wine for the right dish. For more specific notes on the correct service of wine, and the proper selection, see the Wines Chapter, p. 879.

A study of these menus will show how important it is to produce a sensible balance on a menu for a large banquet.

Château de Versailles

Luncheon menu given in honour of
Their Majesties King George VI and Queen Elizabeth
Thursday, 21 of July 1938

Menu

Les Perles Fraîches de Sterlett — *Fresh Caviar*
Le Melon Frappé — *Chilled Melon*

Le Xérès Mackenzie "Amontadillo Grande Réserve"

Les Délices du lac d'Annecy à la Nantua — *Fillets of Lake Annecy Trout à la Nantua*

Le Chevalier Montrachet 1926

Les Mignonettes d'Agneau Trianon — *Small Noisettes of Lamb Trianon*

Le Magnum du Château La Mission Haut Brion 1920

TURBAN OF SOLE FILLETS

1. Prepare some flattened sole fillets and thin slices of salmon, all neatly and evenly cut. Butter a ring mould and lay the sole fillets and slices of salmon round it alternately with the ends hanging over the edge.

2. Using a forcing bag with a large tube, fill the ring mould with forcemeat. Tap on the table several times to distribute the forcemeat evenly and fold the ends of the fillets over into the centre.

3. Poach in the oven in a *bain-marie*, leave to stand for a short time, turn out on to a round dish and wipe away any liquid that escapes.

LINING A MOULD WITH ASPIC

1. Set the mould in finely crushed ice and chill well.

2. Fill the mould up to the top with cold aspic.

3. When the inside of the mould is coated with a layer of aspic about $\frac{1}{5}$-inch thick, pour off the remainder. Leave the mould on ice until it is to be used.

POACHED EGGS IN ASPIC

1. Line the bottom of individual egg moulds (*cocottes*) with a thin layer of aspic. Using a knife or cutter, shape pieces of poached leek, truffle, egg white, sweet pepper, tomato, etc. to make a pattern as desired.

2. Decorate the bottom of the moulds, dipping each piece of garnish in aspic to make it adhere immediately.

3. Trim the poached eggs, place them in the moulds, fill up with cold aspic on the point of setting and place in the refrigerator until set.

POACHED EGGS IN ASPIC

4. The finished eggs after unmoulding.

ANNA POTATOES

1. Peel the potatoes and trim them to a round shape.

2. Cut into thin slices with a knife or slicer.

ANNA POTATOES

3. Butter a special mould or *sauté* pan well, arrange the sliced potatoes in overlapping circles and season and sprinkle each layer with melted butter. Bake in a moderately hot oven.

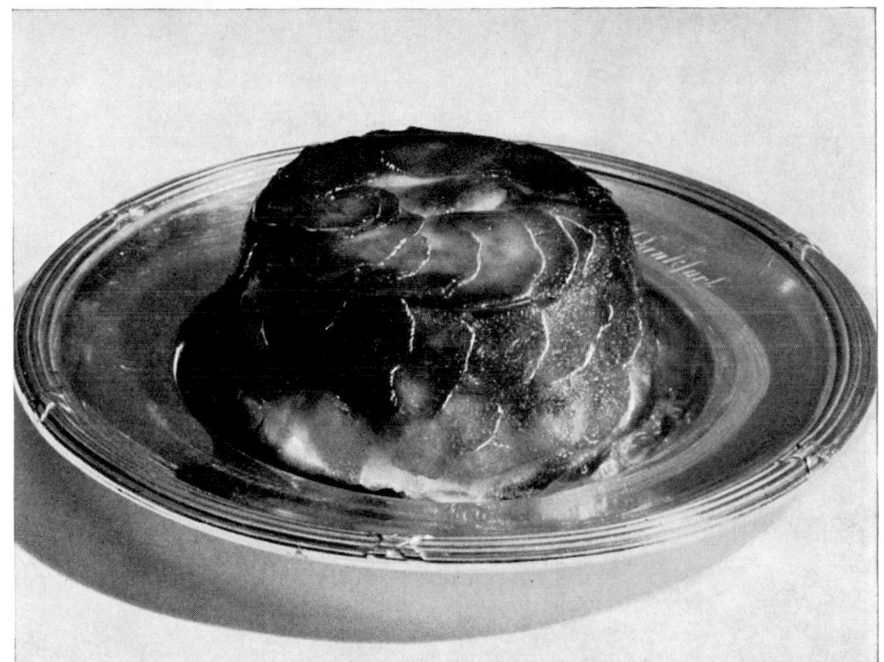

4. Press the top lightly, turn out on to a lid, drain off the butter and place on a round serving dish.

JOINTING A CHICKEN FOR SAUTÉ CHICKEN

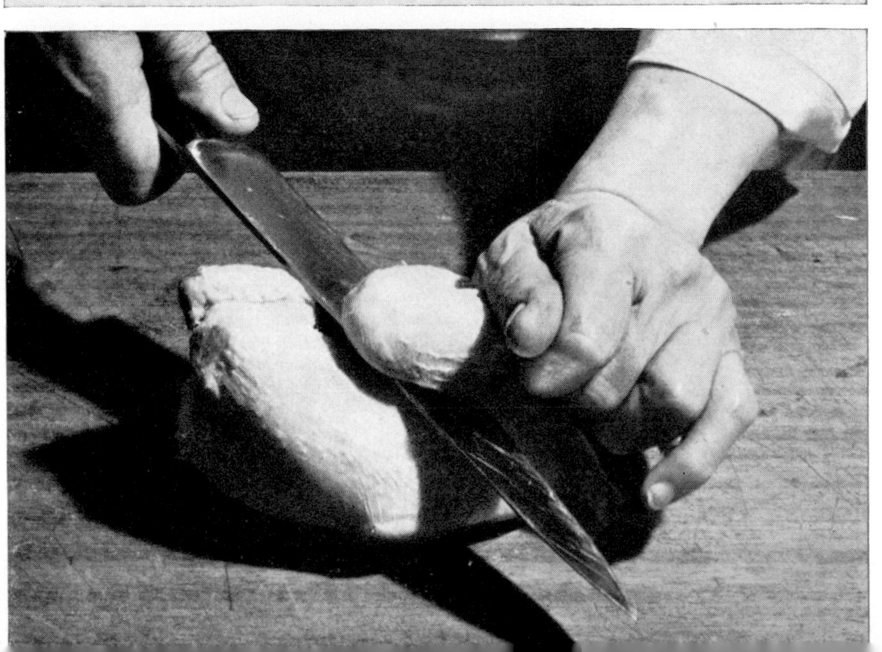

1. Insert the knife between the breast and the leg.

JOINTING A CHICKEN FOR SAUTÉ CHICKEN

2. Lift the leg up and cut through the joint.

3. and 4. Detach the leg completely from the body of the bird.

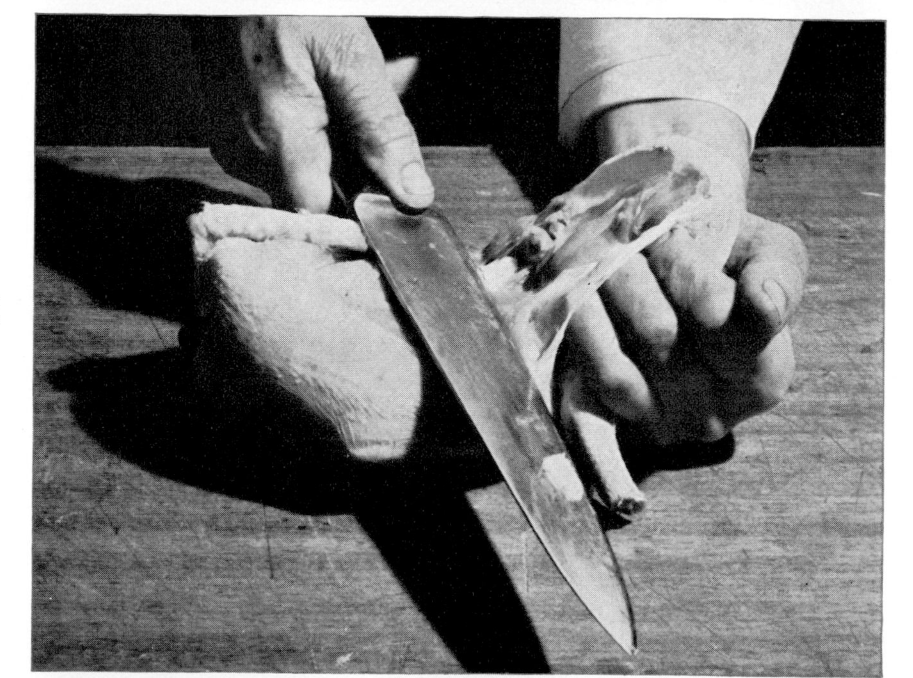

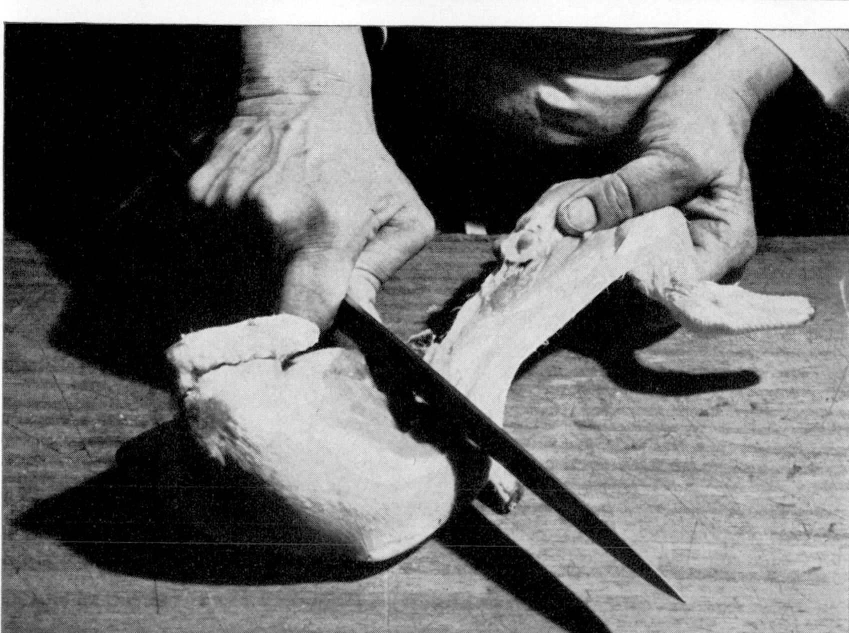

JOINTING A CHICKEN FOR SAUTÉ CHICKEN

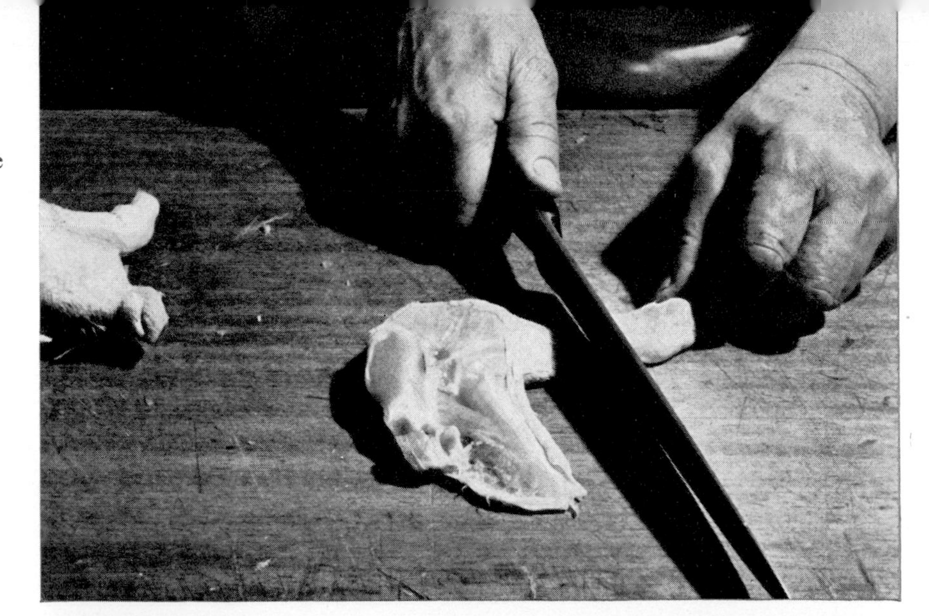

5. Cut off the bone at the end of the drumstick.

6. Press the meat back off the drumstick.

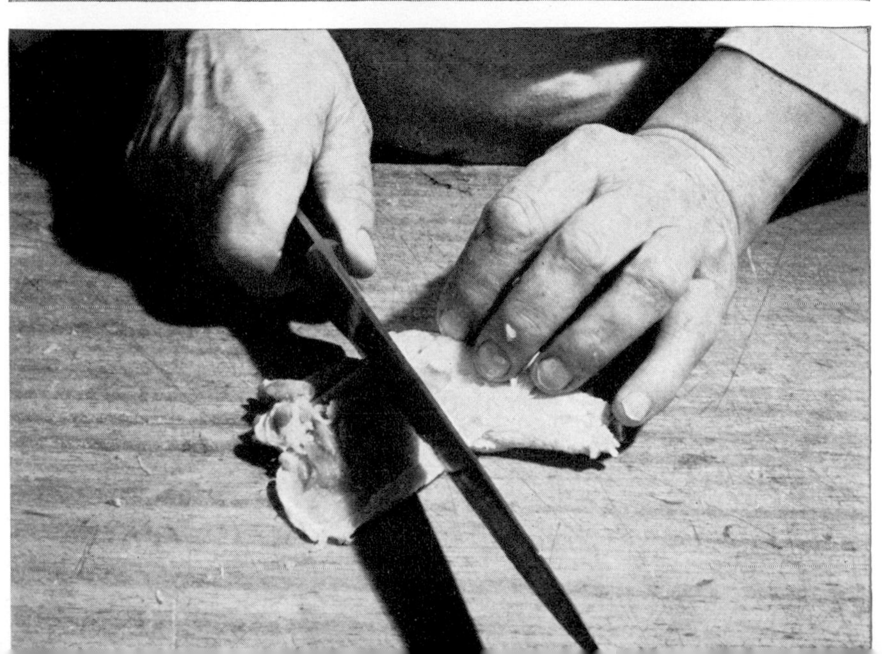

7. Break off the leg bone at the joint.

JOINTING A CHICKEN FOR SAUTÉ CHICKEN

8. Push the meat at the top of the thigh back a little and scrape off the bone.

9. Remove the bone. Repeat the procedure with the other leg.

10. Pull the wing away from the body.

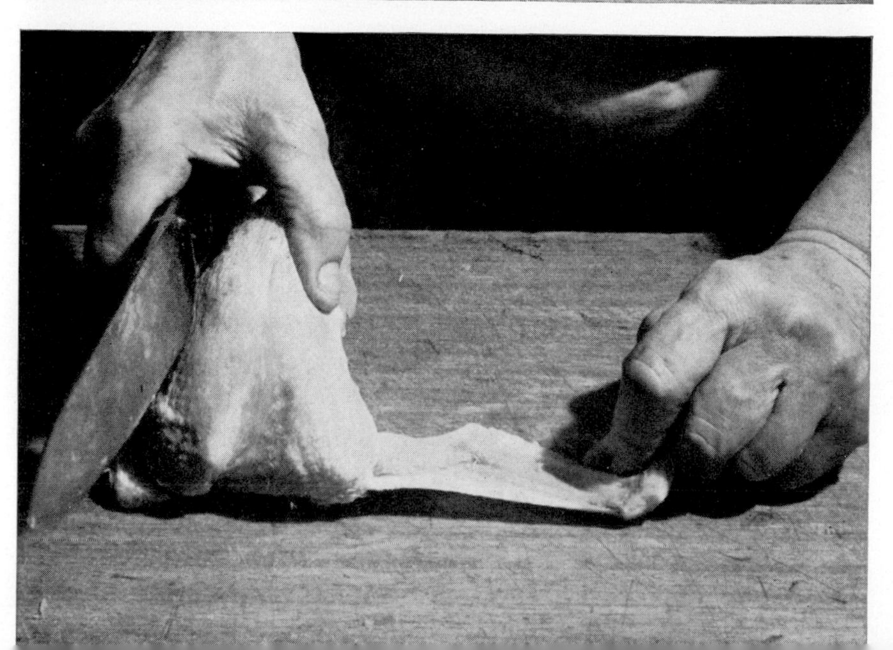

JOINTING A CHICKEN FOR SAUTÉ CHICKEN

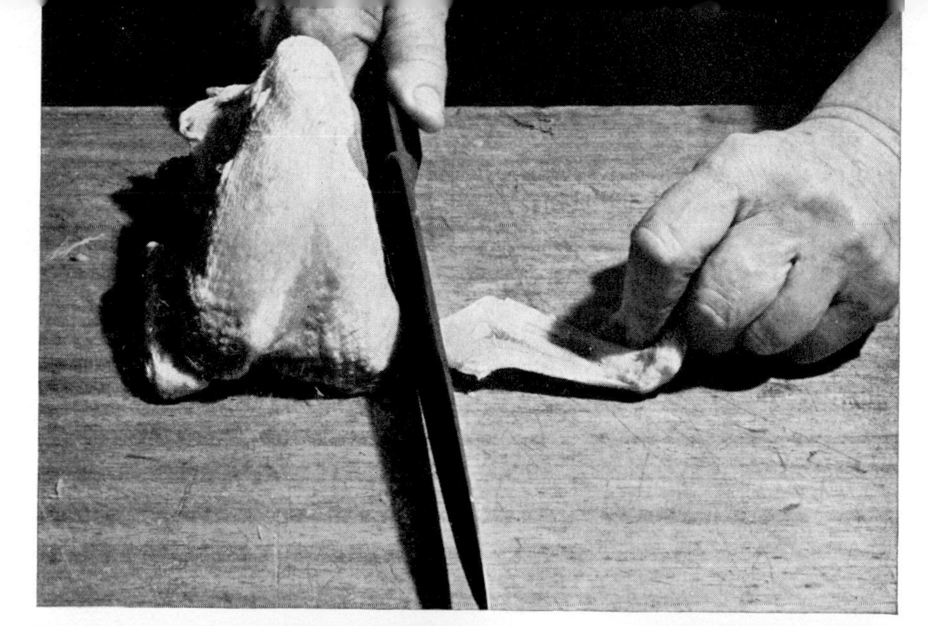

11. Cut off the wing.

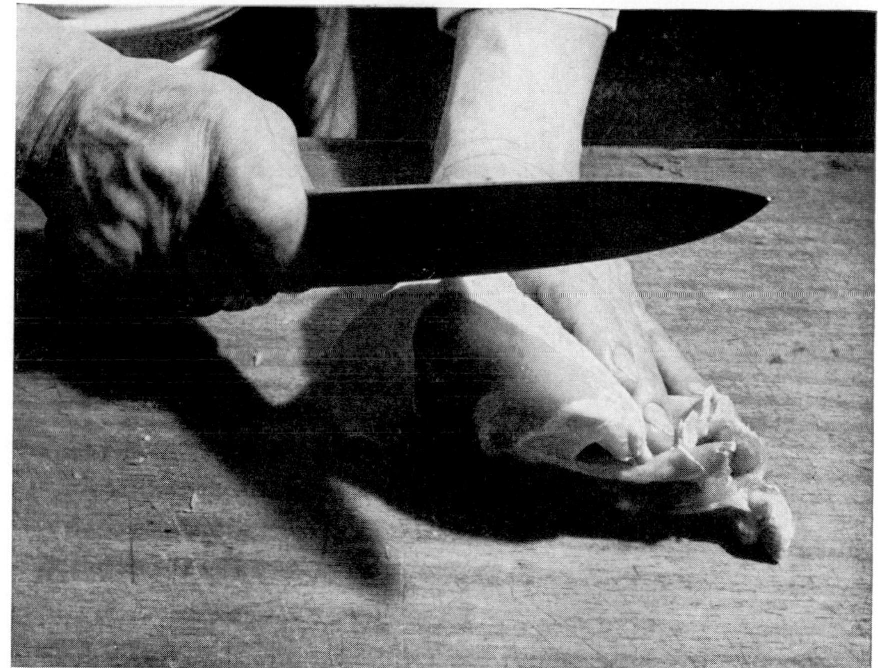

12. Cut into the centre of the breast from the front.

13. Cut into each half of the breast, keeping the knife parallel with the breast-bone.

JOINTING A CHICKEN FOR SAUTÉ CHICKEN

14. Detach both halves of the breast.

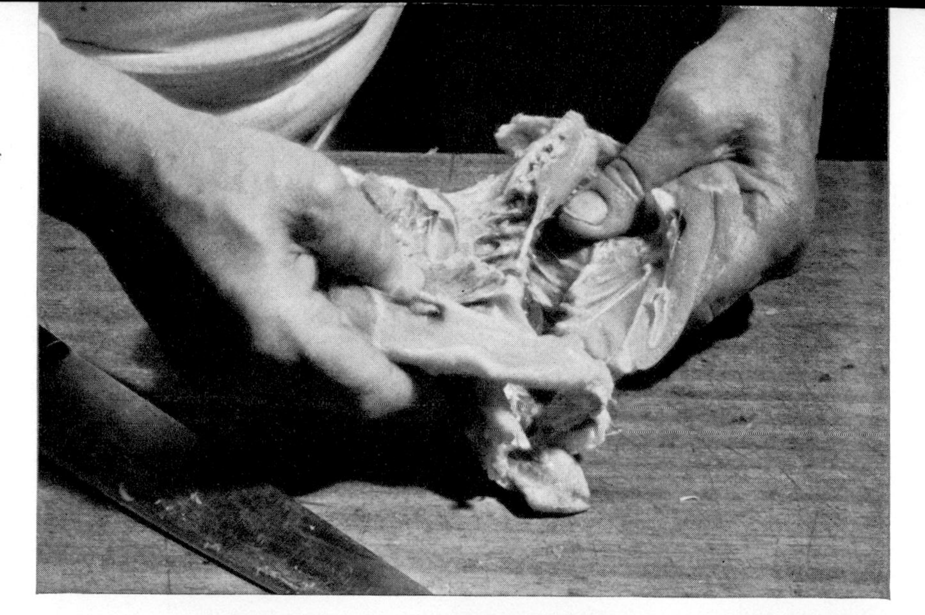

15. Pull them off the bone.

16. Neatly trim the lower part of each half-breast.

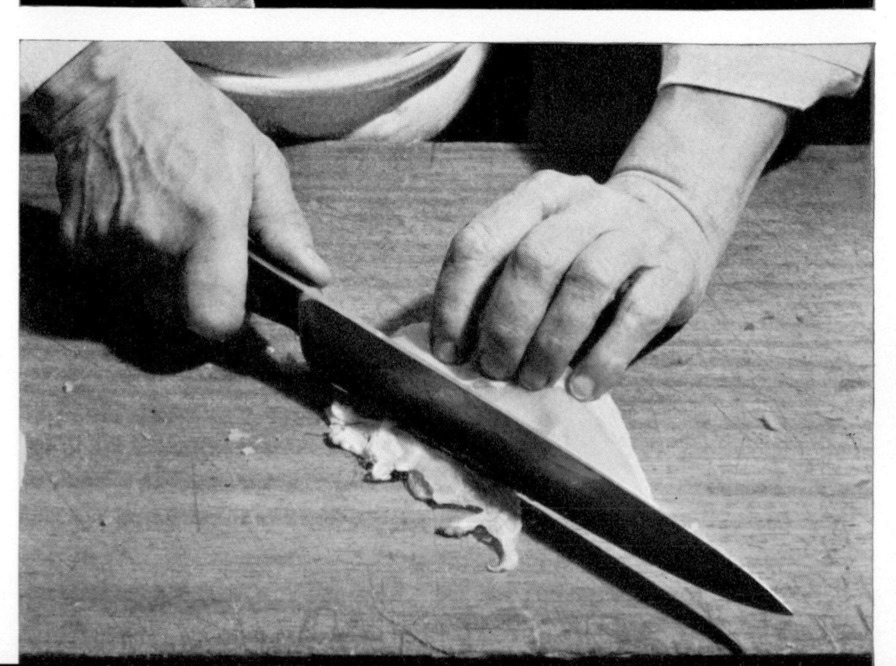

CARVING POULTRY (ROAST DUCK)

Except for very small birds, all types of poultry are prepared in the same way. The illustrations show how to carve a duck.

1. Place the roast duck on a hot-plate.

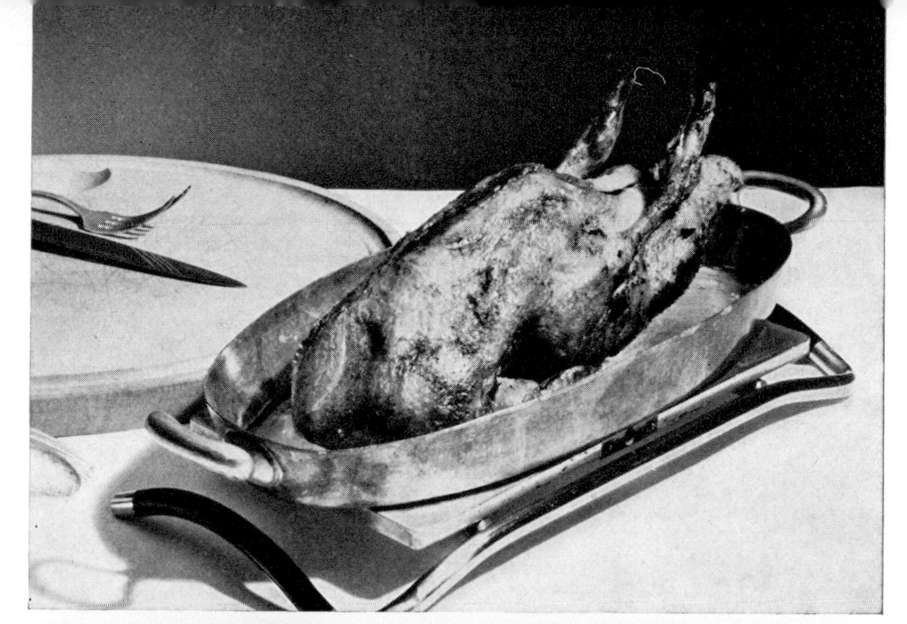

2. Insert the point of the carving knife into the neck and the fork into the opening between the breast and the leg and hold the duck up at right angles to the dish to drain away any remaining juices.

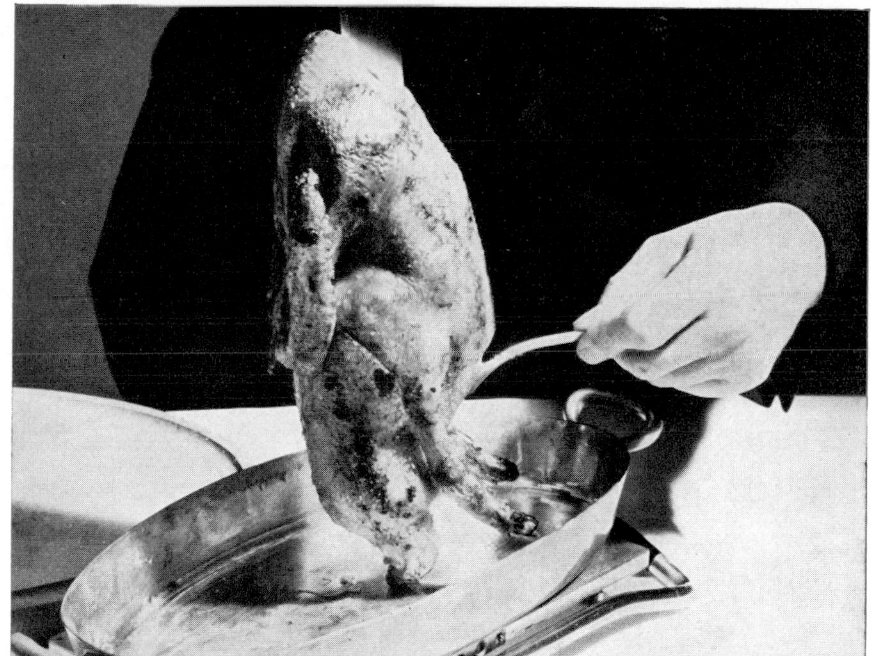

3. Place the duck on the carving board, ease the wing away from the body with the fork and sever at the second joint.

CARVING POULTRY (ROAST DUCK)

4. Turn the duck on its side, insert the fork into the leg joint and pull the legs up a little to cut through the skin, running the knife round the contours of the legs.

5. Prise the legs away from the body completely and pull free of the upper joint, detaching the remaining meat with the knife.

6. Cut off the bone at the end of the drumstick with the knife.

CARVING POULTRY (ROAST DUCK)

7. Sever the leg at the joint, keeping the knife parallel to the bone of the drumstick. Repeat the procedure with the other leg.

8. Turn the duck with the neck end towards you and make a transverse cut behind the tail so that the breast can be carved more easily.

9. Run the knife along the breastbone as far as the top of the junction with the wing and cut through the joint, then repeat on the other side.

CARVING POULTRY (ROAST DUCK)

10. Turn the duck on its side, insert the fork between the wing and the breast-bone and raise the breast off the carcase, first on one side and then on the other, carefully detaching the meat with the knife.

11 and 12. Holding the knife quite flat, cut each half of the breast into slices of the required thickness.

CARVING POULTRY (ROAST DUCK)

13. Scoop out the two small ovals of flesh on the back of the carcase with the knife.

14. Make a transverse cut to sever the tail from the carcase and cut the tail into two.

15. Separate the very crisp skin of the neck from the carcase.

VEAL OLIVES

1. Flatten out slices of veal fillet, spread with forcemeat, sprinkle with finely chopped onions and parsley and cover with half a slice of ham.

2. Roll up the slices of veal and tie.

SERVING OYSTERS

Open the oysters with a machine or a special knife. Arrange on crushed ice with the round shell uppermost and garnish with lemon. Serve with brown bread and butter, or with the bread already sliced and buttered.

Les Timbales de Cailles
Farcies à la Talleyrand

Timbales of Stuffed Quails
à la Talleyrand

Hospices de Beaune "Cuvée Charlotte Dumay" 1915

Les Aiguillettes de Caneton
Rouenais à la Montmorency
Salade Gauloise

Slices of Rouennais Duck
à la Montmorency
French Salad

Le Corton Grancey 1919; Magnum du Château Rothschild 1918

Le Granité au Lanson 1921

Champagne Sorbet

Le Suprême de Poularde de Bresse
avec les Pointes d'Asperges à l'Etuvée

Breast of Bresse Chicken
with Asparagus Tips

Le Château Yquem 1921

Les Truffes à la Mode du Périgord

Truffles in Sauce Périgord

Le Magnum du Château Latour 1904

La Mousse Glacée Singapour
Les Pêches de Montreuil Princess
Les Frivolités

Ice Cream Mousse Singapore
Montreuil Peaches Princess-style
Petits Fours

Wines

Le Magnum de Champagne Pol Roger 1911
Le Magnum de Champagne C. H. Mumm 1911
Le Champagne Louis Roederer 1904
Le Champagne Veuve Clicquot 1900
Le Champagne Pommery 1895

c

The White House

State Dinner given in Honour of
Princess Margaret and Lord Snowdon
17th November 1965

Menu

Atlantic Pompano Amandine

Roast Pigeon White House-style
Artichokes with Vegetable Purée
Palm Heart Salad

Brie Cheese

Praline Ice Cream

Inaugural Luncheon for the
Escoffier Museum, Monday, 2nd May 1966
prepared by Maitre Gaston Puget at his Restaurant
"Le Petit Brouant", 4b rue Gustave Deloye in Nive

Menu

Le cocktail de homard	*Lobster Cocktail*
La mostelle de la Baie d'Anges soufflée	*Angel Bay Fish soufflé*
La volaille G. Puget *Les petits pois de Nice au beurre* *Les fromages de France*	*Chicken à la G. Puget* *Nice-style Buttered Peas* *A selection of French cheeses*
Les fraises Melba *Les mignardises*	*Strawberry Melba* *Petits Fours*

Wines

Moët et Chandon (magnum) 1961
Corton Charlemagne 1964
Château Grancey 1959
Château Yquem 1959

•

Coffee

A selection of French liqueurs

The Royal Dinner for the Nobel Prize-winners
and prominent Members of the Fine Arts and Sciences
11th December 1964

Menu

Consommé Double *Pailettes d'Or*	*Rich Consommé* *Cheese Straws*
Suprême de sole Homardine *Riz Creole*	*Fillets of Sole Homardine* *Creole Rice*
Selle de chevreuil Grand-Veneur	*Saddle of Venison Grand-Veneur*
Feuilletée au Roquefort	*Puff Pastry with Roquefort*
Sorbet de mandarines	*Tangerine Sorbet*

Wines

La Ina
Krug Brut Réserve
Château Cheval Blanc 1950
Rebello Valente Vintage 1943

Dinner
given by Her Majesty Queen Elisabeth II
in Honour of Dr. Heinrich Lubke, President of the Federal Republic of Germany,
during her stay in Germany

Menu

Homard d'Heligoland Thermidor	*Heligoland Lobster Thermidor*
Asperges d'Ingelheim *Sauce Mousseline*	*Ingelheim Asparagus* *Mousseline Sauce*
Venaison Grand Veneur *Chanterelles, Haricots Verts au Beurre*	*Saddle of Venison Grand Veneur* *Mushrooms and Buttered French Beans*
Mangues à la Romanoff	*Mangoes Romanoff*

Wines

Graacher Himmelreich Auslese 1959
Kreuznacher Narrenkappe Spätlese 1959
Château Rauzan Gassies Margaux 1955
Veuve Clicquot 1955

Hotel Dan Carmel, Haifa, Israel

Dinner given in Honour of His Majesty King Baudoin I
during his visit to the Holy Land

Menu

Saumon fumé Belle-Vue	*Smoked Salmon Bellevue*
Consommé Double	*Rich Consommé*
Foie Gras Grillé sur Toast	*Grilled Foie Gras on Toast*
Filet Rôti à l'Andalouse	*Roast Fillet of Beef Andalusian-style*
Salade de Laitue	*Green Salad*
Crêpes Suzette	*Crêpes Suzette*

Hotel Hilton, Amsterdam

Gala Dinner

given by Queen Juliana of the Netherlands in Honour of her daughter
Princess Beatrix of the Netherlands and Klaus von Amberg
8th March 1966

Menu

Délices de la Mer du Nord	*Sea Food*
Consommé à l'Estragon	*Tarragon Consommé*
Selle de Veau à l'Orange	*Saddle of Veal with Oranges*
La Bienvenue Neerlandaise	*Sorbet with Calvados in Nougat Shells*
Friandises	*Friandises*
Demi-Tasse	*Coffee*

Wines

Pouilly Fuissé 1962
Château Batailly 1959
Piper Heidsieck brut extra 1961

LUNCHEON MENUS

The appreciation of the composition of a menu requires not only a knowledge of cooking but a knowledge of food. A knowledge of the basic principles implicit in gastronomy is essential to produce a menu wherein the dishes will blend together in harmony.

Study the following menus and note the balanced composition of the meal, following the general principles of menu planning as detailed on pages 8–14. Remember that a menu should reflect not only the chef's culinary abilities but also the spirit of the occasion for which the menu is planned. It should reflect the time of the year, and feature sensibly chosen fruit and vegetables, fish and game in season.

The following selection of menus, many of which are actual recipes chosen from *L'Art culinaire moderne*, take these basic considerations into account and should be used as examples of the way in which a host of correctly balanced and exciting menus can be made up from the recipes of this book.

Spring

Cocktail d'écrevisses	*Crayfish Cocktail*
Escalope de veau à l'Anglaise *Morilles à La Crème* *Pommes sautées*	*Escalope of Veal English-style* *Mushrooms in Cream Sauce* *Sauté Potatoes*
Beignets aux pommes	*Apple Fritters*
———	———
Omelette Archiduc	*Archduke Omelette*
Entrecôte Marchand-de-vin *Chou-fleurs sauté au beurre* *Pommes nouvelles rissolées*	*Entrecôte steak Marchand-de-vin* *Glazed Cauliflower* *Sauté New Potatoes*
Ananas Marina	*Pineapple Marina*
———	———
Asperges en Branches *aux sauces Hollandaise,* *Vinaigrette et Mayonnaise*	*Asparagus with Hollandaise, Vinaigrette* *and Mayonnaise Sauce*
Côtelettes d'agneau Sevigné	*Lamb Cutlets Sevigné*
Plateau de fromages	*Cheese Platter*
Sabayon Gritti-Palace	*Zabaione Gritti-Palace*
———	———

Spring—*contd.*

Croquettes de poisson, *Sauce tomates*	*Fish Croquettes* *Tomato Sauce*
Foie de veau Bercy *Epinards en Branches* *Purée de pommes de terre Mousseline*	*Calf's Liver Bercy* *Leaf Spinach* *Mashed Potatoes*
Coupe glacée à la Mexicaine	*Mexican Ice Cream Coupe*

Summer

Melon et jambon de Parme	*Melon and Parma Ham*
Coq au Riesling *Girolles aux Fines Herbes*	*Capon in Riesling* *Mushrooms with Mixed Herbs*
Crème Beau-Rivage	*Crème Beau-Rivage*

Oeufs en Gelée à la Jeannette	*Jellied Eggs Jeannette*
Tournedos Masséna *Pommes noisette*	*Tournedos steak Masséna* *Noisette Potatoes*
Plateau de fromages	*Cheese Platter*
Fraises Chantilly	*Strawberries with Whipped Cream*

Crudités	*Vegetable Hors d'œuvre Salads*
Pigeonneaux aux Petits Pois *Pommes Macaire*	*Pigeons with green peas* *Macaire Potatoes*
Plateau de fromages	*Cheese Platter*
Abricots Monte-Cristo	*Apricots Monte-Cristo*

Cuisses de grenouilles sautées Fines Herbes	*Frogs' Legs with Mixed Herbs*
Côtes de veau Bonne Femme	*Veal cutlets Bonne Femme*
Mousse aux framboises	*Raspberry Mousse*

Autumn

Avocat de Fruit de Mer — *Avocado with Seafood*

Côtes de porc aux Pommes — *Pork Chop with apples*
Choux de Bruxelles Sautés — *Glazed Brussels Sprouts*
Pommes Château — *Château Potatoes*

Mousse au Chocolat — *Chocolate Mousse*

Oeufs Brouillés à la Portugaise — *Scrambled Eggs with Tomatoes*

Aiguillette de bœuf à la Flamande — *Braised Topside of Beef Flamande*

Plateau de fromages — *Cheese Platter*

Tarte aux Pêches — *Peach Tart*

Pamplemousses Farcis — *Stuffed Grapefruit*

Sauté de veau Bourguignonne — *Veal Stew à la Bourguignonne*

Plateau de fromages — *Cheese Platter*

Savarin au Rhum — *Savarin with Rum*

Champignons Pimentés à la Grècque — *Mushrooms with Peppers*

Pilaf de volaille à l'Orientale — *Pilaf of Chicken à l'Orientale*

Plateau de fromages — *Cheese Platter*

Croûtes à l'Ananas — *Pineapple Croûte*

Winter

Escargots à la Dijonnaise	*Snails à la Dijonnaise*
Gigot de mouton à l'Anglaise, Sauce au câpres	*Boiled Leg of Mutton with Vegetables and Caper Sauce*
Plateau de fromages	*Cheese Platter*
Pommes Bonne Femme	*Baked Apples*

Potage Chevrière	*Goatherd Soup*
Filet mignon de porc au Calvados *Cardons au jus* *Pommes à la Lyonnaise*	*Pork Fillet with Calvados* *Braised Cardoons* *Lyonnaise Potatoes*
Bread and Butter Pudding	*Bread and Butter Pudding*

Coquilles Saint-Jacques à la Diable	*Devilled Scallops Saint-Jacques*
Queue de bœuf en Hochepot	*Oxtail Casserole*
Plateau de fromages	*Cheese Platter*
Macédoine de fruits	*Chilled Fruit Salad*

Spaghetti alla Vongole	*Spaghetti with Mussels*
Filet de bœuf Sauté Strogonoff	*Fillet of Beef Strogonoff*
Oranges Ilona	*Oranges Ilona*

DINNER MENUS

Spring

Consommé aux Perles du Japon	*Consommé with Tapioca*
Filet de colin Bercy	*Fillet of Hake Bercy*
Poulet en Cocotte à la Paysanne *Salade Mercédès*	*Chicken in Cocotte à la Paysanne* *Mercedes Salad*
Mon Rêve	*Mon Rêve*

Coquilles de langouste	*Scallops of Rock Lobster*
Potage Germiny	*Cream of Sorrel Soup*
Ris de veau Braisés Comtesse *Cèpes à la Bordelaise*	*Braised Sweetbreads Comtesse* *Sautéed Mushrooms*
Vacherin Meringué	*Meringue Vacherin*

Saumon fumé, crème de raifort *Toast et beurre*	*Smoked Salmon and Horseradish Cream* *Toast and Butter*
Crème d'Asperges	*Cream of Asparagus Soup*
Suprêmes de volaille Maryland	*Breasts of Chicken Maryland*
Bavarois Praliné	*Praline Bavarian Cream*

Céleri à la Grècque	*Greek-style Celery*
Quenelles de brochet à la Lyonnaise	*Pike Quenelles à la Lyonnaise*
Filet de veau en Croûte *Salade Béatrix*	*Veal Fillet in a Pastry Crust* *Beatrix Salad*
Soufflé Elvire	*Soufflé Elvira*

Summer

Consommé Madrilène	*Consommé Madrilène*
Truite de rivière aux Amandes	*River Trout with Almonds*
Canard en Compôte *Salade de cœurs de laitue*	*Stewed Duck with Mushrooms and Onions* *Lettuce Salad*
Biscuit glacé Napolitain	*Ice Cream Gâteau Neapolitain*

Rouget à l'Orientale	*Red Mullet à l'Orientale*
Suprêmes de volaille à la Crème de Noisette	*Chicken Breast in Hazelnut Sauce*
Fonds d'artichauts Argenteuil	*Artichoke Bottoms with Asparagus Tips*
Framboises Erimar	*Raspberries Erimar*

Consommé de volaille	*Jellied Chicken Consommé*
Cuisses de grenouilles à la Périgourdine	*Frogs' Legs Perigourdine*
Côtelettes de chevreuil Châtelaine *Nouilles au buerre*	*Cutlets of Venison Châtelaine* *Buttered Noodles*
Fraises Cardinal	*Strawberries Cardinal*

Bisque d'Ecrevisses	*Crayfish Soup*
Omble chevalier, sauce Mousseline *Pommes à la Vapeur*	*Char with Mousseline Sauce* *Steamed Potatoes*
Gelinotte Rôtie à la Russe *Petits pois à la Française*	*Roast Hazelhen with Sour Cream Sauce* *Green Peas à la Française*
Petits soufflés glacés aux Abricots	*Small Apricot Ice Cream Soufflés*

Crème de Laitue	*Cream of Lettuce Soup*
Barbue à l'Amiral	*Brill à l'Amiral*
Suprême de pintadeau aux Lychées	*Breast of Guinea Fowl with lychees*
Salade Lorette	*Lorette Salad*
Charlotte Royale	*Charlotte Royale*

Oeufs de caille aux Cœurs de Palmiers	*Quails' Eggs with Palm Shoots*
Potage Cardinal	*Fish Soup Cardinal*
Filet de bœuf Richelieu	*Fillet of Beef Richelieu*
Salade d'endives	*Chicory Salad*
Pêche Melba	*Peach Melba*

Crème à la Châtelaine	*Cream of Artichoke Soup*
Filets de sole Saint Germain	*Fillets of Sole St. Germain*
Côtelettes de lièvre Pojarski	*Hare Cutlets Pojarski*
Pommes Lorette	*Loretto Salad*
Blanc-Manger aux Avelines	*Hazelnut Blancmange*

Crème Andalouse	*Andalusian Cream Soup*
Merlan Bercy	*Whiting Bercy*
Rognonnade de veau	*Roast Boned Loin of Veal*
Céléri en branches Braisé	*Braised Celery*
Pommes Fondantes	*Fondant Potatoes*
Poires Schouvaloff	*Pears Schouvaloff*

Winter

Potage Darblay	*Darblay Soup*
Quenelles de carpe Saxonne	*Carp Quenelles à la Saxe*
Perdreau sur Canapés *Cœurs de laitue* *Purée de pommes de terre à la Crème*	*Roast Partridge on Canapé* *Lettuce Salad* *Mashed Potatoes with Cream*
Oranges en Surprise	*Surprise Oranges*

Pâté de lapin	*Rabbit Pâté*
Matelote de Moselle	*Fish Stew à la Moselle*
Poulet de grain Crapaudine *Pommes Allumettes* *Salade Waldorf*	*Spatchcock Spring Chicken* *Matchstick Potatoes* *Waldorf Salad*
Crème à la Vigneronne	*Wine-Flavoured Cream*

Potage Jacqueline	*Jacqueline Soup*
Soufflé d'épinards *à la Florentine*	*Florentine Spinach Soufflé*
Oison à l'Allemande *Pommes Dauphine*	*Gosling à l'Allemande* *Dauphine Potatoes*
Mandarines Côte d'Azur	*Tangerines Côte d'Azur*

Consommé à la Parisienne	*Consommé Parisian*
Filet de flétan Mornay	*Fillet of Halibut Mornay*
Faisan rôti *Pommes Chips* *Salade Niçoise*	*Roast Pheasant* *Chipped Potatoes* *Salad Niçoise*
Poires Géraldine	*Pears Geraldine*

SPECIAL DINNER MENUS

Spring

Parfait de foie gras *Toast et beurre*	*Foie Gras Parfait* *Toast and Butter*
Consommé de volaille	*Chicken Consommé*
Queues d'écrevisses *à la Mode du Couvent de Chorin*	*Crayfish Tails à la Chorin*
Bécasse Sautée au Champagne *Salade Mimosa*	*Woodcock sautéed in Champagne* *Mimosa Salad*
Citrons Givrés	*Frosted Lemons*

Summer

Hors d'œuvre Riche	*Rich Hors d'Oeuvre*
Consommé froid au Xérès	*Cold Consommé with Sherry*
Filets de sole Nabuchu	*Fillets of Sole Nabuchu*
Selle de chevreuil Belle-Créole	*Saddle of Venison Belle-Creole*
Melon Majestic	*Melon Majestic*

Autumn

Caviar Beluga Malossol	*Beluga Caviar Malossol*
Consommé de gibier	*Pheasant Consommé*
Truite saumonée, sauce Hollandaise *Pommes à la Vapeur*	*Sea Trout, sauce Hollandaise,* *Steamed Potatoes*
Suprême de poularde *à l'Espagnole*	*Chicken Breast à l'Espagnole*
Mousse glacée à la Favorite	*Ice Cream Mousse à la Favorite*
Mignardises	*Petit Fours*

Winter

Huîtres au citron	*Oysters on the Half Shell*
Tortue claire	*Clear Turtle Soup*
Homard Thermidor	*Lobster Thermidor*
Râble de lièvre Diane *Cœurs de laitues aux Fines Herbes*	*Saddle of Hare Diane* *Lettuce Salad with Mixed Herbs*
Gâteau glacé à la Japonaise	*Ice Cream Gateau Japonaise*

Reveillon de Noël I

Salade de homard en Noix de Coco

Consommé aux nids de hirondelles

Darne de saumon Foyot

Suprêmes de dindonneau Tamerlan
Salade Américaine

Parfait glacé du Père Noël

Christmas Dinner I

Lobster Salad in a Coconut Shell

Birds' Nest Soup

Salmon Steak Foyot

Turkey Breasts Tamerlan
American Salad

Father Christmas Ice Cream Parfait

Reveillon de Noël II

Consommé de gibier
Allumettes au Parmesan

Vol-au-vent de filets
de sole La Vallière

Oie à l'anglaise
Salade Beaucaire

Cœurs de palmiers à la Milanaise

Christmas pudding
Brandy Sauce

Christmas Dinner II

Game Consommé
Parmesan Straws

Vol-au-vent of Fillets of
Sole La Vallière

Stuffed Goose
Beaucaire Salad

Palm Shoots à la Milanaise

Christmas Pudding
Brandy Hard Sauce

Reveillon de Nouvel An

Huîtres de Colchester
Tartines buerrées
de pain de seigle

Crème Capucine

Filets de turbot Chauchat

Selle de chevreuil Windsor

Salade Belle-Hélène

Soufflé glacé au Grand-Marnier

Mignardises

New Year's Eve Dinner

Colchester Oysters
Rye Bread and Butter

Cream of Mushroom Soup

Fillets of Turbot Chauchat

Saddle of Venison Windsor

Salad Belle-Helénè

Ice Cream Soufflé Grand Marnier

Petits Fours

Diner de Gala

Médallions de foie gras Tosca

Potage aux huîtres

Ris de veau Demidoff

Selle de marcassin Rôtie
Purée de marrons, pommes beignets

Langouste en Bellevue

Ananas Edouard VII.

Gala Dinner

Medallions of Foie Gras Tosca

Oyster Soup

Braised Sweetbreads Demidoff

Roast Saddle of Young Wild Boar
Chestnut Purée, Potato Fritters

Rock Lobster en Bellevue

Pineapple Edward VII.

Diner de Mariage

Cocktail de Melon au Porto

Crème Duquinha

Truite saumonée Doria

Selle d'agneau Richelieu

Suprêmes de caneton
aux Oranges en Gelée

Soufflé Amandine,
sauce au Porto

Wedding Dinner

Melon Cocktail with Port

Cream Duquinha

Sea Trout Doria

Saddle of Lamb Richelieu

Breasts of Duckling
with Orange in Aspic

Almond Soufflé with
Port Wine Sauce

TRAINING AND EDUCATION

A survey of the structure of education and training in the hotel and catering industry, giving details of the courses and training schemes available.

There are over 200 colleges throughout the country offering some sort of course for the hotel and catering industry. These range from the two universities with hotel and catering management departments to those colleges offering part-time cookery courses.

Immediately after the war there were only two colleges offering hotel courses—the Westminster Hotel School and the Scottish Hotel School, Glasgow. The number of technical colleges now offering catering courses reflects the growth of the industry and its importance in the country's economy. The industry now earns more than £100 million in overseas currency from tourists and foreign business men.

Since the war, these colleges have produced trained people for every section of the industry—hotel and restaurants, industrial catering, school meals service, colleges and universities, pubs and clubs. At any one time, there are about 20,000 young people on part- and full-time courses for the industry though the annual output is under half this figure.

These courses are aimed at most categories of staff—cooks, waiters, housekeepers, bar and cellar staff, supervisors and managers, are both part-time and full-time, and range from a few days to several years. Most of the major courses last at least one year.

The hotel and catering industry has traditionally obtained most of its trained staff from the further education system; although some large companies have taken care to introduce training schemes, the industry has depended mostly on the colleges for its trained personnel.

Now that the Hotel and Catering Industry Training Board has been established, an opportunity will be given to all employers to train their staff to recognised standards.

The Board, which was established in November 1966, has three main purposes:

1. To provide the right quality of training.
2. To ensure sufficient trained staff at all levels.
3. To spread the cost of training more evenly among employers.

The Board was the seventeenth to be set up by the Minister of Labour, but the first to cover a service industry—all the other Boards covered manufacturing and production industries.

Each Board operates independently, under the overall guidance of the Ministry. Board's members are appointed by the Ministry of Labour and they consist of equal numbers of employer and employee representatives together with a smaller number of educationalists. The HCITB has seven employers, seven employee representatives (trade union officials) and four educationalists which makes it one of the biggest Boards. Each Board sets up its own Committee structure and appoints its own staff.

Boards are financed by the industry to which they are connected. They raise a levy from employers, usually based on a percentage of their annual payroll, and, in return, award grants for approved training. No Board can make employers train their staff; they stimulate training by extracting a levy from employers and by giving grants only to those employers who carry out approved training. An employer who does not train pays a levy but receives no grant. Employers with a payroll of less than £4,000 are excluded from paying levy but can 'opt in' to the scheme if they wish.

Through its Levy and Grant Schemes the Board seeks to encourage as many employers as possible to train if a training need is proven. Its regional training teams, working from eight regional offices covering England, Scotland and Wales, are available to help and advise employers on their training problems.

The Board's training recommendations are now beginning to emerge and approximately twelve new career courses from Cookery to Housekeeping will be published in 1970. These courses will be fully under way in partnership with Colleges of Further Education by September 1971. Management training recommendations are now being fully validated and their publication is scheduled for early 1971.

The Board's regional advisory staff have been responsible for the registration of trainees under the Board's Registration Scheme, which lays down criteria for establishing specific standards. Registration, formerly for Cooks on the two and four-year schemes, has been extended to: Food Service Personnel (Three new City & Guilds Courses), Post College Students, Management Trainees and Trainees taking industrial training as part of a block release or sandwich course.

The Board has continued to encourage the formation of Group Training Schemes, which considerably helps the small employer. The number of Group Training Schemes with near national territorial coverage is now approximately 40. Each Group Training Scheme has a Group Training Officer and these Groups between them employ nearly 50,000 employees.

For further information on any of the Training Board's activities contact: The Information Officer, Hotel & Catering Industry Training Board, P.O. Box 18, Ramsey House, Central Square, Wembley, Middlesex, HA9 7AP. Telephone 01-902-8865.

Entry to the Industry

Many of the people now working in the industry entered the industry when they left school and worked their way up, without the benefit of formal college training or a formal training programme. Most young people entering the industry now do so through college or a company training scheme. At present there are courses available which cover all levels of the industry, from the degree course in hotel and catering administration at the Universities of Strathclyde and Surrey to the City and Guilds 147 basic cookery course for chefs.

The University of Surrey course and that of the Scottish Hotel School, University of Strathclyde are suitable for those who are aspiring to top management in the industry. Both demand at least two GCE "A" levels as entrance qualifications.

At a somewhat lower level is the Higher National Diploma in Hotel and Catering Administration, a three year sandwich course which demands five GCE subjects from a specified list, including one "A" level, or a pass in the OND for entrance requirements.

The Ordinary National Diploma in Hotel and Catering Operations is a two year full time course requiring four GCE "O" levels, three from a specified list, for entrance, and aims to give a thorough grounding in catering to those who wish to prepare themselves for supervisory levels in the industry following appropriate industrial experience.

The HND and OND are administered by the Hotel and Catering Institute in conjunction with the Department of Education and Science (for England and Wales), and the Scottish Education Department (for Scotland).

The membership examination of the Hotel and Catering Institute is designed for those in the industry who wish to complement their industrial experience and development. The examination consists of two parts: the intermediate includes the technical knowledge required by a manager, while the final incorporates the administrative subjects. Entrance requirements for the intermediate examination are four GCE "O" levels, three of which must be chosen from a specified list. A pass in the intermediate examination or equivalent qualification is necessary for entrance into the final examination.

The HCITB and the City and Guilds of London Institute jointly administer courses in crafts such as food service and hotel reception. Cookery examinations for the industry are administered by the City and Guilds. There are five examinations varying from the City and Guilds 147, the basic cookery course, to the City and Guilds 353, a course in kitchen supervision.

The Higher National Diploma in Institutional Management and the Oridnary National Diploma in Institutional Housekeeping and Catering are administered jointly by the Department of Education and Science and the IMA. Two further courses are the IMA Certificate in Institutional Management (One-year Abridged course) and the IMA Matron-Housekeeper's Certificate, both of which are administered by the IMA. The former course is designed for men and women over 25 years of age with good professional qualifications or considerable practical experience, who wish to enter the field of institutional management, while the latter course is popular with girls who wish to work with children.

In addition, there are facilities available for some post-graduate training. Lasting from one day to a few months, these courses can cover individual subjects from an appreciation of work study, or financial accounting, to a longer course devoted to the principles of management. A management development programme of short one-week residential courses leading to the award of the University Certificate is offered by the hotel and catering management department of the University of Surrey. Postgraduate studies leading to higher degrees by research may be undertaken at the Universities of Strathclyde and Surrey.

The Universities of Strathclyde (the Scottish Hotel School) and Surrey and some Polytechnics and technical colleges run a variety of short, part-time courses in varying subjects of interest to management of the industry, i.e. personnel management, work simplification and housekeeping. These, and some other colleges, also organise seminars, work shops and one-day conferences in management subjects.

Most of the Industry's Career (Apprentice) training is now under the administration of the Hotel Catering Industry Training Board—Registered Trainees. All trainees on these schemes are registered with the Board and their training follows a recognisable pattern leading to joint certification by the Board and the City and Guilds of London Institute. All of them are given day release or block release to attend college.

Details of Catering Courses

DEGREE COURSE IN HOTEL AND CATERING ADMINISTRATION, UNIVERSITY OF SURREY

Degree courses are now offered by the University of Strathclyde (Scottish Hotel School) and the Department of Hotel and Catering Management, University of Surrey. The entrance qualifications are of university standard, i.e. at least two GCE "A" levels. The Surrey course lasts four years, of which three terms (i.e. one year) are spent working in an industrial establishment. It has been conceived as a combination of business, technical and general education. In its vocational content, it is directed towards the management of hotel and catering services in a broad sense with no pronounced specialisation towards any particular section of the industry.

The structure and general content of the course are as follows:

	Common Core Studies (Whole Stage)	*Long Options* (3 or 4 terms)	*Short Options* (1 term)
Stage 1			
Terms 1-2	Accounting 1 Economics 1 Law 1 Foods and Beverages Food Preparation Food Science 1 General Studies 1		
Stage 2			
Terms 3-5	Accounting II Economics II Law II Administration Catering Operation Food Science II	General Studies II Languages	Advanced Food Preparation Business Statistics Industrial Orientation Manpower Mechanised Accounting Purchasing Technical French Work Study
Ind Stage			
(12 months)	INDUSTRIAL TRAINING		

Stage 3			
Terms 6-9	Industrial Management Catering Administration Environmental Studies	Languages and Accounting II Food Technology Hotel administration Nutrition Tourism	Stage 2 Short Options and Business Promotion Electronic Data Processing Ergonomics Market Research Operational Research Organisation & Method Personnel Administration

The award of the University is a B.Sc. Honours Degree.

B.A. COURSE IN HOTEL MANAGEMENT, SCOTTISH HOTEL SCHOOL, UNIVERSITY OF STRATHCLYDE

This is a full-time three-year course leading to the B.A. degree for the student intending to enter the field of Hotel and Catering Management and Tourism and which permits the selection of a curriculum that will meet these vocational needs and be academically sound. Depending on his interests, the student may combine with the specialist subjects of hotel and catering management a choice from subjects such as Accountancy, Business Economics or Administration.

The course for the B.A. degree consists of thirteen classes to be taken over three years with two main fields of study (1) Hotel and Catering Management and (2) other business or Arts subjects. At least eight classes from the thirteen must be selected from the three classes in Hotel Operations, the three classes in Catering, the two classes in Catering Technology, Planning and Development (Hotels and Catering), Services Planning (Hotels and Catering) and Tourism I and II. The remainder of classes may be made up from a variety of classes offered by the School of Business and Administration or from the School of Arts and Social Studies and including Modern Languages.

The University's Scottish Hotel School embodies residential facilities at Ross Hall, Crookston, and the course also provides for practical hotel laboratory activity in kitchens, restaurant, front office, reception, hotel housekeeping department, food stores, bars and wine cellars to support studies in hotel administration. Students are also required to undertake periods of applied study in the hotel industry and these are normally each of ten weeks' duration and ordinarily take place during the summer vacation at the end of the first and second academic sessions.

The School normally has some 130 students and there is residential accommodation for 87 male students. Normally, all male students are resident during their first year.

HIGHER NATIONAL DIPLOMA IN HOTEL CATERING ADMINISTRATION (England and Wales)

Aim. To give a sound technical education to students who aspire to ultimate positions of responsibility in this industry. It is expected that after appropriate industrial experience they would be responsible for the work of a number of section heads, supervisors and departmental heads who in turn directly supervise others.

Entry Requirements. Five GCE subjects from a specified list* including one "A" level, or a pass in the OND.
Nature. A three year sandwich course, eight months of which will be spent in industry. The subjects studied include food and beverage operations, accommodation operations, planning establishments and maintenance, economics, accounting, law, business administration and applied science.

ORDINARY NATIONAL DIPLOMA IN HOTEL CATERING OPERATIONS (England and Wales)

Aim. To provide a sound basic technical education for those who, following experience in the industry, aspire to positions of supervisory responsibility.
Entry Requirements. Four GCE "O" levels, three of which must be chosen from a specified list* of academic subjects.
Nature. A two year full time course. Subjects include food and beverage preparation and service, accommodation operations, applied science, bookkeeping and costing, legal aspects and business economics. At the end of the first year students have the option of specialising in either food and beverage preparation or accommodation operations.

H.N.D. IN CATERING AND HOTELKEEPING (Scotland)

Aim. The Scottish HND has aims similar to those above for England and Wales.
Entry Requirements. The normal qualification for admission to the HD1 stage of the Scottish Higher National Diploma course is one of the following:

(a) the Scottish Certificate of Education with passes in five different subjects of which two must be on the Higher Grade and one of the Higher Grade passes must be taken from the subjects listed in groups (i), (ii) and (iii) below. In addition there must be a pass in a subject from each of the groups (i), (ii) and (iii).
(b) any other qualification acceptable to the Joint Committee in Catering and Hotel Keeping.

Nature. The Scottish National Diploma Course consists of three stages known as HD1, HD2, and HD3 with two periods of industrial training, each of at least 12-14 weeks, one between the HD1 and HD2 and HD3 stages.

O.N.D. IN CATERING AND HOTELKEEPING (Scotland)

Aim. Similar to the aim of the OND for England and Wales.
Entry Requirements. The normal qualification for admission to the OD1 stage of the Ordinary Diploma course is one of the following:

(a) The Scottish Certificate of Education with "O" Grade passes in:
 (i) English
 (ii) one subject from Anatomy Physiology and Health, Biology, Botany, Chemistry, Mathematics, Physics, Zoology

**List of Specified subjects:* English Language, English Literature, Mathematics, Geography, History, Modern Language, Classical Language, and one approved Science Subject.
In addition to the above mentioned subjects, Economics will be accepted for the HND. For both OND and HND courses, sociology and up to two approved science subjects may be offered.
—C.S.E. Grade 1 is considered equivalent to G.C.E. "O" Level.—Subjects must include a subject testing command of English.

(iii) one subject from Economic Organisation, Geography, History, Modern Studies, Principles of Accounts, a modern language
(iv) one subject of the student's own choice, which may or may not be taken from those listed above
(b) any other qualification acceptable to the Joint Committee in Catering and Hotel Keeping.

Nature. The Ordinary National Diploma Course consists of two stages known as OD1 (Phase 1) and OD2 (Phase 3) with a period (Phase 2) of at least twelve weeks in the Catering and Hotel Industry between these two stages.

MEMBERSHIP EXAMINATION OF THE INSTITUTE

The examination is principally designed for those in industry who wish to complement their industrial experience and development. The membership examination consists of two parts; the intermediate includes the technical knowledge required by a manager, whilst the final incorporates the administrative subjects.

Intermediate Examination

Aim. To provide a sound knowledge of the technical aspects of hotel and catering operations.
Entry Requirements. Four GCE "O" level passes, three of which must be chosen from a specified list.* Those over 21 may apply for a relaxation of this condition. Also see General Catering Course.
Nature. A student would normally expect to complete this course in three years on a part-time basis. The subjects include preparation and service of food and beverage, food hygiene and nutrition, provision and service of accommodation, bookkeeping and food and beverage control.

Final Examination

Aim. To give those in industry an opportunity of obtaining a fundamental knowledge of the administrative aspects of hotel and catering operations.
Entry requirements. A pass in the intermediate examination or an equivalent qualification, or have been granted exemption from the intermediate in recognition of industrial experience.
Nature. Normally a two-year part-time course. The subjects studied include provision of food and beverage, planning and provision of accommodation, law for the hotel and catering industry, accounting, economic aspects of the hotel and catering industry and introduction to management.

TWO YEAR CATERING COURSE

Many colleges offer a two-year catering course, as distinct from the two-year General Catering Diploma Course. It is difficult to lay down the general principles applying to this course because they vary from college to college. In most cases, however, they are intended for chefs and cooks. Some colleges put the course on to a broader basis, and introduce elements of other crafts—e.g. waiting—and describe the course as a "basic catering course".

The majority of the courses are directed towards the kitchen, and lead to the City and Guilds 151 examination. Some colleges arrange for their students to take the City and Guilds 147 at the end of the first year and the 151 at the end of the second year, but the trend nowadays is to ignore the 147 examination and concentrate on the 151 for the second-year examination. Other examinations taken on the course often include the HCI Nutrition and Hygiene certificates. Age of entry to the course is usually 16 years and no "O" levels are required, although most colleges insist that candidates sit an entrance examination.

FOOD SERVICE CERTIFICATE

This course is intended primarily for young entrants to the industry. It includes an introduction to the hotel and catering industry, particularly food service; the skills necessary for the development of a career in food service and general studies.

ALCOHOLIC BEVERAGE CERTIFICATE

Intended for those who have completed the Food Service Certificate and have a minimum of six months further experience in the industry. The course includes the skills needed to sell and serve wines, alcoholic beverages and associated products, plus an introduction to certain aspects of the supervisor's role.

ADVANCED SERVING TECHNIQUE CERTIFICATE

Intended for those who have completed the Food Service Certificate and have a minimum of six months' further experience. The course includes the skills required in a range of advanced serving techniques, plus an introduction to certain aspects of the supervisor's role.

HOUSEKEEPING CERTIFICATE

This certificate is normally taken during a two-year full-time catering course, but a number of colleges offer a two-year part-time course in this subject. There is a three-hour examination and an assessed practical test.

NUTRITION CERTIFICATE

This certificate is normally taken as part of a two-year full-time catering course but some colleges offer a one-year part-time course. There is a two-hour examination.

HYGIENE CERTIFICATE

This certificate is normally taken as part of a two-year full-time catering course, but some colleges offer a one-year part-time course. There is a two-hour examination.

HOTEL RECEPTION COURSE

A block release course of 540 hours in college and a minimum of 360 hours planned experience in industry. Alternatively, colleges may offer this course on a one-year full-time basis. The course comprises a knowledge of reception, business practice, bookkeeping, calculations, legal requirements and other subjects relevant to the work of a hotel receptionist.

City and Guilds Courses

The City and Guilds of London Institute have for many years offered examinations in cookery for the hotel and catering industry, and these examinations are now standard qualifications for chefs in the industry. Five examinations in catering subjects are presently offered.

CITY AND GUILDS 147. BASIC COOKERY FOR THE CATERING INDUSTRY

1. Purpose of the Scheme. This is intended to meet the needs of apprentice cooks and others in the school meals service, hospitals, hotels, restaurants, industrial canteens and H.M. forces. The emphasis in the scheme is on basic cooking methods and skills and provides a basis for more detailed study of particular aspects of catering in subsequent advanced courses. The course of study and examinations are intended to be complementary to organised practical training, and it is this course which apprentices usually take in their first two years in technical college training.

The course includes a general introduction to the catering industry; commodities; use of cook's tools; basic stocks; basic sauces and their derivatives; gravies; simple soups; fish; larder work; cooking of meats; potatoes, vegetables; egg, cheese and farinaceous dishes; puddings and sweets; simple cake and biscuit mixtures; simple yeast mixtures; breakfast dishes; beverages; menu planning; heat and fuels; safety and fire precautions; working methods.

2. Curriculum. Courses should cover the following:

A—Cookery Theory and Practice
B—Related Studies (simple nutrition and hygiene)

In addition, courses should, wherever possible, include general studies.

3. Course of Study. The scheme has been designed so that courses can be organised on a variety of types of day, evening and block release, or a combination of these.

Not less than 430 hours should be devoted to theoretical and practical work on the syllabuses. Their allocation will depend upon the ages, qualifications and experience of the students, and is entirely at the discretion of the principal of the college.

As the syllabuses indicate, the content of the course is directly related to practical work which is an essential component. Visits to places of interest and co-operation with local caterers, catering organisations and student employers will be essential if maximum advantage is to be derived from the course.

4. Examinations. The examinations offered by the City and Guilds of London Institute will comprise:

Written paper—2 hours—Cookery Theory and Related Studies.
Practical test—3 hours—Basic Cookery.

Both the written and the practical test must be taken in the same year.

5. Entry to Examination. Candidates to be accepted for examination must *either* have satisfactorily completed the course of study, including practical work, *or* have been granted permission by the City and Guilds of London Institute to take the examination as external candidates.

6. Award of Certificates. Results in the examination as a whole will be issued in four classes, and for the individual parts of the examination in eight grades. The relationship between grades and classes is:

Pass with Distinction	—	Grades 1 and 2
Pass with Credit	—	Grades 3 and 4
Pass	—	Grades 5 and 6
Fail	—	Grades 7 and 8

Each candidate will receive a record of performance giving his result in terms of class and grade. Candidates who are successful in both the written and practical examinations in the same year will receive a certificate showing the class of their result in the examination as a whole.

7. Prize. The following prize is offered to candidates who are eligible under General Regulations:

COOKS' COMPANY

no single prize to exceed five guineas.

8. General Studies. In addition to the subjects covered in the curriculum, students will also need to express themselves clearly in both written and spoken English. The contribution that can be made to their education as a whole and to their personal development by a course in general studies is thus of special importance, and it is hoped that all colleges preparing students for the Institute's examinations by part-time day or evening classes will include general studies in the courses they provide. The Institute will not, however, examine in these subjects or require completion of a course in them as a condition of eligibility for its examinations under this scheme.

Syllabus: A—Cookery Theory and Practice

Candidates will be expected to have a knowledge of requirements in relation to cooking for large as well as small numbers and in particular the adoption of methods, garnishing and finish required in large-scale cookery. Attention should be given to correct seasoning, flavouring, consistency, presentation and portioning. Particular attention should also be given throughout the course to the importance of cleanliness and hygiene and to safe practices and the prevention of accidents. In addition, candidates will be expected to make the necessary simple calculations in work on, for example, commodities and recipes.

Only the basic French culinary terms understood in all branches of cookery will be expected for examination purposes.

(a) *General introduction to the Catering Industry*, including a broad survey of the different types of catering establishments.

(b) *Commodities.*

(c) *Use of cook's tools.* Choice, care, use and maintenance of knives and other hand tools; knife drill. Choice, care and use of mechanical equipment and of large-scale equipment.

(d) *Basic stocks.* White (fond blanc) beef or veal; brown (fond brun) beef or veal; chicken (fond de volaille); fish (fond de poisson).

(e) *Basic sauces and their derivatives.* Roux (white, blond, brown); white (Béchamel, Velouté) and brown (Espagnole) and tomato sauces.

(f) *Gravies.* Roast (rôti); thickened (jus lié).

(g) *Simple soups.* Broth; purée; cream (roux and liaison); pulse and fresh vegetable.

(h) *Fish.* Choice, cleaning and preparation, including filleting; methods of cooking; boiling (bouillir), poaching (pocher), shallow and deep frying (meunière et frite), grilling (griller). Use of frozen fish.

(i) *Larder work.*

(a) Simple butchery; use of by-products; choice of joints and cuts; simple boning, carving and preparation; preparation of pies and puddings.

(b) Hors d'œuvre. Preparation of grapefruits, simple hors d'œuvre, simple salads and mayonnaise.

(c) Sandwiches and sandwich fillings.

(j) *Cooking of meats.* Boiling; joints and accompaniments. Stewing; hot-pots, Irish stew, white stews (fricassée, blanquette), brown stews (navarin, sauté), ragôut. Roasting and braising; joints and accompaniments. Grilling and shallow frying: chops, steaks, liver, mixed grills. Preparation of re-heated dishes (rechauffée). Cooking of pies and puddings.

(k) *Potatoes.* Boiled, roast, fried, mashed (purée) and other simple varieties such as sautée, macaire, duchesse, fondante, croquette, boulangère.

(l) *Vegetables.* Preparation and cooking of fresh, frozen and dried vegetables and accompaniments.

(m) *Egg, cheese and farinaceous dishes.* Simple egg dishes, including omelettes, soft and hardboiled eggs, scrambled, poached and fried eggs, œufs sur le plat, œufs en cocotte. Welsh rarebit, spaghetti and macaroni dishes.

(n) *Puddings and sweets (entremets).* Pastry (various), suet, short, sugar, full puff, rough puff or flaky. Use of pastry in making simple sweets such as flans, pies, tarts and tartlets, bouchée and turnovers. Milk puddings; rice, semolina, egg custard, crème caramel, bread and butter. Steamed puddings; suet and sponge, spotted dick, orange or jam sponge and accompaniments. Steamed or boiled fruit puddings, apple or rhubarb. Stewed fruits, fresh and dried.

Simple cold sweets; trifles, bavarois, fools, fresh fruit salad, junket.

Pancakes and fritters. Simple baked sweets, Eve's pudding, apple charlotte. Sweet sauces.

(o) *Simple cake and biscuit mixtures.* Rubbing-in, creaming, whisking and melting methods.

(p) *Simple yeast mixtures.* Bread rolls and bun dough.

(q) *Breakfast dishes.* Preparation, cooking and presentation of usual breakfast dishes.

(r) *Beverages.* Tea, coffee, cocoa.

(s) *Menu planning.* Basic principles affecting menus with special relevance to the work of the cook, i.e. commodities available, variety, colour and texture, loading of equipment, staffing and timing, costs.

(t) *Heat and fuels.* Basic principles; conduction, convection and radiation; economic use of common fuels, including gas and electricity.

(u) *Safety and fire precautions.* Common hazards and simple precautions.

(v) *Water.* Supply of water from mains and cisterns. Cocks and taps.

(w) *Working methods.* Working methods to ensure economy of time, labour and materials.

Syllabus: B—Related Studies

1. Simple nutrition

2. Hygiene including personal, food and kitchen hygiene.

CITY AND GUILDS 441. GENERAL CATERING COURSE

1. Purpose of the Scheme. This scheme for a one year full-time general course in catering subjects and related examination has been designed to meet the needs of young people who, on leaving school, wish to enter the catering industry. It is intended to further the education and development of the student by providing a broad basis of study which will give him an introduction to the nature of openings in the industry and the skills necessary in those occupations so that each individual may be guided to an appropriate course of further training and education.

As an integral part of the course, each student will aim at achieving a recognisable level of performance in tasks as identified by the Hotel and Catering Industry Training Board.

2. Course of Study. The scheme has been devised on the assumption that students will attend a one-year full-time course of not less than 1,000 hours' duration.

The course comprises Food Production and Service, Accommodation Services and General Studies. Applied Science and Business Studies have not been shown as separate subjects as these should form an integral part of the prescribed course. It is recommended that the greater number of hours of the course be devoted to Food Production and Service. As far as possible all sections of the syllabus should be studied in a practical way from the point of view of a person who is required to perform the function, and also to develop the student's attitude to efficient work. The allocation of hours for the scheme as a whole takes into account the need to include General Studies (see paragraph 3 below).

Visits to a variety of catering establishments will considerably assist the student's understanding of the industry. Wherever possible it is recommended that such visits be included as part of the course, together with talks by representatives from various sections of the industry.

3. General Studies. General Studies form an integral part of the course which has been so devised as to leave time available for this purpose. Attention is drawn to the then Ministry of Education's Report "General Studies in Technical Colleges" published by HMSO in 1962.

Suggestions as to the topics which might be covered in this field have been made in the Notes for Guidance (see paragraph 12 below).

General Studies will not be examined by the Institute, but will form part of the College assessment.

4. Approval of Courses. Courses must be initially approved by the Institute and application should be made on Form 441/A, obtainable from the City and Guilds of London Institute, 76 Portland Place, London, WIN 4AA at least six months before the start of the first course. Courses will not be approved unless there are adequate facilities for both the theoretical and practical work.

The scheduling of a class on Form 12 by a technical college does not constitute an application for approval.

After obtaining approval for a course, centres proposing to submit for the examination should notify the City and Guilds of London Institute of their courses of study annually on Form 12.

5. Selection of Students for Courses. No specific educational qualifications are required for entry to the course, the selection of students being entirely at the discretion of the college authorities.

6. Eligibility for Entry to the Examination. Candidates must have attended an approved course of study at a further education establishment.

Local Secretaries will be required to certify on Form CS that all candidates will have completed the college course.

7. External Candidates. No external candidates (that is those who have not completed a college course) will be accepted for this examination.

8. Examination Overseas. This examination will NOT be held outside the United Kingdom and Eire.

9. Examination. The examination will comprise the following:

441-1-01	1st written paper	2 hours
441-1-02	2nd written paper	2½ hours
441-1-03	Project	College assessment
441-1-04	Practical Subjects	

Candidates will be required to satisfy the examiners in all parts of the examination in the same year.

The two written papers will cover all sections of the syllabus: the first paper will comprise multiple choice questions only, the second paper short answer and essay type questions. Each candidate will be required to undertake a project on a topic related to the course. It should be in the form of a report/essay of approximately 1,000/1,500 words and may be illustrated. It will be assessed by the College.

A college assessment for each candidate, based on the year's work in practical subjects, is also required. The assessments for both the project and practical subjects are to be submitted on Form 441/CA by the 15th of June in the year of the examination. Full details regarding assessment may be found in Notes for Guidance (see paragraph 12 below).

The City and Guilds of London Institute reserves the right to send its own assessor to visit colleges by arrangement in order to co-ordinate standards of assessment.

10. Examination Results. Each candidate will receive a record of perfomance giving the class of result in the examination as a whole; there are four classes—"Passed with Distinction", "Passed with Credit", "Passed" and "Failed"; an indication of performance in the separate parts of the examination given in grades; there are 8 grades, grade 1 being the highest of six "pass" grades and grades 7 and 8 being "fail" grades.

11. Award of Certificates. The General Catering Course Certificate will be awarded to candidates successful in the examination. The certificate will indicate the candidate's class of result in the examination as a whole.

12. Notes for Guidance. Notes for the guidance of lecturers concerned with this course are available upon application to the Institute and these should be read in conjunction with the syllabuses. The notes cover such topics as course assessment, the project and recommendations regarding the teaching of all sections of the syllabuses and General Studies.

SYLLABUSES

Food Production and Service

(Aim: to introduce and provide an understanding of the basic technical skills and related subjects in the preparation and service of food to meet the needs of the customer.)

The purpose of food, the study of food commodities and their behaviour in storage and during preparation. Food preservation. The care and control under hygienic conditions of food and non-alcoholic beverages. Cookery: the application of cooking processes and the changes occurring during these in differing groups of commodities (meat and poultry, fish, fruit and vegetables, dairy produce and dry goods) in order to achieve particular characteristics in the end product. Characteristics in terms of quantity, cost and nutritional value; appearance, consistency, texture, flavour, palatability and temperature.

The general responsibilities of the food server to the customer. Attitude and approach, methods, techniques and skills needed to meet varying customer requirements. The customer's needs for knowledge of the food to be served, methods of conveying information about the food available.

The kitchen service of food. Quality and portion control. Food presentation and portioning. Choice of food in relation to cost, choice of recipe, recipe balance and type of end product required.

An appreciation of the application of differing types of food service.

The selection and use of equipment in relation to its effectiveness in meeting the customer's requirements; its routine care, maintenance and cleaning; its safe, hygienic and economic operation.

Fuels in use for cooking and holding food.

Food and personal hygiene. Causes of food poisoning.

The maintenance of records in the main aspects of food production and service.

Accommodation Services

(Aim: To introduce and provide an understanding of the basic technical knowledge for the routine care, cleaning and maintenance of residential accommodation, kitchen, dining and ancillary areas and to recognise, in the practical situation, the required standards of cleanliness and maintenance.)

The necessity for staff to anticipate the needs of their customers and an appreciation of the responsibilities of staff concerned with the routine care, cleaning and maintenance of residential accommodation, kitchen, dining and ancillary areas. Cleaning routines, organisation and method of work; daily, weekly, monthly, special cleaning, block and unit cleaning.

Cleaning agents, basic principles of detergency and disinfection.

Cleaning agents in common use applied to flooring, floor and wall coverings, furniture, fittings, fabrics and metals; their effectiveness, cost and safety.

Hygiene regulations. Disposal of waste.

Safety and fire precautions.

Equipment and methods used for cleaning, heating, lighting and ventilation; its choice, cost, care and effectiveness.

The maintenance of records in the main aspects of accommodation services.

CITY AND GUILDS 151. COOKERY FOR THE HOTEL AND CATERING INDUSTRY

1. Purpose of the Scheme. Students taking the course should have previously followed the course in either subject 147 or some other course of instruction of equivalent standard, for example—subject 150.

There are two 151 courses:—

Section One is aimed particularly at commercial establishments such as hotels and restaurants.

Section Two, is aimed at large-scale welfare and industrial catering establishments.

2. Curriculum. The course should cover the following curriculum which provides for alternative options as follows:

Cookery for the Hotel and Catering Industry (Hotels and Restaurants)

(a) Cookery theory and practice (including répertoire, French terms, and garnishes)
(b) Related Studies

Cookery for the Hotel and Catering Industry (Welfare and Industrial Establishments)

(a) Cookery, Theory and Practice

(b) Related Studies

3. Course of Study. 3.1. The scheme has been designed for flexible adaptation to various forms of part-time study. It is envisaged that the majority of students will attend part-time day or block release courses, or a combination of these.

It is recommended that on part-time day-release courses a minimum of 432 hours should be available for theoretical and practical work on the syllabuses for either option—Hotels and Restaurants, or Welfare and Industrial Establishments. Any allocation for general studies should be in addition to this. For block release courses the minimum number of hours available will be greater. Where students have already satisfactorily completed one of the options and wish to enter for the other option, it is envisaged that a course of part-time study of approximately 216 hours would be necessary to cover the additional work, practical and theoretical, required.

If colleges wish to provide a combined course covering the syllabuses for both options, it is envisaged that a considerable further allocation of time will be required such as would be available on a block release course organised over two years. Candidates who have satisfactorily completed such a course would be permitted to take the examinations for both options in the same year.

3.2. The selection of students for courses is entirely at the discretion of the college authorities. It is, however, recommended that students should previously have passed the Institute's examination in 147—Basic Cookery for the Catering Industry—or some other examination or test of equivalent standard, e.g., a corresponding examination of a Regional Examining Body.

4. Examination. 4.1. The examination offered annually by the Institute will provide alternative papers, as follows:

Cookery for the Hotel and Catering Industry (Hotels and Restaurants)
Written paper (3 hours' duration)
Practical test (4 hours' duration)

Cookery for the Hotel and Catering Industry (Welfare and Industrial Establishments)
Written paper (3 hours' duration)
Practical test (4 hours' duration)

Candidates must enter both the written paper and the practical test for the examination selected.

4.2. The practical test papers will provide for an actual examination period of four hours. The work performed during this time will be designed to test the candidates' planning of the cooking programme and cooking methods and skills. Prior to the examination, candidates will be required to plan their order of work, order the ingredients and commodities required, and carry out the necessary mise-en-place.

5. Entry to Examination. Candidates to be accepted for examination must *either* have satisfactorily completed the course of study, including the necessary practical work, *or* have been granted permission by the City and Guilds of London Institute to take the examination as an external candidate.

6. Award of Certificates. Results in the examination as a whole will be issued in four classes, and for the individual parts of the examination in eight grades. The relationship between grades and classes is:

Pass with Distinction	—	Grades 1 and 2
Pass with Credit	—	Grades 3 and 4
Pass	—	Grades 5 and 6
Fail	—	Grades 7 and 8

Each candidate will receive a record of performance giving his result in the terms of class and grades. Candidates who pass both the appropriate written paper and practical test in the same examination will receive a certificate showing the class of result in the examination as a whole and also the option offered, that is Hotels and Restaurants or Welfare and Industrial Establishments.

7. Prize. The following prize is offered to candidates eligible under General Regulations:

COOKS' COMPANY

no single prize to exceed seven guineas.

8. General Studies. In addition to the subjects covered in the curriculum, students will also need to acquire some measure of skill in communication. The contribution that can be made to their education as a whole and to their personal development by a course in English and general studies is thus of special importance, and it is hoped that all colleges preparing students for the Institute's examinations by part-time day classes or by block release will include English and general studies in the course they provide. The Institute will not, however, examine in these subjects, or require completion of a course in them as a condition of eligibility for its examinations.

Syllabus: Section I (Hotels and Restaurants)

Teaching should be on the assumption that the student is competent in basic trade cookery and should be directed towards the cultivation of professional skills and methods, so as to enable work of good finish to be produced with the minimum of time and labour.

Students should be made aware of the relationship of their practical skills to kitchen organisation (including the parti system), equipment, tools and materials used, and the mise-en-place. They will be expected to show a sound grasp of the principles of trade cookery and hygiene, to have an understanding of food values, a knowledge of menu composition and costing in so far as they affect the work of the practising cook, and an adequate acquaintance with French culinary terms and garnishes. The theory taught should be closely related to the daily work of the cook, and should provide an understanding of the principles underlying the craft. Students should also learn to appreciate the artistry involved in cookery, and should gain some understanding of the derivation of dishes and the evolution of the craft of professional cookery.

A—Cookery, Theory and Practice

The principles of cookery already mastered in the previous course (either for Subjects 147 or 150) should now be applied in the wider range of work in this syllabus.

Candidates will be expected to acquire a broader répertoire of basic dishes and to develop the ability to make use of textbooks and works of reference so that they may exploit fully the range of garnishes and derivative sauces. An appreciation of individual dishes in particular and classic dishes in general should be integrated with this study, and should aid the development of pride of craft.

Candidates should be taught something of the origin of the better-known classic dishes, so that they may have an understanding of menu terminology and the way in which the cookery répertoire has been developed over the years.

Sauces. Further derivatives from the basic sauces: Veloutés, including chaud-froid, and demi-glace, including chaud-froid, Warm egg sauces, e.g. Hollandaise and derivatives. Derivatives of mayonnaise.

Potages (*Soups*). Consommés, hot and cold; extension of répertoire of cream soups. Unclassified soups, e.g. Oxtail, Mock Turtle, Cock-a-Leekie, Mulligatawny, Minestrone.

Oeufs (*Eggs*). Extension of répertoire of egg dishes, to include œuf mollet and further varieties, e.g. en cocotte and sur le plat. Sweet and Spanish-type omelettes.

Pâtés Alimentaires (*Farinaceous Dishes*). Extension of répertoire, to include Ravioli, Gnocchi, Nouilles and Garnishes, including Bolonaise, Milanaise, Italienne, Napolitaine.

Riz (*Rice*). Pilaff, Risotto.

Poissons (*Fish*). Extension of répertoire of fish dishes to cover more advanced treatment of cheaper fish, and also to include simple methods with Sole, Turbot, Salmon, Trout, Scallops, Crab, Lobsters, Whitebait. Similar application to fish covered in the previous syllabuses for Subjects 147 and 150, e.g. choice, cleaning and preparation, including filleting, methods of cooking; bouillir (boil), pocher (poach), meunière (shallow fry), frire (deep fry), griller (grill).

Entrées and Relevés. Volaille (*Chicken*). Poché, fricassée, poêlé, en casserole, en cocotte, vol-au-vent, émincé. The types of dishes will be standard and simple examples of the various forms, such as Chasseur in the case of Poulet sauté, or Bonne Femme in the case of Poulet en casserole.

Bœuf (*Beef*). Braising, e.g. à la mode; boiling, e.g. bœuf bouilli à la française. Smaller cuts, grilling and sauté, e.g. tournedos, entrecôtes. Appropriate simple garnishes such as Vert Pré or Niçoise. Other beef entrées, e.g. Carbonnade de bœuf Flamande.

Agneau et Mouton (*Lamb and Mutton*). The larger cuts: legs and shoulders, e.g. Boulangère and farcies. The smaller cuts; noisettes, côtelettes, with appropriate simple dressings such as Clamart, Chump chop Champvallon.

Veau (*Veal*). Escalopes and côtelettes, with simple garnishes, e.g. Viennoise or Marsala. Goulash à la Hongroise. Fricassée, Blanquette.

Gibier (*Game*). Jugged Hare, Salmis.

Jambon et Porc (*Ham and Pork*). Braised ham, simply served, e.g. with Madeira sauce. Pork cutlet, simply garnished, e.g. Charcutière.

Abafs (*Offal*). Sauté of Kidneys, simply garnished, e.g. Turbigo, Ris de veau braisés and panés. Ox Tongue, simply garnished, e.g. Florentine.

Diverses (*Miscellaneous*). Saucisses au vin blanc, Kebab, Choucroûte garnie, Bitok.

In the service of entrées, candidates will be expected to be familiar with the principal garnishes, such as Bouquetière, Printanier, Dubarry, Chasseur, Duxelle, Réforme, Italienne and Soubise.

Rôtis (*Roasts*). Extension of répertoire, to include all joints of veal, beef, mutton, lamb and pork. Poultry; chicken, turkey, duck, goose. Game; pheasant, grouse, partridge. Correct accompaniments and appropriate garnishes.

Légumes (*Vegetables*). Extension of répertoire, to include, for example, Chou-fleur Polonaise, Tomates farcies, Duxelle, Petits Pois à la française, Celeri braisé, Courgettes farcies. Simple treatment of asperges, aubergines, artichauts (Globe), endives.

Pommes de terre (*Potatoes*). Extension of répertoire, to include common derivatives from Duchesse base. All varieties of deep fry (except soufflé). Pommes Parisiennes. Maître d'Hôtel.

Salades (*Salads*). Appropriate type, use and dressings of salads with hot roasts and cold dishes.

Hors d'œuvre. (*Hors d'œuvre*). Service and accompaniments for single hors d'œuvre, e.g. Smoked Salmon, Smoked Trout, Potted Shrimps. Preparation of pâté. Preparation of a variety of meat, fish and vegetables for composite hors d'œuvre, e.g. Chou-fleur à la Grecque, Riz Orientale, Bismarck Herring, Beef Ravigotte, Canapés à la Russe. All fruits and juices used as appetisers.

Bonne Bouche (*Savoury*). All savouries usually served.

Pâtes (*Pastes*). Extension of répertoire, to include choux (uses for Profiterolles, Beignets, Eclairs). Application of Puff Pastry in Palmiers, D'Artois, Chausson, Vol-au-Vent, Bouchées, Fleurons. Pâte à Savarin.

Entremets chauds (*Sweets, hot*). Extension of répertoire to include the greater variety of crêpes, e.g. Normande. Pouding Soufflé and Milk Pudding Soufflé. Sauce Sabayon.

Entremets froids (*Sweets, cold*). Extension of répertoire to include a variety of simple gâteaux, such as Moka and au Chocolat. Simple sweets containing ices and jellies.

Syllabus: B—Related Studies

1. Menu Composition
2. Food Values
3. Costing
4. Organisation
5. Equipment
6. Hygiene

Section II (Welfare and Industrial Establishments)

Teaching should be on the assumption that the student is competent on the level of Scheme 147—Basic Cookery for the Catering Industry. Students should be taught the relationship of their practical skills to the day-to-day running of the kitchen and to the equipment, tools and materials used. They will be expected to show a sound grasp of the principles of cookery as applied to large-scale food production, to have an understanding of food values and the nature of food commodities, and a knowledge of menu composition and costing in so far as they affect the work of the practising cook. Theoretical course work should be closely related to the daily work of the cook, and should give the student an understanding of the principles underlying the craft. Students should also learn to appreciate the artistry involved in cookery, and should gain some understanding of the derivation of dishes.

Throughout the course the students should be taught to understand the cook's role in controlling food quality, and to develop and practice an objective assessment of food through all stages of kitchen operations, from the receipt of the raw, pre-prepared or processed food commodities up to the time of kitchen service. This will involve the study of food commodities in terms of types, grades, composition, and also the fundamental changes which take place during storage, preparation, cooking and kitchen service. The finished product must be acceptable in terms of colour, finish, presentation, flavour, consistency, texture, palatability, temperature and nutritional value, all of which must be within the context of hygienic and safe working.

Syllabus: A—Cookery, Theory and Practice

Sauces. Brown sauces (including devilled and piquante), white sauces (including cheese, egg, parsley, anchovy, mustard, onion), and miscellaneous sauces (including tomato, Hollandaise, mayonnaise and salad dressings). Techniques of large-scale sauce production and the ingredients used, with particular emphasis on current methods and the use of natural cooking liquors and thickening agents. Adaption and extension of the basic sauces, using simple ingredients, including the use of convenience foods, e.g. concentrated packet or tinned soups and pre-prepared stocks. Comparison of different techniques. Adaptations of derivative sauces, e.g. piquante sauce from a brown sauce. Use of sauces as extenders and liaison agents, e.g. sauce used as a base for a soufflé. Preparation of cold sauces and their uses in cold buffet work—chaud-froid.

Soups. Clear, oxtail, mock turtle, cock-a-leekie, mulligatawny, and minestrone soups. Making of inexpensive soups from raw materials. Use of pre-prepared and packet soups and convenience foods; comparison of time, quality and cost with dishes produced by traditional methods. Preparation of garnishes. Use of mechanical aids in cutting, sieving and pulverising raw materials and convenience foods. Basic proportions of garnish to liquid. Recipe balance. Use of factory-prepared stock bases and cooking liquids.

Egg Dishes. Simple methods of cooking eggs by large-scale methods; scrambled, poached, boiled and fried. Use and nutritional value of eggs as breakfast, lunch, and supper dishes with appropriate accompanying garnishes, and their presentation as in large-scale catering establishments, e.g. curried eggs, salads. Use of eggs in pies and open tarts, sweet and savoury omelettes and soufflés. Use of processed eggs.

Rice and Pastas. Preparation of dishes using rice and Italian pastas in savoury forms, including their use as lunch and supper dishes, as accompanying dishes and as substitutes for potatoes. Use of prepared and packet pasta, e.g. ravioli, spaghetti.

Fish. Basic methods and preparation of fish dishes by boiling, poaching, shallow frying, deep frying, grilling, oven-baking and oven-frying. Use of fish liquors in sauces accompanying fish dishes used in large-scale catering. Filleting and portioning of common fish, e.g. plaice, herring, cod. Use of smoked fish, e.g. kippers, smoked haddock. Use of frozen fish and canned fish in hot and cold dishes. Use of fish in composite dishes.

Poultry. Chicken, turkey and duck: simple dishes using all methods of cooking. Different forms in which chicken may be obtained, e.g., segments. Use of poultry giblets and trimmings. Use of poultry in composite dishes, e.g. pies. Use of canned and frozen poultry.

Meat. Veal, beef, mutton, pork, lamb and offal: use of all cuts and types, with emphasis on inexpensive cuts and methods of cooking them. Use and treatment of frozen, chilled, imported and canned meat. Different cuts and joints in which meat may be obtained, their quality, relative prices, uses and preparation for dishes, e.g., steak, chop, boned, shoulder and leg.

Salads. Preparation of composite salads. Use of salads as main dishes, as appetiser courses, and as accompaniments to cold and hot dishes. Treatment and correct preparation of all salad ingredients. Use of vegetables and fresh fruit.

Sandwiches. Preparation and presentation of different types of sandwich, for all occasions, e.g. traditional, open, rolled neapolitan.

Snacks and Savoury Dishes. Methods of production and forms of presentation of savoury dishes as a light meal and as a course in a formal meal.

Vegetables. Preparation and cooking by varied large-scale methods of fresh vegetables in season. Batch cookery for staggered meal service. Comparison of time, efficiency and cost of vegetables, preparation by hand and by mechanical methods. Emphasis on good finish and presentation, and on preservation of flavour, texture, and nutritive value. Varied treatment of frozen, canned and dried vegetables. Service of vegetables with stuffings and sauces.

Potatoes. Application of various methods of potato cookery to large-scale production. Use of dehydrated and other forms of prepared potato.

Pastry. Production methods of basic pastes (short, sugar, flaky, rough-puff, puff, hot water), using manual techniques. Use of pastry in a variety of attractive and practicable dishes of good finish for large-scale catering.

Hot and Cold Sweets. Methods of production for large-scale catering (including the use of mechanical aids where applicable), of simple gâteaux, steamed and baked sponges, milk puddings, fruit pies, flans and cold sweets. Comparison of dishes produced from raw materials and from materials obtained in commercial convenience forms, e.g. cakes and pudding mixes, sauces, pastes, jelly crystals.

Syllabus: B—Related Studies

1. Applied Food Values
2. Portioning and Portion Control

Kitchen Practice

3. Use and Care of Equipment
4. Hygiene
5. Routines for Safety

CITY AND GUILDS 152. ADVANCED COOKERY FOR THE HOTEL AND CATERING INDUSTRY

1. Purposes of the Scheme. The standard of practical work required in this examination is similar to the work of a chef de parti in a first class hotel, restaurant or club. The syllabus has been drawn up by the Institute's advisory committee on hotel cookery and has been approved by the British Hotels and Restaurants Association. The scheme has been designed for flexible adaption to various forms of part-time study. It is recommended that a minimum of 240 hours part-time study should be allocated to theoretical and practical work on the syllabuses.

2. Courses of Study. It is expected that the facts and classic principles of cookery and basic recipes will have been previously acquired by the student and the syllabus is planned accordingly.

3. Curriculum. Courses should include the following curriculum:

A—Cookery Theory and Practice

B—Related Studies

4. Examinations. 4.1. The examination in Advanced Cookery for the Hotel and Catering Industry offered annually by the Institute will comprise:

Written Paper (three hours)

Practical Test (five hours)

4.2. The Practical examinations will be conducted by examiners appointed and paid by the Institute. Details of the arrangements for these examinations, and the list of utensils and equipment which must be provided by the college authorities for each candidate, will be sent to examination centres by the Institute.

Candidates will be required to carry out a given menu of four or five courses of four covers each and will be required to submit a written plan of work and list the quantities of ingredients they propose to use. This will be forwarded together with the candidate's marks to the Institute.

Candidates may bring to the practical test any cookery books or notes for reference. The choice of service dishes for the presentation of the various foods will be left to the candidate.

5. Entry to Examination. Candidates to be accepted for the examination must have either satisfactorily completed the appropriate course of study, including the necessary practical work, *or* have been granted permission by the Institute to take the examination as external candidates. Local Secretaries will be required on Form CS (i) to certify that all internal candidates entered will have completed the college course and (ii) to give a list of all external candidates entered.

6. Award of Certificates. Results in the examination as a whole will be issued in four classes, and for the individual parts of the examination in eight grades. The relationship between grades and classes is:

Pass with Distinction	—	Grades 1 and 2
Pass with Credit	—	Grades 3 and 4
Pass	—	Grades 5 and 6
Fail	—	Grades 7 and 8

Each candidate will receive a record of performance giving his result in terms of class and grades. Candidates passing the written paper and practical test in the same examination will receive a certificate showing the class of result in the examination as a whole.

7. Prize. The following prize is offered to candidates eligible under General Regulations:

COOKS' COMPANY

no single prize to exceed ten guineas.

Syllabus

It is expected that the facts and classic principles of cookery, and basic recipes, will have been previously acquired by the student; teaching should therefore be directed to the understanding of the numerous extensions. The memorising of actual recipes is not required, but students will be expected to know the composition of classical dishes, garnishes and sauces, together with methods of preparation and timing. They must have an appreciation of the work of the various departments of the cuisine, and the management principles involved in the efficient control and economy of these departments. A knowledge is required of menu composition, recipe balance, quality of ingredients, methods of cooking and of service, food costing, portion control and kitchen percentages.

Particular attention must be given throughout the course to the importance of safe practice and the prevention of accidents.

A—Cookery Theory and Practice

Soups. Preparation and service of: consommé and other clear soups, e.g. petite marmite, madrilene; methods of clarifying, garnishes, use of essences.

Egg Dishes. Preparation and service of all types of egg dishes.

Farinaceous Dishes. Preparation and service of all types of farinaceous dishes.

Potato Dishes. Preparation and service of all types of potato dishes.

Vegetables. Preparation and service of all types of vegetables as a course and as garnishes.

Savoury Soufflés. Preparation and service of all types of savoury soufflés and extensions.

Larder Preparation. All aspects of larder work (including fish, poultry and game, hors d'œuvre, cold buffet work, salads).

Fish Dishes. Preparation and service of all types of fish, e.g. round, flat, shell, smoked, using the following methods—grilling, poaching, deep-frying, shallow-frying, braising, baking, boiling. Use of appropriate garnishes and sauces in hot and cold dishes.

Main Dishes. Preparation, cooking and serving of all types of meat (cured and uncured), poultry, game and offal—roasting, poêling, sauté, grilling, white and brown braising, poaching, deep-frying, stewing and boiling. Different types of, and selective use of, appropriate garnishes.

Sweet Dishes. Methods of preparation and service of the following:

(a) All types of pastes.

(b) Various types of hot sweets (with accompanying appropriate sauces), soufflé puddings, soufflés (various), beignets (various), pancakes, sweet omelettes, rice dishes.

(c) Various cold sweets using fruit; soufflés, crème caramel, bavarois and charlottes, mousses, rice dishes.

Savouries. Methods of preparation and service of various types of savouries.

Syllabus: B—Related Studies

1. Introductory Aspects, including the history of catering and current and future trends
2. Food Costing, Portion and Quality Control
3. Use of Equipment
4. Hygiene

CITY AND GUILDS 353. KITCHEN SUPERVISION AND ORGANISATION

1. Purpose of the Scheme. This scheme for part-time courses and related examinations in Kitchen Supervision and Organisation has been adopted by the Institute on the recommendation of its Advisory Committee for Catering Subjects. It is designed to give an understanding of the problems of organisation and the underlying principles to potential supervisors and those already engaged in kitchen supervision. The supervisor must have an adequate knowledge of cookery, and the aim of this scheme in Kitchen Supervision and Organisation is to provide knowledge of, and practice in, supervisory duties in the day-to-day running of a kitchen in a catering organisation.

2. Courses of Study. 2.1. The scheme has been designed for flexible adaptation to various forms of part-time study. It is envisaged that the majority of students will attend part-time day or block-release courses, or a combination of these.

Where courses are organised on a part-time basis, it is strongly recommended that wherever possible some short residential periods, e.g. weekends, should be arranged for the discussion groups and similar activities so important on this type of course.

2.2. It is recommended that a minimum of 240 hours' part-time study should be available for theoretical and practical work on the syllabuses. The subject matter of the scheme is essentially practical, and students should have practice in the main techniques of decision-making in the organisation and supervision of the kitchen and other sections concerned.

In addition to lectures, courses should include practical projects, discussion groups and visits to local catering organisations. The aim should be to illustrate the general principles outlined in the syllabuses. Discussion groups can be of great value to the more mature students for whom this scheme is intended and will be particularly valuable in a course of this nature where the students may come from different sections of the catering industry. In discussion it should be emphasised that although there may be differences in the various sections of the industry, the general applications of the principles and techniques of supervision are essentially similar.

2.3. The selection of students for courses under this scheme is entirely at the discretion of college authorities. It is, however, recommended that they should have reached the standard of the scheme 151—Cookery for the Hotel and Catering Industry, and have had sufficient appropriate experience within the catering industry to benefit from the course.

3. Curriculum. Courses should cover the following subjects;

(a) Elements of supervision
(b) Economic and financial aspects of supervision
(c) Personnel aspects
(d) Work organisation and control

Institutional Management Association Examinations

H.N.D. IN INSTITUTIONAL MANAGEMENT

Purpose of the Course. The aims of this three-year sandwich course is to give a sound technical education to students who wish, ultimately, to assume positions of managerial responsibility in the domestic administration of residential and catering establishments such as: University Halls of Residence, College of Education, Residential and Day Schools, The School Meals Service, Residential Clubs, Hospitals and Industry. The course will bear special relation to the various aspects of living and working in a community.

Content of Course. The subjects to be studied are: Management Studies, Business Studies, General Studies, Food Service, House Services and Applied Science.

Entry Qualifications. In England and Wales the General Certificate of Education in five subjects including four from a specified list*, one of which must be at Advanced level. The subjects *should* include a Science subject and *must* include a subject testing command of English. For Scotland similar qualifications in the Scottish Certificate of Education are required. Further information may be obtained from the IMA, Swinton House, 324 Grey's Inn Road, London, W.C.1 or The Scottish Association for National Certificates and Diplomas, 38 Queen Street, Glasgow, C.1.

O.N.D. IN INSTITUTIONAL HOUSEKEEPING AND MANAGEMENT

Purpose of the Course. The aim of the two-year, full-time course is to give a sound, basic, technical education to students who wish ultimately to assume positions of supervisory responsibility in residential or other large institutions in the School Meals Service or in other catering establishments. It is envisaged that those holding this award may reach the senior administrative posts after some years of practical experience.

Content of Course. Subjects to be studied: Business Studies, English and Social Studies, Catering, Food Preparation and Service, Institutional Housekeeping and Applied Science.

Entry Qualifications. The General Certificate of Education at Ordinary level or the CSE Grade 1 pass, in *four* subjects, three of which shall be chosen from the above list. The subjects *must* include a subject testing command of English. Similar passes in the SCE are required for the Scottish Scheme.

THE IMA CERTIFICATE IN INSTITUTIONAL MANAGEMENT

This is a one-year abridged course designed to help meet the current shortage of trained women in institutional management. The course extends over three

***English Language, English Literature, Mathematics, Sociology, Geography, History, Modern Language, Classical Language and up to *two* approved Science subjects *or* the O.N.D. in Institutional Housekeeping and Catering.**

terms and includes some vacation work. Entry qualifications are a minimum age of 25 years although university graduates under that age may be admitted to the course. Professional qualifications or considerable practical experience will also be needed.

The syllabus covers domestic administration, large-scale cookery and catering, science applied to health, accounting and business affairs, first aid and home nursing. The examination takes the form of a college assessment and report, based on an internal examination, a short study or essay or a chosen subject and a viva voce.

IMA MATRON—HOUSEKEEPERS CERTIFICATE

This course is designed to enable students to take on responsibilities of the matron housekeeper in small communities of children in which the organisation approximates as nearly as possible to that of a home.

Students must be 17 years of age, and entrance qualifications will be at least three "O" levels. The course consists of two years' full-time work (including practical work in boarding schools or hospitals) and a third year in industry. Examinations are held at the end of the second year, with a viva voce at the end of the third year.

The National Trade Development Association Courses

The National Trade Development Association is the organising and examining body for two courses of training for the licensed trade—the licensed house training course and the licensed trade catering course.

LICENSED HOUSE TRAINING COURSE

The licensed house training course is a part-time course for licensees, their staff and aspiring entrants. Minimum age of acceptance is 18 years and the minimum total period of instruction is 80 hours.

The subjects covered include: Brewing (six hours); brewery cellar management (three hours); cooperage (three hours); bottling (six hours); licensed house cellar management (six hours); bar dispense (nine hours); catering (10 hours); records and wages (nine hours); wines and spirits (nine hours); licensing laws (six hours); hygiene, food and drug regulations (five hours); furnishing and fittings (three hours); revision (six hours).

The licensed trade diploma examination is taken at the end of the course.

LICENSED TRADE CATERING COURSES

This part-time course has been designed for licensees and their wives to give them a knowledge essential for successful catering in the average public house. This includes the use of first-class foods, simply prepared, well displayed snacks and sandwiches, the use of convenience foods, the business man's lunch and the smaller type of functions in club rooms. The course does not intend to teach classical cookery. The minimum period of instruction is 69 hours.

Part I—This consists of demonstrations only in five three-hour periods. It provides an introduction and is also a short complete course.

Part II—This part consists of demonstrations followed by practical cookery. Twenty, three-hour periods cover the preparation and service of stocks, sauces and soups, sandwich and pastry making, various meat, fish and savoury dishes, omelettes, sweets. There is a three-hour practical examination and the two-hour theory examination. Successful candidates are awarded a diploma.

Chef Training

There are two national training programmes—one lasting two years, the other four years. Both of these combine practical training in industry with further education at technical college. Trainee chefs and cooks acquire skill and knowledge by working side by side with experienced craftsmen in their daily work. Both schemes are administered by the Hotel and Catering Industry Training Board.

Registered trainees attend classes in their working time without loss of pay for one day a week or its equivalent. They may attend block-release courses where these are available. This may mean, for example, that they attend a technical college for up to eighteen weeks in one or more blocks between October and March instead of day-release throughout the year.

At present the two programmes are related to the industry's national cookery examinations—the City and Guilds of London Institute 147 examination (Basic Cookery for the Catering Industry) and the City and Guilds 151 examination (Cookery for the Hotel and Catering Industry). The trainee will take the C & G 147 at the end of the second year and the C & G 151 examination at the end of the fourth year. On the four-year training programme, he will have to pass the practical part of the C & G 147 examination before he can go on to the third and fourth years.

Establishments operate either the two- or four-year training programme. Some establishments only require their trainees to reach the standard of the C & G 147 examination and do not have the facilities for training to the more advanced level. A trainee engaged on the two-year programme at such an establishment can, however, be transferred to an employer operating the four-year period of training providing he passes the C & G 147 practical examination at the end of the second year. For the next two years, he studies for the C & G 151 examination and will take this at the end of the fourth year.

The Board keeps a register of all trainees and of firms able and willing to provide training under the conditions laid down by the Board.

Two-year training
This programme aims to provide for the planned basic training for boys and girls wishing to become chefs and cooks in every section of the industry. Training normally begins at school-leaving age but there is no upper age limit for entry. As in both programmes, the first three months is a period of probation.

FOUR YEAR CHEF TRAINING SCHEME

The four year chef's trainee scheme is open to all young people of school-leaving age, although older people are accepted. Trainees are taken on by establishments willing and able to train to the standards laid down by HCITB, and the Board maintains a record of trainees as well as of suitable establishments.

A three-month probationary period is required for all trainees (which is included in the four years training period), and all trainees are given release, without loss of pay, for one day per week for technical college training. In some areas, notably in the south-west, this release takes the form of a block release period in the winter months, where trainees attend technical college full-time, and work full-time during the summer months.

During the four years, trainees generally cover the following departments:—

Butchery Preparation. The various types of meat. Storage, quality, uses and weights of various cuts and preparation for kitchen. Source and preparation of offals. Production and use of by-products.

Fish Preparation. The various types of fish. Storage, quality, uses and weights of various cuts and preparation for kitchen. Preparation and filleting (where appropriate) of all fish including shellfish.

Poultry and Game Preparation. The various types of poultry and game, including hare and rabbit; storage, quality, seasons, uses. Preparation (cleaning and trussing) for the kitchen.

Larder. Preparation and service of: Hors d'œuvres and appetisers. Mayonnaise and vinaigrette sauce groups. Salads of all types. Cold buffet work. Sandwiches. Appropriate dishes, including pies, for the kitchen. Oysters. Cheeses. Decorative napkin folding.

Soup Corner. Methods and preparation of: The various stocks used for soups (meat, fish, poultry, game). Clear soups, broths, purées, veloutés, cream soups, with their accompaniments and service.

Roast and Grill Corner. Methods, preparation, service of and recipes for all roast meat joints and garnishes. All roast game and poultry dishes and garnishes. Deep frying. Fritters. Grills and garnishes. Savouries and canapés. Carving.

Vegetables, Eggs and Farinaceous. Preparation, cooking and service of: all root vegetables; all green vegetables; the mushroom family; (for these three, also attention to seasons, quality, storage, etc.). Pulses; potato variations; frozen vegetables; various types of egg dishes; farinaceous products.

Fish Corner. Preparation, cooking and service of fish of all types, including shellfish where applicable, using the following methods: poaching, frying, baking, grilling, steaming, meunière, court-bouillon. Appropriate sauces and garnishes.

Sauce Corner. Various types of roux and their preparation. Preparation and cooking of espagnole, demi-glace, velouté, jus lié, meat glaze. Other basic sauces and derivatives. All types of entrées and their preparation and cooking, with particular attention to the culinary processes.

Pastry. Preparation, cooking and service of: various types of pastry. Sponges, cakes, yeast mixtures. Various types of pudding mixtures. Hot and cold sauces. Hot and cold sweets. Compôtes and fruit dishes. Various types of ices. Soufflés. Dessert fruits, including season and quality. Elementary sugar work to include decoration. Special pastry dishes.

Historical Summary

Strangely enough the history of the Cookery and Food Association might well be considered longer than the history of the hotel and catering industry itself as the industry is constituted today. Certainly the roots of the Association are closely intertwined with those of our modern industry. It was only around the turn of the century that luxury hotels really developed in such a way as to attract ladies as well as gentlemen for social pleasure as distinct from brief sojourns necessitated by travel. Other sections of our industry are, in present form, of even more recent origin, for some important branches of catering such as in schools and industry have only emerged as well-defined separate fields of enterprise in recent years.

Great catering figures of Britain's past like Alexis Soyer and Eustace Ude gained much of their fame in clubs and private houses rather than in hotels or commercial or welfare catering. With the emergence of famous names in the hotel, restaurant and catering world like César Ritz, Auguste Judah, Auguste Escoffier and Herman Senn we come to the beginnings of our industry's history as we know it today. At the same time the origins of the oldest association devoted to the advancement of catering and culinary arts, the Cookery and Food Association came into being.

The Association was founded in 1885 in the Palace of St. James's by Eugene Pouard and has never lost its Royal connections, for successive Queen Mothers have been its Patron. It has also become traditional that Masters of the Royal Household with their national interest in culinary matters and catering should preside over the Association. The Association was specially enrolled in 1887 by the Lords of the Treasury and enjoyed the special patronage of the Worshipful Company of Cooks and of the Lord Mayor of London.

From its earliest days the Association has striven to raise the standard of catering wherever possible. Apart from teaching cookery to young boys the Association has sent teachers into the poorer parts of our cities to teach housewives how to produce nutritious meals as economically as possible, for malnutrition was rife at the end of the last century and beginning of the present.

Membership has traditionally included the great names of each generation—Pouard, Senn, Escoffier, Ritz, Reeves-Smith, Towle, Cedard, Kriens, Gouffe, Menager, Salmon, Vincent and many others. So important was the work of the Association considered that in the earlier part of this century the list of Patrons included over two hundred names of the crowned heads of Europe, princes and members of nobility.

The Soho school of cookery was opened in the last century and developed to such an extent that the LCC took it over and opened The Hotel and Catering Department of the Westminster Technical College in 1910. Thus the first college of this kind in this country was born and has since formed the pattern for over one hundred and twenty full-time catering colleges, with many other schools and colleges taking catering as part of their curriculum.

The Association also organised schools of cookery in hospitals commencing with one in Brompton Hospital, London in 1900, and a few years later had thirty-eight schools throughout the country. In 1934 the Chairman, Herman Senn presented the 10,000th certificate in hospital cookery. A speciality was the class for ships' cooks and cooks for the armed services. During the First World War the Association was approached by the government to find and train over a thousand cooks for the services. The Association Chairman was also appointed as inspector of H.M. Prison Catering. Again the Association assisted the government by providing the necessary information for rationing in times of necessity.

In 1941 the Association yet again rendered service to the government through its senior officers foremost of whom was Isidore Salmon (later Sir Isidore) in promulgating the Army Catering Corps. Indeed one of the Association members became the first Commandant of the Army Catering Corps whilst many other Association members became senior officers. Since that date the Commandant of the Army Catering Corps has always been an ex-officio member of the Association Management Committee as are the catering chiefs of the other two services.

Present Developments

Today the industry is justly proud not only of the colleges but of the fact that there are two chairs of hotel management and catering, at Strathclyde and Surrey Universities, where degree courses are run. Over twenty thousand students attend annually at these colleges.

Recently the Association has taken a step envisaged by its founding fathers in establishing the grade of Fellow for qualified members who have been at least five years in membership and otherwise satisfy the Association's requirements. There are six degrees of membership—Governor (GCFA), Fellow (FCFA), Full Member (MCFA), Associate Fellow (AFCFA), Associate (ACFA), and Licentiate (LCFA). The grades of Associate Fellow and Associate are intended for those persons not directly engaged in catering but who are persons of repute and standing in related industries and professions. The goal of obtaining the Association's letters of qualification act as a stimulus to those interested in training either full- or part-time particularly on the culinary side, and helps to dignify the higher level of craft work. The Association with its long-standing prestige behind it also confers the oldest established and most honoured gastronomic distinctions in this country—the Order of Merit and the Cordon Rouge.

Salon Culinaire

The first Salon Culinaire was held in 1885 and apart from the war years became an annual event until in 1935 it was merged with the great catering exhibition in London internationally known as "HOTELYMPIA".

Today the Salon is greater than ever, having both junior and senior sections with so many entries that many hundreds of qualifying competitions are held in different parts of the country. The fullest co-operation is given at these exhibitions by the Association, Culinaire Francaise and the Chefs of the Cooks Circle.

In addition to the huge exhibition in London there are a great number of Salons Culinaires that take place in provincial centres throughout the country, at which members give a great deal of their time in order to promote the objects of the Association.

Craft Guild of Chefs

In 1966 the Craft Guild of Chefs was born as a result of talks between the Hotel and Catering Institute, the Worshipful Company of Cooks and the Cookery and Food Association. The Guild will pick up the threads where the Worshipful Company of Cooks left off several hundred years ago and every chef will carry a passport giving details of his training and experience. A young man obtaining his 151 City and Guilds certificate will be eligible for Associate membership and will receive promotion through Craftsman and Master Craftsman as he progresses with his craftsmanship.

The Association's objects are "The Advancement of the Art and Science of Cookery and Food", and this means that a great number of people within the industry are eligible for membership. It is the one Association where managing director, chef, head waiter, vinter, Somalier, carver, the teacher, etc., and all others concerned can discuss their problems around the one table.

Services to Members

This work of examining in cookery and in conferring qualifications and honours goes on and is linked with the advancement of culinary science as the main purpose behind the CFA. But there are, of course, many other ways in which the CFA seeks to serve and link together its members. It has a monthly Review, *Food and Cookery,* now in its sixtieth year and which features articles of interest to those in cookery and catering generally as well as members in particular. CFA arranges visits and outings for its members whilst the annual dinner-dance has long had a wonderful reputation as a unique social and gastronomic occasion. An appointments bureau and a technical advice centre is administered from the head office, 185, Piccadilly, London, W.1. There is a fine library there which contains not only modern catering works but rare volumes of the past and whose shelves yield much information of the Association's own venerable history.

The Association has gained more members this year than in any other one year of its previous history, and believing that its strength lies in the vigorous personal support of members it offers a welcome to all who share its ideals and are suitably qualified. It wants maximum support for the concept of good cookery and kitchen training as the basis of sound catering and as a necessary part in the qualifications of all caterers. For this reason the Committee of Management has decided that for a limited, interim period those who were already over twenty-five on 1st July, 1957 may be elected without passing this examination prescribed for younger applicants but on the basis of experience, in order that older persons trained before the full organisation of technical education may still gain membership during this period of expansion. Indeed, CFA does not merely live on tradition for though it undoubtedly has a great past, it has a vigorous present and can be assured a destiny in the future of the great industry it is proud to serve.

The Association has its headquarters at Charis House, 54, Lyford Road, Wandsworth Common, London, S.W.18, which is also the headquarters of the Salon Culinaire, Craft Guild of Chefs and the Review which is published monthly for the Association.

Acknowledgments

The publishers are very grateful to the following for their help in compiling this material:

The City and Guilds of London Institute, 76, Portland Place, London, W.1, for permission to reprint material from copies of the regulations and syllabuses for the Institutes' catering courses, 147, 150, 151, 152 and 353.

HAROLD E. TAYLOR of the Cookery and Food Association, Charis House, 54, Lyford Road, London, W.1, for supplying the article and information on the Cookery and Food Association.

The publishers would also like to thank Professor JOHN FULLER formerly of Strathclyde University's Scottish Hotel School, Ross Hall, Crookston Road, Glasgow, S.W.2, for co-ordinating the material supplied.